P9-EDM-365

ITALIAN WINES 2000

LE GUIDE DEL GAMBERO ROSSO
Gambero Rosso Editore

Slow Food Arcigola Editore

39

italianwines

2000

ITALIAN WINES 2000

IS THE ENGLISH LANGUAGE EDITION OF VINI D'ITALIA 2000 BY
GAMBERO ROSSO EDITORE AND SLOW FOOD EDITORE

GAMBERO ROSSO EDITORE
VIA A. BARGONI, 8 - 00153 ROMA
TEL. 39-6-58310125 - FAX 39-6-58310170
E-MAIL: gambero@gamberorosso.it

SLOW FOOD ARCIGOLA EDITORE
VIA MENDICITÀ ISTRUITA, 45 - 12042 BRA (CN)
TEL. 39-172-412519 - FAX 39-172-411218
E-MAIL: info@slowfood.it

EDITORIAL STAFF FOR THE ORIGINAL EDITION

CHIEF EDITORS
DANIELE CERNILLI AND CARLO PETRINI

SENIOR EDITORS
GIGI PIUMATTI AND MARCO SABELLICO

TECHNICAL SUPERVISION
ERNESTO GENTILI, VITTORIO MANGANELLI
FABIO RIZZARI AND SANDRO SANGIORGI

MEMBERS OF THE FINAL TASTING PANELS
DARIO CAPPELLONI, GIULIO COLOMBA, GIANNI FABRIZIO,
GIACOMO MOJOLI, MARCO OREGGIA, PIERO SARDO

CONTRIBUTORS
NINO AIELLO, GILBERTO ARRU, ANTONIO ATTORRE, PAOLO BATTIMELLI,
ENRICO BATTISTELLA, ALBERTO BETTINI, BRUNO BEVILACQUA, WALTER BORDO,
MICHELE BRESSAN, DANIELE CERNILLI, VALERIO CHIARINI, ANTONIO CIMINELLI,
GIULIO COLOMBA, MASSIMO DI CINTIO, MASSIMO DOGLIOLO, GIANNI FABRIZIO,
MAURIZIO FAVA, EGIDIO FEDELE DELL'OSTE, NICOLA FRASSON, ERNESTO GENTILI,
VITO LACERENZA, GIANCARLO LO SICCO, VITTORIO MANGANELLI, GIACOMO MOJOLI,
MARCO OREGGIA, MARIO PAPANI, STEFANO PASTOR, NEREO PEDERZOLLI, CARLO PETRINI,
GUIDO PIRAZZOLI, GIGI PIUMATTI, MARIO PLAZIO, FABIO RIZZARI, LEONARDO ROMANELLI,
GIOVANNI RUFFA, MARCO SABELLICO, SANDRO SANGIORGI, PIERO SARDO, DIEGO SORACCO,
HERBERT TASCHLER, MASSIMO TOFFOLO, PAOLO TRIMANI, ANDREA VANNELLI,
RICCARDO VISCARDI, MASSIMO VOLPARI, ALBERTO ZACCONE

WITH SPECIAL THANKS TO
FRANCESCO ANNIBALI, ALESSANDRO BULZONI, REMO CAMURANI, DARIO CAPPELLONI,
ROBERTO CASULLO, SERGIO CECCARELLI, MARINO DEL CURTO, STEFANO FERRARI,
DAVIDE GANDINO, FABIO GIAVEDONI, MARCO LISI, ENZO MERZ,
DANNY MURARO, DUILIO MURARO, NICOLA PERULLO, SILVANO PROMPICAI,
PIER PAOLO RASTELLI, MARINO POERIO, VALENTINO RAMELLI, GABRIELE RICCI ALUNNI,
HELMUT RIEBSCHLEGER, GAETANO ROTOLO, PAOLO VALDASTRI, VALERIO ZORZI.

EDITORIAL ASSISTANTS
MARCO OREGGIA AND UMBERTO TAMBURINI

EDITORIAL COORDINATOR
GIORGIO ACCASCINA

LAYOUT
FABIO CREMONESI

TRANSLATIONS COORDINATED AND EDITED BY
KAREN CHRISTENFELD

TRANSLATORS
M. ASHLEY, L. BAILHACHE, M. BENSON, M. DOUGAN, A. L. MILLER

PUBLISHER
GAMBERO ROSSO, INC.
636 BROADWAY - SUITE 1219 - NEW YORK, NY 10012
TEL. 212- 253-5653 FAX 212 253-8349 - E-MAIL: gamberousa@aol.com

DISTRIBUTION:
USA AND CANADA BY ANTIQUE COLLECTOR'S CLUB, MARKET STREET INDUSTRIAL PARK,
WAPPINGER FALLS, NY 12590, USA;
UK AND AUSTRALIA BY GRUB STREET, THE BASEMENT, 10 CHIVALRY ROAD,
LONDON SW11 1HT, UK.

COPYRIGHT© GAMBERO ROSSO EDITORE SRL - ROMA - ITALY
ALL RIGHTS RESERVED. NO PART OF THIS PUBLICATION MAY BE REPRODUCED, STORED IN A
RETRIEVAL SYSTEM OR TRANSMITTED BY ANY FORM OR BY ANY MEANS: ELECTRONIC,
ELECTROSTATIC, MAGNETIC TAPE, MECHANICAL, PHOTOCOPYING, RECORDING OR
OTHERWISE WITHOUT WRITTEN PERMISSION FROM THE PUBLISHER.
GAMBERO ROSSO IS A REGISTERED TRADE MARK

ITALIAN WINES 2000 WAS CLOSED SEPTEMBER 30, 1999

PRINTED IN ITALY BY TIPOGRAFICA LA PIRAMIDE - VIA ANTON MARIA VALSALVA, 34 - ROMA

CONTENTS

INTRODUCTION

The third edition in English of Italian Wines (which corresponds to the 13th edition of the Guida Vini d'Italia), published by Gambero Rosso and Slow Food, bears on its cover the momentous date 2000 and is, indeed, the last of the century and of the millennium. It also registers the highest number of Three Glasses yet awarded: 182. At the same time it consolidates the leading position of a book, its judgments and the two organizations that together have produced it. For both Gambero Rosso and Slow Food Arcigola, the Guide is one of the most important of their endeavors, the one that introduced them first to an audience of wine lovers and then to the public in general. At the inception of the Guide we never imagined we should be printing 50 thousand copies in Italian alone, ten times more than the first edition, which came out in November 1987. With the 25 thousand copies of the German edition, published by Hallwag, and the more than 20 thousand of Italian Wines 2000, it makes a total of almost 100 thousand copies, which is not at all bad for a book that deals exclusively with Italian wines and costs $24.95 or £15.99 in bookshops. It is now hard to find a wine enthusiast, a responsible wine merchant or a serious Italian wine producer who does not have a copy of the Guide somewhere or other. But the phenomenon is no longer confined to wine professionals. Our sense of having arrived becomes very real when, in wineshops or at the outlets that some producers have at their wineries, we see customers arrive holding our book in their hands and asking for Three Glass wines. This award system, by the way, has an immediate comprehensibility that has given it the sort of success enjoyed by the "Trois Etoiles" of the Guide Michelin. From 1988 to 1994, in the course of seven editions, the producers we reviewed went from 450 to about 1,000, the wines from 1,500 to more than 5,000. In those days no producer was allowed more than one Three Glass award a year. This was perhaps somewhat artificial, but it meant, in those early years, that we could underscore the importance of the award by limiting the number of winners, an old stratagem that worked well enough until we saw that we were in danger of hurting the reputation of some of the leading producers. From the very start our aim has been to promote a renaissance of Italian wine. The leading figures in this renaissance include Elio Altare, Giorgio Rivetti, Domenico Clerico, Silvio Jermann, Giovanni Manetti, Paolo De Marchi, Federico Carletti, Alois Lageder and Maurizio Zanella. These are now all famous names, but they were not nearly so well known 13 years ago, and it would not be very far from the truth to say that the Guide and its Three Glasses have contributed to their success. Our policy changed in 1995: no more limits, and indeed Gaja won four Three Glasses, Altare three and Zanella two. Meanwhile the Guide really started to take off: we reached a printing of 20 thousand around then, and the German edition sold more than 10 thousand. It was doing quite well. Between 1995 and 1999 there wasn't much else. The Italian wine world turned increasingly to the Guide as its major reference work. Now, with the 2000 edition, this position is to a great extent confirmed: the Guide makes a significant difference to the behavior of the market for premium Italian wines. For us it is a dream come true. For Gambero Rosso and Slow Food it is a mainstay, a pièce de résistance, essential to the image and credibillity of two organizations that are eminently successful and, indeed, even fashionable, after the Salone del Gusto in 1998 and the establishment of the Gambero Rosso Channel in July 1999, a pair of enterprises that have succeeded in shaking the drowsy world of the food and wine media to its foundations. But the Guide is still the Guide. This year our work went particularly well. In our comparative blind tastings, organized according to wine category, we tasted almost 20 thousand samples. The first stage determines the cream of the crop, which consisted this year of 609 wines that made it to the final rounds, held at four different places. The panels of tasters then increased to about 10 judges each: our publishers, assistant publishers, freelance and staff contributors from some of the regions providing most wines to the final stage. In Rome, in Bra at the headquarters of Slow Food Arcigola, at Colloredo di Montalbano in Friuli and at Soave in the Veneto, 182 wines were chosen to receive our highest award, Three Glasses. This award is not based on the absolute value of the various wines, but rather on their fidelity to the best characteristics of their category, as well as the quality of the vinification technique employed in their production and the balance of their component parts as perceived by the examining eye, nose and palate. The award may be considered the fruit of a series of parallel stages, since it does not seem feasible to us to compare wines of different categories, from different places, grapes and vintages. This fundamental approach holds true as well in the cases of those wines that received Two Glasses, One Glass or just a mention. The perceived harmony of the wines, fidelity to the character of their "terroir" and grapes, competence in vinification and good judgment about aging in barrel and bottle are the standards by which the panels made their assessments. Naturally a certain flexibility in applying these criteria is necessary, given the great diversity of the wines under examination. This year, in addition to Three Glasses, and to the Stars assigned to those producers who have amassed at least ten Three Glass awards over the years (Gaja has two Stars, having collected 21, and 14 other producers have one Star), we have again chosen the Wines of the Year, the Winery of the Year and the Oenologist of the Year. There are now four wines, one in each of four categories. The prize for "Bubbly" Wine of the Year goes to the Franciacorta Satèn '95 from the Ca' del Bosco. We chose as the best white wine the Vintage Tunina '97 from the Vinnaioli Jermann. The best red wine is the Barbera d'Alba Vigneto Gallina '97 from La Spinetta, the fruit of a vintage which is, to say the least, legendary in the history of this "humble" Piedmontese grape. The best dessert wine is the Colli Orientali del Friuli Picolit '97 from the Rocca Bernarda. The Winery of the Year is the Cantina Produttori di San Michele Appiano/Sanct Michael Eppan, in Appiano/Eppan in Alto Adige. The Oenologist of the Year is Carlo Ferrini, who has racked up 23 Three Glass awards in the last three years, and is the consultant oenologist for, among others, Barone Ricasoli, Castello di Fonterutoli, Poliziano, Tenuta del Terriccio, San Fabiano Calcinaia, La Brancaia, Fattoria Le Corti, Casanova di Neri, Riecine and La Massa, all of which are renowned Tuscan producers. Lastly, a word about the number of Three Glass awards: 182, which is more than ever before and brings the total number assigned in the course of 13 editions of the Guide to 1,054. Too many? We don't think so. In the current context of vast improvement in the world of Italian wine, we do not believe that the list of top wines should be shorter.

Daniele Cernilli and Carlo Petrini

THREE GLASS AWARDS 2000

VALLE D'AOSTA

VALLÉE D'AOSTE CHARDONNAY CUVÉE FRISSONIÈRE LES CRETES CUVÉE BOIS '97	LES CRÊTES	17

PIEDMONT

ASTI DE MIRANDA METODO CLASSICO '97	GIUSEPPE CONTRATTO	48
BARBARESCO BRICCO ASILI BRICCO ASILI '96	BRICCO ROCCHE – BRICCO ASILI	54
BARBARESCO COSTA RUSSI '96	GAJA	30
BARBARESCO FAUSONI VIGNA DEL SALTO '96	SOTTIMANO	114
BARBARESCO RABAJÀ '96	BRUNO ROCCA	33
BARBARESCO SERRABOELLA '96	F.LLI CIGLIUTI	110
BARBARESCO SORÌ SAN LORENZO '96	GAJA	30
BARBARESCO VIGNETO BRICH RONCHI '96	ALBINO ROCCA	33
BARBARESCO VIGNETO GALLINA VÜRSÙ '96	LA SPINETTA	50
BARBERA D'ALBA ASILI BARRIQUE '97	CASCINA LUISIN	28
BARBERA D'ALBA BRIC LOIRA '97	CASCINA CHICCO	44
BARBERA D'ALBA GIADA '97	ANDREA OBERTO	85
BARBERA D'ALBA MARUN '97	MATTEO CORREGGIA	44
BARBERA D'ALBA SUPERIORE '97	GALLINO	46
BARBERA D'ALBA SUPERIORE '97	HILBERG PASQUERO	120
BARBERA D'ALBA VIGNA GATTERE '97	MAURO MOLINO	84
BARBERA D'ALBA VIGNA POZZO '97	GIOVANNI CORINO	81
BARBERA D'ALBA VIGNETO DELLA CHIESA '97	F.LLI SEGHESIO	103
BARBERA D'ALBA VIGNETO GALLINA '97	LA SPINETTA	50
BARBERA D'ALBA VIGNETO POZZO DELL'ANNUNZIATA RIS. '96	ROBERTO VOERZIO	89
BARBERA D'ALBA VITTORIA '97	GIANFRANCO ALESSANDRIA	95
BARBERA D'ASTI BRICCO BATTISTA '97	GIULIO ACCORNERO E FIGLI	140
BARBERA D'ASTI COSTAMIÒLE '97	PRUNOTTO	26
BARBERA D'ASTI SUPERIORE GENERALA '97	BERSANO	115
BARBERA D'ASTI SUPERIORE MONTRUC '97	FRANCO M. MARTINETTI	135
BARBERA DEL MONFERRATO RIVALTA '97	VILLA SPARINA	77
BAROLO BRIC DËL FIASC '95	PAOLO SCAVINO	56
BAROLO BRICCO FIASCO '95	AZELIA	53
BAROLO BRICCO LUCIANI '95	SILVIO GRASSO	83
BAROLO CEREQUIO '95	MICHELE CHIARLO	41
BAROLO MONVIGLIERO '95	F.LLI ALESSANDRIA	138
BAROLO PAJANA '95	DOMENICO CLERICO	96
BAROLO SPERSS '95	GAJA	30
DOLCETTO D'ALBA BARTUROT '98	CA' VIOLA	105
DOLCETTO DELLE LANGHE MONREGALESI IL COLOMBO '98	IL COLOMBO - BARONE RICCATI	95
DOLCETTO DI DOGLIANI SIRÌ D'JERMU '98	F.LLI PECCHENINO	67
DOLCETTO DI DOGLIANI VIGNA DEL PILONE '98	SAN ROMANO	68
LANGHE ARBORINA '97	ELIO ALTARE	79
LANGHE DARMAGI '96	GAJA	30
LANGHE LARIGI '97	ELIO ALTARE	79
LANGHE ROSSO BRUMAIO '97	SAN FEREOLO	68
LANGHE ROSSO LUIGI EINAUDI '97	PODERI LUIGI EINAUDI	66
LANGHE ROSSO MONPRÀ '97	CONTERNO FANTINO	98
LANGHE PAITIN '97	PAITIN	113
LANGHE ROSSO SEIFILE '96	FIORENZO NADA	137
LOAZZOLO PIASA RISCHEI '96	FORTETO DELLA LUJA	91
MONFERRATO ROSSO PIN '97	LA SPINETTA	50
MONFERRATO ROSSO SONVICO '97	CASCINA LA BARBATELLA	115
ROERO RÒCHE D'AMPSÈJ '96	MATTEO CORREGGIA	44
GIUSEPPE CONTRATTO M. CL. BRUT RIS. '95	GIUSEPPE CONTRATTO	48

LOMBARDY

FRANCIACORTA COLLEZIONE BRUT '94	CAVALLERI	172
FRANCIACORTA BRUT COMARÌ DEL SALEM '93	UBERTI	175
FRANCIACORTA GRAN CUVÉE BRUT '95	BELLAVISTA	171
FRANCIACORTA BRUT SATÈN	MONTE ROSSA	165

FRANCIACORTA SATÈN '95	CA' DEL BOSCO	172
VALTELLINA SFORZATO CANUA '97	CONTI SERTOLI SALIS	189
VALTELLINA SFURSAT 5 STELLE '97	NINO NEGRI	165

TRENTINO

GIULIO FERRARI '91	FERRARI	212
SAN LEONARDO '96	TENUTA SAN LEONARDO	195
TRENTINO PINOT GRIGIO '98	CESCONI	200
TRENTO METHIUS BRUT RIS. '92	F.LLI DORIGATI	203

ALTO ADIGE

A. A. CABERNET SAUVIGNON CASSIANO '97	GRAF ENZENBERG TENUTA MANINCOR	225
A. A. CABERNET CASTEL SCHWANBURG '96	CASTELLO SCHWANBURG	236
A. A. CABERNET MUMELTERHOF RIS. '97	CANTINA PRODUTTORI SANTA MADDALENA	220
A. A. CABERNET '97	POPPHOF - ANDREAS MENZ	233
A. A. CABERNET-MERLOT AUHOF '97	BARON WIDMANN	231
A. A. CHARDONNAY CORNELL '97	CANTINA PRODUTTORI COLTERENZIO	228
A. A. CHARDONNAY ST. VALENTIN '97	CANTINA PRODUTTORI SAN MICHELE APPIANO	217
A. A. GEWÜRZTRAMINER KOLBENHOF '98	HOFSTÄTTER	240
A. A. GEWÜRZTRAMINER ST. VALENTIN '98	CANTINA PRODUTTORI SAN MICHELE APPIANO	217
A. A. GOLDMUSKATELLER PASSITO SERENADE '95	CANTINA VITICOLTORI DI CALDARO	224
A. A. LAGREIN SCURO UNTERMOSERHOF RIS. '97	GEORG RAMOSER	222
A. A. MERLOT BRENNTAL '97	CANTINA PRODUTTORI CORTACCIA	230
A. A. MERLOT FREIBERG '97	CANTINA PRODUTTORI MERANO	234
A. A. SAUVIGNON ST. VALENTIN '98	CANTINA PRODUTTORI SAN MICHELE APPIANO	217
A. A. VAL VENOSTA RIESLING '98	TENUTA FALKENSTEIN	236

VENETO

AMARONE DELLA VALPOLICELLA CLASSICO ACINATICO '95	ACCORDINI	273
AMARONE DELLA VALPOLICELLA CLASSICO '95	ALLEGRINI	248
AMARONE DELLA VALPOLICELLA CLASSICO CAMPO DEL TÌTARI '96	LUIGI BRUNELLI	274
AMARONE DELLA VALPOLICELLA CLASSICO MAZZANO '93	MASI	270
AMARONE DELLA VALPOLICELLA CLASSICO PERGOLE VECE '95	LE SALETTE	249
AMARONE DELLA VALPOLICELLA VIGNETO DI MONTE LODOLETTA '93	ROMANO DAL FORNO	250
CABERNET SAUVIGNON CAPITELLO '97	TENUTA S. ANTONIO	246
COLLI EUGANEI ROSSO GEMOLA '97	VIGNALTA	283
FRATTA '97	MACULAN	245
IL ROSSO DELL'ABBAZIA '97	SERAFINI & VIDOTTO	266
LA POJA '95	ALLEGRINI	248
ROSSO DELLA FABRISERIA '97	F.LLI TEDESCHI	276
SOAVE CLASSICO SUPERIORE CONTRADA SALVARENZA VECCHIE VIGNE '98	SANDRO E CLAUDIO GINI	261
SOAVE CLASSICO SUPERIORE VIGNETO CALVARINO '98	LEONILDO PIEROPAN	281
ALBION CABERNET SAUVIGNON VILLA NOVARE '97	CAV. G.B. BERTANI	263

FRIULI VENEZIA GIULIA

BRAIDE ALTE '97	LIVON	351
CAPO MARTINO '97	VINNAIOLI JERMANN	328
COF CHARDONNAY VIGNETO RONC DI JURI '97	DORIGO	300
COF PICOLIT '97	ROCCA BERNARDA	342
COF ROSAZZO BIANCO TERRE ALTE '97	LIVIO FELLUGA	311

COF ROSSO SACRISASSI '97	LE DUE TERRE	344
COF TOCAI FRIULANO '98	MIANI	301
COLLIO CHARDONNAY MONTE CUCCO '97	TENUTA VILLANOVA	329
COLLIO PINOT BIANCO AMRITÀ '97	MARIO SCHIOPETTO	304
COLLIO PINOT GRIGIO '98	ISIDORO POLENCIC	314
COLLIO SAUVIGNON '98	RONCO DEI TASSI	316
COLLIO SAUVIGNON '98	RUSSIZ SUPERIORE	303
COLLIO SAUVIGNON ASCEVI '98	ASCEVI - LUWA	347
COLLIO SAUVIGNON DE LA TOUR '98	VILLA RUSSIZ	305
COLLIO SAUVIGNON RONCO DELLE MELE '98	VENICA & VENICA	325
FRIULI ISONZO SAUVIGNON '98	RONCO DEL GELSO	317
FRIULI ISONZO SAUVIGNON PIERE '97	VIE DI ROMANS	337
MONTSCLAPADE '96	GIROLAMO DORIGO	300
RONCO DEI ROSETI '94	LE VIGNE DI ZAMÒ	334
VINTAGE TUNINA '97	VINNAIOLI JERMANN	328

EMILIA ROMAGNA

ALBANA DI ROMAGNA PASSITO SCACCO MATTO '96	FATTORIA ZERBINA	366
COLLI BOLOGNESI CABERNET SAUVIGNON SEL. '97	VALLONA	364
COLLI BOLOGNESI CABERNET SAUVIGNON BONZARONE '97	TENUTA BONZARA	369
COLLI PIACENTINI CABERNET SAUVIGNON LUNA SELVATICA '97	LA TOSA	378
MALVASIA PASSITO VIGNA DEL VOLTA '97	LA STOPPA	373
MARZIENO RAVENNA ROSSO '97	FATTORIA ZERBINA	366

TUSCANY

BATÀR '97	AGRICOLA QUERCIABELLA	419
BOLGHERI ROSSO SUPERIORE PALEO '96	LE MACCHIOLE	385
BOLGHERI SASSICAIA '96	TENUTA SAN GUIDO	386
BRANCAIA '97	LA BRANCAIA	394
BRUNELLO DI MONTALCINO POGGIO ALL'ORO RIS. '93	CASTELLO BANFI	429
BRUNELLO DI MONTALCINO SCHIENA D'ASINO '93	MASTROJANNI	441
BRUNELLO DI MONTALCINO VIGNA SPUNTALI '93	TENIMENTI ANGELINI–VAL DI SUGA	446
CABERNET SAUVIGNON '96	ISOLE E OLENA	383
CABREO LA PIETRA '97	RUFFINO	475
CAMARTINA '95	AGRICOLA QUERCIABELLA	419
CASALFERRO '97	BARONE RICASOLI	409
CEPPARELLO '97	ISOLE E OLENA	383
CERVIOLO ROSSO '97	SAN FABIANO CALCINAIA	397
CHIANTI CLASSICO GIORGIO PRIMO '97	LA MASSA	466
CHIANTI CLASSICO VIGNA DI FONTALLE RIS. '95	MACHIAVELLI	486
CHIANTI RUFINA MONTESODI '97	MARCHESI DE' FRESCOBALDI	406
FONTALLORO '95	FATTORIA DI FELSINA	401
GALATRONA '97	FATTORIA PETROLO	427
GISÈLE '97	LA RAMPA DI FUGNANO	491
IL CARBONAIONE '96	PODERE POGGIO SCALETTE	418
IL FUTURO '95	COLOMBAIO DI CENCIO	410
LA VIGNA DI ALCEO '97	CASTELLO DEI RAMPOLLA	468
LE STANZE '97	POLIZIANO	460
LIVERNANO '97	LIVERNANO	478
LUENZO '97	VINCENZO CESANI	489
LUPICAIA '97	TENUTA DEL TERRICCIO	399
PODERE IL BOSCO '97	TENIMENTI D'ALESSANDRO	404
ROMITORIO DI SANTEDAME '97	RUFFINO	475
ROSSO DI SERA '97	FATTORIA POGGIOPIANO	487
SAFFREDI '97	LE PUPILLE	423
SASSELLO '97	CASTELLO DI VERRAZZANO	420
SIEPI '97	CASTELLO DI FONTERUTOLI	393
SOLAIA '96	MARCHESI ANTINORI	405
SOLENGO '97	TENUTA DI ARGIANO	428
SYRAH '97	VILLA PILLO	414

TZINGANA '97	MONTE BERNARDI	468
VIN SANTO '89	AVIGNONESI	450
MARCHE		
CHAOS MARCHE ROSSO '97	FATTORIA LE TERRAZZE	523
KURNI '97	OASI DEGLI ANGELI	516
VERDICCHIO DEI CASTELLI DI JESI CLASSICO SUPERIORE CONTRADA BALCIANA '97	SARTARELLI	526
VERDICCHIO DEI CASTELLI DI JESI CLASSICO SUPERIORE PODIUM '97	GIOACCHINO GAROFOLI	519
UMBRIA		
ARMALEO '97	PALAZZONE	542
CERVARO DELLA SALA '97	CASTELLO DELLA SALA	537
MERLOT '97	LA PALAZZOLA	545
SAGRANTINO DI MONTEFALCO '96	CÒLPETRONE	537
SAGRANTINO DI MONTEFALCO 25 ANNI '96	ARNALDO CAPRAI - VAL DI MAGGIO	539
LAZIO		
MONTIANO '97	FALESCO	554
ABRUZZO		
CHARDONNAY MARINA CVETIC '97	GIANNI MASCIARELLI	566
MONTEPULCIANO D'ABRUZZO VILLA GEMMA '94	GIANNI MASCIARELLI	566
CAMPANIA		
CAMPANARO '98	FEUDI DI SAN GREGORIO	581
FIANO DI AVELLINO PIETRACALDA VENDEMMIA TARDIVA '98	FEUDI DI SAN GREGORIO	581
MONTEVETRANO '97	MONTEVETRANO	579
VIGNA CAMARATO '95	VILLA MATILDE	571
PUGLIA		
PRIMITIVO DI MANDURIA ZINFANDEL '98	SINFAROSA	591
SALICE SALENTINO ROSSO DONNA LISA RIS. '95	LEONE DE CASTRIS	599
VIGNA DEL FEUDO '97	FELLINE	597
SICILY		
CHARDONNAY '98	PLANETA	621
CONTESSA ENTELLINA CHIARANDÀ DEL MERLO '98	TENUTA DI DONNAFUGATA	613
MOSCATO PASSITO DI PANTELLERIA MARTINGANA '96	SALVATORE MURANA	618
SANTA CECILIA '97	PLANETA	621
LITRA '97	ABBAZIA SANTA ANASTASIA	609
PASSITO DI PANTELLERIA SOLIDEA '98	D'ANCONA	619
SARDINIA		
ALGHERO MARCHESE DI VILLAMARINA '95	TENUTE SELLA & MOSCA	626
TURRIGA '94	ANTONIO ARGIOLAS	634

WINERY OF THE YEAR

CANTINA PRODUTTORI SAN MICHELE APPIANO		217

OENOLOGIST OF THE YEAR

CARLO FERRINI

THE YEAR'S BEST WINES

THE BUBBLY		
FRANCIACORTA SATÈN '95	CA' DEL BOSCO	172
THE WHITE		
VINTAGE TUNINA '97	VINNAIOLI JERMANN	328
THE RED		
BARBERA D'ALBA VIGNETO GALLINA '97	LA SPINETTA	50
THE SWEET		
COF PICOLIT '97	ROCCA BERNARDA	342

THE STARS

Two years ago we decided to introduce a new symbol, joining our traditional wine Glasses, in recognition of the best Italian wineries. The Star is conferred on those producers who have received our Three Glasses at least ten times and is, we feel, a clear indication of consistency of quality at the highest level. Angelo Gaja is the only one to have two Stars, and he is well ahead of the producers next in line, Ca' del Bosco and Elio Altare, who have collected 16 Three Glasses each. Thirteen Three Glasses have been given to three renowned producers: Allegrini and Jermann, who with their two Three Glasses each join the Fattoria di Felsina, which this year is making do with one award. La Spinetta, which last year wasn't even in this company, has jumped in at 12 with its three Three glasses, thus joining Castello di Fonterutoli and Paolo Scavino, each of which has advanced by one more point. Aldo Conterno is still at 11, but now accompanied by Domenico Clerico and Vie di Romans. And here are the new entries (apart from La Spinetta), who have reached ten Three Glasses: Antinori, Bellavista, Castello della Sala, Ferrari, Girolamo Dorigo (two Three Glasses this year), Mario Schiopetto and Tenimenti Ruffino (two Three Glasses this year). There is no change in the position of Castello di Ama, Giacomo Conterno, Fontodi and Josko Gravner. Two final comments: first, if we were to add Antinori's collection of Three Glasses to those of Castello della Sala, which have been calculated separately (although the estate belongs to the Antinoris), the total would entitle them to two Stars. The second comment is that there are lots of producers on the brink of earning their first Star.

★★

25
ANGELO GAJA (Piemonte)

★

16
CA' DEL BOSCO (Lombardia)
ELIO ALTARE (Piemonte)

13
ALLEGRINI (Veneto)
FATTORIA DI FELSINA (Toscana)
VINNAIOLI JERMANN (Friuli Venezia Giulia)

12
CASTELLO DI FONTERUTOLI (Toscana)
LA SPINETTA (Piemonte)
PAOLO SCAVINO (Piemonte)

11
ALDO CONTERNO (Piemonte)
DOMENICO CLERICO (Piemonte)
VIE DI ROMANS (Friuli Venezia Giulia)

10
BELLAVISTA (Lombardia)
CASTELLO DELLA SALA (Umbria)
CASTELLO DI AMA (Toscana)
GIACOMO CONTERNO (Piemonte)
GIROLAMO DORIGO (Friuli Venezia Giulia)
FERRARI (Trentino)
FONTODI (Toscana)
JOSKO GRAVNER (Friuli Venezia Giulia)
ANTINORI (Toscana)
MARIO SCHIOPETTO (Friuli Venezia Giulia)
TENIMENTI RUFFINO (Toscana)

A GUIDE TO VINTAGES, 1970-1997

	BARBARESCO	BRUNELLO DI MONTALCINO	BAROLO	CHIANTI CLASSICO	VINO NOBILE DI MONTEPULCIANO	AMARONE
1970	●●●●	●●●●	●●●●	●●●●●	●●●●	●●●●
1971	●●●●	●●●	●●●●●	●●●●●	●●●●	●●●●
1972	●	●	●	●●	●	●
1973	●●	●●●	●●	●●	●●●	●●
1974	●●●●	●●	●●●●	●●●	●●●	●●●●
1975	●●	●●●●●	●●	●●●●	●●●●	●●●
1976	●●	●	●●	●●	●●	●●●●
1977	●●	●●●●	●●	●●●●	●●●●	●●●
1978	●●●●●	●●●●	●●●●●	●●●●●	●●●●●	●●●
1979	●●●●	●●●●	●●●●	●●●●	●●●●	●●●●
1980	●●●●	●●●●	●●●●	●●●●	●●	●●●
1981	●●●	●●●	●●●	●●●	●●●	●●●
1982	●●●●●	●●●●●	●●●●●	●●●●	●●●●	●
1983	●●●●	●●●●	●●●●	●●●●	●●●●	●●●●●
1984	●	●●	●●	●	●	●●
1985	●●●●●	●●●●●	●●●●●	●●●●●	●●●●●	●●●●
1986	●●●	●●●	●●●	●●●●	●●●●	●●●
1987	●●	●●	●●	●●	●●	●●
1988	●●●●●	●●●●●	●●●●●	●●●●●	●●●●●	●●●●●
1989	●●●●●	●●	●●●●●	●	●	●●
1990	●●●●●	●●●●●	●●●●●	●●●●●	●●●●●	●●●●●
1991	●●●	●●●	●●●	●●●	●●●	●●
1992	●●	●●	●●	●	●	●
1993	●●●	●●●●	●●●	●●●●	●●●●●	●●●●
1994	●●	●●●	●●	●●	●●	●●
1995	●●●●●	●●●●●	●●●●●	●●●●●	●●●●●	●●●●
1996	●●●●●	●●●	●●●●●	●●●	●●●	●●●
1997	●●●●●	●●●●●	●●●●●	●●●●●	●●●●●	●●●●●

HOW TO USE THE GUIDE

KEY

○ WHITE WINES
● RED WINES
⊙ ROSÉ WINES

RATINGS

LISTING WITHOUT A GLASS SYMBOL:
A WELL MADE WINE
REPRESENTATIVE OF ITS CATEGORY

🍷
ABOVE AVERAGE TO GOOD IN ITS CATEGORY, EQUIVALENT TO 70-79/100

🍷🍷
VERY GOOD TO EXCELLENT IN ITS CATEGORY, EQUIVALENT TO 80-89/100

🍷🍷🍷
OUTSTANDING WINE IN ITS CATEGORY, EQUIVALENT TO 90-99/100

(🍸, 🍸🍸, 🍸🍸🍸) THE WHITE GLASSES REFER TO RATINGS GIVEN IN PREVIOUS EDITIONS OF THE GUIDE, AND WHICH ARE CONFIRMED WHERE THE WINES IN QUESTION ARE STILL DRINKING AT THE LEVEL FOR WHICH THE ORIGINAL AWARD WAS MADE

STAR ★

GIVEN TO ALL THOSE ESTATES WHICH HAVE WON AT LEAST TEN THREE GLASS AWARDS

GUIDE TO PRICES (1)

1 UP TO $ 8 AND UP TO £6
2 FROM $ 8 TO $ 12 AND FROM £ 6 TO £ 8
3 FROM $ 12 TO $ 18 AND FROM £ 8 TO £ 11
4 FROM $ 18 TO $ 27 AND FROM £ 11 TO £ 15
5 FROM $ 27 TO $ 40 AND FROM £ 15 TO £ 20
6 MORE THAN $ 40 AND MORE THAN £ 20

(1) Approx. retail prices in USA and UK

ASTERISK *

INDICATES ESPECIALLY GOOD VALUE FOR MONEY

NOTE

PRICES REFER TO RETAIL AVERAGES. INDICATIONS OF PRICES FOR OLDER VINTAGES INCLUDE APPRECIATION WHERE APPROPRIATE

ABBREVIATIONS

A.A.	Alto Adige
Cl.	Classico
C.S.	Cantina Sociale
Cant.	Cantina
Cast.	Castello
C. Am.	Colli Amerini
COF	Colli Orientali del Friuli
Cons.	Consorzio
Coop.Agr.	Cooperativa Agricola
DOC:	initials standing for Denominazione di Origine Controllata. The term refers to classic quality wines made in traditional wine-making areas where production is regulated by law.
DOCG:	initials standing for Denominazione di Origine Controllata e Garantita. Like DOC, but subject to more rigorous governmental controls. The wines are tasted before bottling, and numbered official seals are applied to each bottle.
M.	Metodo
M.to	Monferrato
O. P.	Oltrepò Pavese
P.R.	Peduncolo Rosso
P. d. V.	Prosecco di Valdobbiadene
Rif. Agr.	Riforma Agraria
Sel.	Selezione
Sup.	Superiore
T.	Terre
T.d.F.	Terre di Franciacorta
Ten.	Tenute
Tenim.	Tenimenti
V.	Vigna
Vign.	Vigneto
V. T.	Vendemmia Tardiva

VALLE D'AOSTA

The Valle D'Aosta was, apart from Basilicata, the only region in Italy not to have ever won Three Glasses. That situation has now been remedied. A wine from this region, the smallest in Italy but one with a strong wine-producing tradition, stood out at our final tastings and walked off with the prize. This could act as an inspiration for the whole wine sector here, which includes only ten or so private producers and six cooperative wineries. The big winner was the top local producer, Les Crêtes at Aymavilles, whose Chardonnay fermented and aged in oak can compete with the very best wines from all over Italy. And we're particularly pleased that the Three Glasses went to Costantino Charrère's estate, which was established ten years ago as a partnership between the Vai brothers, noted restaurateurs, Vincenzo Grosjean and Charrère himself with the aim of making great wines. The first few years were needed to understand the potential of their vineyards, their chosen grape varieties and their production techniques – the latter are particularly inspired by Burgundy – and it is only now that they begin to reap the fruit of all their hard work. Our congratulations to this estate which, even in this mountainous region where every inch of land has to be reclaimed from the rock, has managed to make a place for itself in the Italian and international markets. But this is not the only news: this edition of the Guide contains more reviews of local producers, and there is at last an "Other Wineries" section, with further suggestions for getting to know the wines of the region. In the lower part of the valley, which stretches from Donnas to the gates of Aosta, the winery with most strings to its bow is still La Crotta di Vegneron at Chambave, which has again produced a couple of Two Glass wines and continues to be the best interpreter of Moscato, in both the Passito (raisin wine) and dry versions. We've reviewed more of the producers clustered around the city of Aosta; apart from the Institut Agricole, which continues to fulfill its dual role of research and successful production, two small private estates have been included: one belongs to the Grosjean brothers, the other to Renato Anselmet. We were particularly impressed by Anselmet's well-thought-out determination to achieve excellence. This year he presented a splendid oak-matured Chardonnay which came pretty close to the Les Crêtes version at our tastings. The Charrère family's wines, which are all red, are perfectly reliable and getting better. In the upper valley, between Aosta and Mont Blanc, we have dedicated a debut review to a young producer who, at the almost prohibitive altitude of nearly 1000 meters above sea level, grows grapes with which he succeeds in making a good Pinot Gris. There's also some news from near Morgex: the Cooperative has added a late-harvest wine to its traditional range. Wine production in this zone is definitely not at a standstill, and the Cooperatives are also starting to experiment with new approaches in order to make a name for themselves. Here is just one of many possible examples: the Caves de Donnas will come out next year with a Donnas wine aged in barriques.

AOSTA

Institut Agricole Régional

Reg. La Rochere, 1/A
11100 Aosta
tel. 0165/553304

Of the wines presented this year by the Institut Agricole, we preferred those in the standard range (which are not matured in wood) to the "superior" barrique-aged selections. We were particularly struck by the '98 whites: they are full-bodied, alcohol-rich wines. The almost golden-hued Müller Thurgau displays fruity scents on a background of varietal aromatic notes; the meaty palate seems almost sweet, and the fruit is echoed on the long finish. The Petite Arvine, a brilliant deep straw yellow in the glass, is excellent too. The very elegant nose releases well-defined notes of fruit and Alpine flowers, and the palate again shows the richness characteristic of this year's whites. The very interesting Pinot Gris comes from a particular vineyard 700 meters above sea level on the hillside above Aosta, which has endowed it with lots of alcohol. It's a good wine with great character. The best of the unoaked reds is definitely the Petit Rouge: it has a purplish color, a youthful grapey bouquet, medium body and good balance. Of the wood-aged whites we draw your attention to the Élite, made from viognier, which is less dominated by oak than the monovarietal sauvignon, La Comète; among the reds, the Vin du Prévôt (25% merlot, 50% cabernet sauvignon and 25% cabernet franc) and the Trésor du Caveau (100% syrah) were both very successful. The former shows full-bodied fruit well amalgamated with the wood, while the latter offers characteristic varietal tones, with definite spicy notes setting off the toasty oak-derived nuances.

●	Trésor du Caveau '97	▼▼	4
○	Vallée d'Aoste Müller Thurgau '98	▼▼	3*
○	Vallée d'Aoste Petite Arvine '98	▼▼	3
●	Vin du Prévôt '97	▼▼	4
○	Élite '97	▼	4
○	La Comète '97	▼	4
●	Vallée d'Aoste Petit Rouge '98	▼	3
○	Vallée d'Aoste Pinot Gris '98	▼	3
●	Trésor du Caveau '96	▽▽	4
○	Vallée d'Aoste Chardonnay Barrique '96	▽▽	4
●	Vin du Prévôt '96	▽▽	4

AYMAVILLES (AO)

Costantino Charrère

Fraz. du Moulins, 28
11010 Aymavilles (AO)
tel. 0165/902135

The wines from his own estate as well as those from Les Crêtes confirm that Costantino Charrère is the top producer in the Valle d'Aosta. At his own property, however, he makes exclusively red wines, mostly from indigenous – and in some cases, almost extinct - grape varieties. All four of the bottles presented this year were first in their various categories, with a special commendation for Les Fourches, but the undoubted star is still the Vin de La Sabla. This is a big red made from the local fumin and petit rouge grapes and aged in 900-liter chestnut barrels. The dense, almost opaque color gives the first hint of this wine's potential. The well-nigh perfect bouquet displays notes of spice and black pepper, while the tannins are smooth and well integrated with the highly concentrated fruit on the palate. In short, this is a red with a great future, but it is already thoroughly enjoyable. The equally good grenache-based Les Fourches still seems a little immature, but with a proper amount of bottle age it will certainly express its full potential. The Prëmetta, always an interesting wine, is pale, almost rosé-like, in color. There's an immediate impact on the not very broad palate, and the finish is lightly spicy and a little too noticeably tannic. The last and simplest of their wines, the Torrette, is well worth its One Glass.

●	Vin de La Sabla '98	▼▼	4
●	Vin Les Fourches '98	▼▼	4
●	Vallée d'Aoste Prëmetta '98	▼	4
●	Vallée d'Aoste Torrette '98	▼	3
●	Vallée d'Aoste Prëmetta '97	▽▽	4
●	Vin de La Sabla '97	▽▽	4
●	Vin Les Fourches '97	▽▽	4
●	Vallée d'Aoste Torrette '97	▽	3

AYMAVILLES (AO)

LES CRÊTES
LOC. VILLETOS, 50
11010 AYMAVILLES (AO)
TEL. 0165/902274

There is a further reason for celebration on the tenth anniversary of Les Crêtes: their Chardonnay Cuvée Bois has walked off with Three Glasses. This estate has yet again shown itself to be the best producer in the Valle d'Aosta. The quality of its wines can be explained, first of all, by their vineyard management (high-density plantings, very low yields and excellent exposures), and then by their careful skill in not wasting any of the excellent qualities of their raw material during vinification. The cellar and the vineyards here are the realm of Costantino Charrère, who has succeeded in this past decade in optimizing the potential of the zone. This year's wines are very good indeed, and the Chardonnay Cuvée Bois is the top of the range. It's a modern Chardonnay, vinified and aged in barriques, with a richness and style reminiscent of the great Burgundians: a big but not disproportionate wine that succeeds in combining great elegance with fullness of body. The perfect bouquet reveals oak well integrated with the fruit; the almost monumental palate is both rich and well balanced with a hint of vanilla on the finish which gives the wine a touch of softness. The two whites vinified in stainless steel are also excellent. We slightly preferred the Petite Arvine, which shows a little more personality on both nose and palate. The two "important" reds (the Fumin and the Coteau La Tour) are very interesting. The former, made from the typical local grape called fumin, displays pronounced smoky aromas, with marked woodland scents as well. The syrah-based Coteau La Tour has an almost purple hue and a peppery palate. The Pinot Noir and the Torrette got One Glass but no more.

○	Vallée d'Aoste Chardonnay Cuvée Frissonière Les Crêtes Cuvée Bois '97	▼▼▼	5
○	Vallée d'Aoste Chardonnay Cuvée Frissonière Les Crêtes '98	▼▼	4
●	Coteau La Tour '97	▼▼	4
●	Vallée d'Aoste Fumin Vigne La Tour '97	▼▼	4
○	Vallée d'Aoste Petite Arvine Vigne Champorette '98	▼▼	4
●	Vallée d'Aoste Pinot Noir Vigne La Tour '98	▼	4
●	Vallée d'Aoste Torrette Vigne Les Toules '98	▼	3

CHAMBAVE (AO)

LA CROTTA DI VEGNERON
P.ZZA RONCAS, 2
11023 CHAMBAVE (AO)
TEL. 0166/46670

La Crotta di Vegneron was founded in 1985 with the aim of raising high the banner of the two subdenominations Chambave and Nus. Year after year, this is the cooperative which best interprets the wines of the Valle d'Aosta, and it has upon occasion come very close to obtaining Three Glasses. They stake the most on wines made from moscato, the grape par excellence of Chambave. This year's two versions have again easily pocketed Two Glasses each. The Chambave Moscato Passito has a brilliant yellow color with golden highlights; an intensely floral bouquet unfolds attractively into varietal aromatic notes; the palate is velvety and harmonious, with a light vein of acidity on the finish giving it very good length. The dry version, the Chambave Muscat, is equally good: great depth is apparent on both the nose, where aromatic notes outweigh the fruity tones, and in the mouth, where it is succulent and concentrated. Their star red, the Fumin, didn't do as well, but certainly did not disgrace itself. The nose did not shine, but the wine showed better on the palate, where the structure of the fruit held its own against the oak-derived vanilla. The appealing Nus Malvoisie Flétri, their other raisin wine, is made from pinot gris, which is known up here, as in the nearby Valais, as malvoisie. The agreeable Müller Thurgau '98 completes the series of One Glass wines. These are the cooperative's top labels; their other selections are merely worthy of mention; a few, like the white-vinified Pinot Noir, were rather banal.

○	Vallée d'Aoste Chambave Moscato Passito '97	▼▼	5
○	Vallée d'Aoste Chambave Muscat '98	▼▼	3*
●	Vallée d'Aoste Fumin '97	▼	3
○	Vallée d'Aoste Müller Thurgau '98	▼	3
○	Vallée d'Aoste Nus Malvoisie Flétrì '97	▼	4
○	Vallée d'Aoste Nus Malvoisie '98		3
○	Vallée d'Aoste Chambave Moscato Passito '96	▽▽	5
○	Vallée d'Aoste Nus Malvoisie Flétrì '96	▽	4
●	Vallée d'Aoste Fumin '95	▽	4
●	Vallée d'Aoste Fumin '96	▽	4

INTROD (AO)

EMILIA MILLET
FRAZ. JUNOD, 4
11010 INTROD (AO)
TEL. 0165/95067 - 0165/955437

The winds of change have been blowing even in the Valle d'Aosta. In this region, dominated by cooperatives which, apart from their socializing function, make it possible for the extremely fragmented local viticulture to survive, a few small private estates are emerging and making their mark with wines of high quality. This is the case with the winery of Emilia Millet, which has, for some years now, presented an excellent Pinot Gris. This is a small producer with a current output of only 3,000 bottles a year. The well-situated vineyards in the hills around Introd, at between 800 and 900 meters above sea level, are particularly suited to growing pinot grigio and müller thurgau. Emilia's son Marco Martin divides his time between the Region of Valle d'Aosta, for which he is oenological consultant, and the family winery. Results are more than satisfactory, and this year's wine confirms the positive impressions we had gleaned from previous vintages. The Pinot Gris Lo Triolet '98 has a straw-yellow color and a delicate, elegant bouquet ranging from the sweeter scents of Alpine flowers to the tartness of citrus fruit. On the palate it lacks the body of wines obtained from vineyards at lower altitudes, but it's succulent and well-balanced, with clean, fresh acidity on the finish.

O Vallée d'Aoste Pinot Gris Lo Triolet '98	🍷	3

MORGEX (AO)

CAVE DU VIN BLANC DE MORGEX
ET DE LA SALLE
CHEMIN DES ILES, 19
FRAZ. LA RUINE
11017 MORGEX (AO)
TEL. 0165/800331

The Cave du Vin Blanc de Morgex, taking full advantage of the positive '97 vintage, has released a new wine, called Chaudelune. Using blanc de Morgex grapes, as in all their offerings, but picked late and therefore very ripe, they have produced a more complex white wine than usual, with greater body and about 15° of alcohol. Just a handful of bottles of this experimental wine were made (about 500), but the encouraging results should lead to further experiments. Indeed, it is most unusual at Morgex, a village 1000 meters high with a view of Mont Blanc, to produce dry wines rich in alcohol and complexity, so this success is something to build on in the future. The Blanc de Morgex et de La Salle is as enjoyable as ever. Very pale in color, it offers delicate, fruity and very lightly yeasty aromas; the extremely well-executed palate lacks the decisive personality of the Chaudelune; the succulent and fairly intense finish is rounded off by a touch of acidity. The Spumante Metodo Classico, which vaunts DOC status as a Vallée d'Aoste Blanc de Morgex et de La Salle, is worthy of note.

O Chaudelune Vendemmia Tardiva	🍷	4
O Vallée d'Aoste Blanc de Morgex et de La Salle '98	🍷	3
O Vallée d'Aoste Blanc de Morgex et de La Salle Metodo Classico		4

QUART (AO)

F.LLI GROSJEAN
FRAZ. OLLIGNAN, 1
11020 QUART (AO)
TEL. 0165/765283

The five Grosjean brothers, Vincenzo, Piergiorgio, Marco, Fernando and Eraldo, have taken over their father Delfino's winery – although he remains active in the enterprise - and are going all out for quality. The estate is located in the commune of Quart, just outside Aosta, at altitudes which vary between 500 and 650 meters above sea level. From their own six hectares under vine, plus some grapes bought in from other local growers, the Grosjeans produce about 45 thousand bottles of wine a year, of six different kinds. They are still using the cellar built in 1969, when Delfino started making wine; however, new and more spacious premises, which will also be more in keeping with their current aims, are planned for the near future. Production is overseen by Vincenzo Grosjean, who, among other things, is a consultant oenologist for the Region, while Eraldo and Fernando look after the vineyards and sales. The best of the wines presented this year was the '97 Fumin; this is an oak-matured red whose bouquet displays light animal tones; it is on the palate that the wine expresses its full potential, from its rich, mouth-filling and already well-balanced fruit through to its finish, distinguished by smooth tannins. The late-harvested Petite Arvine is almost as good; it does not have a particularly full bouquet, but the palate shows excellent structure. The "normal" Petite Arvine is simpler but very quaffable. The Torrette and the Gamay, two '98s, are both appealing, with their immediate fragrances and still grapey palates, while the barrique-aged Pinot Noir is a little disappointing.

●	Vallée d'Aoste Fumin '97	🍷🍷	4
●	Vallée d'Aoste Gamay '98	🍷	3
○	Vallée d'Aoste Petite Arvine '98	🍷	3
○	Vallée d'Aoste Petite Arvine Vendemmia Tardiva '97	🍷	4
●	Vallée d'Aoste Torrette '98	🍷	3
●	Vallée d'Aoste Pinot Noir Élevé en Barrique '97		4

VILLENEUVE (AO)

RENATO ANSELMET
FRAZ. LA CRETE, 46
11018 VILLENEUVE (AO)
TEL. 0165/95217

Renato Anselmet, a retired Electricity Board technician, has run this small winery since 1978 with the help of his son Giorgio, the cellarmaster at the Cooperativa Onze Communes, and this year they have presented a really excellent wine. With their hectare and a half of vineyards between Saint-Pierre and Villeneuve plus some grapes they acquire, they produce around 12 thousand bottles a year. There are, however, plans for expansion afoot: these regard the cellar, which at the moment is functional if a bit rough-and-ready (the barrique room, though, is made of stone and very charming), and also involve the acquisition of new vineyards which will give the Anselmets, in a couple of years' time, an annual production of some 25 thousand bottles. As we said above, one of this year's three wines won (and very easily) Two Glasses, whereas the other two, an oak-aged Pinot Noir and a traditional Torrette, were not quite so successful. The Chardonnay '98 was fermented and matured in barriques, and the nose signals its qualities. On the palate it is rich and almost velvety, with the wood perfectly blended with the fruit. The Torrette, although simpler, seemed slightly better than the other red, the Pinot Noir, which revealed a not absolutely clean bouquet and a somewhat unbalanced palate where the body isn't big enough to stand up to the excessive wood. We didn't get to try the Torrette Superiore, which is still maturing, or a sweet wine made from semi-dried pinot gris, which had not yet been bottled at the time of our tastings.

○	Vallée d'Aoste Chardonnay Élevé en Fût de Chêne '98	🍷🍷	4
●	Vallée d'Aoste Torrette '98	🍷	3
●	Vallée d'Aoste Pinot Noir Élevé en Fût de Chêne '98		4

OTHER WINERIES

The following producers obtained good scores in our tastings with one or more of their wines:

PROVINCE OF AOSTA

Dino Bonin, Arnad, tel. 0125 966067
Vallée d'Aoste Arnad-Montjovet Sup. '97

Cooperativa La Kiuva, Arnad, tel. 0125/966351
Vallée d'Aoste Arnad-Montjovet '98,
Vallée d'Aoste Petite Arvine '98

Cooperativa Caves des Onze Communes
Aymavilles, tel. 0165/902912
Vallée d'Aoste Müller Thurgau '98,
Vallée d'Aoste Torrette Sup. '97

Enzio Voyat
Chambave, tel. 0166 46139
La Gazzella Moscato '97,
Vino Passito Le Muraglie

Caves Cooperatives de Donnas
Donnas, tel. 0125/82096
Vallée d'Aoste Donnas '96

Diego Curtaz
Gressan, tel. 0165/251079
Vallée d'Aoste Torrette '98

Maison Albert Vevey
Morgex, tel. 0165/808930
Vallée d'Aoste Blanc de Morgex
et de La Salle '98

PIEDMONT

This year Piedmont has won no fewer than 50 Three Glass awards, thus accomplishing the most brilliant feat since the first Guide to Italian Wines was published in 1988. For the first time not even Tuscany comes near to rivaling this performance. Piedmont has made incredibly rapid viticultural progress and its potential is such that the region has every chance of retaining pole position for the next few years. For four years now the harvest has yielded an unbeatable crop, which in the skillful hands of traditional wineries and of the producers from the new generation has given rise to increasingly interesting wines that can compete with the best on the international market. The task of the tasting panel charged with awarding Three Glasses was by no means easy this year; the mediocre vintage represented by the Barolo '95 had to vie with the outstanding vintages for Barbaresco ('96), Barbera ('96 and '97) and Langhe and Monferrato ('97), not to mention the '98 Dolcettos. Even in the case of Barolo, however, with skillful vineyard management and far lower yields per hectare than the upper limit dictated by the regulations, winegrowers have succeeded in obtaining first-rate results. But it was the Barbera which really astounded our tasters. This variety, until a few years ago wrongly considered a poor relation of the celebrated nebbiolo, now plays a vital role in the regions's economy, thanks to the farsightedness of a number of producers, first and foremost Giacomo Bologna. Rigorous selection in the vineyards, very high concentrations and a modern vinification style with an eye to tradition, have all combined to enable this grape to yield great wines.

The adaptability of barbera is also evident in wines which are the result of a blend of several varieties, so this grape is increasingly used to obtain first-class cuvées. The Langhe Rossos of Bruno Nada, Conterno Fantino and Nicoletta Bocca, and the Monferrato Rosso of Sonvico della Barbatella are convincing proof of how the barbera grape can endow wines with great balance and personality. This wonderful region's great good fortune, especially in the area comprising the provinces of Cuneo, Asti and Alessandria, is its extraordinary number of grape varieties. While only a few years ago international grapes like cabernet, syrah and merlot were considered indispensable, there is now a general awareness of the great potential of native varieties, which accords well with the recognition that the vineyard is the essential foundation for the production of great wines. Of course it's not all smooth sailing: in these last few months the difficult situation of the moscato grape and of Asti has further deteriorated, while in some other winegrowing areas (Gattinara, Ghemme and Canavese) no Three Glass wine has emerged, but on the whole, oenological Piedmont is in flourishing health. What will happen next year, when we shall have the wines of three truly historic vintages ('96, '97 and '98) to review, we cannot even begin to imagine.

AGLIANO TERME (AT)

Roberto Ferraris

Via Dogliano, 33
14041 Agliano Terme (AT)
tel. 0141/954234

This small estate, bought in 1922 by Stefano Ferraris, father of the present owner Achille, has earned a place in the Guide with its Barbera d'Asti Nobbio '97, a full-bodied wine with plenty of character. The cellar obtains its raw material from seven hectares of vineyard, producing around 15 thousand bottles annually. The property includes arable land as well as vines and is at present run by Achille, his wife Bruna Molinari and one of their three children, Roberto, who divides his time between the cellar, the vineyard and marketing. The output consists mainly of Barbera, with some Grignolino and Dolcetto completing the range, while technical advice comes from the oenologist Giuliano Noè. The Nobbio '97, the Barbera in question, shows an intense garnet-ruby color with a decidedly dense rim; the broad, pleasantly ripe nose is enhanced by a well-judged use of wood and offers hints of berry jam with toasty, spicy notes. The powerful palate tends towards a broad softness and is underpinned by noble tannins and substantial alcohol which lend punch to the long, fruity and spicy finish.

● Barbera d'Asti Nobbio '97	▼▼	3*

AGLIANO TERME (AT)

Agostino Pavia e Figli

Fraz. Bologna, 33
14041 Agliano Terme (AT)
tel. 0141/954125

This estate, owned by Agostino, Giuseppe and Mauro Pavia, is in the heart of the most sought-after area for Barbera d'Asti. And it is Barbera d'Asti which is the keynote of the winery's range. Three versions were presented this year, and with a vintage like '97 we were frankly expecting a better performance from this promising producer. As a general conclusion, we can say no more than that the wines are correctly made and display good varietal character but are not in any way memorable. The Blina, with a brilliant, medium intense color, is fresh and fruity on the nose with the typical note of cherry well to the fore, while the palate is rounded, fresh, and clean easy drinking, with the right fruit and body for a medium-structured wine. The Barbera d'Asti Moliss, again '97, is similar to the Blina, but less full and intense, with a marked angularity due to the acidity. However the biggest disappointment comes from what should be the jewel of the winery, the barrique-aged Barbera d'Asti Superiore La Marescialla '97. Medium-deep in color, it has a still closed nose and a not entirely flawless bouquet, with burnt notes detracting from the vanilla of the wood; the palate is rather meagre and distinctly lacking in balance due to the acidity. Finally, the '98 vintage of the Grignolino d'Asti, another traditional wine from this cellar, is somewhat faded in color, with a typical nose disclosing geraniums; the palate offers good fruit but is on the lean side.

● Barbera d'Asti Bricco Blina '97	▼	3
● Barbera d'Asti Moliss '97	▼	3
● Barbera d'Asti Sup. La Marescialla '97	▼	4
● Grignolino d'Asti '98		3
● Barbera d'Asti Sup. La Marescialla '96	▽▽	4
● Barbera d'Asti Bricco Blina '96	▽	2
● Barbera d'Asti Sup. La Marescialla '95	▽	4

AGLIANO TERME (AT)

TENUTA GARETTO
S. S. ASTI MARE, 30
14041 AGLIANO TERME (AT)
TEL. 0141/954068

This farm, surrounded by about 12 hectares of vineyard to which four more will soon be added, has belonged to the Garetto family since 1849. It lies in one of the most prized zones for the barbera grape, which is why this variety is grown in just over 80% of the estate's vineyards. The rest was planted in the '70s and includes grignolino, freisa, ruché, dolcetto and cortese, which will gradually be phased out by the young owner, Alessandro. As with other producers of the Asti area, the determination to move with the times, replacing the traditional demijohn with bottles, has rapidly taken over here, unhindered by clashes between the generations. In 1996, when he was only 21, Alessandro took over the management of the estate, assisted by Lorenzo Quinterno, an oenologist from Canale. His decision gradually to give up the sale of bulk wine and limit the number of wines produced, restoring to Barbera the right of seniority which it deserves, represented a turning-point for the estate. Yields in the vineyards were restricted and vinification carried out according to modern criteria (hygiene in the cellar, temperature control and use of the barrique). Today Alessandro produces three different versions of Barbera d'Asti, which make up only around 30 thousand bottles a year: Tra Neuit e Dì, half of which is matured in stainless steel and the other half in large barrels, In Pectore, aged in 25-hectoliter Slavonian oak barrels, and Favà, barrique-aged for 13 months. The easy drinkability of the first and the elegant austerity of the second contrast with the powerful fruity aromas and inviting harmonious flavors of the third. The Chardonnay too, fermented and aged in new barriques for nine months without racking, is very well-balanced on both nose and palate.

● Barbera d'Asti Sup. Favà '97	🍷🍷	4
● Barbera d'Asti Sup. In Pectore '97	🍷🍷	3*
● Barbera d'Asti Tra Neuit e Dì '97	🍷	3
○ Piemonte Chardonnay Diversamente '98	🍷	4

AGLIÈ (TO)

CIECK
S.DA BARDESONO
FRAZ. S. GRATO
10011 AGLIÈ (TO)
TEL. 0124/32225 - 0124/330522

Remo Falconieri and Lodovico Bardesono are presenting two reds and four different Erbaluce di Caluso wines: the barrique-aged Calliope, the Vigna Misobolo, the San Giorgio Spumante Brut and the Passito Alladium. The first, an intense straw yellow, discloses a broad, well-evolved nose with scents of white flowers, vanilla, tropical fruit and fennel; the palate (soft, fruity, firm and progressive) has a bitterish note on the finish. The pale straw-colored Vigna Misobolo '98 displays fermentation-derived aromas of apple and banana on the nose; the palate leads smoothly into the finish with fresh notes on the aftertaste. The Alladium Passito '94 has a luminous amber-gold hue and a complex bouquet offering soft, mature tones of dried fruit and raisins with heady notes, while the sweet, medium-intense palate offers a lingering finish that mirrors the bouquet. The San Giorgio Brut, straw-colored with greenish tints, offers a fruity, floral bouquet with a certain finesse; the palate is enjoyable, although exuberantly fizzy. The Cieck Rosso '97 is a pleasantly rustic wine whose good concentration is evident from the intense garnet-ruby color. The nose reveals hints of hay and coffee with jammy notes, while the vigorous palate is rather lively in character. The Canavese Rosso, derived from neretto di San Giorgio, offers pleasant, faintly forward aromas while the palate, although aggressive, is perfect for offsetting a rich meal.

○ Erbaluce di Caluso Calliope '97	🍷🍷	3*
○ Caluso Passito Alladium Vigneto Runc '94	🍷	4
● Canavese Rosso '98	🍷	3
● Canavese Rosso Cieck '97	🍷	3
○ Erbaluce di Caluso Spumante Brut S. Giorgio	🍷	4
○ Erbaluce di Caluso Vigna Misobolo '98	🍷	3
○ Erbaluce di Caluso Spumante Brut S. Giorgio '91	🍷🍷 (white glasses)	4

ALBA (CN)

CERETTO
LOC. S. CASSIANO, 34
12051 ALBA (CN)
TEL. 0173/282582

The Ceretto company comprises the estates of Rossana (Alba), Blangé (Vezza and Castellinaldo), Arbarei (Albaretto Torre), Bernardina Monsordo and I Vignaioli di Santo Stefano (under the management of Ceretto). It would take at least two pages of the Guide to give an exhaustive description of all the wines produced by these estates and so we must limit our evaluations. The Dolcetto Rossana '98 is intense and fruity, with only faintly perceptible notes of alcohol on the nose. The Blangé '98 is as amazing as ever: the number of bottles released for sale continues to rise every year but the quality, unbelievably, maintains its high level. Greenish gold in hue, slightly effervescent, with honeyed scents and vivid, lingering flowery notes, followed by a fragrant palate with flavors of apple and white plum: this is the recipe for a successful wine. The house Metodo Classico, the La Bernardina Brut '94, which has proved to be one of the best versions ever, deserves a good write-up: it is a characterful wine with a very fine perlage, a color tending towards gold and a fresh, citrus-flavored drinkability with an impressive structure underlying its softness. This superb Spumante was a hair's breadth short of Three Glasses. Another good wine is the Cabernet La Bernardina '96, which promises well for the future: we were impressed by its warmth and power, the nose offers just the right herbaceous and spicy notes, and it's substantial enough in body to be the envy of certain much-touted Bordeaux wines. The Chardonnay La Bernardina '97 is rich and intensely varietal in character, although we would have liked a little more grip.

● Dolcetto d'Alba Rossana '98	🍷🍷	4
○ La Bernardina Brut '94	🍷🍷	5
● Langhe Cabernet La Bernardina '96	🍷🍷	6
○ Langhe Arneis Blangé '98	🍷	4
○ Langhe Chardonnay La Bernardina '97	🍷	6
● Langhe Cabernet La Bernardina '95	🍷🍷 (outline)	6
○ Langhe Chardonnay La Bernardina '96	🍷🍷 (outline)	5
● Monsordo Rosso La Bernardina '93	🍷🍷 (outline)	6
○ La Bernardina Brut '93	🍷 (outline)	5
● Monsordo Syrah La Bernardina '95	🍷 (outline)	6

ALBA (CN)

LANO
S.DA BASSO, 38
FRAZ. S. ROCCO SENO D'ELVIO
12051 ALBA (CN)
TEL. 0173/286958

Gianluigi Lano's story is similar to that of many other young growers of the Langhe. Having left the family home at an early age to become a factory worker, he decided in 1992 to return to the farm and take up his father's work. Now aged 39, he has perforce limited experience, with the first bottles dating from 1993, but with help from the family and his wife Daniela Marcarino, and backed by the technical assistance of consultant Gianfranco Cordero, he does a brilliant job of running his six hectares under vine. The old vineyards, grassed over and cultivated following the most natural methods possible, are divided between San Rocco Seno d'Elvio, Treiso and Altavilla. Our only criticism is that Gianluigi perhaps expends time and energy in attempting too great a variety of labels, although it has to be admitted that quality is at a more or less constant level throughout the vast range. At the top of the line is the Fondo Prà '97, a Barbera aged in partly new barriques, which with its wonderful, harmonious, velvety finish, the depth and complexity of its bouquet recalling cherries and damp earth, outperforms the less powerful and balanced '96 version. We were also impressed by the Dolcetto Ronchella, a selection of the estate's best dolcetto grapes; it displays clean and inviting notes of ripe fruit (blackberry jam), with a good lingering softness. The Barbaresco offers a complex nose (dark chocolate, tobacco, spice and red fruit) but falls away somewhat on the palate which, although pleasingly long, is still over-rough. The Favorita and the Barbera are both enjoyable easy drinking, the Barbera slightly less so. The still Freisa is an interesting wine, full-bodied and fragrant, but unfortunately not made every year.

● Barbera d'Alba Fondo Prà '97	🍷🍷	4
● Dolcetto d'Alba Ronchella '98	🍷🍷	3*
● Barbaresco '96	🍷	5
● Barbera d'Alba Fondo Prà '96	🍷	4
● Dolcetto d'Alba '98	🍷	3
○ Langhe Favorita '98	🍷	3
● Langhe Freisa '97	🍷	3
● Barbera d'Alba '97		3

ALBA (CN)

Pio Cesare
Via Cesare Balbo, 6
12051 Alba (CN)
tel. 0173/440386

This estate's most important wines, the Barolo and Barbaresco crus, have a feature in common even though they come from widely differing vintages: they reveal a new-styled softness and a smooth density on the nose deriving from an advanced stage of grape ripeness. In the Barbaresco Bricco '95 this is even more marked, to the extent that the berry aromas have an almost overripe note; the color is a dark garnet while the diffused warmth on the palate merges excellently with the generous, lightly-textured structure. The use of oak seems to be increasingly successful, probably the result of a blend of old and new wood. The Barolo from the Ornato vineyard in Serralunga is ample and voluptuous with a rounded harmony which makes it enjoyable to drink now; of an invitingly deep color, it offers hints of black cherry and herbs. Altogether it is much better than what we thought possible from the '95 vintage. The basic version, too, is among the most reliable of its kind. This Barolo, rich in nuances, does not have the concentration of the cru but echoes its finesse, perfect correspondence of nose and palate and satisfying length. The basic version of the Barbaresco performed rather disapppointingly considering the promising conditions of the '96 vintage: it is technically above reproach and offers interesting aromas, but the palate lacks character. We were impressed by the Barbera Fides with its opulent generosity and complex, intriguing array of perfumes. The less demanding Nebbiolo, Dolcetto and Barbera are also successful, while the Chardonnay PiodiLei is, as usual, an excellent wine.

●	Barbaresco Bricco '95	▼▼	6
●	Barbera d'Alba Fides '96	▼▼	5
●	Barolo '95	▼▼	6
●	Barolo Ornato '95	▼▼	6
○	Langhe Chardonnay PiodiLei '97	▼▼	5
●	Barbera d'Alba '97	▼	4
●	Dolcetto d'Alba '98	▼	4
●	Langhe Rosso Il Nebbio '98	▼	4
●	Nebbiolo d'Alba '97	▼	4
○	Piemonte Chardonnay L'Altro '98	▼	4
●	Barolo Ornato '85	▽▽▽	6
●	Barolo Ornato '89	▽▽▽	6
●	Barbaresco Bricco '93	▽▽	6
●	Barolo Ornato '90	▽▽	6
●	Barolo Ornato '93	▽▽	6

ALBA (CN)

Poderi Colla
Fraz. S. Rocco Seno d'Elvio, 82
12051 Alba (CN)
tel. 0173/290148

The Cascine Drago property, where the Colla family have their offices, cellar and museum, is the heart of this estate. It comprises 25 hectares, of which 10 are under vine, overlooking an attractive landscape of vineyards, woods, old farmhouses and quiet country lanes: an out-of-the-way location, hardly cheek to jowl with the celebrated crus of the Langhe, but one which exercises extraordinary charm. It is the birthplace of Piedmont's first "super red" table wine, the Bricco del Drago, created in 1969 by Luciano De Giacomi from 85% dolcetto and 15% nebbiolo. The '96 version is garnet-ruby in color, austere on the nose, with notes of wild cherry and undergrowth, and long, powerful and wonderfully robust on the palate. We liked the Nebbiolo d'Alba '97 with its scents of violet and pine, and the Barbera '97 from the Roncaglia estate in Barbaresco is even better. It is deep ruby in color and fruity on the nose, with a very characteristic hint of spice, and there's a long, plummy finish on the palate well sustained by a vigorous bite of acidity. The estate's top wine is the Barbaresco Tenuta Roncaglia: aged in partly new large oak barrels, it has elegance as its keynote, in keeping with the estate style. It's the quintessence of a Langhe wine, full of inner strength, with noble aromas of red berries and violets and a mouth-filling, balanced palate well-supported by tannins which still need to mature. Less balance is shown by the Barolo Bussia Dardi Le Rose '95, which is feeling the effects of a difficult year: it is vigorous but could do with more fruit. The Sanrocco '98, a blend of pinot nero, riesling and chardonnay, is the best version we have ever tasted, with fragrant spicy aromas and an enjoyable smokiness on the finish. Lastly, the Bonmé, an aromatized moscato with hints of tropical fruit, is a wine that always captivates.

●	Barbaresco Tenuta Roncaglia '96	▼▼	6
●	Langhe Bricco del Drago '96	▼▼	4
○	Bonmé	▼▼	4
●	Barolo Bussia Dardi Le Rose '95	▼▼	6
●	Barbera d'Alba Tenuta Roncaglia '97	▼▼	4
○	Langhe Sanrocco '98	▼	3
●	Nebbiolo d'Alba '97	▼	4
●	Barbaresco Tenuta Roncaglia '93	▽▽	5
●	Barbaresco Tenuta Roncaglia '95	▽▽	5
●	Barolo Bussia Dardi Le Rose '93	▽▽	5
●	Barolo Bussia Dardi Le Rose '94	▽	5
●	Langhe Bricco del Drago '95	▽	4

ALBA (CN)

PRUNOTTO
REG. S. CASSIANO, 4/G
12051 ALBA (CN)
TEL. 0173/280017

The sensation caused by last year's version has been repeated by the Barbera d'Asti Costamiòle '97. Its stature is heralded by the color, a dense garnet-ruby with a compact rim; the bouquet is deep and rich, yet refined and harmonious, delectably redolent of berries both red and black mingling with lively notes of pepper and tobacco in a broad framework which reveals traces of smoke and menthol. In the mouth it is very concentrated, broad, solid and unhesitating right up to the wonderfully long finish, lent depth by noble, powerful tannins. The Barolo Bussia, another premium wine, is concentrated and youthful to look at: the nose displays black currant, blackberry and toasted coffee with intriguing hints of undergrowth, and is followed by a rich, sumptuous palate well supported by a firm phenolic structure and ending on a beautifully lingering finish. The Barbaresco Bric Turot, an entirely new wine from this estate which belongs to the Antinoris, is of a dense garnet-ruby color; vivid hints of faded violet emerge over soft, creamy raspberry notes, while the palate is deep, rich and generous with very mellow tannins reappearing on the long finish of violets and caramel. The Barbera Pian Romualdo, deep garnet in hue, displays fresh notes of cherry and black currant over spicy, earthy nuances; the substantial palate has a faintly perceptible acidity, powerful tannins and a lingering licorice finish. The Dolcetto Mosesco is deep-colored; the slightly rustic nose is swiftly redeemed by a sumptuous entry on the palate, which is broad and vigorous in character. A series of very reliable basic wines ends the range: a bold Barbera, and then a Barolo and a Barbaresco, both balanced and varietal wines.

● Barbera d'Asti Costamiòle '97	🍷🍷🍷	6
● Barbaresco Bric Turot '96	🍷🍷	6
● Barbera d'Alba Pian Romualdo '97	🍷🍷	4
● Barolo Bussia '95	🍷🍷	6
● Dolcetto d'Alba Mosesco '98	🍷🍷	4
● Barbaresco '96	🍷	5
● Barbera d'Alba '97	🍷	3
● Barolo '95	🍷	5
● Barbera d'Asti Costamiòle '96	YYY	6
● Barolo Bussia '85	YYY	6
● Barolo Cannubi '85	YYY	6
● Barbaresco Montestefano '93	YY	5
● Barolo Bussia '93	YY	6
● Nebbiolo d'Alba Occhetti '96	YY	4

ALFIANO NATTA (AL)

TENUTA CASTELLO DI RAZZANO
FRAZ. CASARELLO, 2
15021 ALFIANO NATTA (AL)
TEL. 0141/922124 - 0141/922426

Augusto Olearo, the owner of this estate, is an enthusiastic promoter of Monferrrato and its wines, particularly Barbera, the real protagonist in these parts. To this end he often organizes cultural and artistic events, attracting a large public. Only estate-grown grapes are vinified here and the 35 hectares of vineyard are cultivated without the use of weed-killers, chemical fertilizer or pesticides. Of the total output of 150 thousand bottles, a good 100 thousand contain Barbera, and it is a Barbera, the Vigna del Beneficio, that has earned Two Glasses. The grapes are picked late, in the second half of October; maceration on the skins lasts from 25 to 30 days and the wine is aged in Allier oak barriques for one year. The wine is an extraordinary dense dark ruby in color with aromas of sour cherry, plum, leather and vanilla; rich and intense on the palate, it is enlivened by a characteristic streak of acidity, with the wood still slightly over-evident on the finish. We liked the Barbera Campasso, also made from a late harvest but aged in traditional oak barrels. Of an intense ruby hue, it has aromas of plum, very ripe cherry, coffee and resin; the well-structured palate is broad, round, meaty and mouth-filling. La Leona is a Barbera to be enjoyed now all through the meal: it is oak-aged for three months and is correctly made, fruity and vinous. L'Onero, made from pinot nero and presented for the first time, still needs some adjusting.

● Barbera d'Asti Sup. Vigna del Beneficio '97	🍷🍷	4
● Barbera d'Asti La Leona '98	🍷	2*
● Barbera d'Asti Sup. Campasso '97	🍷	3
● Monferrato Rosso Onero '97		5
● Barbera d'Asti Sup. Campasso Vigna di Ca' Farotto '96	Y	3
● Barbera d'Asti Sup. Vigna del Beneficio '96	Y	4

ALICE BEL COLLE (AL)

Ca' Bianca
Reg. Spagna, 58
15010 Alice Bel Colle (AL)
tel. 0144/55843

Founded at the beginning of the '50s near Alice Bel Colle, Ca' Bianca recently became part of the Gruppo Italiano Vini. The area under vine is about 40 hectares, but there is a land reclassification plan under which ten more will be added. The estate can also count on three more hectares at La Morra in the Langhe, and vineyards in the Gavi zone, and winemaker Marco Galeazzo has a fully equipped modern cellar to work with. Half of the 500 thousand bottles produced annually are Barbera, the rest are Dolcetto, Moscato and Brachetto. The wines we tasted were carefully executed and of a high standard. The Barbera, barrique-aged for eight months, offers aromas of coffee, vanilla, black cherry and raspberry; the acidity typical of this variety marries well with the succulent fruit on a warm, intense palate. The Barolo displays a medium-intense ruby hue; scents of faded violet, rose and ripe plum emerge on the nose, while the well-structured, mouth-filling, fruity palate leads onto a soft, dry, rather short finish. The Gavi, 20% late-harvested and barrique-aged, is straw-colored with a greenish tinge; the nose offers hints of ripe fruit and white flowers with underlying woody notes; it is followed by a corresponding, rich, intense palate. The Moscato is a delicious wine with aromas of citrus, sage and tomato leaf; in the mouth it is rich, long, perfectly balanced and sweet but not cloying.

●	Barbera d'Asti '97	🍷🍷	3*
●	Barolo '95	🍷	5
○	Gavi '98	🍷	3*
○	Moscato d'Asti '98	🍷	3

ASTI

Rovero F.lli
Fraz. S. Marzanotto, 216
14050 Asti
tel. 0141/592460

With so many vineyards in enviable sites crowding the charming slopes of San Marzanotto and Mongardino, it seems a mystery that this area, so full of potential, should so far have yielded such disappointing results. The reason is that modern production strategies are making little headway here and the old demand for quantity is still the dominant factor. However, the Rovero brothers have proved that they can combine respect for local tradition with intelligent innovation. One example is the Monferrato Bianco Sauvignon '98, of an intense straw color, which reveals typical varietal aromas mingling with crusty, yeasty notes; the palate is impressive for its rich fruit, fatness and lingering finish. The Monferrato Rosso Pinot Nero '97 represents another departure from tradition: it shows a good, deep color, and wood to the fore at the first impact on the nose, with black currant following; the palate is round, well-balanced and fairly substantial but freshness is lacking. The Monferrato Rosso Cabernet '96 has a lovely deep color and a strongly varietal nose in which sweet pepper is the keynote; green tones also dominate the palate, accompanied by an astringent sensation; the wine has good body and a medium long finish. Moving on to the traditional sector, we have the Grignolino d'Asti Vigneto La Casalina: the Roveros do very well with this kind of characteristically varietal wine. The '98 vintage is intense in color, with flowery aromas (rose) and a satisfying palate with the typical astringency. The Barbera d'Asti Vigneto Gustin '97 is an excellent example of a modern Barbera, fresh and full-flavored with plenty of fruit; it has an intense color, fruity aromas and good straightforward drinkability.

○	Monferrato Bianco Sauvignon '98	🍷🍷	3*
●	Barbera d'Asti Vigneto Gustin '97	🍷	3
●	Grignolino d'Asti Vigneto La Casalina '98	🍷	3
●	Monferrato Rosso Cabernet '96	🍷	4
●	Monferrato Rosso Pinot Nero '97	🍷	3
●	Barbera d'Asti Rouvé '95	🍸	4
●	Barbera d'Asti Rouvé '96	🍸	4

BARBARESCO (CN)

Ca' Romé - Romano Marengo

Via Rabajà, 36
12050 Barbaresco (CN)
tel. 0173/635126

The Marengo family estate is still undergoing the slow process of restructuring, the most important aspect being the acquisition of vineyards, and indeed almost the entire output of Ca' Romé now comes from their own vines. Young Giuseppe's numerous trips abroad to study top wineries ensure that cellar practices are kept up to date: the number of barriques is increasing and the temperature is always controlled during fermentation. Paola's passion for wine-making and her father Romano's experience complete the picture of a family committed to creating wines faithful to their native territory but also capable of competing on the international market. This year we found the Barbera and the Barbaresco Maria di Brun particularly interesting. The first has the advantage of the splendid '97 vintage, and is deep and concentrated in color with broad, fruity aromas mingling with vanilla followed by a warm, lingering palate. The second reveals the substance of the great wines of Alba, with a garnet-red color and aromas of red fruit with balsamic nuances; the palate is concentrated and already harmonious: Two Glasses to each of them, thoroughly deserved. The Barolo Ceretta, complex and elegant, scores only slightly less. The basic Barbaresco and the Barolo Rapet earn points for being clean, correctly-made wines, even if they offer nothing out of the ordinary in taste and aroma, and the Da Pruvé, a classic blend of 80% nebbiolo and 20% barbera, is in the same category.

● Barbaresco Maria di Brun '96	🍷🍷	6
● Barbera d'Alba La Gamberaja '97	🍷🍷	5
● Barbaresco '96	🍷	6
● Barolo Rapet '95	🍷	6
● Barolo Vigna Ceretta '95	🍷	6
● Da Pruvé '97	🍷	5
● Barbaresco Maria di Brun '95	♀♀	5
● Barbera d'Alba La Gamberaja '96	♀	4
● Barolo Rapet '93	♀	5

BARBARESCO (CN)

Cascina Luisin

Via Rabajà, 23
12050 Barbaresco (CN)
tel. 0173/635154

The great vintages of '96 and '97 have really given of their best in these two outstanding versions of Barbera Asili from the Minuto family. The '96 is impressive, but its successor of the following year, besides confirming the Minutos' skill as wine-makers, surpasses it in finesse. The dense garnet hue of this '97 heralds a rich texture; the bouquet is elegant, broad and complex, displaying faint mineral notes, clearly-defined hints of red and black berries and soft minty and custardy undertones. Robust tannins and warm, powerful alcohol on the superb, concentrated palate enhance its broad progress and lend depth to a long finish reminiscent of fruit and cocoa. Another excellent wine is the Barbaresco Sorì Paolin, of a ruby-garnet color; the broad, enticing nose offers ripe notes of leather and jam which mingle harmoniously with the smooth oak-derived aromas; in the mouth a firm phenolic structure lends density to the broad texture, leading into a long, lingering finish. The Barbaresco Rabajà, almost its equal in quality, has a good deep color and displays finesse on the nose, with hints of wild berries, almond and violet; the substantial palate has strong tannins; caramel and green notes appear on the finish. The excellent Barbera Asili '98 is rich in hue with distinct notes of black currant and blackberry; the full-bodied palate has an enlivening vibrancy which in no way mars its balance. Lastly, the Dolcetto Trifüla is pleasantly rustic in character. Our congratulations to this family which, well out of the limelight, has by dint of steady hard work achieved its aim of creating wines of international stature!

● Barbera d'Alba Asili Barrique '97	🍷🍷🍷	4
● Barbaresco Rabajà '96	🍷🍷	5
● Barbaresco Sorì Paolin '96	🍷🍷	5
● Barbera d'Alba Asili '98	🍷🍷	3*
● Barbera d'Alba Asili Barrique '96	🍷🍷	4
● Dolcetto d'Alba Trifüla '98	🍷	3*
● Barbaresco Rabajà '95	♀♀	5
● Barbaresco Sorì Paolin '95	♀	5

BARBARESCO (CN)

TENUTE CISA ASINARI
DEI MARCHESI DI GRESY
VIA RABAJÀ, 43
12050 BARBARESCO (CN)
TEL. 0173/635222

The opportunity of making a great Barbaresco and exploiting to the full the potential of his vineyards was one not to be missed, and for Alberto di Gresy the '96 vintage was the jumping-off point for a new bid for quality. In our opinion the house style, which is refined while remaining faithful to tradition, is not changing, but from our tastings it is evident that the wines are again beginning to show their former distinctive personality. The Campo Gros, which contains the very best the Martinenga vineyard has to offer, is of a very high standard; the garnet color has a typical mature tone, while the bouquet discloses enticing complex aromas of flowers and licorice; gradual unfolding of flavor is the key to the development on the palate, which is well underpinned by a vigorous and lasting tannic component. While the Camp Gros represents the benign austerity of the nebbiolo grape, the basic version has a more decisive, concentrated character. It is an intense garnet in color, offering dense, dark fruit on the nose; in the mouth it opens out to reveal length and balance while maintaining a supple progress well supported by the tannins. The more "modernist" Gajun is not so demanding, but it lacks the richness of the other two. We were encouraged by the performance of the Virtus, made from cabernet and barbera, a warm red whose most outstanding virtue is the articulated flavor that more than makes up for a certain lightness of body. The Nebbiolo Langhe '98 is subtle and delightful, but we were a little disappointed by the Villa Martis, a blend of barbera and nebbiolo with a rather short palate. Of the whites, we liked the green, crisp Sauvignon and the fresh Chardonnay '98, but the Chardonnay Gresy '97 is the prisoner of its oak.

● Barbaresco Camp Gros '96	🍷🍷	6
● Barbaresco Martinenga '96	🍷🍷	6
● Langhe Rosso Virtus '96	🍷🍷	5
● Barbaresco Gaiun '96	🍷	6
● Dolcetto d'Alba Monte Aribaldo '98	🍷	3
○ Langhe Chardonnay '98	🍷	3
○ Langhe Chardonnay Gresy '97	🍷	5
● Langhe Nebbiolo Martinenga '98	🍷	4
● Langhe Rosso Villa Martis '96	🍷	4
○ Langhe Sauvignon '98	🍷	4
● Barbaresco Gaiun '85	YYY	6
● Barbaresco Camp Gros '90	YY	6
● Barbaresco Gaiun '95	YY	6
● Barbaresco Martinenga '95	YY	5

BARBARESCO (CN)

GIUSEPPE CORTESE
VIA RABAJÀ, 35
12050 BARBARESCO (CN)
TEL. 0173/635131

The extension of the cellar is almost completed, which will mean that every stage of production can be more rationally organized, from fermentation to bottling and subsequent storage. Piercarlo Cortese, flanked by his father Giuseppe and his mother Rosella, is in charge of every aspect of production, from vineyard management to vinification; every year he turns out wines that are, at the very least, good, and, in the case of the Barbaresco made from grapes grown in the prized Rabajà vineyard, achieve real excellence. The Chardonnay '98, although not without varietal character, is not on a par with the rest of the range and therefore only gets a mention. The Dolcetto is pleasantly grapey and fragrant, with acidity and tannins in good balance. The basic Barbera unfolds on the nose with fresh, fruity, lingering aromas; the palate is slightly diminished by a rather lean structure. The barrique-aged Barbera Morassina, dark ruby in color, offers notes of oak-derived vanilla, which, in the mouth, help to soften the acidity typical of this variety. The Nebbiolo is not just the younger brother of Barbaresco but displays its own appealing personality on both nose and palate: alcohol, acidity and tannins underpin well-defined notes of faded rose and licorice. The Barbaresco Rabajà is of a ruby hue verging on garnet; the red berry fragrance, while not broad, is clearly defined, while the palate reveals robust tannins and an imposing structure.

● Barbaresco Rabajà '96	🍷🍷	5
● Barbera d'Alba '97	🍷	3
● Barbera d'Alba Morassina '97	🍷	4
● Dolcetto d'Alba Trifolera '98	🍷	3
● Langhe Nebbiolo '97	🍷	4
○ Langhe Chardonnay '98		3
● Barbaresco Rabajà '95	YY	5
● Barbera d'Alba Morassina '96	Y	4

★ ★ Gaja

Via Torino, 36/A
12050 Barbaresco (CN)
tel. 0173/635158

Once again the nebbiolo grape plays the leading role in the superb range presented by Gaja. Wines like the Chardonnay, the Sauvignon, the Sito Moresco blend and the Barbera score as well as ever, but the Cabernet Darmagi, by dint of power and finesse, is the only one to hold its own against the regal progress of the classic Langhe greats. The Barolo Sperss is almost arrogantly successful in its reaction to the uncertainties of the '95 vintage: its concentrated color has by now achieved legendary status, while the intriguing bouquet offers contrasting, wonderfully deep aromas. The powerful extracts and tannins just add to the pleasure of the palate, which is a model of solidity; the oak articulates the progression of the flavor, at the same time allowing scope for a perfect correspondence to the nose and a mouth-filling density. The Barbaresco Sorì San Lorenzo offers a more mineral note on the nose: the complex bouquet opens out with perfect harmony while its rich tonality has an all-enveloping quality repeated on the palate, whose dynamic force unfolds in an irresistible crescendo leading up with wonderful balance to the finish. The Barbaresco Costa Russi is warm and voluptuous; the ripeness of the fruit seems almost Mediterranean and the bouquet is delightfully seasoned by hints of herbs and spices; the flavor develops along firmly expressive and highly satisfying lines, with tannins beating time while softness embellishes. The basic Barbaresco is a successful wine and the fascinating Sorì Tildìn is riper than ever before.

●	Barbaresco Costa Russi '96	▼▼▼	6
●	Barbaresco Sorì S. Lorenzo '96	▼▼▼	6
●	Barolo Sperss '95	▼▼▼	6
●	Langhe Darmagi '96	▼▼▼	6
●	Barbaresco '96	▼▼	6
●	Barbaresco Sorì Tildìn '96	▼▼	6
○	Langhe Chardonnay Gaia & Rey '97	▼▼	6
●	Barbaresco '94	▽▽▽	6
●	Barbaresco Costa Russi '95	▽▽▽	6
●	Barbaresco Sorì S. Lorenzo '95	▽▽▽	6
●	Barbaresco Sorì Tildìn '93	▽▽▽	6
●	Barolo Sperss '93	▽▽▽	6
○	Chardonnay Gaia & Rey '94	▽▽▽	6
●	Langhe Darmagi '94	▽▽▽	6

I Paglieri

Via Rabajà, 8
12050 Barbaresco (CN)
tel. 0173/635109

The shrewd Alfredo Roagna is still one of the mainstays of wine-making in the Langhe. In over 20 years of activity he has seen plenty of experimenting, some turning out successfully and some ending in ignominious failure. His severe notions about crus and riservas, which he has not seen fit to change, have not made him very popular with his fellow producers, so, from his farmhouse retreat in Barbaresco, he looks after his 14 hectares with his son Luca and other members of the family. This year, with the help of the '95, '96 and '97 harvests, they have presented a first-class range of wines. In this traditional list, where the great Langhe varieties reign almost supreme, the Solea, made mainly from barrique-fermented Chardonnay, is a real rarity. The '97 vintage, while preserving a strong mineral note which makes it immediately recognizable, is less creamy and harmonious on the palate than the '96. Neither does the Barolo La Rocca e La Pira '95, with its harsh tannic component, soar to great heights. With the Opera Prima and the two Barbarescos things begin to look up. The former, an assemblage of barbera and nebbiolo from different vintages, offers a complex nose and a long, smooth finish dominated by tobacco and spice. The Barbaresco '96 mingles balsamic aromas with a fragrance of dried flowers, and the palate, with its remarkably well-articulated flavors and rounded tannins, is even more intriguing. The Barbaresco Crichët Pajé, once again a DOCG after 18 years' absence, is the real "grand cru" of the estate. A beautifully intense garnet color heralds a fine, complex nose revealing notes of violet and licorice, and a long and velvety palate.

●	Barbaresco '96	▼▼	6
●	Barbaresco Crichët Pajé '96	▼▼	6
●	Opera Prima XIII	▼▼	5
●	Barolo La Rocca e La Pira '95	▼	6
○	Langhe Solea '97	▼	5
●	Barbaresco Ris. '90	▽▽	6
●	Barbaresco Ris. '93	▽▽	6
●	Barolo La Rocca e La Pira Ris. '93	▽▽	6
●	Crichët Pajé '88	▽▽	6
●	Crichët Pajé '89	▽▽	6
●	Barbaresco '93	▽	6
●	Barbaresco '95	▽	6
●	Barolo La Rocca e La Pira '93	▽	6
●	Opera Prima XII	▽	5

BARBARESCO (CN)

MOCCAGATTA
VIA RABAJÀ, 24
12050 BARBARESCO (CN)
TEL. 0173/635152 - 0173/635228

The Minuto brothers are back in the forefront with two stunning wines on which, as soon as they had first-rate material to work with, they were able to lavish all their renowned skill and long experience in wine-making. The bottles in question are the Barbaresco Bric Balin and the Barbera Basarin, two wines as different in expression as they are alike in the happy combination of factors which called them into being. Originating from two outstanding harvests, they were vinified with the most up-to-date techniques and aged in new barriques to enhance their varietal character and captivating density. The Barbaresco shows admirable restraint: the impact on the nose is gentle, then expands and gains in complexity, as flowery nuances with spicy notes and red fruit are emphasized by the sweet oak; the entry on the palate is smooth and reassuring, with the flavor growing in intensity as it develops and the tannins playing the lead on the rich, significant finish. The Barbera is more immediate in character: its vitality is evident in the deep ruby color and the profusion of aromas in continual evolution; acidity is at the center of the wonderfully mouth-filling palate. The Moccagatta range is further graced by the Barbaresco Cole, which for the last couple of vintages has been improved by maturation in new oak: its intense color, attractive liveliness on the nose and good density on the palate are the ideal combination for a red of no great complexity which is however highly enjoyable. The standard Barbaresco Basarin earns One Glass: although the nose is not flawlessly balanced, the palate shows impressive structure.

●	Barbaresco Cole '96	🍷🍷	6
●	Barbaresco Bric Balin '96	🍷🍷	6
●	Barbera d'Alba Basarin '97	🍷🍷	5
●	Barbaresco Basarin '96	🍷	6
●	Barbera d'Alba '98	🍷	4
○	Langhe Chardonnay '98	🍷	3
○	Langhe Chardonnay Buschet '97	🍷	5
●	Barbaresco Bric Balin '90	🍸🍸🍸	6
●	Barbaresco Bric Balin '93	🍸🍸	6
●	Barbaresco Bric Balin '95	🍸🍸	6
●	Barbaresco Cole '93	🍸🍸	6
●	Barbaresco Cole '95	🍸🍸	6

BARBARESCO (CN)

CASCINA MORASSINO
VIA OVELLO, 32
12050 BARBARESCO (CN)
TEL. 0173/635149

The Bianco family's small estate, covering five hectares of the Ovello vineyard at Barbaresco, has produced some excellent wines, with a Barbera at the top of the list winning Two very full Glasses. An impenetrable garnet color with a dense rim precedes a broad and fascinating nose with hints of red fruit, mint and smoke; the entry on the splendid palate is rich and firm and the progress well-articulated by impressive tannins, leading into a long, lingering finish. Among the Barbarescos our favorite was the Ovello Ventimesi, which displays a garnet-ruby hue with a slightly faded rim. The subtly forward nose offers a wide array of aromas: coffee, vanilla, leather, jam and toasty notes. In the mouth it is ample and robust, with the vigorous tannins lending dryness to the lingering finish, where the toastiness of the new wood reappears. The Dolcetto is firm and pleasingly rustic, intense in color, and enriched with notes of earth and red berries on the nose; the substantial palate shows good grip and a dry, tannic finish that mirrors the bouquet. The Barbaresco Ovello is less elegant on the nose than the Ventimesi but offers a well-structured, somewhat austere palate with a satisfying finish. The basic Barbaresco shows a not very vivid ruby color and a forward nose with notes of leather, hazelnut and dried flowers; the palate has medium body and a distinctly aggressive tone. A correctly made Nebbiolo ends our review.

●	Barbaresco Ovello Ventimesi '96	🍷🍷	6
●	Barbera d'Alba '97	🍷🍷	4
●	Barbaresco '96	🍷	5
●	Barbaresco Ovello '96	🍷	5
●	Dolcetto d'Alba '98	🍷	3
●	Langhe Nebbiolo '97		4
●	Barbaresco Ovello '95	🍸	5
●	Barbera d'Alba '96	🍸	4

BARBARESCO (CN)

WALTER MUSSO
VIA D. CAVAZZA, 5
12050 BARBARESCO (CN)
TEL. 0173/635129

With the '96 vintage Walter Musso was again able to achieve some excellent results with his Barbaresco wines: the Pora, in particular, stood out at our tastings as one of the most convincing Barbarescos of this vintage. We found all the other wines presented by Musso of more than satisfying quality except for the Chardonnay, which strikes us as being produced to make up the list rather than with any real enthusiasm. The Freisa, lively and effervescent, has light scents of strawberry and an enjoyable, undemanding drinkability. The Dolcetto, a purplish-ruby in color, releases exuberant, strongly-defined fruity aromas; the palate is medium-bodied with acidity and tannins still fairly marked. The Barbaresco Rio Sordo, Two Glasses fully deserved, is especially attractive on the nose, which offers enchanting fruity and balsamic notes that reappear on the palate; here the wine, rather understated in structure, opens out with elegance and balance. We also unhesitatingly awarded Two Glasses to the Barbaresco Pora, which is more complex than the Rio Sordo in both aroma and taste: the nose reveals faded roses, red fruit, licorice and balsamic nuances, while acidity and tannins merge perfectly on the full-bodied palate.

● Barbaresco Pora '96	TT	4
● Barbaresco Rio Sordo '96	TT	4
● Dolcetto d'Alba '98	T	3
● Langhe Freisa '98		3
● Barbaresco Bricco Rio Sordo '93	YY	4
● Barbaresco Pora '95	Y	4
● Barbaresco Rio Sordo '95	Y	4

BARBARESCO (CN)

PRODUTTORI DEL BARBARESCO
VIA TORINO, 52
12050 BARBARESCO (CN)
TEL. 0173/635139

The winery of the Produttori del Barbaresco is rightly esteemed by a wide public of Italian and foreign wine-lovers, who compete particularly for the sought-after Barbaresco crus. The grapes produced by member growers go in part to make up the basic Barbaresco, but some are vinified separately and marketed as Riservas under the labels of celebrated crus: Rabajà, Ovello, Rio Sordo, Montefico, Asili, Montestefano, Pajé and Moccagatta. These wines are impeccably made and in top vintages frequently achieve real excellence. From the '95 vintage the Produttori have come up with an especially good Barbaresco Rio Sordo which is a model of this great Piedmontese red: the color is ruby tending towards garnet, the broad and lingering aromas suggest roses and wild berries; the palate displays remarkable concentration, distinct tannins and an enjoyable licorice finish. We found the Moccagatta even better, deeper-hued and offering very intense, clean aromas; it is unusually full-bodied on the palate, where the tannins have merged smoothly with the wood. The three other crus are just a step below: the Ovello is noteworthy for its delightful aromas, the Montefico displays elegance and balance and the Rabajà is rather light on both nose and palate. In comparison the Barbaresco '96 shows up quite well, particularly because of its superior structure; it unexpectedly went off with One Glass.

● Barbaresco Vigneti in Rio Sordo Ris. '95	TT	5
● Barbaresco Vigneti in Moccagatta Ris '95	TT	5
● Barbaresco Vigneti in Rabajà Ris. '95	T	5
● Barbaresco Vigneti in Montefico Ris. '95	T	5
● Barbaresco Vigneti in Ovello Ris. '95	T	5
● Barbaresco '96	T	5
● Barbaresco Vigneti in Moccagatta Ris. '90	YY	6
● Barbaresco Vigneti in Montestefano Ris. '90	YY	6

BARBARESCO (CN)

Albino Rocca
Via Rabajà, 15
12050 Barbaresco (CN)
tel. 0173/635145

Angelo Rocca, one of the friendliest people in the Langhe, hasn't been at all changed by success and is so unassuming in character that he has stuck to last year's prices for his '96 and '97 Barbarescos, thereby forgoing a considerable increase in his returns. As of this year he is managing about 10 hectares under vine, including a small site planted to nebbiolo bordering Gaja's Sorì Tildin, which will bring the annual output up to a little over 65 thousand bottles. His professional skills have full scope in the cellar, where everything is in place to produce the best wines possible: stainless steel fermentation vats specifically designed for a greater extraction of desirable phenolics and a spotlessly clean, functional barrel-room for maturation in wood. For three years now he has given up stabilization by means of refrigeration, and none of his wines are subjected to clarification or filtration, in order to avoid detrimental effects on their quality. The wines speak for themselves: the cellar has turned out a really superb range. Of the two types of Cortese we preferred the barrique-fermented and -aged version with its toasty, nutty aromas, hints of acacia blossom and creaminess; the basic version has the appeal of simplicity. The Vignalunga is the archetypical Dolcetto d'Alba with its fresh, fruity aromas and succulent palate. The Barbera Gepin is further up in the hierarchy: intense, fruity aromas (cherry jam) emerge on the nose with fresh balsamic notes; the harmonious palate is rich and mouth-filling. The Barbaresco Vigneto Loreto, less explosive in aroma, has a powerful, expressive palate; the Brich Ronchi, on the other hand, has difficulty in restraining its spontaneous, fruity exuberance which intensifies the velvety sensations on the long finish. This wine wins Three Glasses hands down.

●	Barbaresco Vigneto Brich Ronchi '96	🍷🍷🍷	5
●	Barbaresco Loreto '96	🍷🍷	5
●	Barbera d'Alba Gepin '97	🍷🍷	4
●	Dolcetto d'Alba Vignalunga '98	🍷🍷	3*
○	Langhe Bianco La Rocca '98	🍷🍷	4
○	La Rocca '98	🍷	3
●	Barbaresco Vigneto Brich Ronchi '93	🍸🍸🍸	6
●	Barbaresco Loreto '95	🍸🍸🍸	6
●	Barbaresco Vigneto Brich Ronchi '95	🍸🍸	6
●	Barbaresco Loreto '94	🍸🍸	5
●	Barbaresco Loreto '93	🍸🍸	5
●	Barbera d'Alba Gepin '96	🍸	4

BARBARESCO (CN)

Bruno Rocca
Via Rabajà, 29
12050 Barbaresco (CN)
tel. 0173/635112

Over the last ten years Barbaresco has seen an encouraging upsurge in quality after an alarming period in the doldrums. Bruno Rocca played a leading role during this time, being one of the very few producers to react to a sort of general inferiority complex towards the Barolo area, and the wines produced by him in the past are still models of finesse and capacity for evolution. Today Bruno is one of the most skillful interpreters of an exquisite fusion of respect for the raw material and the exigencies of innovation, of which the most exciting result is a stunning Rabajà '96. The color of this Barbaresco already gives an idea of its imposing structure, while the nose gradually releases an enticing profusion of flowery, toasty notes culminating in a heady sensation of wonderful depth. The mineral note and warm, fruity aromas are perfectly reflected on the intense and long palate, where soft alcohol and powerful extract are harmoniously balanced. The Barbaresco Coparossa, a worthy second-in-command, reveals an intense color and a wide array of aromas, with notes of mint, cocoa and cherry to the fore; the palate, although without the concentration of the Rabajà, displays a highly distinctive aromatic finish. This year's tour de force is confirmed by the best Chardonnay ever produced by Rocca: the oak is more successfully judged than before and a warm opulence contrasts intriguingly with an invigorating freshness. The splendid Barbera is exemplary in the clarity of its bouquet and the voluptuous, enticing smoothness of the palate.

●	Barbaresco Rabajà '96	🍷🍷🍷	6
●	Barbaresco Coparossa '96	🍷🍷	6
●	Barbera d'Alba '97	🍷🍷	4
○	Langhe Chardonnay Cadet '98	🍷🍷	4
●	Dolcetto d'Alba Vigna Trifolé '98	🍷	3
●	Barbaresco Rabajà '88	🍸🍸🍸	6
●	Barbaresco Rabajà '89	🍸🍸🍸	6
●	Barbaresco Rabajà '93	🍸🍸🍸	6
●	Barbaresco Coparossa '95	🍸🍸	6
●	Barbaresco Rabajà '90	🍸🍸	6
●	Barbaresco Rabajà '92	🍸🍸	6
●	Barbaresco Rabajà '94	🍸🍸	6
●	Barbaresco Rabajà '95	🍸🍸	6
●	Barbera d'Alba '96	🍸	4

BARBARESCO (CN)

RINO VARALDO
VIA SECONDINE, 2
12050 BARBARESCO (CN)
TEL. 0173/635160

This year Pier Mario Varaldo and his sons Rino and Michele have come up with two Barbarescos which both won Two Glasses; indeed the outstanding Bricco Libero missed Three Glasses by a hair's breadth, and on the same level is a highly concentrated, seductive Barbera; meanwhile it's difficult to find fault with the Barolo. The Barbaresco Bricco Libero, garnet-ruby in color with a slightly faded rim, offers enticing fruity aromas (strawberry and raspberry) with hints of tobacco and menthol; the rich texture of the palate merges with its powerful structure in harmonious progression, while smooth tannins underlie the warm, long finish. The Barbera, of an impenetrable purple-garnet hue, offers a complex, elegant array of aromas of blackberry, strawberry, cherry, vanilla and leather; the palate captivates with its rich fruit and powerfully structured, noble tannins, which lend punch to the long, lingering finish. The Barbaresco Sorì Loreto displays jammy notes with leather and dried flowers on the nose; the palate is ample and chewy with impressive tannins and a very long finish, on which hints of licorice appear. The Barolo, garnet in color with a wide orange rim, offers aromas of wild berries and spice; in the mouth its smooth progress is well-articulated by dry but not rasping tannins. Finally, the Freisa and the Dolcetto are properly made, light-hearted wines.

●	Barbaresco Bricco Libero '96	🍷🍷	6
●	Barbaresco Sorì Loreto '96	🍷🍷	6
●	Barbera d'Alba '97	🍷🍷	5
●	Barolo Vigna di Aldo '95	🍷🍷	6
●	Dolcetto d'Alba '98		3
●	Langhe Freisa '98		3
●	Barbaresco La Gemma '95	🍸🍸	5

BAROLO (CN)

F.LLI BARALE
VIA ROMA, 6
12060 BAROLO (CN)
TEL. 0173/56127

In the successful series of wines presented by this Barolo winery two stand out, winning Two Glasses each: a rich, full-bodied Barbera and an inviting, fruity Barbaresco. The latter is ruby-garnet in color with a faded rim and a rich profusion of ripe fruit with spicy undertones on the nose; the palate, not particularly powerful, progresses confidently, leading into a finish with a faintly perceptible bitterish twist. The Barbera Preda is of a purplish-rimmed, ruby-garnet hue; the nose offers hints of violets, red and black fruit and tobacco leaf. The rich, dense palate has a well-judged vein of acidity and elegant tannins which lend vigor to the lingering finish. The Barolo Bussia Riserva '93, coming in just behind the above, is garnet-tinged ruby red with a slightly faded rim and displays composite, forward aromas with notes of leather, jam and mint; the palate has good firm body and a powerful phenolic structure. Notes of cocoa and jam appear on the finish. The garnet-colored Dolcetto Costa di Rose offers aromas of blackberry, cherry, tobacco and menthol over faint mineral tones; plenty of body lends roundness to the palate, offsetting a marked bite of acidity and assertive tannins. To end the list, the straightforward, correct Chardonnay Bussia, pale straw in color, offers fermentation-derived aromas and a smooth, graceful palate.

●	Barbaresco '95	🍷🍷	5
●	Barbera d'Alba Vigna Preda '97	🍷🍷	4
●	Barolo Bussia Ris. '93	🍷	6
●	Dolcetto d'Alba Costa di Rose '98	🍷	3
○	Langhe Chardonnay Bussia '98		3
●	Barolo Castellero '93	🍸🍸	5
●	Barbaresco Rabajà Ris. '93	🍸	5

BAROLO (CN)

Giacomo Borgogno & Figli

Via Gioberti, 1
12060 Barolo (CN)
tel. 0173/56108

The name of this winery covers over two centuries of the history of wine, and, what's more, of wine of high quality, if it is true that Czar Nicholas II, known to be fond of a really good bottle, was offered a Borgogno Barolo from the 1861 vintage when he visited Racconigi Castle in 1907. The entire Boschis family has a hand in the running of the estate: Giorgio (general administration and marketing), Cesare (oenologist), Franco and Chiara (vineyard management), taking care to keep up the old traditions, are all involved in continuing the activity started back in 1761. For the production of its Barolo the estate does not favor any particular cru, because it believes that the subtle variations in expression of the different hills and vineyard sites contribute to the wine's harmony. Cannubi, Cannubi Boschis, Liste, Brunate and San Pietro are the highly prized zones from which, in good vintages, the Borgogno Barolo Classico is made. The Barolo Classico of the '95 vintage that we tasted was matured in large wooden barrels and then spent some time in bottle. It has a garnet color faintly tinged with orange and aromas reminiscent of flowers (violet), fruit (prune) and spice; these are echoed on the palate which reveals a delicate structure in which the tannins are just noticeable. The basic version offers a faintly ripe nose recalling preserves, cloves and cinnamon, and alcohol announces its presence. We liked the Barbera '98 with its attractive bouquet of spicy notes and wild berries, which carries through onto the straightforward and delightfully fresh palate. The Chinato is an interesting aromatized wine that follows a venerable Piedmontese tradition. It is now almost impossible to find any for sale in a shop, but bottles from very good vintages can be bought at the estate.

● Barbera d'Alba '98	▼	3
● Barolo '95	▼	6
● Barolo Classico '95	▼	6
● Dolcetto d'Alba '98		3
● Barolo Classico '93	▽▽	6
● Barolo '89	▽	6
● Barolo '93	▽	5
● Barolo Classico '88	▽	6
● Barolo Classico '89	▽	6
● Barolo Classico Ris. '90	▽	6
● Barolo Liste '88	▽	6
● Barolo Liste '89	▽	6

BAROLO (CN)

Giacomo Brezza & Figli

Via Lomondo, 4
12060 Barolo (CN)
tel. 0173/56354 - 0173/56191

A total of 100 thousand bottles of Barolo, Nebbiolo, Barbera, Dolcetto, Freisa and Chardonnay is the average production of this winery, founded in 1885. Ninety percent of the vineyards are located in the Barolo district, and it is with this great Piedmontese red that the estate identifies. Planting density is as high as 4,000 vines per hectare, with yields at about 6,000 kilos; the alcoholic fermentation takes place in steel vats and the malolactic in concrete before the wine goes into large oak barrels. We tasted an interesting series of wines this year, starting with the Nebbiolo Santa Rosalia, which displays distinctive flowery aromas mingling with faint spicy notes; the palate is warm, graceful and faintly tannic. The Barolo Cannubi was not quite as good as we had hoped; the nose, redolent of violets, hay and cloves, is pleasing, but the palate is rather short and shows a marked bitterish note. Traditional ruby in color, the Barbera Muscatel offers fresh, fruity aromas of cherry which carry through onto the light and unassuming palate. The Cannubi cru has a fragrance of ripe fruit and needs to age some more to achieve perfect harmony on the palate. It still holds its place as one of the best Barberas of the area. The Dolcetto, highly varietal in aroma, is vinous in character with notes of cherry and almond; the nicely corresponding palate is dry and reveals good length.

● Barbera d'Alba Cannubi '96	▼▼	4
● Barbera d'Alba Muscatel '96	▼	4
● Barolo Cannubi '95	▼	6
● Dolcetto d'Alba S. Lorenzo '98	▼	4
● Nebbiolo d'Alba Santa Rosalia '97	▼	4
● Barbera d'Alba Cannubi '95	▽▽	4
● Barolo Cannubi '90	▽▽	6
● Barolo Cannubi '93	▽▽	6
● Barolo Castellero Ris. '90	▽▽	6
● Barolo Sarmassa '91	▽▽	6
● Barolo Sarmassa '94	▽▽	6
● Barolo Sarmassa Ris. '90	▽▽	6
● Barolo Bricco Sarmassa '93	▽	6

BAROLO (CN)

MARCHESI DI BAROLO
VIA ALBA, 12
12060 BAROLO (CN)
TEL. 0173/564400

This is one of the most important wineries of the Langhe, above all for its Barolo, and much of the credit is due to Roberto Vezza, the oenologist who has for years skillfully handled both the wines destined for mass distribution and the estate's small batches of Riserva. An interesting Barolo from the '95 vintage comes from the Sarmassa vineyard, which is close to the Cerequio and faces south and southeast; a deep, dark ruby in color, it offers aromas of raspberry and blackberry with sweet spicy notes and a minty finish; the palate is superbly soft, rich and long. The garnet-hued Cannubi reveals raspberry and licorice on the nose but is not as rich on the palate. The Estate Vineyard, which owes its difference in style to barrique-aging, is still somewhat closed on the nose, although hints of quinine and licorice are noticeable; it has already achieved a greater balance than the other two between soft tannins and alcohol. The Barolo Vintage, rather forward, the Coste di Rose, fruity but lacking in complexity, and the Barbaresco Vintage '95 did not perform quite so well. The Dolcetto Madonna di Como was excellent, offering ripe aromas of plum jam and a dense, well-balanced palate, as was the Barbera Ruvei, with aromas of cherries steeped in alcohol, and plenty of body. Neither the Dolcetto Boschetti, which lacks balance, nor the Barbera Paiagal, somewhat tired and meagre on the palate, was up to its usual standard. We liked the Moscato Zagara, with its aromas of ripe pear and honey, and the straightforward, properly made Gavi.

●	Barbera d'Alba Ruvei '97	🍷🍷	3*
●	Barolo Cannubi '95	🍷🍷	6
●	Barolo Estate Vineyard '95	🍷🍷	6
●	Barolo Sarmassa '95	🍷🍷	6
●	Dolcetto d'Alba Madonna di Como '98	🍷🍷	3*
●	Barbaresco Vintage '95	🍷	5
●	Barbera d'Alba Paiagal '96	🍷	4
●	Barolo Coste di Rose '95	🍷	5
●	Barolo Vintage '95	🍷	6
●	Dolcetto d'Alba Boschetti '98	🍷	3
○	Gavi del Comune di Gavi '98	🍷	4
○	Moscato d'Asti Zagara '98	🍷	3
●	Barolo Estate Vineyard '90	YYY	6
●	Barolo Millenium '90	YY	6

BAROLO (CN)

BARTOLO MASCARELLO
VIA ROMA, 15
12060 BAROLO (CN)
TEL. 0173/56125

Bartolo Mascarello's name is almost synonymous with one of Italy's most famous winegrowing areas, the Langhe. It is intimately bound up with the achieved independence of good small producers, who in the latter half of the 20th century were the driving force behind the rise to fame of Langhe wines. The Barolo from this estate is produced according to traditional precepts, such as that of blending the grapes from different crus into an assemblage comprising all the various characteristics of the Cannubi, San Lorenzo, Rué and Rocche vineyards. The grapes are of top quality, and cellar practices, also traditional, include a long maceration on the skins and the use of large barrels. The '95 vintage in the Langhe was not so friendly to Barolo as had been hoped, and Bartolo Mascarello's version, slightly less impressive than the '93 and '90 vintages, reflects the consequences of this difficult year. It is ruby-colored with flashing garnet tints and an orange rim; the nose displays the evolved tone typical of this estate's Barolos, together with hints of puréed strawberry and raspberry, dried flowers and tar. In the mouth it is solid and rich-textured, with a slight rigidity of development owing to the austere structure; the finish shows the length and harmony of a first-class wine. The Dolcetto '97, ruby-garnet in color, is somewhat rustic on the nose and firm and chewy on the palate.

●	Barolo '95	🍷	6
●	Dolcetto d'Alba '97	🍷	4
●	Barolo '83	YYY	6
●	Barolo '84	YYY	6
●	Barolo '85	YYY	6
●	Barolo '89	YYY	6
●	Barolo '88	YY	6
●	Barolo '90	YY	6
●	Barolo '93	YY	6
●	Barbera d'Alba Vigna S. Lorenzo '95	Y	4

BAROLO (CN)

E. PIRA & FIGLI
VIA VITTORIO VENETO, 1
12060 BAROLO (CN)
TEL. 0173/56247

This historic winery, which has belonged to the Boschis family since the beginning of the '80s, is in the center of Barolo. The resurgence of the estate, whose original name has been retained out of respect for the Pira family and the past, is due to Chiara, who, having completed her course in business studies, has been managing the estate full-time since 1990. Guided and helped at the beginning by the group of producers known collectively as Langa In, she succeeded after very few years in providing a clear example of her concept of Barolo: a powerful and elegant wine. The grapes all come from the legendary Cannubi cru, so highly prized that past generations would use just a little of its fruit in assemblages with that of other less celebrated vineyards. The Cannubi grapes yield richly perfumed wines, and their potential when vinified unblended is easy to imagine; when this is combined with avant-garde cellar techniques, a fairly short maceration and the exclusive use of new barriques for maturation, it is clear that we are to be treated to a masterly interpretation of one of the last Barolos of the millennium. When tasted, the Cannubi '95 certainly didn't fall short of our expectations: the color is a deep garnet-ruby; the elegant, enticing bouquet offers an attractive fruitiness merging with sweet notes of vanilla and hints of cocoa, leading into an explosion of sensations on the warm, vigorous and corresponding palate. All in all, it seems a successful compromise between an admirably smooth vinification and the nature of the terroir.

● Barolo Cannubi '95	🍷🍷	6
● Barolo '94	YYY	5
● Barolo Ris. '90	YYY	6
● Barolo '93	YY	5

BAROLO (CN)

GIUSEPPE RINALDI
VIA MONFORTE, 3
12060 BAROLO (CN)
TEL. 0173/56156

This winery, already attractive 70 years ago when it was built, has now been further improved with the addition of new underground barrel rooms for aging the wine in large Slovenian oak barrels. There has been an important change in production policy too, although here you will find no impulsive concessions to innovation: the cellar has no space dedicated to either rotary fermenters or barriques. Instead, Beppe Rinaldi has been persuaded by the outcome of harvests over the last decade that the time has come to abandon single vineyard bottlings of Barolo in favor of assemblages from different vineyards belonging to the estate. Having noted in magnificent vintages like '97 and '98 a certain lack of freshness even from legendary sites such as Brunate and Cannubi, Rinaldi has decided to add the Barolo from two other vineyards that yield a higher acidity, thus creating two new labels: Brunate-Le Coste and Cannubi S. Lorenzo-Ravera. The results are interesting, although we were not of the party that thought the Riserva Brunate, which has given so much pleasure over the years to Barolo lovers on both sides of the Atlantic, was in need of improving additions. In the '95 vintage we have a slight preference for the Barolo Brunate-Le Coste, which shows an already fairly open bouquet with deep notes of faded violet and ripe plum and a faint tarriness. Tannins dominate the palate, which reveals good complexity on the finish, although it still lacks elegance. The Cannubi S. Lorenzo-Ravera, which is evolving along the same lines but with a touch more acidity on the palate, is a good example of a young Barolo.

● Barolo Brunate-Le Coste '95	🍷🍷	5
● Barolo Cannubi S. Lorenzo-Ravera '95	🍷🍷	5
● Barolo '90	YY	6
● Barolo '91	YY	6
● Barolo Brunate '90	YY	6
● Barolo Brunate '91	YY	6
● Barolo Brunate '92	YY	6
● Barolo Brunate-Le Coste '94	YY	6
● Barolo Brunate-Le Coste '93	YY	6
● Barolo Cannubi S. Lorenzo-Ravera '93	Y	6

BAROLO (CN)

LUCIANO SANDRONE
VIA ALBA, 57
12060 BAROLO (CN)
TEL. 0173/56239

The Barbera d'Alba '97 is a wine of great stature, displaying fresh aromas on a broad, well-balanced nose and a really impressive structure. The dense ruby-garnet color with a slight rim is an indication of its rich texture; the nose offers elegant red and black fruit, fresh leaves and creaminess over faint undertones of spice and sweet pastry; after a full-bodied entry on the palate, the broad, confident progress is well-articulated by robust tannins which round out the long, lingering, licorice-toned finish. This is one of the best versions of Barbera ever to have come from the Sandrone winery. The Barolo, just as good, is once again the standard-bearer of the estate: dark ruby in color, it displays a deep, harmonious bouquet composed of blackberry, ripe plum, mint, coffee and vanilla with intriguing animal scents; the palate offers a captivatingly rich body which unfolds generously, offering abundant, rounded tannins followed by a long finish with notes of mint and licorice. This year's version of the excellent Dolcetto d'Alba is once again one of the best on the market. We awarded One Glass unhesitatingly to the Nebbiolo d'Alba Valmaggiore, named after its vineyard near Vezza d'Alba in the Roero zone. Its good ruby color with an orange-tinged rim is followed by a soft fragrance of vanilla, raspberry and violet mingling with faint balsamic nuances; the palate, although not particularly powerful, is substantial and well-balanced with a convincing finish and notes of cocoa emerging on the aftertaste.

Barbera d'Alba '97	▼▼	4
Barolo Cannubi Boschis '95	▼▼	6
Dolcetto d'Alba '98	▼▼	3
Nebbiolo d'Alba Valmaggiore '97	▼	5
Barolo '83	∇∇∇	6
Barolo '84	∇∇∇	6
Barolo Cannubi Boschis '85	∇∇∇	6
Barolo Cannubi Boschis '86	∇∇∇	6
Barolo Cannubi Boschis '87	∇∇∇	6
Barolo Cannubi Boschis '89	∇∇∇	6
Barolo Cannubi Boschis '90	∇∇∇	6
Dolcetto d'Alba '97	∇∇	3
Barolo Cannubi Boschis '93	∇	5

BAROLO (CN)

GIORGIO SCARZELLO E FIGLI
VIA ALBA, 29
12060 BAROLO (CN)
TEL. 0173/56170

During a recent blind tasting we once again discovered Giorgio Scarzella's extraordinary ability to get the very best out of his vineyard in Merenda (just next door to Cerequio) when the vintage permits. His Barolo '89 turned out to be one of the best of all from that auspicious year, offering a range of aromas of rare complexity. These aromas can all be traced to the nebbiolo grape, because in this cellar the use of small French oak casks for Barolo is absolutely banned. It is true that a few 600-liter barrels have found their way in, but they are destined solely for the Barbera d'Alba, which is decidedly less rich in aroma and can therefore benefit from this type of maturation in wood. The Barolo '95 needs more bottle aging, since the tannins are still over-evident on the palate and the nose is rather closed. The Barbera d'Alba '97 is a wine with structure rather than finesse and already displays a highly enjoyable and seductive drinkability; a rustic, herbaceous tone gives it personality without depriving it of charm. The Dolcetto, in the same style, already offers well-harmonized aromas with subdued notes of red fruit; the tannins are very well-evolved and it is the richness of the fruit that gives the palate its solidity and grip, leading into a finish with undertones of bitter almond. One of the many things we like about Giorgio Scarzella is his decision to name the wines according to what they are, without adding any creative flourishes, which are, at best, superfluous and misleading.

Barbera d'Alba '97	▼▼	4
Barolo '95	▼▼	6
Dolcetto d'Alba '97	▼	3
Barolo '93	∇∇	6
Barolo Vigna Merenda '90	∇∇	6
Barolo '91	∇	6

BAROLO (CN)

TENUTA LA VOLTA - CABUTTO
VIA S. PIETRO, 13
12060 BAROLO (CN)
TEL. 0173/56168

From its 13 hectares under vine this estate produces an average of not more than 40 thousand liters of wine per year, with Barolo accounting for the lion's share (20 thousand bottles), Dolcetto and Barbera representing a good proportion (about 15 thousand bottles each) and the Vendemmiaio completing the range. The vineyards are in the high part of Barolo, where the magnificent, decaying Castello della Volta overlooks a sweeping vista of treasured vines. The Dolcetto '98 is especially intense in color with aromas of very ripe fruit and dried petals and a medium-structured palate dominated by the bitterish note typical of this variety. The Vendemmiaio '96, with the characteristic not very deep color of the nebbiolo grape, displays quite a pronounced woody tone with a streak of acidity to remind us that there's some barbera in the blend. Along much more traditional lines, the Barolo '95 shows a rather forward bouquet and pronounced tannins on a palate which still needs to find its balance. All in all, these are wines not meant to give instant pleasure, but which unfold with time, after spending a few years in the cellar. This style of wine is very popular with quite a number of foreign customers, who manage to secure a sizeable quantity of the bottles released every year, often visiting the attractive winery in order to do so. We also liked the Barbera d'Alba Superiore Bricco delle Viole, although it is perhaps just a little on the lean side considering the potential of the vintage.

●	Barbera d'Alba Sup. Bricco delle Viole '97	🍷	4
●	Barolo Vigna La Volta '95	🍷	5
●	Dolcetto d'Alba La Volta '98	🍷	3
●	Langhe Rosso Vendemmiaio '96	🍷	5
●	Barolo Riserva del Fondatore '90	YY	6
●	Barbera d'Alba Sup. Bricco delle Viole '96	Y	4
●	Barolo '93	Y	5

BAROLO (CN)

G. D. VAJRA
VIA DELLE VIOLE, 25
LOC. VERGNE
12060 BAROLO (CN)
TEL. 0173/56257

The warm and fat Chardonnay, with an alcoholic strength of 14°, is extremely likeable, offering uncomplicated aromas of yeast and linden blossom which owe nothing to any type of wood maturation, as the wine is unoaked. The only jarring note is a faint bitterness on the finish which detracts from the overall harmony. When we retasted the Riesling '97 we found it really delightful, with delicate mineral aromas that reappear on the aftertaste enhanced by an appealing note of white flowers in which faint echoes of the typical petroleum can already be detected. The reds, direct in character rather than complex, reveal an enjoyable drinkability. The Barolo Bricco delle Viole '95, still clearly youthful and very fruity, needs to be left alone for a few more years. The house champion, the Dolcetto d'Alba Bricco delle Viole, wasn't available in time for our tastings, but since it is a long-lived wine we shall be in good time when we review it next year. Apart from the functional stainless steel vats and numerous barrels of varying sizes, the cellar has an unusual charming feature: we were lucky enough to witness the sun's rays shining through the stained glass windows, filling the vinification area with warm, vivid hues of blue and gold in a truly unique spectacle. You shouldn't miss it, but do make sure that the weather is fine!

●	Barolo Bricco delle Viole '95	🍷🍷	6
○	Langhe Chardonnay '98	🍷🍷	4
●	Dolcetto d'Alba '98	🍷	3
●	Langhe Freisa Kyè '97	🍷	5
●	Barbera d'Alba '97	🍷	3
●	Barbera d'Alba Bricco delle Viole '93	YY	5
●	Barolo '93	YY	5
●	Barolo Bricco delle Viole '91	YY	4
●	Barolo Bricco delle Viole '94	YY	5
●	Dolcetto d'Alba Coste & Fossati '97	YY	4
○	Langhe Bianco '97	YY	4

BASTIA MONDOVÌ (CN)

BRICCO DEL CUCÙ
FRAZ. BRICCO, 21
12060 BASTIA MONDOVI (CN)
TEL. 0174/60153

About ten years ago, when Giuseppe Sciolla reached the age of 70 and began to show signs of slowing down, his son Dario had to decide whether to continue as a municipal employee and sell the family winery, or ábandon a safe job and take up the business himself. He made up his mind to give it a go, and helped by his parents he took over the management of the Bastia property, consisting of 15 hectares near the Sacrario dei Partigiani. Besides the eight hectares under vine, almost all dolcetto and at altitudes of between 450 and 500 meters above sea level, Dario owns seven hectares planted with hazelnuts. After a lifetime spent among demijohns, it was not easy for Giuseppe to change course, so it was with some diffidence that Dario began bottling in 1992, gradually reaching his present annual output of about 40 thousand bottles. Old habits die hard, especially when your cellar lacks the appropriate equipment, the old wooden casks are still firmly in use and prices are getting too high for your old customers. But Dario is now on the right track, carrying out a drastic selection of the crop by removing excess bunches. The resulting high quality, combined with modest prices, has turned this estate into one of the best in Italy if it's value for money you're after. The Langhe Dolcetto offers fruity aromas and a long, powerful palate, while the Dogliani, more elegant on the nose (bitter almond and red berries), still seems very young on the palate. The Bricco San Bernardo, from a 40-year-old vineyard, was fermented and matured in cask; the aromas recall plum preserves, while the concentration and dense fruit in the mouth promise a really wonderful future.

●	Dolcetto di Dogliani '98	🍷🍷	3*
●	Dolcetto di Dogliani Sup. Bricco S. Bernardo '98	🍷🍷	3*
○	Langhe Bianco '98	🍷	3
●	Langhe Dolcetto '98	🍷	2

BORGONE SUSA (TO)

CARLOTTA
VIA CONDOVE, 61
10050 BORGONE SUSA (TO)
TEL. 011/9646150

It is fairly easy to get to the Carlotta estate; if you follow state highway 24 for the Valle di Susa and take the turn-off for Borgone you will see it in front of you, surrounded by the fine terraced vineyard known as Costadoro. This tiny winery, which produces about 5,000 bottles from little more than one hectare of vineyard, came into being ten years ago thanks to Carla Cometto. Helped by her very likeable husband, she reorganized her grandfather's old vineyards and began vinifying and bottling the first vintages, mainly as a hobby. With time, the wines met with acclaim from both local restaurateurs and wine lovers from all over Italy, who were eager to sample wines reminiscent of a vanished rural past and on the verge of extinction. The recent official recognition of the Valsusa DOC further encouraged the family, who in the meantime had acquired a small vineyard of rare charm situated on a very steep slope entirely terraced in stone, just below the hamlet of Ramats di Chiomonte: the Roche du Bau ('the wolf's fortress'). When opened, the Costadoro '98, a blend of barbera, ciliegiolo and neretta cuneese, releases fruity aromas (blueberry) with a faint balsamic note; the palate is satisfyingly fruity, dense and soft. The slightly more straightforward Vignacombe '98, a blend of lesser-known DOC-authorized native varieties, offers a delicate, vinous nose with black cherry and fresh herbal notes; a refreshing crisp acidity emerges on the nicely balanced palate. The well-structured Rocca del Lupo '98, made from barbera and avanà, is behind the other wines; despite its 14° of alcohol it has not succeeded in integrating the high acidity, which makes the wine over-hard but undoubtedly long-lasting.

●	Valsusa Costadoro '98	🍷🍷	4
●	Valsusa Rocca del Lupo '98	🍷	3
●	Valsusa Vignacombe '98	🍷	4
●	Valsusa Costadoro '97	🍷🍷 (outline)	4

BRA (CN)

ASCHERI
VIA PIUMATI, 23
12042 BRA (CN)
TEL. 0172/412394

The reliable range presented by the Ascheri family consists of a series of Langhe wines completed by the Montalupa Rosso and Bianco (based respectively on syrah and viogner) from Bra. The Rosso, offering the typical aromas of the variety, is a lively, generous wine with a broad, chewy palate. The ruby-garnet color with a purplish rim is followed by a bouquet of berries, leafy tones, cocoa, pepper and undergrowth, while the tannins evolve perfectly on the ample, even palate and notes of licorice appear on the long, lingering finish. The straw-colored Bianco reveals apricot and flowery aromas; the nicely textured palate is fresh and silky. The two Barolos both earn a Glass. The ruby-garnet Sorano offers hints of red fruit, dried flowers, tar and walnut on the nose, followed by a mouth-filling palate, not particularly powerful but satisfying and long. The Vigna dei Pola, of a slightly faded ruby hue with an orange tinge, has a fairly intense and heady bouquet with notes of strawberry, raspberry, leather and spice; the palate is well-structured and only slightly marred by a faint streak of acidity. The Dolcetto Sorano, made with grapes from Serralunga, is pleasantly rustic in character and displays fruity, spicy and earthy aromas; the substantial palate has a light tartness and a dry, modulated finish. To end with, the Barbera Vigna Fontanelle shows finesse on the nose and balance on the palate.

●	Montalupa Rosso '97	▼▼	5
●	Barbera d'Alba Vigna Fontanelle '98	▼	4
●	Barolo Vigna dei Pola '95	▼	6
●	Barolo Vigna Sorano '95	▼	6
●	Dolcetto d'Alba Podere di Sorano '98	▼	3
○	Montalupa Bianco '98	▼	5
●	Montalupa Rosso '96	▽▽	4
●	Barolo Vigna Farina '93	▽	5
●	Rocca d'Auçabech '93	▽	4
●	Verduno Pelaverga Costa dei Faggi '95	▽	3

CALAMANDRANA (AT)

MICHELE CHIARLO
S. S. NIZZA-CANELLI, 99
14042 CALAMANDRANA (AT)
TEL. 0141/769030

Passionate involvement and hard work are the crucial factors at the Chiarlo winery, located at the heart of an area renowned and esteemed the world over. When you visit the estate at Calamandrana what impresses you is the balance with which it is managed. Priority is given to the care of the vineyards, where they seek particularly to bring out the characteristic qualities of the grapes, but the cellar also plays its part, of course. It was the task of Roberto Bezzato, the young oenologist who recently died, to co-ordinate the various stages so that everything functioned perfectly. More and more investments are being made in the Barbera, linking the winery with its origins. The results can be seen in the Valle del Sole '96, which did extremely well, quite making up for the absence of the more ambitious La Court: it is the best version ever produced. Its ruby color indicates vitality and concentration; the nose is immediate and enticing and precedes an exceptionally enjoyable palate which vaunts an enchanting evenness. The Barolo Cerequio, with an unusually deep color for a '95, is splendid in its progression: its aromas have an attractive density that effortlessly harmonizes with the oak, and its solid structure leads into a perfectly corresponding finish. The Barbaresco Asili, equally successful although in a lower key, is notable for its distinct earthiness; the rather light palate is redeemed by its satisfying length. The late-harvest Moscato Smentiò '98 deserves more than just a brief mention. Of a bright golden color, it is redolent of ripe peach with intriguing hints of saffron; the entry on the palate is characterized by heady notes of sage, followed by a fat but satisfying mid palate.

●	Barolo Cerequio '95	▼▼▼	6
●	Barbaresco Asili '96	▼▼	6
●	Barbera d'Asti Sup. Valle del Sole '96	▼▼	4
○	Gavi Fornaci di Tassarolo '96	▼▼	5
○	Moscato d'Asti Smentiò '98	▼▼	4
●	Monferrato Countacc! '96	▼▼	5
●	Langhe Barilot '96	▼	5
○	Monferrato Plenilunio '97	▼	4
●	Barolo Cannubi '90	▽▽▽	6
●	Barolo Cerequio '88	▽▽▽	6
●	Barolo Cerequio '93	▽▽▽	6
●	Barbera d'Asti Sup. La Court '96	▽▽	5

CALOSSO (AT)

SCAGLIOLA
FRAZ. S. SIRO, 42
14052 CALOSSO (AT)
TEL. 0141/853183

The Scagliola brothers' estate near the village of Calosso is claiming more and more of our attention. It is also an example which many producers of the Asti area, who rub along in a routine fashion, would do well to follow. It started up many years ago with the usual mixed farming, then began to specialize in the production of moscato grapes, and several years back these enterprising brothers began to chafe at their role of vineyard laborers. Thus it was that they began to produce and bottle the best of the Moscato as the Volo di Farfalle selection, of which the '98 version is once again among the finest of its kind: rich on the nose, fat and long but at the same time fresh and enjoyable on the palate. However, one can't live on Moscato alone so the estate has decided to go in for reds as a serious commitment, with new plantings of barbera and other red varieties. The results confirm that Maggiorino and Mario really know what they're about in both vineyard and cellar. Last year's Barbera d'Asti SanSì made a good impression: this has been more than borne out by the '97 version which came within an inch of Three Glasses: the color is brilliant, deep and intense, the fruit on the nose is ennobled by a masterly use of French oak, and the palate is warm, mouth-filling and very long-lasting. The good Chardonnay Casot dan Via needs just a little more body to achieve real excellence. Last but not least, it should be remembered that all the Scagliola wines are really good value for money.

●	Barbera d'Asti SanSì '97	🍷🍷	4
○	Moscato d'Asti Volo di Farfalle '98	🍷🍷	3*
●	Barbera d'Asti '98	🍷	3
○	Moscato d'Asti '98	🍷	3
○	Piemonte Chardonnay Casot dan Vian '98	🍷	3
●	Barbera d'Asti SanSì '96	🍷🍷 (white)	4
●	Barbera d'Asti SanSì '95	🍷 (white)	4

CALOSSO (AT)

TENUTA DEI FIORI
VIA VALCALOSSO, 3
REG. RODOTIGLIA
14052 CALOSSO (AT)
TEL. 0141/826938 - 0141/966500

Walter Bosticardo, a vigneron based near Calosso, is a singular character. We first got to know this creative and eccentric man through his unusual Pensiero, a "metodo classico" spumante made from moscato grapes. His ability as a wine-maker was confirmed by the Moscato d'Asti Rairì, the Chardonnay Al Sole and the Barbera Vigneto del Tulipano Nero. None of these showed up this year: it is in keeping with Walter's character to perform a sleight of hand, causing the wines one knows, and has been expecting, to disappear, and presenting entirely new ones in their stead. But each time he manages to surprise us with an original and wonderful bottle, and this year it is the Monferrato Rosso Cabernet Sauvignon '96, an outstanding wine, almost Californian in style, which really impressed us. Of an almost impenetrable garnet color, it offers a warm, elegant nose with evident peppery notes; the palate has sweet, almost chewy fruit and is substantial and powerful: this is a young wine with a great future. We were rather disappointed, on the other hand, by the Barbera, particularly as it's a '97. The sample we tasted has a good color but not entirely clean aromas, recalling burnt rubber at the first impact on the nose (with aeration, however, the fruit takes over); the palate displays good texture and balance but lacks fullness and is rather short. We shall have to wait for the Vigneto del Tulipano Nero cru. Lastly, the Gamba di Pernice '97, an exclusive specialty of Calosso, is an aromatic red table wine of a dark garnet color: the impact on the palate is decidedly inadequate but the nose offers intriguing notes of green peppercorn and spice.

●	Monferrato Rosso Cabernet '96	🍷🍷	4
●	Barbera d'Asti '97	🍷	3
●	Gamba di Pernice '97	🍷	3
●	Monferrato Rosso '95	🍷🍷 (white)	4
●	Barbera d'Asti Vigneto del Tulipano Nero '96	🍷 (white)	4
●	Barbera d'Asti Vigneto del Tulipano Nero '95	🍷 (white)	3
○	Pensiero '91	🍷 (white)	5

CAMINO (AL)

TENUTA GAIANO
VIA TRINO, 8
15020 CAMINO (AL)
TEL. 0142/469440

This estate is situated in the foothills on the right bank of the Po, facing the rice paddies, and here Pier Iviglia and Gigi Lavander continue to make good Monferrato wines, with the technical assistance of Giovanni Bailo. Here there is no chopping and changing in style nor, perhaps because of an intimate knowledge of what is going on in France, is there any uneasy sense of inferiority or feverish xenophilia: the estate's preference is still firmly for exploiting all the potential of native varieties. The complexity of the barbera grape, the uniqueness of grignolino, the entirely Piedmontese versatility of freisa, the explosive aromas combined with the body of ruché all make up such a cornucopia that it's hardly necessary to consider foreign fruit. This year the Barbera del Monferrato Gallianum again won Two Glasses, fully deserved thanks in part to its ruby color and clean aromas, with plenty of attractive fruit. It is an austere wine, full-bodied, harmonious, long and satisfying: here at last is a big, classic, non-barriqued Barbera at an extremely reasonable price. The Grignolino '98, which benefited from the same favorable ripening conditions as its immediate predecessor, offers soft tones that will seem unusual to traditional Grignolino fans; nevertheless the exceptional light ruby color and intense aromas of spice and fruit may surprise newcomers to this wine because of the tannic dryness of the palate. Talking of surprises, we had another one when we tasted the Birbarossa, a rich, elegant blend of aromatic red varieties (including a good proportion of brachetto). It is a fine, bright ruby in color, and the nose offers notes of licorice, dried roses and spice; the warm palate has an appealing astringency and adequate body.

●	Barbera del M.to Gallianum '97	TT	3*
●	Birbarossa '98	T	3
●	Grignolino del M.to Casalese '98	T	3
●	Barbera del M.to Gallianum '96	YY	2
●	Barbera del M.to Vigna della Torretta '96	YY	4

CANALE (CN)

CASCINA CA' ROSSA
LOC. CASE SPARSE, 56
12043 CANALE (CN)
TEL. 0173/98348 - 0173/98201

Angelo Ferrio has proved to be one of the best producers of Roero reds: two of them, the Barbera Mulassa and the Roero Audinaggio, have been unhesitatingly awarded Two Glasses. The first is a dense garnet red, with a very slight rim which is a clear indication of its rich texture; the bouquet displays admirable finesse and evolves gradually in the glass, offering aromas of red and black fruit, tobacco, coffee, green leaves and mint. The palate is rich, broad and solid; very elegant tannins lend firmness to the long finish. The Audinaggio is ruby-colored with an orange tinge; with its wide array of fragrant aromas the nose is intriguing and delectable, offering traces of ripe fruit, pepper and mint mingling with forward hints of dried flowers. In the mouth it may not display great power, but it has harmony and evenness with a corresponding, graceful finish. One Glass goes to the Arneis Merica '98, greenish straw yellow in color and uncomplicated in fragrance, with notes of apricot and grass; this simplicity is repeated on the palate, where a crisp, silky development makes it enjoyably drinkable. The Birbét Dolce, made from brachetto, has a lovely purplish cherry color with a delicately aromatic nose and a sweet, lively palate followed by notes of rose and banana on the finish. The basic Roero, simple and undemanding, is light, pleasant drinking.

●	Barbera d'Alba Vigna Mulassa '97	TT	4
●	Roero Vigna Audinaggio '97	TT	5
●	Birbét Dolce '98	T	3
●	Roero '98	T	3
○	Roero Arneis '98	T	3
○	Roero Arneis Merica '98	T	3
●	Roero Vigna Audinaggio '96	YYY	5

CANALE (CN)

CASCINA CHICCO
VIA VALENTINO, 144
12043 CANALE (CN)
TEL. 0173/979069

The more Marco and Enrico Faccenda's experience grows the more they seem to learn, and indeed this year the two brothers have come up with a series of splendid wines. We'll start with the Roero Valmaggiore '97, which won Two Glasses hands down. The color is an intense ruby-garnet; the rich and immediate nose offers hints of violet, blackberry and raspberry enhanced by elegant spicy and leafy notes; the rich, well-structured palate unfolds in a voluptuous progression leading into a long-reverberating finish of violet and cocoa underpinned by austere, powerful tannins. But the estate's real champion, which easily won it Three Glasses, is the Barbera Bric Loira. In the glass it shows an extremely dense ruby color tending towards garnet; the generous and dashing bouquet offers notes of cherry, plum and rosemary with hints of spice and pepper; in the mouth it is fat and ample, and the lingering finish mirrors the bouquet, perfectly blending the wood and the fruit: a small masterpiece. The basic Barbera displays a ruby-garnet hue and aromas of cherry, mint and spice; on the substantial palate a faint streak of acidity is just perceptible. The Nebbiolo Mompissano is vivid in color and fruity on the nose, with a full, lingering palate. The Arneis offers a fragrance of pear, chamomile and crusty bread; the palate is balanced and corresponding. The smoothly drinkable Favorita reveals delicate scents of russet apple and almond. The two Birbéts, made from brachetto, are both good wines.

●	Barbera d'Alba Bric Loira '97	▼▼▼	4
●	Barbera d'Alba '98	▼▼	3*
●	Nebbiolo d'Alba Mompissano '97	▼▼	4
●	Roero Valmaggiore '97	▼▼	4
●	Birbét Dolce '98	▼	3
●	Birbét Secco '98	▼	3
○	Langhe Favorita '98	▼	3
○	Roero Arneis '98	▼	3
●	Barbera d'Alba '97	▽▽	3
●	Barbera d'Alba Bric Loira '96	▽▽	4

CANALE (CN)

MATTEO CORREGGIA
VIA S. STEFANO ROERO, 124
12043 CANALE (CN)
TEL. 0173/978009

This year there is an important newcomer to the wines of the Correggia family: the Roero Ròche d'Ampsèj, the world-beating result of Matteo's experiments in a style of production which is new to him. The former rich fruitiness of aroma and voluptuous softness in the mouth have given way to a bouquet of less immediacy and a palate where a powerful structure and balance of forces are the keynote; it's an interpretation of nebbiolo which, without losing sight of the Langhe tradition, shows it in a modern perspective, by means of a longer maceration on the skins, an extra year of maturation and the use of new wood. The estate's crus, however, are always characterized by the raw material, as can be seen from the impenetrable garnet color and the deep, slowly unfolding bouquet, with flowery, fruity, spicy, and balsamic notes and faint mineral traces. The broad, vigorous palate culminates in an incredibly long finish, where the powerful alcohol and austere tannins are perfectly blended. The Barbera Marun offers aromas of red fruit, coffee, tobacco and menthol; the palate is broad, confident, solid and concentrated and without a harsh note; the very long finish emphasizes the nobility of the tannins. The Nebbiolo La Val dei Preti offers a nose ranging from hints of black fruit to soft, creamy, minty notes; the palate reveals a wonderfully mouth-filling, meaty roundness and a solid phenolic structure. Two easily-earned Glasses for the basic reds: the fruity, elegant Roero and the vigorous Barbera. Lastly, One Glass each goes to the Anthos (a dry brachetto) and to the Arneis.

●	Barbera d'Alba Marun '97	▼▼▼	5
●	Roero Ròche d'Ampsèj '96	▼▼▼	6
●	Nebbiolo d'Alba La Val dei Preti '97	▼▼	5
●	Barbera d'Alba '98	▼▼	3
●	Roero '98	▼▼	3
●	Anthos '98	▼	3
○	Roero Arneis '98	▼	3
●	Barbera d'Alba Bricco Marun '95	▽▽▽	4
●	Barbera d'Alba Marun '96	▽▽▽	4
●	Nebbiolo d'Alba La Val dei Preti '96	▽▽▽	4
●	Nebbiolo d'Alba La Val dei Preti '95	▽▽	4

CANALE (CN)

DELTETTO
C.SO ALBA, 33
12043 CANALE (CN)
TEL. 0173/979383

Vintages like '97 and '98 have helped to improve the wines of Roero, whose steady upward surge seems to be uninterrupted, but we must not forget the skill and ability of the numerous producers of this zone for whom quality is the first priority. One of these is Antonio Deltetto, who has presented an excellent range. This year all his reds have been awarded Two Glasses: the Roero Braja '97, the Roero Madonna dei Boschi '97 and the Barbera Bramè '97. The first, our favorite, has a faint orange rim on a garnet base; the nose is broad and complex, offering black fruit, violets, mint and leather enhanced by a toastiness indicative of a well-judged use of wood; the rich, broad palate has austere tannins and creamy notes on the ample, lingering finish. The Madonna dei Boschi, ruby-garnet in color, is slightly less concentrated. The nose is characterized by strawberry, blueberry and spice, while the slightly unsettled palate offers a composed, balanced finish with echoes of coffee. The young, forceful character of the Barbera Bramè is heralded by its color, purplish glints on a garnet ground; its aromas of caramel, blackberry and black cherry derive from the satisfactory blending of wood and fruit; it is broad and firm on the palate. The Arneis S. Michele has a rather lean nose with notes of lemon and green apple; the palate is invigorating and satisfyingly long. We liked the fruity and flowery Chardonnay and its straightforward palate. To end the list, a frank Favorita and a properly made Arneis Daivej.

●	Barbera d'Alba Bramè '97	🍷🍷	4
●	Roero Braja '97	🍷🍷	4
●	Roero Madonna dei Boschi '97	🍷🍷	4
○	Langhe Chardonnay '98	🍷	3
○	Langhe Favorita S. Michele '98	🍷	3
○	Roero Arneis Daivej '98	🍷	3
○	Roero Arneis S. Michele '98	🍷	3
●	Roero Madonna dei Boschi '96	🍷🍷 (empty)	4

CANALE (CN)

FUNTANIN
VIA TORINO, 191
12043 CANALE (CN)
TEL. 0173/979488

The wines presented by Bruno and Piercarlo Sperone are numerous and of a high standard. The Roero Superiore Bricco Barbisa and the Barbera d'Alba Superiore both win Two full Glasses. The first is ruby-garnet in color with an orange rim; red fruits, spice and undergrowth emerge on the nose with hints of fur; the generous body of the palate counteracts the tannins; these give punch to the finish, which offers toasty notes. The ruby-garnet Barbera displays strawberry, black cherry, vanilla and spice on the nose; it reveals a rich palate, with a confident impact and a long finish articulated by well-modulated tannins. Two Glasses also go to the splendid Arneis Pierin di Soc, straw-colored with a faint greenish tinge; the nose, broad and aristocratic, offers hints of apple, apricot, white flowers and grapefruit peel; the palate has a silky, delicate, but invigorating consistency with a refreshing bite of acidity; the citrus peel re-emerges on the ample finish. The barrique-aged Chardonnay Papé Bianc releases aromas of apricot, anise and vanilla; the palate could do with a touch more freshness. The Favorita has delicate, distinct aromas and is nicely flavored and balanced on the palate. The enjoyable Rosso Menico displays fruity aromas and a vigorous palate. To end the list, a pleasant red made from brachetto (a traditional variety here) which has been called L'Innominabile (the Unnameable) in protest against the authorities who have not granted the Roero producers the DOC status which would allow them to display the name of the variety on the label.

●	Barbera d'Alba Sup. '97	🍷🍷	4
○	Roero Arneis Pierin di Soc '98	🍷🍷	3
●	Roero Sup. Bricco Barbisa '97	🍷🍷	5
○	Langhe Chardonnay Papé Bianc '96	🍷	4
○	Langhe Favorita '98	🍷	3
●	Langhe Rosso Menico '97	🍷	4
●	L'Innominabile '98		3
○	Roero Arneis '98		3
●	Barbera d'Alba '96	🍷🍷 (empty)	3

Filippo Gallino

Fraz. Valle del Pozzo, 63
12043 Canale (CN)
tel. 0173/98112

The two Gallino reds, the Roero Superiore and the Barbera d'Alba Superiore, have for some years been among the finest in the area, and Filippo, Maria and their son Gianni (who share the work in the vineyards and the cellar) did not miss an opportunity like that of the '97 vintage for a further boost in quality. This year both the Barbera and the Roero are splendid, and the former has come in first and won Three Glasses. Of an intense ruby color verging on garnet, it offers clearly defined aromas of black and red fruit (blackberry, plum and cherry) with undertones of violet, herbs and tar. The palate is full-bodied and rich, excellently supported by the solid structure, and the wine is articulated both on the finish and all through its progress in the mouth, harmoniously counterbalancing the warmth of the alcohol with the astringent (but noble) tannic component. This is a superb wine, perhaps a little rustic, but you will be won over by its great personality. The Roero reveals a dense garnet color with an orange-tinged compact rim; the broad, enticing nose offers scents of violet, red fruit, mint and custard with complex undertones of leather and coffee; the rich, balanced palate is well supported by the phenolic structure, which lends plenty of bite to the wonderfully long finish. The pale straw-colored Arneis, with delicate yeasty aromas and notes of banana and apple, deserves One Glass; with its easy, undemanding drinkability it is an excellent match for light, vegetable-based starters or delicate fish courses. A properly made Birbét Dolce ends the list.

●	Barbera d'Alba Sup. '97	🍷🍷🍷	4
●	Roero Sup. '97	🍷🍷	4
○	Roero Arneis '98	🍷	3
●	Birbét Dolce '98		3
●	Barbera d'Alba Sup. '96	🍷🍷 (empty)	4
●	Roero Sup. '96	🍷🍷 (empty)	4

CANALE (CN)

Malvirà

Via S. Stefano Roero, 144
Loc. Case Sparse
12043 Canale (CN)
tel. 0173/978145

Every year the Damonte family estate comes up with a range of really superb wines. This year the top of the line, the Roero Superiore, scored very high marks: a very intense ruby-garnet in color, it offers a broad, complex nose with red and black fruit, tobacco, menthol, toasty notes and intriguing animal scents; the impact on the palate is concentrated and meaty, and it opens out into a long, corresponding finish nicely articulated by the robust tannins. The S. Gugliemo (from barbera, nebbiolo and bonarda) was even better: it shows a very dense garnet hue with a firm rim; the elegant nose releases notes of strawberry, raspberry and plum with complex undertones of leather and cocoa; the full, solid palate vaunts a very long finish in which creamy, balsamic notes emerge. This red was the best from the Malvirà winery, and came very close to winning Three Glasses. The basic Roero has an attractive bouquet of berries, mint, peach and pepper; in the mouth it is soft and substantial with noble tannins on the long finish. The Arneis Saglietto, vinified in wood, and the Arneis Trinità stand out among the whites: the first offers a mouth-filling richness, although the nose is still rather closed, while the second, straw-colored with a greenish tinge, has fresh aromas of peach and lemon with floral hints and hay. The palate is silky, with full, lively flavors ending on a long, seductive finish. The Arneis Renesio with its scents of lily-of-the-valley and fruit followed by a balanced, medium-long palate, was not quite so good. The '97 version of the Tre Uve (arneis, sauvignon and chardonnay) is less successful than the previous vintage: although it has plenty of body, it is diminished by over-pronounced wood. Two One Glass winners end the list: a robust Barbera and a cheerful Favorita.

●	Langhe Rosso S. Guglielmo '97	🍷🍷	5
○	Roero Arneis Trinità '98	🍷🍷	3
○	Roero Arneis Saglietto '98	🍷🍷	4
●	Roero Sup. '96	🍷🍷	5
●	Barbera d'Alba '98	🍷	4
●	Birbét Dolce '98	🍷	3
○	Langhe Bianco Tre Uve '97	🍷	4
○	Langhe Favorita '98	🍷	3
●	Roero '97	🍷	4
○	Roero Arneis Renesio '98	🍷	3
●	Roero Sup. '90	🍷🍷🍷 (empty)	5
●	Roero Sup. '93	🍷🍷🍷 (empty)	5
○	Langhe Bianco Tre Uve '96	🍷🍷 (empty)	4
●	Langhe Rosso S. Guglielmo '96	🍷🍷 (empty)	5
●	Roero Sup. '95	🍷🍷 (empty)	4

CANALE (CN)

MONCHIERO CARBONE

VIA S. STEFANO ROERO, 2
12043 CANALE (CN)
TEL. 0173/95568

Marco Monchiero, the mayor of Canale, has adopted a successful style for his range of excellent wines, midway between tradition and innovation. The most interesting of the series, the Barbera d'Alba MonBirone, is intense ruby-garnet in color with a youthful, purplish tinge to the rim; the nose is broad and delicate, with aromas of violet, wild cherry, raspberry, vanilla and spice. Its impact on the palate is rich and generous, and it progresses smoothly, leading to a persistent finish which reveals toasty notes given by the new wood. We also liked the Roero Srü, ruby crossed with garnet in hue with a slightly faded rim. It offers an elegant, varied and enticing nose: delicious aromas of berries mingle with balsamic, spicy tones and mineral traces in a sumptuous bouquet. The well-articulated palate is broad and firm, leading into a long, smooth finish with hints of raspberry on a spicy background. The barrique-fermented Tamardì '97, from arneis (75%) and chardonnay, is as good as the '96. Of a golden straw color, it reveals aromas of peach and banana over pronounced woody notes, and a smooth and silky palate with admirable balance. The Arneis, green-tinged straw in color, releases a fragrance of apricot and tropical fruit; the palate is light and subdued, with a medium-long finish.

●	Barbera d'Alba MonBirone '97	🍷🍷	4
●	Roero Srü '97	🍷🍷	4
○	Langhe Bianco Tamardì '97	🍷	4
○	Roero Arneis '98	🍷	3
●	Barbera d'Alba MonBirone '96	YY	4
●	Roero Srü '96	YY	4
●	Roero Sup. '95	YY	4
○	Langhe Bianco Tamardì '96	Y	4

CANALE (CN)

MARCO E ETTORE PORELLO

C.SO ALBA, 71
12043 CANALE (CN)
TEL. 0173/978080 - 0173/979324

With a good vintage like '97 to work with, Marco Porello, a graduate of the Alba school of oenology with lots of experience despite his youth, has easily claimed Two Glasses for his Roero Bric Torretta and the consequent cachet for his entire range of reliable good wines. The prize-winner is modern in conception and reveals the personality and expressiveness of nebbiolo combined with a well-judged use of new wood and skilled, careful vinification. The result is a firm ruby color verging on garnet which gives an idea of the structural solidity to follow; the broad aromas range from raspberry to vanilla, cocoa and clove. The even palate shows the promised good consistency, and is only very slightly unsettled; the long finish is invigorated by prominent but noble tannins. We liked the Barbera Bric Torretta '97, ruby-garnet in color with a rather mature rim; it displays moderately heady tones of cherries steeped in alcohol, with balsamic and spicy notes, in a dry, well-ordered bouquet. The palate is robust in character and full-bodied, with hints of violets on the austere finish. The Arneis Vigneto Camestrì '98 is just a little below par: of a slightly deep straw color, it offers aromas of very ripe fruit, herbs and wildflowers; the palate, which shows a certain lack of freshness, is reasonably firm with a faintly bitterish note on the finish.

●	Roero Bric Torretta '97	🍷🍷	4
●	Barbera d'Alba Bric Torretta '97	🍷	3
○	Roero Arneis Vigneto Camestrì '98	🍷	3
●	Birbét Secco '98		2
●	Barbera d'Alba Bric Torretta '96	Y	3
●	Roero Bric Torretta '96	Y	3

CANELLI (AT)

CASCINA BARISEL
REG. S. GIOVANNI, 2
14053 CANELLI (AT)
TEL. 0141/824849

This attractive Canelli estate makes its first appearance in the Guide this year. It covers four hectares of vineyard from which about 20 thousand bottles are produced, divided between the two varieties most typical of this area: Moscato and Barbera. Enrico Penna and his wife Elda bought the property in 1965, and as of 1985 their sons Franco and Fiorenzo have enthusiastically taken charge of, respectively, marketing and wine-making. The Barbera La Cappelletta, 2,500 bottles from a vineyard planted in 1955, would alone justify this debut in the Guide. It shows an intense ruby-garnet color and is broad and harmonious on the nose, offering hints of berries, violet and coffee as well as toasty notes; the soft and mouth-filling palate vaunts a progression well-regulated by a full body which underpins it right through to the long finish, where notes of cocoa appear. The Moscato, greenish glints on a straw-coloured ground, has an elegant, clearly-defined bouquet with broad aromas of tropical fruit, jasmine, crusty bread and peach; the palate is rich and fat, with a delicate effervescence that most effectively offsets the sweetness, and the elegant, lingering finish is enhanced by an enjoyable freshness. We mention the simple and cheerful Barbera, characterized by a robust palate and a certain finesse on the nose. Cascina Barisel also includes a stable which was used for raising cattle until last year, but now houses only rabbits and chickens. It would seem that the estate's future is in wine: there is plenty of enthusiasm and no lack of results.

●	Barbera d'Asti Sup. La Cappelletta '96	🍷🍷	4
●	Barbera d'Asti Barisel '98	🍷	3
○	Moscato d'Asti '98	🍷	3

CANELLI (AT)

GIUSEPPE CONTRATTO
VIA G. B. GIULIANI, 56
14053 CANELLI (AT)
TEL. 0141/823349

This year Contratto has scored a double success: in addition to the De Miranda, the Brut '95 has also received our highest award. The estate now bears the palm as Piedmont's top producer of sparkling wines, and this is not all they produce. The credit should undoubtedly go to Carlo and Antonella Bocchino, brother and sister, the owners also of the well-known Canelli distillery that bears their name, who have guided the estate in its policy of aiming for the highest quality, making considerable investments in property and manpower, and to Giancarlo Scaglione, who skillfully gave concrete shape to this policy by creating wines of great personality and undeniable excellence. The opulent De Miranda '97 is warmly redolent of anise, sage and honey; the seductive palate is wonderfully supported by a perfect effervescence and finishes on long, vibrant notes of apricot preserve. The Metodo Classico Brut '95 is in a different class from previous vintages with its admirable balance on nose and palate. A full-bodied sparkler, it is old gold in color with a very fine perlage; the broad, lingering bouquet with notes of toasty bread, white flowers, damson and green apple is followed by an explosive palate offering hints of citrus, ripe fruit and biscuit. The Barbera Solus Ad, blessed by a unique year, '97, is also among the best of its class. Deep purple in color, it displays still slightly green aromas of vanilla, undergrowth and spice, and a rich palate with exceptional body underpinned by considerable acidity and some nicely ripened fruit. The Chardonnay La Sabauda '97 offers good balance, and the Barolo Tenuta Secolo '95 shows character, an intense bouquet and a faintly perceptible roughness to be imputed to the tannins.

○	Asti De Miranda Metodo Classico '97	🍷🍷🍷	5
○	Spumante Metodo Classico Brut Ris. Giuseppe Contratto '95	🍷🍷🍷	4
●	Barbera d'Asti Solus Ad '97	🍷🍷	6
●	Barolo Cerequio Tenuta Secolo '95	🍷🍷	6
○	Piemonte Chardonnay La Sabauda '97	🍷	5
○	Asti De Miranda Metodo Classico '96	ΥΥΥ	5
●	Barbera d'Asti Solus Ad '95	ΥΥ	5
●	Barbera d'Asti Solus Ad '96	ΥΥ	5
●	Barolo Cerequio Tenuta Secolo '93	ΥΥ	6
○	Spumante Metodo Classico Brut Ris. Giuseppe Contratto '94	ΥΥ	5

CANELLI (AT)

LUIGI COPPO E FIGLI
VIA ALBA, 66
14053 CANELLI (AT)
TEL. 0141/823146

The Coppo brothers' winery, which today is still in the avant-garde, was one of the very first in Monferrato to embrace a modernizing philosophy and breathe new life into the languishing style of the wines of this area. The Coppos learned through experience how to use new French wood while preserving the characteristics of their terroir. The Pomorosso '96 is one of their most representative wines and a perfect expression of the Coppo style. It has an intense ruby color and a nose of great finesse, with spicy notes of vanilla, pepper and juniper mingling with aromas of ripe red fruit. The palate reveals elegance, rather than the explosive impact of other Barberas, but is almost unrivalled in length. Its younger brother, the Camp du Rouss '97, is slightly overpowered by the vigor of this vintage: it shows a violet hue, a faint rusticity in its aromas of cherry and fresh herbaceous notes, and a finish just a bit unbalanced by alcohol. The Monteriolo '97 is excellent: indeed each version of this chardonnay seems better than the last; it shows character both in its greenish-gold color and on the nose, which offers notes of toasty bread, vanilla, white flowers and tangerine. A good bite of acidity underpins the exceptionally sweet fruit on the palate. The Costebianche '98 is among the best ever made, fruity in aroma and delightful in the mouth, and the Brut Riserva '94 is also one of the best of its kind. It reveals power and structure, with enjoyable citrus aromas and yeasty notes on the nose and a long finish in the mouth with echoes of ripe citron. The Alterego '97, from barbera and cabernet, dense in hue, offers aromas of pepper and grass; the palate is suitably tannic, with a pleasant sensation of licorice on the finish.

●	Barbera d'Asti Camp du Rouss '97	🍷🍷	4
●	Barbera d'Asti Pomorosso '96	🍷🍷	6
●	Monferrato Rosso Alterego '96	🍷🍷	6
○	Piemonte Chardonnay Monteriolo '97	🍷🍷	6
○	Piemonte Chardonnay Costebianche '98	🍷🍷	4
○	Brut Riserva Coppo '94	🍷🍷	5
●	Barbera d'Asti Pomorosso '90	ΥΥΥ	5
●	Barbera d'Asti Pomorosso '95	ΥΥ	6
○	Brut Riserva Coppo '90	ΥΥ	5
○	Piemonte Chardonnay Monteriolo '96	ΥΥ	5
○	Piero Coppo Brut Riserva del Fondatore '86	ΥΥ	6

CANELLI (AT)

VILLA GIADA
REG. CEIROLE, 4
14053 CANELLI (AT)
TEL. 0141/831100

The Faccio family seems to have a special feeling for the barbera grape, perhaps the variety most typical of this zone near Asti: each of the estate's three Barberas has in fact carried off Two Glasses. The Bricco Dani '97, with its richness and charm, was only just short of Three; of a dense ruby-garnet color, it has a broad and enticing nose with very ripe red fruit, pepper, menthol and custard; the palate is full-bodied and sumptuous, and vaunts an effortless progression; the substantial structure supports the finish, where warm alcohol emerges, mingling with fresh balsamic notes. The Bricco Dani '96 has a youthful, compact rim on a garnet ground; the nose offers fruity aromas blending with pronounced wood-derived balsamic notes; the palate is beautifully concentrated, and the dry finish reveals a hint of cherry. The Barbera La Quercia '97, of a vivid color with an orange rim, has a broad bouquet of vanilla, cherry and spice; the palate is graceful and invigorating, and wood has the upper hand on the medium-long finish. The '96 version has a harmonious nose that shows finesse; the concentrated palate is lent vigor by a lively acidity and prominent tannins. The good Passito Val di Gala, from moscato grapes, offers hints of peach, sage and quince, while the sweet, almost fat palate is nicely counterbalanced by a crisp freshness. The Barbera Vivace Vezzosa, the Gamba di Pernice and the Chardonnay Bricco Mané are all properly made wines.

●	Barbera d'Asti La Quercia '97	🍷🍷	4
●	Barbera d'Asti Sup. Bricco Dani '96	🍷🍷	4
●	Barbera d'Asti Sup. Bricco Dani '97	🍷🍷	4
●	Barbera d'Asti La Quercia '96	🍷	4
●	Gamba di Pernice '97	🍷	3
○	Val di Gala Passito	🍷	5
●	Barbera del M.to Vezzosa Vivace '98		2
○	Piemonte Chardonnay Bricco Mané '98		3
●	Barbera d'Asti Sup. Bricco Dani '95	ΥΥ	4

CAREMA (TO)

Cantina dei Produttori
Nebbiolo di Carema
Via Nazionale, 28
10010 Carema (TO)
tel. 0125/811160

The winegrowers of this area, the gateway to the Valle d'Aosta, have an immensely tricky terroir to cope with. Precipitous mountain slopes are the natural setting in which these dedicated growers, spurred on by their love for their native territory, cultivate small plots wherever it is possible to create a pergola of nebbiolo vines. Access to the vineyards is only on foot and all vineyard work must be done by hand. In addition, the Alpine climate is known for its severity; indeed, it has given rise to the invention of the "pilun", a characteristic stone structure which supports the pergolas and supplies a valuable reserve of extra warmth to help ripen the grapes. This year the white-labeled Carema Carema, the winery's top selection, was not presented, so we had another taste of the '93, which we reviewed last year, and found it not diminished a whit: the harmony between freshness and evolution on the nose is perfectly intact and the palate still shows a delightful progression in which the austerity of the nebbiolo grape coexists with a carefully wrought balance, making for pleasurable drinking. This year we were offered the basic Carema, of a rather light ruby color with a wide orange rim; the bouquet is distinctly forward, with hints of jam and leather mingling with mineral undertones. The palate has medium body with fairly assertive tannins and a finish that echoes the nose.

●	Carema '95	▼	4
●	Carema Carema '90	▽▽	5
●	Carema Carema '93	▽▽	4

CASTAGNOLE LANZE (AT)

★ La Spinetta
Via Annunziata, 17
14054 Castagnole Lanze (AT)
tel. 0141/877396

The Rivetti brothers felt that they needed more scope than Castagnole Lanze and Moscato d'Asti provided, and so it was that, having proved their worth in 1989 with their first premium red, the Pin, from barbera, nebbiolo and cabernet, they were unable to resist trying their hand at Barbaresco. And now, after a trial vintage in 1995, the dynamic Giorgio, who within the space of a few years has doubled the size of the estate, bringing it up to the present 70 hectares under vine, has scored a real triumph with the outstanding '96 vintage, producing two Barbarescos of world-beating class. The Gallina offers an extremely harmonious and intense nose, with hints of red berries to which very delicate spicy notes add complexity; the soft, velvety palate reveals incredible length with just a trace of wood which will blend in with time. The Starderi, which is very nearly on the same level, has a wonderful intense color and a very elegant nose, on which a faint toastiness mingles perfectly with the fruity aromas; the palate displays exceptional structure, powerful and soft at the same time. To complete the collection of aces presented by the Rivettis, we have the Barbera Gallina and the Pin, both from the celebrated '97 vintage. The first even manages to outstrip last year's achievement, with explosive aromas of cherries and plum preserves; the richness of extract on the palate is such that it outweighs the acidity typical of this variety. The Pin displays its customary stellar standard, with more body and smoothness than usual, conclusive evidence of the phenomenal performance of the '97 vintage in Piedmont. A trio of Three Glasses for a winery that's going from strength to strength!

●	Barbaresco Vigneto Gallina Vürsù '96	▼▼▼	6
●	Barbera d'Alba Vigneto Gallina '97	▼▼▼	5
●	Monferrato Rosso Pin '97	▼▼▼	5
●	Barbaresco Vigneto Starderi Vürsù '96	▼▼	6
○	Moscato d'Asti Bricco Quaglia '98	▼▼	3
●	Barbera d'Asti Ca' di Pian '98	▼	4
●	Barbera d'Alba Vigneto Gallina '96	▽▽▽	5
●	Monferrato Rosso Pin '94	▽▽▽	5
●	Monferrato Rosso Pin '95	▽▽▽	5
●	Monferrato Rosso Pin '96	▽▽▽	5
●	Pin '90	▽▽▽	6
●	Pin '93	▽▽▽	6

CASTEL BOGLIONE (AT)

Araldica Vini Piemontesi
Via Albera, 19
14040 Castel Boglione (AT)
tel. 0141/762354

This winery, which includes the three cooperatives Antica Contea di Castelvero, Cantina di Mombaruzzo and Cantina di Ricaldone, offers a wide and varied range. The wine that proved most interesting is the Nebbiolo Castellero: the color is a youthful, intense ruby, while the broad, enticing nose offers hints of red fruit, peach and undergrowth with faint balsamic traces. The palate is ample in body, with barely perceptible tannins lending substance to the long finish, where peach and cocoa emerge. The Barbera Rive is intense garnet in color and releases ripe fruity, balsamic and spicy aromas; in the mouth it is satisfyingly rich, with an only slightly noticeable acidity and a long finish characterized by fresh balsamic notes. The Barbera Ceppi Storici is somewhat light in color, with rich aromas of vanilla, cocoa, jam and pepper; the palate reveals good body and balance. The Chardonnay Roleto has a straightforwardly varietal character, with aromas of hazelnut, acacia blossom and banana; in the mouth it is very soft and smooth. The pale straw-colored spumante, Brut Alasia, offers fruity notes and fermentation-derived aromas followed by a medium-firm palate; it has plenty of fizz and an uncomplicated finish. The Renero reveals aromas of red fruit and aromatic herbs; the palate is not particularly demanding and the finish echoes the bouquet. Two Moscatos deserve our mention: the Muscaté Sec, dry, pleasantly aromatic and excellent as an aperitif, and the sweet Moscato d'Asti Alasia.

● Langhe Nebbiolo Castellero Poderi Alasia '97	🍷🍷	4
● Barbera d'Asti Rive Poderi Alasia '97	🍷	3
● Barbera d'Asti Sup. Ceppi Storici '97	🍷	3
● Monferrato Rosso Renero Poderi Alasia '97	🍷	4
○ Moscato d'Asti Alasia '98	🍷	3
○ Muscaté Sec Alasia '98	🍷	2*
○ Piemonte Brut Poderi Alasia '96	🍷	4
○ Piemonte Chardonnay Roleto Poderi Alasia '97	🍷	4

CASTEL BOGLIONE (AT)

Cascina Garitina
Via Gianola, 20
14040 Castel Boglione (AT)
tel. 0141/762162

The Morino family's Barbera Neuvsent '96, a confirmation of the quality of the Garitina wines, fully deserves its Two Glasses. The color is a vivid ruby-garnet with a narrow rim; the nose is broad and distinctive, offering notes of strawberry and blueberry with sweetly spicy and balsamic hints; the development on the palate is rich, ample and invigorating, and the dry finish ends on a nicely blended, lingering note of fruit and spice. The Barbera Bricco Garitta '97 displays a dense garnet hue; on the broad nose notes of menthol, vanilla and white pepper are counterbalanced by aromas of raspberry and cherry. The palate is firm, ample and concentrated, with a confident progression; the tannins are faintly perceptible on the warm, lingering finish. The Monferrato Rosso Amis (50% barbera, 40% pinot nero and 10% cabernet) is ruby verging on garnet in color; its complex and original nose offers aromas of strawberry, black currant, rhubarb, tobacco and dried herbs; in the mouth it is robust and chewy, broad in character and well-articulated by pronounced but noble tannins; vigor and deep notes of licorice characterize the finish. The Brachetto Niades, purple-cherry in color, displays the aromas typical of the variety, with notes of mint and rose underlying fruity sensations; the sweet palate is well balanced by an exuberant effervescence and the finish is rough but enjoyable. Lastly, the Barbera Il Morinaccio is well made, pleasantly rustic, light on the palate and enlivened by a slight sparkle.

● Barbera d'Asti Sup. Neuvsent '96	🍷🍷	4
● Monferrato Rosso Amis '97	🍷🍷	3*
● Barbera d'Asti Bricco Garitta '97	🍷	3
● Barbera del M.to Vivace Il Morinaccio '98	🍷	2*
● Brachetto d'Acqui Niades '98	🍷	3
● Barbera d'Asti Sup. Neuvsent '95	🍸	4

CASTELLINALDO (CN)

Teo Costa

Via S. Salvario, 1
12050 Castellinaldo (CN)
tel. 0173/213066

Roberto and Marco Costa produce their wine from about 20 hectares under vine located at an altitude of between 250 and 300 meters above sea level. We'll begin with the Roero Superiore Batajot, named after the vineyard near Castagnito that the grapes come from. Garnet-tinged ruby in color, the wine offers distinctive, enticing aromas, with notes of blackberry and raspberry, menthol, resin and fur; there is a smooth, solid progression on the not particularly rich but beautifully balanced palate, leading into an invigorating, even finish. The Castellinaldo Barbera d'Alba, although still good, as usual, hasn't made the most of the '97 vintage and is less well-defined than it has been. The Nebbiolo, on a slightly lower level, shows an almost transparent ruby color and a rather simple bouquet with hints of red fruit and spice; the medium-firm, well-composed palate leads to a pleasantly dry finish. We liked the Arneis Serramiana and the admirable finesse of its fruity, flowery fragrance; the palate, ample and modulated, is followed by an articulated finish. The less successful Arneis Ajnaldi Bianc has a deep straw hue; the fruit on the nose is somewhat overwhelmed by the aromas of vanilla and caramel given by new wood; the smooth, soft palate has medium body.

●	Castellinaldo Barbera d'Alba '97	🍷	4
●	Nebbiolo d'Alba Bricco Costa '97	🍷	4
○	Roero Arneis Serramiana '98	🍷	3
●	Roero Sup. Vigneto Batajot '97	🍷	4
○	Roero Arneis Ajnaldi Bianc '98		4
●	Castellinaldo Barbera d'Alba '95	🍷🍷 (prev.)	4
●	Castellinaldo Barbera d'Alba '96	🍷🍷 (prev.)	4

CASTELLINALDO (CN)

Stefanino Morra

Via Castagnito, 22
12050 Castellinaldo (CN)
tel. 0173/213489

Stefanino Morra's estate has won Two Glasses for each of its top reds, the Roero Superiore '97 and the Castellinaldo Barbera d'Alba '97. This year the Roero is in the lead, with a dense ruby-garnet color as the first indication of its excellence; the nose is redolent of fruit (strawberry and plum), with complex spicy hints of clove and vanilla mingling with balsamic notes (menthol); the palate is really impressive: vigorous from the start, it shows a broad and gradual development that continues smoothly right through to the long finish, which is well supported by firm, noble tannins. The Castellinaldo Barbera d'Alba, almost as impressive, has a still faintly purple rim on a good ruby-garnet base; the nose offers red fruit, spice and toasty aromas, while the rich, firm palate develops confidently, followed by a dry, just slightly acidic finish. The enjoyable and undemanding Arneis '98 shows a straw color of medium intensity and clean, simple aromas of banana, apple, herbs and wildflowers; its light, graceful palate suggests that it could be an ideal aperitif on a warm summer evening, or a good accompaniment to a light vegetable antipasto. To end the list, the basic Barbera has a light ruby hue; it offers simple, immediate aromas of cherry, raspberry and almond followed by a light and graceful palate. The estate's top white, the cask-aged Arneis Vigneto S. Pietro, is absent this year.

●	Castellinaldo Barbera d'Alba '97	🍷🍷	5
●	Roero Sup. '97	🍷🍷	4
●	Barbera d'Alba '97	🍷	4
○	Roero Arneis '98	🍷	4
●	Castellinaldo Barbera d'Alba '96	🍷🍷 (prev.)	4
●	Roero Sup. '96	🍷🍷 (prev.)	4

CASTELNUOVO DON BOSCO (AT)

CASCINA GILLI
VIA NEVISSANO, 36
14022 CASTELNUOVO DON BOSCO (AT)
TEL. 011/9876984

Among the wines Gianni Vergano presented this year we particularly liked the Barbera d'Asti Vigna delle More. This full-bodied and robust Two Glass wine displays an intense ruby-garnet hue with a purple rim and an exuberant, pleasantly rustic bouquet with notes of hay, raspberry and black currant on a damp earth background; the palate is energetic, with tannins and crisp acidity emerging on the lingering finish. The Malvasia, the traditional local sweet wine, is as appealing as ever, displaying fresh, fruity aromas, a velvety palate and a delightfully sweet finish. The two Freisas each win a Glass. The lively Luna di Maggio, of a purplish garnet color, offers clean aromas of red fruit, almond and crusty bread; in the mouth it is attractively effervescent and dry, and the harmonious finish mirrors the bouquet. The elegant Vigna del Forno is ruby-garnet in color with a slightly faded purplish rim; the nose, simple but not lacking in character, releases scents of strawberry, cherry, yeast and black pepper, while the satisfyingly full-flavored palate, enlivened by a light acidity, has a long, faintly bitterish finish. The good Monferrato Rosso (barbera and freisa), of a medium-intense ruby hue, offers straightforward fruity and spicy aromas with balsamic notes; the palate is reasonably firm, with a dry tannic component and a fairly long finish revealing aromatic nuances. The Chardonnay, of a very light straw color, has rather overpowering fermentation-derived aromas and a fairly intense palate which could do with a touch more finesse.

●	Barbera d'Asti Vigna delle More '98	🍷🍷	3*
●	Malvasia di Castelnuovo Don Bosco '98	🍷🍷	3
●	Freisa d'Asti Luna di Maggio '98	🍷	3
●	Freisa d'Asti Vigna del Forno '98	🍷	3
●	Monferrato Rosso '98	🍷	3
○	Piemonte Chardonnay '98		3

CASTIGLIONE FALLETTO (CN)

AZELIA
VIA ALBA-BAROLO, 53
12060 CASTIGLIONE FALLETTO (CN)
TEL. 0173/62859

There are many ways in which a first-rate producer can show his skill, but the ability to make the most out of the meagre potential that a difficult vintage offers is perhaps the most striking. Luigi Scavini, sharing the honors with his wife and his mother, had already produced a small miracle with the Bricco Fiasco '94 (you should taste it now: it is superb), but he has surpassed himself with the '95, creating a red of astonishing finesse and power. The dense structure of the wine is already revealed by its color, a deep and impenetrable garnet; the broad, expressive nose offers an astounding variety of aromas, with well-defined ripe fruit at its core, surrounded by scents of spice, flowers and licorice. Vigorous tannins underpin the entry on the palate, which is followed by a full development and a grand finale, echoing the bouquet. The Barolo San Rocco, whose greatest charm is its beguiling length, makes a splendid debut: its concentrated color corresponds to the powerful flavor, while the nose displays the intense mineral quality typical of the wines of Serralunga, home to this newly purchased vineyard. The top Azelia wines all reveal an impeccable use of oak and a rare balance. The intense and characteristic Dolcetto from the highly prized Montelupo precincts, does not let down the side. It has a dense-textured palate and a rich, lively nose. If the '96 Barbera showed greater finesse, with a consequent splendid evolution, the '97 version conquers thanks to its mature strength and captivating exuberance.

●	Barolo Bricco Fiasco '95	🍷🍷🍷	6
●	Barbera d'Alba Vigneto Punta '97	🍷🍷	4
●	Barolo S. Rocco '95	🍷🍷	6
●	Dolcetto d'Alba Bricco dell'Oriolo '98	🍷🍷	3*
●	Barolo '95	🍷	6
●	Barolo '91	YYY	6
●	Barolo Bricco Fiasco '93	YYY	6
●	Barbera d'Alba Vigneto Punta '96	YY	4
●	Barolo Bricco Fiasco '94	YY	6
●	Barolo Bricco Fiasco Ris. '90	YY	6
●	Barolo Bricco Fiasco '90	Y	6

CASTIGLIONE FALLETTO (CN)

BRICCO ROCCHE - BRICCO ASILI

VIA MONFORTE, 63
12060 CASTIGLIONE FALLETTO (CN)
TEL. 0173/282582

The wineries in Castiglione Falletto and Barbaresco are the most prized possesions in the oenological empire of the Ceretto brothers. The Bricco Asili '96, a world-beating cru, won Three Glasses hands down, bringing to mind another unforgettable vintage,'89. Ruby-garnet in color, it boasts impressive concentration and fruit and vivid, intense aromas of red berries, violet and tobacco; with its dense, succulent palate it is a truly elegant, soft wine. The other Barbaresco, the Faset, has good fruit, character, robust tannins and length, but lacks the enchanting balance that makes the Asili a great wine. The top Barolo of the house, the Bricco Rocche, is produced only in the best vintages: the '95, a superb version of this cru, of an almost blue dark ruby color, shows powerful aromas of tar and hedgerow and well-integrated tannins in the mouth; it finishes on a note of licorice and ripe plum. The Prapò '95 is another excellent interpretation of this vintage: it is slightly less smooth than the Rocche, but reveals the same long, powerful finish. The Brunate, traditionally the softest house Barolo, is a rather atypical version, more power-driven than usual, with an intensely spicy nose, and alcohol in command of the finish on the palate. All in all, Bricco Rocche and Bricco Asili have come up with a range of austere reds of stunning quality; nature played its part by blessing the nebbiolo grape with two outstanding vintages, but so did the ever-increasing dedication of the Ceretto brothers, supported by Giacolino Gilardi, to the two standard-bearing wines of the Langhe.

● Barbaresco Bricco Asili Bricco Asili '96	▼▼▼	6
● Barbaresco Faset Bricco Asili '96	▼▼	6
● Barolo Bricco Rocche Bricco Rocche '95	▼▼	6
● Barolo Brunate Bricco Rocche '95	▼▼	6
● Barolo Prapò Bricco Rocche '95	▼▼	6
● Barbaresco Bricco Asili Bricco Asili '85	▽▽▽	6
● Barbaresco Bricco Asili Bricco Asili '86	▽▽▽	6
● Barbaresco Bricco Asili Bricco Asili '88	▽▽▽	6
● Barbaresco Bricco Asili Bricco Asili '89	▽▽▽	6
● Barolo Bricco Rocche Bricco Rocche '89	▽▽▽	6
● Barolo Brunate Bricco Rocche '90	▽▽▽	6
● Barolo Prapò Bricco Rocche '83	▽▽▽	6
● Barbaresco Bricco Asili Bricco Asili '95	▽▽	6
● Barolo Brunate Bricco Rocche '94	▽▽	6

CASTIGLIONE FALLETTO (CN)

BROVIA

VIA ALBA-BAROLO, 54
12060 CASTIGLIONE FALLETTO (CN)
TEL. 0173/62852

This year Brovia has again released the full battery of its Barolos, after refusing to bottle anything from the '94 vintage. Nor was much selection possible with the '95, thanks to hailstorms on this side of the valley. Nevertheless the considerable experience of the Brovias was put to good use, and the results were better than we expected. The Barolo Ca' Mia is the fruit of a more modern interpretation than usual; it shows a medium-intense garnet color; the nose is characterized by a varied and captivating freshness, with notes of rose and cherry; the palate vaunts an admirably well-defined, balanced development. The Barolo Villero, also somewhat light in color, is more complex and articulated; the nose offers attractive, dense, jammy aromas over which subtle, intriguing flowery notes emerge with nuanced delicacy. After a meaty entry on the palate, smooth tannins favor an even and long development. The least fortunate of the Barolos is the Rocche dei Brovia: we didn't find the usual richness on the nose, and, after an encouraging attack on the palate, there was a sort of falling off. At the time of our tastings the numerous, eagerly awaited Dolcettos, which this estate usually does very well, were not yet available, but we hope to be able to describe them in next year's Guide. The Barbera Sorì del Drago will also be reviewed next year.

● Barolo Ca' Mia '95	▼▼	6
● Barolo Villero '95	▼▼	6
● Barolo Rocche dei Brovia '95	▼	6
● Barolo Monprivato '90	▽▽▽	6
● Barolo Garblèt Sué '91	▽▽	5
● Barolo Rocche dei Brovia '89	▽▽	6
● Barolo Rocche dei Brovia '90	▽▽	6
● Barolo Rocche dei Brovia '91	▽▽	6
● Barolo Rocche dei Brovia '93	▽▽	5
● Barolo Villero '93	▽▽	5
● Dolcetto d'Alba Solatìo '96	▽▽	4
● Barbera d'Alba Sorì del Drago '96	▽	4

CASTIGLIONE FALLETTO (CN)

Cantina Terre del Barolo

Via Alba-Barolo, 5
12060 Castiglione Falletto (CN)
tel. 0173/262053

For the cooperative winery Cantina Sociale Terre del Barolo this is definitely the year of Dolcetto, of which they have presented numerous versions from both the Alba and the Diano appellations with some extremely satisfying results. The Diano d'Alba Sorì Bricco del Ciabot '98, for example, is all body and vigor, with a medium-intense garnet color and a nose offering aromas of berries, almond and spice laced with light, attractive herbal notes. The full-bodied palate and noticeable tannins make this a pleasingly forceful wine. The Dolcetto d'Alba Castello has a good dense color and aromas of red fruit and pepper; it is substantial on the palate and well-defined, with a deeply satisfying finish. The Dolcetto Diano d'Alba from the Cascinotto vineyard and the one from Sorì Montagrillo are both pleasantly rustic, robust wines: the first offers a nose of medium finesse followed by a good, full palate, while the second, with faint animal notes over the fruit on the nose, is solid and concentrated in the mouth. The Dolcetto Raviole is more cheerful and immediate. The excellent Barbera Sorì Roncaglia, ruby-garnet in color with a faintly orange rim, shows a broad and captivating nose with notes of plum and blackberry preserves, fresh leaves, violet and toastiness. The impact on the palate is rich, with a lively bite of acidity that lends freshness to the intense, smooth finish. The Barolo di Castiglione Falletto '95, slightly faded in color, has a forward bouquet with hints of dried flowers and spice over faint briny nuances; the well-structured palate is almost austere in character.

● Barbera d'Alba Sorì Roncaglia '97	▼▼	3*
● Diano d'Alba Sorì Bricco Ciabot '98	▼▼	3*
● Dolcetto d'Alba Vigneti Castello '98	▼▼	3*
● Barolo di Castiglione Falletto '95	▼	5
● Diano d'Alba Vigneti Cascinotto '98	▼	3
● Diano d'Alba Sorì Montagrillo '98	▼	3
● Dolcetto d'Alba Raviole '98	▼	3
● Barbera d'Alba Sorì Roncaglia '96	▽▽	3
● Barolo Baudana Ris. '90	▽	5
● Barolo Castello Ris. '90	▽	5
● Barolo Codana Ris. '90	▽	5
● Barolo di Castiglione Falletto '93	▽	4

CASTIGLIONE FALLETTO (CN)

Cascina Bongiovanni

Via Alba-Barolo, 4
12060 Castiglione Falletto (CN)
tel. 0173/262184

It is clear that Davide Mozzoni has a great passion for wine, furthered by his recent theoretical studies, but even more by an inquiring mind, constantly urging him on to make even better wines. The three hectares of vineyard in Pernanno which belong to his aunt yield about 20 thousand bottles, and with the addition of grapes from surrounding vineyards he reaches an annual production of 30 thousand. This year's wines once again prove young Davide's skill in the cellar, where he handled the vinification of the Barolo Pernanno '95 perfectly. Aromas of ripe fruit, mint and well-judged wood emerge on the nose; the attractive fruitiness is at home on the palate as well, lingering right up to the long, soft finish with hints of licorice. The extremely well-made basic Barolo is a simpler wine; it has all the character you would want but lacks the finesse and complex elegance offered by the Pernanno. The Langhe Falletto '97, a blend of barbera, nebbiolo and cabernet sauvignon, is excellent, as usual, elegance being its strong suit, as was not the case with the overpowering '96 version. Deep ruby in color with a purple tinge, it releases aromas of toasty oak and cherries steeped in alcohol which still need to amalgamate; the palate is soft and vigorous with a sweet, succulent finish. This is an excellent compromise between the sweetness of ripe barbera, the impetuosity of young nebbiolo and the aromatic character of cabernet sauvignon. The Dolcetto '98, whose aromas need some more bottle age, ends the list.

● Barolo Pernanno '95	▼▼	5
● Langhe Rosso Faletto '97	▼▼	5
● Barolo '95	▼	5
● Dolcetto d'Alba '98	▼	4
● Barolo '93	▽▽	4
● Langhe Rosso Falletto '96	▽▽	5
● Barolo '94	▽	5

CASTIGLIONE FALLETTO (CN)

F.lli Cavallotto
Tenuta Bricco Boschis
Via Alba-Monforte
Loc. Bricco Boschis
12060 Castiglione Falletto (CN)
tel. 0173/62814

The Barolo Vignolo '93, from the family property in the lower part of Castiglione near the hamlet of Garbelletto, is the best wine presented this year by the Cavallotto brothers. This red perfectly expresses the estate's philosophy of production: first and foremost, the wines should be released for sale only when they have acquired a mature harmony; the secondary precepts are long maceration and then aging in large Slovenian oak barrels. The resulting wine reflects the qualities of the '93 vintage, which was certainly not remarkable, but did yield grapes with a good overall balance, which the Cavallottos have turned to excellent advantage. The distinct garnet color of the wine is followed by a nose offering the classic hints of steeped flowers alternating with spicy notes; the palate reveals a pervasive softness with an enjoyable sensation of warmth, good length and a satisfying finish. The attractively complex Barolo Bricco Boschis '95 is admirable for both the clear correspondence between nose and palate, and the solid body which, although not very concentrated, is extremely well distributed. The Barbera Vigna del Cuculo has made progress since the '96 version: the aromas here are well blended with the oak, and the full-bodied, exuberant palate shows better balance. The good Dolcetto Vigna Melera is distinguished this year by an appealing delicacy on the palate and clear, fragrant aromas. Lastly, the Langhe Nebbiolo '96 has, at its tender age, apparently already reached the point of being past its best.

●	Barolo Bricco Boschis '95	▼▼	6
●	Barolo Vignolo Ris. '93	▼▼	6
●	Dolcetto d'Alba Vigna Melera '97	▼	3
●	Barbera d'Alba Vigna del Cuculo '97	▼	4
●	Langhe Nebbiolo '96		3
●	Barolo Vigna S. Giuseppe Ris. '89	▽▽▽	6
●	Barolo Colle Sud-Ovest Ris. '90	▽▽	6
●	Barolo Colle Sud-Ovest Ris. '91	▽▽	6
●	Barolo Vigna S. Giuseppe Ris. '90	▽▽	6
●	Barolo Vigna S. Giuseppe Ris. '93	▽▽	6
●	Barolo Vigna Sud-Ovest Ris. '89	▽▽	6
●	Barolo Vignolo Ris. '89	▽▽	6
●	Barolo Vignolo Ris. '90	▽▽	6
●	Barolo Bricco Boschis '94	▽	5

CASTIGLIONE FALLETTO (CN)

★ Paolo Scavino
Via Alba-Barolo, 59
12060 Castiglione Falletto (CN)
tel. 0173/62850

Paolo Scavino is one of the top winegrowers of the Langhe in terms of consistency of quality, meticulousness and overall skill. His well-balanced, extraordinarily characterful wines seem to have won him an annual subscription to Three Glasses. This year the Dolcetto does not come only from the Fiasc vineyard, but also from a new one of about two hectares recently purchased at Castiglione Falletto. The wine is ruby tending towards violet in hue, releases clean aromas of plum jam and licorice, and seems to caress the palate with its silkiness and substance. The very soft and concentrated Barbera in Carati '96 is an attractive wine with 14° of alcohol; the nose offers fruity notes of cherry jam, and there are admirable soft tannins on the palate. Of the four '95 Barolos our favorite was the Fiasc: very deep-hued, it offers intense aromas of overripe fruit and spicy notes of cinnamon; the explosively powerful palate reveals the usual tremendous charge of tannins, crucial to its future positive development: a glorious Three Glass wine that brilliantly overcame the difficulties of its vintage, which was not a blessing in many zones of the Langhe. The elegant, spicy Cannubi does not lack character; the Rocche has a very complex nose, flowery, fruity and heady; the palate is still rather hard and has yet to find its balance. The basic Barolo '95, made with grapes from all the estate plots, ends the list. It is notable for an easy drinkability combined with a not too punishing price.

●	Barolo Bric dël Fiasc '95	▼▼▼	6
●	Barbera d'Alba Affinata in Carati '96	▼▼	5
●	Barolo Cannubi '95	▼▼	6
●	Barolo Rocche dell'Annunziata '95	▼▼	6
●	Dolcetto d'Alba '98	▼▼	4
●	Barolo '95	▼	6
●	Barolo Bric dël Fiasc '90	▽▽▽	6
●	Barolo Bric dël Fiasc '93	▽▽▽	6
●	Barolo Cannubi '91	▽▽▽	6
●	Barolo Cannubi '92	▽▽▽	6
●	Barolo Rocche dell'Annunziata '93	▽▽▽	6
●	Barolo Rocche dell'Annunziata Ris. '90	▽▽▽	6
●	Barolo Cannubi '93	▽▽	6

CASTIGLIONE FALLETTO (CN)

VIETTI
P.ZZA VITTORIO VENETO, 5
12060 CASTIGLIONE FALLETTO (CN)
TEL. 0173/62825

This year the battery of wines presented by Mario Cordero and Luca Corrado includes three Barbera d'Astis of excellent quality, which come from the six hectares of vineyard they have acquired at Agliano: the Tre Vigne, the Crena and the Quorum. The last one is the result of a project involving, besides Vietti, the wineries of Prunotto, Braida, Coppo, Chiarlo and the Berta distillery and is discussed on p. 122. Two full Glasses go to the Tre Vigne, ruby-garnet in color with a firm, youthful rim; the nose is broad and mature in tone with notes of violet, red fruit and vanilla; the palate is satisfying and reveals an acidic bite that does not disturb its ample progression; the finish, characterized by hints of cocoa, is long. The Barbera La Crena, not quite so rich, offers hints of cherry, coffee and white pepper and a substantial, balanced palate. And now for the Langhe wines: the Barbera Scarrone proved excellent, of a particularly dense garnet hue and redolent of ripe blackberry, black currant, tobacco and menthol with faint animal nuances; the richness promised by the color is found on the palate, with a velvety, broad progression leading into a very long finish with nicely blended fruity and spicy notes. The most successful of the Barolos is the Lazzarito: its aromas range from fruity and floral to spicy and mineral; the well-articulated palate has a long, corresponding finish. The two other Barolos are good, with the more vigorous Rocche performing better than the Brunate, which is perhaps just past its best. The Barbaresco Masseria, soft and creamy in fragrance, is rich and robust on the palate. A simple, fruity Arneis and a smooth and pleasing Nebbiolo end the list.

● Barbaresco Masseria '96	▼▼	6
● Barbera d'Alba Scarrone '97	▼▼	4
● Barbera d'Asti La Crena '97	▼▼	5
● Barbera d'Asti Tre Vigne '97	▼▼	4
● Barolo Lazzarito '95	▼▼	6
● Barolo Rocche '95	▼▼	6
● Barolo Brunate '95	▼	6
● Langhe Nebbiolo Perbacco '97	▼	4
○ Roero Arneis '98	▼	4
● Barolo Rocche di Castiglione '85	▽▽▽	6
● Barolo Rocche di Castiglione '88	▽▽▽	6
● Barolo Villero '82	▽▽▽	6
● Barbaresco Masseria '95	▽▽	6
● Barolo Lazzarito '93	▽▽	6
● Barolo Villero Ris. '90	▽▽	6

CASTIGLIONE TINELLA (CN)

CAUDRINA - ROMANO DOGLIOTTI
S.DA CAUDRINA, 20
12053 CASTIGLIONE TINELLA (CN)
TEL. 0141/855126

This year the Dogliotti family estate has produced 150 thousand bottles of Moscato, divided between the two crus and the Asti Spumante, and 7,500 bottles of Barbera d'Asti La Solista from their recently purchased vineyard at Nizza. This is a simple, traditional Barbera, unoaked and ready to drink; it shows a quite intense ruby color with a youthful rim and a still grapey nose offering notes of cherry and almond with faint green undertones: an eminently satisfying wine, in which the directness of the palate is not in conflict with its meaty consistency. We particularly liked the Moscato La Caudrina, which has a deep, golden-straw hue; the ripe, well-defined nose displays aromas of white- and yellow-fleshed fruit, elder blossom and honey, while the palate is rich and full with a light effervescence and a finish of delightful finesse. The other Moscato cru, La Galeisa, has a less expressive nose: the varietal fragrance does emerge with finesse, but rather timidly; the palate shows satisfying structure. The excellent Asti La Selvatica offers aromas of nectarine, sage and lemon on the nose, with faint green notes; the development of the palate is full and even and leads to a crisp, lingering finish. Vineyards have been rented at Ottiglio and Nizza in order to add new wines to the estate's range. Further details will be revealed in next year's Guide.

○ Asti La Selvatica '98	▼▼	4
○ Moscato d'Asti La Caudrina '98	▼▼	3*
● Barbera d'Asti La Solista '98	▼	3
○ Moscato d'Asti La Galeisa '98	▼	4

CASTIGLIONE TINELLA (CN)

ICARDI

VIA BALBI, 30
LOC. S. LAZZARO
12053 CASTIGLIONE TINELLA (CN)
TEL. 0141/855159

Claudio and Ornella Icardi's wines reflect a carefully articulated plan to establish an estate style with certain distinctive features: they have chosen to vinify very ripe grapes, producing wines that are characterized by a pronounced fruitiness and a well-judged use of new wood; they aim for elegance and an enjoyable, ready drinkability rather than for imposing structure. The wines react well to a certain amount of aging, but they are pleasantly approachable right from the start. Of their wide range, we particularly liked the Chardonnay and the Monferrato Bianco (a blend of chardonnay and sauvignon), which stand out because of their well-defined aromas of ripe fruit and their not inconsiderable structure, the Pinot Nero Nej, which perfectly expresses the varietal characteristics of a grape which is notoriously temperamental and difficult to work with, and the Pafoj (a Piedmontese dialect expression meaning "we're no fools"), a Nebbiolo lent grace by the classic touch of the winery: each of these won Two Glasses. The Dolcetto, the Barbera and the Nebbiolo Surìsjvan, on a slightly lower level, are nevertheless characterized by attractive aromas and good balance on the palate. The Moscato d'Asti La Rosa Selvatica is slightly cloying, while the Barolo Parej (from the Piedmontese "you must make it like this"), a debutant whose grapes come from La Morra, overplays the immediacy of the palate at the expense of the classic nuances of the great Langhe red and does not live up to its somewhat pompous name.

●	Langhe Rosso Nej '97	🍷🍷	4
●	Langhe Rosso Pafoj '98	🍷🍷	6
○	Monferrato Bianco Pafoj '98	🍷🍷	5
○	Piemonte Chardonnay Surìssara '98	🍷🍷	4
○	Moscato d'Asti La Rosa Selvatica '98	🍷	3
●	Barbera d'Alba Surì di Mù '97	🍷	4
●	Barolo Parej '95	🍷	6
●	Dolcetto d'Alba Rousori '98	🍷	3
●	Langhe Nebbiolo Surìsjvan '97	🍷	4
●	Langhe Rosso Pafoj '97	🍸🍸	6
●	Monferrato Rosso Cascina Bricco del Sole '96	🍸	5

CASTIGLIONE TINELLA (CN)

LA MORANDINA

VIA MORANDINI, 11
12053 CASTIGLIONE TINELLA (CN)
TEL. 0141/855261

Our congratulations to Giulio and Paolo Morando, who seized the occasion of the wonderful '97 vintage to produce a Barbera Varmat of great stature, earning Two full Glasses at our tastings! Intense garnet in hue with a firm, narrow rim, it has a deep, complex nose with inviting hints of blackberry, black currant and cherry and an intriguing undertone of tobacco and menthol; this richness reappears on the palate, where the entry is concentrated, the ample progression is articulated by ripe tannins, and the long, vigorous finish reveals notes of violet and cocoa. The more direct Barbera Zucchetto shows a medium-intense ruby color and a bouquet of raspberry, wild cherry and pepper; the palate is light and easy but not unsatisfying, and the finish is reasonably long. The successful Moscato d'Asti '98 offers a deepish straw color and a very well-defined, ripe fragrance of peach, tropical fruit, honey and white flowers. The meaty, fat palate is nicely supported by balanced effervescence and crisp acidity; fruity fragrances reappear with sage on the long, delicate finish. Our review of the wines from this attractive estate ends with the Langhe Chardonnay '98, a clean, perfectly executed wine; pale straw in color, it has undemanding fermentation-derived aromas and a light, crisp, balanced palate.

●	Barbera d'Asti Varmat '97	🍷🍷	4
○	Moscato d'Asti '98	🍷🍷	3*
●	Barbera d'Asti Zucchetto '97	🍷	4
○	Langhe Chardonnay '98	🍷	3
●	Barbera d'Asti Varmat '96	🍸🍸	4
●	Barbera d'Asti Zucchetto '96	🍸	3

CASTIGLIONE TINELLA (CN)

ELIO PERRONE
S.DA S. MARTINO, 3
12053 CASTIGLIONE TINELLA (CN)
TEL. 0141/855803

The Moscato Clarté is again an excellent wine, among the best of its category, and this year the Perrones are also presenting an interesting Barbera Grivò. This wine, of an intense ruby color verging on garnet, has broad aromas with notes of red fruit, leather, pepper and coffee; the substantial and firm palate develops smoothly through to the warm, lingering finish. The Clarté has a greenish straw color and a deliciously fresh nose with hints of citrus, white flowers and summer fruit with aromatic notes; it is rich and full in the mouth, with the slightest fizziness and appropriate acidity which regulates the progression and gives freshness to the long finish. The Moscato Sourgal, of a very pale straw color, with aromas of peach, sage and elderberry, is leaner but graceful; the palate is smooth and moderately effervescent and the finish, though not very long, is elegant. The attractive, barrique-fermented Chardonnay Char-de S. '97 is golden-straw in hue and offers an interesting if somewhat wood-dominated nose, with scents of banana, flowers and honey and toasty notes; the palate is mouth-filling, and a tendency towards flatness is kept in check by a pleasant underlying succulence; the enjoyable finish offers notes of fruit and vanilla. Lastly, the Dolcetto Giulin, ruby-garnet in color with a faintly faded rim, has a slightly rustic nose and a medium-firm palate.

●	Barbera d'Asti Grivò '97	▼▼	4
○	Moscato d'Asti Clarté '98	▼▼	3*
○	Char-de S. '97	▼	4
○	Moscato d'Asti Sourgal '98	▼	3
●	Dolcetto d'Alba Giulin '98		3
●	Barbera d'Asti Grivò '96	▽	4

CASTIGLIONE TINELLA (CN)

PAOLO SARACCO
VIA CIRCONVALLAZIONE, 6
12053 CASTIGLIONE TINELLA (CN)
TEL. 0141/855113

The Langhe Bianco Graffagno, from Rhine riesling, chardonnay and sauvignon, has a markedly individual personality which bears witness to Paolo Saracco's determination and experimental flair. The wine shows a medium-intense straw color and an intriguing nose with tropical fruit and crusty bread mingling with faint mineral nuances. The soft and substantial palate develops smoothly through to an intense and corresponding finish. The Chardonnay Bianch du Luv, of a full straw-yellow hue, displays broad, complex aromas of white-fleshed fruit, anise and sweet pastry together with toasty notes. The nicely textured palate develops along ample lines, leading into a lingering finish where wood is slightly overbearing. Both the Moscatos are good, although the Autunno is less expressive than usual; it is straw-colored with a faint greenish tinge; the nose, while not particularly intense, is delicate and graceful, offering notes of peach and rose mingled with fermentation-derived aromas; in the mouth it is smooth and even with a decided fizziness and a fragrant, aromatic finish. The basic Moscato, pale straw in hue, offers a delicately varietal bouquet of fruity, and floral scents blended with herbal notes; delicacy reappears on the subtle, balanced palate, and the finish, although not very long, reveals charm. The Chardonnay Prasuè, of a green-tinged pale straw hue, offers not very intense aromas of fruit and flowers and a light, refreshing palate.

○	Langhe Bianco Graffagno '97	▼▼	4
○	Langhe Chardonnay Bianch del Luv '97	▼▼	4
○	Moscato d'Asti Moscato d'Autunno '98	▼▼	3
○	Langhe Chardonnay Prasuè '98	▼	3
○	Moscato d'Asti '98	▼	3
○	Langhe Bianco Graffagno '96	▽▽	3
○	Langhe Chardonnay Bianch del Luv '96	▽▽	4

COCCONATO D'ASTI (AT)

BAVA
S.DA MONFERRATO, 2
14023 COCCONATO D'ASTI (AT)
TEL. 0141/907083

The Bava brothers Roberto, Giulio and Piero have produced no fewer than three Two Glass Barberas from the '96 vintage: the Stradivario, the Piano Alto and the Arbest. The first is ruby-garnet in color with a faintly orange rim; the nose offers well-balanced fruit and wood in the form of toasty notes, cherry, blackberry, black currant and vanilla. The palate displays a good texture and robust structure with a restrained but enlivening acidity, and appropriate tannins on a lingering finish. The Barbera Piano Alto (from newly purchased vineyards in Agliano), making its first appearance, has an intense garnet hue and a characterful nose: mineral and balsamic aromas are laced with hints of black fruit and undergrowth; the broad, concentrated palate is nicely balanced by an invigoratingly tangy structure and boasts a long, intense finish. The Arbest, equally dense in hue with a slightly faded rim, releases jammy notes, tar and clove on the nose; the powerful palate is mouth-filling and the integrated tannins lend depth to the long licorice finish. Two Glasses also go to the Bianco Alteserre, of a clear straw color; aromas of tropical fruit, sage and vanilla blend with a faintly briny undertone; it is rich and even in the mouth, and shows crispness and a lingering finish. The Malvasia di Castelnuovo Don Bosco, ruby-purple in hue, offers a clean, enjoyable nose with scents of rose, pear, peach and lemon peel. The palate has a pronounced effervescence and a corresponding finish with a light tannic tone. To end the list, the Moscato Bass Tuba, deep straw in color, has opulent but not cloying aromas of peach, vanilla and sage; the sweet, harmonious palate offers a refreshing sparkle.

● Barbera d'Asti Sup. Arbest '96	🍷🍷	4
● Barbera d'Asti Sup. Piano Alto '96	🍷🍷	5
● Barbera d'Asti Sup. Stradivario '96	🍷🍷	5
○ Monferrato Bianco Alteserre '97	🍷🍷	4
○ Moscato d'Asti Bass Tuba '98	🍷	3
● Malvasia di Castelnuovo Don Bosco '98	🍷	2
● Barbera d'Asti Sup. Stradivario '95	♀	5
○ Giulio Cocchi Brut '90	♀	4

COSSOMBRATO (AT)

CARLO QUARELLO
VIA MARCONI, 3
14020 COSSOMBRATO (AT)
TEL. 0141/905204

For many wine drinkers, Grignolino means a pale rosé with a nice fragrance and not much weight, to be drunk cool, preferably in summer, with a plate of prosciutto and salami: an undemanding, second-rate wine. Among the few winegrowers who are trying to change this image, Carlo Quarello has been for years a major force. A highly cultured man with delightful manners, he manages year after year to produce a really intriguing wine that will even improve and develop with a few years' aging. His vineyards near Alfiano Natta on the border between the provinces of Asti and Alessandria, are planted to grignolino and, to a lesser extent, barbera and nebbiolo. The Grignolino Cré Marcaleone '98 is already promising at first sight, with its ruby-red hue tending towards rosé; the nose is still rather closed, but intense and satisfying fruit is detectable; in the mouth the wine reveals all its personality, with a splendid structure underpinned by hefty tannins and appropriate acidity. Our advice is to wait a few months, or even a few years, in order to appreciate all of its many qualities. This year the Crebarné, 70% barbera and 30% nebbiolo, is also highly successful. The captivating bouquet boasts broad aromas of red berries, and the palate, although still a little rough-edged, is full of succulent fruit.

● Monferrato Rosso Crebarné '97	🍷🍷	4
● Grignolino del M.to Casalese Cré Marcaleone '98	🍷🍷	3*
● Grignolino del M.to Casalese Cré Marcaleone '97	♀♀	3
● Crebarné '96	♀	4

COSTA VESCOVATO (AL)

LUIGI BOVERI
VIA XX SETTEMBRE, 6
FRAZ. MONTALE CELLI
15050 COSTA VESCOVATO (AL)
TEL. 0131/838165

Luigi Boveri has staked his all on producing excellent wines. Results seem to favor him and we feel sure that other winegrowers with a similar dedication will emerge in the Tortona area. The estate has an annual output of about 25 thousand bottles from its eight hectares under vine, all with very good exposure, and the cellar has recently been rendered absolutely up-to-the-minute: this is a winery which is looking to the future. As far as the wines go, Luigi's efforts are concentrated mainly on Barbera, and his best wine was in fact the Vignalunga, a Barbera dei Colli Tortonesi from very old vineyards which was matured in barriques for 15 months. Of a very deep ruby hue, it releases dense aromas of red fruit, with cherry to the fore; the structure is good and the entry on the palate soft and fruity, but the wood still needs to assimilate better on the finish. The unoaked Poggio delle Amarene has an impenetrable, almost black color and offers very ripe black cherry and coffee on the nose. The attack on the palate is sweetish but the effect is nicely counterbalanced by a bite of acidity on the finish. Another wine we liked was the Leopoldo, made from Rhine riesling grown in a vineyard planted by Luigi's grandfather over 50 years ago. An attractive straw color precedes a leafy fragrance with faint mineral and aromatic notes; the palate offers an enjoyable crisp acidity and good length. The appealing Cortese Vigna del Prete, of a pale straw hue, is redolent of chamomile and has a light, inviting palate. We should mention that '98 is the first vintage of the Timorasso, which we shall be tasting next year.

●	Colli Tortonesi Barbera Vignalunga '97	🍷🍷	4
●	Colli Tortonesi Barbera Poggio delle Amarene '97	🍷	3
○	Colli Tortonesi Cortese Vigna del Prete '98	🍷	2*
○	Colli Tortonesi Bianco Leopoldo '97	🍷	3

COSTIGLIOLE D'ASTI (AT)

PIETRO BENOTTO
FRAZ. S. CARLO, 52
14055 COSTIGLIOLE D'ASTI (AT)
TEL. 0141/966406

Costigliole d'Asti is the home of good Barbera in the Asti area, and the Benotto brothers are skilled growers of this variety. The three Barberas they presented this year are all excellent and two of them have won Two Glasses. The Barbera Superiore Rupestris '97, ruby-garnet in color with a youthful rim, has a broad, decidedly forward nose, revealing toasty notes, jam, clove and tar; the rich, firm, dry palate reveals the use of the barrique, and the smooth progression is underpinned by plenty of grip; fruit and spice emerge on the warm, lingering finish. The richness of the very successful Barbera Superiore Vigneto Casot '97 is heralded by the dense ruby-garnet hue. The bouquet unfolds gradually, with hints of ripe cherry, cocoa and sweet spice mingling with balsamic notes; the palate reveals a dense consistency with a slightly unsettled acidity, while the long finish offers red fruit and cocoa. The Barbera Superiore Balau '97, a simpler, less demanding wine, is a medium-intense ruby red verging on garnet; the direct but not deficient fragrance includes notes of cherry and raspberry with hints of vanilla, cocoa and leather, and the palate is quite satisfying.

●	Barbera d'Asti Sup. Rupestris '97	🍷🍷	4
●	Barbera d'Asti Sup. Vigneto Casot '97	🍷🍷	3*
●	Barbera d'Asti Sup. Balau '97	🍷	3
●	Barbera d'Asti Sup. Rupestris '96	🍷🍷 (outline)	4

COSTIGLIOLE D'ASTI (AT)

PODERI BERTELLI
FRAZ. S. CARLO, 38
14055 COSTIGLIOLE D'ASTI (AT)
TEL. 0141/966137

This winery produces a wide range of wines unusually divided between those traditional to the area (Barbera) and a larger group made from imported varieties. The oenologist Maurizio Nervi is in charge of the activities of what can only be described as an experimental laboratory. Some of the wines are released in a limited number of bottles and hence are difficult to find. However it isn't all experimentation: quality is certainly not lacking, as our tasting panel discovered. And now for the wines. The Sauvignon Fossaretti does not overemphasize its varietal notes, which merge well with the wood within a satisfying overall structure. The Chardonnay Giarone, whose aromas still need to evolve, is almost exaggeratedly rich and opulent. The San Marsan Bianco, a blend of marsanne and roussanne, has an intense, complex nose offering fruity, flowery aromas, and shows great possibilities for aging. The Barbera Giarone brings out all the best qualities of this wine, having tamed the acidity, which can be excessive, by means of some time spent in wood. Each of these wines easily won Two Glasses. Half a step down we find the Barbera San Antonio, more modern in style, the San Marsan Rosso (syrah), the Barbera Montetusa and the Cabernet Fossaretti. The Plissé Traminer is rather disapppointing, having performed better on previous occasions; the '98 version, although it has immediacy, lacks depth on the nose and is also slightly cloying: we'll be tasting it again in the future.

●	Barbera d'Asti Giarone '97	🍷🍷	5
○	Monferrato Sauvignon Fossaretti '97	🍷🍷	5
○	Piemonte Chardonnay Giarone '97	🍷🍷	5
○	S. Marsan Bianco '98	🍷🍷	5
●	Barbera d'Asti Montetusa '97	🍷	5
●	Barbera d'Asti S. Antonio '97	🍷	5
●	Monferrato Cabernet Fossaretti '97	🍷	5
●	S. Marsan Rosso '97	🍷	5
○	Plissé Traminer '98		5

COSTIGLIOLE D'ASTI (AT)

CASCINA CASTLÈT
S.DA CASTELLETTO, 6
14055 COSTIGLIOLE D'ASTI (AT)
TEL. 0141/966651

The winery of Mariuccia Borio, who is assisted by the young and competent oenologist Giorgio Gozzelino, has its foundations in a respect for tradition. The grapes cultivated here are the typical local ones, barbera and moscato (and experiments are under way to reintroduce the uvalino grape); the old vineyards have a limited yield, of high quality; there is no haste to modify vinification techniques, although the use of small barrels is not unknown. The 15 hectares under vine, partly estate-owned and partly rented, yield about 130 thousand bottles annually. The Barbera d'Asti '98 is the prototype of an undemanding wine sustained by a lively acidity, to be drunk when young. Six months in oak allow the Barbera Litina to acquire greater complexity, with intriguing vinous and fruity notes. The Passum is made from selected batches of barbera grapes that are allowed to dry, endowing the wine with characteristic overripe notes of cooked fruit and hints of spice. The Policalpo, the most successful of their reds, is a blend of barbera and 20% cabernet sauvignon; the toastiness and vanilla aromas of new wood mingle with notes of ripe red fruit and develop on the palate with good balance and length. Of the two versions of Moscato we prefer the Avié, a Passito (raisin wine), sweet but not cloying, that goes well with herbed cheeses, liver paté and desserts. A fragrant, fruity and floral Moscato d'Asti ends the list.

●	Monferrato Rosso Policalpo '97	🍷🍷	4
○	Piemonte Moscato Passito Avié '97	🍷🍷	5
●	Barbera d'Asti '98	🍷	3
●	Barbera d'Asti Sup. Litina '97	🍷	3
●	Barbera d'Asti Sup. Passum '97	🍷	5
○	Moscato d'Asti '98		3
●	Barbera d'Asti Sup. Passum '96	🍸	4
●	Monferrato Rosso Policalpo '96	🍸	4

COSTIGLIOLE D'ASTI (AT)

SCIORIO
VIA ASTI-NIZZA, 87
14055 COSTIGLIOLE D'ASTI (AT)
TEL. 0141/966610

With each edition of the Guide new wineries make their appearance, and this is one of the most interesting factors in the developing world of Italian wine. This year's Guide includes the debut entry of Sciorio, which has swept onto the stage with a series of splendid wines. The Gozzelino brothers Mauro and Giuseppe seem to have a very clear idea of how to achieve excellence in both vineyard and cellar, and the samples we tasted from the barrel of the wines due to be released next year demonstrate the consistency in quality of this small estate. The property, which is to be extended, consists of four hectares planted to barbera, cabernet sauvignon and chardonnay; in the cellar they make an intelligent use of large barrels, as well as new and once-used barriques which soften and round out the wines. The three versions of Barbera '96 are characterized by substantial alcohol well supported by exceptional structure; the basic version is matured in large barrels, while the Barrique and the Reginal spend about 10 months in barriques. All three are captivating with their partly expressed aromas of red fruit, and fill the mouth with concentrated, succulent fruit; each also boasts an extraordinarily long finish. The Barrique version reveals more vanilla, the Reginal is softer and more expressive, and the basic version has power and balance. The Antico Vitigno '96, a fat, opulent cabernet-based red, displays silky tannins and great breeding. The Bianco Sciorio (100% chardonnay) '97 is good, but the '98, tasted from the barrel, promises to be better.

●	Antico Vitigno '96	🍷🍷	4
●	Barbera d'Asti '96	🍷🍷	3*
●	Barbera d'Asti Barrique '96	🍷🍷	4
●	Barbera d'Asti Reginal '96	🍷🍷	4
○	Bianco Sciorio '97	🍷	4

CUCCARO M.TO (AL)

LIEDHOLM
VILLA BOEMIA
15040 CUCCARO M.TO (AL)
TEL. 0131/771916

Carlo Liedholm, son of the great soccer coach Niels, has been running this modern estate since 1973. Production really got under way in 1985, when the cellar was built and Donato Lanati became the consultant oenologist. Today the 70 thousand bottles made annually from the 12 hectares of vineyard are mainly destined for the foreign market. The Bianco della Boemia '98 is not yet ready and will be reviewed next year; the '97 version, when re-tasted, proved to be in need of more time in the bottle. The Rosso della Boemia '96 (a blend of 40% barbera, 40% pinot nero, 15% cabernet and 5% bonarda), earns One full Glass; because of a problematic harvest the wine is not so imposing as previous versions; also it has spent only one year in barrique instead of the usual two. However it is still an interesting wine, elegant rather than powerful in character, with the characteristics of the pinot nero outweighing the other varieties in the blend. The medium-intense color is followed by a nose that offers delicate, enjoyable aromas such as red currant; the palate is elegant and echoes the bouquet. The Barbera Tonneau, a selection of the best grapes that spends 12 months in 700-liter tonneaux, wins Two Glasses. This dark wine offers aromas of black cherry, plum and coffee, with somewhat pronounced wood; the palate, although not very long, has good body. Lastly, the simple and quaffable Grignolino is worthy of mention.

●	Barbera d'Asti Tonneau '97	🍷🍷	4
●	Rosso della Boemia '96	🍷	4
●	Grignolino del M.to Casalese '98		3
●	Rosso della Boemia '90	🍸🍸	5
●	Rosso della Boemia '91	🍸🍸	5
○	Bianco della Boemia '97	🍸	3

DIANO D'ALBA (CN)

CLAUDIO ALARIO
VIA SANTA CROCE, 23
12055 DIANO D'ALBA (CN)
TEL. 0173/231808

Claudio Alario's modern style is based on a rich softness of aroma, a concentrated texture and a discerning use of wood in an overall context indissolubly linked with the richness of the raw material. An example is the Dolcetto Costa Fiore, which is densely garnet-colored; the nose offers sweet notes of dark fruit preserves which contrast delightfully with the dry nuances of coffee and toastiness; further hints of resin and vanilla lend extraordinary breadth to the aromatic structure of this wine. The same sumptuous texture emerges on the palate, supported by a solid body with impressive tannins, which also lend vigor to the long finish. The Nebbiolo Cascinotto is similar: it is an intense, youthful ruby in color, and offers hints of sweet spice and eucalyptus, and toasty and jammy notes on the nose; the rich palate progresses in a gradual crescendo thanks to the powerful tannins and long finish. The newcomer is a Barolo, the Riba, of an intense, ruby-garnet color; the nose discloses sweet notes of caramel, coffee custard and raspberry with faint animal undertones, while the well-structured palate has plenty of body and a long, austere finish with echoes of fruit and cocoa. Lastly, One full Glass each goes to the Barbera Valletta, with a slight acidity on the palate, and to the mouth-filling Dolcetto Montagrillo.

●	Barolo Riba '95	🍷🍷	5
●	Dolcetto di Diano d'Alba Costa Fiore '98	🍷🍷	3
●	Nebbiolo d'Alba Cascinotto '97	🍷🍷	4
●	Barbera d'Alba Valletta '97	🍷	4
●	Dolcetto di Diano d'Alba Montagrillo '98	🍷	3
●	Barbera d'Alba Valletta '96	YY	4
●	Nebbiolo d'Alba Cascinotto '96	Y	4

DIANO D'ALBA (CN)

BRICCO MAIOLICA
VIA BOLANGINO, 7
FRAZ. RICCA
12055 DIANO D'ALBA (CN)
TEL. 0173/612049

The Accomo family is engaged both in producing good wine and in rearing cattle (for which they have received several prizes at the Fiera del Bue of Carrù), with satisfying results in both fields. This year the estate's top Dolcetto, the Sörì Bricco Maiolica, gets Two Glasses hands down. The dense ruby-garnet color with a firm rim heralds its concentration; the nose is broad and complex, with ripe black fruit, mint, undergrowth and cocoa; the rich, soft but firm palate reveals vigorous tannins that underpin the long, intense, fruity and spicy finish. The excellent basic Dolcetto is ruby-garnet in hue with a purple rim; it has simple but intense aromas of cherry, raspberry and licorice, followed by well-judged tannins on the substantial palate; balsamic nuances emerge on the lingering finish. The Lorié, from pinot nero, earns Two Glasses: of a ruby-garnet color, it offers broad, seductive aromas of raspberry, black currant and custard with undertones of hay and leather; the palate unfolds and expands into a powerful finish on a licorice and cocoa note. The ruby-garnet Nebbiolo d'Alba Il Cumot is nearly as good. The nose discloses coffee, toasty notes, vanilla, and raspberry and red currant jam; it is full and concentrated on the palate, with noble tannins and a fairly long finish which is slightly overpowered by the wood. The attractive Bianco Rolando, with a fruity and flowery fragrance, is free and easy and succulent. To end the list, the Barbera Vigna Vigia is a likeable wine with moderate finesse on the nose and a full, satisfying palate.

●	Dolcetto di Diano d'Alba Sörì Bricco Maiolica '98	🍷🍷	3*
●	Langhe Rosso Lorié '96	🍷🍷	5
●	Barbera d'Alba Vigna Vigia '97	🍷	4
●	Dolcetto di Diano d'Alba '98	🍷	3
○	Langhe Bianco Rolando '98	🍷	3
●	Nebbiolo d'Alba Il Cumot '97	🍷	4
●	Dolcetto di Diano d'Alba Sörì Bricco Maiolica '97	YY	3
●	Nebbiolo d'Alba Il Cumot '96	YY	4

DOGLIANI (CN)

Marziano ed Enrico Abbona

Via Torino, 242
12063 Dogliani (CN)
tel. 0173/70484

On the Dogliani wine horizon a new star is appearing. Within the space of a very few years Marziano Abbona, thanks to the advice of the expert young wine-maker Beppe Caviola, has made swift progress, and he now offers a range of really splendid wines. From their 32 hectares of producing vineyards (which will increase to 36 in a few years' time) the Abbona family (Marziano is flanked by his daughters Mara and Lorena, while the youngest, Cristina, has begun her studies in oenology), make three versions of Dolcetto di Dogliani, a Barolo, a Barbaresco, a Barbera d'Alba, a Langhe Rosso and a white from chardonnay. We'll start with the standard-bearing Dolcettos. The Papà Celso, so named in honor of Marziano's father, comes from the venerable Doriolo vineyard, which includes some 50-year-old vines, and is a glorious wine, with a bouquet of admirable finesse (blackberry and cherry) and a well-balanced palate on which all components are beautifully blended. It seems almost sweet, and is enhanced by its full body and high alcohol (14.5°). The Bricco San Bernardo is nearly as good, its only defect being a little hardness. The basic Dolcetto, fragrant and easily quaffable, is named after its vineyard, the Vigna Muntà. A superb performance also comes from the historic wines of the Langhe, the Barbaresco and the Barolo. The four hectares of the Faset vineyard have yielded a first-rate Barbaresco '96 which displays all the excellent qualities of its vintage and is among the finest of its category. The Barolo Terlo Ravera '95 and the Barbera d'Alba Rinaldi '98 are also first-rate. The Chardonnay Alzavola is an agreeable wine, while the Rosso Rico, a blend of barbera and cabernet sauvignon, is still in need of fine-tuning (too much wood).

● Barbaresco Faset '96	▼▼	5
● Barbera d'Alba Rinaldi '98	▼▼	4
● Barolo Vigneto Terlo Ravera '95	▼▼	6
● Dolcetto di Dogliani Bricco S. Bernardo '98	▼▼	3*
● Dolcetto di Dogliani Papà Celso '98	▼▼	4
● Dolcetto di Dogliani Vigna Muntà '98	▼	3
○ Langhe Chardonnay Alzavola '98	▼	3
● Langhe Rosso Rico '97	▼	5
● Dolcetto di Dogliani Papà Celso '97	▽▽	3
● Barbaresco Faset '95	▽	5
● Barolo Vigneto Terlo Ravera '94	▽	5

DOGLIANI (CN)

Francesco Boschis

Fraz. S. Martino di Pianezzo, 57
12063 Dogliani (CN)
tel. 0173/70574

Francesco and Simona Boschis, helped by their sons Marco and Paolo, devote all their energies to producing Dolcetto di Dogliani, the appellation which has brought fame to this town only a few kilometers away from the world-famous Barolo zone. However, Dogliani's winegrowers did not lose heart and over the last few years have achieved success without the king of wines, basing their ascent on their own excellent red. From their almost ten hectares under vine the Boschis family produces about 40 thousand bottles a year, of which at least 30 thousand are Dolcetto, and, since they know what they're about among the vines and the vats, they make reliable, characterful wines. Of their many, perhaps even too many, versions of Dolcetto di Dogliani, our favorite is still the Vigna dei Prey, which is highly representative of the local Dolcetto; it is clean and harmonious on the nose, still dominated by vinous aromas, and unfolds on the palate with pleasing fullness; the delightful finish reveals a distinct note of almond. The San Martino is slightly harder and less elegant, while the Pianezzo fails to redeem its marked rustic character. The Barbera d'Alba Le Masserie '97, from a vineyard in Roddino, fully exploits the potential of its vintage: red fruit and spices are perceptible in a fine, lingering bouquet; the palate, although rich in fruit, still needs to integrate the over-harsh wood-derived tannins, but age should take care of the problem and establish a general balance. The lightly bubbly Freisa Bosco delle Cicale deserves a mention.

● Barbera d'Alba Vigna Le Masserie '97	▼▼	4
● Dolcetto di Dogliani Vigna dei Prey '98	▼	3*
● Dolcetto di Dogliani Vigna Sorì S. Martino '98	▼	3
● Dolcetto di Dogliani Pianezzo '98		3
● Langhe Freisa Bosco delle Cicale '98		3
● Barbera d'Alba Vigna Le Masserie '95	▽	3

DOGLIANI (CN)

Quinto Chionetti e Figlio

B.ta Valdiberti, 44
12063 Dogliani (CN)
tel. 0173/71179

From the height of San Luigi, the hilltop where his vineyards and cellar are located, Quinto Chionetti somewhat incredulously surveys the great commotion in the wine world of Dogliani. The idea of splitting the DOC into two sub-appellations, with a Dolcetto to be styled simply Dogliani and released a year later, does not seem to find favor with him. He is also strongly opposed to the use of barriques for Dolcetto. It has to be said that Quinto is probably right on the second point, since the attempts carried out so far have yielded inconclusive and not entirely satisfactory results. With regard to the subdivison of the DOC, we think that the arguments in favor carry some weight, but Quinto's comments should nevertheless be taken into serious consideration. He has always believed in Dolcetto and made wonderful examples of it, even when quantity and generous yields were what counted in Dogliani, rather than wines with structure and richness. His two crus, by now legendary, are back again this year to prove he was right to persevere. The Briccolero '98, intense ruby in color with a cherry cast, displays an austere, elegant nose dominated by spicy notes, red berries and blackberry. The succulent palate reveals all the inner strength of Chionetti's best interpretations and shows a beautiful balance between fruit and acidity, followed by a finish on a wild cherry note. The San Luigi '98, its twin brother, is, as always, a little lacking in concentration, but has all its customary drinkability. The finish discloses a lightly smoky and delightful mineral note which makes it vaguely exotic.

●	Dolcetto di Dogliani Briccolero '98	▼▼	3
●	Dolcetto di Dogliani S. Luigi '98	▼▼	3
●	Dolcetto di Dogliani Briccolero '96	▽▽	3
●	Dolcetto di Dogliani S. Luigi '96	▽	3

DOGLIANI (CN)

Poderi Luigi Einaudi

B.ta Gombe, 31/32
Cascina Tecc
12063 Dogliani (CN)
tel. 0173/70191

It was a thrilling moment when the tasting panel, uncloaking the bottles, discovered that the Langhe Rosso Luigi Einaudi '97 had earned one of the highest scores ever achieved. This is the logical climax to the expansion and restructuring which Dr. Ruffo, who is an engineer, and his wife Paola Einaudi have been carrying out over the years with enthusiastic dedication, and thus an estate closely identified with the Langhe triumphantly enters the elite circle of top wineries. The amazing Three Glass winner is made from 30% cabernet and 30% nebbiolo with barbera and merlot making up the rest, and it simply explodes on the palate. Of a deep ruby-violet color, it has a spicy bouquet of cinnamon and pepper with a light balsamic nuance; the warm, long, vibrant palate ends on a delightful mineral note. The Barolo Cannubi '95, from the celebrated parcel of land bought last year from Gancia, has body and power; scents of rose and red fruit on the nose are followed by a robust palate with slightly excessive tannins but with a heady aftertaste of licorice. The excellent Vigna Meira '98, made from tocai pinot gris of undoubted Alsatian ancestry and locally planted at least since the end of the 19th century, offers finesse on the nose and dense fruit. The impressively concentrated and alcohol-rich (14°) Barbera '97 reveals the hand of Caviola, the new consultant oenologist at Einaudi and a real Barbera wizard. The Barolo Costa Grimaldi '95, slightly less meaty than the Cannubi, displays good finesse and length on the palate. The two Dolcetto di Dogliani crus are superb: the Filari '97 displays depth, sinew and a succulent, faintly tannic finish. The Vigna Tecc '97, which is not quite so complex, has lingering fruity aromas and echoes of spice and ripe cherry on the palate.

●	Langhe Rosso Luigi Einaudi '97	▼▼▼	5
●	Barolo Cannubi '95	▼▼	6
●	Dolcetto di Dogliani I Filari '97	▼▼	4
●	Dolcetto di Dogliani Vigna Tecc '97	▼▼	4
●	Piemonte Barbera '97	▼▼	4
○	Vigna Meira Bianco '98	▼▼	4
●	Barolo Costa Grimaldi '95	▼	6
●	Dolcetto di Dogliani '98	▼	3
●	Barolo Cannubi '94	▽▽	6
●	Dolcetto di Dogliani I Filari '96	▽▽	4
●	Dolcetto di Dogliani Vigna Tecc '96	▽▽	3
●	Langhe Rosso Luigi Einaudi '96	▽	5
●	Piemonte Barbera '96	▽	3

DOGLIANI (CN)

F.LLI PECCHENINO
B.TA VALDIBÀ, 59
12063 DOGLIANI (CN)
TEL. 0173/70686

Attilio and Orlando Pecchenino were among the first to believe in Quinto Chionetti's teaching that Dolcetto di Dogliani was capable of holding its own against the great reds of Piedmont. Their conviction was such that they made considerable investments both in land and in the cellar; indeed they converted an old farmhouse and completely re-equipped it. This year the Sirì d'Jermu has again won our highest award and by now it will be clear even to the most skeptical observer that this is not just a flash in the pan. Its power, complexity and balance are unparelleled in their intensity. This is a wine created in the vineyard, rather than in the cellar, and the wonderfully ripe, concentrated fruit plays a decisive role. The color is dense and impenetrable; the austere, lingering nose offers aromas of ripe red berries mingling with spicy notes from the perfectly-gauged and unintrusive wood. The palate is dense and mouth-filling, with a mellowness lasting right through to a finish characterized by delightful mineral notes. The "normal" version, the Dolcetto S. Luigi '98, is excellent too. It has a beautiful deep bluish-ruby hue and offers lively fruity aromas with faintly smoky nuances. The palate is long, vibrant and sinewy, with notes of blackberry and pencil lead emerging on the finish. The Bricco Botti '97, on the other hand, is slightly unbalanced: despite its impressive fruit it has not managed to assimilate the penetrating new wood. The extremely attractive Chardonnay Vigna Maestro '98 could do with a little more concentration in order to express all the charm promised by the fruit.

●	Dolcetto di Dogliani Sirì d'Jermu '98	▼▼▼	4
●	Dolcetto di Dogliani Bricco Botti '97	▼▼	5
●	Dolcetto di Dogliani S. Luigi '98	▼▼	3*
○	Langhe Chardonnay Vigna Maestro '98	▼	4
●	Dolcetto di Dogliani Sirì d'Jermu '96	▽▽▽	4
●	Dolcetto di Dogliani Sirì d'Jermu '97	▽▽▽	4
●	Dolcetto di Dogliani Bricco Botti '96	▽▽	4
●	Langhe La Castella '96	▽▽	4
●	Langhe La Castella '95	▽▽	4

DOGLIANI (CN)

PIRA
B.TA VALDIBERTI, 69
12063 DOGLIANI (CN)
TEL. 0173/78538

The Pira family, taking advantage of the favorable '97 and '98 vintages, has presented a wide and interesting range of successful wines, with some really excellent Langhe and Dogliani bottles. An example is the Dolcetto di Dogliani Bricco dei Botti, which earns Two Glasses: it has a dense garnet color with a very narrow rim and a highly expressive, very charming bouquet that offers notes of red berry and cocoa and faint, intriguing undertones of damp earth; the palate has all the concentration promised in the glass, and displays a rich, ample texture enhanced by the powerful phenolic structure. The basic Dolcetto di Dogliani, which is very nearly as good, shows a full ruby-garnet hue with a purple rim and aromas of blackberry, plum and menthol enriched by light hints of leather. The dense palate has a slightly tangy vigor, and a solid layer of noble tannins lends firmness to the long, fruity finish. Two Glasses also go to the Barbera Vendemmia Tardiva, ruby-colored with hints of dark garnet, which offers aromas of black fruit, tobacco and spice on a faintly mineral background; the palate is soft and concentrated with a very long finish and just perceptible tannins. The Barbera Briccobotti displays a pleasantly rustic fragrance and a good robust palate. The Barbera Vigna Fornaci, a mature wine with good consistency, has slightly overbearing wood on the nose but is very inviting on the palate.

●	Barbera d'Alba Vendemmia Tardiva '97	▼▼	4
●	Dolcetto di Dogliani '98	▼▼	4
●	Dolcetto di Dogliani Vigna Bricco dei Botti '98	▼▼	4
●	Barbera d'Alba Vigna Fornaci '97	▼	4
●	Piemonte Barbera Briccobotti '97	▼	4
●	Barbera d'Alba Vendemmia Tardiva '95	▽▽	4
●	Dolcetto di Dogliani Vigna Bricco dei Botti '97	▽▽	3
●	Barbera d'Alba Vendemmia Tardiva '96	▽	4
●	Barbera d'Alba Vigna Fornaci '96	▽	3
●	Piemonte Barbera Briccobotti '96	▽	4

DOGLIANI (CN)

SAN FEREOLO
B.TA VALDIBÀ, 59
12063 DOGLIANI (CN)
TEL. 0173/742075

For Nicoletta Bocca 1999 will be a year to remember. The arrival of her baby, Pietro, in May undoubtedly put everything else in the shade, including matters such as wine scores, wine writers and the market. However, time passes and a few years hence Pietro will be gratified to know that his birth coincided with an outstanding tribute to the family winery. Having won Three Glasses last year for her Dolcetto, Nicoletta has repeated her success this time with the Barbera Il Brumaio. Let there be no misunderstanding: the San Fereolo '98 is a superb Dolcetto; the color is a dense ruby, almost violet, and the aromas are intense and austere, with those mineral tones that seem to be the personal stamp of Nicoletta's wines. The grapes come from six hectares in Valdiberti and Santa Lucia and yield 25 thousand bottles of this wine, after 15% of it has spent some time in new seven-hectoliter tonneaux. But the power and personality of the Barbera simply astonished the tasting panel. It has distinct varietal aromas, with pronounced notes of sour cherry and plum, an unbelievably intense bluish-ruby color and a wonderfully sinewy body. The sweet fruit, lent subtlety by the merest hint of new wood (30%), is characterized by almondy flavors and mineral notes that enhance the palate. Credit is due to a unique year for the barbera grape, but also to the 40-50-year-old Austri vineyards with a natural yield of 4,000 kilos per hectare, and credit is due to the estate's technical staff: Francesco Stralla, who saved these vineyards from being uprooted with the devotion of a genetic scientist, and Federico Curtaz and Beppe Caviola, wizards in the vineyard and in the cellar. And to Nicoletta Bocca, of course, the heart and soul of this enterprise, who combines wholehearted commitment with a restless search for improvement.

● Langhe Rosso Brumaio '97	🍷🍷🍷	4
● Dolcetto di Dogliani S. Fereolo '98	🍷🍷	4
● Dolcetto di Dogliani S. Fereolo '97	♀♀♀	4
● Il Brumaio '95	♀♀	4
● Langhe Rosso Brumaio '96	♀♀	4

DOGLIANI (CN)

SAN ROMANO
B.TA GIACHELLI, 8
12063 DOGLIANI (CN)
TEL. 0173/76289

Bruno Chionetti is one of the "Dogliani boys", i. e. the group of young winegrowers who gambled on Dolcetto's chances of being included among the great red wines of Piedmont. Bruno left his job and his home, moving to the land where he cultivates the vine and vinifies its fruit and, four years on, we can say that he has won his wager. His top cru, the Vigna del Pilone '98, has received Three Glasses for the second year running. This confirms the greatness of Dolcetto itself, provided it is in the hands of someone who knows how to get the most out of it. Bruno thins the crop and vinifies with the object of extracting all that the grape can yield without disturbing its balance. This '98 vintage has power and character, but manages to preserve an astonishing drinkability: ruby-violet in color with an inky cast, it has rich and lingering aromas; the herbaceous note of a young wine is noticeable but not disturbing, and is followed by sour cherry, undergrowth and green peppercorn. The opulent palate shows lots of succulent fruit and a finish of overwhelming sweetness well supported by an aristocratic structure. The standard Dolcetto '98 is slightly less concentrated, but how wonderfully fragrant it is, on both nose and palate! The barrique-aged Vigna del Pilone '97 does not perform so well: the wood is over-pronounced and the secondary tannins on the finish are not well assimilated. We mustn't leave out the exceptional Langhe Rosso '98, from freisa, barbera and pinot nero, which shows remarkable concentration and balance; unfortunately this is a unique appearance, since the freisa has been uprooted.

● Dolcetto di Dogliani Vigna del Pilone '98	🍷🍷🍷	4
● Dolcetto di Dogliani '98	🍷🍷	3*
● Langhe Rosso '98	🍷🍷	4
● Dolcetto di Dogliani Sup. Vigna del Pilone '97	🍷	4
● Dolcetto di Dogliani Vigna del Pilone '97	♀♀♀	3
● Dolcetto di Dogliani Vigna del Pilone '96	♀♀	3

FARA NOVARESE (NO)

DESSILANI
VIA CESARE BATTISTI, 21
28073 FARA NOVARESE (NO)
TEL. 0321/829252

Enzio Lucca's estate makes its debut in the Guide with some impressive wines, including two excellent Faras: the Caramino and the Lochera. The winery began bottling under its own label in1892 and has an annual output of 500 thousand bottles, produced from 150 hectares of vineyard. They are cultivated according to the rules of organic farming with advice from the Universities of Piacenza and Milan. Enzio is an oenologist and is in charge of the technical side himself, while Raffaella Ramaioli is responsible for estate administration. The Caramino is ruby-garnet in color with a faintly orange rim; the subtly forward bouquet, of an admirable overall finesse, releases notes of raspberry jam, menthol and vanilla. The palate is immediately rich and concentrated, and on the long, lingering finish hints of cocoa and licorice emerge on a background of noble tannins. The Lochera, only slightly less good, is, like the Caramino, partially aged in barriques; it has a youthful rim on a ruby-garnet ground, while the nose offers scents of strawberry, raspberry, tobacco and custard. The broad and solid palate leads into a deeply satisfying finish that harmoniously blends fruit and spice. The Gattinara is warm and substantial in the mouth; the complex, forward nose displays aromas of jam, sweet biscuits and leather. Two other properly made wines end the list: the Laio, a dried-grape wine from greco, and a rather rustic Spanna.

● Fara Caramino '95	🍷🍷	4
● Fara Lochera '95	🍷🍷	4
● Gattinara '93	🍷	5
○ Laio '96	🍷	6
● Colline Novaresi Spanna '97		3

FARIGLIANO (CN)

ANNA MARIA ABBONA
FRAZ. MONCUCCO, 21
12060 FARIGLIANO (CN)
TEL. 0173/797228

When, towards the end of the '80s, Anna Maria Abbona and her husband Franco Schellino decided to leave their respective jobs and their house in Belvedere to move to the old family farm, their friends and relations thought they were out of their minds. Today, their return to this hillside property, abandoned during the '70s as a result of the slump in agriculture, has proved itself a successful venture. Little by little, Anna Maria and Franco first bought or replanted new vineyards and then remodeled and extended the family cellar. They cultivate eight hectares under vine, including two old vineyards planted to barbera and dolcetto which were grafted by Anna Maria's grandfather between 1936 and 1943, all situated on the same hillside at an altitude of between 550 and 490 meters. Their range consists of three Dolcettos and a Langhe Rosso: the Langhe Dolcetto, made with grapes from the youngest vineyards with the least favorable exposures, the Sorì dij But, from the Botti site, the Maioli, from the oldest vines situated in the subzone of the same name, and the Langhe Cadò, a blend of 85-90% barbera, aged in tonneaux, with unoaked dolcetto. The Dolcetto Langhe, fruity and quaffable, is an enjoyable everyday wine, while the Sorì dij But boasts a fuller body and greater finesse, without sacrificing any of its drinkability. The Maioli, on a level with the great Doglianis, has a beautifully dense color and great structure, to which the exceptionally sweet alcohol and the dry extract add grace; it ends on a long, fascinating finish. The Langhe Rosso, at least for the moment, is equally powerful and slightly more complex, but reveals less harmony on the palate.

● Dolcetto di Dogliani Maioli '98	🍷🍷	3*
● Dolcetto di Dogliani Sorì dij But '98	🍷🍷	3*
● Langhe Rosso Cadò '97	🍷🍷	4
● Langhe Dolcetto '98	🍷	2*

FARIGLIANO (CN)

GIOVANNI BATTISTA GILLARDI
CASCINA CORSALETTO, 69
12060 FARIGLIANO (CN)
TEL. 0173/76306

What with the completion of their new and more spacious storage cellar, and their ability to exploit to the full two historic vintages, the Gillardis have come up with three premium wines. None of them made it into the very top group, but the goal is getting nearer with every year that passes. This is in part due to the excellent work of Pinuccia and Giovanni Gillardi, who look after the vineyards almost as if they were their children. This means that the grapes are of first-rate quality, and can be transformed into excellent wines by the skilled hands of Giacolino, the Gillardi's son and the winery's oenologist. Another great virtue of this family is their avoidance of the latest oenological fashions; neither do they show any tendency to add new labels to their range of wines. They continue to produce just three, on which they lavish the greatest care. The very successful '97 version of the Harys, a monovarietal syrah, reveals great structure and an enchanting palate with considerable fruit and a long finish. The deep, impenetrable, violet-tinged color introduces a mineral nose, with hints of pepper and spice; the only jarring note in this complex wine is the slightly astringent finish. Of the two Dolcettos, we again prefer the Cursalet, from the estate's best cru, as it's fuller and shows a fine, balanced texture. The Vigneto Maestra, which easily scores Two Glasses, is, on the other hand, grapier and more easily quaffable, but it is nevertheless an excellent example of a Dolcetto di Dogliani, a fragrant wine just right for copious drinking throughout the meal.

●	Dolcetto di Dogliani Cursalet '98	▼▼	3*
●	Dolcetto di Dogliani Vigneto Maestra '98	▼▼	3*
●	Harys '97	▼▼	6
●	Dolcetto di Dogliani Cursalet '97	▽▽	3
●	Harys '95	▽▽	5
●	Harys '96	▽▽	5
●	Dolcetto di Dogliani Vigneto Maestra '97	▽	3
●	Harys '93	▽	5

FRASSINELLO M.TO (AL)

CASTELLO DI LIGNANO
REG. LIGNANO
15035 FRASSINELLO M.TO (AL)
TEL. 0142/334529 - 0142/925326

Giuseppe Gaiero, whose family has been at Casale Monferrato since the '50s, feels that the promotion of his wines is strongly linked with that of the land. The efforts of people like him and Ugo Bertana, his co-worker, represent the groundwork behind the growth of this zone. His output of 50 thousand bottles comes from the ten hectares of vineyard surrounding the castle. Among the wines we tasted, the barrique-aged Barbera Vigna Stramba stood out. Its color is a fairly intense ruby-violet; the nose offers aromas of ripe plum, coffee and licorice and the palate is well balanced and very meaty. The good Barbera Valisenda shows a round and fruity palate and aromas of ripe black cherry, plum and coffee. A new wine, the Lhennius, takes its name from the builder of the castle; it is made from barbera (60%), cabernet (25%) and pinot nero (15%), and half of the blend is aged in large barrels. Spice and red berries emerge on the nose, and the complex palate shows good structure, but the finish is rather brusque. The agreeable Grignolino Vigna Tufara shows spicy and flowery aromas and a typically tannic palate with a bitterish note on the finish. The Grisello, a blend of equal parts of cortese and sauvignon, offers generous scents of green apple and leaves, and an enjoyably crisp and intense palate.

●	Barbera d'Asti Vigna Stramba '97	▼▼	4
●	Monferrato Rosso Lhennius '97	▼▼	4
●	Barbera del M.to Valisenda '97	▼	3*
●	Grignolino del M.to Casalese Vigna Tufara '98	▼	3
○	Monferrato Casalese Grisello '98	▼	3
●	Barbera d'Asti Vigna Stramba '96	▽	3

GATTINARA (VC)

Antoniolo

C.so Valsesia, 277
13045 Gattinara (VC)
tel. 0163/833612

Rosanna, Alberto and Lorella Antoniolo have presented four versions of Gattinara, a celebrated long-lived Piedmontese wine made from nebbiolo. The Castelle displays a ruby hue verging on garnet with an orange rim; the nose offers a pleasant forwardness revealed both in the aromas of strawberry and raspberry jam and in the austere tones of leather and dried flowers; the richly textured palate culminates in a long finish with fruity tones on a solid phenolic structure. The Vigneto Osso S. Grato, ruby-garnet in color with a slightly faded rim, offers ripe, complex aromas of jam, coffee and undergrowth and faint mineral nuances; it is ample in the mouth, with noticeable tannins on the corresponding and long finish. The lesser concentration of the S. Francesco is already apparent from its color, a light ruby with an orange tinge; the bouquet includes fruit steeped in alcohol and sweet biscuits, with underlying animal notes. The palate is good, and the finish is enlivened by alcohol and tannins. The basic Gattinara, of an almost transparent ruby color, offers delicate scents of dried violets, red fruit and spice; the palate shows good balance and there are hints of cocoa on the finish. To close, the pale straw-colored Erbaluce di Caluso earns a Glass; its delicate secondary aromas of apple and yeast are followed by a smooth, undemanding palate.

●	Gattinara Vigneto Castelle '95	🍷🍷	5
●	Gattinara Vigneto Osso S. Grato '95	🍷🍷	5
○	Erbaluce di Caluso '98	🍷	3
●	Gattinara '95	🍷	4
●	Gattinara Vigneto S. Francesco '95	🍷	5
●	Gattinara S. Francesco '90	♀♀	5
●	Gattinara Vigneto Castelle '90	♀♀	5
●	Gattinara Vigneto Osso S. Grato '93	♀♀	5

GATTINARA (VC)

Nervi

C.so Vercelli, 117
13045 Gattinara (VC)
tel. 0163/833228

Carla Ferrero and Giorgio Agliata are the enthusiastic managers of this Gattinara winery which produces 90 thousand bottles a year. The star of local viticulture is the nebbiolo grape, whose cultivation in this rocky terrain is accompanied by numerous difficulties and which yields one of the Piedmontese wines that enjoy worldwide prestige: Gattinara. Compared with the nebbiolo-based wines of the Langhe, such as Barolo and Barbaresco, the ones from northern Piedmont are more austere, because of the climate, of course, but also as a result of local tradition. This estate's Gattinaras are no exception to the general rule, being dry wines that make no concessions to opulence and base their appeal on a rigorous clarity of structure. This year the only wine we tasted was the cru Vigneto Molsino '95, and it won Two Glasses, confirming the excellent impression made by its predecessor last year. It shows an orange rim on an almost transparent base; the unusually charming nose offers enticing aromas of dried flowers, berry jam, leather and tar, shot through with a mysterious brininess. The palate is meaty from the start and reveals austere but noble tannins that lend depth to the very long cocoa-toned finish.

●	Gattinara Vigneto Molsino '95	🍷🍷	4
●	Gattinara Vigneto Molsino '93	♀♀	4
●	Gattinara '91	♀	4
●	Gattinara '93	♀	4

GATTINARA (VC)

GIANCARLO TRAVAGLINI
S.DA DELLE VIGNE, 36
13045 GATTINARA (VC)
TEL. 0163/833588

The 300 thousand bottles annually produced from Giancarlo Travaglini's 32 hectares under vine do a lot to ensure the lasting fame of Gattinara. The wines are traditional but obtained with the help of modern technology, and many bottles find their way abroad. The Gattinara Riserva '95, a blend of several crus, is a highly successful example of the house style. It has a dark garnet color with a wide orange rim and its complexity is immediately revealed on the nose. Soft, modern tones of vanilla and menthol mingle with the old-fashioned austerity of the local nebbiolo, expressed as forward notes of leather, dried flowers and jam. The palate, underpinned by an impressive phenolic structure and generous alcohol, is firm and demanding and scoffs at opulence; the finish is not remarkable for length but is intense and licorice-toned. The basic Gattinara '96, ruby-hued with a garnet cast, has a simpler bouquet than the Riserva; the wine is not so imposing but is definitely sunnier and more direct and offers the same breadth and satisfying complexity, as befits a Gattinara. Enchanting notes of raspberry and strawberry are enriched by hints of leather and rhubarb on a balanced and graceful nose; the palate reveals grip and substance and is warm, mouth-filling and satisfying.

●	Gattinara Ris. '95	▼▼	5
●	Gattinara '96	▼	4
●	Gattinara '93	▽▽	4
●	Gattinara '94	▽▽	4
●	Gattinara Ris. '93	▽▽	5
●	Gattinara Ris. Numerata '88	▽▽	5
●	Gattinara Ris. Numerata '89	▽▽	5
●	Gattinara Ris. Numerata '90	▽▽	5

GAVI (AL)

NICOLA BERGAGLIO
LOC. PEDAGGERI, 59
FRAZ. ROVERETO
15066 GAVI (AL)
TEL. 0143/682195

The village of Rovereto, in a schematic diagram of the Gavi district, might figure as the historic nucleus of the appellation. It is not by chance that the township of Gavi, tin conjunction with the local tourism board, holds the annual Festa del Vino right here. Tradition also tends to mean reliability, and this is the case with Gianluigi Bergaglio's estate, which has been producing wine for generations and has been bottling Gavi since 1969, a full 30 years. (It would be interesting to hold a vertical tasting to test the capacity for development and longevity of wines that popular prejudice has always held to be short-lived.) The 12 hectares of vineyard also play their part by yielding grapes of prime quality. This esteemed family-run and tradition-driven estate produces Gavi and only Gavi: 65 thousand reliable bottles with two historic labels, standard and Minaia. The Minaia '98, straw-colored with a greenish tinge, offers rich and lingering fruity aromas with apple to the fore; it is highly enjoyable in the mouth, where it reveals its usual good structure, remarkable softness and pleasant echoes of vanilla. There is less acidity than in last year's version, and this takes its toll in crispness and length. The basic Gavi has a lovely greenish-straw color, intense and brilliant. The nose offers floral and mineral notes, while the keynote on the palate, as with its elder brother, is softness. Crispness, however, is also in evidence here, together with some succulence and moderate length.

○	Gavi del Comune di Gavi '98	▼	3
○	Gavi del Comune di Gavi Minaia '98	▼	3

GAVI (AL)

Gian Piero Broglia
Tenuta La Meirana
Loc. Lomellina, 14
15066 Gavi (AL)
tel. 0143/642998 - 0143/743267

Piero Broglia is constantly improving his winery. His ability as an entrepreneur is evident not only from the prestige and international reputation which the estate enjoys, but even more from his capacity to understand the market and his decision to make quality his goal both in the more traditional estate wines and in his plans for the future, which include native red varieties with a long history and great potential. Meanwhile his whites have done beautifully, starting with the excellent Gavi DOCG Bruno Broglia '97, a blend of Gavi aged in stainless steel with a small percentage of the same wine matured in barriques: a triumph of harmony and balance. The intense, lively golden straw color introduces a very complex and richly fragrant nose with hints of honey, flowers, pineapple, grapefruit and white-fleshed fruit. The succulent, rich, dense, almost sweet palate is wonderfully crisp and fairly long. The Gavi Villa Broglia '98, of a brilliant greenish straw color, has unusual, intense and clean aromas reminiscent of peach. The palate is moderately rich and extremely harmonious. The equally enjoyable Gavi La Meirana, of a lively deep straw color, displays ripe fruity aromas with mineral notes, all mirrored on the immediate, refreshing and fairly long palate. The slightly fizzy Gavi Roverello '98 is a pleasant wine with some structure; a much greater effervescent elegance is to be found in the Extra Brut '92, which offers a fine perlage, fresh yeasty aromas of great distinction, a lovely creaminess and good length. A final mention is due the table wine Le Pernici Rosso, partly made from the rare and very old native variety dolcetto dal raspo rosso.

○	Gavi di Gavi Bruno Broglia '97	▼▼	4
○	Gavi del Comune di Gavi La Meirana '98	▼	3
○	Gavi del Comune di Gavi Villa Broglia '98	▼	3
○	Gavi Spumante Extra Brut '92	▼	4
○	Gavi del Comune di Gavi Roverello '98		3
●	Le Pernici Rosso		3
○	Gavi di Gavi Bruno Broglia '96	▽▽	4
○	Gavi di Gavi Bruno Broglia '95	▽	4

GAVI (AL)

Cascina S. Bartolomeo
Cascina S. Bartolomeo, 26
Loc. Valleggie
15066 Gavi (AL)
tel. 0143/643180

The Bergaglio family of S. Bartolomeo has, since 1916, managed everything on the estate by itself, or very nearly. They do gladly accept the advice of the experienced and able oenologist Giuliano Noè, but it was they who built their new cellar, and very well too. They also did very well with the three wines submitted for tasting this year, although without the high points of the '97s. The Gavi Etichetta Nera '98 presents an inviting appearance with its deep straw color; the warm and intense nose offers aromas of flowers and ripe fruit, nicely paving the way for a crisp, enjoyable palate; succulence and medium body lead into an unusual finish with notes of pear. Although it was probably tasted too soon, the Gavi Cappello del Diavolo '98, partially aged in wood, shows a straw color with a vivid greenish tinge; the initial fermentation-derived aromas, which indicate a need for more bottle age, give way to notes of flowers, bitter almond and vanilla; the palate reveals moderate structure and softness nicely counterbalanced by appropriate crispness, with a fairly long finish. The basic Gavi '98, pale straw in hue with attractive bright greenish flashes, offers aromas of white flowers and herbs with overtones of hay; the full, impressive palate displays good body and a medium finish with satisfying bitterish notes.

○	Gavi del Comune di Gavi '98	▼	3
○	Gavi del Comune di Gavi Cappello del Diavolo '98	▼	4
○	Gavi del Comune di Gavi Etichetta Nera '98	▼	3

GAVI (AL)

Castellari Bergaglio
Fraz. Rovereto, 136
15066 Gavi (AL)
tel. 0143/644000

The hilly slope known as Pessenti at Rovereto di Gavi is wedged in between the main valley of the Lemme and the small stream of the Mesima, which separates it from Tassarolo. This is where Wanda Castellari and her son Marco have their estate, which continues to vinify only cortese grapes: a monovarietal production which is absolutely faithful to the land and to the tradition of four generations, but with five different labels representing differing techniques in vineyard and cellar. In our opinion the decision to postpone the release of the oak-aged Gavi Pilìn, which for two consecutive years figured among the top wines of the appellation, is laudable. The Vignavecchia derives from vines with low yields and well-ripened grapes, which accumulate concentration from a month's pre-drying in crates; unlike the Pilìn, it completes its vinification cycle exclusively in steel. The color is a good, deep, lively straw yellow; the intense nose offers aromas of fresh butter and fruit, including citrus; the well-structured palate is fat, soft, citric and faintly astringent. The Fornaci, a celebrated Tassarolo cru, makes its debut with Two well-earned Glasses: inviting to look at with its intense straw color enlivened by brilliant green glints, it is deep and characterful on the nose, disclosing complex mineral notes, ripe fruit and wildflowers; the palate has lots of wonderful fruit but we would have liked a little more length on the finish. The Gavi Rolona has a distinctly greenish cast and a varietal nose on which wildflowers, apple and citron emerge; an attractive crispness rules the roost on a palate of non-obtrusive body. The youthful, lively green tinge in the color of the Brise '98, a lightly sparkling Gavi with a good prise de mousse, goes well with the yeastiness and fruit of the wine, whose freshness is enhanced by the effervescence.

○ Gavi Fornaci '98	🍷🍷	3*
○ Gavi del Comune di Gavi Rolona '98	🍷	3
○ Gavi Rovereto Vignavecchia '98	🍷	4
○ Gavi Brise '98		3
○ Gavi Rovereto Pilìn '95	ŸŸ	4
○ Gavi Rovereto Pilìn '96	ŸŸ	4

GAVI (AL)

Il Rocchin
Loc. Vallemme, 39
15066 Gavi (AL)
tel. 0143/642228

The Zerbo family estate, which combines winegrowing with cattle rearing, is situated on the left bank of the river Lemme near an ancient church, the Pieve Lemurina of Gavi. It is a real "particolare", which in local terminology means a freehold farm independent of the estates of the nobility and the old landed properties of the district. Its debut in the Guide is the consequence of a new approach to vineyard and cellar management under the guidance of Mario Ronco, who aims for lower yields per hectare and riper grapes in order to achieve a greater concentration of aroma and more structure. After an excellent '97 vintage, they did very well in '98, hence our interest in their range of wines, which are also very good value for money. The estate red is produced from the vineyards lying within the Dolcetto di Ovada DOC zone. It has a deep ruby color with youthful violet highlights and offers a typical fruity bouquet of cherry with jammy, spicy overtones; the entry on the palate is warm and soft, followed by appropriate tannins and good length; the crisp acidity should ensure a long life. The Gavi selection, the Vigna del Bosco '98, of a good deep straw color, has a delightful note of overripe fruit and herbaceous, balsamic and resinous nuances; the impressive structure and good body guarantee its admirable persistence, which is enlivened by a pleasing crispness. It is a fine demonstration of what the cortese grape is capable of in this vintage. The basic Gavi, elegant in character and a classic of its kind, offers a fresh, full palate after the characteristic aromas of flowers and citrus fruit with typical notes of bitter almond.

○ Gavi del Comune di Gavi Vigna del Bosco '98	🍷🍷	3*
● Dolcetto di Ovada '98	🍷	3
○ Gavi del Comune di Gavi '98	🍷	3

GAVI (AL)

La Chiara

Loc. Valleggie, 24/2
15066 Gavi (AL)
tel. 0143/642293

Roberto Bergaglio's estate continues to produce well-executed, reliable wines. The oenologist Giancarlo Scaglione showed his customary ability in his handling of the excellent crop from the '97 and '98 vintages. The recognition of the DOCG has been a further boost to incentive all over the area, and the desire to excel is gradually becoming apparent not only in the vineyards and cellars, but also in increasing efforts in the field of public relations and guest accommodation. The estate style has always been based on solid worth derived from hard work, professional skill and quality. Last year we wrote enthusiastically about the Gavi Groppella '96, which catapulted La Chiara into the Guide with Two well-deserved Glasses. The element of surprise is of course missing this year and in fact we were curious to find out if it was not just a flash in the pan. However it won't be necessary to wait for posterity to confirm our verdict which is once again unhesitatingly positive. The Vigneto Groppello '97, vinified Burgundy-style with fermentation and aging in small oak, confirms its excellence with its deep, brilliant amber-yellow color heralding pronounced toasty aromas with bitter notes and flowery scents. The palate displays great power with a rich softness and an exceptionally long finish, in which the wood still has a tendency to dominate. The straw-colored basic Gavi '98 is a good representative of the appellation; the satisfactory nose is followed by a sweet entry on the palate, which quickly gives way to a remarkable crispness.

○	Gavi del Comune di Gavi Vigneto Groppella '97	🍷🍷	4
○	Gavi del Comune di Gavi '98		3

GAVI (AL)

La Giustiniana

Fraz. Rovereto, 5
15066 Gavi (AL)
tel. 0143/682132

The three types of soil in the Gavi zone are red alluvial clay, brown and blackish conglomerates from marine deposits, and white or grey alternating sand and marl. La Giustiniana, the historic 18th century estate of an ancient line of Genoese doges, is the largest winery of the appellation and the only one to include all three geological zones, represented in vinous form under the three labels of Montessora, Centurionetta and Lugarara. This not only gives experts and wine lovers the chance to have a horizontal tasting, assessing year by year the perceptible changes wrought by the variation in soil, but also means that any one of the three crus can come out on top, depending on the climatic conditions of the vintage. In '98 it was the Montessora, of a vivid, intense straw colour, which stood out. Rather closed at first, the nose gradually opens out into a truly exquisite array of aromas of herbs, flowers and apple. The palate is notably crisp but has good structure and plenty of flavor, with an elegant, bitterish finish: an impressive, traditional Gavi. The Lugarara is also a deep straw in color, with intense fruity aromas and balsamic notes. Plenty of body and good structure characterize the palate, which is harmonious, correspondingly fruity, appropriately crisp and fairly long. The Centurionetta also deserves a Glass, with its bright, lively straw color and intense aromas of yeast, flowers and citrus fruit. The entry on the palate is full and harmonious and the finish adequate. From the twin estate at Strevi, Contero, which is also under the management of Enrico Tomalino, we liked the Brachetto Spumante, a delicate bubbly with clearly defined scents of rose and violet, the still Brachetto, this year too among the best expressions of the DOCG, and the Asti with its unmistakable varietal aromas.

○	Gavi del Comune di Gavi Montessora '98	🍷🍷	4
○	Asti Contero '98	🍷	3
●	Brachetto d'Acqui Contero '98	🍷	4
●	Brachetto d'Acqui Spumante Contero '98	🍷	4
○	Gavi del Comune di Gavi Centurionetta '98	🍷	4
○	Gavi del Comune di Gavi Lugarara '98	🍷	4
○	Moscato d'Asti Contero '98		3
○	Roverì '98		3

GAVI (AL)

La Scolca

Fraz. Rovereto
15066 Gavi (AL)
tel. 0143/682176

La Scolca confirms its place as one of the top producers of the appellation, and Giorgio Soldati and his co-workers are making important decisions and considerable investments for the future. This year the sparkling wines are again at the head of the line. We'll start with the delicate, complex Soldati Gavi Brut, which has a very fine, dense bead and herbaceous aromas with notes of crusty bread, yeast and flowers; the harmonious palate displays good balance and length. On the same level, the Soldati Brut '90 has a soft, mellow palate that displays great finesse with good dosage and sweet notes of wood-derived vanilla. The non-vintage Soldati Brut offers biscuity, spicy aromas on the nose, while the palate is notably full and complex. The Brut Nature '87 shows a very fine perlage and an attractive golden hue, but the finesse of its creamy palate is masked by the wood. One Glass each goes to the non-vintage Gavi Pas Dosé, with its scents of crusty bread, flowers and apple and its creamy palate, and to the new Rosé Brut, onion-skin pink in color, which is redolent of strawberry and raspberry and is acidic but pleasant on the palate. Of the non-sparkling Gavis our favorite is the Gavi La Scolca: of a pale straw color with a greenish tinge, it has a clean citron fragrance, succulence and a good crisp note. The Valentino '98, of a deep, lively straw color, is just as good: the attractive nose with ripe fruit and mineral notes is followed by good body with appropriate crisp acidity and a long, fruity finish. The new Pinot Nero '97 already deserves One full Glass for its good, deep ruby color and intriguing hints of cherry and green hazelnut; the palate, still rather dumb owing to its youth, reveals bitter notes.

○	Soldati La Scolca Gavi Brut	🍷🍷	4
○	Soldati La Scolca Spumante Brut '90	🍷🍷	6
○	Gavi La Scolca '98	🍷	4
○	Gavi Valentino '98	🍷	3
●	Pinot Nero '97	🍷	4
○	Soldati La Scolca Brut	🍷	4
⊙	Soldati La Scolca Brut 2000 Rosé	🍷	4
○	Soldati La Scolca Brut Nature '87	🍷	5
○	Soldati La Scolca Gavi Pas Dosé	🍷	4
○	Soldati La Scolca Spumante Brut '87	🍸🍸	5
○	Gavi dei Gavi Etichetta Nera '97	🍸	5

GAVI (AL)

Morgassi Superiore

Loc. Case Sparse Sermoria, 7
15066 Gavi (AL)
tel. 0143/642007

The Piacitelli estate now regularly produces wines of consistently high quality, thanks in part to the assistance of the oenologist Giancarlo Scaglione. The Tamino '97, from 100% syrah, has a wonderful opaque ruby-black color followed by an intense and original nose offering notes of fruit, spice and caramel with toasty hints. The impressively structured palate, although it still has some rough edges, is warm, dry, succulent and extremely long. The Arbace '96, a blend of barbera and cabernet sauvignon of a classic ruby color, also earns Two Glasses; the French grape contributes intense peaty and vegetal aromas with distinct notes of coffee. The palate, harmonious and fresh with well-judged tannins, shows moderate length. The Gavi '98, of a classic pale straw color, offers briny and mineral notes on the nose; characteristic crispness is evident on the palate, upheld by good body and adequate length. The Fiordiligi '97, a deep straw-colored chardonnay with a youthful greenish tinge, would have scored Two Glasses for its delicate varietal aromas and fresh, dense, long palate, were it not for its over-pronounced wood. The Pistrice '98, from cortese and chardonnay, has a light greenish-straw color and releases flowery aromas with mineral hints; with its medium length and fresh succulent palate it is a very enjoyable, undemanding wine. The bright golden Cherubino '97, made from viognier, offers sweet aromas of wood and spice; the palate is rich but lacks length.

●	Arbace '96	🍷🍷	5
●	Tamino '97	🍷🍷	6
○	Cherubino '97	🍷	5
○	Gavi del Comune di Gavi '98	🍷	4
○	Piemonte Chardonnay Fiordiligi '97	🍷	4
○	Pistrice '98	🍷	3
○	Cherubino '96	🍸🍸	5
●	Tamino '96	🍸🍸	5
●	Arbace '95	🍸	4

GAVI (AL)

VILLA SPARINA
FRAZ. MONTEROTONDO, 56
15066 GAVI (AL)
TEL. 0143/633835

Federico Curtaz, who supervises the vineyards, and Beppe Caviola, in charge in the cellar, work with a well-organized team co-ordinated by Mario Moccagatta. Yields per hectare are ruthlessly restricted, and the idea of starting with super-concentrated grapes with the aim of producing a Gavi rivaling the world's great whites has proved a successful gamble. However the top wine of the estate, and the most interesting, does not come from Gavi but from the Rivalta property in the Acqui zone, which concentrates on reds. The Moccagattas, thanks to the skill of their two experts, have progressed from the production of reliable but characterless wines to really wonderful bottles, and have achieved the concentrations necessary for their wines to compete with the best in Italy. One example is the Barbera del Monferrato Rivalta '97. We had never tasted such a big, opulent, but at the same time elegant Barbera in this area. Its Three Glasses are a thoroughly deserved triumph for the Moccagatta family. The two Dolcettos are also very good, the d'Giusep perhaps slightly better than the Bric Maioli. However there are other surprises in store: the Gavi Monterotondo '97 is the perfect embodiment of the ideas behind the estate's new approach to production, which Mario Moccagatta's sons, Stefano and Massimo, were the keenest to put into practice. Starting with its brilliant golden color, it is at the top of its category; for a few seconds the intense honeyed, buttery note prevails over the flowers and tropical fruit, which then emerge, well-balanced by the aromas of toasty wood; tertiary aromas are just perceptible, promising long and positive development. The palate, fat and velvety but satisfyingly fresh, leads into an impressive finish. The Pas Dosé '92 again scores Two full Glasses, while the Müller Thurgau, a stranger in these parts, earns One ample Glass.

●	Barbera del M.to Rivalta '97	🍷🍷🍷	5
●	Dolcetto d'Acqui Bric Maioli '98	🍷🍷	3*
●	Dolcetto d'Acqui Sup. d'Giusep '98	🍷🍷	4
○	Gavi Cremant Pas Dosé '92	🍷🍷	5
○	Gavi del Comune di Gavi '98	🍷🍷	3*
○	Gavi di Gavi Monterotondo '97	🍷🍷	5
○	Monferrato Müller Thurgau '98	🍷	4
●	Dolcetto d'Acqui Sup. d'Giusep '97	🍸🍸	4
○	Gavi Cremant Pas Dosé '90	🍸🍸	5
○	Gavi di Gavi La Villa '97	🍸🍸	4
●	Barbera del M.to Rivalta '96	🍸🍸	6

GHEMME (NO)

ANTICHI VIGNETI DI CANTALUPO
VIA MICHELANGELO BUONARROTI, 5
28074 GHEMME (NO)
TEL. 0163/840041

Alberto Arlunno's '94 Ghemmes, although feeling the effects of a poor vintage, should not be underrated. The Collis Carellae has a ruby-garnet color with an orange rim introducing a pleasantly forward nose with hints of cocoa, leather, spice and jam. The palate immediately reveals a good structure; stark, noble tannins lend it austerity, and the finish, which echoes the bouquet, is long. The Collis Breclemae, of an intense ruby-garnet hue, offers more intriguing aromas: notes of red fruit mingle with hints of tar, undergrowth and dried flowers on a complex and enticing nose. The not very powerful palate reveals pronounced tannins that make the wine a good match for rich dishes. The almost transparent ruby-colored basic Ghemme offers a fruity, spicy nose and a dry, medium-firm palate. The Agamium is an undemanding red, somewhat austere in character. The Carolus, a white made from greco, chardonnay and arneis, has fermentation-derived aromas with fresh hints of aromatic herbs and citrus fruit; the palate is generous and well-balanced. The Villa Horta, from vespolina, and the Primigenia, from uva rara, nebbiolo and vespolina, are two pleasantly rustic reds. The Mimo, a nebbiolo-based rosé, is agreeably quaffable.

○	Carolus '98	🍷	2
●	Colline Novaresi Agamium '97	🍷	3
●	Ghemme '94	🍷	4
●	Ghemme Collis Breclemae '94	🍷	5
●	Ghemme Collis Carellae '94	🍷	5
●	Villa Horta '98	🍷	2
⊙	Colline Novaresi Il Mimo '98		2
●	Primigenia '98		2
●	Ghemme Collis Breclemae '90	🍸🍸	5
●	Ghemme Collis Breclemae '91	🍸🍸	4
●	Ghemme Collis Carellae '90	🍸🍸	5
●	Ghemme Signore di Bayard '93	🍸🍸	5
●	Ghemme Collis Carellae '91	🍸	4

INCISA SCAPACCINO (AT)

ERMANNO E ALESSANDRA BREMA
VIA POZZOMAGNA, 9
14045 INCISA SCAPACCINO (AT)
TEL. 0141/74019 - 0141/74617

Ermanno Brema, having cleverly acquired one of the most sought-after sites for Barbera, the Bricco Nizza, has now decided to concentrate his efforts on the cellar. With the help of his friend the oenologist Giancarlo Scaglione, he has made a start on both the buildings and the equipment, and at the same time introduced the use of the barrique for the top house reds. As a consequence his wines, above all the Barberas, display a greater finesse than was their wont, thanks to an equilibrum which succeeds in subduing the raw material, which tends to be strong and unruly at Brema. The Bricconizza '97, in its debut appearance, is a wine with an astonishing density of fruit and persistence of flavor which only just missed Three Glasses: the still rather closed nose, with prominent balsamic and peppery notes, precedes a rich and succulent palate with a long finish reminiscent of licorice and ripe cherry. Le Cascine '97, a Barbera deriving from the best of the estate's various vineyards, is a very similar wine, perhaps slightly rougher-edged, as it has some not yet perfectly assimilated secondary tannins. The lightly fizzy Barbera Monferrato Vigna Castagnei '98, one of the best of its type, is as enjoyable and straightforward as ever: it offers aromas of raspberry and a fresh hint of strawberry on the finish. The Dolcetto d'Asti Vigna Impagnato '97 has a wonderful deep violet color, a nose with fairly prominent wood and good concentration. The brightly cherry-hued Grignolino d'Asti Bric le Rocche '97 is fragrant and succulent; it offers intense aromas with citrus notes and a good balance between acidity and tannins.

●	Barbera d'Asti Sup. Bricconizza '97	🍷🍷	5
●	Barbera d'Asti Sup. Le Cascine '97	🍷🍷	4
●	Dolcetto d'Asti Vigna Impagnato '97	🍷🍷	3
●	Barbera del M.to Vigna Castagnei '98	🍷	3
●	Grignolino d'Asti Bric le Rocche '97	🍷	3
●	Dolcetto d'Asti Vigna Impagnato '96	YY	3
●	Barbera d'Asti Sup. Le Cascine '96	Y	4

IVREA (TO)

FERRANDO E C.
VIA TORINO, 599
10015 IVREA (TO)
TEL. 0125/641176

Three of Luigi Ferrando's wines, the Caluso Passito, the Erbaluce Cariola and the Carema Etichetta Nera, are particularly successful. The first has an unusual deep golden hue; the nose offers aromas of peaches in syrup, dried fruit and leather, while the palate, appealingly rich, soft and sweet, progresses smoothly to a lingering finish that mirrors the bouquet. The Erbaluce di Caluso Cariola, of a deep straw color, offers a generous, intense nose with hints of apple, tropical fruit and hazelnut; the mouth-filling palate is well balanced by a lively acidity which keeps it from being heavy, and the long, corresponding finish displays floral hints of lily of the valley. The Carema Etichetta Nera revives the splendor of the best vintages: it is a powerful, full-bodied red, a truly excellent example of the appellation. The basic Erbaluce offers a satisfying intensity on the nose, with aromas of apricot and apple and floral notes; the substantial palate, heralded by the rich straw color, is enlivened by a pronounced crisp acidity, and the lingering finish reveals faintly forward tones. The good Solativo, a dried-grape wine from erbaluce, is a little less expressive than the Caluso Passito: the nose offers notes of leather and dried fruit and the palate a rich sweetness followed by a warm, corresponding finish. The Carema Etichetta Bianca, of an almost transparent ruby color, displays notably fresh aromas with hints of strawberry, blueberry and rhubarb; the palate, while not powerful, is firm and agreeable.

●	Carema Etichetta Nera '95	🍷🍷	6
○	Caluso Passito Vigneto Cariola '94	🍷🍷	6
○	Erbaluce di Caluso Cariola '98	🍷🍷	4
●	Carema Etichetta Bianca '95	🍷	5
○	Erbaluce di Caluso '98	🍷	3
○	Solativo '97	🍷	5
●	Carema Etichetta Nera '90	YY	6
●	Carema Etichetta Bianca '90	Y	5

LA MORRA (CN)

★ ELIO ALTARE
CASCINA NUOVA, 51
FRAZ. ANNUNZIATA
12064 LA MORRA (CN)
TEL. 0173/50835

For many years now Elio Altare has been a benchmark for a whole group of Langhe winegrowers. His generous nature has often prompted him to give a hand to emerging producers and set them on the road to excellence. Now he has succeeded in realizing one of his dreams: the cultivation and vinification of the grapes from one of the best and most highly prized subzones of the Barolo appellation, Brunate. Although he was not helped by the vintage (violent hailstorms ravaged La Morra on the 3rd and 4th of August 1995), a significant difference is immediately apparent between the new Brunate, which was a hair's breadth short of Three Glasses, and the Barolo Arborina, although the latter is still an excellent wine. Compared to its stablemate, the Brunate has greater finesse and complexity on the nose, as well as superior length and balance. The basic Barolo is refined, elegant and never weighty. Backed up by the fabulous '97 harvest, the real house jewels are the Langhe Rossos: Larigi (a monovarietal barbera), Arborina (a monovarietal nebbiolo) and La Villa (a blend of barbera and nebbiolo). As the barbera grape was the star of the '97 vintage, our preference is for the Larigi, which displays the personality and power of an absolute champion. The Arborina, true to its origins, offers dense-textured, soft tannins, enhanced by the extraordinary complexity of nose and palate belonging to this variety: a wine which aging will render sublime. The La Villa reveals a density and length which it has never before achieved. Unfortunately the tasting of Altare's new wine, a blend of all the varieties he grows, from dolcetto to cabernet sauvignon, has had to be put off for another year.

● Langhe Arborina '97	▼▼▼	6
● Langhe Larigi '97	▼▼▼	6
● Barbera d'Alba '98	▼▼	4
● Barolo '95	▼▼	6
● Barolo Brunate '95	▼▼	6
● Barolo Vigneto Arborina '95	▼▼	6
● Dolcetto d'Alba '98	▼▼	4
● Langhe La Villa '97	▼▼	6
● Barolo Vigneto Arborina '93	▽▽▽	6
● Langhe Arborina '96	▽▽▽	6
● Langhe Larigi '94	▽▽▽	6
● Langhe Larigi '95	▽▽▽	6
● Vigna Arborina '90	▽▽▽	6
● Vigna Arborina '93	▽▽▽	6
● Vigna Larigi '90	▽▽▽	6

LA MORRA (CN)

RENATO RATTI ANTICHE CANTINE
DELL'ABBAZIA DELL'ANNUNZIATA
FRAZ. ANNUNZIATA, 7
12064 LA MORRA (CN)
TEL. 0173/50185

Pietro and Giovanni Ratti, with the assistance of Massimo Martinelli, have again presented a vast range of wines from their two wineries at Annunziata di La Morra and Costigliole d'Asti. The three best are the Nebbiolo, the Dolcetto Colombè and the Villa Pattono. The first, a good example of a Nebbiolo d'Alba, comes from the celebrated Ochetti cru and offers strong varietal aromas, good balance and a lingering finish. The Colombè, vinous, fruity, medium-bodied and still a little astringent, is an immensely quaffable wine. The Villa Pattono, 70% barbera with some merlot and cabernet sauvignon, is elegant and balanced: the acidity of the barbera is toned down by maturation in wood, which has conferred soft, sweet tannins. The nose is still rather reticent but does reveal attractive notes of ripe red fruit. The Cabernet I Cedri and the Monferrato Rosso (merlot) are well-gauged wines with no excesses; they want only more intensity and length on nose and palate. The Barbera Torriglione, partly overwhelmed by the exuberance of the grape, displays an over-prominent acidity and harshness. Of the two Barolos we prefer the concentrated, expressive Marcenasco: the palate, while not imposing in structure, reveals characteristic notes of rose with hints of licorice. The Rocche has fewer strings to its bow, its appeal being mostly in its broad, heady aromas.

● Dolcetto d'Alba Colombè '98	▼▼	3*
● Monferrato Villa Pattono '97	▼▼	5
● Nebbiolo d'Alba Ochetti '97	▼▼	4
● Barbera d'Alba Torriglione '97	▼	4
● Barolo Marcenasco '95	▼	6
● Barolo Rocche Marcenasco '95	▼	6
● Monferrato I Cedri '97	▼	5
● Monferrato Rosso '97	▼	5
● Barolo Rocche Marcenasco '83	▽▽▽	6
● Barolo Rocche Marcenasco '84	▽▽▽	6
● Barolo Conca Marcenasco '93	▽▽	6
● Barolo Rocche Marcenasco '90	▽▽	6
● Monferrato Villa Pattono '96	▽▽	4
● Monferrato I Cedri '96	▽	4
● Monferrato Merlot '96	▽	4

LA MORRA (CN)

BATASIOLO
FRAZ. ANNUNZIATA, 87
12064 LA MORRA (CN)
TEL. 0173/50130 - 0173/50131

In the last edition of the Guide we noted a decline in quality from this estate, but this year the Dogliani family is back in form with a series of excellent wines. The Barbera d'Alba Sovrana is an example: its broad, soft-toned and harmoniously blended aromas of fruit and wood and its concentrated palate easily earned it Two Glasses. It shows a ruby-garnet hue with a slightly faded rim and aromas of cherry, caramel, mint and custard; pronounced tannins in the mouth offset the soft body, and the lingering finish echoes the bouquet. The deep golden Muscatel Tardì is a delicious dessert wine: the broad nose, with hints of ripe fruit, hazelnut cream and dates, precedes a dense and concentrated palate with plenty of sinew and a warm, long finish. The '95 Barolos were very good, starting with the vivid-hued Corda della Briccolina, which offers ample aromas of jam, dried flowers and sweet biscuits together with toasty notes on the pleasantly forward nose. The palate is broad and meaty, with just perceptible tannins and a nicely lingering finish. The Boscareto displays marked spicy notes on a forward nose, followed by a rather austere palate. The basic version is not in the least inferior, showing plenty of fruit on the nose and an enjoyably soft palate. One Glass goes to the Barolo Riserva '93, with its slightly heady aromas and somewhat over-austere palate, and to the Barbaresco '96, which offers simple aromas with balsamic notes to the fore. The list ends with the pleasant and forceful Dolcetto Bricco Vergne.

●	Barbera d'Alba Sovrana '97	🍷🍷	4
●	Barolo '95	🍷🍷	6
●	Barolo Boscareto '95	🍷🍷	6
●	Barolo Corda della Briccolina '95	🍷🍷	6
○	Piemonte Moscato Passito Muscatel Tardì '97	🍷🍷	5
●	Barbaresco '96	🍷	6
●	Barolo Ris. '93	🍷	6
●	Dolcetto d'Alba Bricco Vergne '98	🍷	4
●	Barolo Corda della Briccolina '88	YYY	6
●	Barolo Corda della Briccolina '89	YYY	6
●	Barolo Corda della Briccolina '90	YYY	6
●	Barolo Corda della Briccolina '93	YY	6
●	Barolo Bofani '93	Y	5
●	Barolo Boscareto '93	Y	6

LA MORRA (CN)

ENZO BOGLIETTI
VIA ROMA, 37
12064 LA MORRA (CN)
TEL. 0173/50330

Enzo Boglietti's unpredictable and strong-willed personality is reflected in the intensity that distinguishes his wines. He believes in a minimum of human intervention in wine-making, feeling that only a few operations need to be carried out on what nature offers him: the most important element, for him, is balance. This is how we understand the distinctly different styles of two wines that have made him famous: the Barbera Vigna dei Romani and the Langhe Rosso Buio. In the former we find all the power and irrepressible exuberance of the '97 vintage only partially toned down by fermentation and barrique maturation; the nose, characterized by dense black fruit laced with hints of coffee, releases a full, enveloping sensation; the palate reveals the body and length conferred by superb raw material and is enlivened by the classic acidic bite on the finish. The Buio, from barbera blended with a little nebbiolo, is more reserved and mature in tone: its finesse emerges in the floral hints on the nose, in the enticing softness of the palate and the lingering creaminess on the finish. Boglietti is helped by his brother Gianni; together they now manage ten hectares of vineyards scattered over the area between La Morra and Serralunga, taking in Monforte on the way. However, Enzo's main concern is still the nebbiolo for the two Barolos. We liked both the '95s, slightly preferring the Case Nere. This wine is of an intense hue and offers broad aromas and a satisfyingly rich development on the palate. The delicate and undemanding Brunate reveals an intriguing nose. We greatly admired the Dolcetto Tigli Neri, with its unusual richness of fragrance and characterful palate.

●	Barbera d'Alba Vigna dei Romani '97	🍷🍷	5
●	Barolo Vigna Case Nere '95	🍷🍷	6
●	Dolcetto d'Alba Tigli Neri '98	🍷🍷	4
●	Langhe Rosso Buio '97	🍷🍷	5
●	Barolo Brunate '95	🍷	6
●	Dolcetto d'Alba '98	🍷	3
●	Barbera d'Alba Vigna dei Romani '94	YYY	4
●	Barbera d'Alba Vigna dei Romani '96	YY	4
●	Barolo Vigna Case Nere '94	YY	5
●	Langhe Rosso Buio '96	YY	5
●	Barolo Vigna delle Brunate '94	Y	5

LA MORRA (CN)

GIANFRANCO BOVIO
B.TA CIOTTO, 63
FRAZ. ANNUNZIATA
12064 LA MORRA (CN)
TEL. 0173/50190 - 0173/50604

Some dramatic changes are taking place this year at the Bovio estate. The energetic Gian, not content with having transformed the restaurant into a veritable gastronomic and oenological temple with banqueting rooms for large groups, other more secluded areas and a wonderful wineshop, has begun constructing a monumental cellar. But the news is not limited to his building plans: Gian has decided to call in the assistance of Beppe Cavioli as consultant oenologist. Although the results will really be perceptible only after a few vintages, this year's Dolcetto already encourages blitheness. The wine immediately reveals its potential in its color, ruby with intense garnet highlights; the nose, impressive in impact, releases hints of ripe strawberry, raspberry, pepper and tobacco; the palate, solid and smooth, leads into a lingering licorice finish. The Barolo Vigneto Gattera '95, like the Vigneto Arborina, shows the effects of a vintage not notably favorable to the winegrowers of Annunziata. We prefer the Gattera, which is less austere and more softly fruity. The Barbera Il Ciotto '98, appealing as usual, is ruby in color with a settled rim and shows finesse if not great intensity on the nose, with its hints of violet, red fruit and pepper; the palate is fairly dense and structured and boasts a deeply satisfying finish. The Barbera Reja Veja, almost transparent in the glass, has not made the most of the superb '97 vintage: it wants more density and less wood.

● Barolo Vigneto Gattera dell'Annunziata '95	▼▼	6
● Dolcetto d'Alba Vigneto Dabbene dell'Annunziata '98	▼▼	3*
● Barbera d'Alba Il Ciotto '98	▼	3
● Barbera d'Alba Regia Veja '97	▼	4
● Barolo Vigneto Arborina dell'Annunziata '95	▼	6
● Barolo Vigneto Arborina dell'Annunziata '90	▽▽▽	6
● Barolo Vigneto Arborina dell'Annunziata '93	▽▽	6
● Barolo Vigneto Gattera dell'Annunziata '93	▽▽	6

LA MORRA (CN)

GIOVANNI CORINO
FRAZ. ANNUNZIATA, 24
12064 LA MORRA (CN)
TEL. 0173/50219 - 0173/509452

Every member of the Corino family has contributed to the improvement of the estate, which over the last ten years has been extended, little by little, to encompass the present 15 hectares under vine. By dint of unremitting hard work, Renato and Silvano, together with their father Giovanni, have repeated last year's coup with the stunning Barbera Vigna Pozzo '97. Its nearly impenetrable ruby-purple hue and almost unctuous aspect are normal for a vintage which was anything but normal. The nose reveals intense aromas of cherry jam made more intriguing by a faint, sweet echo of vanilla, while, on the palate, incredibly succulent fruit manages to subdue the typical acidity of the grape, resulting in a long and velvety finish. However, in recent years the mainstay of the Corino winery has been Barolo. Despite an uphill start thanks to the hailstorms of August 3rd and 4th, 1995, a new Barolo, from the Arborino vineyard of La Morra, appears in this year's Guide together with our old friends the Vigna Giachini and the Vigneto Rocche. For the moment, although time could transform it, the Vigna Giachini is a little less elegant and harmonious because of somewhat dry tannins. The Arborina and the Vigneto Rocche, on the other hand, are almost neck and neck. The former is a little softer and less intense, with powerful aromas of red fruits; the latter is more austere both on the nose, which shows a marked spicy note, and on the palate, which boasts a notably rich and powerful tannic finish. Following in the wake of these thoroughbreds, the Dolcetto has a more immediate and carefree charm, while the Barbera needs more time to acquire balance.

● Barbera d'Alba Vigna Pozzo '97	▼▼▼	5
● Barolo Arborina '95	▼▼	6
● Barolo Vigneto Rocche '95	▼▼	6
● Dolcetto d'Alba '98	▼▼	3*
● Barbera d'Alba '98	▼	3
● Barolo Vigna Giachini '95	▼	6
● Barbera d'Alba Vigna Pozzo '96	▽▽▽	4
● Barolo Vigna Giachini '89	▽▽▽	6
● Barolo Vigneto Rocche '90	▽▽▽	6
● Barolo Vigna Giachini '90	▽▽	6
● Barolo Vigna Giachini '93	▽▽	6
● Barolo Vigneto Rocche '93	▽▽	6
● Barolo Vigneto Rocche '94	▽▽	5

LA MORRA (CN)

Dosio
Reg. Serradenari, 16
12064 La Morra (CN)
tel. 0173/50677

Beppe Dosio shows great skill in all the wines of his vast range, which includes the classics of the Langhe and of Roero, as well as international varieties and more or less experimental blends. This year the traditional Langhe wines were our favorites, particularly the Dolcetto Nassone and the Barolo Fossati, which won Two Glasses each. The first, is highly varietal in character, showing a dark purplish hue, vinous aromas with rich red fruit and a mouth-filling, richly succulent palate with a nice balance between tannins and acidity. The Barolo Fossati '95, ruby-garnet in color, is redolent of prune and dried roses with fresher notes of berries; the palate is warm, full-bodied and long. The other Barolo, a '93 Riserva, displays a stunning brilliant ruby color; it opens out well on the nose but falls away on the palate, which is slightly disjointed and forward. The Momenti, a blend of equal parts of nebbiolo and barbera, needs further adjustment: its potential is evident, but it loses points for its excessive harshness. The Barbera has a very attractive bouquet with enjoyable fruity notes, but in the mouth it lacks intensity and length.

● Barolo Fossati '95	🍷🍷	5
● Dolcetto d'Alba Nassone '98	🍷🍷	3*
● Barbera d'Alba Sup. '97	🍷	4
● Barolo Ris. '93	🍷	6
● Langhe Momenti '97	🍷	4
● Barolo Fossati '94	ΥΥ	5
● Barolo Fossati '93	Υ	5
● Eventi '96	Υ	4

LA MORRA (CN)

Gianni Gagliardo
B.ta Serra dei Turchi, 88
Fraz. Santa Maria
12064 La Morra (CN)
tel. 0173/50829

This year Gianni Gagliardo's estate makes its debut in the Guide. It has an annual output of about 250 thousand bottles and cultivates 20 hectares under vine, which will soon increase to 28; the rest of the grapes are bought in from growers of long-standing reliability. Recently Gianni entrusted the cellar to his firstborn, Stefano, and the vineyards to his second son, Alberto, so that he himself is able to dedicate more time to the business side. The family looks after three separate vineyard areas: the first, at Monticello d'Alba in the Roero zone, provides their favorita grapes; the second, near Alba, between Montelupo Albese and Diano d'Alba, is planted to dolcetto, and the third, producing nebbiolo and barbera, is scattered throughout the entire Barolo zone. One of the particularly interesting wines they presented this year is the Barolo Preve, a skillful assemblage of nebbiolo grapes from the vineyards of Serra dei Turchi di Santa Maria at La Morra, and Moriondino at Castiglione Falletto. Aged in 500- and 700-liter tonneaux, it is elegant rather than powerful on the nose, with a nice harmony between spicy notes and fruity aromas (red berries), while the palate, still a bit rough, is very lively. Another excellent wine is the Batié, a younger brother of the Barolo which undergoes a shorter and cooler maceration process. The wine seems sweet and harmonious, thanks to the French oak, without sacrificing its good solid fruit. The Dolcetto d'Alba Paulin, rustic rather than refined, shows notably intense aromas of plum and strikingly powerful tannins on the finish. One Glass each also goes to the two Favoritas, the more easily quaffable Casà and the fleshier Neirole.

● Barolo Preve '95	🍷🍷	6
● Batié '95	🍷🍷	5
● Dolcetto d'Alba Paulin '98	🍷	4
○ Langhe Favorita Casà '98	🍷	4
○ Langhe Favorita Neirole '97	🍷	4

LA MORRA (CN)

SILVIO GRASSO
CASCINA LUCIANI, 112
FRAZ. ANNUNZIATA
12064 LA MORRA (CN)
TEL. 0173/50322

This year Federico and Marilena Grasso have presented three outstanding Barolos. We'll begin with the superb Bricco Luciani, which after an interval of five years has again won Three Glasses. It has a dense ruby-garnet hue with a firm, narrow rim; the ample, harmonious nose, with perfectly blended fruit and wood, releases aromas of jam and licorice with balsamic and spicy notes that together show great elegance. In the mouth the wine immediately reveals its concentration, breadth and rich profusion of integrated tannins; these emerge with power and without harshness on the mid palate and lend punch to the long finish. The faintly forward hint that marks the Barolo Ciabot Manzoni is heralded by the orange rim on its garnet color; bitterish rhubarb and quinine tones characterize the nose, together with black fruit and toasty notes. On the palate the ample texture and sweetness of extract reveal its relationship to the Bricco Luciani. The basic Barolo is very dense in color, with a firm rim; the notes of jam, toasty coffee and eucalyptus are a further indication of richness; it develops along soft, ample lines on the palate, supported by an imposing structure, and the lingering finish reveals notes of licorice and cocoa. Spicy oak-derived tones blend delightfully with varietal fruit on the nose of the Barbera Fontanile, and the palate is very harmonious; only the distinctive personality of a real star is wanting. Of the two base wines we preferred the very characteristic Dolcetto; the Barbera, although pleasant, seems to lack structure.

●	Barolo Bricco Luciani '95	🍷🍷🍷	6
●	Barbera d'Alba Fontanile '97	🍷🍷	4
●	Barolo '95	🍷🍷	5
●	Barolo Ciabot Manzoni '95	🍷🍷	6
●	Dolcetto d'Alba '98	🍷🍷	3*
●	Barbera d'Alba '98	🍷	3
●	Barolo Bricco Luciani '90	🍸🍸🍸	6
●	Barbera d'Alba Fontanile '96	🍸🍸	4
●	Barolo Bricco Luciani '93	🍸🍸	6
●	Barolo Ciabot Manzoni '90	🍸🍸	6
●	Barolo Ciabot Manzoni '93	🍸🍸	6
●	Barolo Ciabot Manzoni '94	🍸🍸	6
●	Barolo Bricco Luciani '94	🍸	6

LA MORRA (CN)

MARCARINI
P.ZZA MARTIRI, 2
12064 LA MORRA (CN)
TEL. 0173/50222

For almost ten years Luisa Bava and her husband Manuel Marchetti have been running this historic winery with its breathtaking view over Castiglione Falletto and Serralunga. There are just over 12 hectares under vine, of which almost two thirds are in the Brunate and La Serra vineyards and planted to nebbiolo. Among the other plots, we shall never tire of mentioning the small Bosco di Berri vineyard, planted to dolcetto on ungrafted rootstock that escaped phylloxera, and yielding about 1,500 bottles a year of a wine that is among the best of its category. At the moment, the '98 version is not very forthcoming on the nose, but with the enlightened patience required by a great wine one finds it gradually unfolding with fruity notes of raspberry and spicy licorice tones; in the mouth it shows satisfying breadth and subtlety which enhance the powerful structure. The rather simpler and more rustic Dolcetto Fontanazza '98, with its not very ripe fruity aromas, is nevertheless good. The particularly successful Nebbiolo Lasarin '98 shows the rich, powerful body of its vintage and the attractive fruit (strawberry and raspberry) and hefty tannins of its grape. The '95 vintage, troubled by violent hailstorms at the beginning of August, has deprived the two Barolos of their customary richness and succulence. The Brunate, offering distinct aromas of fresh mint, black currant and strawberry, is diminished by harsh and bitter tannins on the finish. The Serra is more agreeable, although less complex on the nose (raspberry and citrus peel), and the palate develops more smoothly to a warm, medium-long finish. The Moscato offers a remarkable lingering sensation of ripe yellow peach. The Barbera Camerano '98 was still in cask when we were at our tastings, so it will be reviewed at a later date.

●	Barolo La Serra '95	🍷🍷	6
●	Dolcetto d'Alba Boschi di Berri '98	🍷🍷	4
●	Langhe Nebbiolo Lasarin '98	🍷🍷	4
●	Barolo Brunate '95	🍷	6
●	Dolcetto d'Alba Fontanazza '98	🍷	3
○	Moscato d'Asti '98	🍷	3
●	Barolo Brunate Ris. '85	🍸🍸🍸	6
●	Dolcetto d'Alba Boschi di Berri '96	🍸🍸🍸	4
●	Barbera d'Alba Ciabot Camerano '97	🍸🍸	4
●	Barolo Brunate '90	🍸🍸	6
●	Barolo Brunate '93	🍸🍸	6
●	Barolo La Serra '93	🍸🍸	6
●	Dolcetto d'Alba Boschi di Berri '97	🍸🍸	4

LA MORRA (CN)

Mario Marengo
Via XX Settembre, 32
12064 La Morra (CN)
tel. 0173/50127

The Marengo family has for many years divided its time between laboring in the vineyard and their hardware store. For over a century they have owned a small vineyard of about one and a half hectares in the sought-after Brunate cru at La Morra. But the present owner's grandfather Giacomo, who was a blacksmith by trade, bought a small ironmonger's shop in the center of La Morra, and for years this distracted the family from viticulture, relegating the celebrated vineyard to the status of a hobby. Nevertheless they never entirely ceased producing Barolo, and today Mario, a dedicated collector, has a series of wines stored in his cellar which bear witness to the long-established connection betweem the Marengos and the vines of Brunate. Mario's son Marco has some idea of what the Brunate property represents, and now it looks as if, thanks in part to the boom in the Barolo area, and certainly thanks to strong encouragement from friends (Elio Altare first of all, and then Marco De Grazia), he has decided to take the plunge. The two hectares under vine (besides the cru already mentioned, the estate also owns half a hectare at Vergne, in the Bricco delle Viole zone) yield at the moment just about 8,000 bottles. To add to the attractions, two additional hectares will shortly be planted. The other real problem that the enthusiastic Marco will have to face is the lack of a proper cellar. At the moment his father makes do with the restricted but functional existing cellar, where he vinifies a few thousand bottles of an enjoyable, light and drinkable Dolcetto and not quite 5,000 bottles of Barolo Brunate, which maturation in new barriques renders soft and harmonious without in the least diminishing the enchanting fragrance that only the Brunate cru can give.

●	Barolo Brunate '95	🍷🍷	5
●	Dolcetto d'Alba '98	🍷	3

LA MORRA (CN)

Mauro Molino
B.ta Gancia, 111
Fraz. Annunziata
12064 La Morra (CN)
tel. 0173/50814

Success has not changed Mauro Molino. We remember him at the start of his career when his concern was to keep the family vineyards going somehow, and today he has become one of the best producers of the area. His wines receive meticulous care and the resulting quality is stupendous. We can best describe the Barbera Vigna Gattere as possessing an extraordinary spontaneity, which rather than overwhelming us with power and warmth, offers a delightful overall harmony. The very dark ruby color introduces aromas in which the spicy oak and dense fruit are perfectly blended; a wonderful freshness appears on the palate, where the structure reveals its strength in a continuing crescendo with a long, satisfying finish. Greater austerity characterizes the Acanzio, a striking example of harmony, richness of aroma and characterful flavor: while the nebbiolo grape confers dryness on the palate and a floral nose, the barbera brims over with vitality. The two '95 Barolos, one as good as the other, also share some characteristics; the more forward Conca shows its maturity in its color and in the sweetness of its tannins; the Gancia, which is still developing, is complex on the nose and long on the palate. The Chardonnay is fundamentally sound but does not yet have the elegance that would transform it. Lastly, the Dolcetto is straightforward and easy to drink.

●	Barbera d'Alba Vigna Gattere '97	🍷🍷🍷	5
●	Barolo Vigna Conca '95	🍷🍷	6
●	Barolo Vigna Gancia '95	🍷🍷	6
●	Langhe Rosso Acanzio '97	🍷🍷	5
●	Dolcetto d'Alba '98	🍷	3
○	Langhe Chardonnay Livrot '98	🍷	4
●	Barbera d'Alba Vigna Gattere '96	🍸🍸🍸	5
●	Acanzio '95	🍸🍸	4
●	Barolo Vigna Conca '93	🍸🍸	5
●	Barolo Vigna Conca '94	🍸🍸	5
○	Langhe Chardonnay Livrot '97	🍸🍸	4
●	Langhe Rosso Acanzio '96	🍸🍸	5

LA MORRA (CN)

MONFALLETTO
CORDERO DI MONTEZEMOLO
FRAZ. ANNUNZIATA, 67/BIS
12064 LA MORRA (CN)
TEL. 0173/50344

Monfalletto, a fair-sized estate in Langhe terms, with 25-30 hectares under vine, has made a leap up in quality, launching a new phase and a new, successful style of production. The barriques, arranged on raised platforms in the cellar, now number 600, and it is here that 50-60% of the '95 Barolos are aged. The Enrico VI '95, made exclusively from the michet subvariety grown in the Villero cru at Castiglione Falletto, is elegant and intense, with spicy notes that don't muffle the attractive red fruit on the nose; the palate is austere and has a fairly long finish. This Barolo stands up to the best of the vintage. The Monfalletto reveals earthy notes and a marked toastiness, followed in the mouth by rather dry, rasping tannins imputable to hail in early August. The Barbera d'Alba '97 offers intense aromas with toasty notes alongside hints of cherry; the palate is mouth-filling, sweet and lingering. The Nebbiolo '98 underperforms last year's version; it reveals captivating notes of red fruit and violet, but the palate, although powerful, is rough-edged and lacks balance. The Curdè is an extremely well-made pinot nero, 1,500 bottles strong, rich in the fruity aromas and animal notes typical of the variety, mouth-filling, sweet and lingering on the finish. The properly executed and quaffable Dolcetto '98 is very dark, juicy, mouth-filling and long. The Langhe Bianco '98, of a delightful lively straw color, reveals fruity aromas with hints of white flowers, notably acacia: delicate notes of pear on the palate lead into a sweet, long finish. The Elioro '97, an almost golden barriqued chardonnay, reveals woody notes with aromas of honey; the palate is so rich that it verges on heaviness.

●	Barbera d'Alba '97	🍷🍷	4
●	Barolo Enrico VI '95	🍷🍷	6
●	Barolo Monfalletto '95	🍷🍷	6
○	Langhe Bianco '98	🍷🍷	3*
●	Langhe Rosso Curdè '97	🍷🍷	5
○	Langhe Chardonnay Elioro '97	🍷	4
●	Dolcetto d'Alba '98	🍷	3
●	Langhe Nebbiolo '98	🍷	4
●	Barolo Enrico VI '90	♀♀	6
●	Barolo Enrico VI '93	♀♀	5
●	Barolo Enrico VI '94	♀♀	5
●	Barolo Monfalletto '90	♀♀	6
●	Barolo Monfalletto '93	♀♀	5
●	Barolo Monfalletto '94	♀	5

LA MORRA (CN)

ANDREA OBERTO
VIA G. MARCONI, 25
12064 LA MORRA (CN)
TEL. 0173/509262

Year after year we are amazed by the excellence of the wines from the Oberto estate which started out unobtrusively in the mid '80s and is now one of Piedmont's top producers. If the Obertos are people of few words, notwithstanding their warm hospitality, their wines, once in the glass, do more than speak for themselves. We feel that there is little more to say about the Barbera Giada '97 once it has been said that it is not only one of the best of the vintage, but perhaps one of the best produced in recent years. It is made with grapes from a more than 60-year-old vineyard in the hamlet of Boiolo, between Brunate and Rocche dell'Annunziata. Its concentration already shows in its almost impenetrable dark ruby color; the nose reveals fruity aromas of cherry jam and spicy notes of licorice and vanilla with toasty coffee. The palate is an explosion of sweet, mouth-filling sensations in perfect harmony, and as caressing as velvet right up to the long, warm, succulent finish. The Langhe Fabio '97, a nebbiolo-barbera blend, is similarly vinified: after 18 months in new barriques the aromas of vanilla and coconut tend to outweigh the red berries. The wine is boisterous and still very youthful on the palate, with a Barolo-like structure and density. The two Barolos, the Albarella and the Rocche, are both '95s and very good: the first is elegant and can already, at its tender age, be drunk with pleasure, and the second reveals the finesse, breadth and depth of its superb cru. Of the three '98 Dolcettos, we preferred the richness, concentration and structure of the San Francesco to the elegance of the Vantrino Albarella; the basic version aims less high but is nevertheless decidedly enjoyable. The same goes for the Barbera Boiolo '98, which is full-bodied and pleasingly soft.

●	Barbera d'Alba Giada '97	🍷🍷🍷	5
●	Barolo Vigneto Albarella '95	🍷🍷	6
●	Barolo Vigneto Rocche '95	🍷🍷	6
●	Dolcetto d'Alba Vigneto S. Francesco '98	🍷🍷	3*
●	Langhe Fabio '97	🍷🍷	5
●	Barbera d'Alba Vigneto Boiolo '98	🍷	3
●	Dolcetto d'Alba '98	🍷	3
●	Dolcetto d'Alba Vigneto Vantrino Albarella '98	🍷	3
●	Barbera d'Alba Giada '96	♀♀♀	5
●	Barolo Vigneto Rocche '90	♀♀	6
●	Barolo Vigneto Rocche '93	♀♀	6
●	Barolo Vigneto Rocche '94	♀♀	6
●	Langhe Fabio '96	♀♀	5

LA MORRA (CN)

F.LLI ODDERO

VIA S. MARIA, 28
12064 LA MORRA (CN)
TEL. 0173/50618

The cabernet-based Langhe Rosso Furesté '97 is a wine with a powerful structure; of a dense garnet hue with a narrow rim, it releases an unusual bouquet of black fruit preserves, licorice, rhubarb, tobacco leaf and vanilla; rich and ample on the palate, it displays pronounced tannins which lend punch to the very long, corresponding finish. The Barolo Vigna Rionda also earns Two Glasses: its garnet-tinted ruby color is followed by a pleasantly forward bouquet in which briny, pungent notes emerge over aromas of jam, pepper and leather. The palate, slightly austere in tone, has good body and a lingering finish with notes of licorice. The basic Barolo is of a medium-intense color verging on garnet and offers aromas of jam and licorice laced with creamy notes; the palate has lots of body, with a faintly perceptible tannic note on the remarkably long finish. One full Glass goes to the Dolcetto, with its intense garnet hue and highly individual bouquet revealing berries, mint and juniper; the dry, forceful palate leads into a deeply satisfying finish. The Barbera d'Alba '98 offers notes of tar and iodine on a fruity, spicy nose; the palate is chewy and somewhat austere. The Chardonnay Collaretto, of a deep straw color with golden highlights, shows a good broad nose with tropical fruit, green leaves and smoky notes; the robust palate has a fresh bite of acidity and lingering tones of flowers and hazelnut on the finish.

●	Barolo '95	▼▼	5
●	Barolo Vigna Rionda '95	▼▼	5
●	Langhe Furesté '97	▼▼	4
●	Barbera d'Alba '98	▼	3
●	Dolcetto d'Alba '98	▼	3
○	Langhe Chardonnay Collaretto '98	▼	3
●	Barolo Vigna Rionda '89	▽▽▽	6
●	Barolo Vigna Rionda '90	▽▽	6
●	Barolo Vigna Rionda '93	▽▽	5
●	Barolo Rocche dei Rivera '93	▽	5
●	Langhe Furesté '96	▽	4

LA MORRA (CN)

F.LLI REVELLO

FRAZ. ANNUNZIATA, 103
12064 LA MORRA (CN)
TEL. 0173/50276

In this winery the Revello brothers' drive towards innovation, backed up by Beppe Caviola, lives side by side with the surrounding environment, i. e. the Annunziata zone with its incredible aptitude for yielding elegant, scented wines. The '95 wines were a real test of ability, since a very promising vintage had been jeopardized by violent hailstorms. The Revellos managed extremely well, presenting very harmonious wines that compensate for lack of concentration with graceful balance. The basic Barolo has a well-defined bouquet which, although not rich, is inviting and even; the aromas follow through perfectly on a palate also enhanced by sweet tannins. The Giachini shows the color of a mature wine; the warm aromas unfold gradually with underlying notes of fruit compote and dried flowers; the palate is broad and even and the finish pleasingly clean. The most exciting of their wines is the extraordinarily rich Barbera Ciabot du Re, overflowing with vitality deriving from the acidity and still slightly dominated by the oak; it has wonderfully exuberant aromas and is a first-rate example of enthrallingly sustained tension on the palate. The dark violet color, dense aromas and vivid, lingering finish merge in a magnificently harmonious whole. An echo of this great wine can be seen in the highly successful Barbera '98, which has not yet acquired complexity but is eminently quaffable.

●	Barbera d'Alba '98	▼▼	3*
●	Barbera d'Alba Ciabot du Re '97	▼▼	5
●	Barolo '95	▼▼	5
●	Barolo Giachini '95	▼▼	6
●	Dolcetto d'Alba '98	▼▼	3*
●	Barolo '93	▽▽▽	6
●	Barbera d'Alba Ciabot du Re '95	▽▽	4
●	Barbera d'Alba Ciabot du Re '96	▽▽	4
●	Barolo Vigna Giachini '94	▽▽	5
●	Barolo '94	▽	5

LA MORRA (CN)

ROCCHE COSTAMAGNA
VIA VITTORIO EMANUELE, 8
12064 LA MORRA (CN)
TEL. 0173/509225

The most important wines from this historic estate, with Barolo at their head, are meant to be enjoyed unhurriedly, after they have aged in the bottle; tasted young they do not always reveal all their many-faceted qualities. But this year Alessandro Locatelli has come up with a Barolo Bricco Francesco '95 which not only promises great future development, but manages to please the most demanding palates right away. Deriving from one of the legendary Annunziata crus, the Rocche, it has a ruby color tending towards garnet and offers an ample, seductive bouquet of spice, tobacco, dried roses and red fruit, while the full-flavored palate ends on an intriguing note of licorice. Taste it now, or, better yet, leave it in the cellar for a few years; you will certainly be rewarded with a wine of greater complexity and balance. The Barolo Rocche from the same vintage does not perform so well; it has good structure but is unlikely to develop as interestingly, as its nose is dumb and not very rich. The Roccardo, a Nebbiolo of more immediate and undemanding appeal, nevertheless shows some personality and a fairly rich, articulated palate. The Dolcetto and the Barbera are, as usual, well made and enjoyable. Meanwhile we are patiently awaiting the release of the new Barbera Rocca delle Rocche.

●	Barolo Rocche dell'Annunziata Bricco Francesco '95	🍷🍷	6
●	Barbera d'Alba Annunziata '97	🍷	4
●	Barolo Rocche dell'Annunziata '95	🍷	6
●	Dolcetto d'Alba '98	🍷	3
●	Langhe Roccardo '98	🍷	4
●	Barolo Rocche dell'Annunziata '93	YY	5
●	Barbera d'Alba Annunziata '96	Y	4
●	Barolo Vigna Francesco '93	Y	5

LA MORRA (CN)

AURELIO SETTIMO
FRAZ. ANNUNZIATA, 30
12064 LA MORRA (CN)
TEL. 0173/50803

The '95 Barolos are not among the estate's best. However, we know that vintages vary, and even in lesser years the Settimos manage to produce clean, distinctive wines that in no way disgrace themselves. An example is the Barolo Rocche '95, which, if not exceptional, is a perfectly sound wine. It is ruby-garnet in hue with a wide orange rim and offers a slightly heady bouquet with hints of strawberry, raspberry, leather and mint; the medium-bodied palate has somewhat austere tannins that lend a dry tone to the finish. The basic Barolo, of an almost transparent ruby hue tending towards brick-red, shows a forward nose with aromas of jam, dried flowers and leather; there is not much concentration on the palate and the finish lacks length. The Barolo Riserva '93 is richer and more expressive, revealing a vivid color and pronounced aromas of berries and licorice mingling with distinct briny notes. The palate has plenty of body with stern but not overpowering tannins and an enjoyable lingering finish. Lastly, the Nebbiolo is ruby verging on garnet in hue and displays a pleasantly rustic, uncomplicated fragrance of fruit, hay and violet; the fairly meaty palate shows charm on the finish.

●	Barolo '95	🍷	5
●	Barolo Ris. '93	🍷	5
●	Barolo Rocche '95	🍷	5
●	Langhe Nebbiolo '97	🍷	4
●	Barolo '93	YY	5
●	Barolo Rocche '89	YY	6
●	Barolo Rocche '93	YY	5
●	Barolo Rocche '90	Y	6
●	Barolo Rocche Ris. '90	Y	6

LA MORRA (CN)

MAURO VEGLIO
LOC. CASCINA NUOVA, 50
12064 LA MORRA (CN)
TEL. 0173/509212

The wines Mauro Veglio has presented this time are not quite up to last year's glories, but it could hardly be otherwise, since the '95 vintage (the Barolos) suffered from a violent hailstorm that saved its worst bursts for Annunziata. The Barbera Cascina Nuova '97, within in an inch of Three Glasses, is very similar to its illustrious predecessor: it has a promising depth of color and prominent fruity aromas in a warm, striking bouquet which is perhaps not yet fully expressed. The palate, too, suggests that there is room for improvement: the oak is pronounced but is counterbalanced by the rich, succulent body which rallies with encouraging vitality. The Barbera '98, which resembles the Cascina Nuova in tone, is, of course, less complex in bouquet but shows the same full body and sinew on the palate. The Barolo Gattera is the most successful of the three Barolos, with its good balance, highly original bouquet and nicely concentrated palate, giving a satisfying sensation of completeness. The Barolo Rocche and the Barolo Arborina reveal a rather monotonous development on the nose, characterized by a distinct note of hay; the palate offers more warmth than real density. Lastly, the lively, satisfying Dolcetto is an impeccable example of its kind.

● Barbera d'Alba '98	TT	3*
● Barbera d'Alba Cascina Nuova '97	TT	5
● Barolo Gattera '95	TT	5
● Dolcetto d'Alba '98	TT	3*
● Barolo Arborina '95	T	5
● Barolo Rocche '95	T	6
● Barbera d'Alba Cascina Nuova '96	YYY	4
● Barbera d'Alba Cascina Nuova '95	YY	4
● Barolo Vigneto Arborina '94	YY	5
● Barolo Vigneto Rocche '93	YY	5
● Barolo Vigneto Rocche '94	YY	5

LA MORRA (CN)

ERALDO VIBERTI
B.TA TETTI, 53
FRAZ. SANTA MARIA
12064 LA MORRA (CN)
TEL. 0173/50308

The Barbera Vigna Clara '97 is a wine with powerful structure and great balance. The favorable vintage and Enzo's rigor in reducing vineyard yields meant that only the best grapes found their way into the cellar. Tasting this Barbera shows that the raw material, far from being wasted, was exploited to the full by unusually skillful vinification. The wine has an intense ruby-garnet color with a very dense rim; the nose offers an excellent ample bouquet, with aromas of berries, cocoa and menthol mingling with toasty notes. On the palate the massive body is immediately evident and the mid palate, although characterized by a slightly acid bite, is ample right through to the lingering, fruity finish. The Barolo '95, of a medium-intense ruby color with a firm orange rim, shows a pleasantly forward bouquet of raspberry and redcurrant jam, custard and leather mingling with fleeting hints of tar and dried flowers. The substantial palate is somewhat austere thanks to a slightly over-assertive acidity, and balsamic and spicy notes characterize the lingering finish. Once again Enzo Araldo has shown he knows how to make fine wines. What's more, since he has not allowed himself to be dazzled by fashion or quick returns, he is one of the few remaining Langhe producers who have not extended their range of wines or annually invented a new cru-of-the-year.

● Barbera d'Alba Vigna Clara '97	TT	4
● Barolo '95	TT	6
● Barolo '93	YYY	6
● Barbera d'Alba Vigna Clara '93	YY	4
● Barbera d'Alba Vigna Clara '95	YY	4
● Barolo '90	YY	6
● Barolo '91	YY	5
● Barolo '94	YY	5

LA MORRA (CN)

GIANNI VOERZIO
S.DA LORETO, 1/BIS
12064 LA MORRA (CN)
TEL. 0173/509194

This year Franca and Gianni Voerzio have presented an exciting range of wines, starting with the Barolo La Serra '95. The color is dense and vivid, heralding an exquisitely elegant nose redolent of ripe fruit and spice nicely counterbalanced by balsamic oak-derived notes. The entry on the palate immediately reveals its rich texture, while the firm, almost austere character is evidence of a powerful structure. The Serrapiù, from nebbiolo and barbera, is very nearly as good: the progression on the palate is ample and invigorating right through to the lingering finish, which is slightly masked by the wood. The delightfully sweet bouquet, on the other hand, offers delicate notes of spice, black currant and blueberry. The Barbera and the Nebbiolo are both named Ciabot della Luna and are both excellent wines. The former has a compact rim on a rich ruby base, followed by a warm, stylish bouquet with hints of blackberry, pepper and tobacco; it is full and vigorous on the smooth palate, and has a nicely lingering finish. The Nebbiolo, along the same lines, reveals green notes on a good firm fruity background on the nose and is broad on the palate, with a note of freshness that makes it particularly easy to drink. Freshness is the keynote of the Roero white, the simple, fruity Arneis Bricco Cappellina; the nose is characterized by hints of white-fleshed fruit and chamomile. The equally successful Freisa Sotto i Bastioni is a Voerzio classic, not a very powerful red but especially pleasant in summer, drunk at cellar temperature.

●	Barbera d'Alba Ciabot della Luna '97	🍷🍷	4
●	Barolo La Serra '95	🍷🍷	6
●	Langhe Nebbiolo Ciabot della Luna '97	🍷🍷	4
●	Langhe Rosso Serrapiù '97	🍷🍷	5
●	Langhe Freisa Sotto i Bastioni '98	🍷	4
○	Roero Arneis Bricco Cappellina '98	🍷	4
●	Barbera d'Alba Ciabot della Luna '96	🍷🍷 (white)	4
●	Barolo La Serra '93	🍷🍷 (white)	6
●	Langhe Rosso Serrapiù '96	🍷🍷 (white)	4
●	Barolo La Serra '94	🍷 (white)	5
●	Langhe Nebbiolo Ciabot della Luna '96	🍷 (white)	4

LA MORRA (CN)

ROBERTO VOERZIO
LOC. CERRETO, 1
12064 LA MORRA (CN)
TEL. 0173/509196

Roberto Voerzio, undoubtedly one of the ablest winegrowers of his generation and a fierce upholder of the importance of terroir, laboring in the vineyard and, in particular, very hard pruning and crop thinning, has scored a success at the first go: the release on the market of the Barbera d'Alba Vigneto Pozzo '96, whose price rivals that of the great wines of Bordeaux, is an event that cannot be ignored. From a small parcel of land, planted to barbera a few years back with rigorous attention to quality (very high plant density, low-vigor rootstock and selection of low-yielding clones), he has produced an outstanding wine unbelievably high in extract. Its black color is quite impenetrable; the intense and elegant nose combines succulent ripe fruit (very ripe cherry and plum) with complex notes of sweet spice and a delightfully refreshing distinct menthol tone. The entry on the palate is almost palpably chewy, and no sense of heaviness mars the lingering finish enhanced by perfect acidity. This year the Brunate is missing from the usual trio of Barolo crus, since the grapes were decimated by hail when at an advanced stage of ripeness: it was therefore not produced. The two survivors are very similar: elegant and complex on the nose (the Cerequio more balsamic, the La Serra spicier), and powerful if a little harsh on the palate. The Vignaserra, a skillful blend of nebbiolo and barbera, slightly underperforms last year's superb version; it certainly does not lack its customary richness, but has not yet achieved perfect balance on either nose or palate. To end the list, the Dolcetto Priavino '98 gives us no cause to regret the excellent '97, and the Chardonnay is bowing out with the '98.

●	Barbera d'Alba Vigneto Pozzo dell'Annunziata Ris. '96	🍷🍷🍷	6
●	Barolo Cerequio '95	🍷🍷	6
●	Barolo La Serra '95	🍷🍷	6
●	Dolcetto d'Alba Priavino '98	🍷🍷	4
○	Langhe Chardonnay Fossati Roscaleto '98	🍷🍷	5
●	Vignaserra '97	🍷🍷	5
●	Barolo Brunate '89	🍷🍷🍷 (white)	6
●	Barolo Brunate '90	🍷🍷🍷 (white)	6
●	Barolo Brunate '93	🍷🍷🍷 (white)	6
●	Barolo Cerequio '88	🍷🍷🍷 (white)	6
●	Barolo Cerequio '90	🍷🍷🍷 (white)	6
●	Barolo Cerequio '91	🍷🍷🍷 (white)	6
●	Vignaserra '96	🍷🍷🍷 (white)	5

LESSONA (VC)

SELLA
VIA IV NOVEMBRE, 110
13060 LESSONA (VC)
TEL. 015/99455

The Sella family winery, whose oenological and administrative departments are entrusted to Giancarlo Scaglione and Pietro Marocchino respectively, has presented a very successful range this year: three typical local wines – two Lessonas and a Bramaterra, have received Two Glasses. The Lessona Il Chioso, the most appealing, shows a fine, intense ruby-garnet color; soft notes of ripe raspberry and red currant mingle with hints of violet and spice in a broad, harmonious bouquet. The palate, after a full-bodied and rich entry, grows more austere as it progresses, revealing a solid phenolic structure that lends severity to the lingering licorice finish. The good basic Lessona shows a wide orange rim on a ruby-garnet base; the aromas, although not particularly intense, show breadth and finesse and nicely blended fruit and spice; the slight headiness is reminiscent of fruit steeped in alcohol and gingers up the spice. The captivating palate offers immediately mouth-filling fruit that lasts right through to the long, corresponding finish characterized by a dry tannic note. The Bramaterra '95, of a dark garnet hue tinged with orange, offers a well-defined, faintly heady bouquet of red and black fruit, dried flowers and leather. The palate displays good concentration and, as it progresses, a powerful tannic structure emerges, pervading the corresponding finish.

●	Bramaterra '95	🍷🍷	4
●	Lessona Il Chioso '95	🍷🍷	4
●	Lessona '95	🍷	4
●	Lessona S. Sebastiano allo Zoppo '93	🍷 (white glass)	4

LOAZZOLO (AT)

BORGO MARAGLIANO
REG. S. SEBASTIANO, 2
14050 LOAZZOLO (AT)
TEL. 0144/87132

The Galliano family has long been established in the isolated hills of Loazzolo; the first purchase of land dates back to 1750, when they bought the house where they live to this day and where the cellar is situated. Carlo and Giuseppe now look after 14 hectares of vineyard divided between two properties, Maragliano and Crevoglio, both near Loazzolo. The Gallianos grow only three varieties, moscato bianco, pinot nero and chardonnay, from which they produce about 70 thousand bottles annually. After selling his moscato grapes for years to Cinzano, Giuseppe Galliano began to vinify his own grapes and to sell the wine in bulk, while waiting for his son Carlo, who got his diploma from the Scuola Enologica of Alba in 1990, to enter the business. In 1991 bottles made their first appearance and from then on have ruled the roost. Their most important wine, not in terms of quantity (average production is barely 2,500 half bottles), but of prestige, is the Loazzolo. The nose offers delicate notes of dried apricot and custard, while the perfect balance of sweetness and acidity on the palate indicates that this is a late-harvest wine rather than an understated version of a Passito (only 10% of the grapes are dried); here Carlo was looking for elegance rather than power. In addition to a pleasantly rich, enjoyable Moscato d'Asti, a delightful non-DOC version is produced, the El Calié, which is sweeter and less alcoholic (only 3%). Of the two Chardonnays we preferred the partially barrique-aged Marajan, richly redolent of honey and acacia blossom. The two sparkling wines are further evidence of an excellent cellar technique: the Brut '95, which is Metodo Classico, and the long-Charmat-method non-vintage Brut.

○	Giuseppe Galliano Brut '95	🍷🍷	4
○	Loazzolo Borgo Maragliano Vendemmia Tardiva '96	🍷🍷	5
○	Piemonte Chardonnay Marajan '97	🍷🍷	4
○	El Calié '98	🍷	3
○	Giuseppe Galliano Chardonnay Brut	🍷	3
○	Moscato d'Asti La Caliera '98	🍷	3
○	Piemonte Chardonnay Crevoglio '98	🍷	3

LOAZZOLO (AT)

FORTETO DELLA LUJA
CASA ROSSO, 4
REG. BRICCO
14050 LOAZZOLO (AT)
TEL. 0141/831596

The Scaglione family estate is brilliantly run by the younger generation: Gianni, with an excellent grounding in agronomy, looks after the vineyards and cellar, while his sister Silvia is responsible for management and marketing. The main parental contribution is the technical expertise of their father Giancarlo, one of the most renowned oenologists in Piedmont. Forteto della Luja consists of about seven and a half hectares under vine divided between Loazzolo and Santo Stefano Belbo. From the vineyards in the area of San Maurizio at Santo Stefano Belbo they produce about 13 thousand bottles of Moscato d'Asti Piasa San Maurizio, outstanding for the fragrance of its varietal aromas. In our opinion the Le Grive '97, an interesting barrique-aged blend of barbera and pinot nero, was better than usual, without soaring to great heights; it has a not particularly dense ruby color, elegant aromas of strawberry and raspberry and fair balance. The wines for which the estate and the area of Loazzolo are deservedly famous are, however, the Passitos (raisin wines), of which only a few thousand bottles are produced. The Brachetto Pian dei Sogni offers powerful aromas rich in scents of dried flowers and candied fruit, followed by a balanced body and lingering finish. The Loazzolo Piasa Rischei '96 is a different story: it is made from moscato grapes, half of which are picked at the beginning of November when noble rot has made its beneficial mark, while the other half are left to dry on bamboo mats for over two months. After fermenting for about two years in new barriques, the resultant nectar releases a myriad of intoxicating scents of dried fruit and spice, and slips caressingly over the palate without a jot of superfluous sweetness.

○ Loazzolo Piasa Rischei '96	**YYY**	6
● Piemonte Brachetto Forteto Pian dei Sogni '97	**YY**	5
● Monferrato Rosso Le Grive '97	**Y**	4
○ Moscato d'Asti Piasa S. Maurizio '98	**Y**	3
○ Loazzolo Piasa Rischei '93	YYY	6
○ Loazzolo Piasa Rischei '94	YYY	6
○ Loazzolo Piasa Rischei '95	YYY	6
● Piemonte Brachetto Forteto Pian dei Sogni '95	YY	5

LU M.TO (AL)

TENUTA S. SEBASTIANO
CASCINA S. SEBASTIANO, 41
15040 LU M.TO (AL)
TEL. 0131/741353

Roberto De Alessi, the owner of this attractive estate, is full of enthusiasm for this land and its wines. His six hectares planted to cortese, grignolino, moscato and, above all, barbera yield about 25 thousand bottles. Roberto, who looks after the cellar himself, had Donato Lanati's assistance for the wines presented this year; next year we shall be tasting the results of Mario Ronco's (the new consultant oenologist) advice. All the wine is made exclusively from estate-grown grapes and is sold without the mediation of middlemen, direct contact with the customer being preferred. We very much liked the excellent Barbera Mepari, dedicated to Roberto's father. It has a very intense ruby hue and an attractive bouquet of cherry and spice, mirrored on the long, soft palate, which reveals a satisfying balance between fruit and wood. The quite intriguing Grignolino displays floral aromas of rose and geranium and fruity notes of sour cherry; the palate reveals softness, very mellow tannins and characteristic spicy notes. The Monferrato Casalese Bianco, from cortese grapes macerated for 12 hours on the skins, shows a fine straw color, intense flowery scents and an enjoyable, balanced palate with an appropriate finish. They also produce a small quantity of a late-harvested Moscato, fermented and matured in barriques, which is not sweet but is worthy of mention.

● Barbera del M.to Mepari '97	**YY**	3*
○ Monferrato Casalese Cortese '98	**Y**	2*
● Piemonte Grignolino '98	**Y**	2*

MANGO (CN)

Cascina Fonda
Loc. Cascina Fonda, 45
12056 Mango (CN)
tel. 0173/677156

The Barbero family's Vendemmia Tardiva is again a wine with great personality. One should not be led astray by the name: the overripening is not excessive and the wine is not still but lightly sparkling; the fact that it is a borderline wine between two different categories means, in this case. that it combines freshness and maturity, richness and a ready drinkability, in a general context of harmony and originality. The '98 version has an attractive straw color; the bouquet offers hints of peach and ripe tropical fruit, tomato flower and candied citrus peel with delicate underlying hints of extreme ripeness. The concentrated texture is immediately enlivened by an exuberant but pleasant effervescence, which lends unexpected freshness to the palate, and the finish is very long and corresponding. The excellent Moscato, of an intense straw color, has a full, straightforward nose with notes of yellow peach, tangerine peel and elderblossom; the marked fizziness of the palate harmonizes with its mouth-filling body and distinct sweet note, while fruity, floral tones emerge on the lingering finish. The Asti has a dry nose blending aromatic character with fermentation-derived nuances, while the palate is captivating in its full-flavored and refreshing drinkability. The Brachetto reveals aromas of rose, peach and lemon in a bouquet of medium finesse, followed by an enjoyable palate. The Barbera Vigna Bruseisa shows a nearly transparent garnet-tinged ruby hue, while sweet hints of fruit and coffee emerge on the nose; the palate is fairly substantial and well balanced. The Dolcetto Brusalino is a properly executed and straightforward wine.

○	Moscato d'Asti '98	TT	3*
○	Moscato d'Asti Vendemmia Tardiva '98	TT	4
○	Asti '98	T	3
●	Barbera d'Alba Vigna Bruseisa '97	T	4
●	Piemonte Brachetto '98	T	3
●	Dolcetto d'Alba Brusalino '98		3
○	Vendemmia Tardiva '97	YY	3

MANGO (CN)

Sergio Degiorgis
Via Circonvallazione, 3
12056 Mango (CN)
tel. 0141/89107

The Bricco Peso, a cru from this small estate in the hills of Mango, is once again an excellent Dolcetto. Like last year's, it has won Two Glasses, but this year they are overflowing. The nose is not particularly complex but is exceptionally broad and gracefully varietal, with intense, fruity notes of sour cherry and red currant to the fore, and hints of almond, spice and licorice lending depth. The palate offers the best that a Dolcetto can give, starting with the sumptuous concentration heralded by the dense ruby-garnet color with a narrow purplish rim. The entry is robust and invigorating; a lively bite of acidity accompanies the progression, while plenty of characterful tannins give it body. The wonderfully long finish echoes the rich fruity notes, enriched by intriguing balsamic nuances. So Sergio and Patrizia were right to attempt an important Dolcetto in this part of the world, which tends to be known for its Moscato rather than for its red wines. The Moscato d'Asti Sorì del Re is, in fact, excellent, offering rich fruity aromas ranging from peach to baked pear; the palate is opulent, full-bodied, lingering and agreeably harmonious. Lastly, the simple basic Dolcetto is a well-made wine.

●	Dolcetto d'Alba Bricco Peso '98	TT	4
○	Moscato d'Asti Sorì del Re '98	TT	3
●	Dolcetto d'Alba '98		3
●	Dolcetto d'Alba Bricco Peso '97	YY	3

MOASCA (AT)

PIETRO BARBERO
CASCINA LA GHERSA
V.LE S. GIUSEPPE, 19
14050 MOASCA (AT)
TEL. 0141/856012

The barrique-aged Barbera La Vignassa, deriving from an old vineyard with very low yields, is Massimo Barbero's top bottle, and the '97 vintage does not fail to win the customary Two Glasses, thanks to the richness of aroma and concentrated extract of this impressive and sumptuous wine. Ruby-garnet in color, it offers an ample and complex bouquet of red and black fruit preserves, tobacco leaf, caramel and toasty notes; the substantial palate is enlivened by a vibrant acidic bite that ensures an excellent progression and refreshes the vigorous, lingering finish. The Bianco Sivoy, of a pale straw color, is a captivating wine; the nose reveals finesse and delicacy, with notes of fruit and white flowers; the palate, while not powerful, is crisp and silky, with a pleasing succulence and a long, corresponding finish. We liked the Gavi Il Poggio, pale straw with a greenish cast; its fresh, fruity aromas include hints of peach, apple, herbs and lemon; the palate is light but satisfying, and the finish, although not very long, leaves its own personal stamp. The Barbera Verlenga, of an almost transparent ruby color, has a nose of moderate finesse with notes of red fruit, good body on the palate, with acidity just perceptible, and a faintly bitterish but very satisfying finish. The more straightforward Barbera Camparò shows grip and an agreeable quaffability. .

●	Barbera d'Asti Sup. La Vignassa '97	TT	5
○	Monferrato Bianco Sivoy '97	TT	3
●	Barbera d'Asti Sup. Bricco Verlenga '97	T	4
●	Barbera d'Asti Sup. Camparò '97	T	3
○	Gavi di Rovereto Vigna Il Poggio '98	T	3
●	Barbera d'Asti Sup. La Vignassa '96	YY	5
●	Barbera d'Asti Sup. Bricco Verlenga '96	Y	4
●	Barbera d'Asti Sup. Camparò '96	Y	3

MOMBELLO M.TO (AL)

FELICE COPPO
CASCINA COSTE, 15
15020 MOMBELLO M.TO (AL)
TEL. 0142/944503

The news at the Coppo estate is that the Bastiàn Cuntrari is changing its old appellation of Barbera del Monferrato to become a "table wine", in order not to be tied to the rules of a particular DOC. However, the love and attention that Felice lavishes on this jewel of his are unchanged. Production is still very limited, but now reaches almost 8,000 bottles; just under one hectare of land came into production in 1998, right next to the old vineyard whose oldest vines date back to 1942. Research indicates that this zone is the warmest in Piedmont, and therefore ideal for barbera. Felice has decided to turn his attention to another variety as well, which, it seems, will be able to make the most of this hilly terrain and the qualities it imparts to wine: merlot. This grape, unlike barbera, is very low in acidity, has less astringent tannins, and yields more complexity of bouquet. It will go into the blend of the Bastiàn Cuntrari from now on, since this tiny new vineyard of little over half a hectare comes into partial production with the '99 vintage. As far as this year is concerned, we tasted an excellent Bastiàn Cuntrari '98, which offers the usual powerful fruit but without sufficient complexity to go with it. Although the wine seems as enjoyable as ever, it is a little on the rustic side, but we're quite willing to bet on its evolution.

●	Bastiàn Cuntrari '98	TT	5
●	Bastiàn Cuntrari Tipe III '95	YY	5
●	Barbera del M.to Bastiàn Cuntrari '97	YY	5
●	Bastiàn Cuntrari '93	YY	5

MONCALVO (AT)

CASCINA ORSOLINA
VIA CAMINATA, 28
14036 MONCALVO (AT)
TEL. 0141/917277

Just beyond the township of Moncalvo is a little valley where, over two centuries ago, near a little Romanesque church, the Orsolina farmhouse was built. Attracted by the peaceful surroundings, the Denegri family bought it in 1988 with the idea of escaping from Turin at weekends and relaxing away from the noise of the city. It would have been a real pity to neglect the vineyards which have always covered these gently rolling hills, and so in 1993 young Michele Denegri decided to redo the cellar and start producing wine again. After a little initial uncertainty, the Cascina Orsolina seemed to find its feet. Today Michele manages the estate from New York, where he has started up a new business in catering, but he frequently returns to Italy to make sure, together with his father, that everything is functioning as it should. As for the day-to-day running of the place and the solving of any pressing problems, Michele can rely on the professional skill and disinterested assistance of Gianni Rossi, who is guided by the oenologist Donato Lanati in the cellar. The leading role in the 15 hectares of vineyard is naturally played by the barbera grape. About 30 thousand bottles are produced of the Barbera Bricco dei Cappuccini, which is barrique-aged for 18 months; the grapes from this cru have been vinified separately since the '94 vintage. The '96 version, less lively on the nose and palate, is outclassed by the ample fruit and succulent softness of the '97. For the Monferrato Rosso Sole as well (50% barbera, 25% merlot and 25% pinot nero), the '97 vintage, with its exuberant, irrepressible fruit (cherry and red currant), overshadows the more timid and restrained '96. The rich, buttery Chardonnay Rosanna and the more quaffable Grignolino San Giacu and Barbera Caminata are also good wines.

●	Barbera d'Asti Sup. Bricco dei Cappuccini '97	🍷🍷	4
●	Monferrato Rosso Sole '97	🍷🍷	4
●	Monferrato Rosso Sole '96	🍷	4
●	Barbera d'Asti Caminata '97	🍷	3
●	Barbera d'Asti Sup. Bricco dei Cappuccini '96	🍷	4
●	Grignolino d'Asti S. Giacu '98	🍷	3
○	Piemonte Chardonnay Rosanna '97	🍷	4

MONCHIERO (CN)

GIUSEPPE MASCARELLO E FIGLIO
VIA BORGONUOVO, 108
12060 MONCHIERO (CN)
TEL. 0173/792126

The '94 vintage was not a fair test of the Mascarello estate's top wine. The Barolo Monprivato, from near Castiglione Falletto, has never had a powerful structure or exuberant character, but the hardships of that harvest punished it severely. Nevertheless, Mauro Mascarello has managed to create an enjoyable red which has now reached its peak. It has a pale garnet hue; the nose reveals notes of leather, steeped flowers and licorice, while the pronounced tannins on the palate are accompanied by substantial alcohol; it is not remarkably long and the finish reveals a slight dryness. The basic Barolo, probably a blend of the Villero and Santo Stefano di Perno crus, is similar; a note of fruit steeped in alcohol with a touch of clove emerges on the rather light nose; the palate is somewhat lean, while the tannins are softer than the Monprivato's and the finish is rather short. The Barbera is a traditional interpretation that emphasizes acidity and ripe aromas; the result is a forceful, rather aggressive red which may develop further, acquiring greater harmony. The rich-hued Dolcetto d'Alba has an unsettled nose and a characterful, persistent palate.

●	Barbera d'Alba Codana '96	🍷	5
●	Barolo '94	🍷	5
●	Barolo Monprivato '94	🍷	6
●	Dolcetto d'Alba '97	🍷	4
●	Barolo Monprivato '85	🍷🍷🍷 (white)	6
●	Barolo Monprivato '89	🍷🍷 (white)	6
●	Barolo Monprivato '90	🍷🍷 (white)	6
●	Barolo Villero '93	🍷🍷 (white)	6
●	Barbera d'Alba Codana '95	🍷 (white)	4
●	Barolo Monprivato '93	🍷 (white)	6
●	Barolo S. Stefano di Perno '93	🍷 (white)	6

MONDOVÍ (CN)

IL COLOMBO - BARONE RICCATI
VIA DEI SENT, 2
12084 MONDOVI (CN)
TEL. 0174/41607 - 0174/43022

Last year, when Adriana and Carlo Riccati won Three Glasses for the first time, numerous readers and even a fair number of tasters were surprised. How could such a young winery, working with a "plebeian" variety in an area better known for its beef and dairy products than for serious wine, show so well? And how could they repeat the triumph this year? There is nothing miraculous about it: the answer can be found in the dedication and self-sacrifice of everyone who works at Il Colombo, seeking to glorify one grape variety, dolcetto. With considerable difficulty, Carlo and Adriana managed to buy a hectare and a half of land above the Vigna Chiesetta. They planted one hectare of this plot, using the replanting rights that came with a poorly positioned vineyard which had been uprooted and whose grapes they had never vinified. With meticulous care and saintly patience they look after the vines, which have already been subjected to hard winter pruning; the crop is further reduced by thinning the excess bunches, leaving a maximum of six or seven per vine. The lower half of the bunches is cut away and foliage is removed so as to prevent damp from getting in. This is how you make a great wine and how Il Colombo, many of whose grapes were sun-wrinkled at harvest time, has succeeded, with its notes of chocolate and plum and its overwhelming softness, in outdoing even the '97 version. The Vigna della Chiesetta won us over with its aromas of black berries, almond and quinine, not to mention its rich palate and agreeably tannic finish.

● Dolcetto delle Langhe Monregalesi Il Colombo '98	🍷🍷🍷	3*
● Dolcetto delle Langhe Monregalesi Vigna della Chiesetta '98	🍷🍷	3*
● Dolcetto delle Langhe Monregalesi Il Colombo '97	🍸🍸🍸	3
● Dolcetto delle Langhe Monregalesi Il Colombo '96	🍸🍸	3

MONFORTE D'ALBA (CN)

GIANFRANCO ALESSANDRIA
LOC. MANZONI, 13
12065 MONFORTE D'ALBA (CN)
TEL. 0173/78576 - 0173/787222

The secret of Gianfranco Alessandria's success is his ability to follow advice without losing sight of his own ideas. His works as closely with the expert oenologist Beppe Caviola as ever, but his wines reveal a stubborn independence that gives you a perfect picture of the ambitions of this generous, dedicated and somewhat reserved winegrower. The Barbera Vittoria '97 is one of the most sensational wines from this memorable vintage: its concentration is not just a simple fact but is transformed into a fascinating, warm sensuality. The very appearance of this red with its impenetrable density is striking; its deep, enticing aromas display an unimaginable variety of nuances arising from the perfect merging of the fruit with the oak; an unexpected mineral nuance ushers in the corresponding palate. The impact in the mouth is an overwhelming explosion of power and the palate develops ceaselessly right up to the wonderfully intense aromas on the finish. His extraordinary ability to interpret different styles is also apparent in the Barolo San Giovanni '95, an excellent example of symmetry and balance: a full ripeness emerges on the nose, while the smoothness of the tannins is one of the most interesting aspects of the palate; the well-articulated, even structure has its counterpart in a medium density and a satisfyingly long, refreshing finish. The Dolcetto and the basic Barbera are two intense wines represented at their best: both have richness of aroma and personality; the first is more incisive and elegant, while the second displays a marked vitality.

● Barbera d'Alba Vittoria '97	🍷🍷🍷	5
● Barbera d'Alba '98	🍷🍷	3*
● Barolo S. Giovanni '95	🍷🍷	6
● Dolcetto d'Alba '98	🍷🍷	3*
● Barolo '95	🍷	5
● Barbera d'Alba Vittoria '96	🍸🍸🍸	4
● Barolo '93	🍸🍸🍸	5
● Barolo '94	🍸🍸	5

MONFORTE D'ALBA (CN)

Bussia Soprana

Loc. Bussia Soprana, 87
12065 Monforte d'Alba (CN)
tel. 039/305182

Of the wines presented by Silvano Casiraghi and Guido Rossi, the one which impressed us most was the Barbera d'Alba Vin del Ross '97, with its richness and ripeness co-existing with a remarkable clean elegance. The wine, an intense ruby-garnet in color with a mature rim, offers aromas of red and black fruit preserves, leather and coffee with an undertone of dried violet; the impact on the palate is rich and the development ample, confident and well-regulated by soft and close-knit tannins, leading into a very long, highly satisfying finish in which the solidity of the tannins and the warm strength of the alcohol mingle with notes of fruit and spice. The Barolo Mosconi, one of the historic crus of Monforte and the latest acquisition of Bussia Soprana, has a garnet-tinged ruby hue of medium intensity; the nose is immediately interesting, releasing aromas of violet, berries, licorice and spice; the palate is broad and substantial, if not outstandingly powerful, with sweet tannins and an excellent finish. The Barolo Bussia, with a wide orange rim on a garnet base, has a slightly piquant nose with notes of red fruit, pepper, coffee and tar; in the mouth, aggressive tannins slightly detract from the harmony, but the intensely fruity finish is a satisfying conclusion.

●	Barbera d'Alba Vin del Ross '97	🍷🍷	5
●	Barolo Mosconi '95	🍷🍷	6
●	Barolo Bussia '95	🍷	6
●	Barbera d'Alba Vin del Ross '96	YY	5
●	Barolo Vigna Colonnello '93	YY	6
●	Barolo Bussia '93	Y	5
●	Barolo Bussia '94	Y	6

MONFORTE D'ALBA (CN)

★ Domenico Clerico

Loc. Manzoni, 67
12065 Monforte d'Alba (CN)
tel. 0173/78171

Backed up by his experience and the relative good luck that spared part of Monforte d'Alba from the scourge of hail, Domenico has not made a wrong move and has presented a superb range of wines which make him one of the most unfailingly reliable producers of the Langhe. It should be mentioned that he has been lucky enough to find an exceptional co-worker, Massimo Conterno, who not only assists him but can, in his absence, be counted on to carry out the day-to-day work in the cellar carefully and thoroughly. Among the newcomers is a Langhe Dolcetto, which places the estate among the top producers of this category. The Visadì offers a nose in which the young, vinous aromas of the grape blend perfectly with the more complex, spicy oak-derived notes; the palate, of a rare softness, is rendered lingering and velvety by the wood. We were also impressed by the new Barbera d'Alba Trevigne '97, with its sweet vanilla notes and its good structure that already makes it delightful to drink. The two Barolos and the Arte are still Domenico's real pride and joy, and in this edition of the Guide the Barolo Pajana '95 bears the palm. It offers intense aromas that already show great complexity, and the oak, although perceptible, is not dominant; the pronounced tannins of the nebbiolo grape blend with the rich, succulent fruit on the full-bodied palate. The Arte is not behind by much; here the hardness and austerity of nebbiolo is counterbalanced by the freshness and fruit of barbera, resulting in an unusually perfect equilibrium. The more austere Barolo Ciabot Mentin Ginestra is among the finest of the appellation from a vintage which has not always fulfilled its early promise.

●	Barolo Pajana '95	🍷🍷🍷	6
●	Barbera d'Alba Trevigne '97	🍷🍷	4
●	Barolo Ciabot Mentin Ginestra '95	🍷🍷	6
●	Langhe Arte '97	🍷🍷	5
●	Langhe Dolcetto Visadì '98	🍷🍷	3*
●	Arte '90	YYY	5
●	Arte '93	YYY	5
●	Barolo Ciabot Mentin Ginestra '85	YYY	6
●	Barolo Ciabot Mentin Ginestra '89	YYY	6
●	Barolo Ciabot Mentin Ginestra '92	YYY	5
●	Barolo Pajana '90	YYY	6
●	Barolo Pajana '91	YYY	6
●	Barolo Pajana '93	YYY	5
●	Langhe Arte '96	YYY	5
●	Barolo Pajana '94	YY	5

★ Giacomo Conterno

Loc. Ornati, 2
12065 Monforte d'Alba (CN)
tel. 0173/78221

Throughout the eventful career of Barolo over the last few years, Giovanni Conterno's winery has represented an important guideline for anyone who values tradition and reliability. The approach to production is probably taking on a more modern emphasis here too, but it is happening so gradually that the change is barely perceptible. The most youthful wines of the range adhere strictly to a distinctly Langhe style of expression, while the interpretation of Barolo is authoritative. But let's consider them one by one. The Freisa, endowed with its usual easy-going appeal, is not up to the '97: it wants a touch more concentration, but has, on the other hand, a ready drinkability which is irresistible. The Barbera, underpinned by its proverbial acidity and showing excellent follow-through on the palate, will probably acquire greater balance and a better-defined bouquet, but its exuberant vitality, which we have found so attractive even in maturer vintages, is all there. The Dolcetto offers impeccably clean aromas in which a marked green note emerges; the impact on the palate, less overwhelming than usual, is followed by a notably well-articulated structure which guarantees balance and length. And so we come to the Barolo '95, which is a lot better than its vintage gave us reason to hope. Intense garnet in color, the Cascina Franca is a complex, intriguing wine whose finest aromas, the result of a blending of the fully mature nebbiolo with the wood of large casks, are apparent only after the most careful attention; the floral tone reappears on the mouth-filling, tannic, harmonious and long palate.

Wine	Glasses	
● Barolo Cascina Francia '95	🍷🍷	6
● Barbera d'Alba '98	🍷🍷	4
● Dolcetto d'Alba '98	🍷	4
● Langhe Freisa '98	🍷	4
● Barolo Cascina Francia '85	YYY	6
● Barolo Cascina Francia '87	YYY	6
● Barolo Cascina Francia '89	YYY	6
● Barolo Cascina Francia '90	YYY	6
● Barolo Monfortino Ris. '74	YYY	6
● Barolo Monfortino Ris. '82	YYY	6
● Barolo Monfortino Ris. '85	YYY	6
● Barolo Monfortino Ris. '87	YYY	6
● Barolo Monfortino Ris. '88	YYY	6
● Barolo Monfortino Ris. '90	YYY	6

MONFORTE D'ALBA (CN)

Paolo Conterno

Via Ginestra, 34
12065 Monforte d'Alba (CN)
tel. 0173/78415

Paolo Conterno, who is helped in the cellar by his son Giorgio, has about seven hectares under vine, of which five are in production, situated in that wonderful corner of the Langhe, Ginestra at Monforte. At least half of the 30 thousand bottles he produces contain Barolo; a small quantity of these are Riserva, which is bottled only in the best years after almost five years' aging in large oak barrels. This year we tasted a splendid Barolo Riserva '93: it has a ruby hue tending towards garnet and its strong point is its breadth of aroma, with notes of vanilla, licorice, clove and minty herbs and undertones of bitter cherry; the palate is warm, noble and long with robust but well-assimilated tannins. The Barolo Ginestra '95 shows greater depth of color; the nose, still youthful and somewhat closed, displays an attractive fresh and fruity, almost vinous tone with hints of licorice; a profusion of tannins on the finish is accompanied by succulence and some warmth. The dark purple Dolcetto '98 offers clean, vinous aromas with hints of cherry jam; the hardness of the palate is due to abundant tannins and acidity. The Barbera '97, aged for one year in 35-hectoliter oak barrels, has a garnet-tinged ruby hue; the rather dumb nose offers notes of leather and oak, while the prominent acidity on the palate overpowers the sweet alcohol, resulting in a still somewhat rough-edged wine.

Wine	Glasses	
● Barolo Ginestra '95	🍷🍷	6
● Barolo Ris. Ginestra '93	🍷🍷	6
● Barbera d'Alba Ginestra '97	🍷	4
● Dolcetto d'Alba Ginestra '98	🍷	3
● Barolo Ginestra '94	YY	5
● Barbera d'Alba Ginestra '96	Y	4

★ PODERI ALDO CONTERNO

Loc. Bussia, 48
12065 Monforte d'Alba (CN)
tel. 0173/78150

In the summer of '95 the釀Conternos were getting ready to accommodate their great nebbiolo grapes in their completely re-equipped vinification cellar, when a succession of hailstorms decimated their best vineyards, drastically reducing the possibility of creating the wines they had hoped for. The Barolo della Vigna Colonnello was simply not produced, and it was unreasonable to expect anything out of the ordinary from the Cicala and the Bussia Soprana, but the skill of Aldo and Stefano, helped by Franco and Giacomo, achieved two notable reds which give an idea of the expected quality even if they do not fully represent it. We liked the Cicala for its straightforward aromas and full-bodied flavor; it does not show the breadth of a great wine, but is vigorous and lingering. The Bussia Soprana, more subdued in tone, is characterized by a scent of new hay, while the palate reveals pronounced tannins and a delicate, lingering finish. Three excellent wines come from the '97 vintage. The elegant and seductive Favot, from 100% nebbiolo aged in new barriques, unfolds gradually; it represents the less austere side of this Langhe grape, but retains its striking complexity. The Barbera Conca Tre Pile reveals its maturity in its garnet hue; the fragrance offers hints of jam and spice, while the palate progresses smoothly, with well-restrained acidity, right through to the enjoyable finish. The Chardonnay Bussiador has its customary powerful structure; the nose is still dominated by oak, but notes of white-fleshed fruit are beginning to emerge; the entry on the palate is remarkably dense and a harmonious warmth spreads smoothly, underpinned by the crescendo of the finish. The white Printanié is reliable and the Dolcetto has been properly made.

●	Barbera d'Alba '97	🍷🍷	4
●	Barolo Cicala '95	🍷🍷	6
○	Langhe Chardonnay Bussiador '97	🍷🍷	5
●	Langhe Nebbiolo Favot '97	🍷🍷	6
●	Barolo Bussia Soprana '95	🍷	6
●	Dolcetto d'Alba '98	🍷	3
○	Langhe Bianco Printanié '98	🍷	4
●	Barolo Gran Bussia Ris. '88	YYY	6
●	Barolo Gran Bussia Ris. '89	YYY	6
●	Barolo Gran Bussia Ris. '90	YYY	6
●	Barolo Vigna Colonnello '88	YYY	6
●	Barolo Vigna Colonnello '89	YYY	6
●	Barolo Vigna Colonnello '90	YYY	6
●	Barolo Cicala '93	YY	6
●	Barolo Romirasco '93	YY	6

MONFORTE D'ALBA (CN)

CONTERNO FANTINO

Via Ginestra, 1
Loc. Bricco Bastia
12065 Monforte d'Alba (CN)
tel. 0173/78204

The outstanding excellence of this estate is apparent not only in the undeniable quality of the raw material but above all in the impeccable interpretation of all the wines. This year, favored by a propitious harvest as well, the Dolcetto and the Barbera were splendid too; and if the Barolo '95 did not scale the highest peak, it was left to another wine to represent the top of the line: a world-beating version of the Monprà. A blend of barbera and nebbiolo with 10% cabernet sauvignon, the Monprà embodies the best of the wonderful '97 vintage; its deep color is a reminder of the limited yields in the vineyard, while the richness of well-defined and elegant aromas tell of a perfect microclimate; all the density and intense warmth on the palate have perfectly assimilated the oak, which plays an active role in a satisfying and dynamic overall context. The two Barolos are twinned in quality if not in nature. The Sorì Ginestra is at an interesting stage of its evolution: its aromas of fruit steeped in alcohol blend with the wood-derived vanilla; the structure does not display great power, but is nicely balanced. The Vigna del Gris, whose greater vitality is evident in the color, offers aromas of blackberry and herbs; the palate is mouth-filling and quite long. The Chardonnay is undergoing further maturation, so was unavailable, while the Barbera has now attained considerable complexity, supported by a deep and articulated palate. The Dolcetto too, the result of a successful coordination of hard work in the vineyard and great skill in the cellar, is very good.

●	Langhe Rosso Monprà '97	🍷🍷🍷	5
●	Barbera d'Alba Vignota '98	🍷🍷	4
●	Barolo Sorì Ginestra '95	🍷🍷	6
●	Barolo Vigna del Gris '95	🍷🍷	6
●	Dolcetto d'Alba Bricco Bastia '98	🍷🍷	3*
●	Barolo Sorì Ginestra '86	YYY	6
●	Barolo Sorì Ginestra '90	YYY	6
●	Barolo Sorì Ginestra '91	YYY	6
●	Langhe Rosso Monprà '95	YYY	5
●	Monprà '94	YYY	6
●	Barolo Sorì Ginestra '94	YY	6
●	Barolo Vigna del Gris '93	YY	6

MONFORTE D'ALBA (CN)

Alessandro e Gian Natale Fantino
Via G. Silvano, 18
12065 Monforte d'Alba (CN)
tel. 0173/78253

The Fantino brothers, Alessandro and Gian Natale, are passionately committed to their small estate in Dardi. From their seven hectares under vine they produce about 20 thousand bottles of typical Langhe wines: Barbera, Dolcetto and Barolo. And it is in the vineyard, tended like a garden, with low yields per hectare and absolutely no use whatever of harmful chemicals, that the Fantinos lay the foundations for the creation of first-class wines. These wines are made in a magnificent cellar, which has been reconstructed in an old building in the historic center of the village and fitted out with everything necessary, without resorting to the most elaborate modern equipment. The Barolo Vigna dei Dardi '95, a wine which combines tradition and innovation to perfection, displays a ruby-garnet color with a faintly orange rim; the complex nose is slightly heady, with hints of red fruit, dried violet, leather and pepper; the palate has good concentration, while the progression is not powerful but is soft and ample; the lingering, corresponding finish shows admirably smooth tannins and warm alcohol. The new version of the Nebbiolo Passito, the only one of its kind in the Langhe, is excellent too; while the nose is still a little dumb, in search of proper balance, the full, austere palate expresses all the potential of the nebbiolo grape. The Barbera Vigna dei Dardi '97, of a medium-intense ruby hue with a slightly faded rim, has a ripe bouquet that shows finesse; the satisfying palate offers an enjoyable bite of acidity and a lingering, fruity finish. The almost transparent ruby-colored Dolcetto '98 has some attractive fruit on the nose, which perhaps lacks intensity; the palate is light and well-balanced and the finish, if not overlong, is well ordered and corresponding.

● Barolo Vigna dei Dardi '95	▼▼	6
● Nebbiolo Passito Vigna dei Dardi '96	▼▼	6
● Barbera d'Alba Vigna dei Dardi '97	▼	3
● Dolcetto d'Alba '98		3
● Barolo Vigna dei Dardi '93	▽▽	5
● Nebbiolo Passito Vigna dei Dardi '94	▽▽	5
● Barbera d'Alba Vigna dei Dardi '96	▽	3
● Barolo Vigna dei Dardi '94	▽	5
● Nebbiolo Passito Vigna dei Dardi '93	▽	4

MONFORTE D'ALBA (CN)

Attilio Ghisolfi
Reg. Bussia, 27
Cascina Visette
12065 Monforte d'Alba (CN)
tel. 0173/78345

Gian Marco, with the help of his father Attilio and the advice of his friend Beppe Caviola, looks after the five hectares of vineyard that border the Bussia zone and are planted to nebbiolo, barbera, dolcetto and freisa. These yield the classic Langhe wines and also the Carlìn, a blend of nebbiolo and freisa. This year's wines were among the best in the area, revealing powerful structure and good balance. The Dolcetto '98 has a deep ruby color shot through with purple; the nose, still a little closed, gradually releases notes of red fruit, while the mellow, tannic palate is underpinned by appropriate acidity. The impressively powerful alcohol and solid body of the Barbera Vigna Lisi make it already intriguing, even if the nose is still immature; the wood is noticeable but not over-pronounced. The Carlìn offers fascinating aromas that include the characteristic fruit of the freisa grape; the young tannins are still in evidence on the lingering palate. To end the list, the Barolo Bricco Visette, 80% of which is aged in large barrels and 20% in barriques, is a striking example of elegance and harmony: the structure is more than satisfying, despite the awkward '95 vintage, and the nose offers intense, inviting notes of rose, red berries and vanilla, all perfectly mirrored on the soft, well-balanced palate with no hint of harshness.

● Barbera d'Alba Vigna Lisi '97	▼▼	4
● Barolo Bricco Visette '95	▼▼	5
● Langhe Rosso Carlìn '97	▼▼	4
● Dolcetto d'Alba '98	▼	3*
● Barbera d'Alba Vigna Lisi '96	▽▽	4
● Barolo Bricco Visette '93	▽▽	5
● Langhe Rosso Carlìn '96	▽▽	4
● Barolo Bricco Visette '94	▽	5

MONFORTE D'ALBA (CN)

ELIO GRASSO
LOC. GINESTRA, 40
12065 MONFORTE D'ALBA (CN)
TEL. 0173/78491

Marina and Elio Grasso can relax with regard to the future of their winery, since their son Gianluca, aged 24, now works full-time on the estate. The cellar, which has recently been restructured and is still not quite finished, is among the most interesting in the area from the point of view of efficiency and position, and the vineyards cover almost 14 hectares. Production at the moment is a little over 30 thousand bottles. In 1995 Elio made three Barolos: the Riserva Runcot, which will be released next year, the Ginestra Casa Maté and the Gavarini Vigna Chiniera, each of which won Two Glasses. The Casa Maté, deriving from predominantly clayey soil, displays aromas of black berries, chocolate and eucalyptus, followed by a rich, powerful palate. The soil from which the Vigna Chiniera springs is sandy, with some limestone and tufa, and the wine shows an attractive color and aromas of cherry and sweet spice; the palate is elegant, refined and dense-textured. The appealing Barbera Vigna Martina '96 reveals toasty hints and ripe fruit on the nose; characteristic acidity and marked vigor make the palate a little hard still, but the excellent structure conferred by a superb vintage will allow it time to smooth its rough edges. The Dolcetto '98 has an appealing palate, with notes of red fruit, rose and almond. Lastly, the Chardonnay '97, although it spends from six to eight months in barriques, is rather simple and does not seem to have gained much from the wood.

●	Barbera d'Alba Vigna Martina '96	▼▼	4
●	Barolo Gavarini Vigna Chiniera '95	▼▼	6
●	Barolo Ginestra Vigna Casa Maté '95	▼▼	6
●	Dolcetto d'Alba Gavarini Vigna dei Grassi '98	▼	3
○	Langhe Chardonnay Educato '97	▼	4
●	Barolo Gavarini Vigna Chiniera '89	▽▽▽	6
●	Barolo Ginestra Vigna Casa Maté '90	▽▽▽	6
●	Barolo Ginestra Vigna Casa Maté '93	▽▽▽	5
●	Barolo Gavarini Vigna Chiniera '93	▽▽	5
●	Barbera d'Alba Vigna Martina '95	▽	4

MONFORTE D'ALBA (CN)

GIOVANNI MANZONE
VIA CASTELLETTO, 9
12065 MONFORTE D'ALBA (CN)
TEL. 0173/78114

Giovanni Manzone produces an interesting range of wines not only from the point of view of quality but also because of its originality: he is the only winegrower to vinify the white variety of the rossese grape and one of the few producing a blend made up of barbera, nebbiolo and dolcetto. However, it is Barolo, of which there are several different versions, which plays the leading role. The Gramolere '95 wins Two Glasses thanks to the exuberance of its fruity, spicy aromas and the excellently balanced palate. The Bricat selection is even better, deriving greater complexity and structure from higher-lying vineyards. Of a deep, orange-tinged ruby color, it reveals an austere and stilll somewhat reserved nose; the palate unfolds gradually and suggests that the wine will age well. The Riserva '93, which almost got Two Glasses, is slightly forward in tone, although it confirms Giovanni's skill in vinification. The excellent Dolcetto, with an intense ruby hue and complex, lingering aromas, is a wine for keeping. The Rosserto, from the '96 vintage, is made from white rossese: Giovanni produces an unusual and fascinating wine which could easily be taken for a red. Complex on nose and palate, it displays floral and citrus notes supported by a more than satisfying structure, and is quite surprising in the unorthodox choice of dishes it gracefully accompanies. The Tris, from equal parts of barbera, nebbiolo and dolcetto, has made progress since last year's version, now successfully blending the varietal characteristics of its three grapes. We were rather disappointed by the Barbera '95, which seems too forward even in color and is dominated by acidity on the palate.

●	Barolo Gramolere '95	▼▼	5
●	Barolo Gramolere Bricat '95	▼▼	5
●	Langhe Rosso Tris '96	▼▼	4
○	Rosserto	▼▼	4
●	Barbera d'Alba La Serra '95	▼	4
●	Barolo Gramolere Ris. '93	▼	6
●	Dolcetto d'Alba '98	▼	3*
●	Barolo Gramolere '93	▽▽	5
●	Barolo Gramolere Bricat '94	▽▽	5
●	Barolo Gramolere Ris. '90	▽▽	6
●	Barolo Gramolere '94	▽	5

MONFORTE D'ALBA (CN)

Monti

Loc. S. Sebastiano, 39
Fraz. Càmia
12065 Monforte d'Alba (CN)
tel. 0173/78391

Pier Paolo Monti, a young (just 33) building contractor, is passionate about wine and, having bought a farm in 1996, he was able to set up a winery from scratch. This brief introduction helps to explain why this is one of the new jewels of Piedmontese wine-making. Although the cellar has so far produced and marketed only 2,500 bottles of Barbera '97 (all sold, by the way), everything has been set in motion for an annual output in the near future of 25 thousand bottles, subdivided into four different wines. As of the '99 harvest, the pre-existing barbera vineyard at San Martino is joined in production by new vines, all planted in '97 and covering altogether less than one hectare: one plot is planted to cabernet sauvignon in San Martino, one to merlot in the Val di Sacco zone, two to chardonnay in the Val di Sacco and Camie zones and one to Rhine riesling in Camie. In addition, starting in '99, two small vineyards of nebbiolo and barbera, planted respectively in 1981 and 1960 and located in Bussia, have come under estate management. The cellar is equipped to meet all the winery's needs, and includes horizontal and vertical fermentation vessels, custom-made stainless steel vats for aging and a fully air-conditioned barrel cellar. The Barbera will shortly be flanked by a white from chardonnay and riesling, a red from merlot and cabernet with small amounts of nebbiolo, and a Barolo. For the time being we must be content with the Barbera, whose concentration, harmony and personality (fruity and complex) place it very close to the best from this vintage.

●	Barbera d'Alba '97	ΨΨ	4

MONFORTE D'ALBA (CN)

Armando Parusso

Loc. Bussia, 55
12065 Monforte d'Alba (CN)
tel. 0173/78257

Marco and Tiziana Parusso have finally managed to map out the future of their estate by means of a compromise between tradition and innovation. For certain wines the maceration period has been reduced in order to increase the fruit and softness, while others, such as Dolcetto, are aged in barriques, used ones if possible, to enhance their fragrance. Let's consider the wines. We awarded Two Glasses to the Bianco Bricco Rovella, made from sauvignon and characterized by notes of tropical fruit and sweet spice; although underpinned by powerful alcohol it does not lack freshness, which presages very well. The Rosso Bricco Rovella (nebbiolo, barbera and cabernet sauvignon) reveals fruity aromas of cherry and black currant, while the substantial palate has sweet, succulent tannins; this is a more elegant interpretation than last year's explosive and impressive version. From the Bussia vineyards we have the Barolo Vigna Rocche and the Barolo Vigna Munie; the first, from marly soil, is a subtle, silky, soft and elegant wine with a lingering finish; the second, decidedly more robust and forceful, with rougher tannins and notes of chocolate, comes from clayey soil mixed with tufa. This year the Mariondino and the Piccole Vigne are a little behind the others; they are pleasantly spicy but not as rich. The Dolcetto '98, a fresh, vinous wine reminiscent of raspberry candy, and the Barbera '98, warm and mature with hints of blackberry jam, are both impeccably made.

●	Barolo Bussia Vigna Munie '95	ΨΨ	6
●	Barolo Bussia Vigna Rocche '95	ΨΨ	6
○	Langhe Bianco Bricco Rovella '98	ΨΨ	5
●	Langhe Rosso Bricco Rovella '97	ΨΨ	5
●	Barbera d'Alba Ornati '98	Ψ	4
●	Barolo Mariondino '95	Ψ	6
●	Barolo Piccole Vigne '95	Ψ	5
●	Dolcetto d'Alba Piani Noci '98	Ψ	3
●	Langhe Rosso Bricco Rovella '96	ΥΥΥ	5
●	Barolo Bussia Vigna Munie '93	ΥΥ	5
●	Barolo Bussia Vigna Rocche '93	ΥΥ	5
●	Barolo Bussia Vigna Rocche '94	ΥΥ	5
●	Barolo Mariondino '90	ΥΥ	6
○	Langhe Bianco Bricco Rovella '97	Υ	4

MONFORTE D'ALBA (CN)

Podere Rocche dei Manzoni

Loc. Manzoni Soprani, 3
12065 Monforte d'Alba (CN)
tel. 0173/78421

The energy and enthusiasm of Valentino Migliorini are clearly evident from the most recent enterprises at the winery. The modernization of the cellars is now completed, and they are functional as well as very impressive to look at; the estate has been extended by the acquisition of the Pianpolvere Soprano vineyard, and, finally, all the wines presented this year are super. We applaud the decision to delay the release of three such important wines as the Quatr Nas (Three Glasses last year), the Chardonnay L'Angelica and the Pinot Nero, which are held to be in need of further maturation. But now for the wines that were presented. The two bubblies are, as usual, excellent, the Brut Zero being more powerful and immediate and the Riserva Elena more delicate and elegant. Of the three Barolos, the Big, which offers an attractive blending of fruit and wood, is for the moment the best balanced. The S. Stefano gives a glimpse of great potential and unfolds slowly in the glass with complex and intriguing aromas. The Barolo Vigna d'la Roul reveals enjoyable toasty and spicy notes. All in all, these are three outstanding interpretations of Barolo which demonstrate Valentino's skill in vineyard management and vinification. The Bricco Manzoni, leader of all the nebbiola-barbera blends of the Langhe, combines an impressive structure underpinned by smooth tannins with ample, lingering aromas of red fruit and barrique-derived notes of vanilla. Both Barberas are successful, but we have a slight preference for the Sorito Mosconi, elegant on the nose and concentrated on the palate. The La Cresta is still dominated by toasty, smoky notes that partially mask the varietal aromas of the grape.

●	Barbera d'Alba Sorito Mosconi '97	🍷🍷	5
●	Barbera d'Alba Vigna La Cresta '97	🍷🍷	5
●	Barolo Vigna Big '95	🍷🍷	6
●	Barolo Vigna Cappella di S. Stefano '95	🍷🍷	6
●	Barolo Vigna d'la Roul '95	🍷🍷	6
●	Bricco Manzoni '96	🍷🍷	5
○	Valentino Brut Zero Ris. '95	🍷🍷	5
○	Valentino Ris. Elena '93	🍷🍷	5
●	Barolo Vigna Big Ris. '89	YYY	6
●	Barolo Vigna Big Ris. '90	YYY	6
●	Barolo Vigna d'la Roul Ris. '90	YYY	6
●	Langhe Rosso Quatr Nas '96	YYY	6
○	Valentino Brut Zero Ris. '93	YYY	5

MONFORTE D'ALBA (CN)

Ferdinando Principiano

Via Alba, 19
12065 Monforte d'Alba (CN)
tel. 0173/787158

Ferdinando Principiano, held to be one of the emerging Barolo talents in the Langhe, has had as his tutors some of the most exacting winegrowers of the area, the makers of recent local history. From them he learned that awkward harvests can be useful lessons and that one must rise above the bad hand dealt by the weather and turn every possibility to account in one's interpretation of the vintage. The successful Barolo '94, which is developing in the bottle, is echoed by the '95, which on the face of it appeared an easier wine to handle, but which, according to Principiano, posed a series of unexpected problems. He was wise enough not to push extraction to extremes, and not to attempt at all costs to achieve the power of the '93 version, and the result is a red of remarkable finesse. The color is intense and, above all, lively, due largely to the use of barriques; the oak merges nicely with the fruit on the rich nose, with notes of violet and herbs, and the complex whole becomes increasingly deep and fascinating. The palate is classic: entry, mid palate and finish are all coordinated by the structure of the tannins; the dense body and warm alcohol provide a wonderfully mouth-filling sensation. The profound tannic force, typical of the wines from the Boscareto cru, could not have been handled better and perfect harmony has been achieved. The Barbera La Romualda is of an amazing color and reveals immediacy of fragrance on both nose and palate. The fruit is a little too opulent for elegance, but this is one of their best versions yet.

●	Barbera d'Alba La Romualda '96	🍷🍷	5
●	Barolo Boscareto '95	🍷🍷	5
●	Barolo Boscareto '93	YYY	6
●	Barbera d'Alba Pian Romualdo '93	YY	5
●	Barbera d'Alba Pian Romualdo '94	YY	5
●	Barbera d'Alba Pian Romualdo '95	YY	5
●	Barolo Boscareto '94	YY	6
●	Dolcetto d'Alba Sant'Anna '97	Y	3

MONFORTE D'ALBA (CN)

Flavio Roddolo
Loc. Sant'Anna, 5
Bricco Appiani
12065 Monforte d'Alba (CN)
tel. 0173/78535

Flavio Roddolo has come up with some truly spectacular wines over the years, such as the legendary Dolcetto '90. The '98 version looks like rivaling it, despite its youth and humble origins in what violent hail halfway through June turned into a lean year. However, it is precisely this promising richness of structure that has prompted Flavio Roddolo to delay bottling, so we shall be reviewing it in next year's Guide. The Bricco Appiani '96, of which 500 bottles were made in its debut year, is a superb red from 100% cabernet sauvignon. Flavio gets quite carried away when he vinifies this strange small grape with its thick, dark skin. Of a dense ruby color in the glass, it releases varietal aromas of small red berries and undergrowth that made us think of France; the entry on the palate is soft and velvety, with smooth tannins, and the finish offers the harder sensations typical of this area. The Nebbiolo d'Alba, spicy and powerful on the palate and undoubtedly one of the best of the vintage, and the dark-hued Barbera d'Alba, with notes of cherries steeped in alcohol and a warm finish, are both excellent, as is their wont. The Barolo '95, of which only 1,200 bottles were produced because of the hail, is closed and austere, with notes of red fruit and dry herbs: the rough, hard palate cannot fail to improve with proper bottle aging.

● Bricco Appiani '96	**YY**	6
● Nebbiolo d'Alba '97	**YY**	4
● Barbera d'Alba '97	**YY**	4
● Barolo '95	**Y**	5
● Barbera d'Alba '96	YY	3
● Barolo '93	YY	5
● Nebbiolo d'Alba '96	YY	4
● Barolo '94	Y	5

MONFORTE D'ALBA (CN)

F.lli Seghesio
Fraz. Castelletto, 20
12065 Monforte d'Alba (CN)
tel. 0173/78108

Aldo and Riccardo Seghesio have succeeded in drawing out all that the various vintages had to offer, in the wines they've presented this year. Credit is due to the superb position of their vineyards and to their confident skill in the cellar: this is particularly evident in their expert use of wood, which always blends well with the wine and never masks it. They are back in the realm of Three Glasses with their extraordinary Barbera Vigneto della Chiesa '97; of a dark, almost impenetrable color, it opens gradually in the glass, releasing sensational fruity and balsamic aromas; the palate develops with elegance, revealing all its power and harmony; the masterly handling of new wood, in which the wine spent 18 months, is evident. The Barolo La Villa '95, from a vintage which at the time was somewhat overrated, has its place among the limited number of really good ones. The color is ruby verging on garnet; the nose displays complex aromas including spicy and toasty notes, red fruit and faded rose; the palate, soft and mouth-filling, is underpinned by crisp acidity. The Dolcetto '98 offers finesse and immediate appeal rather than power; raspberry and attendant berries emerge on the nose, and tannins are well to the fore but not aggressive in the mouth; this wine can be enjoyed right away, but it should be even better with time. The intriguing Bouquet '97 (merlot, cabernet sauvignon and nebbiolo) has also benefited from the excellent vintage, thus revealing yet again the Seghesios' wine-making expertise.

● Barbera d'Alba Vigneto della Chiesa '97	**YYY**	4
● Barolo Vigneto La Villa '95	**YY**	6
● Bouquet '97	**YY**	5
● Dolcetto d'Alba Vigneto della Chiesa '98	**YY**	3*
● Barolo Vigneto La Villa '91	YYY	5
● Barbera d'Alba Vigneto della Chiesa '96	YY	4
● Barolo Vigneto La Villa '90	YY	6
● Barolo Vigneto La Villa '93	YY	5
● Barolo Vigneto La Villa '94	YY	5
● Bouquet '96	YY	5

MONLEALE (AL)

Vigneti Massa

P.zza G. Capsoni, 10
15059 Monleale (AL)
tel. 0131/80302

Walter Massa has always been a firm believer in the winegrowing potential of the Tortona district. This conviction of his about a territory which until a few years ago marketed good grapes rather than wine may have made some people take him for a madman, but he took no notice, simply insisting that Tortona's limits were not in its land but in its inhabitants. The zone is at last showing its potential, and no longer through Massa's wines alone: today a large group of young and competent winegrowers have their sights firmly set on quality, with the two flagships, Barbera and Timorasso, in the forefront. Of the Barberas presented we were particularly impressed by the Bigolla. A barriqued wine, it shows an impenetrable ruby-purple color and dense, complex aromas followed by a palate of tremendous breadth and meatiness. The Barbera Monleale, traditional in style, and the Sentieri, with its explosive fruit, are both very good. The Cerreta (the new name for the Vecchia Cerreta), a blend of 50% barbera, 20% nebbiolo and 10% each of cabernet, croatina and freisa, is excellent, as usual: it is complex, elegant and rounded, with good structure and aromas of cherry and raspberry. The Croatina Pertichetta, the Freisa Pietra del Gallo and the Cortese Dueterre are all fine examples of their categories. The Costa del Vento is made exclusively from timorasso, a white grape native to this area yielding wines that benefit from some aging. The nose reveals aromas of peach, apricot and tropical fruit with faint mineral notes. The palate is long, very powerful and enjoyable, although the marked rotundity and fleshiness characteristic of this vintage deprive it for the moment of the finesse shown by previous versions.

●	Colli Tortonesi Bigolla '97	🍷🍷	5
●	Colli Tortonesi Cerreta '97	🍷🍷	5
●	Colli Tortonesi Monleale '97	🍷🍷	4
●	Piemonte Barbera Sentieri '98	🍷🍷	3
○	Colli Tortonesi Timorasso Costa del Vento '97	🍷	4
●	Colli Tortonesi Croatina Pertichetta '97	🍷	4
●	Colli Tortonesi Freisa Pietra del Gallo '98	🍷	3
○	Piemonte Cortese Dueterre '98	🍷	3
●	Piemonte Barbera Campolungo Vivace '98		3
○	Piemonte Cortese Casareggio '98		3
●	Bigolla '96	🍸🍸	5

MONTÀ D'ALBA (CN)

Giovanni Almondo

Via S. Rocco, 26
12052 Montà d'Alba (CN)
tel. 0173/975256

Domenico Almondo, the mayor of Montà d'Alba, has presented a series of very attractive wines. The debutant Barbera d'Alba Valbianchera has won Two Glasses straight off. It has a lovely ruby-garnet color with a firm rim; the broad, inviting nose offers notes of ripe cherry, coffee, tobacco, menthol and cocoa; the palate is concentrated and the impact vigorous and refreshing, and noble tannins emerge on the lingering finish. The yet better Roero Bric Valdiana '97 displays an intense ruby hue verging on garnet with a faint orange tinge on the rim; the nose offers aromas of red fruit and mint, with notes of chocolate and custard. The remarkably balanced palate is underpinned by the phenolic structure, which in its turn is offset by the softness of the body; harmony characterizes the long, vigorous finish as well. The Arneis Bricco delle Ciliegie, of a clear straw color, offers hints of apple, banana and vanilla; the silky palate is enlivened by a delightful succulence leading into a lingering finish that mirrors the bouquet. To end the list, the Arneis Vigne Sparse shows a deep straw color and a faintly forward nose offering notes of ripe fruit, hay and wildflowers; the palate is fairly firm and restrained, and the graceful, easy finish makes this wine a particularly good match for light, vegetable-based starters and delicate-flavored fish.

●	Barbera d'Alba Valbianchera '97	🍷🍷	4
○	Roero Arneis Bricco delle Ciliegie '98	🍷🍷	4
●	Roero Bric Valdiana '97	🍷🍷	4
○	Roero Arneis Vigne Sparse '98	🍷	3
●	Roero Bric Valdiana '96	🍸🍸	4

MONTEGROSSO D'ASTI (AT)

TENUTA LA MERIDIANA
FRAZ. TANA, 5
14048 MONTEGROSSO D'ASTI (AT)
TEL. 0141/956172 - 0141/956250

Giampiero Bianco has presented a new wine: the Rivaia, a barrique-aged blend of barbera and nebbiolo with a small amount of cabernet franc. It is ruby in hue with garnet highlights; the nose is fairly forward and heady, offering notes of hay, fruit steeped in alcohol and spice with balsamic nuances; the palate is ample and well balanced with robust tannins and a nicely lingering finish. The Barbera Bricco Sereno, from an old vineyard, is ruby tending towards garnet in color with a slightly faded rim; the nose reveals notes of cherry, mint and spice, while the palate has plenty of body with lively acidity and a long finish with a lingering cocoa tone. The Monferrato Bianco Vigneti Delizia e Collina, from chardonnay, favorita and cortese, has a very light straw color and mainly fermentation-derived aromas with hints of chamomile and quince; the palate is fairly firm and restrained and the moderately fresh finish does not disappoint. The Grignolino Vigna Maestra shows a vivid cherry color and good varietal character on the nose (white pepper, peanut and dried herbs); the palate is dry and straightforward with a crisp tone and a corresponding finish. Two indubitably well executed wines end the list: the undemanding Barbera d'Asti le Gagie and the sweet, lively red, Vigneti del Malaga.

●	Barbera d'Asti Sup. Bricco Sereno '96	▼	4
●	Grignolino d'Asti Vigna Maestra '98	▼	3
○	Monferrato Bianco Vigneti Delizia e Collina '98	▼	3
●	Monferrato Rosso Rivaia '96	▼	5
●	Barbera d'Asti Le Gagie '97		3
●	Vigneti del Malaga '98		3
●	Barbera d'Asti Sup. Bricco Sereno '95	▽	4

MONTELUPO ALBESE (CN)

CA' VIOLA
VIA LANGA, 17
12050 MONTELUPO ALBESE (CN)
TEL. 0173/617570

In the hands of Beppe Caviola, Dolcetto reveals its true calling, acquiring a personality which places it firmly among the classic Langhe wines. His Barturot has the virtue of combining stunning concentration with an irresistibly enjoyable charm; its capacity to develop does not hinder its ready drinkability, since the incisive tannins of its native soil blend with an enticing, modern density of flavor. The varietal characteristics of this grape, never very ample, reveal an unexpected richness; the very intense color heralds a long, vivid structure. This '98 is a really great Dolcetto, perhaps one of the best ever made, and it once again wins Three Glasses hands down. The Bric du Luv, prototype of a great Barbera, is opulent and full of vitality: its dense texture is not simple concentration but a profusion of extract and aromas regulated by emphatic, well-integrated wood. The color is impenetrable and the ripe expressiveness of the grape emerges on the nose, whose seductive development is followed by a rich, silky, even palate. The basic version of the Dolcetto is immediate and vinous on the nose; the palate not only has lots of body, but is fresh and joyous in tone. By dint of making his Rangone, Caviola is beginning to get the measure of his pinot nero; this increasingly elegant wine is shedding some of its rough edges and gaining depth. There is still a long way to go, but Caviola has many years before him and he also has the assistance of a first-rate vineyard manager, Maurizio Anselma.

●	Dolcetto d'Alba Barturot '98	▼▼▼	4
●	Dolcetto d'Alba '98	▼▼	3*
●	Langhe Rosso Bric du Luv '97	▼▼	5
●	Langhe Rosso Rangone '97	▼▼	5
●	Dolcetto d'Alba Barturot '96	▽▽▽	4
●	Langhe Rosso Bric du Luv '95	▽▽▽	5
●	Langhe Rosso Bric du Luv '96	▽▽▽	5
●	Dolcetto d'Alba Barturot '97	▽▽	4
●	Langhe Rosso Rangone '96	▽▽	5

MONTELUPO ALBESE (CN)

DESTEFANIS
VIA MORTIZZO, 8
12050 MONTELUPO ALBESE (CN)
TEL. 0173/617189

The winery of Marco Destefanis, a young winegrower of under thirty with his life before him, has earned its debut in the Guide with easy assurance. It is a small estate on which three generations work together: Marco's grandfather Francesco, who way back in 1945 began selling wine in bulk, his father Giuseppe, who in the second half of the '70s started to market it in bottle, and Marco himself, who has been handling the vinification for almost ten years. He doesn't have the very latest in modern equipment, but, by dint of unassuming, ceaseless effort, and with the help of the new stainless steel fermentation vessels which have replaced the fiberglass vats, he has presented an admirable range of wines. In these parts, of course, Dolcetto is the lead player, and Destefanis makes almost 20 thousand bottles of the basic Dolcetto d'Alba, which is more than two-thirds of the total production. This wine, which is really excellent value for money, makes up for the slight spikiness of the palate with a delightfully clean and enjoyable nose characterized by attractive floral aromas and a distinct note of bitter almond typical of the variety. The Dolcetto Monia Bassa, the top estate wine, derives from a superbly situated vineyard planted in 1945. The nose offers sweet scents of blackberry jam enhanced by complex smoky notes, while the soft, firm succulence of the palate subdues its powerful tannins. Both the Nebbiolo and the Chardonnay, which is 70% barrique-fermented, are admirable: the former for the complex, fascinating sensations it offers and the latter for its harmony and finesse. The Barbera and the basic Chardonnay are only slightly less interesting.

●	Dolcetto d'Alba Vigna Monia Bassa '98	🍷🍷	3*
○	Langhe Chardonnay Barrique '98	🍷🍷	3*
●	Nebbiolo d'Alba '97	🍷🍷	4
●	Barbera d'Alba '98	🍷	3
●	Dolcetto d'Alba '98	🍷	3
○	Langhe Chardonnay '98	🍷	2

MONTEU ROERO (CN)

CASCINA PELLERINO
LOC. SANT'ANNA
12040 MONTEU ROERO (CN)
TEL. 0173/978171 - 0173/979083

In the space of 15 years Luciano Bono has succeeded in transforming a semi-derelict farm into a first-class winegrowing estate: 30 to 35 thousand good bottles are now produced annually from about six hectares of land. Luciano's son Cristian has inherited his father's passion for this work, and dedicates all his professional skill to the estate. Next harvest time, a new underground cellar will start functioning. We'll begin with the excellent Roero Superiore Vicot, whose concentration can be guessed from its intense ruby-garnet color; the ample, balanced nose offers hints of cherry, raspberry and cocoa with toasty notes and a mineral undertone; the progress on the palate is broad and confident, nicely articulated by the well-judged tannins that lend a pleasing dryness to the lingering finish. The Barbera Gran Madre, ruby verging on garnet in hue, displays attractive aromas of red fruit, mint and tar; the slightly acidic palate is firmly supported by its full body. The pleasantly rustic basic Roero has an appealingly firm, vigorous palate. The Arneis Boneur offers well-blended fruity and vegetal aromas and a graceful, silky palate. Lastly, the Arneis Passito Poch ma Bon (in dialect 'what little there is is good') has a faintly heady bouquet of candied fruit and sweet biscuits; the palate is sweet and fleshy, with a well-judged crispness that lends charm to the walnut tone of the finish.

●	Barbera d'Alba Sup. Gran Madre '97	🍷🍷	4
●	Roero Sup. Vicot '97	🍷🍷	4
○	Arneis Passito Poch ma Bon '97	🍷	4
●	Roero '97	🍷	3*
○	Roero Arneis Boneur '98	🍷	3

MONTEU ROERO (CN)

ANGELO NEGRO & FIGLI

FRAZ. SANT'ANNA, 1
CASCINA RIVERI
12040 MONTEU ROERO (CN)
TEL. 0173/90252

The 200 thousand bottles produced annually by Giovanni Negro, mayor of Monteu Roero (for the fourth time), very worthily represent the wines of his native territory in the world at large. The Roero Superiore Sodisfà has made a very successful debut. The deep, vivid garnet color is followed by complex and fascinating aromas with distinct fruity notes (black cherry and plum) and intriguing hints of mint. The palate is rich and ample and the crescendo development gives full expression to its vigorous, refreshing character, leading to a long and corresponding finish. The Roero Prachirosso '97 is definitely less concentrated. The Barbera d'Alba Bric Bertu '97, on the other hand, is a remarkable wine and the star of the estate; it shows great personality and a perfect balance between wood and structure. The Nicolon, a basically simple wine, is pleasingly fresh and easy to drink. The excellent amber-hued Passito Perdaudin, from arneis, reveals spicy and balsamic notes enhanced by hints of leather and candied fruit on the nose; the palate is sweet, ample, vigorous and even; the long, intense and corresponding finish offers notes of dried fruit. The Bonarda Bric Millon gets One full Glass: the intense ruby-garnet color youthfully tinged with purple is followed by aromas of black fruit, almond and cocoa; the soft, rich palate leads to an intense, lingering finish punctuated by well-judged tannins. Another newcomer is the Arneis Gianat, which takes its place beside the Perdaudin and the basic version.

●	Roero Sup. Sodisfà '96	🍷🍷	4
○	Perdaudin Passito '96	🍷🍷	6
●	Barbera d'Alba Bric Bertu '97	🍷🍷	4
●	Barbera d'Alba Nicolon '97	🍷	3
●	Piemonte Bonarda Bric Millon '97	🍷	3
○	Roero Arneis '98	🍷	3
○	Roero Arneis Perdaudin '98	🍷	4
○	Roero Arneis Gianat '98	🍷	4
○	Langhe Favorita '98		3
●	Roero Prachiosso '97		4
●	Barbera d'Alba Bric Bertu '96	🍸🍸	4
●	Barbera d'Alba Nicolon '96	🍸🍸	3

MORIONDO (TO)

TERRE DA VINO

VIA ROMA, 50
10020 MORIONDO (TO)
TEL. 011/9927070

Year after year the 20 wineries making up the Terre da Vino offer a yet better range of wines. Bruno Cordero, the young oenologist in charge of production, has created two successful Barolos this time, the Paesi Tuoi and the Poderi Parussi, both of which won Two Glasses. The first, ruby-garnet in color with a compact rim, shows a good impact on the nose with strawberry, black currant, coffee and licorice notes over faint undertones of leather; the palate is mouth-filling, intense and regulated by soft tannins which lend power to the long, licorice finish. The Poderi Parussi, of an intense ruby-garnet hue with a dense rim, offers scents of fresh red fruit, sweet spice and mint; the palate, similar to the Paesi Tuoi's, displays ample body, smooth tannins and a lingering finish. The Barbera d'Asti La Luna e i Falò, again very good, first reveals its richness in its color; the nose releases notes of blackberry, raspberry and mushroom with light underlying balsamic nuances; the palate is balanced and long. The excellent Langhe Rosso La Malora looks dense in the glass; the complex aromas of black fruit, tobacco leaf, sweet pastry and undergrowth are followed by an elegant and deeply satisfying palate. One full Glass goes to the Gavi Masseria dei Carmelitani, straw-colored with a greenish tinge; the fresh fragrance of peach, citrus rind and banana precede a silky, succulent palate with a lingering, fruity finish. The other wines listed also fully deserve One Glass apiece for their clearly expressed varietal character. The opening of new premises in Barolo is planned for next year.

●	Barbera d'Asti La Luna e I Falò '97	🍷🍷	4
●	Barolo Paesi Tuoi '95	🍷🍷	5
●	Barolo Poderi Parussi '95	🍷🍷	5
●	Langhe Rosso La Malora '97	🍷🍷	4
●	Dolcetto di Ovada Tenuta Magnona '98	🍷	3
○	Gavi del Comune di Gavi Masseria dei Carmelitani '98	🍷	3
○	Gavi del Comune di Gavi Ca' da Bosio '98	🍷	3
○	Piemonte Chardonnay Rocche di Ricaldone '98	🍷	3
○	Piemonte Chardonnay Tenuta Magnona '98	🍷	3
●	Barbera d'Asti La Luna e I Falò '96	🍸🍸	4

MORSACO (AL)

La Guardia
Reg. La Guardia
15010 Morsasco (AL)
tel. 0144/73076

The Priarone family estate represents a benchmark for quality in the Ovada district and fulfills the important role of ambassador for Dolcetto d'Ovada to the world at large. The range of wines produced from the 32 hectares under vine is almost too vast. The Dolcetto Bricco Riccardo lacks the structure of previous versions, but pleasant aromas of sour cherry and almond emerge on a somewhat rustic nose; the palate is fresh and enjoyable. We must, however, unfortunately report a certain inconsistency of quality between one bottle and another of the Bricco Riccardo. The Dolcetto Il Gamondino, on the other hand, shows a greater concentration, starting with the color. We particularly liked the Sacro e Profano, 65% cabernet and 35% barbera, which spends 18 months in barriques: it has improved considerably and won Two full Glasses. Of a dark almost impenetrable color, it displays distinct aromas of sweet pepper, red currant and vanilla; the palate is rich, dense, soft and complex. The excellent Chardonnay Butàs, of which 30% is fermented in wood, has a complex bouquet of banana, grapefruit, tangerine and hazelnut; the palate is fat and lingering. The Gavi Camghé is varietal and well executed; it offers intense aromas and a soft, lingering palate not without a refreshing acidity. The barriqued Dolcetto Villa Delfini is rather understated and needs further maturation. The two sweet wines are appealing: the Figlio di un Bacco Minore, a non-sparkling Brachetto, and the Moscato Passito, aged in used barriques. To end the list, we mention the Barbera La Vigna di Dante and the Cortese La Vigna di Lena.

●	Monferrato Rosso Sacro e Profano '97	🍷🍷	5
○	Piemonte Chardonnay Butàs '98	🍷🍷	4
●	Dolcetto di Ovada Sup. Il Gamondino '97	🍷	4
●	Dolcetto di Ovada Sup. Vigneto Bricco Riccardo '97	🍷	4
●	Dolcetto di Ovada Villa Delfini '97	🍷	4
●	Figlio di un Bacco Minore '98	🍷	4
○	Gavi Camghé '98	🍷	4
○	Piemonte Moscato Passito '96	🍷	5
●	Barbera del M.to La Vigna di Dante '97		4
○	Cortese dell'Alto M.to La Vigna di Lena '98		3

MURISENGO (AL)

Isabella
Via Gianoli, 64
Fraz. Corteranzo
15020 Murisengo (AL)
tel. 0141/693000

After a few years of waiting in the wings in the "Other Wineries" section, the Isabella estate now makes its debut in the Guide. This attractive Murisengo winery has been making wine since the 19th century, but it only began bottling towards the end of the 1970s, when Gabriele Calvo, the present owner and an oenologist with a diploma from the school at Alba, took over. Today Isabella is an up-to-date estate, very well equipped and well organized, with a production capacity of about 110 thousand bottles from 22 hectares under vine out of a total of 52 hectares. The vines are mostly barbera, and are on average 20 years old. And we found that, in fact, Barbera, in which Gabriele is a firm believer, has given the most satisfying results. The Bric Stupui '97, which spends a year in barriques used once or twice before, is a really excellent wine; it shows an impenetrable black-ruby color, and, on the nose, notes of ripe sour cherry, plum, eucalyptus and spice. It performs just as well on the palate, where it is immediately rich, dense, succulent and warm, with perfectly judged oak. The Truccone, which ages for a year in large casks, is more simple and direct in style but is nevertheless admirable: of an intense ruby color with a nose offering hints of red fruit, it has a very fruity, meaty, warm and rounded palate. The good Freisa Sobric displays a quite intense color and aromas of raspberry, red currant, violet and spice; the palate, with lots of fruit and a typically tannic, bitterish finish, is very enjoyable.

●	Barbera d'Asti Bric Stupui '97	🍷🍷	4
●	Barbera d'Asti Truccone '97	🍷	3
●	Monferrato Freisa Sobric '98	🍷	3

MURISENGO (AL)

LA ZUCCA
VIA SORINA, 53
FRAZ. SORINA
15020 MURISENGO (AL)
TEL. 011/8193343

The flourishing Murisengo estate of Ester Accornero, a passionate producer of wine, makes its debut in the Guide this year. For centuries the vine has prospered on the charming slopes of this zone, whose soil is mainly composed of marine deposits. Ester's ambition is to bring out the characteristics and spirit of this territory through her wines and other typical products. The estate has five hectares under vine (two more will shortly come into production), yielding some 25 thousand bottles a year, with the help of the consultant oenologist Donato Lanati. The vineyards planted to barbera are 40-50 years old and excellently situated. Two full Glasses go to the Barbera Martizza, a selection of their very best grapes aged for about a year in tonneaux and barriques. It presents an intense ruby color and a powerful, well-structured, fat, warm and lingering palate. Coffee and spicy wood-derived notes are prominent on the nose, with an undertone of cherry. The unoaked Barbera del Monferrato 'I Sulì, from the prized Ca' di Srù vineyard, is pleasant and well executed. The color is a medium-intense ruby; ripe cherry and red currant emerge on the nose with hints of white pepper, while the palate offers sweet, fresh fruit: this wine is altogether less demanding and easier drinking than the Martizza. Lastly, the Freisa, a refreshing, fruity, varietal wine, gets One Glass.

●	Barbera del M.to Martizza '97	🍷🍷	5
●	Barbera del M.to 'I Sulì '97	🍷	4
●	Freisa d'Asti '98	🍷	3

NEIVE (CN)

PIERO BUSSO
B.TA ALBESANI, 8
12057 NEIVE (CN)
TEL. 0173/67156

On Piero Busso's estate there is a general air of renewal: the reconstruction of the barrel-rooms, begun last year, is now nearly finished and the labels have been cleverly redesigned by Massimiliano Frezzato, a young cartoonist from Turin. This year we are unable to review the Langhe Bianco, which starting in '98 will be called Bianco di Busso, because Piero has decided to delay bottling this very good vintage. Of the wines we tasted, the Barbaresco Vigna Borgese '96 and the Barbera '97 were particularly rewarding. The first, of a somewhat dark, very dense ruby color, is wonderfully concentrated; the nose offers earthy aromas of damp leaves on a background of red fruit, while the palate shows a captivating softness and well assimilated abundant smooth tannins leading into a long, rich finish. The Barbera Vigna Majano '97 has never been so good; the color is a deep, dense ruby; the nose reveals fruity aromas of wild cherry perfectly blended with the spicy wood-derived notes; the palate is clean, fruity and warm, with just the right bite of characteristic refreshing acidity. Despite its 13% of alcohol, the Dolcetto '98 is still hard; echoes of fresh almond linger on the palate. Lastly, the Nebbiolo '97 gets only One Glass because the nose, with its berry and rose aromas, is not entirely flawless; the palate is well balanced thanks to its smooth tannins and good body.

●	Barbaresco Vigna Borgese '96	🍷🍷	5
●	Barbera d'Alba Vigna Majano '97	🍷🍷	4
●	Barbaresco Bricco Mondino '96	🍷	5
●	Dolcetto d'Alba Vigna Majano '98	🍷	3
●	Langhe Nebbiolo '97	🍷	4
●	Barbaresco Vigna Borgese '95	🍸🍸	5
○	Langhe Bianco '97	🍸🍸	3
●	Barbera d'Alba Vigna Majano '96	🍸	3

NEIVE (CN)

CASCINA VANO
LOC. RIVETTI, 9
12057 NEIVE (CN)
TEL. 0173/677705 - 0173/67263

Beppe has always vinified and sold wine in bulk to private customers, bottling just a small part of the Barbaresco since the early '70s. In 1993 his son Bruno, having finished his oenological studies in Alba, began to take a hand in the running of the cellar, and as the years went by more and more of the wine went into bottles, of which they now fill a total of 20 thousand a year. The grapes come from eight hectares of vineyard, two of which are rented, mainly near Neive. Vinification is decidedly modern in style, with brief maceration and aging in tonneaux and new barriques for the barbera, while the nebbiolo is aged in once-used barriques and sometimes in large casks. The Barbaresco '96, from the Serraboella and Ca' Nova vineyards, shows a very lively ruby color tinged with garnet; distinct aromas of cherry and licorice are followed by attractively mouth-filling fruit on the palate, while the robust body bodes well for its future evolution. The Barbera '97, which also won Two Glasses, is very good value for money; it offers fresh, vinous aromas and notes of bitter cherry with an undertone of vanilla; in the mouth it is soft and warm. The hard, youthful Dolcetto '98, from the Basarin vineyard, rates One Glass, as does the Moscato '98, with its intense fragrance of pear and honey, its delicate effervescence and its dry, palate-cleaning finish.

●	Barbaresco '96	🍷🍷	5
●	Barbera d'Alba '97	🍷🍷	3*
●	Dolcetto d'Alba '98	🍷	3
○	Moscato d'Asti '98	🍷	3

NEIVE (CN)

F.LLI CIGLIUTI
VIA SERRA BOELLA, 17
12057 NEIVE (CN)
TEL. 0173/677185

Renato Cigliuti's '96 Barbaresco has carried off Three Glasses, just like the '83 and the '90. The color is an intense ruby verging on garnet with a youthful rim; the broad, complex and delightful nose offers notes of cherries steeped in alcohol, cocoa and coffee with intriguing animal undertones; the palate, which is ample and meaty right from the start, shows a broad mid palate well articulated by noble, powerful tannins that lead confidently to the long and satisfying finish on a note of cocoa. The Langhe Rosso Bricco Serra should also not be missed: it displays a concentrated garnet hue with a narrow rim and scents of plum and very ripe red currant over hints of custard, green leaves and menthol; the sumptuousness apparent to the eye and nose emerges on the palate, where the entry is rich and mouth-filling and the development is opulent if not particularly powerful; tannins show their vigor on the finish. The excellent Barbera d'Alba Serraboella '97 has an intense ruby-garnet color with a still purplish rim; the generous, highly expressive nose offers hints of very ripe berries, leather, rosemary and dry grass; the palate has a lively acidity which in no way diminishes the full body and solid phenolic structure; the finish is warm, dry and lingering.

●	Barbaresco Serraboella '96	🍷🍷🍷	6
●	Barbera d'Alba Serraboella '97	🍷🍷	4
●	Langhe Rosso Bricco Serra '97	🍷🍷	5
●	Barbaresco Serraboella '90	🍷🍷🍷 (outline)	5
●	Barbaresco Serraboella '93	🍷🍷 (outline)	5
●	Barbaresco Serraboella '95	🍷🍷 (outline)	5
●	Langhe Rosso Bricco Serra '96	🍷 (outline)	5

NEIVE (CN)

FONTANABIANCA
FRAZ. BORDINI, 15
12057 NEIVE (CN)
TEL. 0173/67195

Aldo Pola and Bruno Ferro have all the basic requirements for success: the zone where the estate lies is undoubtedly one of the best, and in the cellar they have the skilled assistance of Beppe Caviola as consultant oenologist. The output is about 50 thousand bottles and Silvano Formigli with his Selezione Fattorie takes care of the marketing. We'll begin with the Barbaresco Sorì Burdin '96, ruby-garnet in color with an orange rim; the nose is broad and faintly forward in tone, with notes of raspberry, red currant, leather and dried flowers; the palate is nicely concentrated and possesses a firm phenolic structure that invigorates the lingering licorice finish. The basic Barbaresco is nearly as good, and also rates Two Glasses. It has a garnet-tinged ruby hue and offers aromas of fruit steeped in alcohol, mint and cocoa over faint woody nuances; the palate is rich and vigorous, and the powerful finish is enhanced by a delightful note of cocoa. The Dolcetto Bordini '98, which reveals its power straightaway in its intense ruby-garnet color, is a well-structured, characterful wine; mint and marjoram are in evidence on the nose over a ground of cherry and almond. The development on the palate is rich and fairly ample, with a faintly noticeable acidity and a finish made dry by pronounced tannins. To end the list, the Chardonnay Montesommo shows a rich straw color; the nose is dense with notes of herbs and hazelnut over well-blended fruity and floral tones, while the medium-bodied palate is silky and balanced.

●	Barbaresco '96	🍷🍷	5
●	Barbaresco Sorì Burdin '96	🍷🍷	5
●	Dolcetto d'Alba Bordini '98	🍷	3
○	Langhe Chardonnay Montesommo '98	🍷	4
●	Barbaresco Sorì Burdin '95	🍷🍷 (outline)	5

NEIVE (CN)

GASTALDI
VIA ALBESANI, 20
12057 NEIVE (CN)
TEL. 0173/677400

After making his fans wait for a year by delaying the presentation of his new wines, Bernardino Gastaldi has come up with a series of distinctly successful bottles. We'll start with the Bianco '97, a blend of chardonnay and sauvignon with an especially rewarding palate that can hold its own with the best to be found on the home market. The nose is just a little unsettled, needing a few more months in bottle to find its balance. The Gastaldi Rosso '93, released after a full five years' aging in stainless steel, also proves to be excellent. It is a dark garnet in color with aromas of dried violet and ripe red fruit and an exceptionally long, enthralling palate: an impeccable Rosso, very nearly as well-structured as the memorable '88 and '89. Incidentally, nothing has ever been heard of a '90 version: who knows if Gastaldi is preparing a surprise for the new millennium? The Barbaresco '95, which offers a good bouquet in which clean wood is still evident, does not have much structure or length. The Dolcetto is extremely attractive, showing none of the rather glib vinous and youthful tones often found in this kind of wine; the clean fruity nose is mirrored by a good firm palate on which the tannins are still faintly perceptible; the finish is enjoyable and decidedly dry. It should be remembered that the Dolcetto, like the Bianco, comes from a vineyard near Rodello, a much sought-after zone for this grape.

●	Dolcetto d'Alba Moriolo '98	🍷🍷	4
●	Gastaldi Rosso '93	🍷🍷	6
○	Langhe Bianco '97	🍷🍷	5
●	Barbaresco '95	🍷	6

NEIVE (CN)

BRUNO GIACOSA
VIA XX SETTEMBRE, 52
12057 NEIVE (CN)
TEL. 0173/67027

The Barbaresco S. Stefano '96, ruby-garnet in color with a slightly faded rim, offers red fruit, leather, undergrowth, spice and dried flowers on the nose; the progression is austere on the full-bodied, confident palate and the long finish displays fruity and balsamic tones. This is an outstanding wine in its category and will undoubtedly give of its best with time. The same goes for the Barolo Falletto, which has a wide rim on a garnet ground; the faintly forward nose reveals aromas of jam, pepper and dried flowers with an unusual almost salty note; the development on the palate is well balanced right through to the lingering finish. This interpretation does not offer easy appeal, but can be counted on to express all its potential with the right amount of aging. The Dolcetto d'Alba Basarin displays a rather faded ruby color; the somewhat rustic nose releases notes of berries and sweet pastry; the palate, with agreeable tannins and a sustaining warmth on the finish, is satisfyingly full. The ruby-orange basic Barbaresco offers a slightly heady bouquet with hints of red fruit, spice and yeasty dough; the tannins are just perceptible on the medium-bodied palate and the finish echoes the bouquet. The Arneis, straw-colored with a greenish cast, displays aromas of peach, apricot and banana on a straightforward, inviting nose. It is enjoyable drinking thanks to its crisp, mouth-filling palate. The Spumante Extra Brut '95 has aromas of fruit in syrup and custard that carry through onto the balanced palate. Lastly, the Nebbiolo has a nose of moderate finesse and a rather simple palate.

●	Barbaresco S. Stefano '96	▼▼	6
●	Barolo Falletto '95	▼▼	6
●	Barbaresco '96	▼	6
●	Dolcetto d'Alba Basarin '98	▼	4
●	Nebbiolo d'Alba Valmaggiore '97	▼	4
○	Roero Arneis '98	▼	4
○	Spumante Extra Brut '95	▼	5
●	Barolo Collina Rionda '82	▽▽▽	6
●	Barolo Rocche di Castiglione Falletto '85	▽▽▽	6
●	Barbaresco S. Stefano '95	▽▽	6
●	Barolo Collina Rionda '93	▽▽	6
●	Barolo Falletto '93	▽▽	6

NEIVE (CN)

GIACOSA F.LLI
VIA XX SETTEMBRE, 64
12057 NEIVE (CN)
TEL. 0173/67013

This year Valerio and Silverio Giacosa, with their respective sons Maurizio and Paolo, have presented two quintessential Langhe wines that have won Two Glasses each: the Barbaresco Rio Sordo '96 and the Barolo Vigna Mandorlo '95. The first, of an attractive ruby-garnet color with a very firm rim, has a pleasantly forward nose with notes of cocoa, dried flowers and leather. The palate has grip right from the start and its satisfying body makes itself felt all the way through to the austere and lingering finish. The intense ruby-garnet Barolo Vigna Mandorlo offers a harmonious bouquet of mint, berries and custard over a subtle and complex blending of animal and mineral nuances with their hints of leather and earth. The palate is full and rich, with noble tannins and substantial alcohol giving punch to the lingering finish. The excellent Chardonnay Ca' Lunga, of a rich straw color, has an intriguing nose enhanced by well-judged new wood: aromas of tropical fruit, hazelnut, white flowers and vanilla emerge. The palate, if not particularly powerful, is soft and broad and offers a satisfying finish. Both the Dolcettos, the Madonna di Como and the San Rocco Seno d'Elvio, are good. The first shows a dense ruby hue with a purplish rim; aromas of bitter cherry, raspberry and almond precede a substantial palate with a just perceptible acidity and a slightly harsh-edged fruity finish. The second, lighter and more straightforward, has a purple rim on a ruby base; the nose offers fruit and rhubarb, while the palate is light but sound. The Barbera Maria Gioana, the Barolo Bussia and the Chardonnay Rorea are all good too.

●	Barbaresco Rio Sordo '96	▼▼	6
●	Barolo Vigna Mandorlo '95	▼▼	6
●	Barbera d'Alba Maria Gioana '97	▼	4
●	Barolo Bussia '95	▼	6
●	Dolcetto d'Alba Madonna di Como '98	▼	3
●	Dolcetto d'Alba S. Rocco Seno d'Elvio '98	▼	3
○	Langhe Chardonnay Ca' Lunga '97	▼	4
○	Langhe Chardonnay Rorea '98		3
●	Barbaresco Rio Sordo '95	▽▽	5
●	Barbera d'Alba Maria Gioana '96	▽	4

NEIVE (CN)

UGO LEQUIO

VIA DEL MOLINO, 10
12057 NEIVE (CN)
TEL. 0173/677224

This young Neive winery fully deserves its first appearance in the Guide. Ugo Lequio, who was born on the Prinsi di Neive farm where his family has always produced Nebbiolo and Dolcetto, vinifies the grapes he buys in the area, mainly from the Gallina cru. His first job was as an agent for a big Langhe winery in Brianza; in 1982 he decided to buy wine in bulk and then bottle and market it under the La Sandrina label. The profit margins of the time were so good that in a few years he was able to equip his cellar for vinification, and with the '86 vintage he began making his own wine. Today he has at his disposal some fine stainless steel vats, a few barriques and, above all, large new Slovenian oak barrels with a capacity of 13 to 25 hectoliters. His Barbaresco Gallina '96 outstripped many celebrated names at our tastings and delighted everyone. Of an intense deep ruby color, it has an ample, complex nose with spicy notes of licorice, pepper, leather and even rose; the explosive palate is warm, dense and full of personality, and leads into a sweet, lingering finish. The Barbera '97, which is just as good, displays a lovely vivid color; despite its youth, it releases vinous and well-defined aromas of cherry jam; it is gentle and velvety on the palate, displaying a wonderful softness and remarkable length. The Langhe Arneis '98, of a very intense hue, is unusually rich in alcohol (13.6%); the nose is reminiscent of apple and dried mint, while the palate is fat and the finish bitterish.

● Barbaresco Gallina '96	🍷🍷	5
● Barbera d'Alba Gallina '97	🍷🍷	4
○ Langhe Arneis '98	🍷	3

NEIVE (CN)

PAITIN

VIA SERRA BOELLA, 20
12057 NEIVE (CN)
TEL. 0173/67343

This family winery, in which Secondo and his sons Silvano and Giovanni are assisted by their consultant oenologist Beppe Caviola, is maintaining its high standards. It is situated on the hillside of Serra Boella at Neive and includes ten hectares that yield 50-60 thousand bottles. The wines presented this year are superb, starting with the Paitin '97, 5,000 bottles of a blend of nebbiolo and barbera with a little cabernet sauvignon and syrah, all aged in new and used barriques. The color is extremely dark, and intense aromas of vanilla and red fruit meld with the spiciness of the oak; the full-bodied, concentrated, meaty palate is lingering and various, with a solid structure and excellent balance: Three Glasses without a murmur. The Barbaresco '96 (18 thousand bottles) scored nearly as high: aged partly in barriques and partly in large Slovenian oak barrels, it shows finesse on the nose, with wonderful floral aromas enhanced by the oak; the palate is appealingly complex and reveals excellent body, an austerity imparted by tannins and acidity, and a long and powerful finish. Another first-class wine is the Dolcetto '98, half of which is aged in large old casks: it is very intense in color and the elegant and harmonious nose offers vinous and fruity aromas, while the palate is powerful, rich and meaty but still a little austere; more time in the bottle can do it nothing but good. The Campolive '97, a blend of steel-aged sauvignon (65%) with barrique-fermented chardonnay, also performs well: it has abundant toasty, spicy aromas with fresh balsamic notes, and a refined and structured palate with a balanced finish. The Barbera '97 is simpler and coarser, with a lack of balance due to its substantial alcohol.

● Langhe Paitin '97	🍷🍷🍷	5
● Barbaresco Sorì Paitin '96	🍷🍷	6
○ Campolive Bianco '97	🍷🍷	4
● Dolcetto d'Alba Sorì Paitin '98	🍷🍷	3*
● Barbera d'Alba Campolive '97	🍷	4
● Barbaresco Sorì Paitin '95	🍷🍷🍷	5
● Barbaresco Ris. '90	🍷🍷	6
● Barbaresco Sorì Paitin '93	🍷🍷	6
● Barbaresco Sorì Paitin '94	🍷🍷	5
● Langhe Paitin '95	🍷🍷	5
● Langhe Paitin '96	🍷🍷	5
● Barbera d'Alba Campolive '96	🍷	4

NEIVE (CN)

SOTTIMANO
LOC. COTTÀ, 21
12057 NEIVE (CN)
TEL. 0173/635186

Within the space of a few years the quality of the wines from this estate has risen considerably, as can be seen from the impressive collection of Glasses. This is due to young Andrea's active role in the winery, to the technical assistance of Beppe Caviola and to Rino's firm belief that if one wishes to make a champion wine, yields must be reduced in the vineyard. The nine hectares under vine currently in production yield 40-50 thousand bottles. Three different Barbaresco crus, from the '96 vintage this time, have been presented, and with the addition of the Pajorè vineyard next year there will be four. The Currà offers aromas of red fruit, cinnamon, licorice and fresh vanilla, which reappear on the extremely well-balanced palate. The Cottà, more forward in color, has a spicy bouquet with citrus rind and leather; the rich, close-knit and very intense palate displays a lingering softness. The more opulent color of the Fausoni is an indication of the greater power and richness to be found on the palate, thanks to prominent tannins and enveloping warmth; the aromas, still reticent, are of spice, dried mint and chocolate. The Barbera Pairolero '97, which boasts 14% of alcohol, comes from the Gavello and Currà vineyards and is a dark ruby red in the glass; the rather closed but concentrated bouquet suggests blueberry, beeswax and vanilla; these are mirrored on the palate with velvety softness. Of the two '98 Dolcettos we preferred the Cottà, although it is less typical: with its roundness and concentrated fruit it is a splendid wine with a sweet licorice finish. The unusual Maté '98 (a dry Brachetto) has characteristic varietal aromas and a warm, powerful palate.

●	Barbaresco Fausoni Vigna del Salto '96	▼▼▼	5
●	Barbaresco Cottà Vigna Brichet '96	▼▼	5
●	Barbaresco Currà Vigna Masué '96	▼▼	5
●	Barbera d'Alba Pairolero '97	▼▼	4
●	Dolcetto d'Alba Cottà '98	▼▼	3*
●	Dolcetto d'Alba Bric del Salto '98	▼	3
●	Maté '98	▼	3
●	Barbaresco Currà '95	▽▽	5
●	Barbaresco Pajoré Vigna Lunetta '95	▽▽	5
●	Barbaresco Brichet '95	▽	5
●	Barbera d'Alba Pairolero '96	▽	4

NEVIGLIE (CN)

F.LLI BERA
CASCINA PALAZZO, 12
12050 NEVIGLIE (CN)
TEL. 0173/630194

The Beras have been producing some very good red wines for a number of years, but never before have they achieved the excellence shown by these two reds: Two full Glasses for both the Langhe Sassisto '96 and the Barbera d'Alba '97! The first, from 75% barbera with nebbiolo, has a dense garnet color with a narrow rim; the broad, harmonious nose displays aromas of red currant, blueberry, mint, pepper and cocoa; the palate is immediately ample and concentrated, and the solid progression is well articulated by noble tannins that lend volume to a finish that lingers on a note of licorice. The Barbera, of an intense ruby-garnet hue, offers hints of black fruit, coffee, cocoa and licorice on the nose; the palate is broad and substantial with pronounced tannins and a modulated, long finish. The Nebbiolo '95, dense and vivid in color, reveals rich aromas of spice, jam, coffee and eucalyptus; it is full and robust on the palate, with vigorous tannins and a finish on which toasty nuances and licorice emerge. The basic Moscato has a little more personality than the selection this year; this is due to its well-expressed nose, with notes of tropical fruit, elderblossom, pennyroyal and sage, and to a mouth-filling palate ending on a long, elegant finish. One fully deserved Glass goes all the same to the Moscato Su Reimond, which is slightly lighter on the nose than usual, although it very elegantly offers delicate aromas of white-fleshed fruit, wild herbs and lily of the valley followed by a silky and even palate and a finish that perfectly mirrors the bouquet. An enchanting Brut Metodo Classico and a correct Asti Spumante end the list.

●	Barbera d'Alba '97	▼▼	3*
●	Langhe Sassisto '96	▼▼	4
○	Asti Cascina Palazzo '98	▼	3
○	Bera Brut	▼	4
●	Langhe Nebbiolo '95	▼	4
○	Moscato d'Asti '98	▼	3
○	Moscato d'Asti Su Reimond '98	▼	3
●	Barbera d'Alba Sassisto '95	▽	4

NIZZA M.TO (AT)

Bersano
P.zza Dante, 21
14049 Nizza M.to (AT)
tel. 0141/720211

Change is in the air at the Bersano winery: there are some new highly prized vineyards, new bottles and labels, new wines and a new consultant oenologist, the distinguished Giuliano Noè. The boost given to the estate by the owners, in particular by Ugo Massimelli, and by the general manager Nico Conti, with co-workers Piersandro Sandri and Massimiliano Diotti, is making itself felt. And the results are most gratifying: the Barbera Generala '97 has won Three Glasses. This is an extraordinary event, if you think of the winery's policies of only a few years back: production geared to quantity, aggressive marketing strategies and correct but run-of-the-mill wines. This Barbera, a wine of breeding, elegance and sinew, is the exact opposite, and superbly expresses its terroir. It is dense ruby in color, and offers an intense bouquet of still very youthful spicy and balsamic aromas; on the palate it is mouth-filling and well balanced, and ripe cherry characterizes the extremely long finish. The Pomona '97, a blend of cabernet and barbera, is almost as good; opaque in the glass, it releases scents of green grass and red fruit; chocolate and ripe plum appear on the ample and caressing palate. We liked the Gavi di Gavi Raggio; the '98 version shows character, density and a fragrance of white flowers on the nose; these reappear on the finish together with a hint of almond. The Brachetto d'Acqui Castelgaro has always been one of the best of its kind; the '98 is redolent of sweet spice and rose, while the palate has good varietal character and an inviting succulent finish. The Barbera Cremosina '97 is properly made but does not do full justice to this unique vintage.

●	Barbera d'Asti Sup. Generala '97	▼▼▼	6
●	Brachetto d'Acqui Castelgaro '98	▼▼	4
○	Gavi del Comune di Gavi Marchese Raggio '98	▼▼	4
●	Monferrato Pomona '97	▼▼	6
●	Barbera d'Asti Cremosina '97	▼	4
●	Barbera d'Asti Sup. Generala '96	▽▽	5
●	Barbera d'Asti Cremosina '96	▽	4
●	Pomona '96	▽	6

NIZZA M.TO (AT)

Cascina La Barbatella
S.da Annunziata, 55
14049 Nizza M.to (AT)
tel. 0141/701434

The Monferrato hills, straddling the provinces of Turin, Asti and Alessandria, are a rich and privileged corner of the world, a panorama of ploughed fields, poplar groves, vineyards and farmhouses alternating with windswept vistas of wheat and corn. To Angelo Sonvico, a true Lombard and a bookmaker by trade with a love of nature and the world of wine, it must have seemed the ideal spot for getting the Milanese smog out of his system. Thus it was that in 1982, trusting in the skill of his friend Giuliano Noè, the expert Monferrato oenologist, he went ahead and bought this hillside estate just outside Nizza Monferrato with the intention of producing a great red wine. Almost twenty years have passed since then, and Angelo and Giuliano have produced not one but several great reds: indeed with the outstanding performance of the Sonvico '97 they are close to winning a star, the symbol conferred on wineries that have collected ten Three Glasses. The estate's standard-bearer shows a deep ruby-red color; the enticing bouquet offers a profusion of intense aromas in which hints of blackberry, bitter cherry, black currant, spice and coffee emerge; the palate echoes them all and is balanced, aristocratic and long. The two monovarietal Barberas, La Vigna dell'Angelo and La Barbatella, are also superb. The first, revealing good impact and length on the nose, mingles fresh notes of berries with enticing hints of spice, followed by a rich and even palate. The second, almost as good, offers intense fruity aromas; the clean, mouth-filling palate is eminently satisfying. The Bianco Noè, with a fresh fragrance of wild herbs and flowers, has been put slightly out of kilter by a prominent citric note.

●	Monferrato Rosso Sonvico '97	▼▼▼	6
●	Barbera d'Asti La Barbatella '98	▼▼	4
●	Barbera d'Asti Sup. La Vigna dell'Angelo '97	▼▼	6
○	Monferrato Bianco Noè '98	▼	4
●	Barbera d'Asti Sup. La Vigna dell'Angelo '96	▽▽▽	6
●	La Vigna di Sonvico '90	▽▽▽	6
●	La Vigna di Sonvico '93	▽▽▽	6
●	La Vigna di Sonvico '94	▽▽▽	6
●	La Vigna di Sonvico '95	▽▽▽	6
●	La Vigna di Sonvico '96	▽▽▽	6
●	Barbera d'Asti Sup. La Vigna dell'Angelo '95	▽▽	5

SCARPA - ANTICA CASA VINICOLA
VIA MONTEGRAPPA, 6
14049 NIZZA M.TO (AT)
TEL. 0141/721331

The production philosphy that has always informed Mario Pesce's winery is by now legendary. No concessions are made to latter-day trends, either in the vineyard (where traditional varieties continue to hold sway) or in the cellar, where not a barrique can be found, or indeed any other modern 'frippery'. Long maceration, long maturation in cask and in bottle, flavors and aromas that make no concessions to the so-called "international taste": this is what lies behind Scarpa's wines. We'll begin with the Grignolino d'Asti S. Defendente '97, which shows a pale color already tending towards orange tones and a forward bouquet with dried flowers to the fore. Next comes the table wine Rouchet, from ruché grapes. The '98 version, of an intense, brilliant color, has a warm, elegant, aromatic bouquet; it is soft in the mouth but lacks sinew. The dry Brachetto, a traditional local wine now very hard to find, has always been one of the estate's mainstays. The '98 maintains customary high standards: it shows a vivid ruby hue and an intensely floral (rose) and aromatic (pepper) bouquet, while the impact on the palate is correspondingly well-sustained. The Nebbiolo d'Alba is another classic of the estate, which also has vineyards in the Langhe. We close with the Barberas: two examples were presented, both from the '96 vintage and both intended to be kept for a long time. At the moment, the I Bricchi di Castelrocchero shows a more attractive bouquet, pleasantly fruity with a light note of spice; the palate, however, displays a rather marked acidity. The La Bogliona is less appealing on the nose, which is dominated by wood (large casks), but it's richer and meatier on the palate, and should round out better with time.

●	Rouchet Bricco Rosa '98	▼▼	6
●	Barbera d'Asti Sup. I Bricchi di Castelrocchero '96	▼	5
●	Barbera d'Asti Sup. La Bogliona '96	▼	6
●	Brachetto Secco La Selva di Moirano '98	▼	6
●	Grignolino d'Asti S. Defendente '97	▼	5
●	Nebbiolo d'Alba Bric du Nota '97	▼	5
●	Rouchet Bricco Rosa '90	▽▽▽	6
●	Barbera d'Asti Sup. La Bogliona '95	▽▽	5
●	Barolo Tettimora '88	▽▽	6
●	Rouchet Bricco Rosa '96	▽▽	5
●	Rouchet Bricco Rosa '97	▽▽	6

FRANCO E MARIO SCRIMAGLIO
VIA ALESSANDRIA, 67
14049 NIZZA M.TO (AT)
TEL. 0141/721385 - 0141/727052

The Scrimaglio winery has in recent years become one of the most active and enterprising in the Nizza Monferrato area, presenting new products, some of which come from the estate farm, and, in a variety of ways, promoting the area in general. They have presented a wide range of wines, and we shall start with the Monferrato Bianco Bricco Sant'Ippolito '98, made from sauvignon. It shows a moderately intense color and a pleasant bouquet, first distinctly grassy and then enriched by fresh, fruity notes (melon); the palate is very varietal and immediate, and the wine is easily quaffable. The best of this year's reds is the Barbera d'Asti Acsé, with its youthful, brilliant garnet hue; the fruity bouquet precedes a nicely rounded, full, lingering palate, underpinned by a good acidic bite. The Barbera d'Asti Superiore Bricco Sant'Ippolito '97, an inviting and intensely fruity red, is not to be despised either: the palate is clean and straightforward, although not particularly full-bodied and somewhat dominated by acidity. The Barbera d'Asti Superiore Croutin '96 did really quite well, given its mediocre vintage. The color is not very deep and the nose, closed at first, reveals a balsamic note followed by some good fruit; the palate shows substance and a finish with noticeable acidity. The direct and characteristic Barbera d'Asti Superiore Vigneto RoccaNivo '97, although not remarkable for its structure, offers a definitely satisfying palate. The list ends with the table wine Futuro, a white blend: it shows good balance and an agreeable palate, with a bitterish note on the finish.

●	Barbera d'Asti Sup. Acsé '97	▼▼	6
●	Barbera d'Asti Sup. Bricco S. Ippolito '97	▼	4
●	Barbera d'Asti Sup. Croutin '96	▼	5
●	Barbera d'Asti Sup. Vigneto RoccaNivo '97	▼	3*
●	Barbera del M.to Vivace Il Matto '98	▼	3*
○	Futuro	▼	3
○	Monferrato Bianco Bricco S. Ippolito '98	▼	4
●	Barbera d'Asti Sup. Croutin '90	▽▽	5
●	Barbera d'Asti Sup. Croutin '95	▽	5

NOVELLO (CN)

ELVIO COGNO
LOC. RAVERA, 2
12060 NOVELLO (CN)
TEL. 0173/744006

This Novello winery, brilliantly run by Walter Fissore and his wife Nadia, offers a range of highly reliable wines. All four presented this year have scored about 80 out of 100 points, and in some cases considerably more. The Langhe Rosso Montegrilli '97 displays an intense ruby-garnet hue and a profusion of fruity sensations on the nose, enhanced by intriguing spicy and animal hints: aromas of blackberry and ripe raspberry mingle with licorice and leather in an inviting bouquet, while the solid, ample palate leads into a lingering finish with a violet accent. The Dolcetto d'Alba Vigna del Mandorlo, of a dense garnet color, offers a delightful bouquet with soft, ripe tones of cherry, tobacco, licorice and sun-warmed grass; the rich and concentrated palate develops smoothly through to the long finish where pleasant, dry tannins emerge. The excellent Barolo Ravera '95 manages to combine freshness and character on a full-bodied and beautifully balanced palate. The Barbera Bricco dei Merli, medium-intense ruby in color, is still rather dominated by wood on the nose but succeeds all the same in revealing notes of red fruit, coffee and spice. The palate is broad and substantial and the finish long, with hints of cherry and cocoa. The native variety nas-cetta has yielded a wine with subtle, delicate aromas of apple, banana and dried herbs; the restrained silky palate finishes on notes of fruit and anise.

●	Barbera d'Alba Bricco dei Merli '97	▼▼	4
●	Barolo Ravera '95	▼▼	6
●	Dolcetto d'Alba Vigna del Mandorlo '98	▼▼	3
●	Langhe Rosso Montegrilli '97	▼▼	5
○	Nas-Cetta '98	▼	4
●	Barbera d'Alba Bricco del Merlo '95	▽▽	4
●	Barbera d'Alba Bricco del Merlo '96	▽▽	4
●	Barolo Ravera '93	▽▽	5
●	Dolcetto d'Alba Vigna del Mandorlo '97	▽▽	3
●	Langhe Rosso Montegrilli '96	▽▽	5

NOVI LIGURE (AL)

CASCINA DEGLI ULIVI
S.DA MAZZOLA, 12
15067 NOVI LIGURE (AL)
TEL. 0143/744598

It cannot be said that Stefano Bellotti lacks determination: having solved the bureacratic problems of recent years, he has now begun to offer country accommodation at Cascina degli Ulivi, with the family directly responsible for the restaurant and the six rooms. In perfect keeping with the estate philosophy, a vineyard has been planted in one of the best crus of Tassarolo to the rare dolcetto dal raspo rosso, here known as nibiô. The Nibiô '97 is, in fact, the wine we enjoyed most: its not excessively purplish ruby color is that of the best Dolcettos; the bouquet is very broad and satisfying and the warm, long palate reveals a perfect harmony between pleasing tannins and crisp acidity. The Barbera Piemonte Mounbè is a reasonable wine; aromas of toffee appear on the otherwise not particularly distinctive nose, and the palate is soft and enjoyable. Of the three interpretations of the cortese grape, the Montemarino '97 lives up to its cru, offering notable balsamic and smoky notes, borrowed perhaps from the unusual wood of the large barrels. The nose offers characteristic aromas of flowers and citrus fruit; the fresh, resinous palate has plenty of body and a long, pleasantly bitter finish. The old Filagnotti vineyard has yielded a straw-colored Gavi '98 with a vivid greenish cast; the nose offers hints of almond and mineral notes; the palate is satisfying but less structured than in the past. The Gavi Ulivi '98 displays delightful freshness underpinned by appropriate acidity and is a classic example of its appellation. The L'Amoroso, a partially fermented red, is an ideal dessert wine.

●	Monferrato Dolcetto Nibiô '97	▼▼	3*
○	Gavi I Filagnotti '98	▼	3
○	Gavi Montemarino di Tassarolo '97	▼	3
○	Gavi '98	▼	3
●	Piemonte Barbera Mounbè '98	▼	3
●	L'Amoroso '98		3

IL VIGNALE
VIA GAVI, 130
15067 NOVI LIGURE (AL)
TEL. 0143/72715

The Cappellettis' estate, with ten hectares of vineyard near the old road leading from Novi Ligure to Gavi, on a beautiful hillside that once belonged to the Lomellina property of the Marquises of Raggio, makes its debut in the Guide this year. The meticulous care of the owners and the oenological skill of the technical expert Bassi have contributed to decidedly successful results, with a consistently high level that over the years has brought its reward. Piero, who is up to the task, takes care of business, while a flock of wild geese is responsible for weeding between the rows. The estate's top wine, of which 45 thousand bottles are produced, is the Gavi DOCG Vigne Alte, which had already shown unexpected richness of aroma and elegance in '97. Careful selection in the vineyard and the harvesting of perfectly ripe grapes have resulted in an excellent '98 version too. Of a pale straw color, it has an ample and intense bouquet of flowers, tropical fruit and banana; the palate does not disappoint: it is full-flavored, soft, crisp and lingering. The Gavi Vilma Cappelletti '98 selection undergoes a long period of lees contact, and a small amount of the wine spends time in oak tonneaux; aromas of pear and tropical fruit emerge on the nose, while a pleasing freshness and well-judged acidity on the palate bring forth hints of green apple; the palate is fat and satisfyingly long. The Monferrato Rosso di Malì '97, from cabernet sauvignon and pinot nero, is aged in oak casks; it has a pale ruby color and offers varietal herbaceous aromas; the medium-bodied palate is vegetal and tannic.

○ Gavi Vigne Alte '98	ŸŸ	4
○ Gavi Vilma Cappelletti '98	Ÿ	4
● Monferrato Rosso di Malì '97	Ÿ	4

NOVI LIGURE (AL)

LAURA VALDITERRA
S.DA MONTEROTONDO, 75
15067 NOVI LIGURE (AL)
TEL. 0143/321451

Laura Valditerra has been managing her estate in the Gavi zone by herself for several years. The winery, on the road for Monterotondo, has eight hectares of vineyard surrounded by woods; a small lake adds further charm. Her Tenuta Rombetta's Gavi has been noticed at our tastings for quite some time; now it makes its debut in the Guide thanks to its consistent quality and the excellent results of her '98, of which she has presented more than one version. A Gavi DOCG selection is in fact making its first appearance and we were able to taste it in advance (it will be released well after this edition goes to press). The straw color with brilliant greenish highlights indicates its extreme youth, while aromas of resin and honey blend well with the wood; notes of apple and white flowers complete the delightful bouquet and precede a fresh, rich, fat palate with plenty of body and excellent balance; the finish is appropriately long. The Gavi Valditerra '98 has the classic pale straw color with a green tinge. The nose is intense and aristocratic, with floral and herbaceous notes mingling with mineral nuances; it has satisfying body and structure, followed by a long finish with a fresh anise tone.

○ Gavi Selezione Valditerra '98	ŸŸ	3*
○ Gavi Valditerra '98	Ÿ	3

PIOBESI D'ALBA (CN)

Tenuta Carretta

Loc. Carretta, 2
12040 Piobesi d'Alba (CN)
tel. 0173/619119

The Miroglio family winery divides its production between Roero wines and those of the Langhe. This year two Langhe wines came out on top: the Barbaresco Cascina Bordino and the Barolo Cannubi. The first is ruby-garnet in color with a wide orange rim and an intense bouquet of raspberry, tobacco leaf and licorice; the rich, broad palate progresses evenly to the dry, licorice finish. The garnet-tinged ruby-colored Barolo offers a harmonious nose with notes of berries, dried flowers, spice and marzipan. The palate is soft and harmonious, and the tannins blend nicely with the alcohol on the lingering finish. The very good Dolcetto first reveals its concentration in its garnet color; the nose is deep, broad and pleasantly rustic, with aromas of red and black fruit, undergrowth, spices and menthol; the soft, substantial palate leads into a long, fruity, faintly bitter finish. Another excellent wine is the Bric Quercia: it releases a forward fragrance of jam, leather, wood, vanilla and toasted coffee; the rich, forceful palate has a long, vigorous finish. The Roero Superiore displays scents of red currant, raspberry, green leaves and coffee custard; the palate has good body with extremely lively tannins and a rather short finish. The Arneis Vigna Canorei is below par: the nose is inexpressive, the palate medium-bodied and the finish over in a trice. The Favorita is well executed.

●	Barbaresco Cascina Bordino '96	TT	5
●	Barolo Vigneti in Cannubi '95	TT	6
●	Langhe Bric Quercia '97	TT	4
●	Dolcetto d'Alba Vigna Tavoleto '98	T	3
●	Roero Sup. Bric Paradiso '97	T	4
○	Roero Arneis Vigna Canorei '98		4
○	Langhe Favorita '98		3
●	Barolo Vigneti in Cannubi '93	YY	5
●	Roero Sup. Bric Paradiso '96	YY	4
●	Barbaresco Cascina Bordino '93	Y	5
●	Barbaresco Cascina Bordino '95	Y	5
●	Barolo Vigneti in Cannubi '94	Y	5

PRASCO (AL)

Verrina - Cascina Tornati

Via S. Rocco, 14
15010 Prasco (AL)
tel. 0144/375745

The Ovada zone has great potential for Dolcetto, but this is not always exploited in the cellar. As yet there are only a few estates that seem able to get the best out of the raw material and present interesting, well-made wines of consistent quality. Among these, one of the most prominent is Nicolò Verrina's Cascina Tornati, which produces about 50 thousand bottles from ten hectares under vine. The Dolcetto Oriali, deriving from 30-year-old vineyards, is vinified and aged in tanks; starting this year about 10% of dolcetto dal peduncolo rosso, previously vinified separately to obtain a sweet wine, will go into it. The Oriali, a lovely intense ruby in color, offers a dense, broad, round, meaty palate with lots of fruit and good length, its only flaw being a slightly sweetish attack; the rich bouquet displays ripe sour cherry, strawberry, raspberry, red currant and almond. The Dolcetto Semonina, similarly vinified and aged, is less demanding but still satisfying and comme il faut. Its color is a purplish ruby; the aromas resemble those of the Oriali, but are slightly less ample: cherry, red currant, raspberry, almond and pepper are to the fore. It is extremely enjoyable, fresh and varietal on the palate, with a pleasantly bitter finish. We liked the ruby-hued Barbera, with its vinous aromas in which violet, ripe cherry and plum emerge, and the fruity palate with a refreshing acidity. The crisp and carefree Cortese is also worthy of mention.

●	Dolcetto di Ovada Vigna Oriali '98	TT	3*
●	Barbera del M.to '98	T	2*
●	Dolcetto di Ovada Podere Semonina '98	T	3
○	Cortese dell'Alto M.to '98		2
●	Dolcetto di Ovada Vigna Oriali '97	YY	2

PRIOCCA (CN)

CASCINA VAL DEL PRETE
S.DA SANTUARIO, 2
12040 PRIOCCA (CN)
TEL. 0173/616534

Bartolomeo Roagna, his wife Carolina and their sons Luigi and Mario have owned the eight hectares of vineyard at the Cascina Val del Prete since 1977. From this year's range we were particularly impressed by the Barbera d'Alba Superiore Carolina, which spends a certain amount of time in wood. It introduces itself with a rather intense ruby-garnet color sporting a faintly orange rim; the bouquet, modern in style, offers notes of cherry, raspberry, violet, rosemary and vanilla, while the palate has a good, rich body; the development is not particularly powerful but is solid and even; vigorous, austere tannins lend grip to the lingering finish. This is a perfect wine to accompany rich, hefty meat courses. The Nebbiolo d'Alba Vigna di Lino '97 has a ruby hue verging on garnet with a slightly forward rim; the elegant nose reveals notes of red fruit and leather; the palate, while perhaps less concentrated than the '96's, is admirably balanced and restrained. The Arneis '98, an undemanding but enjoyable wine, shows a vivid straw-yellow color and aromas of very ripe fruit and white flowers on the nose; the palate is smooth and agreeable.

●	Barbera d'Alba Sup. Carolina '97	▼▼	4
●	Nebbiolo d'Alba Vigna di Lino '97	▼	4
○	Roero Arneis '98	▼	3
●	Barbera d'Alba Sup. Carolina '96	▽▽	4
●	Nebbiolo d'Alba Vigna di Lino '96	▽▽	4

PRIOCCA (CN)

HILBERG PASQUERO
VIA BRICCO GATTI, 16
12040 PRIOCCA (CN)
TEL. 0173/616197

The Pasquero property, like that of many farmers, has only a small proportion of its land under vine, the rest being devoted to orchards and vegetables. Michele, a qualified agronomist, manages, together with his wife Annette Hilberg and his mother Clementina, just three hectares of vineyard scattered around Priocca and Castellinaldo. This extreme fragmentation of the land and the attendant geological differences have enabled him to establish which soils have the greatest affinity with which Roero varieties, and then to make intelligent use of his terrain. Today, partly through necessity and partly through choice, he looks after one and a half hectares of barbera, one of brachetto and half a hectare of nebbiolo. Thus this is, in terms of wine, a tiny estate: it produces around 6,000 bottles, while the rest is still sold in bulk. The estate strategy of focusing on quality by means of rigorous pruning is backed up by Michele's decision to follow the (EEC-approved) dictates of organic farming. And now for the wines, which are a revelation, one of the greatest surprises of the year. The Barbera d'Alba Superiore '97 is in every respect one of the best we tasted for this edition of the Guide, and, at the debut appearance here of this estate, wins Three Glasses with flying colors. Great density is already apparent in the color; the bouquet (red currant, cherry, cinnamon and cocoa) is extraordinary in its intensity and concentration, and the characteristics of the palate can be summed up in one word: stunning. It belongs to the category of those wonderful Barberas you can almost chew as well as drink, that the '97 vintage was so generous with. The Nebbiolo and the Vareij, an aromatic blend of barbera and brachetto, are only a little less rich and dense. The delightful basic Barbera is a bargain.

●	Barbera d'Alba Sup. '97	▼▼▼	4
●	Nebbiolo d'Alba '97	▼▼	4
●	Vareij '98	▼▼	3*
●	Barbera d'Alba '97	▼	4

ROCCAGRIMALDA (AL)

CASCINA LA MADDALENA
LOC. PIANI DEL PADRONE, 258
15078 ROCCAGRIMALDA (AL)
TEL. 0143/876074

With its debut in the Guide, La Maddalena introduces readers to Roccagrimalda, the heart of Dolcetto d'Ovada country. It only took a few years for Cristina Bozzano and Anna Poggio to give expression to the huge potential of the zone and this variety, which in few other parts of Piedmont enjoys such wonderful exposure and long-established tradition. Giovanni Bailo, a rising oenologist who has had valuable experience in Tuscany as well as around Alessandria, has given a distinctive mark of quality to the wines, working with grapes from old vineyards. We'll begin with the amazing Bricco Maddalena '97, a monovarietal barbera which for some reason is presented as a Monferrato Rosso. It shows a wonderful dark-ruby color, vivid and brilliant; the generous, rich and intense bouquet with notes of geranium and ripe red fruit gradually develops aromas of cherry preserves, stewed plums, cocoa, pepper and spice, while the palate is imposing, rich and authentic. An exemplary balance between alcohol and acidity, combined with powerful structure, seems to promise longevity accompanied by improvement. The Bricco del Bagatto, a Dolcetto that has spent time in new wood, has a dense ruby color with youthful purplish highlights; the nose is broad and vinous, offering aromas of red fruit, cherries steeped in alcohol and sweet pastry; it is a powerful wine with lots of body and grip and a soft, lingering palate. It is perhaps the best interpretation of the Ovada appellation we tasted this year. The Barbera Monferrato La Maddalena '97 is also rewarding, with its frank aromas of red fruit and jam and some herbaceous notes; the palate is refreshing and long. The basic Dolcetto also gets One full Glass; it has a highly satisfying nose and is dry and full-flavored in the mouth, showing good tannins and a subtle bitter finish.

● Dolcetto di Ovada Bricco del Bagatto '98	🍷🍷	4
● Monferrato Rosso Bricco Maddalena '97	🍷🍷	5
● Barbera del M.to La Maddalena '97	🍷	3
● Dolcetto di Ovada '98	🍷	3

ROCCHETTA TANARO (AT)

BRAIDA
VIA ROMA, 94
14030 ROCCHETTA TANARO (AT)
TEL. 0141/644113

The Asti area is one of the most highly prized for the cultivation of the barbera grape. Giacomo Bologna, known as Braida, was fully aware of this, and used to compare the potential of these hills and this variety with the celebrated terroir of Burgundy where pinot noir reigns supreme. It is hard to say if Barbera d'Asti is really comparable; on the other hand we can confidently state that at the Bolognas' winery, where Giovanni paved the way with courage and foresight, his wife and children are following in his footsteps and continuing to reap success. The family has achieved some outstanding results with this legendary wine; with rigorously selected grapes from vines of varying ages, three crus are produced: Ai Suma, the only one to undergo malolactic fermentation in barriques, Bricco dell'Uccellone and Bricco della Bigotta. All are of high quality, but the Ai Suma selection seemed the best. The intense ruby-red in the glass heralds captivating aromas of sweet spice and ripe fruit; the concentrated and even palate shows balance and great length. The Bricco dell'Uccellone does almost as well, offering an intense and lingering bouquet of fruit with toasty notes, mirrored on the dry, even and elegant palate. The Bricco della Bigotta offers fragrant and graceful aromas followed by a palate which is fresh and delicate rather than rounded and powerful. The lightly sparkling La Monella has an imperfect nose, while the Bacialé (barbera and pinot nero) is good but not very complex. The most interesting wine from the Serra dei Fiori property is, once again, the white blend Il Fiore. The Brachetto d'Acqui, the Grignolino and the Moscato d'Asti are all worthy of mention.

● Barbera d'Asti Ai Suma '97	🍷🍷	6
● Barbera d'Asti Bricco dell'Uccellone '96	🍷🍷	6
● Barbera d'Asti Bricco della Bigotta '96	🍷	6
● Barbera del M.to La Monella '98	🍷	3
● Dolcetto d'Alba Serra dei Fiori '98	🍷	3
○ Langhe Bianco Il Fiore '98	🍷	3
○ Langhe Chardonnay Asso di Fiori '98	🍷	5
● Monferrato Rosso Il Bacialé '98	🍷	4
● Barbera d'Asti Ai Suma '89	🍷🍷🍷 (empty)	6
● Bricco dell'Uccellone '91	🍷🍷🍷 (empty)	6
● Barbera d'Asti Ai Suma '95	🍷🍷 (empty)	6
● Barbera d'Asti Ai Suma '96	🍷🍷 (empty)	6

ROCCHETTA TANARO (AT)

HASTAE
P.ZZA ITALIA, 1/BIS
14030 ROCCHETTA TANARO (AT)
TEL. 0141/644113

Six Piedmontese producers, four from the Asti area and two from the Langhe, have joined forces to produce a great wine from barbera. This enterprise, begun in 1997, seems on the face of it to be a publicity stunt or a purely commercial venture. Instead, famous names in the world of wine like Chiarlo, Coppo, Bologna, Vietti, Antinori and Berta (a producer of grappa) felt the need to make a joint effort and relaunch the name of Barbera d'Asti in style. The profits from the sale of this lot of bottles will in fact be used to promote the image of a zone which until a few years ago was a backwater, but is now seething with activity, as a result, amongst other things, of investments on the part of many estates. This new enterprise, which has been the subject of heated discussion, will be a boost to the whole area. To move on to the wine, all the prerequisites for creating a great red, capable of holding its own with the best bottles anywhere, are there. To start with, the estates whose grapes go into the production of this Barbera are among the best in the land; next, the chosen oenologist is Riccardo Cotarella, who is, to say the least, distinguished. The result of the first bottling, an assemblage of Barberas produced individually by each of the estates, has turned out to be more than promising. The wine, named Quorum, has the attributes of a great red, with perfect harmony between nose and palate; it could perhaps do with a little more body to counterbalance the still slightly exuberant woody note. We eagerly await the new version, which is entirely vinified by Riccardo Cotarella.

● Barbera d'Asti Quorum '97	🍷🍷	6

RODELLO (CN)

MOSSIO F.LLI
VIA MONTÀ, 12
12050 RODELLO (CN)
TEL. 0173/617149

Traditionally the vineyards of Montelupo and Rodello are considered to have a special aptitude for the dolcetto grape, which as far as winegrowing is concerned is virtually a monoculture here. It was also traditional for the grapes to be sold to reliable wineries farther afield, and not to build cellars for vinification or bottling on the spot. However, new producers are emerging, although more gradually than in the territory of Barolo and Barbaresco: the Mossio brothers are a praiseworthy example and have earned a profile in the Guide. From 12 hectares of land, of which a large proportion has been planted in excellent sites in recent years, their winery makes only two wines. The basic Dolcetto has a deep ruby color, moderately intense and very clean aromas, and a fresh, captivating, undemanding palate. The more concentrated purplish-blue-tinged Dolcetto d'Alba Bricco Caramelli offers notes of ripe fruit on the nose and a delightfully mouth-filling palate, powerful enough to overshadow the characteristic dolcetto tannins. Quality has been their aim for many years, but with the '98 vintage we can confirm that the Mossios have in fact achieved excellence, chiefly due to restricted yields and greater skill in vinification. This is a very welcome debut in the Guide, and should be an encouragement to the whole area.

● Dolcetto d'Alba Bricco Caramelli '98	🍷🍷	3*
● Dolcetto d'Alba '98	🍷	3

RODELLO (CN)

VITICOLTORI ASSOCIATI DI RODELLO
VIA MONTÀ, 13
12050 RODELLO (CN)
TEL. 0173/617159 - 0173/617318

In 1976 five winegrowers decided to join forces in order to do their best for Piedmont's classic everyday wine, Dolcetto. Their property consists of about 12 hectares at an altitude of 400-500 meters. The grapes come from four separate crus, and the differences in the soils (tufa, clay) and in exposure (eastern, southern, western) are carefully considered, to allow each wine to preserve the characteristics of its terroir. Wood, whether large or small, is not allowed in: vinification takes place exclusively in stainless steel, so the resulting wines are all firmly linked to the qualities of the grape. Our favorite of the wines we tasted was the Dolcetto Vigna Deserto: the color is attractive and vivid, and the distinct aromas of cherry and hints of woodland are mirrored on the warm, dry palate of this delightfully drinkable red. The Vigna Buschin has a fresh bouquet and a dry, fruity palate of simple but coherent structure. The Vigna Campasso reveals characteristic vinous aromas and a warm, appropriately tannic palate with a light pleasant note of almond. The last of the selections is the Vigna San Lorenzo, which is elegant and well balanced in the mouth. The agreeable basic version offers classic vinous and fruity aromas followed by a simple but correct palate with rather prominent tannins. The Barbera did well too: ruby-red in color, it is redolent of ripe fruit, echoed on a warm palate which is slightly lacking in structure.

●	Dolcetto d'Alba Vigna Deserto '98	🍷🍷	3*
●	Barbera d'Alba '98	🍷	2
●	Dolcetto d'Alba '98	🍷	2
●	Dolcetto d'Alba Vigna Buschin '98	🍷	3
●	Dolcetto d'Alba Vigna Campasso '98	🍷	3
●	Dolcetto d'Alba Vigna S. Lorenzo '98	🍷	3

ROSIGNANO M.TO (AL)

VICARA
CASCINA MADONNA DELLE GRAZIE, 5
15030 ROSIGNANO M.TO (AL)
TEL. 0142/488054

This winery, founded in 1992 and now at its seventh vintage, is definitely on the rise, thanks in part to the arrival two years ago of the expert oenologist Mario Ronco. The 42 hectares under vine yield some 200 thousand bottles a year. The Rubello is again the top of the line, but this year it is flanked by the Cantico della Crosia. The first, a blend of 80% barbera, 15% cabernet and 5% nebbiolo, shows a good deep color and notes of cherry and coffee on the nose; the palate is generous, balanced and structured, evincing a well-gauged use of barriques, where the wine spends 12 months. The second is a selection of the best barbera grapes and has a very intense ruby hue, a nose somewhat overpowered by the wood of the barriques which it calls home for a year, and a warm and structured palate. The Barbera Superiore, aged in large casks, is a satisfying, fruity, rounded wine, enjoyably redolent of bitter cherry, while the Volpuva, a pleasant easy-drinking Barbera, is well executed. The intriguing Grignolino, of a lively cherry color, releases clean, intense aromas of white pepper, clove, rose and geranium, and is soft and fruity in the mouth. The appealing Nettare del Paradiso is sweet but not cloying and, although it has plenty of fizz, it offers a delicate bouquet with the varietal aromas of the moscato grape. A last mention goes to the attractive and quaffable Freisa.

●	Barbera del M.to Cantico della Crosia '97	🍷🍷	4
●	Monferrato Rubello '97	🍷🍷	4
●	Barbera del M.to Sup. '97	🍷	3
●	Barbera del M.to Volpuva '98	🍷	3
●	Grignolino del M.to Casalese '98	🍷	3
○	Nettare del Paradiso	🍷	3
●	Monferrato Freisa '98		3
●	Monferrato Rubello '96	🥂🥂	5
●	Barbera del M.to Cantico della Crosia '96	🥂	4
●	Barbera del M.to Sup. '96	🥂	3
○	Monferrato Bianco Airales '97	🥂	3

S. GIORGIO CANAVESE (TO)

ORSOLANI
VIA MICHELE CHIESA, 12
10090 S. GIORGIO CANAVESE (TO)
TEL. 0124/32386

The Orsolani family produces wonderfully rich wines from the erbaluce grape. This year the Erbaluce La Rustìa performed slightly below its usual standard, while the Brut Nature '94 and the Caluso Passito La Rustìa bear witness to the quality of one of the most important wineries of northern Piedmont. The Brut Nature, an elegant sparkling wine with a delicately forward tone, shows an intense straw color with a fine perlage; the inviting bouquet offers hints of apricots in syrup and white blossom with briny and smoky undertones; the exuberant effervescence on the palate does not detract from its evenness, to which the generous, soft body contributes; the dry, lingering finish echoes the bouquet. The Caluso Passito La Rustìa is the most interesting wine of its kind, steadily maintaining its distinctive qualities of breadth and crispness. The '94 version boasts a vivid, intense amber hue; the nose is well-defined and frank, with notes of tamarind, plum, dried fig and leather; the entry on the palate is sweet, but counterbalanced by perfect acidity, and walnut and dried fruit emerge on the very long finish. The Erbaluce di Caluso La Rustìa, of a decided straw color, has a rich bouquet of fermentation-derived aromas and fruity and floral tones; the palate is substantial and mouth-filling, with an acidic bite lending freshness and charm. The fruity Vignot S. Antonio, with a soft palate and a modulated finish, ends the list.

○	Brut Nature Cuvée '94	🍷🍷	4
○	Caluso Passito La Rustìa '94	🍷🍷	5
○	Caluso Bianco Vignot S. Antonio '97	🍷	4
○	Erbaluce di Caluso La Rustìa '98	🍷	3
○	Caluso Passito La Rustìa '93	🍸🍸	5
○	Brut Nature Cuvée '92	🍸	4

S. MARTINO ALFIERI (AT)

MARCHESI ALFIERI
CASTELLO ALFIERI
14010 S. MARTINO ALFIERI (AT)
TEL. 0141/976288

Marchesi Alfieri is one of the historic estates of Piedmont. It was here that in the first half of the 19th century Count Camillo Benso di Cavour, guided by the French oenologist Oudart, chose one of the estate's vineyard sites to introduce the cultivation of pinot nero. The San Germano sisters, the owners of the property, commemorate the event with one of their wines, the Monferrato Rosso San Germano, a rare example of a Piedmontese Pinot Nero that reflects the style of its Burgundian cousins. From its color, ruby with a marked orange rim, you might think the wine forward, but on the nose it immediately reveals notes of red berries followed by more complex aromas of leather and chocolate. The palate is perhaps a little too austere and wood-dominated. The two versions of Barbera d'Asti, the result of two completely different approaches, are extremely interesting. The fresher, more readily drinkable La Tota '97 is characterized by fruity aromas (cherry and blackberry) and a very inviting succulence, with a good structure not at all overpowered by the acidity. The estate's top selection, the Alfiera, is much more complex and important, and on a level with the best Barberas of Asti and the Langhe. The range is completed by an attractive Grignolino and two well-made Monferrato wines, a white and a red, which are excellent value for money. Since January 1999 the cellar has been in the hands of the oenologist Mario Olivero, renowned for his success with the wines of Col d'Orcia at Montalcino; he is assisted by the advice of the consultant Giancarlo Scaglione.

●	Barbera d'Asti Alfiera '96	🍷🍷	5
●	Barbera d'Asti La Tota '97	🍷🍷	4
●	Monferrato Rosso S. Germano '95	🍷	5
●	Barbera d'Asti Alfiera '93	🍸🍸	5
●	Barbera d'Asti La Tota '96	🍸🍸	4
●	Barbera d'Asti Alfiera '94	🍸	5

S. MARZANO OLIVETO (AT)

ALFIERO BOFFA
VIA LEISO, 50
14050 S. MARZANO OLIVETO (AT)
TEL. 0141/856115

The Alfiero Boffa estate is a historic feature of the Nizza area. For some years Rossano, oenologist and representative of the most recent generation of the family, has been at work here, and modernization is going full steam ahead. The pride of the estate is the Vigne Uniche line, a series of single-vineyard wines deriving from the best old vineyards. Barbera plays the leading role, appearing in no fewer than four versions. We'll start with the Barbera d'Asti Vigna Muntrivé '97, from a vineyard in San Marzano Oliveto planted in 1935: its garnet hue is elegant, concentrated and dense; the varietal nose displays notable cherry; the palate is well balanced, immediate, frank and very long. The equally intriguing Barbera d'Asti Vigna More '97, from a vineyard in Nizza Monferrato, also shows an intense garnet color; the bouquet of cherry and blackberry is enriched by an attractive spicy note; the palate is soft, round, very fruity, even and rather long. A half step below, the Barbera d'Asti Vigna Cua Longa '97, from a site in San Marzano, offers tobacco and green notes on the nose, but is not so dense-textured as the others. The Barbera d'Asti Collina della Vedova '96 is clearly the fruit of a lesser vintage: the color is not so rich, the oak is in evidence on the aromatic nose, and the palate is not so full-bodied and has a bitterish, slightly astringent finish. Our review ends with the Velo di Maya '96, a barbera-based table wine whose intense garnet color is followed by a rather faded bouquet with herbal notes that reappear on the somewhat harsh palate.

● Barbera d'Asti Vigna More '97	🍷🍷	4
● Barbera d'Asti Vigna Muntrivé '97	🍷🍷	4
● Barbera d'Asti Collina della Vedova '96	🍷	4
● Barbera d'Asti Vigna Cua Longa '97	🍷	4
● Monferrato Rosso Velo di Maya '96		5
● Barbera d'Asti Collina della Vedova '95	🍷🍷 (white)	4
● Barbera d'Asti Vigna More '96	🍷🍷 (white)	3
● Barbera d'Asti Vigna Cua Longa '96	🍷 (white)	3

S. MARZANO OLIVETO (AT)

CASCINA L'ARBIOLA
REG. SALINE, 56
14050 S. MARZANO OLIVETO (AT)
TEL. 0141/856194

The Cascina L'Arbiola, thanks to the passionate commitment and investments of the Terzano family, has built up over recent years a wide range of wines, from the traditional local wines (Moscato and Barbera) to new creations based on imported white and red varieties, some of which have not yet been released. For the moment Barbera is center stage, with the Asti Superiore La Romilda '97 in the star role. It presents a medium-intense brilliant ruby color; the nose is at first closed and rather heady, but then slowly reveals good fruity aromas (red berries and blackberries); the palate is mouth-filling, round, balanced and very long. The other two Barberas have obviously been made for immediate pleasure but are less interesting, particularly since they are the fruit of the splendid '97 and '98 vintages. The Carlotta '97, pale in color, has a clean, fruity bouquet but is rather lean. The same goes for the Barbera del Monferrato L'Arbiolin '98, which seems very like a nouveau with its fruity fragrance (cherry and banana) and simple immediacy; it does better on the nose than on the palate, where it lacks sinew. The Monferrato Bianco Le Clelie '98 is on the whole a successful wine; the moderately intense straw color is followed by a pleasant floral bouquet with notes of tropical fruit and melon; the palate shows balance and medium body underpinned by appropriate acidity and succulence. The Moscato d'Asti Ferlingot '98 has more body than freshness.

● Barbera d'Asti Sup. La Romilda III '97	🍷🍷	4
● Barbera d'Asti La Carlotta '97	🍷	4
○ Monferrato Bianco Le Clelie III '98	🍷	4
○ Moscato d'Asti Ferlingot '98	🍷	3
● Barbera del M.to L'Arbiolin '98		3
● Barbera d'Asti Sup. La Romilda II '96	🍷🍷 (white)	4

CA' D'GAL

S.DA VECCHIA, 108
FRAZ. VALDIVILLA
12058 S. STEFANO BELBO (CN)
TEL. 0141/847103

In a zone that traditionally yields first-rate Moscato, the Boido family is no exception. Side by side with good wines like their Dolcetto and Chardonnay they have presented two lovely Moscatos from the '98 vintage: an elegant and fascinating Vigna Vecchia and a generous, energetic Vigneti Ca' d'Gal. The former, of a medium-intense straw color, shows a stylish and subtle nose that repays attention: hints of white-fleshed fruit and flowers mingle with highly individual notes of citrus fruit and nutmeg in an almost subdued but richly nuanced bouquet; the palate reveals good substance with a definite acidic bite that effectively counterbalances the sweet tone; the effervescence is restrained, and the graceful finish has a fruity tone. The Vigneti Ca' d'Gal, of a very light straw color, has a varietal nose which is more clearly defined and less demanding than the Vigna Vecchia's: it offers, without heaviness, scents of peach, lily of the valley, sage and fresh grapes; the palate is well delineated and very satisfying, with a delicate perlage and a corresponding finish that reveals a pronounced but not excessive sweet note. The Dolcetto '98 has a medium-intense ruby hue generously tinged with garnet; the nose offers aromas of blueberry, black currant, menthol and pepper; the palate does not reveal great structure but is admirably balanced and favors easy drinking. Lastly, the Chardonnay has an attractive palate and a nose slightly dominated by fermentation-derived aromas.

○	Moscato d'Asti Vigna Vecchia '98	🍷🍷	4
●	Dolcetto d'Alba '98	🍷	3
○	Moscato d'Asti Vigneti Ca' d'Gal '98	🍷	3
○	Langhe Chardonnay '97		3
●	Langhe Pian del Gäje '96	🍸	4

PIERO GATTI

LOC. MONCUCCO, 28
12058 S. STEFANO BELBO (CN)
TEL. 0141/840918

Again this year Piero decided to forgo the DOCG label so that he could harvest his grapes when he saw fit. By starting a little early he manages to gather the crop at the right stage of ripeness before any of the fragrance of the grape is sacrificed to excessive maturation. The Moscato has a green-tinged pale straw color and offers fresh, delicate notes of peach, pear, wildflowers and aromatic herbs on the nose; it shows the same freshness on the palate, together with a delicate attack and a balanced progression which is delightfully punctuated by a restrained effervescence. The finish is long, charming and modulated. We also liked the Brachetto, cherry-hued with a purple tinge; the bouquet is not over-fresh but shows finesse, with its notes of pear, peach and rose; the fresh and pleasantly fizzy palate has an underlying dry tone that characterizes the graceful, corresponding finish. The simple and rather vinous Freisa La Violetta has a slightly bubbly rustic palate with restrained acidity.

○	Piemonte Moscato '98	🍷🍷	3
●	Piemonte Brachetto '98	🍷	4
●	Langhe Freisa La Violetta '97		4

S. STEFANO BELBO (CN)

SERGIO GRIMALDI - CA' DU SINDIC
LOC. S. GRATO, 15
12058 S. STEFANO BELBO (CN)
TEL. 0141/840341

Of a total production of 40 thousand bottles, Grimaldi fills 30 thousand with Moscato. Oenological skill is revealed when, on tasting the wine, we discover the personality of this Moscato, which derives not only from the special aptitude of these hills for the variety but also, and this should not be underestimated, from the care and expertise lavished on it by this family. The '98 version is warm and intense, and shows an attractive rich straw color; the nose offers hints of white- and yellow-fleshed fruit, wildflowers and faint, pleasantly rustic hints of geranium on a delicately overripe bouquet; the palate is full and well-defined, sweet and strong in character but kept in line by the combined action of acidity and carbon dioxide; the balanced finish reveals notes of fruit and honey. The Piemonte Brachetto '98 is cherry-colored with a generous purplish cast; ripe fruit and dried rose petal characterize the nose; the sweet, medium-bodied palate is immediately balanced by the exuberant effervescence, and the straightforward, modulated finish offers mingled fruity and floral tones. The carefree Barbera Vivace shows a transparent ruby hue; the nose has medium finesse, offering simple, fresh aromas of fruit and almond, followed by an agreeable, direct and moderately fizzy palate with a graceful finish.

○	Moscato d'Asti Ca' du Sindic '98	🍷	3
●	Piemonte Brachetto Ca' du Sindic '98	🍷	3
●	Piemonte Barbera Vivace '98	🍷	2*

S. STEFANO BELBO (CN)

I VIGNAIOLI DI S. STEFANO
FRAZ. MARINI, 12
12058 S. STEFANO BELBO (CN)
TEL. 0141/840419

This time I Vignaioli di Santo Stefano have not presented their Moscato Passito, which is released only in the best years; nevertheless the Moscato d'Asti and the Asti Spumante '98 are excellent wines, among the best of their respective categories, and they have both won Two Glasses. The first, with a delicately overripe tone on the nose, has a deep straw, almost golden color; the rich, ample nose, of impeccable cleanness and finesse, releases scents of very ripe peach and apricot, grapefruit rind and white flowers. The palate is soft and rich, with a delicate effervescence effectively offsetting the sweetness, so that the progress is smooth and even, right through to the long, subtle finish. The Asti Spumante '98, of a light straw color, has a graceful bouquet of ripe white- and yellow-fleshed fruit laced with delightful hints of lemon. On the palate the wine performs at its best: its solid texture is immediately revealed, enhanced by sweetness, in its turn offset by the well-gauged, restrained effervescence; the finish is lingering, corresponding and deeply satisfying.

○	Asti '98	🍷🍷	4
○	Moscato d'Asti '98	🍷🍷	4
○	Piemonte Moscato Passito	🍷🍷 (white)	5

S. STEFANO BELBO (CN)

TENUTA IL FALCHETTO
VIA VALLE TINELLA, 16
FRAZ. CIOMBI
12058 S. STEFANO BELBO (CN)
TEL. 0141/840344

The vast and reliable range of wines presented by the Forno family this year boasts a few peak products which rise above One Glass; among these are the two versions of Barbera Superiore, the Bricco Paradiso and the Lurei. The first, of a medium-intense ruby-garnet hue, has aromas ranging from berries to menthol and coffee; the palate displays plenty of body and a certain acidity, which is toned down on the warm, lingering finish. The Lurei, of an almost transparent ruby color with garnet highlights, mingles soft notes of raspberry and cream with complex mineral hints of damp earth. In the mouth it is robust and balanced, revealing a light tannic vein and ending on a nicely expressed fruity and spicy finish. We particularly liked the Chardonnay Incompreso '97 with its intense straw color and aromas of candied orange peel, vanilla and white-fleshed fruit; the ample, pleasantly overripe bouquet is followed by a generous, concentrated palate that maintains its freshness throughout; woody notes are somewhat prominent on the finish. The Dolcetto Soulì Braida '98 has excellent body and a bouquet of medium finesse. The Arneis, with fresh aromas of herbs, rather unripe peach and citrus peel, is smooth and soft in the mouth with an enjoyable succulence and a lingering finish. Both the Moscatos are good, but our preference was for the Tenuta del Fant with its full, fresh interpretation of the varietal aromas of the grape. Lastly, the Barbera Zio Rico is properly executed.

●	Barbera d'Asti Sup. Bricco Paradiso '97	🍷🍷	4
●	Barbera d'Asti Sup. Lurei '97	🍷🍷	3
○	Langhe Chardonnay Incompreso '97	🍷🍷	4
●	Dolcetto d'Alba Soulì Braida '98	🍷	3
○	Langhe Arneis '98	🍷	3
○	Moscato d'Asti Tenuta dei Ciombi '98	🍷	3
○	Moscato d'Asti Tenuta del Fant '98	🍷	3
●	Barbera d'Asti Vigna Zio Rico '98		3

SAREZZANO (AL)

MUTTI
LOC. S. RUFFINO, 49
15050 SAREZZANO (AL)
TEL. 0131/884119

The Mutti winery, under the guidance of Dino, has marketed good wines in bottle since the end of the '60s. The real turning-point, with a consequent profile in the Guide, came when Dino's son Andrea entered the business; with a degree in agricultural sciences behind him, he devoted his energies to the vineyards and to the study of the techniques adopted by the leading producers of the Langhe, the Collio zone and Burgundy. The ten hectares under vine yield up to 30 thousand bottles. The very successful Barbera S. Ruffino, presented as a Colli Tortonesi Rosso, spends at least a year in barriques and shows an intense dark color; ripe cherry, coffee and spice emerge on the nose, while the palate is warm and structured. The excellent Rosso Rivadestra, 90% cabernet sauvignon, also spends a year in barriques; it has an intense ruby hue and a bouquet of ripe red fruit, almond and spice; the palate is rich, warm and meaty. The barrique-aged Bianco Rivadestra, from 90% chardonnay and 10% sauvignon, displays an attractive golden straw color, while the nose offers clean, intense aromas in which the wood is noticeable but not excessive; the rich, full palate has a slightly bitter finish imparted by the wood. The interesting Castagnoli, a monovarietal timorasso of a lively golden straw color, releases scents of peach and honey with mineral notes, while the palate is fat and very well structured.

●	Colli Tortonesi Rosso Rivadestra '97	🍷🍷	4
●	Colli Tortonesi Rosso S. Ruffino '97	🍷🍷	4
○	Colli Tortonesi Bianco Castagnoli '97	🍷	3
○	Colli Tortonesi Bianco Rivadestra '97	🍷	3

SCURZOLENGO (AT)

CANTINE SANT'AGATA
REG. MEZZENA, 19
14030 SCURZOLENGO (AT)
TEL. 0141/203186

The Cavallero family has presented a delicious range of wines this year, starting with the two made from ruché grapes, the Rosso Genesi and the Ruché 'Na Vota. The former, from ruché and barbera left to dry in crates and barrique-aged, is making its first appearance, and the appearance is almost transparently ruby; notes of partially-dried red fruit and pepper appear on the nose; the rich, full-bodied palate shows vigorous tannins and a long moderately aromatic finish with a fruity barbera tone. The 'Na Vota, a characteristic, generous Ruché, is notable for the finesse and delicacy of its fragrance, featuring rose, pepper and almond harmoniously blended with fruit. On the palate it is soft, warm and relatively ample. Two Glasses each go to the Barbera Cavalé and the Superiore '97. The Cavalé, of a very intense ruby-garnet hue, is quite forward on the nose as a result of deliberate overripening: red fruit, menthol, cocoa and tobacco are all suggested. The development on the palate is rich and even, with very smooth tannins lending body to the exceptionally long finish. The Barbera Superiore has a color of medium intensity; the ripe bouquet includes hints of berries and spice, and is followed by a substantial, full-bodied palate. The Barbera Piatin, with a slightly acidic palate, shows a touch less finesse on the nose. To end the list, the Bianco Ciarea, the Grignolino Miravalle and the Rosso Monterovere all show attractive personality.

●	Barbera d'Asti Sup. '97	🍷🍷	3*
●	Barbera d'Asti Sup. Cavalé '97	🍷🍷	4
●	Monferrato Rosso Genesi '96	🍷🍷	5
●	Ruché di Castagnole M.to 'Na Vota '98	🍷🍷	4
●	Barbera d'Asti Sup. Piatin '97	🍷	4
●	Grignolino d'Asti Miravalle '98	🍷	3
○	Monferrato Bianco Ciarea '98	🍷	3
●	Monferrato Monterovere '97	🍷	4
●	Barbera d'Asti Sup. Cavalé '96	🍸🍸	4
●	Ruché di Castagnole M.to 'Na Vota '97	🍸🍸	4
●	Barbera d'Asti Sup. Piatin '96	🍸	3

SERRALUNGA D'ALBA (CN)

LUIGI BAUDANA
FRAZ. BAUDANA, 43
12050 SERRALUNGA D'ALBA (CN)
TEL. 0173/613354

Luigi Baudana and his wife Fiorina, after their period at the Enoteca Regionale in Grinzane, have decided to devote themselves full-time to the family estate, consisting of four and a half hectares in the Baudana vineyard. Two and a half of these are planted to dolcetto and the rest are divided between nebbiolo, barbera and chardonnay; this is because, until about ten years ago, for a small farm with few commercial outlets, dolcetto was more profitable than other varieties. The upshot is that Luigi's Dolcetto annually earns a place among the best of the area. The most successful wine this year is the deep ruby-hued Dolcetto Sorì Baudana; the nose offers fresh, elegant notes of steeped cherry and almond, followed by a warm, soft, dense palate with good tannins and a soft, dry finish. The Barbera Donatella '97, which shows the effects of a violent hail storm at an advanced stage of the growth cycle, has fairly good balance but is not as rich as the '96; it does earn One full Glass, however. The two good whites are the fresh, yeasty Langhe Chardonnay and the new Langhe Lorenso, a barriqued blend of sauvignon and chardonnay with aromas of tropical fruit and a strong toasty note, good structure and well-judged acidity.

●	Dolcetto d'Alba Sorì Baudana '98	🍷🍷	3*
●	Barbera d'Alba Donatella '97	🍷	4
●	Dolcetto d'Alba '98	🍷	3
○	Langhe Bianco Lorenso '98	🍷	4
○	Langhe Chardonnay '98	🍷	3
●	Barbera d'Alba Donatella '96	🍸🍸	4

SERRALUNGA D'ALBA (CN)

CAPPELLANO
VIA ALBA, 13
FRAZ. BRUNI
12050 SERRALUNGA D'ALBA (CN)
TEL. 0173/613103

Teobaldo Cappellano is firmly linked to tradition: his family has been in the area since the 17th century, and one of Cavour's estate managers referred to a winegrower named Cappellano in Serralunga. Nevertheless Teobaldo is not unwilling to try out the most recent innovations. When you listen to him expound his vinification philosophy, you often get the impression of a dual personality: the public persona is one of the most conservative producers of the Langhe, sworn enemy of the infamous barrique; but his more conflicted and perhaps more genuine nature is open to experimenting with new methods. All of this is expressed in his wines. He too has realized the important role of the vineyard, its exposure and the management of the various stages of the growth cycle. The great upsurge in quality here coincided with the release of the first bottles from the Gabutti cru. Every year this Serralunga estate comes up with at least one really interesting wine: from Barolo to Barbera, taking in Dolcetto, the enormous potential of the vineyard bought at the end of the '80s makes itself felt. The two Barolos presented this year both derive from the Otin Fiorin vineyard in the Gabutti cru, and in both of them, although the wood has not yet finished integrating, the excellence of the raw material is evident. Neither wine had any trouble winning Two Glasses, but our preference was for the Franco di Piede selection, made with grapes from vines not hit by the phylloxera plague. This Barolo, of an intense garnet color with an orange rim, is still evolving on the nose, which is currently rather dominated by alcohol and ripe fruit. The palate is splendid: it offers already well-defined structure and character, and an enticing succulence gives it length and restrains the exuberance of the wood. The other version has only slightly less body and finesse.

●	Barolo Otin Fiorin Collina Gabutti '95	▼▼	6
●	Barolo Otin Fiorin Collina Gabutti Franco '95	▼▼	6
●	Barolo Otin Fiorin Collina Gabutti '90	▽▽▽	6
●	Barolo Otin Fiorin Collina Gabutti '91	▽▽	6
●	Langhe Rosso Augusto '96	▽▽	4
●	Barbera d'Alba Gabutti '95	▽	4
●	Barbera d'Alba Gabutti '96	▽	4
●	Barolo Otin Fiorin Collina Gabutti '93	▽	6
●	Barolo Otin Fiorin Collina Gabutti '94	▽	5

SERRALUNGA D'ALBA (CN)

FONTANAFREDDA
VIA ALBA, 15
12050 SERRALUNGA D'ALBA (CN)
TEL. 0173/613161

At Fontanafredda, which belongs to the Monte dei Paschi bank, the new management headed by Gian Minetti is beginning to show results: as of the '99 vintage the cellar is in the capable hands of Daniele Drocco, who has already proved his ability at the Antinoris' Prunotto winery. This new oenologist has found things in a flourishing state of health, beginning with the two Metodo Classico sparkling wines. The Gatinera Brut Talento '90 shows a rich straw color and hints of apple, lemon rind and vanilla on the nose; the palate is ample, with plenty of fizz and an intense, lingering finish. The pale straw-colored Contessa Rosa Nuovo Millennio '93 (produced to celebrate the year 2000) offers a bouquet with some finesse and notes of white-fleshed fruit, citrus and yeast; the smooth, slightly dry palate has a moderately lingering finish. The good Barbera Papagena displays a garnet-tinged ruby hue with a faintly faded rim; the nose reveals cherry, blackberry, pepper, undergrowth and mint, while the palate has body and balance. Of the '95 Barolos, the Galarej releases aromas of jam, dried flowers and licorice; acidity is just perceptible on the palate, and the finish is reasonably firm. The La Villa, a little more forward and spicy on the nose, has a lean palate with slightly prominent tannins; the spicy notes of the bouquet are echoed on the finish. The Vigna La Rosa displays earthy nuances over hints of jam and leather, and a moderately intense palate with a pronounced tannic note and an austere finish. Lastly, the Barbaresco Coste Rubìn and the two Dolcettos, the Diano d'Alba Vigna La Lepre and the Dolcetto d'Alba Treiso, are unquestionably well made.

●	Barolo Vigna La Rosa '95	▼▼	6
○	Contessa Rosa Brut Nuovo Millennio '93	▼▼	4
○	Gatinera Brut Talento '90	▼▼	5
●	Barbaresco Coste Rubìn '96	▼	5
●	Barbera d'Alba Papagena '96	▼	4
●	Barolo Galarej '95	▼	6
●	Barolo La Villa '95	▼	6
●	Diano d'Alba Vigna La Lepre '98	▼	3
●	Dolcetto d'Alba Treiso '98	▼	3
●	Barolo La Villa '93	▽▽	6
●	Barolo Vigna Lazzarito Ris. '90	▽▽	6
●	Barbaresco Coste Rubìn '95	▽	5
●	Barolo Vigna La Delizia '93	▽	6

SERRALUNGA D'ALBA (CN)

GABUTTI - FRANCO BOASSO
B.TA GABUTTI, 3/A
12050 SERRALUNGA D'ALBA (CN)
TEL. 0173/613165

Here in the heart of Serralunga one is completely surrounded by vineyards. The Boassos own four hectares at Gabutti and Parafada: in the former, barbera and nebbiolo are grown and in the latter, dolcetto. Anyone expecting to find in this year's range the customary hardness of this corner of the Langhe will be amazed by the smooth tannins of the '98s. The Dolcetto d'Alba Vigna Parafada is superb: of a deep ruby hue with purple highlights, it releases intense, vinous aromas of raspberry jam mingling with delightful varietal notes of almond; the rich full body and the smoothness of the dense-knit impressive tannins add to the attractions of the palate. It's a small masterpiece, and at a very reasonable price. The Barbera d'Alba from the Gabutti vineyards is almost as good; the color is less lively and the still heady nose is redolent of cherry; marked acidity on the very warm palate suggests the need for more bottle age. The Barolo Gabutti '95, presented several times at blind tastings during the year, came very close to Two Glasses; its intense garnet color heralds a rich wine with a bouquet of cherry, licorice and quinine; dry, impressive but not entirely blended tannins emerge on the warm palate.

● Dolcetto d'Alba Vigna Parafada '98	🍷🍷 (black)	3*
● Barbera d'Alba '98	🍷 (black)	3
● Barolo Gabutti '95	🍷 (black)	5
● Barolo Gabutti '90	🍷🍷 (white)	5
● Barolo Gabutti '93	🍷🍷 (white)	5

SERRALUNGA D'ALBA (CN)

ETTORE GERMANO
B.TA CERRETTA, 1
12050 SERRALUNGA D'ALBA (CN)
TEL. 0173/613528 - 0173/613112

Many changes have taken place at the Germanos', the first being the definitive transfer of ownership from Ettore to his son Sergio, who as sole proprietor can finally concentrate on production without bureaucratic irritation. Next, work has at last been completed on the renovation and extension of the cellar, which now includes a separate barrel-room for barriques and tonneaux destined for the wines of a more modern style. Lastly, to our delight, some of Sergio's vines were spared by the hailstorms, as can be seen above all in the wonderful Barbera Vigna della Madre '97, which missed Three Glasses by a hair's breadth. Its deep color precedes a not yet very intense nose that nevertheless offers finesse and plenty of fruit with a pleasing touch of wood; the palate is rich, soft and powerful but not overbearing, and leads to an elegant, lingering finish. Of the two '95 Barolos, 6,000 bottles altogether, we preferred the Cerretta, intense and stylish on a nose that is modern but not to excess, with its notes of spice and licorice; the powerful, dense, long palate has remarkable body, although it needs a little more time to mellow. The Prapò, aged in large casks, is more austere in tone, with hints of quinine mingling with red fruit in the bouquet; in the mouth it is somewhat harsh and severe. There are two '98 Dolcettos: the Pra di Pò is very dark and dense in color, and still closed and coarse on the palate, but with its richness and length it should be lovely in a couple of years' time. The Lorenzino, with greater finesse and less density, is pleasant on the palate. Lastly, the Balàu '97 has an intense, complex bouquet of red fruit and spice; the rich palate reveals the characteristic varietal notes; this is a wine that should improve greatly.

● Barbera d'Alba Vigna della Madre '97	🍷🍷 (black)	4
● Barolo Cerretta '95	🍷🍷 (black)	6
● Barolo Prapò '95	🍷🍷 (black)	5
● Dolcetto d'Alba Vigneto Pra di Pò '98	🍷🍷 (black)	3*
● Langhe Rosso Balàu '97	🍷🍷 (black)	4
● Dolcetto d'Alba Vigneto Lorenzino '98	🍷 (black)	3
○ Langhe Chardonnay '98	🍷 (black)	3
● Barolo '93	🍷🍷 (white)	5
● Barolo Cerretta '93	🍷🍷 (white)	6
● Barolo Cerretta '94	🍷🍷 (white)	5
● Dolcetto d'Alba Vigneto Pra di Pò '97	🍷🍷 (white)	3

Luigi Pira

Via XX Settembre, 9
12050 Serralunga d'Alba (CN)
tel. 0173/613106

Under the brilliant management of Giampaolo Pira this estate now produces almost 40 thousand bottles from its seven hectares under vine, all situated in the most highly prized crus of Serralunga. Until a few years ago the sale of wine in bulk represented the main source of income; only recently did the 27-year-old Giampaolo, with the backing of his father and his brother Romolo, decide to make a bid for quality by reducing yields in the vineyard and properly equipping the cellar. In keeping with the advice of Beppe Caviola, he does not mean to do away with the vinification techniques of his predecessors but simply to update them, so as to produce wines that lose none of their salient characteristics but are softer from the start. At present the 6,000 bottles of Margheria '95 and the 8,000 of Marenca '95 have undergone much shorter macerations followed by maturation in large oak barrels; only about 10% is aged in new barriques. Unfortunately these two wines show dry, astringent tannins on the finish, demonstrating how improbable it is, in a vintage hit by late hailstorms, to produce really outstanding bottles. The Margheria displays attractive personality, although it is not over-elegant on the nose; the Marenca has greater finesse of bouquet, with distinct balsamic notes, and more mouth-filling body, which masks the tannins by softening their harshness to a certain extent. The Dolcetto is powerful, very long and in need of more time, which is business as usual at Serralunga. Starting with the '97 vintage, these two crus will be joined by a few bottles from the Vigna Rionda, aged in new French oak tonneaux.

● Barolo Vigna Marenca '95	🍷🍷	6
● Barolo Vigna Margheria '95	🍷	6
● Dolcetto d'Alba '98	🍷	3

Vigna Rionda - Massolino

P.zza Cappellano, 8
12050 Serralunga d'Alba (CN)
tel. 0173/613138

When young Franco, a skilled oenologist and sensitive wine-taster, made his appearance in the cellar, the level of quality here was given a further boost, as he worked with tact and good sense alongside his father Giovanni and his uncle Renato. For the first time the Barbera Vigneto Margheria made a really favorable impression at our tastings, turning out indeed to be an amazing wine. Of a dense dark ruby hue with a purplish cast, it offers a still closed bouquet of quinine, ink and blackberry jam with spicy, smoky notes of new oak; in the mouth it is rich, dense and succulent, the tannins are smooth and the finish very long. The Barolo Margheria '95 also performed extremely well; aromas of wild strawberry, chocolate and sweet vanilla precede a soft, round palate of remarkable elegance and finesse. The Parafada expresses the Serralunga terroir with its hints of ripe fruit, tobacco, earth and fennel seed; the explosive palate has impressive tannins and the long finish is remarkably warm. We were not quite so impressed by the Barolo '95, which is pleasantly fruity but reveals very dry tannins, or the Vigna Rionda Riserva '93, which has been impoverished by too much maturation. The hard and characterful Dolcetto '97 and the lush Moscato '98, refreshing and never cloying, are both good.

● Barbera d'Alba Margheria '97	🍷🍷	4
● Barolo Parafada '95	🍷🍷	6
● Barolo Margheria '95	🍷🍷	6
● Barolo '95	🍷	5
● Barolo Vigna Rionda Ris. '93	🍷	5
● Dolcetto d'Alba Barilot '97	🍷	3
○ Moscato d'Asti '98	🍷	3
● Barolo Parafada Ris. '90	ΥΥΥ	6
● Barolo Vigna Rionda Ris. '90	ΥΥΥ	6
● Barolo Parafada '90	ΥΥ	6
● Barolo Vigna Parafada '93	ΥΥ	6
● Barolo Vigna Rionda '93	ΥΥ	6
● Barolo Vigneto Margheria '90	ΥΥ	6
● Barolo Vigneto Margheria Ris. '90	ΥΥ	6

SERRALUNGA DI CREA (CN)

TENUTA LA TENAGLIA
S.DA SANTUARIO DI CREA, 6
15020 SERRALUNGA DI CREA (AL)
TEL. 0142/940252 - 0142/940546

La Tenaglia is undoubtedly one of the finest winegrowing estates of the area, thanks to the well-sited vineyards, the cellar and the energy and passion which Delfina Quattrocolo dedicates to her wines. Erica Nobbio, Delfina's daughter, also makes good use of the expert assistance of Curtaz and Pagli. The oaked Chardonnay Oltre '97 shows a lovely rich gold color, and, on the nose, finesse and intensity with its notes of citrus and hazelnut enhanced by wood in the process of assimilation; the palate is warm, fat, soft and very succulent. The Barbera Emozioni is as good as the '96; the intense ruby hue precedes aromas of red fruit and jam; the palate is fresh but rather tannic, and the moderatley long finish reveals a bitter note. The Paradiso '97, from syrah, has an amazing almost black ruby color; the intense and vegetal bouquet is followed by a warm, powerful palate with excellent structure and length but, as yet, less than perfect balance. We had another taste of the Barbera Giorgio Tenaglia '97 after it had had another year's maturation and it shows what La Tenaglia can do with the barbera grape; it displays a classic ruby color and a fresh, medium-bodied and succulent palate. The Grignolino '98, of a wonderful, vivid light red color, has a peppery fragrance and a rich, warm, harmonious palate. The Barbera Bricco Crea '98, aged in stainless steel, is spicy, vinous, long and, as usual, enjoyable. The basic Chardonnay, varietal and redolent of banana, is easy to drink.

●	Barbera d'Asti Emozioni '97	🍷🍷	6
●	Paradiso '97	🍷🍷	5
○	Piemonte Chardonnay Oltre '97	🍷🍷	6
●	Barbera d'Asti Bricco Crea '98	🍷	3
●	Grignolino del M.to Casalese '98	🍷	3
○	Piemonte Chardonnay '98	🍷	4
●	Barbera d'Asti Emozioni '96	♀♀	5
●	Paradiso '96	♀♀	5
●	Barbera d'Asti Giorgio Tenaglia '97	♀	4

SPIGNO M.TO (AL)

CASCINA BERTOLOTTO
VIA PIETRO PORRO, 70
15018 SPIGNO M.TO (AL)
TEL. 0144/91223 - 0144/91551

Cascina Bertolotto, at Spigno between upper Monferrato, the Langhe and the Ligurian Appennines, has 15 hectares of vineyard whose microclimate is felicitously influenced by the altitude and by beneficial sea breezes that blow away harmful mildews. The La Muïëtte, the estate's top Dolcetto, is highly individual in character: the grapes, in fact, are left for a few days in wooden crates before fermentation, which takes place in a traditional vat. The '97 vintage is unfortunately not a match for its predecessors, especially the excellent '95. It has a pale ruby color and a bouquet of almond, bitter cherry, red currant and balsamic nuances deriving from overripeness; the medium-bodied palate is fruity and lingering. The Dolcetto La Cresta maintains its usual standard from its attractive ruby-violet hue through to its structured, fruity and long palate. The Barbera I Cheini, whose grapes, picked at the beginning of November, come from a 60-year-old vineyard, earns One Glass: both nose and palate reveal the marked overripeness of the fruit. The unconventional La Tia, from brachetto grapes, and the appealing Cortese Il Barigi are worthy of mention. The Vin Bianc is an interesting wine that should be very rewarding for the estate: it is produced only in the best years from late-harvested moscato grapes that are left to dry on racks for two weeks; old gold in color with amber highlights, it offers a rich, warm and sweet but never cloying palate.

●	Barbera del M.to I Cheini '97	🍷	4
○	Cortese dell'Alto M.to Il Barigi '97	🍷	3
●	Dolcetto d'Acqui La Cresta '98	🍷	3
●	Dolcetto d'Acqui La Muïëtte '97	🍷	4
●	La Tia Brachetto Secco '97	🍷	4
○	Vin Bianc '95	🍷	4
●	Dolcetto d'Acqui La Muïëtte '96	♀♀	4

STREVI (AL)

BANFI VINI
VIA VITTORIO VENETO, 22
15019 STREVI (AL)
TEL. 0144/363485

Banfi is known as the biggest estate of Montalcino, but it also has a significant property in Piedmont ("our second self", as it is described in the estate's brochure), with a particularly interesting location, i. e. away from the limelight of the Langhe. The choice was hardly a matter of chance, since it comprises the three DOCGs of the province of Alessandria: Brachetto d'Acqui, Moscato d'Asti and Gavi. Here even the sophisticated customer can be certain of finding what he seeks without being bankrupted by exorbitant prices. A good example is the Banfi Brut '95, with its golden color and fine perlage. It has an ample bouquet of honey, crusty bread, dried fruit and vanilla, while the palate is mellow, harmonious and admirably lingering. The Gavi Vigna Regale '97 (from the estate at Novi Ligure) aims at finesse and harmony, starting with the aromas of ripe fruit, pear, sweet citrus and vanilla. The Brachetto Spumante '98 shows what this variety is capable of when vinified with skill: it displays finesse, a fragrance of roses and a restrained sweetness lent elegance by a balanced effervescence. The Acqui Brachetto Vigneto La Rosa, fresh, mellow and sweet but not cloying, is among the best of its category. The intensely ruby-red Dolcetto d'Acqui Ardì has an attractive, fruity nose following through well on the palate, which is supported by well-judged tannins and good length. The Argusto was masked by prominent wood at our tastings and gets just One Glass, unlike the '96. The Gavi Principessa Gavia shows good varietal character and fresh citrus notes.

○	Gavi Vigna Regale '97	two black glasses	4
○	Talento Banfi Brut Metodo Classico '95	two black glasses	4
●	Acqui Brachetto d'Acqui Vigneto La Rosa '98	one black glass	4
○	Asti '98	one black glass	3
●	Brachetto d'Acqui Spumante '98	one black glass	4
●	Dolcetto d'Acqui Ardì '98	one black glass	3
●	Dolcetto d'Acqui Argusto '97	one black glass	4
○	Gavi Principessa Gavia '98		3
●	Dolcetto d'Acqui Argusto '96	two white glasses	4

STREVI (AL)

MARENCO
P.ZZA VITTORIO EMANUELE, 10
15019 STREVI (AL)
TEL. 0144/363133

This modern winery at Strevi has again presented a reliable range, but without the high points we had hoped for. Their 60 hectares under vine currently yield 300 thousand bottles, mainly of Moscato and Brachetto. The consultant agronomist is Federico Curtaz, and the oenologist Donato Lanati. Sweet wines are the estate's forte, particularly the enjoyable, well-made Moscato Scrapona; it shows a lovely straw yellow color and a bouquet of peach and flowers; the sweet palate has good length and a fine effervescence. The Brachetto Il Pineto, in the same style but not quite at the same level, rather reluctantly releases its characteristic fragrance of roses; in the mouth it is balanced and lingering. The Dolcetto Marchesa displays a moderately intense purplish ruby hue and marked aromas of almond and red currant; the good fruity palate leads to a slightly dry finish. The Chardonnay Galet, of a medium-intense straw color, offers concentrated scents of banana and other tropical fruit; the palate is soft and simple and rather dominated by the wood. The Carialoso, obtained from a rare native variety called carica l'asino, has a balanced palate and unusual vegetal aromas. The slightly bubbly Cortese Valtignosa is well executed, crisp and quaffable. Lastly, the simple, pleasant Barbera Bassina is also worthy of mention.

●	Brachetto d'Acqui Il Pineto '98	one black glass	4
○	Cortese dell'Alto M.to Valtignosa '98	one black glass	3
●	Dolcetto d'Acqui Marchesa '98	one black glass	3
○	Moscato d'Asti Scrapona '98	one black glass	3
○	Piemonte Chardonnay Galet '98	one black glass	3
●	Barbera d'Asti Bassina '97		3
○	Carialoso '98		3
●	Barbera d'Asti Ciresa '96	one white glass	3

TASSAROLO (AL)

CASTELLO DI TASSAROLO
CASCINA ALBORINA
15060 TASSAROLO (AL)
TEL. 0143/342248

Tassarolo, which was described in 1656 in one of the Emperor Ferdinand III's documents as "a strong castle full of good wine, grain, meat and cheese of every kind", has been linked with the name of the Spinola family since 1367. The Tassarolo branch was powerful enough to be granted the privilege of coining money, which they continued to do until the 17th century, and they played a not indifferent part in international history. Feudal holdings are a thing of the past and the large landed estate was to a great extent parceled out in the 19th century, but the Cascina Alborina continues to do honor to family tradition with the help of the oenologist Agostino Berruti. There are 18 hectares under vine planted to barbera, cortese and some rather untraditional foreign varieties. The Rosso Castello di Tassarolo '96 is a blend of cabernet sauvignon (80%) and barbera which matures for a year in barriques and a year in the bottle. Of a vivid ruby color with a garnet tinge, it offers an intense nose of moderate finesse, with aromas of sweet wood shading into stewed fruit, fur and spice. Notes of grass and coffee grounds emerge distinctly on the medium-bodied, fresh and astringent palate. It promises great things for the future. The basic Gavi Tassarolo S '98 offers an intense, refined bouquet of toasted almond with hints of banana and citronella, and a crisp and acidulous but not very long palate. The Gavi Castello di Tassarolo '98, partially matured in French and American barriques, reveals vanilla and citrus fruit on the nose with tangerine peel to the fore. It has a marked freshness and an enjoyable palate, but the structure is too lean for it really to shine. The cuvée Ambrogio Spinola, semillon and sauvignon blanc, will be presented next year.

●	Rosso Castello di Tassarolo '96	▼▼	4
○	Gavi Castello di Tassarolo '98	▼	4
○	Gavi Tassarolo S '98		3
●	Rosso Castello di Tassarolo '95	▽	4
○	Gavi Castello di Tassarolo '97	▽	4
○	Gavi Vigneto Alborina '96	▽	4

TORINO

FRANCO M. MARTINETTI
VIA S. FRANCESCO DA PAOLA, 18
10123 TORINO
TEL. 011/8395937

The greatest asset of such wines as the Sul Bric and the Barbera Montruc is probably their clearly defined linearity. This should not be confused with simplicity. They are wines of great breadth and complexity, which still manage to be essentially but sumptuously consistent. The Barbera Montruc, for example, is everything that a Barbera can be, nothing less and nothing else. It has an intense ruby-garnet color and "luminous" aromas of red currant, cherry, pepper and mint shot through with a light, intriguing mineral note that makes the bouquet wonderfully expressive. On the palate the ample body is admirably kept in line by crisp sinew, and tannins lend volume to the long, fruity and spicy finish. The Sul Bric, from barbera and cabernet, has a dense almost garnet hue and a harmonious bouquet of black fruit, leather and damp earth; the palate is generous and juicy, with a solid but not overbearing structure followed by a very long finish that echoes the bouquet. The extremely attractive Gavi Minaia displays a deep straw color and aromas of ripe apricot, citrus peel, eucalyptus and pistachio; the palate immediately reveals substance and freshness in subtle and elegant equilibrium. The Barbera Bric dei Banditi has a firm rim on a ruby ground with garnet highlights; the fruity bouquet releases balsamic and spicy notes, and the palate, balanced and reasonably full-bodied, leads into a pleasantly dry, fruity finish.

●	Barbera d'Asti Sup. Montruc '97	▼▼▼	5
●	Barbera d'Asti Bric dei Banditi '98	▼▼	4
○	Gavi Minaia '97	▼▼	5
●	Monferrato Rosso Sul Bric '97	▼▼	6
●	Barbera d'Asti Sup. Montruc '96	▽▽▽	5
●	Sul Bric '94	▽▽▽	5
●	Sul Bric '95	▽▽▽	5
●	Barbera d'Asti Sup. Montruc '93	▽▽	5
●	Barbera d'Asti Sup. Montruc '95	▽▽	5
○	Gavi Minaia '96	▽▽	4
●	Monferrato Rosso Sul Bric '96	▽▽	5
●	Sul Bric '93	▽▽	5

TREISO (CN)

Orlando Abrigo
Fraz. Cappelletto, 5
12050 Treiso (CN)
tel. 0173/630232

The Montarsino is at the moment the only Barbaresco cru released by the Abrigo family; their other vineyard, the Rongallo, was too old and has been completely replanted: it will come into production again in 2001. Montarsino is a 27-year-old vineyard on a steep slope at Treiso, bordering Alba, which was bought by the Abrigos in 1995. The Barbaresco it yields, 40% barrique-aged, has a ruby-garnet color with a very firm rim; the bouquet is admirably ample and faintly dominated by the wood, and releases notes of jam, cocoa, hay and sweet spice; the palate is meaty and just a bit acidic at mid palate, but firm and even. The lingering licorice finish is nicely underpinned by pronounced but noble tannins. The Rosso Livraie, a monovarietal merlot making its debut, is of an opaque garnet hue with a very narrow purplish rim; the immediately varietal nose offers well-defined notes of tobacco leaf, leather and damp earth on a soft background of strawberry, black currant and custard; the generous and concentrated palate reveals a vigorous structure that lends punch to the long, corresponding finish. The golden Chardonnay Rocca del Borneto offers an intriguing bouquet of ripe apple and apricot, vanilla and white flowers; the palate shows a full body, crisp sinew and a finish on which the notes of caramel imparted by the new wood just manage to have the upper hand. The Dolcetto Vigna dell'Erto displays moderate finesse on the nose and a pleasantly rustic palate, highly satisfying in texture. Lastly, the properly executed Freisa is a simple wine with a mouth-cleansing palate.

●	Barbaresco Vigna Montarsino '96	🍷🍷	5
○	Langhe Chardonnay Rocca del Borneto '96	🍷🍷	4
●	Langhe Rosso Livraie '96	🍷🍷	4
●	Dolcetto d'Alba Vigna dell'Erto '98	🍷	3
●	Langhe Freisa '98		3
●	Barbaresco '95	YY	5
●	Barbaresco Vigna Pajoré '94	YY	5
●	Barbera d'Alba Vigna Roreto '96	Y	3

TREISO (CN)

Ca' del Baio
Via Ferrere, 33
12050 Treiso (CN)
tel. 0173/638219

The two Barbarescos produced by the Grasso family are from the Asili cru and the '95 versions were responsible for the estate's debut in the Guide last year. This year is the turn of the '96s, and they proved even better at our tastings. The Asili '96, aged in traditional barrels, was outstanding and won Two overflowing Glasses. The intense ruby-garnet color with a very narrow rim prefigures the wine's concentration, while the articulated, complex nose is notable for finesse; aromas of raspberry and violet merge beautifully with notes of earth and pepper and a faint ground bass of caramel. The palate is immediately rich, ample and solid, with no harshness of any sort, and the very long licorice finish is lent depth by a profusion of noble tannins. The Asili Barrique is very nearly on the same level: a faintly orange rim tops a ruby-garnet base; aromas of berry jam, rosemary, menthol and tar precede the concentrated, broad and even palate, which boasts a very long, corresponding finish with nuances of cocoa and fruit preserves. The rewarding Chardonnay '98, of a rich straw color, has a bouquet characterized by barrique-derived scents together with notes of white flowers, banana and apple and undertones of sweet pastry. The palate is mouth-filling and structured and the finish is slightly overpowered by wood. Our review ends with the properly made and pleasant Nebbiolo and Moscato.

●	Barbaresco Asili '96	🍷🍷	5
●	Barbaresco Asili Barrique '96	🍷🍷	5
○	Langhe Chardonnay '98	🍷	4
●	Langhe Nebbiolo '98		4
○	Moscato d'Asti '98		3
●	Barbaresco Asili '95	YY	4
●	Barbaresco Asili Barrique '95	YY	5

TREISO (CN)

FIORENZO NADA
LOC. ROMBONE
12050 TREISO (CN)
TEL. 0173/638254

Bruno Nada's wines have always been so good that restaurateurs and wine merchants have for years been clamoring to have their meagre consignments increased. Bruno, well aware that a good vineyard is the first prerequisite for a great wine, has calmly been expanding his estate, buying up plots of land little by little so that he now produces about 30 thousand bottles annually. But the output could not be increased without extending the cellar, which with its new premises for vinification and maturation is even more attractive than before, not to mention more functional. Having set everything in order, Bruno has now come up with a Seifile '96 that combines power, elegance and fruit and wins Three Glasses hands down. This blend of nebbiolo and barbera has frequently been excellent, but with this wonderful vintage it reaches the summit: it is massive, but with finesse, revealing ample, fruity and wide-ranging aromas lightly enhanced by the oak. The palate is mouth-filling without excessive lushness, full of fruit and perfectly balanced, with a well-defined and very long finish. The Barbaresco '96, whose palate is a model of power and opulence, just misses Three Glasses; the nose is clearly in need of further evolution, being rather closed although impeccably clean. The Dolcetto '98 is very good too: it's not particularly fruity or excessively crisp and vinous, but it's well made, stylish, not too powerful and very easy to drink.

● Langhe Rosso Seifile '96	🍷🍷🍷	6
● Barbaresco '96	🍷🍷	6
● Dolcetto d'Alba '98	🍷	4
● Langhe Rosso Seifile '95	YYY	5
● Seifile '93	YYY	6
● Barbaresco '90	YY	6
● Barbaresco '91	YY	6
● Barbaresco '92	YY	6
● Barbaresco '93	YY	6
● Barbaresco '94	YY	6
● Barbaresco '95	YY	6
● Dolcetto d'Alba '97	YY	3
● Seifile '92	YY	6
● Seifile '94	YY	5

TREISO (CN)

PELISSERO
VIA FERRERE, 19
12050 TREISO (CN)
TEL. 0173/638136 - 0173/638430

Giorgio Pelissero's wines are amassing Glasses right and left, thanks to the balanced and modern style he succeeds in imparting to them. The '96 Barbaresco Vanotu, while not like the glorious '95, is still a superb wine. Its ruby-garnet hue with a brick-red rim is followed by a broad, captivating bouquet in which the new-wood-derived tones need further integration; aromas of vanilla, coffee, cherry jam and cocoa are in evidence. The palate is rich and soft, with impressive tannins and a long, intense finish on a licorice note. The basic Barbaresco, a little less intense in color, offers scents of berries and pepper with toasty notes on a marked balsamic background; the palate, full-bodied and broad-textured, is articulated by invigorating tannins that lend punch to the cocoa-toned finish. The excellent Dolcetto Augenta has a dense garnet color and a bouquet of great personality that releases notes of black fruit, mint, licorice and coffee; the rich, close-knit palate develops and expands, underpinned by powerful, noble tannins all the way through to the extremely long licorice-toned finish. The Dolcetto Munfrina is more straightforward, with a fruity and spicy nose and a robust palate. The substantial Barbera I Piani shows sweet tones on the nose and ample softness on the palate. A very well-balanced Nebbiolo and a properly made Favorita end the list.

● Barbaresco '96	🍷🍷	6
● Barbaresco Vanotu '96	🍷🍷	6
● Barbera d'Alba I Piani '98	🍷🍷	4
● Dolcetto d'Alba Augenta '98	🍷🍷	4
● Dolcetto d'Alba Munfrina '98	🍷	3*
○ Langhe Favorita '98	🍷	3
● Langhe Nebbiolo '98	🍷	4
● Barbaresco Vanotu '95	YYY	5
● Barbaresco '95	YY	5
● Barbaresco Vanotu '90	YY	5
● Barbaresco Vanotu '93	YY	5
● Barbera d'Alba I Piani '97	YY	3

TREISO (CN)

VIGNAIOLI ELVIO PERTINACE
LOC. PERTINACE, 2
12050 TREISO (CN)
TEL. 0173/442238

After a few years' absence this historic winery is back in the Guide, under the management of the young Cesare Barbero: credit is due chiefly to an excellent Barbaresco '96 from the Castellizzano cru which wins Two Glasses with flying colors. The 14 member growers cultivate a total of 80 hectares under vine and annually produce about 170 thousand bottles. Cesare personally supervises work in the vineyards, since there's no other way of making great wines. The Barbaresco Castellizzano lords it over the other estate crus with its complex and intriguing floral and fruity bouquet; the full, warm palate shows still slightly astringent tannins and the finish offers notes of licorice and tar. A little below the Castellizzano are the Nervo and the basic version, both of which, although a bit lacking in concentration and complexity, offer pleasant balsamic and fruity tones. The Marcarini, rather lean on nose and palate, is worthy only of mention. One Glass each goes to the fragrant and vinous Dolcetto Castellizzano and to the Pertinace, a blend of nebbiolo, barbera and cabernet that reveals satisfying fruity aromas with notes of vanilla. A Barbera d'Asti, from vineyards purchased at Agliano, is to be released in the near future.

● Barbaresco Castellizzano '96	🍷🍷	5
● Barbaresco '96	🍷	5
● Barbaresco Nervo '96	🍷	5
● Dolcetto d'Alba Castellizzano '98	🍷	3
● Langhe Pertinace '96	🍷	4
● Barbaresco Marcarini '96		5

VERDUNO (CN)

F.LLI ALESSANDRIA
VIA BEATO VALFRÉ, 59
12060 VERDUNO (CN)
TEL. 0172/470113

Gian Alessandria's wines show a fine balance between modernity and tradition; they are made from first-class raw material, the fruit of low yields and careful vineyard management. For the first time in his life, this unassuming winegrower has walked off with Three Glasses. Not only is the Barolo an absolute gem, but the Barbera '97 is also one of the best to be found. The former presents an ample and highly individual bouquet, with hints of berry jam, cocoa, eucalyptus and clove. The palate is as amply rich as the dense ruby-garnet color would lead you to suppose; the powerful entry and austere and solid mid palate lead into a consistent, long and deeply satisfying finish, where smooth tannins play the leading role. The Barbera, of an impenetrable garnet color with a very narrow purplish rim, offers a bouquet full of charm and personality: soft tones of vanilla and red currant and blackberry jam blend perfectly with pungent hints of tobacco leaf and toastiness; the overall impression is complex and inviting. On the palate abundant fruit and ample softness, nicely regulated by a powerful structure, create an enthralling progression that culminates beautifully in a very long, corresponding finish. The Pelaverga is an attractive, undemanding wine of an almost transparent ruby hue; the nose reveals delicate aromas of berries and pepper; the smooth palate has vigorous tannins and a warm finish. A Dolcetto of a garnet-tinged ruby color with faintly rustic aromas and a full body ends the list.

● Barolo Monvigliero '95	🍷🍷🍷	5
● Barbera d'Alba '97	🍷🍷	4
● Dolcetto d'Alba '98	🍷	3
● Verduno Pelaverga '98	🍷	3
● Barolo Monvigliero '93	🍷🍷 (outline)	5

VERDUNO (CN)

Bel Colle
Fraz. Castagni, 56
12060 Verduno (CN)
tel. 0172/470196

Paolo Torchio's '96 Barbaresco has won Two brimful Glasses; forceful and elegant, it declares its intensity in its ruby-garnet color with a slightly faded rim. The pronounced soft fruity tones on the nose blend with complex notes of pepper and leather and briny nuances; the soft and richly fruity entry on the palate emphasizes a phenolic structure that is solid and vigorous without harshness; the long noble finish shows depth. The Barolo Monvigliero '95 displays an almost transparent garnet-tinged ruby color and a restrained, harmonious bouquet with hints of strawberry, raspberry, rhubarb and dried flowers; the soft texture of the palate reveals robust tannins that carry through to a lingering, corresponding finish. When we'd finished with these two champions we found we also liked the less demanding wines. The Dolcetto, made with grapes from Verduno, is ruby-garnet in color with a good firm rim; the nose releases fresh aromas of cherry, blackberry and violet with spicy nuances, while the palate is full-bodied and soft, with caressing tannins on the lingering finish. The Favorita, of a pale straw color, has a simple and inviting nose with hints of fruit candy and wild herbs; the smooth, silky palate mirrors the fresh and balanced bouquet. The characteristic and well-made Pelaverga offers a light and delicious palate with typical fruity and spicy tones. The Nebbiolo, fruity and floral with a pleasant rusticity, is characterized by prominent tannins on the palate.

●	Barbaresco '96	🍷🍷	5
●	Barolo Monvigliero '95	🍷🍷	5
●	Dolcetto d'Alba '98	🍷	3
○	Langhe Favorita '98	🍷	3
●	Nebbiolo d'Alba Bricco S. Cristoforo '97	🍷	4
●	Verduno Pelaverga '98	🍷	3
●	Barolo Vigna Monvigliero '93	🍸🍸	5
●	Barbaresco '95	🍸	5

VERDUNO (CN)

Commendator G. B. Burlotto
Via Vittorio Emanuele, 28
12060 Verduno (CN)
tel. 0172/470122

Giuseppe Alessandria, Marina Burlotto and their son Fabio have presented a series of excellent wines: the Barbera d'Alba Boscato and the Langhe Bianco Dives, both from the '97 vintage, win Two full Glasses each. The former, of an intense ruby-garnet color with a firm purple rim, offers a deep, dense nose with notes of red currant, sour cherry, pepper, menthol and almond; the palate is rich and broad, displaying noble tannins followed by a warm and powerful finish permeated with mineral notes and hints of melted licorice. The Dives, from sauvignon, shows an attractive golden color. The bouquet, whose varietal character is enhanced by aging in new wood, offers a wide array of aromas including tomato leaf, tropical fruit, vanilla, peach skin and ripe grape. The rich, broad and light palate leads into a fresh and quintessentially varietal finish. The three Barolos get One Glass each. The Cannubi displays an intense garnet color, while the nose offers briny notes with spicy hints; the palate is well-structured, with mildly aggressive tannins on the finish. The Monvigliero has a fruity bouquet with notes of quinine and citrus peel; the palate is fairly substantial and slightly harsh in tone. The basic version has a lightly heady bouquet and a medium-bodied palate. A characteristic and inviting Pelaverga and a rustic but agreeable Dolcetto end the list.

●	Barbera d'Alba Vigneto Boscato '97	🍷🍷	3*
○	Langhe Bianco Dives '97	🍷🍷	4
●	Barolo '95	🍷	5
●	Barolo Vigneto Cannubi '95	🍷	6
●	Barolo Vigneto Monvigliero '95	🍷	6
●	Dolcetto d'Alba Vigneto Neirane '97	🍷	3
●	Verduno Pelaverga '98	🍷	3
●	Barbera d'Alba Vigneto Boscato '96	🍸	3
●	Barolo Vigneto Monvigliero '93	🍸	5

VERDUNO (CN)

CASTELLO DI VERDUNO
VIA UMBERTO I, 9
12060 VERDUNO (CN)
TEL. 0172/470125 - 0172/470284

This year Gabriella and Franco Bianco have presented a range of admirable wines, with both the Barbarescos performing well, the Rabajà rather better than the Faset. The former, of a nearly transparent ruby hue tinged with garnet, has a rather forward bouquet characterized by hints of jam, licorice, leather and dried flowers; it is not powerful on the palate but is nicely balanced and appropriately tannic; the finish shows some finesse, with nuances of cocoa and fruit steeped in alcohol. The Faset, which is a little less expressive, has a wide orange rim on a medium-intense ruby base; it is not particularly powerful on the distinctly forward nose; the palate is austere, fairly substantial and long enough. The good Barolo Massara, ruby-garnet in hue with an orange rim, reveals jammy notes and mineral and iodine undertones; the palate shows sufficient intensity and solid but not excessive tannins leading into an elegant, not very long finish. The Barolo Monvigliero, of a quite transparent ruby color with a broad orange rim, has a bouquet of medium finesse; the palate lacks breadth, so the tannins are fairly prominent; the finish reveals notes of wood and licorice. The most successful wine is still the Pelaverga di Verduno; it is most unusual, with spicy aromas, a delightful, lingering palate and a peppery finish. Lastly, the Barbera Bricco del Cuculo is not over-elegant on the nose but is redeemed by a characterful and highly satisfying palate.

● Barbaresco Vigna Rabajà '96	🍷🍷	5
● Verduno Pelaverga '98	🍷🍷	4
● Barbaresco Vigna Faset '96	🍷	5
● Barbera d'Alba Bricco del Cuculo '97	🍷	4
● Barolo Monvigliero '95	🍷	6
● Barolo Vigna Massara '95	🍷	6
● Barbaresco Rabajà '93	🍸🍸	5
● Barbaresco Rabajà '95	🍸🍸	5
● Barolo Monvigliero '90	🍸🍸	5
● Barolo Monvigliero '93	🍸🍸	5
● Verduno Pelaverga '97	🍸🍸	4
● Barbaresco Vigna Faset '93	🍸	5
● Barolo Massara '93	🍸	5

VIGNALE M.TO (AL)

GIULIO ACCORNERO E FIGLI
CA' CIMA, 1
15049 VIGNALE M.TO (AL)
TEL. 0142/933317

Ermanno and Massimo Accornero, who have confirmed the stature of the Grignolino and the Barbera, are making considerable investments to modernize their estate. Mario Ronco is proving himself to be a first-rate oenologist, and the first-rate team at Ca' Cima has pulled a winner out of the hat. The Barbera Bricco Battista '97, a nearly perfect wine, is the first in the Casale zone to be awarded Three Glasses. It is a pleasure to behold with its opaque inky ruby color, while the nose releases wonderful notes of cherry preserves, stewed prunes and spice; it explodes on the rich, soft palate, revealing satisfying tannins and a very long finish. Each time it appeared at a tasting it scored over 90 points. The Centenario '96, of a lovely intense ruby hue, is very broad, with aromas of herbs and sweet spice; it shows great body and structure, a delightful succulence and a long finish. The rustic Barbera Giulìn '97 again displays good varietal character, with aromas of cooked red fruit. The Grignolino Bricco del Bosco '98, of a light rosé color, stands out for its abundant fruit and freshness. The Accorneros also produce Malvasia di Casorzo: the still version, the Brigantino '98, is very highly perfumed, not at all cloying, and pleasingly quaffable. This year's new offering is the Casorzo Passito Pico '97, named after the counts Pico Pastrone of Casorzo. Barrique-aged for a year and sold in half bottles, it has varietal aromas joined by notes of hazelnut and vanilla; the dry palate makes it an ideal wine for sipping slowly on its own or with sweet biscuits.

● Barbera d'Asti Bricco Battista '97	🍷🍷🍷	4
● Monferrato Rosso Centenario '96	🍷🍷	5
● Barbera del M.to Sup. Giulìn '97	🍷	3
● Casorzo Brigantino '98	🍷	3
● Casorzo Passito Pico '97	🍷	5
● Grignolino del M.to Casalese Bricco del Bosco '98	🍷	3
● Barbera del M.to La Mattacchiona '98		3
● Monferrato Freisa La Bernardina '98		3
● Barbera d'Asti Bricco Battista '96	🍸🍸	4
● Barbera del M.to Sup. Giulìn '96	🍸	3
● Monferrato Rosso Centenario '95	🍸	5

VIGNALE M.TO (AL)

BRICCO MONDALINO

REG. MONDALINO, 5
15049 VIGNALE M.TO (AL)
TEL. 0142/933204

To make a Grignolino of high quality requires a great deal of effort which does not often seem warranted by its earnings, but this is nonetheless Mauro Gaudio's ambition. The potential of this variety, which has always been widespread in the Monferrato zone, can be appreciated by anyone who tastes the Bricco Mondalino cru from the '98 vintage. Made from selected grapes picked slightly overripe, it has, amazingly, more than 14% alcohol. The color, too, an attractive ruby of medium intensity, indicates a most unusual Grignolino, while the palate is another surprise: full, powerful and fruity, with a typical tannic punch on the finish. Hints of rose, strawberry, ripe cherry and spice emerge in the intense and complex bouquet. The normal Grignolino cannot compete with the cru, but it is still very pleasant with its cherry hue, aromas of geranium, strawberry and almond, and its fresh, fruity palate. And now for the Barberas. The new unoaked Gaudio Amilcare selection is very successful: of a fairly intense ruby color, it displays aromas of ripe cherry, plum and raspberry; the palate is soft, fruity and elegant. The Gaudium selection, an assemblage of the best barriques of the Bergantino cru bottled only in magnums, is of a similar quality, while the dark ruby-garnet Barbera d'Asti Il Bergantino, barriqued for a year, scores a little below it. It reveals aromas of very ripe red fruit and leather, followed by a full, soft palate. The Freisa offers a fragrance of raspberry and red currant, but also a rather strong sulfurous note; the juicy palate leads to a pleasantly dry, bitterish finish. The good Malvasia, of a vivid, brilliant color, is redolent of rose, violet and pear, all mirrored on the exuberantly fizzy palate.

●	Barbera d'Asti Sel. Gaudium Magnum '97	🍷🍷	6
●	Barbera del M.to Sel. Gaudio Amilcare '98	🍷🍷	4
●	Grignolino del M.to Casalese Bricco Mondalino '98	🍷🍷	3*
●	Barbera d'Asti Il Bergantino '97	🍷	4
●	Grignolino del M.to Casalese '98	🍷	3
●	Malvasia di Casorzo Molignano '98	🍷	3
●	Monferrato Freisa La Monferrina '98	🍷	3
●	Grignolino del M.to Casalese Bricco Mondalino '97	🍸🍸	3
●	Barbera d'Asti Il Bergantino '96	🍸	4

VIGNALE M.TO (AL)

COLONNA

CA' ACCATINO, 1
FRAZ. S. LORENZO
15049 VIGNALE M.TO (AL)
TEL. 0142/933239

Alessandra Colonna, president of the new Vini del Monferrato Casalese Consortium, attributes the success of her estate to her commitment and a passion for her work: good land, investments and untiring effort are the surest way of producing excellent wine. Many changes are taking place, both in the cellar and in the selection of wines. Next year will see the release of the Alessandra, the new barriqued Barbera which is expected to be the estate's top wine. Meanwhile we must be content with the fine range presented this year. The Barbera Monferrato La Rossa '97 is an example of how the equilibrium between acidity and alcohol can lend a ready drinkability to full-bodied wines without the mediation of bubbles. The Grignolino del Monferrato Casalese, the real standard-bearer of the area, is excellent for the second year running. The '98 version, called Sansìn, offers varietal aromas, good balance and satisfying tannins that result in a long, clean finish. The Monferrato Rosso Il Bigio '97, a monovarietal pinot nero, shows an even garnet color; the nose reveals notes of strawberry and cooked fruit, while the palate is attractive but a little short. The Piemonte Chardonnay Armonia '98 displays an attractively vivid straw color, a lovely simple fragrance of overripe fruit, and exemplary balance in the mouth. The Monferrato Rosso Mondone '96, an assemblage of cabernet sauvignon, pinot nero and barbera, was conceived as a wine for the international market; a bouquet of jam and grass is followed by a medium-bodied, coffee-toned and extremely fresh palate underpinned by impressive tannins.

●	Monferrato Rosso Mondone '96	🍷🍷	5
●	Barbera del M.to La Rossa '97	🍷	3
●	Grignolino del M.to Casalese Sansìn '98	🍷	3
●	Monferrato Rosso Bigio '97	🍷	3
○	Piemonte Chardonnay Armonia '98	🍷	3
●	Monferrato Rosso Bigio '96	🍸	3
●	Monferrato Rosso Mondone '95	🍸	5

VINCHIO (AT)

Cantina Sociale
di Vinchio e Vaglio Serra
Reg. S. Pancrazio, 1
14040 Vinchio (AT)
tel. 0141/950903

The Cantina Sociale di Vinchio e Vaglio Serra is generally associated with its top wine, the Barbera d'Asti Vigne Vecchie, which is the resullt of the rigorous selection that this cooperative winery requires from its member growers. It is hardly surprising that, with the outstanding '97 vintage, this wine has gathered up Two Glasses. The ruby hue is tinged with garnet shading to orange; the complex bouquet includes notes of berry jam, licorice and spice with a faint mineral undertone; the entry on the palate is full-flavored, and ample body is revealed with the progression, leading to an intense, lingering finish on a note of fruit and spice. The good Freisa '98 releases lively aromas of red fruit, menthol, pepper and hazelnut; the substantial palate, rather austere in character, has a dry, lingering finish. The Cortese dell'Alto Monferrato Dorato, of a very pale straw color, is redolent of white-fleshed fruit, wildflowers, anise and lemon; the palate does not disappoint, being fresh and smooth, and quite delightful on the finish. The ruby-orange Barbera d'Asti Superiore '97 offers a bouquet of medium finesse with fruity and spicy notes; the balanced palate is rendered dry on the finish by a tannic presence. Three lightly bubbly wines, the simple and undemanding Cortese, the light-hearted, quaffable Barbera del Monferrato Vivace and the basic Barbera d'Asti with its good bite of acidity, are all very well executed.

●	Barbera d'Asti Sup. Vigne Vecchie '97	🍷🍷	5
●	Barbera d'Asti Sup. '97	🍷	3
○	Cortese dell'Alto M.to Dorato '98	🍷	3
●	Monferrato Freisa '98	🍷	3
●	Barbera d'Asti '98		3
●	Barbera del M.to Vivace '98		3
○	Cortese dell'Alto M.to '98		2
●	Barbera d'Asti Sup. Vigne Vecchie '96	YY	5
●	Barbera d'Asti Sup. Vigne Vecchie '95	Y	4

VIVERONE (BI)

La Cella di S. Michele
Via Cascine di Ponente, 21
13886 Viverone (BI)
tel. 0161/98245

The Enrietti family, whose estate is splendidly perched on the slopes of the Serra d'Ivrea overlooking Lake Viverone, produces admirably consistent wines. This year there are once again two different interpretations of the erbaluce grape: the sparkling Brut Cella Grande di S. Michele and the Erbaluce di Caluso Cella Grande, which this time has benefited from a brief spell in new barriques, and each wine won One full Glass. The first, a spumante made by the long Charmat method (about eight months of aging on the lees), shows a pale straw color and a fairly fine perlage; the nose is simple but satisfying, offering hints of banana, candied almonds, apple and jasmine; the palate reveals intensity and a refreshing sparkle; the finish clearly and fully mirrors the bouquet. The richly straw-colored Erbaluce di Caluso Cella Grande '98 displays ample and harmonious aromas of tropical fruit, vanilla and sweet tobacco. The good fruit on the palate is underpinned by crisp acidity and followed by a lingering finish, only just dominated by a note of caramel from the essentially well-judged wood. Meanwhile, in the cellar, a Metodo Classico Spumante '97 is awaiting dégorgement, and a late-harvested '96 vintage (erbaluce, of course) is about to be bottled. And we eagerly await both interesting newcomers, which we'll be describing in next year's Guide.

○	Brut Cella Grande di S. Michele	🍷	3
○	Erbaluce di Caluso Cella Grande '98	🍷	3

OTHER WINERIES

The following producers obtained good scores in our tastings with one or more of their wines:

PROVINCE OF ALESSANDRIA

Paolo Poggio
Brignano Frascata, tel. 0131/784929
Colli Tortonesi Barbera Derio '97

La Centuriona, Gavi, tel. 0143/648884
Gavi del Comune di Gavi '98

Produttori del Gavi, Gavi, tel. 0143/642786
Gavi del Comune di Gavi Etichetta Nera '98

Santa Seraffa, Gavi, tel. 0143/643600
Gavi del Comune di Gavi Ca' di Maggio '96

Casalone, Lu M.to, tel. 0131/741280
Barbera d'Asti Ruber Millo '97

Cantina Sociale Tre Castelli
Montaldo Bormida, tel. 0143/85136
Dolcetto di Ovada Sup. Colli di Carpeneto '97

Cascina Perpetua, Novi Ligure, tel. 0143/61191
Gavi '98

Vigne del Pareto
Novi Ligure, tel. 010/8398776
Gavi Vigna del Pareto '98

Rossi Contini, Ovada, tel. 0143/833696
Monferrato Rosso Cras Tibi '97

Colle Manora
Quargnento, tel. 0131/219252
Monferrato Bianco Mimosa Collezione '98

Tenuta Migliavacca
S. Giorgio M.to, tel. 0142/781761
Grignolino del M.to Casalese '98

La Zerba, Tassarolo, tel. 0143/342259
Gavi di Tassarolo '98

Livio Pavese, Treville, tel. 0142/487215
Monferrato Rosso Montarucco '96

Cascina Alberta
Vignale M.to, tel. 0142/933313
Grignolino del M.to Casalese '98

Il Mongetto
Vignale M.to, tel. 0142/933469
Barbera d'Asti Vigneto Guera '97

PROVINCE OF ASTI

dacapo, Agliano Terme, tel. 0141/964921
Barbera d'Asti Vigna dacapo '97

Trinchero, Agliano Terme, tel. 0141/954016
Barbera d'Asti Vigna del Noce '96

Vittorio Bera, Canelli, tel. 0141/831157
Moscato d'Asti '98

Marco Maria Crivelli
Castagnole M.to, tel. 0141/292533
Ruché di Castagnole M.to '98

G. L. Viarengo e Figlio
Castello di Annone, tel. 0141/401131
Barbera d'Asti Il Falé '97

Villa Fiorita
Castello di Annone, tel. 0141/401231
Barbera d'Asti Sup. Il Giorgione '96

Renaldo Graglia
Castelnuovo Don Bosco, tel. 011/9874708
Freisa d'Asti Vigneto Bric du Linger Parlapà '97

Renzo Beccaris
Costigliole d'Asti, tel. 0141/966592
Barbera d'Asti Sup. S. Lorenzo '97

Luigi Nebiolo
Costigliole d'Asti, tel. 0141/966030
Barbera d'Asti '96

Rosso, Costigliole d'Asti, tel. 0141/968437
Barbera d'Asti Sup. Cardin '97

Gazzi, Nizza M.to, tel. 0141/793512
Barbera d'Asti Praiot '98

Guasti, Nizza M.to, tel. 0141/721350
Barcarato '96

Lanunsiò, Nizza M.to, tel. 0141/721531
Barbera d'Asti Lanunsiò '97

Castello del Poggio
Portacomaro, tel. 0141/202543
Barbera d'Asti Val del Temp '97

Ca' d'Carussin
S. Marzano Oliveto, tel. 0141/831358
Monferrato Rosso Signorotto '97

Mondo, S. Marzano Oliveto, tel. 0141/834096
Barbera d'Asti Vigna del Salice '97

PROVINCE OF CUNEO

Silvano e Elena Boroli, Alba, tel. 0173/35865
Moscato d'Asti Aureum '98,
Dolcetto d'Alba Madonna di Como '98

Poderi Sinaglio, Alba, tel. 0173/612209
Dolcetto di Diano d'Alba Sorì Bric Maiolica '98

Mauro Sebaste, Alba, tel. 0173/262954
Barolo Prapò '95

Cantina del Pino, Barbaresco, tel. 0173/635147
Dolcetto d'Alba '98

Carlo Giacosa, Barbaresco, tel. 0173/635116
Barbaresco Montefico '96

La Ca' Növa, Barbaresco, tel. 0173/635123
Barbaresco Montefico '96

Montaribaldi, Barbaresco, tel. 0173/638220
Barbera d'Alba dü Gir '97

Ronchi, Barbaresco, tel. 0173/635156
Barbaresco '96

Damilano, Barolo, tel. 0173/56105
Barolo '95

Sylla Sebaste, Barolo, tel. 0173/56266
Barolo Bussia '95

Luca Abrate, Bra, tel. 0172/415254
Barbera d'Alba Castelvé '97

Cornarea, Canale, tel. 0173/979091
Roero Arneis '98

Marsaglia, Castellinaldo, tel. 0173/213048
Nebbiolo d'Alba S. Pietro '97

Gigi Rosso
Castiglione Falletto, tel. 0173/262369
Dolcetto di Diano d'Alba Moncolombetto '98

Paolo Monte, Diano d'Alba, tel. 0173/69231
Diano d'Alba Cascina Flino Vigna Vecchia '98

Oddero, Diano d'Alba, tel. 0173/69169
Dolcetto di Diano d'Alba Sorì Sorba '98

Celso Abbona, Dogliani, tel. 0173/70668
Dolcetto di Dogliani 'L Sambù '98

Mario Cozzo, Dogliani, tel. 0173/70571
Dolcetto di Dogliani Vigna Pregliasco '98

La Fusina, Dogliani, tel. 0173/70488
Dolcetto di Dogliani Vigna Muntà '98

Bruno Porro, Dogliani, tel. 0173/70371
Dolcetto di Dogliani Ribote '98

Eraldo Revelli, Farigliano, tel. 0173/797154
Dolcetto di Dogliani '98

Accomasso, La Morra, tel. 0173/50843
Barolo Rocche '95

Erbaluna, La Morra, tel. 0173/50800
Barbera d'Alba La Bettola '98

Stroppiana, La Morra, tel. 0173/50169
Barolo '95

Viberti, La Morra, tel. 0173/50374
Barolo '95

Cascina Pian d'Or, Mango, tel. 0141/89440
Moscato d'Asti Bricco Riella '98

Podere Ruggeri Corsini
Monforte d'Alba, tel. 0173/78625
Barbera d'Alba Armujan '97

Taliano, Montà d'Alba, tel. 0173/976512
Roero '97

Cantina del Glicine
Neive, tel. 0173/67215
Barbaresco Marcorino '96

Castello di Neive
Neive, tel. 0173/67171
Barbaresco La Rocca di S. Stefano '96

Cascina Crosa, Neive, tel. 0173/67376
Barbaresco '96

Parroco di Neive
Neive, tel. 0173/67008
Barbaresco Vigneto Gallina '96

Roberto Sarotto, Neviglie, tel. 0173/630228
Enrico I '96

Ada Nada, Treiso, 0173/638127
Barbaresco Valeirano '96

PROVINCE OF TORINO

Cooperativa della Serra
Piverone, tel. 0125/72166
Erbaluce di Caluso '98

LIGURIA

In the last two vintages, which, while not earth-shattering, were certainly positive, wine-making in Liguria has shown definite signs of improvement, due to better vineyard management and superior cellar technique. Everything would seem admirable, were it not for a certain sameness resulting from a technical level that not many producers have yet managed to go beyond; there is even a tendency for the differences between Pigato and Vermentino to be blurred, which means that the individual characteristics of each varietal have not yet been highlighted. The solution may lie in clonal selection, which is still virtually unheard of here. Are the costs just too high for small estates and insensitive regional authorities? Maybe, but the impasse has to be overcome somehow. It is worth remembering that the interest in Ligurian wine in general is on the increase and that pigato has great potential: it is a unique indigenous variety, grown nowhere else. Then there's the question of rising prices: this might be the moment for regulation. But general considerations aside, the outlook that emerged from our tastings this year was positive, with well-known producers, in both the Levante and the Ponente, strengthening their positions, and the appearance on the scene of some new names. There were also a few attempts to turn out fashionable and easily marketable wines, but they were greeted with about as much enthusiasm as they deserve. Let's get down to details. Close to the stratosphere we found the Solitario '97, creation of Vladimiro Galluzzo, a stubborn and individualistic "vigneron" who has gradually succeeded in producing one of the region's best reds. The Rossese di Dolceacqua Bricco Arcagna is keeping it company; this is an aristocratic, elegant wine from Terre Bianche, an estate which also produced good results with their Arcana blends, both red and white. We are already used to the splendid performances of Pigato Russeghine, for which we offer our compliments to Riccardo Bruna, and we are delighted to welcome Fausto De Andreis and his excellent Spigàu to the Guide. We should like to emphasize, too, the quality of Vio's Pigato, as well as that of the Cascina Terre Rosse, which gains high praise for its Le Banche blend as well. The Colli dei Bardellini winery has worked a little magic with its special selections, Pigato Vigna La Torretta and Vermentino Vigna U Munte, while Emanuele Trevia has presented a trio of treats: Vermentino, Eretico Vermentino and Eretico Pigato; the latter two were fermented and aged in barriques. We saw an excellent interpretation of their Vignamare blend from the Lupi brothers, the charms of whose basic Vermentino should also be remembered. Tenuta Giuncheo won Two Glasses with a pair of Vermentinos, including the Eclis selection; our congratulations to the village of Castelnuovo Magra, both for Ottaviano Lambruschi's two Vermentino selections, Costa Marina and Sarticola, and for the Vermentino made by Giorgio Tendola at Il Torchio. We dedicate our final fanfare to an extraordinary wine, the Cinque Terre Sciacchetrà '96, and to its headstrong producer Walter De Battè. Cheers!

ALBENGA (SV)

ANFOSSI

VIA PACCINI, 39
FRAZ. BASTIA
17030 ALBENGA (SV)
TEL. 0182/20024

In July '98, after working together for years, Mario Anfossi and Paolo Grossi transformed their association into a registered partnership; fortunately nothing essential changed; they simply renewed their determination to produce good wines and excellent delicacies. This estate is, in fact, an ideal destination for the food- and wine-loving traveler: it offers olive oil, olives (both in brine and as paste), tender baby artichokes and sun-dried tomatoes in olive oil (delicious!), basil cream and the traditional pesto. The wines are no less significant in quality and in quantity (indeed within the next three years production should increase from the present 50 thousand bottles to about 70 thousand). But let's get down to the wines we tasted. After twelve months' bottle aging the cru Pigato le Caminate has now been released. As evidence of its brief maceration on the skins it displays a fine deep straw-yellow color in the glass; it has an appealing bouquet, reminiscent, at least initially, of acacia honey, then suggesting yellow flowers and tropical fruit. The well-balanced, rounded and lingering palate is underpinned by good acidity: it missed Two Glasses by a shadow. The standard Pigato scored a little lower; a rather pale straw hue is followed by faint and simple floral aromas, which carry through onto the agreeable palate: undemanding easy drinking. The straw yellow Vermentino is rather better: a delicate bouquet of mineral notes, meadow flowers, citron, apple and banana is echoed on a palate well supported by acidity.

○ Riviera Ligure di Ponente Pigato '98	🍷	3
○ Riviera Ligure di Ponente Pigato Le Caminate '97	🍷	3
○ Riviera Ligure di Ponente Vermentino '98	🍷	3

ALBENGA (SV)

FAUSTO DE ANDREIS

REG. RUATO, 4
FRAZ. SALEA
17030 ALBENGA (SV)
TEL. 0182/21175

Fausto de Andreis runs his estate with an appealing combination of modesty and conviction. His determination to rediscover the idiosyncrasies of traditional Pigato without copying its faults, and to push it beyond the limits of a merely "sound" wine, has led to some quite painful decisions, ultimately involving having to do without DOC status. The result is called Spigaù, with an "S" in front of the dialect spelling of Pigato. Fausto playfully suggests that the invading consonant stands for splendid, staggering, super or stunning. Made from pigato grapes, the wine comes from just one hectare of luxuriant vines and is vinified with a few days' skin contact, a sojourn on the lees, rackings and a gentle fining. It is never put into its simple, unpretentious bottles earlier than August! We also tasted the '97, which left us virtually speechless except for these few words: attractive in the glass, rich and noble on the nose, it makes a great impression on the palate with its fleshiness and balance. The '98 vintage is also very well executed, to the advantage of the cleanness and harmony of the wine. It has a deep straw hue and an intense, lingering nose, in which flowery and fruity notes meld with hints of mint, sage, honey and white pepper, all mirrored on the structured palate crowned by excellent aromatic length and an attractively bitterish finish.

○ Spigàu '98	🍷🍷	3*

ALBENGA (SV)

CASCINA FEIPU DEI MASSARETTI
LOC. MASSARETTI, 8
FRAZ. BASTIA
17030 ALBENGA (SV)
TEL. 0182/20131

There have been some minor changes at the winery of Pippo Parodi, legendary standard-bearer of Ligurian wine. He has planted some more pigato (on a hectare of his own and a hectare of rented land), which will lead to a slight increase in production and greater potential for selection. "Old" Pippo has never believed in using barriques to make Pigato, and his son-in-law Mirko, who is now managing the estate, has come to be of the same mind. In all honesty, we also think that those toasty oak-derived notes get in the way of the characteristic self-expression of this wine on both nose and palate. In future they will probably use their barriques for the red table wine, whereas they are now studying the possibility of giving the Rossese greater body with a small dollop of syrah. The Pigato, Cascina Feipu's real bread-and-butter wine, did not manage to repeat its Two Glass performance of last year. It displays a straw-yellow color of middling intensity; the bouquet yields fresh vegetal scents blended with fruity nuances of apricot, pineapple and apple, and lighter notes of honey and musk, all perfectly echoed on the well-balanced, attractively dry palate that slightly emphasizes alcohol; the finish is crisp, clean and even, but not particularly long. The Riviera Ligure di Ponente Rossese deserves its honorable mention: fresh, delicate scents of berries characterize the nose of this decidedly quaffable wine. Olive oil and olives in brine are the estate's other products.

○ Riviera Ligure di Ponente Pigato '98	🍷	4
● Riviera Ligure di Ponente Rossese '98		3

ALBENGA (SV)

LA VECCHIA CANTINA
VIA CORTA, 3
FRAZ. SALEA
17030 ALBENGA (SV)
TEL. 0182/559881

Salea, a hamlet of scattered but dense properties set amongst vineyards and olive groves, is one of the wine-producing satellites of Albenga, along with Bastia, Campochiesa, Ortovero and Vendone. Umberto Calleri is a leading player in the saga which unfolds, accompanied by constant hard labor, on his four hectares of red, clayey soil, the ideal environment for pigato and vermentino. From these rows of Guyot-trained vines come excellent grapes which Calleri's proven wine-making alchemy, a mixture of technical expertise and country wisdom, succeeds in transforming into satisfying wines. His is a straightforward policy: to aim for body and structure rather than for easy, charming but often ephemeral perfumes. This, then, is the small estate which has accustomed us to successfully executed wines we could count on; we were therefore somewhat perplexed by a Pigato which was a bit below par. An attractive deep straw color introduces not very elegant aromas of overripe fruit; the palate has similar problems and the wine is still a bit unbalanced. The stylish, well-judged Vermentino, straw yellow in hue, boasts a fruity fragrance with hints of rosemary and wood resins, all mirrored on the palate, which is underpinned by a pleasant acidity that emphasizes the fruit. This crisp yet soft, medium-bodied wine is both even and long, and will rightly gain lots of admirers, thanks to its easy, natural style and appealing quaffability.

○ Riviera Ligure di Ponente Vermentino '98	🍷	4
○ Riviera Ligure di Ponente Pigato '98		4

CAMPOROSSO (IM)

Tenuta Giuncheo
Loc. Giuncheo
18033 Camporosso (IM)
tel. 0184/288639

Arnold and Monica Schweizer had the good sense to purchase this estate and Marco Romagnoli, who is in charge of vines and cellar, really knows his business. The combined force of ability, intuition and business sense, together with the advice of the first-rate oenologist Donato Lanati could only lead to an upswing. Meanwhile work is proceeding apace: there are new plantings, small plots being turned over to innovative systems, experimental vineyards using environmentally friendly methods, etc. But let's see about the wines. The extremely appealing basic Vermentino is a model of its type, thanks to the breadth of its fragrance and the harmony of its structure: the nose offers, in succession, notes of broom, eucalyptus, undergrowth and honey; the palate shows perfect balance between acidity and body on the one hand, and smoothness and length on the other. The single-vineyard Le Palme is also successful: its fresh, fruity and sweet (honey and candy) scents introduce a full, soft and characterful palate. The Vermentino Eclis, which will be released in the spring of the year 2000, is the fruit of rigorous grape selection and vinification "sur lie" in new barriques. Golden yellow in color, it offers an unusually intense nose and equally remarkable length on the palate, which is crisp, though with well-defined structure, and displays an elegant almondy finish. Lastly, the Rosseses: the inviting Pian del Vescovo, a very good example of this DOC wine, has slightly sweet oak-derived notes on the nose, as well as hints of underbrush and woodland fruit; the satisfying palate is soft, succulent and delicately warm. The basic Rossese, with its more straightforward style, is well executed and easy drinking.

○	Riviera Ligure di Ponente Vermentino '98	🍷🍷	3*
○	Riviera Ligure di Ponente Vermentino Eclis '98	🍷🍷	5
○	Riviera Ligure di Ponente Vermentino Le Palme '98	🍷	4
●	Rossese di Dolceacqua '98	🍷	3
●	Rossese di Dolceacqua Vigneto Pian del Vescovo '98	🍷	4
●	Rossese di Dolceacqua Vigneto Pian del Vescovo '97	🍸	4

CASTELNUOVO MAGRA (SP)

Giacomelli
Via Palvotrisia, 134
19030 Castelnuovo Magra (SP)
tel. 0187/674155

The walls and towers of Castelnuovo Magra, built by Genoese and Pisans, date back to the 12th century; and we recommend a visit to the municipal wine cellar, the only one of its kind in Liguria, as a first step into the world of local wine. This is the world in which, after his university studies, Roberto Giacomelli passionately immersed himself. His property covers a total of six hectares, including a small olive grove. The vineyards, located at an altitude of about 200-250 meters, are near Castelnuovo Magra and Ortonovo; they have splendid southern and southeastern exposures and are planted to a density of some 4,000 Guyot-trained vines per hectare. The varieties are traditional to the Lunigiana district: vermentino, albarola, trebbiano, sangiovese and canaiolo. Concentrating on careful vineyard management (yields are kept quite low) and taking advantage of the advice of the oenologist Bacigalupi, Roberto produces roughly 23 thousand bottles a year, split between Rosso, Bianco and Vermentino. At our tastings it was the monovarietal wine that particularly impressed us. It has a deep straw color and attractive, aromatic scents of Mediterranean undergrowth combined with verdant, wild herb notes. The dry, delicate, fairly fat, even and harmonious palate has a typical almondy finish. The Giacomellis also produce a small quantity of extra virgin olive oil – using the traditional method – from the frantoio, pendolino and lavagnina olive varieties.

○	Colli di Luni Vermentino '98	🍷	3
○	Giacomelli Bianco '98		2
●	Giacomelli Rosso '98		2

Il Torchio

Via Provinciale, 202
19030 Castelnuovo Magra (SP)
tel. 0187/674075

An interesting range of wines was presented this year, starting with the Vermentino, which carried off Two Glasses: its bright appearance and deep straw color herald an attractive and intriguing bouquet of wildflowers and captivating herbal notes (sage). The palate is rich and silky, well-balanced and tightly knit, with a characteristic long almondy finish. The passionate dedication of Giorgio Tendola, the owner of the estate, has also brought about the rebirth of Linero, a wine praised by such writers (and connoisseurs) as Mario Soldati and Gianni Brera. A blend of vermentino, a little trebbiano and albarola, it displays a marked straw-yellow color and a distinct aromatic bouquet in which rosemary, broom, mimosa and nuances of star anise stand out; these are all perfectly mirrored on the well-balanced palate, which offers a fresh, bitterish finish. Giorgio, with his usual blend of energy and appealing exuberance, and with the assistance of Bacigalupi, the expert oenologist from the Riviera di Levante, is working on producing a top-notch red. The '96 vintage version, although denser than its predecessors, is not yet what they have in mind. On the nose it offers somewhat muted notes of spice, flowers and jam, all carrying through onto a palate which does not yet display sufficient structure or the complexity that characterizes "great" red wines.

○	Colli di Luni Vermentino '98	🍷🍷	3*
●	Colli di Luni Rosso '96	🍷	3
○	Linero '98	🍷	3

Ottaviano Lambruschi

Via Olmarello, 28
19030 Castelnuovo Magra (SP)
tel. 0187/674261

The Lambruschi estate is a touchstone for viticulture in the Ligurian Levante. Ottaviano (the traditionalist) and Fabio (the innovator) together make it possible to produce wines of considerable quality. Their five hectares are planted to white grapes, together with a small amount of sangiovese, merlot, canaiolo and cabernet sauvignon. The samples we tasted this year were excellent. The two Vermentino crus, Costa Marina and Sarticola, galloped into the Two Glass category. The former, of a deep straw color, has an elegant and distinctive bouquet, with vegetal, floral and citrus scents all bound together by a delicate honeyed note. The dry, full and crisp palate boasts a good balance between acidity and softness and the finish is pleasingly bitter. The Sarticola offers a deep color and an impressive fragrance of enchanting fruity (apple and peach), balsamic and wildflower notes, which carry through onto the warm, fairly powerful and concentrated palate. The basic Vermentino is more straightforward; sulfurous notes still muffle the nose, which doesn't have the intensity of its bigger brothers. It is well-balanced and refreshing in the mouth, simple in structure and light-hearted in style, but the bitter note on the finish is perhaps a bit too pronounced. The Ottaviano Lambruschi, which will be released at a later date, is now made from wine matured in stainless steel blended with a small amount that has been aged in oak. We'll be talking about it next year.

○	Colli di Luni Vermentino Costa Marina '98	🍷🍷	3*
○	Colli di Luni Vermentino Sarticola '98	🍷🍷	3*
○	Colli di Luni Vermentino '98		3

CHIAVARI (GE)

ENOTECA BISSON
C.SO GIANELLI, 28
16043 CHIAVARI (GE)
TEL. 0185/314462

Thanks to a recently purchased small additional vineyard, Piero Lugano now owns about six and a half hectares of land. With this new acquisition Piero can be even less dependent on grapes from other growers and can allow himself more rigorous grape selection. His intention is to reduce the range and increase the quality of the wines he offers. Turning to the wines we tasted, we note with pleasure that the Acinirari, while not extremely complex, is reminiscent of its Two Glass predecessors of a few years ago; the '97 version came awfully close to that level again with its warm amber color and rich, attractive nose with distinct notes of raisins and honey; the palate, which faithfully echoes the bouquet, is fairly simple in structure, and has a very clean finish. The Caratello, with its not very expressive nose and light structure in the mouth, is less interesting. The good Vermentino Vigna Erta displays aromatic notes of Mediterranean underbrush; the palate shows fair balance, with a slightly pronounced acidulous vein. The long list of wines ends with the Vermentino Monte Bernardo, the Bianchetta U Pastine, the Musaico (made from dolcetto grapes and offered also in a briefly oak-aged version), the Marea and the refreshing Ciliegiolo.

○	Acinirari '97	🍷	5
○	Caratello '97	🍷	4
○	Golfo del Tigullio Bianchetta Genovese U Pastine '98	🍷	3
●	Golfo del Tigullio Rosso Musaico '98	🍷	3
○	Golfo del Tigullio Vermentino Monte Bernardo '98	🍷	3
○	Golfo del Tigullio Vermentino Vigna Erta '98	🍷	3
⊙	Golfo del Tigullio Ciliegiolo '98		3
○	Golfo del Tigullio Vermentino '98		3
○	Marea '98		3

DIANO CASTELLO (IM)

MARIA DONATA BIANCHI
VIA DELLE TORRI, 16
18010 DIANO CASTELLO (IM)
TEL. 0183/498233

Emanuele Trevia, scrupulous professional that he is, does not like to rest on his laurels. He has recently purchased a single 10-hectare plot at Diano Aretino, which involved him in long-drawn-out negotiations and a sizeable outlay of funds. For now, he has an experimental vineyard planted to merlot and cabernet sauvignon, and there are some other projects on the boil. But then, Trevia, with his research into new vinification techniques and lots of successful experiments yielding white wines with aging potential and character, has got us used to successful results. So it's only reasonable to expect the best from the new varieties as well. But coming back to the present, each of the wines currently available has its own personality (a further indication of the reliable house technique), and they all did very well. The elegant and enchanting Vermentino shows a deep straw yellow color; the rich, captivating nose already reveals floral and balsamic notes with hints of citrus fruit; the generous, concentrated and soft palate is characterized by excellent balance. The Pigato scored a little bit lower: it is fruity and aromatic, dry but soft, with its usual bitter undertone and a few rough edges that need smoothing. The barrique-vinified Ereticos show that they've been properly brought up: the brown-labeled Pigato is golden yellow in colour and has a broad well-blended bouquet and an appealing, full-bodied and even palate. The Vermentino has a green label; its brilliant hue is matched by good depth on the nose, with intense and persistent aromas ranging from flowers to vanilla and coffee, all echoed on the full, soft palate.

○	Eretico Pigato '97	🍷🍷	5
○	Eretico Vermentino '97	🍷🍷	5
○	Riviera Ligure di Ponente Vermentino '98	🍷🍷	4
○	Riviera Ligure di Ponente Pigato '98	🍷	4
○	Eretico Vermentino '96	🍸🍸	5
○	Eretico Pigato '96	🍸	5

DOLCEACQUA (IM)

GIOBATTA MANDINO CANE
VIA ROMA, 21
18035 DOLCEACQUA (IM)
TEL. 0184/206120

The notes of the various tasters (many of them German-speaking) who visit this winery usually include comments on the delicate yet characteristic bouquets of the wines, as well as positive – and frequently extremely enthusiastic – remarks about the palates. The reason is to be found in the modern Rossese di Dolceacqua, of which Mandino Cane has been both pioneer and promoter; he has played a not insignificant role in restoring breeding to a wine which is innately noble but had been debased by primitive wine-making practices. It is a challenge, a dream towards the realization of which he continues to strive, brimful of youthful enthusiasm despite his grey hair, and which has led him to plant new vines. Among the innovations, there is even a small experimental vineyard planted to syrah which is beginning to bear fruit. The forte and also the pride of the estate are still the few thousand bottles of Dolceacqua Superiore, divided between two special selections: Vigneto Arcagna and Vigneto Morghe, the two most propitious zones in the whole district. The Morghe cru comes out on top again in the '98 version: it is not so markedly superior as it was last year, but the difference is still appreciable. This lovely wine, of a fairly light ruby color, offers fruity aromas of black currant and strawberry as well as hints of rose and sweet violet; the substantial and succulent palate reveals good balance and a bitterish undertone. The attractive Arcagna displays appropriately varietal fruity and resinous aromas; after a soft and intriguing entry on the palate it develops smoothly with finesse and warmth.

●	Rossese di Dolceacqua Sup. Vigneto Morghe '98	▼▼	4
●	Rossese di Dolceacqua Sup. Vigneto Arcagna '98	▼	4
●	Rossese di Dolceacqua Sup. Vigneto Morghe '97	▽▽	4
●	Rossese di Dolceacqua Sup. Vigneto Arcagna '97	▽	4

DOLCEACQUA (IM)

TERRE BIANCHE
LOC. ARCAGNA
18035 DOLCEACQUA (IM)
TEL. 0184/31426

The cellar and some of the vineyards are on the loose limestone soil of the hillside of Arcagna, which enjoys excellent exposure in a legendary zone for the production of Rossese di Dolceacqua; the winery, now one of the established estates in the westmost part of the Ponente, was founded a dozen years ago to make this wine. The dedicated and resolute Franco Laconi looks after the vines and the cellar, while his brother-in-law (the owner of Terre Bianche), Paolo Rondelli, is in charge of sales and of running the country hostelry. The grapes they grow are vermentino, pigato, cabernet sauvignon and, naturally, rossese. But let's examine the wines one by one. The excellent barrique-aged Bricco Arcagna is a red of real breeding with good aging potential, but also perfectly enjoyable now. Of a deep ruby color, it has a rich and complex nose and a silky palate of exemplary balance and good length. The Arcana Rosso, made from rossese and cabernet sauvignon, is slightly less richly structured; both its appearance and its bouquet are inviting, and it shows good evolution on the palate, as well as personality and an attractive finish. The Arcana Bianco, a blend of vermentino and pigato, reveals elegant aromas of ripe peach, pear and honey interwoven with toasty oak-derived notes, all invitingly echoed on the even palate where body and acidity are in perfect harmony. And now for the Pigato: the bouquet opens a little bashfully to show fresh, fruity and lightly aromatic notes; in the mouth it offers admirable succulent acidity, fair substance and undemanding quaffability. The Vermentino, though a bit vegetal on the nose, is properly made and has a supple and well-balanced palate. The basic Rossese di Dolceacqua is simple in character and dominated by alcohol on the palate.

○	Arcana Bianco '97	▼▼	5
●	Arcana Rosso '97	▼▼	5
●	Rossese di Dolceacqua Bricco Arcagna '97	▼▼	5
○	Riviera Ligure di Ponente Pigato '98	▼	4
○	Riviera Ligure di Ponente Vermentino '98	▼	4
●	Rossese di Dolceacqua '98		4
○	Arcana Bianco '96	▽▽	5
●	Arcana Rosso '96	▽▽	5
●	Rossese di Dolceacqua Bricco Arcagna '95	▽▽	5
●	Rossese di Dolceacqua Bricco Arcagna '96	▽▽	5

FINALE LIGURE (SV)

CASCINA DELLE TERRE ROSSE
VIA MANIE, 3
17024 FINALE LIGURE (SV)
TEL. 019/698782

Once again Cascina delle Terre Rosse has offered a fine range of wines divided amongst the major local DOCs and creatively named blends and monovarietals. The particularly successful Pigato vaunts a fresh richness on the nose, with hints of aromatic herbs, citrus fruit, broom, yellow plum and apricot, all reflected on a palate that shows extraordinary substance, thanks to rich alcohol and the perfectly judged harmony among its components. The attractive Vermentino combines scents of herbs and wildflowers with fruity notes and a lightly aromatic vein; it displays sound structure, good length and a soft, elegant finish. Le Banche is the result of a very rigorous selection of pigato and vermentino grapes fermented and aged in barriques. The wine offers an appealing array of aromas, with particularly delightful hints of vanilla, peaches in syrup and white chocolate. The silky, mellow palate has a long finish supported by the well-judged balance of fruit and oak. The natural, elegant and enchanting Acerbina is made from lumassina grapes that have been hard-pruned and skillfully vinified; clean, well-defined varietal aromas introduce a pleasantly acidulous, fairly stylish palate. The Solitario, made mostly from grenache and rossese, is their newly conceived red: its concentrated color precedes a delicate nose that releases notes of wild strawberry, black currant and raspberry and a touch of spice. The soft entry on the palate leads to a warm and mouth-filling mid palate; the gentle tannins allow the elegant fruit to show through and linger on the long finish. Well done, Vladimiro Galluzzo!

○	Le Banche '97	🍷🍷	5
○	Riviera Ligure di Ponente Pigato '98	🍷🍷	4
●	Solitario '97	🍷🍷	6
○	L'Acerbina '98	🍷	3*
○	Riviera Ligure di Ponente Vermentino '98	🍷	4
○	Passito Terre Rosse '95	🍸	6
●	Riviera Ligure di Ponente Rossese '97	🍸	4

IMPERIA

COLLE DEI BARDELLINI
VIA FONTANAROSA, 12
LOC. S. AGATA
18100 IMPERIA
TEL. 0183/291370

The '98 vintage was definitely a good one for this estate. With diligent vineyard management and the expert guidance of the oenologist Giuliano Noè, they have won Two Glasses each for their two special selections, the Vermentino Vigna U Munte and the Pigato Vigna La Torretta. The intensely straw-colored Vermentino has a fresh, moderately intense and persistent bouquet with balsamic and floral notes and a hint of honey. After a good entry on the palate it develops smoothly, showing balance and varietal character, and the finish is supported by a citrus tone. The Pigato is more complex: deep in color, it is at first a little bit reticent on the nose; opening notes of spice and vanilla give way to scents of yellow flowers and tropical fruit. These carry through perfectly onto the silky, soft and well-balanced palate, loaded with almost chewable fruit; the long finish is delightfully clean. The basic Pigato also showed well: it has a pale straw yellow hue tinged with light green, and primarily fruity aromas of medium intensity, suggestive of apple and, characteristically, peach. Perfect balance has not yet been achieved on a palate slightly dominated by acidity. The pleasant basic Vermentino has a fresh green fragrance and is undemandingly easy to drink. The success of this winery is due in no small measure to Pino Sola, well-known wine merchant and restaurateur from Genoa, who gracefully combines the management of the estate with a passion for wine.

○	Riviera Ligure di Ponente Pigato Vigna La Torretta '98	🍷🍷	4
○	Riviera Ligure di Ponente Vermentino Vigna U Munte '98	🍷🍷	4
○	Riviera Ligure di Ponente Pigato '98	🍷	4
○	Riviera Ligure di Ponente Vermentino '98		3

ORTONOVO (SP)

La Pietra del Focolare

Via Dogana, 209
19034 Ortonovo (SP)
tel. 0187/662129

Stefano Salvetti, who is assisted by his wife Laura, owes his love for the countryside to two people: his grandfather Armando, who passed down his love of nature and the good but simple life, and Ottaviano Lambruschi, standard-bearer of excellence in viticulture, who has imbued him with a passion for this profession, which is composed of hard labor and sacrifice but is, if performed well, deeply satisfying. Salvetti's small estate yields about 3,500 bottles of two Vermentino crus: the Solarancio and the Becco. The former comes from Sarticola and Bacchiano, near Castelnuovo Magra; the plant density is 8,000 vines per hectare, at an altitude of about 220 meters. The latter is from Becco, near Ortonovo, where the altitude is only 40 meters. The Vermentino Becco, which remains on its lees for around ninety days, was not yet ready for tasting, so we are reviewing only the Solarancio. Its yield per hectare is only 4,000 kilos of grapes, which then ferment at a temperature of about 18° C, remaining in contact with the skins for 12 hours. The resulting wine has an extremely attractive richness: it is intense in color and offers harmonious and well-knit scents of flowers, honey, exotic fruit (pineapple) and citrus peel; a good, weighty entry in the mouth leads to a silky, warm and soft mid palate; this is a satisfying wine despite the presence of a very small amount of residual sugar.

○	Colli di Luni Vermentino Solarancio '98	🍷	3

PIEVE DI TECO (IM)

Tommaso e Angelo Lupi

Via Mazzini, 9
18026 Pieve di Teco (IM)
tel. 0183/36161 - 0183/291610

This winery is located in the heart of the Arroscia valley. Its vineyards (whether owned or rented) are renowned for their position and microclimatic peculiarities. Grapes are supplied in part by growers with whom the Lupis have a close working relationship. In a good year they produce 120 thousand bottles, a substantial quantity by Ligurian standards. Our tastings bear witness to the work they have put into their wine-making. The basic Vermentino presents aromatic and fragrantly fruity scents; acidity and alcohol are well judged, and it offers solid structure and richness as well on the palate. The good special selection Le Serre releases light, delicate varietal aromas as a prelude to a crisp, soft and reasonably concentrated palate. The Pigatos, though clean, straightforward and well executed, are less substantial than last year's versions. The basic one, which is still a bit vegetal on the nose, concentrates on freshness and balance rather than on complexity. The more interesting Le Petraie offers distinct scents of citrus fruit and aromatic herbs. On the palate it is succulent, fruity and of medium density. The Vignamare, a partly barrique-fermented blend of pigato and vermentino, displays a broad floral and fruity fragrance, and rich, concentrated and evenly evolving fruit on the palate, as well as a long, lingering finish. Among the reds we particularly liked the Ormeasco Le Braje: it has good supple, rounded fruit and a bouquet reminiscent of cherry and blackberry.

○	Riviera Ligure di Ponente Vermentino '98	🍷🍷	4
○	Vignamare '97	🍷🍷	4
●	Riviera Ligure di Ponente Ormeasco Sup. Le Braje '97	🍷	4
○	Riviera Ligure di Ponente Pigato '98	🍷	4
○	Riviera Ligure di Ponente Pigato Le Petraie '98	🍷	4
○	Riviera Ligure di Ponente Vermentino Le Serre '98	🍷	4
●	Riviera Ligure di Ponente Ormeasco Sup. Le Braje '96	🍸🍸	4
●	Rossese di Dolceacqua '97	🍸	4

RANZO (IM)

A Maccia

Via Umberto I, 56
Fraz. Borgo
18028 Ranzo (IM)
tel. 0183/318003

The guiding hand at A Maccia is the graceful yet firm hand of a woman. Some time ago Loredana Faraldi took over the reins from her mother Fernanda, although she continues to heed her recommendations and advice. The estate vineyards are at Fighi Gianch, Cian du Beu and Curnai, all of them excellent hillside sites at an altitude of about 200 meters in the vicinity of Ranzo, a particularly felicitous area for producing Pigato. The estate was established a dozen or so years ago and has always aimed at excellence, with continually improving vineyard management and, as far as possible, organic farming methods. Thus their grapes are of appropriate quality, and vinification is directed by the oenologist Trevia. We should like to stress the reliability of A Maccia's wines, which have always been good and sometimes are excellent. The '98 Pigato displays its usual straw color, while the nose is characterized by sweet, powdery scents with hints of tropical fruit (pineapple), white plum and musk; a dryness on the palate is supported by reasonable fruit and a marked acidulous vein. This vintage is definitely not remarkable for its structure: the general impression is of a wine that is certainly enjoyable, but perhaps a bit over-confected. The succulent and fruity Rossese is, once again, very inviting. Loredana Faraldi has opened up a tiny estate shop, where one can buy directly at the winery: not only wine, but also a good extra virgin olive oil, olives in brine and olive paté.

○ Riviera Ligure di Ponente Pigato '98	🍷	3
● Riviera Ligure di Ponente Rossese '98	🍷	3

RANZO (IM)

Bruna

Via Umberto I, 81
Fraz. Borgo
18028 Ranzo (IM)
tel. 0183/318082

Behind the bottles that emerge from this estate are passionate devotion and self-sacrifice; this is all the more true because Liguria is a region that doesn't give away anything to anyone. Riccardo Bruna looks after four hectares of vineyards (divided up between several prime zones) with meticulous care and rigorous pruning to reduce yields. He then carries out a further selection of the grapes and divides them according to their vineyard of origin: those from Ortovero are for the Villa Torrachetta and the ones from Ranzo go into Le Russeghine. His aim is to produce notable wines, each of which retains its own individual characteristics and typical varietal qualities, with an added touch of elegance and personality. We recently carried out a small vertical tasting of the Le Russeghine selection, starting with the latest vintage and going back to the '94. We can say that the tasting was very satisfying, and that it revealed a potential for development over time which was unthinkable for this type of wine even a few short years ago. Thus Bruna is again clearly shown to be a leading producer of Pigatos that can stand aging. This year, as always, we particularly enjoyed the Pigato Le Russeghine, with its intense and persistent varietal fragrance; on the palate it offers a robust structure with good fruit and satisfying length. The Torrachetta doesn't shy at comparison with its more renowned stable-mate: it has a delicate bouquet with suggestions of yellow peach and musk and balsamic notes. The palate is crisp and easy, if a little lacking in flesh.

○ Riviera Ligure di Ponente Pigato Le Russeghine '98	🍷🍷	3*
○ Riviera Ligure di Ponente Pigato Villa Torrachetta '98	🍷	3
○ Riviera Ligure di Ponente Pigato Le Russeghine '97	🍷🍷 (outline)	3

RIOMAGGIORE (SP)

Walter De Battè
Via Pecunia, 168
19017 Riomaggiore (SP)
tel. 0187/920127

Walter's vineyards, divided among small strips of terracing, are located in the Cinqueterre right above Riomaggiore; they enjoy excellent south-southeastern exposure and the vines are trained according to the local "low canopy" system. Walter has a particular liking for the bosco grape and he has replanted principally to this variety rather than to albarola or vermentino. He keeps his yields extremely low and he was the first in the area to use barriques, demonstrating that small casks, if used well, can add positive notes both to the dry white and to Sciacchetrà; he also introduced virtually unknown wine-making practices here, such as lees stirring and malolactic fermentation. His wines, of which he makes about 3,000 bottles, do not need to be drunk up in a hurry: indeed, the years tend to be kind to them. The Cinque Terre '98, of a lovely deep straw hue, needs more time to acquire its customary harmony on the nose: the oak, at least initially, somewhat masks its delicately floral and marine tones as well as an inviting nuance of acacia honey. The bouquet is mirrored on the even and long palate. The sweet version also won Two Glasses. De Battè's Sciacchetrà is not a wine to knock back without thinking: its intense amber color leads into an elegant yet forceful nose with aromas of cocoa, nuts and dried apricots blended with lively spicy notes. The palate displays remarkable concentration and full body, and its sweetness never becomes cloying thanks to underpinning acidity and tannins which provide excellent balance.

○ Cinque Terre '98	🍷🍷	4
○ Cinque Terre Sciacchetrà '96	🍷🍷	6
○ Cinque Terre '97	🍷🍷 (white)	4
○ Cinque Terre Sciacchetrà '95	🍷🍷 (white)	6

VENDONE (SV)

Claudio Vio
Fraz. Crosa, 16
17030 Vendone (SV)
tel. 0182/76338

Once again this year, unfortunately, fire destroyed a great many hectares of forest in Liguria. Apart from the damage to the natural environment, those who suffer most are the people who work in these areas: farmers and vignerons, in fact, must deal not only with the vicissitudes of nature but with the stupidity of man as well. At Vendone, a characteristic hilly corner of Liguria, Claudio Vio had to work long and hard to prevent the pyromaniacs from literally sending the fruits of a good vintage up in smoke. He dedicatedly and skillfully cultivates about two hectares of land planted almost entirely to pigato and vermentino, plus a small percentage of red grapes which, together with a few white ones, go to make up a light and unpretentious wine called Ronco Brujau. But the winery's real strength lies in the traditional local varieties: both pigato and vermentino succeed, year in and year out, in giving excellent results, be it thanks to the terroir or to the ability of the grower. In the last vintage, Vio was working with excellent raw material, so his wines did particularly well at our blind tastings. The Pigato came in first: it has a clear and inviting deep straw yellow color, and its quite complex bouquet opens with delicate scents of peach, apple and apricot which then combine with seductive aromatic and floral notes, all following through onto the dry but rounded, warm and silky palate; the succulent finish is attractively reminiscent of bitter almond. The Vermentino is very good; although its nose (banana and wildflowers) is understated, the palate shows good backbone, softness and length, as well as just perceptible alcohol.

○ Riviera Ligure di Ponente Pigato '98	🍷🍷	3*
○ Riviera Ligure di Ponente Vermentino '98	🍷	3

OTHER WINERIES

The following producers obtained good scores in our tastings with one or more of their wines:

PROVINCE OF GENOVA

F.lli Parma
Ne, tel. 0185/337073
Golfo del Tigullio Vermentino I Canselé '98
Bianchetta Genovese Vigna dei Parma '98

PROVINCE OF IMPERIA

Antonio Perrino
Dolceacqua, tel. 0184/206267
Rossese di Dolceacqua '98

Lorenzo Ramò
Pornassio, tel. 0183/33097
Riviera Ligure di Ponente Ormeasco '98
Riviera Ligure di Ponente
Ormeasco Sciac-trà '98

PROVINCE OF LA SPEZIA

Fattoria Il Chioso
Arcola, tel. 0187/986620
Colli di Luni Vermentino Stemma '98
Merlot del Melo '97

La Colombiera
Castelnuovo Magra, tel. 0187/675655
Colli di Luni Rosso Terrizzo '97

Cooperativa Agricola di Riomaggiore, Manarola, Corniglia, Vernazza e Monterosso
Riomaggiore, tel. 0187/920435
Cinque Terre
Costa de Campu di Manarola '98

Forlini e Cappellini
Riomaggiore, tel. 0187/920496
Cinque Terre '98

Il Monticello
Sarzana, tel. 0187/621432
Colli di Luni Vermentino '98

Santa Caterina, Sarzana, tel. 0187/610129
Colli di Luni Vermentino '98

PROVINCE OF SAVONA

Cantine Calleri, Albenga, tel. 0182/20425
Riviera Ligure di Ponente
Vermentino I Musazzi '98
Riviera Ligure di Ponente
Pigato Saleasco '98
Riviera Ligure di Ponente Pigato '98

LOMBARDY

If we were to look at the Three Glass wines only – seven of them this year as opposed to nine in '99 – we might be tempted to say that Lombardy is on a downswing. In fact it's far from it! There are eight more reviews this time, and even so we feel we haven't dedicated enough space to one of the oenologically most dynamic regions of the north. The Lombards would seem to have realized that there is vast, indeed almost limitless potential in their land. This is, of course, not the enchanted south, where the sun always shines (or almost always), but the wealth at their disposal, in terms of soil and microclimate, in such areas as the Oltrepò, the Valtellina and Garda, to name only a few macro-zones, is really remarkable. Not to mention the fact that Milan, with its renowned State University School of Agriculture, whose influence is felt in every aspect of viticulture throughout Italy, is virtually around the corner. Many prospective producers, seeing the results that attentive zone-oriented agriculture has succeeded in bringing forth even in the most far-flung regions, have set out to work in their own zones. It's a slow process at first, but when it gets going it can have astonishing effects on the quality of the wine. So they're not being caught napping in Lombardy. Our hats are off to Franciacorta for a start, and particularly the most distinguished labels. Five great Franciacortas won top honors, but a good three or four others came very close indeed. It just confirms once again that this district is on the cutting edge of wine-making in the region. The Oltrepò, on the other hand, the other great wine-making plain up here, has produced scattered results. There are a number of newcomers and many estates have improved considerably, but there is no sense of a master plan to upgrade the enire area. Where are the great metodo classico spumantes that the Oltrepò could so clearly give us? You could count the existing examples on the fingers of one hand, and you might even have a finger or two left over. This is somewhat distressing when you think that almost all the Italian pinot nero for spumante grows right here. Paradoxically it is the fruity whites and the semi-sparkling wines made from local grapes such as barbera and bonarda that are most consistent and representative. There's a lot of talk about great reds and great whites, but you might have some trouble finding them. The Valtellina will be working towards an important transformation in the next few years: they're going to replant most of their vineyards, since many of the vines are rather long in the tooth. Given the current general excellence, this process should have stupendous results once it is well under way, if it is accompanied by some modernization of cellar technique. The eastern part of Lombardy is sailing along in its customary top form, although this year it didn't capture Three Glasses. But that's just a question of vintages.

ADRO (BS)

COLA
VIA SANT'ANNA, 22
25030 ADRO (BS)
TEL. 030/7356195

Cola, a small estate in Adro that doesn't make more than 70 to 80 thousand bottles a year, maintains a high standard that makes it a point of reference for all of Franciacorta. Battista Cola and his son Stefano work the vines themselves on their 12 hectares of land on Adro's Monte Alto, and with the advice of the oenologist Alberto Musatti they produce a range of still wines and Franciacortas with evident care. Their star is once again the Franciacorta Extra Brut in its '95 version, one of the best vintage wines of the whole district. The complex bouquet is elegant and harmonious, rich in notes of yeast and vanilla with a delicate toasty quality that doesn't cover the fruit. Dense, structured and complex, yet elegant on the palate, it offers a fine, caressing effervescence and a long finish. The Franciacorta Brut is soft, full-bodied and stylish; just a slightly longer finish would have secured it Two Glasses. Next time. Moving to the still wines, we would point out the good T. d. F. Bianco '97 from the Tinazza vineyard, another estate classic, with perhaps a slightly intrusive note of new oak. We must say we expected something better from the Rosso Tamino '97. It has a lovely ruby hue and a soft bouquet of ripe black berries, but in the mouth we find a pleasing freshness and undemanding quaffability rather than substance and complexity. Both T. d. F. Rosso '97s are worthy of mention.

○	Franciacorta Extra Brut '95	🍷🍷	4
○	Franciacorta Brut	🍷	4
○	T. d. F. Bianco V. Tinazza '97	🍷	3
●	T. d. F. Rosso Tamino '97	🍷	3
●	T. d. F. Rosso '97		2
○	Franciacorta Brut	YY	4
○	Franciacorta Extra Brut '92	YY	4
○	Franciacorta Extra Brut '94	YY	4
○	T. d. F. Bianco Sel. '93	YY	4
○	T. d. F. Bianco Sel. '94	YY	3
○	T. d. F. Bianco V. Tinazza '95	YY	3
○	T. d. F. Bianco '97	Y	2*
●	T. d. F. Rosso '93	Y	3
●	T. d. F. Rosso '95	Y	2*
●	T. d. F. Rosso Tamino '95	Y	3

ADRO (BS)

CONTADI CASTALDI
VIA COLZANO, 32
LOC. FORNACI
25030 ADRO (BS)
TEL. 030/7450126

In the course of a few short years Contadi Castaldi has become one of the most important wineries of Franciacorta. It is to this zone what a "négociant-manipulant" is in Champagne. In addition to the grapes from various leased vineyards, this well-known firm (a part of the holding company Terre Moretti which also includes Bellavista) vinifies grapes from dozens of growers whose viticultural labors it supervises throughout the year. At the helm of Contadi Castaldi is the young and brilliant manager Martino De Rosa, while the distinguished oenological scientist Mario Falcetti directs the technical side. The most important fruit of this collaboration is a Franciacorta, the Brut Magno '95, bottled only in magnums, and one of the very best to be found. Its color is a brilliant greenish straw and it shows a fine and persistent bead; it opens on the nose with notes of apple, white peach and ripe apricot and is soft and fleshy in the mouth, where the peach and apricot are very cleanly echoed, together with hints of yeast, kiwi, litchi and fresh fruit cocktail. Next comes the exquisitely elegant Franciacorta Satèn, all soft tones of ripe white-fleshed fruit, herbs and vanilla, with great finesse and overall stylishness. The Terre di Franciacorta Bianco Mancapane '97 is rich, succulent and fruity; if food were scarce you could just about spread it on a piece of bread and forget your hunger, it's so delightful, soft and balanced. High marks also for the excellent Franciacorta Zéro and the extremely pleasant sweet Pinodisé.

○	Franciacorta Magno Brut '95	🍷🍷	6
○	Franciacorta Satèn	🍷🍷	5
○	Franciacorta Zéro	🍷🍷	5
○	Pinodisé	🍷🍷	6
○	T. d. F. Bianco Mancapane '97	🍷🍷	5
○	Franciacorta Brut	🍷	4
⊙	Franciacorta Rosé	🍷	5
○	Franciacorta Brut	YY	4
⊙	Franciacorta Rosé	YY	5
○	Franciacorta Satèn	YY	5
○	Pinodisé	YY	5
○	T. d. F. Bianco '96	YY	3*
○	Franciacorta Zéro	Y	5
○	T. d. F. Bianco '97	Y	3
●	T. d. F. Rosso '96	Y	3

ADRO (BS)

CORNALETO
VIA CORNALETO, 2
25030 ADRO (BS)
TEL. 030/7450507 - 030/7450565

Luigi Lancini's winery, situated among the beautful vineyards of Monte Alto di Adro, continues to uphold its high standards. Its excellent exposure and its soil rich in pebbly "corna" ("horns" in the local Brescian dialect--hence the name of the estate) are, perhaps, the secret of the quality of these wines. But one needs more than good land. To make wines like these - the excellent vintage Pas Dosé '90, for example, which we tasted this year - one needs clear ideas and plenty of energy. Luigi has these in abundance, and also the advice of the oenologist Cesare Ferrari. The Pas Dosé '90 has a lovely bright straw color with a light green tinge, enticingly intense aromas of ripe fruit and herbs, with sage to the fore, and a delightful note of vanilla, all of which carry through to the fresh and fruity, full, balanced and soft palate, with a long finish besides. The Brut is up to standard, but hasn't made it to Two Glasses. Among the still wines we would mention the T.d.F. Rosso Poligono '95, which has a good concentrated color, sweet scents of berries and ripe plum, and a rounded softness in the mouth with well integrated tannins. The Rosso Baldoc '95 is pleasant and correctly made but without much body. The T.d.F. Rosso '96, with its evolved and vegetal notes, and the T.d.F. Rosso Sarese are less interesting. This year we did not try the whites, but they are usually good.

○	Franciacorta Pas Dosé '90	🍷🍷	5
○	Franciacorta Brut	🍷	5
●	T. d. F. Rosso Baldoc '95	🍷	4
●	T. d. F. Rosso Poligono '95	🍷	4
●	T. d. F. Rosso '96		3
●	T. d. F. Rosso Sarese '95		4
○	Franciacorta Brut '89	🍷🍷	5
○	Franciacorta Extra Brut	🍷🍷	4
○	T. d. F. Bianco V. Saline '92	🍷🍷	4
○	T. d. F. Bianco V. Saline '93	🍷🍷	4
●	T. d. F. Rosso Poligono '90	🍷🍷	3*
○	T. d. F. Bianco Corno Nero '93	🍷🍷	4
○	T. d. F. Bianco V. Saline '94	🍷🍷	3
●	T. d. F. Rosso Cornaleto '90	🍷🍷	3
○	T. d. F. Bianco '97	🍷	3

BEDIZZOLE (BS)

CANTRINA
VIA COLOMBERA, 7
25081 BEDIZZOLE (BS)
TEL. 030/6871052

Cantrina is a small estate with six of its seven hectares under vine. Established in 1990, it makes about 10 thousand bottles of wine from its riesling, chardonnay, pinot nero, merlot and groppello grapes. Since quantity is limited, it perforce must aim at quality (a preference here in any case). Of the four wines presented at our tastings this year, two received Two Glasses, a third came awfully close and the fourth was at the very least worthy of mention. We'll start with the Garda Pinot Nero Corteccio '97. The grapes themselves were extremely rich (the yield was 1.5 kilograms per vine); they were macerated on their skins for eight days, fermentation was carefully controlled and the wine spent a year in barriques, six months in steel vats and another six in the bottle before the market got a first look at it. This Pinot Nero has a good garnet color (though the variety has few of those reddening pigments called anthocyanins), a clear fragrance of black currant jam, and is succulent, harmonious and elegant to the palate. The white Sole '96 seemed excellent as well. It is made from sauvignon (60%) and semillon grapes which were dried for five months before gentle pressing. The must started fermentation in steel vats and was transferred to barriques to finish the process and rest for 18 months. It has a brilliant golden color, a complex bouquet with notes of vanilla, raisin and ripe meadow mushroom, and a gracefully pleasing palate. The Garda Chardonnay '97 is somewhat dominated by wood: a sweet spicy tone almost drowns out the excellent varietal notes. The Garda Riesling Renano '98 is still a bit closed to the nose but should improve in the bottle.

●	Garda Pinot Nero Corteccio '97	🍷🍷	4
○	Sole '96	🍷🍷	4
○	Garda Chardonnay '97	🍷	2*
○	Garda Riesling '98		2

BRONI (PV)

CANTINA SOCIALE DI BRONI
VIA SANSALUTO, 81
27043 BRONI (PV)
TEL. 0385/51505

The Cantina Sociale di Broni, established in the early 1960s, is one of the largest and most modern wineries in the Oltrepò Pavese: 500 member growers provide some 100 thousand quintals of grapes harvested from about a thousand hectares of vines to produce 12.5 million liters of white, red, rosé and sparkling wines sold at eminently reasonable prices, given their quality. The mildly fizzy Barbera '98 is particularly successful. It has a light, ruddy foam and a fragrant, grapy bouquet with touches of carnation and wild blackberry; in the mouth it's dry with no hint of harshness, clean and harmonious, with a good acid thrust. The Pinot Grigio '98 is somewhat light in color, delicately flowery to the nose, and crisp, distinct and succulent on the palate. The straightforward and fragrant lightly sparkling '98 Bonarda has an attractive almondy finish. The monovarietal Pinot Nero Brut Classico '95, from grapes grown in the Scuropasso Valley, is a little thin but pleasingly frank, and dominated by notes of hazelnut and crusty bread attributable to two years on its refermentation lees in the bottle. The mildly bubbly Riesling Italico '98 is simple, fresh and succulent if perhaps a bit green. The naturally fizzy Moscato '98, while not very rich, does offer distinct aromas of peach and sage, and is a pleasure to drink (especially considering its extremely low price). The Buttafuoco, 80% croatina and 20% uva rara, and the white and lightly bubbly Pinot Nero in bianco are both decent.

●	O. P. Barbera '98	🍷🍷	2*
●	O. P. Bonarda '98	🍷	2*
○	O. P. Moscato '98	🍷	1*
○	O. P. Pinot Grigio '98	🍷	2
○	O. P. Pinot Nero Brut Cl. '95	🍷	3
○	O. P. Riesling Italico '98	🍷	2*
●	O. P. Buttafuoco '97		2
●	O. P. Pinot Nero in bianco '98		2

CANNETO PAVESE (PV)

F.LLI GIORGI
VIA CAMPONOCE, 39/A
27044 CANNETO PAVESE (PV)
TEL. 0385/262151

This is the debut in the Guide of Fratelli Giorgi, established in 1870 and now run by the brothers Gianfranco, the oenologist, and Antonio, in charge of marketing. In their three large cellars in Camponoce, Casa Chizzoli and Vigalone, all near Canneto in the Oltrepò hills, a considerable amount of good wine is made. Their Sangue di Giuda '98, from croatina (80%), barbera (10%), uva rara, ughetta and pinot nero grown in sandy, limestone-rich earth, is made in a traditional fashion. It's a sweet, fizzy deep purple wine with the distinctly grapy aroma of must and an intensely fruity taste. The Bonarda La Brughera '98 has a similar style. Produced exclusively from croatina grapes from the La Brughera vineyard on a hillside near Canneto, it has a red mousse, a dark ruby hue, aromas of almond and black cherry and a full body with a vein of light sweetness which contrasts well with its bitter, subtly tannic finish. This is an up-to-date version of the traditional Bonarda. The Buttafuoco '97, on the other hand, is a dry red, matured in barrels of Slavonian oak and in barriques. A blend of barbera, croatina, uva rara and pinot nero from the Casa del Corno vineyard near Stradella, it is of a garnet-tinged ruby color, with a well-defined nose of jam and spice (vanilla, cinnamon, clove). In the mouth it is dry and still a bit rough because of its tannins, but they should smooth out in the not too distant future. The Pinot Grigio '98 is the most interesting of the whites, simple, well-balanced, and admirably fresh and succulent. The spumantes don't do quite as well: the Brut classico '94 is too far along, and the Charmat method Incontro is clean but hasn't much character.

●	O. P. Bonarda La Brughera '98	🍷🍷	2*
●	O. P. Sangue di Giuda '98	🍷🍷	2*
●	O. P. Buttafuoco Casa del Corno '97	🍷	3
○	O. P. Pinot Grigio '98		2

CANNETO PAVESE (PV)

Bruno Verdi
Via Vergomberra, 5
27044 Canneto Pavese (PV)
tel. 0385/88023

Young Paolo Verdi is as determined as ever to make superlative wines. The Rosso Riserva Cavariola, his standard-bearer, is living up to its reputation. The grapes from the '96 harvest (60% croatina, 20% uva rara, 15% vespolina, 5% barbera) were macerated for a good while, and 20% of the must finished fermenting in Allier barriques. The wine, which matured in new or once-used small barrels or in Slavonian oak casks, is warm, robust, harmonious and elegantly full-bodied. High marks also for the lightly fizzy, fragrant and fruity Bonarda '98. The fine cold-macerated Riesling Renano Vigneto Costa '98 stands out among the whites. It has a greenish gold color and a clearly varietal nose and is, in the mouth, full-bodied and elegant, with an acid impetus, lacking in the '97, that gives it its delightful freshness. Down a step we find the Pinot Grigio '98, pleasingly direct, with a slight citric edge. The Moscato Vivace '98 (90% moscato, 10% malvasia di Candia, from Volpara) is not disappointing; it offers a bouquet of sage and orange blossom with a hint of musk, while in the mouth it is sweet and enticing, finishing on a note of peach and apricot. Returning to the reds, the Buttafuoco '96 (croatina, barbera and uva rara), aged for a year in Slavonian oak, is full-bodied and robust, but also a little harsh because of untamed tannins. The Sangue di Giuda Dolce Paradiso '98, a lightly fizzy red dessert wine, is worthy of mention. A promising piece of news to finish with: Paolo has planted, on the Scuropasso side of Broni, a vineyard of pinot nero from which he hopes to make a great red wine. We look forward to it.

●	O. P. Bonarda '98	▼▼	3*
○	O. P. Riesling Renano Vigneto Costa '98	▼▼	3*
●	O. P. Rosso Cavariola Ris. '96	▼▼	4
●	O. P. Buttafuoco '96	▼	3
○	O. P. Moscato '98	▼	3
○	O. P. Pinot Grigio '98	▼	3
●	O. P. Sangue di Giuda Dolce Paradiso '98		3
●	O. P. Barbera '90	▽▽	3*
●	O. P. Bonarda '93	▽▽	3*
○	O. P. Moscato '95	▽▽	2*
○	O. P. Riesling Renano Vigneto Costa '96	▽▽	3*
●	O. P. Rosso Cavariola Ris. '90	▽▽	4

CAPRIOLO (BS)

Lantieri de Paratico
Via Paratico, 50
25031 Capriolo (BS)
tel. 030/736151

The Lantieri de Paratico family has deep and ancient roots in Franciacorta. They were among the first here to use the classic method in making effervescent wines, which they have been doing in their beautiful cellar in Capriolo since the early 1870s. In recent years their Franciacorta and Terre di Franciacorta labels have been much applauded. They are well-executed perfect representatives of their native soil, as a taste of the Franciacorta Brut '96 will show you. It has a very lively straw color and intense, sweet, enticing aromas featuring peach jam and milk toffee. The notable elegance and balance on the palate are evidence of an attentive "prise de mousse", and the crisp finish is elegantly vanilla-laden. In other words, altogether marvelous. The Brut Arcadia '95 is on the same level. It's a new cuvée made from chardonnay (70%) and pinot nero and its fortes are fresh herbal and fruity aromas and a soft, richly structured, elegant and persistent palate with a delectable note of sage on the finish. This is an ideal Franciacorta for drinking with the local pasta dishes with their tomato-free sauces. The T.d.F. Bianco Colzano '97, full-bodied but a bit too woody, and the Franciacorta Extra Brut, which seemed to us to be a bit thinner than previous versions, are perfectly acceptable. The T.d.F. Rosso Colzano '97 is not quite up to snuff.

○	Franciacorta Brut '96	▼▼	5
○	Franciacorta Brut Arcadia '95	▼▼	5
○	Franciacorta Extra Brut	▼	5
○	T. d. F. Bianco Colzano '97	▼	4
●	T. d. F. Rosso Colzano '97		4
○	Franciacorta Brut '90	▽▽	4
○	Franciacorta Brut '91	▽▽	4
○	Franciacorta Brut '94	▽▽	5
○	Franciacorta Extra Brut	▽▽	4
○	T. d. F. Bianco Colzano '95	▽▽	3*
○	Franciacorta Brut '89	▽	5
○	Franciacorta Extra Brut '94	▽	3
●	T. d. F. Rosso '96	▽	3
●	T. d. F. Rosso Colzano '96	▽	4

CAPRIOLO (BS)

RICCI CURBASTRO
VIA ADRO, 37
25031 CAPRIOLO (BS)
TEL. 030/736094

In every edition of the Guide we find ourselves congratulating Riccardo Ricci Curbastro for some new important position he has attained as well as for the quality of his wines. This year we offer our best wishes to Riccardo, a past president of the Consorzio Vini Franciacorta, for becoming the president of Federdoc, a national association that coordinates the activities of all the consortiums formed to safeguard Italian wine. Our tastings were very positive again this time, and the best wine he made, together with the oenologist Alberto Musatti, is, in our opinion, the Franciacorta Satèn. It has a brilliant straw color with just a thought of green, and shows a fine, dense, long-lasting perlage. The nose evinces soft, almost sweet notes of ripe white-fleshed fruit and vanilla, and on the palate it is full-bodied, fat and structured, with a dry crispness that shades into delicate bitterish tones. The structure, fleshiness and fullness of its finish make it an ideal Franciacorta at table, as is the soft and fruity Franciacorta Démi Sec, elegant and full-bodied with a trace of fresh herbs. The altogether well-balanced Franciacorta Brut is very good as well, but the Extra Brut '95 seems a little thinner than in the past. The Pinot Nero '96 stands out among the still wines. It is very well executed, and the hints of blueberry, raspberry and black currant are nicely blended with the barrique-derived wood. The Terre di Franciacortas are interesting, and so is the Brolo dei Passoni '96, an elegant sweet wine made from partly dried chardonnay.

○	Brolo dei Passoni '96	🍷🍷	5
○	Franciacorta Satèn	🍷🍷	4
●	Pinot Nero Sebino '96	🍷🍷	5
○	Franciacorta Brut	🍷	4
○	Franciacorta Démi Sec	🍷	4
○	Franciacorta Extra Brut '95	🍷	5
○	T. d. F. Bianco '98	🍷	2*
○	T. d. F. Bianco Vigna Bosco Alto '97	🍷	4
●	T. d. F. Rosso Santella del Gröm '96	🍷	4
○	Franciacorta Brut Magnum '91	🍷🍷 (empty)	5
○	Franciacorta Extra Brut '93	🍷🍷 (empty)	4
○	Franciacorta Satèn	🍷🍷 (empty)	4
○	Franciacorta Satèn '92	🍷🍷 (empty)	4
○	Franciacorta Satèn '93	🍷🍷 (empty)	4
●	Pinot Nero Sebino '95	🍷🍷 (empty)	4

CASTEGGIO (PV)

RICCARDO ALBANI
VIA SAN BIAGIO, 46
27045 CASTEGGIO (PV)
TEL. 0383/83622

Riccardo Albani is a young wine producer who knows what he wants. He doesn't flounder in a multitude of different wines as often happens in the Oltrepò, but concentrates on making a few kinds as well as he can, and that turns out to be very well. His vines cover about 15 hectares on the hills near Casteggio (200 to 250 meters above sea level), mostly in La Casona, a small valley near the Ceresino woods and a very propitious spot both for climate and for soil, which is quite various (from dense clay to limestone and even loose and pebbly textures), imparting various aromas to the grapes. These last are Rhine riesling, bonarda, barbera, uva rara and pinot nero. The greenish gold Riesling '98 is very graceful and harmonious, with elegant floral and mineral tones and excellent length. The '97 version is agreeable, but less richly fruity. The Rosso Riserva Vigne della Casona '96, whose grapes (mostly barbera but also uva rara and pinot nero) grew on old vines, was aged in wood and then for a year in the bottle before being offered for sale. It has a dark garnet hue, a distinct bouquet of jam and spice, and a full-bodied, austere palate. The lightly effervescent Bonarda '98 is fragrant, fruity and clean, with alcohol, acidity, and tannins in good balance. The Pinot Nero '98, in its debut appearance, has an appealing lively color and an intense nose of black currant and sweet spice. In the mouth it's still sharp, but it shows excellent structure: with some more bottle age it should turn into a remarkable wine.

●	O. P. Bonarda '98	🍷🍷	3*
●	O. P. Pinot Nero '98	🍷🍷	4
○	O. P. Riesling Renano '98	🍷🍷	3*
●	O. P. Rosso Vigna della Casona Ris. '96	🍷🍷	4
○	O. P. Riesling Renano '97	🍷	3
●	O. P. Rosso Vigna della Casona Ris. '95	🍷	4

CASTEGGIO (PV)

FRECCIAROSSA

VIA VIGORELLI, 141
27045 CASTEGGIO (PV)
TEL. 0383/804465

Thanks to Pietro Calvi di Bergolo's energetic organizational and marketing prowess, and the great competence of oenologist Franco Bernabei, the wines of Frecciarossa are returning to their glory days. This historic estate in Casteggio (it goes back to the 18th century) is still staking its all on a small number of wines, and they're getting better and better. The first example is the Riesling Renano '98, made from grapes grown on old vines (3,000 vines per hectare) and new ones (4,800 per hectare). After cold maceration on the skins for 24 hours, it's fermented at a temperature kept at 18-20°C. It has a greenish gold color and a clearly varietal nose of apple, lemon balm, rose and flint, and a decidedly richer and more harmonious palate than the '97; it still has a good acid thrust, but there's more fullness and grace. The Riserva Villa Odero '94 is very good as well. A blend of croatina, barbera and uva rara left on their skins for two weeks of controlled maceration, it is aged partly in Slavonian oak barrels and partly in barriques for two years, then for another ten months in the bottle before going to market. The red Le Praielle '97 is better than last year's version. It is made like the Riserva but spends less time in the wood (10-12 months) and bottle (4 months) before being sold. It's still a little hard, but should acquire harmony and fullness with time. The brick-red Pinot Nero '95, with its elegant nose of black currant and spice, is soft and ripe and can be drunk right now.

○	O. P. Riesling Renano '98	▼▼	4
●	O. P. Rosso Villa Odero Ris. '94	▼▼	4
●	O. P. Pinot Nero '95	▼	4
●	O. P. Rosso Le Praielle '97	▼	3
●	O. P. Pinot Nero '91	▽▽	5
●	O. P. Rosso '90	▽▽	5
●	O. P. Rosso Villa Odero '89	▽▽	5
●	O. P. Rosso Villa Odero '91	▽▽	4
●	O. P. Rosso Villa Odero Ris. '90	▽▽	5
●	O. P. Pinot Nero '90	▽	5
●	O. P. Pinot Nero '93	▽	4
●	O. P. Pinot Nero '94	▽	4
●	O. P. Rosso Le Praielle '96	▽	4
●	O. P. Rosso Villa Odero Ris. '91	▽	4
●	O. P. Rosso Villa Odero '92		0

CASTEGGIO (PV)

LE FRACCE

VIA CASTEL DEL LUPO, 5
27045 CASTEGGIO (PV)
TEL. 0383/804151

In last year's Guide we said that for some time now Francesco Cervetti, Le Fracce's technical director, has been luckier with his whites than with his reds. This year, though, he didn't put a foot wrong. Four wines were presented, two whites and two reds, and each came home with Two Glasses. The Pinot Grigio '98, made from organically grown grapes, as for that matter are all their wines, is as robust (13.9% alcohol) as it is elegant; it's also succulent and harmonious, and richly redolent of acacia flowers. The Riesling Renano '98, from the vines of the San Biagio and Mairano vineyards at an altitude of 250-300 meters, is not a lesser wine. Greenish gold in color, with a fragrance of apple and wild peach, it is both fuller-bodied and more graceful than its predecessor of a year ago. The Cirgà '97, made from croatina, barbera and pinot nero, is excellent. The bunches of grapes, harvested in the middle of October, underwent a two-week maceration in their skins. Of a deep ruby hue, it has a nose of ripe grape and prune, with a hint of dried violet. The palate is dry, warm (14.5% alcohol), robust but also velvety, with a long finish. More time in the bottle should give it further cohesion. The Bonarda La Rubiosa '98 is living up to its reputation. Made from well-ripened grapes, it underwent a second fermentation in pressure tanks the February following its harvest. It's a lightly sparkling, mouth-filling and concentrated wine with an exuberant fragrance.

●	O. P. Bonarda La Rubiosa '98	▼▼	3*
○	O. P. Pinot Grigio '98	▼▼	3*
○	O. P. Riesling Renano '98	▼▼	3*
●	O. P. Rosso Cirgà '97	▼▼	4
●	O. P. Bonarda '94	▽▽	4
●	O. P. Bonarda '95	▽▽	4
○	O. P. Pinot Grigio '93	▽▽	4
○	O. P. Pinot Grigio '95	▽▽	4
○	O. P. Pinot Grigio '97	▽▽	4
○	O. P. Riesling Renano '96	▽▽	4
●	O. P. Rosso Bohemi '90	▽▽	5
●	O. P. Rosso Cirgà '90	▽▽	5
●	O. P. Rosso Cirgà '91	▽▽	5
○	O. P. Riesling Renano '97	▽	4
●	O. P. Rosso Cirgà '96	▽	5

CASTEGGIO (PV)

TENUTA PEGAZZERA
LOC. PEGAZZERA
27045 CASTEGGIO (PV)
TEL. 0383/804646

Tenuta Pegazzera is one of the most beautiful estates in the Oltrepò Pavese. Formerly owned by the Almo Collegio Borromeo of Pavia, it is on the road that climbs, among the vines, from Casteggio to Montalto. The nucleus of the estate is a splendid 18th century villa with its own private chapel, venerable park and Italian-style garden full of roses. Their vines cover approximately 50 hectares and are supervised by the agronomist Pierluigi Donna, who follows European Union standards for organic farming. The vaulted brick cellar with its modern equipment is in the hands of the notably experienced oenologist Corrado Cugnasco, who is also the technical consultant for several spumante producers in Franciacorta. So it's hardly surprising that the most successful wine made here at the moment is the Brut Classico '92. Pinot nero and chardonnay went into it, and it had 36 months on its lees. A pale golden color with a greenish tinge and an extremely fine and long-lasting perlage are the prelude to a subtle yet penetrating bouquet of crusty bread, laurel, apple and musk. The dry but not punitive palate is mature yet firm and elegantly mouth-filling. The good, garnet-hued Pinot Nero '97 has a distinct aroma of black currant jam, and a soft, nicely evolved palate with a well-judged bitterish finish. The Moscato Naturale '98 is very fragrant, fresh and fruity, with hints of sage and rosewood. The white-vinified Pinot Nero in bianco '98 is pleasingly direct and faintly fizzy. The Oltrepò Pavese Rosso Cardinale is correctly made, but perhaps a bit thin. The cardinal in question is of course Carlo Borromeo.

○	O. P. Pinot Nero Brut Cl. '92	🍷🍷	4
○	O. P. Moscato '98	🍷	3
●	O. P. Pinot Nero '97	🍷	3
○	O. P. Pinot Nero in bianco '98		3
●	O. P. Rosso Cardinale '97		3

CASTEGGIO (PV)

RUIZ DE CARDENAS
STRADA ALLA MOLLIE, 35
27047 CASTEGGIO (PV)
TEL. 0383/82301

When he planted his five hectares of vines, Ruiz de Cardenas made a firm decision: only pinot nero (clones from Burgundy for the reds and from Champagne for the sparklers and the whites) and chardonnay (clones from Champagne). Then he entrusted these vines to the agronomist Giuseppe Zatti, and the small but very well-equipped cellar to the oenologist Giancarlo Scaglione. The idea was to make excellent wine and hang the expense. In the past their efforts have not always been crowned with success, but this year it's a different story. The spumante classico Brut Réserve '93 (two parts chardonnay to one of pinot nero), produced only in excellent years, with a minimum of 48 months on its lees, is lovely to look at and offers a complex fragrance of sweet spice (part of the base wine was fermented in oak from Allier and Vosges), honey, Golden Delicious apple and black currant and then a long aristocratic palate. The Extra Brut '94 is a simpler wine. The Pinot Nero Brumano '96 takes its name from a vineyard on a Casteggio slope. The grapes were fermented with 10 days of maceration, then left to age for a year in small French barrels, and for another year and a half in the bottle. It was worth the trouble. It's a lovely velvety Pinot Nero with a bouquet of black currant jam, leather and wild game, and it's ready to drink. The Baloss '97 is admirable too. It's another pinot nero, but it had a shorter maceration (one week), and was aged in steel to keep its varietal aromas intact.

○	O. P. Brut Cl. Réserve '93	🍷🍷	4
●	O. P. Pinot Nero Baloss '97	🍷🍷	3*
●	O. P. Pinot Nero Brumano '96	🍷🍷	4
○	O. P. Extra Brut Cl. '94		4
●	O. P. Pinot Nero Brumano '92	🍸🍸	4
○	O. P. Extra Brut Cl.	🍸	4
●	O. P. Pinot Nero '94	🍸	3

CAZZAGO S. MARTINO (BS)

MONTE ROSSA
FRAZ. BORNATO
VIA MARENZIO, 14
25040 CAZZAGO S. MARTINO (BS)
TEL. 030/725066

Monte Rossa is one of the stars of the Franciacorta wine scene again this year. Indeed, one should say the Italian wine scene, given the spectacular performance of the bubblies from Paolo Rabotti and Paola Rovetta's estate, (which is in the capable hands of their son Emanuele). The general excellence of their production becomes immediately evident as soon as you open any bottle of their wine, still or sparkling. This year we were, surprisingly, bewitched at once by their Franciacorta Satèn. This is a kind of wine that is catching on among producers up here, made to be soft and enchanting, and hence strikingly pleasing right away. However their Satèn has something more going for it. An incredibly elegant bouquet of very ripe white-fleshed fruit, featuring quince, apricot, damson and Golden Delicious apple blended with delicate hints of vanilla and fresh medicinal herbs, leads to a soft and alluring entry on the palate; this soon develops with lots of body, structure, rich fruit and a velvety caressing mousse which, as it fades, leaves a note of ripe fruit and honey: Three very well-deserved Glasses. The Cabochon '94 came quite close: it is elegant, mouth-filling, round and harmonious, but perhaps just a shade too mature for its years. The Franciacorta Brut, for its part, is one of the best of the standard wines we've tasted this year, and the Sec is a fascinating soft blend of ripe fruit, vanilla and elegant sweetness. The Rosé and the two still Terre di Franciacortas are very good too.

○	Franciacorta Satèn	▼▼▼	5
○	Franciacorta Brut	▼▼	4
○	Franciacorta Brut Cabochon '94	▼▼	5
○	Franciacorta Sec	▼▼	4
⊙	Franciacorta Rosé	▼	4
○	T. d. F. Bianco Ravellino '98	▼	3
●	T. d. F. Rosso Cep '96	▼	3

CHIURO (SO)

NINO NEGRI
VIA GHIBELLINI, 3
23030 CHIURO (SO)
TEL. 0342/482521

The Sfursat 5 Stelle '97 made by the oenologist Casimiro Maule is at the very least a candidate for inscription in the book of great Italian red wines, and is without doubt the best red ever made in the Valtellina. Of course it gets Three Glasses. It has the best characteristics of all its greatest predecessors of the past decade. For a start, the use of wood in this wine seems perfect: there is a magic balance between balsamic aromas and notes of ripe red berries. In the mouth it is dense and extraordinarily broad, with evident but nicely amalgamated fruit, and soft, smooth, well-judged tannins on an extremely elegant finish. Nino Negri has presented two new interpretations, both modern and stylish, of his traditional Sassella and Inferno; even their labels have been carefully redesigned. The wood-aged Sassella Le Tense '96, of which 40,000 bottles were made, has a captivating fragrance of fruit and spice, followed by a round, structured and remarkably long palate. The elegant Inferno Mazer '96 is, at last, an original and brilliant version of this variety. The Grumello Vigna Sassorosso '95 seemed properly executed, harmonious and easy to drink, and I Grigioni '98 has a clean bouquet and is agreeably grapy and well made. Although it deserves its Two Glasses, the Ca' Brione '98 is not quite as good as last year's. Still it has a fruity nose with a touch of minerals, and an enchanting palate with good length.

●	Valtellina Sfursat 5 Stelle '97	▼▼▼	6
●	Valtellina Sup. Inferno Mazer '96	▼▼	4
●	Valtellina Sup. Sassella Le Tense '96	▼▼	4
○	Vigneto Ca' Brione Bianco '98	▼▼	4
●	Valtellina Sup. Grumello Vigna Sassorosso '95	▼	4
○	Vigneto I Grigioni '98	▼	3
●	Valtellina Sfursat 5 Stelle '89	▽▽▽	5
●	Valtellina Sfursat 5 Stelle '94	▽▽▽	5
●	Valtellina Sfursat 5 Stelle '95	▽▽▽	5
●	Valtellina Sfursat 5 Stelle '96	▽▽▽	5
●	Valtellina Sfursat 5 Stelle '88	▽▽	5
●	Valtellina Sfursat 5 Stelle '90	▽▽	6

CHIURO (SO)

ALDO RAINOLDI
VIA STELVIO, 128
23030 CHIURO (SO)
TEL. 0342/482225

The renovation of his cellar and a heavy investment in new equipment have, not surprisingly, had their effect. In Valtellina, where the standard bottles, and even the riservas, are not always produced with the necessary attention, the overall improvement of Peppino Rainoldi's wines is really striking. It's a sign not only of careful grape selection but also that the cellar technique at this winery is now on a par with some of the most advanced winemaking in the country. Their star, of course, is the Sfurzat Ca' Rizzieri '96, an excellent wine, even if it's not as glorious as last year's. The nose is notably mature and warm, with notes of quinine and enticing hints of spice, while the palate is dense, well-defined and increasingly captivating. The Sfurzat '96 is more traditional, with its richly oaky fragrance which is gradually acquiring balance. In the mouth it is clean, intense and underpinned by an all-encompassing softness. The Crespino '96 has an elegant nose, though it is not, perhaps, so long and soft as last year's version. The really admirable Sassella Riserva '94 is an authentic nebbiolo: ruby-hued and redolent of tobacco, it offers good structure and well-integrated tannins in the mouth. The good Inferno Riserva '94 is firm and ripe on the palate. The wood-fermented Inferno '95 has a seductive bouquet, but the oak needs further smoothing if there is to be balance in the mouth. The Ghibellino '97 may even be too concentrated; the nose is elegant and the palate long and overwhelming.

● Valtellina Sfurzat '96	YY	5
● Valtellina Sfurzat Ca' Rizzieri '96	YY	6
● Valtellina Sup. Crespino '96	YY	5
● Valtellina Sup. Inferno Ris. '94	YY	4
● Valtellina Sup. Sassella Ris. '94	YY	4
○ Bianco Ghibellino '97	Y	4
● Valtellina Sup. Inferno Ris. Barrique '95	Y	5
● Valtellina Sfurzat Ca' Rizzieri '95	yyy	5
● Valtellina Sfurzat '94	yy	4
● Valtellina Sup. Crespino '95	yy	4
● Valtellina Sup. Inferno Ris. '89	yy	4
● Valtellina Sup. Inferno Ris. Barrique '89	yy	5
● Valtellina Sup. Inferno Ris. Barrique '94	yy	4
● Valtellina Sup. Inferno Ris. Barrique '90	yy	4
● Valtellina Sup. Sassella '90	yy	4

CICOGNOLA (PV)

MONTERUCCO
VALLE CIMA, 38
27040 CICOGNOLA (PV)
TEL. 0385/85151

Roberto Valenti's estate, Monterucco, lies at the beginning of the Scuropasso Valley on the first slopes, near Cigognola, Broni, Canneto and Castana. It has 15 hectares of intelligently cultivated vineyards growing in calcareous marly soil, and a cellar well equipped with stainless steel vats, barrels and barriques. We greatly admired his fizzy '97 Barbera. It has a clear ruby color, an evanescent red mousse, an intense fragrance of grapes and mature fruit and a full-bodied, straightforward, succulent palate. It's ready for drinking now, but could easily last for a good while. The Brut Classico is elegantly mouth-filling. It has a light straw hue, a fine dense perlage and evident aromas of toasted bread, dry bay leaf and Golden Delicious apple. The dry, mature but firm palate has a distinct toasted almond finish. It's at its peak. The Metellianum Riserva '96, a blend of barbera, uva rara and croatina traditionally fermented and aged in barriques, is vigorous but rather rustic, with noticeable tannins. It's a promising start but it wants more elegance and harmony. The semi-sparkling Sangue di Giuda '98 is dark purple with a violet mousse. A very clear fragrance of must leads to a sweet taste of ripe grapes. The Buttafuoco Sanluigi '97 and the fizzy white-vinified Pinot Nero in bianco I Primi Fiori '98 are both worthy of mention.

● O. P. Barbera '97	YY	2*
○ O. P. Brut Classico '93	YY	4
● O. P. Rosso Metellianum Ris. '96	Y	3
● O. P. Sangue di Giuda '98	Y	2*
● O. P. Buttafuoco Sanluigi '97		3
○ O. P. Pinot Nero in bianco I Primi Fiori '98		3

COCCAGLIO (BS)

Tenuta Castellino
Via S. Pietro, 46
25030 Coccaglio (BS)
tel. 030/7721015

The Bonomi family, at its Castellino estate in Coccaglio, produces excellent Franciacortas and some fine still wines too. This year their Satèn '94 leads the way, demonstrating once again how well-suited the area is for producing this wine from the chardonnay grape. Castellino's Satèn has a lovely brilliant straw color, an unctuous, sweet and harmonious nose, and a structured, full-bodied and elegant palate. A retasting of the Brut '93 confirmed that it's splendid, crisp, inviting and still young. The Franciacorta Brut '95 easily carried off One full Glass. The T.d.F. Bianco Solicano, one of the historic labels of the house, is in tip-top form in its '97 version, with a thoroughly winning fresh fragrance of tropical fruits, and a perfectly clean palate, mouth-filling, long and fleshy, with a fresh citric note for balance. However, the T. d. F. Bianco '97 is barely acceptable and the red Capineto '96 is very disappointing. We expected better still wines (apart from the Solicano) from this estate.

○	Franciacorta Satèn	🍷🍷	5
○	T. d. F. Bianco Solicano '97	🍷🍷	4
○	Franciacorta Brut '95	🍷	4
●	Capineto '96		4
●	T. d. F. Rosso '97		3
○	Franciacorta Bianco '94	YY	3*
○	Franciacorta Bianco Ris. '91	YY	4
○	Franciacorta Bianco Solicano '92	YY	4
○	Franciacorta Bianco Solicano '93	YY	4
○	Franciacorta Brut '93	YY	5
○	Franciacorta Crémant	YY	5
○	Franciacorta Satèn '92	YY	4
○	Franciacorta Satèn '93	YY	5
○	T. d. F. Bianco Solicano '95	YY	3*
○	T. d. F. Bianco Solicano '96	YY	4

COCCAGLIO (BS)

Lorenzo Faccoli & Figli
Via Cava, 7
25030 Coccaglio (BS)
tel. 030/7722761

The Faccolis have one of the smallest estates in Franciacorta, but it's certainly not one of the least important. Lorenzo, a winegrower from the Marche, came to Lombardy in the '60s to establish a winery, and in the next ten years he began to bottle and sell his own wines. Today his sons Gian Mario and Claudio work with him and together they produce a carefully made range of Franciacortas, the strong point of which is its consistent quality. In fact each year their wines get better, as is happily exemplified by their Franciacorta Extra Brut '89, which shined at our tastings this year. It has an attractive brilliant golden straw color and an amazingly unctuous, full, dense and mature nose enriched by notes of yeast and toasted bread. In the mouth it is elegant, ample and soft, not very powerful but refined, complex and continuous. The Franciacorta Brut is as good as usual, lean, crisp, very easy to drink and richly fruity. The Extra Brut, while good, is less appealing, particularly on the somewhat ill-defined nose, with vegetal and rather too forward notes. But the excellent T.d.F. Bianco '98 is fresh, fruity and pleasingly full-bodied.

○	Franciacorta Extra Brut '89	🍷🍷	6
○	Franciacorta Brut	🍷	4
○	Franciacorta Extra Brut	🍷	4
○	T. d. F. Bianco '98	🍷	3
○	Franciacorta Brut	YY	4
○	Franciacorta Extra Brut	YY	4
⊙	Franciacorta Rosé	Y	4
○	T. d. F. Bianco '93	Y	2*
○	T. d. F. Bianco '94	Y	2*
○	T. d. F. Bianco '96	Y	2*
○	T. d. F. Bianco '97	Y	3

CODEVILLA (PV)

MONTELIO
VIA D. MAZZA, 1
27050 CODEVILLA (PV)
TEL. 0383/373090

Mario Rosa Sesia's historic estate (it celebrated its 150th birthday in 1999) is gaining ground. Using the grapes harvested on the 27 hectares under vine and his considerable skill as an oenologist, with an assist from some good wood in the cellar, Mario Maffi has further improved the top reds and whites. The oak-aged Comprino '97, made from merlot planted half a century ago, has a ruby color with shades of garnet. The complex bouquet reveals hints of raspberry jam, ripe hay and spice, and the palate is warm, vigorous and persisistent. The '97 Barbera (with 15% croatina) can't be faulted: it's richer, spicier and more harmonious than it has been in the past. Already excellent, it is bound to improve in the bottle. The good Bianca La Giostra '98 is made from slightly overripe müller thurgau grapes cold-macerated on their skins for 24 hours. Bright gold in the glass, it has an intense and captivatingly aromatic nose, and a full-bodied, soft but crisp, fruity and elegant palate. The Müller Thurgau '98 is less complicated but extremely enjoyable. Other whites worthy of note from this harvest are the fruity and succulent Riesling Italico and the limpid, clean Cortese '98 with its faint hint of green apple and almond on the finish. Moving on to the reds, the fizzy Bonarda '98 is well-balanced and reminiscent of black cherry; the Oltrepò Pavese Rosso '97 is graceful and well-developed; the Comprino '96 has matured and confirms our favorable verdict in last year's Guide. The effervescent Rosato '98 is fresh and quaffable. The Brut La Stroppa '97 (60% chardonnay, 40% cortese), refermented in pressure tanks, is soft and clean.

●	Comprino Rosso '97	🍷🍷	4
○	Müller Thurgau La Giostra '98	🍷🍷	4
●	O. P. Barbera '97	🍷🍷	3*
○	Brut La Stroppa	🍷	4
○	Müller Thurgau '98	🍷	3
●	O. P. Bonarda '98	🍷	3
○	O. P. Cortese '98	🍷	3
○	O. P. Riesling Italico '98	🍷	3
⊙	O. P. Rosato '98	🍷	3
●	O. P. Rosso '97	🍷	3
●	Comprino Rosso '90	🍷🍷 (outline)	4
●	Comprino Rosso '90	🍷🍷 (outline)	4
●	Comprino Rosso '95	🍷🍷 (outline)	4
●	O. P. Pinot Nero '90	🍷🍷 (outline)	4
●	O. P. Pinot Nero '93	🍷🍷 (outline)	4

CORTEFRANCA (BS)

BARONE PIZZINI PIOMARTA
LOC. TIMOLINE
VIA BRESCIA, 5
25050 CORTEFRANCA (BS)
TEL. 030/984136

Things are looking very good at this Cortefranca estate, and not for the first time. The last vintage of the Franciacorta Bagnadore 1° hadn't yet come out, so we tried the excellent '93 again and found, if possible, even more finesse and balance. It still charms with its fine perlage and the delicacy it manages to offer together with good structure. And their new and very fresh Satèn confirms their excellent reputation. It has a pale straw color, very fine perlage, and a soft and sweet nose with notes of white peach and vanilla and a final fresh hint of citrus. In the mouth it produces soft tones of ripe white-fleshed fruit and yeast, carrying through masterfully to a long finish. But their basic Brut is just as good. It has a brilliant pale straw hue and a ripe, rounded fragrance with creamy tones of yeast and the honeyed nuances of the chardonnay grape. The elegant palate is characterized by a caressing mousse, crispness and harmonious fruit, including delicate hints of the tropical variety. Among the still wines, the Polzina '97 has good fruit and reasonable structure, and the San Carlo '97, a new red made from cabernet sauvignon (55%) and merlot, came very close to receiving Two Glasses. The Bianco '98, as usual, is fresh, properly made and pleasant, and the Rosso '97 drinks well enough although it is a little thin.

○	Franciacorta Brut	🍷🍷	4
○	Franciacorta Satèn	🍷🍷	5
⊙	Franciacorta Rosé	🍷	4
○	T. d. F. Bianco '98	🍷	3
○	T. d. F. Bianco Polzina '97	🍷	4
●	T. d. F. Rosso San Carlo '97	🍷	4
●	T. d. F. Rosso '97		3
○	Franciacorta Brut	🍷🍷 (outline)	4
○	Franciacorta Brut Bagnadore V '93	🍷🍷 (outline)	5
○	Franciacorta Extra Brut Bagnadore V '92	🍷🍷 (outline)	5
○	T. d. F. Bianco '96	🍷🍷 (outline)	3*
○	T. d. F. Bianco Pulcina '95	🍷🍷 (outline)	3*
●	T. d. F. Rosso San Carlo '96	🍷🍷 (outline)	4

CORTEFRANCA (BS)

F.LLI BERLUCCHI
LOC. BORGONATO
VIA BROLETTO, 2
25040 CORTEFRANCA (BS)
TEL. 030/984451

Fratelli Berlucchi is one of the best-known wine names of Franciacorta. They produce some 300 thousand bottles a year from their vines and cellar in Borgonato di Cortefranca. Their Brut is one of the most consistent wines we have tasted in the area. Fruit of Pia Donata Berlucchi's administrative abilities and Cesare Ferrari's oenological gifts, this Franciacorta is admirable for its structure, body and elegance. The '95 version, which is definitely up to snuff, has an appealing and brilliant greenish straw-yellow hue and fresh aromas of yeast, vanilla and white-fleshed fruit, with just a hint of citrus peel. In the mouth it is lean, refined and caressing. This year, to celebrate three decades of producing DOC wines, they're offering a special vintage bubbly, the excellent 30 anni di Doc '93. It has the concentration of the best vintages (a characteristic which does not get at all in the way of a softness of tone and general crispness which are typical of Berlucchi Franciacortas) and an elegant more mature finish: a really good wine. Their Satèn makes its debut this year. This is a new kind of chardonnay-based spumante which is becoming popular up here. Their version is well made, soft and fresh, but it doesn't have all the refinement that typifies this producer. The Rosé, as usual, is interesting. It has a good full body, balance and crispness, and offers a rich raspberry note. Among the still wines we can recommend the unctuous and full-bodied Bianco Dossi delle Querce '96 with its abundant tones of sweet, ripe white-fleshed fruit, while the T.d.F. Bianco and Rosso once again do not seem on the same level as their other labels.

○ Franciacorta 30 anni di Doc '93	▼▼	6
○ Franciacorta Brut '95	▼▼	5
⊙ Franciacorta Rosé '95	▼	5
○ Franciacorta Satèn '95	▼	6
○ T. d. F. Bianco Dossi delle Querce '96	▼	4
○ T. d. F. Bianco '98		3
● T. d. F. Rosso '97		3
○ Franciacorta Brut '91	▽▽	4
○ Franciacorta Brut '92	▽▽	4
○ Franciacorta Brut '93	▽▽	4
○ Franciacorta Brut '94	▽▽	4
⊙ Franciacorta Rosé '92	▽▽	4
⊙ Franciacorta Rosé '94	▽	3
● T. d. F. Rosso '95	▽	2*

CORTEFRANCA (BS)

GUIDO BERLUCCHI & C.
LOC. BORGONATO
P.ZZA DURANTI, 4
25040 CORTEFRANCA (BS)
TEL. 030/984381 - 030/984293

Guido Berlucchi & C. is one of the most important Italian producers of sparkling wine, and few Italian labels are so widely known abroad. Franco Ziliani, the heart and soul of the winery, has come a long way since the early '60s. He has taught the Italians to drink bubbly, and has created a solid and trustworthy firm. These days he is assisted by his children Arturo, an oenologist, Paolo, who handles the business side, and Cristina, who is in charge of public relations. Berlucchi & C., which produces several million bottles a year, has an absolutely state-of-the-art cellar and buys grapes and base wines from the best "bubbly" zones, from Franciacorta to Alto Adige and the Oltrepò Pavese. This year's Cellarius Brut is as good as ever. It has a brilliant green-tinged pale straw color, a fine perlage and creamy mousse. To the nose it offers notes of ripe fruit and flowers with vanilla to finish. In the mouth it's crisp and caressing, with lots of fruit, body and balance. It makes an excellent aperitif, but it stands up to a meal as well. The Max Rosé is very interesting too, with its lovely berry scent and softness on the palate, but so are all the others: the vintage '93, delicate in body but very elegant, the extremely dry Brut Extrême, and of course their old standby the Cuvée Imperiale Brut, rich in notes of yeast and toasted bread. The Ziliani family also runs the Antica Cantina Fratta at Monticelli Brusati, which offers two very good Franciacortas: the Brut and the vintage '95.

○ Cellarius Brut Ris.	▼▼	5
○ Franciacorta Antica Cantina Fratta '95	▼▼	5
○ Franciacorta Brut Antica Cantina Fratta	▼▼	4
○ Bianco Imperiale	▼	3
○ Cuvée Imperiale Brut	▼	4
○ Cuvée Imperiale Brut '93	▼	5
○ Cuvée Imperiale Brut Extrême	▼	4
⊙ Cuvée Imperiale Max Rosé	▼	4
○ T. d. F. Bianco Antica Cantina Fratta '98	▼	3
○ Cellarius Brut Ris.	▽▽	5
○ Franciacorta Brut Antica Cantina Fratta	▽▽	4

CORTEFRANCA (BS)

MONZIO COMPAGNONI
FRAZ. NIGOLINE
C.DA MONTI DELLA CORTE
25040 CORTEFRANCA (BS)
TEL. 030/9884157

Marcello Monzio Compagnoni has for several years now run two different wineries. The original one is in Cenate Sotto in the province of Bergamo. In Franciacorta, on the other hand, he has leased a winery from the Barons Monti della Corte, and here he produces local Doc and Docg wines. We found the Franciacortas particularly successful this year, most of all the Satèn, which is soft and elegant with hints of white-fleshed fruit jam and vanilla on the nose. The delicate vanilla and toasty notes on the elegant and long palate do not overwhelm the underlying clean fruit. The Franciacorta Extra Brut reflects a careful use of new wood for the base wine and is rich, complex and harmonious, although just a touch forward, and perhaps there was a slightly enthusiastic application of sweetening "liqueur de dosage". The Franciacorta Brut has density and body, but is not so stylish as the other two and has been marked accordingly. The two '97 T.d.F.s, the Bianco Ronco della Seta, fruity and notably full-bodied, but with new wood a little too evident, and the balanced and clean Rosso Ronco della Seta, are both interesting. The T.d.F. Bianco Ronco della Seta '98 is fresh, mouth-filling and richly fruity and closes the Franciacorta chapter with honor. Turning to the Valcalepio wines, we admired the Bianco Colle della Luna '98, brilliant greenish gold in color with a fresh and distinct bouquet of apricot and peach and a crisp, balanced, aromatic, elegant and delicate palate. The excellent Rosso di Nero '97 is a stylish and characteristic pinot nero, and the Moscato Don Quijote '96 is a delectable "passito" (dried grape wine).

○	Franciacorta Extra Brut	▼▼	5
○	Franciacorta Satèn	▼▼	5
○	Moscato di Scanzo Don Quijote '96	▼▼	5
●	Rosso di Nero '97	▼▼	5
○	T. d. F. Bianco Ronco della Seta '98	▼▼	4
○	Colle della Luna Bianco '98	▼	4
●	Colle della Luna Rosso '98	▼	4
○	Franciacorta Brut	▼	5
●	Rosso di Luna '97	▼	5
○	T. d. F. Bianco Ronco della Seta '97	▼	5
●	T. d. F. Rosso Ronco della Seta '97	▼	4

CORVINO SAN QUIRICO (PV)

TENUTA MAZZOLINO
VIA MAZZOLINO, 26
27050 CORVINO SAN QUIRICO (PV)
TEL. 0383/876122

Sandra Braggiotti's Tenuta Mazzolino is back in the Guide in grand style. The estate covers 20 hectares, of which 14 are under vine, in old Mazzolino near Corvino San Quirico. Meticulous care in the cultivation of the grapes (no chemical fertilizers, and a bare minimum of anti-parasitical treatment), and sensible application of a well-balanced blend of innovative and traditional oenological techniques (barriques of Allier, Tronçais and Nevers oak are among the features of the more than 150-year-old cellar) have enabled her to produce some splendid wines. The pride of the estate is its Noir, made solely from ripe pinot nero grapes fermented and aged for a year in French oak. The '95 vintage has a clear garnet color, a bouquet of vanilla, black currant and raspberry and a velvety and aristocratic palate. The harmonious and distinctly varietal Pinot Nero '96 and the '94 version of the same, now at its peak, are less complex but still admirable. The dark ruby Cabernet Sauvignon Corvino '97 has a broad fragrance of raspberry jam and undergrowth and is vigorous and well-balanced in the mouth. The Blanc '96, a monovarietal chardonnay which is cold-macerated, then fermented and matured for almost a year in barriques and tonneaux from Allier and Tronçais, and aged for a further year in the bottle, was presented in two versions. The '96 is more evolved and harmonious, offering notes of honey and vanilla and elegant nuances of acacia and artemisia flowers, peach and Golden Delicious apple. Wood still has the upper hand in the '97 but it's a very promising wine. The acceptable Bonarda '98 finishes on a distinctly bitterish note.

○	O. P. Chardonnay Blanc '96	▼▼	4
●	O. P. Pinot Nero '96	▼▼	4
●	O. P. Pinot Nero Noir '95	▼▼	5
○	O. P. Chardonnay Blanc '97	▼	4
●	O. P. Bonarda '98		3
●	O. P. Cabernet Sauvignon Corvino '97		4
●	O. P. Pinot Nero '94		4
●	O. P. Pinot Nero Noir '89	▽▽	6
●	O. P. Pinot Nero Noir '90	▽▽	6
●	O. P. Barbera '95	▽	3
●	O. P. Cabernet Sauvignon Corvino '94	▽	4
●	O. P. Pinot Nero Noir '93	▽	6
●	O. P. Rosso Terrazze '95	▽	3

DESENZANO DEL GARDA (BS)

PROVENZA
VIA DEI COLLI STORICI, 13
25015 DESENZANO DEL GARDA (BS)
TEL. 030/9910006 - 030/9910014

Provenza, the Contato family's estate, includes 30 hectares of vineyards surrounding their farmhouse, Maiolo e Molino, in the midst of the Lugana plain. The vines are grown according to essentially organic principles, with treatments based on prevention of disease that take advantage of a sophisticated satellite system of weather forecasting. And from their good grapes come good wines. The first of these is the special selection Lugana Ca' Molini '97, vinified with cold skin contact and aged for six months in new French barriques. It has a lovely straw color, a broad bouquet of honey, flowers and sweet spice, and a full-bodied, crisp and harmonious palate with an elegant almondy finish that includes a faint hint of oak. A good but simpler wine is the Lugana Ca' Maiol '98. The Negresco '96 just fell short of Two Glasses. This blend of groppello, cabernet sauvignon and marzemino matured for a year in barriques has a dark ruby hue, a broad fragrance of berries and, in the mouth, roundness and balance. The Brut Ca' Maiol, a "metodo classico" bubbly that includes 10% chardonnay, is, after 36 months spent on its yeasts, without doubt pleasant; but, it is so graceful, simple and seductive that it rather resembles their other spumante, the charmat method Lugana Brut Sebastian. Their Sol Doré '95, the last in this admirable series, is a sweet white wine, made from trebbiano and chardonnay grapes dried until February, which was aged in the wood for two years.

○	Lugana Cà Molin '97	🍷🍷	4
○	Lugana Brut Cl. Cà Maiol '94	🍷	4
○	Lugana Brut Sebastian '97	🍷	3
○	Lugana Cà Maiol '98	🍷	3
●	Negresco '96	🍷	4
○	Sol Doré '95	🍷	5
○	Lugana '93	♀	4
○	Lugana Brut Sebastian	♀	5
○	Sol Doré '92	♀	5

ERBUSCO (BS)

★ BELLAVISTA
VIA BELLAVISTA, 5
25030 ERBUSCO (BS)
TEL. 030/7760276

Again this year Bellavista won a round of applause with a Franciacorta of incredible elegance and finesse: their Gran Cuvée Brut '95, another perfect example of the unmistakable Bellavista style. It has a brilliant and lively straw color shot through with a light greenish tinge. From among the rounded vanilla scents which characterize it there emerge notes of biscuit, pastries and fruit cocktail and delicate vegetal nuances. The palate is harmonious, exquisite and balanced, and there's good structure too. It has a fine dense perlage that caresses the palate, and the finish, with fruit and vanilla to the fore, seems to go on indefinitely. It is a little masterpiece. The Satèn will win you over with its aromas of fresh fruit and notes of citron and of orange peel. In the mouth it demonstrates delicacy, a perfectly judged "dosage", harmony and length. The Gran Cuvée Pas Operé has delicious tones of fresh brioche, butter, white peach and vanilla. This year's Franciacorta Rosé, pale in hue and redolent of dried rose petals and red berries, seems better than the previous version. The Cuvée Brut is as good as ever. The Terre di Franciacorta Uccellanda '96, an excellent chardonnay, is one of the best they have ever made. Aromas of grapefruit, kiwi, pineapple and passion fruit blend elegantly with toasty tones of new wood, and it all carries through to the meaty, soft and full structure on the palate. Their other splendid white, the Convento dell'Annunciata '96, has abundant notes of apricot, peach and aromatic woods, and is fleshy and harmonious in the mouth.

○	Franciacorta Gran Cuvée Brut '95	🍷🍷🍷	6
○	Franciacorta Brut	🍷🍷	4
○	Franciacorta Gran Cuvée Pas Operé '93	🍷🍷	5
⊙	Franciacorta Gran Cuvée Rosé	🍷🍷	4
○	Franciacorta Gran Cuvée Satèn	🍷🍷	5
●	Solesine '96	🍷🍷	5
○	T. d. F. Bianco Convento dell'Annunciata '96	🍷🍷	5
○	T. d. F. Uccellanda '96	🍷🍷	5
○	T. d. F. Bianco '98	🍷	4
●	T. d. F. Rosso '97	🍷	4
○	Franciacorta Extra Brut Vittorio Moretti Ris. '91	♀♀♀	6
○	Franciacorta Gran Cuvée Brut '93	♀♀♀	5

ERBUSCO (BS)

★ Ca' del Bosco
Via Case Sparse, 20
25030 Erbusco (BS)
tel. 030/7766111

In the Guide's 13 years of tastings we have seen, together with the charismatic Maurizio Zanella, the rise in quality of his wines, of Franciacorta wines generally, and also, thanks to people like him, the progress that Italian wine has made in the world's opinion. Maurizio is always a step or two ahead of all the others. He has produced the best Franciacortas there are, and also great reds and very great whites: not bad, considering that his winery first opened its doors in the late 1970s. Once again this year the best bubbly we tasted is his. The spectacular Franciacorta Satèn '95, a prodigy of finesse and complexity, is absolutely and irresistibly seductive, with its soft tones of vanilla and fresh fruit pervaded by notes of mint, gooseberry and ripe apricot. It has the incontrovertible elegance of a real thoroughbred, and also astonishing length. The Cuvée Annamaria Clementi '92 is velvety, captivating, elegant and fleshy, with woody aromas perfectly integrated with the wine's own fragrance. Its very fine, dense and extremely persistent perlage dissolves into a stylish creamy effervescence on the palate. Only the slightest forward nuance kept it from getting a Third Glass. The other Franciacortas, from the Brut '95 with its note of beautifully defined and elegant fruit, to the crisp, refined and extremely well-balanced Dosage Zéro, are up to their usual high standards. The stars among the still wines are the excellent Chardonnay '97, which suffers only from the not very felicitous vintage, and the Pinèro '97, which is in great form and gives us a little foretaste of the '98, which is said to be a knockout.

○	Franciacorta Satèn '95	TTT	5
○	Franciacorta Brut '95	TT	5
○	Franciacorta Cuvée Annamaria Clementi '93	TT	6
○	Franciacorta Dosage Zéro '95	TT	5
●	Maurizio Zanella '96	TT	6
●	Pinèro '97	TT	6
○	T. d. F. Chardonnay '97	TT	6
○	Elfo 8	T	5
○	Franciacorta Brut	T	4
○	T. d. F. Bianco '98	T	4
●	T. d. F. Rosso '97	T	4
○	Franciacorta Cuvée Annamaria Clementi '91	YYY	6
○	T. d. F. Chardonnay '96	YYY	6

ERBUSCO (BS)

Cavalleri
Via Provinciale, 96
25030 Erbusco (BS)
tel. 030/7760217

Cavalleri in Erbusco is a star of the first order in the firmament of Franciacorta. This year Giovanni Cavalleri, the owner, and also president of the local Consorzio di Tutela, an association set up to regulate and safeguard regional wines, sent 10 different wines to our tastings. This in itself is no small matter. It betokens a producer with the ability and concentration to harvest, vinify and age a great number of different base wines. And perhaps this is the particular strength of this winemaker, who has hit the bullseye with his Brut Collezione '94, winning his fourth well-deserved Three Glasses. This Collezione '94 is extremely elegant, harmonious, refined and full on the nose, and in the mouth it's absolutely, splendidly well-balanced and captivating, and soft and caressing at the same time. The perlage is amazingly fine and as a result the mousse is caressingly creamy; vanilla sees it out. The excellent Satèn has a sweet and fruity bouquet; on the palate it exemplifies the best qualities of this type of wine with its notes of dry ripe white-fleshed fruit and a remarkable overall elegance. The pale pink Rosé has a rich red berry fragrance . The Pas Dosé '94 has repeated last year's success: a complex and compelling Franciacorta, which is both many-faceted and crisply agreeable. The Brut Blanc de Blancs is, as usual, a little gem. This time it has elegant, soft aromas of brioche and butter and, on the palate, complex notes of fruit and spice. Among the still wines, we particularly admired the Bianco Seradina '97, which has great softness and pleasing notes of new wood underpinned by an ample and well-balanced structure.

○	Franciacorta Collezione Brut '94	TTT	6
○	Franciacorta Cremant Satèn	TT	5
○	Franciacorta Brut	TT	5
○	Franciacorta Pas Dosé '94	TT	5
○	T. d. F. Bianco Serandina '97	TT	5
●	Corniole Merlot '96	T	4
⊙	Franciacorta Collezione Rosé '94	T	6
○	T. d. F. Bianco Rampaneto '97	T	4
●	T. d. F. Rosso '97	T	4
●	T. d. F. Rosso Tajardino '96	T	5
○	Franciacorta Collezione Brut '86	YYY	6
○	Franciacorta Collezione Brut '93	YYY	6
●	Corniole Merlot '95	YY	4
⊙	Franciacorta Collezione Rosé '93	YY	6
○	Franciacorta Pas Dosé '93	YY	5

ERBUSCO (BS)

FERGHETTINA
VIA CASE SPARSE, 4
25030 ERBUSCO (BS)
TEL. 030/7760120 - 030/7268308

A few years ago Roberto Gatti created his own winery, and today, with 40 hectares of vineyards (including those he owns and the ones he leases), from which he makes about 150 thousand bottles of wine a year, he runs one of the most dynamic estates in Franciacorta. In a part of the country better known for white wines and classic method bubblies Roberto has come up with what we feel is definitely the best red in the area: his Merlot Sebino '96. It has a dark ruby hue, an intense, warm nose of sweet ripe blackberry, plum and black currant with nuances of tobacco, toasted wood and vanilla. The palate is concentrated, round, fleshy and rich in fruity merlot tones, finishing with a light vegetal hint that shades off into sweet fruit and delicate new oak. Not bad at all! But it shouldn't distract us from the fact that Roberto, now assisted by his daughter Laura, who is studying viticulture and oenology at the University of Milan, also makes excellent whites and Franciacortas. Their Brut is elegant, full-bodied, crisp and fruity, richly redolent of white flowers, and pleasingly pervaded by vanilla in the mouth. The Satèn, a newcomer, is soft, rich in fruit and nicely elegant. The T.d.F. Rosso is good, and a retasting of the chardonnay Bianco Favento '97 confirms its breeding and excellent balance. The T.d.F. Bianco '98 didn't have to strain to get its Two Glasses and its place among the best wines of its kind this year. That's all for the moment. We must wait for the new wines, including the vintage Franciacorta, which are still doing their time in the cellar.

○	Franciacorta Brut	**YY**	4
○	Franciacorta Satèn	**YY**	4
●	Merlot Sebino '96	**YY**	4
○	T. d. F. Bianco '98	**YY**	3*
●	T. d. F. Rosso '97	**Y**	3
○	Franciacorta Brut	YY	4
○	T. d. F. Bianco '95	YY	2*
○	T. d. F. Bianco Favento '97	YY	4
●	T. d. F. Rosso Merlot '95	YY	4
○	T. d. F. Bianco '96	Y	2*
○	T. d. F. Bianco '97	Y	3
○	T. d. F. Bianco Favento '96	Y	3
●	T. d. F. Rosso '93	Y	2*
●	T. d. F. Rosso '95	Y	2*
●	T. d. F. Rosso '96	Y	3

ERBUSCO (BS)

ENRICO GATTI
VIA METELLI, 9
25030 ERBUSCO (BS)
TEL. 030/7267999 - 030/7267157

Lorenzo Gatti and Enrico Balzarini, who are brothers-in-law, and their respective wives Sonia and Paola (Lorenzo's sister) are a hardworking foursome who have always wanted their winery to be one of the best in Franciacorta. And it is. Now they would like it to be one of the elite cult wineries and, thanks to their splendid vines and not indifferent abilities in the cellar, they are coming perilously close to their goal. Try, for example, the Gatti Bianco '97, a monovarietal chardonnay. It has an intense and brilliant greenish straw color and a complex, fresh, soft and fruity nose with a subtle, not at all overbearing note of vanilla . In the mouth it pulls out all the stops: the softest notes of fruit typical of a good Chardonnay, as well as characteristic hints of butter, hot brioche, honey and white chocolate are all there. It is a marvelous wine, and available at a very fair price. On the bubbly front, their Franciacorta Brut is outstanding, with its delightful nuances of toasted bread and ripe fruit on the nose, and structure and body, together with fine, dense perlage and creamy mousse on the palate. They have also done well with the Gatti Rosso '97, a cabernet sauvignon which is a little vegetal because of a somewhat unpropitious vintage but is beautifully executed, and the pleasing Terre Rosso '97. Among the very few '98 Terre Biancos to have deserved One Glass is, naturally enough, the Gatti version.

○	Franciacorta Brut	**YY**	4
○	Gatti Bianco '97	**YY**	4
●	Gatti Rosso '97	**Y**	4
○	T. d. F. Bianco '98	**Y**	3
●	T. d. F. Rosso '97	**Y**	3
○	Franciacorta Brut	YY	4
○	Gatti Bianco '96	YY	4
●	Gatti Rosso '90	YY	5
●	Gatti Rosso '91	YY	4
●	Gatti Rosso '95	YY	4
●	Gatti Rosso '96	YY	4
○	T. d. F. Bianco '94	YY	2*
○	T. d. F. Bianco '95	YY	2*
○	T. d. F. Bianco '96	YY	2*
●	T. d. F. Rosso '95	YY	2*

ERBUSCO (BS)

PRINCIPE BANFI
VIA ISEO, 20
25030 ERBUSCO (BS)
TEL. 030/7750387

We loved the Franciacortas from Principe Banfi, Roberto Principe's handsome 10-hectare estate, 9 hectares of which are under vine. The Extra Brut boasts a splendid bouquet of delicately aromatic medicinal herbs, white-fleshed fruit, clean yeasty notes and a fresh hint of citrus. In the mouth it is crisp, elegant and harmonious, rich in fine fresh vegetal nuances, fruity and long, with lots of structure and finesse and a vanilla and floral finish: a model of subtle and measured elegance. This is a Franciacorta that seduces you with its style and balance, as does their other bubbly, the Brut, which offers intense, full aromas with ripe fruit again to the fore, and a structured, harmonious palate featuring fresh notes of peach and yeast and a long, pleasing vanilla finish. It is further along than the Extra Brut but has greater structure. The T.d.F. Bianco '97, which we reviewed last year, is holding its own, and the fresh and fruity T.d.F. Bianco '98 is good too. The less interesting T.d.F. Rosso '97 is a bit thin and astringent.

○	Franciacorta Brut	🍷🍷	5
○	Franciacorta Extra Brut	🍷🍷	5
○	T. d. F. Bianco '98	🍷	3
●	T. d. F. Rosso '97		3
○	Franciacorta Brut	YY	5
○	Franciacorta Brut	YY	4
○	Franciacorta Extra Brut	YY	5
○	T. d. F. Bianco '96	YY	3*
○	T. d. F. Chardonnay Pio IX '96	YY	4
○	T. d. F. Chardonnay Pio IX '97	Y	4
●	T. d. F. Rosso '92	Y	2*
●	T. d. F. Rosso '93	Y	2*
●	T. d. F. Rosso '95	Y	3

ERBUSCO (BS)

SAN CRISTOFORO
VIA VILLANUOVA, 2
25030 ERBUSCO (BS)
TEL. 030/7760482

San Cristoforo is an old acquaintance, often praised as the source of clean, intense and mouth-filling Terre di Franciacortas which are good value for money (even the Rosso, a category that doesn't tend to do all that well in Franciacorta). Bruno Dotti and his wife Claudia, working with great dedication (Bruno came to wine-making after leaving a previous career), make the most of their 10 hectares of vines, and of their modern cellar, just recently completed. But making good still wines doesn't seem to have been enough for Bruno, who has always had a passion for sparkling Franciacorta. And this year the Dottis have presented an excellent Brut, produced with the help of the oenologist Alberto Musatti. This is a Franciacorta with a lovely brilliant straw color. It opens on the nose with intense fresh notes of apricot, apple and peach, with a hint of vanilla that comes to the fore after a few seconds. It would have been hard to resist the excellent structure and full body on the exuberant and crisp palate, the fine mousse and the overall harmony. This is a really splendid debut. Bruno has also made a good merlot, his San Cristoforo Uno '96, which has good structure and delicate herbaceous and vegetal tones. The T.d.F. Rosso '97 is good, and the T.d.F. Bianco '98 is among the best whites of the area and certainly deserves its Two Glasses.

○	Franciacorta Brut	🍷🍷	4
○	T. d. F. Bianco '98	🍷🍷	3*
●	San Cristoforo Uno	🍷	4
●	T. d. F. Rosso '97	🍷	3

ERBUSCO (BS)

UBERTI
VIA E. FERMI, 2
25030 ERBUSCO (BS)
TEL. 030/7267476

Once again Eleonora and Agostino Uberti have walked off with Three Glasses. Nothing new there, you may think, but there is! It wasn't their Magnificentia, a Satèn which for years has been among the best Franciacortas available, but their "cuvée prestige", the classic Comarì del Salem '93, that hit the jackpot. In fact the by now legendary '88 version of this Franciacorta was the first of their wines to be thus honored, and the '93 is not a lesser wine. This is immediately clear: all you need do, when you've finished admiring the extraordinarily fine perlage, is to lift the glass to your nose, and you'll be astonished by the intensity and complex elegance of its bouquet, in which fresh yeasty nuances blend with notes of toasted bread, ripe fruit, flowers and subtle sage, shading off into round tones of vanilla, exactly comme il faut. The equally satisfying palate is elegant, structured, persistent and perfectly balanced, and it finishes, like the nose, on a soft, mature note. The Magnificentia lives up to its reputation, although aromas of ripe tropical fruit and tea biscuits fresh from the oven are followed by a slightly too forward palate. The T.d.F Bianco Maria Medici '97 is one of the best Lombard whites this year and is captivating in its crispness and concentrated and clean fruitiness. The equally interesting wood-aged Bianco dei Frati Priori '97 is elegantly structured and well-balanced. All their other wines are excellent as well.

○	Franciacorta Brut Comarì del Salem '93	▼▼▼	6
○	Franciacorta Francesco I Brut	▼▼	5
○	Franciacorta Magnificentia	▼▼	6
○	T. d. F. Bianco dei Frati Priori '97	▼▼	5
○	T. d. F. Bianco Maria Medici '97	▼▼	4
○	Franciacorta Francesco I Extra Brut	▼	5
⊙	Franciacorta Francesco I Rosé	▼	5
○	Franciacorta Extra Brut Comarì del Salem '88	▽▽▽	6
○	Franciacorta Magnificentia	▽▽▽	5
○	Franciacorta Magnificentia	▽▽▽	5
○	Franciacorta Magnificentia	▽▽▽	5
○	Franciacorta Brut Comarì del Salem '91	▽▽	5
●	T. d. F. Rosso dei Frati Priori '94	▽▽	4
●	T. d. F. Rosso dei Frati Priori '95	▽▽	4

GODIASCO (PV)

CABANON
LOC. CABANON
27052 GODIASCO (PV)
TEL. 0383/940912

For the third year in a row, the Cabanon Blanc is the best of the wines from Elena Mercandelli's estate, some 20 hectares of vines cultivated according to organic principles. The '98 was made from sauvignon grapes grown on quite infertile calcareous soil at an altitude of about 300 meters, pressed as whole bunches, and fermented for a long time at a low temperature. The result is a wine of a brilliant pale straw hue with a nose of pineapple, litchi, passion fruit and flint; on the palate it's full, crisp and fruity. The Riesling Renano, which had 24 hours of cold skin contact to enrich its color, perfume and taste, is almost as good. The Pinot Grigio '98, from the well-ventilated mid-slope Vignossa vineyard, is flowery and rich in structure and just missed Two Glasses: it needs more time to develop, particularly in the mouth. Among the reds, the Syra's '97 stands out. It was made from syrah grapes grown on the poor rocky soil of the Gerbidi vineyard and picked very ripe. The wine, matured in oak after malolactic fermentation and bottled the September after the harvest, emerges vigorous and rich in smooth tannins, and has well-defined varietal notes of chocolate and roasted coffee. The soft and full-bodied fizzy Bonarda '98, made from very ripe grapes, is worthy of mention. The Barbera Prunello '96 has lovely structure. It's a pity that both bottles we tasted had a strong scent of sulfur.

○	O. P. Riesling Renano '98	▼▼	3*
○	Opera Prima Cabanon Blanc '98	▼▼	3*
○	O. P. Pinot Grigio '98	▼	3
●	Syra's '97	▼	5
●	O. P. Bonarda Vivace '98		3
●	O. P. Bonarda Ris. '91	▽▽	4
○	O. P. Pinot Grigio '93	▽▽	4
○	O. P. Riesling Renano '93	▽▽	4
●	O. P. Ris. Bonarda '90	▽▽	4
●	O. P. Rosso Ris. Infernot '91	▽▽	5
●	O. P. Rosso Ris. Infernot '90	▽▽	5
●	O. P. Rosso Vino Cuore '91	▽▽	4
○	Opera Prima Cabanon Blanc '93	▽▽	4
○	Opera Prima Cabanon Blanc '96	▽▽	4
○	Opera Prima Cabanon Blanc '97	▽▽	4

GRUMELLO DEL MONTE (BG)

CARLOZADRA
VIA GANDOSSI, 13
24064 GRUMELLO DEL MONTE (BG)
TEL. 035/832066 - 035/830244

Carlo Zadra never disappoints. Of the six wines he presented at our tastings three were awarded Two Glasses, while the other three got One full Glass each. His top spumante classico is the Carlozadra Tradizione vintage '92, a cuvée of chardonnay, pinot nero and pinot meunier from Trentino aged for a year in the wood and then left on its yeasts for nearly six years. The possessor of a very fine perlage and a brilliant golden yellow color, it has an ample, complex nose of spice cake, vanilla and black currant. In the mouth it's mature but quite firm and harmonious, and it has a light touch of sweetness that adds to its grace. The Nondosato '94, of which only 5 thousand bottles were made, has a very different but equally admirable style. Made from chardonnay and pinot nero grown in the gravelly soil of the central Valdadige Trentina, it's a dry,clean and elegant wine. His Liberty, on the other hand, is soft, fruity and flowery: an enchanting blanc de blanc from chardonnay and pinot bianco, which spent much less time (about 22 months) on its yeasts. The range of bubblies closes with the Brut '95: this is a blend of chardonnay, pinot nero and pinot bianco grapes from the upper reaches of Trentino which was "dégorgé" in mid-July '98 and is outstanding for its finesse. There are also two still wines: the Donna Nunzia Moscato '98 (2,500 bottles), which is dry and very aromatic, and the Don Lodovico Pinot Nero '97 (3 thousand bottles), which was aged in the wood for a year. It has pronounced varietal tones and a rather intense color, something not often found in wines made from this grape.

○	Carlozadra Cl. Brut '95	▼▼	4
○	Carlozadra Cl. Brut Nondosato '94	▼▼	5
○	Carlozadra Cl. Extra Dry Tradizione '92	▼▼	5
○	Carlozadra Cl. Extra Dry Liberty	▼	4
●	Don Ludovico Pinot Nero '97	▼	4
○	Donna Nunzia Moscato Giallo '98	▼	3
○	Carlozadra Cl. Brut '93	▽▽	5
○	Carlozadra Cl. Brut '92	▽▽	4
○	Carlozadra Cl. Brut Nondosato '91	▽▽	4
○	Carlozadra Cl. Brut Nondosato '92	▽▽	5
○	Carlozadra Cl. Extra Dry Tradizione '91	▽▽	5
○	Carlozadra Cl. Gran Ris. '87	▽▽	6
●	Don Ludovico Pinot Nero '93	▽▽	4

GRUMELLO DEL MONTE (BG)

TENUTA CASTELLO DI GRUMELLO
VIA FOSSE, 11
24064 GRUMELLO DEL MONTE (BG)
TEL. 035/4420817 - 035/830244

The most important vineyard on Cristina Kettliz's Tenuta Castello di Grumello (37 hectares, of which 20 are planted in vines), is the Colle del Calvario, which takes its name from an 18th century church. Here, on land with good exposure and poor soil, grow the cabernet sauvignon and merlot which go into their top wine. The '96 was produced from bunches of grapes (75% cabernet) picked between October 8 and 11 and macerated for 16 days; the wine was aged for a year in barriques, a quarter of which were new. Of a deep garnet hue, it is distinctly redolent of black cherry jam and prune, shading off into sweet spices. The palate is dry, full-bodied, warm and, as a result of well-judged tannins, austere, and it's long as well. This wine should get better, particularly in the mouth, with more bottle age, but it's already very good as it is. Indeed Colle del Calvario's tendency to improve with age is evident from the Riserva '93, which has acquired greater complexity and completeness with its years in the bottle. The Valcalepio Rosso '97 is pleasant, but it has developed too quickly; the agreeable Valcalepio Bianco '98 has a citric tang. The Aurito '97, a monovarietal chardonnay fermented and aged for eight months in barriques of Alliers oak, would have been a superb wine if the massive wood didn't cover the varietal aromas, which had enough trouble with the hot summer of '97. Hence it falls short of Two Glasses. The Moscato Nero Passito '96 is graceful and harmonious, but we'd have liked a more decided aromatic charge.

●	Valcalepio Rosso Colle del Calvario '96	▼▼	4
○	Chardonnay della Bergamasca Aurito '97	▼	4
○	Valcalepio Bianco '98		3
●	Valcalepio Moscato Nero Passito '96	▼	4
●	Valcalepio Rosso '97		3
○	Aurito '92	▽▽	4
○	Chardonnay della Bergamasca Aurito '96	▽▽	4
●	Valcalepio Rosso Colle del Calvario '90	▽▽	4

MONTALTO PAVESE (PV)

Ca' del Ge'

Loc. Ca' del Gé, 5
27040 Montalto Pavese (PV)
tel. 0383/870179

Enzo Padroggi's Ca' del Ge' includes 22 hectares of his own vineyards and a further 15 hectares that he rents on the hillsides of Montalto Pavese. It produces about 150 thousand bottles of wines of greatly varying quality and price. Of the 16 samples presented at our tastings, some are excellent and others left us wondering. But let's get started. The Riesling Italico '98 is rich and quite delightful, with a fragrance of fresh roses and flint that definitely reminds one of Rhine riesling: Two Glasses. The Müller Thurgau '98 is very graceful and lingering: One full Glass (and nearly Two). Very high marks for the Oltrepò Pavese Pinot Nero Spumante Classico '92, with its notes of butter and biscuit, mature but still quite firm: Two Glasses. The Croatina Rivuné Pasì '91, from croatina grapes allowed to dry on the vine and then harvested at the end of November, is as sweet and dense as jam, a pleasing example of its kind: One high-scoring Glass. The Moscato '98 is fragrant, agreeable and fat; the white-vinified Pinot Nero in bianco '98 is refined, fresh and clean; the red Pinot Nero Albaron '96 is not really recognizably varietal, but is full-bodied and well-balanced; the Chardonnay '98 is simple but clean and graceful: One Glass apiece. The Moscato Spumante, the Barbera, the Bonarda and the Uva Rara Raretto, all '98s, are acceptable. On the other hand, we feel we fully understand why their Dolcetto Passito '97 is called "Tormento" (torment): rarely have we tasted such a tannic wine. The Passito Padren '97, a blend of riesling (90%) and cortese picked in November and deliberately aerated during vinification, is not a great deal better: very bitter licorice is what it suggests.

○	O. P. Pinot Nero Brut Cl. '92	🍷🍷	3*
○	O. P. Riesling Italico '98	🍷🍷	2*
●	Croatina Rivuné Pasì '91	🍷	5
○	Müller Thurgau del Casteggiano '98	🍷	2*
○	O. P. Chardonnay '98	🍷	2*
○	O. P. Moscato '98	🍷	2*
●	O. P. Pinot Nero Albaron '96	🍷	3
○	O. P. Pinot Nero in bianco '98	🍷	2*
●	O. P. Barbera '98		2
○	O. P. Moscato Spumante '98		2
●	O. P. Barbera Vigna Varmasi '90	🍸🍸	4
●	O. P. Barbera Vigna Varmasi '95	🍸	4
●	O. P. Bonarda '95	🍸	3
●	Tormento Rosso '93	🍸	4
●	Tormento Rosso '95	🍸	5

MONTALTO PAVESE (PV)

Doria

Casa Tacconi, 3
27040 Montalto Pavese (PV)
tel. 0383/870143

The Dorias of Montalto have been regaining ground since last year, and have made it back up to Two Glasses with their white Pinot Nero in bianco Querciolo '97. The grapes were grown in volcanic limestone soil with a southwest exposure and were given a gentle pressing; the must fermented in barriques from the Massif Central and stayed in the wood for over six months. Its color is light and luminous, its broad bouquet offers notes of artemisia, musk and vanilla (the wood is just a little too noticeable), and the palate is dry, soft but substantial, elegant and lingering. Equally high marks went to the Bonarda '98, which has been given a light fizz by a brief second fermentation in pressure tanks. Purple in hue, it has a fragrant bouquet of plum, almond and ripe yellow peach, and a dry, full-bodied, straightforward and fruity palate with a pleasing bitterish undertone. The Roncobianco Riesling '97 isn't bad either. It is 50% cold-macerated, and a part of the must finishes its fermentation in barriques and in 350-liter oak casks; then the wine rests on its fine lees until the following spring. It has a greenish straw-yellow hue and an intense aroma of herbs and exotic fruit, and it's mouth-filling and harmonious, with a light honey undercurrent. The tasty Dado, a semi-sparkling pinot nero (70%) and riesling italico, has a fresh aroma of sage and a gracefully fruity palate. Some bottle age has greatly improved the Roncorosso Vigna Siura '96, a blend of barbera, croatina and uva rara left for a year in barriques, while the Pinot Nero Querciolo '96 has kept well and is now at its peak. We were rather disappointed by the two "metodo italiano" bubblies made from pinot nero, the Baroness and the Querciolo Brut. They can (and should) do better.

●	O. P. Bonarda '98	🍷🍷	3*
○	O. P. Pinot Nero in bianco Querciolo '97	🍷🍷	4
○	O. P. Pinot Nero in bianco Dado '98	🍷	3
○	O. P. Riesling Renano Roncobianco V. Tesi '97	🍷	4
●	AD '95		5
○	O. P. Pinot Nero Brut	🍸🍸	4
●	O. P. Pinot Nero Querciolo '91	🍸🍸	5
●	O. P. Pinot Nero Querciolo '93	🍸🍸	5
●	O. P. Pinot Nero Querciolo '95	🍸🍸	5
●	O. P. Rosso Roncorosso V. Siura '93	🍸🍸	4
●	O. P. Rosso V. del Masö '91	🍸🍸	4

MONTICELLI BRUSATI (BS)

La Montina
Via Baiana, 17
25040 Monticelli Brusati (BS)
tel. 030/653278

La Montina in Monticelli Brusati belongs to the brothers Giancarlo, Vittorio and Alberto Bozza. The estate includes some 20 hectares under vine, and in recent years it has achieved quite a high standard. Not surprisingly we again enjoyed our tastings of their offerings this year. We were most pleased by the Franciacorta Brut '95, a wine of unquestionable breeding. It is made from a cuvée of chardonnay (65%) and pinot nero, and exhibits a fine, dense and continuous perlage. The nose is agreeably fruity and floral, and in the mouth there is a tone of elegant, complex maturity not unconnected with a fresh acid tang and good extract. The Satèn also pocketed Two Glasses for grace and softness, aromas of white-fleshed fruit and medicinal herbs, and roundness and body in the mouth. Further excellent wines are the eccentric Franciacorta Rosé Demi Sec, with its sweet notes of faded rose petals, and the Franciacorta Brut, with lots of ripe exotic fruit aromas (pineapple and banana), and balance in the mouth, although a little more crispness wouldn't have hurt. The Franciacorta Extra Brut has a crisper and drier nature, but it manages to be soft and fruity at the same time. The interesting and well-made T.d.F. Bianco Palanca '98 is structured and fragrant, but we found the two T.d.F. Rossos, the standard '97 and the special selection Rosso dei Dossi '97, somewhat under par.

○ Franciacorta Brut '95	🍷🍷	5
○ Franciacorta Satèn	🍷🍷	4
○ Franciacorta Brut	🍷	4
○ Franciacorta Extra Brut	🍷	4
⊙ Franciacorta Rosé Demi Sec	🍷	4
○ T. d. F. Bianco Vign. Palanca '98	🍷	3
● T. d. F. Rosso '97		3
● T. d. F. Rosso dei Dossi '97		3
○ Franciacorta Brut	YY	4
○ Franciacorta Brut '91	YY	4
○ Franciacorta Brut '94	YY	5
○ Franciacorta Crémant	YY	4
○ Franciacorta Extra Brut	YY	4
○ Franciacorta Satèn	YY	4
● T. d. F. Rosso dei Dossi '96	Y	3

MONTICELLI BRUSATI (BS)

Lo Sparviere
Via Costa, 2
25040 Monticelli Brusati (BS)
tel. 030/652382

Its 25 hectares under vine and annual production of over 110 thousand bottles definitely remove this estate from the realm of the amateur venture. In the last few years Ugo Gussalli Beretta, a name to conjure with in the business world of Brescia, and his wife Monique Poncelet have definitely decided to make a go of it with Lo Sparviere and its wines. This time the Franciacorta Extra Brut carried off Two Glasses for being an exceptionally well-made and elegant bubbly. Although it's an extra brut, it is fairly soft and seems to have gobbled up all six grams of sugar that are the dosage limit for this category. A rich and structured base wine and a brief sojourn in wood before the "prise de mousse" did the rest, giving us a Franciacorta with enchanting notes of vanilla and peach and apricot jam. It's a long-lasting, full-bodied wine and a particular pleasure at table. The oenologist Francesco Polastri has also presented a Franciacorta Brut which is agreeable and properly put together, but not such a triumph as his Extra Brut. The Rosso Il Sergnana '96 stands out amongst the Terre di Franciacortas: it's soft and full-bodied, rich in noble tannins and intense berry notes, and lingering. The barrique-aged T.d.F. Bianco '96 seemed a little too forward and tired. The Terre di Franciacorta '98 is worthy of mention.

○ Franciacorta Extra Brut	🍷🍷	5
○ Franciacorta Brut	🍷	4
○ T. d. F. Bianco Barrique '96	🍷	4
● T. d. F. Rosso '96	🍷	4
○ T. d. F. Bianco '98		2
○ Franciacorta Brut	YY	4
○ Franciacorta Extra Brut	YY	4
○ T. d. F. Bianco Ris. '95	YY	3*
○ T. d. F. Bianco '96	Y	2*
○ T. d. F. Bianco '97	Y	3
● T. d. F. Rosso Vino del Cacciatore '95	Y	3

MONTICELLI BRUSATI (BS)

VILLA

FRAZ. VILLA
25040 MONTICELLI BRUSATI (BS)
TEL. 030/652329 - 030/6852305

This lovely estate in Monticelli Brusati belongs to Alessandro Bianchi and boasts about 26 hectares of vineyards that have been converted to high-density plantings and are kept well turfed. The yield is low (not over 80 quintals per hectare), and the grapes are picked by hand and placed in plastic boxes. Ermes Vianelli is in charge of producing their approximately 170 thousand bottles, assisted by the valuable advice of the oenologist Corrado Cugnasco. There is a vast range of Franciacortas and still wines, and the pick of the lot this time is the superb Franciacorta Selezione Vita Nova Brut '93, a special edition of about 750 jeroboams made to celebrate the end of the millennium. This is one of the best Franciacortas we tasted this year. Its great finesse and elegance are suggested as soon as you see its extremely fine perlage, the result of a full five years on its yeasts before dégorgement. It has a harmonious bouquet of fresh fruit, mint, sage and yeast, and is perfectly balanced, remarkably full-bodied and lingering on the palate, where it finishes with delightful vanilla nuances. It's a splendid wine, although rather a dear one. Many of the same qualities can however be found in the Satèn, which is one of the best of its kind. It displays sweet aromas of butter and warm brioche, a prelude to distinct, crisp notes of tropical fruit on the rounded, fruity and very delicate palate. All the other Franciacortas and the still wines from this estate are excellent.

○	Franciacorta Cuvette Sec '95	🍷🍷	5
⊙	Franciacorta Rosé Démi Sec '95	🍷🍷	5
○	Franciacorta Satèn Brut '95	🍷🍷	5
○	Franciacorta Vita Nova Brut '93	🍷🍷	6
○	Franciacorta Brut '95	🍷	4
○	Franciacorta Extra Brut '95	🍷	4
○	T. d. F. Marengo '97	🍷	4
○	T. d. F. Pian della Vigna '98	🍷	4
●	T. d. F. Rosso '97	🍷	3
●	T. d. F. Rosso Gradoni '96	🍷	4
○	Franciacorta Brut '93	🍸🍸	4
○	Franciacorta Brut '94	🍸🍸	4
○	Franciacorta Brut Sel. '92	🍸🍸	6
○	Franciacorta Cuvette '93	🍸🍸	5
○	Franciacorta Extra Brut '94	🍸🍸	4

MONTÙ BECCARIA (PV)

VERCESI DEL CASTELLAZZO

VIA AURELIANO, 36
27040 MONTÙ BECCARIA (PV)
TEL. 0385/262098 - 0385/60067

The Vercesis of Castellazzo (the ancient Beccaria castle which was frequently destroyed and rebuilt, then transformed into a Barnabite monastery in the 16th century) again have reason to be proud of their Pinot Nero Luogo dei Monti, this time of two successive vintages, the '96 and the '97. The first, an elegant wine aged for 12 months in French barriques, has a properly evolved bouquet with rich tertiary aromas of roasted coffee beans, sweet spice and black currant, and should be getting even better on the palate: Two Glasses without strain. The second, which is more concentrated, promises very well indeed but needs a few more months' rest in the bottle. The Orto di San Giacomo '96, an Oltrepò Pavese Rosso made from a blend of bonarda, barbera, pinot nero and cabernet sauvignon, is a complete success. Aged in medium-toasted barriques for a year, it is deep ruby in hue and intensely redolent of prune and almond. The palate is vigorous, warm and full-bodied. Their other Oltrepò Rosso, the Pezzalunga '98 (barbera, croatina and uva rara) has an agreeably immediate fragrance, but should nevertheless last well for some time. The Bonarda Fatila '96, which matured for a few months in wood and a few years in the bottle, is full-bodied and shows just the right amount of tannin. The lightly fizzy Bonarda '98 is an easy tipple with a violet and black cherry nose. The Gugiarolo '97, made from selected, white-vinified pinot nero, has a compound fragrance of apple, peach and wildflowers, and a dry, firm, lingering palate. As usual the Vespolino'98, made from the grape of the same name (which grows on the Novara slopes as well), is quite delightful. It's a quaffable red with a characteristic green peppercorn nose.

●	O. P. Pinot Nero Luogo dei Monti '96	🍷🍷	4
●	O. P. Rosso Orto di S. Giacomo '96	🍷🍷	4
●	O. P. Bonarda '98	🍷	3
●	O. P. Bonarda Fatila '96	🍷	4
○	O. P. Pinot Nero in bianco Gugiarolo '97	🍷	3
●	O. P. Pinot Nero Luogo dei Monti '97	🍷	4
●	O. P. Rosso Pezzalunga '98	🍷	3
●	Vespolino Rosso '98	🍷	3
●	O. P. Bonarda Fatila '90	🍸🍸	4
●	O. P. Bonarda Fatila '91	🍸🍸	4
●	O. P. Pinot Nero Luogo dei Monti '95	🍸🍸	4

MONZAMBANO (MN)

La Prendina - La Cavalchina

Loc. La Prendina
46040 Monzambano (MN)
tel. 045/516002

Once again La Prendina's best wine is Il Falcone, which has become a Garda DOC with this vintage ('96), after some years as an Alto Mincio IGT. This estate, the property of the Piona family, which also owns La Cavalchina in Custoza, includes 27 hectares under vine on the morainal Mantovan hills near Lake Garda. The Falcone vineyard, planted in '65, covers 2.66 propitiously situated hectares where cabernet sauvignon and merlot (10%) are particularly successful. The '96 has opted for elegance rather than vigor; it was aged for four months in steel, 12 in small oak barrels and another year in the bottle, and is garnet-tinged ruby in the glass, and redolent of vanilla, jam and ripe hay; on the palate it is warm and soft but very firm. Its finesse and harmony have won it Two Glasses. The Merlot Garda '96 has developed well in the bottle, confirming the One full Glass it got last year. Turning to the whites, we tasted the Riesling '98, which offers a good nose with distinct mineral notes, and a fairly citric palate with appropriate length. But their top white is the Sauvignon Garda '98, produced with brief skin contact and deliberate aeration of the must. Of a light golden hue, it has a compound fragrance (pineapple, melon, a faint hint of grass) and a soft but crisp, full-bodied, fruity palate. The attractive Pinot Bianco '98 is slightly redolent of green tobacco leaf. Of the wines from La Cavalchina, the excellent barrique-aged Bianco di Custoza Amedeo '98 is a Two Glass winner. It reveals an intriguing floral fragrance and a smooth, delightful structure. All their other wines are interesting.

○	Bianco di Custoza Amedeo '98	▼▼	3*
●	Cabernet Sauvignon Alto Mincio Il Falcone '96	▼▼	4
○	Garda Sauvignon '98	▼▼	3*
●	Bardolino Sup. Santa Lucia Cavalchina '97	▼	3
○	Bianco di Custoza Cavalchina '98	▼	2*
○	Garda Pinot Bianco '98	▼	2*
○	Garda Riesling '98	▼	3
⊙	La Rosa Cavalchina '98	▼	4
○	Le Pergole del Sole Cavalchina '97	▼	6
○	Garda Pinot Grigio '98		2
●	Cabernet Sauvignon Alto Mincio Il Falcone '95	▽▽	4

MORNICO LOSANA (PV)

Ca' di Frara

Loc. Casa Ferrari, 1
27090 Mornico Losana (PV)
tel. 0383/892299

Luca Bellani's Ca' di Frara has given an excellent performance. Established in 1905, the winery has 28 hectares of its own under vine and markets 260 thousand bottles of wine, some produced here and some brought in from elsewhere. The top of the range, as usual, is the Pinot Grigio: the '98 vintage, made from overripe grapes, has a lightly green-tinged golden color, an intense fragrance of rose and pineapple, and a full-bodied, fat, powerful and very long-lasting palate. Within an ace of it is the Pinot Nero Il Raro '97, made from three different clones vinified traditionally and aged for 12 months in barriques. The vanilla serves to bring out a broad fragrance of black currant jam, followed by a soft, rich palate. Next comes the Riesling (both Rhine and italico) Apogeo '98, made from late-harvested, cold-macerated grapes. A green-gold hue leads into a complex bouquet of flowers (lemon balm, linden blossom), fruit (apple) and mineral notes, followed by an elegant, sinewy palate. The Oltrepò Pavese Rosso Io '97, matured in Slavonian oak casks, is very woody, but there's also ripe cherry and blackberry to be found, and it has remarkable structure. The mouth-filling, graceful and extremely aromatic Il Raro Bianco is made from malvasia di Candia grown in sandy soil with crystalline chalk outcrops. The barrique-aged Chardonnay '98 has enticing hints of honey, sweet spice and gooseberry, but it's a little short. We were disappointed by the two Bonarda La Casetta '97s, one still, one a little fizzy: they were both less direct than we'd have wished. On the other hand, Il Frater Riserva '97, which we had found immature and "smothered" by wood, is decidedly improved: bottle aging has been good for it.

○	O. P. Malvasia Il Raro '98	▼▼	4
○	O. P. Pinot Grigio V. T. '98	▼▼	4
●	O. P. Pinot Nero Il Raro '97	▼▼	4
○	O. P. Riesling Apogeo '98	▼▼	3*
●	O. P. Rosso Io '97	▼▼	4
○	O. P. Chardonnay '98	▼	3
○	O. P. Chardonnay '97	▽▽	3
○	O. P. Pinot Grigio V. T. '95	▽▽	4
○	O. P. Pinot Grigio V. T. '97	▽▽	4
○	O. P. Riesling Renano '95	▽▽	3
●	O. P. Bonarda '96	▽	3
○	O. P. Chardonnay '96	▽	3
●	O. P. Pinot Nero Il Raro '94	▽	4
○	O. P. Riesling Renano '97	▽	3

OME (BS)

MAJOLINI
VIA PRATO, 15
25050 OME (BS)
TEL. 030/652161

As far as we're concerned, Majolini in Ome has made more progress recently than any other estate in Franciacorta. And we think you'll be favorably impressed too after (or while) tasting their splendid Franciacorta Brut '92, which boldly takes its place amongst the best we tasted this year. It has a vivid straw color with brilliant gold highlights, and its opening on the nose is intense, elegant and full, with complex notes of ripe white-fleshed fruit, followed by more evolved toasty tones and delicate mineral nuances. On the palate it is dense, mouth-filling, rounded and fleshy, with evolved tones that are not in the least troubling, but progress with fascinating complexity. It's well-balanced, fresh and perfectly constructed, and finishes to great effect on broad vanilla and toasty oak notes. Their standard Franciacorta Brut is particularly successful as well, meaty and stylish, and winking familiarly at the vintage bottle to which it is evidently so closely related. Two agreeable and well-made examples of their Terre di Franciacorta are the Bianco Ronchello '98, with good structure and rich fruit, and the Rosso Dordaro '96, a fairly full-bodied red with soft tannins and a moderate amount of fruit, but finishing on a slightly bitter note. The T.d.F. Rosso Ruc di Gnoc '97 and the T.d.F Bianco '98 are a step below them.

○	Franciacorta Brut	🍷🍷	4
○	Franciacorta Brut '92	🍷🍷	5
○	T. d. F. Bianco Ronchello '98	🍷	4
●	T. d. F. Rosso Dordaro '96	🍷	4
○	T. d. F. Bianco '98		3
●	T. d. F. Rosso Ruc di Gnoc '97		4
●	T. d. F. Rosso Dordaro '90	🍸🍸	4
●	T. d. F. Rosso Ruc di Gnoc '91	🍸🍸	4
○	Franciacorta Brut	🍸	5
○	T. d. F. Bianco Ronchello '92	🍸	4
●	T. d. F. Bianco Ronchello '93	🍸	4
●	T. d. F. Rosso Ruc di Gnoc '92	🍸	4

PASSIRANO (BS)

MARCHESI FASSATI DI BALZOLA
VIA CASTELLO, 2
25050 PASSIRANO (BS)
TEL. 02/8692132 - 02/72003611

Marquis Leonardo Fassati di Balzola and his wife Cecilia are both agronomists and own various estates that they manage directly, as well as acting as consultants for many other producers. From the vineyards surrounding the castle of Passirano they make admirable Franciacortas and Terre di Franciacortas with the help of the oenologist Corrado Cugnasco. This year both of their Franciacortas, the Brut and the Extra Brut, did very well indeed at our tastings. The Brut is elegant, graceful, soft and sweet on the nose, with delightful notes of apricot, peach and vanilla. In the mouth it is caressing and elegant, revealing a good "prise de mousse" (although a few more months on its yeasts would probably have done it some good), and it has a long, stylish finish with a good vanilla aftertaste. The Extra Brut, of a lovely bright pale straw hue with a delicate greenish tinge, has a fine dense perlage, a creamy mousse, mellow notes of ripe fruit and sweet hints of brioche and butter. On the palate it offers a good acid thrust, and is dry but at the same time soft, fruity and full-bodied, finishing on a vanilla and fresh almond note. The two Terre di Franciacortas, the Rosso '97 and the Bianco '98, are fresh, fruity and properly made, although a little thin.

○	Franciacorta Brut	🍷🍷	5
○	Franciacorta Extra Brut	🍷🍷	5
○	T. d. F. Bianco '98		2
●	T. d. F. Rosso '97		2
○	Franciacorta Extra Brut	🍸🍸	4
○	Franciacorta Brut	🍸	4
○	T. d. F. Bianco '97	🍸	3
○	T. d. F. Bianco Vigna Medes '95	🍸	4

PASSIRANO (BS)

IL MOSNEL
FRAZ. CAMIGNONE
VIA BARBOGLIO, 14
25040 PASSIRANO (BS)
TEL. 030/653117 - 030/654236

This year Il Mosnel has presented an excellent range of Franciacortas. Giulio and Lucia Barzanò have worked hard in these few years to turn this into a top-level estate and, to judge from our tastings, they haven't labored in vain. One of their most interesting wines this time is a special cuvée for the year 2000, a vintage '90 that has rested on its yeast all this while, waiting for dégorgement. It has a brilliant pale straw color, an elegant, aristocratic bouquet with complex vegetal notes, hints of white-fleshed fruit jam and delicate nuances of spice and vanilla. The palate is stylish, harmonious and fruity with a long, freshly vegetal finish. The Franciacorta Extra Brut is as good as it has ever been, with lots of aromas of patisserie and candied peel and, in the mouth, a velvety, captivating softness, underpinned by a lovely crisp tone and good structure. The Brut '91 is round, harmonious and refined, showing remarkable balance and freshness, while the Brut Etichetta Blu offers elegant yeasty and toasty aromas and a fruity palate where peach predominates. The Brut Nouvelle Cuvée, with its good structure, fine mousse and soft ripeness, has won itself Two Glasses too. The most striking of the still wines this time is the T.d.F. Campolarga '98, with its richly fresh and intense bouquet of white-fleshed fruit and flowers, and lovely structure and concentration in the mouth. All their other wines are top-flight as well; we particularly mention the chardonnay-based Passito Sebino '97 because of its elegance.

○	Franciacorta Brut	▼▼	4
○	Franciacorta Brut '91	▼▼	5
○	Franciacorta Brut Nouvelle Cuvée	▼▼	4
○	Franciacorta Brut Sel. 2000 '90	▼▼	6
○	Franciacorta Extra Brut	▼▼	4
○	T. d. F. Chardonnay Campolarga '98	▼▼	3*
○	Passito Sebino '97	▼	4
●	T. d. F. Rosso '97	▼	3
●	T. d. F. Rosso Fontecolo '95	▼	4
○	Franciacorta Brut	▽▽	4
○	Franciacorta Brut '90	▽▽	5
○	Franciacorta Brut '91	▽▽	5
○	Franciacorta Brut Nouvelle Cuvée	▽▽	4
○	T. d. F. Bianco Sulìf '97	▽▽	4
●	T. d. F. Rosso Fontecolo '93	▽▽	4

POLPENAZZE DEL GARDA (BS)

CASCINA LA PERTICA
FRAZ. PISCEDO
25040 POLPENAZZE DEL GARDA (BS)
TEL. 0365/651471

After a year's absence Ruggero Brunoni's Cascina La Pertica is back in the Guide. The estate covers 35 hectares, 5 of which are olive groves, while 15 are vineyards, planted to varieties both local (groppello, marzemino, barbera, sangiovese, erbamat, tocai...) and "international" (chardonnay, sauvignon, cabernet merlot...), which yield 60-70 thousand bottles a year. The reds elbowed their way to the front of all the wines produced by the oenologist Franco Bernabei, and the first in line is the Riserva del Garda Bresciano '96, a blend of groppello, marzemino, barbera, sangiovese and cabernet sauvignon vinified in the traditional manner and then part barrel- and part barrique-aged. Dark ruby with a purple tinge in the glass, it is redolent of red berries and vanilla; the palate is full-bodied, warm, harmonious and firm, with a distinct and pleasingly persistent jammy undertone. It earns its Two Glasses. The red Le Zalte '95, made from cabernet (both sauvignon and franc) and merlot and barrique-aged for 10 months, is deep garnet in hue and has a definite fragrance of undergrowth and spice, but it's rather harsh to the taste because of untamed tannins; with more harmony it would have scored higher. The Garda Classico Groppello '98, 10% of which matured in large barrels, is clearly heady, fragrant and fruity, with a restrained bitterish undertone that accentuates its succulence. Lagging somewhat behind, the Chiaretto '98 would have benefited from greater vigor and more intense fruit. Just as we went to press we retasted Le Zalte Rosso '97 and found our earlier doubts resolved: it is now an elegant and concentrated red wine.

●	Le Zalte Rosso '97	▼▼	4
●	Garda Bresciano Rosso Le Sincette Ris. '96	▼▼	3*
●	Garda Bresciano Groppello '98	▼	2*
●	Le Zalte Rosso '95	▼	4
⊙	Garda Bresciano Chiaretto Le Sincette '98		2
○	Le Sincette Brut M. Cl.	▽▽	5
●	Le Zalte Rosso '90	▽▽	4
●	Le Zalte Rosso '92	▽▽	4
●	Le Zalte Rosso '94	▽▽	4
●	Garda Bresciano Groppello '96	▽	3
●	Garda Bresciano Rosso Le Sincette '94	▽	3
●	Le Zalte Rosso '93	▽	4

PONTIDA (BG)

CANTINA SOCIALE VAL SAN MARTINO
VIA BERGAMO, 1195
24030 PONTIDA (BG)
TEL. 035/795035

Pontida is well known as the place where Alberto da Giussano took his famous oath before confronting Frederick Barbarossa at the battle of Legnano in 1176, but it's also well known to the wine lovers of Bergamo and thereabouts as the site of the Cantina Sociale Val San Martino. Here a small number of winegrowers stubbornly strive to produce the best wine they're capable of, with really encouraging results. The first example of these extremely positive developments is their Valcalepio Rosso Riserva '95, made with cabernet and merlot from the Colle Pasta (a one-hectare vineyard near Torre dei Roveri with a yield limited to a maximum of 70 quintals) and aged for 18 months in 24-hectoliter Allier oak barrels. Bright garnet-hued, with a distinct black cherry jam and licorice nose, it has a ripe, well-supported, warm and harmonious palate and didn't have to strain at all to get its Two Glasses. The Valcalepio Bianco '98 is just as good of its kind. The component chardonnay and pinot grigio underwent a light maceration to achieve a straw yellow hue, an intensely varietal nose and a full-bodied crisp palate. The Incrocio Manzoni 6.0.13 (a hybrid of pinot bianco and Rhine riesling) is just a bit lean, but it has quite a delightful nose with hints of rose, banana and apple. The Valcalepio Rosso '97, cold-blended cabernet and merlot briefly matured in wood, and the Cabernet della Bergamasca '97 from the vineyards near Pontida, Palazzago and Mapello, with a delicate clean fragrance of undergrowth and freshly mown grass, are not at all bad. When you think that this cooperative puts out quite a number of bottles (between 15 thousand and 40 thousand a year), and that the prices are eminently affordable, it becomes even clearer that these are wines worth trying.

○	Valcalepio Bianco '98	🍷🍷	2*
●	Valcalepio Rosso Ris. '95	🍷🍷	3*
●	Cabernet della Bergamasca '97	🍷	2*
○	Incrocio Manzoni 6.0.13 '98	🍷	2*
●	Valcalepio Rosso '97	🍷	2*
○	Chardonnay della Bergamasca '98		2

PROVAGLIO D'ISEO (BS)

BERSI SERLINI
VIA CERRETO, 7
25050 PROVAGLIO D'ISEO (BS)
TEL. 030/9823338

At Provaglio d'Iseo there's an estate, Bersi Serlini, with, at its center, a 15th century farmhouse surrounded by beautiful vineyards. Here the Bersi Serlinis follow the precepts of modern organic farming, and have already established themselves as good and reliable producers. This time they have presented a pair of excellent Franciacortas, two different vintages of their Brut Cuvée Millennio. The '93 has a lovely bright straw yellow hue and full, elegant and harmonious aromas of yeast, Golden Delicious apple and peach, with a hint of vanilla. On the palate it offers a mouth-filling body, fine balance between fruit and acidity and a general complexity that makes it particularly enticing, with nuances of white-fleshed fruit jam and butter and elegant toasty notes. It's delightful and altogether mature, as is the previous vintage, the '92, which has even more intense fruit, distinct notes of acacia honey and the same elegance. Their standard Franciacorta Brut wins Two Glasses again this year. It has its customary green-tinged bright straw yellow color, a nose rich in sweet yeasty and vanilla notes, and admirable harmony, structure and softness of mousse on the palate. There is lots of acidity, and it could develop for a few more years in the bottle. A confirmation of the durability of the Bersi Serlinis' Franciacortas: we had another taste of the '92 vintage, which has evolved very elegantly. The attractive sweet Nuvola Démi Sec, one of their classics, is an excellent accompaniment to a barely seared fresh foie gras served in its pan with figs and grapes. The T.d.F. Bianco '98 is perfectly acceptable.

○	Franciacorta Brut	🍷🍷	5
○	Franciacorta Brut Cuvée Millennio '92	🍷🍷	6
○	Franciacorta Brut Cuvée Millennio '93	🍷🍷	6
○	Nuvola Démi Sec	🍷	5
○	T. d. F. Bianco '98	🍷	2*
○	Franciacorta Brut	YY	4
○	Franciacorta Brut '90	YY	5
○	Franciacorta Brut '91	YY	5
○	Franciacorta Brut '91	YY	4
○	Franciacorta Extra Brut	YY	5
○	Franciacorta Extra Brut '92	YY	5
○	Nuvola Démi Sec	YY	5
●	T. d. F. Rosso '95	Y	5

ROCCA DE' GIORGI (PV)

ANTEO
LOC. CHIESA
27043 ROCCA DE' GIORGI (PV)
TEL. 0385/48583 - 0385/99073

Anteo's wines, which are indubitably improving, do show some inconsistency: together with interesting bottles there are some that need more attention. This year's most successful wine is the Quattro Marzo '98, named after the date when its bottling began (March 4). It's an original blend of chardonnay (40%), pinot nero (40%) and Rhine riesling, from Guyot-trained and spur-pruned cordon-trained vines grown on calcareous marly hillsides. The bunches were cooled to 8°C for 24 hours; subsequent vinification featured gentle pressing and cryomaceration, and the wine fermented partly in steel, partly in small oak barrels. Of a bright straw yellow hue, it is redolent of peach and wildflowers, with oak-derived toasty and vanilla notes; on the palate it is dry, crisp and succulent. Close behind it are the Pinot Nero in bianco Il Floreale (with 20% chardonnay), which is a white-vinified semi-sparkler, the Ca' dell'Oca bianco '96, which spent six months in barriques, the red Giublot '96, a blend of cabernet sauvignon, pinot nero and bonarda aged for 15 months in Allier and Nevers barriques, and the pleasingly fruity, lightly fizzy Bonarda '98 from Rovescala Staffolo. Another good one is the partly wood-aged Pinot Nero Brut Classico '94 Selezione del Gourmet (20% chardonnay). We found two other spumantes, the Pinot Nero Martinotti and the standard Pinot Nero Brut Classico, less successful but still worthy of mention. The further attention we mentioned earlier is, however, indispensable for the Nature and, most particularly, for a strange sparkling rosé with an aroma we were simply unable to identify.

○	Quattro Marzo Bianco '98	🍷🍷	3*
●	Giublot '96	🍷	4
●	O. P. Bonarda Staffolo '98	🍷	3
○	O. P. Pinot Nero Brut Cl. Sel. Gourmet '94	🍷	5
●	O. P. Pinot Nero Il Floreale '98	🍷	3
○	O. P. Pinot Nero in bianco Ca' dell'Oca '96	🍷	4
○	O. P. Pinot Nero Brut Cl.		4
○	O. P. Pinot Nero Brut Martinotti		3
○	O. P. Pinot Nero in bianco Ca' dell'Oca '95	🍸🍸	4
●	O. P. Pinot Nero Ca' dell'Oca '93	🍸	4
●	O. P. Bonarda Vivace '97		3

RODENGO SAIANO (BS)

MIRABELLA
VIA CANTARANE, 2
25050 RODENGO SAIANO (BS)
TEL. 030/611197

This year Mirabella's extra brut, the Nondosato, did not win Two Glasses, but their classic Franciacorta Brut did. It has a brilliant straw yellow hue, minute and persistent bubbles, and soft fresh aromas of ripe white-fleshed fruit, with light hints of tropical fruit and a touch of citrus peel that makes it vivid, refreshing and enchanting. On the palate it's soft, rounded and shot through with a crisp, well-balanced acidity, and the fruit blends perfectly with notes of yeast and toasted bread. But Franciacorta is not all that Mirabella offers. One of the partners is the set designer Enrico Job, who is married to the director Lina Wertmüller. And a set of sparkling wines is dedicated to her, one of which, the Wertmüller Brut, has walked off with Two Glasses this time, thanks to its lovely smooth roundness, remarkably fine perlage, softly floral tone and long finish. Compared with the previous version the Franciacorta Nondosato '92 seemed slightly under par. Of course it had to cope with a less felicitous year, and it is elegant and well-balanced, but also leaner and less structured than the '91. The Franciacorta Rosé has a lovely brilliant pale pink hue and a delicate palate with soft, inviting notes of wild berries. Of the still wines we admired the T.d.F. Bianco '97 from the Palazzina vineyard, which has a faint but elegant floral nose with fresh notes of bouncing Bet and lavender, and is dry and light-bodied. The T.d.F. Bianco '98 and the two reds, the T.d.F. '97 and the special selection Maniero '97, are all less interesting.

○	Franciacorta Brut	🍷🍷	4
○	Wertmüller Brut	🍷🍷	5
○	Franciacorta Non Dosato '92	🍷	5
○	T. d F. Bianco Palazzina '97	🍷	4
○	T. d F. Bianco '98		3
●	T. d F. Rosso '97		3
●	T. d F. Rosso Maniero '97		4
○	Franciacorta Brut	🍸🍸	4
○	Franciacorta Brut '90	🍸🍸	5
○	Franciacorta Non Dosato '91	🍸🍸	5
○	T. d F. Barrique '95	🍸🍸	4
○	T. d F. Bianco '96	🍸	3
○	T. d F. Bianco '97	🍸	3
●	T. d F. Rosso Barrique '95	🍸	4
○	Wertmüller Brut	🍸	4

ROVESCALA (PV)

F.LLI AGNES
VIA CAMPO DEL MONTE, 1
27040 ROVESCALA (PV)
TEL. 0385/75206

These are real Bonarda specialists. Cristiano, an agronomist, and Sergio, who looks after the business end, members of a family that has been involved in wine-making since time immemorial, have chosen to devote themselves primarily to red wine, and in particular to Bonarda, which means the croatina grape, another native of Rovescala. Their Bonardas are among the very best in the Oltrepò Pavese: dark, rich, concentrated, perhaps just a bit rustic, but in the most wholesome and excellent way. The semi-sparkling Cresta del Ghiffi '98 is made with overripe grapes from a vineyard planted in the mid '50s; wood is eschewed in its preparation, so as not to disturb the varietal aromas of blackberry, vineyard peach and almond. The Campo del Monte '98, from a hilltop vineyard, has also acquired some bubbles from a light refermentation in glass vessels, but it ages in oak barrels before being bottled. The Millenium '97 is extremely concentrated, heady (over 14% alcohol) and ripe. Possessione del Console (from pignolo, a venerable croatina clone) and Vignazzo, both '98s, are somewhat in the shadow of the first three wines, but they're attractive all the same. The Poculum '97, named after the ancient Roman goblet, is very good. It's made from a selection of the best grapes grown in their 10 hectares of vineyards, and is a fine red for aging, with notes of licorice and vanilla revealing its sojourn in French barriques. Last but not least, the Loghetto '98, made from grapes lightly dried in boxes, tastes of honey locust and black cherry and has that highly prized bittersweet undertone that the natives hereabouts perceive as almondy.

●	Loghetto '98	🍷🍷	3*
●	O. P. Bonarda Campo del Monte '98	🍷🍷	3*
●	O. P. Bonarda Cresta del Ghiffi '98	🍷🍷	3*
●	O. P. Bonarda Millenium '97	🍷🍷	5
●	Poculum '97	🍷🍷	4
●	Loghetto '97	🍷	3
●	O. P. Barbera '98	🍷	2*
●	O. P. Bonarda Possessione del Console '98	🍷	3
●	O. P. Bonarda Vignazzo '98	🍷	3
●	O. P. Bonarda Campo del Monte '97	🍷🍷 (outline)	3
●	O. P. Bonarda Possessione del Console '97	🍷🍷 (outline)	3

ROVESCALA (PV)

MARTILDE
FRAZ. CROCE, 4/A/1
27040 ROVESCALA (PV)
TEL. 0385/756280

Antonella Tucci's Martilde estate covers 18 hectares of land around Rovescala, the birthplace of the bonarda-croatina grape, in the first terraced hillsides of the Oltrepò, an area particularly favorable to the production of red wine. The vineyards are in the process of being replanted, with an average density of 3,500-4,000 vines per hectare, and the idea is eventually to have 15 hectares under vine. Training has tended to follow the simple Guyot system, but low spur-pruned cordon training is gaining ground, limiting the number of buds. Cultivation follows organic principles (minimal use is made of chemicals). The cellar is well equipped, including 50- and 25-hectoliter stainless steel vats, oak barrels from the Massif Central and Allier oak barriques. Annual production at the moment reaches about 40 thousand bottles of reds and whites, with imaginative labels featuring cats and horses. Starting with the red wines, we particularly liked the full-bodied and harmonious Bonarda '98, with its clean and distinctive varietal aromas. We were also struck by the Pinot Nero Martuffo '96, now at its peak, with a toasty and black currant jammy bouquet, and soft and firm on the palate. An extremely successful white is the Riesling Italico Gelo '98, perfumed and so soft as to seem almost fat. The Malvasia Piume '98 is fragrant and clean; the Barbera Diluvio '95 is agreeable despite its noticeable acidity; the Bonarda Zaffo '93 is quite mature and should be drunk up.

●	O. P. Bonarda '98	🍷🍷	3*
●	O. P. Pinot Nero Martuffo '96	🍷🍷	4
○	O. P. Riesling Italico Gelo '98	🍷🍷	3*
●	O. P. Barbera Diluvio '95	🍷	4
●	O. P. Bonarda Zaffo '93	🍷	4
○	O. P. Malvasia Piume '98	🍷	4

S. GIULETTA (PV)

ISIMBARDA
FRAZ. CASTELLO
27046 S. GIULETTA (PV)
TEL. 0383/899256

In last year's Guide we predicted an improvement from this estate, formerly the property of the marquises Isimbardi and now belonging to Luigi Meroni, but we didn't need a crystal ball. The great care lavished on the vines and the enthusiasm of the young oenologist Gian Giacomo Liberali have borne fruit. The top of their range is currently the Barbera '98, made only from barbera grown in the Picco dei Giganti Guyot-trained vineyard with a yield of less than two kilos per vine. Vinification followed by a slight second fermentation in a pressure tank have produced a wine with a creamy mousse, a violet-tinged dark purple hue and a broad heady bouquet of ripe fruit and bitter spice; the palate is robust, straightforward and harmonious, with a firm, full body. A more or less equally laudable wine is the Oltrepò Pavese Rosso '96, a blend of barbera, croatina, uva rara and pinot nero, grown in the Vigna del Tramonto in Mornico Losana (it seems a pity not to use the vineyard name on the label), matured partly in 25-hectoliter barrels and partly in once-used barriques. At the moment the wood still has the upper hand over the varietal notes, but the wine is developing well. Another red worthy of note is the Bonarda Vivace '98 from the Ronco dei Torti vineyard, made from very ripe grapes that are allowed to macerate for 4-5 days at 28°C. Refermentation in pressure tanks takes place the following spring, and the result is a dark Bonarda, redolent of cherry and hazelnut, with a vigorous, dry but not harsh palate that offers the characteristic bitterish finish. The Riesling Vivace '98, made from both riesling italico and Rhine riesling and 50% cryomacerated, is pleasing, crisp and easy to drink.

●	O. P. Barbera '98	🍷🍷	3*
●	O. P. Bonarda Vivace '98	🍷🍷	3*
●	O. P. Rosso '96	🍷🍷	3*
○	O. P. Riesling '98	🍷	3
●	O. P. Bonarda Vivace '97	🍸	3
○	O. P. Pinot Nero in bianco '96	🍸	3
○	O. P. Riesling Italico '96	🍸	3
○	O. P. Riesling V. Belvedere '97	🍸	3

S. MARIA DELLA VERSA (PV)

LA VERSA
VIA CRISPI, 15
27047 S. MARIA DELLA VERSA (PV)
TEL. 0385/798411

La Versa is back in the Guide again. This is a vast and important wine organization with 750 shareholding partners, 480 estates, 1,300 hectares under vine, 106 thousand quintals of grapes brought in, 7 million bottles of wine and spumante and 200 thousand bottles of monovarietal grappa sold. The technical staff now boasts the presence of the expert oenologist Carmelo Simoncelli, (who used to be in charge of the cellar at the Istituto di San Michele all'Adige), working side by side with Corrado Cavallo to give a further boost to the quality of their products. Meanwhile we were very favorably impressed by the Lacrimae Vitis La Soleggia '95, a white moscato passito made from semi-dried grapes grown on Guyot-trained vines, yielding only 45 quintals per hectare, on clay and limestone soil in the Alta Valle Versa. The bunches, once selected, were left to dry on cane mats until December. After gentle pressing and fermentation at a low temperature, the wine aged for 14 months in little Allier oak barrels and for 6 months in the bottle. Bright golden yellow in hue, it has a broad complex bouquet with notes of musk, vanilla, nutmeg, sage and rosewood, and a sweet aristocratic palate that can hold its own even with a chocolate-based dessert. The Brut Classico is decidedly good, although a bit lean. It was "cellared in 1996" (which does not imply a vintage bubbly) and "dégorgé" in spring '99. The sweet Croatina Spumante '98, which has a fragrance all its own, and the Pinot Nero Brut '96, a clean, crisp Charmat-method bubbly, are both admirable. Of the semi-sparkling wines, the Riesling Italico '98 and the Malvasia '98 are good drinking, while the Chardonnay '98 stands out among the still whites.

○	O. P. Moscato Passito Lacrimae Vitis '95	🍷🍷	5
○	O. P. Brut '98	🍷	3
○	O. P. Brut M. Cl.	🍷	4
○	O. P. Chardonnay '98	🍷	3
●	O. P. Croatina Spumante	🍷	3
○	O. P. Malvasia '98	🍷	2*
○	O. P. Riesling Italico '98	🍷	2
●	O. P. Bonarda '98		2
○	O. P. Moscato Passito Lacrimae Vitis '92	🍸🍸	6
○	O. P. Moscato Passito Lacrimae Vitis '93	🍸🍸	6
●	O. P. Pinot Nero Vigna del Ferraio '93	🍸🍸	4

S. PAOLO D'ARGON (BG)

CANTINA SOCIALE BERGAMASCA
VIA BERGAMO, 10
24060 S. PAOLO D'ARGON (BG)
TEL. 035/951098

The Cantina Sociale Bergamasca in S. Paolo d'Argon, very near Bergamo, opened its doors in 1962. It now has 150 member growers, who cultivate 100 hectares of vines, and is the major producer of Valcalepio DOC. Managed by the oenologist Sergio Cantoni and directed by Count Bonaventura Grumelli Pedrocca (of ancient country lineage), it boasts up-to-the-minute technology that allows them to exploit to the full both their reds and their whites. Among the latter the Valcalepio Bianco '98 stands out. It's a blend of pinot bianco, pinot grigio and chardonnay and offers a lovely straw color and a dry, soft, crisp and fruity palate. The fresh and simple Pinot Bianco della Bergamasca '98 (150 thousand bottles) is good too, with its very clean fruity and herbal notes. The most successful of the reds is the Valcalepio Riserva '95, mostly cabernet sauvignon with some merlot, aged for three years in 25-hectoliter French oak barrels. It has a brilliant garnet color, an enchanting bouquet of jam and spice (vanilla, licorice, cinnamon) and a warm, succulent, ripe palate. With some more structure it would have had Two Glasses. Lastly, the Valcalepio Rosso '97, a blend of separately fermented cabernet sauvignon and merlot, has a fruity, heady fragrance, clean if not very intense, and a juicy, well-balanced taste.

○	Valcalepio Bianco '98	two black glasses	2*
○	Pinot Bianco della Bergamasca '98	one black glass	2*
●	Valcalepio Rosso Ris. '95	one black glass	3
●	Valcalepio Rosso '97		2

SCANZOROSCIATE (BG)

LA BRUGHERATA
VIA MEDOLAGO, 47
24020 SCANZOROSCIATE (BG)
TEL. 035/655202

La Brugherata seems more like a botanical garden than a wine estate: rose bushes, lavender, rosemary, myrtle and arbutus surround the vines, which are cared for like garden plants, all overlooked by one of the northernmost olive groves in Italy. There are even two palms, and then cherry, apricot and almond trees. It's hard to believe you're just a few kilometers from Bergamo and near the A4, the busiest highway in the country. Yet right here, thanks to the enthusiasm of Patrizia Merati, the owner, and to the dedication of both the oenologist Sergio Cantoni and the agronomist Pierluigi Donna, some of the most interesting wines of Valcalepio come into being. The top of this year's list is the Vescovado '98, a chardonnay and pinot bianco blend that gets Two full Glasses for its shining golden hue, intense fragrance of white flowers and apple, and rich, succulent, elegant and fruity palate. Close behind it is the Valcalepio Rosso Vescovado '96, merlot and cabernet sauvignon blended after fermentation and matured for eight months in Allier oak. It has a pleasing hint of black cherry with an undertone of vanilla. The Valcalepio Rosso Riserva Doglio '95, less concentrated than the excellent '94, is good, if not exciting; it should hold up still for a while, but it is evolving rapidly. The Bianco d'Alberico '98 however, a monovarietal oak-fermented chardonnay, is remarkable, with its well-judged notes of spice (licorice and cinnamon) bringing out all the fruit. Finally, the rare Moscato Nero di Scanzo Passito '96 has improved with bottle aging, becoming more harmonious and complete.

○	Bianco di Alberico '98	two black glasses	4
○	Valcalepio Bianco Vescovado '98	two black glasses	3*
●	Valcalepio Rosso Vescovado '96	two black glasses	3*
●	Valcalepio Rosso Ris. Doglio '95	one black glass	4
●	Valcalepio Rosso Ris. Doglio '94	two white glasses	4
●	Moscato di Scanzo Passito '96	one white glass	6
○	Valcalepio Bianco Vescovado '97	one white glass	3
●	Valcalepio Rosso '95	one white glass	3

SIRMIONE (BS)

Ca' dei Frati
Fraz. Lugana
Via Frati, 22
25010 Sirmione (BS)
tel. 030/919468

In a great year a great cru can give rise to a really remarkable wine; hence the trebbiano di Lugana grapes selected from the Brolettino vineyard in '95 have produced the best Lugana we have ever tasted, the Brolettino Grande Annata '95. The perfect bunches, picked at the peak of ripeness, have brought forth a white wine of great breeding, as rich as it is elegant, which spent 14 months in French barriques (half new and half once used) and was then bottle-aged. Of a shining green-gold color, it has a notably complex flowery and spicy bouquet and is ripe and very firm, harmonious and full-bodied with an extremely long aromatic finish. What a pity there's so little of it available! The Pratto '97, a blend of trebbiano di Lugana, chardonnay and sauvignon, has not repeated the success of the previous vintage: during the final ripening of the grapes there was insufficient variety in temperature (a very hot year), which cut into its fragrance. So it has to "make do" with just Two Glasses this time. Two other wines at the same level are the Lugana Brolettino '97 and the Tre Filer '96, a sweet white made from grapes shriveled by botrytis cinerea (noble rot) and matured in oak. The Lugana I Frati '98 is good, as is its wont, and the Chiaretto is agreeable, although we'd have liked more fruit. The Bordeaux blend Ronchedone is over-evolved, hence less successful.

○ Lugana I Frati '98	▼▼	3*
○ Lugana Il Brolettino '97	▼▼	4
○ Lugana Il Brolettino Grande Annata '95	▼▼	5
○ Pratto '97	▼▼	5
○ Tre Filer '96	▼▼	5
⊙ Garda Bresciano Chiaretto '98	▼	3
○ Pratto '96	▽▽▽	4
○ Lugana Il Brolettino '95	▽▽	4
○ Lugana Il Brolettino '96	▽▽	4
○ Pratto '95	▽▽	4
○ Tre Filer '90	▽▽	5
○ Tre Filer '92	▽▽	5
○ Tre Filer '94	▽▽	5
○ Tre Filer '95	▽▽	5

TEGLIO (SO)

Fay
Loc. S. Giacomo
Via Pila Caselli, 1
23030 Teglio (SO)
tel. 0342/786071

There have been some big changes at Sandro Fay's. Firstly, Marco and Elena, the two children of the oenologist-mayor of Teglio, have taken over responsibility for running the estate: Marco is to be the oenologist, while Elena will be in charge of marketing and promotion. But that's not all. The viticultural potential of this well-known house is being exploited by a recent replanting of many of the vines according to a new and rational system. The idea is to create little crus within a roughly five-hectare area of the Valgella DOC subzone. Their bottles have a new look too, more restrained and stylish. At our tastings we were struck by the ability of one of their wines to provide a modern interpretation of a terroir. This is the Valgella Carteria '96, well-constructed and direct in fragrance, and concentrated and round on the palate, with a long finish. The Valgella Ca' Morei '96, their old mainstay, is still being "reformulated": there is evidence of new wood put to good use, it's soft on the palate with hints of sweetness, but it wants a little more fruit and density. The Sassella Glicine '96 is maintaining standards; it is fruitily fragrant and slips down with no trouble at all. The Sforzato '96 has a definite character all its own, but overripe nuances are too perceptible. This rich and structured wine deserves greater aromatic cleanliness.

● Valtellina Sup. Valgella Carteria '96	▼▼	4
● Valtellina Sforzato '96	▼	5
● Valtellina Sup. Sassella Il Glicine '96	▼	4
● Valtellina Sup. Valgella Ca' Morei '96	▼	4
● Valtellina Sforzato '89	▽▽	5
● Valtellina Sforzato '94	▽▽	4
● Valtellina Sup. Sassella Il Glicine '94	▽▽	4
● Valtellina Sup. Valgella Ca' Morei '90	▽▽	5
● Valtellina Sup. Valgella Ca' Morei '92	▽▽	4

TIRANO (SO)

Conti Sertoli Salis
P.zza Salis, 3
23037 Tirano (SO)
tel. 0342/710404

That Valtellina has been making a lot of progress is plain for all to see, but that it can now be compared to the best the country has to offer is largely thanks to Sforzato. Claudio Introini, the fine oenologist at Sertoli Salis, one of the most splendid estates, historically and architecturally, in Italy, makes the Sforzato Canua out of nebbiolo that he dries on special racks and, in its '97 version, it's a masterpiece of elegance. Hence we have a new Three Glass wine, and one whose harmoniousness and general finesse capture your attention as soon as you inhale. It comes from a great vintage, and its attack on the palate is a striking fusion of smoothness and vigor, developing with depth, soft tannins and rich, succulent fruit. The '96 Canua, although less brilliant, has a spicy nose with notes of black cherry in spirits and a decided, structured and round palate, where wood and the semi-dried fruit have struck a good balance. The Saloncello '97, which is rather hard to find, has toasty aromas and is round in the mouth. The fruitily fragrant '98 Saloncello is distinctive and long-lasting on the palate. We found the Corte della Meridiana '96 less good than the last vintage; the excellence of its raw material is apparent, but the bouquet is not perfectly balanced. The Valtellina '97 is straightforward and slightly tart, but fresh; the '98 was still green at tasting time. The Torre della Sirena '98, which has become a classic of stylishness and quaffability, is floral and notably mouth-filling.

●	Valtellina Sforzato Canua '97	▼▼▼	6
●	Valtellina Sforzato Canua '96	▼▼	6
●	Il Saloncello '97	▼	4
●	Il Saloncello '98	▼	4
○	Torre della Sirena '98	▼	4
●	Valtellina '97	▼	3
●	Valtellina Sup. Corte della Meridiana '96	▼	5
●	Valtellina '98		3
●	Valtellina Sforzato Canua '94	▽▽	5
●	Valtellina Sforzato Canua '95	▽▽	5
●	Valtellina Sup. Corte della Meridiana '94	▽▽	4
●	Valtellina Sup. Corte della Meridiana '95	▽▽	4

TORRICELLA VERZATE (PV)

Monsupello
Via San Lazzaro, 5
27050 Torricella Verzate (PV)
tel. 0383/896043

The troika consisting of Carlo Boatti, patriarch, Pierangelo, his dynamic son, and the agronomist Paolo Fiocchi, who brilliantly manages the 40 hectares of estate vines, just does better and better. They make an annual average of 195 thousand bottles of different white and red wines and 35 thousand bottles of spumante classico, and you'd be hard put to find a single one that has gone wrong. Here's a very brief summary of the wines we liked most. The Chardonnay Senso '97, aged in French barriques, is continuing to mature in the bottle, acquiring yet more complexity. It's the best chardonnay we tasted from the Oltrepò. All their '98 still whites are very richly structured; they include a particularly succulent Pinot Grigio with aromas of hay and walnut skin, a Sauvignon that tastes of litchi and, ever so slightly, tomato leaf, and a Riesling Renano with elegant floral and mineral notes. The best of the sparkling wines is the Pinot Nero Brut Classico '93, graceful and elegantly mouth-filling. The non-vintage Nature and Brut, both from pinot nero, show traces of their recent "dégorgement", but should soon be in good form. Of the reds, the lightly sparkling Great Ruby '98 is noteworthy: it shows vibrancy, and definition on the nose. The fizzy and succulent Barbera Magenga is in a slightly sulfurous phase. The Bonarda Vivace '98 is a harmonious and straightforward wine. The two Pinot Nero I Germoglis, one white, one rosé and both with a sparkle, are fruity easy tipples. Dolce Carlotta (named after a little granddaughter) is a tasty, agreeable sweet red semi-sparkler. To end the list, we again found La Cuenta Passito Giallo '95 excellent.

○	O. P. Chardonnay '98	▼▼	3*
○	O. P. Chardonnay Senso '97	▼▼	4
●	O. P. Croatina Dolce Carlotta '98	▼▼	3*
○	O. P. Pinot Grigio '98	▼▼	3*
○	O. P. Pinot Nero Brut Cl. '93	▼▼	4
○	O. P. Riesling Renano '98	▼▼	3*
●	O. P. Rosso Great Ruby '98	▼▼	3*
○	O. P. Sauvignon '98	▼▼	3*
●	O. P. Barbera Magenga '98	▼	3
●	O. P. Bonarda Vivace '98	▼	3
○	O. P. Pinot Nero Brut Cl.	▼	4
○	O. P. Pinot Nero Nature Cl.	▼	4
○	O. P. Pinot Nero in bianco I Germogli '98	▼	3
⊙	O. P. Pinot Nero Rosato I Germogli '98	▼	3
○	La Cuenta '95	▽▽	6

VILLA DI TIRANO (SO)

TRIACCA
VIA NAZIONALE, 121
23030 VILLA DI TIRANO (SO)
TEL. 0342/701352

Domenico Triacca can be said to have won his wager. His clonal selections of the nebbiolo grape and the concrete results he obtained from experimental plantings demonstrate his great talent and determination. In confirmation of his magic touch in the vineyard, we tasted a really extraordinary Sauvignon Del Frate '98. It's an exceptional white wine, especially since this is red country up here. Intensely golden-hued, it releases a fragrance of tropical fruits and is dense and meaty in the mouth, with a rich, long finish. The Prestigio '96 is increasingly learning to hit its stride and should be getting even stronger. It's made from nebbiolo which has been allowed to dry a little on its broken-off shoots and is elegant and spicy on the nose, and rich in extract, round and distinctly fruity in the mouth. The properly made Sassella '96 is somewhat tannic. The Riserva Triacca '95, definitely out of the common run, intensely fragrant, and soft on the palate, came very close to getting Two Glasses. The interesting Valtellina La Gatta '96 was fruity on the nose, with nuances of freshly mown hay, and dry and substantial in the mouth. Lastly, the complex Sforzato '96 has a well-balanced and clean bouquet and is structured, round and lingering.

○	Sauvignon Del Frate '98	▼▼	4
●	Valtellina Prestigio '96	▼▼	5
●	Valtellina Sforzato '96	▼▼	5
●	Valtellina Casa La Gatta '96	▼	3
●	Valtellina Sup. Ris. Triacca '95	▼	4
●	Valtellina Sup. Sassella '96	▼	3
●	Valtellina Prestigio '89	▽▽	4
●	Valtellina Prestigio '94	▽▽	4
●	Valtellina Prestigio '95	▽▽	4
●	Valtellina Sforzato Il Corvo '94	▽▽	4
●	Valtellina Sup. Ris. Triacca '90	▽▽	4
●	Valtellina Sup. Ris. Triacca '91	▽▽	4
●	Valtellina Sup. Ris. Triacca '94	▽▽	4
●	Valtellina Sup. Sassella '89	▽▽	4
●	Valtellina Tradizione '91	▽▽	3

ZENEVREDO (PV)

TENUTA IL BOSCO
LOC. IL BOSCO
27049 ZENEVREDO (PV)
TEL. 0385/245326

There was a brilliant performance at this year's tastings by Tenuta il Bosco, the Oltrepò estate of the Zonin family. Their red Teodote, which was presented last year as Barbera DOC dell'Oltrepò and has now become a "table wine", easily took Two Glasses. Bunches of croatina, barbera and uva rara from the La Ginestra vineyard are vinified in small modern rotovats, with delicate maceration on the skins and a light second fermentation. The wine, matured in steel, has a deep ruby hue, a fruity, spicy fragrance and a full-bodied, concentrated, harmonious palate, concluding with a bitterish almond note. The decidedly improved semi-sparkling Malvasia '98, made with malvasia di Candia from the San Zeno and Laghetto vineyards, undergoes a light "prise de mousse" in a pressure tank. It is richer in both color and aroma (with hints of acacia flowers and musk) than in the past, and softer, spicier and more graceful on the palate. The best of the spumantes is the Brut Classico Regal Cuvée, made from pinot nero and bottle-aged for more than four years. Pale yellow in color, with a fine perlage, it has a broad bouquet of flowers (hawthorn, artemisia), rusk, laurel and apple; in the mouth it is dry, but not too dry, fruity and elegant. The vintage Brut Il Bosco '92 (85% pinot nero, 15% chardonnay), which we had already tasted for some of our previous editions, has a stylish nose with distinct hints of crusty bread and a clean and pleasing palate. The agreeable Pinot Nero Brut Philéo, a product of the long Charmat method, is fragrant, soft, crisp and fruity, and goes down very easily as well. Their old standby, the semi-sparkling Bonarda '98, successful as usual, is stylish and graceful.

○	O. P. Brut Cl. Regal Cuvée	▼▼	4
○	O. P. Malvasia '98	▼▼	3*
●	Teodote '97	▼▼	4
●	O. P. Bonarda '98	▼	2*
○	O. P. Pinot Nero Brut Philéo	▼	3
○	O. P. Brut Cl. '92	▽▽	2*
○	O. P. Moscato '95	▽▽	2*
●	O. P. Barbera Teodote '96	▽	4
●	O. P. Bonarda '95	▽	2*
●	O. P. Bonarda Vivace Poggio Pelato '97	▽	2*
○	O. P. Pinot Nero in bianco Vivace '97	▽	2*

OTHER WINERIES

The following producers obtained good scores in our tastings with one or more of their wines:

PROVINCE OF BERGAMO

Il Calepino
Castelli Calepio, tel. 035/847178
Il Calepino Brut Classico Ris. Fra Ambrogio '92

Joaninus de Pedrinis
Carobbio degli Angeli, tel. 035/953576
Moscato Rosso Bettinus Passito '97

Tenuta degli Angeli
Carobbio degli Angeli, tel. 035/951489
Brut Classico degli Angeli

Caminella
Cenate Sotto, tel. 035/941828
Valcalepio Bianco Ripa di Luna '98,
Verde Luna Bianco '97

La Carnosella
Grumello del Monte, tel. 035/832012
Valcalepio Moscato Passito '95

Bonaldi Cascina del Bosco
Sorisole, tel. 035/571701
Valcalepio Bianco '98

La Tardela
Torre de' Roveri, tel. 035/580172
Valcalepio Rosso '96

PROVINCE OF BRESCIA

Tognazzi
Caionvico, tel. 030/2692695
Botticino Vigna Colio '96

Redaelli de Zinis
Calvagese Riviera, tel. 030/501001
Chiaretto Garda '98

CastelFaglia
Cazzago San Martino, tel. 059/908828
Franciacorta Brut Monogram

Guarischi
Cazzago San Martino, tel. 030/7250838
Franciacorta Brut

Agricola Gatta,
Cellatica, tel. 030/2772950
Febo Chardonnay '97

Cooperativa Vitivinicola Cellatica Gussago
Cellatica, tel. 030/2522418
Franciacorta Brut

Ronco Basso, Coccaglio, tel. 030/7721689
Franciacorta Brut

Riccafana, Cologne, tel. 030/7156797
Franciacorta Brut

Barboglio de' Gaioncelli
Cortefranca, tel. 030/9826831
Franciacorta Brut,

Visconti
Desenzano del Garda, tel. 030/9120681
Lugana Sant' Onorata '98,

Spia d'Italia, Lonato, tel. 030/9130233
Extra Brut Classico '95,

Cantine Valtenesi - Lugana
Moniga del Garda, tel. 0365/502002
Lugana '98

Castelveder
Monticelli Brusati, tel. 030/652308
Franciacorta Brut '94

Vezzoli
Palazzolo sull'Oglio, tel. 030/738018
Franciacorta Brut

Le Marchesine
Passirano, tel. 030/657005
Franciacorta Brut Secolo Novo

Fraccaroli
Peschiera del Garda, tel. 045/7550949
Lugana Vigna Campo Serà '96

Bottarelli
Polpenazze del Garda, tel. 0368/674059
Garda Marzemino Bersanino di Picedo '95

Cascina Nuova
Poncarale, tel. 030/2540058
Capriano del Colle Bianco '98

Le Chiusure
Portese di San Felice Benaco,
tel. 0365/626243
Campei Benaco Rosso '97

Tenuta Roveglia, Pozzolengo, tel. 030/918663
Lugana Vigne di Catullo '97

Pasini Produttori
Raffa di Puegnago, tel. 030/266206
Garda Classico Il Renano '98

Ca' Lojera
Rovizza di Sirmione, tel. 045/7551901
Lugana Vigna Silva '97

PROVINCE OF MANTOVA

Dondino, Cavriana, tel. 0376/82231
Garda Cabernet Sauvignon '98

Lebovitz, Governolo, tel. 0376/668115
Lambrusco dei Concari '98

Spezia, Stefano
Mariana Mantovana, tel. 0376/735012
Lambrusco Etichetta Blu '98

Ricchi, Monzanbano, tel 0376/800238
Cabernet Alto Mincio '96

Gozzi - Colombara
Olfino di Monzambano, tel. 0376/800377
Garda Cabernet '98

Cantina Sociale Quistello
Quistello, tel. 0376/618118
Lambrusco Mantovano Banda Blu '98,
Lambrusco Mantovano Banda Rossa '98

Ca' Roma
Volta Mantovana, tel. 0376/604450
Cabernet Alto Mincio '98

Reale, Volta Mantovana, tel. 0376/83409
Garda Colli Mantovani Rubino '98

PROVINCE OF MILANO

Panigada - Banino
San Colombano al Lambro, tel. 0371/89103
San Colombano Banino Vigna La Merla '98

Riccardi, Enrico
San Colombano al Lambro,
tel. 0371/897381
San Colombano Rosso I Chiostri '96

PROVINCE OF PAVIA

Percivalle, Borgo Priolo, tel. 0383/871293
O. P. Barbera Demetra '98

Barbacarlo, Broni, tel. 0385/51212
O. P. Barbacarlo '97

Giorgi, Luigi, Broni, tel. 0385/51495
Croatina Laetitia '98

Montagna, Broni, tel. 0385/51028
O. P. Sauvignon '98

Travaglino, Calvignano, tel. 0383/872222
O. P. Cabernet Sauvignon '96

Fiamberti
Canneto Pavese, tel. 0385/88019
O. P. Buttafuoco Vigna Solenga '98,

C. S. Casteggio, Casteggio, tel. 0383/806311
O. P. Cabernet Sauvignon '98

Castidio Ballabbio
Casteggio, tel. 0383/82566
O. P. Rosso Narbusto '97

Ca' Montebello, Cigognola, tel. 0385/85182
O. P. Barbera '98

La Costaiola
Montebello della Battaglia, tel. 0383/83169
O. P. Pinot Nero Bellarmino '97

Casa Ré
Montecalvo Versiggia, tel. 0385/99986
O. P. Chardonnay '98

Torti, Dino
Montecalvo Versiggia, tel. 0385/951000
O. P. Barbera '97

Dellafiore
Montù Beccaria, tel. 0385/60040
O. P. Barbera '98

Castello di Luzzano
Rovescala, tel. 0523/863277
O. P. Barbera '98

Vanzini
San Damiano al Colle, tel. 0385/75019
O. P. Barbera Vigna Preda '96

Podere S. Giorgio, S. Giuletta, tel. 0383/899168
O. P. Bonarda '98

Torrevilla, Torrazza Coste, tel. 0383/77520
O. P. Bonarda La Genisia '97

PROVINCE OF SONDRIO

Mamete Prevostini, Mese, tel. 0343/41003
Valtellina Superiore Sassella Sommarovina '96

TRENTINO

A white, a red, and two spumantes: four wines from Trentino – only four – have managed to stand out with all their exuberant vitality and breeding, examples of elegance in a decidedly international style. Two of them are quite new to such high honors: Dorigati of Mezzocorona's spumante Methius and the Pinot Grigio made by the Cesconis on their Lavis hillside estate. Then the repeat performances: the Giulio Ferrari '91 Riserva del Fondatore, which would appear to have signed on permanently for Three Glasses, and San Leonardo, made by Carlo Guerrieri Gonzaga, who has succeeded in making a first-class wine despite the unfortunate effects of the '96 vintage on all reds, not only in Trentino. So these are the four Trentino wines that bear the palm. Many in the wine world, and a number of discriminating wine lovers, may feel that Trentino wine has not received the recognition it deserves. Hence we would like to point out that all the wines (and there were more than 260 of them) that made it to our tastings made a good showing, seemed free of defects and were well received. But very few indeed seem to excel in breeding or distinctive personality. In other words they were good, occasionally even excellent, but not exciting wines, and most of their producers will be happy with that and feel that they made the right choices. Particularly those wine-makers (and they are the vast majority) who are primarily interested in high earnings from their vineyards. These returns are virtually guaranteed by the extremely dynamic, efficient and commercially powerful wine cooperatives, which are keen on keeping or increasing their share of the market, but are unfortunately not particularly inclined to take risks on a special small production with a limited potential market, however much the resulting wines would show what Trentino is capable of and earn it the respect it deserves. The year 2000 should bring serious reform to local wine-making. The Associazione Trentina Vini will be safeguarding quality, while the Istituto del Vino Trentino will be concerned only with sales promotion. For this little revolution to get going, it will be necessary to forge an alliance for that purpose among wine cooperatives, businessman in the field, oenologists and independent wine-makers. These last, who produce only about 5% of the total, are understandably hesitant. And then too, a number of cooperatives sell vast amounts abroad of excellently made but increasingly characterless wines. Commercial success makes for contentment among the managers of the co-ops and the member growers, who, thanks to profit-sharing, aim only to produce grapes in quantity, keeping just under the prescribed upper limits of the Doc regulations. ESAT (the agency for agricultural development in this province, which has a total of 8,800 hectares under vine and almost 9,000 wine-makers) keeps trying to spread the gospel, but it still falls on deaf ears: farmers, reduce your yields per hectare, follow the regulations, start creating the conditions for excellence in your vineyards. Otherwise the Trentino wines with "soul" will be fewer and fewer, as the breed is undermined by increasing uniformity of taste and by international competition. Which is just what we found at our tastings.

ALA (TN)

La Cadalora
Fraz. Santa Margherita
38060 Ala (TN)
tel. 0464/696300

In Trentino dialect "Cadalòra" means home of the "ora", the south wind that blows from Lake Garda, a beneficial breeze that conditions the local climate, especially in the valleys next to the lake. And in the very heart of the valley that links Rovereto to the province of Verona, the Tomasi family has been cultivating its vineyards for six generations. They own some ten hectares of vines, distributed among the sunny slopes of Ala on the left bank of the Adige river, with traditional varietals and some experimentation with old rootstocks, such as a red grape which is near extinction, the casetta or foia tonda. They mean to create a wine unlike anything we've seen for a long time, redolent and tasting of cherries. Past and future: an oenological heritage that Mario Tomasi has been nurturing with the help of his young sons Tiziano and Rodolfo. And the results have not been long in coming. Their wines are definitely getting better and better, showing solid structure and aromas of unusual complexity, compared with their fellows. But that's not all. The Tomasis have chosen to hold back their wines from the market for a time, in order to bring out specific qualities in them. We particularly admired their Trentino Pinot Grigio '98, which is very characteristic of its grape, with scents of wildflowers and flint and a dry palate with a lovely balance of acidity and roundness, leading to a long finish. The Trentino Sauvignon '98 (a fine nose, but a tart palate), the Trentino Chardonnay '98 and the Trentino Marzemino San Valentino '98 are just as good, if slightly less seductive. Another red, a blend called Majere '97, would perhaps profit from further aging.

○	Trentino Pinot Grigio '98	▼▼	3*
●	Majere '97	▼	4
○	Trentino Chardonnay '98	▼	3
●	Trentino Marzemino San Valentino '98	▼	3
○	Trentino Sauvignon '98	▼	3

AVIO (TN)

Cantina Sociale di Avio
Via Dante, 14
38063 Avio (TN)
tel. 0464/684008

The quality of this dynamic wine cooperative in the Vallagarina is improving by leaps and bounds. Last year it was an attractive newcomer to the Guide, and now it more than fulfills its promise. All the wines they have presented are of remarkable quality. Whether this is the result of a commitment on the part of all 450 member growers to produce grapes only in the best plots, or whether it can be traced to the particular competence of the cellar staff directed by the young but supremely qualified oenologist Alfonso Iannielli, the fact is that their wines are very good indeed. Consider the Riserva '96 version of their Trentino Rosso, a Bordeaux blend which could hold its own with the best Italian wines, thanks to its enormous power combined with grace, qualities that place it well ahead of the pleasing non-riserva version we first tasted last year. We were very favorably impressed by the Trentino Pinot Nero '97, with its delightful aromas of black cherry, and a palate reminiscent of vanilla and cocoa. The distinctly traditional Trentino Marzemino '98 displays an intense color tinged with violet and good correspondence between nose and palate. The interesting Trentino Enantio '98, a wine produced only in the Vallagarino, is made from a particular variety of lambrusco (with serrated leaves) which produces a full-bodied and dark, yet fruity and quaffable red. Their whites are good examples of their kinds, from the Chardonnay to the Pinot Grigio, but special mention should be made of their Trentino Bianco blend, golden in hue, succulent and long-lasting, and of a final treat, the Vendemmia Tardiva 11 Novembre '97, made from chardonnay, sauvignon and traminer. It's a rich, harmonious, lingering late vintage white which will last for years: a wine that will just go on improving, like the winery that made it.

○	11 Novembre '97	▼▼	4
●	Trentino Pinot Nero '97	▼▼	3*
●	Trentino Rosso Ris. '96	▼▼	4
●	Trentino Enantio '98	▼▼	2*
○	Trentino Bianco '97	▼	2*
●	Trentino Marzemino '98	▼	2*
○	Trentino Pinot Grigio '98	▼	2*
●	Trentino Rosso '96	▽▽	3*
○	Trentino Bianco '96	▽	2*
●	Trentino Marzemino '97	▽	2*
○	Trentino Pinot Grigio '97	▽	2*
●	Trentino Pinot Nero '96	▽	3

AVIO (TN)

TENUTA SAN LEONARDO
FRAZ. BORGHETTO
LOC. SAN LEONARDO, 3
38060 AVIO (TN)
TEL. 0464/689004 - 0464/689000

San Leonardo has become legendary, and not only amongst the wines of Trentino, where it is essentially unrivaled. It's a first-class wine from any point of view and firmly linked to the land that produces it, the Campi Sarni which were already dedicated to viticulture before the last millennium. The Marquises Guerrieri Gonzaga, whose family has been here for about the same amount of time, lavish loving care on the vines on their splendid estate on the banks of the Adige river, and it shows. Thus, despite the fact that '96 was not a stellar vintage, their grapes did not disappoint. They have produced a wine with depth and complexity, whose typical faintly herbaceous allure blends perfectly with aromas of eucalyptus, wild blackberry and black cherry, all elegantly knit together by a harmonious vinification in wood which has intensified the considerable personality of the wine. It is of a dark, deep, almost opaque ruby color, and is just as engrossing in the mouth, where it keeps developing, showing both energy and profundity at the same time, as well as a rich, velvety, lingering softness. The Trentino Merlot '97 is also a wine of great breeding and was presented, as usual, together with the older San Leonardo. Thanks to a favorable vintage it is an excellent red, vinified in the same manner as its legendary older brother.

●	San Leonardo '96	TTT	5
●	Trentino Merlot '97	TT	3*
●	San Leonardo '88	YYY	5
●	San Leonardo '90	YYY	5
●	San Leonardo '93	YYY	5
●	San Leonardo '94	YYY	5
●	San Leonardo '95	YYY	5
●	San Leonardo '91	YY	5
●	Trentino Cabernet '91	YY	4
●	Trentino Cabernet '93	YY	3*
●	Trentino Cabernet '94	YY	3*
●	Trentino Merlot '92	YY	3*
●	Trentino Merlot '95	YY	3*
●	Trentino Merlot '96	YY	3*
●	Villa Gresti '93	YY	3*

CALLIANO (TN)

VALLIS AGRI
VIA VALENTINI, 37
38060 CALLIANO (TN)
TEL. 0464/834113

Vallis Agri is the feather in the cap of SAV – the Società Agricola Vallagarina, a cooperative consortium with activities as diverse as cheese-making and viticulture. The grapes come from their 210 member growers, who have all agreed to abide by the same rules for cultivation, chemical treatment and yield per hectare. Vinification takes place in the appropriately remodeled 17th century Palazzo Valentini, which boasts up-to-the-minute oenological equipment capable of bringing out the best qualities of the various zones of origin of the grapes gathered, in the case of individual crus, from miniscule plots of land. Here is a quick glance at this year's roster, starting with a pleasing Trentino Cabernet Sauvignon Riserva Sant'Ilario '95, which is mature and well-defined, with an intense and clear bouquet and a fruity palate whose structure suggests it's a wine for keeping. The Trentino Marzemino is definitely up to standard, both in the more highly prized versión made from grapes grown in Ziresi, the legendary area on the banks of the Adige where this variety has always done best, and in the more immediate version to be drunk young, almost like a nouveau. Their two blends are also successful and well-balanced. The interesting white Aura '98 is made from sauvignon and chardonnay, has good body and is fairly harmonious and long. To round off the list, special praise for the Trentino Moscato Giallo '98, which is pleasurable in every way.

●	Trentino Cabernet Sauvignon Sant'Ilario '95	TT	4
●	Trentino Marzemino dei Ziresi '98	TT	3*
○	Aura '98	T	3
○	Trentino Moscato Giallo '98	T	3
○	Trentino Pinot Grigio '98		3
●	Trentino Marzemino dei Ziresi '96	YY	3*
○	Trentino Moscato Giallo '97	YY	3*
●	Paris '93	Y	4
●	Trentino Cabernet '90	Y	4
●	Trentino Cabernet '92	Y	4
●	Trentino Marzemino dei Ziresi '93	Y	4
●	Trentino Marzemino di Isera '91	Y	4
●	Trentino Rosso '91	Y	4
●	Trentino Rosso '94	Y	4

CIVEZZANO (TN)

MASO CANTANGHEL
LOC. FORTE
VIA MADONNINA, 33
38045 CIVEZZANO (TN)
TEL. 0461/859050

Every year, but particularly when there's a good vintage, Piero Zabini decides to amaze us with something new. The latest is a sauvignon with the momentous name of Solitaire, an indicator of the sheer obstinacy of the wine-maker, who wants to do everything exactly his own way: a loner, in short. This wine, from the '98 vintage, has character, lovely aromatic tonalities, a delicious honeyed palate and a structure that will keep it going for years in the bottle. Zabini has always been a red specialist (his Pinot Nero is still one of the best in the region), but he has proven himself a dab hand at whites as well. His Trentino Chardonnay Vigna Piccola '98 is very good, perhaps even the most exciting of all the wines from this little estate on the slopes between Trento and the Valsugana, where an evocative Austro-Hungarian fort has been transformed into the cellar, its mighty cannons making way for the barriques. Among the other reds, we make special mention of the Trentino Merlot Tajapreda '98, which won us over with its vast array of aromas and flavors, with wild berries to the fore. The more complex and elegant Trentino Cabernet Sauvignon Rosso di Pila '97 is also more "difficult"; it is even more concentrated than before, with a spicy nose, well-balanced, rounded tannins and a characteristic bitter chocolate finish. These are very distinctive wines, to be tasted with attention, and not necessarily in solitude.

●	Trentino Cabernet Sauvignon Rosso di Pila '97	🍷🍷	5
○	Trentino Chardonnay Vigna Piccola '98	🍷🍷	4
●	Trentino Pinot Nero '97	🍷🍷	5
○	Trentino Sauvignon Solitare '98	🍷🍷	4
●	Trentino Merlot Tajapreda '98	🍷	3
○	Trentino Bianco Forte di Mezzo '97	🍷🍷 (white)	3*
●	Trentino Cabernet Sauvignon Rosso di Pila '95	🍷🍷 (white)	5
●	Trentino Cabernet Sauvignon Rosso di Pila '96	🍷🍷 (white)	5
○	Trentino Chardonnay Vigna Piccola '97	🍷🍷 (white)	4
●	Trentino Merlot Tajapreda '97	🍷🍷 (white)	3*

FAEDO (TN)

GRAZIANO FONTANA
VIA CASE SPARSE, 9
38010 FAEDO (TN)
TEL. 0461/650400

The '98 vintage was not kind to the wine-makers of the Faedo hillsides. The distinctiveness of the grapes has not come through. As a result, we have less harmonious, slightly discontinuous, very vegetal and somewhat coarse wines. This vintage was particularly hard on those producers who work the vines in the most direct and simple ways, respecting seasonal progression and never "forcing" the harvest or tampering with it by using fancy cellar techniques. Thus Graziano Fontana was not able to repeat his two little masterpieces from the previous vintage, a Trentino Chardonnay and a Trentino Sauvignon of lovely freshness and dense texture on the palate. But he has nevertheless produced two '98 whites which are more than well-made, typically piquant and fruity. The succulent and vigorous Trentino Müller Thurgau '98 is good too, and one of the most interesting wines from the Alpine regions. The Trentino Traminer Aromatico '98, on the other hand, is slightly bitter, its characteristic spicy note is too faint, its acidity too noticeable. Fortunately the two reds are another story altogether. For one thing, they're '97s, and that was a fantastic year, even on this high hill overlooking San Michele all'Adige. The Trentino Lagrein '97 is concentrated in appearance and in its aromas, which, while not very forward, are varied and inviting, with a lovely base of ripe fruit. The Trentino Pinot Nero '97 is inviting too, and elegant, with a light but well-balanced structure and full body. A final note (and a positive one): Graziano Fontana has finished constructing his fine new cellar in the midst of his vineyards. It will allow him to make substantial improvements in vinification techniques without, however, betraying traditional country methods or counting on any assistance beyond what a good vintage can offer.

●	Trentino Lagrein di Faedo '97	🍷🍷	4
○	Trentino Chardonnay '98	🍷	3
○	Trentino Müller Thurgau '98	🍷	3
●	Trentino Pinot Nero '97	🍷	4
○	Trentino Sauvignon di Faedo '98	🍷	3
○	Trentino Traminer Aromatico '98		3
○	Sauvignon di Faedo '95	🍷🍷 (white)	3*
○	Trentino Chardonnay '97	🍷🍷 (white)	3
●	Trentino Lagrein di Faedo '95	🍷🍷 (white)	3*
●	Trentino Lagrein di Faedo '96	🍷🍷 (white)	3*
○	Trentino Müller Thurgau '96	🍷🍷 (white)	3*
○	Trentino Müller Thurgau '97	🍷🍷 (white)	3*
●	Trentino Pinot Nero '94	🍷🍷 (white)	4*
○	Trentino Sauvignon di Faedo '96	🍷🍷 (white)	3*
○	Trentino Sauvignon di Faedo '97	🍷🍷 (white)	3*

FAEDO (TN)

POJER & SANDRI
LOC. MOLINI, 6
38010 FAEDO (TN)
TEL. 0461/650342

Mario Pojer and Fiorentino Sandri have presented three wines which, while excellent, have not quite made it to Three Glasses. This is a shame, because the two versions of Faye, one red (which has been a winner more than once) and one white, are really splendid, with almost imperceptible shortcomings due entirely to the somewhat disappointing '96 vintage. The Faye Rosso, a Bordeaux blend with small additions of lagrein and syrah, has a style all its own, with aromas of lead pencil and eucalyptus leading to a palate of citron, black currant and chocolate, with slightly rough tannins. The Faye Bianco, mostly chardonnay, has a nose that makes it seem like a herbal tea, and delicious ripe apple flavors; it's fleshy, full-bodied, harmonious and long-lasting. The third outstanding bottle is Essenzia, the prototype of Trentino late harvest wines copied by many wine-makers, although precious few have managed to reproduce such concentration of bouquet and palate. It's powerful but elegant and shows great intensity throughout. Aromatic force and balance, obtained with the help of a text-book oenological technique, are, indeed, typical of all their DOC Trentino wines, from the Schiava to the Pinot Nero (of which they make two versions, one light and easy and the other important and complex), and from the Müller Thurgau to the Chardonnay, without forgetting the Nosiola, Sauvignon and Traminer: all maintain very high standards. And since they are not given to resting on their laurels, Pojer & Sandri have remodeled an old estate in nearby Cembra, in the Val Bona, and will soon be offering the first results, made from old grape varieties in danger of extinction. We'll be writing about this again.

○	Bianco Faye '96	**YY**	4
○	Essenzia Vendemmia Tardiva '98	**YY**	4
●	Rosso Faye '96	**YY**	5
○	Trentino Chardonnay '98	**YY**	3*
○	Trentino Müller Thurgau '98	**YY**	3*
○	Trentino Nosiola '98	**YY**	3*
●	Trentino Pinot Nero Ris. '96	**YY**	4
○	Trentino Traminer '98	**YY**	3*
●	Rosso Faye '93	YYY	5
●	Rosso Faye '94	YYY	5
○	Essenzia Vendemmia Tardiva '97	YY	4
●	Rosso Faye '95	YY	5
●	Trentino Pinot Nero Ris. '93	YY	5
●	Trentino Pinot Nero Ris. '95	YY	5
○	Trentino Sauvignon '97	YY	4

ISERA (TN)

CANTINA D'ISERA
VIA AL PONTE, 1
38060 ISERA (TN)
TEL. 0464/433795

The watchword of this fine wine cooperative is "Reform in order to strengthen tradition!". It may seem paradoxical but it is the operational philosophy of Mauro Baldessari, director of this cooperative which has 200 member growers, virtually all the farmers of Isera. Reform means introducing new growing techniques and experimenting with improved strains of marzemino, thus returning to a genuinely characteristic wine which really represents the land it springs from. In other words, it should be full-bodied and fruity, inviting and graceful but with lots of structure. Every aspect of the winery has been overhauled: the buildings have been enlarged, the use of wood has been encouraged and marketing has been undertaken farther afield, so that the fame of Marzemino may spread well beyond the borders of Trentino. Their hopes have not been disappointed. Their '98 Marzeminos, both the normal version and the green-labeled special selection, have lovely fruity bouquets and palates, and show lots of character: rich, fresh, well-defined, fruity, harmonious wines that don't put a foot wrong. There is also an excellent debut performance from their Trentino Rebo, a hybrid of marzemino and merlot. It's a pleasing soft wine that's easy to get into. The Bordeaux blend Trentino Rosso Novecentosette '96 is an elegant homage to the year the coop was founded (1907); both it and the interesting Trentino Merlot '98 are on the right path and should improve with a little bottle aging. To finish off, the other wines are both pleasant and affordable, especially the crisp and quaffable Moscato Giallo '98.

●	Trentino Marzemino Etichetta Verde '98	**YY**	3*
●	Trentino Rebo '98	**YY**	3*
●	Trentino Rosso Novecentosette '96	**YY**	3*
●	Trentino Marzemino '98	**Y**	2*
●	Trentino Merlot '98	**Y**	3
○	Trentino Moscato Giallo '98	**Y**	3
●	Trentino Marzemino Etichetta Verde '96	YY	3*
●	Trentino Marzemino Etichetta Verde '97	YY	3*
●	Trentino Merlot '95	YY	2*
●	Trentino Rosso Novecentosette '95	YY	3*

ISERA (TN)

DE TARCZAL
LOC. MARANO
38060 ISERA (TN)
TEL. 0464/409134

Old documents suggest that this estate may have been the first in the Vallagarina to receive official permission to make wine. Thus the de Tarczals are a historic wine-making family. Armed with these traditions, Ruggero de Tarczal presents himself as a modern wine producer, determined to relaunch the already distinguished image of his wines and of Isera, the home of Marzemino par excellence. And his Husar, as he calls his special selection Marzemino, is again at the top of the list of this Trentino specialty. Made from grapes harvested in late October '98, it is a ruby-colored, deep violet-tinged wine that offers an intense nose as well, with sweet violets to the fore, and a full-bodied, savory and velvety palate. The attractive special selection Trentino Merlot Campiano '97 is characteristically herbaceous, with a faint and pleasing bitterish undertone. And theTrentino Cabernet Franc '97 has a brilliant ruby hue and a hay fragrance, and is slightly tannic but successful on the palate. Ruggero de Tarczal is devoted to his reds; only in great years does he make his Bordeaux blend Pragiara, but he doesn't neglect a classic Trentino Cabernet Sauvignon, which, in its '97 version, shows both garnet and granite, i.e. solidity in both color and structure. It's a warm, appropriately tannic, harmonious wine with a long finish. To complete the range, the Trentino Pinot Bianco '98, straw yellow with green highlights, offers aromas and flavors that recall the Golden Delicious apple, the typical Trentino fruit.

●	Trentino Marzemino di Isera Husar '98	TT	4
●	Trentino Merlot Campiano '97	TT	4
●	Trentino Cabernet Franc '97	T	3
●	Trentino Cabernet Sauvignon '97	T	3
○	Trentino Pinot Bianco '98	T	3
●	Trentino Marzemino di Isera '96	YY	3*
●	Trentino Marzemino di Isera Husar '97	YY	4
●	Trentino Cabernet Sauvignon '95	Y	3
○	Trentino Chardonnay '97	Y	2*
●	Trentino Marzemino di Isera '97	Y	3
●	Trentino Merlot d'Isera '95	Y	3

ISERA (TN)

ENRICO SPAGNOLLI
VIA G. B. ROSINA, 4/A
38060 ISERA (TN)
TEL. 0464/409054

Their commitment to vinifying grapes that have for the most part been acquired "in the field" as if they came from their own vineyards, in order to produce wines with character and lots of substance, has placed the Spagnolli family in the front ranks of the small independent wine-makers of Trentino. They have also acquired the art of selection, of knowing how to assess raw material, through keen negotiation year after year, vintage by vintage, with the growers of the Vallagarina. So for some years now Luigi Spagnolli, known as Gigi, wine technician and patient oenological experimenter, has been presenting a varied range of wines, all of which are well made, of a distinctive style, well-defined and clean. The Bordeaux blend Trentino Rosso Tebro '97 is elegant, properly amalgamated and satisfying, with just enough spice to add complexity. The Trentino Pinot Nero '97 is also more than pleasant: it's produced from grapes grown fairly high up, so as to make the most of the altitudinous temperature swings and give elegance to the wine. It has a subtle fragrance and is delicate and a little tannic. The Marzemino, the flagship of the winery, is as attractive as ever. The Trentino Traminer Aromatico '98 (wanting only fleshiness) and the Trentino Moscato Giallo '98 (a wine that deserves more attention in Trentino) are again interesting and pleasing. The other Trentino DOC wines from this vintage are average but all well made: the lean and intentionally tart Chardonnay, the vivacious Müller Thurgau and the light Nosiola.

●	Trentino Pinot Nero '97	TT	4
●	Trentino Rosso Tebro '97	TT	4
●	Trentino Marzemino '98	T	3
○	Trentino Moscato Giallo '98	T	3
○	Trentino Müller Thurgau '98	T	3
○	Trentino Traminer Aromatico '98	T	3
○	Trentino Chardonnay '98		3
○	Trentino Nosiola '98		3
●	Trentino Rosso Tebro '96	YY	4
○	Trentino Traminer Aromatico '97	YY	3*
○	Trentino Moscato Giallo '97	Y	3
○	Trentino Müller Thurgau '97	Y	3
○	Trentino Nosiola '97	Y	3
●	Trentino Pinot Nero '96	Y	4

LASINO (TN)

F.LLI PISONI
LOC. PERGOLESE
VIA S. SIRO, 9
38070 LASINO (TN)
TEL. 0461/564106 - 0461/563216

Steadfastness is the special strength of the Pisonis, who by now constitute a dynasty of wine-growers in Trentino. Their estate goes back to the Middle Ages, when the land with its Mediterranean climate was already used for viticulture. This steadfastness has been maintained throughout all these centuries and handed down from generation to generation: brothers, cousins, children and grandchildren are all united in their passion for oenology (they've been attending the distinguished Istituto Agrario in San Michele all'Adige for some generations already) and by a daily dedication to the vines. It's an estate that follows the full cycle of wine-making. They cultivate the vineyards spread out on the slopes surrounding their cellar, they make use of every part of the grape, bottle their wines and make spumante (they were among the first in Trentino to do so according to the classic method). In the new cellar that they have just finished building, Marco and Stefano produce a vast and straightforward range of wines. They are experimenting with syrah and with some unusual blends (chardonnay, sauvignon and moscato; syrah and pinot nero) and new, perhaps at times questionable vinification methods (they subject the delicate nosiola to wood), but they are determined to rise to the challenge, and with each of their wines. The Trentino Nosiola '98 is lean and well made, the Trentino Bianco San Siro '98 is equally fragrant, and the Trentino Rebo '97 is delicately tannic. One wine, however, almost beggars belief: the Trentino Vino Santo, vintage '90, the only one to be pressed at Easter (hence the name), from dried nosiola grapes. It's a full-bodied, absolutely distinctive dessert wine, as rare as it is delicious. Last of all, the Trento Talento Brut is not very complex, but attractive all the same.

○ Trentino Vino Santo '90	🍷🍷	5
○ Trentino Bianco San Siro '98	🍷	3
○ Trentino Nosiola '98	🍷	3
● Trentino Rebo '97	🍷	4
○ Trento Talento Brut	🍷	4

LASINO (TN)

PRAVIS
VIA LAGOLO, 28
38076 LASINO (TN)
TEL. 0461/564305

For a quarter of a century the Pravis estate has been carefully making wine from its own vineyards, segregating the grapes according to the plot where they were grown. The commitment and tenacity of the three partners have resulted in wines which, although simple, are very distinctive. The new millennium's first harvest will be transformed into wine in their modern completely underground cellar, which is near completion on the hill that leads to Castel Madruzzo. Vines with old local grapes (groppello) grow side by side with international varieties not usually found in Trentino, one of which has gone to make the very successful syrah called Syrae '97. Ruby-hued and tinged with purple, it has a forward bouquet of fruit preserved in spirits, and an extremely captivating energy on the palate. Another excellent wine is their Trentino Cabernet Fratagranda '97, a very supple and well-structured red with lightly spicy aromas and a palate reminiscent of pepper, but also of cherry and black currant; the only drawback is a faintly vegetal note, which is virtually unavoidable in Trentino reds. The lively and eloquently straightforward Trentino Nosiola Le Frate '98 is a classic of its kind; the Trentino Müller Thurgau San Thomà '98 is graceful and appropriately tart, while the Trentino Pinot Grigio Polin '98 combines delicacy of fragrance with exuberance of taste. Of their other wines the red Trentino Rebo Rigotti '97 is the best example of the unaffected and spontaneous Pravis style, but we can't finish our review without a few words about the miraculous Vino Santo Le Arele '84, seductive, warm and sun-drenched, with flavors that summon up the sensual delight produced by one's first taste of ripe grapes as a child.

● Syrae '97	🍷🍷	4
● Trentino Cabernet Fratagranda '97	🍷🍷	4
● Trentino Rebo Rigotti '97	🍷🍷	3*
○ Vino Santo Le Aréle '84	🍷🍷	5
○ Trentino Müller Thurgau St. Thomà '98	🍷	3
○ Trentino Nosiola Le Frate '98	🍷	3
○ Trentino Pinot Grigio Polin '98	🍷	3
○ Soliva '97	🍷🍷 (outline)	4
● Syrae '95	🍷🍷 (outline)	4
● Syrae '96	🍷🍷 (outline)	4
● Trentino Cabernet Fratagranda '95	🍷🍷 (outline)	4
● Trentino Cabernet Fratagranda '92	🍷🍷 (outline)	4
○ Trentino Nosiola Le Frate '97	🍷🍷 (outline)	3*
○ Vino Santo Le Aréle '83	🍷🍷 (outline)	5

LAVIS (TN)

NILO BOLOGNANI
VIA STAZIONE, 19
38015 LAVIS (TN)
TEL. 0461/246354

This is not Happy-Go-Lucky Hall. In this winery every detail is lovingly looked after, nothing is left to chance: they want to be sure of producing first-class wine. Diego Bolognani and his brothers keep a tight rein on their cellar, but they are always willing to consider other points of view. This year once again they are offering whites only, all recognizably in the Bolognani style: clean, subtle and harmonious. The one we liked most was the Trentino Sauvignon '98, a rich, unusually fleshy white with a lingering bouquet and a long finish, characteristic varietal aromas of citron and elderberry and tasty mineral tones. But the Trentino Müller Thurgau '98, which was rated one of the most representative of its grape at the annual international exhibition dedicated to this variety at Cembra, also seemed notably fragrant, as well as elegantly various on the palate. Next comes the typical Trentino Chardonnay '98, with delicate hints of pineapple and green apple, showing pleasing tartness, definition and substance. The last three were perfectly satisfactory and recognizable Trentino DOC wines: the Pinot Grigio (a little stalky, due perhaps to the vintage), the Moscato Giallo (one of the best, as usual) and the pale, limpid, easily quaffable and very enjoyable Nosiola.

O Trentino Müller Thurgau '98	🍷🍷	3*
O Trentino Nosiola '98	🍷🍷	3*
O Trentino Sauvignon '98	🍷🍷	3*
O Trentino Chardonnay '98	🍷	3
O Trentino Moscato Giallo '98	🍷	3
O Trentino Pinot Grigio '98	🍷	3
O Müller Thurgau della Val di Cembra '95	🍸🍸	3*
O Müller Thurgau della Val di Cembra '96	🍸🍸	3*
O Trentino Moscato Giallo '96	🍸🍸	3*
O Trentino Moscato Giallo '97	🍸🍸	3*
O Trentino Müller Thurgau '97	🍸🍸	3*
O Trentino Pinot Grigio '96	🍸🍸	3*
O Trentino Sauvignon '97	🍸🍸	3*

LAVIS (TN)

CESCONI
LOC. PRESSANO
VIA MARCONI, 39
38015 LAVIS (TN)
TEL. 0461/240355

The year 1998 will be engraved on the memories of the Cesconis, four young brothers who, together with their parents, look after the family vineyards in Pressano, on the Lavis hillside, and in Ceniga di Drò, near Lake Garda. It will be unforgettable because after a mere four vintages they have risen to an easy Three Glasses with their Pinot Grigio. Of course no one is really surprised, because they have been improving at a breathtaking rate. All their wines have been profusely praised, putting much of the competition in the shade. This excellent Trentino Pinot Grigio '98 has a golden hue, with just the faintest copper tinge, and notes of pear, ripe fruit and even a delicious jasmine fragrance on the nose. Its entry on the remarkably harmonious palate is powerful and it opens out evenly and firmly. The Trentino Sauvignon '98, with its elegant notes of elderberry and geranium and a captivating crispness featuring succulent rennet apple flavors, and also their most recent wine, Olivar, a briefly barriqued blend of pinot bianco, chardonnay and pinot grigio with very little sauvignon, displaying notes of grapefuit, chamomile and medicinal herbs on the nose and warmth, breadth and length on the palate, are both admirable. The Trentino Traminer '98 is clear-cut, cleanly aromatic, spicy and smoothly piquant, although a bit thin, perhaps because the vines are still quite young. Two full Glasses for the Pinot Bianco too, with its well-dosed acidity and dense, full-bodied, fleshy texture. Last but not least, the Trentino Nosiola '98 is a straightforward wine that hold its own with a distinctive style and aromatic range.

O Trentino Pinot Grigio '98	🍷🍷🍷	4*
O Olivar '98	🍷🍷	4
O Trentino Nosiola '98	🍷🍷	3*
O Trentino Pinot Bianco '98	🍷🍷	4
O Trentino Sauvignon '98	🍷🍷	4
O Trentino Traminer Aromatico '98	🍷🍷	4
O Sauvignon Atesino '96	🍸🍸	3*
O Trentino Chardonnay '97	🍸🍸	3
O Trentino Pinot Bianco '96	🍸🍸	3*
O Trentino Pinot Bianco '97	🍸🍸	3*
O Trentino Pinot Grigio '96	🍸🍸	3*
O Trentino Pinot Grigio '97	🍸🍸	3*
O Trentino Traminer Aromatico '96	🍸🍸	3*
O Trentino Traminer Aromatico '97	🍸🍸	3*
O Trentino Sauvignon '97	🍸	3

LAVIS (TN)

LA VIS
VIA CARMINE, 12
38015 LAVIS (TN)
TEL. 0461/246325

When this benchmark Trentino winery did not win even one Three Glass award this year, we were the first to be staggered. And La Vis had four really likely candidates. But although they didn't make it to the finish, no blame should be meted out to the wines or, least of all, to those in charge of the winery, a cooperative that can safely be called the best in the region. Their Ritratto '97, a blend of teroldego and lagrein, is marvelous, with an extraordinary richness of bouquet featuring mineral and minty notes, a lovely deep scarlet ruby color and an easy quaffability. The Trentino Cabernet Ritratti '97 is full-bodied and powerful, the Trentino Merlot Ritratti soft and sensual, the Trentino Pinot Nero Ritratti elegant, with rare finesse. And furthermore, the Ritratto Bianco may well be the most successful chardonnay and pinot bianco blend in Trentino, with its extraordinary harmony between acidity and fruit. The excellent Mandolaia '98, a late harvest of various aromatic white varieties, is harmonious, lingering and unforgettable. Two other wines in the Ritratti series, the Trentino Pinot Grigio '98 and the inviting Trentino Chardonnay '98, both have distinctive personalities. And all their other wines, from the aromatic Trentino Müller Thurgau Maso Roncador '98 to the characteristic special Sorni, in both its Bianco and Rosso versions, are forceful, very good wines at very good prices. Lastly, we can toast to perfection with the successful Trento Arcade Brut. So hats off to La Vis all the same!

O Mandolaia '98	🍷🍷	5
O Ritratto '97	🍷🍷	4
● Ritratto '97	🍷🍷	5
O Sorni Bianco '98	🍷🍷	3*
O Trento Brut Arcade	🍷🍷	4
● Trentino Cabernet Sauvignon Ritratti '97	🍷🍷	4
O Trentino Chardonnay Ritratti '98	🍷🍷	4
● Trentino Merlot Ritratti '97	🍷🍷	4
O Trentino Müller Thurgau Maso Roncador '98	🍷🍷	3*
O Trentino Pinot Grigio Ritratti '98	🍷🍷	4
● Trentino Pinot Nero '97	🍷🍷	2*
● Ritratto '91	🍷🍷🍷 (white)	4

LAVIS (TN)

MASO FURLI
LOC. PRESSANO
38015 LAVIS (TN)
TEL. 0461/240667

We're pleased to say that Lavis and its vine-covered slopes have offered us an extraordinary newcomer: Maso Furli, a tiny estate (four hectares) that belongs to the Zanoni family, wine-growers from way back and, more recently, wine-makers as well. The sons of the family, Marco and Giorgio, decided to try managing every phase of the work themselves, from vines to cellar, and their debut has been more than encouraging. Indeed their three white wines (we'll have to wait until next year for their red, a Bordeaux blend) have become gems you won't want to miss. They make three Trentino DOC wines, a Chardonnay, a Traminer and a Sauvignon, just 12 thousand bottles in all, containing important wines with unmistakable character. We were excited by the Trentino Sauvignon '98 with its distinct aromas of fig and elderberry, because its entry on the palate is broad, fleshy and densely packed, it shows a masterful alcoholic balance as it develops and it boasts a long finish. The Trentino Traminer '98 is also a splendid wine, very aromatic and intense, not awfully complex in structure but subtly spicy and seductive with a sweet but by no means cloying finish. It's a sign that the Zanonis know what they're about at every stage of the way. Last of all is the Trentino Chardonnay '98, a little behind the others, with a properly concentrated bouquet and an agreeable harmoniousness in the mouth, although the finish is somewhat impaired by sustained acidity. But it hardly seems to matter. They've done a wonderful job and we congratulate them.

O Trentino Sauvignon '98	🍷🍷	3*
O Trentino Traminer Aromatico '98	🍷🍷	3*
O Trentino Chardnnay '98	🍷	3

LAVIS (TN)

CANTINA SEBASTIANI
VIA G. CLEMENTI, 31
38015 LAVIS (TN)
TEL. 0461/246315

The Sebastiani winery – a family enterprise that goes back some 50 years – makes its return to the Guide. The two young Sebastiani brothers, Dario (oenologist) and Roberto, have moved their cellars from Lavis to Ravina di Trento and, after a couple of years of finding their feet, are once again producing wines of character. The Sebastianis are able to produce a considerable range of wines, not least because their vineyards are located throughout the Trentino region: from the hills of the valley of Cembra, renowned for its aromatic whites, to the Rotaliana Plain, the prinipal Teroldego area. And it is with this full-bodied wine that the Sebastiani brothers have made their big comeback to the local wine-making scene. The deep, dense ruby-toned '98 Teroldego Rotaliano is characterful and intense on the nose, and rounded and complex in the mouth, with a characteristic hint of bitterness and a good finish. Another skilfully produced wine is the Sorni Rosso '98, obtained from teroldego and lagrein grapes ripened on the slopes of Lavis near the village of Sorni. Fruity, with low tannin, this is a graceful, quaffable wine with fresh flavors and a hint of raspberry on the nose. The whites – and the Nosiola and Müller Thurgau in particular – also testify to the beneficial effects of technical innovation on wine production methods. The Nosiola, pale straw in color, has a typical hazelnut aroma, which is echoed on the tasty palate. The Müller Thurgau has a harmonious bouquet and is lightly fruity, dry and vigorous in the mouth. The Schiava is engaging and eminently drinkable, the Pinot Grigio and Chardonnay straightforward and properly made.

●	Teroldego Rotaliano '98	▼▼	3*
○	Trentino Müller Thurgau '98	▼	3
○	Trentino Nosiola '98	▼	3
●	Trentino Sorni Rosso '98	▼	3
○	Trentino Chardonnay '98		3
○	Trentino Pinot Grigio '98		3
●	Valdadige Schiava '98		2
○	Chardonnay Atesino Dario Sebastiani '94	▽▽	3*
●	Teroldego Rotaliano '93	▽▽	2*
●	Maset '91	▽	4
●	Maset '92	▽	3
●	Schiava Valdadige '94	▽	2*
●	Teroldego Rotaliano Vigna Donati '91	▽	3

MEZZOCORONA (TN)

MARCO DONATI
VIA CESARE BATTISTI, 41
38016 MEZZOCORONA (TN)
TEL. 0461/604141

Marco Donati is a likeable and astute wine-maker. Apart from his patient research into innovative wine-making techniques, he has done much to improve cultivation methods in the vineyards surrounding his lovely family farmhouse in the heart of the district known as the Campo Rotaliano. The Donatis have been making wine since 1863 and devote their best efforts to Teroldego, especially to their Sangue di Drago (Dragon's Blood). The '97 version has a very intense blood-red color, aromas of blackberry and raspberry with notes of vanilla (the wine is fermented in oak barrels), and a full-bodied, flavorsome and compelling palate with a characteristic berry – particularly strawberry – finish . The non-riserva Teroldego, a very fruity and lively wine, should be drunk young. Their Vino del Maso seemed interesting too: a blend of lagrein, teroldego and merlot, it balances elegance with power. The '97 Cabernet Sauvignon, a fairly uncomplicated red made from selected grapes grown on the Trento hillside, made a reasonable impression. Turning to the whites, the Terre del Noce, a blend of sauvignon, chardonnay and moscato giallo, stood out on account of its aromatic, intense and distinctive fragrance. The other Trentino DOC wines were characteristic and distinctly varietal, from the tasty Chardonnay to the succulent Nosiola, while the Moscato Rosa, although not especially concentrated, and the fresh Lagrein, a rosé, deserve special mention. Lastly, we point out a lively spumante classico produced at Roveré della Luna by Marco Donati together with a friend, Marco Cristoforetti, using only chardonnay grown especially for this "bubbly".

●	Teroldego Rotaliano Sangue di Drago '97	▼▼	4
○	Terre del Noce Bianco '98	▼▼	4
●	Teroldego Rotaliano '98	▼	3
○	Trentino Chardonnay '98	▼	3
⊙	Trentino Lagrein Rosato '98	▼	3
●	Trentino Moscato Rosa '98	▼	3
○	Trentino Nosiola '98	▼	3
●	Vino del Maso Rosso '98	▼	3
●	Teroldego Rotaliano Sangue di Drago '96	▽▽	4
○	Terre del Noce Bianco '95	▽▽	3*
○	Terre del Noce Bianco '96	▽▽	3*
●	Teroldego Rotaliano '96	▽	3

MEZZOCORONA (TN)

F.lli Dorigati
Via Dante, 5
38016 Mezzocorona (TN)
tel. 0461/605313

Patience, a well-known virtue, also has its rewards. Certainly it has contributed to the success of the spumante that the brothers Carlo and Franco Dorigati, with their friend Enrico Paternoster, have finally offered to an eager public. Their Methius '92 was a clear-cut success in all our tastings. The ten thousand bottles of this spumante classico were made from chardonnay and pinot nero grown high on the hillsides around Lavis, where the three wine-makers select their grapes. More than four years in the bottle have balanced and harmonized all the different components. The result is that this is one of the best Talento Trento DOC spumantes we have ever tasted. Of a brilliant straw color, it has a decided and varying aroma with hints of spice and resin, and a fine, seductive mousse, not aggressive in the least, leaving a lingering soft sensation in the mouth. But these Dorigatis, the fourth generation of wine-makers here, also make good reds, particularly Teroldego, both the traditional version, violet-hued, fragrant and harmonious, and the Riserva Diedri '97, which suggests a careful hand with the wood, and offers a granite nature with its garnet color. The fresh and easy-to-drink Rebo '97, the mature and balanced '98 Chardonnay, the Pinot Grigio '98, succulent and velvety, and the traditional Lagrein rosato '98 are all very good. This last is called Kretzer after the wicker baskets the peasants once used to filter pressed grapes when they wanted to make a very light-colored wine.

○	Trento Methius Ris. '92	🍷🍷🍷	5
●	Teroldego Rotaliano Diedri Ris. '97	🍷🍷	5
●	Trentino Rebo '97	🍷🍷	3*
●	Teroldego Rotaliano '98	🍷	3
○	Trentino Chardonnay '98	🍷	3
⊙	Trentino Lagrein Rosato '98	🍷	3
○	Trentino Pinot Grigio '98	🍷	3
●	Teroldego Rotaliano '97	🍸🍸	3*
●	Teroldego Rotaliano Diedri Ris. '94	🍸🍸	5
●	Teroldego Rotaliano Diedri Ris. '96	🍸🍸	5
○	Trento Methius Ris. '90	🍸🍸	5
○	Trento Methius Ris. '91	🍸🍸	5

MEZZOCORONA (TN)

MezzaCorona
Via IV Novembre, 127
38016 Mezzocorona (TN)
tel. 0461/605163 - 0461/616399

Mezzacorona knows no limits. It attacks the wine market on a global scale, determined to be known as one of its leading lights. Its power is based on the enthusiasm of its managers and the loyalty of its more than 1300 member growers, who cultivate 2000 hectares of vineyards, making them unrivaled in Trentino. There is something of the great industrial group about this winery, as it diversifies its production according to grape type, and places the final product on some specific part of its vast market. To be as competitive as possible, they have not only revamped their image, but also the character of their wines. First an old friend: the spumante Rotari (and we await large quantities of riservas that are yet to appear) is well-placed to contend with other well-known "bubblies" on the market, especially abroad, according to the plans of Fabio Rizzoli, the "boss" of this cooperative. Their '98 Teroldego, despite the vast number of bottles produced, is characteristic, unmistakably itself, grapy, well-balanced and an excellent bargain. Among the wines destined to be sold on a wide scale, the '98 Pinot Grigio is varietal, has the right touch of acidity and a vegetal nuance together with soft notes of pear before its pleasingly bitterish finish, while the delicate and quaffable Chardonnay '98 was very good indeed. The Cabernet Sauvignon and the Merlot from '97 seem almost twins, both offering lively, well-defined aromas, with berries to the fore. The Cabernet, however, has a bit more body, which is just as it should be. The young Lagrein '98 and the simple but tasty Pinot Nero '97 are two authentic examples of traditional Trentino wines.

○	Trento Rotari Brut Arte Italiana	🍷🍷	3*
●	Teroldego Rotaliano '98	🍷	2*
●	Trentino Cabernet Sauvignon '97	🍷	3
○	Trentino Chardonnay '98	🍷	2*
●	Trentino Merlot '97	🍷	3
○	Trentino Pinot Grigio '98	🍷	2*
●	Trentino Pinot Nero '97	🍷	3
●	Trentino Lagrein '98		3
●	Teroldego Rotaliano Ris. '94	🍸🍸	3*
●	Teroldego Rotaliano Ris. '96	🍸🍸	3*
●	Trentino Cabernet Sauvignon Oltresarca '94	🍸🍸	3*
○	Trentino Traminer Aromatico '97	🍸🍸	3*
○	Trento Rotari Brut Arte Italiana	🍸🍸	3*
○	Trento Rotari Brut Ris. '94	🍸🍸	4

MEZZOLOMBARDO (TN)

Barone de Cles
Via G. Mazzini, 18
38017 Mezzolombardo (TN)
tel. 0461/601081

The history of Trentino is intertwined with this estate. The Barons Cles were already producing wine from the hillside vines around Castel Cles in the 14th century. The vineyards nearest the castle, which is still family property, have made way for lush orchards. The de Cles family is without a doubt the Trentino wine-maker with the longest history, and this tradition is continued by the Barons Michele, Guido and Leonardo. Their vines are mostly teroldego, the most authentically local grape, and their plots are the best in the area. For several years now they have been concentrating on quality and the wines reflect this decision. The Teroldego Rotaliano Maso Scari '97 is fragrant, intense and concentrated. Of course there is still room for improvement, but it is already decidedly pleasurable and very convincing. Their Lagrein '97 is also interesting, but does not yet offer the enticingly mouth-filling lagrein that you can sometimes find in Alto Adige. The same is true of the Merlot '97, which is clean and straightforward but not very distinctive. Among the whites, we tried a flavorful '98 Chardonnay with pleasant hints of fresh banana, and a tasty, succulent Pinot Grigio '98.

●	Teroldego Rotaliano Maso Scari '97	🍷🍷	4
●	Trentino Lagrein '97	🍷	3
○	Trentino Pinot Grigio '98	🍷	3
○	Trentino Chardonnay '98		3
●	Trentino Merlot '97		3
●	Teroldego Rotaliano Maso Scari '96	♀♀	3*
●	Trentino Lagrein '96	♀	3
○	Trentino Moscato Giallo '96	♀	3
○	Trentino Traminer '96	♀	3

MEZZOLOMBARDO (TN)

Cantina Rotaliana
C.so del Popolo, 6
38017 Mezzolombardo (TN)
tel. 0461/601010

Very pleasant surprises are rather rare at our tastings. But we had one when we tried the wines of this well-established cooperative, which has always concentrated primarily on producing Teroldego. All of the wines they presented were good, with two exceptions, which were excellent. The first of these was the Teroldego produced from the first crop from a new experimental vineyard in Mezzolombardo, one hectare known locally as the "Clesure", in the heart of the village. It's a spot long dedicated to the vine, which has always flourished. Wine technicians from the nearby Istituto Agrario di San Michele and from the cooperative itself identified some special clones and rootstocks, which have already produced results as surprising as they are encouraging: these wines (which are not yet commercially available) will have people talking! Furthermore, their other wines seem to have benefited from all this experimentation. The normal Teroldego '98 is amongst the most clean-cut and successful of its kind, while the '96 Riserva again fully merits its Two Glasses. The dark-hued Lagrein '97, with a traditional fermentation in large wooden barrels, is good too. It's a wine that should last, and if it is somewhat less elegant than its counterparts from Alto Adige, it is very well made. The '98 whites are also pleasing. The Pinot Grigio, the Pinot Bianco and the Chardonnay are all fresh, clean and quaffable, and they are good value for money as well. This winery is on the rise. Further progress is to be expected when their new cellar is finished and when the experiments in progress come to fruition.

●	Teroldego Rotaliano '98	🍷🍷	2*
●	Teroldego Rotaliano Ris. '96	🍷🍷	3*
○	Trentino Chardonnay '98	🍷	2*
●	Trentino Lagrein '97	🍷	3
○	Trentino Pinot Bianco '98	🍷	2*
●	Teroldego Rotaliano '97	♀♀	2*
●	Teroldego Rotaliano Ris. '93	♀♀	3*
●	Teroldego Rotaliano Ris. '95	♀♀	3*
○	Trentino Pinot Bianco '96	♀♀	2*
●	Teroldego Rotaliano '96	♀	2*
●	Teroldego Rotaliano '94	♀	2*
●	Teroldego Rotaliano Ris. '94	♀	3
○	Trentino Chardonnay '97	♀	2*
●	Trentino Lagrein Tait '95	♀	3
●	Trentino Moscato Rosa '97	♀	4

MEZZOLOMBARDO (TN)

FORADORI
VIA DAMIANO CHIESA, 1
38017 MEZZOLOMBARDO (TN)
TEL. 0461/601046

The name Foradori immediately suggests Teroldego and vice versa. Elisabetta Foradori comes up with a great wine only when Teroldego makes it possible. The promising '97 vintage should have produced wonders. But it didn't. Elisabetta made her wine with confident determination, sure that she had done everything possible, and that the result would be all she hoped. And it is an excellent red, but it lacks that extra something that would turn it into an absolute champion. Let it be understood, the Granato '97 is unquestionably a splendid Teroldego, technically faultless and of really high quality. But still, if only by a hair's breadth, it fails to reach the level of the world's great reds. Perhaps next time. The regular Teroldego '98 has maintained its usual high standards. Full-bodied and elegantly tannic, it offers a mixture of richly fruity aromas and tastes with the varietal vigor typical of this grape, which is justly considered the best of the native Trentino varieties. The two '97 reds, Karanar and Ailampa, are very good. They are experimental blends, including petit verdot and syrah, and only bottled in good years. They are both juicy, spicy wines and still too young to be easily understood, but they display considerable structure, resulting from a very patient vinification in wood. The Myrto '98, her only white, has wonderful body and a delicious bouquet. Its three components, chardonnay, pinot bianco and sauvignon, were individually fermented in steel vats, and then matured in small barrels of new oak.

●	Ailampa '97	**YY**	4
●	Granato '97	**YY**	5
●	Karanar '97	**YY**	4
○	Myrto '98	**YY**	3*
●	Teroldego Rotaliano '98	**YY**	3*
●	Granato '91	YYY	5
●	Granato '93	YYY	5
●	Granato '96	YYY	5
●	Teroldego Rotaliano Sgarzon '93	YYY	4*
●	Teroldego Rotaliano Sgarzon '94	YYY	4*
●	Teroldego Rotaliano '97	YY	3*
●	Teroldego Rotaliano Sgarzon '96	YY	4

NOGAREDO (TN)

CASTEL NOARNA
FRAZ. NOARNA
VIA CASTELNUOVO, 1
38060 NOGAREDO (TN)
TEL. 0464/413295 - 167/348809

Nogaredo is not only known for being the site of Mozart's first Italian concert, but is now increasingly associated with wine. This is due in part to Marco Zani, a young hotel-keeper, promoter of tourism and enthusiastic wine-maker. In the course of very few years, he has acquired skill in both vineyards and cellar, and has produced some excellent wines worthy of the ancient castle in whose shadow they come into being, and that seem to link past and future. The foremost wine produced here is called Romeo, his nickname in the family. It is a Bordeaux-style red that has been getting better year by year. The enticing '96, which is still developing, is soft, with lovely silky tannins, and harmonious, even though the year was not a very felicitous one. The wood-fermented Chardonnay Campo Grande '97 is also decidedly good. Its subtly fruity bouquet also offers hints of milk and vanilla. The entry on the palate is well articulated, and then it is ample, persistent and extraordinarily soft. The Bianco di Castelnuovo '97, a completely barrique-vinified blend of chardonnay, sauvignon, traminer and Rhine riesling, is much more aromatic but shows the same powerful structure. Rich, mouth-filling, and fragrant, it is one of the whites that really stood out in our tastings. Fresh, fruity and quick to please, the Mercuria '98 is a fairly simple but well-balanced cabernet sauvignon. The Nosiola '98, made from very old native rootstock in a plot next to the almost thousand-year-old castle, is fresh, succulent and just tart enough.

○	Bianco di Castelnuovo '97	**YY**	4
●	Trentino Cabernet Romeo '96	**YY**	4
○	Trentino Chardonnay Campo Grande '97	**YY**	4
○	Trentino Nosiola '98	**YY**	3*
●	Trentino Cabernet Sauvignon Mercuria '98	**Y**	3
○	Bianco di Castelnuovo '96	YY	3*
●	Trentino Cabernet Romeo '93	YY	4
●	Trentino Cabernet Romeo '94	YY	4
●	Trentino Cabernet Sauvignon Mercuria '97	YY	3*
○	Trentino Chardonnay '97	YY	3*
●	Valdadige Schiava Scalzavacca '95	YY	3*

NOGAREDO (TN)

LETRARI
PALAZZO LODRON, 4
38060 NOGAREDO (TN)
TEL. 0464/411093 - 0464/414147

The Letraris have decided to celebrate the inauguration of their beautiful new cellar in the year 2000, which they mean to make much of. For one thing, they will be honoring their father, Leonello, the founder of the winery, who has just finished the fiftieth consecutive harvest under his direct supervision. For some time now he has been sharing responsibility with his children, Paolo, Emilio and Lucia, but he has kept a good grip on the reins. Together they have decided to reduce the number of different kinds of wines they produce, and to concentrate on producing wines of distinction. Hence the other great event of the new millenium is to be the debut of Ballistarius, a Bordeaux-style red currently engaged in its maturation. In the meanwhile we can happily turn our attention to their spumante, both the normal Brut, and the Riserva, which are excellent as usual. The Brut has a lovely straw color enlivened by the fine perlage pervading the wine's dense structure. To the nose it offers distinct aromas of apples and freshly-baked bread; in the mouth it is fresh, well-balanced and persistent. The Brut Riserva '95 is much richer and more intense, and has a full, natural softness that makes its development on the palate particularly satisfying. As for the traditional still whites, the tasty and varietal Pinot Bianco '98 and the Chardonnay from the same year were quite attractive. The two red '98s, the Marzemino and the Lagrein, are again very good, both well-balanced and grapy, but the Cabernet Riserva '95 is, perhaps, a little disappointing.

●	Trentino Marzemino '98	▼▼	3*
○	Trento Brut Letrari	▼▼	4
○	Trento Brut Letrari Ris. '95	▼▼	4
●	Trentino Cabernet Ris. '95	▼	4
○	Trentino Chardonnay '98	▼	3
●	Trentino Lagrein '98	▼	3
○	Trentino Pinot Bianco '98	▼	3
○	Trentino Bianco Saccardo '96	▽▽	3*
●	Trentino Marzemino Sel. '97	▽▽	3*
●	Trentino Moscato Rosa '93	▽▽	6
●	Trentino Moscato Rosa '94	▽▽	6
●	Trentino Moscato Rosa '95	▽▽	6
●	Trentino Rosso Maso Lodron '95	▽▽	3*
○	Trentino Sauvignon '97	▽▽	3*
○	Trento Brut Letrari '94	▽▽	4

NOMI (TN)

LUCIANO BATTISTOTTI
VIA III NOVEMBRE, 21
38060 NOMI (TN)
TEL. 0464/834145

Everything in Nomi reminds one of wine: rows of vines that find their way into courtyards, the local roads, that skirt the edges of the vineyards, and the wine cellars which, in this town, are almost as numerous as the houses. In one of these, on the narrow street that leads from the main square towards the fields in the direction of Rovereto, we find Battistotti, a winery that has been active for a hundred years or more and is currently run by the brothers Enzo, Elio and Luciano. Into their cellar come grapes they choose and buy for the most part in the vineyards of the Vallagarina, but they also make special crus with the grapes from their own tiny holdings. Their principal focus is on Marzemino. They are in the classic area for this grape, and Luciano Batistotti, since he is an oenologist and in charge of the cellar, makes it according to his own way of thinking. Trentino folk tend to consider Marzemino their wine, and they want it fresh, fruity and easy to drink. His style is somewhat different, and he produces a more complex, almost an important red. In the '98 version an often aggressive spikiness has been softened into a graceful persistence on the palate. The Battistotti are a red-loving family, and they've been devoting some attention to their Bordeaux-style wine, the Rosso Savignam '97. (The name is a play on words involving the grape, cabernet sauvignon, and the minute village the grapes come from, Savignano). The '97 vintage shows breeding, structure and quaffability. The '98 whites are also interesting: the Chardonnay and the Müller Thurgau are rich in fragrance if somewhat less so in body.

●	Trentino Marzemino '98	▼▼	3*
●	Rosso Savignam '97	▼	3
○	Trentino Chardonnay '98	▼	3
○	Trentino Müller Thurgau '98	▼	3
●	Trentino Marzemino '96	▽▽	3*
●	Trentino Marzemino '97	▽▽	3*
●	Trentino Moscato Rosa '97	▽▽	5
○	Trentino Müller Thurgau '97	▽▽	3*
●	Rosso Savignam '96	▽	3
●	Trentino Cabernet '96	▽	3
○	Trentino Chardonnay '96	▽	3
●	Trentino Merlot '96	▽	3

NOMI (TN)

CANTINA SOCIALE DI NOMI
VIA ROMA, 1
38060 NOMI (TN)
TEL. 0464/834195

Here's another newcomer to our guide: a small cooperative with fewer than 180 member growers, founded just before 1960 to make, mostly, red wines. They grow merlot in particular. In the beginning they took advantage of the vigor of this noble vine, but they have come to realize that it is important to produce less, in order to do better. And in the course of very few years they have become one of the best producers of this celebrated wine in Trentino. Thanks to a drastic reduction in yields, careful fermentation in wood and above all the excellent '97 vintage, they have produced a fantastic Merlot Le Campagne. Of a dense, concentrated and impenetrable red hue, it offers a range of aromas including cocoa, leather and ripe blackberries as well as the classic note of pencil lead. In the mouth it is substantial and robust but also soft and very pleasing. That they have a magic touch in this cellar, which is directed by the oenologist Christian Scrinzi, is also clear from their Bordeaux-style offering, the Résorso '97, an elegant red with a rich and well-balanced structure. There is also a white Résorso, a wood-fermented blend of chardonnay and pinot bianco, which, however, leaves room for improvement. Our compliments for the delicious '98 Marzemino Le Fornas and the tasty Pinot Bianco Valbone '98. The wines of their traditional range, the Pinot Grigio, Chardonnay, Müller Thurgau and the easy-to-drink Merlot are well made and very affordable. Another bit of news: this cooperative has recently agreed to join forces with a Sicilian winery. Talk about covering the whole field!

● Trentino Merlot Le Campagne '97	▼▼	4
● Trentino Rosso Résorso '97	▼▼	4
● Trentino Marzemino Le Fornas '98	▼	3
○ Trentino Pinot Bianco Valbone '98	▼	3
○ Trentino Bianco Résorso '97		3
● Trentino Merlot '98		2

ROVERÉ DELLA LUNA (TN)

GAIERHOF
VIA IV NOVEMBRE, 51
38030 ROVERÉ DELLA LUNA (TN)
TEL. 0461/658514

The Togn family's modern winery deservedly reappears in this year's Guide. For the coming millennium they offer wines with more personality which reflect the land they spring from, on the border between Trentino and Alto Adige. They put their money on their whites in particular, without, however, completely ignoring their reds. Their '98 Müller Thurgau dei Settecento made a notable impression in our tastings. Produced from a selection of grapes grown on the higher slopes, it has a distinctly greenish hue and a well-defined and many-faceted floral fragrance with a subtle, enticing note of nutmeg. The delectable palate recalls tropical fruit, pineapple and banana. Another excellent white is the Sorni Bianco '98 Maso Poli, a special selection from the fifteen hectares the Togns bought in the 1970s on the Lavis hills. The result of a knowing blend of chardonnay, müller thurgau and nosiola fermented in oak, it is succulent and fresh, an agreeable combination of tangy and softer touches. The other wines, from the Traminer to the Pinot Nero, up to the Teroldego, the Merlot and the Marzemino, point up the general trustworthiness of this wine-maker. A last sweet note: their Moscato Rosa '97 is sensual, perfumed, intense and harmonious. It's an extraordinary wine that the Togns make with exceptional skill.

● Trentino Moscato Rosa '97	▼▼	4
○ Trentino Müller Thurgau dei Settecento '98	▼▼	3*
● Teroldego Rotaliano '97	▼	3
● Trentino Pinot Nero Maso Poli '97	▼	4
○ Trentino Sorni Bianco '98	▼	3
○ Trentino Traminer Aromatico '98	▼	3
○ Trentino Chardonnay '98		3
○ Trentino Sorni Bianco Maso Poli '93	▽▽	4
● Teroldego Rotaliano '93	▽	2*
● Teroldego Rotaliano '94	▽	3
● Trentino Moscato Rosa '93	▽	4
● Trentino Pinot Nero '92	▽	3
● Trentino Pinot Nero '95	▽	3

ROVERETO (TN)

BALTER

VIA VALLUNGA ILA, 26
38068 ROVERETO (TN)
TEL. 0464/430101

One of the most dynamic estates in the Trentino is run by Nicola Balter, a young entrepreneur who inherited his father's passion for viticulture. In his ancient watchtower, built many years ago to guard the Rovereto valley, he makes wine only with those grapes he harvests from his adjacent vineyards, some ten hectares surrounded by medieval walls. His work is completely engrossing and dictates the rhythms of his life and his wines are definitely on an upswing. Let's begin with his spumante, the Trento Balter Brut. It has great finesse, a very characterful bouquet, a smooth and fascinating palate with a creamy mousse perfectly blended with the harmonious, almost sweet structure and an extremely lively finish. This is a wine that missed Three Glasses only by a whisker, and that just because of the hardships of this vintage, which was unforgiving here in the Trentino. The '98 whites are pleasant, (speaking of which, his Clarae '97 blend will come out in 2000, after patient bottle aging), ample and lingering on the nose with notes of both apple and mature fruit. The most successful ones are the Chardonnay, promising in every way, and the Sauvignon, mellow in the mouth, with a grapefruit and vanilla finish. The Traminer is nicely spiced and aromatically well-defined, but slightly lacking in body. In conclusion, the Rossinot '98 deserves special mention. It's a light, grapy, easily drinkable red that isn't at all banal, perhaps because it's an unusual mixture of schiava, lagrein, and pinot nero.

● Trentino Cabernet Sauvignon '96	🍷🍷	4
○ Trentino Sauvignon '98	🍷🍷	3*
○ Trento Balter Brut	🍷🍷	4
● Rossinot '98	🍷	2*
○ Trentino Chardonnay '98	🍷	3
○ Trentino Traminer Aromatico '98	🍷	3
○ Clarae '95	YY	4
○ Clarae '96	YY	4
● Trentino Cabernet Sauvignon '91	YY	4
● Trentino Cabernet Sauvignon '95	YY	4
○ Trentino Chardonnay '97	YY	3
○ Trento Balter Brut	YY	4

ROVERETO (TN)

LONGARIVA

LOC. BORGO SACCO
VIA ZANDONAI, 6
38068 ROVERETO (TN)
TEL. 0464/437200

For the last 23 harvests, Marco Manica and his wife Rosanna have been in charge of all phases of their wine-making, and they produce 13 different wines. With hard work and dedication they have achieved notable results, and have every right to hope for even more gratifying ones. Our tastings revealed that all their wines are well made, clear-cut and satisfying, and it's not by chance that lots of them have easily won Two Glasses. The Sauvignon Cascari '98 came very close indeed to receiving Three. It has a rich elderberry fragrance that dominates notes of nettle, fig and citrus. In the mouth there's an explosion of flavor with notable complexity as well: it's mellow, splendidly crisp and underpinned by plenty of alcohol. The standard Pinot Grigio '98 offers an elegantly intense aromatic medley of spice and fruit, and it's complicated, appropriately acidulous and long-lasting on the palate. The concentrated Merlot Tovi '96, with its pronounced ripe berry fragrance, and the Rosso Tre Cesure '96, a Bordeaux blend, with its vivacious nose and intriguing palate, are both excellent. The Pinot Nero Zinzéle '95, on the other hand, offering ripe red berries on the nose and harmony and great delicacy in the mouth, suffers only from the youth of its vines. The fresh, intense and violet-tinged Marzemino has a pleasantly bitter finish. The tasty Pinot Grigio Graminé is as easy to drink as ever. The remaining '98s, the Chardonnay Perer and the Pinot Bianco Pergole, are lessons in wine-making.

○ Pinot Grigio '98	🍷🍷	3*
○ Sauvignon Cascari '98	🍷🍷	4
● Trentino Merlot Tovi '96	🍷🍷	4
● Trentino Rosso Tre Cesure '96	🍷🍷	4
○ Pinot Grigio Graminè '98	🍷	4
○ Trentino Chardonnay Perer '98	🍷	4
● Trentino Marzemino '97	🍷	3
○ Trentino Pinot Bianco Pergole '98	🍷	4
● Trentino Pinot Nero Zinzèle '95	🍷	4
● Trentino Cabernet Sauvignon Marognon Ris. '94	YY	4
● Trentino Cabernet Sauvignon Marognon Ris. '95	YY	4
● Trentino Merlot Tovi Ris. '95	YY	4

ROVERETO (TN)

ARMANDO SIMONCELLI
LOC. NAVESEL, 7
38068 ROVERETO (TN)
TEL. 0464/432373

Despite a certain perversity in the weather, Armando Simoncelli has produced some good wines with the '98 vintage, so he can feel encouraged to continue in his direct, spontaneous wine-making ways. His wines have both character and style. They are, indeed, simple, but also immediate and decisive. The Lagrein '98 is easy to drink, clearly youthful both in its vivid ruby color and in its pleasing impact in the mouth. This is a wine to be enjoyed young, but you shouldn't ask too much of it. The Marzemino '98 seemed excellent to us, with its broad fruity fragrance enriched by characteristic notes of sweet violet. It's attractive on the palate too, with the light touch of astringency inherited from the grape. Both the Bordeaux-style Navesel '96, named after the ancient river port, and the Cabernet '98 very nearly received Two Glasses. The first has a deep garnet hue and heady aromas of raspberry and black currant, with perhaps an excessively herbaceous accent, but lots of intensity and finesse. The other red, the Cabernet, is intriguingly dark-hued, gracefully fragrant and then structured and almost hot in the mouth. The whites pay a heavier price to the vintage. The Chardonnay plays its best cards when it reveals delicate aromas of citrus fruit and a frankly tangy succulence in the mouth. The Pinot Bianco has a somewhat acidulous nature, witness its almost sour hint of unripe apple. However the spumante Trento Brut is decidedly more interesting. It is pleasingly aromatic and has a full-bodied and enchanting palate, a creamy mousse and a succulent finish.

●	Trentino Lagrein '98	🍷🍷	3
●	Trentino Marzemino '98	🍷🍷	3*
○	Trento Brut M. Cl.	🍷🍷	4
●	Trentino Cabernet '98	🍷	3
○	Trentino Chardonnay '98	🍷	3
●	Trentino Rosso Navesèl '96	🍷	4
○	Trentino Pinot Bianco '98		3
○	Trentino Chardonnay '94	YY	3*
○	Trentino Chardonnay '95	YY	3*
●	Trentino Lagrein '97	YY	3*
●	Trentino Marzemino '96	YY	3*
●	Trentino Marzemino '97	YY	3*
○	Trentino Pinot Bianco '95	YY	3*
●	Trentino Rosso Navesèl '91	YY	3*
●	Trentino Rosso Navesèl '97	YY	3*

S. MICHELE ALL'ADIGE (TN)

AZIENDA VITIVINICOLA DELL'ISTITUTO
AGRARIO PROVINCIALE
VIA EDMONDO MACH, 2
38010 S. MICHELE ALL'ADIGE (TN)
TEL. 0461/615252

The wines presented at our tastings this year by this historic producer are properly made, as usual, but they seemed somewhat less convincing than they have been in the past. This is disappointing considering their provenance: a school which has long been a model, highly imitated in Italy and abroad, of wine-making efficiency and oenological experimentation. Probably the wines have suffered from some organizational uncertainties, which indirectly impinged upon the choices made by the oenologist-professors. To avoid a decline in quality, the administrative council has now made some significant changes and has appointed Enrico Paternoster head of the cellar. A former Istituto student, he quickly became a fine oenologist and a successful wine-maker despite his youth, and the immediate future of this historic institution is in his hands. As for the wines themselves, made before Paternoster's appointment, it is again the Bordeaux-style Castel San Michele '96 that stands out, for its tastiness and sinew, and its successful marriage of firm tannins and notable alcohol. This good red is flanked by the pleasing Rebo '98 (from the first name of the well-known viticultural scientist Rigotti, who worked at the institute in the '30s), and two other good wines, the grapy Lagrein and the soft Merlot, both '97s. The other bottles are well made and average, with a nod going to the Sauvignon.

●	Trentino Lagrein '97	🍷	4
●	Trentino Merlot '97	🍷	4
●	Trentino Rebo '98	🍷	3
●	Trentino Rosso Castel San Michele '96	🍷	4
○	Trentino Sauvignon '98		3
○	Prepositura Atesino '96	YY	3*
○	Spumante Riserva del Fondatore '89	YY	5
●	Trentino Castel San Michele '93	YY	4
●	Trentino Merlot '95	YY	4
●	Trentino Merlot '96	YY	4
●	Trentino Rebo '97	YY	3*
●	Trentino Rosso Castel S. Michele '95	YY	4

S. MICHELE ALL'ADIGE (TN)

Endrizzi

Loc. Masetto
38010 S. Michele all'Adige (TN)
tel. 0461/650129

Endrizzi's historic stone cellar with its little oenological museum will soon be flanked by a modern building currently under construction. Christine and Paolo Endrici will be able to make the most of their material and further raise the quality of their wines. These two young wine-makers, both enthusiasts of avant-garde art, have meanwhile presented the results of recent vintages. Most of their grapes are selectively bought from nearby growers, while some come from their own vineyards on the Faedo hillside on the way to Castel Monreale. The special selection Teroldego Maso Camorz, profiting from the fabulous '97 vintage, is bursting with strength: a dark ruby color, both dense and brilliant, a concentrated bouquet of violet, eucaplyptus, berries and cocoa and, in the mouth, denseness, structure and great length. The Endricis believe particularly in their Pinot Nero Pian di Castello '97, an exemplar of harmony and elegance, and in its potential for improvement as the vines acquire more age. The Masetto Nero '97, an old family label, has a new wine inside which is made this time from a blend of cabernet sauvignon, merlot and lagrein. It's even now ready to drink, attractive to look at and soft to the nose and mouth, with a long corresponding finish. The whites, among which the succulent Pinot Grigio '98 stands out, are all crisp and tasty. The Trento Brut '95 spumante, the highly prized Moscato Rosa '96 and the standard Cabernet are all good.

●	Teroldego Rotaliano Maso Camorz '97	🍷🍷	4
●	Trentino Pinot Nero Pian di Castello '97	🍷🍷	4
●	Masetto Nero '97	🍷	4
●	Trentino Moscato Rosa '96	🍷	5
○	Trentino Pinot Grigio '98	🍷	3
○	Trento Brut M. Cl. '95	🍷	4
●	Trentino Cabernet Sauvignon '97		3
○	Trentino Chardonnay '98		3
●	Teroldego Rotaliano Sup. Sel. '96	🍸🍸	4
○	Trentino Bianco Masetto '97	🍸🍸	4
○	Trentino Chardonnay Tradizione '95	🍸🍸	3*
●	Trentino Moscato Rosa Collezione '94	🍸🍸	5

S. MICHELE ALL'ADIGE (TN)

Zeni

Fraz. Grumo
Via Stretta, 2
38010 San Michele all'Adige (TN)
tel. 0461/650456

The Zeni brothers, Andrea and Roberto, began making wine in the mid-'70s. White wine enthusiasts initially, they have become increasingly interested in reds. And now they are placing heavy bets on them, particularly on their Teroldego. They want to demonstrate with this wine that they have really come of age, oenologically speaking. So they waited patiently while the teroldego they picked in '95 matured in small oak barrels until they felt that they had a wine that is powerful, absolutely distinctive and worthy of the new millennium. It has the color of ripe pomegranate seeds and is dense and velvety. Its delightfully broad spicy bouquet is interlaced with liquorice and strawberry, while it is warmly seductive on a palate underpinned by richness of extract. This is one of the best Trentino reds of recent years. The normal Teroldego merits applause as well. This '98 is pleasurable and delicate, full-bodied and at the same time easy to drink. Their Pinot Nero Spiazol is another proof of their magic touch. A ruby-hued wine of medium intensity, it offers a classic bouquet with a characteristic note of black currant, and is well-balanced and enjoyable to drink. The Moscato Rosa, for some time one of the family jewels, has a scent of rosebuds in the vintage '98 and a deliberately simple palate. Among the whites, the delectably varietal Pinot Bianco Sortì '98 is worthy of special mention: there are hints of apple and medlar on the nose and it's rich, enticing and complete on the palate. The Sauvignon showed off well too with its distinct elderflower fragrance and admirable tastiness. The Müller Thurgau is crisp and characteristically fruity, while the subtle Nosiola has the required touch of green hazelnuts.

●	Teroldego Rotaliano Pini '95	🍷🍷	4
●	Trentino Pinot Nero Spiazol '97	🍷🍷	4
●	Teroldego Rotaliano '98	🍷	3
●	Trentino Moscato Rosa '98	🍷	4
○	Trentino Müller Thurgau '98	🍷	3
○	Trentino Nosiola '98	🍷	3
○	Trentino Pinot Bianco Sortì '98	🍷	4
○	Trentino Sauvignon '98	🍷	3
●	Teroldego Rotaliano '97	🍸🍸	4
●	Teroldego Rotaliano Pini '93	🍸🍸	4
○	Trentino Müller Thurgau La Croce '97	🍸🍸	4
●	Teroldego Rotaliano '96	🍸	4
●	Trentino Moscato Rosa '96	🍸	4
●	Trentino Moscato Rosa '97	🍸	4

SEGONZANO (TN)

BARONI A PRATO
FRAZ. PIAZZO, 44
38047 SEGONZANO (TN)
TEL. 0461/686241

When you enter this splendid estate, the country residence of the noble Barons a Prato, you feel the charm of times past. This is a place where every possible effort is made to safeguard an oenological tradition which has been nurtured in a little-known corner of the Val di Cembra for a century. It was right here in Segonzano that Dürer, clearly also enchanted by the spot, painted one of his famous canvases. Giovanni Napoleone a Prato, who founded the winery almost a hundred years ago, (after his studies in Dresden, Vienna and Klosterneuburg, and further investigation of the vineyards of France, Spain, Tunisia and Sicily), introduced the pinot nero grape, (then improperly called Borgogna), and also cabernet, to Segonzano. Flanking these vines, which have now been cultivated for three generations, they have also planted chardonnay, to take advantage of the volcanic soil kindly deposited by glaciers past. Ferdinando a Prato is in charge of every stage of the wine-making, although he is giving more responsibility these days to a young oenologist, his son Paolo. With a very personal style these two continue to produce wine in a thoroughly traditional way, and the wines show breeding as well as originality. Our most delightful surprise was provided by the Cabernet '97 (made from franc and sauvignon), fermented in small wooden barrels. Intensely ruby-hued, it is fragrant, soft, indeed almost velvety, and has well-balanced tannins and a long finish. The interesting Pinot Nero from the same year is harmonious and finishes beautifully. The only white made on this reliable estate, the Chardonnay '98, has the slightly spiky quality so typical of Trentino.

● Trentino Cabernet '97	🍷🍷	4
○ Trentino Chardonnay '98	🍷	2*
● Trentino Pinot Nero '97	🍷	3

TRENTO

CAVIT - CONSORZIO
DI CANTINE SOCIALI
FRAZ. RAVINA
VIA PONTE, 31
38040 TRENTO
TEL. 0461/381711

Cavit consistently has a decisive effect on the lives of thousands of winegrowers. It's a consortium that makes the most of the best that its member growers produce, and it markets an enormous amount of wine under its own label. Once again this year the wines they presented at our tastings showed a faultless technique, a distinct aromatic tone and admirable body. They did well in comparative tastings with the same kinds of wine produced by respectable small growers. This just goes to show that you can make good wine in large (or shall we say vast) quantities. Yet we must admit that these wines often seem to lack a certain extra charm, that touch of elegance that makes all the difference. This slight want of style is unfortunately common among the wines of Trentino. However lots of good news emerged from tasting their wide range of bottles this year. Their spumantes are very good, beginning with the successful classic Trentino Brut Firmato, which is clean and harmonious. The whites, vinified with great care, all have an excellent clean aromatic freshness, and are more than acceptable on the palate. The Teroldego Maso Cervara '96 is one of the best in the province, with its brilliant ruby color and intense bouquet of berries. The native varieties are characteristic and easy to drink. This is especially true of the two tasty Marzeminos, one made with grapes from Maso Romani and the other from Ziresi, the legendary Vallagarina vineyard.

● Teroldego Rotaliano Maso Cervara '96	🍷🍷	4
○ Trentino Chardonnay Maso Torresella '98	🍷🍷	4
● Trentino Marzemino Maso Romani '97	🍷🍷	4
○ Trentino Vino Santo '92	🍷🍷	5
○ Trento Brut Firmato	🍷🍷	3*
○ Trento Graal Brut Ris. '95	🍷🍷	4
● Trentino Cabernet Sauvignon '97	🍷	3
● Trentino Marzemino Ziresi '98	🍷	4
● Trentino Pinot Nero Maso San Valentino '97	🍷	3
● Trentino Rosso Quattro Vicariati '95	🍷	4
○ Trento Graal Brut Ris. '93	🍷🍷🍷	4*

★ FERRARI
FRAZ. RAVINA
VIA DEL PONTE, 15
38040 TRENTO
TEL. 0461/972311 - 0461/922500

Spumante makers are, one might say, in a ferment at the approach of the millennial celebrations. For the Lunelli brothers, however, festive toasting is nothing new: indeed with their Ferrari spumante they dominate the Italian market for top-flight "bubbly". This they do with a series of typically Trentino spumantes, all of them enchanting. The most important of these is their Riserva named after Giulio Ferrari, a Trentino native who, more than a century ago, was one of the very first in Italy to stake his all on the future of classic spumante. The Giulio Ferrari '91, as soon as it was opened, again confirmed the unquestionable quality of this Trento DOC. It is a marvel of finesse with the vigor of one of the great mature white wines. The complex bouquet includes notes of vanilla, herbs and honey, and it's a knockout on the palate: powerful, dense, creamy and yet crisp, with a very long finish, succulent and inviting. Their Brut Perlé '95, of which many thousands of bottles are produced using state-of-the-art oenological techniques, is also extremely attractive. It has a wealth of yeasty aromas of bread just out of the oven and notes of ripe fruit, and in the mouth it has a seductive nobility. This is a spumante that can be favorably compared with more famous and dearer "bubblies". Quality and quantity happily coexist at the Lunellis', partly because of their strict attention to every facet of their wine-making but partly also because of their pride in producing excellent spumante not just for the happy few. All of their other spumantes were excellent too: decidedly harmonious, elegant and full-bodied; they're hard to beat, and that includes their prices!

○ Giulio Ferrari '91	▼▼▼	6
○ Trento Brut Maximum	▼▼	4
○ Trento Brut Perlé '95	▼▼	5
⊙ Trento Brut Rosé	▼▼	4
○ Trento Ferrari Incontri	▼▼	3*
○ Trento Démi Sec	▼	4
○ Giulio Ferrari '86	▽▽▽	6
○ Giulio Ferrari '88	▽▽▽	6
○ Giulio Ferrari '89	▽▽▽	6
○ Giulio Ferrari '90	▽▽▽	6
○ Giulio Ferrari '87	▽▽	6
○ Trento Brut Perlé '91	▽▽	5
○ Trento Brut Perlé '93	▽▽	5
○ Trento Brut Perlé '94	▽▽	5
○ Trento Ferrari Incontri	▽▽	3*

TRENTO

LE MERIDIANE
LOC. CASTELLER, 6
38100 TRENTO
TEL. 0461/920811

On the Casteller, Trento's splendid vineyard-covered hill overlooking the Adige plain, in a space they have dug out for it in the midst of their terraced vines, stands the winery of Le Meridiane, a relatively new producer which has for some years been in the forefront of Trentino wine-making. We tasted six of their wines and found that standards are being maintained, but we had hoped for something even better. The wines seem properly made and develop well, but in several cases the finish is somewhat disappointing. The wine that did best is their Teroldego Atesino '96, an unusual offering because this is not classic teroldego-growing country. Deeply colored and concentrated, richly fragrant, round in attack, almost silky in the tannins which potentiate a palate that grows into a long finish, it's a really interesting wine. The Merlot Riserva San Raimondo '96 is vigorous and fresh. Dark ruby in hue, it displays a tantalizing range of aromas from blackberry to cocoa, and is soft and persistent in the mouth. The San Bartolomeo Riserva '96 struck us as less successful. Intensity isn't wanting, there are pleasing hints of chocolate, the structure on the palate is fine, but as it develops there are off-tastes that get in the way. And now for the whites: two Sauvignons are on offer. One, the Sauvignon Atesino '97, is full-bodied and harmonious, with delicate notes of elderberry and sage, broad, supple and lingering. The other Sauvignon, the Trentino DOC, is much more fragrant, pleasingly crisp and quaffable, but it is rather lean by comparison. The Chardonnay '97 is decent. We hope for pleasant surprises next year.

○ Sauvignon Atesino '97	▼▼	4
● Teroldego Atesino Cernidor '96	▼▼	4
● Trentino Merlot Vigneto San Raimondo Ris. '96	▼▼	4
● Trentino Cabernet Sauvignon Vigneto San Bartolomeo Ris. '96	▼	4
○ Trentino Sauvignon '97	▼	3
○ Trentino Chardonnay '97		3
● Trentino Cabernet Sauvignon Vigneto San Bartolomeo Ris. '94	▽▽	4
● Trentino Cabernet Sauvignon Vigneto San Bartolomeo Ris. '95	▽▽	4
● Trentino Merlot Vigneto San Raimondo Ris. '95	▽▽	4

TRENTO

LUNELLI
FRAZ. RAVINA
VIA DEL PONTE, 13
38040 TRENTO
TEL. 0461/972311

In Trentino Lunelli is synonymous with spumante. Their success has been such that they've been able to enter the lists with other kinds of wine as well; thus, in addition to their lively bubbly gems, they offer various whites and reds that are full-bodied, structured, mature and likely to age well over time. This is the origin of the Lunelli estate, the brainchild of Mauro, principally, with the help of his young nephew Marcello, who is also an oenologist with a special interest in agronomy. Together they identified the most promising vineyards in the Adige valley, bought them and replanted them, suiting themselves in the choice of grape varieties, planting and training systems and cultivation techniques. Thus they have produced five wines, one from each vineyard. The whites are not new to us. The two '97 chardonnays, Villa Margon and Villa Gentilotti, once again display personality, lovely structure, an inviting bouquet and a long rich finish. So the real news – and good news too – is the reds. Last year saw the virtually unheralded arrival of Maso Le Viane '95, a successful Bordeaux-style red. The '96 vintage is concentrated, has a wide range of aromas and seems to promise a long future, although the youth of the vines makes itself felt. But we've saved the best for last: the Pinot Nero Maso Montalto '96, made from grapes grown in a vineyard fairly high up on Trento's mountain, Monte Bondone. This is an elegant and really well-made wine. Its ruby hue could be more intense and brilliant, but its bouquet is stylish, with classic wild berry aromas, and on the palate it is soft and fruity and, to say the very least, enchanting.

○	Trentino Chardonnay Villa Gentilotti '97	YY	4
○	Trentino Chardonnay Villa Margon '97	YY	4
●	Trentino Pinot Nero Maso Montalto '96	YY	4
●	Trentino Rosso Maso Le Viane '96	Y	5
○	Trentino Chardonnay Villa Gentilotti '96	yy	4
○	Trentino Chardonnay Villa Margon '96	yy	4
●	Trentino Rosso Maso Le Viane '95	yy	4
○	Trentino Sauvignon Villa San Nicolò '97	yy	4

VOLANO (TN)

CONCILIO
ZONA INDUSTRIALE 2/4
38060 VOLANO (TN)
TEL. 0464/411000

Concilio is a name to be reckoned with in Trentino. It was founded in 1860 by Angelo Grigolli and has grown over the years, thanks to the dedication of other enterprising wine-producing families. Now Concilio, apart from being one of the most important wineries in Trentino, is a corporation, composed of not only the families that have long been involved, but also a group of Trentino wine-makers with combined holdings of almost 500 hectares of choice vineyards that guarantee quality as well as quantity. The wines have character and a modern style, and even the graphics on the bottle have received careful attention. To turn to the most interesting wines: the mellow Chardonnay '98, with its lovely bouquet and harmonious, full-bodied, inviting palate, is one of the best Trentino wines to emerge from our tastings. Another delightful surprise was the Pinot Grigio '98, a graceful white with a by no means negligible force, a distinct pear flavor and a long finish. Further whites: the Traminer Aromatico is clear-cut and harmonious, while the Sauvignon'98 is slightly less successful because of a leanness that its vintage may explain. But it's a different story, and a more successful one again, for the reds. The Merlot Novaline '96, a Riserva which has for some years been the apple of their eye, is a really all-around, rich, broad and balanced wine. The Cabernet Sauvignon '96, another worthy Riserva, fragrant and lingering, comes close to Two Glasses, which its brother, the Mori Vecio '97, wins. The latter was one of the first Bordeaux-style wines to appear in Trentino and is soft, full-bodied and easy to drink.

○	Trentino Chardonnay '98	YY	3*
●	Trentino Merlot Novaline Ris. '96	YY	4
○	Trentino Pinot Grigio '98	YY	3*
●	Trentino Rosso Mori Vecio '97	YY	4
●	Trentino Cabernet Sauvignon Ris. '96	Y	4
○	Trentino Traminer Aromatico '98	Y	3
○	Trentino Sauvignon '98		3
●	Trentino Cabernet Sauvignon Ris. '95	yy	4
●	Trentino Marzemino Mozart '97	yy	3*
●	Trentino Merlot Novaline Ris. '91	yy	4
●	Trentino Merlot Novaline Ris. '94	yy	4
●	Trentino Merlot Novaline Ris. '95	yy	4
○	Trento Angelo Grigolli Ris.	yy	5

OTHER WINERIES

The following producers in the province of Trento obtained good scores in our tastings with one or more of their wines:

Alessandro Secchi
Ala, tel. 0464/696647
Corindone Rosso '97

Madonna delle Vittorie
Arco, tel. 0464/505542
Trentino Chardonnay '98

Maso Roveri
Avio, tel. 0464/684395
Trentino Pinot Bianco '98

Vallarom
Avio, tel. 0464/684297
Questa importante azienda ha cambiato conduzione e responsabili di cantina. Aspettiamo i nuovi risultati.

Cantina di Toblino
Calavino,
tel. 0461/564168
Trentino Cabernet '97,
Trentino Nosiola '98

Gino Pedrotti
Cavedine, tel. 0461/564123
Trentino Cabernet '97,
Trentino Vino Santo '88

Pelz & Piffer
Cembra, tel. 0461/683051
Trentino Pinot Nero '97

Maso Bergamini
Cognola,
tel. 0461/983079
Trentino Lagrein '97,
Trentino Moscato Rosa '98,
Trentino Pinot Nero '98

Arcangelo Sandri
Faedo, tel. 0461/650935
Trentino Müller Thurgau '98

Villa Piccola
Faedo,
tel. 0461/650420
Trentino Pinot Nero '97

Renzo Gorga
Folgaria, tel. 0464/721161
Trentino Marzemino '97

Abate Nero
Gardolo, tel. 0461/246566
Trento Brut,
Trento Extra Brut,
Trento Extra Dry

La Vigne
Isera, tel. 0464/433182
Fior di Ciliegio '96

Casata Monfort
Lavis, tel. 0461/241484
Trentino Lagrein '97,
Trentino Traminer Aromatico '98

Molino dei Lessi
Lavis, tel. 0461/870275
Cabernet Sauvignon dei Sorni '97

Vignaioli Fanti
Lavis, tel. 0461/240809
Incrocio Manzoni '98,
Portico Rosso '96

Maso Martis
Martignano, tel. 0461/820394
Trentino Chardonnay '98,
Trento Brut '96

Cipriano Fedrizzi
Mezzolombardo, tel. 0461/602328
Teroldego Rotaliano '97

Grigoletti
Nomi, tel. 0464/834215
Gonzialer '95,
Retiko '97,
Trentino Merlot '97

Dalzocchio
Rovereto, tel. 0464/413461
Trentino Chardonnay '98

Frasnelli-Sartori
San Michele all'Adige, tel. 0461/650413
Spumante Brut '92,
Trentino Bianco '98,
Trentino Müller Thurgau '98

Giulio Poli
Santa Massenza, tel. 0461/350443
Schiava Valle dei Laghi '98

Bailoni, Trento, tel. 0461/911842
Blu Perla '97,
Trentino Cabernet '97

ALTO ADIGE

Burgundy, plus Alsace, plus a touch of Bordeaux and just a dash of the Loire: this isn't the recipe for an oenological cocktail of dubious taste, but it could be the goal of Alto Adige viticulture, one of the major agricultural resources of the region. One should, however, add to the characteristics of those four French regions the great wealth of more or less indigenous grape varieties that are certainly not to be sniffed at: lagrein, the schiavas, even gewürztraminer which, since it means "the spicy one from Termeno" in German, must have some local origins, even if not all ampelographers are prepared to recognize them. The Alto Adige, then, is one of the great homelands of viticulture, and this year it offered not just historical and cultural evidence, but also a quantity of wine whose average quality is perhaps among the highest in the whole of Italy. This is the result of a felicitous combination of private wineries and first-rate cooperatives, as well as talented oenologists, the "Kellermeisters", who are undoubtedly among the best around today (and not just in Italy). Such men as Hans Terzer, Helmuth Zozin, Willi Sturz and Celestino Lucin, just to mention the first who spring to mind and not necessarily the best, are now all part of Europe's wine-making Olympus. But that's not all. The data that the Guide offers us this year are indicative of a sector whose growth in terms of quality is exponential. No fewer than 15 wines earned Three Glasses (last year there were only 10). And 52 wineries have their own profile, four more than in '99. Of over 400 samples tasted, more than 90% rated at least One Glass. These are impressive figures indeed, and give an idea of the now widespread and constant quality. Furthermore, we have awarded an Alto Adige winery, the Cantina Produttori di San Michele Appiano/Sanct Michael Eppan, the title of Winery of the Year: indeed three of their wines earned Three Glasses, a triumph for this fine cooperative winery but also for the region's wine producers as a whole. Even five years ago all of this would have been unimaginable. So what has taken place in this brief period? Above all, production has become much less provincial. Today Alto Adige wines have established themselves throughout Italy and they are no longer exported merely to German-speaking countries. They're to be found in Great Britain and in the United States, partly because they are made mainly from grape varieties that are well known in those countries, like chardonnay, sauvignon, cabernet sauvignon, pinot nero and now merlot as well. Then too, they are starting to show a recognizable character, which is determined by their terroir but also reflects the fact that yield per vine is being reduced and that, alongside the traditional pergola training, producers are starting to plant Guyot-trained vineyards. All of these factors make it easy for us to foresee a brilliant future for the wine of this region. It will not be Burgundy, plus Alsace, plus a touch of Bordeaux and just a dash of the Loire, as we suggested to begin with: it will be unabashedly Alto Adige/Südtirol, one of Europe's great wine regions.

ANDRIANO/ANDRIAN (BZ)

Cantina Produttori Andriano

Via della Chiesa, 2
39010 Andriano/Andrian (BZ)
tel. 0471/510137

In a region full of cooperative wineries, the Cantina Produttori di Andriano is the oldest, having been established in 1893. Its 140 member growers, led by their dynamic president, Konrad Matha, have decided to pursue a policy of steady progress and constant quality. The Cantina, with its 140 hectares of vines currently in production, is not one of the biggest in the zone; however, Matha says, "Better a little bit less, but a little bit better". And we agree, because the Produttori di Andriano succeed every year in making us sit up and take notice of at least a couple of their wines. The three stupendous bottles from the Tor di Lupo range greatly impressed us yet again this time. The barrique-aged Chardonnay Tor di Lupo '97 displays a golden straw color, an intense, fine and fruity bouquet, and rich, soft ripe fruit on the palate. It is an exciting wine, as is the Sauvignon Tor di Lupo Preciosa '98 with its elegant varietal aromas of sage and peach and its soft, well-balanced and highly appealing palate. The Lagrein Tor di Lupo '98 too is true to form with its very intense ruby-garnet hue, its broad gamut of berry scents and its excellent structure and extract counterpointed by measured, unobtrusive oak. Among the other wines we found the Merlot Siebeneich '97 particularly worthy of note: it has an intense, complex nose, very attractive fruit on the palate and a long finish. Lastly, we should like to mention a few very enjoyable, well-made whites: the Gewürztraminer, the Chardonnay, the basic Sauvignon and the Müller Thurgau, all '98s. The Schiava Santa Giustina '98 is, however, - like many other Schiavas from this vintage – unfortunately not a very worthy example of its type.

○	A. A. Chardonnay Tor di Lupo '97	▼▼	4
●	A. A. Lagrein Scuro Tor di Lupo '97	▼▼	4
●	A. A. Merlot Siebeneich '97	▼▼	4
○	A. A. Terlano Sauvignon Preciosa Tor di Lupo '98	▼▼	3*
○	A. A. Chardonnay '98	▼	2*
○	A. A. Gewürztraminer '98	▼	2*
●	A. A. Schiava S. Giustina '98	▼	2*
○	A. A. Terlano Sauvignon '98	▼	2*
●	A. A. Lagrein Scuro Tor di Lupo '91	▽▽	4
●	A. A. Lagrein Scuro Tor di Lupo '94	▽▽	4
●	A. A. Lagrein Scuro Tor di Lupo '95	▽▽	4
●	A. A. Schiava S. Giustina '97	▽▽	2*
○	A. A. Terlano Sauvignon Cl. '95	▽▽	3*
○	A. A. Terlano Sauvignon Cl. '96	▽▽	3*

APPIANO/EPPAN (BZ)

Josef Brigl

Fraz. Cornaiano
Via S. Floriano, 8
39057 Appiano/Eppan (BZ)
tel. 0471/662419

This large and famous Alto Adige winery makes its debut in the Guide this year thanks to a range of wines which may not show recognizable personality but are unquestionably flawlessly executed. The intriguing Sauvignon '98 displays a quite varietal bouquet and a linear and concentrated palate underpinned by an appealing (and characteristic) delicately acidulous note. The very attractive and quaffable Santa Maddalena Reierhof Monika Brigl '98 is a pleasant, light, medium-bodied and well-balanced red. The successful Lago di Caldaro Scelto Haslhof '98 is a little more decided and concentrated than the Santa Maddalena. It offers an intensely fruity and vinous nose and a rounded, velvety palate with the slightest hint of bitterness on the finish. The Pinot Nero Haslhof '97 is the product of a distinctly propitious year but doesn't show the complexity one expected: hence just One Glass. Nevertheless Brigl has four wines listed below, and at last this important regional winery has its own profile in the Guide: good news for all wine lovers.

○	A. A. Sauvignon '98	▼▼	3*
●	A. A. Lago di Caldaro Scelto Haslhof '98	▼	3
●	A. A. Pinot Nero Haslhof '97	▼	4
●	A. A. Santa Maddalena Reierhof Monika Brigl '98	▼	3
⊙	A. A. Lagrein Rosato '97	▽▽	3*
○	A. A. Gewürztraminer '97	▽	3
●	A. A. Santa Maddalena Reierhof Monika Brigl '97	▽	3

APPIANO/EPPAN (BZ)

CANTINA PRODUTTORI SAN MICHELE
APPIANO/ST. MICHAEL EPPAN
VIA CIRCONVALLAZIONE, 17/19
39057 APPIANO/EPPAN (BZ)
TEL. 0471/664466

Three Three Glass wines and five others that have won Two Glasses; six with the asterisk indicating value for money: if this isn't the Winery of the Year we don't honestly know what should be. And furthermore, amazing to relate, we are talking about a cooperative winery: the best in Italy and perhaps the world. The people who are responsible for all this, apart from all the member growers, are the president Anton Zublasing and the Kellermeister (the German term seems appropriate here) Hans Terzer, the white wine expert par excellence in Alto Adige, and creator of some extraordinary wines. The Sauvignon Sanct Valentin '98 shows the usual marvelous concentrated varietal aromas of peach and elderflower and a soft, absolutely delectable palate. The Gewürztraminer, another Sanct Valentin '98, is the best they've ever made and the best of the region. An aromatic, almost mineral fragrance precedes a decided and concentrated palate. The barrique-aged Chardonnay Sanct Valentin '97 magically combines richness of extract with an elegance that is easier to obtain in these parts. But that's not all: you should try the Riesling Montiggl '98, the Sauvignon Lahn '98 and the Pinot Bianco Schulthauser '98, all reasonably priced wines produced in some quantity and able to satisfy the most demanding expert as well as the "normal" consumer. The Pinot Grigio Sanct Valentin '97 and the Comtess '98, a delicious, aromatic sweet white made from semi-dried gewürztraminer grapes, just missed out on a third Glass. Our enthusiasm wanes slightly for the merely sound Chardonnay Merol '98 and for the Pinot Nero Riserva '97, from which we expected quite a bit more.

○	A. A. Chardonnay St. Valentin '97	🍷🍷🍷	4*
○	A. A. Gewürztraminer St. Valentin '98	🍷🍷🍷	4*
○	A. A. Sauvignon St. Valentin '98	🍷🍷🍷	4*
○	A. A. Pinot Bianco Schulthauser '98	🍷🍷	3*
○	A. A. Pinot Grigio St. Valentin '97	🍷🍷	4
○	A. A. Riesling Montiggl '98	🍷🍷	3*
○	A. A. Sauvignon Lahn '98	🍷🍷	3*
○	Comtess '98	🍷🍷	5
○	A. A. Chardonnay Merol '98	🍷	3
●	A. A. Pinot Nero Ris. '97	🍷	5
○	A. A. Sauvignon St. Valentin '94	🍸🍸🍸	4*
○	A. A. Sauvignon St. Valentin '95	🍸🍸🍸	4*
○	A. A. Sauvignon St. Valentin '96	🍸🍸🍸	5
○	A. A. Sauvignon St. Valentin '97	🍸🍸🍸	5

APPIANO/EPPAN (BZ)

CANTINA PRODUTTORI SAN PAOLO/
KELLEREIGENOSSENSCHAFT ST. PAULS
VIA CASTEL GUARDIA, 1
39050 APPIANO/EPPAN (BZ)
TEL. 0471/662183

We were delighted by this year's wines from this cooperative winery, which were better than ever before and show that San Paolo is entering the top rank of Alto Adige producers. We were particularly impressed by the two Pinot Biancos, the really amazing standard version and the Plötzner, both '98s. The former is one of the best of its type, not least because it offers such remarkable value for money. The most impressive of the reds seemed to us to be the full-bodied and concentrated Merlot DiVinus '97 and the Lagrein Exklusiv '96, which, though from a rather lackluster vintage, displayed good varietal characteristics and tannins that were neither bitter nor harsh. We found the Sauvignon Gfilhof '98, which was very appealing but offered slightly diluted varietal qualities, and the Pinot Nero DiVinus '97 not quite at the same level. The latter is the fruit of a really propitious vintage but did not show the concentration and rich bouquet we rather expected: a good red wine, but a bit one-dimensional. This criticism does not detract in the slightest, however, from the overall quality of a winery which, we repeat, is now one of the leading producers in this extraordinary region.

●	A. A. Lagrein Scuro Exklusiv Gries Ris. '96	🍷🍷	5
●	A. A. Merlot DiVinus '97	🍷🍷	5
○	A. A. Pinot Bianco '98	🍷🍷	3*
○	A. A. Terlano Pinot Bianco Exklusiv Plötzner '98	🍷🍷	4
●	A. A. Pinot Nero DiVinus '97	🍷	5
○	A. A. Sauvignon Exklusiv Gfilhof '98	🍷	4
●	A. A. Lagrein Scuro Exklusiv Gries Ris. '95	🍸🍸	4
○	A. A. Pinot Grigio Exklusiv Egg-Leitn '97	🍸🍸	4
○	A. A. Terlano Pinot Bianco Exklusiv Plötzner '97	🍸🍸	4

APPIANO/EPPAN (BZ)

KÖSSLER - PRAECLARUS
SAN PAOLO/ST. PAULS
39057 APPIANO/EPPAN (BZ)
TEL. 0471/660256 - 0471/662182

The first-class range presented by Kössler-Praeclarus reveals once again that this winery has been undergoing a definite change of direction in the last few years. From being essentially a sparkling wine producer, in fact, it has enlarged its repertoire to include a whole series of very fine reds. But it has never done as well with them as this year, partly because of the release of the splendid '97s, the fruit of a superb vintage. The excellent '97 Lagrein Scuro shows substantial body and concentration. The Merlot Tschiedererhof '97, the best version yet of this red, with a broad, varietal nose and marked but yielding tannins on the palate, just missed Three Glasses. There were good performances once again from the Cabernet-Merlot St. Pauls '97, now a regular Two Glass winner, and from the Pinot Nero '97, one of the best of its type and year. The sparkling Praeclarus Brut, with its delicate, yeasty aromas and elegant, well-balanced flavor, is very good, as usual, but it wants a little more body. This is definitely a winery to watch out for in future, considering the constant progress it has made over the last few years and its ever-growing sureness of hand in dealing with decidedly difficult grape varieties, lagrein and pinot nero in particular.

●	A. A. Cabernet-Merlot S. Pauls '97	▼▼	5
●	A. A. Lagrein Scuro '97	▼▼	4
●	A. A. Merlot Tschidererhof '97	▼▼	5
●	A. A. Pinot Nero '95	▼▼	5
○	A. A. Spumante Praeclarus Brut	▼▼	5
●	A. A. Cabernet '96	▼	4
●	A. A. Cabernet-Merlot '93	▽▽	4
●	A. A. Cabernet-Merlot St. Pauls '96	▽▽	5
●	A. A. Lagrein Scuro '95	▽▽	4
○	A. A. Spumante Praeclarus Extra Brut '93	▽▽	5
○	A. A. Spumante Praeclarus Noblesse '90	▽▽	5

APPIANO/EPPAN (BZ)

STROBLHOF
VIA PIGANO, 25
39057 APPIANO/EPPAN (BZ)
TEL. 0471/662250

Stroblhof is getting better all the time: in the last couple of years a great deal has changed in terms of the reliability and average quality of their wines. Previously they were in the Guide one year and out the next, and even in good years there might be technical quibbles. Besides, for every high point (the Pinot Nero Strahler Riserva '90, for example), there were many disappointments. But now the wines are good even in indifferent vintages and they all seem very well executed. Try, if it ever comes your way, the '98 Gewürztraminer. It very nearly walked off with Three Glasses, making it to the finals and only being eliminated in the very last round. But you should also taste the '96 Pinot Nero Riserva, produced in a vintage that was anything but outstanding, yet an exemplarily varietal wine: only a slightly dilute palate reveals the mediocrity of the year. And the Pinot Bianco Strahler '98 is a minor classic of South Tyrolean wine-making. It reveals a delicately fruity, elegant and fragrant bouquet and a full, well-balanced and very stylish palate. A further revelation is its price, which is very reasonable indeed. These are three excellent wines, further evidence that the winery is making great progress: all very encouraging.

○	A. A. Gewürztraminer '98	▼▼	4
○	A. A. Pinot Bianco Strahler '98	▼▼	3*
●	A. A. Pinot Nero Ris. '96	▼▼	5
○	A. A. Gewürztraminer '97	▽▽	4
○	A. A. Pinot Bianco Strahler '97	▽▽	3*
●	A. A. Pinot Nero Ris. '91	▽▽	4
●	A. A. Pinot Nero Strahler Ris. '90	▽▽	5
○	A. A. Chardonnay '97	▽	4
●	A. A. Pinot Nero Ris. '93	▽	4
●	A. A. Pinot Nero Ris. '95	▽	5

BOLZANO/BOZEN

CANTINA CONVENTO MURI-GRIES
P.ZZA GRIES, 21
39100 BOLZANO/BOZEN
TEL. 0471/282287

This review of the wines from the Abbey of Muri-Gries is in a minor key. In fact, they sent us only their basic range for tasting this year, since the Lagrein Riserva '97, unquestionably their standard-bearer, had not yet been bottled. It should be borne in mind, however, that Muri-Gries is the producer par excellence of Lagrein, which it takes to great, yet traditional, heights. But let's get back to what we actually tasted this year. The Lagrein Rosato '98 was pleasant, fruity, quaffable and, although perhaps a little straightforward and yeasty, well executed. The standard version of Lagrein Scuro, the '98, was a bit better: it offered an intense fruity bouquet with a reasonably concentrated black currant scent, and a substantial palate with marked and still abundant tannins. We felt we were drinking a very young wine that still had some rough edges to smooth out. The very light hint of bitterness in the aftertaste gave an impression of slight over-extraction. Lastly, the Moscato Rosa '97 is a respectable version of one of the classic wines of this zone: it shows a well-defined aromatic fragrance, but no great weight on the palate and a slightly bitterish tone on the finish.

⊙	A. A. Lagrein Rosato '98	🍷	3
●	A. A. Lagrein Scuro Gries '98	🍷	4
●	A. A. Moscato Rosa '97	🍷	5
●	A. A. Lagrein Abtei Ris. '96	YYY	5
●	A. A. Cabernet Ris. '91	YY	5
●	A. A. Lagrein Abtei Ris. '92	YY	5
●	A. A. Lagrein Abtei Ris. '94	YY	5
●	A. A. Lagrein Ris. '90	YY	4
●	A. A. Lagrein Scuro Gries '95	YY	4
●	A. A. Lagrein Scuro Gries '97	YY	2*
●	A. A. Lagrein '91	Y	4
●	A. A. Lagrein '92	Y	4

BOLZANO/BOZEN

CANTINA DI GRIES
P.ZZA GRIES, 2
39100 BOLZANO/BOZEN
TEL. 0471/270909

The Cantina di Gries succeeded in winning a whole cupboardful of Glasses in this addition of the Guide. This is the best-ever performance for a producer considered until recently a major player only for its Lagrein. This year, however, it astonished us with a Merlot, the Siebeneich Riserva '97, which came within an inch of Three Glasses and is one of the very best in its category. It is an absolutely splendid red, soft, concentrated and elegant, with intense varietal scents along with tobacco and violet notes. The two '96 Lagrein Riservas were almost of the same standard: the Grieser Prestige Line – more modern in style – and the Baron Carl Eyrl which seems a shade more traditional, especially in its high polyphenolic content, which makes it just a little rougher on the palate. The '98 Mauritius, a blend based predominantly on merlot and lagrein, was excellent, and the Santa Maddalena mit Gütesiegel '98 was very good of its type: it has a fragrant nose with marked fruity and vinous notes, and is easy and inviting to drink. All the other wines were satisfactory, and the Terlano Pinot Bianco '98 deserves a special mention: it missed Two Glasses by just a whisker.

●	A. A. Lagrein Scuro Grieser Baron Carl Eyrl Ris. '96	🍷🍷	5
●	A. A. Lagrein Scuro Grieser Prestige Line Ris. '96	🍷🍷	5
●	A. A. Merlot Siebeneich Prestige Line Ris. '97	🍷🍷	5
●	A. A. Santa Maddalena mit Gütesiegel '98	🍷🍷	3*
●	Mauritius '96	🍷🍷	6
⊙	A. A. Lagrein Rosato Pischlhof '98	🍷	3
●	A. A. Santa Maddalena Cl. Tröglerhof '98	🍷	3
○	A. A. Terlano Pinot Bianco '98	🍷	4
●	A. A. Lagrein Scuro Grieser Baron Carl Eyrl Ris. '95	YY	5

BOLZANO/BOZEN

CANTINA PRODUTTORI
SANTA MADDALENA
VIA BRENNERO, 15
39100 BOLZANO/BOZEN
TEL. 0471/972944

There is really very little we need to add to what you can see at the bottom of the page. We should just point out that all the evidence keeps confirming that the Cantina Produttori di Santa Maddalena has become one of the top producers in Alto Adige. This year they almost outdid themselves. All the wines were at the very least good, and many were really outstanding. Apart from the Three Glasses won yet again by the Cabernet Mumelterhof – the '97 version, a real Titan of a wine – it must be said that the Chardonnay Kleinstein '98 came within a hair's breadth of joining it. And at its price it is one of the biggest bargains to be had among the whites of the Alto Adige. And how about the basic Santa Maddalena Classico '98, which is deliciously fruity and a delight to drink, ideal for serving with the zone's traditional "speck" (a cured smoky ham)? Then there is the Lagrein Taberhof Riserva '97, whose Two Glasses are definitely overflowing: it is a powerful yet elegant red which has been really excellent for some years now. Or consider the Santa Maddalena Huck am Bach '98, with its intense and very elegant vinous bouquet and its soft, highly concentrated palate with a delicious, delicately bitter finish. The simpler wines – the Sauvignon Mockhof, the Valle Isarco Müller Thurgau and the Gewürztraminer, all whites from the '98 vintage – were simply good.

●	A. A. Cabernet Mumelterhof '97	🍷🍷🍷	5
○	A. A. Chardonnay Kleinstein '98	🍷🍷	3*
●	A. A. Lagrein Scuro Perlhof '97	🍷🍷	4
●	A. A. Lagrein Scuro Taberhof Ris. '97	🍷🍷	5
●	A. A. Pinot Nero Ris. '97	🍷🍷	5
●	A. A. Santa Maddalena Cl. Huck am Bach '98	🍷🍷	4
●	A. A. Santa Maddalena Classico '98	🍷🍷	3*
○	A. A. Sauvignon Mockhof '98	🍷	3
○	A. A. Valle Isarco Müller Thurgau '98	🍷	3
○	A. A. Gewürztramier '98		3
●	A. A. Cabernet Mumelterhof '94	🍸🍸🍸	3*
●	A. A. Cabernet Mumelterhof '95	🍸🍸🍸	4*
●	A. A. Lagrein Scuro Taberhof Ris. '95	🍸🍸🍸	4*

BOLZANO/BOZEN

EGGER-RAMER
VIA GUNCINA, 5
39100 BOLZANO/BOZEN
TEL. 0471/280541

For three generations now, the Egger-Ramer family has been dedicated to growing vines in the classic production zones for Santa Maddalena and Lagrein. Toni Egger-Ramer's way of working is based on long-standing family traditions and a wealth of personal experience – although, until ten years ago, the winery was geared towards high-volume production and wholesale marketing. With singularly good timing, the owner then decided to embark on a new path, leading towards quality, and the successes of the last few years have shown how wise he was. The Lagrein and the Santa Maddalena are the real standard-bearers of the house. The Lagrein Grieser '97 from the Kristan vineyard (1.5 hectares, with vines up to 35 years old) was, once again, one of the best Lagreins we tasted from the zone. Traditional in style, it is aged, after 15 days' fermentation on the lees, for 12 months, partly in large casks and partly in barriques. On the nose it displays intense berry scents as well as very fine balsamic notes and a perfectly judged hint of oak . Its full body, power, concentration and persistence are equally impressive and exciting on the palate. The Lagrein Grieser Kristan Riserva '96 is similar in style, but because it is from a less good vintage it lacks the precision and inherent quality of its "younger brother". We should also like to mention the '98 Santa Maddalena Classico, a delicious, easy-drinking red with a very fruity and fragrant bouquet.

●	A. A. Lagrein Grieser Kristan '97	🍷🍷	3*
●	A. A. Lagrein Grieser Kristan Ris. '96	🍷🍷	5
●	A. A. Santa Maddalena Cl. '98	🍷	3
●	A. A. Lagrein Grieser Kristan '96	🍸🍸	3*
●	A. A. Lagrein Grieser Kristan Ris. '95	🍸🍸	5
●	A. A. Santa Maddalena Cl. '97	🍸🍸	3*

BOLZANO/BOZEN

Franz Gojer Glögglhof

Fraz. St. Magdalena
Via Rivellone, 1
39100 Bolzano/Bozen
tel. 0471/978775

Just three wines were presented by Franz Gojer this year - and they were three little gems, in spite of the fact that they were from less than glorious vintages. Only really good vineyard management, with yields kept rigorously low and ruthless selection of the best bunches for vinification, can produce results like these. The Lagrein Riserva '96 is a dream: it reached our Three Glass finals (the first wine of Gojer's to do so), and is one of the top wines in its category. It is a monumental characteristic red with a very concentrated purplish ruby color and intense aromas of black currant and blueberry. But, above all, it is amazingly full-bodied, with perhaps just a little touch of harshness that goes with extreme youth: this is a wine that is certainly destined to see out the first five years of the new Millennium without straining in the least. Then there are the two Santa Maddalenas: the basic one, which is fragrant, very charming and highly quaffable, and the more concentrated and potentially long-lived Rondell. Both are medium-bodied reds from the '98 vintage, and both are delicious wines which can be drunk throughout a meal, but which show at their very best when drunk at cellar temperature with cold smoked meats, and speck in particular. They are straightforward, traditional wines perfectly interpreted.

●	A. A. Lagrein Scuro Ris. '96	🍷🍷	5
●	A. A. Santa Maddalena Cl. '98	🍷🍷	3*
●	A. A. Santa Maddalena Rondell '98	🍷🍷	3*
●	A. A. Lagrein Scuro Ris. '95	🍸🍸	4
●	A. A. Santa Maddalena Cl. '95	🍸🍸	3*
●	A. A. Santa Maddalena Cl. '97	🍸🍸	3*
●	A. A. Santa Maddalena Rondell '93	🍸🍸	4
●	A. A. Santa Maddalena Rondell '95	🍸🍸	3*
●	A. A. Lagrein Scuro '96	🍸	3
●	A. A. Lagrein Scuro '97	🍸	3
●	A. A. Lagrein Scuro Ris. '96	🍸	4
●	A. A. Santa Maddalena Rondell '96	🍸	3
●	A. A. Santa Maddalena Rondell '97	🍸	3

BOLZANO/BOZEN

Thomas Mayr e Figli

Via Mendola, 56
39100 Bolzano/Bozen
tel. 0471/281030

This winery is dedicated to the red wines of the Bolzano district, particularly Santa Maddalena. In other words, you'd have a hard time finding any grapes other than schiava and lagrein in their cellar, and the results are consistent and dependable, even in lesser vintages. We therefore beg your indulgence while we plead the cause of this estate, a true standard-bearer for local tradition and terroir. This year, indeed, we are helped in our task by the wines, as the range, though small, is of considerable interest. The Lagrein Scuro S. (for "Selezione", perhaps?) from the '97 vintage, an excellent year for this type of wine, is particularly good. It reveals, apart from a very concentrated color, characteristic and well-defined varietal aromas of black currant, blueberry and violet. On the palate, apart from a slight and not unexpected youthful lack of polish, it displays notable body and structure and also remarkable length. The Santa Maddalena Rumplerhof '98 is fragrant, intensely fruity and easy to drink, making it one of the best examples of its type in this vintage. The other three wines are well made and appealing, although simpler; a special mention must go to the light, quaffable and inexpensive '98 Schiava.

●	A. A. Lagrein Scuro S. '97	🍷🍷	4
●	A. A. Santa Maddalena Cl. Rumplerhof '98	🍷🍷	3*
⊙	A. A. Lagrein Rosato '98	🍷	3
●	A. A. Lagrein Scuro '98	🍷	3
●	A. A. Schiava '98	🍷	2*
●	A. A. Lagrein Scuro '93	🍸🍸	3*
●	A. A. Lagrein Scuro '95	🍸🍸	3*
●	A. A. Lagrein Scuro Ris. '92	🍸🍸	5
●	A. A. Lagrein Scuro Ris. '94	🍸🍸	4
●	A. A. Lagrein Scuro Ris. '96	🍸🍸	4
●	Creazione Rosa '95	🍸🍸	5
●	A. A. Santa Maddalena Cl. Rumplerhof '97	🍸	3

BOLZANO/BOZEN

HEINRICH PLATTNER - WALDGRIESHOF
SANTA GIUSTINA, 2
39100 BOLZANO/BOZEN
TEL. 0471/973245

A fantastic Lagrein Scuro Riserva '97 dominates the range of wines presented this year by the famous winery at Santa Giustina. Heinrich Plattner has, therefore, had his revenge for our assertion in last year's Guide that he was, above all, a great interpreter of cabernet sauvignon. Lagrein is definitely a more traditional, and indeed more appropriate, wine for the zone, and Plattner's is truly monumental: it easily reached our finals and came within an ace of winning Three Glasses. It has everything that a great Lagrein should have, including a slight rustic earthiness, which detracts, even if only to a tiny extent, from its balance on the palate. The extremely intriguing '98 Pinot Grigio is a fruity, varietal, soft and fairly concentrated white which is, incidentally, offered at a very fair price indeed. A similar comment can be made about the Santa Maddalena Classico '98, which may not be extraordinarily complex (which one wouldn't really expect this type of wine to be, anyway), but is admirably well executed and delightfully fragrant. The Moscato Rosa '97 is also one of the best wines in its category. This is a very difficult wine to produce, but Plattner's displays all the aromatic qualities that belong to this varietal. The list is completed by the Cabernet Sauvignon '97, slightly disappointing given our high expectations (but we must consider its extreme youth), and the Terlano Pinot Bianco '98, which seemed to us to be the least impressive wine in the range.

● A. A. Lagrein Scuro Ris. '97	TT	5
● A. A. Moscato Rosa '97	TT	5
○ A. A. Pinot Grigio '98	TT	3*
● A. A. Santa Maddalena Cl. '98	TT	3*
● A. A. Cabernet Sauvignon '97	T	5
○ A. A. Terlano Pinot Bianco '98	T	4
● A. A. Cabernet Sauvignon '94	YY	5
● A. A. Cabernet Sauvignon '95	YY	5
● A. A. Cabernet Sauvignon '96	YY	5
● A. A. Lagrein Scuro '93	YY	4
● A. A. Lagrein Scuro '95	YY	4
● A. A. Lagrein Scuro Ris. '96	YY	4
○ A. A. Terlano Pinot Bianco '94	YY	4
● A. A. Moscato Rosa '96	Y	5
● A. A. Santa Maddalena Cl. '97	Y	3

BOLZANO/BOZEN

GEORG RAMOSER
LOC. S. MADDALENA
39100 BOLZANO/BOZEN
TEL. 0471/975481

Just last year he made his debut in the Guide, but young Georg Ramoser, vigneron of the Untermoserhof estate at Santa Maddalena, has not stopped there but has gone shooting up to the top. With two of his wines, Georg has recently stunned the world of wine, and not just in Alto Adige. With his first-ever Merlot, the '95, (from a mere half hectare or so of vines planted in 1992) he obtained his first notable success. In a Europe-wide tasting with famous Bordeaux wines, this red left a couple of its more illustrious French rivals in its wake; it is unusual in its richness, depth, ripeness, softness and length. The Merlot Riserva '97 is also a stunner. It has an intense ruby hue and a complex bouquet of blackberry, pencil lead and well-balanced oak. On the palate it is very full and concentrated, with close-knit, elegant tannins and a very impressive finish. This Merlot is a great wine, as is the Lagrein Riserva '97, which stood out at our tastings above all the other Lagreins from the zone. A deep ruby in color, it displays a fine, elegantly fruity bouquet, with well-integrated notes of new oak. The palate is concentrated, soft, sensuous, sweetly ripe and extremely persistent: there is nothing more we need to say. It just has to be tasted, this magnificent Lagrein from the Untermoserhof, but also the Santa Maddalena Classico '98, the other real house specialty. Of a brilliant intense ruby color, it has very fresh, lively fruit on the nose, and an intense, well-defined juicy palate. Congratulations, Georg!

● A. A. Lagrein Scuro Untermoserhof Ris. '97	TTT	4*
● A. A. Merlot Untermoserhof Ris. '97	TT	5
● A. A. Santa Maddalena Cl. Untermoserhof '98	TT	3*
● A. A. Lagrein Scuro Untermoserhof Ris. '95	YY	5
● A. A. Lagrein Scuro Untermoserhof Ris. '96	YY	4
● A. A. Merlot Untermoserhof '97	YY	5
● A. A. Santa Maddalena Cl. Untermoserhof '97	YY	3*

BOLZANO/BOZEN

HANS ROTTENSTEINER
VIA SARENTINO, 1/A
39100 BOLZANO/BOZEN
TEL. 0471/282015

The Santa Maddalena Premstallerhof, one of the stars of this small winery, made a good showing in this '98 version. No Pinot Grigio, indeed no white wines at all, at least among the samples that Rottensteiner chose to present to us: there were just four of his wines for us to judge, but they were four excellent proofs of the absolute reliability of this estate. The Schiava Gentile Kristplonerhof '98 is straightforward but very well made. It has a characteristic fragrant nose with fruity and delicately herbaceous notes, and the palate is light, appealing and very varietal. The Lagrein Grieser Select Riserva '96 is a great wine. As we have already said a number of times, this was not a very good vintage, but with the right procedures – particularly in the vineyard – it could be induced to yield some excellent results, as in this case. Neither richness nor concentration is in short supply. Much the same sort of thing can be said of the '96 Cabernet Select, another of this estate's classic wines. It may not have the structure of the '95, but the difference is not all that marked and all of the best varietal qualities are clearly and impressively expressed. This was a very good performance altogether, and Anton Rottensteiner is clearly one of the very best producers in the Bolzano area.

●	A. A. Cabernet Select '96	🍷🍷	5
●	A. A. Lagrein Scuro Grieser Select Ris. '96	🍷🍷	4
●	A. A. Schiava Gentile Kristplonerhof '98	🍷	2*
●	A. A. S. Maddalena Cl. Premstallerhof '98	🍷	3
●	A. A. Cabernet Select Ris. '90	🍷🍷 (white)	5
●	A. A. Cabernet Select Ris. '91	🍷🍷 (white)	4
●	A. A. Cabernet Select Ris. '93	🍷🍷 (white)	5
○	A. A. Chardonnay Select '90	🍷🍷 (white)	5
●	A. A. Lagrein Grieser Select Ris '94	🍷🍷 (white)	4
●	A. A. Lagrein Grieser Select Ris. '95	🍷🍷 (white)	4

BRESSANONE/BRIXEN (BZ)

KUEN HOF - PETER PLIEGER
LOC. MAHR, 110
39042 BRESSANONE/BRIXEN (BZ)
TEL. 0472/850546

Peter Plieger is one of the most dedicated and talented producers in the whole of Alto Adige, and his wines this year did not disappoint us. Plieger is also a standard-bearer of the problematic Isarco Valley zone, the northernmost vinegrowing area in the whole of Italy. The conditions are those of real northern viticulture (the situation is very similar to that of the Wachau in Austria or the Valais in Switzerland), so the varieties and vinification techniques used must be chosen accordingly; and here Plieger really shines. This year we tasted three of his wines, all '98s. They do make us wonder how Plieger manages to obtain such concentration under such difficult climatic conditions. His Sylvaner is just superb. It has power, well-structured fruit and an evident acidulous note which, however, does not get in the way or deprive the wine of body or richness. The bouquet is floral, delicately aromatic, and very elegant. One can say much the same about the Veltliner, which has a nose dominated by particularly well-defined floral and citrus notes. The Gewürztraminer is also notably aromatic and concentrated; this grape has found, as if by magic, a home away from home in these parts.

○	A. A. Valle Isarco Gewürztraminer '98	🍷🍷	4
○	A. A. Valle Isarco Sylvaner '98	🍷🍷	4
○	A. A. Valle Isarco Veltliner '98	🍷🍷	4
○	A. A. Valle Isarco Sylvaner '97	🍷🍷 (white)	4
○	A. A. Valle Isarco Veltliner '93	🍷🍷 (white)	4
○	A. A. Valle Isarco Veltliner '97	🍷🍷 (white)	4
○	Kaiton '97	🍷🍷 (white)	4
○	A. A. Valle Isarco Gewürztraminer '97	🍷 (white)	4

CALDARO/KALTERN (BZ)

CANTINA VITICOLTORI DI
CALDARO/KALTERN
VIA DELLE CANTINE, 12
39052 CALDARO/KALTERN (BZ)
TEL. 0471/963149

The Cantina Viticoltori di Caldaro has always been particularly renowned for its Cabernet Riserva, one of the best reds of the Alto Adige, but they did not release a '96 because the vintage was not considered worthy of such an outstanding wine. Taking its place as the star turn this year, however, is a sweet, aromatic white, the Serenade '95, made from semi-dried moscato giallo grapes, a wine of extraordinary breeding and concentration. But the rest of the range was really remarkable as well, starting with the simpler wines like the Lago di Caldaro Scelto Pfarrhof '98 (the best of its type) and the Sauvignon Premstallerhof '98, in which some varietal characteristics are sacrificed on the nose in order to achieve, by means of more marked ripeness, greater power and concentration on the palate. The red and white Campaner wines, a '96 Cabernet Sauvignon and a '98 Gewürztraminer, again showed well. The former contains, among others, the grapes that normally go into the Cabernet Riserva. Last but not least, the Chardonnay Wadleith '98 displays its usual excellent rich, rounded palate, and a particularly well-defined fruity, varietal bouquet overlaid with a delicate but perceptible vanilla tone.

○	A. A. Goldmuskateller Passito Serenade '95	TTT	6
●	A. A. Cabernet Sauvignon Campaner Ris. '96	TT	5
○	A. A. Chardonnay Wadleith '98	TT	4
○	A. A. Gewürztraminer Campaner '98	TT	4
●	A. A. Lago di Caldaro Pfarrhof '98	TT	4
○	A. A. Pinot Bianco Vial '98	TT	4
●	A. A. Pinot Nero Ris. '97	TT	5
●	A. A. Pinot Nero Saltnerhof '97	TT	5
○	A. A. Sauvignon Premstalerhof '98	TT	4
○	A. A. Gewürztraminer '98	T	3
●	A. A. Cabernet Sauvignon Ris. '93	YYY	5
●	A. A. Cabernet Sauvignon Ris. '95	YYY	5

CALDARO/KALTERN (BZ)

CASTEL SALLEGG - GRAF KUENBURG
V.LO DI SOTTO, 15
39052 CALDARO/KALTERN (BZ)
TEL. 0471/963132

We only actually judged three wines from this estate: others were presented, but in the form of barrel samples that displayed all the faults of excessively young wines, so we shall taste them again next year. We were impressed by the three wines we did try, however, an indication that the progress we noted last year has now become part and parcel of the ethos of this historic and prestigious Alto Adige producer. The Merlot '97 is very good. It shows the power and richness that the Caldaro sub-zone is capable of yielding in its reds: intense varietal aromas with hints of tobacco, pencil lead and berries, a characterful, concentrated and already quite soft palate and remarkably fine tannic structure. It earned Two Glasses with ease. The Gewürztraminer '98 is decidedly interesting, with its characteristic aromatic bouquet and, thanks in part to a little residual sugar, a strikingly full flavor. The Terlano Pinot Bianco '98 is sound, and quite varietal on the nose, but certainly not huge in terms of body. The celebrated Moscato Rosa, from the '95 vintage, was a bit below par. The bottles we were sent for tasting seemed somewhat forward on the nose. This may have been caused by rather disappointing corks, so we'll suspend judgment.

○	A. A. Gewürztraminer '98	TT	4
●	A. A. Merlot '97	TT	5
○	A. A. Terlano Pinot Bianco '98	T	4
●	A. A. Cabernet '90	YY	4
●	A. A. Cabernet '95	YY	5
○	A. A. Gewürztraminer '97	YY	3*
●	A. A. Lago di Caldaro Scelto Bischofsleiten '93	YY	4
●	A. A. Merlot '95	YY	5
●	A. A. Moscato Rosa '91	YY	6
●	A. A. Moscato Rosa '93	YY	6
●	A. A. Moscato Rosa '90	YY	6
○	A. A. Pinot Grigio '93	YY	4

Graf Enzenberg
Tenuta Manincor

S. Giuseppe al Lago, 4
39052 Caldaro/Kaltern (BZ)
tel. 0471/960043

The sub-zone of Caldaro is one of the most enchanting winegrowing areas of Alto Adige. The vineyards sweep down to the shores of the small lake, a sort of Mediterranean enclave in the middle of the Tyrolean mountains, and bask in an ideal microclimate for making fine, full-bodied reds and occasionally also for growing aromatic varieties like moscato rosa and gewürztraminer. One of the most handsome properties is the Tenuta Manincor of Graf (Count) Enzenberg. It is a fine estate, but this year it's also a great and delightful surprise, since it waltzed off with Three Glasses for its masterly Cabernet Cassiano '97, perhaps the year's best red in the whole of Alto Adige. This is a massive and extremely concentrated wine, with dense tannins that are, however, completely enveloped by the soft, velvety fruit on the palate. Our tasting panel was simply stunned, and gave it the ovation inspired only by the very finest of wines. This is a really remarkable success for a winery which last year was not even in the Guide. Besides this monument of, and to, wine-making in the Alto Adige, there is also an excellent Lago di Caldaro '98, a soft, quaffable, inviting wine, ideal for serving at cellar temperature with the best local speck (a smoky prosciutto). The very impressive Pinot Nero '97 comes from the splendid sub-zone of Mason, the best of all for this variety. The range is completed by the Terlano Pinot Bianco '98, which, with its fruity and slightly acidulous palate, shows clearly that the estate's true vocation is to make red wines.

●	A. A. Cabernet Sauvignon Cassiano '97	▼▼▼	5
●	A. A. Lago di Caldaro Scelto '98	▼▼	4
●	A. A. Pinot Nero Mason '97	▼▼	5
○	A. A. Terlano Pinot Bianco '98	▼	4

CALDARO/KALTERN (BZ)

Kettmeir

Via delle Cantine, 4
39052 Caldaro/Kaltern (BZ)
tel. 0471/963135

After a year in the "purgatory" of the "Other Wineries" section this large winery owned by the Marzotto-Santa Margherita group is back in the Guide. It has returned with a series of successful wines that reveal good cellar technique, pleasing qualities and a ready availability on the market. These are all points to be considered, because even if they are in part unconnected with the intrinsic quality of the wines, they do make a difference to would-be consumers. But let's get down to detail. The Cabernet Maso Castello '95 showed especially well: it has body, and particularly well-defined varietal characteristics on the nose. The Pinot Grigio Reinerhof '98 is good yet again; this is perhaps their most representative wine, always keeping up standards even in lesser years. The Chardonnay Reinerhof '98 was more than satisfactory, and the Gewürztraminer '98 was actually a pleasant surprise: it is varietal and well executed, if a little lacking in body. Since the Guide came into being, this is Kettmeirs' best range, a fact that is certainly worthy of note.

●	A. A. Cabernet Sauvignon Maso Castello '95	▼▼	4
○	A. A. Chardonnay Reinerhof '98	▼	3
○	A. A. Gewürztraminer '98	▼	3
●	A. A. Lago di Caldaro Classico '98	▼	3
○	A. A. Pinot Grigio Reinerhof '98	▼	3
●	A. A. Cabernet Sauvignon Maso Castello '92	▽▽	4
○	A. A. Chardonnay Maso Reiner '95	▽▽	3*
●	A. A. Cabernet Sauvignon Maso Castello '91	▽	3
○	A. A. Pinot Grigio Maso Reiner '96	▽	3
○	A. A. Pinot Grigio Maso Reiner '97	▽	3
○	A. A. Sauvignon '96	▽	3

CALDARO/KALTERN (BZ)

PRIMA & NUOVA/ERSTE & NEUE
VIA DELLE CANTINE, 5
39052 CALDARO/KALTERN (BZ)
TEL. 0471/963122

Wines you can count on: that could be the motto of this splendid cooperative winery at Caldaro. And you can see why if you glance at the bottom of the page. Of the nine samples presented, seven won Two Glasses, a remarkable achievement that completely overshadows the fact that none of the wines made it to Three. From the vast and excellent range we've selected a few bottles that are particularly worthy of comment. The excellent Chardonnay Salt '98 displays delicate vanilla and fruity tones on the nose and a positive, concentrated palate; besides, it's quite a bargain. The very good Lago di Caldaro Scelto Puntay '98 is one of the best wines in its category: it is vinous yet fruity, and deliciously quaffable. The '98 vintage of the Gewürztraminer Puntay, one of their top wines, did not reconquer the Three Glasses that the '97 got last year, but it did very well all the same. It reveals some residual sugar within an imposing structure that seems, however, less concentrated than its predecessor's. Then there is the, as usual, exuberantly fruity and delicious Pinot Bianco Brunar '98 and the Anthos '96, a very elegant, aromatic sweet white. Among the still quite youthful reds, both the Cabernet Puntay '96 and the Pinot Nero Mezzan '97 are well made and varietal, if not overwhelmingly full-bodied.

●	A. A. Cabernet Puntay '96	**YY**	4
○	A. A. Chardonnay Salt '98	**YY**	3*
○	A. A. Gewürztraminer Puntay '98	**YY**	4
●	A. A. Lago di Caldaro Scelto Puntay '98	**YY**	3*
○	A. A. Pinot Bianco Brunar '98	**YY**	3*
●	A. A. Pinot Nero Mezzan '97	**YY**	4
○	Anthos '96	**YY**	6
○	A. A. Pinot Bianco Puntay '98	**Y**	3
○	A. A. Sauvignon Stern '98	**Y**	3
○	A. A. Gewürztraminer Puntay '97	YYY	4*
●	A. A. Cabernet Puntay '94	YY	5
●	A. A. Cabernet Puntay '95	YY	5
●	A. A. Lago di Caldaro Scelto Leuchtenburg '97	YY	4

CARDANO/KARDAUN (BZ)

JOSEPHUS MAYR
ERBHOF UNTERGANZNER
VIA CAMPIGLIO, 15
39053 CARDANO/KARDAUN (BZ)
TEL. 0471/365582

Josephus Mayr is a role model for the young winegrowers of Alto Adige. He works at his Unterganzner farm (which has belonged to his family since 1629) in Cardano, at the easternmost end of the Bolzano basin, cultivating his six hectares of vineyards situated right by the banks of the Isarco. Josephus is a vigneron who knows what he's about, and he's about it from dawn till dusk. In his quest for quality he follows organic farming methods and rigorously reduces yields. (And, incidentally, we are quite curious about his olive oil, too, which comes from the very first olive grove in Alto Adige, where, over the last two years, he has planted and nurtured about a hundred trees.) Concentration and depth: these are definitely the main characteristics of all of his wines. For proof, just taste his Lamarein '97, a table wine made in part from semi-dried lagrein grapes. Though still very youthful and firmly tannic, it displays extraordinary concentration on both nose and palate. The Lagrein Scuro '98 is similarly full-bodied, powerful and rich, and it offers a particular strawberry note. The Unterganznerhof blend, the Composition Reif '97, also has a very deep, concentrated ruby color. This is a soft, full-bodied table wine with close-knit tannins and a stunning finish. Two other classics in Josephus Mayr's range are his Lagrein Rosé '98, sporting extremely delicate fruity aromas and an elegant structure – definitely one of the best rosés from the Alto Adige -, and his stupendous Santa Maddalena Classico '98, a small masterpiece from a vintage that did not really favor this kind of wine.

⊙	A. A. Lagrein Rosato '98	**YY**	2*
●	A. A. Lagrein Scuro '98	**YY**	3*
●	A. A. Santa Maddalena Cl. '98	**YY**	3*
●	Composition Reif '97	**YY**	5
●	Lamarein '97	**YY**	5
●	A. A. Cabernet Sauvignon '95	YY	5
●	A. A. Cabernet Sauvignon '96	YY	5
⊙	A. A. Lagrein Rosato V. T. '97	YY	4
●	A. A. Lagrein Scuro Ris. '93	YY	5
●	A. A. Lagrein Scuro Ris. '94	YY	5
●	A. A. Lagrein Scuro Ris. '95	YY	5
●	A. A. Lagrein Scuro Ris. '96	YY	5
●	Composition Reif '95	YY	5
●	A. A. Lagrein Scuro '97	Y	3
●	A. A. Santa Maddalena Cl. '97	Y	3

CERMES/TSCHERMS (BZ)

GRAF PFEIL WEINGUT KRÄNZEL
VIA PALADE, 1
39010 CERMES/TSCHERMS (BZ)
TEL. 0473/564549

Which is the best Schiava in all of Alto Adige? The answer is to be found in the cellar of the Kränzel estate at Cermes, not far from Merano. It is a delicious fruity Schiava, with scents that seem the very essence of red currant and mountain herbs, and a full but not heavy palate: a thorough delight. This is a wine to be drunk in industrial quantities, as Nereo Pederzolli, the well-known Italian television commentator on matters agricultural (and long-time contributor to the Guide) would say. Faced with a wine like this, he could very easily lose his sang-froid because, as he is wont to comment, quality is fine, but quantity isn't bad either! But moving on to more complex wines, we find that the Kränzel estate can hold its own in this category too. Indeed their Pinot Bianco probably beats every other one in the region. The '98 made it to our finals and missed Three Glasses by a whisker. It is a very fruity and varietal white with a structure not usually to be found from this grape. The Dorado '97, again from pinot bianco grapes (but this time semi-dried), made a fine showing in the sweet wine section. It too displays excellent body and it's not at all cloying. We were, however, somewhat puzzled by the '97 Pinot Nero, from which we expected far more. Instead it was merely satisfactory and showed signs of overripeness on the nose.

○ A. A. Pinot Bianco Et. Nera '98	🍷🍷	4
● A. A. Schiava '98	🍷🍷	3*
○ Dorado '97	🍷🍷	5
● A. A. Pinot Nero '97	🍷	5
○ A. A. Pinot Bianco '95	🍷🍷 (empty)	4
○ A. A. Pinot Bianco '96	🍷🍷 (empty)	4
● A. A. Pinot Nero '95	🍷🍷 (empty)	5
○ A. A. Sauvignon '95	🍷🍷 (empty)	4
○ Dorado '94	🍷🍷 (empty)	5
○ Dorado '95	🍷🍷 (empty)	5
● Sagittarius '95	🍷🍷 (empty)	5
● Sagittarius '96	🍷🍷 (empty)	5
● A. A. Meranese Hügel '95	🍷 (empty)	3
● A. A. Meranese Hügel '97	🍷 (empty)	3

CHIUSA/KLAUSEN (BZ)

CANTINA PRODUTTORI VALLE ISARCO/
EISACKTALER
LOC. COSTE, 60
39043 CHIUSA/KLAUSEN (BZ)
TEL. 0472/847553

We were expecting a confirmation of recently achieved good levels, and instead we found a delightful surprise! The Cantina Produttori Valle Isarco is set to take a leading role in the Alto Adige wine-making scene and the range it presented this year shows it. We'll start with the only red, the Valle Isarco Klausner Laitacher, a blend of schiava, lagrein and portugieser. It is just a medium-bodied red, certainly, but its bouquet is remarkably fragrant and its flavor is delicate, stylish and thoroughly enjoyable. Then there is a trio of Sylvaners, of which one, the Dominus '98, is even aged in barriques: an experiment, however, with which we are not in total agreement. The Sylvaner in the Aristos line, on the other hand, is excellent: elegant, powerful and concentrated. The '98 Pinot Grigio is very good, too, but this is nothing new. The distinct varietal aromas of pear are evident and well expressed, and the palate is full-flavored and reasonably concentrated. The Müller Thurgau Aristos '98 is stunning – perhaps the best in its category this year. There is not much more to add, except that this cooperative stands out for the breadth and truly laudable reliability of the range it offers and for the excellent value for money of all its wines. And these are no small matters.

● A. A. Valle Isarco Klausener Laitacher '98	🍷🍷	3*
○ A. A. Valle Isarco Müller Thurgau Aristos '98	🍷🍷	3*
○ A. A. Valle Isarco Pinot Grigio '98	🍷🍷	3*
○ A. A. Valle Isarco Sylvaner Aristos '98	🍷🍷	3*
○ A. A. Chardonnay '98	🍷	2*
○ A. A. Valle Isarco Müller Thurgau '98	🍷	2*
○ A. A. Valle Isarco Sylvaner '98	🍷	2*
○ A. A. Valle Isarco Sylvaner Dominus '98	🍷	3
○ A. A. Valle Isarco Veltliner '98	🍷	3

CORNAIANO/GIRLAN (BZ)

CANTINA PRODUTTORI
COLTERENZIO/SCHRECKBICHL
STRADA DEL VINO, 8
39050 CORNAIANO/GIRLAN (BZ)
TEL. 0471/664246

This is a great repeat performance and further proof that this splendid Alto Adige winery is now one of the most important producers in Italy. You need but look at this year's ratings and recall those of the wines released in previous years (starting with the '90 vintage) to get a good idea of what goes on here. A great deal of the credit is due to their president, Luis Raifer, a leading figure on the Alto Adige wine scene, who has been running this cooperative winery with great intelligence. There were no fewer than nine wines up for judging this year. Our highest award goes to an exemplary version of the Chardonnay Cornell, the '97, fruit of an early and rather good vintage. Its fermentation in small casks can be detected in the still present faint toasty tone and hints of vanilla that lightly veil the intense fruity (plum and pineapple) notes, and bode well for the development on the nose over the next two or three years. On the palate it is fat, powerful and concentrated, with a notable bite of acidity that nicely offsets the rich softness, and the finish is satisfyingly long. There are also excellent versions of the Sauvignon Lafoa '98, the Gewürztraminer Cornell '98, the Chardonnay Coret '98 and the Cornelius Bianco '97. The two premium reds, the Merlot Siebeneich Riserva '96 and especially the Cabernet Sauvignon Lafoa '96, are a bit below par, coming as they did from a not exactly exceptional vintage. The potent and characterful Lagrein Cornell '97 is much more impressive. The Sauvignon Prail and the Pinot Bianco Weisshaus, both '98s, are sound, well made and varietal.

○	A. A. Chardonnay Cornell '97	3 black glasses	5
●	A. A. Cabernet Sauvignon Lafoa '96	2 black glasses	6
○	A. A. Chardonnay Coret '98	2 black glasses	4
○	A. A. Gewürztraminer Cornell '98	2 black glasses	5
●	A. A. Lagrein Cornell '97	2 black glasses	5
●	A. A. Merlot Siebeneich Ris. '96	2 black glasses	5
●	A. A. Moscato Rosa Cornell '97	2 black glasses	6
○	A. A. Sauvignon Lafoa '98	2 black glasses	5
○	Cornelius Bianco '97	2 black glasses	5
○	A. A. Pinot Bianco Weisshaus '98	1 black glass	4
○	A. A. Sauvignon Prail '98	1 black glass	4
●	A. A. Cabernet Sauvignon Lafoa '91	3 white glasses	6
●	A. A. Cabernet Sauvignon Lafoa '92	3 white glasses	6
●	A. A. Cabernet Sauvignon Lafoa '94	3 white glasses	6
●	A. A. Cabernet Sauvignon Lafoa '95	3 white glasses	6

CORNAIANO/GIRLAN (BZ)

CANTINA PRODUTTORI
CORNAIANO/GIRLAN
VIA S. MARTINO, 24
39050 CORNAIANO/GIRLAN (BZ)
TEL. 0471/662403

The Cantina Produttori di Cornaiano is one of the stalwarts of wine-making in Alto Adige. Every year it offers wines that are at the very least well made, thoroughly dependable and available at fair prices. We only wish there were some real champions, prize-winners that really make a name for a producer. We cannot believe that the Cornaiano winery does not have some absolutely first-class lots of wine (perhaps from particular vineyard sites) that could compete with the top bottles of the region. Theirs must, therefore, be a deliberate choice in favor of uniformity and reliability year after year. And it's a perfectly respectable choice, too, although, in our heart of hearts, we would prefer to find a truly outstanding wine under the Cornaiano label. For the moment there is an enjoyable Cabernet Riserva '97, varietal and concentrated, as well as the usual amazing Schiava Gschleier, the '98 this time, a little gem but, nevertheless, still just a Schiava, with the limited structure that such a wine inevitably possesses. Then there is a good Lagrein Riserva '97, one of the best they've ever produced. All in all, not a bad showing, but we know they could do even better.

●	A. A. Cabernet Sauvignon Ris. '97	2 black glasses	5
●	A. A. Lagrein Ris. '97	2 black glasses	5
●	A. A. Schiava Fass N. 9 '98	2 black glasses	3*
●	A. A. Schiava Gschleier '97	2 black glasses	4
○	A. A. Gewürztraminer Optimum '98	1 black glass	3
○	A. A. Pinot Bianco '98	1 black glass	3
○	A. A. Pinot Grigio Vinum '98	1 black glass	3
●	A. A. Pinot Nero Trattmannhof '97	1 black glass	5
○	A. A. Sauvignon Optimum '98	1 black glass	3
●	A. A. Cabernet Optimum '90	2 white glasses	5
●	A. A. Cabernet Optimum '92	2 white glasses	4
●	A. A. Cabernet Optimum '93	2 white glasses	5
●	A. A. Cabernet Optimum '95	2 white glasses	5
●	A. A. Cabernet Sauvignon Ris. '96	2 white glasses	5
●	A. A. Schiava Gschleier '96	2 white glasses	5

CORNAIANO/GIRLAN (BZ)

K. MARTINI & SOHN
VIA LAMM WEG, 28
39050 CORNAIANO/GIRLAN (BZ)
TEL. 0471/663156

Gabriel Martini's range of wines this year is, as always, very good, but there were one or two disappointments in the shape of the Pinot Nero '97 and the Gewürztraminer '98, bottles about which we are reserving judgment. All the others are fine, and the splendid Cabernet-Lagrein Palladium Coldirus '97, a signature wine of this producer, deserves special mention. It provides further evidence of how these two varieties can complement each other, showing noteworthy balance and complexity when blended. The intriguing Lagrein Maturum '97, favored by its vintage, is a powerful, rich red with an unusually concentrated color and the classic bouquet of black currant and ink. The extremely well executed '98 Chardonnay Palladium is less impressive than the '97: it doesn't have the same intensity but does have fairly clear and well-defined varietal aromas. The Lago di Caldaro Classico Felton '98, on the other hand, was up to par and earns One Glass once more thanks to the evident technical skill that went into making it. The sound Lagrein Scuro Rueslhof '97 is less intense than the Maturum and also less suitable for lengthy aging.

●	A. A. Cabernet-Lagrein Palladium Coldirus '97	🍷🍷	5
●	A. A. Lagrein Scuro Maturum '97	🍷🍷	5
○	A. A. Chardonnay Palladium '98	🍷	3
●	A. A. Lago di Caldaro Cl. Felton '98	🍷	3
●	A. A. Lagrein Scuro Rueslhof '97	🍷	5
●	A. A. Cabernet-Lagrein Palladium Coldirus '94	YY	4
●	A. A. Cabernet-Lagrein Palladium Coldirus '95	YY	5
○	A. A. Chardonnay Palladium '97	YY	3*
●	A. A. Lagrein Scuro Maturum '95	YY	5
●	A. A. Lagrein Scuro Rueslhof '95	YY	5

CORNAIANO/GIRLAN (BZ)

JOSEF NIEDERMAYR
VIA CASA DI GESU, 15
39050 CORNAIANO/GIRLAN (BZ)
TEL. 0471/662451

Our congratulations to Josef Niedermayr and to his talented oenologist Lorenz Martini: these names are now synonymous with continuity and quality in the wine world of Alto Adige. This year they have once again presented some fabulous wines. Two of these came within an inch of getting Three Glasses. The '97 Aureus, a passito (raisin wine) made from chardonnay, pinot bianco and sauvignon, is a real treat. It is extraordinarily complex on the nose, with rich notes of noble rot, honey and caramel; the palate displays beautiful balance and restraint. The excellent Lagrein Gries Riserva '96 is one of the very best Lagreins from the Alto Adige. It has a rich ruby hue and a delicate bouquet of fruit with a toasty ground bass. It is powerful, intense and appealingly soft on the palate, and has a long delightful finish. We were impressed by the Euforius '97 as well, the estate's elegant red blend, although it is less vigorous. The successful Santa Maddalena Classico Egger–Larcher Hof '98 is a fruity, soft red with notable structure, and is definitely one of the best examples of its kind from the area. The complex and well-balanced Schiava Ascherhof '98 seemed very enjoyable. As for the other wines, the Lagrein Gries Blacedelle '98 is fair, while the '97 Pinot Nero Riserva was not, at our tastings, fully ready. The estate whites, too, the Sauvignon Lage Naun and the Terlano Hof zu Pramol, both '98s, are properly made.

●	A. A. Lagrein Gries Ris. '96	🍷🍷	4
●	A. A. Santa Maddalena Cl. Egger-Larcher Hof '98	🍷🍷	3*
●	A. A. Schiava Ascherhof '98	🍷🍷	3*
○	Aureus '97	🍷🍷	5
●	Euforius '97	🍷🍷	5
●	A. A. Lagrein Gries Blacedelle '98	🍷	3
●	A. A. Pinot Nero Ris. '97	🍷	3
○	A. A. Sauvignon Lage Naun '98	🍷	4
○	A. A. Terlano Hof zu Pramol '98	🍷	4
○	Aureus '95	YYY	5
●	A. A. Cabernet Ris. '94	YY	5
●	A. A. Lagrein Gries Ris. '95	YY	4
○	Aureus '96	YY	5
●	Euforius '94	YY	5

CORNAIANO/GIRLAN (BZ)

IGNAZ NIEDRIST
VIA RONCO, 4
39050 CORNAIANO/GIRLAN (BZ)
TEL. 0471/664494

Riesling and pinot nero have always been Ignaz Niedrist's favorite grapes, the ones with which this extraordinarily sensitive winegrower is most comfortable. We recall some really intriguing wines he has made from them in the past, a point worth underlining because these are very difficult wines to make and are, to add insult to injury, inevitably compared with the best bottles from the Mosel, Alsace, and Burgundy, which can be discouraging. This year, neither Niedrist's Riesling nor his Pinot Nero seemed as successful as some of their predecessors. Difficult vintages? Perhaps so, although for contrasting reasons: '97 was too hot for the Pinot Nero and in '98 the weather was not constant enough for the Riesling. The upshot: these are well-made wines, but without much varietal character. A splendid Sauvignon '98, however, brings us back to Neidrist's normal high level: it very nearly earned Three Glasses. It's a formidable wine with decidedly varietal aromas: slightly funky and fruity scents, with hints of tomato leaf and white-fleshed peach. On the palate it is full-flavored and deliciously concentrated, showing a tangy acidulous bite. It made us breathe a sigh of relief and gives us good reason to express once again all the admiration we feel for this highly talented producer from Cornaiano.

○	A. A. Terlano Sauvignon '98	🍷🍷	4
●	A. A. Pinot Nero '97	🍷	5
○	A. A. Riesling Renano '98	🍷	4
●	A. A. Pinot Nero '91	YY	5
●	A. A. Pinot Nero '92	YY	4
●	A. A. Pinot Nero '93	YY	4
●	A. A. Pinot Nero '95	YY	4
●	A. A. Pinot Nero '96	YY	4
○	A. A. Riesling Renano '93	YY	4
○	A. A. Riesling Renano '95	YY	4
○	A. A. Riesling Renano '96	YY	4
○	A. A. Riesling Renano '97	YY	4
●	A. A. Lagrein Berger Gei '93	Y	4
●	A. A. Pinot Nero '94	Y	4
○	A. A. Terlano Pinot Bianco '97	Y	4

CORTACCIA/KURTATSCH (BZ)

CANTINA PRODUTTORI CORTACCIA
STRADA DEL VINO, 23
39040 CORTACCIA/KURTATSCH (BZ)
TEL. 0471/880115

Arnold Terzer, the dynamic director of this cooperative winery, should be pleased with the results achieved by his wines in this edition of the Guide. Even without the most representative and prestigious bottle, the Cabernet Freienfeld, which they didn't produce because they didn't consider the '96 vintage up to scratch, they still managed to capture Three Glasses with the Merlot Brenntal '97, and the rest of the range on offer was not at all bad either. It's as if the Inter team had managed to win the championship without Vieri or Ronaldo. The Brenntal, in its third appearance, (the first, the '95, immediately claimed our highest award) has become a real classic of its type. Indeed this '97 proved one of the best Merlots – if not the very best – from Alto Adige. It offers its customary elegantly fruity nose, with faint mineral notes and hints of pencil lead, tobacco and black currant. On the palate it displays extraordinary finesse, and its tannins are rich yet soft, and not at all rough. But for once we should also like to focus on another red from this winery. We are talking about the Cabernet Kirchhügel '97, the "deputy" Freienfeld. This vintage seemed to us the best they've ever produced, and its price is therefore staggeringly modest. All the other wines were good and well made; the Lagrein Scuro Forhof '97, another standard-bearer of this cooperative, deserves special mention.

●	A. A. Merlot Brenntal '97	🍷🍷🍷	5
●	A. A. Cabernet Kirchhügel '97	🍷🍷	4*
●	A. A. Lagrein Scuro Forhof '97	🍷🍷	4
○	A. A. Chardonnay Felsenhof '98	🍷	3
●	A. A. Pinot Nero Fritzen Hof '97	🍷	5
●	A. A. Pinot Nero Vorhof '97	🍷	5
○	A. A. Sauvignon '98	🍷	3
●	A. A. Schiava Grigia Sonntaler '98	🍷	2*
●	A. A. Cabernet Freienfeld '92	YYY	5
●	A. A. Cabernet Freienfeld '95	YYY	6
●	A. A. Cabernet Freienfeld Ris. '90	YYY	6
●	A. A. Merlot Brenntal '95	YYY	5
●	A. A. Cabernet Kirchhügel '96	YY	4
●	A. A. Merlot Brenntal '96	YY	5

CORTACCIA/KURTATSCH (BZ)

Tiefenbrunner

Loc. Niclara
Via Castello, 4
39040 Cortaccia/Kurtatsch (BZ)
tel. 0471/880122

Those two wondeful winegrowers from Cortaccia, Herbert and Cristof Tiefenbrunner, may have presented their best series ever this year: confident technical skill was evident in a vast range of excellent wines, with a few examples of outstanding excellence. There are no Three Glass bottles yet, but it's just a matter of time and good fortune, because they already come very close. This year, though, we offer a recommendation to our readers: try the Lagrein Scuro '97. Not the Riserva 150 Jahre '96, good as it is, but the basic Lagrein, a wine which, incidentally, does not cost a punishing amount of money. It's a stunner. It may lack great complexity, but its structure, concentration and persistence on the palate are those of a real champion. There are few winegrowing areas in the world where you can find red wines of this quality at such good prices. Almost the same thing, mutatis mutandis, might be said about the deliciously fruity and surprisingly full-bodied Chardonnay '98, or about the Gewürztraminer '98, which is aromatic, characteristic and not dominated by residual sugar. Among their other particularly interesting wines, the Moscato Rosa Linticlarus '97, one of the best in its category, should not be neglected. It has the classic bouquet of rose hip, and the palate, not content with being merely sweet, mirrors the elegant fragrance perfectly right on through the finish. All the other wines performed well, and the Linticlarus Cuvée '97 (lagrein and cabernet sauvignon) is in particularly good form.

●	A. A. Cabernet Sauvignon Linticlarus '96	🍷🍷	5
○	A. A. Chardonnay '98	🍷🍷	3*
○	A. A. Gewürztraminer '98	🍷🍷	3*
●	A. A. Lagrein Scuro '97	🍷🍷	4
●	A. A. Lagrein Scuro 150 Jahre Ris. '96	🍷🍷	5
●	A. A. Moscato Rosa Linticlarus '97	🍷🍷	5
●	Linticlarus Cuvée '97	🍷🍷	5
○	A. A. Sauvignon Kirchleiten '98	🍷	3
●	A. A. Cabernet Sauvignon Linticlarus '95	YY	5
●	Linticlarus Cuvée '96	YY	5

CORTACCIA/KURTATSCH (BZ)

Baron Widmann

Via Im Feld, 1
39040 Cortaccia/Kurtatsch (BZ)
tel. 0471/880092

When we happen to sample an extraordinary wine in one of our blind tastings, the excitement of the members of the tasting panel is always palpable. If then, when we uncover the bottles, we find that the producer of the wine is known to be a diligent, skilled and impassioned vigneron, our pleasure and satisfaction at being able to give him our highest award makes up for the fatigue and stress of long hours spent tasting and evaluating wines: in other words, it makes it all seem worthwhile. This was certainly the case with the Cabernet-Merlot Auhof '97 made by Andreas Widmann, a young wine-maker whose blue blood is pumped by a true farmer's heart. This year he has really given us all a superb red, a minor masterpiece of viticulture and wine-making, a dream in a 75cl. bottle. As we write, we recall most vividly the elegantly fruity bouquet, with its notes of pencil lead, black currant, vanilla and, in the background, leather, and then that velvety, well-balanced palate, those even, smooth tannins and the harmonious, aristocratic finish. Andreas' other wines – his fragrant Schiava '98 and his appealing '98 Sauvignon – good as they are, really pale by comparison, so we mention them only briefly. We're left with the memory of that great red wine and the hope that we shall have the chance to taste it many more times.

●	A. A. Cabernet-Merlot Auhof '97	🍷🍷🍷	5
○	A. A. Pinot Bianco '98	🍷	3
○	A. A. Sauvignon '98	🍷	3
●	A. A. Schiava '98	🍷	2*
●	A. A. Cabernet Feld '91	YYY	5
●	A. A. Merlot '93	YYY	5
●	A. A. Cabernet Feld '90	YY	5
●	A. A. Cabernet Feld '93	YY	5
●	A. A. Cabernet Feld '95	YY	5
●	A. A. Cabernet Sauvignon '90	YY	4
●	A. A. Merlot '91	YY	4
●	A. A. Merlot '92	YY	5
●	A. A. Merlot '94	YY	5
●	A. A. Merlot '95	YY	5
●	Rot '95	YY	5

CORTINA/KURTINIG (BZ)

PETER ZEMMER
STRADA DEL VINO, 24
39040 CORTINA/KURTINIG (BZ)
TEL. 0471/817143

Peter Zemmer has produced nothing but Two Glass wines this year: hence it's not just that his range is reliable, but that he has achieved a level of quality that few producers can boast, in Alto Adige or anywhere else. Our only hesitation was about the '97 Chardonnay Barrique, which was simply too young to be evaluated properly. We'll be tasting it again next year. Everything else was unquestionably excellent, starting with the basic Chardonnay '98, the wine that, more than any other, shows how constant Zemmer's high quality is. As usual, it offers a delightfully fruity and varietal nose and very good structure on the palate for its type. It is a stylish, balanced and varietal Alto Adige Chardonnay worth every penny it costs and then some. The admirable Lagrein Scuro '97 made excellent use of its propitious vintage. It is a typical Lagrein: concentrated, powerful, intriguing but not too demanding. The splendid Cabernet–Lagrein '96, meanwhile, was not hampered in the least by a generally not very helpful vintage, further proof of the natural affinity of these two grapes. Lastly, the '97 Merlot is fantastic, full-bodied, deep…a real abundance of riches!

●	A. A. Cabernet-Lagrein '96	▼▼	5
○	A. A. Chardonnay '98	▼▼	3*
●	A. A. Lagrein Scuro '97	▼▼	4
●	A. A. Merlot '97	▼▼	5
●	A. A. Cabernet-Lagrein '95	▽▽	5
○	A. A. Chardonnay '96	▽▽	3*
○	A. A. Chardonnay '97	▽▽	3*
○	A. A. Chardonnay Barrique '96	▽▽	4
●	A. A. Merlot '96	▽	3
○	A. A. Pinot Grigio '96	▽	3
○	A. A. Pinot Grigio '97	▽	3
○	A. A. Riesling '96	▽	3
○	A. A. Sauvignon '96	▽	3

MAGRE/MARGREID (BZ)

ALOIS LAGEDER
TENUTA LÖWENGANG
39040 MAGRE/MARGREID (BZ)
TEL. 0471/809500

For the second year running Alois Lageder saw fit not to send us his wines. In an interview he gave to a German-language Alto Adige weekly he described us as 'arrogant'. And he's absolutely right: we "arrogate" to ourselves the right to express, quite freely, our own opinions. This year, though, for that very reason, we decided to buy his wines from his wine shop in Bolzano, where they had been stored with the same care as those we'd have had, if he'd sent them, from his cellar. And, lest you should think us interested in some sort of revenge, we'll say at once that we found his wines to be very good. Some of them, in fact, were so good that they made it to our final round of tastings. So we hope to be able to gain his trust once more. Arrogant as we are (and who is entirely without faults?), what interests us is first-class wine, and Lageder has been producing some for many years. In our opinion the best one this time is the Cabernet Sauvignon Cor Römigberg '95, a little gem that missed Three Glasses only because the nose was just a bit dumb. These things happen. On the palate, though, it was the equal of a great Bordeaux. The Cabernet Löwengang '95 is a shade more dilute and has a faintly bitter finish. The Sauvignon Lehenhof '97, produced in the Terlano district, is splendid, one of the best from the region: it is varietal, elegant and concentrated, but not particularly full-bodied. The Chardonnay Löwengang '96, the most classic of Lageder's whites, is as good and reliable as ever, though a bit lean, and a little forward on the nose. Lastly, the Pinot Nero Krafuss '96 is pleasant, fairly straightforward, and easy to drink.

●	A. A. Cabernet Löwengang '95	▼▼	6
●	A. A. Cabernet Sauvignon Cor Romigberg '95	▼▼	6
○	A. A. Chardonnay Löwengang '96	▼▼	5
○	A. A. Terlano Sauvignon Lehenhof '97	▼▼	5
●	A. A. Pinot Nero Krafuss '96	▼	4
●	A. A. Cabernet Löwengang '92	▽▽▽	5
●	A. A. Cabernet Sauvignon Cor Romigberg '90	▽▽▽	6
○	A. A. Pinot Bianco Haberlerhof '93	▽▽▽	5
●	A. A. Cabernet Sauvignon Cor Romigberg '93	▽▽	6
●	A. A. Pinot Nero Mazzon Ris. '95	▽▽	5

MARLENGO/MARLING (BZ)

Cantina Produttori Burggräfler

Via Palade, 64
39020 Marlengo/Marling (BZ)
tel. 0473/447137

The Burgraviate is a sub-region of the Alto Adige near Merano; its best-known towns are Marlengo, Lana and Cermes. Here, though quite far north, the south-facing vineyards yield particularly interesting grapes and red wines. The Cantina Produttori Burggräfler is the most important producer in this sub-zone and interprets its classic wines most ably. The star of their range is the Pinot Nero Tiefenthalerhof: it always makes it to our final rounds and, although the '97 is a little less varietal and a little more forward than the '96 and the '95, it is nevertheless one of the best Pinot Neros in Italy for the third year running. But probably the wine most closely associated with this area is the Meranese or Meraner Hügel, a light red made mainly from schiava grapes, hence a member of the large family of schiava-based wines that also includes Santa Maddalena and Lago di Caldaro, among others. The Schickenburg '98 is perhaps the very best example of all. Then there are the cooperative's great red blends: the Cabernet-Merlot, presented for the first time this year, and the classic Lagrein-Cabernet MerVin (a re-tasting for us), both '96s and both elegant, powerful and concentrated; the former is softer, the second more sinewy and tannic. The range is completed by this year's only white, the well-made and fruity, if somewhat straightforward, Pinot Bianco Guggenberg '98.

●	A. A. Cabernet-Merlot '96	2 glasses	5
●	A. A. Meranese Schickenburg '98	2 glasses	3*
●	A. A. Pinot Nero Tiefenthalerhof '97	2 glasses	5
○	A. A. Pinot Bianco Guggenberg '98	1 glass	3
●	A. A. Lagrein-Cabernet MerVin '95	2 glasses (white)	5
●	A. A. Lagrein-Cabernet MerVin '96	2 glasses (white)	5
●	A. A. Meranese Schickenburg '97	2 glasses (white)	3*
●	A. A. Pinot Nero Tiefenthalerhof '94	2 glasses (white)	5
●	A. A. Pinot Nero Tiefenthalerhof '95	2 glasses (white)	5
●	A. A. Pinot Nero Tiefenthalerhof '96	2 glasses (white)	5
○	MerVin '97	2 glasses (white)	5

MARLENGO/MARLING (BZ)

Popphof - Andreas Menz

Mitterterzerstrasse, 5
39020 Marlengo/Marling (BZ)
tel. 0473/447180

Andreas Menz, the owner of the Popphof estate at Marlengo, is definitely one of the surprises of this year's Guide. Wine has been made on the Popphof property since 1592; they have been selling it in bulk since 1722 and bottling since the 19th century. The very traditional labels showing the family's coat of arms continue to bear witness to the estate's long history. Last year we described Andreas Menz's Cabernet as a particularly agreeable discovery amidst the great ocean of fine wines from the Alto Adige. This year it inspired us to go further. The '97 Cabernet, made from 70% cabernet sauvignon and 30% cabernet franc, is a red of great breeding, and there is no doubt about its deserving Three Glasses. It has a brilliant deep ruby color, and an elegant, characteristic bouquet combining fruity and herbaceous notes. It is concentrated and harmonious on the palate, with particularly fine, round, smooth tannins. The vineyards of the Merano basin, rich in slate and clay, certainly offer an excellent foundation for a wine of such elegance, but it would not have been possible without the winegrower's skilled hand in the cellar. We find the same harmony in the Pinot Nero '97. It has a ruby-garnet hue, and its initial delicately floral aromas give way to a fruitier tone (distinct strawberry hints). On the palate it reveals elegant, concentrated fruit and a long, well-defined and even finish. It's a shame about the Pinot Bianco '98: last year it was one of the best of its type, but it did not live up to our expectations this time around.

●	A. A. Cabernet '97	3 glasses	5
●	A. A. Pinot Nero '97	2 glasses	5
●	A. A. Cabernet '95	2 glasses (white)	5
○	A. A. Pinot Bianco '97	2 glasses (white)	3*

MELTINA/MÖLTEN (BZ)

VIVALDI - ARUNDA
CIVICO, 53
39010 MELTINA/MÖLTEN (BZ)
TEL. 0471/668033

No surprising news here: the Vivaldi–Arunda winery confirms its place as the top producer of sparkling wine in the Alto Adige, and does so in such a positive manner as to leave no doubt as to the validity of our claim. The credit for this success goes to Josef Reiterer, a highly talented oenologist and sparkling wine specialist, and also the owner of the estate. Incidentally, while in Alto Adige and some other parts of the world these wines are sold with an Arunda label, in the rest of Italy and elsewhere they are labeled Vivaldi and distribution is handled by Mid of Palermo, making a curious Sicilian-Tyrolean partnership which has had tremendous success. (Is this a recipe that could be followed in other fields as well? Amongst the pioneers of this type of mixture was one of the great figures of the Middle Ages, Frederick II.) But let's consider this year's bubblies, all of them perfectly executed. The Arunda and Vivaldi Extra Bruts, which are very similar (we suspect that they may just have different "dosages"), show all the best qualities of the sparkling wines from this zone, including a not overly full body. The delicate, attractive and creamy Vivaldi Extra Brut Cuvée Marianna is in our opinion the best estate offering. There were no vintage wines available for our tastings, as their release was scheduled for the end of 1999.

○	A. A. Spumante Extra Brut Arunda	🍷🍷	5
○	A. A. Spumante Extra Brut Vivaldi	🍷🍷	5
○	A. A. Spumante Extra Brut Vivaldi Cuvée Marianna	🍷🍷	5
○	A. A. Spumante Brut Vivaldi '93	🍷🍷 (white)	5
○	A. A. Spumante Extra Brut Arunda Ris. '93	🍷🍷 (white)	5
○	A. A. Spumante Extra Brut Vivaldi '95	🍷🍷 (white)	5
○	A. A. Spumante Extra Brut Vivaldi Ris. '87	🍷🍷 (white)	5
○	A. A. Spumante Extra Brut Vivaldi Ris. '89	🍷🍷 (white)	5

MERANO/MERAN (BZ)

CANTINA PRODUTTORI DI MERANO/
MERANER KELLEREI
VIA DI SAN FLORIANO, 8
39012 MERANO/MERAN (BZ)
TEL. 0473/235544

The roster of cooperative wineries in the Alto Adige now has a new leading player. The Cantina Produttori di Merano, in fact, has won Three Glasses with a truly great red, the Merlot Freiberg '97. It is a rounded, concentrated wine with typical scents of tobacco, pencil lead and blackberry and a palate that strikes a fine balance between particularly smooth, velvety tannins and an ample, concentrated body, all given a further hint of freshness by a light and extremely well-integrated tangy note. Elegance is predominant, but also substance, without heaviness or aggression, on the palate, where it develops powerfully to a long corresponding finish. It is difficult to find a Merlot of this quality that eschews overripening and the sometimes rather syrupy characteristics that accompany it: Three Glasses hands down. But that's not all: the Lagrein Segenpichl '97, from a well-nigh legendary vintage for this variety, is excellent as well. It has absolutely no bitter aftertaste, but it does have a vast abundance of fruit on the nose and a richly structured body with marked but fairly smooth tannins; some remaining rough edges are only due to its youth. The Sissi '97 is very satisfying: it is a sweet white with faintly aromatic notes and an elegance conferred by the perfect balance between acidity and residual sugars. The range is completed by the well-made and fruity Chardonnay Graf von Meran '97, which reveals a delicate vanilla bouquet.

●	A. A. Merlot Freiberg '97	🍷🍷🍷	5
●	A. A. Lagrein Scuro Segenpichl '97	🍷🍷	4
○	Sissi '97	🍷🍷	5
○	A. A. Chardonnay Graf Von Meran '97	🍷	4
●	A. A. Cabernet-Merlot Graf Von Meran '95	🍷 (white)	4

MONTAGNA/MONTAN (BZ)

Franz Haas

Via Villa, 6
39040 Montagna/Montan (BZ)
tel. 0471/812280

Last year Franz Haas presented only two wines for our tastings and we registered our disappointment. This time around he sent samples of everything he makes, so at last we can give a more accurate idea of the standard of quality and reliability achieved by this famous winery and its dynamic proprietor. We'll begin with a new wine, the Istante '97, a blend of merlot and cabernet which, at its very first appearance in the Guide, made it all the way to our final rounds and only just missed out on Three Glasses. It is a classic "Bordeaux blend", although not massive in body. What it concentrates on, instead, is elegance and balance. The aromatic and very stylish Moscato Rosa '97 is excellent, as is its wont: it's the best of its kind in Alto Adige. The Pinot Nero '97 is intriguing, which is no surprise either, and the Manna '97, from chardonnay, traminer, riesling and sauvignon, is a little gem in its own way and more impressive every year. Lastly, the basic wines – all '98s – are well-made whites that further confirm the dependability of this estate and the undoubted talent of Franz Haas, a first-class winegrower.

●	A. A. Moscato Rosa '97	▼▼	5
●	A. A. Pinot Nero Schweizer '97	▼▼	5
●	Istante '97	▼▼	5
○	Mitterberg Manna '97	▼▼	5
○	A. A. Gewürztraminer '98	▼	3
○	A. A. Pinot Bianco '98	▼	3
○	A. A. Pinot Grigio '98	▼	3
●	A. A. Merlot Schweizer '93	▽▽	4
●	A. A. Moscato Rosa '94	▽▽	5
●	A. A. Moscato Rosa '96	▽▽	5
●	A. A. Moscato Rosa Schweizer '95	▽▽	5
●	A. A. Pinot Nero '90	▽▽	4
●	A. A. Pinot Nero Ris. '91	▽▽	5
●	A. A. Pinot Nero Schweizer '95	▽▽	5
○	Mitterberg Manna '96	▽▽	5

NALLES/NALS (BZ)

Cantina Produttori Nalles Niclara Magrè/ Kg Nals, Margreid, Entiklar

Via Heilingenberg, 2
39010 Nalles/Nals (BZ)
tel. 0471/678626

The Cantina Produttori Nalles Niclara Magrè has made some great strides forward, partly due, no doubt, to the new young Kellermeister Gerhard Kofler, who, with great passion and energy, has taken over responsibility for the two associated cooperatives which unite the producers of Nalles in the Valle d'Adige and those of Magrè and Niclara in the southern part of Alto Adige. This is the classic zone for the great white wines of the region, and indeed it is in this wide-ranging category that we found the best bottles. The excellent Pinot Grigio Punggl '98, with its intense golden straw color, fresh fruity bouquet (with distinct hints of pear) and full, soft, concentrated structure, is a marvelous example of what this cooperative winery is capable of. The Chardonnay '98 too, fruity and ripe in fragrance and linear and full-flavored on the palate, is one of the best of the range. The Gewürztraminer Baron Salvadori '98, the Pinot Bianco Sirmian '98 and the Terlaner Sauvignon Mantele '98 are all fair and technically faultless, though they could perhaps do with a little more concentration. The fresh and lively Schiava Galea '98, with its elegant fruity aromas and good substance on the palate, is an excellent representative of its category. We found the cooperative's top red, the Cabernet-Merlot Anticus Baron Salvadori '96, however, a bit below par: it is pleasant and well made, but not very impressive.

○	A. A. Chardonnay '98	▼▼	3*
○	A. A. Pinot Grigio Punggl '98	▼▼	3*
●	A. A. Schiava Galea '98	▼▼	3*
●	A. A. Cabernet-Merlot Anticus Baron Salvadori '96	▼	5
○	A. A. Pinot Bianco Sirmian '98	▼	3
○	A. A. Terlano Sauvignon Cl. Mantele '98	▼	4
○	A. A. Gewürztraminer Baron Salvadori '98	▼	3
●	A. A. Cabernet Baron Salvadori '92	▽▽	5
●	A. A. Pinot Nero Baron Salvadori Ris. '90	▽▽	5
○	A. A. Terlano Sauvignon Cl. Mantele '97	▽▽	4

NALLES/NALS (BZ)

Castello Schwanburg
Via Schwanburg, 16
39010 Nalles/Nals (BZ)
tel. 0471/678622

It is something of an understatement to say that we are happy to be able to award Three Glasses once again to Dieter Rudolph Carli's Castello Schwanburg. The regard in which we hold the owner, the historical importance of the winery and the seriousness of an estate that did not release the '95 version of its top wine because it didn't consider it worthy (who else would have done this with such an easily marketable vintage?) all speak for themselves. If we then go on to say that the Cabernet Sauvignon Castel Schwanburg '96 may not be a powerhouse (we are in Terlano after all, not Bolgheri) but has an elegance and balance worthy of a fine red Graves, then everything really falls into place. But what particularly caught our attention this year is the extraordinary excellence of the entire range. Five wines with Two Glasses apiece is a performance that very few producers in Italy can equal. For the first time the Sonnenberg '97 is really impressive; this is an oak-aged Pinot Bianco that we had often found too forward and rather tired. The other whites, on the other hand, repeat splendid performances, the Riesling and the Sauvignon first of all, but also the Pinot Grigio which is perhaps a little simple but is beautifully made, and intensely fruity on the nose. Hats off to a winery that is one of the cornerstones of great wine-making in Alto Adige!

●	A. A. Cabernet Castel Schwanburg '96	3 black glasses	6
○	A. A. Pinot Grigio '98	2 black glasses	4
○	A. A. Riesling '98	2 black glasses	4
○	A. A. Sauvignon '98	2 black glasses	4
○	A. A. Terlano '98	2 black glasses	4
○	A. A. Terlano Pinot Bianco Sonnenberg '97	2 black glasses	5
●	A. A. Cabernet Sauvignon Ris. '96	1 black glass	4
●	A. A. Cabernet Castel Schwanburg '90	3 white glasses	6
●	A. A. Cabernet Castel Schwanburg '93	2 white glasses	5
●	A. A. Cabernet Castel Schwanburg '94	2 white glasses	5

NATURNO/NATURNS (BZ)

Tenuta Falkenstein
Franz Pratzner
Via Argine, 2
39025 Naturno/Naturns (BZ)
tel. 0473/666054

Certain vineyards, from a distance, seem to be quite vertical. When you actually walk through them, however, you recognize that the steepness of the slope was in fact accentuated by perspective. But this is not the case with Franz Pratzner's vineyards near Naturno in the Val Venosta. They really are vertical, and just strolling amidst the vines is an exercise fit for a mountaineer, never mind actually tending them. This doesn't seem to worry Pratzner, though: he does not suffer from vertigo, and he almost skips, sure-footedly, from one row to the next. Grapes cultivated with such dedication could not help but yield outstanding wines and this year Pratzner has presented a truly excellent range. Our favorite is undoubtedly the Riesling '98, the finest example of this varietal yet produced in Italy. It is a white with complex, characteristically mineral aromas together with grapefruit and aromatic herbal notes, and then a positive, concentrated, aristocratic palate underpinned by the classic bite of acidity that all great Rieslings should have, especially when young. The Gewürztraminer '98 is very good, too, although from a zone not known for that variety. The Pinot Bianco '98 is extraordinary, definitely one of the best in its category, with its very marked scents of Golden Delicious apple, fresh almond and white-fleshed peach. The Pinot Nero '97 is less successful: it is certainly sound, but lacks the complexity and elegance which make some wines from this variety among the most sought after in the world.

○	A. A. Val Venosta Riesling '98	3 black glasses	4*
○	A. A. Val Venosta Gewürztraminer '98	2 black glasses	4
○	A. A. Val Venosta Pinot Bianco '98	2 black glasses	3*
●	A. A. Val Venosta Pinot Nero '97	1 black glass	4
○	A. A. Val Venosta Pinot Bianco '97	2 white glasses	3*
●	A. A. Val Venosta Pinot Nero '95	2 white glasses	5
○	A. A. Val Venosta Riesling '96	2 white glasses	4
○	A. A. Val Venosta Riesling '97	2 white glasses	3*
○	Falkensteiner '97	2 white glasses	5

ORA/AUER (BZ)

CLEMENS WALDTHALER
VIA DEL RIO, 4
39040 ORA/AUER (BZ)
TEL. 0471/810182

The wines presented by the Clemens Waldthaler estate this year are all reds, and all very good. The best of the bunch is the Lagrein Scuro '97, which comes from the only zone in the Alto Adige – that of Ora – which can be compared with the Gries district near Bolzano for lagrein-friendly environment. This, combined with favorable weather during the growing cycle in '97, enabled the estate to make a powerful and concentrated red with an intense black currant nose and an impressive structure. The Merlot from the same vintage is excellent too. It offers a well-defined varietal bouquet of tobacco, Parma violet and berries on a light vanilla background. The palate, soft, full-bodied and velvety, has even and close-knit tannins that are not at all aggressive, and the finish is long and persistent. The Cabernet '97, which is well made but not as concentrated, and the Pinot Nero, which does not seem to be a real specialty of this nonetheless admirable winery, are slightly less impressive. Altogether this small but very interesting range fully warrants an individual entry in the Guide.

●	A. A. Lagrein Scuro '97	▼▼	4
●	A. A. Merlot '97	▼▼	4
●	A. A. Cabernet '97	▼	4
●	A. A. Pinot Nero '97	▼	4
●	A. A. Cabernet Raut '95	▽▽	4
●	A. A. Lagrein Scuro Raut '94	▽▽	4
●	A. A. Lagrein Scuro Raut '95	▽▽	4
●	A. A. Cabernet '95	▽	3
●	A. A. Merlot Raut '95	▽	4
○	A. A. Pinot Bianco '96	▽	3
○	A. A. Pinot Bianco '97	▽	3
○	Bianco Grigio Raut '97	▽	4

SALORNO/SALURN (BZ)

HADERBURG
POCHI, 31
39040 SALORNO/SALURN (BZ)
TEL. 0471/889097

The customary irreproachable small range that Haderburg presents each year is even smaller than usual this time. But, most importantly, it is dominated by a sparkling wine that is perhaps the very best bubbly ever produced in Alto Adige. We refer to the Hausmannhof '90, which was on its lees for over eight years before dégorgement. The result is a spumante with a complex bouquet in which mineral and fruity notes coexist in perfect harmony. Its carbon dioxide is so well integrated that all you sense on your tongue is a light, even and very delicate prickle. Its only limitation (a small one) is a less than enormous structure, and that cost it the Three Glasses it was on the point of carrying off. The range of still wines is also good: Haderburg seems to have started focusing on them more seriously in recent years. Perhaps the overall level is not as high as last year's, but this is due mainly to the vintages currently on offer. There are two exceptions, however. The first is the Sauvignon Hausmannhof '97, which impressed us greatly with its firm structure and complex varietal aromas with just a hint of underlying toastiness. The second is the delightfully surprising Gewürztraminer Blaspichl '98, which is aromatic and very varietal. The Chardonnay Stainhauser '98, which is fruity and pleasant but a bit lacking in body, and the Pinot Nero Hausmannhof '96, the fruit of a not very exciting vintage, are simpler wines.

○	A. A. Gewürztraminer Blaspichl '98	▼▼	4
○	A. A. Sauvignon Hausmannhof '97	▼▼	5
○	A. A. Spumante Hausmannhof '90	▼▼	6
○	A. A. Chardonnay Stainhauser '98	▼	4
●	A. A. Pinot Nero Hausmannhof '96	▼	5
●	A. A. Pinot Nero Hausmannhof '95	▽▽	5
○	A. A. Sauvignon Hausmannhof '96	▽▽	5
○	A. A. Spumante Haderburg Pas Dosé '91	▽▽	5

STAVA/STABEN (BZ)

TENUTA UNTERORTL-CASTEL JUVAL
JUVAL, 1B
39020 STAVA/STABEN (BZ)
TEL. 0473/667580

Martin Aurich's name is indissolubly linked not only with the Istituto Sperimentale Laimburg, but also (and increasingly) with this splendid estate in the Val Venosta. Here everything is done by him: he cultivates the vineyards and vinifies the wines, and although the estate belongs to the renowned mountain climber Reinhold Messner, Aurich is the guiding spirit and creative force behind wine production here. And he is a craftsman of extraordinary skill, as his wines clearly testify. The range this year, though small, is excellent. The Riesling seemed to us the most successful of the whites, confirming that this zone in northwestern Alto Adige is definitely the most favorable to this highly aristocratic grape. It shows good varietal aromas, with hints of citrus fruit and mountain herbs, and is full-flavored and just a little tart, thanks to its classic bite of acidity. The straightforward and very good Pinot Bianco '98 is fruity and attractive, not particularly concentrated but extremely well executed. Here too, the distinct acidity should ensure longevity in the bottle. Lastly, the Pinot Nero '97 comes from a hot year that did not, however, in this zone, detract from varietal characteristics. It displays the customary scents of strawberry and lightly balsamic notes. On the palate it is surprisingly well-balanced and concentrated.

○	A. A. Val Venosta Pinot Bianco '98	TT	3*
●	A. A. Val Venosta Pinot Nero '97	TT	5
○	A. A. Val Venosta Riesling '98	TT	4
●	A. A. Val Venosta Pinot Nero '95	YY	5
○	A. A. Val Venosta Riesling '96	YY	4
○	A. A. Val Venosta Riesling '97	YY	4
○	A. A. Val Venosta Pinot Bianco '96	Y	4
○	A. A. Val Venosta Pinot Bianco '97	Y	4
●	A. A. Val Venosta Pinot Nero '96	Y	5

TERLANO/TERLAN (BZ)

CANTINA DI TERLANO
VIA SILBERLEITEN, 7
39018 TERLANO/TERLAN (BZ)
TEL. 0471/257135

The Cantina di Terlano did very well indeed at our tastings this year: almost 90% of the wines it presented earned Two Glasses, a very clear sign of dependably high quality. Our compliments to the ambitious cellarmaster, Hartmann Donà, and to the president, Georg Höller. Their top wine this time is, we think, the Terlano Nova Domus '96. This blend of pinot bianco, chardonnay and sauvignon blanc has a deep golden straw color, a very complex, forward and ample nose, and a rich, full-flavored, powerfully structured palate: a great wine, which deserves a place of honor among the splendid whites long produced by the Cantina di Terlano. Of the two Terlano Sauvignons, the Winkl '98 and the Quarz '97, we slightly preferred the former because of its crispness and varietal characteristics. The Terlano Pinot Bianco Vorberg '96 is very mature, full and rich, and the Gewürztraminer Lunare '97 is really aromatic and well defined, with fine sweet oaky notes. Now for the reds: the Lagrein Porphyr Riserva '97, very true to type, displays an intense ripe blackberry fragrance and a soft, concentrated and elegantly structured palate. To close, the Pinot Nero Montigl '97 shows a brilliant deep ruby color, slightly vegetal aromas with notes of geranium and, on the palate, a full body and good concentration with a long and pleasing finish.

○	A. A. Gewürztraminer Lunare '97	TT	4
●	A. A. Lagrein Porphyr Ris. '97	TT	5
●	A. A. Pinot Nero Montigl '97	TT	5
○	A. A. Terlano Nova Domus '96	TT	5
○	A. A. Terlano Pinot Bianco Vorberg '96	TT	4
○	A. A. Terlano Sauvignon Quarz '97	TT	5
○	A. A. Terlano Sauvignon Winkl '98	TT	5
○	A. A. Terlano Chardonnay Kreuth '97	T	4
○	A. A. Terlano Pinot Bianco '79	YYY	5
○	A. A. Gewürztraminer Lunare '96	YY	4
●	A. A. Lagrein Porphyr Ris. '95	YY	5
○	A. A. Terlano Pinot Bianco '88	YY	5

TERMENO/TRAMIN (BZ)

CANTINA PRODUTTORI DI TERMENO
STRADA DEL VINO, 122
39040 TERMENO/TRAMIN (BZ)
TEL. 0471/860126

It was not just last year's Three Glasses won by the Cabernet Terminum Riserva '95 that placed the Cantina Produttori di Termeno in the very top ranks of Italian producers: it was most particularly the constant and extraordinary quality of its wines and their extremely reasonable prices. The magnificent Gewürztraminer Nussbaumerhof '98 (a wine which has already won several prizes) came within a hair's breadth of Three Glasses. With its intense fruity aromas, its elegant structure and concentrated, full-flavored and attractive palate, it is one of the best wines produced from this grape in the region. It's quite obvious that their oenologist Willi Stürz has, with hard work, skill and passion, discovered the secret of making great wines. This is not true only of his whites, among which we also draw your attention to the delicious Pinot Grigio Unterebnerhof '98 and the refreshing Sauvignon '98, but also of his reds. Indeed, the Lagrein Urbanhof '97 shows great breeding: it has a deep ruby color, an intensely aromatic bouquet with nicely restrained fruitiness, and a soft, velvety palate. The Cabernet Renommée '97, a less demanding wine than the great Terminum (which was not released this year), is very appealing too. The Schiava Hexenbichler '98, a fresh, attractive wine with a typical fruity aroma and good concentration on the palate, is a fine example of a Schiava. The only Pinot Nero, the Schiesstandhof Riserva '97, was well made, linear and perhaps a little too simple. But, faced with such a wealth of stunning wines, we can easily excuse the talented Willi Stürz for this minor lapse.

●	A. A. Cabernet Renommée '97	🍷🍷	3*
○	A. A. Gewürztraminer Nussbaumerhof '98	🍷🍷	4
○	A. A. Gewürztraminer Passito '97	🍷🍷	5
●	A. A. Lagrein Urbanhof '97	🍷🍷	3*
○	A. A. Pinot Grigio Unterebnerhof '98	🍷🍷	4
○	A. A. Sauvignon '98	🍷🍷	4
●	A. A. Schiava Hexenbichler '98	🍷🍷	3*
●	A. A. Pinot Nero Schiesstandhof Ris. '97	🍷	4
●	A. A. Cabernet Terminum Ris. '95	🍷🍷🍷 (white)	5
●	A. A. Lagrein Urbanhof '96	🍷🍷 (white)	3*
●	A. A. Pinot Nero Schiesstandhof '93	🍷🍷 (white)	4
●	A. A. Pinot Nero Schiesstandhof Ris. '96	🍷🍷 (white)	4

TERMENO/TRAMIN (BZ)

PODERI CASTEL RINGBERG
E KASTELAZ ELENA WALCH
VIA A. HOFER, 1
39040 TERMENO/TRAMIN (BZ)
TEL. 0471/860172

Elena Walch did not win Three Glasses this year, but the fact that five wines earned Two Glasses each says a great deal about the standard that this historic and renowned winery has achieved. The best wine in the range this time (with respect to its variety as well) is, in our opinion, the Merlot '98 from the Kastelaz vineyards at Termeno. It is an excellent red, but it's a '96, which was not an altogether propitious vintage for merlot in the Alto Adige; nevertheless it displays quite a complex varietal bouquet and a structure on the palate which may be a tiny bit dilute but is certainly well balanced and elegant. All the whites presented were of considerable interest, including a '98 Gewürztraminer which is less fat and powerful than the '97, a splendid Pinot Bianco Kastelaz '98 (one of the best in its category) and a surprising Pinot Grigio Castel Ringberg '98, extremely varietal and very well executed. The range is completed by the delicious Chardonnay Cardellino '98, a white with exemplary aromas of pineapple and ripe rennet apple, which is well-balanced on the palate and eminently, almost irresistibly, quaffable. And then its price is quite reasonable, which makes it a star in its category. The top reds were not released this year, as Elena Walch preferred to wait and then release a better vintage, the '97; so we have some treats to look forward to, especially the Cabernet.

○	A. A. Chardonnay Cardellino '98	🍷🍷	3*
○	A. A. Gewürztraminer Kastelaz '98	🍷🍷	4
●	A. A. Merlot Kastelaz Ris. '96	🍷🍷	5
○	A. A. Pinot Bianco Kastelaz '98	🍷🍷	4
○	A. A. Pinot Grigio Castel Ringberg '98	🍷🍷	4
○	A. A. Gewürztraminer Kastelaz '97	🍷🍷🍷 (white)	4
●	A. A. Cabernet Sauvignon Castel Ringberg Ris. '92	🍷🍷 (white)	5
●	A. A. Cabernet Sauvignon Castel Ringberg Ris. '93	🍷🍷 (white)	5
●	A. A. Cabernet Sauvignon Castel Ringberg Ris. '95	🍷🍷 (white)	5

TERMENO/TRAMIN (BZ)

HOFSTÄTTER
P.ZZA MUNICIPIO, 5
39040 TERMENO/TRAMIN (BZ)
TEL. 0471/860161

Paolo and Martin Foradori's Hofstätter winery gave what we consider to be its best performance ever at our tastings this year. And this was in spite of the fact that their star wine, the Pinot Nero S. Urbano , was not released in the '96 version, which is rather like winning a soccer championship with only ten men. It all goes to show what remarkable progress has been made by this splendid and famous winery at Termeno. The starring role was taken over by the exceptional Gewürztraminer Kolbenhof '98, a fine, aromatic and very elegant white that offers a well-defined fragrance of rose hip, and a soft, concentrated palate with just the least hint of faint bitterness on the finish. But that's not the half of it. How about the two '98 Pinot Biancos, with the Barthenau in particularly fine form? Or the Pinot Nero Crozzolhof '97, which earned its Two Glasses despite being the estate's third-ranked Pinot Nero? Or the delicate, complex Riesling '98 and the forceful and concentrated Lagrein '97, or, then again, the '97 Cabernet, which is not particularly complex but is perfectly executed? One is spoilt for choice, and even the One Glass wines have been kept back just because of our severity. The Foradoris should be very pleased with themselves and their wines. Hearty congratulations!

○	A. A. Gewürztraminer Kolbenhof '98	🍷🍷🍷	4*
●	A. A. Cabernet '97	🍷🍷	4
●	A. A. Lagrein Scuro '97	🍷🍷	3*
○	A. A. Pinot Bianco '98	🍷🍷	3*
○	A. A. Pinot Bianco Villa Barthenau '98	🍷🍷	4
●	A. A. Pinot Nero Crozzolhof '97	🍷🍷	4
○	A. A. Riesling '98	🍷🍷	3*
○	A. A. Chardonnay '98	🍷	3
●	A. A. Pinot Nero Ris. '96	🍷	4
●	A. A. Pinot Nero S. Urbano '91	ΥΥΥ	6
●	A. A. Pinot Nero S. Urbano '93	ΥΥΥ	6
●	A. A. Pinot Nero S. Urbano '95	ΥΥΥ	6
●	A. A. Pinot Nero S. Urbano '90	ΥΥΥ	6
●	A. A. Pinot Nero S. Urbano '94	ΥΥ	6

VADENA/PFATTEN (BZ)

ISTITUTO SPERIMENTALE LAIMBURG
LOC. LAIMBURG, 6
39051 VADENA/PFATTEN (BZ)
TEL. 0471/969210

The Istituto Sperimentale di Laimburg is one of those rare places in Italy in which viticultural and oenological research and experimentation are carried out according to scientific criteria. Such institutions are much easier to find in France, the United States and Germany than in Italy. Here, research, even in our field, suffers from the same problems that it encounters in the public sector. So Laimburg is all the more to be treasured, not least because the wines it offers each year, produced from grapes grown in its experimental vineyards, are very often extremely good. This year the Chardonay Doa '97, fermented and aged in small casks, came very close to earning Three Glasses. This elegant white offers varietal aromas and well-integrated oak on the nose and a full-bodied, rich and meaty palate. The Riesling '98, a house specialty, did very well too, with its characteristic bouquet and tart, aristocratic palate. The Sauvignon '98 amazed us with its typical funky and fruity notes of white-fleshed peach and elderflower. The Cabernet Riserva is intriguing as well, especially for a '96. It may not knock you over, but a sure hand has produced it. All of the other wines were sound, but we were a little disappointed with the '98 Gewürztraminer, which rated only One Glass; from a wine that won Three Glasses just four years ago, we were hoping for rather more.

●	A. A. Cabernet Ris. '96	🍷🍷	5
○	A. A. Chardonnay Doa '97	🍷🍷	5
●	A. A. Pinot Nero '97	🍷🍷	5
○	A. A. Riesling Renano '98	🍷🍷	4
○	A. A. Sauvignon '98	🍷🍷	4
○	A. A. Gewürztraminer '98	🍷	4
●	A. A. Lagrein Scuro Ris. '96	🍷	4
●	A. A. Moscato Rosa '96	🍷	5
○	A. A. Pinot Bianco '98	🍷	4
○	A. A. Gewürztraminer '94	ΥΥΥ	4*
●	A. A. Cabernet Ris. '92	ΥΥ	5
●	A. A. Cabernet Ris. '93	ΥΥ	5
●	A. A. Cabernet Ris. '94	ΥΥ	5
●	A. A. Lagrein Scuro Ris. '95	ΥΥ	5
●	A. A. Merlot '96	ΥΥ	5

VARNA/VAHRN (BZ)

Cantina dell' Abbazia di Novacella

Via dell'Abbazia, 1
39040 Varna/Vahrn (BZ)
tel. 0472/836189

It was not quite the triumph of last year, but the show given by the Abbazia di Novacella and its "performing artist" Urban von Klebersberg was certainly first-rate, proving once again that there has been a big change at this winery in the last couple of years. Almost all the new wines were whites and '98s, the fruit of a rather tricky vintage in the Valle Isarco that nevertheless yielded some very interesting wines. The best of the lot is the Prepositus '98, an IGT made from a blend of sylvaner (70%), chardonnay (20%) and pinot grigio (10%). Its full flavor and richness of extract perfectly counterbalance the marked note of acidity that characterizes it. The Sauvignon '98, which comes from the estate vineyards south of Bolzano, is not bad either. It does not have the structure or the distinctly varietal bouquet of the '97, but it can hold up its head among its peers. The reds are the again quite delightful Moscato Rosa, characteristic, aromatic and decidedly sweet, and the Lagrein Prepositus '97, a wine of great character, full-bodied and powerful. All the other wines are sound, and the Sylvaner is a little better; this is a typical grape of the Valle Isarco, as well as of various zones in Germany, Austria and Alsace. It has its usual slightly vegetal nose but it lacks the concentration of more felicitous vintages.

●	A. A. Lagrein Prepositus '97	🍷🍷	4
○	A. A. Moscato Rosa '97	🍷🍷	5
○	A. A. Sauvignon '98	🍷🍷	3*
○	Prepositus '98	🍷🍷	4
○	A. A. Valle Isarco Kerner '98	🍷	3
○	A. A. Valle Isarco Müller Thurgau '98	🍷	3
○	A. A. Valle Isarco Sylvaner '98	🍷	3
○	A. A. Sauvignon '97	🍸🍸🍸	4*
●	A. A. Lagrein '93	🍸🍸	3
●	A. A. Moscato Rosa '95	🍸🍸	5
●	A. A. Pinot Nero '95	🍸🍸	4
○	A. A. Valle Isarco Gewürztraminer '97	🍸🍸	4
○	A. A. Valle Isarco Sylvaner '97	🍸🍸	3*

VARNA/VAHRN (BZ)

Köfererhof

Via Pusteria, 3
39040 Varna/Vahrn (BZ)
tel. 0472/836649

The old Köfererhof estate at Varna has been around for more than 850 years. Since 1940 it has been owned by the Kerschbaumer family, and in the 1980s Josef and his son Günther began to rearrange the old vineyards and to plant sylvaner, müller thurgau, kerner and pinot grigio on the land around the farmhouse: poor land, but with good exposure to sunlight. In 1991, after a pause of over thirty years and the construction of a new cellar, Köfererhof started making its own wine again, as it had traditionally done. This wine was initially destined mainly for use in the large "agriturismo" (country guest accommodation) run by the family, but Günther soon realized that his vineyards had more to offer than an unassuming everyday tipple. And his first attempts proved him right. Tasting his wines today (about 18 thousand bottles are filled every year) we feel genuine admiration for the Kerschbaumers. The Pinot Grigio Valle Isarco '98 is one of the best wines made from this variety in Alto Adige. Of a clear golden straw color, it is astonishing both in its intense, stylish and varietal fruit on the nose and in its elegant, lively acidity on the palate. But the Valle Isarco Silvaner '98 and the Valle Isarco Kerner '98 are also thoroughbreds, fruity, fresh and succulent, with good acidity and structure. The Gewürztraminer '98 and the Müller Thurgau '98 still want some of their siblings' backbone, but they are nevertheless well-made and attractive wines.

○	A. A. Valle Isarco Kerner '98	🍷🍷	3*
○	A. A. Valle Isarco Pinot Grigio '98	🍷🍷	3*
○	A. A. Valle Isarco Silvaner '98	🍷🍷	3*
○	A. A. Gewürztraminer '98	🍷	3
○	A. A. Müller Thurgau '98	🍷	3

OTHER WINERIES

The following producers in the province of Bolzano obtained good scores in our tastings with one or more of their wines:

PROVINCE OF BOLZANO

Viticoltori dell'Alto Adige/ Südtiroler Weinbauernverband
Appiano/Eppan,
tel. 0471/666060
A. A. Lagrein Scuro Pischlhof Ris. '95,
A. A. Pinot Bianco Eggerhof Plattenriegl '98

Andreas Berger - Turmhof
Bolzano/Bozen, tel. 0471/288460
A. A. Lagrein Scuro '97,
A. A. Sauvignon '98

H. Lun
Bolzano/Bozen,
tel. 0471/976583
A. A. Gewürztraminer '98,
A. A. Lagrein Scuro Albertus Ris. '96,
A. A. Pinot Bianco '98,
A. A. Pinot Grigio '98

Malojer Gummerhof
Bolzano/Bozen,
tel. 0471/972885
A. A. Lagrein Scuro '96,
A. A. Lagrein Scuro Weingut Rahmhütt '96,
A. A. Merlot '96,
A. A. Pinot Nero '97,
A. A. Santa Maddalena Classico '98,
A. A. Valle Isarco Sylvaner '98

Georg Mumelter
Bolzano/Bozen,
tel. 0471/973090
A. A. Lagrein Scuro Griesbauerhof '97,
A. A. Pinot Grigio Griesbauerhof '98,
A. A. Santa Maddalena Cl. Griesbauerhof '98

Heinrich Rottensteiner
Bolzano/Bozen, tel. 0471/973549
A. A. Lagrein Scuro Grafenleiten '97,
A. A. Santa Maddalena Classico '98,
A. A. Sauvignon '98

Anton Schmid - Oberrautner
Bolzano/Bozen, tel. 0471/281440
A. A. Lagrein Scuro Barrique '97,
A. A. Lagrein Scuro Grieser '97

Loacker Scwarhof
Bolzano/Bozen, tel. 0471/365125
A. A. Lagrein Pitz Thurü '97,
A. A. Pinot Nero Wachstum '97,
Cuvée Jus Osculi '97

Baron Dürfeld de Giovannelli
Caldaro/Kaltern, tel. 0471/962072
A. A. Lago di Caldaro Scelto Cl. Panholzer '98,
A. A. Lago di Caldaro Scelto Keil '98

Peter Sölva & Sohn
Caldaro/Kaltern, tel. 0471/964650
A. A. Gewürztraminer De Silvas '98,
A. A. Lago di Caldaro Scelto Cl. Sup. Peterleiten '98,
De Silvas '97

Kupelwieser
Cortina/Kurtnig, tel. 0471/817143
A. A. Gewürztraminer '98,
A. A. Lagrein Intenditore '97,
A. A. Müller Thurgau '98,
A. A. Pinot Bianco '98,
A. A. Sauvignon Intenditore '98

Cason Hirschprunn
Magré/Margraid, tel. 0471/809500
Mittenberg Cason '96,
Mittenberg Corolle '95,
Mittenberg Etelle '96

VENETO

The Veneto is a region whose potential is widely recognized but not yet fully exploited. If, only a few years ago, we wrote that winery practices here were rather out of date, today virtually every producer's wine-making operations are in line with the most modern standards. What is still lacking among the majority of the Veneto's producers is real proficiency in the matter of viticulture: everyone says that it's just about to take off, yet many producers prefer to invest their financial resources in other ways, of which some are indeed entirely commendable, but which do not help resolve what has, for at least half a century, been the region's main problem. There are some zones, Valpolicella above all, which are experiencing a particularly favorable period, yet the trend towards high quality is not making the decisive and positive progress that one might have expected. The '95 vintage seemed to be the best of the century for Amarone and Recioto, and indeed the wines are very good, but their quality has not improved dramatically over what it was a few years ago when the producers were considerably less well off. Often one gets the impression that the wines are impeccably made, but that one is merely getting an inkling of what the quality of the area and the fruit, in the hands of a skilled producer, might give – and this is not good sign. Also Valpolicella lacks a united purpose which would lead, finally, to the approval of DOCG status for Amarone and Recioto: one can no longer, realistically, make distinctions between the Classico and the surrounding zones, considering the quality now expressed in the latter. Instead of making up their minds to establish serious self-regulated controls on production, a number of wineries, backed up by certain local mayors, are thinking about creating a new consortium to defend the interests of the Classico zone. The Soave zone also has some problems with regard to DOCG approval: here there is still too big a difference in quality between a few wines (whose number, in truth, is constantly growing) and the mediocrity of the sea of Soave one can find all over the world. Naturally the more serious producers want to prevent new regulations from conceding an increase in yields, because what is actually needed is the exact opposite, given the current crisis in the demand for white wines. An area so far untouched by this recession is the Prosecco zone, but we are not the only ones who believe that there is an urgent need for regulations which clarify for the consumer the difference between the wines which come from the undoubtedly superior area between Valdobbiadene and Conegliano, and all the Prosecco produced elsewhere. We are seeing signs of a reawakening, in the provinces of Padua and Vicenza, in producers with increased interest in vine management, but this is actually true of the region as a whole: the difficult '98 vintage in fact highlighted the problems of those who have to purchase grapes, must or wine and are not always able to make the necessary selection. Our final remarks concern the area along the Verona shore of Lake Garda, which is going though a period of stagnation from which it can emerge only if the leading producers are accepted as models and the traditional emphasis on quantity (which in view of the decrease in consumption, appears anachronistic to say the least) is abandoned.

BARDOLINO (VR)

GUERRIERI RIZZARDI
P.ZZA GUERRIERI, 1
37011 BARDOLINO (VR)
TEL. 045/7210028

There is important news about the management of this winery: since '98 operations here have been run by Giuseppe, the son of Countess Cristina. This young man has had considerable oenological experience in California and Australia: his input will therefore be of enormous value to an estate which does not limit itself to the Garda classics, but also tries its hand at international grape varieties and dessert wines. The Amarone '95, which is perhaps benefiting from a slightly longer period of aging, was missing from the wines presented for our tastings. However, the rest of the range was well represented by one of the best-ever versions of the Dogoli, a white vinified in stainless steel, based on dried moscato with some other non-aromatic varieties. Its delicate straw color introduces a nose with a profusion of aromas which, for now, are very youthful but which suggest intriguing maturation potential: notes of citrus fruit, mint, rose and almond are evident on both the nose and the palate; here the flavor evolves nicely, ensuring excellent length and appealing vitality. The Soave Costeggiola is only slightly less successful than the '97. It still has the same good concentration on the nose and characteristically balanced flavor; this year (and this was to be expected) it merely lacked the breadth and vivacity which it often displays. The basic Soave also scored quite well thanks to its appealing, easy-drinking style. The fourth white in the range, the Castello Guerrieri, revealed an interesting combination of freshness and complexity. The performance of the Rosso '94, on the other hand, seemed less impressive.

○	Dogoli Bianco '98	▼▼	3*
○	Castello Guerrieri Bianco '98	▼	3
○	Soave Cl. '98	▼	2
○	Soave Cl. Costeggiola '98	▼	3
●	Valpolicella Cl. Sup. Pojega '97	▼	3
●	Castello Guerrieri Rosso '94		4
●	Amarone della Valpolicella Cl. Calcarole '91	▽	5
●	Amarone della Valpolicella Cl. '94	▽	5
●	Castello Guerrieri Rosso '93	▽	3

BARDOLINO (VR)

F.LLI ZENI
VIA COSTABELLA, 9
37011 BARDOLINO (VR)
TEL. 045/7210022

As was the case last year, Nino Zeni's star wine is his Amarone; nevertheless, there were also some pleasant surprises among the Garda wines, bearing in mind that '98 was a really difficult year for the earlier-maturing grapes. Let us begin with the Chiaretto and the Bianco di Custoza in the Vigne Alte range, which, though delicate as expected, are among the most characterful wines in their respective categories, as is the Garganega from the new Garda DOC. The Bardolino Superiore is good too, though it comes from the richer '97 vintage. We will overlook the Reciotos of the same year, which revealed very dense fruit but which lack the balance that only appropriate aging can give them: we therefore hope to speak about them in the next Guide. The Valpolcellas, the Bardolino and the Soave are sound, but lacking in verve: there is considerable room for improvement here. The Pinot Bianco '95, perhaps the best ever produced by this winery, is seductive, well-balanced and intimate. We come, then, to the three Amarones, which certainly benefited from the excellent '95 vintage: indeed, they all scored very well, but perhaps lacked that special touch of breeding which we might have expected, given that year's fruit. The basic version has a traditional style, with warmth, good structure and ripe fruit on the nose; the finish is not especially long, but it is very clean indeed. The Vigne Alto selection is similarly appealing, while the version aged in barriques has broader structure; it also has a deep color and elegant, ample perfumes; the fruit on the front and middle palate is attractively mellow and leaves a voluptuous aftertaste.

●	Amarone della Valpolicella Cl. '95	▼▼	5
●	Amarone della Valpolicella Cl. Barrique '95	▼▼	6
○	Passito Bianco '95	▼▼	5
●	Amarone della Valpolicella Cl. Vigne Alte '95	▼	6
⊙	Bardolino Chiaretto Cl. Vigne Alte '98	▼	2*
●	Bardolino Cl. Sup. '97	▼	2*
○	Bianco di Custoza Vigne Alte '98	▼	2*
○	Garda Garganega '98	▼	3
●	Bardolino Cl. '98		2
○	Soave Cl. Sup. Vigne Alte '98		3
●	Valpolicella Cl. Sup. Vigne Alte '97		3
●	Amarone della Valpolicella Cl. '88	▽▽▽	6

BASSANO DEL GRAPPA (VI)

VIGNETO DUE SANTI
V.LE ASIAGO, 84
36061 BASSANO DEL GRAPPA (VI)
TEL. 0424/502074

The Vigneto Due Santi estate is only a short distance from the historic center of Bassano, yet here the terrain is decidedly hilly. Indeed, Stefano Zonta's vineyards, which he farms with passion and an ever-increasing wealth of experience, have perfect exposure. Recent vintages have not been kind to our vigneron: hail is the malefactor, and caused major problems right at harvest time. Sadly, therefore, certain wines (like the Prosecco and Malvasia) are slightly under par. The Breganze Bianco showed better: it has a positive nose with scents of peach and green almond and a clean, fresh style; the palate mirrors the bouquet and is underpinned by enchanting structure. The '98 Sauvignon, which Zonta holds in particularly high regard, offered see-sawing results in the course of our various tastings, a sign perhaps that the wine hadn't yet completely settled down in bottle. You can taste the oak, even though it is less marked than in the past, but we found a greater overall harmony and appeal, with attractive sensations of very juicy fruit and evident but well-balanced alcohol. Among the reds, the Breganze '97 deserves only an honorable mention, but the Cabernet Riserva is of the usual high standard. The bluish tones in the color give an indication of the wine's richness. The nose reveals good use of new oak as well as a satisfyingly complex amalgam of sweet spice, red berries, leather and mineral tones. This ripe fruitiness is echoed on the palate along with fine acid-tannin balance, and the finish is excellent and long. The fact that the vines are still relatively young suggests that these wines will improve considerably with future vintages and will thus launch Stefano into the ranks of the Veneto's top producers.

●	Breganze Cabernet Vigneto Due Santi '97	🍷🍷	4
○	Breganze Sauvignon Vigneto Due Santi '98	🍷🍷	4
○	Breganze Bianco '98	🍷	3
●	Breganze Cabernet '97		3
○	Malvasia Campo dei Fiori '98		3
●	Breganze Cabernet Vigneto Due Santi '95	🍸🍸	4
●	Breganze Cabernet Vigneto Due Santi '96	🍸🍸	4
●	Breganze Cabernet '96	🍸	3

BREGANZE (VI)

MACULAN
VIA CASTELLETTO, 3
36042 BREGANZE (VI)
TEL. 0445/873733

Fausto Maculan had no need to demonstrate his skill as a producer, but he has probably never before offered us such a delicious wine to taste. Nature and great technique both contributed towards making the Fratta '97 a fit companion for the world's great reds and earning it Three Glasses. The Fratta has an international style (in the best sense of the term), being made from a blend of 70% cabernet sauvignon and 30% merlot. It shows an impressive gamut of aromas (sweet spice, licorice and berries) and intoxicating power and complexity which do not diminish in the slightest even after a long time in the glass. On the palate it displays amazing balance, creaminess and delicious fruit (the monumental structure notwithstanding) and its finish is every bit as long as expected; the presence of beautifully ripe merlot is fundamental in softening the austerity and tannins of the cabernet. This wine is enjoyable even now, though it will almost certainly improve for a long time yet in the cellars of those who are patient enough to wait for it. The '97 Cabernet Sauvignon Ferrata is, once again, an extremely enjoyable, well-made red, though it does not lack depth either. The Merlot Marchesante is rather too thin, and the oak almost completely overwhelms the fruit. The sweet wines all showed well. The Dindarello '98 gave a brilliant performance and stands out for its delicious freshness. The Torcolato is excellent too, ennobled by an exemplary drying of the grapes, but perhaps just a shade over-alcoholic. The Acininobili reveals rich, sumptuous fruit which requires further aging in order to re-establish a perfect balance.

●	Fratta '97	🍷🍷🍷	6
○	Breganze Acininobili Ris. '97	🍷🍷	6
●	Breganze Cabernet Sauvignon Ferrata '97	🍷🍷	6
○	Dindarello '98	🍷🍷	4
○	Breganze Torcolato '97	🍷🍷	6
○	Breganze Chardonnay Ferrata '97		5
○	Breganze Chardonnay Riale '97		4
●	Breganze Merlot Marchesante '97		6
○	Acininobili '91	🍸🍸🍸	6
●	Cabernet Sauvignon Ferrata '90	🍸🍸🍸	6
●	Cabernet Sauvignon Ferrata '94	🍸🍸🍸	5
●	Breganze Cabernet Sauvignon Ferrata '96	🍸🍸	6
●	Breganze Cabernet Palazzotto '96	🍸	4

CAVAION VERONESE (VR)

LE FRAGHE
LOC. LA COLOMBARA
37010 CAVAION VERONESE (VR)
TEL. 045/7236832

Matilde Poggi has now taken on full responsibility for running the estate, a task she shared until a few years ago with some of her cousins. After a few seasons which she spent reorganizing production, the winery has now offered a really impressive performance and deserves its own full entry. The best results were achieved by two whites and a red, the Quaiare, made from cabernet franc and cabernet sauvignon. The vineyard for this wine is planted with guyot-trained vines which have drastically reduced yields in a zone where the pergola is the most widespread training system. The resulting wine is very encouraging, both now and for the future. It has, in fact, a very deep color and concentrated fruity aromas which successfully absorb the power of the oak. On the palate one finds excellent balance between the extract, alcohol and tannins, while the flavor as a whole develops positively and persistently. A wine that the estate really believes in is the white Garganega. Indeed, this wine, made entirely from the eponymous grape, is very much in the Veronese tradition and comes from a particularly well-suited area for this variety, which has been growing here at least since the end of the 19th century. It has a deep-toned color, while its aromas subtly reveal that it was macerated on the skins and display surprising richness rather than any sort of heaviness. On the palate the wine is broad and soft, showing to some extent the lack of acidity typical of the '98 vintage. The Chardonnay '97 is well-balanced and rather complex, and offers quite positive fruit on the palate; it contains a proportion of barrique-aged wine which has been really well integrated. The classic Garda wines, Bardolino and Chiaretto, are worthy of an honorable mention.

○	Garganega '98	🍷🍷	3*
●	Valdadige Quaiare '96	🍷🍷	4
○	Chardonnay '97	🍷	3
⊙	Bardolino Chiaretto '98		2
●	Bardolino Cl. '98		2

COLOGNOLA AI COLLI (VR)

TENUTA S. ANTONIO
VIA CERIANI, 23
FRAZ. S. ZENO
37030 COLOGNOLA AI COLLI (VR)
TEL. 045/7650383

Tenuta Sant'Antonio, which made its debut in our Guide last year in the role of a favored outsider, now takes its place as a real front runner among the select group of the Veneto's top producers. As usual, the reasons are to be found not only in a couple of the wines just presented but also, and particularly, in the meticulous preparatory work which the Castagnedi family has carried out over the last few years, thereby confirming that the area to the east of Verona is full of wine-making stars; in this case stars who have, on their second appearance in our Guide, obtained a Three Glass rating for their Cabernet Sauvignon Capitello '97. Power is the cardinal feature of the Capitello, a red whose production depends on absolutely rigorous vineyard management. The deep beauty of its color is bewitching. Its wonderfully ample bouquet displays the typical austere directness of the principal Bordeaux grape variety; its hints of dark berries, sweet herbaceousness and marked mineral notes are evident on both the nose and the palate, where the structure of the fruit offers impressive solidity. The '95 Amarone lives up to the promise of our unofficial tastings and reveals itself to be one of the most sought-after and attractive examples of its type. Its color reflects the intensity of all of its taste characteristics. On the nose its fruity notes, splendidly well defined, are accompanied by cocoa and vanilla nuances; on the palate it has a beautifully modulated strength and appealing clean and inviting fruit to which the semi-dried grapes have contributed without causing an excess of alcohol or imperfections of any kind. The Passito Colori d'Autunno shows well once again too: it is less extremely ripe and sweet than last year's, but it is nevertheless full, persistent and perhaps better balanced. The Valpolicella Superiore Monti Garbi is successful, but the Chardonnay a bit less so: the oak is a little too dominant.

●	Cabernet Sauvignon Capitello '97	🍷🍷🍷	5
●	Amarone della Valpolicella Campo dei Gigli '95	🍷🍷	6
○	Passito Colori d'Autunno '96	🍷🍷	5
●	Valpolicella Sup. Monti Garbi '97	🍷	4
○	Chardonnay Vigna Capitello '97		4
●	Cabernet Sauvignon Vigna Capitello '95	🍸🍸	5
○	Passito Colori d'Autunno '95	🍸🍸	4
●	Cabernet Sauvignon Torre dei Mellotti '96	🍸	3
●	Valpolicella Sup. '96	🍸	3

DOLCÉ (VR)

ARMANI
VIA CERADELLO, 401
37020 DOLCÉ (VR)
TEL. 045/7290033

Foja tonda, an indigenous variety of the Val Lagarina (a sub-zone of the Valdadige situated between Rovereto and Dolcé), is a grape which, because it ripens early, is perfectly suited to the cold climate here. Albino Armani, the owner of this estate, has rediscovered this forgotten variety and has enthusiastically set about reviving it. The Foja Tonda '97, aged for 12 months in barrique, offers a warm, concentrated and rounded nose, with good balance between the primary aromas of the fruit and the tertiary oak-derived ones. It is rich and harmonious in the mouth, with an evolving finish that mirrors the bouquet. The estate, which draws on 135 hectares of its own vineyards as well as the fruit of other local growers, bottles only wine made from grapes grown in the best vineyards and from suppliers who adhere to rigorous standards in their cultivation. Careful vineyard management has yielded other good wines as well. We particularly liked the Chardonnay Piccola Botte '98. Its warm, ripe aromas entice you with their depth and volume, tempting you to savor its satisfyingly rich, concentrated fruit and its well-modulated acidity. Armani's other red, the Corvara '96, is made from a blend of cabernet sauvignon, merlot and corvina. It is fresh and appealingly elegant, with good evolution on the palate. The Pinot Grigio Corvara '98 and the Sauvignon Campo Napoleone '98 were both attractive, if somewhat too straightforward.

●	Foja Tonda Rosso '97	🍷🍷	3*
○	Valdadige Chardonnay Piccola Botte '98	🍷🍷	4
●	Corvara Rosso '96	🍷	4
○	Sauvignon Campo Napoleone '98		3
○	Trentino Pinot Grigio Corvara '98		3

FAEDO DI CINTO EUGANEO (PD)

CA' LUSTRA
VIA S. PIETRO, 50
35030 FAEDO DI CINTO EUGANEO (PD)
TEL. 0429/94128

This estate continues to make excellent wines even when the year in question is not outstanding. A case in point: Zanovello and Polastri, the owners, succeeded in producing some interesting and well-defined wines although, indeed, '98 was not a particularly favorable year: rains in September had an adverse effect on the harvesting of the earlier-ripening white varieties. The wines are therefore somewhat more dilute, and the heat of the summer also reduced their acidity. The Incrocio Manzoni '98 displays a pleasingly soft style and its real appeal lies in its intriguing aromatic qualities, while the Chardonnay of the same vintage relies on a broader structure and an attractively evolving finish. The wine that suffered most, on the other hand, was the Colli Euganei Bianco, which was very good last year but shows less concentration this time around. The Cabernet Girapoggio '97 confirmed its quality. It is a richly fragrant red that is elegant and well-structured on the palate (if not particularly deep), and has a long and intense finish. The Colli Euganei Rosso Riserva '97 is delicate and fairly straightforward: we might have expected a little bit more from it. The Sauvignon '98 is a pleasantly surprising new wine: it is green but not one-dimensional on the nose and has a crisp, refreshing flavor. The Fior d'Arancio is considerably improved: it is sweet yet lively, with good persistence and a satisfying touch of complexity.

●	Colli Euganei Cabernet Girapoggio '97	🍷🍷	4
○	Colli Euganei Spumante Fior d'Arancio '98	🍷🍷	3*
○	Colli Euganei Bianco '98	🍷	2*
○	Colli Euganei Chardonnay Vigna Marco '98	🍷	4
●	Colli Euganei Rosso Ris. '97	🍷	3
○	Incrocio Manzoni Vigna Linda '98	🍷	4
○	Sauvignon '98	🍷	3
●	Colli Euganei Cabernet Girapoggio '95	🍷🍷 (outline)	3

FOSSALTA DI PORTOGRUARO (VE)

SANTA MARGHERITA
VIA ITA MARZOTTO, 8
30025 FOSSALTA DI PORTOGRUARO (VE)
TEL. 0421/246111

This is one of the most important names in Italian wine-making. It actually emerged from a recent poll that Santa Margherita is the most widely distributed Italian label in restaurants of the upper middle level throughout the world; a very satisfying statistic for this large and famous company owned by the Marzotto Group. We take note of this fact and congratulate them on their good fortune, but we are bound to say that we would hope for a bit more from the wines that Santa Margherita presents us with each year. In fact, we believe that the company's strategies of communication and promotion, which are among the most effective – if not the most effective – in the wine sector, should be given greater support by the actual quality of the wines on offer. We hasten to say that they are all correct and well made, but we feel the absence of a couple of wines of truly outstanding quality, such as the overwhelming majority of giant Italian wineries now seem capable of producing. So it's just fine that the Versato '97, a pleasant merlot with good body and fairly characteristic aromas, should win a prize at the Banco d'Assaggio at Torgiano, an important national wine competition. Just as it's all well and good that the Cabernet Sauvignon Ca' d'Archi '96 or the Alto Adige Müller Thurgau '98 or the Valdadige Pinot Grigio Impronta del Fondatore '98 should all be undoubtedly very well executed. But we long for more character, more "soul", more concentration and more typically varietal notes. In short, we would like the highly creative and well-distributed publicity to be matched by wines that are really interesting and not just pleasant, well-made and correct.

○	Valdadige Pinot Grigio Impronta del Fondatore '98	▼	3
○	A. A. Müller Thurgau '98	▼	2*
●	A. A. Cabernet Sauvignon Ca' d'Archi '96	▼	3
●	Versato '97	▼	3

FUMANE (VR)

★ ALLEGRINI
CORTE GIARA, 7
37022 FUMANE (VR)
TEL. 045/7701138

The Allegrinis have made an art of semi-drying their grapes, giving the lie to those who maintain that this is merely a means of increasing the sugar level of mediocre fruit. Instead, using extremely modern techniques, they emulate what history has taught the farmers of Valpolicella: to lay down only sound and rigorously selected grapes, impeding the attack of mold during drying in order to give the wine a happy combination of finesse and aging potential. The two Amarones are different, but equally splendid. The refined '94 proffers inviting warmth on the nose, and the fruit evolves beautifully on the palate, while well-defined aromas and an amazing fragrance characterize its brilliant finish. In the majestically rounded and complex '95, the restrained and suggestive strength of flavors redefines one's approach to Amarone and fully lives up to the reputation of the vintage: the measured and gradual progression of aromas and the mouth-filling fruit which make it a delight to drink are just two of its outstanding qualities. The deep, complex sweetness of the Recioto reveals itself with the elegance and restraint of a truly fine wine: its slowness in opening up is then matched by the intensity with which it evolves on the palate. The La Poja, made entirely from corvina grapes, is an indicator for the future of this estate: to make memorable wines even without drying. The balance of this red hinges on the contrast between its seductively soft tones of dark berries and its resolute, vigorous extract; its length of flavor and its solidity suggest an exceptional aging potential. The Palazzo della Torre has never been so good: its masterly balance is an example well worth following.

●	Amarone della Valpolicella Cl. '95	▼▼▼	6
●	La Poja '95	▼▼▼	6
●	Amarone della Valpolicella Cl. '94	▼▼	6
●	Recioto della Valpolicella Cl. Giovanni Allegrini '96	▼▼	6
●	Valpolicella Cl. Sup. La Grola '96	▼▼	4
●	Valpolicella Cl. Sup. Palazzo della Torre '96	▼▼	4
●	Valpolicella Cl. '98	▼	3
●	La Poja '93	▽▽▽	6
●	Amarone della Valpolicella Cl. '93	▽▽▽	6
●	Recioto della Valpolicella Amarone Cl. Sup. '91	▽▽▽	5
●	Recioto della Valpolicella Cl. Giovanni Allegrini '93	▽▽▽	5

FUMANE (VR)

LE SALETTE
VIA PIO BRUGNOLI, 11/C
37022 FUMANE (VR)
TEL. 045/7701027

Franco Scamperle's moment has come: a stunning '95 Amarone rewards his family's efforts and affords recognition for the impeccable operation he has built up with passionate devotion. In the last few years there have been other wines from Le Salette which have just missed out on Three Glasses, but our high esteem for the estate does not spring from these scores. It is, instead, based on two factors: Franco Scamperle's exemplary maintenance of a high level of quality throughout the range and the attention he has always paid to his "lesser" wines. Besides, this time around we were overwhelmed by a truly memorable and elegant red that combines tradition with innovation and has been obtained through ruthless grape selection and absolutely faultless vinification and aging. The wine is called Pergole Vece. Its deep color is accompanied by a complex bouquet that offers a really delightful variety of rich aromas. The entry on the palate is immediately mouth-filling, and then the wine just continues to evolve beautifully, revealing the entire arsenal of elements which make this a truly fine red: tannins, extract, alcohol, glycerine and acidity; this armory will also serve to give the wine remarkable aging potential. We noted the same skillful hand in the Le Traversagne '96, the basic Recioto. Its concentration is evident even from its color, and we particularly enjoyed the richness of its perfumes, its well-balanced sweetness and the length of its flavor. The Amarone La Marega '95 showed well too. It is on a smaller scale than the Pergole Vece, but is similarly elegant and appealing. The '98 Valpolicella is fair, while the Superiore I Progni offers unusual aromas and a well-structured palate.

●	Amarone della Valpolicella Cl. Pergole Vece '95	🍷🍷🍷	6
●	Amarone della Valpolicella Cl. La Marega '95	🍷🍷	5
●	Recioto della Valpolicella Le Traversagne '96	🍷🍷	5
●	Valpolicella Cl. Sup. I Progni '96	🍷🍷	3*
●	Valpolicella Cl. Sup. Ca' Carnocchio '96	🍷	3
●	Valpolicella Cl. '98		2
●	Amarone della Valpolicella Cl. La Marega '94	🍸🍸	5
●	Amarone della Valpolicella Cl. Pergole Vece '93	🍸🍸	6

GAMBELLARA (VI)

LA BIANCARA
C.DA BIANCARA, 8
36053 GAMBELLARA (VI)
TEL. 0444/444244

In the argument between those who attribute the greater importance to the work carried out in the cellar and those who concentrate all their attention on their vines, Angiolino Maule has taken up an uncompromising position. For him, a good wine can only be the logical consequence of hard work in the vineyards, which leads to the grapes being picked at optimum ripeness. In the cellar, therefore, one must simply perform a script that has already been written, with full respect for (and without altering in any way) the raw materials which nature has thought fit to provide. Angiolino confronts this challenge with courage and enjoys the satisfaction of seeing neighboring large and small producers alike follow in his footsteps. His wines proclaim their terroir, whether they be soft like his Reciotos or sinewy like his Gambellaras, and they have never been as good as they are this year. The I Masieri selection stands out for its excellent quaffability and a rich, long aftertaste. The Sassaia is even better: it has enchanting and well-defined aromas and displays the exuberant acidity of garganega, held in check by plump fruit that finishes long and rich. The very successful '96 Recioto seems to be better balanced than the '95. The nose offers us fine, clean, ripe fruit, and good skin maceration is evident. The flavor is harmonious, with a seductive balance between the sugars and the acidity. The Recioto Riserva '92 is a real star. It reveals an opulent, Mediterranean style, but is at the same time unadorned, indeed almost severe; its complex bouquet of dried fruit, fig and sweet spice is set off by rich fruit on the not at all cloying palate, which possesses an almost staggering length.

○	Gambellara Cl. Sup. Sassaia '98	🍷🍷	3*
○	Recioto di Gambellara '96	🍷🍷	5
○	Recioto di Gambellara Ris. '92	🍷🍷	6
○	Gambellara Cl. I Masieri '98	🍷	2*
○	Recioto di Gambellara '95	🍸🍸	5
●	Rosso La Biancara '96	🍸	4

GAMBELLARA (VI)

ZONIN
VIA BORGOLECCO, 9
36053 GAMBELLARA (VI)
TEL. 0444/640111

The greatest source of satisfaction for Franco Giacosa, Technical Director of the Zonin group, isn't the success of Acciaiolo in Tuscany or the fine performance of the wines from Tenuta Il Bosco in the Oltrepò, but rather the first really good showing by the Gambellara Il Giangio, a white from the parent winery. This wine earned One Glass, a rating that may not seem sensational, especially as it is the same as last year's. In fact it is, though, because it signals the beginning of the real upswing in quality that Giacosa so badly wanted to achieve but found so difficult to obtain because of the abundant yields which the vineyards surrounding the company's headquarters had been trained to produce. Once they had tasted the finished product, however, even those growers least willing to reduce production accepted this painful but necessary cure. We all know that garganega does not give easy and immediate whites: this, if you like, is a good thing, because it means Gambellara does not have to compete with "international" stars, but can be allowed to express its frank personality, its clarity of fragrance, composed of few but distinct aromas, and its incisive and fairly rustic structure. There is still considerable room for this white to improve, but Zonin seems to be on the right track, particularly if one compares it to the much simpler '97 version. Of the other Zonin wines, the Prosecco Brut and the Amarone confirm their reliable quality, but the Berengario, the red Bordeaux blend from Friuli, did not quite live up to our expectations. From that region we also have the Ca' Bolani range: the particularly impressive offerings this year are the Sauvignon, with its notable force on the palate, and the Pinot Grigio Aristòs, which is less powerful, but extremely elegant.

○	Friuli Aquileia Sauvignon Ca' Bolani '98	🍷🍷	3*
●	Amarone della Valpolicella Maso Laito '95	🍷	4
●	Berengario '96	🍷	4
○	Friuli Aquileia Pinot Bianco Ca' Bolani '98	🍷	3
○	Friuli Aquileia Pinot Grigio Aristòs Ca' Bolani '98	🍷	3
○	Gambellara Cl. '98	🍷	1*
○	Gambellara Cl. Podere Il Giangio '98	🍷	2*
○	Prosecco Spumante Brut	🍷	2*
●	Amarone della Valpolicella '94	🍸	4
●	Amarone Podere Il Maso '92	🍸	4

ILLASI (VR)

ROMANO DAL FORNO
VIA LODOLETTA, 4
FRAZ. CELLORE
37030 ILLASI (VR)
TEL. 045/7834923

The quest for perfection is a long, perhaps endless process, so Dal Forno does not consider that he has already reached his goal. He feels he is just at the beginning of a path which he can see clearly but which we can hardly glimpse. His wines have a very particular geographical origin. Being a long way from the Valpolicella Classico zone as regards mentality, too, Romano has interpreted tradition in his own way, freeing it from those criteria of "typicity" which he finds too limiting. His wines speak their own clear language: they are individualistic, warm, opulent and sometimes even excessive, but they are never banal and are always instantly recognizable. The rich and glowing Recioto '94 is a case in point: it is certainly no shrinking violet. The Valpolicella Superiore '94 is one of the best of its type: it doesn't try, as in some other vintages, to disguise itself as a small-scale Amarone, but instead succeeds in establishing its own particular identity, in a style that is certainly more immediate and approachable than before. The '93 Amarone is definitely one of Romano's finest wines ever. Here we find his ability to interpret the individual vintage perfectly displayed, as well as his courage to make a marked change in style. The power, the intoxicating richness of fruit and the intensity which we expect from him all remain, but behind all this one finds an extra elegance and freshness which come from meticulous attention to his grapes. The wine, though still slightly dumb on the nose, is already complex, exciting and delicious, with a long finish made even more appealing by an evident hint of residual sweetness. It will be really difficult to resist enjoying it right away, but this Amarone will also develop extraordinary complexity with time.

●	Amarone Vigneto di Monte Lodoletta '93	🍷🍷🍷	6
●	Recioto della Valpolicella Vigneto di Monte Lodoletta '94	🍷🍷	6
●	Valpolicella Sup. '94	🍷🍷	6
●	Amarone Vigneto di Monte Lodoletta '87	🍸🍸🍸	6
●	Amarone Vigneto di Monte Lodoletta '88	🍸🍸🍸	6
●	Amarone Vigneto di Monte Lodoletta '89	🍸🍸🍸	6
●	Amarone Vigneto di Monte Lodoletta '90	🍸🍸🍸	6
●	Amarone Vigneto di Monte Lodoletta '91	🍸🍸🍸	6

ILLASI (VR)

F.lli Giuliari
Loc. Santa Giustina, 3/4
37031 Illasi (VR)
tel. 045/7834143

After its satisfying showing last year, the Giuliari brothers' winery repeats its success with a splendid Amarone '95, thus displaying once again its vocation for making wines which are exciting and pull no punches. Among the many Amarones we tasted, several were excellent, but we rarely came across real intensity of aroma and flavor, as if the year had cast a soporific veil over Valpolicella and made the zone miss out on a really big opportunity. Naturally, this was not the case at this estate, which combines the most rigorous viticultural practices in the eastern Valpolicella area with an innovative approach to vinification. Their Amarone takes on, therefore, a notably complete style: it has excellent depth of color, and its nose opens up to reveal the full rich concentration of the semi-dried grapes. On the palate its fruit is impetuous yet velvety, really full and long; it precisely echoes the bouquet, and the finish is really elegant and persuasive. The broad and lively Cabernet Sauvignon '97 offers excellent flavor, with supple, full-bodied and persistent fruit; the oak is starting to meld with the aromas, which are becoming increasingly interesting, offering a balance of concentrated fruity notes with headier spicy tones. We know that it is not difficult to make a good Cabernet, but often producers go too far and make wines that are over-muscular; this one, however, displays exemplary restraint. Only the Recioto '97 offered a less successful performance than last year; we don't know, at the moment, if this is because of being released too early or if there is actually a problem with the fruit; in any case, the wine is still quite pleasant.

●	Amarone della Valpolicella Cl. '95	🍷🍷	5
●	Cabernet Sauvignon Santa Giustina '97	🍷🍷	5
●	Recioto della Valpolicella '97	🍷	5
●	Amarone della Valpolicella Cl. '93	🍸🍸	5
●	Recioto della Valpolicella '96	🍸🍸	5

ILLASI (VR)

Santi
Via Ungheria, 33
37031 Illasi (VR)
tel. 045/6520077

Santi's decision to postpone the first release of its Amarone Proemio '95 proved to be the right one: this red has benefited from an extra year's aging in bottle and was therefore fully ready at the time of our tastings. Santi maintains that the grapes for this wine come from Valpolicella Classico, though its denomination does not make this claim and so, probably, grapes from the Illasi district are also included. This combination of the two spirits of the Verona area proves itself to be a winning one: there are both a warm fleshiness and silky mineral-toned fruit. Its bright color and its frank spicy perfumes are evidence of the use of new oak, and the entry on the palate is soft and clean. The fruit then evolves elegantly in the mouth and the finish echoes the wine's initial finesse. The only element that seems to need a little fine-tuning is the maturation in barrique: the oak has not yet fully integrated with the fruit. This sensation is also dominant in the Soave Sanfederici, which is certainly obtained from excellent grapes but whose fruit is slightly impoverished by the oak. The Soave Monteforte has undoubtedly been skillfully made, but lacks the touch of liveliness that would enhance its appeal. The very nearly Two Glass Bianco di Custoza has quite accustomed us to its unpredictability. This time it did very well, thanks to the delicious harmony between its aromas and flavor. Turning finally to the reds, we draw your attention to the good showing put up by the modern and voluptuous Valpolicella Le Solane, another example of the attention that Santi devotes to its wines; the wine-making here is in the safe hands of Marco Monchiero, one of Italy's finest oenologists, who has long been connected with the wineries in the Gruppo Italiano Vini.

●	Amarone della Valpolicella Proemio '95	🍷🍷	6
○	Bianco di Custoza I Frari '98	🍷	2*
○	Soave Cl. Monteforte '98	🍷	2*
○	Soave Cl. Sanfederici '98	🍷	3
●	Valpolicella Sup. Le Solane '97	🍷	3
●	Amarone della Valpolicella '90	🍸🍸	5
●	Amarone della Valpolicella '91	🍸	5

ILLASI (VR)

TRABUCCHI
LOC. MONTE TENDA
37031 ILLASI (VR)
TEL. 045/7833233 - 049/650129

We must express our satisfaction at the results of our tastings of this relatively newly-established estate's wines, which seem to have found the reliability they were lacking. The number of Glasses in the grid below is not as significant as the fact that the wines are actually mainly from the '96 vintage, whose mediocrity they manage to conceal pretty well. We can see evidence of this in the two Valpolicellas, which display an excellent level of ripeness that will act as a basis for further maturation. The new Terre del Cereolo, considered the more ambitious wine by the Trabucchis, has a broad traditionally-styled nose: the typical warmth combines with a really notable depth of fruit. The Terre di San Colombano is even better balanced: though concentrated, even in appearance, this Valpolicella shows ideally restrained alcohol, well integrated as it is with the solid, full-bodied fruit. In conclusion, we should like to point out the distinctness of the finish of both the above wines, a quality not always present in previous vintages. The Amarone is spicy, floral and creamy: its rating indicates its success. It doesn't possess enormous structure, but what it has it displays with satisfactory authority. The warmth of the alcohol is perhaps a little too marked, but the finish makes up for this with a delightful echo of the bouquet. We are withholding our judgment on the '96 Recioto as the wine is still not ready for release. The more stable Passito Bianco Sparavieri shows the subtle balance for which it is well known.

●	Amarone della Valpolicella '96	🍷🍷	6
●	Valpolicella Sup. Terre di San Colombano '96	🍷🍷	4
○	Passito Sparavieri '97	🍷	4
●	Valpolicella Sup. Terre del Cereolo '96	🍷	4
●	Amarone della Valpolicella '95	YY	5
●	Recioto della Valpolicella '95	YY	5
●	Amarone della Valpolicella '93	Y	5

LAZISE (VR)

LAMBERTI
VIA GARDESANA
37017 LAZISE (VR)
TEL. 045/7580034

Lamberti did not succeed in repeating its very good performance of last year: its wines were very much affected by the problems of the '98 vintage, so they are merely sound and honest. We must also add that certain reds, like the Amarone, which have done well in the recent past, were not available for tasting, and this also made the general picture less exciting than usual. The best wine is, once again, the Soave Santepietre: it is impeccably made and offers satisfying, well-balanced and reasonably persistent fruit on the palate. The Lugana Oro is in a minor key, though not at all disagreeable: it lacks the incisiveness that has been one of its most appealing features in other vintages. The Chiaretto deserves an honorable mention: it is subtle and delicate, but wants a little more length. The Bardolino, however, reveals greater verve, and the Bianco di Custozas are among the most dependable wines in Lamberti's range. The Orchidea Platino is enjoyable, thanks to its spicily floral nose as well as its supple yet mouth-filling fruit on the palate. The basic version has a more direct appeal: it offers excellent definition on the nose and is crisp and refreshing on the palate. Lastly, the version called Le Galene is rather slight and much too simple to be considered more than sound and neutral.

●	Bardolino Cl. Santepietre '98	🍷	2*
○	Bianco di Custoza Santepietre '98	🍷	2*
○	Bianco di Custoza Orchidea Platino '98	🍷	3
○	Soave Cl. Santepietre '98	🍷	3
⊙	Bardolino Cl. Chiaretto Santepietre '98		2
○	Bianco di Custoza Le Galene '98		2
●	Amarone Corte Rubini '93	Y	5
●	Amarone Corte Rubini '94	Y	5

LAZISE (VR)

Le Tende di Fortuna e Lucillini

Loc. Le Tende
Fraz. Colà
37010 Lazise (VR)
tel. 045/7590748

Mauro Fortuna and Beatrice Lucillini bought this estate about ten years ago. Mauro runs the business full-time, looking after every aspect from the vineyards to the cellar, while Beatrice is in charge of marketing and management. The grapes they vinify, around half of which come from their own vineyards, the other half from external suppliers, yield a total of 100 thousand bottles. The singular position of the estate, straddling the boarder between the Bianco di Custoza and Bardolino DOCs , allows Mauro to experiment with both types of wine and offer an interesting and varied range. The list is rounded off by a pair of more ambitious reds, the Cicisbeo and the Sorbo degli Uccellatori, and by a Bianco Passito, the Amoroso. This year, as always, the Passito is pleasant, but it is a little too light and, on the whole, not as good as in the very best vintages. The Cicisbeo '97, a Bordeaux blend with the addition of a little sangiovese, is the winery's most interesting offering. The complexity and richness of the nose introduce the substantial fruit on the front palate which, supported by the wine's very good structure, gradually evolves to reveal all its stimulating qualities. Of the typical Lake Garda wines we especially liked the Bianco di Custoza Lucillini '98, which is partly fermented and aged in oak and offers a pleasing gamut of aromas, sound structure and a long, attractive finish. The Bianco di Custoza Oro '98 is not as good as in the past, and the rather lackluster Bardolinos probably show the effects of their unfortunate vintage.

●	Cicisbeo '97	▼▼	4
○	Bianco di Custoza Lucillini '98	▼	3
○	Amoroso '97	▼	4
⊙	Bardolino Cl. Chiaretto '98		2
○	Bianco di Custoza Oro '98		2
○	Amoroso '95	▽▽	4
●	Cicisbeo '95	▽▽	4
●	Cicisbeo '96	▽	4
●	Sorbo degli Uccellatori '96	▽	3

MARANO DI VALPOLICELLA (VR)

Giuseppe Campagnola

Via Agnella, 9
Fraz. Valgatara
37020 Marano di Valpolicella (VR)
tel. 045/7703900

The Campagnola family's winery is going through an intense period of reorganization in the quest of higher quality. As could be expected, this transitional phase is marked by some really impressive bottles which alternate with wines that could (and indeed must) improve. Giuseppe, the real driving force in the family business, is taking a leaf out of the top producers' book in order to create an irreproachable range: purchasing vineyards so as to be less dependent on the grapes of other growers, applying more rigorous grape selection and using wine-making methods designed to give cleaner and purer sensations. This is the origin of the Amarone Catarina Zardini '95, a dry, modern version of the Veronese passito (raisin wine). It has an intense red hue, with a positive nose and some complexity in its evolution of flavor; had it caused just a shade more excitement it would have been in line for Three Glasses. The Valpolicella Superiore Le Bine is very good. It too is clean, velvety and vigorous, and displays the typically attractive style of its denomination without any of the unpleasant heaviness sometimes caused by the "ripasso" system (involving the addition of unpressed dried skins from Amarone). Another fine example from the Le Bine line is the Soave, which Campagnola purchases from two of the best producers in that zone: it offers an extremely attractive style which highlights both the lively ripeness of the garganega and the mellow broadness of the chardonnay. The Bianco di Custoza is sound, as opposed to the much-awaited Recioto Casotto del Merlo, which does not seem to have benefited from the positive '97 vintage. Lastly, the Amarone '96, for which our unofficial tastings had given us considerable hopes, is fairly neutral in character and has lost fruit during aging.

●	Amarone della Valpolicella Caterina Zardini '95	▼▼	6
○	Soave Cl. Sup. Le Bine '98	▼▼	2*
●	Valpolicella Cl. Sup. Le Bine '97	▼▼	2*
●	Amarone della Valpolicella '96		4
○	Bianco di Custoza '98		1
●	Amarone della Valpolicella '95	▽	4

Michele Castellani e Figli

Via Granda, 1
Fraz. Valgatara
37020 Marano di Valpolicella (VR)
tel. 045/7701253

Sergio Castellani introduced, with the excellent '95 vintage, a new range of wines called Ca' del Pipa, which includes classic wines from Valpolicella interpreted in an innovative idiom, whereas those in the I Castei line are more firmly anchored to tradition. The results of our tastings were excellent in both cases and are symptomatic of a really exemplary production method, particularly as the estate vinifies its own grapes but also buys in a fair quantity. The Ca' del Pipa Amarone displays prodigious richness and concentration; if we add that it has a freshly aromatic nose and a refined overall harmony, then we have the blueprint for a delicious and intensely-flavored red. The '97 Recioto has an understated sweetness and an inviting fragrance; on the palate it is fresh and, though not especially long, is eminently satisfying. The Amarone Campo Casalin has a deep but mature color; the full, rich nose with its notes of distilled fruit and coffee leads into a broad, positive and seductive flavor. The range of wines from the Valpolicella zone has been enlarged with some actual Valpolicellas, and these are all of a fair standard. In the Ca' del Pipa line, the clean and appealing Superiore '97 is a greater success than the Ripasso '96, which is dominated by the oak and has not really benefited by being refermented on the lees of the Recioto. The Cabernet del Capitel '95 is well made and has a certain verve; the youthful Valpolicella is simple and not particularly ambitious.

● Amarone della Valpolicella Cl. Ca' del Pipa '95	TT	5
● Amarone della Valpolicella Cl. Campo Casalin I Castei '95	TT	6
● Recioto della Valpolicella Cl. Ca' del Pipa '97	TT	5
● Cabernet Sauvignon del Capitel '95	T	4
● Valpolicella Cl. Sup. Ca' del Pipa '97	T	3
● Valpolicella Cl. Sup. Ripasso Ca' del Pipa '96		4
● Amarone della Valpolicella I Castei '94	YY	5
● Recioto della Valpolicella I Castei '96	YY	5

Corte Rugolin

Loc. Rugolin, 1
Fraz. Valgatara
37020 Marano di Valpolicella (VR)
tel. 045/7702153

Marano is becoming a point of reference for the entire Valpolicella zone: hardly a year goes by without a new producer, with his sights set on high quality, emerging from this village. But the even more significant aspect of these new estates is the great emphasis they lay on the importance of their vineyards, which tend to be small in size but managed with a care and attention that are quite unusual for the overproductive area to the west of Verona. Corte Rugolin started up in 1995 as an offshoot of Bruno Coati's winery. It is run by his children Elena and Federico, who share the various aspects of the estate's operations, with the invaluable assistance of the oenologist Luigi Andreoli. They have five hectares under vine and, though these are planted using the traditional Veronese low pergola system, the aim is progressively to reduce their yields. Vinification here is intelligent: it is based on traditional methods without being straitjacketed by them, and in the aging of the wines, too, cleanness is a principal aim. This sensation is to be found in the well-made Valpolicella Superiore, conceived without any intention of making it a big, full-bodied wine but nevertheless fashioned with undoubted skill. This is a lively and delicious red, with soft, measured and gratifyingly warm fruit. We predict that the similarly stylish Recioto '97 will evolve very well in bottle: its promising deep color leads one into broad, sweet, well-balanced fruit on the palate, which perfectly echoes the aromas on the nose and carries on through to a satisfyingly long finish. The Amarone '95 is good, too: it fits nicely into a range of wines intended to give pleasure rather than merely to impress. The Aresco is deep and fascinating, and its flavor evolves irresistibly on the palate: it is a worthy heir to the noble dynasty of white wines made from semi-dried grapes in Valpolicella.

○ Aresco '97	TT	5
● Amarone della Valpolicella Cl. Vigna Monte Danieli '95	TT	6
● Recioto della Valpolicella Cl. '97	TT	5
● Valpolicella Cl. Sup. Ripasso '97	T	4
● Valpolicella Cl. '98		2

F.LLI DEGANI

VIA TOBELLE, 3/A
FRAZ. VALGATARA
37020 MARANO DI VALPOLICELLA (VR)
TEL. 045/7701850

Aldo Degani is a perfect example of the traditional winegrower whose watchwords are self-denial and hard labor, whereas his brother Luca personifies the up-to-date, forward-thinking technician: from this apparent clash of personalities comes a highly successful synergistic team that produces absolutely exemplary wines. The '94 Amarone is one of these, in spite of the disheartening outcome of that vintage generally (but, tricky as it was, it held some splendid surprises in store). According to the Deganis, making the '94 Amarone involved a major cutback in terms of volume. And then, early tastings of the wine were far from encouraging, as the wine seemed indecipherable and unable to find its true style. Now it has opened up completely and boasts a majestic potency. Its opaque garnet color leads on into complex, persistent aromas that remind one that the wine has been made from semi-dried grapes, but that lack the tiredness such wines are unfortunately prone to display. The same lively, clean style is to be found on the palate, where the fruit is sumptuous, mouth-filling and long. If the Amarone is now essentially ready for drinking, the same cannot be said for the Recioto '97, which we shall consequently discuss in next year's Guide. The warmth of the alcohol is the most noticeable element in the Valpolicella Superiore '96, from which, to be honest, we did not expect great things; it does, however, seem better-balanced and more well-knit than the '95 version, and is a good example of a mature, enjoyable red. The '98 Valpolicella is an improvement, too, and has a remarkably appealing style.

● Amarone della Valpolicella Cl. '94	🍷🍷	4
● Valpolicella Cl. '98	🍷	2*
● Valpolicella Cl. Sup. '96	🍷	3
● Amarone della Valpolicella '92	♀♀	4
● Amarone della Valpolicella '93	♀♀	4
● Recioto della Valpolicella '95	♀♀	4
● Recioto della Valpolicella '96	♀♀	4

MARANO DI VALPOLICELLA (VR)

GIUSEPPE LONARDI

VIA DELLE POSTE, 2
37020 MARANO DI VALPOLICELLA (VR)
TEL. 045/7755154

Giuseppe Lonardi divides his time between his winery and the trattoria he runs together with his family. Once upon a time he was principally a restaurateur, but today, encouraged in part by the results he has achieved, he devotes an increasing amount of his attention to making his wines. The cellar, built in the mid-'80s beneath his house, is small but well-equipped and spotless. Half of the 50 thousand bottles he produces come from grapes grown in his own three and a half hectares of vineyards, and the other half from grapes bought in from long-standing suppliers. The Amarone '95, helped by a vintage that many have called historic, displays great vitality on the nose, as well as admirable balance and restraint. On the palate it is warm, attractively deep and very long: a fine example of a wine with fresh, well-structured flavor. The Recioto '97 also showed well: in spite of its slightly excessive sweetness we enjoyed it because of the richness of its perfumes and its good depth on the palate. This year the estate also offered the Recioto Le Arele, named, in dialect, after the racks on which the grapes are dried: this wine matures for about three years, dividing its time between stainless steel, new barriques and bottles. The '95 vintage did not seem entirely successful because it is a bit too light and undemanding. No doubt Giuseppe will succeed in perfecting this wine over the next few years, bringing out its full potential. The Privilegia '96, which had shown well in the previous vintage, was compromised by the less than favorable year, and was rather light and unexciting.

● Amarone della Valpolicella Cl. '95	🍷🍷	5
● Recioto della Valpolicella Cl. '97	🍷	4
● Recioto della Valpolicella Cl. Le Arele '95	🍷	5
● Valpolicella Cl. '98	🍷	2*
● Privilegia '96		4
● Recioto della Valpolicella '96	♀♀	4
● Amarone della Valpolicella '93	♀	5
● Recioto della Valpolicella '95	♀	4

Novaia

Via Novaia, 3
37020 Marano di Valpolicella (VR)
tel. 045/7755129

Novaia is a small estate run by the two Vaona brothers. Cesare (in the vineyards) and Giampaolo (in the cellar) devote every moment of their free time to the estate (they both have other jobs). Furthermore, Giampaolo has a son who is an oenologist, and he too will most likely become involved in the proceedings. The winery, then, is alive and viable, and this is made even more evident by the plans to renew both cellar and vineyards. At the moment only three of the Vaonas's eight hectares of vines are in full production: the others have recently been replanted and will soon start to bear fruit. The wines produced here stand out for their elegant perfumes and the rich concentration on the palate. The Amarone '95, for example, displays really delicious fruit framed in a notable structure, and notes of ripe dark berries alternate with floral scents on the nose; a fine balance is ensured by the wine's fresh acidity. In the Amarone '94 we find the same characteristics, but here the vintage is also of some consequence: the structure is lighter and the well-balanced components are on a more modest scale. The Valpolicella maintains the high Novaia standards, displaying elegant perfumes and deep, warm and evolving fruit on the palate. The restraint with which the "ripasso" technique has been used contributes greater softness without giving the unpleasant heavy notes often found in wines of this type.

● Amarone della Valpolicella Cl. '95	▼▼	4
● Valpolicella Cl. '97	▼▼	2*
● Amarone della Valpolicella Cl. '94	▼	4
● Valpolicella Sup. '96	▽	3
● Amarone della Valpolicella '91	▽▽	5

MARANO DI VALPOLICELLA (VR)

San Rustico

Via Pozzo, 2
Fraz. Valgatara
37020 Marano di Valpolicella (VR)
tel. 045/7703348

The Campagnola brothers' winery proves its quality this year with an excellently made Recioto, designed as a happy combination of the fragrant, early-drinking style generally favored by the Veronese and the sweeter, more complex red for which there is an increasing demand. It displays a deep ruby color with purple highlights. The fruit on the nose is natural and inviting, with hints of jam that are echoed on the palate. The flavor reveals a sweet creaminess which, however, never becomes cloying: indeed, the finish is notable for its fresh, dry and persistent aftertaste. Another well-made wine is the Valpolicella Superiore '96, which confirms last year's rating in spite of the unexciting vintage. Its main characteristic is the liveliness of its bouquet which, though a little heady, offers well-expressed scents of strawberry and red currant. On the palate it is broad and well-structured though not particularly deep, and the finish is well-defined. The wines that raised a few doubts, however, were the Amarones. The one from the estate's celebrated Gaso cru did not confirm the excellent impression made by the basic '94 Amarone last year, so we shall be considering it in the next edition of the Guide. The standard version, on the other hand, is of fair quality: it is not at all unbalanced but neither does it possess the verve that we had hoped for from a '95. Lastly, the youthful Valpolicella '98 was good enough to warrant an honorable mention.

● Recioto della Valpolicella '97	▼▼	4
● Valpolicella Cl. Sup. Vigneti del Gaso '96	▼▼	3*
● Amarone della Valpolicella Cl. '95	▼	4
● Valpolicella Cl. '98		2
● Amarone della Valpolicella Cl. '94	▽▽	4
● Amarone della Valpolicella Cl. Vigneti del Gaso '90	▽▽	5
● Amarone della Valpolicella Cl. Vigneti del Gaso '91	▽▽	5
● Amarone della Valpolicella Cl. '93	▽	4
● Amarone della Valpolicella Cl. Vigneti del Gaso '93	▽	5

MEZZANE DI SOTTO (VR)

Corte Sant'Alda
Via Capovilla, 28
Loc. Fioi
37030 Mezzane di Sotto (VR)
tel. 045/8880006

Valpolicella is an area of great contrasts. Thus alongside magnificent ancient villas you find the encroachments of wild and often unauthorized building speculation, an unsightly blot on some of the district's most beautiful sites. Then, perhaps, you turn a corner and there is no trace left of these eyesores: nature has taken the upper hand once again, and you discover steep hillsides with cultivated terraces; hidden, rounded valleys where the vines are sheltered and the soil is ideal for their growth; and farm cottages and wineries built of stone which seem to be a man-made expression of the countryside around them. As you climb from the plain towards Corte Sant'Alda you become increasingly aware of this natural environment, which Marinella Camerani's wines evoke, as well as much else besides. They reflect the warmth of the sunshine in the hills of Mezzane and they temper it with the fresher, more elegant tones that derive from the altitude of the vineyards. While looking forward to another champion that can repeat the splendor of the Amarone '90, we enjoyed an interesting range of wines. The Valpolicella '98 does not quite avoid a certain rustic quality and the Superiore '96 deserves only an honorable mention, but the Mithas '96 reassures you right from its appearance, which suggests complexity and concentration: it is from a not especially good vintage but succeeds in making you forget it. The Amarone '94, one of the best of its year, has the usual wealth of rounded, alcoholic notes on the nose, which do not prevent it, however, from being graceful and elegant; in the mouth it offers the same sensations, and the fruit evolves nicely, caressing the palate with its velvety tannins and leaving a long finish. The Recioto '96 comes very close to earning Two Glasses thanks to its beautiful balance.

●	Amarone della Valpolicella '94	🍷🍷	6
●	Valpolicella Sup. Mithas '96	🍷🍷	4
●	Recioto della Valpolicella '96	🍷	4
●	Valpolicella '98		3
●	Valpolicella Sup. '96		4
●	Amarone della Valpolicella '90	🍸🍸🍸	6
●	Amarone della Valpolicella '92	🍸🍸	5
●	Amarone della Valpolicella '93	🍸🍸	5
●	Amarone della Valpolicella Mithas '90	🍸🍸	6
●	Recioto della Valpolicella '94	🍸	4
●	Valpolicella Sup. Mithas '94	🍸	4

MIANE (TV)

Gregoletto
Via S. Martino, 1
Fraz. Premaor
31050 Miane (TV)
tel. 0438/970463

Gregoletto is a family-run winery. Luigi, the father, is in overall charge, both in the vineyards and in the cellar, and is helped by his children Giuseppe and Antonella, both qualified oenologists. His other child, Giovanni, looks after the commercial and administrative aspects of the business. The estate grows a third of its grapes itself and the remaining two thirds are purchased from long-standing suppliers. Both the grapes which the Gregolettos produce and those that are bought in come from hillside vineyards. The wine we tasted confirmed last year's trend: we preferred the whites to the reds, which had, in earlier editions of the Guide, stood out as the estate's top wines. Probably this can be put down to the last few vintages, which in this particular area have not been kind to later-ripening varieties. It will be interesting to see how the reds come out when the grapes are as good as the Gregolettos want them. The Colli di Conegliano Albio '98 has elegant floral perfumes, evolves interestingly on the palate and has an excellent finish. A good rich nose and a pleasant flavor are the characteristics of the Prosecco Tranquillo '98, one of the best of its type. The Prosecco Extra Dry, though delicate and appealing, was not up to last year's, and we enjoyed the freshness of the quaffable Verdiso. The Rosso '94 is too mature and has perhaps been released at a time when it is not really showing at its best. The Cabernet is not sufficiently well-modulated for an honorable mention, unlike the Merlot, in which we enjoyed the interesting combination of an undemanding, easy-drinking style and full, satisfying fruit.

○	Colli di Conegliano Bianco Albio '98	🍷🍷	3*
●	Merlot dei Colli Trevigiani '97	🍷	3
○	Conegliano Valdobbiadene Extra Dry	🍷	3
○	Conegliano Valdobbiadene Tranquillo '98	🍷	2
●	Colli di Conegliano Rosso Gregoletto '94	🍷	4
○	Verdiso dei Colli Trevigiani '98	🍷	2*
●	Cabernet '95	🍸🍸	3
●	Rosso Gregoletto '93	🍸🍸	4

MONSELICE (PD)

BORIN
VIA DEI COLLI, 5
35043 MONSELICE (PD)
TEL. 0429/74384

Gianni Borin's winery is one of the most interesting gateways to the Colli Euganei that you can find, prior to losing yourself among vineyards and picturesque old villages. The first Italian vineyard of sizeable dimensions devoted to cabernet was planted in the midst of these conical hills, which reveal their volcanic origins and have been dedicated to viticulture since ancient times. At the entrance to this handsome, recently completed winery, a sign reads "Borin, vini & vigne" (wines and vines), indicating the close relationship between this family and its vineyards, and the Borins' almost total dependence on grapes which they have grown and harvested themselves. The most successful wines are the whites, among which the Colli Euganei Bianco, a blend of garganega, sauvignon and pinot bianco, stands out. It has a broad, pungent nose, and displays intense, rich and attractively exotic fruit on the palate, with a persistent note of bitter almond. The Moscato Fior d'Arancio, definitely one of the best examples of its type, offers exuberant perfumes of flowers and citrus fruit. It is broad and fleshy in the mouth, where the fruit evolves gradually, accompanied by a fine, silky bead of carbon dioxide. The Pinot Bianco, which spends a short time in small oak casks, is interesting too: the palate follows through nicely from the nose and is dense and rounded; its most attractive quality is undoubtedly its beautiful overall balance.

○	Colli Euganei Bianco '98	🍷🍷	2*
○	Colli Euganei Pinot Bianco '98	🍷	2
○	Colli Euganei Spumante Fior d'Arancio '98	🍷	3

MONTEBELLO (VI)

DOMENICO CAVAZZA & F.LLI
VIA SELVA, 22
36054 MONTEBELLO (VI)
TEL. 0444/649166

Cavazza permanently occupies a place in the list of the best producers of the western part of the Province of Vicenza. The wines from this splendid winery at Selva di Montebello all bear the hallmark of extremely correct style, whether they be those in the more commercial lines or the more ambitious selections. Coming to the wines we tasted this year, we have to register a backward step from the standard to which we had become accustomed in recent years. Probably the vintage plays a role, with '96 rather unfavorable for the reds and '98 yielding whites that are low in acidity and, in any case, made from grapes that were plagued by rain at the time of the harvest. The great exception is the Sauvignon, which is refined, long and typical of its variety. The Recioto Capitel S. Libera '97 is, quite rightly, delicate in character, and has been vinified to point up the elegance of the fruit: one could not expect great concentration from it, but its frank, characteristic style is attractive. The Tocai Rosso reveals, even in its color, the light, lively fruit that one expects in this kind of wine. Its delicately spicy nose leads into a fresh, simple palate. The best red this year is the Cabernet Cicogna '96: soft and with a certain amount of body, it is still slightly dominated by the oak but a short time in bottle should allow it to do itself full justice. The Merlot, which impressed us in the '92 and '95 vintages, only gets an honorable mention this time around because of its overly straightforward style. Lastly, we also draw your attention to the herbaceous Cabernet Capitel S. Libera '96.

○	Colli Berici Sauvignon Capitel S. Libera '98	🍷🍷	2*
●	Colli Berici Cabernet Cicogna '96	🍷	4
○	Recioto di Gambellara Capitel S. Libera '97	🍷	4
●	Colli Berici Tocai Rosso '98	🍷	1*
●	Colli Berici Cabernet Capitel S. Libera '96		3
●	Colli Berici Merlot Cicogna '96		4
●	Colli Berici Cabernet Cicogna '95	🍸🍸	4
●	Colli Berici Merlot Cicogna '95	🍸🍸	4
●	Colli Berici Cabernet Capitel S. Libera '95	🍸	3

MONTEBELLO (VI)

DAL MASO
VIA SELVA, 62
36054 MONTEBELLO (VI)
TEL. 0444/649104

This winery, which is making its debut in the Guide, offers two quite distinct lines. On the one hand we find the typical wines of the Gambellara zone, all based on garganega; the Casara Roveri range, on the other hand, comes from the vineyards of the Colli Berici. Here the grapes make "international-style" whites and reds, and the producer has more room to maneuver. From their handsome, well-equipped winery at Montebello, Luigino and Nicola release some 250 thousand bottles a year. The range of wines presented was good, and some of them actually showed real personality rather than just a simple and correct style. The Tocai Rosso is, by its very nature, not an especially richly structured wine, but Dal Maso's is nevertheless one of the best, thanks to the adroitness of the wine-making. We tasted an interesting Chardonnay, also from the Colli Berici, kept in stainless steel, whose clean nose and reasonably long flavor we enjoyed, as well as an oak-aged Chardonnay, the Terra dei Roveri, which, like the Cabernet '97, only gained an honorable mention. The Recioto Riva dei Perari, presented in both its '97 and '98 versions, was satisfying. The vineyard is situated behind the winery, on steep terrain where the vines are planted on terraces and nurtured in such a way as to allow problem-free overripening of the grapes. After a long period of drying for the grapes, the must ferments for several months in barriques: the resulting wine has a handsome, warm golden color. The '97 is interesting, but the '98 is of superior quality, with better-defined aromas, a rich body and a clean, elegant finish. The Sauvignon has an intriguing, complex nose and solidly textured fruit on the palate. It is not yet perfectly well balanced but is nevertheless a wine worth keeping an eye on.

○	Recioto di Gambellara Cl. Riva dei Perari '98	🍷🍷	4
○	Colli Berici Chardonnay Casara Roveri '98	🍷	2*
○	Colli Berici Sauvignon Casara Roveri '98	🍷	2
○	Recioto di Gambellara Cl. Riva dei Perari '97	🍷	2
●	Colli Berici Tocai Rosso '98	🍷	1*
●	Colli Berici Cabernet Casara Roveri '97		3
○	Terra dei Roveri '98		3
○	Gambellara Cl. Vigneti Ca' Cischele '98		1

MONTEFORTE D'ALPONE (VR)

ROBERTO ANSELMI
VIA S. CARLO, 46
37032 MONTEFORTE D'ALPONE (VR)
TEL. 045/7611488

Having carefully studied the Soaves that this winery has produced in the last five years, we have noted how their style has adapted itself to the characteristics of each individual year and has reflected, in a masterly way, the differences between the vintages. Roberto Anselmi, in making his dry wines, has found a way to form his goals each time in absolute harmony with the fruit with which nature has provided him. The Capitel Croce, the Capitel Foscarino and the San Vincenzo offer a perfect snapshot, an exact record of what the harvest has brought in to his presses. With the Recioto, on the other hand, Anselmi operates according to his own instinct: his purpose is quite different and the wine always takes on certain unmistakable features, starting with the color, which has a very rich golden tone with copper highlights. The nose is even more recognizable: with its profusion of hints of candied citrus fruit, spice and macerated herbs, it is reminiscent of the fragrance of a drying loft during grape drying. On the palate, the sweetness is clean and immediately appealing and the fruit is extremely soft on entry, before becoming enlivened by a vibrant acidity. Returning to the Soaves, we highlight the notable performance given by the barrique-aged Capitel Croce '97, perhaps its best ever. The oak is quite noticeable, but well integrated with the fragrant fruit, which loses none of its vaunted attractiveness. The Capitel Foscarino has a delicious, immediate and natural appeal: it displays a full, rich flavor and exciting length. Vitality is also the principal characteristic of the San Vincenzo, which is just a touch less concentrated than the Capitel Foscarino, though similarly fresh and satisfying.

○	Recioto di Soave I Capitelli '97	🍷🍷	5
○	Soave Cl. Sup. Capitel Croce '97	🍷🍷	4
○	Soave Cl. Sup. Capitel Foscarino '98	🍷🍷	4
○	Soave Cl. Sup. San Vincenzo '98	🍷🍷	3*
○	Recioto dei Capitelli '87	YYY	6
○	Recioto dei Capitelli '88	YYY	6
○	Recioto di Soave I Capitelli '93	YYY	6
○	Recioto di Soave I Capitelli '96	YYY	5
●	Realda Cabernet Sauvignon '96	YY	4
○	Soave Cl. Sup. Capitel Croce '96	YY	4
○	Soave Cl. Sup. Capitel Foscarino '97	YY	3

CA' RUGATE

VIA MEZZAVILLA, 12
FRAZ. BROGNOLIGO
37030 MONTEFORTE D'ALPONE (VR)
TEL. 045/6175082

Wine producers have periods of growth and of reflection, of wanting to be innovative and of returning to tradition. Gianni Tessari experiences all these phases simultaneously: his natural empiricism makes him want to take advantage of every possible opportunity to exploit the full potential of the Soave zone and its grapes. The Bucciato is not meant merely to pay homage to the traditional practice of Brognoligo, where white wines have always been fermented on their skins, but is a genuine attempt to extract as broad a range as possible of substances and sensations from garganega. The resulting wine has a vibrant richness even in its appearance; it possesses remarkable depth, and one is aware of a strong, suggestive, stirring character. Its nose displays deep, complex and well-knit aromas, while the palate has an essential, clean, linear quality: it captivates with the strength of its flavor, its mouth-filling roundness and its exceptional length. The Bucciato, then, is not only of historical interest, just as the Soave Monte Alto is not merely a piece of stylistic virtuosity: it is also a white of thrilling finesse in which maturation in barrique has enhanced the garganega's traditional suppleness. It has a brilliant golden color and marked scents of flowers, sweet white-fleshed fruit and walnut. On the front palate, its dense fruit is immediately matched by the acidity which then modulates the wine's wonderfully well-balanced and persistent evolution in the mouth. The appeal of the Monte Fiorentine lies not only in the inviting herbaceous note on the nose but also in its juicy flavor and in the broad, rich aromas one finds on both nose and palate: these qualities make this Soave a rare delight to drink.

O	Soave Cl. '98	🍷🍷	3*
O	Soave Cl. Sup. Bucciato '98	🍷🍷	3*
O	Soave Cl. Sup. Monte Alto '98	🍷🍷	3*
O	Soave Cl. Sup. Monte Fiorentine '98	🍷🍷	3*
O	Recioto di Soave La Perlara '97	🍷	4
O	Soave Cl. Sup. Monte Alto '96	🍷🍷🍷	4
O	Soave Cl. Sup. Monte Alto '97	🍷🍷	4

MONTEFORTE D'ALPONE (VR)

FATTORI & GRANEY

VIA ZOPPEGA, 14
37032 MONTEFORTE D'ALPONE (VR)
TEL. 045/7460041

Giovanni Fattori has a very skillful touch. His Soave, rather than just being true to type or just expressing the quality of excellent grapes, is the perfect expression of Giovanni's precious combination of sensibility and long experience. There are not many producers who manage to impress their own style so clearly on their wine, and Soave does not leave an awful lot of room for maneuver, given the limits imposed on its expressiveness. However, hidden away in the folds of the wine's typically delicate style, we find a refined elegance and a series of nuances which would be insignificant individually, but which, together, create a complex and convincing whole. The color does not give much away: it is a pale straw. Fruity notes dominate initially on the nose, yielding gradually to subtle yet persistent floral scents, underpinned in the background by typical sweet almondy hints. The entry on the palate is beautifully clean, and the fruit then evolves vigorously towards a voluptuous finish. The highly satisfying Pinot Grigio is also beautifully executed. Its style has very little to do with the bone-dry, spare profile one often finds with this type of wine, but instead highlights the softness of its flavor and the broad vitality of its nose. Next to his new cellar, in which Fattori does not limit himself to making his own Soave, but vinifies that of other Veronese producers as well, there is to be a building for the production of a Recioto: we do not yet, however, have any more exact information.

O	Soave Cl. Sup. '98	🍷🍷	3*
O	Pinot Grigio delle Venezie '98	🍷	3

MONTEFORTE D'ALPONE (VR)

Sandro e Claudio Gini
Via G. Matteotti, 42
37032 Monteforte d'Alpone (VR)
tel. 045/7611908

What amazes us more and more each year is the special relationship these producers manage to create with their grapes and their ability to read beyond the technical data, to pick up on every nuance and transfer it to the wine. The Ginis seem to live in symbiosis with nature and this quality comes through in their wines, which, when tasted, always display great personality. Sandro and Claudio Gini produce whites of unique finesse: if they sometimes show an "international" stamp, it is only to a tiny degree: deep down there is a real expressiveness and substance to them which comes form the preferential rapport these two vignerons build up with their fruit. The resounding success of the Soave Salvarenza reveals the extent to which garganega can combine with oak without losing any of its fragrance. The balance between the varietal tones and the spiciness from the wood gives each an enthralling completeness, and the flavor evolves in a beautifully natural and vital way, echoing the aromas on the nose and creating a subtle and satisfying harmony. If the Salvarenza is a stately expression of Soave, the La Froscà offers more juicy and exciting sensations; its seductive appeal stems from its lively and intriguing evenness. It does not show the concentration of the '97, but the clarity of its bouquet and the silky texture in the mouth make it an absolute classic of its kind. The always absolutely reliable basic Soave is supple, complex and intense. A deep, inviting nose characterizes the warm and vigorous Col Foscarin: the Gini brothers have made a sumptuous desert wine without sacrificing the delicate style of Recioto di Soave.

○	Soave Cl. Sup. Contrada Salvarenza Vecchie Vigne '98	🍷🍷🍷	4
○	Recioto di Soave Col Foscarin '96	🍷🍷	6
○	Soave Cl. Sup. '98	🍷🍷	3*
○	Soave Cl. Sup. La Froscà '98	🍷🍷	4
○	Soave Cl. Sup. Contrada Salvarenza Vecchie Vigne '95	YYY	4
○	Soave Cl. Sup. Contrada Salvarenza Vecchie Vigne '96	YYY	4
○	Soave Cl. Sup. La Froscà '97	YYY	4
●	Pinot Nero Sorai Campo alle More '95	YY	5
○	Soave Cl. Sup. Contrada Salvarenza Vecchie Vigne '97	YY	4

MONTEFORTE D'ALPONE (VR)

La Cappuccina
Via San Brizio, 125
Fraz. Costalunga
37030 Monteforte d'Alpone (VR)
tel. 045/6175840 - 045/6175036

At La Cappuccina estate they seem to believe in a responsive versatility, as can be clearly seen in their three top wines: this year, too, their scores were very high. The dissimilarity among them stems not so much from the fact that they are made from different grapes by means of different techniques, as from the Tessaris' strong desire to give each one a very particular and precise style. The Recioto, for example, is an intense and Mediterranean white made from semi-dried grapes, which combines depth and a very appealing, easy-drinking style: the high sugar level and vigorous alcohol assert themselves without overwhelming the fragrance of the bouquet or the freshness of the flavor. In the Cabernet Franc Campo Buri we note the quest for a more subdued and refined style. The deep color has a mature tone, while the nose offers extremely inviting peppery hints which combine with the classic verdant notes of cabernet franc. The most attractive quality on the palate is its silky depth, which is not accompanied by great body, but this is compensated for by its engaging persistence. One is aware of the attractive maturity of the Soave San Brizio as soon as one sees its color. There is an initial hint of oak on the warm, complex nose; sensations of white-fleshed fruit and flowers and an almondy sweetness make the flavor even more captivating, and the finish displays a satisfying completeness. Among the other wines in the range the Soave Fontégo (for which the Tessari siblings, Elena, Pierantonio and Sisto, carried out a traditional vinification on the skins) showed particularly well. It is a ripe, rich white which has been slightly affected by the unfortunate '98 vintage. The basic Soave is delicate and well made.

●	Cabernet Franc Campo Buri '96	🍷🍷	4
○	Recioto di Soave Arzìmo '96	🍷🍷	5
○	Soave Cl. Sup. San Brizio '97	🍷🍷	4
○	Sauvignon '98	🍷	3
○	Soave Sup. '98	🍷	3
○	Soave Sup. Fontégo '98	🍷	3
●	Cabernet Franc Campo Buri '95	YYY	4
○	Recioto di Soave Arzìmo '95	YY	4
○	Soave Cl. Sup. San Brizio '96	YY	4
○	Soave Sup. Fontégo '97	YY	3
●	Cabernet Sauvignon Madégo '96	Y	3

MONTEFORTE D'ALPONE (VR)

UMBERTO PORTINARI

VIA S. STEFANO, 2
FRAZ. BROGNOLIGO
37030 MONTEFORTE D'ALPONE (VR)
TEL. 045/6175087

Beyond the built-up area of Monteforte d'Alpone and sheltered by the hills of the Soave zone lies the small village of Brognoligo. Facing a little square reminiscent of times gone by is Umberto Portinari's diminutive winery, which has little in common with the wineries with impressive gateways or coats of arms over the front door. Yet, on entering this house, you breathe an air of age-old attachment to the land and to human toil as a source of growth and gratification. Umberto came late to wine. He inherited the vineyards, but not the profession, although his knowledge of viticulture dates back to his childhood. However, the call of the land was imperative. Thus began his adventure, made up of diligent and constant hard work in the vineyard, a bit of modern wine-making technology and sensitivity in pruning, in determining the best moment to harvest and in controlling temperatures during vinification. And the wines he produces are like him: they need time to express themselves. They are broad, ripe and never banal; their solid balance makes them forceful and complex. The Recioto, with its deep, licorice-toned nose, is excellent. The broad palate mirrors the bouquet and there is a voluptuous crescendo on the finish. The Soave Vigna Albare, which had already accustomed us to some top-level performances, is very interesting indeed: the "rationalized double ripening" system allows Portinari to obtain ripe, soft fruit combined with freshness and suppleness. The Soave Vigna Ronchetto is more individual: it is traditional and powerful, with the pleasant roughness typical of garganega and a robust, vigorous style on the palate. The only Soave aged in oak, the Santo Stefano, is mature, rich and spicy.

O	Recioto di Soave Oro '97	🍷🍷	5
O	Soave Cl. Vigna Ronchetto '98	🍷🍷	3*
O	Soave Sup. Santo Stefano '97	🍷🍷	4
O	Soave Vigna Albare Doppia Maturazione Ragionata '98	🍷🍷	3*
O	Soave Vigna Albare Doppia Maturazione Ragionata '97	🍷🍷🍷 (white)	3
O	Recioto di Soave '95	🍷🍷 (white)	4
O	Soave Cl. Vigna Ronchetto '97	🍷🍷 (white)	3

MONTEFORTE D'ALPONE (VR)

PRA

VIA DELLA FONTANA, 31
37032 MONTEFORTE D'ALPONE (VR)
TEL. 045/7612125

It is not easy to describe the strength of a great Soave, or at least one cannot do so by merely referring to its weight and size: in fact this white, though it displays its charms in a lively and immediate manner, also seduces one with such intriguing and enticing elegance and suppleness as to require other parameters. So it is not just the amount of its extract which accounts for how good the Monte Grande is, but rather the harmony revealed by all the characteristics one senses, beginning with its brilliant deep straw color. A wonderful scent of almond is at the heart of its bouquet, in which enchanting, clear yet complex aromas confirm the success of this blend of garganega and chardonnay. The tight, delicate fruit on the palate evolves deliciously to a broad, juicy crescendo on the finish. The hand of Flavio Pra, son of Sergio and nephew of Graziano, has had an effect here which we hope will also spread to the winery's other offerings, which are, in fact, a little less exciting than usual this time. The basic Soave earns a decent One Glass thanks to its unquestionable correctness, though it does lack its usual verve. The Soave aged in barrique, the Sant' Antonio, after last year's excellent showing, is still rather closed and we shall hold off judging it until next year. The Recioto '96 is not especially concentrated, but rather light and easy to drink.

O	Soave Cl. Sup. Vigneto Monte Grande '98	🍷🍷	3*
O	Recioto di Soave Le Fontane '96	🍷	5
O	Soave Cl. '98	🍷	3
O	Soave Cl. Sup. Vigneto Monte Grande '97	🍷🍷 (white)	4

NEGRAR (VR)

CAV. G.B. BERTANI
LOC. NOVARE
FRAZ. ARBIZZANO
37020 NEGRAR (VR)
TEL. 045/6011211

Bertani's Albion confirms its status as one of the Veneto's best Cabernets and indeed one of the most interesting from anywhere in Italy. Obtained from the innovative vineyard at Villa Novare, it is the result of the combination of two really favorable factors. The first is the '97 vintage, whose long, undisturbed harvest allowed the skins and seeds to ripen fully, and the other is the ambition and passion of the people who saw it through the various stages of production and decided to make it into a fine wine from Valpolicella rather than the usual, superconcentrated Cabernet. Indeed as well as its predictable deep ruby color, the Albion reveals an unexpected vitality on the nose. Its profusion of scents includes hints of spice, candied fruit, and an elegant mineral note, as well as that touch of decadence which is typical of the Valpolicella zone. The palate provides a delicious mirror image of the bouquet; the tannins are firm, but the flavor is nevertheless creamy and imperturbably long. The lack of an Amarone inevitably made us focus our attention on the Cabernet, but the range of this Arbizzano winery offered some other points of interest as well this year. The Secco Bertani, for example, gave a good account of itself with the '97 version: it displays the characteristic aromas of fruit preserved in alcohol and, though not particularly powerful, envelops the palate with its softness and notable harmony, before rewarding us further with a rich and very persistent finish. The Soave is good, and does not suffer unduly from the problems of the '98 vintage: it may pehaps lack a touch of freshness, but it does reveal appreciable depth. The Bardolino and the Le Lave white are excellently made, and the young Valpolicella and the Superiore '97 both earn honorable mention.

●	Albion Cabernet Sauvignon Villa Novare '97	▼▼▼	5
●	Bardolino Cl. '98	▼	3
○	Soave Cl. Sup. '98	▼	3
○	Le Lave '97	▼	4
●	Valpantena Secco Bertani '97	▼	4
●	Valpolicella Cl. '98		3
●	Valpolicella Sup. '97		3
●	Amarone della Valpolicella '85	▽▽▽	6
●	Amarone della Valpolicella Cl. Sup. '90	▽▽	6
●	Albion Cabernet Sauvignon Villa Novare '96	▽▽	5
○	Catullo Bianco '97	▽▽	3

NEGRAR (VR)

TOMMASO BUSSOLA
VIA MOLINO TURRI, 30
FRAZ. S. PERETTO
37024 NEGRAR (VR)
TEL. 045/7501740

Tommaso Bussola's story is an unusual one: unlike almost all the producers in the zone he did not inherit the family estate, but instead began his experience as a vigneron at an uncle's winery. Perhaps the lack of normal paternal pressure to carry on the family business allowed Tommaso, guided by his great passion for his work, to follow his own path, free from external influences. With the unflagging support of his wife, he has learned to cope, with consummate skill, in the vineyards, the cellar and the accounting office. The estate is located in the foothills of San Peretto, in an ideal zone which the Bussolas have, with great ability, made the most of. This year, too, the wine which impressed us most of all is the Recioto Selezione '96, a real star in its category: overripe and balsamic, it displays perfumes of dried flowers and aromatic herbs which give it an unmistakable style. It is full-bodied and substantial on the palate, yet elegant and beautifully modulated; its complexity succeeds in winning over even the most diffident of tasters. The Valpolicella Superiore '96 is very good indeed: its fruit is rich and fleshy in the mouth, and on the nose it is ripe and warm, with tertiary aromas which promise to evolve even further. The Amarone '95 is excellent, too: it offers the same bouquet as the Recioto. After a good entry on the palate, it opens up with great elegance, becoming warm and mouth-filling, and echoing perfectly the sensations on the nose. The long suit of the basic Recioto '97 is its attractive, easy-drinking style, and it is a rather more straightforward wine.

●	Amarone della Valpolicella Cl. Vigneto Alto '95	▼▼	6
●	Recioto della Valpolicella Cl. '97	▼▼	5
●	Recioto della Valpolicella Cl. Selezione '96	▼▼	6
●	Valpolicella Cl. Sup. '96	▼▼	3*
●	Recioto della Valpolicella '95	▽▽▽	5
●	Amarone della Valpolicella '93	▽▽	6
●	Recioto della Valpolicella '94	▽▽	5
●	Amarone della Valpolicella '94	▽	5

NEGRAR (VR)

Cantina Sociale Valpolicella

Via Ca' Salgari, 2
37024 Negrar (VR)
tel. 045/7500070

The Cantina Sociale in Negrar is doing very well. Only its young Valpolicella seems a little too simple, while the rest of the range reveals notable care. The Valpolicella Superiores, having overcome the problems of the '96 vintage, stand out as characterful and attractive wines: the Vigneti di Torbe version, which displays better integration with the oak than the '95, shows attractive warmth and appealing structure. The Righetti version exhibits an unexpected richness: the alcohol is tempered by the extract and the finish rises to an appealing crescendo of flavor. The Recioto Vigneti di Moron almost earns Two Glasses: it wants, perhaps, just a little aging in bottle in order to express the full potential which the '97 vintage has provided; indeed, the Domini Veneti version, which is in theory a lesser wine, seems broader and more complete, and its rich, voluptuous, rounded fruit asserts itself with remarkable authority. These two wines demonstrate that Recioto, when conceived of as an ambitious red instead of a sweet, fizzy wine, requires a suitable period of bottle-aging in order to become complex and acquire greater harmony between the aromas and the flavors. These problems do not touch the Amarones, both of which have been really well matured. The Vigneti di Jago displays the traditional warmth combined with an elegance that is becoming the hallmark of the Cantina Sociale. Its color is a medium-deep garnet; on the nose it offers distinct mature, spicy hints which are not at all aggressive, and its flavor is persistent and clean. The Amarone Domini Veneti shares many of the aspects just described but has more immediacy; it reveals mouth-filling but less concentrated fruit on the palate.

●	Amarone della Valpolicella Cl. Vigneti di Jago Selezione '95	🍷🍷	5
●	Amarone della Valpolicella Cl. Domini Veneti '95	🍷🍷	4
●	Recioto della Valpolicella Cl. Domini Veneti '97	🍷🍷	4
●	Recioto della Valpolicella Cl. Vigneti di Moron '97	🍷	5
●	Valpolicella Cl. Sup. Righetti '96	🍷	3
●	Valpolicella Cl. Sup. Vigneti di Torbe '96	🍷	3
●	Amarone della Valpolicella Cl. Vigneti di Jago Selezione '93	🍸🍸	5

NEGRAR (VR)

Le Ragose

Via Ragose, 1
Fraz. Arbizzano
37020 Negrar (VR)
tel. 045/7513241

The range presented this year by Le Ragose did not include its top wines: the Amarone '95 was not yet available, while for some years now we have not had the pleasure of tasting the Recioto, of which the estate has, in the past, always taken care to produce an extremely interesting and characterful interpretation. But the Galli family, which is very serious about matters of production, does not kowtow to market demands: it bears them in mind, naturally, as it should, but it never forces the situation and so the Amarone will have to wait until it is good and ready. While we're on the subject of semi-dried grapes, the fruit has not recently shown sufficient concentration to produce a rich, full-bodied sweet wine. It is therefore the Cabernet, which confirms the excellent impression it made last year, that flies the flag for the company's well-structured reds. The version on offer comes from the '96 vintage, which has lent it an elegant and extremely fresh richness on the nose; on the palate, it has a restrained tone, the tannins are barely perceptible and the evolution of the fruit becomes progressively more resolute and persistent. The beauty of this red is that it manages to provide the classically incisive style of the grape variety with a more immediate appeal. The young Valpolicella, which impresses us more each year, is good: it succeeds in matching its fragrance with a touch more substance than is the norm. There is no news at the moment about the Valpolicella Superiore: the new vintages had not yet been released at the time of our final tastings. We'll know more next year.

●	Garda Cabernet Le Ragose '96	🍷🍷	4
●	Valpolicella Cl. '98	🍷	3
●	Amarone della Valpolicella Cl. '88	🍸🍸🍸	5
●	Amarone della Valpolicella Cl. '86	🍸🍸🍸	5
●	Amarone della Valpolicella Cl. '94	🍸🍸	5
●	Amarone della Valpolicella Cl. '91	🍸🍸	5
●	Amarone della Valpolicella Cl. '90	🍸🍸	5
●	Cabernet Le Ragose '95	🍸🍸	4
●	Recioto della Valpolicella '93	🍸🍸	4
●	Cabernet Le Ragose '93	🍸	4

NEGRAR (VR)

GIUSEPPE QUINTARELLI
VIA CERE, 1
37024 NEGRAR (VR)
TEL. 045/7500016

In the pantheon of Italian oenology, Quintarelli is the god of immutability. Don't believe for a moment, however, that his conception of wine-making is unaffected by what is happening around him: his secret, in the fifty years of his career, has been to take on board cultural and technical progress while remaining safely at the helm, foreseeing, in most cases, the themes and values that today we consider fundamental in a first-class wine. His wine is a heritage for everyone to draw on in order to understand the profound wealth of the Valpolicella area and of the production techniques which make this zone unique in the world. At one time, it used to be said that semi-dried grapes removed the territorial stamp, the individuality of a microclimate or of a particular soil formation from the finished wine. However, Quintarelli's first great revelation was to give his wines a new identity charged with potential, linked to the breathtaking sites of his zone and to the hard, mean soils that compose it. Even his experiments with Nebbiolo Passito in the '60s and '70s had, and continue remarkably to display, a spectrum of sensations that reveal a magical link between the Langhe and Valpolicella. We therefore impatiently await the wines which at the time of our tastings were not yet bottled, and grant Bepi the honor of our Empty Glasses: this allows us to give him a full listing in our Guide although we were unable to taste his wines.

● Alzero '90	ΥΥΥ	6
● Amarone della Valpolicella Ris. '83	ΥΥΥ	6
● Amarone della Valpolicella Ris. '85	ΥΥΥ	6
● Amarone della Valpolicella '84	ΥΥΥ	6
● Amarone della Valpolicella '86	ΥΥΥ	6
● Alzero '91	ΥΥ	6
● Amarone della Valpolicella '90	ΥΥ	6
● Amarone della Valpolicella '91	ΥΥ	5

NEGRAR (VR)

VILLA SPINOSA
LOC. JAGO
37024 NEGRAR (VR)
TEL. 045/7500093

For some time now Villa Spinosa has been one of the more promising estates in Valpolicella; not always, however, have the wines performed as well as one therefore expected. This year was once again positive, perhaps thanks to two really successful vintages for the zone (the '95 and the '97); or perhaps, and we sincerely hope that this is the case, because Enrico Cascella, who inherited the estate a little less than ten years ago, has finally succeeded in integrating all the aspects of production. When tasting the wines over the last few years, we have noted that there was certainly no problem with the quality of the fruit; instead there seemed to be insufficient clarity of expression. This time, starting with the Valpolicella Superiore Jago, we perceived an unusual warmth and richness on the palate, well balanced by a marked and appealing fresh acidity. Moreover, the wine, though not outstandingly muscular, asserts itself with surprising persistence. The Recioto is very full-bodied; its depth is not due to the sweetness alone, but also to its complex flavor in which the firm tannins play a decisive role. The color is intense but the bouquet is extremely elegant. The Amarone '95 is made in a traditional style: the alcohol is a constant presence on the nose, but it leaves room for notes of spice and fruit liqueur; on the palate, it is mouth-filling, and the flavor evolves nicely toward a slightly hot finish. The only wine we found unsuccessful was the Valpolicella Superiore Antanel. It does not seem to have benefited from the same care as the preceding wines: it is over-oaked and not properly balanced.

● Amarone della Valpolicella Cl. '95	🍷🍷	6
● Recioto della Valpolicella Cl. '97	🍷🍷	5
● Valpolicella Cl. Sup. Jago '95	🍷	3

NEGRAR (VR)

VIVIANI

VIA MAZZANO, 8
37024 NEGRAR (VR)
TEL. 045/7500286

Claudio Viviani has done his utmost with the '94 vintage and has come up with a wine which is considerably better than one might have expected, given the weather conditions of that year. Let us make one thing clear, though: his Amarone has neither a particularly intense color nor overwhelming concentration, which seductive sensations would have made one suspect that he had resorted to the oenological equivalent of anabolic steroids. The cru Casa dei Bepi '94 displays a harmony based on its intriguing complexity and irresistible finesse. Its bouquet suggests the understated freshness typical of wines from the high-altitude hills of Mazzano; the oak is well integrated too, allowing the softness of the fruit to emerge. On the palate, the wine is sumptuous and long, with an uncommonly easy appeal for an Amarone. The estate's range has been enriched this year by an excellent Valpolicella Superiore '96, which clearly demonstrates how small estates with lots of ambition can compete with the best in this category too. Its bright ruby color introduces a nose and palate which both display evolving full, dense fruit. The finish is rich and clean. The youthful Valpolicella is also a perfect example of its type – it is perhaps the best of the '98 vintage – and shows just the right amount of concentration: its appeal lies not only in its expected freshness, but also in its surprising length. If the much-awaited Recioto Selezione '95 is worthy of longer aging, the '96 is already at just the right point, with an easy-drinking and quite deliciously creamy style.

●	Amarone della Valpolicella Cl. Casa dei Bepi '94	**YY**	6
●	Valpolicella Cl. '98	**YY**	2*
●	Valpolicella Cl. Sup. '96	**YY**	4
●	Recioto della Valpolicella '96	**Y**	5
●	Amarone della Valpolicella Cl. Casa dei Bepi '93	YY	5
●	Recioto della Valpolicella La Mandrela '93	YY	5
●	Amarone della Valpolicella Cl. Ammandorlato '93	Y	4
●	Recioto della Valpolicella '94	Y	4

NERVESA DELLA BATTAGLIA (TV)

SERAFINI & VIDOTTO

VIA ARDITI, 1
31040 NERVESA DELLA BATTAGLIA (TV)
TEL. 0422/773281

What is amazing about Francesco Serafini and Antonello Vidotto is their ability to pursue their own path, seeming almost to ignore whatever attempts to come between them and the realization of their ambitious plans. Neither increasing the area under vine, with the acquisition of new sites in the surrounding hills, nor the projected new cellar, whose realization will keep them busy over the next few years, has distracted them in the least from the preparation of their top wine. And this in a vintage that was very generous but also difficult to interpret, in which the slightest distraction could have made the hard work of an entire year come to nothing. The result of all this dedication is one of the few authentic Bordeaux blends produced in Italy, the Rosso dell'Abazia: this year it is particularly striking in its depth of color and its herbaceous, overripe aromas which then reappear and expand in the dense yet silky texture of the palate. The warm and velvety structure, which develops among hints of spice and red berries, charms us with its persistence and with a measured expression which is the real novelty of the '97. The estate's other great red, the Pinot Nero, is on a par with the best Pinots from anywhere in Italy. Its bouquet offers red berries and spice; it evolves evenly and broadly in the mouth, and reflects the bouquet; the delicate astringency of the tannins leaves the palate clean and dry. The Phigaia is the Rosso's little brother. It is ripe and flowery on the nose, and very elegant and well-balanced on the palate: a real (and successful) combination of complexity and an easy-drinking style.

●	Il Rosso dell'Abazia '97	**YYY**	5
●	Pinot Nero '97	**YY**	5
●	Phigaia After the Red '97	**Y**	4
●	Il Rosso dell'Abazia '93	YYY	5
●	Il Rosso dell'Abazia '94	YYY	5
●	Il Rosso dell'Abazia '95	YYY	5
●	Il Rosso dell'Abazia '96	YYY	5
●	Il Rosso dell'Abazia '92	YY	5
●	Phigaia After the Red '96	YY	4
○	Il Bianco dell'Abazia '97	Y	4

OTTELLA

LOC. OTTELLA, 1
FRAZ. S. BENEDETTO DI LUGANA
37019 PESCHIERA DEL GARDA (VR)
TEL. 045/7551950

Gimè was the word the old-timers in the zone used to use to indicate something that was particularly good. The Gimè '98, the estate's new wine, seems to deserve its name. Made from 60% incrocio Manzoni (which gives excellent results in this zone) and 40% chardonnay, it impressed us with its attractive aromatic qualities as well as its interesting impact on the palate, which leaves a distinct, restrained and elegant aftertaste. Character and quaffability combine in a wine that could improve still further. The attention bestowed on the Gimè has not had an adverse effect on the production of the Luganas, which this year are again among the best. As was the case last year, we actually enjoyed the basic Lugana more than the one from the Le Creete vineyard, whose ambitions of complexity require more time to express themselves. But there is more good news: a new wine, called Il Molceo. It is a Lugana Superiore (a brand-new denomination, this) which ferments in new barriques and then spends a further six months there. Its perfumes reveal the presence of oak, which is, however, not at all overwhelming. The palate offers a broad progression and a good carry-through of the soft, ripe fruit aromas of the bouquet. Among the reds, the Campo Sireso, made from merlot, cabernet sauvignon and corvina, is up to its usual high standard. Its very promising opaque color precedes a nose that has not yet developed great complexity, but is rich and deep. The entry on the palate is satisfying, with its intriguing contrasts between the tannins and the soft fruit, leading to a rising finish. The Rosso Ottella is slight, lean and a bit too acidulous.

●	Campo Sireso '97	🍷🍷	4
○	Gimè Bianco '98	🍷🍷	3*
○	Lugana Sup. Il Molceo '98	🍷🍷	4
○	Lugana '98	🍷	3
○	Lugana Le Creete '98	🍷	3
●	Rosso Ottella '98		3
●	Campo Sireso '95	♀♀	4
●	Campo Sireso '96	♀♀	4

ZENATO

VIA S. BENEDETTO, 8
FRAZ. S. BENEDETTO DI LUGANA
37019 PESCHIERA DEL GARDA (VR)
TEL. 045/7550300

Each year the range from Zenato becomes fuller; thus, after achieving a consistent high quality with its Amarone and Lugana, the estate now also has an excellent Soave which is capable of competing with the best. It comes from one of the finest crus in the Soave district, La Colombara, and is a blend of garganega, trebbiano and chardonnay. This grape mix has made it a complete white, modern in the fragrance of its aromas, but also dense, dynamic, broad and delicate: a very model of harmony. We enjoyed a similarly soft, tasty style in the Valpolicella Superiore Ripassa, which has an invitingly concentrated nose, a broad, supple structure on the palate and a pleasing finish. The Amarone Sergio Zenato, though different from previous versions, is impeccable. We found this '93 more modern in its use of oak and less rich in alcohol than previous versions. It has an extremely clean bouquet, and its aromas of blackberry and black cherry are well defined on the palate as well; the flavor is soft and well-balanced, with good acidity and tannins evident right through to the finish. The basic Amarone is good and more traditional; it just lacks the depth of fruit needed to keep the alcohol at bay. Taking a look at the Santa Cristina wines, we note the minor disappointment of the Cabernet Sauvignon '96, a little reticent to offer its perfumes and too short in flavor. The showing of the barrique-aged Lugana, which is becoming something of a standard-bearer, was more impressive. It is slightly dominated by oak, but its good fruit is evident on both the nose and palate, leaving a sensation on the latter of considerable fullness. The Lugana San Benedetto is reliable, whereas the Santa Cristina version is not as good as usual.

●	Amarone della Valpolicella Sergio Zenato Ris. '93	🍷🍷	6
○	Lugana Sergio Zenato Ris. '97	🍷🍷	4
○	Soave Cl. Sup. Vigneto Colombara '98	🍷🍷	3*
●	Valpolicella Cl. Sup. Ripassa '96	🍷🍷	3*
●	Amarone della Valpolicella Cl. '93	🍷	4
○	Lugana S. Cristina Vigneto Massoni '98	🍷	3
○	Lugana San Benedetto '98	🍷	3
●	Cabernet Sauvignon Santa Cristina '96		4
●	Amarone della Valpolicella Cl. Sergio Zenato '88	♀♀♀	6

PIEVE DI SOLIGO (TV)

CASE BIANCHE
VIA CHISINI, 79
31053 PIEVE DI SOLIGO (TV)
TEL. 0438/841608

A group of white farmhouses lying on a ridge in the hills between Conegliano and Valdobbiadene gives this historic estate its name; it was purchased three years ago by Martino Zanetti, a businessman from Treviso with a passion for the world of wine and, after a few years of settling in, he is starting to see the first results, the fruits of the important programme of renewal directed by the two young oenologists Enrico Moschetta and Lionello Lot. Their work has involved raising the quality of about 32 hectares of vineyards, almost all owned by the estate, as well as a partial restructuring of the cellar. However, the aim is to increase the area under vine and, in the near future, to build a more rationalized vinification cellar. Production, which has settled at around 400 thousand bottles of wine a year, is mainly of Prosecco but also includes some other interesting whites; the reds, on the other hand, still have some way to go. The best wine is the Prosecco Extra Dry, which displays an intense straw color; on the nose we find scents of ripe fruit, while the palate is full, quite long, and well integrated with the carbon dioxide. The Prosecco Brut, with its wonderfully clean bouquet, is inviting; this immediate wine displays quite good body. The Colli di Conegliano Costa dei Falchi and the Chardonnay are promsing. The former offers floral perfumes, and is mouth-filling and well balanced on the palate, with an attractive freshness and a good finish. The Chardonnay reveals a fragrantly fruity nose and similarly aromatic fruit on the palate.

O	Prosecco di Conegliano Extra Dry	🍷🍷	3*
O	Chardonnay '98	🍷	3
O	Colli di Conegliano Costa dei Falchi '98	🍷	3
O	Prosecco di Conegliano Vigna da Cuc Brut	🍷	3
O	Prosecco di Conegliano Brusolè Frizzante		3

PRAMAGGIORE (VE)

RUSSOLO
VIA LIBERTÀ, 36
30020 PRAMAGGIORE (VE)
TEL. 0421/799087

During 2000, the headquarters of this winery will move from Pramaggiore to via San Rocco, 78/A at San Quirino in the province of Pordenone, tel. 0434/919577; this is where the winery's own vineyards and vinification cellar are now. Careful vineyard management and continued up-dating of the winery equipment enabled the range as a whole to perform very well again this year. We'll begin with the Pinot Bianco Ronco Calaj '98, with its fine and varied aromas whose nuances range from the fruity to the floral and which are echoed on the attractive, elegantly evolving palate. Next, the Doi Raps '97, made from sauvignon and pinot bianco: during the harvest two bunches are deliberately left on each vine (hence the name), and these are then picked toward the end of October. The wine produced from them succeeds in combining a rich nose with an equally good, creamy and persistent palate. The Chardonnay I Legni '97, fermented and matured in barriques, succeeds in displaying its abundant sensations gradually and with elegance on both nose and palate. The Pinot Grigio Ronco Calaj '98, on the other hand, was particularly enjoyable for its pleasant scents of Williams pear. The two Sauvignons, the Ronco Calaj and the I Legni, should not be neglected either. The Müller Thurgau did not manage to equal the fine performance the of '97 vintage, unlike the Tocai which, on the other hand, seems to have got better, especially as regards its expression on the nose. The Cabernet I Legni stands out among the reds because of the broad and persistent force of its bouquet, which introduces a body that is not particularly full, but is very fine. The delicate Merlot I Legni is one to watch.

●	Friuli Grave Cabernet I Legni '96	🍷🍷	4
O	Friuli Grave Pinot Bianco Ronco Calaj '98	🍷🍷	3*
O	Doi Raps '97	🍷🍷	4
O	Friuli Grave Chardonnay I Legni '97	🍷	4
●	Friuli Grave Merlot I Legni '96	🍷	4
O	Friuli Grave Pinot Grigio Ronco Calaj '98	🍷	3
O	Friuli Grave Sauvignon I Legni '97	🍷	4
O	Friuli Grave Sauvignon Ronco Calaj '98	🍷	3
O	Friuli Grave Tocai Ronco Calaj '98	🍷	3*
O	Müller Thurgau Mussignaz '98	🍷	3
O	Malvasia Istriana '98		3

REFRONTOLO (TV)

Astoria Vini

Via Crevada, 44
31020 Refrontolo (TV)
tel. 0423/665042

Astoria confirms its place in the Guide, even if the '98 vintage was not a particularly happy one for Prosecco. The wines in the Val de Brun range, made entirely from grapes grown on the estate, were well made and displayed more character than the average large producer's wines. The most difficult test, that of Prosecco Tranquillo, was passed with surprising ease: this still wine, with its bright straw color, was once again one of the best of its type. The fruitiness on the nose opens up to reveal faintly floral and aromatic tones; the flavor is quite forceful and well balanced between softness and liveliness; the interesting finish is tight, long and positively fruity, underlining the skillful blend of prosecco with other varieties and the general quality of the fruit. We find the same sensation when tasting the Prosecco Extra Dry, which has an intriguing nose and offers lively finesse on the palate; the carbon dioxide is subtle and well integrated, while the acidity contributes to the overall freshness, leaving the characteristic softness of this wine the task of righting the balance. Only the finish does not seem up to par. The attractive sweetness of the Cartizze (which is not quite as good as last year's) is not really counterbalanced by its structure, as it was in the previous version, but it is just as complex and interesting on the nose.

○ Cartizze	🍷	4
○ Prosecco di Valdobbiadene Dry Grande Cuvée	🍷	4
○ Prosecco di Valdobbiadene Extra Dry '98	🍷	3
○ Prosecco di Valdobbiadene Tranquillo Vigna Val de Brun '98	🍷	3

REFRONTOLO (TV)

Vincenzo Toffoli

Via Liberazione, 26
31020 Refrontolo (TV)
tel. 0438/894240

Toffoli, one of the most interesting newcomers this year, is a small estate which owns about five hectares of vineyards and rents as many again (all near Refrontolo) and produces no more than 60 thousand bottles. It is only in the last ten years, with the arrival at the winery of the sons of Vincenzo, the head of the family, that interest has shifted towards wine in bottles. Gabriele, one of three brothers, looks after production and sales, while Santo and Luciano dedicate themselves to the vineyards. The consultant oenologist is Daniele Novak. For the moment, all the brothers have a second job (Gabriele is a fireman), which state of affairs was motivated up to now by the need for a sure source of income, but it is becoming increasingly difficult to continue this way. This security, however, has allowed the estate to experiment with methods which are original (but within a context of respect for tradition) without worrying about immediate commercial results. Among their short-term plans is the building of a new cellar with more up-to-date wine-making equipment. Indeed, though the still wines are made on the estate, the production of the sparkling wines is still carried out by others. The Prosecco Extra Dry, one of the most interesting of the year, is spare and clean: it is particularly appealing thanks to the balance of all its elements, starting with the well-integrated mousse. Another wine characterized by notable balance is the inviting Marzemino Passito: warm, silky and yet lively, it displays an exquisitely well integrated sweetness. The Prosecco Passito is delicate and the Tranquillo version is elegant.

○ Prosecco di Conegliano Extra Dry	🍷🍷	3*
● Colli di Conegliano Passito di Refrontolo '98	🍷	4
○ Prosecco di Conegliano Tranquillo '98	🍷	3
○ Prosecco Passito	🍷	4

S. AMBROGIO DI VALPOLICELLA (VR)

Aleardo Ferrari

Via Giare, 15
Fraz. Gargagnago
37020 S. Ambrogio di Valpolicella (VR)
tel. 045/7701379

The Ferrari family has run this estate, which has always been dedicated to the cultivation of vines, since the end of the 18th century; however, Aleardo was the first, in the mid-'80s, when he had left his job in a bank, to dedicate himself full-time to this activity. With the help of his children, he cultivates his seven hectares of vineyards, all with a hillside location in an area noted for being among the best in the zone. In addition to producing the classic grape varieties, he also has a little sangiovese and cabernet. The training system used is the locally favored pergola but gradually, as the vineyards are replanted, the guyot system is being introduced, as it seems to offer a better guarantee of quality. Our tastings of the wines this year confirmed the high level which this estate has been achieving for some time now, although there has been a slight dip in quality since last year. The Amarone '95 did not in fact repeat the notable success of the '94. Once again we find the usual cleanness and the finesse, but without the personality and character which should be typical of such an ambitious wine. Without doubt the Valpolicella Classico Superiore '97 Bure Alto (from the vineyard of the same name) was more impressive. Its deep, warm-toned color tempts you to taste it. Its perfumes are intense and ripe, typical of Valpolicellas made using the "ripasso" technique. These sensations are nicely echoed in the attractive, mouth-filling flavor. The Recioto '97, although it wants more complexity, appealed to us with its lively red berry aromas, its simple and immediate flavor and its overall finesse.

●	Valpolicella Cl. Sup. Bure Alto '97	🍷🍷	4
●	Amarone della Valpolicella '95	🍷	5
●	Recioto della Valpolicella '97	🍷	5
●	Amarone della Valpolicella Cl. '94	🍸🍸	5
●	Amarone della Valpolicella '93	🍸	5
●	Pelara '96	🍸	2
●	Recioto della Valpolicella '96	🍸	4

S. AMBROGIO DI VALPOLICELLA (VR)

Masi

Via Monteleone
Fraz. Gargagnago
37010 S. Ambrogio di Valpolicella (VR)
tel. 045/6800588

At Masi they're not resting on their laurels, but are skillfully nurturing the progress of the wines from Valpolicella which, in the last few years, have made a big leap forward in quality. This is what we gleaned from our tastings, which offered some interesting wines in all categories interspersed with the odd less successful bottle. We'll begin with the latter, which are to be found mainly among the Valpolicellas and the "ripasso" method wines. The Superiore from Serego Alighieri gains no more than a mention: it seemed a bit overwhelmed by the wood and not altogether well-knit on the palate. The Campofiorin '96 is similar in style and has not benefited from refermenting on the Recioto lees. The more serious version, called Il Brolo, is slightly better, but we did not find much concentration or the expected vivacious fruit on the palate. The Bardolino La Vegrona confirms its One Glass status and is the first of a series of very good wines. The Amarone Mazzano '93 duplicates the elegance of the Campolongo, to which we gave Three Glasses last year. It has a bright color and well-defined, ripe perfumes; the evolution on the palate is underpinned by good, deep structure and displays a clean finish which completely echoes the wine's aromatic sensations: it fully deserves its award. The basic '96 Amarone is better than average for the year, and its warm richness is well balanced by its firm structure. The red "table wine" obtained from oseletta and corvina showed splendidly: this Osar, which really impressed us last year too, exemplifies the mouth-filling richness and ripe depth that one finds in the very best wines from Valpolicella. Of the two Reciotos on offer we preferred the deliciously delicate version from Serego Alighieri to the correct Amabile degli Angeli from Masi. The Soave and the Bianco Serego Alighieri were just slightly below par.

●	Amarone della Valpolicella Cl. Mazzano '93	🍷🍷🍷	6
●	Amarone della Valpolicella Cl. '96	🍷🍷	5
●	Osar '96	🍷🍷	6
●	Bardolino Cl. La Vegrona '98	🍷	3
●	Il Brolo di Campofiorin '95	🍷	4
●	Recioto della Valpolicella Cl. Casal dei Ronchi Serego Alighieri '96	🍷	5
○	Soave Cl. Sup. Colbaraca '98	🍷	3
○	Bianco Serego Alighieri '98		3
●	Campofiorin Ripasso '96		4
●	Valpolicella Cl. Sup. Serego Alighieri '96		3

S. AMBROGIO DI VALPOLICELLA (VR)

RAIMONDI VILLA MONTELEONE
FRAZ. GARGAGNAGO
37010 S. AMBROGIO DI VALPOLICELLA (VR)
TEL. 045/7704974

Anthony Raimondi, a professor of juvenile neurosurgery, was born in Chicago, where he worked for a large part of his life. When he was offered a teaching position in Italy, his first thought was to move to Verona. Then he discovered Valpolicella and has never moved from there. He is fortunate that his wife Lucia fully shares his pleasure in a rural lifestyle. In fact, it is she who has taken on the administrative responsibility for the beautiful, small estate which, even before their arrival, had always produced extraordinary grapes. The Raimondis, though they have visited even the most obscure corners of the zone and studied all that there is to know about it, maintain that speaking to farmers in the area was fundamental in their preparation. From the very beginning, around eight years ago, they have been assisted by Celestino Gaspari, who supervises the technical side of their wine-making operation. The style of the wines is in a state of transition and, although Anthony and Lucia know exactly what they want, this unfortunately does not always immediately come through in the finished product: however, the raw materials for producing great quality can be found in many of the wines in their range. The Amarone did not fall victim to the uncertainties of the '94 vintage and displays a rare elegance: it starts slowly but builds to a thrilling crescendo of flavor. This regal power is a feature that we also find in the ripe and successful Passito Bianco, which is impressive both for the clarity of its aromas of candied citrus peel and dried apricot, and for its explosive finish. The Recioto is good, stylish and not especially demanding; the Valpolicella San Vito, an example of a "ripasso" wine whose base wine was already very good and was genuinely enriched by the process, is more complex and captivating. The less ambitious Valpolicella Santa Lena is warm and harmonious.

●	Amarone della Valpolicella '94	🍷🍷	6
○	Passito Bianco di Gargagnago '95	🍷🍷	5
●	Valpolicella Cl. Sup. San Vito '95	🍷🍷	4
●	Recioto della Valpolicella Cl. '95	🍷	6
●	Valpolicella Cl. Sup. Santa Lena '95	🍷	4

S. BONIFACIO (VR)

GIUSEPPE INAMA
VIA IV NOVEMBRE, 1
37047 S. BONIFACIO (VR)
TEL. 045/6101411

Stefano Inama's ambition is to create a new kind of Soave, a third way which bridges the divide between accentuated expression of terroir and a quaffable, immediately pleasing style, which today is the choice of basic traits in the best examples. He has experimented with late-harvesting garganega, that grape's relationship with chardonnay, and fermentation and maturation in new oak. The Soave Du Lot is the most striking result: it has richness, depth and complex, inviting fruit on the nose. On the palate it is both silky and vigorous. The evolution of the flavor is very satisfying, and it leaves a notably clean aftertaste. In the Vigneti di Foscarino we find more alcoholic warmth: it is appealing, even if less elegant than the Du Lot; its structure is just as strong and lingering. This year is distinguished by the return of the basic Soave to a level worthy of Inama's high reputation, and also by the release of two vintages of the barriqued Sauvignon. The '97 has a Mediterranean timbre, a complete aromatic expressiveness and a harmonious softness on the palate. The '98 bowls you over with its freshness, its broad variety of sensations and its really stunning body. As if this were not enough, Inama has decided to try his luck in the Colli Berici district and has made a dry and extremely refined Cabernet called Bradisismo. This name refers to a strip of land near Lonigo where the vineyards are sited and which is subject to the slow movements of the earth's crust for which the geological term is bradyseism. The wine combines a slowly opening and well-defined nose with predictable concentration of color. The relationship between nose and palate is impeccable, as is the combination on the palate of the vitality of the cabernet franc and the density of the cabernet sauvignon. It is a steely red, perhaps a little unyielding, but nonetheless irreproachable.

○	Chardonnay Campo dei Tovi '98	🍷🍷	4
●	Colli Berici Cabernet Bradisismo '97	🍷🍷	6
○	Sauvignon Vulcaia Fumé '97	🍷🍷	5
○	Sauvignon Vulcaia Fumé '98	🍷🍷	5
○	Soave Cl. Sup. Vigneti di Foscarino '98	🍷🍷	4
○	Soave Cl. Sup. Vigneto Du Lot '98	🍷🍷	5
○	Soave Cl. Sup. Vin Soave '98	🍷🍷	3*
○	Chardonnay '98	🍷	3
○	Vulcaia Apres '97	🍷	5
○	Sauvignon Vulcaia Fumé '96	🍸🍸🍸	4
○	Soave Cl. Sup. Vigneto Du Lot '96	🍸🍸🍸	4
○	Soave Cl. Sup. Vigneti di Foscarino '97	🍸🍸	4

S. FIOR (TV)

MASOTTINA
VIA BRADOLINI, 54
LOC. CASTELLO DI ROGANZUOLO
31010 S. FIOR (TV)
TEL. 0438/400775

After an auspicious debut in the Guide last year, Masottina not only reconfirmed its results, but did even better. The credit for this can be divided among the Dal Bianco brothers, Renzo in the vineyards and Adriano and Valerio in the winery, who have assembled a competent technical staff and have availed themselves of the assistance of the consultant Marzio Pol, oenological guru of the Treviso area. The estate produces some two million bottles of reliable quality and tries occasionally to aim for real excellence. This is the case with the Colli di Conegliano Rosso '97, whose color demonstrates its concentration; on the nose, it releases scents of wild berries and bitter cherry which alternate with floral and spicy notes; the oak is not yet fully integrated, but it no doubt will be in time. The palate is dense and tight but could perhaps do with a little more complexity. The Colli di Conegliano Bianco '97, which we tasted and appreciated last year, is in great form: a year in bottle has improved it further, allowing its rich fruit to emerge. We were impressed with the Prosecco Extra Dry, which easily earned a high rating: its perfumes are broad and layered, and it is lively, with good evolution on the palate and well-balanced acidity. The Cartizze is distinguished by the elegance of its perfumes and its attractive quaffability. Among the still white wines, the Incrocio Manzoni showed well, with its appealingly frank aromatic style and its delicate flavor. The Chardonnay and the Pinot Bianco earn an honorable mention, whereas two reds, the Merlot and the Cabernet, are the only jarring notes.

● Colli di Conegliano Rosso '97	▼▼	4
○ Prosecco di Conegliano Extra Dry	▼▼	3*
○ Cartizze	▼	4
○ Incrocio Manzoni 6.0.13 '98	▼	3
○ Pinot Spumante Brut	▼	3
○ Chardonnay del Piave '98		2
○ Pinot Bianco del Piave '98		2
○ Colli di Conegliano Bianco '97	▽	3

S. PIETRO DI FELETTO (TV)

BEPIN DE ETO
VIA COLLE, 32/A
31020 S. PIETRO DI FELETTO (TV)
TEL. 0438/486877

"Croda Ronca", the name given to the Colli di Conegliano Rosso, is the hill where the vineyard is located and indicates a particular rocky formation of soil, rich in minerals and micro-elements. All this seems to benefit the wine which, although it only recently made its debut, already knows that it will become a star. The '96 continues to live up to expectations, and indeed offers greater finesse thanks to the bottle-aging it has now had. The Colli di Conegliano Rosso '97, assisted by its particularly good vintage, has even greater ambitions than the '96: it has an outstanding color and an extremely rich, full, deep nose, with overripe notes of blackberry, cherry and sweet spice. Its powerful and progressive flavor, along with its other characteristics, make it a real thoroughbred. We look forward to tasting the finished wine. De Eto's Colli di Conegliano Bianco '97 is still one of the best of its category, even if it doesn't have the verve of previous versions: its aromatic quality, enhanced by hints of flowers and exotic fruit, and its richness on the palate, with roundedness moderated by a herbaceous freshness, are just two qualities that make tasting this wine a joy. The Proseccos played their part in our tastings, too. The best is the Frizzante (lightly sparkling) version, with its notably clean, refined style. The Prosecco Tranquillo (non-sparkling) is sound, while the Extra Dry expresses its charms very gradually. After a few years' absence, the Faè, the estate's Passito Bianco, returns to the Guide. Although it does not possess great structure, it shows admirable balance and definition of its sensations. The Marzemino Passito has balsamic and fruity notes and a delicate structure. The Incrocio Manzoni 6.0.13 is not as good as earlier versions.

○ Colli di Conegliano Bianco Il Greccio '97	▼▼	3*
○ Faè Passito Bianco '95	▼▼	5
● Colli di Conegliano Passito di Refrontolo '96	▼	4
○ Prosecco di Conegliano Extra Dry	▼	3
○ Prosecco di Conegliano Frizzante	▼	2*
○ Prosecco di Conegliano Tranquillo '98	▼	2
● Colli di Conegliano Rosso '96	▽▽	4
○ Incrocio Manzoni 6.0.13 '97	▽▽	2

S. PIETRO IN CARIANO (VR)

Stefano Accordini
Via Alberto Bolla, 9
Fraz. Pedemonte
37029 S. Pietro in Cariano (VR)
tel. 045/7701733

The Accordini family presented an excellent range this year. Their two most important wines, the Recioto and the Amarone, were among the best we tasted and even their "lesser" bottles did very well. Tiziano Accordini, with the help of his father Stefano in the vineyards and the oenological supervision of his brother Daniele, has taken full advantage of the notable potential of two great vintages, '95 and '97. The Amarone '95 is complex and perfectly structured, with the alcohol beautifully set off by firm tannins and the density of the fruit: a Three Glass wine of magnificent balance. Accordini also wanted to make a sweet wine from semi-dried grapes with exceptional balance but without excessive "recioto-like" flavors and aromas: skillful barrique-aging was a help. This was the origin of Accordini's Recioto '97: it is creamy but not too sweet, with rich, deep perfumes of flowers, herbs and dark berries, and a lively, full and extremely persistent palate. The '97 vintage offered good opportunities for selection for the Valpolicella Superiore as well: it came very close to Two Glasses for its warmth and fine intensity. We shall be following the blend of corvina and the Bordeaux varieties called Passo with some attention: captivating and cleverly executed, it has an elegant bouquet and a pleasing length of flavor; and then it succeeds in concealing the true nature of the '96 vintage, which was certainly not outstanding west of Verona. Lastly, the performance of the Valpolicella '98 was satisfactory. We'll be writing about the Passico Bricco delle Bessole in the next edition of the Guide.

● Amarone della Valpolicella Cl. Acinatico '95	**YYY**	5
● Passo '96	**YY**	4
● Recioto della Valpolicella Acinatico '97	**YY**	4
● Valpolicella Cl. Sup. '97	**Y**	3
● Valpolicella Cl. '98		2
● Amarone della Valpolicella Cl. Vigneto Il Fornetto '93	YYY	5
● Amarone della Valpolicella Cl. Acinatico '91	YY	4
● Amarone della Valpolicella Cl. Acinatico '93	YY	5
● Amarone della Valpolicella Cl. Acinatico '94	YY	5

S. PIETRO IN CARIANO (VR)

Lorenzo Begali
Via Cengia, 10
37020 S. Pietro in Cariano (VR)
tel. 045/7725148

Lorenzo Begali is the appointed heir to the great Veronese viticultural tradition: he is a strong (and strong-willed) farmer who has discovered, at over fifty years of age, how to make the most of his agricultural labors by combining in the cellar the indisputable quality of his fruit with a surprising intuitive gift. This year's wines are, indeed, the result of a rule which has stood him in good stead over the last few years: always try to extract as much as possible from your grapes. This is evident when one retastes the Amarones from lesser vintages like '92 and '91, which not only reveal dependable staying power, but also a splendid capacity to improve. What one also finds in the Amarone '95 is the crystal-clear quality of a perfect year, as if the appropriate balance were already to be found in the grapes themselves. Time has given the nose a certain intriguing complexity without, however, lessening its vigor and natural appeal. The entry on the palate is soft and the warmth of the alcohol immediately fills the mouth but remains very attractive indeed. The fruit evolves unhesitatingly on the palate and closes with exceptional verve. The quality of the Recioto '97 is similar to that of previous vintages: once again we find the force and harmony of a fine wine, preceded by an irrepressible sweetness. The nose displays fruity notes and spicy hints which then carry through attractively onto the palate. Begali's Amarone and Recioto both have palates that show virtuosity and firmness, and they are never at all cloying. The Valpolicella is sound – of average quality for its category – and very well priced.

● Amarone della Valpolicella Cl. Vigneto Monte Ca' Bianca '95	**YY**	5
● Recioto della Valpolicella Cl. '97	**YY**	5
● Valpolicella Cl. '98		2
● Amarone della Valpolicella Cl. '92	YY	4
● Amarone della Valpolicella Cl. '93	YY	4
● Recioto della Valpolicella '95	YY	4
● Recioto della Valpolicella '96	YY	4

S. PIETRO IN CARIANO (VR)

Brigaldara

Via Brigaldara, 20
Fraz. S. Floriano
37029 S. Pietro in Cariano (VR)
tel. 045/7701055

The last few vintages have not allowed Brigaldara to present some of its most representative wines, such as the Valpolicella and the Garganega; on the other hand, we were able to taste an impressive Amarone '95 which clearly indicates the future path for this estate. In fact, Stefano Cesari's efforts to restructure the vineyards have been focused primarily on the indigenous grape varieties; a great deal of his energy has also been channeled into improving the conditions for drying his grapes, with special attention being given to those for his Reciotos. This '95 Amarone may be considered a homage to the estate's past, with an eye to the future. Aided by his colleagues, Cesari has combined the straightforward rustic style which had become his hallmark, with more complex and modern tones. The result is a red that is dense even in appearance; it displays a broad, rich nose, in which one recognizes the excellent ripeness of the grapes; on the palate, the marked tannins hold the softness of the alcohol at bay, while the fruit evolves with good persistence on the palate, leaving an aftertaste that fully echoes the bouquet. The Amarone '94 has, as expected, a lighter style, but is nevertheless enjoyable: the garnet color introduces a nose that shows good balance between the alcohol and jam-like notes. The flavor is round but not very persistent. The Passito Bianco is somewhat perplexing: the oak is too pronounced and it lacks the necessary flesh.

●	Amarone della Valpolicella Cl. '95	▼▼	5
●	Amarone della Valpolicella Cl. '94	▼	5
●	Amarone della Valpolicella Cl. '90	▽▽	5
●	Amarone della Valpolicella Cl. '93	▽▽	5
●	Recioto della Valpolicella '93	▽▽	5
●	Amarone della Valpolicella Cl. '91	▽	5
●	Recioto della Valpolicella '94	▽	5

S. PIETRO IN CARIANO (VR)

Luigi Brunelli

Via Cariano, 10
37029 S. Pietro in Cariano (VR)
tel. 045/7701118

Brunelli's splendid Amarone Campo del Titari is a tribute to his childhood. It takes its name from Brunelli's favorite horse with whom he passed many happy hours roaming the countryside as a boy. It is a stunning wine, which has not been at all adversely influenced by the difficult '96 vintage because Brunelli harvested before the rain. Made from a ruthless selection of grapes before drying, the wine underwent a modern-style vinification and was then aged in new barriques. It was not filtered, so as to maintain all the power and substance with which Nature endowed it. The impressive color is accompanied by scents of fruit that are not the least bit overripe or tired, while mineral hints and notes of cocoa and spice also contribute to its fascinating complexity. The entry on the palate is rich, and then the fruit evolves unhesitatingly and finishes with an invigorating persistence. It fully deserves its Three Glasses. The basic Amarone, which is not far from Three Glasses either, also displays mineral notes on the nose, along with a more traditional density and alcohol level. On the palate, it is mouth-filling and long, and it displays a good capacity for aging. The very attractive young Valpolicella is one of the best of its type. It has a bright color and is spicy and immediate on the nose; on the palate, it is well balanced but perhaps just a shade hot. The Recioto '97 was clearly made from excellent fruit, but its stability in the bottle was not perfect and this affected our evaluation. This is also true of the promising Valpolicella Pa' Riondo '97, which will be judged in the next edition of the Guide.

●	Amarone della Valpolicella Cl. Campo del Titari '96	▼▼▼	6
●	Amarone della Valpolicella Cl. '96	▼▼	5
○	Passito Re Sol '97	▼	4
●	Recioto della Valpolicella Cl. '97	▼	4
●	Valpolicella Cl. '98	▼	2
●	Corte Cariano Rosso '97		3
●	Valpolicella Cl. Sup. '97		3
●	Amarone della Valpolicella Cl. '93	▽▽	5
●	Amarone della Valpolicella Cl. '95	▽▽	5
●	Amarone della Valpolicella Cl. Corte Cariano '90	▽▽	5
●	Recioto della Valpolicella '96	▽	4
●	Recioto della Valpolicella Corte Cariano '95	▽	4

S. PIETRO IN CARIANO (VR)

Angelo Nicolis e Figli

Via Villa Girardi, 29
37029 S. Pietro in Cariano (VR)
tel. 045/7701261

The Ambrosan clearly indicates the change in quality and style that Amarone has gone through: the magic of the semi-dried grapes is still all there, but the wine appears less prone to spoilage and its aging potential is based on a new solidity of structure. At one time, Amarone aged because it was already mature when bottled; Nicolis' wine, on the other hand, has a complete, chiseled style in which the combination of the polyphenols with the other substances does not leave the alcohol exposed to support the wine's entire structure on its own; this style is anything but decadent. Its color is, quite naturally, an opaque ruby. Oak is evident on the nose, but does not overwhelm it; instead, one finds an exemplary freshness with mineral notes and hints of berries and almond. The best of it, however, is the palate, which displays a very attractive tightness of flavor. The bouquet carries through exquisitely, and the fruit evolves with all the vigor that one expects from an Amarone; the finish is of sumptuous length. The Recioto also benefits from this more modern style. Its rich, ripe fruit contrasts splendidly with the lively force of the tannins and the brightness of the acidity, and the wine's intense color, its scents of black cherry and its rounded sweetness are all similarly well-balanced. The basic Amarone is also a great success: it is more charming and immediate than the Ambrosan but no less rich or persistent. The Valpolicella '98 is well made, and rather better than the Valpolicella Superiore, which is still the estate's weak link. From the family's holdings on Lake Garda come contrasting results. The Chiaretto is successful, the Bardolino and the Chardonnay less so.

●	Amarone della Valpolicella Cl. '95	▼▼	5
●	Amarone della Valpolicella Cl. Ambrosan '95	▼▼	6
●	Recioto della Valpolicella '97	▼▼	5
●	Valpolicella Cl. '98	▼	2*
⊙	Bardolino Cl. Chiaretto '98		2
○	Garda Chardonnay '98		3
●	Valpolicella Cl. Sup. '96		3
●	Amarone della Valpolicella Cl. Ambrosan '93	YYY	6
●	Amarone della Valpolicella Cl. '93	YY	5
●	Amarone della Valpolicella Cl. Ambrosan '90	YY	6
●	Recioto della Valpolicella '94	YY	4

S. PIETRO IN CARIANO (VR)

Santa Sofia

Via Ca' Dedé, 61
Fraz. Pedemonte
37020 S. Pietro in Cariano (VR)
tel. 045/7701074

Santa Sofia is going through a delicate phase of improving the quality of its wine. The aim is to keep pace with the growing demand for quality without altering the individual style which has always made Santa Sofia stand out among the medium-to-large Veronese producers. The first encouraging signs come from a Valpolicella Superiore '97 which very nearly earned Two Glasses. It is a red whose nose displays traditional overripe notes: this sensation does not adversely affect the agreeableness of the wine; indeed, it contributes to it by giving it a ripe and appealing harmony. The Recioto is good, too: it has a delicate sweetness and is rather more than just a simple, agreeable wine. In fact, its fruity perfumes offer a certain subtle elegance; if it displayed slightly greater verve on the palate it could even be one of the best of its type. A satisfyingly fresh and lively white is the Bianco di Custoza Montemagrin , which could count on better fruit this year than in '97: this standard-bearer has a bright color, quite a complex nose and positive evolution of flavor. Of the two Soaves, Costalta and Monte Foscarino, we preferred the latter because of the clarity of its expression and its sinuously well-knit style, even though it does rather lack length. The Costalta is overripe and short, while the Amarone '93 is back down to normal: it is an almost transparent red in color, not particularly complex on the nose and very light, though not unpleasant, in flavor. We are counting on the '95 version, which was ready at the beginning of the year 2000, to give us once again the pleasure that we have found in other Santa Sofia Amarones in the recent past.

●	Amarone della Valpolicella Cl. '93	▼	5
○	Bianco di Custoza Montemagrin '98	▼	2*
●	Recioto della Valpolicella '97	▼	5
○	Soave Cl. Monte Foscarino '98	▼	2*
●	Valpolicella Cl. Sup. Monte Gradella '97	▼	3
●	Bardolino Cl. '98		2
●	Amarone della Valpolicella Cl. Gioé '93	YY	5

F.LLI SPERI

VIA FONTANA, 14
FRAZ. PEDEMONTE
37029 S. PIETRO IN CARIANO (VR)
TEL. 045/7701154

Now that the work on the cellar is finished, the members of the Speri family can dedicate themselves full-time to the work which is most important to them – the care of the vineyards. Cellar technology does matter to them also, however, but avant-garde equipment is not used indiscriminately: it is tried out first and only actually used if the results produced are really those that the Speris hope for. Their starting point, however, has always been, and remains, the grapes, the fruit of all their hard work and all their intuition in the vineyard. And how can one object to such convictions after having tasted the memorable Recioto La Roggia '95? Very concentrated and delicate, in spite of its incredible power, it offers scents of overripe red berries together with fine balsamic tones; on the palate all of its exuberant character is released, splendidly kept in line by the dense tannins and by an almost unmatchable elegance; the velvety sensations on the palate seem to go on indefinitely, and the roundness of the finish completes the wine perfectly. In the absence of the Amarone, we tasted the best version ever of the Valpolicella Superiore Sant'Urbano: it is rich and vegetal on the nose and displays fleshy, aromatic fruit on the palate. Its flavor is persistent and well balanced right though to a dry, very clean finish. The Valpolicella Superiore La Roverina '97 stands out for its broad mineral tones that meld with the ripe fruit on the nose; the flavor is full and pleasant. The Recioto I Comunai, unable to ask much from the unpropitious '96 vintage, reveals its best aspects in its delicacy and the balance of its sweetness.

● Recioto della Valpolicella Cl. La Roggia '95	TT	5
● Valpolicella Cl. Sup. Sant'Urbano '95	TT	3*
● Recioto della Valpolicella Cl. I Comunai '96	T	5
● Valpolicella Cl. Sup. La Roverina '97	T	3
● Valpolicella Cl. '98		2
● Amarone della Valpolicella Cl. Vigneto Monte Sant'Urbano '90	YYY	6
● Amarone della Valpolicella Cl. Vigneto Monte Sant'Urbano '93	YYY	5
● Recioto della Valpolicella Cl. La Roggia '94	YYY	5
● Amarone della Valpolicella Cl. Vigneto Monte Sant'Urbano '91	YY	6

F.LLI TEDESCHI

VIA VERDI, 4/A
FRAZ. PEDEMONTE
37029 S. PIETRO IN CARIANO (VR)
TEL. 045/7701487

An improvement in production methods and a growing recognition of what they have available: these are the keys to understanding the recent achievements of the Tedeschis, who are now no longer merely content to produce great classic Valpolicella wines, but have embarked on making an intense and characterful "vino da tavola". Behind the Rosso della Fabriseria is a desire to show the full glory of their grapes, without the interference of the drying process: the grapes from which it is made are not the ones that weren't good enough to be laid down for drying, but are actually probably the estate's prime fruit. Fundamental to the style and success of this wine are the experience of the head of the family, Renzo, and the scrupulousness and experimental bent of his son Riccardo. The length and temperatures of the fermentation, aging in different-sized barrels and the final blend of the various types of corvina: all these factors were at the center of an open and productive family debate. The resulting wine has a deep garnet color; its vigor is not just taken for granted but acts as a vehicle for an admirably even continuity of aromas from the nose through to the palate: a note of sour cherry, hints of vanilla, and sweet floral nuances combine with a broad, tannic structure which confirms the exceptional nature of the grapes used. All in all, this is a really fine Three Glass wine. The Recioto, exemplary in its grace and modernity, was conceived in the same style: rich in color, it offers a complex nose with enchanting fruity tones that are as deep as the spicy and herbal notes are delicate. On the palate, it displays a creamy sweetness which soon gives way to the long and mouth-filling confrontation between the extract and the acidity. The two Amarones are much better than their vintage would lead you to expect: the Monte Olmi came close to winning another Three Glasses.

● Rosso della Fabriseria '97	TTT	5
● Amarone della Valpolicella Cl. '96	TT	5
● Amarone della Valpolicella Cl. Capitel Monte Olmi '96	TT	6
● Recioto della Valpolicella Cl. Capitel Monte Fontana '96	TT	5
● Capitel San Rocco Rosso di Ripasso '96	T	4
● Valpolicella Cl. Capitel delle Lucchine '98	T	2*
● Valpolicella Cl. Sup. Capitel dei Nicalò '96	T	3
● Amarone della Valpolicella Cl. Capitel Monte Olmi '95	YYY	5
● Amarone della Valpolicella Cl. Capitel della Fabriseria '95	YY	6
● Recioto della Valpolicella Cl. Capitel Monte Fontana '95	YY	5

S. PIETRO IN CARIANO (VR)

MASSIMINO VENTURINI
VIA SEMONTE, 20
FRAZ. S. FLORIANO
37020 S. PIETRO IN CARIANO (VR)
TEL. 045/7701331 - 045/7703320

Over the last few years the Valpolicella zone has offered new examples of producers who have decided to look beyond their own area and take on markets other than that for bulk wine or bottles sold at the cellar door. Although this has involved substantial investment of time and money and an important review of production methods, the rewards which have come their way have amply repaid them for their efforts. Daniele and Mirco Venturini inherited their dedication to agriculture from their father Massimino. Starting with that, they have gone on to give free play to their own ambitions, but have never wanted to forget their origins. The Recioto Le Brugnine '95 represents a heartfelt homage to Valpolicella's best traditions. It isn't incredibly concentrated like some notable examples from this vintage: it is more understated and mellower in style, with a balance that links nose and palate with a clear and persistent vein of sweetness. The unexaggerated style of their wines can be appreciated even more in the Valpolicella Superiore, aided and abetted by the lightish '96 vintage. Its medium-deep color precedes a nose that is broad but composed of slight, subtle nuances. After a velvety attack, the evolution on the palate is not particularly long, but it leaves a very positive general impression. We find intensity and warmth displayed without half measures, however, in the Amarone '95, which gives an outstanding performance. Its flavor is tight and persistent, and the strength of the tannins does not succeed in disrupting the notable harmony; the aromas on both nose and palate suggest the ripeness of the fruit and a voluptuous cornucopia of spices. The basic Recioto '97 is, in its simple way, well interpreted, whereas we expected a touch more character from the basic Valpolicella.

● Amarone della Valpolicella Cl. '95	▼▼	5
● Recioto della Valpolicella Cl. Le Brugnine '95	▼▼	5
● Recioto della Valpolicella Cl. '97	▼	4
● Valpolicella Cl. Sup. '96	▼	3
● Valpolicella Cl. '98		2
● Amarone della Valpolicella Cl. '93	▽▽	4
● Amarone della Valpolicella Cl. '94	▽▽	5
● Recioto della Valpolicella Cl. '96	▽▽	4

S. PIETRO IN CARIANO (VR)

VILLA BELLINI
VIA DEI FRACCAROLI, 6
LOC. CASTELROTTO DI NEGARINE
37029 S. PIETRO IN CARIANO (VR)
TEL. 045/7725630

At the southernmost end of the Classico zone, in the midst of the plain to the north of Verona, is the Castelrotto hill, apparently separated from the rest of Valpolicella, but in fact indissolubly linked to the heart of the zone's wine-making tradition. Villa Bellini, rising like a watchtower facing Verona on the southeastern side of this hill, is surrounded by vineyards which have always been considered ideal for making great "passiti" (wines made from semi-dried grapes). And in this splendid setting Cecilia and Marco have made the best Recioto of their brief career as producers. It is a memorable wine: a concentrated color introduces a rich, deep nose with notes of aromatic herbs and ripe red berries; the full flavor and perfect evenness on the long and elegant palate are astonishing, and it seems to caress the entire mouth with its velvety softness. The Amarone is very interesting as well; it has come out of an infelicitous vintage with balance and restraint; its ripe and supple fruit evolves gradually in the mouth. The two Valpolicellas are also good: the Superiore stands out for its characteristic, warm and appealing mineral tone; the standard version is fruity, pleasantly soft and ready to drink. This is the best range from Villa Bellini that we have tasted for some years and the wines that are still maturing also show promise.

● Amarone della Valpolicella Cl. '94	▼▼	5
● Recioto della Valpolicella Cl. '95	▼▼	5
● Valpolicella Cl. Il Brolo '98	▼	3
● Valpolicella Cl. Sup. Il Taso '96	▼	4
● Amarone della Valpolicella '90	▽▽	5
● Amarone della Valpolicella Cl. '93	▽▽	5
● Amarone della Valpolicella Ris. '90	▽▽	5
● Recioto della Valpolicella Amandorlato '90	▽▽	4
● Amarone della Valpolicella '92	▽	4
● Recioto della Valpolicella '93	▽	4

SALGAREDA (TV)

Ornella Molon Traverso
Via Risorgimento, 40
Fraz. Campodipietra
31040 Salgareda (TV)
tel. 0422/804807

Every year we find ourselves singing the praises of Ornella Molon and her husband Giancarlo Traverso, true pioneers of quality in a zone, the Piave, better known for quantity. Their estate produces two lines: one is a special selection obtained from their own 16 hectares of vineyards at Campodipietra; the other, which is more economical, comes from carefully purchased grapes. In the first range, the fine, elegant Traminer particularly stood out. On the nose it expressed its usual intense aromatic character, which then carries through perfectly onto the well-structured palate with its delightful finish. The Sauvignon is extremely quaffable and offers classic herbaceous and mineral scents on the nose: the '98 vintage did not give it much concentration but the wine has good fruit and reasonable length. The Vite Bianca '96, a barrique-aged chardonnay, boasts a fairly complex nose which suggests interesting potential for development; the softness in the mouth is a bit predictable, but nonetheless attractive. The most eagerly-awaited of the reds was the Merlot, which is always noteworthy, but in fact we were amazed by the Cabernet, whose vitality can be guessed from its concentrated hue. The nose reveals a gamut of perfumes ranging from mineral hints to blackberry; on the palate, the solid, well-structured fruit is made even more appealing by its fine depth. The Vite Rossa, a Bordeaux blend with raboso, shows an intense color; its interesting bouquet reveals overripe fruity notes; its flavor is warm and finishes full and long. We'll be writing about the Merlot '96, which was bottled after our tastings, in the next edition of the Guide.

●	Piave Cabernet Ornella '96	TT	4
○	Sauvignon '98	TT	3*
○	Traminer '98	TT	3*
●	Vite Rossa '95	TT	4
○	Vite Bianca '96	T	4
○	Piave Chardonnay '98		3
●	Piave Merlot Ornella '95	YY	4
○	Traminer '97	YY	4

SELVAZZANO DENTRO (PD)

La Montecchia
Via Montecchia, 16
35030 Selvazzano Dentro (PD)
tel. 049/637294

The 15th century winery at the foot of the castle and the 40-year-old vines surrounding Villa Capodilista bear witness to the ancient traditions of this estate which, in the last few years, have been successfully combined with innovation. The young owner, Count Giordano Emo Capodilista, who took over the running of the family winery in 1992, has brought in a number of changes: the staff is young, and vineyard and cellar equipment are kept up-to-the-minute. The wines we tasted reflect a deliberate and measured compromise between the old and the new. A splendid case in point is the '96 Fior d'Arancio Passito, a classic wine of the zone: it offers an elegant and delicious restraint; it is sweet and generous on the finish and is noteworthy for its length, structure and evenness. The Cabernet Franc Godimondo '98, a wine without great pretensions, designed to be drunk young, is sustained by excellent fruit and succeeds absolutely in its intentions: it is simply and directly appealing. We liked the graceful freshness of the Raboso Vendemmia Tardiva, while the Chardonnay '98, though light, is enjoyably delicate and characteristic. Another interesting wine is the Cabernet '96, which is only released as a monovarietal in the best vintages; otherwise it is used in the blend for the Colli Euganei Rosso. The version we tasted this year is lean and pleasing.

○	Colli Euganei Moscato Fior d'Arancio Passito '96	TT	4
●	Colli Euganei Cabernet Bandiera '96	T	3
○	Colli Euganei Chardonnay Montecchia '98	T	3
●	Godimondo Cabernet '98	T	3
●	Raboso '97	T	3

BISSON

VIA BISSON, 17
37038 SOAVE (VR)
TEL. 045/7680775

Bisson is one of this year's new entries. The owner, Lino Battocchia, personally looks after both his seven hectares of vineyard and the wine-making operations, helped by his daughter Stefania, who also takes care of administration and sales. The grapes he grows, garganega (80%), trebbiano, chardonnay and sauvignon, go into making three different types of Soave: the Classico Superiore, obtained form the hillside vineyards, and two Soave DOCs from grapes grown in the plain. These, the Bisson and the Bissoncello, take their names from the two small hills at whose feet the winery lies. The range is completed by two Reciotos, one matured in stainless steel, the other in wood; total production is around 40 thousand bottles. If you visit, you'll find a simple, direct, family atmosphere, and much the same style can be found in the wines, beginning with the Soave Classico Superiore '98. A blend of garganega and trebbiano, it impressed us with the fragrance of its aromas, well coordinated with the similarly lively and well-balanced palate, which displays a lovely harmonious evolution through the finish. The Soave DOC Bissoncello '98 is also more than satisfactory: in this wine, apart from the usual garganega and trebbiano, there is a good dollop of chardonnay. The delicate nose offers scents of fresh fruit and floral notes. On the palate it is quaffable, mouth-filling, well-structured and surprisingly long. The barrique-aged Recioto '96 is warm, medium-sweet and not particularly demanding. Lastly, we should like to underline the excellent value for money of the entire range.

O	Soave Cl. Sup. '98	🍷🍷	1*
O	Recioto di Soave '96	🍷	4
O	Soave Bissoncello '98	🍷	1*
O	Soave Bisson '98		1

SOAVE (VR)

CANTINA DEL CASTELLO

CORTE PITTORA, 5
37038 SOAVE (VR)
TEL. 045/7680093

Situated right in the heart of the small town of Soave itself, the Cantina del Castello has for years now been a godsend for those who love a crisp, clean Soave at a very good price. Arturo Stocchetti, aided by the oenologist Roberto Carcereri, has kept pace with the top producers even with the grapes from a vintage (the '98) which at best can be called capricious. Stocchetti has, in the last few years, gone from purchasing other people's grapes to growing his own: an entirely positive change but one which could not produce immediate results; indeed, this new activity was marked by inevitable organizational difficulties, which now seem to have been overcome. The wine from his Monte Pressoni vineyard easily picked up Two Glasses thanks to its fragrance and depth: it is a typically enjoyable and lively Soave, with good meaty fruit underpinned by crisp acidity. The Soave from the Monte Carniga cru is of a quite different style, although similarly good. It is richer and more complex and seems to be intended for drinkers who like the ripe style of garganega-based wine, which offers particular mineral notes. Both these wines undoubtedly have greater depth and a better-defined style than the '97s. The barrique-aged Soave does not appear to be a complete success, although it shows interesting potential for improvement. The basic Soave is delicate and undemanding; the Recioto is insubstantial and uninspired.

O	Soave Cl. Sup. Monte Carniga '98	🍷🍷	3*
O	Soave Cl. Sup. Monte Pressoni '98	🍷🍷	3*
O	Soave Cl. Sup. Acini Soavi '97	🍷	4
O	Soave Cl. Sup. '98		3
O	Soave Cl. Sup. Monte Pressoni '97	🍷🍷 (outline)	3

SOAVE (VR)

COFFELE

VIA ROMA, 5
37038 SOAVE (VR)
TEL. 045/7680007

The fascination of the Soave zone lies in some of its more important sites, and Castel Cerino is certainly one of them. It is a broad hillside which challenges the garganega grape by providing it with an enviable wealth of micro-elements. This is where the Coffeles' Soaves come from. The wines are definitely as good as last year's, although their style is different. Alberto and his father Beppino have decided to leave out the chardonnay (which they are using to make an excellent monovarietal wine) and have therefore increased, whenever the quality of the grapes has allowed it, the proportion of trebbiano di Soave. Their aim, in the standard Soave and in the Ca' Visco selection, is to return to the idea of a well-defined white with personality, which reveals both surprising immediacy and promising complexity. In the basic Soave one finds, well-integrated in its voluptuous and intriguing bouquet, a more evident fragrance of apple and pear. The palate is forceful and displays an exciting, almost tannic verve, with a finish that is everything one could hope for. The style of the Ca' Visco is more understated. Its broad nose is exquisite; the body is more substantial and well-structured than that of the standard Soave, and it all, together with evenness and length, leads one to think that the wine should have an excellent future. The Chardonnay is deeply appealing: it enchants from beginning to end. The Recioto Le Sponde, with its irresistible perfumes of fresh hazelnut, apricot and melon, displays a remarkable harmony and is a wonderful amalgam of tradition and innovation.

O Chardonnay '98	🍷🍷	3*
O Recioto di Soave Le Sponde '97	🍷🍷	4
O Soave Cl. Sup. '98	🍷🍷	2*
O Soave Cl. Sup. Ca' Visco '98	🍷🍷	3*
O Recioto di Soave Le Sponde '95	♀♀	4
O Soave Cl. Sup. Ca' Visco '97	♀♀	3

SOAVE (VR)

MONTE TONDO

VIA S. LORENZO, 89
37038 SOAVE (VR)
TEL. 045/7680347

At a time when Italian white wines are undergoing something of a crisis in the market-place, what one needs is more estates like Monte Tondo to set an example: this producer has decided to react with determination and drive to a phase in which viticulture in the Soave area appears to have become complacent. There are lots of good vineyard sites between Soave and Monteforte, but many of them are not properly used; instead, they are left to produce very high yields, often even beyond those permitted by the DOC regulations, with a consequent detrimental effect on the quality of the finished wines. This was the starting point for Gino Magnabosco's campaign: from being a simple grape grower he has transformed himself into an impassioned wine-maker. Even if he has not yet received the plaudits of some of his more celebrated colleagues, his high aims, and the efforts he has expended in order to achieve them, certainly warrant his doing so. The Soave Casette Foscarin got a very high score: it has voluptuous depth on the palate allied with irrepressible clarity on the nose. Part of the wine has been aged in oak and one can distinctly taste the presence of chardonnay, but all these elements fuse perfectly. The very inviting Soave Monte Tondo, which very nearly earned Two Glasses with its immediate and fragrant aromas, is less intense on the palate than the Casette Foscarin, but shares its clean, well-balanced style. The Recioto di Soave Spumante is excellently made (for some years now it has been the best in its category), and the Soave Spumante is even more impressive: it is dry, crisp and thoroughly enjoyable, thanks to its supple structure and extreme freshness.

O Soave Cl. Sup. Casette Foscarin '98	🍷🍷	3*
O Soave Spumante Brut '98	🍷🍷	3*
O Recioto di Soave Cl. Spumante '97	🍷	4
O Soave Cl. Sup. Monte Tondo '98	🍷	2*

SOAVE (VR)

Leonildo Pieropan

Via Camuzzoni, 3
37038 Soave (VR)
tel. 045/6190171

Leonildo Pieropan is tireless and meticulous: in the fashioning of his wines one glimpses the manner of a scholar who analyzes the details in order to understand the phenomenon as a whole. Probably Soave and Recioto no longer hold any secrets for him, but his approach does not change: he is always ready to find out about new techniques for protecting his vineyards, he learns from the market without forcing his own style, and when he tastes his wines he displays the healthy dissatisfaction of one who knows that he can still do better. This must all lie behind the Soave La Rocca '97, a wonderful compendium of intensity and balance and a perfect white for anyone who loves persistence and elegance: it has absorbed complexity from being fermented and matured in oak; hence its aromas display a well-modulated wealth of nuances; on the palate, one senses the force of the garganega, its surprising generosity and voluptuous and persistent subtlety. The alter ego of this ripe, multi-faceted wine is the Calvarino, which encompasses all the satisfying qualities a Soave can offer. This year Pieropan has reduced the proportion of trebbiano, a variety that suffered particularly in '98, leaving the garganega to yield all of its juicy roundness. The color shows a promising hint of green; scents of flowers, pear and almond lie at the heart of its deep and intriguing nose. It is forceful on entry, acquiring a stunning, lively and extreme finesse on the palate: it is a wine of great breeding, and Three Glasses belong to it by right. The basic Soave is a delicious small-scale version of the crus. The Recioto is a sweet white with an intoxicating fragrance. The Passito della Rocca is vigorous yet refined, and deliciously yields up all of its potential: its plump richness is contrasted by the vibrant force of its extract, while the finish displays exemplary restraint.

O Soave Cl. Sup. Vigneto Calvarino '98	🍷🍷🍷	4
O Passito della Rocca '96	🍷🍷	6
O Recioto di Soave Le Colombare '96	🍷🍷	4
O Soave Cl. Sup. '98	🍷🍷	3*
O Soave Cl. Sup. Vigneto La Rocca '97	🍷🍷	4
O Passito della Rocca '88	YYY	6
O Passito della Rocca '93	YYY	5
O Passito della Rocca '95	YYY	5
O Soave Cl. Sup. Vigneto La Rocca '95	YYY	4
O Soave Cl. Sup. Vigneto La Rocca '96	YYY	4

SOAVE (VR)

Suavia

Via Centro, 14
Fraz. Fittà
37038 Soave (VR)
tel. 045/7675089

From the hills that wind down towards the plain, as if to separate the territories of Soave and Monteforte, there are some breathtaking views which reveal better than words can the "suave" nature of these sites and of the wine which comes from them. It is on one of these natural terraces that one discovers the Suavia winery, where not even the extension work under way manages to draw one's attention away from the vineyards that surround it. And it is the Tessari family's dedication to these hillsides and their natural potential that makes it possible for them to produce a wine like the Monte Carbonare. The source of its bouquet is deep in the volcanic mineral soil of the hill on which the vineyard is sited. Its palate is that of a great wine: a gradual, constant and elegant evolution, soft but lively, leads to a harmonious vegetal finish. The barrique-aged Soave Le Rive, is very interesting too, and they have waited to release it until it was fully mature: here the fruity and floral scents are already accompanied by tertiary aromas, and the flavor is full and satisfyingly attractive. The basic Soave Classico is also a success: verdant and spicy on the nose, it is supple and perfectly balanced in its straightforward way.

O Soave Cl. Sup. Le Rive '96	🍷🍷	4
O Soave Cl. Sup Monte Carbonare '98	🍷🍷	3*
O Soave Cl. Sup. '98	🍷	2*
O Soave Cl. Sup Monte Carbonare '97	YY	3
O Recioto di Soave La Boccara '95	Y	5

SOMMACAMPAGNA (VR)

Le Vigne di San Pietro

Via S. Pietro, 23
37066 Sommacampagna (VR)
tel. 045/510016

This year the range from this winery is graced by a sweet wine of notable finesse: the Due Cuori. This is a more delicate version of the Mediterranean-style "passito" (raisin wine) Sud, which earned Three Glasses a couple of years ago. It is made from moscato giallo, and has a brilliant warm straw color; its nose offers hints of bergamot, grapefruit and pineapple, as well as a surprising mineral note; this fragrant immediacy is also dominant on the palate, where the definite, plump sweetness is well balanced by an acidity that ensures that the wine does not become cloying. The '96 vintage did not allow Nerozzi to make the Refolà into that complete red which he has been planning for some time: one finds warmth and a good dose of extract, and the oak seems well-integrated, but perhaps it lacks the harmony to tie all these sensations together; besides, the perfumes, though intense, lack a bit of finesse. However, the Refolà is still a very distinctive Cabernet, and will always be the subject of intense debate. The Garda classics are not up to last year's: they are sound and delicate, but without the verve that has enlivened them on other occasions; they are the victims of a year that caused problems for all the earlier-ripening grape varieties. In conclusion, we enjoyed the I Balconi Rossi red, which is agreeable and inviting on the nose, and well balanced and undemanding on the palate.

○	Passito Due Cuori '96	🍷🍷	5
●	Refolà Cabernet Sauvignon '96	🍷🍷	6
●	I Balconi Rossi '97	🍷	3
●	Bardolino '98		3
⊙	Bardolino Chiaretto '98		3
○	Bianco di Custoza '98		3
○	Sud '95	ΨΨΨ	5
●	Refolà Cabernet Sauvignon '93	ΨΨ	6
●	Refolà Cabernet Sauvignon '94	ΨΨ	6

SONA (VR)

Daniele Zamuner

Via Valecchia, 40
37060 Sona (VR)
tel. 045/6081090

We frequently get conflicting signals from this winery, which seems to alternate successful and fascinating wines with decidedly less interesting ones. We refer, in particular, to the Montespada and Valecchia reds, which as of this year include the grape varieties from which they are made in their names. The Montespada selection, from the '98 vintage, offers two light, easy-drinking wines, one a pinot nero and the other a blend of sangiovese and corvina. Under the Valecchia label, on the other hand, there is a Bordeaux-style red and a Sangiovese: although the aim here may be greater character, the wines are unduly dominated by the oak in their bouquets, and are not particularly well-knit on the palate. Just the opposite can be said of the barrique-aged Chardonnay, a model of how oak can improve the complexity of a white which still manages to keep its eminently drinkable style: warmth and energy characterize color, nose and palate. The Bianco di Custoza is good, too, thanks in part to a positive maceration on the skins which has made the aromas more intriguing, the structure on the palate more solid, and the finish longer. The Spumante Extra Brut '93 is very fine; its high score recognizes its overall finesse, as it is not in fact particularly concentrated. The perlage is very fine indeed, the perfumes are complex and well balanced and the flavor lingers. Our judgment of the Spumante Rosé was complicated by the variability of the bottles tasted, a result of the variability of their corks.

○	Spumante Metodo Classico Extra Brut '93	🍷🍷	4
○	Bianco di Custoza '98	🍷	2*
○	Chardonnay Valecchia '97	🍷	3
⊙	Spumante Metodo Classico Brut Rosé '93	🍷	4
●	Rosso Valecchia '94	ΨΨ	3
●	Rosso Valecchia '96	ΨΨ	4
○	Spumante Metodo Classico '91	ΨΨ	4
○	Spumante Metodo Classico Brut '92	ΨΨ	4
○	Spumante Metodo Classico Extra Brut '91	Ψ	4

SUSEGANA (TV)

CONTE COLLALTO
VIA XXIV MAGGIO, 1
31058 SUSEGANA (TV)
TEL. 0438/738241

In the last few editions of the Guide we have mentioned the good results the Collalto estate has achieved by means of improved exploitation of the excellent potential of its vineyards. This year's tastings confirm the positive trend, although we still feel the want of reliably outstanding reds. The work in the vineyards is extremely promising: they are being completely reorganized, with a high density of vines per hectare and consequent low yields, and meanwhile the cellar is being completely re-equipped. In this difficult transitional phase, it is interesting that the Prosecco Extra Dry is once again their best wine: pale straw in color, it displays aromas of almond and pear which are then echoed on the palate. Here the wine evolves well, admirably supported by the carbon dioxide. Sticking to the whites, we found an appealing Incrocio Manzoni 6.0.13 with sweet and delicate perfumes; it is well balanced, restrained and persistent on the palate. The Cabernet Riserva '95 stands out among the reds. It has a fine ruby color, and its concentrated nose reveals scents of red berries and spice; on the palate it is full, soft and elegant, and has a well-balanced finish. The Merlot offers a vinous fragrance and an attractive flavor, while the Wildbacher (a variety found mostly in southern Austria) has a more vigorous nose and a nice supple structure.

●	Piave Cabernet Ris. '95	**YY**	4
○	Prosecco di Conegliano Extra Dry	**YY**	3*
○	Incrocio Manzoni 6.0.13 '98	**Y**	3
●	Piave Merlot '98	**Y**	2*
●	Wildbacher '98	**Y**	3
○	Piave Chardonnay '98		2
●	Piave Cabernet Ris. '94	YY	4
●	Incrocio Manzoni 2.15 '97	Y	3
●	Wildbacher '97	Y	3

TORREGLIA (PD)

VIGNALTA
VIA DEI VESCOVI, 5
FRAZ. LUVIGLIANO
35038 TORREGLIA (PD)
TEL. 0429/777225

The Gemola and the Sirio make Vignalta one of the Veneto's top producers once again this year. The search for quality here includes giving the wines greater character, thus allowing them to emerge from the narrow context of the Colli Euganei and become truly universal wines, without of course losing the individuality they derive from such a viticulturally blessed area. In the Gemola '97 we find all the opulence of merlot, which represents 70% of the blend, combined with the stirring mineral quality of cabernet franc. Its deep ruby color introduces a constantly evolving bouquet with beautifully judged oak. This wealth is mirrored on the palate, which is not at all aggressive, but soft and mouth-filling. The '96 version of the Gemola is a shade less intense, but the sumptuous linear style it has always displayed remains intact. The Sirio, made from moscato bianco, was presented in two versions: the basic one shows its habitual rich varietal character, expressed with great immediacy and well supported by the wine's attractive full-bodied structure. The Oro version displays grater complexity and a full, dense style that is immediately apparent in the glass. Scents of citrus fruit and yellow flowers emerge on the nose. The entry on the palate is broad, as is the progression, in which all the voluptuous sensations of the bouquet reappear. The Colli Euganei Bianco Marlunghe is again irresistibly attractive and supported, despite the poor year, by surprisingly well-structured fruit. The Merlot from the more economical Marlunghe line deserves its One Glass. The barrique-aged Chardonnay is ripe and well made, while the Pinot Bianco is simpler but equally pleasant. The moscato Il Nero is fascinating and really unusual.

●	Colli Euganei Rosso Gemola '97	**YYY**	5
○	Colli Euganei Bianco Marlunghe '98	**YY**	3*
●	Colli Euganei Rosso Gemola '96	**YY**	5
●	Il Nero '97	**YY**	4
○	Sirio '98	**YY**	3*
○	Sirio Oro '98	**YY**	4
○	Colli Euganei Chardonnay '97	**Y**	4
●	Colli Euganei Merlot Marlunghe '98	**Y**	3
○	Colli Euganei Pinot Bianco '98	**Y**	4
●	Colli Euganei Cabernet Ris. '90	YYY	6
●	Colli Euganei Rosso Gemola '95	YYY	5
●	Colli Euganei Rosso Gemola '94	YY	5

DESIDERIO BISOL & FIGLI

VIA FOL, 33
FRAZ. S. STEFANO
31049 VALDOBBIADENE (TV)
TEL. 0423/900138

This year, Bisol successfully experimented with its Prosecco, altering the style of its wines, making them less immediate on the palate, and giving them greater potential complexity. We do not know all the technical particulars that effected this change but, significantly, it coincided with the '98 vintage, one of the most difficult to interpret of recent years. The key is in the ripening of the grapes, that Bisol chose to leave even longer on the vine, and in the fermentation and "prise de mousse", which has also become considerably longer. The first noticeable result is in the style of the Vigneti del Fol, a silky and lively Extra Dry with an elegant nose and a concentrated and lingering flavor: this sparkling wine shows aging potential. The Brut Crede shows some similarity; it displays all the traits of an elegant, well-structured Prosecco, and charming vividly floral-toned perfumes. A ripe richness and complexity are the outstanding characteristics of the creamy and mouth-filling Garnéi, which possesses a perfect balance between sugars and extract. The Prosecco Dry Salis is more immediate: its rich, enveloping sweetness is rendered more harmonious by the good integration of the carbon dioxide. The Cartizze did slightly less well than recent versions, as it lacks the exciting richness on the nose which has often characterized it. The Prosecco Tranquillo suffered more from the summer drought and we found it a bit short, but we should like to note the good showing of the delicate Incrocio Manzoni '96. Lastly, the Pas Dosé '95, stylish, bone-dry and perfectly mature, is really successful.

O	Prosecco di Valdobbiadene Dry Garnéi '98	🍷🍷	4
O	Prosecco di Valdobbiadene Dry Salis	🍷🍷	3*
O	Prosecco di Valdobbiadene Extra Dry Vigneti del Fol '98	🍷🍷	4
O	Talento Pas Dosé '95	🍷🍷	4
O	Cartizze '98	🍷	4
O	Incrocio Manzoni 6.0.13 Perusai '96	🍷	3
O	Prosecco di Valdobbiadene Brut Crede	🍷	3
O	Spumante Jeio	🍷	3
O	Talento Cuvée del Fondatore '92	🍷🍷 (white)	4

F.LLI BORTOLIN SPUMANTI

VIA MENEGAZZI, 5
FRAZ. S. STEFANO
31049 VALDOBBIADENE (TV)
TEL. 0423/900135

What is really unusual about Fratelli Bortolin compared to most producers in the zone is that they not only produce a range of constantly reliable quality, but every year they also release at least one extraordinary wine. This is all thanks to the passion that Valeriano Bortolin, with true rural calm, has managed to pass on to his children, who for some time now have played a pivotal role in the running of the winery. Excellent results can never be taken for granted, since the fruit the Bortolins have to work with is not always of the quality that they hope for, and indeed is a plaything of freaks of the weather. The '98 vintage, for example, saw a very long drought during the month of August which, in the great scheme of things, is almost worse than rain during the harvest (which in fact duly arrived as well). However, the Rù, a Prosecco Extra Dry from the Rua di Feletto zone, has the verve of a great year: its floral perfumes are lifted by a lively freshness; on the palate it is broad, and the balance is enhanced by crisp acidity. The Cartizze is always a touchstone: it has a straw yellow color and a fine perlage. On the nose it displays notes of citrus fruit and white flowers; on the palate it is full, elegant, well-balanced and very long. The Prosecco Extra Dry offers some pungent notes and intense, well-defined aromas which then evolve very enjoyably on the palate; the finish is fresh and delicately almond-toned. The Prosecco Brut is direct and not very demanding; the Brut di Convento, made from chardonnay and prosecco, shows perhaps a little less character than usual. The only wine we really cannot evaluate is the Prosecco Dry, of which we tried several bottles with extremely varying results.

O	Cartizze	🍷🍷	4
O	Prosecco di Conegliano Rù	🍷🍷	3*
O	Prosecco di Valdobbiadene Brut	🍷	3
O	Prosecco di Valdobbiadene Extra Dry	🍷	3
O	Spumante Brut Vigneto del Convento		3

Bortolomiol

Via Garibaldi, 142
31049 Valdobbiadene (TV)
tel. 0423/975794

This is definitely the best year for this producer since its first appearance in our Guide, and it is significant that it should coincide with the '98 vintage, which was certainly not hugely successful in the Prosecco zone. In the last six years the Bartolomiol family has made great efforts to distance itself from the image of a commercial producer, trying instead to convey through its wines a clear picture of the quality of its grapes. It's not such a surprise that the Prosecco Banda Rossa easily won Two Glasses, as it clearly had had ambitions of that sort; what is remarkable is that a number of wines in the range came very close to equaling it, thus making up a very satisfying range indeed. The Frizzante version is more than simply agreeable, making its mark with a delicate variety of aromas and surprising length. The same touch of complexity is to be found in the Prosecco Tranquillo, which is light in body but offers a crescendo on the finish. The showing of the Cartizze was quite unusual: its perfumes are anything but banal, and it is mouth-filling and well-defined on the palate. Only the Prosecco Brut performed below par: rather short in the mouth, it also showed one or two problems on the nose. The stylish basic Prosecco Extra Dry, with its impeccably judged carbon dioxide, is a small-scale version of the Banda Rossa. The latter's richness and vigorous flavors and aromas amazed us: it is certainly a softer Extra Dry than average, but the mellowness is perfectly supported by an ideal structure.

O	Prosecco di Valdobbiadene Extra Dry Selezione Banda Rossa	🍷🍷	3*
O	Cartizze	🍷	4
O	Prosecco di Valdobbiadene Dry	🍷	3
O	Prosecco di Valdobbiadene Extra Dry	🍷	3
O	Prosecco di Valdobbiadene Frizzante Il Ponteggio	🍷	3
O	Prosecco di Valdobbiadene Tranquillo	🍷	3

VALDOBBIADENE (TV)

Canevel Spumanti

Via Roccat e Ferrari, 17
Loc. S. Biagio
31049 Valdobbiadene (TV)
tel. 0423/975940

Just over twenty years after starting up, Canevel is about to move for the second time: they are leaving their headquarters on via Calpiandre to transfer to the hamlet of San Biagio, in the Saccol zone, near the Cartizze vineyards. The offices, the tasting room and all the other places designed to accommodate people have been created from the restructuring of the very old building which was already standing on this hill, whereas the cellar has been purpose-built. Inside the cellar one finds only a part of the equipment that existed previously, while state-of-the-art choices have been made for the new plant, aimed at providing optimum control over all the phases from the arrival of the grapes through to bottling. While looking forward to tasting and evaluating the wines that will be made at the new winery from the next vintage onwards, we tasted a good version of the vintage Dry; this wine, which is delicate on the nose, is very elegant and well-balanced on the palate, revealing excellent integration of the clean, regular mousse. The basic Extra Dry version, which was not unduly affected by the problems of the dread '98 vintage, is also interesting. Its straw yellow color and the perlage which enlivens it both suggest an inebriating freshness; the sweet floral notes on the nose are echoed in the progression of fruit on the palate, which is deliciously enjoyable rather than full-bodied; the finish, with its hints of almond and apple, is enchanting. The Cartizze is good too: here we find an inviting contrast between the ripeness of the nose and the bright freshness of the flavor. The very dry Prosecco Brut is more straightforward but nevertheless tasty, and we particularly enjoyed its finesse.

O	Cartizze '98	🍷	4
O	Prosecco di Valdobbiadene Brut '98	🍷	3
O	Prosecco di Valdobbiadene Extra Dry '98	🍷	3
O	Prosecco di Valdobbiadene Extra Dry Il Millesimato '98	🍷	4
O	Prosecco di Valdobbiadene Tranquillo '98		3

COL VETORAZ

VIA TRESIESE, 1
FRAZ. S. STEFANO
31040 VALDOBBIADENE (TV)
TEL. 0423/975291

This year Col Vetoraz is the best producer in the entire Valdobbiadene area. If we add the sparkling wines in a new line, Rivalta, specially created for the foreign market, to those named after the site of the winery, the results of our tastings become truly triumphant. It is, however, necessary to explain that the partners in Col Vetoraz are Miotto, (the owner of the vineyards), Dall'Acqua, (the oenologist), and De Bortoli, (the director). These last two have created, together with Caldart, who recently left Col Vetoraz, Rivalta, a sort of new company in which grapes are bought in from growers and are vinified at the parent winery here in Santo Stefano. All of Col Vetoraz's sparkling wines showed a character and richness which were quite unexpected after the really rather meagre hopes held out for the '98 vintage. Here Loris Dall'Acqua's role as selector and wine-maker was no doubt crucial. The Prosecco Extra Dry was extraordinarily impressive: bright in color and with a creamy, constant mousse, it offers voluptuous breadth on the nose; on the palate it is soft, full-bodied and persistent. The excellent Prosecco Brut, one of the hardest wines to make this year, is a tiny bit sweeter than usual. The Cartizze is rich and displays more elegance than it did last year. The vintage Prosecco Dry, which reveals a surprising herbaceous tone on the nose, is sinuous, mouth-filling and long. The Rivalta wines offer the same high level of quality; we particularly mention the robust Prosecco Tranquillo.

O Cartizze	🍷🍷	4
O Prosecco di Valdobbiadene Brut	🍷🍷	3*
O Prosecco di Valdobbiadene Dry Millesimato '98	🍷🍷	3*
O Prosecco di Valdobbiadene Dry	🍷🍷	3*
O Prosecco di Valdobbiadene Extra Dry	🍷🍷	3*
O Prosecco di Valdobbiadene Tranquillo Rivalta '98	🍷🍷	3*

VALDOBBIADENE (TV)

NINO FRANCO

VIA GARIBALDI, 147
31049 VALDOBBIADENE (TV)
TEL. 0423/972051

In the last few years, Primo Franco's winery has improved significantly. His decisions to press all the grapes he receives himself and to acquire vineyards in excellent sites have increased his ability to select his grapes, and as a consequence Primo has finally been able to return to the level which he is definitely much more used to. His best wine this year is the Cartizze, in which one finds all the qualities that are typical of his wines: good ripeness, evident even from the color; full, well-evolved richness on the nose; and a less banal flavor than average, underpinned not only by the carbon dioxide but also by lively, dry acidity and by surprising persistence. A Prosecco which, on the other hand, will always give rise to debate – not so much about its quality, but rather about its style – is the Primo Franco: it is particularly intended to have a traditional profile; hence it is warm, mouth-filling and perhaps a bit sedate, but undoubtedly intriguing and evocative. The interpretation of the Prosecco Extra Dry Rustico may be called classic, even in the most modern sense of the term: its scents of fruit are straightforward and very inviting, it is lively on the palate and the perlage is not overdone. The Prosecco Brut, in which one clearly sees the hand of Franco, is captivating: in fact the wine is never bone-dry, but offers its pure flavor with a perfect and pleasurable suppleness. The Prosecco Tranquillo suffered particularly from the difficulties of the '98 vintage, but all the sparkling wines show a well-defined character: this is what we find most encouraging for the future of the winery which, in the '80s, re-invented Prosecco.

O Cartizze	🍷🍷	4
O Prosecco di Valdobbiadene Brut	🍷	3
O Prosecco di Valdobbiadene Dry Primo Franco	🍷	3
O Prosecco di Valdobbiadene Extra Dry Rustico	🍷	3

VALDOBBIADENE (TV)

Le Colture
Via Fol, 5
Fraz. S. Stefano
31049 Valdobbiadene (TV)
tel. 0423/900192

Cesare and Renato Ruggeri, of the Le Colture estate, continue to produce excellent results, in line with their established project to increase quality and quantity. Having started off with seven hectares, they now cultivate about 40, of which 30 actually belong to the estate. Still on the subject of development, the planting of a new vineyard of excellent quality at Rua di Feletto, for the production of a promising Colli di Conegliano Rosso, is of particular interest. For their Prosecco, the Ruggeris have planted their vineyards in a way that is unusual in the Marca Trevigiana area: a high density of vines per hectare, low yields and thinning of the bunches, as well as paying attention to the equilibrium of the vines rather than to individual analytical data. And this year's results are really stunning! The Prosecco Dry Funer displays, along with its delicate perlage, fresh, elegant perfumes with hints of exotic fruit in the foreground; on the palate it is soft, full, and round, and boasts a well-balanced finish. The Cartizze has a complex nose and a well-balanced, silky palate, on which one finds ripe notes with hints of hazelnut; the splendid finish is absolutely clean. The Brut is one of the best of the '98 vintage: it offers a fresh and elegant nose that reveals ripe fruity tones; on the palate its characteristic dry flavor is balanced by a pleasing softness and by very good integration of the carbon dioxide; the finish is elegant. The Prosecco Extra Dry is similarly attractive and interesting, pervaded as it is by fruity tones (apple in particular); on the palate it shows broad, delicately evolving fruit, nicely combined with the carbon dioxide. The finish is well defined and balanced.

O	Cartizze	🍷🍷	4
O	Prosecco di Valdobbiadene Brut	🍷🍷	3*
O	Prosecco di Valdobbiadene Dry Funer	🍷🍷	3*
O	Prosecco di Valdobbiadene Extra Dry	🍷🍷	3*
O	Prosecco di Valdobbiadene Tranquillo Masaré '98		3

VALDOBBIADENE (TV)

Angelo Ruggeri
Via Fol, 18
Fraz. S. Stefano
31049 Valdobbiadene (TV)
tel. 0423/900235

This winery and its six hectares under vine are in the heart of the Prosecco zone: in the vineyards at Fol, Funer and Santo Stefano Remigio and Vittore pick most of the grapes they need. They also have a small vineyard in the hills of Cartizze. The wines of this current vintage confirm their extremely dependable quality: this in a year which, with its rain-plagued harvest, was really not among the easiest to handle. Well-timed picking and expeditious cellar operations, however, enabled them to safeguard the quality of their Prosecco. Again this year, the Dry Funer is their most important wine; the typical flowery nose is enriched by fresh fruity notes; the rich and well-balanced palate reveals a long and enticing finish. The Cartizze, though it did not repeat last year's excellent result, offers a broad and enjoyable spectrum of aromas; it is a little lean of body and this allows the carbon dioxide to become somewhat excessive. The delicacy of its perfumes and its balanced palate mark the Prosecco Extra Dry as an ideal easy-drinking wine; the light body leads to a faultless finish. The wine that suffered most was the Prosecco Brut which, though not unattractive, is too thin.

O	Cartizze	🍷🍷	4
O	Prosecco di Valdobbiadene Dry Funer	🍷🍷	3*
O	Prosecco di Valdobbiadene Extra Dry	🍷	3
O	Prosecco di Valdobbiadene Brut		3

VALDOBBIADENE (TV)

RUGGERI & C.

VIA PRA FONTANA
31049 VALDOBBIADENE (TV)
TEL. 0423/975716

This year marks the tenth harvest that Paolo Bisol has personally managed. His father Giustino bought the share of his partner Luciano Ruggeri in the summer of '89, leaving Paolo responsible for a vintage that was not even particularly memorable. That year the winery received 200 thousand kilos of grapes from some twenty growers: from that moment on the success of their Prosecco grew right along with the growth of the winery, so that in the last harvest the winery pressed almost 1,800,000 kilos obtained from more than 100 suppliers. This fact can be interpreted in many ways, but we note that this increase has been accompanied by a progressive increase in quality, supported by a major investment in wine-making technology. In recent years Ruggeri's most representative wine, the Prosecco Extra Dry Giall'Oro, has once again taken on the best qualities of its type, going beyond a simple, juicy attractiveness: it has acquired complex and rich perfumes and a structure of wonderful persistence and balance. This wine represents a very high standard level of quality. The Dry Santo Stefano shows verve, intensity and a softness that satisfies because it is balanced by an excellent fresh acidity. The '98 vintage was divided in two: before and after the first weekend in October, during which torrential rains fell. The Cartizze della Ruggeri belongs to the first half, as we can tell from the complex variety of its aromas and from its impressive body. The silky, long Prosecco Giustino B is dazzling and worth following in the future. Among the Brut sparkling wines, the improvement of the Chardonnay is encouraging, and the Prosecco is reliable.

O Cartizze	🍷🍷	4
O Prosecco di Valdobbiadene Dry Santo Stefano	🍷🍷	3*
O Prosecco di Valdobbiadene Extra Dry Giustino B. '98	🍷🍷	4
O Prosecco di Valdobbiadene Extra Dry Giall'Oro	🍷🍷	3*
O Chardonnay Brut Metodo Italiano	🍷	3
O Prosecco di Valdobbiadene Brut	🍷	3
O Prosecco di Valdobbiadene Tranquillo Le Bastie '98		3

VALDOBBIADENE (TV)

S. EUROSIA

VIA DELLA CIMA, 2
FRAZ. S. PIETRO DI BARBOZZA
31049 VALDOBBIADENE (TV)
TEL. 0423/973236

Although the press described '98 as a memorable vintage, in the hills around Valdobbiadene the reality was quite different: rains in October had winegrowers, who were already worried by the extremely dry summer, in a panic, and created a vintage that proved very tricky to deal with. Giuseppe Geronazzo, though, certainly didn't let himself get carried away; instead he made the best of the year's fruit by means of even more discriminating purchases from his usual suppliers; then, thanks, to a careful and slow "prise de mousse", he brought out a series of wines whose composure and balance are their most attractive qualities. We'll start with the creamy Cartizze, which displays a very broad floral note and is rich and fleshy in the mouth, with a flavor and texture that broaden out to cover, with great elegance, the entire palate. We could certainly not have done without the mandatory excellent Brut, the real standard-bearer of the company, whose harmony is expressed in its delicacy and well-integrated bubbles. The Extra Dry version is also a success: it is very elegant and ripe on the nose; on the palate it is broad, well balanced, delightfully silky and persistent. The Prosecco Tranquillo is correct, fresh and easy to drink.

O Cartizze	🍷🍷	4
O Prosecco di Valdobbiadene Brut	🍷	3
O Prosecco di Valdobbiadene Extra Dry	🍷	3
O Prosecco di Valdobbiadene Tranquillo		3

VALDOBBIADENE (TV)

TANORÈ

VIA MONT, 4/A
FRAZ. S. PIETRO DI BARBOZZA
31049 VALDOBBIADENE (TV)
TEL. 0423/975770

One of the major problems for producers of Prosecco is maintaining a consistent level of quality: what is needed is the meticulousness, the stubbornness and the dedication which Sergio and Renato Follador bestow on their seven hectares of vines. These are scattered about in the heart of the Cartizze zone, near Santo Stefano, San Pietro and Guia, in some of the most sought-after sites for growing the prosecco grape. The vineyards have excellent sunny exposures and benefit from a dry and windy climate. The Cartizze, the standard-bearer of the estate, again shows that it one of the best and most reliable of its category. It has a handsome brilliant straw color; the nose is rich and attractive with sweet hints of ripe fruit and white flowers; on the palate it is full and elegant, with a very fine mousse and an attractive almond finish. The Prosecco Extra Dry was produced in a normal version and in a special selection. The former displays excellent breadth of aromas with sweet notes of pear and apple; on the palate the wine is soft and round with an elegant and lingering dry finish. The Selezione, designed to be softer, is a little more straightforward than the normal version, and the nose is less broad, but it offers elegance, evenness and balance. The very interesting Prosecco Brut is dry, clean and fresh, and displays a good balance between the body and the carbon dioxide, thus ensuring intensity and length. The Prosecco Tranquillo is sound, but a little too simple.

○	Cartizze	🍷🍷	4
○	Prosecco di Valdobbiadene Extra Dry	🍷🍷	3*
○	Prosecco di Valdobbiadene Brut	🍷	3
○	Prosecco di Valdobbiadene Extra Dry Selezione	🍷	3
○	Prosecco di Valdobbiadene Tranquillo	🍷	3

VALEGGIO SUL MINCIO (VR)

CORTE GARDONI

LOC. GARDONI, 5
37067 VALEGGIO SUL MINCIO (VR)
TEL. 045/7950382

Corte Gardoni confirms its status as the best producer on the Verona side of Lake Garda by virtue of the quality of its wines, its reliability over the last few years, and its attention to detail, which has become proverbial in the zone. The style of the winery can be appreciated in its top wines, like the sweet white and red Bordeaux blend, but it is even more evident in the Custoza and in the Bardolino, easy, light wines, that are, however, anything but banal and indifferent. The basic Bianco di Custoza showed very well once again; it offers a brilliant straw color, while distinct hints of white-fleshed fruit and delicate verdant tones dominate the nose; the gradual evolution on the palate is counterbalanced by a tension which grows progressively towards the extremely attractive finish. The Bardolino le Fontane, a model of dependability even when the vintage is less than good, has a bright pale ruby color; delicate secondary aromas precede a light and fairly long palate. The Passito I Fenili offers fresh notes of peach and hazelnut on the nose, rather than the candied peel and Mediterranean tones it has often displayed in the past; on the palate, in place of the expected density, we find a more straightforward and undemanding structure. The impressive Rosso di Corte, an admirable combination of complexity and immediacy, shows a youthful dark ruby color and an engaging variety of aromas, in which the oak serves to lift the fruit; the progression on the palate is delicious. Finally, we give the Chiaretto and the Bardolino Superiore '97 an honorable mention.

○	Bianco di Custoza '98	🍷🍷	2*
●	Rosso di Corte '96	🍷🍷	4
●	Bardolino Cl. Le Fontane '98	🍷	3
○	I Fenili '95	🍷	4
⊙	Bardolino Chiaretto '98		3
●	Bardolino Sup. '97		3
○	I Fenili '94	ΥΥ	4
●	Rosso di Corte '92	ΥΥ	4

VERONA

F.lli Bolla

P.zza Cittadella, 3
37122 Verona
tel. 045/8670911

For some years now an improved relationship between the technical staff and the management of the company has resulted in a steady increase in overall quality, due also in great part to the incentives to improve grape quality which have been taken advantage of by Bolla's extremely numerous contributing growers, who are to be found in both the Valpolicella and Soave zones. And from this latter zone comes a white wine which quite makes up for the general weakness of the preceding vintage (the '97): the delicate yet mouth-filling Soave Tufaie, which has been skillfully designed to take advantage of the softness and warmth yielded by the '98 vintage, while not allowing the low acidity to make it flabby. In this Tufaie one again senses the characteristics of the Castellaro, Bolla's historic cru, which always yielded particularly delicious wines. The Amarone '95 is supple, clean and inviting; though not the prodigiously warm and vigorous wine one might have expected from such a celebrated year, it is nonetheless a clear example of a happy balance between quality and quantity. Its bright garnet color introduces scents of macerated flowers and distilled fruit, and the supple and harmonious body is the basis of the appeal of the palate. The Recioto della Valpolicella '97 came close to Two Glasses: though it expresses the true value of its fruit, the integration with the new oak still leaves something to be desired. The basic Soave is small-scale but enjoyable; the Merlot and the Chardonnay, on the other hand, showed less character.

●	Amarone della Valpolicella Cl. '95	🍷🍷	5
●	Recioto della Valpolicella Cl. '97	🍷	4
○	Soave Cl. Sup. Tufaie '98	🍷	3
○	Soave Cl. '98		3
●	Amarone della Valpolicella '90	YY	5
●	Amarone della Valpolicella Ris. '89	YY	5
●	Valpolicella Cl. Sup. Le Pojane '95	YY	3

VERONA

Giacomo Montresor

Via Ca' dei Cozzi, 16
37124 Verona
tel. 045/913399

The large Montresor winery produces a total of three and a half million bottles a year and owns 100 hectares of vineyards from which it makes a large part of its wine: the rest comes from purchased grapes. The wines for their top ranges are made exclusively with grapes produced by their four estates, three of which are in the Garda zone, while the fourth is in Valpolicella, at San Peretto di Negrar. It is to Montresor's great credit that it has been able to demonstrate good quality throughout its long and varied list. We'll begin with the basic Bianco di Custoza '98, definitely one of the best in its category. Its inviting nose displays pleasing aromas; on the palate, the wine shows character and structure and has a good, long finish. The Bianco di Custoza Montefiera '98, after a promising fresh and floral nose, disappoints a little on the palate because of an excessive unctuousness that detracts from the elegance of the finish. The satisfying and delicate Soave Classico '98 is attractively balanced. Now for the Valpolicella wines: the Amarone Capitel della Crosara '97 lived up to expectations: it has a concentrated color and a deep nose with notes of ripe red berries and sweet spice; on the palate it is dense, well-balanced and reasonably long. The Recioto Re Teodorico '97, on the other hand, is a bit below par: it seems straightforward on the nose and rather unexciting on the palate. The Cabernet Sauvignon '97 and the Bordeaux blend Santonmìo '96 are interesting and harmonious, if not especially rich.

●	Amarone della Valpolicella Cl. Capitel della Crosara '97	🍷🍷	6
○	Bianco di Custoza '98	🍷🍷	3*
○	Bianco di Custoza Montefiera '98	🍷	3
●	Cabernet Sauvignon Campo Madonna '97	🍷	3
●	Rosso Santomìo '96	🍷	5
○	Soave Cl. '98	🍷	2
●	Recioto della Valpolicella Re Teodorico '97		5
●	Valpolicella Cl. Capitel della Crosara '97		3
●	Amarone della Valpolicella Cl. Capitel della Crosara '95	YY	6

VERONA

PASQUA
VIA BELVIGLIERI, 30
37131 VERONA
TEL. 045/8402111

The good news for Pasqua is provided by one of the Amarones, which entirely fulfills the promise of the great '95 vintage. It carries the Villa Borghetti label and makes up for the uncertain performance of the Amarone Vigneti di Casterna '94. Pasqua gives the wine a modern interpretation which can be seen in the brilliance of its ruby color. The care taken during the drying phase is aimed at preventing this practice from becoming just a way to increase the alcohol level, using it instead as a means of enhancing all the sensations the wine yields. The bouquet is well-delineated, fresh and enveloping. The evolution on the palate is similarly modern: it is smooth, while the softness of the alcohol does not dominate but leaves room for echoes of the bouquet, as well as for firm tannins. Unfortunately the two Valpolicellas, the Superiore Sagramoso and the Classico Villa Borghetti, have suffered from the inimical '96 vintage: they do not rise above the level of simple correctness. The two Soaves, the Montegrande and the Sagramoso, do a little better. Though made in different ways and derived from grapes grown in different sites, they make similar impressions. The former seems more ambitious: it has a fresh and slightly more complex nose and a little more body. The Sagramoso is admirably direct and remarkably delicate on the palate.

●	Amarone della Valpolicella Villa Borghetti '95	🍷🍷	6
○	Soave Cl. Montegrande '98	🍷	3
○	Soave Cl. Sup. Sagramoso '98	🍷	4
●	Valpolicella Cl. Sup. Sagramoso '96		4
●	Valpolicella Sup. Villa Borghetti '96		4
●	Amarone della Valpolicella Vigneti di Casterna '90	🍸🍸	5
●	Morago Cabernet Sauvignon '93	🍸🍸	5
●	Amarone della Valpolicella Vigneti di Casterna '93	🍸	5
●	Amarone della Valpolicella Vigneti di Casterna '94	🍸	5

VIDOR (TV)

ADAMI
VIA ROVEDE, 21
FRAZ. COLBERTALDO
31020 VIDOR (TV)
TEL. 0423/982110

The Adami family has lived since time immemorial near the hills that stretch from Vidor towards Valdobbiadene, passing through Saccol, the Cartizze area and then on through other vineyards until they reach Conegliano Veneto: the head of the clan used to sell grapes and even worked with one of the great Carpenès. But the focus of the family's attention has always been the Giardino di Colbertaldo, a hill that, historically, is the "premier cru" of Prosecco, the emblem of a style and of an excellence that they sought when few even had such an idea, and which continues to inspire Armando and Franco Adami. They were fortunate in having, in Adriano, an enlightened father who permitted them, at the tender age of twenty, to revolutionize the estate and manage it their own way; and Adriano never refused his help and support. The attention dedicated to their wines shows in the impressively consistent quality and the clearly perceptible idea behind each bottle. Let's begin with the splendid Brut, perhaps the most difficult style: it is delicate and floral on the nose, and broad, fragrant and elegant on the palate, with a long and profound almond-toned finish. The ripe and exotic Cartizze is very good too: on the palate it is mouth-filling and rounded, yet fresh at the same time. The Extra Dry is excellent on the palate: it offers notes of apple and hazelnut, and a full flavor underpinned by the perlage. Two notable wines, especially considering the year, are the Incrocio Manzoni, which has never before been so fine and rich in personality, and the Prosecco Tranquillo, which has finally returned to an excellent level. And now finally to the Dry Giardino: sumptuous, long and gradual, it is a perfect Prosecco for those who love understated tones and delicate refinement.

○	Cartizze	🍷🍷	4
○	Prosecco di Valdobbiadene Brut Bosco di Gica	🍷🍷	3*
○	Prosecco di Valdobbiadene Dry Giardino '98	🍷🍷	3*
○	Prosecco di Valdobbiadene Extra Dry dei Casel	🍷🍷	3*
○	Prosecco di Valdobbiadene Tranquillo Giardino '98	🍷🍷	3*
○	Incrocio Manzoni 6.0.13 Le Portelle '98	🍷	3

VIDOR (TV)

De Faveri
Via G. Sartori, 21
Fraz. Bosco
31020 Vidor (TV)
tel. 0423/987673

De Faveri is one of the wineries which dealt best with the complicated '98 harvest: they have produced excellent wines with the grapes picked before the rains and managed to make some quite respectable ones with the fruit picked later in the season. Because of this situation, they have created two lines: the first, in dark bottles, consists of excellent wines, and the second, with the usual label, offers properly made sparkling wines without distinctive character. Lucio De Faveri always aims to make a Prosecco with well-defined perfumes and a clear typicity: few sensations, but distinct ones which, if well balanced, yield an irresistible wine. The Prosecco Dry is in this vein. It is mouth-filling and rich in character; on the nose, it offers the characteristic hints of banana and white flowers; on the rich palate, the residual sugar is nicely balanced by fresh acidity and carbon dioxide, which though forceful does not intrude on the very attractive finish. The Prosecco Brut in the black bottle is again one of the best of its type this year. Its various and complex aromas include white-fleshed fruit, flowers and hazelnut; on the palate, a fine progression leads to a vivid and mouth-filling finish, enhanced by a higher than average residual sugar level for a Prosecco Brut. The Prosecco Extra Dry is the real surprise of the year: usually good but delicate, it demonstrates, in this version, great personality and verve, characteristics which we haven't always found in previous years. The basic Prosecco Brut is true to form, even if the acidity is a little sharp and less controlled than in the special selection.

○ Prosecco di Valdobbiadene Dry Selezione '98	🍷🍷	4
○ Prosecco di Valdobbiadene Extra Dry	🍷🍷	3*
○ Prosecco di Valdobbiadene Dry Brut Selezione	🍷	4
○ Prosecco di Valdobbiadene Brut		3

VIDOR (TV)

Sorelle Bronca
Via Martiri, 20
Fraz. Colbertaldo
31020 Vidor (TV)
tel. 0423/987201 - 0423/987009

The most important items of news at the Sorelle Bronca estate are that the new cellar has been completed and a really interesting red has been released. There were some problems that affected some of the wines, but nothing was so dire as the '98 vintage, which was particularly hard on this estate at Vidor. If the still Prosecco and the semi-sparkling version are a little below par (in the past they were among the best), this cannot be said of the Prosecco Extra Dry, which earns Two Glasses. The bouquet is delicate at first, but it keeps going and grows with time in the glass, revealing an unexpected depth. The wine is light again on the front palate; the perlage is extremely fine and the finish displays exemplary cleanness. The Spumante Metodo Italiano Livio Bronca Brut came very close to earning Two Glasses too: its subtle yeasty hints give way to notes of apple, while the palate reveals harmony and length. The Colli di Conegliano Rosso mentioned in last year's edition of the Guide was in fact a '95: hence this year's wine, from the '96 vintage, is a new release. A deep color introduces a nose with all the richness and depth of an ambitious red, and in which the impetuosity of the Bordeaux grape varieties is combined with the fruitiness of marzemino. The palate is dominated by a sensation of warmth and by the extract which governs the evolution of the flavor; although the wine may be a bit overripe, the overall impression is delightful. The Colli di Conegliano Bianco '98 fully deserves its One Glass.

● Colli di Conegliano Rosso Ser Bele '96	🍷🍷	4
○ Prosecco di Valdobbiadene Extra Dry	🍷🍷	3*
○ Colli di Conegliano Bianco Ser Bele '98	🍷	3
○ Spumante Livio Bronca Brut	🍷	3
○ Prosecco di Valdobbiadene Brut		3
● Colli di Conegliano Rosso '95	🍷 (outline)	3

VIDOR (TV)

SPUMANTI DAL DIN
VIA MONTEGRAPPA, 31
31020 VIDOR (TV)
TEL. 0423/987295

For some years now, Dal Din has presented excellent still wines and slightly less convincing bubblies. This year the situation is completely reversed: the three sparkling wines made from the prosecco are really impressive, while the Colli di Conegliano Bianco, the Prosecco Tranquillo and the Incrocio Manzoni have sunk into the morass of mediocrity that marks Veneto whites from the '98 vintage. Dal Din's standard-bearer, the Prosecco Dry, is designed to be a complete, persistent and elegant wine which is at the same time quite forceful in its flavors and aromas: its sweetness is restrained and the palate echoes the bouquet. The very dry and extremely attractive Prosecco Brut is far from the simple correctness of last year's version; from this kind of wine we do not expect a rich body: its lively and refreshing flavor are what one would hope for. The classic spumante, the Extra Dry, displays elegance and balance; the quite intense color, dotted with fine bubbles, introduces a clearly expressed fragrance and a long palate. The vigorous Cartizze, well balanced and frankly sweet, reveals a delicate structure in line with the possibilities of the vintage; its welcome carbon dioxide is perfecly integrated.

○	Prosecco di Valdobbiadene Dry	🍷🍷	3*
○	Cartizze	🍷	4
○	Prosecco di Valdobbiadene Brut	🍷	3
○	Prosecco di Valdobbiadene Extra Dry	🍷	3

VILLAGA (VI)

CONTE ALESSANDRO PIOVENE
PORTO GODI
VIA VILLA DI TOARA, 14
36020 VILLAGA (VI)
TEL. 0444/885142

The Colli Berici is considered the least exploited zone and the one with the most potential in the entire Veneto, Valpolicella included, and Tommaso Piovene is well aware of it. For the last five years, Piovene, together with his consultant oenologist Flavio Pra, has worked toward improving quality at his family estate at Toara di Villaga. It is a sort of "grand cru" of the zone, consisting of 22 hectares planted to the usual varieties of the Berici, such as garganega and tocai rosso, as well as the classic Bordeaux grapes sauvignon, cabernet and merlot. The management of Piovene's vineyards has become very rigorous, and the consequent yields very low; vinification techniques, which are up-to-the-minute, are aimed at maximizing polyphenolic extraction, and part of the aging takes place in new oak barrels. And indeed we were most impressed by the reds, starting with a spicy and enjoyable Cabernet called Polveriera, which is fragrant, immediate and perfect in its straightforwardness. The more ambitious Cabernet from the Pozzare vineyard iis rich in color. It displays full, ripe scents of dark berries, and is still perhaps a little bit marked by the oak, but the high quality of the fruit comes through all the same. This is not an exemplar of finesse, but there's plenty of body and warmth. The more elegant if less intense Merlot Fra I Broli is the basic version of a varietal on which Piovene and Pra are working hard and in which they have invested great hopes. In fact, the plan for the next year involves the release of a Merlot '98 called Toara, which seemed quite promising in unofficial tastings. The Pinot Bianco is delicate and well put together; the Sauvignon, which is light, but heavy on the alcohol, still needs some fine tuning.

●	Colli Berici Cabernet Pozzare '97	🍷🍷	4
●	Colli Berici Cabernet Polveriera '98	🍷	3
●	Colli Berici Merlot Fra i Broli '97	🍷	3
○	Colli Berici Pinot Bianco Polveriera '98	🍷	3
○	Colli Berici Sauvignon Fostine '98		3

OTHER WINERIES

The following producers obtained good scores in our tastings with one or more of their wines:

PROVINCE OF PADOVA

La Roccola
Cinto Euganeo, tel. 0429/94298
Colli Euganei Fior d'Arancio '98

PROVINCE OF TREVISO

Carpené Malvolti
Conegliano, tel. 0438/410575
Prosecco di Conegliano Dry Oro

Loggia del Colle
Conegliano, tel. 0438/23719
Prosecco di Conegliano Brut

Zardetto
Conegliano, tel. 0438/208909
Prosecco di Conegliano Brut,
Prosecco di Conegliano Extra Dry

La Gioiosa
Crocetta del Montello, tel. 0423/665043
Prosecco di Valdobbiadene Extra Dry,
Cartizze Villa Sandi

Orsola Andreola
Farra di Soligo, tel. 0438/989379
Prosecco di Valdobbiadene Dirupo Extra Dry

Merotto, Farra di Soligo, tel. 0438/898195
Prosecco di Valdobbiadene Dry
Colle Molina,
Prosecco di Valdobbiadene Dry
Primavera di Barbara

Dall'Armellina
Mareno di Piave, tel. 0438/308878
Incrocio Manzoni 6.0.13 '98

Cantina Sociale La Marca
Oderzo, tel. 0422/814681
Prosecco di Valdobbiadene Extra Dry,
Incrocio Manzoni 6.0.13 '98

Rechsteiner
Oderzo, tel. 0422/752074
Piave Cabernet Ris. '95

Nardin
Ormelle, tel. 0422/851002
Lison-Pramaggiore Cabernet Franc '98,
Rosso Vigna Melonetto '96

Sanfeletto
S. Pietro di Feletto, tel. 0438/486832
Prosecco di Conegliano Extra Dry,
Incrocio Manzoni 6.0.13 '98

San Giuseppe
S. Pietro di Feletto, tel. 0438/450526
Prosecco di Conegliano Extra Dry,
Prosecco di Conegliano Frizzante

Vigna Dogarina
Salgareda, tel. 0422/804129
Piave Merlot '98

Bernardi
Susegana, tel. 0438/781022
Incrocio Manzoni Brut

Montesel
Susegana, tel. 0438/781341
Prosecco di Valdobbiadene Extra Dry,
Cabernet del Veneto '98

Bruno Agostinetto
Valdobbiadene, tel. 0423/972884
Prosecco di Valdobbiadene Tranquillo '98

Bellussi, Valdobbiadene, tel. 0423/982147
Prosecco di Valdobbiadene
Extra Dry della Casa,
Prosecco di Valdobbiadene Extra Dry

Cantina Produttori di Valdobbiadene
Valdobbiadene, tel. 0423/982070
Prosecco di Valdobbiadene Brut Val d'Oca,
Prosecco di Valdobbiadene
Extra Dry Val d'Oca

Col de' Salici
Valdobbiadene, tel. 055/291424
Prosecco di Valdobbiadene Brut

Ciodet, Valdobbiadene, tel. 0423/973131
Prosecco di Valdobbiadene Extra Dry,
Cartizze

Drusian, Valdobbiadene, tel. 0423/982151
Prosecco di Valdobbiadene Tranquillo '98

Foss Marai
Valdobbiadene, tel. 0423/900560
Prosecco di Valdobbiadene Extra Dry,
Cartizze

Le Groppe
Valdobbiadene, tel. 0423/972305
Prosecco di Valdobbiadene Extra Dry

Varaschin, Valdobbiadene, tel. 0423/973553
Cartizze

Valdo, Valdobbiadene, tel. 0423/972403
Prosecco di Valdobbiadene Extra Dry
Cuvée del Fondatore,
Prosecco di Valdobbiadene Extra Dry Oro

Bellenda, Vittorio Veneto, tel. 0438/920025
Prosecco di Conegliano Extra Dry Col di Luna

Venegazzù
Volpago del Montello, tel. 0423/870024
Venegazzù Rosso Capo di Stato '97

PROVINCE OF VERONA

Lenotti
Bardolino, 045/7210484
Soave Vigna Capocolle '98,
Bardolino Cl. '98

Villabella
Bardolino, tel. 045/7236448
Bardolino Vigna Morlongo '98

Corte S. Arcadio
Bussolengo, tel. 045/7575331
Bianco di Custoza la Boschetta '98

Tenuta Valleselle - Tinazzi
Cavaion Veronese, tel. 045/7235394
Amarone della Valpolicella La Bastia '95,
Prato del Faggio Ca' de Rocchi '97

Fasoli, Colognola ai Colli, tel. 045/7650741
Recioto di Soave San Zeno '95

Vicentini
Colognola ai Colli, tel. 045/7650539
Soave Sup. '98

Corteforte
Fumane, tel. 045/6839104
Recioto della Valpolicella Amandorlato '94,
Amarone della Valpolicella '95

Le Bertarole
Fumane, tel. 045/6839220
Amarone della Valpolicella '95,
Valpolicella Cl. '98

Paolo Boscaini e Figli
Marano di Valpolicella, tel. 045/6800840
Amarone della Valpolicella
Vigneti di Marano '95,
Soave Cl. Sup. Monteleone '98

Ca' la Bionda
Marano di Valpolicella, tel. 045/6837097
Amarone della Valpolicella '95

Bruno Sartori - La Nave
Mezzane di Sotto, tel. 045/8880089
Soave Sup. '98

Bogoni
Monteforte d'Alpone, tel. 045/6100385
Recioto di Soave '96

Cantina Sociale di Monteforte
Monteforte d'Alpone, tel. 045/7610110
Soave Cl. Sup. Il Vicario '98,
Soave Cl. Sup. Clivus '98

Terre dei Monti
Monteforte d'Alpone, tel. 045/6100867
Soave Cl. Sup. I Righi '98

Mazzi
Negrar, tel. 045/7500136
Valpolicella Cl. '98,
Amarone della Valpolicella
Punta di Villa '95

Sartori
Negrar, tel. 045/7513200
Valpolicella Cl. Sup. Monte Gradella '95,
Amarone della Valpolicella Corte Bra '95

Marcato
Roncà, tel. 045/7460070
Soave '98

Aldegheri
S. Ambrogio di Valpolicella,
tel. 045/6861356
Valpolicella Sup. Ripasso '97,
Amarone della Valpolicella '96

Musella
S. Martino Buon Albergo
tel. 045/994736
Amarone della Valpolicella '95,
Rosso la Musella '96

Paolo Sartori
S. Martino Buon Albergo, tel. 045/8740039
Passito Bianco '96,
Valpolicella Sup. '96

Giuseppe Fornaser
S. Pietro in Cariano, tel. 045/7701651
Amarone della Valpolicella
Monte Faustino '94

Tommasi
S. Pietro in Cariano, tel. 045/7701266
Amarone della Valpolicella '95,
Amarone della Valpolicella Cl.
Ca' Florian Tommasi '95

Tamellini
Soave, tel. 045/6190491
Soave '98,
Soave Cl. Sup. '98

Cantina Sociale di Custoza
Sommacampagna, tel. 045/516200
Bianco di Custoza '98

Albino Piona
Sommacampagna, tel. 045/516055
Passito Bianco La Rabitta '96,
Bianco di Custoza '98

Arcadia
Verona, tel. 045/8204466
Soave Sup. '98

Baltieri, Verona, tel. 045/557616
Valpolicella La Romensa '98

Cantina Sociale della Valpantena
Verona, tel. 045/550032
Amarone della Valpolicella '95,
Valpolicella Sup. '97

Cecilia Beretta
Verona, tel. 045/8402021
Valpolicella Cl. Sup. Roccolo di Mizzole '97

PROVINCE OF VENEZIA

Mosole, Annone Veneto, tel. 0421/310404
Lison-Pramaggiore Tocai '98

Sant'Osvaldo
Annone Veneto, tel. 0422/864046
Lison-Pramaggiore Pinot Grigio '98

Tenuta S. Anna
Annone Veneto, tel. 0422/864511
Grave Friuli Pinot Grigio '98

Santo Stefano
Fossalta di Piave, tel. 0421/67502
Piave Pinot Grigio '98

Mazzolada
Portogruaro, tel. 0421/704646
Lison-Pramaggiore Tocai '98

Teracrea
Portogruaro, tel. 0421/287041
Malvasia di Teracrea '98

PROVINCE OF VICENZA

Bartolomeo da Breganze
Breganze
tel. 0445/873112
Breganze Torcolato '96

Miotti
Breganze, tel. 0445/873006
Breganze Cabernet '97,
Breganze Torcolato '96

Frigo
Cornedo Vicentino, tel. 0445/951334
Colli Berici Rosso del Buielo '96

Iseldo Maule
Gambellara, tel. 0444/444001
Recioto di Gambellara '96,
Gambellara Cl. Gold '98

Da Schio
Longare, tel. 0444/555032
Colli Berici Cabernet '97

Villa dal Ferro - Lazzarini
S. Germano dei Berici, tel. 0444/868025
Colli Berici Pinot Bianco del Rocolo '98

FRIULI VENEZIA GIULIA

Apart from the odd frost and hail shower, the favorable weather held extraordinarily well during the growing season leading up to the '98 grape harvest, right until the beginning of September. In August in particular, the intense heat of the day alternated with cool, and at times rainy, nights, ideal weather for nurturing aromas. The harvest of white and early-maturing red grapes therefore produced truly outstanding wines. Just before mid-September, however, heavy rains began; these lasted for more than two weeks and caused irreparable damage, especially to the red grapes. For this reason, with the exception of the few lucky cases where the grapes were picked no later than Sunday, 13 September, red wines were either not produced at all, or were of a much lower quality than usual. In the following pages you will, however, find some young reds that did well at our tastings. On the price front, we should point out that price lists have officially not been adjusted, but in practice discounting arrangements often reduce costs by 5-20%. This is the result of a contraction of the market caused by a number of factors: these include a shift in consumption toward red wines, and Friuli's image as a wine-producing region, which does not get a lot of support even from the institutions set up for this very purpose. The fact is that Friuli just doesn't make news, because it is already the undisputed leader in the field of Italian white wines. The conviction has also spread, with no real basis in fact, that the wines produced in this region are costly compared with those from other regions. Well, with the odd exception, highly prized wines are also costly wines, all over Italy. It is our impression that Friuli now tends to be very fair in terms of value for money. Twenty wines won Three Glasses and, as always, there is a mixture of repeat performances and first-time winners. Silvio Jermann received this award for two wines, his Vintage Tunina, which got the highest score given to an Italian white this year, and his Capo Martino '97. Girolamo Dorigo made a welcome return to the top, again with two wines, his Chardonnay '97 and his red Montsclapade '96. Wineries that repeated last year's honor include Livio Felluga for his Rosazzo Bianco Terre Alte '97, the Livon brothers for their Braide Alte '97, Miani for the Tocai Friulano '98, Ronco del Gelso, this time for the Sauvignon '98, Russiz Superiore for the Sauvignon '98, Mario Schiopetto for his Pinot Bianco Amrità '97, the Venica brothers for their Sauvignon Ronco delle Mele '98, Gianfranco Gallo's Vie di Romans, which returns with the Sauvignon Piere '97, and Villa Russiz for their Sauvignon de La Tour. Wineries back in the Three Glass group include: Le Vigne di Zamò, for their red Ronco dei Roseti '94 and Fabio Coser's Ronco dei Tassi for the Sauvignon '98. And finally, the debutant winners of Three Glasses, starting with the Ascevi-Luwa winery for their Sauvignon '98, then Flavio Basilicata's Le Due Terre for the Rosso Sacrisassi '97, Isidoro Polencic for his Pinot Grigio '98, the historic Rocca Bernarda winery for an incredible Picolit '97, and Tenuta Villanova for their Chardonnay Monte Cucco '97.

BAGNÀRIA ARSA (UD)

TENUTA BELTRAME
LOC. ANTONINI, 6/8
FRAZ. PRIVANO
33050 BAGNÀRIA ARSA (UD)
TEL. 0432/923670

Year after year this winery, situated between the remains of the ancient Roman city of Aquileia and the star-shaped fortress of Palmanova, continues to improve in quality. The 25 hectares of vineyards, which produce about 140 thousand bottles, are lovingly cultivated by Cristian Beltrame, aided by the oenologist Giuseppe Gollino. The high quality of the Sauvignon, which has become one of the winery's staples, no longer comes as a surprise: it is varietal on the nose, where it displays aromas of elder blossom, tomato, apple and white flowers, all extremely well balanced; in the mouth it opens assertively, but with elegance, to expand on the palate with a note of white fruit in the finish. The Chardonnay is of the same standard, with its striking, intense aromas of apple, barely ripe banana and pineapple. It makes a strong initial impression in the mouth, after which it rounds out to a long banana finish. The Cabernet Sauvignon also won Two Glasses. Its intense purple color, which reveals the youth of the wine, is followed by intense scents of blackberry jam, black currant and hay; its richness in the mouth, unusual for this particular year, is only slightly tempered by tannins that are still a trifle hard. The Merlot, in which the ripe fruit (plum) and the attractive coffee flavors are overshadowed by not yet entirely smooth tannins, came very close to Two Glasses. One full Glass to the Pinot Grigio, which is extremely varietal and has the mineral and green apple aromas typical of this grape: these follow through well on the palate, although the wine is somewhat lacking in overall structure. The Tocai Friulano and the Cabernet Franc are also worth trying. The varietal characteristics come through immediately in the first, with its elegant aromas of bitter almond; these are followed by a simple, albeit well-executed, palate. The second wine, spicy (black pepper) and herbaceous, fades slightly in the mouth.

○	Friuli Aquileia Chardonnay '98	🍷🍷	3*
○	Friuli Aquileia Sauvignon '98	🍷🍷	3*
●	Friuli Aquileia Cabernet Sauvignon '98	🍷🍷	3
●	Friuli Aquileia Cabernet Franc '98	🍷	3
●	Friuli Aquileia Merlot '98	🍷	3
○	Friuli Aquileia Pinot Grigio '98	🍷	3
○	Friuli Aquileia Tocai Friulano '98	🍷	3
○	Friuli Aquileia Pinot Bianco '98		3
●	Friuli Aquileia Refosco P. R. '98		3
●	Pinot Nero '98		3

BAGNÀRIA ARSA (UD)

MULINO DELLE TOLLE
VIA ROMA, 29
LOC. SEVEGLIANO
33050 BAGNÀRIA ARSA (UD)
TEL. 0432/928113

This winery in the Aquileia DOC district, owned by the Bertossi cousins Giorgio, oenologist, and Eliseo, agronomist, is more than merely promising, to judge from the increasing quality of the wines presented at our tastings. The Palmade Bianco, a wine on which they rightly set great store, made a particularly successful debut: a blend of malvasia (briefly wood-aged), sauvignon and chardonnay, it makes a good impact on the nose, with aromas that are fine and elegant notwithstanding the intensity of the fragrance of wildflowers, mint and marjoram; it follows through well on the rich, full and long palate. The Traminer, one of the best of its type, has the characteristic scent of roses with just faint hints of ripe Golden Delicious apple and moss. Overall, it is rich and balanced, although the end result is slightly sweet; lingering fruity tones emerge on the palate, blending in well with the varietal rose notes. The Cabernet Franc, with its fine, fruity nose, plumps more for finesse than for the aggressiveness typical of this grape. The Refosco has decidedly violet tones, and is grapey with hints of spices and rose. It has become traditional for the Mulino delle Tolle to present an interesting Malvasia, and this year is no exception: its fairly intense aromas are reminiscent of ripe pear and citrus fruit; these are echoed very clearly on the palate, which finishes on a predominantly citrus note. Lastly, the Chardonnay and the Merlot, varietal and well made, are also worthy.

○	Friuli Aquileia Bianco Palmade '98	🍷🍷	3*
●	Friuli Aquileia Cabernet Franc '98	🍷	3
●	Friuli Aquileia Merlot '98	🍷	2
●	Friuli Aquileia Refosco P. R. '98	🍷	3
○	Friuli Aquileia Traminer Aromatico '98	🍷	3
○	Malvasia '98	🍷	3
○	Friuli Aquileia Chardonnay '98	🍷	2

BERTIOLO (UD)

CABERT
VIA MADONNA, 27
33032 BERTIOLO (UD)
TEL. 0432/917434

Cabert, a large corporation in the Grave DOC district, vinifies the fruit of some 290 hectares on the Friuli plain. For years their technical staff has been preaching the "gospel" of quality to shareholders, with all that that involves in terms of production methods in the vineyard (lower yields per vine, for example). In the interests of further improvements, particularly in the reds, an external consultancy arrangement was set up fairly recently with established Australian oenologists. This already seems to be bearing fruit, to judge from the distinct leap up in quality in Cabert's wines. We shall start with the Picolit, made from grapes grown in vineyards in the Colli Orientali zone: the nose includes rich but delicate baked apple, candied orange peel, fig and date; all this is echoed in the mouth, which has a long and elegant finish. The Pinot Bianco amazed us with its intense milky, yeasty and ripe apple fragrances; it has a full, rich palate that picks up on the apple flavor, which is just slightly diluted by an acidic finish. And now for the reds: the Cabernet Sauvignon Riserva '94, with its suitably brick red tones, has intense aromas of tobacco, quinine, black pepper and black cherry jam; its balanced palate opens out to fruity flavors, with smooth tannins and a lingering finish. The '96 version of this wine fades just a little in the mouth, where it is not particularly concentrated. To complete an admirable series of Grave wines, the Chardonnay, partly aged in wood, offers aromas of vanilla, ripe banana and milk; the palate, although it reflects the nose, is a bit weaker and not long enough. The Verduzzo Friulano Dolce comes close to One Glass.

●	Friuli Grave Cabernet Sauvignon Ris. '94	🍷🍷	3*
○	Friuli Grave Pinot Bianco '98	🍷🍷	2*
○	COF Picolit '94	🍷🍷	5
●	Friuli Grave Cabernet Sauvignon Ris. '96	🍷	3
○	Friuli Grave Chardonnay '97	🍷	3
○	Friuli Grave Pinot Grigio '98		3
○	Friuli Grave Verduzzo Friulano Dolce '98		3
●	Friuli Grave Cabernet Franc l'Arco '96	🍷 (white)	3

BUTTRIO (UD)

CONTE D'ATTIMIS - MANIAGO
VIA SOTTOMONTE, 21
33042 BUTTRIO (UD)
TEL. 0432/674027

Alberto d'Attimis-Maniago has been renewing the winery's vine stock by replanting a few hectares each year in keeping with modern viticultural criteria. This year some of the new plantings produced excellent wines for this estate in Sottomonte di Buttrio; this is how we explain the leap up in quality we expressed a hope for in last year's Guide. The wine that impressed us most was the Verduzzo Tore delle Signore '98: the lovely golden color offered a foretaste of the fine varietal aromas of baked apple; it holds back initially in the mouth, but then expands on the palate with flavors of candied peel. The warm finish shows characteristic very soft tannins. The Chardonnay is another excellent wine: it is already impressive on the nose, with its rich aromas of ripe apple, pear and mango. Then, on the palate, the refreshing acidity combines with fruity – mainly apricot - notes. The white Vignaricco '94, another really good wine, is a blend of pinot bianco (60%) and chardonnay: it matures in five-hectoliter barrels, then barriques, after which it spends a long time maturing in the bottle. Its golden tones are matched by scents of hazelnut, date and candied apricot: these are echoed very closely on the palate, which opens with flavors of dried fruit and develops into a long finish. The red version, Vignaricco '95, made from cabernet sauvignon, merlot and a little schioppettino, is of lower quality overall. The Pinot Grigio, very nearly a Two Glass winner, has delicate, elegant aromas of ripe pear and dried flowers: we find these again in the mouth, where the wine has a refreshingly acidic finish. The other reds (Merlot, Refosco and Cabernet), all well made, are also good.

○	COF Chardonnay '98	🍷🍷	3*
○	COF Verduzzo Friulano Tore delle Signore '98	🍷🍷	4
○	Vignaricco '94	🍷🍷	4
●	COF Cabernet '97	🍷	3
○	COF Malvasia '98	🍷	3
●	COF Merlot '97	🍷	3
○	COF Pinot Grigio '98	🍷	3
●	COF Refosco P. R. '98	🍷	3
●	Vignaricco '95	🍷	4
○	COF Sauvignon '98		3

BUTTRIO (UD)

★ Girolamo Dorigo
Via del Pozzo, 5
33042 Buttrio (UD)
tel. 0432/674268

We have heard it whispered here and there that the wines made by Girolamo Dorigo and his son Alessio are not what they used to be. We tasted 11 of them: three were contenders for Three Glasses, and all received at least One Glass. The Chardonnay is once again in peak form: warm, velvety, and enticing, it fills the mouth with notes of vanilla, peach and honey and has the right degree of acidity to ensure that it will develop beautifully over the years. The Montsclapade is another satisfying wine: warm and mouth-filling, it has a compelling personality suggestive of licorice, cocoa, plum and black currant. Always fascinatingly elegant and restrained, the Picolit is made from fruit dried naturally on mats for two months, then selected grape by grape and fermented in new wood: it impressed us once again with its green-tinged golden color, its balance on nose and palate, its array of aromas ranging from broom to citrus fruit, vanilla and almond paste, and its enchanting length. The Sauvignon came out well: fermented for the first time from whole, de-stalked grapes, followed by a short time in wood, it has gained in complexity, and its typical tartness is less pronounced. The best sparkling wine of the region, Dorigo Brut '90, is distinguished by clear-cut scents of crusty bread and ripe fruit. Black currant, raspberry and vanilla lend finesse to a surprising Refosco. Lastly, and briefly, the other wines: the Ribolla, elegant and floral; the Pinot Grigio, dry, fruity and fresh; the Verduzzo Ronc di Juri, with honey, thyme and lasting crispness; the Tocai (denied DOC status because of its silicone cork), fruity and even; the Pignolo, powerful and concentrated, but too hard.

●	Montsclapade '96	🍷🍷🍷	6
○	COF Chardonnay Vigneto Ronc di Juri '97	🍷🍷🍷	5
○	COF Picolit Vigneto Montsclapade '97	🍷🍷	6
●	COF Refosco P. R. '96	🍷🍷	5
○	COF Sauvignon '98	🍷🍷	4
○	Dorigo Brut '90	🍷🍷	4
●	COF Pignolo di Buttrio '96	🍷	6
○	COF Pinot Grigio '98	🍷	4
○	COF Ribolla Gialla '98	🍷	4
○	Tocai Friulano '98	🍷	4
○	COF Verduzzo Friulano Vigneto Ronc di Juri '97	🍷	4
●	Montsclapade '92	🍸🍸🍸	6

BUTTRIO (UD)

Davino Meroi
Via Stretta del Parco, 7
33042 Buttrio (UD)
tel. 0432/674025

A lovely surprise from Paolo Meroi! Some may say they can detect the hand of the "maestro of Vicinale", friend and neighbor Enzo Pontoni; but a maestro is meant to teach and serve as an example, and when the process works both sides deserve credit. The Tocai, very concentrated, elegant, rich and fine, develops into a long finish that, notwithstanding the alcohol and the abundant extract, strongly suggests plum and toasted almond. We should remember, anyway, that we are not dealing here with a new arrival on the wine-making scene; for years now Paolo has been presenting wines that are well executed and richly individual. And his other bottles bear this out. The Bianco Blanc di Buri, an assemblage of tocai, chardonnay and malvasia, all fermented in wood, is buttery, floral and fruity; in the mouth it is crisp, consistent, fairly long and slightly tart on the finish. The Ribolla still has the lactic note of good wood-fermented yeasts which doesn't overshadow the fruit but accentuates a softness that is nicely balanced by the lively acidity. The delicate Sauvignon, with its faint fermentative notes, is dry and vigorous, with the lightly toasty flavors that are to some extent the leitmotif of Meroi's wines. The Refosco very nearly won Two Glasses: it has a deep color between ruby and purple; pepper, coffee and red currant on the nose are followed by a palate where alcohol and extract soften the natural roughness of the grape. Finally the new Rosso Ros di Buri, the younger sibling of the Dominin which, with the Picolit and the Verduzzo, will be released later on: garnet-hued, with some bluish traces still, it is more composed in the mouth than on the nose, where slightly unripe fruit clashes somewhat with aromas of sweet sponge cake.

○	COF Bianco Blanc di Buri '98	🍷🍷	4
○	COF Tocai Friulano '97	🍷🍷	4
●	COF Refosco P. R. '97	🍷	5
○	COF Ribolla Gialla '97	🍷	5
●	COF Rosso Ros di Buri '97	🍷	4
○	COF Sauvignon '98	🍷	4
○	COF Picolit '97	🍸🍸	6
●	Dominin '95	🍸🍸	5
●	Dominin '96	🍸🍸	5

BUTTRIO (UD)

Miani
Via Peruzzi, 10
33042 Buttrio (UD)
tel. 0432/674327

Here we are again singing the praises of Enzo the Sublime, the Cantankerous, the Prophet, the Irresponsible... the better you know him, the more epithets you invent. As far as we are concerned, his forthright manner, his wines and the questions he still manages to provoke are quite enough to keep us happy. Tasting the bottles he's presenting this year, for example, we found ourselves wondering if a wine's capacity to mature is a necessary virtue. If wine is this good at the outset, perfectly able to compete on equal terms with the best that's available, Italian and otherwise, then why wait? Not least because supply is low and demand is high. Try this year's Tocai: golden and intense, it has a wealth of aromas, seemingly including everything from plum to honey, Sicilian blood orange, thick cream from Alpine pastures, wild herbs and acacia blossom, from the freshness of young wine to the heady scents of maturity. The palate, as it expands, is full and powerful but never overbearing; it is warm, velvety, extremely long and engrossing. Or else try the Sauvignon, which - we should point out for the record - we tasted freshly drawn from the barrel, when the wood was still intrusive: the same aristocratic nature, the same powerful impact in the mouth, with suggestions of vanilla, honey and apricot, without neglecting the freshness of this grape. And what can we say about the new Refosco, now at last available after 10 years of radical vine management, a wine on the very frontiers of wine-making? What more could anyone do with Refosco? Coffee custard, black currant syrup and vanilla accompany a structured, compact palate that closes on the same fruity notes as the nose. The Bianco was slightly below par - thank goodness, we're all only mortal after all! - and did not quite succeed in matching its maker's usual elegant touch with a sufficiently pronounced body and bouquet.

○	COF Tocai Friulano '98	▼▼▼	6
●	Refosco P. R. Vigna Calvari '96	▼▼	6
○	COF Sauvignon '98	▼▼	6
○	COF Bianco '98	▼	6
○	COF Bianco '96	▽▽▽	5
○	COF Bianco Miani '97	▽▽▽	5
●	COF Merlot '94	▽▽▽	5
●	COF Rosso Miani '96	▽▽▽	5
○	COF Sauvignon '96	▽▽▽	5
○	COF Tocai Friulano '96	▽▽▽	5
○	COF Ribolla Gialla '97	▽▽	5
○	COF Sauvignon '97	▽▽	5
○	COF Tocai Friulano '97	▽▽	5
●	Rosso Miani '95	▽▽	5

BUTTRIO (UD)

Petrucco
Via Morpurgo, 12
33042 Buttrio (UD)
tel. 0432/674387

Husband and wife team Lina and Paolo Petrucco run an estate with about 20 hectares of vineyards that produce some 100 thousand bottles each year, the result of keeping yields per vine and per hectare low, and of extremely rigorous grape selection. Their oenologist Flavio Cabas, who makes excellent use of the winery's up-to-the-minute equipment, deserves special mention. The Sauvignon, made from particularly successful grapes, has a typical nose of elder flower and tomato leaf, all echoed on the palate; rich and luscious, this is a wine for laying down. The Cabernet Franc was a surprise: a grape that usually lacks finesse but which, as vinified by the Petruccos, has intense fruity and spicy aromas, and a persistent palate with perfectly judged tannins. The very varietal Chardonnay offers yeast, with a thread of green notes, on the nose; the harmonious palate is crisp and pleasing. A fine fragrance of melon and pineapple characterizes the Pinot Grigio; it is elegant on the palate and has the right degree of acidity but fades slightly on the finish. The Ribolla Gialla, which merits One full Glass, has a fresh and floral nose with a distinctive note of tobacco leaf; in the mouth it's balanced and well structured, with a combination of fleshiness and acidity that enhances the wine's green apple fruitiness. The Tocai Friulano is almost as good: the intense aromas of apple and fresh fruit salad are followed by a palate that is let down by a slightly excessive acidity. The Picolit, with its sweet palate, is lightened by fresh green scents that make the nose especially lively. Last comes a characteristic Refosco, with its hints of pepper and other spices.

●	COF Cabernet Franc '97	▼▼	3
○	COF Sauvignon '98	▼▼	3
○	COF Chardonnay '98	▼	3
●	COF Merlot Vigna del Balbo '97	▼	4
○	COF Picolit '97	▼	6
○	COF Pinot Grigio '98	▼	3
●	COF Refosco P. R. '97	▼	3
○	COF Ribolla Gialla '98	▼	3
○	COF Tocai Friulano '98	▼	3
●	COF Merlot Vigna del Balbo '96	▽▽	4

CAPRIVA DEL FRIULI (GO)

Castello di Spessa

Via Spessa, 1
34070 Capriva del Friuli (GO)
tel. 0481/639914

Loretto Pali's winery did not quite manage to repeat last year's outstanding performance, but still scored well at this year's tastings. The winery is run by polyglot Patrizia Stekar with the help of Paolo Della Rovere and, in the 30 hectares of vineyards and in the cellar, the oenologist Domenico Lovat. The cellars, centuries old, are worth a visit; they are the most ancient part of this splendid dwelling, which was restored at the end of the 19th century and now includes first-class guest accommodation. But let's move on to the wines. The Pinot Bianco displays its customary elegance, with delicate notes of apple on the nose, a well-structured palate suggestive of a variety of freshly picked ripe fruit, and a long finish dominated by Golden Delicious apple. The Sauvignon gets better month by month, and, when we tasted it, released aromas of sage and elder flower, mirrored on an unexpectedly robust palate which boasted an excellent balance of acidity, richness and alcoholic warmth. In the Tocai Friulano aromas of apple, pear and apple seeds can be detected in the intense, elegant bouquet; in the mouth, a pronounced degree of acidity makes it a little lean; it bears up well, however, thanks to a great structure that comes from substantial extract. The Pinot Grigio doesn't quite make its second Glass, although on the nose it offers an excellent balance and lots of fruit, since some excessive sharpness mars the palate. Acidity is not a problem for the Ribolla Gialla, where it is, on the contrary, an important varietal feature. Here we have another elegant wine, with a bouquet of wildflowers and green apple; it lingers long on the nose and in the mouth.

○	Collio Pinot Bianco '98	🍷🍷	4
○	Collio Ribolla Gialla '98	🍷🍷	4
○	Collio Sauvignon '98	🍷🍷	4
○	Collio Tocai Friulano '98	🍷🍷	4
○	Collio Pinot Grigio '98	🍷	4
○	Collio Pinot Bianco '97	YYY	4
●	Collio Rosso Conte di Spessa '93	YY	5

CAPRIVA DEL FRIULI (GO)

Giovanni Puiatti

Via Aquileia, 30
34070 Capriva del Friuli (GO)
tel. 0481/809922

Giovanni Puiatti produces his wines from his 24 hectares at Romans d'Isonzo, in addition to the four hectares purchased years ago at Ruttars, in the Collio district, and another six rented at Mossa, in the same DOC area. As far as the first holding is concerned, we suspect that results would be better if yields per stock, which at present, according to estate records, are at the limit of the levels laid down by the DOC guidelines, were reduced still more. The Collio Sauvignon P, made from grapes grown in the Ruttars vineyards, is very successful. It has a forthright bouquet of elder flower and sage; on the palate it is rich and complex, with notes of citrus fruit and nectarine, and a very long finish. We feel sure that Giovanni will also be able to obtain a great Pinot Nero from these plots once the vines are old enough; for the time being, however, this wine is not convincing. The Chardonnay has hints of mandarin orange on the nose, together with the varietal vanilla; in the mouth the fruit is supple, crisp and rich in alcohol, while the texture is fine, yet dense. The Pinot Grigio offers aromas of apple and mixed fruit compote; the distinct but well-judged acidity on the palate is balanced by the richness of the fruit. A peppery theme blends with the notes of cherry and plum in the bouquet of the Cabernet Franc Isonzo, all echoed on the fleshy, grassy palate. The Cabernet Sauvignon comes from the Mossa vineyards in Collio country; it has some metallic notes that give a hardness to the otherwise richly fruity palate.

○	Collio Sauvignon P di Puiatti '98	🍷🍷	5
○	Friuli Isonzo Chardonnay '98	🍷🍷	3
○	Friuli Isonzo Pinot Grigio '98	🍷	3
●	Collio Cabernet Sauvignon '98		4
●	Friuli Isonzo Cabernet Franc '98		3

Roncùs

Via Mazzini, 26
34070 Capriva del Friuli (GO)
tel. 0481/809349

We went for a walk with Marco Perco, the life and soul of the Roncùs winery, through his vineyards in Capriva. We were struck not only by the neatness and order of the rows of vines, but also by his original experiments in vine spacing and training, the aim of which is to protect the leaves, which provide energy to the plant, and to ensure that the bunches of grapes receive maximal exposure to the sun. A series of excellent wines have again rewarded his experiments this year. The splendid Sauvignon focuses on richness and ripeness of bouquet, which is dominated by tomato and peach. The delightful entry on the palate is fruity and full, with a distinctive note of mango; a creamy mid palate leads to a long, smoky finish. The intensely ruby-hued Val di Miez is of the same standard; this blend displays rich, complex aromas of coffee, tobacco, quinine and blackberry and black currant jam. The lovely attack on the palate is characterized by fruity notes that continue for quite a while, and the overall structure is good. We know that Marco had high hopes for the Pinot Bianco, but at the time of our tastings it clearly merited One full Glass and nothing more: the fruity bouquet, with notes of citrus, apple and white peach, is echoed in the mouth, where finesse prevails over structure. The Tocai Friulano is another worthwhile wine, with unusual - for this estate - green notes of rue on the nose; it gets much better on the palate, where it displays richness and ripe, persistent fruit followed by a pleasingly refreshing acidic finish.

○ Sauvignon '98	▼▼	4
● Val di Miez '97	▼▼	4
○ Collio Tocai Friulano '98	▼	4
○ Pinot Bianco '98	▼	4
○ Roncùs Bianco '97	▽▽	4
○ Tocai Friulano '97	▽▽	4

Russiz Superiore

Via Russiz, 7
34070 Capriva del Friuli (GO)
tel. 0481/80328 - 0481/99164

In a year in which reds have been "struggling for breath", here are at least five whites elbowing each other for the top marks. Out in front is the Sauvignon, slightly "foreign" in style, with a peach and melon nose followed by a powerful, succulent, warm, long, complex and velvety palate. Next comes the Tocai, with a compelling range of aromas including peach and acacia blossom, leading to a mouth-filling, soft and then crisp palate that finishes on an upbeat of bitter almond. And then the Pinot Bianco: concentrated, dense, long and sinewy, with suggestions of yellow plum and crusty bread. The winery has been thinking of reducing its range of wines, but the fresh, fruity, classic, consistent and eminently quaffable Pinot Grigio seems to have made a deliberate effort to avoid being sidelined. Lastly, the new pinot bianco-based Bianco Russiz di Sore, fermented and matured in a range of different barrels, caught our attention with its aristocratic honey, banana, and hazelnut notes, its long, buttery body and silky, seductive structure; it has considerable potential for improvement over time and promises great things for the future. Among the reds, the best is still the Cabernet Franc: intense and deep in color, it offers red berries and spice on the nose; in the mouth it is meaty and concentrated, with soft tannins and a long finish dominated by tomato leaf. The weighty and austere Rosso degli Orzoni, 80% cabernet sauvignon and 20% merlot and cabernet franc, follows the pattern of previous years; however this version has lots of body but less elegance. We close with the Verduzzo, a fine example of the elegance and finesse that are a hallmark of this estate.

○ Collio Sauvignon '98	▼▼▼	4
○ Collio Bianco Russiz di Sore '98	▼▼	4
● Collio Cabernet Franc '97	▼▼	4
○ Collio Pinot Bianco '98	▼▼	4
○ Collio Pinot Grigio '98	▼▼	4
● Collio Rosso Riserva degli Orzoni '95	▼▼	5
○ Collio Tocai Friulano '98	▼▼	4
○ Verduzzo '98	▼	4
● Collio Merlot '97		4
● Collio Rosso Riserva degli Orzoni '93	▽▽▽	5
● Collio Rosso Riserva degli Orzoni '94	▽▽▽	5
● Collio Cabernet Franc '96	▽▽	4

CAPRIVA DEL FRIULI (GO)

★ MARIO SCHIOPETTO
VIA PALAZZO ARCIVESCOVILE, 1
34070 CAPRIVA DEL FRIULI (GO)
TEL. 0481/80332

Mario Schiopetto, a producer who is never far from the critical limelight, is still out there in the avant-garde, despite his age and painful physical ailments. The hallmark of his work is a combative and creative spirit. He rightly complained that in last year's review we mentioned his use of barriques, a container he has long opposed. And in fact for the two whites, the Pinot Amrità and the Tocai Pardes, and for the reds, Mario uses bigger barrels, which allow less interaction between wine and wood. Once again we found his Pinot Bianco Amrità, the '97 this time, glorious: its dried apple fragrance, with light vanilla and banana notes, precedes a closely textured, structured and complex palate with just the right acidity and alcohol, opening out to a very long, fruity finish. The Pinot Bianco '98 is nearly as good: it displays an elegant nose of Golden Delicious apple; the palate, variegated, mouth-filling and dense, suggests fresh fruit salad with a citrus undertone. The Tocai Friulano '98 is equally successful, starting with its clean, elegant, full, intense and faintly smoky bouquet, echoed on the fine-textured and elegant palate, which reveals an incredibly long finish. The Tocai Friulano Pardes '97, on the other hand, has a very pronounced oak-derived vanilla that, in the mouth, needs further blending with the acidity. The excellent Chardonnay, produced on the Rosazzo estate in the Colli Orientali, displays citrus fruit and custard on the nose and its habitual elegance on the consistent and crisp palate. The Sauvignon is remarkable for length. The Blanc des Rosis, made from tocai, pinot bianco, sauvignon and malvasia, is excellent.

○	Collio Pinot Bianco Amrità '97	🍷🍷🍷	5
○	Blanc des Rosis '98	🍷🍷	4
○	Collio Pinot Bianco '98	🍷🍷	4
○	Collio Sauvignon '98	🍷🍷	4
○	Collio Tocai Friulano '98	🍷🍷	4
○	COF Chardonnay '98	🍷🍷	4
●	Collio Merlot '97	🍷	4
○	Collio Pinot Grigio '98	🍷	4
○	Collio Tocai Friulano Pardes '97	🍷	5
●	Rivarossa '97	🍷	4
○	Collio Pinot Bianco '94	YYY	4
○	Collio Pinot Bianco Amrità '96	YYY	5
○	Collio Sauvignon '97	YYY	5
○	Collio Tocai Friulano '94	YYY	4
○	Collio Tocai Friulano '95	YYY	4

CAPRIVA DEL FRIULI (GO)

VIDUSSI
VIA SPESSA, 18
34070 CAPRIVA DEL FRIULI (GO)
TEL. 0481/80072

Vidussi, which is directed by Antonietta Causero, the widow of Ferruccio Vidussi, includes 25 hectares under vine in the Collio DOC district and seven in the Colli Orientali del Friuli. An enviably consistent quality is due in large measure also to the technical support of the oenologist Paolo Fornasiero. The cellar, mostly underground, was built a few years ago and is highly functional. The Capriva zone, as far as Pradis di Cormons, is the ideal habitat for pinot bianco and should, in our opinion, be dedicated entirely to this grape, which always performs well here. The Pinot Bianco Vidussi is no exception to this rule, with its stylish bouquet of fresh fruit (apple, yellow plum, notes of wild strawberry) that carries through to the substantial, long-lasting palate. The Sauvignon is also strikingly elegant on the nose, which is dominated by elder flowers; the fleshy palate, rich in alcohol and fruit, with a hint of citrus, has a long finish. The Chardonnay came very close to Two Glasses: elegant fruit on the nose (where you can't tell that 10% of the wine spent some time in barriques) followed by citrus fruit, tea, apple, crisp acidity and good length in the mouth. The Collio Bianco also carried off One full Glass. This is an assemblage, made after the alcoholic fermentation, of wines produced from grapes grown in the Ronco Croce Alta vineyard (malvasia istriana, tocai friulano, pinot bianco and sauvignon) and it's elegant, refreshing and mellow in the mouth. The Traminer Aromatico has a pronounced alcoholic content and is fat and dense, almost oily on the palate. In the Merlot '97 we found a fragrance of hay and red berries, and an excellent balance of acidity and tannins.

●	Collio Merlot '97	🍷	3
○	Collio Bianco Ronco Croce Alta '98	🍷	3
○	Collio Chardonnay '98	🍷	3
○	Collio Pinot Bianco '98	🍷	3
○	Collio Sauvignon '98	🍷	3
○	Collio Traminer Aromatico '98	🍷	3
○	Collio Pinot Grigio '98		3
○	Collio Tocai Friulano '98		3
●	COF Refosco P. R. '97	YY	3
●	Ronc dal Rol '96	YY	4

CAPRIVA DEL FRIULI (GO)

VILLA RUSSIZ
VIA RUSSIZ, 6
34070 CAPRIVA DEL FRIULI (GO)
TEL. 0481/80047

It is hard to find new adjectives to describe the incredible skill displayed year after year by Gianni Menotti, the director of this winery belonging to the Istituto Cerruti, a non-profit institution. The ratings at the bottom of the page speak for themselves but, just in case they're not enough for you, go and read some past editions of the Guide, or, better yet, taste the '91s or the Sauvignon de La Tour '88. Said Sauvignon de La Tour - this time the '98 – is yet again the absolute winner, having beaten the Tocai Friulano by a hair's breadth. It boasts an extraordinarily elegant bouquet of elder flower, clear-cut, intense and delicate at the same time, with just a hint of mint; on the densely textured palate it progresses through an exceptionally rich range of fruit, from apple to citrus, and finishes on a salty note. The Tocai Friulano got a very, very high score: aromas of apple, pear and peach skin introduce a fat, concentrated, and intensely fruity palate– a wine that is well worth laying down. The unfailing Pinot Bianco, elegant as always, won Two full Glasses: its considerable structure is underpinned by substantial alcohol. The Ribolla Gialla is distinguished by balance, crispness and a substantial quality not often found in this variety. The Riesling displays – and is one of the few Friuli Rieslings to do so - varietal characteristics as well as plum on the nose and a distant echo of petroleum which, if we know this winery, will emerge with growing intensity in future years. The Sauvignon '98 has clear notes of elder blossom, rue and mint that follow through to a forthright, long palate. Until the Graf de la Tour '97 is ready, red wine is represented by the Merlot and the Cabernet, each of which received "only" One full Glass, as did the Pinot Grigio.

○	Collio Sauvignon de La Tour '98	🍷🍷🍷	5
○	Collio Malvasia Istriana '98	🍷🍷	4
○	Collio Pinot Bianco '98	🍷🍷	4
○	Collio Ribolla Gialla '98	🍷🍷	4
○	Collio Riesling '98	🍷🍷	4
○	Collio Sauvignon '98	🍷🍷	4
○	Collio Tocai Friulano '98	🍷🍷	4
○	Collio Pinot Grigio '98	🍷	4
●	Collio Cabernet '97	🍷	4
●	Collio Merlot '97	🍷	4
●	Collio Merlot Graf de La Tour '93	🍸🍸🍸	5
○	Collio Sauvignon de La Tour '91	🍸🍸🍸	5
○	Collio Sauvignon de La Tour '94	🍸🍸🍸	5
○	Collio Sauvignon de La Tour '97	🍸🍸🍸	5

CARLINO (UD)

EMIRO CAV. BORTOLUSSO
VIA OLTREGORGO, 10
33050 CARLINO (UD)
TEL. 0431/67596

Sergio and Clara Bortolusso are carrying on the family estate formerly run by their late father Emiro, so this debut in the Guide is a triumph due to all of them. The 38 hectares owned by the family, for the most part planted with red wine grapes, are divided between two DOC zones (Annia and Latisana); annual production amounts to about 90 thousand bottles of reliably good wines. Sergio and Clara are personally involved in both vineyard and cellar, where they are assisted by the oenologist Luigino De Giuseppe. The Pinot Bianco is an excellent wine; its not particularly intense color caused us some initial doubts, but they were soon dispelled by the extremely varietal and balanced aromas of green apple and crusty bread; the impressive entry on the palate includes mouth-filling notes of apple and white plum. The Verduzzo Friulano '98, which also deserved its Two Glasses, has a typical golden hue and a delightful nose with complex aromas of candied orange peel and peach; it is not particularly fleshy in the mouth, where its strong suit is fruit. The Malvasia is redolent of star anise and flowers; its even palate finishes with pear and flowers. The Pinot Grigio and the Tocai Friulano got One full Glass each. The former, with typical nuances of onion skin, has a balanced fragrance of white flowers and fruit, a full body and a sweet pear finish. The latter is remarkable for its elegant aromas of ripe apple. The Merlot, in which a rather ordinary nose is followed by a full, rich and structured palate, is worthy of note.

○	Friuli Annia Pinot Bianco '98	🍷🍷	2*
○	Friuli Annia Verduzzo Friulano '98	🍷🍷	3*
○	Friuli Annia Malvasia '98	🍷	2
○	Friuli Annia Pinot Grigio '98	🍷	2
○	Friuli Annia Tocai Friulano '98	🍷	2
●	Friuli Latisana Merlot '98	🍷	2
●	Friuli Annia Cabernet Franc '98		2
●	Friuli Annia Refosco P. R. '97		3

CIVIDALE DEL FRIULI (UD)

DAL FARI

VIA DARNAZZACCO
33043 CIVIDALE DEL FRIULI (UD)
TEL. 0432/731219 - 0432/706726

Renzo Toffolutti's estate is located in the hills above Cividale, a splendid setting. Although not very large, with 12 hectares under vine, it boasts a state-of-the-art cellar. With the help of his wife Laura, Renzo has put together a top-notch team coordinated by an outstanding oenologist, Fabio Coser. Together they have produced an excellent range of wines, the best in recent years. The splendid Pinot Grigio is varietal on the nose, with mineral notes balanced by sweet, ripe fruit; in the mouth it is fat, even and lingering, ripe banana providing the finishing dominant note. The Bianco delle Grazie (chardonnay, tocai friulano, sauvignon and riesling), which is always good, offers delicate aromas of white flowers counterpoised by richer tones of vanilla and apricot, all perfectly mirrored on the elegant rather than concentrated palate with its long fruity finish. The Merlot releases pleasantly varietal scents of ripe red fruit (wild cherry in particular), white pepper and alfalfa; we found the palate impressive, both in its fatness and in the fruity finish in which silky tannins have been well blended. The Cabernet has a slightly rustic plum jam and tobacco bouquet; the palate is not complex and the finish is just a bit diminished by somewhat rough tannins. These same rough tannins also influenced our final assessment of the other blend, the Rosso d'Orsone, which, with its austere, concentrated nose of black cherry jam, coffee, tobacco and mint, had made a favorable first impression. The Chardonnay, some of which spent a little time in barriques, displays aromas of dry flowers and Golden Delicious apple.

○	COF Bianco delle Grazie '97	🍷🍷	4
●	COF Merlot '97	🍷🍷	4
○	COF Pinot Grigio '98	🍷🍷	4
●	COF Cabernet '97	🍷	4
○	COF Chardonnay '98	🍷	4
●	COF Rosso d'Orsone '95	🍷	4
●	COF Schioppettino '97		4
○	COF Tocai Friulano '98		4
○	COF Bianco delle Grazie '96	🍸🍸	4
●	Rosso d'Orsone '93	🍸🍸	4

CIVIDALE DEL FRIULI (UD)

LUCIA GALASSO

STRADA DI PLANEZ, 32
FRAZ. SPESSA
33043 CIVIDALE DEL FRIULI (UD)
TEL: 0432/730292 - 0432/701462

Giovanni Crosato, an oenologist from the Veneto who has come to be so much at home in Friuli that he is now mayor of Dolegna del Collio, has entrusted his wife Lucia Galasso with the running of this estate with its five hectares of hillside vineyards. Giovanni himself deals with the wines, of course, and, as many of the vines are old and since the varieties are many, he has decided to concentrate on blends, which he calls, with a touch of self-deprecating humor, Don. Giovanni. The label depicts Mozart's Don Giovanni, a glass of wine in his hand. The Bianco Don.Giovanni, made from tocai, sauvignon and pinot bianco, easily carried off One Glass, especially thanks to its intense yet elegant bouquet ranging from apple to wildflowers and medicinal herbs; the palate is reminiscent of fresh fruit, with a vein of green acidity. The Rosso Don.Giovanni, made from merlot, cabernet (both sauvignon and franc), refosco and schioppettino, is somewhat lacking in vigor on the palate, while the interesting nose is decidedly complex, with aromas of cherry and black cherry tart. The Rosso DOC Colli Orientali del Friuli '98, 80% merlot and 20% refosco dal peduncolo rosso, has a crisp palate, as might be expected from this vintage, while the nose offers riper aromas of stewed plums and citrus peel. The Cabernet '98 was not particularly intense either, although it earned One Glass; red fruit on the nose is followed by a soft entry on the palate, but the tannins seem rough in the finish, partly as a result of the slightly excessive acidity. The Merlot '98 is admirably long in the mouth, but acidity makes the wine seem thinner than it actually is.

●	COF Cabernet '98	🍷	3
●	COF Rosso '98	🍷	3
○	Il Bianco Don.Giovanni '97	🍷	4
●	Il Rosso Don.Giovanni '97	🍷	4
●	COF Merlot '98		3
○	Il Bianco Don Giovanni '96	🍸🍸	4
●	Il Rosso Don Giovanni '96	🍸	4

CIVIDALE DEL FRIULI (UD)

PAOLO RODARO
VIA CORMONS, 60 - FRAZ. SPESSA
33040 CIVIDALE DEL FRIULI (UD)
TEL. 0432/716066

Meeting Paolo Rodaro in his well-ordered vineyards spread over the Bosco Romagno above Cividale, you realize that his laid-back, detached manner hides an enthusiastic personality constantly seeking improvement. For years now he has been producing wines that are always reliable and excellent value for money, thanks not least to his intuition and technical skill. And Paolo has not let us down this year either. We liked the Chardonnay: the glimmers of gold gave us advance notice that this was a wine of structure, and it is indeed rich on the nose, with notes of banana, mango, broom flowers and tobacco; these follow through on the palate, which has a long and delectable pear finish. The Ronc, made from pinot bianco, chardonnay and tocai friulano, is a new departure for this winery; it strikes you immediately with its elegant yet opulent aromas of banana, mango and dried wildflowers; the fruitiness follows through and fills the mouth, where it is underpinned by a refreshing acidity. The Verduzzo Pra Zenâr is traditional in style: amber in appearance, it has a nose of tea and ripe tropical fruit; it is stunning on the palate where, after an assertive entry, it expands into flavors of dried fruit. The Tocai almost won Two Glasses: the clean bouquet shows varietal and fairly intense aromas of almond and crusty bread, all echoed on the palate. The Sauvignon has a complex nose redolent of ripe tomato, Golden Delicious apple and wildflowers; it makes a lovely entry on the palate, where it is fruity and quite long. The promising fresh mineral and white pear aromas of the Pinot Grigio are reflected on the well-executed if somewhat straightforward palate.

○	COF Chardonnay '98	🍷🍷	3*
○	COF Verduzzo Friulano Pra Zenâr '98	🍷🍷	5
○	Ronc '98	🍷🍷	4
○	COF Pinot Grigio '98	🍷	3
○	COF Ribolla Gialla '98	🍷	3
○	COF Riesling '98	🍷	3
○	COF Sauvignon '98	🍷	3
○	COF Tocai Friulano '98	🍷	3
○	COF Traminer '98	🍷	3
○	COF Sauvignon Bosc Romain '96	YYY	4
○	COF Picolit '97	YY	5
○	COF Verduzzo Friulano Pra Zenâr '97	YY	5

CORMONS (GO)

BRUNO & MARIO BASTIANI
VIA SAVAIAN, 36
34071 CORMONS (GO)
TEL. 0481/60725

Once again Mario Bastiani's traditional winery has shown itself to be a reliable producer of monovarietal white wines. A relative newcomer to his range is the Isonzo DOC Merlot which, with an appropriate amount of bottle age, should be capable of great things. The offerings this year are very good indeed, starting with a big Sauvignon del Collio, of a vivid straw color with a greenish golden tinge; the well-defined and inviting bouquet of elder flower and tomato leaf introduces an even, fleshy and soft palate with a long finish. The Tocai Collio, another Two Glass winner, has a characteristic nose of white flowers and almond with faint yeasty notes; the palate is clear-cut, full-bodied, rich in alcohol, balanced, elegant and clean. The Pinot Bianco Collio, which is just as good, releases stylish aromas of green apple with an underlying citrus tone; the mouth-filling flavors develop into a long, fruity finish. The Pinot Grigio Collio, made from very ripe grapes that are quite noticeable on the nose, seems fresher in the mouth. From their Isonzo vineyards they have produced an interesting Riesling, which shows elegance and a crisp acidity enriched by hints of apple. Lastly, the Merlot '97 also received One Glass: a nose of red fruit compote with some grassy notes is followed by an intense, robustly structured palate with non-aggressive tannins. Mario Bastiani has produced a praiseworthy selection of wines from his almost seven hectares of vineyards in the hills and plains around Cormons.

○	Collio Pinot Bianco '98	🍷🍷	3*
○	Collio Sauvignon '98	🍷🍷	3*
○	Collio Tocai Friulano '98	🍷🍷	3*
○	Collio Pinot Grigio '98	🍷	3
●	Friuli Isonzo Merlot '97	🍷	3
○	Friuli Isonzo Riesling '98	🍷	3

CORMONS (GO)

Borgo del Tiglio

Via S. Giorgio, 71
Fraz. Brazzano
34070 Cormons (GO)
tel. 0481/62166

Nicola Manferrari has caught us off guard: we knew he was good, of course, but we expected him to attack from the Brazzano front, with the Tocai Ronco della Chiesa and the Rosso della Centa. Instead, three staggering broadsides have arrived from the Ruttars and Ca delle Vallate positions, his most recently purchased vineyards, with which he is still experimenting, but which now seem destined for highly aromatic white grapes (Ruttars), and chardonnay (Ca delle Vallate). The Studio di Bianco, a blend of tocai, riesling and overripe sauvignon, has ripe, elegant fruit emerging over light toasty notes; the palate is big, dry, even, balanced and long. The Chardonnay '97 and the Selezione '96, made from the best grapes of that vintage, are no less worthy: the former is buttery, redolent of dried fruit, rich in alcohol and lingeringly fresh – a wine for laying down; the latter is sweeter on the nose, with scents of yellow flowers and dried apricot; a powerful, well-structured wine this, with pronounced but pleasing and well-judged notes of wood. The other contenders are of a similar standard. The Rosso della Centa, the prototype of Nicola's wines, is still impressive, with its almost aristocratic character that makes no concessions to easy charm: the wine is austere, with notes of licorice and jam on the nose, and a full, dry palate with raisin and dried flowers on the finish. The Malvasia is delicious and an ideal accompaniment to any number of foods, with its aromatic herbal and light lactic notes. The Bianco is good as well: almond milk, hazelnut and flint accompany a palate of considerable character. The Tocai is a little under par, but only relatively speaking, because of some slightly pungent notes.

○	Collio Chardonnay '97	🍷🍷	5
○	Collio Chardonnay Selezione '96	🍷🍷	6
○	Collio Malvasia '97	🍷🍷	5
●	Rosso della Centa '94	🍷🍷	6
○	Studio di Bianco '97	🍷🍷	6
○	Collio Tocai Friulano '97	🍷	5
○	Collio Tocai Ronco della Chiesa '90	YYY	5
○	Bianco '96	YY	5
○	Collio Chardonnay '96	YY	5
●	Collio Rosso '93	YY	5
●	Collio Rosso '94	YY	5
●	Rosso della Centa '93	YY	6

CORMONS (GO)

Borgo San Daniele

Via S. Daniele, 16
34071 Cormons (GO)
tel. 0481/60552

Alessandra and Mauro Mauri continue, with their customary enthusiasm and dedication, in their quest for a personal and original style in the wines they make on their small estate near Cormons. A brief summary of their current method: exacting work in the vineyard, late harvesting, renunciation of young, fresh white wines, maceration for the whites as well, controlled minimal aeration on the yeasts, late bottling without sterile filtering, fewer wines available. There are also plans afoot for the future (we tasted an excellent experimental pignolo when we were there). The Arbis Rosso is splendid: an assemblage of cabernet franc and sauvignon which presents its credentials – in the form of an intense ruby color - to the eye, going on to display a complex nose of coffee and black cherry and berry jam, shading off to tobacco and tar. This red does not let you down on the palate either, where, expanding nicely, it reveals a fat and creamy nature with fruit and coffee tones that reappear on the long finish, with very smooth tannins. The excellent Tocai Friulano releases a complex bouquet of delightfully balanced dried flowers, apple, and citrus notes with a buttery yet smoky finish, all mirrored on the entry on a palate which, as it develops, is crisp, succulent and reminiscent of pear, if not particularly long. The Arbis Blanc, made from chardonnay, pinot bianco, tocai and sauvignon, has a pleasingly harmonious fragrance of melon, banana and ripe fruit; these are echoed lingeringly in the mouth and lead to a good finish of dried fruit, but it could be fuller-bodied. The Pinot Grigio is worthy of note.

●	Arbis Rosso '97	🍷🍷	4
○	Friuli Isonzo Tocai Friulano '98	🍷🍷	4
○	Arbis Blanc '98	🍷	4
○	Friuli Isonzo Pinot Grigio '98		4
○	Friuli Isonzo Tocai Friulano '97	YYY	4
○	Arbis Bianco '97	YY	4
●	Gortmarin '94	YY	4
●	Lucky Red '94	YY	4
○	Friuli Isonzo Chardonnay '97	Y	4

CORMONS (GO)

BORIS E DAVID BUZZINELLI
LOC. PRADIS, 22/BIS
34071 CORMONS (GO)
TEL. 0481/62272

The brothers Boris and David Buzzinelli have again proven their ability to produce first-rate wine. Their father Carlo is pleased with the changes they're making , and is helping in the modernization of the cellar; altogether this is one of the most interesting new developments in Pradis di Cormons. In their new cellar Boris and David are investing in the aging process for their two ranges of wine, Carlo Buzzinelli DOC Collio from the Vigneti di Pradis and Bordavi DOC Isonzo from the Cormons plain, with the three additional hectares in the Isonzo zone that entered into production this year, making a total of 45 thousand bottles. First the Collio Bianco Vigneti di Pradis '97, a blend of tocai friulano, malvasia, pinot bianco and sauvignon partly fermented and matured in small oak casks: we were struck by its fruity complexity, both on the nose and in the mouth, where it blends with notes of cream and custard; the wine reveals a dense texture, interesting development potential and substantial alcohol (13.5°). Green tones pervade the elegant and richly fruity bouquet of the Pinot Grigio '98, which is full, harmonious, rich and long on the palate. Any puzzlement we may have felt at the aromas of the Sauvignon was instantly banished by its full-bodied palate, where characteristic elder flower notes come through evenly and at some length. One full Glass for the Pinot Bianco '98, very faintly sulfurous when we tasted it, but successful in balance and structure; this is a wine that tends to do very well on the Pradis slopes. Pear and apple characterize the nose of the Tocai Friulano, which is crisp and full-bodied on its alcohol-rich (13°), fleshy and long palate.

○	Collio Bianco Vigneti di Pradis '97	▼▼	3*
○	Collio Pinot Grigio Vigneti di Pradis '98	▼▼	3*
○	Collio Sauvignon Vigneti di Pradis '98	▼▼	3*
○	Collio Pinot Bianco Vigneti di Pradis '98	▼	3
○	Collio Tocai Friulano Vigneti di Pradis '98	▼	3
●	Collio Merlot Carlo Buzzinelli '94	▽▽	4
●	Collio Merlot Vigneti di Pradis '95	▽	4

CORMONS (GO)

PAOLO CACCESE
LOC. PRADIS, 6
34071 CORMONS (GO)
TEL. 0481/61062

Our review of the estate that belongs to the likeable Paolo Caccese might be entitled "Business as Usual". For years it has been producing a range of wines that are successful, pleasing and, often, really excellent. Yes, we realize that the vines are located on the gentle southern slopes of Pradis, but it should not be forgotten that position isn't everything. And Paolo certainly does not hold back when there is work to be done in the vineyard, be it on foot or on his tractor (and incidentally, the way he drives this vehicle when he sets off to trim his vines is legendary). In the cellar too, he follows the development of the wines closely, assisted by the oenologist Giuseppe Lipari, a celebrated figure in the Friuli wine world. The Pinot Bianco has won Two Glasses again, with its customary fruity elegance, a seductive palate refreshed by just the right degree of acidity, and a long finish. And Two Glasses again go to the Pinot Grigio, which displays well-defined and delicate scents of apple; various fruits come out clearly on the complex, rich and full palate. The hot summer sun was apparently just the thing for the Pinots. There is an interesting harmony on the palate of the Malvasia, with its elegant balance of softness and acidity, and pervasive flowers and fruit. In the Sauvignon the aromas are intense but not excessively so: tomato leaf, elder flower, grapefruit and citron peel. The varietal note in the Riesling is provided by unripe plum, which with time should veer towards petroleum. The La Veronica '97, made from semi-dried malvasia and verduzzo friulano, with a sweet palate reminiscent of apple and hazelnut, is particularly good.

●	Collio Cabernet Franc '98	▼▼	4
○	Collio Pinot Bianco '98	▼▼	4
○	Collio Pinot Grigio '98	▼▼	4
○	Collio Malvasia Istriana '98	▼	4
○	Collio Riesling '98	▼	3
○	Collio Sauvignon '98	▼	4
○	La Veronica '97	▼	5
●	Collio Merlot '98		4
○	Collio Müller Thurgau '98		4
○	Collio Tocai Friulano '98		3

CORMONS (GO)

Cantina Produttori di Cormons

Via Vino della Pace, 31
34071 Cormons (GO)
tel. 0481/60579 - 0481/62471

Two hundred member growers with just under 300 hectares under vine producing about 18 thousand hectoliters, and 22 wines at our tastings: these numbers always make something of an impression, especially up here where the idea that one is "better off alone" seems almost genetically inspired. However, we would like to put one fundamental question to the evergreen Luigi Soini (because you can tell that the same hand has been at work to make all these wines attractive), whose merits are beyond dispute: are all these labels really necessary? But turning to the wines we tasted, we have to acknowledge that eight wines, mainly from the Collio DOC district, were awarded a Glass apiece, and that the whites were far better than the reds. The wine that impressed us most was the Collio Tocai, with a delicate bouquet accompanying a well-balanced palate of average length with the classic notes of wildflowers and bitter almond. Other successful wines from the same DOC are: the Malvasia (a wine with lots of personality that would repay more careful attention), which is dry, not in the least cloying, and displays good green apple notes and a pleasant scent of mallow, the Pinot Grigio, typically varietal on nose and palate; and the Sauvignon, which displays its customary woodland aromas, but is too dilute on the palate. The most successful of the reds is the Collio Cabernet Franc; the best wine they've made from the Isonzo zone is the Bianco Pietraverde.

● Collio Cabernet Franc '97	🍷	4
○ Collio Collio '98	🍷	3
○ Collio Malvasia Istriana '98	🍷	3
○ Collio Pinot Grigio '98	🍷	3
○ Collio Sauvignon '98	🍷	3
○ Collio Tocai Friulano '98	🍷	3
○ Friuli Isonzo Bianco Pietraverde '98	🍷	3
○ Collio Müller Thurgau '98	🍷	3
● Collio Rosso Melograno '98		3
● Friuli Aquileia Refosco P. R. '98		3
● Friuli Isonzo Madreterra '98		3

CORMONS (GO)

Colle Duga

Loc. Zegla, 10
34071 Cormons (GO)
tel. 0481/61177

Those who work in the world of wine will not be surprised by the debut appearance in the Guide of Colle Duga. It is a well-deserved recognition of the dedication shown by Damian Princic and his father Luciano, and of the affectionate advice of many friends, which helped them get off to a good start. Of their 12 hectares six and a half are under vine, producing some 300 hectoliters which became, in this third year of bottling, 12 thousand bottles. The estate is named after the village of Colle Duga, an official name before either Zegla or Plessiva existed. To give you an idea of what we mean about the quality of this producer, suffice it to say that the Chardonnay, the only wine with just One Glass, missed the second one by a hair's breadth. The Tocai Friulano has a lovely intense, lingering, extremely clean and elegant nose, perhaps even better than the palate, which however is succulent, full, long and not very fleshy. The Collio Bianco is excellent, starting with its lively greenish-gold color; aromas of citrus and fresh fruits are echoed on the tightly knit, crisply acidic palate. The Merlot '97 has just come out this year, as soon as it was ready; it displays a grassy fragrance well integrated with the prune-dominated fruit, and a soft and alcohol-rich palate, with a long finish that echoes the bouquet. Lastly, the Chardonnay, with a nose of apple and lemon tea that carries over onto the palate, has a lingering finish. A hearty welcome to a small producer who is wise enough to concentrate on making the most of a limited number of wines!

○ Collio Bianco '98	🍷🍷	3*
● Collio Merlot '97	🍷🍷	4
○ Collio Tocai Friulano '98	🍷🍷	3*
○ Collio Chardonnay '98	🍷	3

CORMONS (GO)

MAURO DRIUS
VIA FILANDA, 100
34071 CORMONS (GO)
TEL. 0481/60998

The wines bearing the Drius label are really wonderful this year. We shall begin with the two Tocais. The Collio version is intense and rich on the nose, which displays well-balanced notes of dried fruit, pear, crusty bread and almond; the attack on the palate is full of lovely fruit, which keeps going through an almondy finish. The Tocai from the Isonzo DOC zone, almost golden in appearance, is intensely redolent of acacia blossom, apple seed and ripe pears; it's broad and long-lasting in the mouth, and the bouquet is mirrored in full. The Pinot Bianco, another Two Glass wine, has a fruity, intense nose with hints of Golden Delicious apple and apricot and graceful notes of wildflowers; these are echoed on the complex and broad palate, which has a citrus finish. The Sauvignon, which stakes everything on ripe fruity tones of pear and tomato, came very close to Two Glasses; the opulent palate reveals ripe apple on the long finish. Riesling is not an easy wine: Mauro proposes a version with a pronounced greenish tinge, followed by a nose and palate of ripe peach and apple; slightly excessive acidity makes it somewhat lean. The Bianco Vìgnis di Sìris, made from a blend of tocai (50%), sauvignon (30%), and pinot bianco (20%), with partial fermentation in wood, is more successful this year. Delicate fruity aromas (pear) and vanilla are the key notes in this wine which, although balanced in the mouth, is slightly lacking in concentration. Fresh floral and fruity scents, in which broom and apple can be detected, characterize the Malvasia, whose palate shows admirably refreshing acidity. The Cabernet, the only red produced by this winery, is simple and varietal.

○	Collio Tocai Friulano '98	🍷🍷	3*
○	Friuli Isonzo Pinot Bianco '98	🍷🍷	3*
○	Friuli Isonzo Tocai Friulano '98	🍷🍷	3*
○	Collio Sauvignon '98	🍷	3
○	Friuli Isonzo Bianco Vìgnis di Sìris '98	🍷	3
●	Friuli Isonzo Cabernet '97	🍷	3
○	Friuli Isonzo Malvasia '98	🍷	3
○	Friuli Isonzo Riesling '98	🍷	3

CORMONS (GO)

LIVIO FELLUGA
VIA RISORGIMENTO, 1
FRAZ. BRAZZANO
34071 CORMONS (GO)
TEL. 0481/60203

Livio Felluga's range of wines seems better every year. This is thanks to the dedication of the entire family, under the guidance of the great Livio, a historic figure in the wine-making world of Friuli. The Terre Alte from the Rosazzo sub-zone is, as always, a glorious wine. It's a blend of sauvignon, pinot bianco and tocai, and once again it's the sauvignon that sets the pace, lending delightful notes of bell pepper and elder flower in a rich, warm cocktail of mixed fruits. It's ready for drinking now, but it has sufficient structure and acidity to take it to peak potential in a few years' time. The series of Two Glass wines opens with a Chardonnay from the Esperto line, the range offering particularly good value for money. Two full Glasses go to the Merlot Riserva Sossò '96: the prune, concentrated blackberry and alcohol on the nose are echoed on the complex palate, which is extraordinarily rich in fruit, with pronounced but nicely smoothed tannins. The Tocai Friulano also filled Two Glasses to overflowing, with its slowly emerging nose of ripe sweet fruit; the soft and entirely successful palate makes this a wine that manages to be both captivating and austere at the same time. The Refosco '96, very intense in hue, boasts aromas of red fruit and citrus fruit tart, and a characteristic very spicy palate with a good balance of tannins and acidity. The lovely new red, Vertigo '97, merlot plus cabernet sauvignon, has dominant notes of custard that leave room for plum and cherry aromas; the mellow and even palate reveals a touch of acidity in the finish. Vanilla, exotic fruit and dried banana characterize the Chardonnay Esperto, an extremely forthright wine.

○	COF Rosazzo Bianco Terre Alte '97	🍷🍷🍷	5
○	Chardonnay Esperto '98	🍷🍷	3*
○	COF Tocai Friulano '98	🍷🍷	4
●	COF Rosazzo Merlot Sossò Ris. '96	🍷🍷	5
●	COF Refosco P. R. '96	🍷🍷	5
●	Vertigo '97	🍷🍷	4
○	COF Pinot Grigio '98	🍷	4
○	COF Sauvignon '98	🍷	4
○	COF Bianco Terre Alte '95	🍷🍷🍷 (prior vintage)	5
○	COF Rosazzo Bianco Terre Alte '96	🍷🍷🍷 (prior vintage)	5
○	Terre Alte '92	🍷🍷🍷 (prior vintage)	5
○	Terre Alte '93	🍷🍷🍷 (prior vintage)	5

CORMONS (GO)

Edi Keber
Loc. Zegla, 17
34071 Cormons (GO)
tel. 0481/61184

Edi Keber is rightly held up as an example of swimming against the current of tradition here in Friuli, with methods that are gaining a foothold in other important wine-producing areas of Italy as well. Instead of increasing the variety of his wines, Edi has opted for two monovarietals and two blends, one white and one red. This means that only four wines are released each year. This time around Edi has not recaptured the Three Glasses he won in last year's Guide for his splendid '97 Tocai. He gets pretty close, though, with - somewhat surprisingly - his Merlot '97, a big wine with red fruit tart on the nose, a rich, soft, warm palate with well-judged wood and a plum and cherry jam finish. All the other red grape varieties are used in the Collio Rosso, but great things were not to be expected from the '98 harvest, which was adversely affected by the rain. The prevailing note is black cherry; the acidity, which makes itself felt, is not yet well amalgamated with the sweetness and glycerin, hence just One little Glass at this stage. Edi's whites are, however, still great. The Collio Bianco '98 gets better with each month that passes and we would not be surprised if in 2000 we were to regret our decision to award it "only" Two Glasses. Apple, peach leaf and mineral notes appear clearly on the nose; after an elegant attack the palate expands into a rich fruitiness; it has acidity, structure and a piquant, alcohol-rich finish. The Tocai Friulano '98, nearly as good, is elegant and fresh on the nose, with notes of apple and flint; the palate is extraordinarily long and even.

○ Collio Bianco '98	🍷🍷	4
● Collio Merlot '97	🍷🍷	5
○ Collio Tocai Friulano '98	🍷🍷	4
● Collio Rosso '98	🍷	4
○ Collio Tocai Friulano '95	🍸🍸🍸	4
○ Collio Tocai Friulano '97	🍸🍸🍸	4
● Collio Merlot '95	🍸🍸	4
● Collio Rosso '97	🍸🍸	4
○ Collio Tocai Friulano '96	🍸🍸	4
● Collio Merlot '96	🍸	4

CORMONS (GO)

Renato Keber
Loc. Zegla, 15
34071 Cormons (GO)
tel. 0481/61196

Renato Keber cultivates 13 hectares of vineyards on the hills near Cormons and produces about 80 thousand bottles each year, mainly for the domestic market. His work in vineyard and cellar is aimed at producing long-lasting wines and our tastings suggest that he has not worked in vain. This choice of his means that he has to release his wines rather late, so this year only one of the '98s was available for our consideration. The wines fermented and matured in wood go by the name of Grici, a Slovene term meaning peaks or summits, hence the highest and most highly prized vines. Beli Brici means white peaks, which is meant to suggest hillsides covered with flowering cherry trees, a classic Cormons landscape; it is also the name of the Collio Bianco '97, made mainly from pinot bianco, chardonnay and ribolla gialla. Very elegant on the nose, with mixed fruits and vanilla, it has a pronounced acidity that thins the palate. The Tocai '97 has an intense and complex nose and shows structure and length in the mouth, while the Grici version of the same year has very pronounced wood, which does not altogether mask the underlying fruity richness. The Tocai Friulano '98 displays concentrated aromas of pear and exotic fruit and a crisp, consistent, warm and long palate. In the bouquet of the Chardonnay Grici '97 we noted vanilla, custard, yeast and citrus fruit; in the mouth we detected pineapple and a refreshing acidity. The Merlot Grici '97, a great wine that is getting even better, boasts a fragrance of prune, blackberry and sweet black cherry; the soft and velvety palate is elegant, full-bodied and rich in alcohol. The Pinot Grigio and the Sauvignon almost captured One Glass.

○ Collio Tocai Friulano '98	🍷🍷	3*
● Collio Merlot Grici '97	🍷🍷	5
○ Collio Tocai Friulano '97	🍷🍷	3*
○ Collio Bianco Beli Grici '97	🍷	4
○ Collio Chardonnay Grici '97	🍷	4
○ Collio Tocai Friulano Grici '97	🍷	4
○ Collio Pinot Grigio '97		4
○ Collio Sauvignon '97		4

CORMONS (GO)

La Boatina
Via Corona, 62
34071 Cormons (GO)
tel. 0481/60445

La Boatina returns to the Guide with full honors this year, thanks to a series of distinguished wines. Loretto Pali's estate covers almost 60 hectares, 20 of which are under vine on the last gentle slopes of the Collio, near the boundary with the Isonzo district. This winery too (like Pali's Castello di Spessa) is managed by Patrizia Stekar, calls on the services of Paolo Della Rovere and, in vineyard and cellar, of the oenologist Domenico Lovat. The pick of the lot is the Pinot Bianco: straw-hued with a distinct greenish tinge, this wine has an elegant fruity nose; complex, broad and long in the mouth, it reveals a graceful undertone of apple. The Collio Bianco Pertè, made from pinot bianco, tocai friulano, sauvignon and a touch of picolit, also won Two Glasses for the harmony and finesse it manages to show together with its intense fruity aromas and considerable alcohol. The Picol Maggiore '94, a Bordeaux-style blend from a year that was not one of the best for Friuli reds, has good structure and offers a fair degree of complexity on the nose; the grassy flavor of cabernet franc is clearly discernible on the palate. The Pinot Grigio offers a notably appealing fruity nose; the palate is agreeably reminiscent of apricot, and perfectly judged acidity makes it refreshing and lengthens the finish. The Tocai has some lactic aromas in the bouquet, while the palate is decidedly fruity and fairly long. The very varietal Chardonnay is pleasing and well balanced; apple and yeast appear in the bouquet and the palate is admirably even. Although acidity is typical of this grape, there's a bit much of a good thing in the Ribolla Gialla, making the palate a little lean; it is generally well made, however, and nice with fish.

○	Collio Bianco Pertè '98	🍷🍷	4
○	Collio Pinot Bianco '98	🍷🍷	3
○	Collio Chardonnay '98	🍷	3
○	Collio Pinot Grigio '98	🍷	3
●	Collio Rosso Picol Maggiore '94	🍷	4
○	Collio Tocai Friulano '98	🍷	3
○	Collio Ribolla Gialla '98		3

CORMONS (GO)

Magnàs
Via Corona, 47
34071 Cormons (GO)
tel. 0481/60991

There have been many new developments in the Magnàs establishment, starting with the birth of Giovanni, a lovely bouncing pink and white baby boy who is curious to explore everything daddy Andrea does in the fields, the cellar and the stables, which have been owned by the family for several generations. The second new development is that they have decided to shut the no longer profitable stables and to open a country guesthouse instead. In the cellar the Merlot '97 is maturing in the bottle after six months in wood: this selection from that splendid vintage will be available in 2000. Meanwhile work proceeds on the three hectares of vineyards owned by the family in the Isonzo zone. But let's move on to the wines that we tasted, all of them white. Out in front is the Pinot Bianco, satisfying, long and full of personality; the complex fresh fruit bouquet is echoed on the enormous, rich, delicious, elegant and tightly knit palate. Next comes a series of One Glass wines, beginning with the Chardonnay, which is a little weak on the nose, but once again full-bodied and fat in the mouth, with well amalgamated fruit and yeast. The same nose-mouth relationship is present in the Tocai Friulano, but the harmonious, even, succulent and soft palate is even more successful. In the Pinot Grigio notes of apple and yeast create a well-balanced bouquet, while the palate reveals pear, apple and a crisp acidity that underpins the finish. An excess of acidity diminishes the palate of the Sauvignon, which is nevertheless distinctly deserving of note.

○	Friuli Isonzo Pinot Bianco '98	🍷🍷	3*
○	Collio Tocai Friulano '98	🍷	3
○	Friuli Isonzo Chardonnay '98	🍷	3
○	Friuli Isonzo Pinot Grigio '98	🍷	3
○	Friuli Isonzo Sauvignon '98		3

CORMONS (GO)

ROBERTO PICECH
LOC. PRADIS, 11
34071 CORMONS (GO)
TEL. 0481/60347

The Picech family has been working this land, on the hills of Pradis di Cormons, since the 1920s. They started out as share-croppers, but as a result of the peasant struggles of the period Egidio, known as "il ribèl", was able to buy the property. Today his son Roberto manages the five hectares of vineyards and, in true farming tradition, has not forgotten his parents: a hedgehog on the label, which bears the caption "the vines of the rebel" is dedicated to his father, with his prickly personality. The Collio Bianco Jelka is named after his mother. This wine, made from tocai, malvasia and ribolla, the traditional Collio Bianco blend, is sure to develop with time; it has remarkable length and, although some of it spends a little time in wood, you can't tell when you taste it, so great is the impact of ripe fruit and alcohol. The bouquet of the Malvasia suggests wildflowers and jasmine, with some notes of apple; the entry on the palate is rich and full, but the finish is a little less generous. Fresh green apple and plum are the keynote scents of an elegant Pinot Bianco, and the palate is beautifully balanced between acidity and fruit. The Collio Rosso, a blend of merlot, cabernet sauvignon and cabernet franc, was macerated for 16 days and, at the end of January 1999, was transferred to barriques, where it remained for just five months because, as we have pointed out elsewhere, this was a harvest plagued by unwelcome rains. The resultant wine is, however, satisfying, grapey and long, with fresh cherries on the nose and carrying through onto the palate. The Tocai Friulano suffers from a certain lack of balance, but still deserves a mention.

○ Collio Bianco Jelka '98	🍷	4
○ Collio Malvasia '98	🍷	3
○ Collio Pinot Bianco '98	🍷	3
● Collio Rosso '98	🍷	4
○ Collio Tocai Friulano '98		3
● Collio Cabernet Sauvignon '95	ŸŸ	4
○ Passito di Pradis '96	ŸŸ	6
● Collio Cabernet Sauvignon '96	Ÿ	4
● Collio Merlot '96	Ÿ	4

CORMONS (GO)

ISIDORO POLENCIC
LOC. PLESSIVA, 12
34071 CORMONS (GO)
TEL. 0481/60655

This estate is the biggest surprise in our Friuli pages this year, having coolly walked off with Three Glasses for an incredible Pinot Grigio. But first a bit of background: Isidoro Polencic, together with his children Elisabetta and Michele, manages 22 hectares of vineyards, almost all in the Collio DOC zone (10% of his vines are in the Isonzo DOC). The practical cellar, built in the early '80s, is not strained by the vinification and storing of the approximately 1,500 hectoliters of wine produced each year. And so to the Pinot Grigio: it's white-vinified and has an exceptionally fruity nose with clear notes of pear and apple accompanied by hints of herbs, green bark and honey; it explodes on the opulent, velvety palate, where acidity and dense fruit live in perfect harmony, and closes with an excellent long finish; in short, it won over even those of us who are not at all keen on pinot grigio. Meanwhile Two full Glasses were assigned to the Pinot Bianco, which has a decidedly elegant fragrance of apples; in the mouth it reveals complexity, softness, dense texture and a really long finish. The Tocai Friulano, which is just as good, displays an enticing nose with hints of tobacco leaf; the palate shows good acidity and a solid, concentrated structure, with pear and almond leaf to close. The indisputably varietal Sauvignon boasts aromas of bell pepper and tomato leaf; the mouth, luscious, rich and soft, has a balanced acidity and pronounced flavors of peach and grapefruit. The Oblin Blanc, made from chardonnay, ribolla and sauvignon, has an intense bouquet of custard, honey and vanilla; wood has the upper hand on the palate. The Pinot Nero is fairly varietal and has struck a balance between wood and fruit.

○ Collio Pinot Grigio '98	🍷🍷🍷	3*
○ Collio Pinot Bianco '98	🍷🍷	3
○ Collio Sauvignon '98	🍷🍷	3
○ Collio Tocai Friulano '98	🍷🍷	3
● Collio Pinot Nero '97	🍷	4
○ Oblin Blanc '97	🍷	5
○ Collio Bianco '98		3
● Friuli Isonzo Cabernet Sauvignon '97		4
● Oblin Ros '96		5
○ Oblin Blanc '96	ŸŸ	5

CORMONS (GO)

Alessandro Princic
Loc. Pradis, 5
34071 Cormons (GO)
tel. 0481/60723

Here is a great winery, diligently run by the appealing Sandro Princic, son of the legendary Doro, one of the fathers of serious wine production in Friuli. Sandro does not miss the mark with any of his wines, and the minimum grade they obtained this year was just short of Two Glasses. By the way, we erroneously spoke of a Merlot '97 in last year's Guide: we meant the '96. So we'll start with the real '97, their only red, and a full and powerful wine; the nose suggests a sweet red berry tart and raisins; the excellent, long and rounded palate opens out into a symphony of fruit with a hint of tar. Once again the top wine is the luscious and rich Pinot Bianco, which is so concentrated that it seems to have spent some time in wood; the elegant, generous and fully ripe apple on the nose opens slowly in the mouth, to be joined by delicate yeast and vanilla on the finish. The Tocai is splendid, as is its wont; a powerful, complex and rich nose with hints of green almond introduces the opulent and even palate with its vegetal overtones. We were surprised by how much the Sauvignon had developed since some tastings a few months earlier: we now found it unexpectedly varietal in its elder flower fragrance, and substantial and structured on the palate, which is typical of Sandro's style. What a pity that he has produced so few bottles of the Malvasia! All the flowers that bloom in the spring are in the bouquet, together with yellow plum, and the palate is alcohol-rich, luscious, and enduringly fruity. Lastly, the Pinot Grigio, the only wine not to win Two Glasses, albeit by a hair's breadth: it has a complex nose, with pear, apple and linden blossom to the fore, and a varietal palate, with mineral notes and hints of red and pink plum; acidity is kept in its place and the finish is fleshy.

○ Collio Malvasia '98	▼▼	4
● Collio Merlot '97	▼▼	4
○ Collio Pinot Bianco '98	▼▼	4
○ Collio Sauvignon '98	▼▼	4
○ Collio Tocai Friulano '98	▼▼	4
○ Collio Pinot Grigio '98	▼	4
○ Collio Pinot Bianco '95	▽▽▽	4
○ Collio Tocai Friulano '93	▽▽▽	5
○ Collio Pinot Bianco '97	▽▽	4
● Collio Merlot '96	▽	4

CORMONS (GO)

Dario Raccaro
Via S. Giovanni, 87/b
34071 Cormons (GO)
tel. 0481/61425

In keeping with his disciplined approach, Dario Raccaro did not present all his red wines at our tastings; being a white wine specialist, he said, he did not want us to review wines, however excellent, of which very few bottles are available. In any case, on the basis of the wines we did manage to taste, we have to compliment Dario on his oenological gifts. He is a small producer, but he has the good fortune to cultivate, in addition to the few hectares he actually owns, a plot he rents on the hills of Brazzano, a great environment for tocai; indeed we've been singing the praises of his version for the past couple of years. So let's have a look at the Tocai Friulano vintage '98. Its nose is almost austere, yet elegant, with clear notes of pear and peach leaf; after a sottovoce attack on the palate it develops fullness and warmth, to close with a very long finish; even as it sits in the glass it gets better, so it seems quite reasonable to predict further improvement with more bottle age. The Merlot '97 has a splendid nose redolent of plum tart, tar, herbs and flowers; the fat, warm, full, spicy and lingering palate boasts well-integrated tannins. This is a wine that will be difficult to keep, because it is so delightful for present drinking. The Collio Bianco, half tocai and half malvasia and sauvignon, has a nose dominated by apple and pear; a slightly pronounced acidity makes the palate seem thinner than it actually is. The Malvasia's substantial alcohol declares itself on the nose, along with a rich infusion of herbs; it's all mirrored on the palate, where the excellent entry evolves into a yellow plum and herbal finish.

● Collio Merlot '97	▼▼	3
○ Collio Tocai Friulano '98	▼▼	3
○ Collio Bianco '98	▼	3
○ Collio Malvasia '98	▼	3
○ Collio Tocai Friulano '97	▽▽	3
● Friuli Isonzo Cabernet Franc '97	▽▽	3

CORMONS (GO)

RONCADA
LOC. RONCADA, 5
34071 CORMONS (GO)
TEL. 0481/61394

This winery, which the Mattioni family has owned since 1953, cultivates 22 hectares of vineyard, all in the low-lying part of the Collio zone. There is evidence that grapevines were already growing at Roncada in the late 19th century; indeed the family villa, which dates from then, was equipped with the cellars that are still in use today. Since 1982 the uncommonly patient and tenacious Oscar Biasi has been the estate oenologist. Fourteen different wines are produced, and the best of them this time is the elegant, intensely fruity, harmonious, dense and long Pinot Bianco. This is followed by a series of One Glass winners, starting with the Chardonnay, which has a complex, clean bouquet and vegetal overtones on the palate. Next comes the Ribolla Gialla, which combines scents of fresh fruit with green leaf tones; the varietal palate, with its distinct acidity, is delicately appley. In the Riesling Italico the prevailing aroma is beeswax, which is transformed into honey on the palate, together with mixed fruit salad. White flowers and straw characterize the nose of the Tocai and carry through onto the full-bodied and long palate. The red wines spend some time in 7 quintal barrels: the best are the Cabernet Franc and the Franconia. The former is grapey, with notes of wild cherry and freshly cut grass on the nose and dry tannins on the palate, which is dominated by varietal grassy flavors. In the Franconia a faint note of black cherry emerges on the nose; the palate is refreshing, supple, fruity and appealing.

○	Collio Pinot Bianco '98	🍷🍷	3
●	Collio Cabernet Franc '97	🍷	3
○	Collio Chardonnay '98	🍷	3
○	Collio Ribolla Gialla '98	🍷	3
○	Collio Riesling Italico '98	🍷	3
○	Collio Tocai Friulano '98	🍷	3
●	Franconia '97	🍷	3
●	Collio Cabernet Sauvignon '97		3
○	Collio Malvasia '98		3
○	Collio Müller Thurgau '98		3
○	Collio Sauvignon '98		3
○	Collio Pinot Grigio '98		3

CORMONS (GO)

RONCO DEI TASSI
LOC. MONTE, 38
34071 CORMONS (GO)
TEL. 0481/60155

Another triumph for Fabio Coser with his Sauvignon, which won him star status in our first Guide! Before we move on to the wines, however, here are a few background notes on Ronco dei Tassi. This estate, the property of Fabio and his wife, covers seven hectares of vines a short distance from the cellar, on the north-eastern slopes of Monte Quarin, the hill overlooking Cormons. Here Fabio, who is one of the most skilled oenologists to have migrated from the Veneto to Friuli, is embarking on major restructuring to create more practical working and storage spaces. The Cjarandon '97, mainly merlot and cabernet sauvignon, is currently maturing in barriques and is very promising indeed. But a wine that is already living up to its promise is the Sauvignon '98: golden-hued, it releases a well-defined bouquet of elder flower, tomato leaf and sage, all mirrored on the stunning palate, which is luscious and richly fruity, with apple and peach to the fore, and has a delicious, succulent and piquant finish. The Collio Bianco Fosarin, an assemblage of tocai friulano and malvasia istriana matured in stainless steel, and wood-aged pinot bianco, has a delicate, elegant and complex nose of fresh mixed fruit with a hint of banana; the soft and alcohol-laden palate is extraordinarily rich and lingering. The excellent bouquet of the Pinot Grigio, an elegant balance of pear, apple and yellow plum, carries through to a succulent palate with well-dosed alcohol. The Tocai Friulano was aged in lightly toasted wood and is meant to improve with bottle age; the soft and fruity nose with faint notes of vanilla is echoed on the quite full and structured palate. Further compliments to Fabio for his decision to limit his range to just a few labels, in marked contrast to most other Friuli wine producers.

○	Collio Sauvignon '98	🍷🍷🍷	3*
○	Collio Tocai Friulano '98	🍷🍷	3*
○	Collio Bianco Fosarin '98	🍷🍷	4
○	Collio Pinot Grigio '98	🍷🍷	3*
○	Collio Bianco Fosarin '96	YYY	4
○	Collio Bianco Fosarin '97	YY	4
●	Collio Rosso Cjarandon '96	YY	4
●	Collio Rosso Cjarandon '95	Y	4

CORMONS (GO)

RONCO DEL GELSO

VIA ISONZO, 117
34071 CORMONS (GO)
TEL. 0481/61310

Once again, Giorgio Badin has claimed his place in the ranks of Three Glass winners; indeed a trio of his wines made it to the final round, confirming his reputation as a top-rate wine-maker. His hyperoxygenation technique sets the seal on his diligent, painstaking work in the vineyard and enables him to produce intensely colored, incredibly long-lived white wines, as we have been able to confirm in numerous vertical tastings. And since this year the quality of the reds was also beyond dispute, the prize awarded to the Sauvignon should in fact be extended to the winery as a whole. After a few seconds in the glass this lemony yellow Sauvignon releases intense aromas of sage and elder flower; but the palate is the real knockout, luscious, full-bodied, broad, soft and very long, with a smoky note; this is a wine to watch over the years. The powerful, structured Tocai Friulano is splendid, as usual; its aromas range from apple to green banana, citrus fruit and fig leaf; the soft and full-bodied palate seems to go on for ever. The other showpiece, the Isonzo Bianco Làtimis '98, a blend of tocai, pinot bianco and late-harvested riesling, displays a concentrated and complex nose, dominated by ripe yellow fruit (peach and plum); these notes are echoed faithfully on the palate, with its balanced acidity and succulence and notes of overripe fruit on the finish. The Chardonnay, very similar in style to the other wines, has an astonishingly warm, full structure; alcohol contributes nicely to the roundness in the mouth. Much the same sort of thing takes place in the Pinot Grigio, for which the use of barriques has been so clever that you can't tell it spent any time there at all. We were very pleasantly surprised, not so much by the richly spiced Cabernet Franc, but by the Merlot, which has had some trouble in recent years but is now clearly on its way back up to the top.

○ Friuli Isonzo Sauvignon '98	🍷🍷🍷	4
○ Friuli Isonzo Bianco Làtimis '98	🍷🍷	4
● Friuli Isonzo Cabernet Franc '98	🍷🍷	4
○ Friuli Isonzo Chardonnay '98	🍷🍷	4
● Friuli Isonzo Merlot '97	🍷🍷	5
○ Friuli Isonzo Pinot Grigio Sot lis Rivis '97	🍷🍷	4
○ Friuli Isonzo Tocai Friulano '98	🍷🍷	4
○ Friuli Isonzo Tocai Friulano '95	🍷🍷🍷 (white)	5
○ Friuli Isonzo Tocai Friulano '97	🍷🍷🍷 (white)	4
○ Isonzo Tocai Friulano '94	🍷🍷🍷 (white)	5
○ Friuli Isonzo Bianco Làtimis '97	🍷🍷 (white)	4

CORMONS (GO)

LAURA SREDNIK

VIA PRADIS, 1
34071 CORMONS (GO)
TEL. 0481/61943

After last year's listing in the Other Wineries section, the estate run by agronomist Laura Srednik – with a decisive contribution from her father Giovanni in the vineyards – has returned to the front ranks with a full review. That temporary relegation to the minor leagues was due to a performance which, while generally satisfactory, had only one real high point , a Two Glass Pinot Grigio; the fact is that the competition in Friuli is getting really fierce! Here, then, is Laura's riposte, starting with a great Chardonnay. The clean and varietal bouquet includes notes of yeast and fresh apple; the soft, rich and full palate is characterful and long. Elegant elder blossom dominates the nose of the Sauvignon, together with distinct notes of tomato leaf; these follow through on the stylish and complex palate. The Tocai Friulano offers a fragrance of hay and straw with an underlying pear tone; in the mouth it seems well-executed, clean, substantial and rather long. The Merlot '97 makes the grade as a result of its intensely fruity palate and slightly dry tannins; the complex aromas range from wild cherry to plum and alcohol. The Ribolla Gialla, intensely redolent of fruit rather than flowers, has a slightly overpronounced acidity that makes for a bitterish finish. The Pinot Bianco and the Pinot Grigio present the same problem, but are otherwise very good. The Müller Thurgau, with its remarkably refreshing nose and palate, is simple but appealing.

○ Collio Chardonnay '98	🍷🍷	3
● Collio Merlot '97	🍷	3
○ Collio Sauvignon '98	🍷	3
○ Collio Tocai Friulano '98	🍷	3
○ Collio Müller Thurgau '98		3
○ Collio Pinot Bianco '98		3
○ Collio Pinot Grigio '98		3
○ Collio Ribolla Gialla '98		3

CORMONS (GO)

OSCAR STURM
LOC. ZEGLA, 1
34071 CORMONS (GO)
TEL. 0481/60720

Oscar and Dunja Sturm have again shown that they know what they're about. Consistent painstaking work on their 12 hectares under vine and in their modern and spacious cellar produces excellent results, at times even quite surprising ones, but there are never unpleasant surprises. The Sauvignon, usually their top wine, got off to quite a muted start at first trial in the cellar. Later, when our comparative blind tastings took place, it had developed a good bit, and it's by no means unthinkable that it will have quietly turned into a Two Glass wine by the time this review is published. Tomato leaf and yellow peach had come through more clearly on the nose, while grapefruit and nectarine could be detected on the fat, structured, decidedly varietal and long palate. However, it comes nowhere near the surprise of the year, the Chardonnay '98, which carried off Two Glasses full to overflowing: golden-hued, with a complex, rich and elegant bouquet, it displays such lush and fruity substance in the mouth that the distinct acidity is powerless to cut into its body and depth. The Pinot Grigio, another Two Glass winner, has a nose of mixed and tropical fruits, a sure sign of grapes picked really ripe; the full, intense but not at all heavy palate boasts a long finish. In the Merlot Andritz, named after the Styrian village the family originally came from, the oak has been completely absorbed, leaving the way open for blackberries and cherry tart to emerge on the complex, mouth-filling, agreeably robust palate that just goes on and on. The Tocai is both elegant and intense; the Refosco, with its alcohol-rich aromas of cherry and custard, makes a soft entry on the palate and closes with dry tannins.

○	Chardonnay Andritz '98	🍷🍷	3
○	Collio Pinot Grigio '98	🍷🍷	3
●	Merlot Andritz '96	🍷🍷	4
○	Collio Sauvignon '98	🍷	3
○	Collio Tocai Friulano '98	🍷	3
●	Refosco P. R. '97	🍷	3
●	Cabernet Franc '97		3
○	Chardonnay Andritz '97	ΥΥ	3

CORMONS (GO)

SUBIDA DI MONTE
LOC. MONTE, 9
34071 CORMONS (GO)
TEL. 0481/61011

Gigi Antonutti's sons Cristian and Andrea have given a new vitality to this winery. Cristian is in charge of production and Andrea looks after the commercial side. Soon the results of their dedicated labors in vineyard and cellar will be plain for all to see in the form of two special selections from the '99 vintage, a Merlot and a Chardonnay. For the time being, we have limited ourselves to the currently available bottles, produced from the eight hectares they own and the two they rent. The Sauvignon '98 is very successful: pronounced aromas of tomato leaf and bell pepper introduce a lingeringly fruity palate underpinned by impressive acidity. The Rosso Poncaia '96, a blend of merlot, cabernet sauvignon and cabernet franc, spent 20 months in barriques and five-hectoliter tonneaux. Blackberry and wood define the nose, while the palate is complex, rich, long and fairly full-bodied. We were more impressed by the Cabernet Franc '98, which has turned out very well despite an unpropitious vintage: the luscious cherry tart bouquet is followed in the mouth by wild cherries steeped in alcohol. In the Pinot Grigio we preferred the intense and complex nose to the succulent, easy palate. Two classic '98s, the Merlot and the Tocai, are well made, fairly varietal and worthy of note.

○	Collio Sauvignon '98	🍷🍷	3
●	Collio Cabernet Franc '98	🍷	4
○	Collio Pinot Grigio '98	🍷	3
●	Collio Rosso Poncaia '96	🍷	5
●	Collio Merlot '98		3
○	Collio Tocai Friulano '98		3
○	Collio Bianco Sotrari '97	ΥΥ	4
●	Collio Cabernet Franc '97	ΥΥ	4
●	Collio Cabernet Ris. '95	ΥΥ	5
●	Collio Merlot Ris. '95	ΥΥ	4

CORMONS (GO)

FRANCO TORÒS
LOC. NOVALI, 12
34071 CORMONS (GO)
TEL. 0481/61327

The collection of Glasses awarded to Franco Toròs, the affable winemaker from Novali di Cormons, is growing apace with the increase in cellar space for the maturing of his special selections. Furthermore the vines he replanted a few years ago are now producing, so, weather permitting, his grapes keep getting better. And what with the limited yields per hectare, the full ripening of the grapes for the '98 whites and the debut of the Merlot '97, we were simply not able to award less than One Glass to any of his wines. This Merlot '97, a selection of which will come out in 2000, has an intense, full and richly fruity bouquet; the concentrated and lingering palate dominated by cherry and ripe blackberry displays pronounced but elegant tannins. The Tocai Friulano is redolent of pear and almond leaf; the luscious, inviting palate is dense and mouth-filling from start to finish. Aromas of yeast, dried flowers, quince jam and Golden Delicious apple appear in the Chardonnay '98; the substantial alcohol is largely masked on the palate by an acidity that emerges particularly on the finish. The Pinot Grigio has an intensely fruity, concentrated fragrance and a dense, structured and long palate with notes of apple and citrus fruit. The Chardonnay Riserva '97 shows well-integrated wood, sweet fruit and average length. Elder flowers characterize the nose of the Sauvignon, which has an admirable balance of fruit and acidity in the mouth. The Pinot Bianco displays an elegant fragrance of apple and a crisp and individual palate. We tasted the Cabernet Franc '97 again and found it even better than before.

○	Collio Chardonnay '98	🍷🍷	4
●	Collio Merlot '97	🍷🍷	3*
○	Collio Pinot Grigio '98	🍷🍷	4
○	Collio Tocai Friulano '98	🍷🍷	3*
○	Collio Chardonnay Ris. '97	🍷	4
○	Collio Pinot Bianco '98	🍷	4
○	Collio Sauvignon '98	🍷	4
●	Collio Cabernet Franc '97	🍸	4

CORMONS (GO)

VIGNA DEL LAURO
LOC. MONTE, 38
34070 CORMONS (GO)
TEL. 0481/60155

The Vigna del Lauro label now refers to the fruit of different vineyards, but it is still Fabio Coser who directs operations, most importantly in the cellar. He has rented about seven hectares in the renowned Lucinico, San Floriano del Collio and Cormons zones and has, with his practiced hand, succeeded in creating a series of excellent wines, including a One Glass Merlot '98, which is doubly admirable, since '98 was a disaster for this variety and Fabio had in any case started looking after the vines relatively late in the year. Let's start then with this wine, the runt of the litter: a black cherry fragrance introduces a gentle entry on the palate, where it expands with freshness, fruit and average length. Several steps up the ladder we find the Collio Bianco, made from tocai friulano, malvasia istriana and pinot bianco; the elegant bouquet is a delicate blend of apple, pear and yellow plum, while the palate is intense, full, structured and well-balanced between acidity and substantial alcohol. The Coser touch is quite evident also in the Pinot Grigio's elegant, complex and rich fragrance, which is echoed on the succulent palate, with its long appley finish. The Sauvignon wears its varietal characteristics on its sleeve, starting with its elder blossom, nettle and grapefruit nose, followed by the lovely fruity richness of the palate, with its intense impact and supporting acidity. And, to finish, the Tocai Friulano: fruity, dry aromas of peach and almond lead to an enticing entry on a palate that reveals itself as very soft, fleshy, long, alcohol-rich and both extremely elegant and mouth-filling. This is a truly excellent wine.

○	Collio Bianco '98	🍷🍷	3*
○	Collio Pinot Grigio '98	🍷🍷	3*
○	Collio Sauvignon '98	🍷🍷	3*
○	Collio Tocai Friulano '98	🍷🍷	3*
●	Collio Merlot '98	🍷	4
○	Collio Pinot Bianco '97	🍸🍸	3
○	Collio Pinot Grigio '97	🍸🍸	3
○	Collio Sauvignon '97	🍸🍸	3

VALENTINO BUTUSSI

VIA PRA' DI CORTE, 1
33040 CORNO DI ROSAZZO (UD)
TEL. 0432/759194

The architectural attractions of this winery are matched by its admirable wines. Its name is a homage to 89-year old Valentino Butussi, Angelo's father and the guiding spirit of a whole family of dedicated wine-makers: not just Angelo's wife, but his children too (Filippo, Erika, and Tobia) are already hard at work here, whether in the vineyards, in the cellars, or in the office. Their youngest child, the 14-year-old Mattia, is just starting his oenological studies in Cividale. The family has 12 hectares under vine: five in the Colli Orientali district and seven in Grave. The well-balanced Pinot Grigio is unusually elegant for this grape and offers pleasant fruity notes and considerable length. The complex and broad bouquet of the Tocai Friulano includes distinct aromas of pear and apple seed; the palate is even and succulent, with a good acidic structure and substantial fruit. The quite complex Chardonnay displays flowers, fruit and yeast on the nose; the very ripe yellow-fleshed fruit on the harmonious and balanced palate seems to come through even more clearly on the long finish. The Sauvignon, after some initial toasty notes, displays well-defined aromas of tomato leaf and elder blossom, all echoed on the palate, which, in typical Butussi style, enjoys a particularly harmonious balance of fruit and crisp acidity. The Ribolla Gialla falls just short of its second Glass; this inviting wine is redolent of green apple, and is extraordinarily appealing in the mouth. Unexpectededly noticeable toasty notes work somewhat to the disfavor of the concentrated Pinot Bianco; its fruit does however manage to emerge, and its finish is very long. This excellent range ends with the Verduzzo Friulano and the Cabernet Sauvignon, which are also worthy of mention.

○	COF Chardonnay '98	🍷🍷	3*
○	COF Pinot Grigio '98	🍷🍷	3*
○	COF Sauvignon '98	🍷🍷	3*
○	COF Tocai Friulano '98	🍷🍷	3*
○	COF Pinot Bianco '98	🍷	3
○	COF Ribolla Gialla '98	🍷	3
●	COF Cabernet Sauvignon '97		3
○	COF Verduzzo Friulano '98		3

CA DI BON

VIA CASALI GALLO, 1
33040 CORNO DI ROSAZZO (UD)
TEL. 0432/759316

In keeping with their traditional practice, Gianni and Ameris Bon still prudently bottle only some of the wine obtained from their vineyards in the three DOC districts of Colli Orientali del Friuli, Grave and Collio; a substantial part of their production finishes on the bulk wine market or else in the outlet they have opened at San Giovanni al Natisone. The white Ronco del Nonno, a blend of pinot bianco, sauvignon and tocai friulano with an elegant fresh apple fragrance and a fat, full, glycerin-rich palate pervaded by ripe fruit, is particularly successful. The Chardonnay testifies to their oenological skills: composite and pleasant both on the nose and in the mouth, it boasts substantial fruit and an inviting finish. The Pinot Grigio has all the characteristics of this favorable vintage: a concentrated and intense bouquet of dried flowers and ripe fruit that follows through onto a fat palate with notes of pear and apple; what it lacks in elegance it makes up for with meaty richness. Those are the Two Glass wines, and now for the One Glass winners: the Tocai Friulano was nearly in the first category because of its full, fine, floral nose mirrored on its intense, harmonious palate. The Pinot Bianco has a hint of pear and a crispness well balanced by alcoholic warmth, while the varietal notes of the Sauvignon come through without undue pushing. The Cabernet Franc displays attractive aromas of rose and cherry, and substance in the mouth. The Schioppettino offers fresh aromatic herbs, cherry and rose on both nose and palate.

○	Chardonnay '98	🍷🍷	3*
○	COF Pinot Grigio '98	🍷🍷	3*
○	Ronco del Nonno '98	🍷🍷	3*
●	COF Merlot '98	🍷	3
○	COF Pinot Bianco '98	🍷	3
●	COF Schioppettino '98	🍷	3
○	COF Tocai Friulano '98	🍷	3
●	Friuli Grave Cabernet Franc '98	🍷	3
○	Friuli Grave Sauvignon '98	🍷	3
●	COF Refosco P. R. '97	🍷🍷 (white)	3

CORNO DI ROSAZZO (UD)

EUGENIO COLLAVINI
LOC. GRAMOGLIANO, 2
33040 CORNO DI ROSAZZO (UD)
TEL. 0432/753222

Manlio Collavini's winery has made a notable leap forward this year. Since the estate comprises just a few hectares, he is obliged to buy grapes. Between 25 and 30% of these currently come from vines that are either planted at a high density per hectare, or are over 20 years old. The most impressive wine this time is the Collio Chardonnay dei Sassi Cavi Collezione Privata '98, fermented and matured in barriques: the wine wears its wood with nonchalance, displaying varietal yeast and crusty bread on the nose; the agreeable green note in the mouth is matched by an elegance reminiscent of pinot bianco. The other Chardonnays we tasted were also very good. The Collio dei Sassi Cavi '97, with its soft, round palate, has fruit that stands out over a base of vanilla. The Friuli Isonzo '98, of which 150 thousand bottles were produced, releases a complex and harmonious fragrance; apricot and banana characterize the velvety and long palate, on which a note of vanilla is barely perceptible. The Sauvignon Collezione Privata '98, partly fermented in barriques, should absorb the toasty notes into the bouquet over time; in the mouth it is already luscious and elegant, with yellow-fleshed peach lingering all the way through to the long finish. The Tocai della Collezione Privata is another very, very good wine, with sweet scents of apple jam, a remarkable balance between fleshiness and acidity on the palate and a richly fruity finish. The Merlot Collezione Privata '97, with plum and berry tart on the nose, shows massive structure. The Grigio Spumante, an appealing Charmat-method bubbly made from chardonnay, prosecco and pinot, completes the series of Glass winners.

○ Collio Chardonnay dei Sassi Cavi '97	🍷🍷	4
○ Collio Chardonnay dei Sassi Cavi Collezione Privata '98	🍷🍷	4
○ Collio Sauvignon Collezione Privata '98	🍷🍷	4
○ Collio Tocai Friulano Collezione Privata '98	🍷🍷	4
○ Friuli Isonzo Chardonnay dei Sassi Cavi '98	🍷🍷	3*
● Collio Merlot Collezione Privata '97	🍷	4
○ Il Grigio Spumante	🍷	3
○ Collio Pinot Grigio Collezione Privata '98		4
○ Collio Sauvignon Blanc '98		3
● Collio Merlot Conte di Cuccanea '96	♀	4

CORNO DI ROSAZZO (UD)

ADRIANO GIGANTE
VIA ROCCA BERNARDA, 3
33040 CORNO DI ROSAZZO (UD)
TEL. 0432/755835

Adriano Gigante is one of the leading figures – and current Vice President - of the Colli Orientali del Friuli Consortium. The wines he produces from his 11 or so hectares of vineyards have been of a consistently high standard for many years, and recent vintages have done nothing to damage his fine reputation. Indeed the best wines we tasted were the Chardonnay '98 and the Merlot '97. The former introduces itself with notes of flint and sweet fruit and hints of honey, all echoed on the fleshy and quite international palate. The Merlot has a grassy vein, but sweet and lingering grapiness gets the upper hand; the tannins are still a little astringent on the palate but will probably soften sooner rather than later. In the Tocai Friulano '98 we noted a delightful scent of wild strawberries on a base of pear and apple; Golden Delicious apple emerges clearly on the palate. The Sauvignon, which is fatter, displays the varietal elder blossom combined with a complex, soft fruitiness. The Verduzzo Friulano is fairly characteristic: rennet apple on the nose is followed by a palate that seems sweeter, fatter and more elegant than average; it is just a trifle tannic and has a very pronounced apple flavor. The Picolit '97 was a disappointment after last year's: it lacked balance on both nose and palate. The red wines, the Schioppettino and the Refosco, both '97s, and the Cabernet Franc '98, are well made and worthy of note.

○ COF Chardonnay '98	🍷🍷	3*
● COF Merlot '97	🍷🍷	3*
○ COF Sauvignon '98	🍷	3
○ COF Tocai Friulano '98	🍷	3
○ COF Verduzzo Friulano '97	🍷	3
● COF Cabernet Franc '98		3
○ COF Picolit '97		5
● COF Refosco P. R. '97		4
● COF Schioppettino '97		4

CORNO DI ROSAZZO (UD)

PERUSINI

VIA TORRIONE, 13
LOC. GRAMOGLIANO
33040 CORNO DI ROSAZZO (UD)
TEL. 0432/675018

The historic Perusini estate on the slopes of Corno di Rosazzo is managed personally by Teresa Perusini, who received a degree in humanities, specialized in the arts and has worked extensively as a restorer. She is flanked in the winery by her husband, the engineer Giacomo de Pace, who comes from a farming family. The two of them have been running the estate, which they inherited from Giampaolo Perusini, since 1985. It was Giampaolo who carried out the first selections of his own vines, encouraging only the most suitable ones. This operation, performed on the ribolla and the merlot, has been taken up again by Teresa, with immediately apparent and admirable results. Indeed, as in previous years, the Ribolla Gialla has conquered Two Glasses; apple, jasmine and acacia flower characterize the nose; the even, rich and lingering palate reveals perfectly judged acidity. The Merlot Nero '97, made from the fruit of shoots from a vine planted in 1944, is also maintaining high standards: a fragrance of chocolate and warmed red berries introduces a mellow, silky, soft and long palate that has no toasty notes revealing the time it spent in wood. The Pinot Bianco is redolent of apple and tropical fruit; in the mouth it is warm, rich in glycerin and generously fruity. We weren't altogether happy with the nose of the Pinot Grigio, despite its complexity, but we were delighted by the rich, close-textured, warm and structured palate. Of the basic reds, both the Merlot '98 and the compact Cabernet '98 deserve One Glass; the former is warm, intense and reminiscent of wild cherry and blackberry, while the hay, green leaf and black cherry tart bouquet of the Cabernet precedes a good tannic structure on the palate.

● COF Merlot Nero '97	▼▼	4
○ COF Pinot Bianco '98	▼▼	3
○ COF Pinot Grigio '98	▼▼	3
○ COF Ribolla Gialla '98	▼▼	3
● COF Cabernet '98	▼	3
● COF Merlot '98	▼	3
● COF Merlot Nero '96	▽▽	4
○ COF Ribolla Gialla '97	▽▽	3
○ COF Picolit '97	▽	5

CORNO DI ROSAZZO (UD)

LEONARDO SPECOGNA

VIA ROCCA BERNARDA, 4
33040 CORNO DI ROSAZZO (UD)
TEL. 0432/755840

We begin our review with some very sad news: Alexander Trolf, the young Austrian oenologist who had been working with Graziano Specogna for several years, has died in a tragic road accident. We all regret his passing. Although heavy of heart, Graziano, a man of character, has rolled up his sleeves and carried on working, helped and well advised by Valdino Diust. A great Merlot '97 was revealed at our tastings: very intense ruby in color, it introduces its bouquet with aromas of chocolate and coffee, pleasantly interlaced with notes of cherry jam and quinine; a lovely spicy tone reveals dominant black pepper, and the whole is extremely well balanced and carries through onto the warm palate which has a delightful finish where cherry and coffee re-emerge. Of the One Glass wines we particularly liked the Verduzzo Friulano. Its golden appearance hints at the power and substance to come; and indeed the intense bouquet of baked apple and candied citrus peel is followed by a palate that is both powerful and rather elegant; the finish is not particularly long. The delectable and opulent palate of the Picolit suggests orange and baked apple. The barrique-aged Chardonnay is good, as usual; the oak is responsible for the aromas of vanilla, coffee, ripe banana and tobacco; the impressive attack on the palate counterbalances a relative lack of length. In what would seem to be its customary style, the Tocai is hurt by a not yet balanced nose and helped by a palate that offers everything it has: fleshiness, warmth, breadth and a ripe fruitiness that goes on and on. The Cabernet has a delicate nose of plum jam, black currant and tobacco; it is straightforward in the mouth, and finishes on a note of wild cherry. The Sauvignon and Refosco are good wines too.

● COF Merlot '97	▼▼	4
● COF Cabernet '97	▼	4
○ COF Chardonnay '97	▼	4
○ COF Picolit '98	▼	5
● COF Refosco P. R. '97	▼	4
○ COF Sauvignon '98	▼	3
○ COF Tocai Friulano '98	▼	3
○ COF Verduzzo Friulano '98	▼	3
● COF Cabernet '96	▽▽	4
● COF Merlot '95	▽	4
● COF Merlot '96	▽	4

ANDREA VISINTINI

VIA GRAMOGLIANO, 27
33040 CORNO DI ROSAZZO (UD)
TEL. 0432/755813

The consistently high quality associated with Oliviero Visintini, the driving force behind the winery that he runs with his father Andrea and his sister Cinzia, is confirmed by this year's wines. Oliviero loves his work and the wines he produces and, although he knows he should reduce the number of labels, he can't bring himself to eliminate any of them. The problem is further complicated by the fact that he has built up a friendly relationship with many of his customers, and would feel he was betraying their trust if he stopped making any of their favorites. We should also note that his pricing policy shows exemplary prudence and respect for the consumer. The Sauvignon, an excellent wine, offers characteristic scents of tomato leaf; on the palate, where it makes a decisive but by no means intrusive entry, it develops evenly through to a long finish with an undertone of citrus. The Pinot Bianco del Collio has considerable elegance on the nose, with clear notes of apple and fresh fruit; in the mouth it manages to combine a mellow, full structure with an agreeable vein of acidity. The Ribolla Gialla is also extremely varietal; wild flowers, wisteria and yellow plum dominate the nose and are echoed on the forthright, long palate, underpinned by well-judged acidity. Visintini's Traminer Aromatico is one of the few in Friuli to be fully recognizably varietal, in particular on the palate, where notes of tropical fruit and candied citrus peel are accompanied by refreshing acidity. It was not easy to make good reds from the '98 vintage; Oliviero, however, has succeeded in producing a Merlot with excellent concentration on the nose, although in the mouth the wine does not quite live up to expectations. For the first time this winery has used small barrels to produce a wine, the Merlot Il Barrique '97: a spicy bouquet with notes of medicinal herbs and red berries precedes a palate that is full-bodied, if not elegant.

○	Collio Pinot Bianco '98	🍷🍷	3*
○	COF Ribolla Gialla '98	🍷🍷	3*
○	COF Sauvignon '98	🍷🍷	3*
●	COF Merlot '98	🍷	3
●	COF Merlot Il Barrique '97	🍷	3
○	COF Traminer Aromatico '98	🍷	3
○	COF Pinot Grigio '98		3
○	COF Riesling '98		3
○	COF Verduzzo Friulano '98		3
○	Collio Tocai Friulano '98		3
○	COF Sauvignon '97	🍷🍷 (white)	3
○	Collio Pinot Bianco '97	🍷🍷 (white)	3
○	Collio Tocai Friulano '97	🍷🍷 (white)	3

CORNO DI ROSAZZO (UD)

ZOF

VIA GIOVANNI XXIII, 32/A
33040 CORNO DI ROSAZZO (UD)
TEL. 0432/759673

Daniele Zof, who got his degree in oenology from the prestigious Istituto di Cividale del Friuli in 1990, has taken over full responsibility for wine-making at the estate established by his father Alberto in 1984. He is still young and knows that he needs to build up experience, but we have to admit that his wine is getting better and better, as a quick glance at this year's Glasses will tell you. And while we're admitting things, we may as well mention our own fallibility: for example, in last year's review we discussed a supposed '96 Va' Pensiero, which was really vintage '95. So we make our public apologies, and present our impressions of the real Va' Pensiero '96, a blend of merlot and cabernet franc with a small percentage of cabernet sauvignon: the resultant wine has a concentrated bouquet dominated by plum, undergrowth and bitter chocolate, a palate with a fine balance of body, crispness, complex fruit and tannins, and a really long finish. We were delighted by the Pinot Bianco '98, with its brilliant hue and elegant notes of apple and vanilla on the nose, mirrored on a palate where they blend harmoniously with a satisfying structure and an acidity that supports the long finish. The Bianco Sonata '98 includes amongst its intense and elegant aromas notes of fresh fruit and infusions of medicinal herbs; the soft and even palate expands on the finish. The Tocai Friulano also offers a general elegance that enhances the dense, rich, fruity and long-lasting structure. The Cabernet Franc '98 surprised us with hints of cherry tart and red berries instead of the usual rustic grassiness. Last of the series, the Merlot is balanced and substantial, with a concentrated wild berry fragrance.

○	COF Bianco Sonata '98	🍷🍷	3
○	COF Pinot Bianco '98	🍷🍷	3
●	Va' Pensiero '96	🍷🍷	4
●	COF Cabernet Franc '98	🍷	3
●	COF Merlot '98	🍷	3
○	COF Tocai Friulano '98	🍷	3
○	COF Pinot Grigio '97	🍷🍷 (white)	3
○	COF Tocai Friulano '97	🍷🍷 (white)	3
●	Va' Pensiero '95	🍷🍷 (white)	4

DOLEGNA DEL COLLIO (GO)

Ca' Ronesca

Loc. Lonzano, 27
34070 Dolegna del Collio (GO)
tel. 0481/60034

Vine renewal continues apace at Ca' Ronesca and new experiments are under way (see our comments on the Saramago below); this was, in addition, an essentially positive year, but we still await further progress. The grapes that make up the Saramago are mostly picolit and riesling, with smaller quantities of malvasia and verduzzo; some are dried on the vine, and some on mats; all of them are selected by hand from the best bunches. The wine presents aromas of rose hip, ripe orange and raisin, and a pleasing palate that is sweet without cloying. The Pinot Grigio, which is back up to its former heights, offers an elegant and delicate bouquet with hints of apricot, wisteria and rose, all perfectly mirrored on the palate, where the fruit expands, accompanied by mineral notes. No wood is used to enhance the varietal characteristics of the Picolit: the not very intense fragrance is fairly floral; the palate is more successful, with its attractive candied orange peel entry and its long, sweet finish. The Sauvignon from the Ipplis holding, on the other hand, has a more impressive nose, which is intense, rich and reminiscent of tomato, elder blossom, ripe Golden Delicious apple and dried wildflowers; the fruity palate suggests pear. One full Glass goes to the Cabernet Franc, with its fairly intense scents of cut grass, red berries and black pepper; the palate is harmonious and well-balanced, and spice is noticeable on the finish. The oak-derived vanilla in the appealing Marnà blends well with the elegant white plum fruitiness; the Pinot Bianco and the Tocai are definitely worthwhile.

○	Collio Pinot Grigio '98	🍷🍷	3*
○	Saramago '97	🍷🍷	4
○	COF Picolit '97	🍷	5
○	COF Sauvignon Podere di Ipplis '98	🍷	4
○	Collio Bianco Marnà '97	🍷	4
●	Collio Cabernet Franc '97	🍷	4
○	Collio Pinot Bianco '98	🍷	3
○	Collio Tocai Friulano '98	🍷	3
●	Sariz '95	🍷	4
○	Collio Chardonnay '98		3
○	Collio Tocai Friulano '97	🍷🍷 (prev.)	3

DOLEGNA DEL COLLIO (GO)

Giovanni

Loc. Mernico, 7
34070 Dolegna del Collio (GO)
tel. 0481/60549

Roberto Ferreghini's winery, named after his father Giovanni, enters the Guide accompanied by the celebratory clinking of many Glasses. The estate covers seven hectares under vine, soon to be ten. Half the vineyards are in the Collio district, half in the Colli Orientali del Friuli a hundred meters away, just over the Judrio river. Annual production, which is 60% white, is of 40 to 50 thousand bottles divided among 14 different labels. Last year they were in the Other Wineries section, but they have really astonished us this time around with their incredible Merlot '97, which very nearly won Three Glasses. It displays aromas of red fruits and licorice, with an excellent woody undertone; the even, fat, structured, full-bodied and long palate shows inviting tannins. The merlot- and refosco-based Rosso Giovanni, which spent 14 months in 20-quintal oak barrels, is almost as good: the concentrated, fruity nose has a harmonious note of hay and spice; the palate is mellow, rich in glycerin, full of substantial fruit and both tannic and soft. The Pinot Bianco has an uncommon fullness of flavor and combines the rich notes of apple and pear with a warm, rounded structure. The Merlot '96, the product of a relatively poor vintage, is another excellent wine: complex and long, it is held back by a hint of volatile acidity. The Cabernet Franc '97 is similar in quality; the varietal notes in its complex bouquet have a certain elegance; the tannins are well integrated into the fat palate. The splendid palate of the Pinot Grigio is both elegant and full, and offers a fruity softness; the clean Tocai Friulano has average length and a lovely clear pear fragrance. The simple and properly made Sauvignon shows just a hint of bell pepper.

●	COF Rosso Giovanni '97	🍷🍷	4
●	Collio Merlot '97	🍷🍷	4
○	Collio Pinot Bianco '98	🍷🍷	3*
●	Collio Cabernet Franc '97	🍷	4
●	Collio Merlot '96	🍷	4
○	Collio Pinot Grigio '98	🍷	3
○	Collio Tocai Friulano '98	🍷	3
○	COF Sauvignon '98		3

La Rajade
Loc. Restocina, 12
34070 Dolegna del Collio (GO)
tel. 0481/639897

Romeo Rossi, the young wine-maker who runs La Rajade, is accumulating precious experience, thanks in part to the advice of Professor Zironi from the University of Udine. He has presented a range of excellent wines from the almost seven hectares that belong to the estate and some rented vineyards. The terrain reaches the Slovenian border and is all steeply sloping, which means that it requires a lot of hard work. This year Romeo has presented just one red wine from the '98 vintage, a fair Cabernet Franc with some lactic notes on the nose and pronounced tannins and acidity in the mouth. This demonstrates the wisdom of the decision not to bottle most of the '98 reds, which were badly hurt by rains during the harvest. We eagerly await the Merlot and the Stratin '97, which will be released early in 2000. The Sauvignon '98 is highly distinguished, as is its wont; intense aromas of elder blossom, tomato leaf and peach follow through beautifully onto the forthright, rich palate. The Tocai reminds you that this variety is a close relation of the sauvignon; it has the family vegetal nose with notes of nettle and a hint of tomato leaf, followed by a soft entry on the palate, which departs fat and succulent, with a final echo of green pepper. After an initial faint sulfurous note the Chardonnay opens up with sweet floral and distant citrus scents; it is mouth-filling and long. The Collio Bianco Caprizzi di Marceline ("caprice of Marcellina", Romeo's grandmother), is made from malvasia, ribolla, tocai, sauvignon, verduzzo and, in our opinion, chardonnay. It is somewhat muffled by overbearing toasty oak, but complex fruitiness and a balanced acidity manage to make their presence felt. It may not have been quite ready when we tasted it, and it should, we think, improve.

○ Collio Chardonnay '98	TT	4
○ Collio Sauvignon '98	TT	4
○ Collio Tocai Friulano '98	TT	3*
○ Collio Bianco Caprizzi di Marceline '96	T	4
● Collio Cabernet Franc '98		3
○ Caprizzi di Marceline	YY	4

DOLEGNA DEL COLLIO (GO)

Venica & Venica
Via Mernico, 42
Loc. Cero
34070 Dolegna del Collio (GO)
tel. 0481/60177 - 0481/61264

If anyone in Italy can be considered a sauvignon specialist, Gianni and Giorgio Venica can, without the shadow of a doubt. These two immediately likeable brothers are aided by Gianni's wife, the energetic Ornella, who is in charge of public relations and certainly seems to know what she's about. The estate produces two monovarietal Sauvignons, the standard one and the version made from grapes grown in the Ronco delle Mele vineyard, which has a nearly northern exposure and a supplementary irrigation system that keeps aromas intact even through punishingly hot, dry summers. The vintage '98 is, like its predecessors, extraordinary, with the characteristic, intense and elegant fragrance of elder blossom, peach leaf and bell pepper echoed beautifully on the palate, which has a full-bodied entry, an opulent, concentrated development and an absolutely delectable finish. The simpler version offers a concentrated nose of elder blossom and yellow peach skin; a lovely evenness on the palate leads into a distinctly nectarine-toned finish. The same grape has the upper hand in the complex fruity bouquet, dominated by elder flower and tomato leaf, of the Prime Note '97, a blend of chardonnay, tocai friulano, sauvignon and ribolla gialla; the complex, broad and very rich palate makes an extraordinary impact, displaying citrus fruit, peach, wild flowers and apple. The Vignis is made from chardonnay, tocai and sauvignon picked from various plots when fully ripe; it has aromatic and wild strawberry notes. Other excellent wines are the warm, soft Tocai, the elegant, fleshy Pinot Bianco with its citrus finish, and the crisp Pinot Grigio.

○ Collio Sauvignon Ronco delle Mele '98	TTT	4
○ Collio Pinot Bianco '98	TT	4
○ Collio Pinot Grigio '98	TT	4
○ Collio Sauvignon '98	TT	4
○ Collio Tocai Friulano '98	TT	4
○ Prime Note '97	TT	4
○ Collio Chardonnay '98	T	4
○ Vignis '97	T	4
● Collio Merlot Perilla '95		5
● Collio Rosso delle Cime '95		5
○ Collio Pinot Bianco '96	YYY	4
○ Collio Sauvignon Ronco delle Mele '97	YYY	4
● Collio Merlot Perilla '94	Y	5

DUINO-AURISINA (TS)

KANTE
LOC. PREPOTTO, 3
FRAZ. S. PELAGIO
34011 DUINO-AURISINA (TS)
TEL. 040/200761

In the last few years Kante has had to shoulder a heavy burden of investment in both vineyard and cellar (and you should have a look at them, if, that is, you manage to find yourself a slot among Edi's numerous engagements), a fact which, like it or not, conditions both production and commercial decisions. And yet the appealing Edi Kante continues to collect a rich array of Glasses. He would seem to have settled permanently into his role as "beacon of the Carso", not least because his extensive experimentation with native grape varieties is beginning to bear fruit. Apropos of which, notwithstanding his stated intention to stop making Terrano, he is still producing it, to our great delight; it may never become a Château Ausone, but if the cuisine of the Carso calls for a red that cuts through rich, fat food, and is full and aggressive like the winters around these parts, let's hope it's as good as this one, with its rich notes of raspberry, vanilla custard and pepper. Among the other wines, the Chardonnay is again fascinating; an elegant and aromatic nose is the prelude to the customary full, dry, long and alcohol-rich palate with a fruity tone reminiscent of green banana and melon. Wisteria introduces an excellent, sweet and winning Malvasia, and then reappears on the refreshing palate, where well-judged alcohol takes the edge off the acidity. Sour plum and apple stand out on the nose of the green-tinged Vìtovska, which is free and easy and not as delicate as it seems in the mouth. We close with another classic, the Sauvignon, which testifies to Edi's unfailingly elegant hand; his skill with oak has allowed him to create a fresh and fruity wine that is lifted out of the ordinary by its lactic notes and the softness of its mellow structure.

○	Carso Chardonnay '97	⚲⚲ (black)	5
○	Carso Malvasia '97	⚲⚲ (black)	5
○	Carso Sauvignon '97	⚲⚲ (black)	5
○	Carso Vìtovska '97	⚲⚲ (black)	5
●	Carso Terrano '95	⚲ (black)	4
○	Chardonnay '90	⚲⚲⚲	4
○	Chardonnay '94	⚲⚲⚲	4
○	Sauvignon '91	⚲⚲⚲	4
○	Sauvignon '92	⚲⚲⚲	4
○	Carso Chardonnay '96	⚲⚲	4
○	Carso Sauvignon '96	⚲⚲	4

FAEDIS (UD)

PAOLINO COMELLI
VIA DELLA CHIESA, 8
LOC. COLLOREDO
33040 FAEDIS (UD)
TEL. 0432/711226 - 0432/504973

The notary Pierluigi Comelli has put together a fine team which produces good results year after year. But then the expertise of Fabio Coser and the increasing skill of Roberto Ottogalli, the winery's oenologist, are beyond question. Comelli's drive, and his strong will to succeed, can upon occasion clash with the rhythms imposed by agriculture and oenology. We were impressed by the Tocai Friulano '98, in particular by its substantial nose dominated by a pleasing and elegant apple fragrance; the structure in the mouth is less concentrated than might be expected, but we are nevertheless dealing here with an excellent wine. The intensely ruby-hued Merlot '97 has a grassy vein and a faint, not unpleasant hint of the stable in its fragrance; these testify to a complexity that translates into a dense, full-bodied palate with notes of cherry and baked plum, well-rounded tannins and a long finish. The Pinot Grigio has a strikingly elegant nose, with fruit salad under the sway of an agreeable apple note; the palate is substantial, rich, crisp and soft. The Sauvignon, far from being aggressive, could almost be described as faint on the nose, at least during our tastings, but the palate shows body and a good balance between acidity and richness. The clean and enchanting Chardonnay displays average complexity on the properly executed and long palate. The Bianco Locum Nostrum, which refers to the name the patriarchs of Aquileia gave to Colloredo di Soffumbergo, is made from barrique-fermented chardonnay and sauvignon; the splendid color is followed by a nose of ripe white- and yellow-fleshed fruit; citrus notes in the mouth reveal a slightly pronounced acidity. The Rosso Soffumbergo '97, a Bordeaux blend with tannins that are still rough and astringent, is worthy of note.

●	COF Merlot '97	⚲⚲ (black)	3
○	COF Tocai Friulano '98	⚲⚲ (black)	3
○	COF Bianco Locum Nostrum '97	⚲ (black)	4
○	COF Chardonnay '98	⚲ (black)	3
○	COF Pinot Grigio '98	⚲ (black)	3
○	COF Sauvignon '98	⚲ (black)	3
●	COF Rosso Soffumbergo '97		4

FARRA D'ISONZO (GO)

Borgo Conventi

Strada Colombara, 13
34070 Farra d'Isonzo (GO)
tel. 0481/888004

There have been many new developments this year in the Vescovo household, and hence also in "Master Gianni's" winery, starting with his close collaborators: his daughter Barbara will look after business and public relations together with Gianni himself, whose expertise is renowned; Erica, his second daughter, will be in charge of the cellar and production, while the oenologist Paolo Corso supervises the work in both vineyard and cellar, together with Alberto Toso. The last piece of news is that Gianni is organizing a second auction (the first was for the '88 vintage), this time for the Braida Nuova 2000, which will naturally involve everyone. But let's get down to the wines. The Chardonnay Colle Russian '97, which was in the running for Three Glasses, is really extraordinary. We were struck by the sweet fruit on the nose, nicely amalgamated with wisely judged wood that underpins the great length of the full and even palate. We found the fragrance of the Collio Chardonnay '98 almost austere; on the palate it opens slowly but is definitely promising: it should develop and improve over time. The Braida Nuova '96, a Bordeaux-style blend, is clearly the child of an ungenerous vintage; on the nose it has notes of custard, but also of unripe blackberry, all echoed in the mouth, where the fruit is pervaded by a vein of acidity which however supports the long and appealing finish. The stylish Collio Merlot from the most recent vintage has cherry tart to the fore on the nose and a fair tannic structure on the palate. The Cabernet Sauvignon and the Schioppettino, both '98s from the Isonzo DOC district, also deserve mention.

○	Collio Chardonnay Colle Russian '97	🍷🍷	4
●	Braida Nuova '96	🍷	5
○	Collio Chardonnay '98	🍷	4
●	Collio Merlot '98	🍷	4
○	Collio Tocai Friulano '98		4
●	Friuli Isonzo Cabernet Sauvignon Braida Colombara '98		4
●	Friuli Isonzo Schioppettino La Colombara '98		4
●	Braida Nuova '91	YYY	6
●	Braida Nuova '93	YY	5
●	Braida Nuova '94	YY	5
●	Braida Nuova '95	YY	5

FARRA D'ISONZO (GO)

Casa Zuliani

Via Gradisca, 23
34070 Farra d'Isonzo (GO)
tel. 0481/888506

Claudio Tomadin, director of marketing for Bruna Zuliani's winery, told us that a couple of bad hail showers at the end of May and the beginning of August had adversely affected the quality of this year's wines, especially the Sauvignon. However, we have to give this winery credit for the good standards - albeit in a minor key - it has managed to maintain in such an inauspicious year. From its 14 hectares of vines, some in the Collio district, some in Isonzo, the winery has selected a few very successful wines, starting with the barrique-aged Merlot Gospel '97 (musical names are frequently in evidence) from the Collio. Hints of spicy stewed bell peppers on the nose are overlaid by intense fruitiness; the palate displays a compact structure, good balance, and pervasive grassy and fruity notes; the peppers are echoed appealingly on the finish. The '98 Chardonnay dell'Isonzo came very close to Two Glasses: its golden tones serve as an overture to varietal aromas of crusty bread and yeast, followed by a dense-textured palate supported by appropriate acidity. The Chardonnay Collio '98 is less varietal but equally successful: clear notes of pineapple lead on to an elegance that goes nicely with the substantial structure in the mouth. The Pinot Bianco is redolent of peach and fresh apple, beautifully mirrored on a palate with a long finish. The Pinot Grigio is, not unusually, less stylish, but it compensates quite satisfactorily with distinct apple aromas and a succulent palate. The Cabernet Sauvignon Fandango del Collio did very well, and the Sauvignons, one from Collio and the other from Isonzo, and also the Tocai Friulano, are all definitely worthy of mention.

●	Collio Merlot Gospel '97	🍷🍷	4
●	Collio Cabernet Sauvignon Fandango '97	🍷	4
○	Collio Chardonnay '98	🍷	3
○	Collio Pinot Bianco '98	🍷	3
○	Collio Pinot Grigio '98	🍷	3
○	Friuli Isonzo Chardonnay '98	🍷	3
○	Collio Sauvignon '98		3
○	Collio Tocai Friulano '98		3
○	Friuli Isonzo Sauvignon '98		3
●	Collio Cabernet Franc Habanera '96	Y	3
●	Collio Merlot Gospel '96	Y	4

FARRA D'ISONZO (GO)

COLMELLO DI GROTTA

VIA GORIZIA, 133
34070 FARRA D'ISONZO (GO)
TEL. 0481/888445

As of the spring of '99, Luciana Bennati, the founder of this wine estate covering some 15 hectares under vine in the Collio and Isonzo del Friuli DOC districts, is no longer with us. However, almost as a last homage, a range of really splendid wines has emerged from the Colmello di Grotta cellar, which is in the capable hands of Fabio Coser. The top of the line this year is the Isonzo Cabernet Sauvignon '97; fermented in stainless steel and aged in wood, it reveals intense, complex and lingering aromas of fruit steeped in alcohol and antique furniture, which are perfectly mirrored on the substantial, fleshy, mouth-filling and long palate. The excellent Pinot Grigio also comes from the Isonzo DOC district; a richly fruity and remarkably complex nose accompanies an even palate that shows good balance between acidity and warm alcohol. The Collio version has a little too much acidity, and is leaner in the mouth as a result. The partly wood-fermented Collio Chardonnay has a captivating bouquet that includes a hint of vanilla; its harmonious and complex palate gives it an edge on the Isonzo Chardonnay, a denizen of stainless steel. Vines that have seen some 30 summers lend an extra dimension to the Tocai Friulano Collio, with its dry, succulent, complex and clean-tasting palate that displays a characteristic almondy note on the finish. The Collio Bianco Rondon '98, a blend of steel-fermented pinot grigio and sauvignon and barrique-fermented chardonnay, a wine made for keeping a while, is reminiscent of vanilla as well as apricot, banana and green apple. Of the other wines, all One Glass winners, the generous and full-bodied Collio Merlot '97, from very high-density vines, deserves special mention; the nose combines creaminess with concentrated fruit.

○	Collio Chardonnay '98	🍷🍷	3*
○	Collio Tocai Friulano '98	🍷🍷	3*
●	Friuli Isonzo Cabernet Sauvignon '97	🍷🍷	3*
○	Friuli Isonzo Pinot Grigio '98	🍷🍷	3*
○	Collio Bianco Rondon '98	🍷	3
●	Collio Merlot '97	🍷	4
○	Collio Pinot Grigio '98	🍷	3
○	Collio Sauvignon '98	🍷	3
○	Friuli Isonzo Chardonnay '98	🍷	3
○	Friuli Isonzo Sauvignon '98	🍷	3

FARRA D'ISONZO (GO)

★ VINNAIOLI JERMANN

VIA MONTE FORTINO, 21
FRAZ. VILLANOVA
34070 FARRA D'ISONZO (GO)
TEL. 0481/888080

Silvio Jermann, more than anyone else, represents Friuli oenology. Say what you like of his wines, but one thing is certain: you can find them all over the world. Although he still has some years to go before he hits 50, Silvio has built up a vast amount of experience, and not just in Italy, so current achievements are the result of years and years of work. In his spectacular cellar and estate every last detail is looked after, and his appealing, fresh, and long-lasting wines are a reflection of their creator. Once again, Jermann has hit two bull's-eyes, missing a third by a shadow ("As usual!" we can hear him saying). Let's consider the Vintage Tunina '97, a blend of chardonnay, sauvignon, picolit and some aromatic varieties, which emphatically confirms its reputation as an even and mouth-filling top-flight wine; an enormous and complex bouquet with notes of tomato leaf and mixed fruit introduces a palate that could be described as an unending symphony of fruit on a rich, elegant and fleshy body. And then there's the Capo Martino '97, made from tocai and pinot and aged in oak that you simply cannot detect, so overwhelming is the extraordinary fruity richness of the wine. "Complex", "concentrated", "fat", "extremely rich", "warm", "elegant" and "full of extract" are some of the comments it provoked from our tasters. Once again the Dreams, vintage '97 this time, doesn't quite make it to the top ranks, but is excellent nonetheless; it's both fruity and floral and shows well-dosed wood, softness, lots of body and a succulent, piquant finish. Of the monovarietals, the Chardonnay made us sit up and take notice, and the Afix Riesling, the Pinot Grigio and the Vinnae are all very successful.

○	Capo Martino '97	🍷🍷🍷	6
○	Vintage Tunina '97	🍷🍷🍷	6
○	Chardonnay '98	🍷🍷	4
○	Pinot Grigio '98	🍷🍷	4
○	Riesling Afix '98	🍷🍷	4
○	Vinnae '98	🍷🍷	4
○	Were Dreams, Now It Is Just Wine! '97	🍷🍷	6
○	Pinot Bianco '98	🍷	4
●	Red Angel '98	🍷	4
○	Sauvignon '98		4
○	Capo Martino '93	YYY	6
○	Vintage Tunina '94	YYY	6
○	Vintage Tunina '95	YYY	6
○	Vintage Tunina '96	YYY	6

FARRA D'ISONZO (GO)

VITTORIO PUIATTI
VIA DANTE, 69
34070 FARRA D'ISONZO (GO)
TEL. 0481/809922

We're delighted by Vittorio Puiatti's well-deserved return to the Guide. His is a great name in the wine-making world, and not just in Friuli, since Vittorio has worked in various Italian regions during his long career. In Friuli he runs the Farra d'Isonzo winery, which buys its grapes in from growers who are well aware that their produce will be examined carefully to see that it comes up to high standards. Of the wines we tasted this year, we were particularly impressed by the Chardonnay '98, which spent its time exclusively in stainless steel and did not undergo malolactic fermentation. (Indeed it's advisable not even to utter the word "wood" around Puiatti.) This harmonious wine is one of his classics; notes of yeast and banana on the nose precede a fruity, elegant and long palate with considerable but well-judged acidity. The Chardonnay Archetipi '96 comes a few points lower down the scale, but is an admirable wine, although it should be drunk up in a hurry. Varietal characteristics come through clearly and it has a long palate. The Ribolla Gialla, with its characteristic nose of fresh fruit and wildflowers, shows remarkable balance between acidity and green apple in the mouth, together with lots of substance and great length. The Pinot Grigio, which is better on the nose than in the mouth, offers a wealth of fruity aromas, but has less body than might have been expected. A faint fragrance of elder blossom and pronounced acidity characterize the Sauvignon; the medium-bodied Merlot '96 is redolent of undergrowth and wild cherry tart.

○	Collio Chardonnay '98	TT	3
○	Collio Chardonnay Archetipi '96	T	5
○	Collio Pinot Grigio '98	T	3
○	Collio Ribolla Gialla '98	T	3
●	Collio Merlot '96		4
○	Collio Sauvignon '98		3

FARRA D'ISONZO (GO)

TENUTA VILLANOVA
VIA CONTESSA BERETTA, 29
FRAZ. VILLANOVA
34070 FARRA D'ISONZO (GO)
TEL. 0481/888593

"On the 5th of April, 1499, while the excitement generated by Columbus' recent discovery of the New World continued to make people all over Europe dream of adventure, wealth and glory... the Tenuta Villanova first saw the light, in Farra d'Isonzo, Italy..." So begins the press release announcing the celebrations for the 500th anniversary of Tenuta Villanova. We consider the Yuletide release of a very limited number of bottles of wood-aged red Fraja '95 and a 20-year-old Fraja grappa to be an even more appropriate celebratory event. We have contributed to the festivities at this winery, which is directed by Paolo Cora, by assigning Three Glasses to a stupendous Chardonnay Monte Cucco. Indeed, there were by chance actually two wines contending for the top grade in this anniversary year. But back to the Chardonnay: the intense and elegant nose displays notes of ripe apricot, banana and yeast; the palate, after an impressive entry, is even, full-bodied and extraordinarily balanced, with sweet fruit that reappears on the long finish. The other excellent and very characterful wine is the Sauvignon Monte Cucco '98, which boasts distinct aromas of elder blossom and tomato leaf; a full and opulent attack is followed by an incredible expansion on the palate and a lingering finish. In the Tocai Friulano Isonzo we again find a particularly harmonious and complex bouquet, which is fruity (pear and apple) rather than floral, with a fresh vegetal vein that enhances, instead of diminishing, the richness of the wine. The Pinot Grigio Collio is characterized by a fruity entry on the even and long palate. The concentrated Menj Rosso, made from merlot, cabernet franc, cabernet sauvignon and petit verdot, is redolent of cherries steeped in alcohol and hay.

○	Collio Chardonnay Monte Cucco '97	TTT	4
○	Collio Sauvignon Monte Cucco '98	TT	4
○	Friuli Isonzo Tocai Friulano '98	TT	3
○	Collio Pinot Grigio '98	T	3
●	Menj Rosso '96	T	3
●	Collio Pinot Nero Monte Cucco '95		5
○	Collio Chardonnay Monte Cucco '96	YY	4
○	Collio Sauvignon Monte Cucco '96	YY	4
○	Collio Tocai Friulano '97	YY	3
○	Menj Bianco '97	YY	3

GONARS (UD)

DI LENARDO
VIA BATTISTI, 1
FRAZ. ONTAGNANO
33050 GONARS (UD)
TEL. 0432/928633

Massimo di Lenardo never fails to surprise us: first by imparting his own personal style to the business side of his winery and then, not content with this, by taking charge, as of this year, of the wine-making, with the help of a team of experts. Changes are usually detrimental to quality at the outset, so we expected the wines to be somewhat undefined this time. Instead we were confronted with Di Lenardo's best year yet. So let's get down to the wines. The Tocai Friulano is excellent, as is its wont: its intense bouquet is reminiscent of crusty bread, ripe pear and sage; it enters the mouth with attractive varietal notes of almond and develops lusciously into a long, lingering finish. The equally admirable Chardonnay Musque suggests with its intense aromas of banana and tropical fruit that this is a concentrated wine, and indeed, after an entry on the palate which is notable for finesse, it expands into an opulent mid palate with appropriate echoes of banana, and then just keeps going. The Ronco Nolè, a Bordeaux-style blend, shows that it's possible to make a first-rate red wine in the Grave district: nicely balanced notes of chocolate and coffee emerge on a background of black cherry jam. One Glass wines worthy of note include the Pinot Bianco, with its delicate fragrance of white flowers and apple; a curious vanilla tone appears on the straightforward and fairly persistent palate. Le Madri, a blend of pinot bianco, sauvignon and tocai, is the first offering in their new Santa Pazienza range, which will be dedicated to affordable excellence. The refreshing and fruity bouquet and palate of this debutant were immediately appealing. For reasons of space, we make just a brief mention of the elegant and varietal Sauvignon, and of the Merlot, which comes into its own on the palate.

○	Friuli Grave Chardonnay Musque '98	🍷🍷	3*
○	Friuli Grave Tocai Friulano '98	🍷🍷	3*
●	Ronco Nolè '97	🍷🍷	3*
●	Friuli Grave Cabernet '98	🍷	3
●	Friuli Grave Merlot '98	🍷	3
○	Friuli Grave Pinot Bianco '98	🍷	3
○	Friuli Grave Sauvignon Blanc '98	🍷	3
○	Le Madri Santa Pazienza '98	🍷	2*
○	Friuli Grave Chardonnay Woody '98		3
○	Friuli Grave Pinot Grigio '98		3

GORIZIA

ATTEMS CONTE DOUGLAS
VIA GIULIO CESARE, 36/A
FRAZ. LUCINICO
34170 GORIZIA
TEL. 0481/390206

Count Douglas Attems was the head - and guiding light - of the Collio wine consortium for decades; in accepting his resignation, the producers opted unanimously to appoint him honorary president. Free of the day-to-day pressures of running the Consorzio, the 85-year old Douglas Attems can finally devote his time to the winery, with the help of his daughter Virginia, who got her degree in modern languages and is determined to give this historic estate a new lease on life. Virginia, who is now the head of the board of managers, insisted on having Fabio Coser as oenologist. The winery owns some 30 hectares under vine in the Collio district, as well as a couple of hectares in the Isonzo zone; together, these produce about 150 thousand bottles per year. The very successful Sauvignon Ronco Pelicans is soft, rich and well balanced, with clear scents of elder blossom and a long fruity finish. The Ribolla Gialla and the Malvasia Ronco Bratinis are two wines that almost won Two Glasses, both made from native grape varieties; the crisp and elegantly floral Ribolla Gialla is underpinned by a characteristic acidity, and the Malvasia has an excellent bouquet and admirable length. The Pinot Grigio Ronco Pelicans, with its distinct notes of apple and a perfect correspondence between nose and palate, has just a little too much acidity on the finish. The Tocai Friulano Ronco Rupis is succulent, clean and rather full-bodied, while the Collio Bianco Vintage Castel Pubrida, made from tocai, malvasia, ribolla gialla and riesling italico, falls just short of One Glass. Although the year was a poor one for reds, those produced by this winery, including the Vintage Castel Pubrida, a blend of merlot and cabernet franc, got One Glass each.

○	Collio Sauvignon Ronco Pelicans '98	🍷🍷	4
●	Collio Cabernet Franc Ronco Trebes '98	🍷	4
○	Collio Malvasia Ronco Bratinis '98	🍷	4
●	Collio Merlot Ronco Bratinis '98	🍷	4
○	Collio Pinot Grigio Ronco Pelicans '98	🍷	4
○	Collio Ribolla Gialla Ronco Bratinis '98	🍷	4
●	Collio Rosso Vintage Castel Pubrida '98	🍷	4
○	Collio Tocai Friulano Ronco Rupis '98	🍷	4
○	Ribolla Gialla Brut		4

GORIZIA

FIEGL
LOC. LENZUOLO BIANCO, 1
FRAZ. OSLAVIA
34170 GORIZIA
TEL. 0481/31072

The Pinot Grigio makes an elegant first impression, wafting notes of wild herbs and distant hints of honey; then, in the mouth, we find the classic fresh, fruity, rather neutral, fine-textured and bitterish wine. A similar tale can be told of the Pinot Bianco, which has, however, a slightly riper fragrance and a more rounded palate. The Ribolla is, as we might expect, vigorous, a little uncouth, but also forthright and long, the ideal accompaniment for fish dishes (cooked without tomato). The successful Sauvignon displays aromas of tomato leaf and rue that re-emerge on the rather long finish after a refreshing entry and a textbook development on the palate. The same goes for the Leopold Blanc, based on sauvignon, tocai, ribolla and pinot bianco, which comes on like a pleasing alcoholic infusion of herbs and cane sugar; it develops consistently in the mouth, showing the acid notes that seem to characterize all the Fiegl wines. The red version, Leopold Rosso, a blend of merlot and cabernet franc, is somewhat disappointing; after scents of slightly stewed fruit, this wine is a little too sharp-edged and roughly tannic on the palate. We preferred the Merlot, with its nose reminiscent of walnut skin and red currant; after a soft attack it has a dry mid palate, returning to rather light fruit on the finish. Their range is properly made, varied and traditional. But from the brothers Alessio, Giuseppe and Rinaldo Fiegl, who run this 25-hectare property dating back to 1782, we've been hoping for something more, not least because all the evidence at our disposal – the quality of the cellar, the terroir, their ability and previous vintages – leads us to believe that they have it in them to do better.

● Collio Merlot '97	🍷	4
○ Collio Pinot Bianco '98	🍷	3
○ Collio Pinot Grigio '98	🍷	3
○ Collio Ribolla Gialla '98	🍷	3
○ Collio Sauvignon '98	🍷	3
○ Leopold Cuvée Blanc '97	🍷	4
● Leopold Rosso '94	🍷	5
○ Collio Chardonnay '98		3
○ Leopold Cuvée Blanc '96	ϒϒ	4
● Leopold Rosso '93	ϒϒ	5

GORIZIA

LA CASTELLADA
FRAZ. OSLAVIA, 1
34170 GORIZIA
TEL. 0481/33670

If we were to rank the producers in the Guide according to the proportion of Glass-winning wines they have produced over the years, Giorgio and Nicolò Bensa's estate would certainly be very near the top, both because their wines are always well made, and because they have deliberately limited their range to just a few distinctive bottles, a trend that we hope will be more widely followed, and not only in Oslavia. You'll find no review of their red this year: so little of it was produced that they opted not to present it, and we were also unable to acquire the Bianco Selezione. We did, however, taste the Sauvignon, which was immediately recognizable as such. (It is La Castellada policy to produce monovarietal wines, with the exception of ribolla, only in outstanding years.) A bouquet of elder blossom, apricot, honey and vanilla with lactic tones introduces an impressive palate that develops in a smooth yet clearly distinguishable sequence of sensations. From the initial warmth of the alcohol it passes to the velvety softness of the structure; then, by way of contrast, the crispness of the acidity kicks in, followed by the juicy fleshiness of the fruit, with a finish that mirrors the nose. The same hand can be discerned in the Bianco, a barrique-fermented blend of tocai friulano, pinot grigio, chardonnay and a small amount of sauvignon; the nose, with its hints of mint and pineapple, is almost austere, and is reflected on the palate, which is immediately powerful and harmonious; although very long, it doesn't hold together perfectly in the finish because of too much toasty oak. The house style is also evident in the Ribolla: lactic aromas again, together with fresh fruity scents of yellow plum; again the palate is first creamy, then sinewy, then persistent, with dominant wood on the finish.

○ Bianco della Castellada '97	🍷🍷	5
○ Collio Ribolla Gialla '97	🍷🍷	5
○ Collio Sauvignon '97	🍷🍷	5
○ Bianco della Castellada '92	ϒϒϒ	6
○ Bianco della Castellada '94	ϒϒϒ	6
○ Bianco della Castellada '95	ϒϒϒ	6
○ Collio Chardonnay '94	ϒϒϒ	6
○ Collio Sauvignon '93	ϒϒϒ	6
○ Bianco della Castellada '96	ϒϒ	5
○ Collio Ribolla Gialla '96	ϒϒ	5
● Rosso della Castellada '94	ϒϒ	6

GORIZIA

PRIMOSIC
VIA MADONNINA DI OSLAVIA, 3
FRAZ. OSLAVIA
34170 GORIZIA
TEL. 0481/535153

Things are not going altogether smoothly in the neighborhood of Oslavia, so we're particularly thankful for producers like the Primosic family, who can always be counted on to produce good wines. And in fact, this year Silvestro, Marko and Boris are again taking home quite a nice collection of Glasses. We'll start with our favorite, the Ribolla Gialla, which has the intense color that betrays some time spent in wood; a nose of milk, honey, and flowers introduces the impressive palate where acidity and alcohol blend with vanilla and elder blossom. The Picolit, a classic, elegant wine, a little heady and floral on the nose, expands into a mellow, sweetish palate. The well-made, crisp, dry and lively Sauvignon has a lingering finish on a note of green. The pronounced alcohol of the Chardonnay, while it masks to some extent the aromas of hazelnut and banana, does provide a good counterbalance to the persistent and vigorous acidity. The Klin, a blend of chardonnay, sauvignon and ribolla fermented and matured in new barriques and then bottle-aged, although admirably dense-textured, sacrifices some of its length and follow-through from nose to palate to the intrusive wood. The coppery-hued Pinot Grigio, with its rather faint bouquet of white flowers and crusty bread, and an equally light palate, what with the warmth of the alcohol and the citric finish, is altogether a bit small. The Merlot has not yet found itself: this year's version still has the dense and even texture of the '95, but some discordant notes on both nose and palate get in the way.

○	Collio Chardonnay Gmajne '98	🍷🍷	4
○	Collio Picolit Ris. '95	🍷🍷	6
○	Collio Ribolla Gialla Gmajne '98	🍷🍷	4
○	Collio Sauvignon Gmajne '98	🍷🍷	4
●	Collio Merlot Ris. '96	🍷	4
○	Collio Pinot Grigio Gmajne '98	🍷	4
○	Klin Ris. '96	🍷	4
○	Collio Chardonnay Gmajne '97	YY	4
●	Collio Merlot Ris. '95	YY	4
○	Collio Ribolla Gialla Gmajne '96	YY	4

GRADISCA D'ISONZO (GO)

MARCO FELLUGA
VIA GORIZIA, 121
34072 GRADISCA D'ISONZO (GO)
TEL. 0481/99164 - 0481/92237

Marco Felluga is not just the landmark figure known to us all: he is also the creator of one of the most significant and best-functioning wine-producing groups in Italy. The winery which bears his name could be considered the mother house or, in less religious terms, group HQ. The Marco Felluga estate has grapes of its own, from the Carantan and Molamatta vineyards, and grapes bought in from its long-time grower-suppliers, whose ties with the winery are so close that they follow its lead even in vine planting and training. Felluga always markets a wide range of good, reliable wines. This year we particularly liked the Carantan, with an appealing cherry note accompanying the typical cabernet franc characteristics in a long, complex palate that closely echoes the nose. The whites, which are all vinified with skin contact, also made a good showing, as can be seen from the crisp, fruity and elegant Pinot Grigio and the eminently drinkable Tocai, with its charming floral notes. Further successes are the white Molamatta, a blend of ribolla, tocai and pinot bianco, with 10% of wood-fermented pinot, which is just a touch leaner than in previous years, the simple and straightforward Sauvignon, the somewhat neutral but well-executed Pinot Bianco and the Chardonnay, with its fresh apple tone. The Cabernet and the Sauvignon are worthy of mention; the pleasingly aristocratic Moscato Rosa, a wine for special occasions, is the best of its kind to be found in the region.

●	Carantan '96	🍷🍷	5
○	Collio Chardonnay '98	🍷	4
○	Collio Pinot Bianco '98	🍷	4
○	Collio Pinot Grigio '98	🍷	4
○	Collio Tocai Friulano '98	🍷	4
○	Molamatta '98	🍷	4
⊙	Moscato Rosa '98	🍷	5
●	Collio Cabernet '97		4
○	Collio Sauvignon '98		4
●	Collio Merlot '97	YY	4

MANZANO (UD)

Bandut

Via Orsaria, 32
33044 Manzano (UD)
tel. 0432/740315

As of this year the paths of Giorgio and Elisabetta Colutta have divided, these two cousins having chosen different directions for the future. Giorgio Colutta has kept the Bandut name and about ten hectares of the estate, to which he has added two that he rents. He is aiming ambitiously high, as he is the first to admit, but he is firmly determined to pursue excellence and we shall be following his progress with interest. For now we shall review the best wines presented this time, most of which won One Glass. The white-vinified Pinot Grigio has attractive notes of apple and pear both on the nose and in the mouth; the finish is underpinned by an agreeable acidity. The bouquet of the Pinot Bianco offers unusual notes of tropical and citrus fruit; the dense-textured palate shows excellent balance between acidity and fruit. By now we are used to the finesse and elegance of the Colli Orientali del Friuli Bianco Nojâr, (the word for walnut in Friuli dialect), made from ribolla gialla and chardonnay; a fragrance of wildflowers and apple introduces a harmonious, crisp palate with a long finish. Two red wines also made the grade: the Refosco dal Peduncolo Rosso '97 displays aromas of red berry tart with a vein of licorice, which carry through onto the spicy palate; the Rosso Selenard '97, a schioppettino and pinot nero blend, releases a bouquet of medicinal herbs, cherry and black cherry; the even palate exhibits pronounced and not fully tamed tannins. The Chardonnay '98 is redolent of dried flowers but lacks focus in the mouth, while the effects of an unpropitious vintage can be seen in the imperfect balance of the Merlot '98.

○	COF Bianco Nojâr '98	🍷	4
○	COF Pinot Bianco '98	🍷	3
○	COF Pinot Grigio '98	🍷	3
●	COF Refosco P. R. '97	🍷	3
●	COF Rosso Selenard '97	🍷	4
○	COF Chardonnay '98		3
●	COF Merlot '98		3

Walter Filiputti

P.zza dell'Abbazia, 15
Loc. Rosazzo
33044 Manzano (UD)
tel. 0432/759429

Walter Filiputti is forging ahead. But then anyone who knows this controversial character will have observed his driving ambition to become one of the recognized leaders of Friuli wine-making. And it must be admitted that his intuition and excellent palate enable him to create innovative blends with great potential. The wines Filiputti presented at our tastings this year did very well indeed. The top bottle is the Picolit Riserva '97, made from grapes left to dry until the beginning of December and then fermented and aged in 110-liter casks: a fragrance of custard, banana and apricot jam is followed by a concentrated, sweet and alcohol-rich palate with masses of sweet fruit and extraordinary length. The late-harvested Picolit '97 is sweet, elegant, structured, full, soft, harmonious and lingering. The Bianco Poiesis (which means "something created" in Greek), a blend of tocai, chardonnay, pinot bianco and just a little picolit, manages to combine elegance and complexity with breadth and substance. The successful Pinot Grigio '98 is fat, full, and fruity, with agreeable toasty notes. The 906 Ronco dei Benedettini '97 (906 is the number of years since the monks entered the Abbey of Rosazzo; the next version should be 907), made from merlot from 50-year old vines with a touch of cabernet franc, is a big wine offering undergrowth, red berry tart, smooth tannins, a full body and length. We reserve judgment on the Ronco degli Agostiniani and the Ronco del Monastero until we can make a fuller assessment; the Pignolo needs more time to mature.

●	COF 906 Ronco dei Benedettini '97	🍷🍷	6
○	COF Bianco Poiesis '98	🍷🍷	4
○	COF Picolit '97	🍷🍷	5
○	COF Picolit Ris. '97	🍷🍷	6
○	COF Pinot Grigio '98	🍷🍷	4
○	COF Bianco Ronco degli Agostiniani '97	🍷	5
○	COF Bianco Ronco del Monastero '98	🍷	4
○	COF Ribolla Gialla '98	🍷	4
●	COF Rosso Pignolo '96	🍷	6
●	Broili di Filip		4
●	Pignolo '95	ΥΥ	6

MANZANO (UD)

Le Vigne di Zamò

Via Abate Corrado, 4
Loc. Rosazzo
33044 Manzano (UD)
tel. 0432/759693

Last year the new administrative offices of this winery came into operation, with splendid guest accommodation in the annex. And now the brothers Pierluigi and Silvano Zamò have inaugurated their huge new underground cellar, and are presenting all their wines under a single imprint. Our good wishes have happily taken the form of a Three Glass award for the fabulous Ronco dei Roseti '94, a Bordeaux-style blend with the addition of some local varieties. A bouquet of red berry tart blended with elegant notes of tar and licorice is a prelude to a concentrated, complex and powerful palate with lots of body, structure and tannin, as well as the acidity that was a feature of the vintage but in this case is not at all displeasing. Next in line is the classic Bianco Ronco delle Acacie, made from chardonnay, tocai and pinot bianco fermented separately in barriques, where they also complete their malolactic fermentation. Aromas of banana, yeast and ripe melon carry through onto the crisp and fruity palate. The Tocai Vigne Cinquant'anni, made from grapes grown on selected old vines on the hills near Buttrio (the name means 50-year-old vines), impressed us very favorably with its richly fruity, full and open fragrance and its complex, crisp, even and lingering palate. Jasmine and tropical fruit characterize the nose of the Malvasia; in the mouth we found an excellent balance between acidity and fruit. The golden Pinot Bianco Tullio Zamò '95 shows its wood but is still an excellent and harmonious wine, with aromas of vanilla, apple and banana. The Pinot Bianco '98 offers a fresh fragrance of green apple and lemon grass, a softly fruity palate and an elegant finish. The Verduzzo, with a touch of sweetness, is more successful on the nose than in the mouth, while the Merlot follows through beautifully.

●	Ronco dei Roseti '94	🍷🍷🍷	5
○	COF Bianco Ronco delle Acacie '96	🍷🍷	4
○	COF Malvasia '98	🍷🍷	4
●	COF Merlot '97	🍷🍷	4
○	COF Pinot Bianco '98	🍷🍷	4
○	COF Pinot Bianco Tullio Zamò '95	🍷🍷	4
○	COF Tocai Friulano Vigne Cinquant'Anni '97	🍷🍷	4
○	COF Verduzzo Friulano '94	🍷🍷	4
○	COF Bianco Vino di Lâ '98	🍷	3
●	COF Cabernet '97	🍷	4
○	COF Ribolla Gialla '98	🍷	4
●	Pignolo '95	🍷	6
●	Tazzelenghe '94	🍷	6

MANZANO (UD)

Ronchi di Manzano

Via Orsaria, 42
33044 Manzano (UD)
tel. 0432/740718

Although Roberta Borghese, the owner of Ronchi di Manzano (45 hectares of vineyards and 10 of olive groves) has not won another Three Glasses this time, it must be admitted that she came very close with the Merlot Ronc di Subule '97: a spicy fragrance of berries and wild cherry and plum tart is mirrored on the smoothly and astringently tannic palate with its long finish. Unlike most producers in Friuli, Roberta seems to have specialized in red wines, for which she maintains an extremely low yield per vine and per hectare. And indeed the Cabernet Franc, despite the youth of the vines, releases a concentrated fragrance of red berries, followed by a dense, richly fruity and intense palate with lots of structure and alcohol as well as smooth tannins. The Cabernet Sauvignon, with more pronounced wood on its nose and palate, is equally good; this is a rich, full-bodied wine, with dominant cherry and spice. The Refosco, strikingly dense in color, lives up to expectations: although oaky notes are still in evidence, this wine is fat, structured, mouth-filling and even, with distinct notes of pepper, wild cherry and prune. From her vines in Rosazzo Roberta produces the Rosazzo Rosso: here too wood stands out clearly on the nose, but it is on the palate that this wine, which has great potential for development, expresses its power and richness and shows quite well-integrated tannins. Some of the whites too are extraordinarily harmonious and rich, starting with the Chardonnay, fermented and matured in 26-liter barrels of French oak; then there is the Rosazzo Bianco, which spends time in barrels of varying sizes, and the Verduzzo, matured in 113-liter barrels.

●	COF Cabernet Franc '97	🍷🍷	4
●	COF Cabernet Sauvignon '97	🍷🍷	4
○	COF Chardonnay '98	🍷🍷	4
●	COF Merlot Ronc di Subule '97	🍷🍷	5
●	COF Refosco P. R. '97	🍷🍷	4
○	COF Rosazzo Bianco '98	🍷🍷	4
○	COF Rosazzo Picolit '97	🍷🍷	5
●	COF Rosazzo Rosso Ronc di Rosazzo '97	🍷🍷	4
○	COF Verduzzo Friulano Ronc di Rosazzo '97	🍷🍷	4
●	COF Merlot '97	🍷	4
○	COF Pinot Grigio '98	🍷	4
○	COF Tocai Friulano Sup. '98	🍷	4
●	COF Merlot Ronc di Subule '96	YYY	5

MANZANO (UD)

RONCO DELLE BETULLE
VIA A. COLONNA, 24
LOC. ROSAZZO
33044 MANZANO (UD)
TEL. 0432/740547

Of course it would be nice to have a sort of subscription to Three Glasses, but in the long run this would remove the element of surprise that is one thing we can be sure of in the unpredictable world of wine. This consideration serves to remind us that what counts is not so much winning Three Glasses, as creating a solid tradition of excellence. With her "10-hectare passion", as she calls it, located in the Rosazzo subzone, Ivana Adami is achieving just this. The appealingly fleshy and even Tocai boasts balance and fruity freshness. The Pinot Grigio releases mineral aromas just a little tainted by sulfur; the palate is agreeably fresh and long. The other Pinot, with its clean fragrance of Golden Delicious apple, is softer and more elegant thanks to its generous alcohol. The warm and fruity Narciso Bianco, a blend of chardonnay and sauvignon, is fairly substantial, creamy and soft, although a bit forward. The reds are good too. The Narciso, maintaining high standards, displays cherry tart and macaroon on the nose; after a balanced and fairly substantial attack it evolves to a mid palate where the tannins are a little too noticeable, although soft (quite promising for future development) and then on to a fruity finish that mirrors the bouquet. The Franconia is a wine worth tasting; made from the grape of the same name, it does not, admittedly, have many competitors, but some comparisons with wines from farther north have confirmed its value; the palate opens on notes of blackberry and ink, then becomes increasingly grapey and fresh, but at the same time meaty and mouth-filling. The Cabernet Sauvignon is another success.

●	COF Rosazzo Narciso Rosso '96	🍷🍷	5
○	COF Tocai Friulano '98	🍷🍷	4
●	Franconia '97	🍷🍷	4
●	COF Cabernet Sauvignon '97	🍷	4
○	COF Pinot Bianco '98	🍷	4
○	COF Pinot Grigio '98	🍷	4
○	COF Rosazzo Narciso Bianco '97	🍷	4
○	COF Rosazzo Picolit '98	🍷	6
○	COF Rosazzo Ribolla Gialla '98		4
●	Narciso Rosso '94	🍷🍷🍷	5
○	COF Tocai Friulano '97	🍷🍷	3
○	COF Narciso Bianco '96	🍷	4

MANZANO (UD)

TORRE ROSAZZA
LOC. POGGIOBELLO, 12
33044 MANZANO (UD)
TEL. 0432/750180

You need but glance at the bottom of the page to see that Torre Rosazza, owned by Genagricola, makes good wines. The agronomist Claudio Flaborea and the oenologist Giovanni Tomadoni are determined to make them even better, but in the wake of the extensive recent replanting they are dealing with vines that are not yet mature enough to produce outstanding results. The Merlot L'Altromerlot '96 is again very good. Once the alcoholic and malolactic fermentations have taken place the wine is transferred to barriques, where it is left to mature for as long as is necessary, which is never less than 15 months. Intense and well-delineated aromas of plum and cherry are followed by a forceful entry on the palate; the fruit in the bouquet emerges again as the wine unfolds, together with a note of licorice and characterful tannins. The elegant fresh apple on the nose of the Pinot Bianco reappears on the palate enriched by fresh fruits and a distant hint of peach, all underpinned by a crisp acidity. The Sauvignon is redolent of tomato leaf and faint elder blossom and has an attractively forthright and even palate: One very full Glass. The round and easy Pinot Grigio did equally well thanks to its unusual elegance on the nose and a palate that skillfully combines acidity and mellowness. The considerable alcohol in the intense Verduzzo Friulano seems to smother the fruit, while the well-structured Refosco shows characteristic spicy notes. The wood in the Tocai Friulano is not fully balanced; the refreshing Merlot '98 is reminiscent of black cherry and is just a bit too tangy.

●	COF Merlot L'Altromerlot '96	🍷🍷	5
○	COF Pinot Bianco '98	🍷🍷	3
○	COF Pinot Grigio '98	🍷	3
●	COF Refosco P. R. '97	🍷	3
○	COF Sauvignon '98	🍷	3
○	COF Verduzzo Friulano '97	🍷	4
●	COF Merlot '98		3
○	COF Tocai Friulano '98		3
●	COF Cabernet Sauvignon Ronco della Torre '95	🍷🍷	4
●	COF Merlot L'Altromerlot '94	🍷🍷	5
●	COF Merlot L'Altromerlot '95	🍷🍷	5

MARIANO DEL FRIULI (GO)

EDDI LUISA

VIA CORMONS, 19
LOC. CORONA
34070 MARIANO DEL FRIULI (GO)
TEL. 0481/69680

The whole Luisa family works with a passion on their 45-hectare estate in the Isonzo Doc district, with father Eddi and mother Nella helping their two sons Michele (oenologist) and Davide (agronomist). The picture is completed by a well-equipped up-to-the-minute cellar and a surprising (given the youth of the two "technicians") skill in the use of wood. The soil around Corona might have been designed for producing red wines, rich as it is in iron and aluminum. We'll start with the Merlot, which is intense, yet balanced and stylish; aromas of quinine, rose hip, mint, coffee and spice precede a powerful entry on the palate, where it develops with elegant fruity notes of wild cherry. The Cabernet Franc has a distinctly fruity bouquet with well-blended notes of coffee, quinine and violet; on the palate, after a good fruity entry, vanilla and coffee fuse on the long finish. The key features of the Refosco are milky coffee, blackberry jam and pepper. Another wine from the same range, the Cabernet Sauvignon, just missed winning Two Glasses; its complex, warm aromas of chocolate, black cherry and rose hip together with distinctive candied orange reappear on the not very long or fleshy palate. The excellent Cabernet Sauvignon from the standard range confirms the winery's gift for red wines: extremely varietal, it has beautifully blended fruity, grassy and spicy notes. And what of the whites? The Pinots deserve One full Glass apiece. The Grigio has an attractive bouquet and luscious tropical fruit well balanced with floral notes on the palate. The Bianco has the same white peach and crusty bread on the palate that it releases on the nose. The Sauvignon is a good wine too.

●	Friuli Isonzo Cabernet Franc I Ferretti '97	🍷🍷	4
●	Friuli Isonzo Cabernet Sauvignon '97	🍷🍷	3
●	Friuli Isonzo Merlot I Ferretti '97	🍷🍷	4
●	Friuli Isonzo Refosco P. R. I Ferretti '97	🍷🍷	4
●	Friuli Isonzo Cabernet Sauvignon I Ferretti '97	🍷	4
○	Friuli Isonzo Pinot Bianco '98	🍷	3
○	Friuli Isonzo Pinot Grigio '98	🍷	3
○	Friuli Isonzo Sauvignon '98	🍷	3
○	Friuli Isonzo Chardonnay '98		3

MARIANO DEL FRIULI (GO)

MASUT DA RIVE

VIA MANZONI, 82
34070 MARIANO DEL FRIULI (GO)
TEL. 0481/69200

This historic winery in the Isonzo DOC district is deservedly back in the Guide. Masut da Rive is the nickname of the Gallo family, which has been running this 18-hectare estate for many years. Everything revolves around the evident enthusiasm and passion for experimentation of young Fabrizio, who follows the vinification and maturation processes personally. Fabrizio is convinced that quality should be pursued at all costs, with all that this entails: hyperoxygenation of the must, with a very limited use of sulfur dioxide, modern vine planting and training methods and constant renewal of the vines. The result is an excellent range of wines. We were struck by the intensely ruby red Cabernet Sauvignon; on the nose blackberry and cherry jam, tobacco and white pepper are presented with finesse and elegance, to reappear at the entry on the palate, with a wild cherry note that lingers through the warm, creamy mid palate. A marvelous wine! The Merlot, with an elegant fleshiness that indicates richness, releases aromas of plum and blackberry jam, quinine, tobacco, chocolate, coffee and mint. In the mouth it's perhaps a bit straightforward, but very attractive all the same. And now for the whites. The excellent oak-fermented Chardonnay Maurùs is redolent of vanilla, ripe banana and dried flowers, which are all fully mirrored in the mouth, where a pleasing, long finish is under the influence of banana and tea. The Tocai Friulano has a Mediterranean tone, thanks to its scents of crusty bread and distinctive apricot. The Sauvignon has a particularly well-matched nose and palate, while the Pinot Bianco is varietal and properly made.

●	Friuli Isonzo Cabernet Sauvignon '97	🍷🍷	3*
○	Friuli Isonzo Chardonnay Maurùs '97	🍷🍷	4
●	Friuli Isonzo Merlot '97	🍷🍷	3
○	Friuli Isonzo Sauvignon '98	🍷🍷	3
○	Friuli Isonzo Tocai Friulano '98	🍷🍷	3
●	Friuli Isonzo Cabernet Franc '97	🍷	3
○	Friuli Isonzo Pinot Bianco '98	🍷	3
○	Friuli Isonzo Pinot Grigio '98	🍷	3
○	Friuli Isonzo Chardonnay '98		3

MARIANO DEL FRIULI (GO)

★ VIE DI ROMANS
LOC. VIE DI ROMANS, 1
34070 MARIANO DEL FRIULI (GO)
TEL. 0481/69600

Gianfranco Gallo's wines have the curious tendency to divide their numerous admirers into factions that demonstrate a passionate and unwavering loyalty to their favorite bottle. As a result, before the Guide comes out there is an annual feverish ferment, typical of quite another endeavor, about which will win, place or show. This year it was the Sauvignon Piere that took Three Glasses, and everybody wins: the nose starts off a little closed, but opens out immediately like a peacock's tail with warm scents of elder blossom, white peach and fresh cream; in the mouth the wine expands smoothly from one sensation to the next, long and mellow, with a grace found only in great wines. This time the Vieris came in second, but only by a neck: as usual it is long and elegant, with a well-matched nose and palate; lactic and fruity aromas are in evidence, but it's less substantial than the Piere. The '97 vintage was great for pinot grigio, witness the Dessimis: the classic, green-tinged straw color introduces a fruity and intense nose and a concentrated, succulent and very elegant palate. The Flors di Uis, a blend of chardonnay and malvasia with full malolactic fermentation, with the addition of riesling, is reminiscent of apple and cinnamon; this is an exceptionally harmonious wine, but recent versions had led us to expect greater concentration and a more complex bouquet. The powerful and dense Chardonnay has a bitter finish, a little roughness on the palate and an off note on the nose which keep it from making a better showing.

O	Friuli Isonzo Sauvignon Piere '97	🍷🍷🍷	4
O	Friuli Isonzo Chardonnay Vie di Romans '97	🍷🍷	4
O	Friuli Isonzo Pinot Grigio Dessimis '97	🍷🍷	4
O	Friuli Isonzo Sauvignon Vieris '97	🍷🍷	4
O	Friuli Isonzo Bianco Flors di Uis '97	🍷	4
O	Friuli Isonzo Bianco Flors di Uis '96	999	4
O	Friuli Isonzo Chardonnay '91	999	4
O	Friuli Isonzo Sauvignon Piere '93	999	4
O	Friuli Isonzo Sauvignon Vieris '95	999	4
O	Friuli Isonzo Sauvignon Vieris '92	999	4
O	Friuli Isonzo Sauvignon Vieris '93	999	4

NIMIS (UD)

DARIO COOS
VIA RAMANDOLO, 15
33045 NIMIS (UD)
TEL. 0432/790320

Dario Coos, the most important and modern producer of Verduzzo di Ramandolo, is composing a series of "variations on a theme", i.e. some admirable experiments in how to get the most out of a white grape that has a lot in common with red ones, starting with a skin rich in mouth-puckering tannins. This is the feature that makes this wine immediately recognizable, but it has also been a limit to its excellence. Hence we welcome Dario's attempts – and anyone else's too – to give greater elegance to a wine that is not to everyone's liking. The most promising path would appear to involve drying the grapes, perhaps after late harvesting, followed by fermentation and long aging in small wooden barrels. Dario's young Ramandolo Il Longhino '98, which has known only stainless steel, is redolent of honey and grass; these both turn up again on the classic palate dominated by baked apple; one's tongue does tend to stick to one's upper palate. The golden-toned Ramandolo '97, from grapes picked at the beginning of November, offers a sequence of apple, raisin and honey on the nose; it is sweet and alcohol-rich in the mouth, with some notes of crispness and varietal tannins. The Ramandolo Romandus '97 is the excellent result of careful mat-drying of the grapes; of a brilliant golden hue, it wafts concentrated scents of raisin, dried fruit and toffee apple which carry through onto a fleshy, sweet and balanced palate with enough volatile acidity to keep it from cloying, and with a hint of noble rot and tannins under control. Lastly, the Picolit Romandus '96, with its intense greeny-golden yellow color, has a rich bouquet of very ripe and dried fruit; there's a great concentration of fruit on the thick, sweet, dense and almost unctuous palate.

O	COF Picolit Romandus '96	🍷🍷	6
O	COF Ramandolo Romandus '97	🍷🍷	6
O	COF Ramandolo '97	🍷	5
O	COF Ramandolo Il Longhino '98	🍷	4
O	COF Ramandolo '96	99	5

PAVIA DI UDINE (UD)

BASTIANICH

V.LE GRADO, 4
FRAZ. LAUZACCO
33050 PAVIA DI UDINE (UD)
TEL. 0432/675612

Lidia Bastianich and her son Giuseppe run not just one but four restaurants in Manhattan, as well as one in Kansas City, Missouri. The family idée fixe is high quality, whatever their activity; thus, after years of working together with Valter Scarbolo, Lidia and Giuseppe decided to buy just over five hectares under vine on the slopes near Buttrio, in the the midst of the Colli Orientali del Friuli DOC zone. For the time being they use Scarbolo's cellar for vinification, where they have the advice of the consultant oenologist Maurizio Castelli. Waine Young, who assists the Bastianich family in selecting the wines for their American restaurants, is also active in the winery. Because of the rains, it was not possible to gauge the full potential of the red grapes in this first harvest, but the white ones produced excellent results. The Vespa, a blend of barrique-aged chardonnay and picolit with sauvignon matured in stainless steel, is a great success. The bright green-gold color introduces a fragrance of citrus fruit, custard, milk and dried flowers; the extraordinarily complex palate is both crisp and fleshy, with a long, fruity finish. The Bastianich idea for the Tocai Friulano Plus was to blend this classic Friuli wine with over 10% of a late-harvested version. The nose has, indeed accentuates, the varietal notes of apple seed and almond, and the palate is excitingly full-bodied and characteristic. The Pinot Grigio, with its notes of pear and apple and a honeyed tone, climbs ever closer to Two Glasses. Lastly, the standard version of the Tocai Friulano took home One full Glass.

○ COF Tocai Friulano Plus '98	🍷🍷	4
○ Vespa '98	🍷🍷	4
○ COF Pinot Grigio '98	🍷	4
○ COF Tocai Friulano '98	🍷	4

PAVIA DI UDINE (UD)

PIGHIN F.LLI

V.LE GRADO, 1
FRAZ. RISANO
33050 PAVIA DI UDINE (UD)
TEL. 0432/675444

This year the Pighin winery opted to amaze us with a couple of extremely well-made wines from Grave del Friuli, one of which, the Chardonnay, is tremendously good value for money. It is not easy to hit the high notes when you are responsible for 140 hectares of vineyards in the Grave DOC district and 30 in the Collio, with correspondingly large production levels, so we have to give oenologist Paolo Valdesolo credit for creating wines that are generally well executed, and occasionally really splendid. It's a pity that the Collio vineyards are laid out in the old style, with an eye more to quantity than to quality, but the winery plans to improve them, with denser plantings. And so to the Grave Chardonnay: we were struck by the substantial, rich nose of this wine, with its characteristic toffee note; the intensely fruity palate was equally good, with classic hints of crusty bread and an impressive length. The Collio Pinot Bianco comes in second but is splendid nonetheless, offering delicate scents of apple with a hint of peach leaf, and an elegant, full and harmonious palate. The incredibly well-defined aromas of green pepper and tomato leaf in the Grave Sauvignon are echoed on the glycerin-rich palate, with green notes accenting the finish. The Sauvignon from the Collio district is less aggressive and intense, but still varietal, with an attractive fatness on the palate. A dense-textured palate characterizes their key wine, the Grave Pinot Grigio. The Grave Merlot '97 has a nose of fresh red fruit and undergrowth; the red fruit reappears on the palate, with a hint of juniper. The fruit of the Merlot Collio '97 is put in the shade by slightly rough tannins, while the Barredo, a substantial red blend, is full-bodied and long.

○ Collio Pinot Bianco '98	🍷🍷	3*
○ Friuli Grave Chardonnay '98	🍷🍷	3
○ Friuli Grave Sauvignon '98	🍷🍷	3
● Baredo '95	🍷	4
● Collio Merlot '97	🍷	3
○ Collio Pinot Grigio '98	🍷	3
○ Collio Sauvignon '98	🍷	3
● Friuli Grave Merlot '97	🍷	3
○ Friuli Grave Pinot Grigio '98	🍷	3

PAVIA DI UDINE (UD)

SCARBOLO
V.LE GRADO, 4
FRAZ. LAUZACCO
33050 PAVIA DI UDINE (UD)
TEL. 0432/675612 - 0432/675150

Valter Scarbolo's winery uses grapes produced in about nine hectares of vineyards that, in the case of the youngest vines, reach a density of 5,000 plants per hectare. Valter, an oenologist who is also a pork butcher and restaurateur, is well aware that the way to improve quality is by reducing yields, and he applies this philosophy to his wine-making. This makes for a very interesting range, with wines produced on the plains that can stand comparison with their usually more structured hill-grown rivals. He is assisted in the cellar by Emilio Del Medico, a young but highly skilled oenologist, and draws on the advice and wide-ranging experience of the excellent consultant Maurizio Castelli. Over a series of tastings we have been increasingly impressed by the Chardonnay '98, which is both intense and elegant on the nose; fat in the mouth, it offers pronounced fruit (ripe apple) and a hint of yeast, and its fresh acidity comes through particularly on the finish. The Tocai Friulano is more appealing on the nose than in the mouth, where the acidity seems to undermine its complexity; on the nose, however, it is elegant and complex, with clear scents of pear and apple. The Sauvignon, not at all aggressive, shows finesse in its bouquet of tomato leaf and elder blossom; the balanced palate has the right degree of acidity and considerable length. In the Pinot Grigio we find hints of caramel on the nose and a little rustic roughness on the palate. The Merlot '98 is something of a surprise, having done quite well in such a poor year for reds: the nose is reminiscent of wax furniture polish and berries, with an undertone of citrus fruit; these follow through on the tannic and lingering palate.

○	Friuli Grave Chardonnay '98	🍷🍷	3*
●	Friuli Grave Merlot '98	🍷	3
○	Friuli Grave Pinot Grigio '98	🍷	3
○	Friuli Grave Sauvignon '97	🍷	3
○	Friuli Grave Tocai Friulano '98	🍷	3
●	Friuli Grave Merlot '97	♀♀	3
●	Friuli Grave Merlot Campo del Viotto '95	♀	4

PINZANO AL TAGLIAMENTO (PN)

ALESSANDRO VICENTINI ORGNANI
VIA SOTTOPLOVIA, 2
FRAZ. VALERIANO
33090 PINZANO AL TAGLIAMENTO (PN)
TEL. 0432/950107

Alessandro Vicentini Orgnani, a young but well-established Friuli winegrower, makes good use of his terrain and of the occasional help of Fabio Coser, and so has presented another range of excellent wines this year. This was an impressive vintage for whites, with the Pinot Bianco and the Chardonnay, both from the Braide Cjase line, for which partial use of barriques is envisaged, leading the way. The Pinot impressed us immediately with its rich varietal scents of ripe apple perfectly balanced with mango, vanilla and dried flowers. The Chardonnay exhibits an intense and harmonious nose of banana and mango; the keynote of the palate is elegance, which helps make up for the slight lack of concentration. The Pinot Grigio offers fine aromas of ripe white-fleshed fruit and broom flowers, which are echoed on the palate, where fruit has the upper hand and the finish is not very long. The Pinot Grigio Braide Cjase is another good wine: its attractive complex scents of white plum, wisteria and vanilla precede a not particularly concentrated palate where white plum is overlaid by wood-derived vanilla notes. The Tocai has an excellent bouquet, with varietal notes of almond accompanied by white flowers and rue; these are found again on the elegant, balanced palate, with a refreshing acidity on the finish. The Sauvignon, which has long been a dependable wine, has not let us down this time either: the standard version is agreeably redolent of elder flower with a light note of rose hip; the Braide Cjase has, in addition, attractive ripe fruit well blended with vanilla on both nose and palate.

○	Friuli Grave Chardonnay Braide Cjase '98	🍷🍷	3*
○	Friuli Grave Pinot Bianco Braide Cjase '98	🍷🍷	3*
○	Friuli Grave Pinot Grigio '98	🍷	3
○	Friuli Grave Pinot Grigio Braide Cjase '98	🍷	3
○	Friuli Grave Sauvignon '98	🍷	3
○	Friuli Grave Sauvignon Braide Cjase '98	🍷	3
○	Friuli Grave Tocai Friulano '98	🍷	2
●	Friuli Grave Cabernet Sauvignon '97		3

POVOLETTO (UD)

Teresa Raiz
Via della Roggia, 22
Loc. Marsure di Sotto
33040 Povoletto (UD)
tel. 0432/664144

The Tosolini brothers' winery hasn't done this well for years. This is good news, not least because their production is so large (250 thousand bottles) compared to the Friuli average. They vinify grapes grown on their own property as well as some grown in rented vineyards; when necessary they also buy in grapes from other growers. Two excellent wines won Two Glasses each. The first was the Chardonnay Le Marsure, which is intense, complex and elegant on the nose, with varietal hints of yeast and crusty bread; the dense-textured, persistent palate is lightened by a fresh acidity that lends it great appeal. The Tocai Friulano, the other particularly impressive wine, offers a marked fragrance of Golden Delicious apple on an extremely enticing background of citrus fruit, all echoed on the long, even palate, with a vegetal note accentuated by pronounced acidity. The Sauvignon has an attractively concentrated nose that suffered somewhat at our tastings from a touch of sulfur undoubtedly destined to disappear before long. If we had judged this wine just by its palate, which is mellow, full, fat, and complex with a beautiful balance between acidity and alcohol, it would have scored a great deal higher. The Decano Rosso `96, made from cabernet sauvignon, cabernet franc and merlot, has a bouquet of well-judged wood and fully ripe red fruit leading to a complex palate with tannins a bit accentuated by acidity. The two Cabernets did well too; we had a slight preference for the grapey Grave version, with notes of bell pepper on the nose; there is some astringency on the palate, for which the tannins can be held responsible. The Cabernet dei Colli Orientali del Friuli is reminiscent of ripe fruit.

○ COF Tocai Friulano '98	🍷🍷	3
○ Friuli Grave Chardonnay Le Marsure '98	🍷🍷	3
● COF Cabernet '98	🍷	3
● COF Rosso Decano Rosso '96	🍷	5
○ COF Sauvignon '98	🍷	4
● Friuli Grave Cabernet Le Marsure '98	🍷	3
○ COF Pinot Grigio '98		3
○ Friuli Grave Pinot Grigio '98		3
● Decano Rosso '95	🍸	5

PRADAMANO (UD)

Fantinel
Via Cussignacco, 80
33040 Pradamano (UD)
tel. 0432/670444

Under the watchful eye of the young Marco Fantinel, improvement and enlargement are continuing apace. A new winery was purchased recently in Friuli: the objective here will be very high standards, to be pursued with the help of excellent consultant oenologists, and a start has already been made. But what of the wines that were actually presented? There has definitely been a further marked improvement, although results are still somewhat uneven. The first Two Glass wine from the Fantinel winery is the Collio Pinot Bianco: straw-colored with golden highlights, it offers intense, elegant fragrances of vanilla, white flowers and ripe pear, which follow through on the fleshy palate, where the ripe pear in particular lingers at length; vanilla rules the long finish. Then there are the admirable reds. The nose of the Cabernet Sauvignon offers a good balance between fruit (black cherry and plum) and spice; it enters the mouth with the same fruit, and develops into a long coffee finish. The Merlot releases very rustic grassy and animal aromas; after a fruity attack on the palate it offers length and very soft tannins. The Refosco has scents of plum, cherry, red currant and sage; the palate, although not particularly concentrated, is attractively fruity and long. The Brut produced by this winery traditionally offers notes of dried fruit and nuts: this year too, attractive walnut, date and yeasty bread characterize both nose and palate. The Picolit, probably tasted on an off day, was slightly discordant.

○ Collio Pinot Bianco Vigneti Sant'Helena '98	🍷🍷	4
○ Fantinel Brut '95	🍷	4
● Friuli Grave Cabernet Sauvignon Vigneti Sant'Helena '97	🍷	4
● Friuli Grave Merlot Vigneti Borgo Tesis '97	🍷	3
● Friuli Grave Refosco P. R. Vigneti Sant'Helena '97	🍷	4
○ Collio Chardonnay Vigneti Sant'Helena '98		4
○ COF Picolit '98		5

PRATA DI PORDENONE (PN)

VIGNETI LE MONDE

VIA GARIBALDI, 2
LOC. LE MONDE
33080 PRATA DI PORDENONE (PN)
TEL. 0434/626096 - 0434/622087

A visit to Piergiovanni and Antonella Pistoni's estate is always a very agreeable experience. As you approach it from the road you get a good view of the well-preserved 18th-century farmhouse. Piergiovanni and his oenologist Luigi Franco, who has practically grown up in this winery, produce good wines. This year two in particular stood out: the Pinot Grigio and the Cabernet Franc. The first has staked everything on finesse: attractive mineral, pear and white flower notes on the nose are pleasingly mirrored on the well-balanced palate. The Cabernet Franc has characteristic grassy scents balanced with notes of ripe plum and, towards the end, roasted coffee; the palate is predominantly fruity, with a top note of plum. Another appealing wine is the Sauvignon, produced with selected native yeasts: it has attractive varietal scents of ripe tomato. The white blend, Bianco, a new departure for this winery, is an assemblage of tocai (70%), chardonnay (20%) and sauvignon (10%). The immediate impression on the nose is of tomato leaf and broom; after a lovely and promising fruity entry on the palate, there is not much of a finish. The two important house reds, the Querceto and the Cabernet Riserva, are very pleasing. The first, a typical Bordeaux blend, releases grassy notes of new-mown hay that blend well with hints of plum, blackberry and tobacco; the agreeable grassiness of cabernet franc dominates a palate where the tannins are still somewhat rough. The Cabernet offers striking, not altogether characteristic fruity aromas (merlot): these follow through in the mouth, with tannins that are still a trifle hard but will undoubtedly be softened by a few months' aging.

○	Friuli Grave Bianco '98	🍷	3
●	Friuli Grave Cabernet Franc '97	🍷	3
●	Friuli Grave Cabernet Ris. '95	🍷	4
○	Friuli Grave Pinot Grigio '98	🍷	3
○	Friuli Grave Sauvignon '98	🍷	3
●	Querceto '95	🍷	4
●	Friuli Grave Cabernet Sauvignon '97		3
○	Friuli Grave Chardonnay '98		3
●	Friuli Grave Pinot Nero '97		3
●	Friuli Grave Cabernet Franc '96	🍷🍷 (empty)	3
●	Friuli Grave Refosco P. R. '97	🍷 (empty)	3
●	Querceto '94	🍷 (empty)	4

PREMARIACCO (UD)

DARIO E LUCIANO ERMACORA

VIA SOLZAREDO, 9
FRAZ. IPPLIS
33040 PREMARIACCO (UD)
TEL. 0432/716250

For more than twenty years the brothers Dario and Luciano Ermacora have been vinifying the grapes from their lovely, well-ordered 15-hectare estate on the hills near Ipplis. With this solid experience behind them, they are well placed to pursue innovative approaches based on mature judgment rather than a reckless thirst for adventure. This leads each year to the creation of a range of reliably good wines. The '97 Merlot is particularly successful: after an initial rustic moment the bouquet releases pronounced grassy scents that gradually make way for ripe fruit and mint; the palate is not particularly complex, but it echoes the nose and is agreeable. The extremely characteristic Tocai offers intense, balanced aromas of bitter almond and green apple. The Verduzzo Friulano, 15-20% of which spent some time in barriques, came close to Two Glasses: attractively golden in appearance, it has an elegant nose with keynotes of baked apple, ripe white plum and Golden Delicious apple. The palate is fat, with an appealing cooked apple tone; it finishes on a distinct note of candied orange peel with refreshing acidity. The Sauvignon, which stakes all on the finesse and elegance of its elder flower and ripe pear nose, merits One full Glass: it has a fleshy, broad and reasonably long palate with an agreeable reappearance of pear on the finish. The Pinot Bianco has distinctive golden highlights, and a bouquet of ripe fruit and hazelnut; in the mouth it is fruity and not particularly full, but there's a lovely citrus finish. The last three wines, all worthy of note, are the very varietal Refosco, the Cabernet Sauvignon and the Pinot Grigio, which has been thinned by excessive acidity.

●	COF Merlot '97	🍷🍷	3
○	COF Pinot Bianco '98	🍷	3
○	COF Sauvignon '98	🍷	3
○	COF Tocai Friulano '98	🍷	3
○	COF Verduzzo Friulano '98	🍷	3
●	COF Cabernet Sauvignon '97		3
○	COF Pinot Grigio '98		3
●	COF Refosco P. R. '97		3

PREMARIACCO (UD)

Fiore dei Liberi

Via Case Sparse, 21
Fraz. Ipplis
33040 Premariacco (UD)
tel. 0432/716501

In its second year of bottling, the Case Sparse – Fiore dei Liberi estate makes a masterly entry into the ranks of first-class producers. Purchased in 1991 by Giancarlo and Simone Tognacchini, the vineyards have been laid out anew on truly spectacular terraces and provided with an emergency drip irrigation plant. The cellar was completed in 1997; although it is perfectly equipped for vinifying "international" varieties, the principal aim here is to raise high the banner of the region's native wines. In 1998 they purchased a further plot of land, bordering on the existing property, which means that the vines now extend over about 12 hectares. Simone Tognacchini, the agronomist, manager and head of production, benefits from the celebrated expertise of the consultant oenologist Luca D'Attoma, and is further helped in the cellar by Renato Cozzarolo. The best wine we tasted was the white assemblage, Le Pleiadi '98, based on wood-aged tocai friulano with sauvignon, picolit and a very small percentage of other white grapes. The fragrance is intense and complex, a blend of fresh ripe fruit; the palate has a green note, with a luscious, rich consistency and a long finish. The good Ribolla Gialla is also full and soft and more fruity (apple and peach) than floral on the nose. The bouquet is mirrored on the even and long palate, which vaunts a proper varietal acidity. The Pinot Bianco, redolent of apple and jasmine, is distinguished by the elegance of its fruity palate, with a successful balance of sweetness and acidity. The Schioppettino, reminiscent of cherry and new grass on the nose, bears the signs of a difficult vintage for reds. The cabernet and merlot blend, Rosso Cassiopea, with its unresolved conflict between acidity, tannins and lactic creaminess, is perhaps still too young.

○	COF Bianco Le Pleiadi '98	▼▼	4
○	COF Ribolla Gialla '98	▼▼	3
○	COF Pinot Bianco '98	▼	3
●	COF Rosso Cassiopea '97		4
●	COF Schioppettino '98		3

PREMARIACCO (UD)

Rocca Bernarda

Via Rocca Bernarda, 27
Fraz. Ipplis
33040 Premariacco (UD)
tel. 0432/716273

Finishing the review of this winery in last year's Guide we wrote, "The estate is devoting considerable attention to its Picolit, a great local tradition". This attention has already led to a Picolit, the '97, that merits, without the shadow of a doubt, Three Glasses. The able manager Mario Zuliani told us that they are still investing, to extend the vineyards from which this Friuli wine – which, it seems, was first grown on the land around this castle, the Rocca Bernarda – is obtained. Although Marco Monchiero, their oenologist, is not from Friuli himself, he shows a distinct aptitude for this particular wine. Its bouquet leaps from the glass almost before you have raised it to your nose, releasing scents of candied peel (orange and mandarin orange) followed by dried fruit (date and fig) and almond, and a closing note of dried wildflowers. These are echoed on the sweet entry on the palate, where it develops with luscious elegance into a long-lingering finish of candied fruit, with apricot, orange, date, fig and honey standing out. The '96 version gets Two full Glasses: old gold in color, it has a nose of apricots steeped in alcohol and ripe banana, which follow through nicely in the mouth. The Merlot Centis has a rich and complex fragrance, with notes of quinine, coffee and chocolate; this complexity is echoed on the palate, where the wine is long, warm, creamy and harmonious. The Pinot Grigio, another great wine, vaunts intense aromas of dried flowers, ripe Golden Delicious apple and hazelnut; it is fat and opulent on the palate, where nuts and ripe fruit re-emerge. The Sauvignon is redolent of pear, ripe tomato and yellow flowers. Reasons of space allow us only to mention the Chardonnay, the Tocai Friulano and the Ribolla Gialla, each of which earned One full Glass.

○	COF Picolit '97	▼▼▼	6
●	COF Merlot Centis '97	▼▼	4
○	COF Picolit '96	▼▼	6
○	COF Pinot Grigio '98	▼▼	3
○	COF Chardonnay '98	▼	3
○	COF Ribolla Gialla '98	▼	3
○	COF Sauvignon '98	▼	3
○	COF Tocai Friulano '98	▼	3
●	COF Merlot Centis '95	▽▽	4
●	COF Merlot Centis '96	▽▽	4
○	COF Picolit Ris. '94	▽▽	6

PREMARIACCO (UD)

SCUBLA
VIA ROCCA BERNARDA, 22
FRAZ. IPPLIS
33040 PREMARIACCO (UD)
TEL. 0432/716258

It would seem that Roberto Scubla has opted to reduce the number of wines he produces, and to concentrate his energies on just a few monovarietals and some blends. He has finally completed the renovation of his cellar, which gives him an underground barrel-room for barriques and a well-laid-out loft, where he dries the grapes used to make his wonderful Verduzzo Graticcio. Fermented and aged in barriques, this wine has the color of old gold and aromas of peach blossom, dried fig, raisins, citrus fruit, almond paste, custard and alcohol; in the mouth it is sweet, fat, dense, almost unctuous, powerful, round, focused, mellow and extremely long. The Tocai, a classic of this winery, has an elegant, fruity nose, while the palate exhibits a fine balance of acidity and alcohol, as well as notable length. The mellow Pinot Bianco, another of Scubla's classics, is even and full-flavored, with a finish that combines power and elegance. We were also impressed by the Bianco Speziale, a blend of pinot, tocai and sauvignon, because of its complex nose with Golden Delicious apple to the fore, and its pleasing and intensely fruity palate that echoes the bouquet, carrying it through onto the finish. And now the reds: the Merlot confirms its position as Scubla's key wine: enticing aromas of cherry, wild berries and blackberry herald a broad and full-bodied palate, with fairly marked wood and pronounced tannins that will stand the wine in good stead as it develops. Excessive acidity has marred the palate of the Sauvignon, a wine that Scubla generally does a much better job with. Lastly, the Cabernet Sauvignon has substantial alcohol and a raspberry fragrance, together with a vegetal note.

○ COF Bianco Speziale '98	🍷🍷	4
● COF Merlot '97	🍷🍷	4
○ COF Pinot Bianco '98	🍷🍷	4
○ COF Tocai Friulano '98	🍷🍷	4
○ COF Verduzzo Friulano Graticcio '97	🍷🍷	5
● COF Cabernet Sauvignon '97	🍷	4
○ COF Sauvignon '98	🍷	4
○ COF Bianco Pomédes '97	YY	4
● COF Merlot '96	YY	4

PREPOTTO (UD)

IOLE GRILLO
LOC. ALBANA, 60
33040 PREPOTTO (UD)
TEL. 0432/713201

Grillo, a small and very interesting winery, is a newcomer to the Guide. Purchased in 1974 by Iole Grillo, the eight hectares under vine are now managed personally by her daughter Anna Muzzolini with the help, in both vineyard and cellar, of the skillful and diligent oenologist Lino Casella. At the moment they produce no more than 22 thousand bottles annually, but they could certainly produce more. As is the custom up here, numerous grape varieties are grown: five red and six white. The red wines all spend some time in 5-hectoliter oak barrels. We'll start with the great Tocai Friulano '98, from hillside vineyards with a yield of 32 hectoliters per hectare. This explains why, even though the mineral notes are not strongly expressed on the nose, the palate is fat, substantial, mouth-filling and remarkably long. Malolactic fermentation has given the Pinot Grigio a creamy nose with distinct scents of milk; the palate exhibits substantial structure and a lovely creaminess, the result of an even lower yield per hectare (27 hectoliters). The Sauvignon, from vineyards on the plain, has characteristic aromas of ripe bell pepper, with a hint of geranium. The '97 vintage produced successful reds here, starting with the Merlot: a fragrance of ripe red fruit and cherry and plum tart precedes a palate of great length. The Refosco has a complex and not quite elegant nose; it enters the mouth on a note of leather and continues with fruit steeped in alcohol: this is a dry and rustic but nevertheless harmonious wine. To round up, the intriguing Schioppettino displays a spicy nose of black pepper, rosemary and thyme; the pepper re-emerges on the palate, along with wild and black cherries.

○ COF Tocai Friulano '98	🍷🍷	3*
● COF Merlot '97	🍷	3
○ COF Pinot Grigio '98	🍷	3
● COF Refosco P. R. '97	🍷	3
○ COF Sauvignon '98	🍷	3
● COF Schioppettino '97	🍷	3

PREPOTTO (UD)

LA VIARTE
VIA NOVACUZZO, 50
33040 PREPOTTO (UD)
TEL. 0432/759458

La Viarte, spring, or life renewed, is the name Giuseppe Ceschin chose for his planned 21 hectares of terraces carved from the basin lying between Prepotto and Corno di Rosazzo. Today, Giuseppe and his wife Carla are flanked in the winery by their son Giulio: this family continuity, together with the consistent quality of the wines, is the most obvious sign that the planning stage is comfortably in the past and the family can now begin to consider its "tradition". We very much liked the Liende, made from tocai, pinot bianco, sauvignon and riesling, with a challenging bouquet in which the sauvignon predominates over hazelnut cream and yeast; the palate is soft, long and structured. We were equally impressed by the Chardonnay: grown on lower-lying ground and fermented in wood, it is sweet and fruity, with good, pronounced flavors that closely echo the nose. The same high quality can be found in the Siùm, made from verduzzo and picolit grapes dried naturally, given a long fermentation in barriques, left on its lees for over a year and aged in the bottle for at least six months; the resultant wine is fat, almost unctuous, with enticing scents of dried apple, apricot, walnut and fig, and a mouth-filling and honeyed palate with a vigorous counterpoint of acidity. The successful Pinot Bianco displays appealing almond and fruit; after a sweet, warm entry on the palate it shows a straightforward development, delicate and never harsh. The Sauvignon is, as usual, very characteristic; we are always on safe ground with this eminently drinkable, crisp and fruity wine. Last in the list, the Tocai, with its classic bouquet and palate: this wine is reasonably mouth-filling, but not very strong.

○ COF Bianco Liende '97	▼▼	4
○ COF Chardonnay '97	▼▼	4
○ COF Pinot Bianco '98	▼▼	4
○ Siùm '96	▼▼	5
○ COF Sauvignon '98	▼	4
○ COF Tocai Friulano '98	▼	4
○ COF Pinot Grigio '98		4
○ COF Ribolla Gialla '98		4
○ COF Bianco Liende '96	▽▽	4
● Roi '94	▽▽	4
○ Siùm '95	▽▽	5
● COF Schioppettino '95	▽	4

PREPOTTO (UD)

LE DUE TERRE
VIA ROMA, 68/B
33040 PREPOTTO (UD)
TEL. 0432/713189

In view of the commitment and diligence with which Flavio and Silvana Basilicata have been working for a long time, their achievement this year was in some respects inevitable: the four wines they presented have won a truly impressive array of glasses. Their little estate close by the Judrio river includes about seven hectares under vine. The particularly felicitous '97 vintage allowed the Basilicatas to present a Picolit Implicito and a Pinot Nero, instead of dedicating those grapes to the Sacrisassi blends. And it's just this Rosso Sacrisassi, a blend of refosco and schiopettino of which about 7,000 bottles are produced, that bears the palm. The grapes come from vineyards with a yield per hectare of less than 5,000 kilos and are harvested in the second week of October; the wine spends 20 months in barrels and in barriques of French and Slovenian oak. The fruity and creamy bouquet offers notes of plum tart, blackberry and pink peppercorns; in the mouth this extremely long wine displays character and complexity, with pronounced, but not hard, tannins, and a dense texture from which berries, black cherry, pepper and cinnamon emerge. The incredible Picolit Implicito requires close attention; then it unveils all its great complexity: the nose is reminiscent of apricots steeped in alcohol, banana, honey, milk and vanilla; in the mouth it exhibits ripe fruit and almond paste, accompanied by felicitous acidity on the long finish. The Pinot Nero is right on target this year: its austere nose, with bitter chocolate and tar, is echoed on the mellow palate, together with cherries in syrup, well-judged tannins and acidity. To finish, the Bianco Sacrisassi, made from tocai, sauvignon and ribolla gialla, has aromas of tomato leaf, bell pepper, almond and jasmine, with an undertone of clove; the softness of this wine is proof against its acidity.

● COF Rosso Sacrisassi '97	▼▼▼	4
○ COF Bianco Sacrisassi '97	▼▼	4
● COF Pinot Nero '97	▼▼	5
○ Implicito '97	▼▼	6
○ Implicito '96	▽▽	6
● Sacrisassi Rosso '96	▽▽	4
● Sacrisassi Rosso '94	▽	4

PREPOTTO (UD)

PETRUSSA
VIA ALBANA, 49
33040 PREPOTTO (UD)
TEL. 0432/713192

The brothers Gianni and Paolo Petrussa never seem to put a foot wrong. It's a pity that, among all their good bottles, there are no Two Glass wines this year, but the Verduzzo Pensiero '96 did come very close: of the color of old gold, it has a broad, creamy bouquet with a wealth of very ripe fruit, including apple, fig and candied citrus peel, as well as nougat; these are echoed on the palate, which has considerable freshness, notwithstanding the wine's alcoholic warmth, residual sugar and hint of noble rot. The Tocai Friulano is appealing, as usual: its intense fruit scents follow through nicely onto the even palate, where acidity underpins a long finish. The Pinot Bianco displays a fragrance of mint, chamomile and tobacco leaf; the harmonious and pleasing palate offers a blend of apple and pear with notes of apricot and peach. The Bianco Petrussa '97, about half tocai friulano with a mixture of pinot bianco, sauvignon and chardonnay, has a lovely golden hue and scents of fully ripe fruit; in the mouth it is complex, warm, firmly structured, dense in texture and persistent. Scents of smoke and elder flower characterize the nose of the Sauvignon and appear again on the palate, where this reasonably long wine exhibits nicely balanced acidity and fruit. The reds all fall short of One Glass, but the Schioppettino, a typical wine of the Albana and Prepotto zones, almost got it, thanks in particular to its jammy nose with lactic notes, and to the new wood that is still fairly pronounced; in the mouth, where noble and rustic notes alternate, it is a trifle discordant, and closes on a dry finish. The Rosso Petrussa '96, and the '98 Merlot and Cabernet, the products of poor vintages for the grapes in question, are simpler wines.

○	COF Bianco Petrussa '97	🍷	4
○	COF Pinot Bianco '98	🍷	3
○	COF Sauvignon '98	🍷	3
○	COF Tocai Friulano '98	🍷	3
○	Pensiero '96	🍷	4
●	COF Cabernet '98		3
●	COF Merlot '98		3
●	COF Rosso Petrussa '96		4
●	COF Schioppettino '96		4
●	COF Cabernet '97	🍷🍷	3
●	COF Rosso Petrussa '95	🍷🍷	4
○	Pensiero '95	🍷🍷	4

PREPOTTO (UD)

RONCO DEL CASTAGNETO
VIA RONCHI, 73
33040 PREPOTTO (UD)
TEL. 0432/713072

Ronco del Castagneto has been hovering in the wings for several years, and this time it has succeeded in reappearing in the Guide. Meanwhile it has changed hands, passing from Tino Parrasia to Stefano Traverso, the twenty-year-old son of Ornella Molon and Giancarlo Traverso, well-known winegrowers from the Veneto. And, as might be expected, the overall approach to production has also changed, although the wines we tasted this year were of course the fruit of the work carried out under the previous ownership. The important new developments are that Stefano intends to move to Friuli, and that he will have the benefit of the advice of the great Tuscan oenologist Luca D'Attoma. The new team will still be able to call on Lauro Iacolettig's expert help in the cellar and in the vineyard. The Tocai Friulano won us over with its fragrance of tea and apple; the intense palate exhibits substantial fruit enriched by notes of fresh citrus on the finish. The Chardonnay displays a concentrated, forthright nose with notes of yeast and crusty bread; it is complex and richly fruity in the mouth, with substantial alcohol. The Pinot Grigio shows an unusually elegant bouquet, with clean scents of apple and pear, all mirrored on the even, mouth-filling, dense-textured and long palate. The Ribolla Gialla is shy at first, but after some time in the glass it unveils its aromas of yellow plum enriched by an agreeable citric acidity. Both the Sauvignon and the moscato rosa-based Petali di Rosa are somewhat simpler. The estate's main project for the coming years is to narrow down the range of red grape varieties to make perhaps just one wine, Schioppettino: this typical Prepotto wine has a refreshing style, ideal for summer drinking. We look forward to tasting it.

○	COF Chardonnay '98	🍷🍷	3
○	COF Pinot Grigio '98	🍷🍷	3
○	COF Tocai Friulano '98	🍷🍷	3
○	COF Ribolla Gialla '98	🍷	3
○	COF Sauvignon '98		3
⊙	Petali di Rosa '98		4

RONCHI DEI LEGIONARI (GO)

TENUTA DI BLASIG
VIA ROMA, 63
34077 RONCHI DEI LEGIONARI (GO)
TEL. 0481/475480

The picture presented this year by Elisabetta Bortolotto Sarcinelli's Tenuta di Blasig is good but not exciting. Perhaps the reason is to be found in the vineyards, where the vines have low density planting with a high yield per stock, which makes concentrated, meaty, rich wines an unlikely outcome. However, the use of wood for the reds in the Gli Affreschi line has led to some good results. The wood in question is in the form of barrels of 30 hectoliters for the Merlot and of 55 hectoliters for the Cabernet, with further aging in classic barriques. The Merlot offers aromas of cherry tart and grapes preserved in alcohol, which are perfectly mirrored on the reasonably structured palate. The Cabernet came close to Two Glasses with its bouquet of custard, wood and red currant jelly; the complex and persistent palate is slightly jarred by a pronounced acidity. Of the refreshing whites we particularly enjoyed the Malvasia, which offers elegant, distinct notes of apple on the nose that return on the palate and continue, underpinned by appropriate acidity, all the way through the long finish. In the Chardonnay we found a marked lack of continuity between the nose and the palate: the ripe melon and grapefruit aromas are followed by a simple, even palate where ripeness threatens to become overripe. We could not expect an outstanding Merlot from the '98 vintage, and in fact the bouquet of this wine, cherries steeped in alcohol and undergrowth, is better than the palate, in which the fruit is overwhelmed by the tannins.

● Friuli Isonzo Cabernet Gli Affreschi '97	🍷	4
○ Friuli Isonzo Chardonnay '98	🍷	3
○ Friuli Isonzo Malvasia '98	🍷	3
● Friuli Isonzo Merlot Gli Affreschi '97	🍷	4
● Friuli Isonzo Merlot '98		3
○ Friuli Isonzo Tocai Friulano '98		3
○ Falconetto Bianco '97	🍷🍷 (white)	4

S. CANZIAN D'ISONZO (GO)

LORENZON
VIA CA' DEL BOSCO, 6
LOC. PIERIS
34075 S. CANZIAN D'ISONZO (GO)
TEL. 0481/76445

Enzo Lorenzon's winery cultivates almost 160 hectares of vineyards, with production divided between the I Feudi di Romans line, with about 15 hectares, and the Borgo dei Vassali line, from the vineyards nearest to the modern cellar. Enzo's son Davide, an oenologist, works alongside his father in the cellar, while his other son, Nicola, is in charge of the orchards. Again this year the wines from the I Feudi di Romans line are generally fresh, always at least well executed and sometimes decidedly good. The Malvasia Istriana, with scents of dried flowers and apple, is very attractive on the palate, thanks to its lovely balance of ripe fruit and acidity; the long finish makes you want to have another sip. In the Pinot Grigio the aromas are reminiscent of yellow plum and, again, apple; these are echoed on the palate, which vaunts a balanced acidity. This year's Tocai Friulano is a reminder that this grape is related to sauvignon: indeed it even shows a faint note of tomato leaf; this is echoed in the mouth, where one finds good weight and evenness. There is apple on the nose of the Pinot Bianco, but also yeast and crusty bread, almost as though the pinot bianco vines were mixed with chardonnay, which is not such an uncommon occurrence in Friuli. The Alfiere Rosso DOC, a blend of refosco, cabernet franc and merlot aged in 30-hectoliter oak barrels for six months, is redolent of hay, damp mown grass and black cherry; in the mouth the grassiness of the cabernet franc accentuates the wine's personality. Finally, two wines that are well made if somewhat simple also deserve a mention: the Merlot, with its pronounced fruit and soft tannins, and the Cabernet Sauvignon.

● Friuli Isonzo Alfiere Rosso I Feudi di Romans '97	🍷	3
○ Friuli Isonzo Malvasia Istriana I Feudi di Romans '98	🍷	3
● Friuli Isonzo Merlot I Feudi di Romans '98	🍷	3
○ Friuli Isonzo Pinot Bianco I Feudi di Romans '98	🍷	3
○ Friuli Isonzo Pinot Grigio I Feudi di Romans '98	🍷	3
○ Friuli Isonzo Tocai Friulano I Feudi di Romans '98	🍷	3
● Friuli Isonzo Cabernet Sauvignon I Feudi di Romans '98		3

S. FLORIANO DEL COLLIO (GO)

Ascevi - Luwa

Via Uclanzi, 24
34070 S. Floriano del Collio (GO)
tel. 0481/884140

Marjan Pintar's estate, in which he is helped by his children Luana (in the cellar) and Walter (in the vineyard), has changed its name to formalize the fact that it produces two different lines. The Ascevi label is dedicated to the more structured wines, obtained from late harvesting of the grapes (sauvignon and ribolla gialla) or from cryomaceration for up to 36 hours (sauvignon, pinot bianco and chardonnay) or from a short time in wood (Vigna Verdana) or, yet again, from a long time on the lees (tocai). The easy-drinking line is called Luwa, and is based on grapes from less clayey terrain between San Floriano and Monte Calvario which are vinified solely in stainless steel. This is, all considered, an excellent winery, which, far from the limelight, has been making steady progress, witness the Three Glasses we awarded to the stunning Sauvignon Ascevi, Marjan's real passion. Its nose of flowers and yellow-fleshed fruit precedes a powerful, structured, warm palate that mirrors the floral theme, with acidity to help support the not inconsiderable length. The splendid Col Martin, a blend of sauvignon, tocai and pinot grigio with the sauvignon as the leading player, offers pleasing notes of elder blossom and peach. Nor are the other wines mere walk-ons: the graceful and elegant Vigna Verdana, made from sauvignon, chardonnay and ribolla, with exotic fruit and long-lasting freshness; the Pinot Bianco, with its satisfyingly complex flavors and concentrated white plum aromas; the two Chardonnays, both showing scents of tropical fruit echoed on the long, crisp palate; the Sauvignon Luwa, full-flavored and intense, with sage and elder flowers on nose and palate; and, to finish, the two Pinot Grigios, with their enchanting fragrances.

○	Collio Sauvignon Ascevi '98	🍷🍷🍷	3*
○	Bianco Col Martin Luwa '98	🍷🍷	4
○	Collio Chardonnay Ascevi '98	🍷🍷	3*
○	Collio Pinot Bianco Ascevi '98	🍷🍷	3
○	Collio Ribolla Gialla Luwa '98	🍷🍷	3*
○	Collio Sauvignon Luwa '98	🍷🍷	3
○	Vigna Verdana Ascevi '98	🍷🍷	4
○	Collio Chardonnay Luwa '98	🍷	3
○	Collio Pinot Grigio Ascevi '98	🍷	3
○	Collio Pinot Grigio Luwa '98	🍷	3
○	Collio Tocai Friulano Luwa '98	🍷	3
●	Le Vigne '96		4

S. FLORIANO DEL COLLIO (GO)

Borgo Lotessa

Loc. Giasbana, 23
34070 S. Floriano del Collio (GO)
tel. 0481/390302

Borgo Lotessa is located on the high ground surrounding the villages of Lotessa and Crussoli almost at the Slovenian border. The owners, Pia Pettarin and Salvatore Fratepietro, have about 15 hectares under vine near Mossa and Giasbana. Their family-run estate involves the efforts of husband and wife as well as the two children, Roberto, who is playing a growing role in the technical management of the cellar under the watchful eyes of the oenologist Fabio Coser, and Raffaella, who deals with the commercial side. The wines are good and well made, although the winery undoubtedly has the potential to do even better things. The Margravio Bianco '96 is an excellent wine, made from three varieties (sauvignon, pinot grigio and chardonnay) vinified separately and then fermented in barriques. Its gold-tinged straw color introduces a bouquet with a good balance between fruity, woody and fat, almost buttery scents. The delicious palate has notes of white chocolate over ripe fruit. We awarded One full Glass to both the Pinot Grigio and the Chardonnay. The first shows a light and varietal coppery glint and an elegant bouquet: we detected peach and white flowers; in the mouth it offers agreeably lingering ripe fruit and mineral notes. The moderately intense Chardonnay has a simple nose of green apple, but comes into its own on the crisp and quite long palate. The Sauvignon also won One Glass, with its floral scents and a faint note of tomato. The Rosso Poggio Crussoli '97, a mainly merlot-based blend characterized by strawberry and blueberry jam, is a new development for Borgo Lotessa. In addition there's a whole range of other wines worthy of note.

○	Il Margravio Bianco '96	🍷🍷	4
●	Collio Merlot '98	🍷	3
●	Rosso Poggio Crussoli '97	🍷	3
○	Collio Chardonnay '98	🍷	3
○	Collio Pinot Grigio '98	🍷	3
○	Collio Sauvignon '98	🍷	3
○	Collio Pinot Bianco '98		3
●	Friuli Isonzo Cabernet Sauvignon '98		3
●	Il Margravio Rosso '96		4
●	Friuli Isonzo Cabernet Sauvignon '96	🍷🍷 (outline)	3

DRAGA - MIKLUS
LOC. SCEDINA, 8
34070 S. FLORIANO DEL COLLIO (GO)
TEL. 0481/884182

The estate that Milano Miklus runs with his family has made a well-deserved return to the Guide. It covers nine hectares under vine near San Floriano del Collio, in the area known as Draga. Starting this year, Milano has introduced a new line, called Miklus, the family surname: this is a selection of the best lots obtained by vinifying selected grapes from a few particular vineyards. The top wine this year is the Pinot Grigio Miklus. The fine, elegant nose, with more apple than pear, is echoed deliciously in the mouth, where it develops evenly, showing a soft, inviting structure. The successful golden-hued Picolit Miklus has a very characteristic fruity elegance on the nose; on the palate it is soft and sweet, with varietal apple notes and wood that, despite the wine's seven months in barrels, is not at all intrusive. The Ribolla Gialla '98 also wins One Glass, thanks to its aromas of wildflowers and fresh herbs that carry through well onto the properly acidic palate. The Chardonnay has a fairly forthright fragrance of soaked bread crust and a refreshing palate. Both the Pinot Grigio '98, interesting on the nose but rather simple thereafter, and the Sauvignon, which lacks varietal notes in its bouquet and is perhaps too soft and alcohol-accented on the palate, came just short of One Glass. The same score was given to the Sauvignon Miklus, with its nose of vanilla and ripe apricot and its straightforward palate. To finish, the Cabernet Sauvignon Miklus '97 is redolent of cherries steeped in alcohol but shows a very simple palate.

○	Collio Pinot Grigio Miklus '98	🍷🍷	4
●	Collio Cabernet Sauvignon Miklus '97	🍷	4
○	Collio Chardonnay '98	🍷	4
○	Collio Picolit Miklus '98	🍷	6
○	Collio Ribolla Gialla '98	🍷	4
○	Collio Pinot Grigio '98		4
○	Collio Sauvignon '98		4
○	Collio Sauvignon Miklus '98		4

CONTI FORMENTINI
VIA OSLAVIA, 5
34070 S. FLORIANO DEL COLLIO (GO)
TEL. 0481/884131

The Conti Formentini estate, established in 1520, is now part of the Gruppo Italiano Vini. Marco Monchiero, a Piedmontese who for some years now has been equally at home making white wine in Friuli, has been hired as the winery's consultant oenologist. The cellar has a production potential of over 300 thousand bottles per year; the grapes they vinify are purchased in the zone and carefully selected, so as to guarantee high quality. The best wine this year is the Merlot Tajut (a Friulian dialect word meaning wine goblet); on the nose it displays aromas of undergrowth and leather, with notes imparted by big wooden barrels; these all follow through onto the fat, structured and lingering palate. Scents of cherries steeped in alcohol can be detected in the complex and richly fruity Pinot Nero Torre di Borea. The Pinot Grigio is redolent of pear, although other fruits emerge as well; it does better in the mouth, where it is salty and substantial, and yet elegant. The bouquet of the Tocai Friulano has a stylish note of apple as well as wildflowers; these are perfectly mirrored on the even, succulent palate, which displays a varietal bitter almond on the finish. The Chardonnay is another forthright wine, with characteristic scents of dried flowers and crusty bread, a crisp palate suggestive of Golden Delicious apple and an agreeably inviting finish. Lastly, the Sauvignon is reminiscent of fig leaf and tomato leaf, with notes of green pepper emerging on the finish: this agreeable and not at all aggressive wine is very good to dine with.

●	Collio Merlot Tajut '97	🍷🍷	4
○	Collio Chardonnay '98	🍷	3
○	Collio Pinot Grigio '98	🍷	3
●	Collio Pinot Nero Torre di Borea '95	🍷	4
○	Collio Sauvignon '98	🍷	3
○	Collio Tocai Friulano '98	🍷	3
○	Collio Chardonnay Torre di Tramontana '97	🍷🍷 (white)	4

S. FLORIANO DEL COLLIO (GO)

MUZIC
LOC. BIVIO, 4
34070 S. FLORIANO DEL COLLIO (GO)
TEL. 0481/884201

The secret of this little family-run estate lies in the quiet but determined character of Giovanni Muzic, the owner, who works in both vineyards and cellar. There are ten hectares under vine in the Collio DOC district and two more in the Isonzo del Friuli DOC. The structural alterations to the premises (creation of a cellar for vinification and a second one for aging), and further investments to improve the quality of the wines (substitution of all the cement vats with stainless steel), are evident signs of a commitment to excellence. We were impressed by the Isonzo Merlot Primo Legno '96, produced from grapes grown on the plain; fermented and matured for 12 months in small oak casks and then aged for at least a further 18 in the bottle, it has attractive wood, tar and black cherry on the nose, with a concentrated flavor of undergrowth and a good structure in the mouth. The very well-made Chardonnay Collio '98, with its characteristic aromas of yeast and crusty bread, has good fruit on the palate which, although full-flavored, is not particularly long. The Ribolla Gialla is also very interesting, thanks to its array of elegant fruity scents, all echoed on the palate, which is dry and shows characteristic varietal acidity on the finish. The Collio Pinot Grigio, which offers a distinct apple fragrance with an almost toasty undertone, makes a decisive entry on the palate and develops smoothly with lots of fruit, only to fade slightly on the finish. The Collio Sauvignon has more personality, with characteristics notes of sage and tomato leaf on the nose; in the mouth we noted a balanced acidity. The Cabernet Sauvignon and the Tocai del Collio, like the Isonzo Merlot '97, came very close to getting One Glass.

○ Collio Chardonnay '98	🍷🍷	3
● Friuli Isonzo Merlot Primo Legno '96	🍷🍷	4
○ Collio Pinot Grigio '98	🍷	3
○ Collio Ribolla Gialla '98	🍷	3
○ Collio Sauvignon '98	🍷	3
○ Collio Tocai Friulano '98	🍷	3
● Collio Cabernet Sauvignon '97		3
○ Collio Picolit '97		5
● Friuli Isonzo Cabernet Franc '97		3
● Friuli Isonzo Merlot '97		3

S. FLORIANO DEL COLLIO (GO)

MĂTIJAZ TERCIC
VIA BUKUJE, 9
34070 S. FLORIANO DEL COLLIO (GO)
TEL. 0481/884193

Work never stops at Matijaz Tercic's, either on his four hectares under vine or in the cellar. We are anxiously awaiting the Collio Merlot '97 and the Collio Chardonnay '98, which are currently taking their ease in five French barriques: their release is planned for September 2000. A change in the general marketing schedule for all the wines is imminent, with the whites to be available in June and the reds in September. Because of a replanting program, the additional 8,000 meters of vineyard planted to chardonnay and merlot will not lead to an increase in production (a steady 20-22 thousand bottles). Matijaz is spending a lot of time on local grape varieties, like ribolla gialla, which he wants to show off to their greatest advantage. He did well last year to hold back the Chardonnay '97, which has now developed very well: the vanilla derived from light-toasted wood can still be detected on the nose, but it doesn't cover the fruit and yeast; the full, fat and soft palate has a properly dry fruity finish. There's another very good performance from the Vigna degli Orti, an assemblage of tocai friulano, malvasia istriana and Rhine riesling; its pale tones herald an elegant nose, which offers intense aromas of fresh fruit, with apple to the fore; the acidity on the palate is perfectly balanced by its opulence, and fruit informs the long finish. The Sauvignon, which we may have tasted before it had a chance to settle, was not notably varietal but was impeccably made; in the Ribolla Gialla very ripe fruit and intense acidity have not quite come to terms on the palate.

○ Collio Chardonnay '97	🍷🍷	3
○ Vino degli Orti '98	🍷🍷	3
○ Collio Ribolla Gialla '98		3
○ Collio Sauvignon '98		3
○ Vino degli Orti '97	🍸🍸	3
● Collio Merlot '95	🍸	3

S. FLORIANO DEL COLLIO (GO)

FRANCO TERPIN

LOC. VALERISCE, 6/A
34070 S. FLORIANO DEL COLLIO (GO)
TEL. 0481/884215

In the past we have said that it seems to be Franco Terpin's policy to take one small step at a time, but this year we must acknowledge that he has made some real leaps forward. He has rented a new cellar for vinification in the Dolegna del Collio area where, by the way, the Ribolla Gialla '97, to be bottled in 2000, is maturing in wooden barrels. In the San Floriano house-cum-winery, which is now utterly inadequate for Terpin's production requirements, he will see people and sell wine. Everything he presented this year did well, particularly the Collio Bianco, made from chardonnay, sauvignon and pinot grigio: despite intense toasty notes, which are especially evident on the nose, the wine shows lots of fruit, which explodes on the finish and should become more marked over time. The very well-executed Chardonnay has a clean and extremely varietal bouquet, and is full-bodied, dense-textured and very long and fruity on the excellent palate. The Sauvignon would be just as good as the Chardonnay if it had a more concentrated bouquet; characteristic notes of elder flower rule the roost on the fleshy and alcohol-rich palate. The Pinot Grigio also wins One very full Glass: the elegant yet intense nose offers notes of apple and tropical fruit together with wildflowers, all mirrored on the rich, even and very long palate. The Ribolla is fresh, simple and gracefully tangy, while the Cabernet, half cabernet franc and half cabernet sauvignon, is mildly reminiscent of red berries.

○	Collio Bianco '97	YY	5
○	Collio Chardonnay '98	YY	3
○	Collio Pinot Grigio '98	Y	3
○	Collio Sauvignon '98	Y	3
●	Collio Cabernet '97		4
○	Collio Ribolla Gialla '98		3

S. GIORGIO DELLA RICHINVELDA (PN)

FORCHIR

VIA CIASUTIS, 1
FRAZ. PROVESANO
33095 S. GIORGIO DELLA RICHINVELDA (PN)
TEL. 0427/96037

Forchir, whose more than 200 hectares under vine on the Friuli plain are scattered near the villages of Felettis, Barbeano and Gorizzo, produces about 800 thousand bottles a year. Its considerable size has been no hindrance to a series of innovations involving the red wines in particular. With the '98 vintage, in fact, the changeover to Guyot training, with consequent lower yields, was completed in all the red grape vineyards; it was also decided that at least a part of each of the reds should pass some time in barriques or 30-hectoliter barrels. What they have in mind, as the oenologist Bianchini told us, is to impart greater complexity and structure to the wines. And as far as the Merlot '98 is concerned, this goal has already been achieved in the first year. The purplish red color reveals the youth of the wine; a fairly intense bouquet displays balanced and very elegant notes of black cherry jam and coffee, which follow through to the entry on the palate, where red berries appear as well; the mid palate is fleshy, but the tannins on the finish need further integration. The other reds (Cabernet Sauvignon and Refosco) deserve a mention but cannot yet be described as excellent. We have long admired Forchir's Sauvignon, but this year's version really struck us with its intense, complex green scents of bell pepper and tomato leaf in perfect harmony with more rounded notes of ripe pear. The properly executed and varietal Chardonnay, with its characteristic banana and apple fragrance, fell just short of One Glass. The Tocai, Traminer and Pinot Grigio are all worthy of note.

●	Friuli Grave Merlot '98	YY	2*
○	Friuli Grave Sauvignon '98	YY	3*
●	Friuli Grave Cabernet Sauvignon '98	Y	2
○	Friuli Grave Chardonnay '98		3
○	Friuli Grave Pinot Grigio '98		3
●	Friuli Grave Refosco P. R. '98		2
○	Friuli Grave Tocai Friulano '98		2
○	Friuli Grave Traminer '98		3

S. GIOVANNI AL NATISONE (UD)

ALFIERI CANTARUTTI
VIA RONCHI, 9
33048 S. GIOVANNI AL NATISONE (UD)
TEL. 0432/756317

Antonella Cantarutti is now firmly at the helm of this estate, and this has enabled her to launch a wide-ranging program of agronomic, commercial and structural innovations: she is taking more account of the market in her wine-making choices and is also doing over the cellar. These changes have required considerable effort, but were an ineluctable precondition for going beyond the anonymous wines that the estate has in fact now left behind it. And speaking of wines, those that impressed us most this year were, first, the new Bianco Canto, which combines the characteristic rusticity and power of tocai with the aromatic notes of sauvignon and the elegance of pinot bianco: the pear and faint almond notes on the nose are echoed on the soft, crisp palate; the wine would be perfect if it lasted longer. Next, the Schioppettino, in its first year as a monovarietal, was another surprise: its purplish color is of moderate intensity but the bouquet vaunts a remarkable and enchanting complexity with notes of vanilla and raspberry, which follow through on the full-bodied and harmoniously developing palate. The well-designed Solivo and Poema both nearly won Two Glasses. The former, made from barrique-fermented pinot bianco with tocai and riesling, is a little reluctant to display its fresh herbal aromas. The latter, made from merlot, cabernet franc, schioppettino and tazzelenghe, offers aromas of cherry and pepper; the attack on the palate is soft, and the mid-palate dryness is a result of pronounced tannins. Both have good development potential, as indicated by recent tastings of the '96 vintage. To finish, the Grave Chardonnay deserves special mention.

○	COF Bianco Canto '98	▼▼	3*
●	COF Schioppettino '97	▼▼	4
○	COF Bianco Solivo '97	▼	4
●	COF Rosso Poema '97	▼	5
○	Friuli Grave Chardonnay '98	▼	3
●	COF Cabernet Sauvignon '96		3
●	COF Cabernet Sauvignon '97		3
●	COF Rosso Poema '96	▽▽	4
●	COF Merlot Carato '93	▽	4

S. GIOVANNI AL NATISONE (UD)

LIVON
VIA MONTAREZZA, 33
FRAZ. DOLEGNANO
33048 S. GIOVANNI AL NATISONE (UD)
TEL. 0432/757173 - 0432/756231

The Livon group seems to be settling down with its three wineries in Friuli and one in Tuscany, but the usual numerous wines continue to emerge and win the usual numerous Glasses, so what can we say? The champion is once again the Braide Alte, made from chardonnay, sauvignon, picolit and moscato giallo: butter, honey, grass and apple are the prelude to an ample, balanced, fat and long palate with the bouquet reflected on the finish. The Chardonnay offers tropical and citrus fruit on the nose; the palate, almost sweet at first, shows a creamy texture and a succulent and unhurried finish. The Ribolla is all herbs and flowers: the characteristic acidity in the mouth is nicely counterbalanced by alcohol and a fairly dense structure. The Tocai seems to be under the misapprehension that it is a Sauvignon, with its notes of peach and tomato leaf. Of the two Merlots, the younger is better: intense and concentrated, it is a little gamey on the nose, but should evolve well, thanks to its powerful palate and tannins; the '96 is agreeably fruity, although simpler, but perhaps a trifle too harsh in the mouth. The Sauvignon, with its peach, citrus and green notes, the Cabernet, absolutely classic in style, and the Refosco, which is redolent of black cherry and pepper but has the usual roughness on the palate, are a worthy accompaniment to the more prestigious group described above. The Tiareblù needs to be considered separately: this is a Bordeaux-style blend that has not yet found its feet; the '95 version is rough-edged and lacks the softness that in previous vintages managed to play down the strong tannic element. To close on a sweet note, the Verduzzo Casali Godia, a quintessentially Friulian wine, is again irreproachable.

○	Braide Alte '97	▼▼▼	5
○	COF Verduzzo Friulano Casali Godia '97	▼▼	4
○	Collio Chardonnay Braide Mate '97	▼▼	5
●	Collio Merlot Tiare Mate '97	▼▼	5
○	Collio Ribolla Gialla Roncalto '98	▼▼	4
○	Collio Tocai Friulano Ronc di Zorz '98	▼▼	4
●	Collio Cabernet Franc Arborizza '96	▼	4
●	Collio Merlot Tiare Mate '96	▼	5
●	Collio Refosco P. R. Riul '96	▼	4
○	Collio Sauvignon Valbuins '98	▼	4
●	Tiareblù '95	▼	5
○	Braide Alte '96	▽▽▽	5
○	Collio Sauvignon Valbuins '96	▽▽▽	4

S. GIOVANNI AL NATISONE (UD)

RONCO DEL GNEMIZ
VIA RONCHI, 5
33048 S. GIOVANNI AL NATISONE (UD)
TEL. 0432/756238

The Ronco del Gnemiz wines are genuine, distinct and easy to interpret; they are often the subject of lively discussion, but this regards the degree of excellence of the wine in question. Serena Palazzolo, who runs the winery together with Gabriele, works with commitment and passion, but also without the worries of some years ago. As usual, the golden-hued Chardonnay was our favorite, although this latest version doesn't aim for the stars, seemingly content with just being an excellent wine. A balanced, intense bouquet of very ripe banana and apricot with a ground bass of custard is echoed on the palate, which is, perhaps, a touch too tangy. The Tocai has a lightly honeyed nose; the palate is similar, but better on the whole; this almost exaggeratedly long wine should develop very well. Although the wood in the bouquet of the Rosso del Gnemiz '96 is certainly pronounced, aromas of red berry tart and undergrowth still manage to emerge distinctly; the bouquet is mirrored on the even, well-structured and full-bodied palate, which shows nicely smoothed tannins. The Schioppettino '97 is intense and grapey on the nose, and clear notes of blueberry appear in the mouth; here, tannins and wood are over-represented, and the balance between acidity and alcohol is not yet perfect. The Sauvignon, too, needs more time to achieve better balance, but the essential elements are all there: aromas of sage and nectarine, acidity, fatness and concentration. The Pinot Grigio, with pronounced apple scents and an even and medium-bodied palate, falls just short of One Glass.

○	COF Chardonnay '97	🍷🍷	5
○	COF Tocai Friulano '98	🍷🍷	4
●	Rosso del Gnemiz '96	🍷🍷	5
○	COF Sauvignon '98	🍷	4
●	COF Schioppettino '97	🍷	5
○	COF Pinot Grigio '98		4
○	Chardonnay '90	🍷🍷🍷	6
○	COF Chardonnay '91	🍷🍷🍷	6
○	COF Chardonnay '96	🍷🍷	5
○	Müller Thurgau '97	🍷🍷	4
●	Rosso del Gnemiz '95	🍷🍷	5
●	Rosso del Gnemiz '94	🍷	5

S. GIOVANNI AL NATISONE (UD)

VILLA CHIOPRIS
VIA MONTAREZZA, 33
FRAZ. DOLEGNANO
33048 S. GIOVANNI AL NATISONE (UD)
TEL. 0432/757173

Grave del Friuli is a fairly extensive zone; the 20 hectares of this estate are at the eastern edge, where the flood-plain terrain is loose and rich in ferrites, and the soil and climatic conditions have elements of both the Colli Orientali and Isonzo districts. This winery, which belongs to the Livon group, lends its name to their less challenging and more easily quaffable – but by no means ordinary or unexciting – line: the wines are all made from grapes picked by hand and from musts cold-macerated in the press, drained and fermented at a low temperature in stainless steel, then matured on the lees for several months (the whites) or fermented on their skins at controlled temperatures and then matured in stainless steel (the reds). We were all pleasantly surprised by the Chardonnay, which offers notes of ripe fruit, yeast and yellow flowers on the nose; the full-flavored and pleasing palate is underpinned by an agreeable vein of acidity. The Pinot Grigio is some way behind it, but still quite good, with its fruity, delicate and straightforward aromas. The equally worthy Sauvignon is rather acidic and not particularly full-bodied, but it offers attractive notes of mint and peach. The Cabernet Sauvignon, which is somewhat monotonous, needs improvement, as does the Tocai, which is no more than acceptable.

○	Friuli Grave Chardonnay '98	🍷🍷	3
○	Friuli Grave Pinot Grigio '98	🍷	3
○	Friuli Grave Sauvignon '98	🍷	3
○	Friuli Grave Tocai Friulano '98		3
●	Friuli Grave Cabernet Sauvignon '98		3

S. LORENZO ISONTINO (GO)

Lis Neris - Pecorari

Via Gavinana, 5
34070 S. Lorenzo Isontino (GO)
tel. 0481/80105

Three ranges: the first, with only the name of the grape variety, is vinified in steel; the second, with the name of the grape and of the vineyard from which most of the grapes derive, is made from an assemblage of wines fermented in wood and stainless steel; the third contains single-vineyard selections fermented in wood that bear on their labels either an invented name or the name of the vineyard. Now that we have a scorecard, here are the results of the tastings. The Sauvignon Picòl is a wonderful wine, with an impressive nose, both complex and elegant, and a long-lasting, structured palate that shows sinew within the proper limits. The Dom Picòl, another sauvignon, is not far behind: it reveals ripe apricot on the fresh, velvety palate, with lactic tones that want more time in the bottle. Of the Pinot Grigios, the simplest version is very good: sweet and floral, with a delicate but lingering note of Williams pear. The intermediate one, the Gris, is very good as well: after a velvety start with a note of softness, it opens out to be aromatic, long and rich in alcohol. The third, and new, version is the Confini, a late-harvested pinot grigio with small amounts of riesling, traminer and malvasia: high in residual sugar, it needs a little fine-tuning of both the aromas and the balance on the palate. The Chardonnay Sant'Jurosa is no disappointment, especially in the mouth, where it opens to a full-bodied, firm and, as usual, close-knit texture; it is better than its near namesake, which is a little more dilute, with a touch of acidity and a note of wet rag that undermine its elegance.

○	Friuli Isonzo Chardonnay St. Jurosa '97	▼▼	4
○	Friuli Isonzo Pinot Grigio '98	▼▼	4
○	Friuli Isonzo Pinot Grigio Gris '97	▼▼	4
○	Friuli Isonzo Sauvignon Dom Picòl '97	▼▼	4
○	Friuli Isonzo Sauvignon Picòl '98	▼▼	4
○	Tal Lûc '97	▼▼	6
○	Confini '97	▼	5
○	Friuli Isonzo Chardonnay Jurosa '97	▼	4
○	Friuli Isonzo Sauvignon Dom Picòl '96	▽▽▽	4
○	Isonzo Chardonnay St. Jurosa '96	▽▽	4
●	Isonzo Rosso Lis Neris '95	▽	5

S. LORENZO ISONTINO (GO)

Pierpaolo Pecorari

Via Tommaseo, 36/c
34070 S. Lorenzo Isontino (GO)
tel. 0481/808775

Two new developments: the attractively renovated old farm building, transformed into a barrel-room for barriques, and the Refosco. This is intense in color, with an equally concentrated bouquet of vanilla and sour cherry and a palate that's caught in the fray between the hard notes of the tannin and the soft texture of the alcohol and extract. The wines are presented with a new, slightly surreal label, featuring themes from Beethoven. But to get back to the content, a point worth remembering is that the selections, which bear a vineyard name, are fermented and aged in 500-liter barrels; the regular vintage wines have only the name of the grape and spend their time in stainless steel. The Chardonnay opens with pronounced toasty notes that make way for dried apricot; on the palate it is elegant, warm, long and nicely supported by refreshing acidity. The very successful Merlot, of a dark ruby hue with a purplish rim, is particularly interesting for its soft tannin, spice, black currant, tobacco and considerable alcohol. The Pinot Grigio Olivers has a very concentrated color and a warm and heady fragrance of fresh herb tisane. The other Pinot, more easily quaffable, is dry, characteristic, not overbearing and a good accompaniment to various kinds of food. The Pratoscuro, made from stainless- steel-aged müller thurgau and wood-aged riesling, was less pleasing than in previous years: it has the usual elegant initial notes (pear), but it soon loses balance, both on the nose and in the mouth. The standard Sauvignon, with a classic crispness, natural and unfettered, seemed better and more harmonious than the more prestigious Kolàus.

○	Chardonnay Soris '97	▼▼	5
●	Merlot Baolar '96	▼▼	5
○	Pinot Grigio Olivers '96	▼▼	5
○	Sauvignon '98	▼▼	4
○	Pinot Grigio '98	▼	4
○	Pratoscuro '97	▼	4
●	Refosco P. R. '96	▼	6
○	Sauvignon Kolàus '97	▼	5
○	Sauvignon Kolàus '96	▽▽▽	5
○	Pratoscuro '96	▽▽	4

SACILE (PN)

VISTORTA
BRANDINO BRANDOLINI D'ADDA
VIA VISTORTA, 87
33077 SACILE (PN)
TEL. 0434/71135

The two 2nd century Roman capitals that marked the boundaries of the farm properties of the period bear witness to the ancient origins of the village of Vistorta, on the border between Friuli and the Veneto. This little village still has interesting historical monuments such as the Torre Colombaia from the 13th century and the little 15th century church. At the end of the 19th century Guido Brandolini, who had retired to his estate at Vistorta, built the splendid villa with barn and farmhouses. This estate, which now covers 220 hectares, of which 16 are under vines, is managed by Brandino Brandolini d'Adda, who has set himself the goal of producing, in Friuli, only merlot. The clones for the most recent plantings are from Bordeaux and add to the complexity of the vineyards, with their vines planted in past decades and now acclimatized to the local terroir. The winery has as consultant Georges Pauli, the oenologist of Château Gruaud-Larose. Anyone who tastes this Merlot will notice that a non-Friulian hand had the making of it. Some of the credit should certainly go to the clayey terrain, similar to that of Bordeaux, to the densely planted vines and to the cellar techniques, which include an extensive use of wood. In addition to tasting the `97, we had another taste of the '96 vintage; this has improved, as we have often found when even earlier years were tasted again. But to go back to the latest release: the color is a ruby red of medium intensity; from the characteristically complex bouquet red berries, licorice and grass emerge by turns; the palate is excellent – dense, rich, elegant and soft – with tannins clearly present but not hard, and with a long, full finish.

●	Friuli Grave Merlot '97	🍷🍷	4
●	Friuli Grave Merlot '95	🍷🍷 (white)	4
●	Friuli Grave Merlot '96	🍷 (white)	4

SAGRADO (GO)

CASTELVECCHIO
VIA CASTELNUOVO, 2
34078 SAGRADO (GO)
TEL. 0481/99742

Gianni Bignucolo, the manager and oenologist of this winery, emphasizes the quality of the '95s. From that vintage they have now released the Sagrado Rosso, a blend of cabernet franc and cabernet sauvignon, matured first in barrique and then in French tonneaux for over three years. The name is that of the village where the vineyards are located, and the wine is excellent: of an intense ruby hue, it releases aromas of red berry tart, herbs and dry leaves; these follow through perfectly onto the palate, which shows good weight, character, rich alcohol and length. But the real pièce di résistance turned out to be the Cabernet Franc '96, which spent a year in French barriques followed by another year in 15-25-hectoliter barrels of Slavonian oak: a bouquet of blackberry, mushroom and undergrowth heralds a full, dense and complex entry on the palate, followed by a mid palate with soft tannins, warm alcohol and rich fruit. A fresh, characterful white also won Two Glasses: the Sauvignon '98, with an elder flower bouquet which is mirrored on a palate further enriched by nectarine and peach leaf. The Turmino '96, 70% terrano and 30% cabernet, is redolent of red berry liqueur; with its substantial palate it is a good match for the dishes from the Carso, as is the Terrano '98, with its characteristic rough rusticity, and its tart grapiness and toasty notes. The acidity on the palate accentuates the roughness of the tannins in the Cabernet Sauvignon '96, which is austere and powerful on the nose, and also in the Refosco '96, with its spice and undergrowth. The Malvasia Istriana and the Traminer Aromatico are good too.

●	Carso Cabernet Franc '96	🍷🍷	4
○	Carso Sauvignon '98	🍷🍷	3*
●	Sagrado '95	🍷🍷	5
●	Carso Cabernet Sauvignon '96	🍷	4
○	Carso Malvasia Istriana '98	🍷	3
●	Carso Refosco P. R. '96	🍷	4
●	Carso Rosso Turmino '96	🍷	3
○	Carso Traminer Aromatico '98	🍷	3
●	Terrano '98	🍷	3
○	Carso Pinot Grigio '98		3
●	Carso Rosso Turmino '95	🍷🍷 (white)	4
●	Terrano '97	🍷 (white)	4

SPILIMBERGO (PN)

BORGO MAGREDO
VIA BASALDELLA, 5
LOC. TAURIANO
33097 SPILIMBERGO (PN)
TEL. 0427/51444

Last year's poor vintage, instead of provoking patient resignation, provided a strong impetus for innovation. During '98 there were changes in cellar procedures with the arrival of the oenologist Luca Zuccarello; the new modus operandi is intended to demonstrate that the Grave district can produce admirable reds. The affable manager Piero Totis told us about their acquiring new, less productive clones of merlot and cabernet sauvignon and of the purchase of new vinification equipment. The Tocai Friulano is a splendid wine: the complex and intense nose suggests white-fleshed fruit and almond, all echoed on the long palate, which finishes on a very attractive acidic note conducive to further sips. The Sauvignon, which displays fairly intense and harmonious aromas of pear, apple, ripe bell pepper and dried flowers, almost touched Two Glasses; the lovely initial fruit on the palate fades a little on the finish. The Sauvignon Braida Curta (the Braida line features wines partly fermented in barriques) is characterized by promising notes of butter, tomato and white plum, which carry through well onto the not particularly dense palate. The Moscato Rosa is well made, as it is every year; with its fragrance of date, fig and berry jam in perfect harmony with the scent of faded roses, it is an instantly appealing wine, and the follow-through from nose to palate is pleasurable as well. There is also a good range of reds. The Merlot Braida Moral offers an excellent nose and palate with coffee, pepper and grassy and fruity notes all well blended. A slightly rough tannic finish diminishes the Refosco, which otherwise makes a good impression with its scents of spice (pepper), blackberry and plum. The Cabernet Franc gets One full Glass.

○	Friuli Grave Tocai Friulano '98	🍷🍷	2*
●	Friuli Grave Cabernet Franc '98	🍷	2
●	Friuli Grave Merlot Braida Moral '97	🍷	3
⊙	Friuli Grave Moscato Rosa Braida delle Rose '98	🍷	3
○	Friuli Grave Pinot Grigio '98	🍷	3
●	Friuli Grave Refosco P. R. '98	🍷	3
○	Friuli Grave Sauvignon '98	🍷	3
○	Friuli Grave Sauvignon Blanc Braida Curta '98	🍷	3
○	Friuli Grave Sauvignon Braida Vieri '97	🍷	3
●	Friuli Grave Pinot Nero '98		2

SPILIMBERGO (PN)

PLOZNER
VIA DELLE PRESE, 19
FRAZ. BARBEANO
33097 SPILIMBERGO (PN)
TEL. 0427/2902

The Plozner estate covers 70 hectares under vine on the infertile alluvial plain near Spilimbergo, typical Grave DOC terrain. It produces some 700 thousand bottles a year. The steadfast and determined Valeria Plozner runs the whole show. The results prove that she and the expert oenologist Francesco Visentin, who quietly helps turn out fine, well-made wines year after year, are on the right track. The Sauvignon is certainly more than merely well made. About 40 thousand bottles of this splendid wine, which is no letdown after last year's excellent version, were produced. It boasts an elegant bouquet with complex, varietal notes of tomato leaf, elder flower and peach; the palate, after a lovely entry, is fruity, rich and long. The two Chardonnays, the standard and Riserva versions, get One full Glass apiece. The former offers scents of apple, pineapple, banana and white flowers, all mirrored in the mouth, where apple takes the upper hand. The partly barrique-fermented Riserva opens with aromas of banana, pineapple and candied fruit, which gradually give way to attractive vanilla scents. The two Pinot Grigios are excellent. The first, a Riserva produced from selected grapes, has a very good nose with an intense fragrance of ripe pear which reappears on the fairly long palate. The standard Pinot Grigio offers appealing aromas of pear and apple seed and a concentrated palate. Of the reds, the Refosco did quite well: very intense ruby red in the glass, it shows pronounced spice that lords it over the ripe fruit on the nose; the palate releases notes of coffee and pepper on the attractive finish. The Pinot Bianco and the Cabernet Sauvignon are worthy of note.

○	Friuli Grave Sauvignon '98	🍷🍷	3
○	Friuli Grave Chardonnay '98	🍷	3
○	Friuli Grave Chardonnay Ris. '96	🍷	4
○	Friuli Grave Pinot Grigio '98	🍷	3
○	Friuli Grave Pinot Grigio Ris. '97	🍷	4
●	Friuli Grave Refosco P. R. '97	🍷	3
●	Friuli Grave Cabernet Sauvignon '98		3
○	Friuli Grave Pinot Bianco '98		3

TALMASSONS (UD)

MANGILLI
VIA TRE AVIERI, 12
FRAZ. FLUMIGNANO
33030 TALMASSONS (UD)
TEL. 0432/766248

The Mangilli winery has at its command about 25 hectares of terrain divided between Grave (20 hectares), Collio (four hectares) and little plots at Nimis, where the Refosco and the Ramandolo are produced. The oenologist Adriano Teston personally supervises the various holdings, vinifying the best batches in the quest for excellence. In recent years the young Carlo Perissinotto has been playing an increasingly active part in the management of the winery, to take some of the pressure off his very busy father Francesco. Undoubtedly this year has seen a marked upward leap in the quality of the 150 thousand bottles produced. Particular praise goes to the Sauvignon '95, described on the label as "must from partly fermented grapes". It shows a lovely golden yellow color, and a delightful bouquet of rich and complex scents of candied citrus peel, dried flowers and ripe apricot; these are echoed very closely on the fat, warm palate which adds distinct notes of butter and tropical fruit. The Grave Sauvignon is splendid too: varietal on the nose, it is refreshing on the agreeably sage-accented palate. The Pinot Bianco, another noteworthy wine, has delicate, appealing scents of white flowers and peach, followed by a full, fleshy palate. The Collio Sauvignon confirms the producer's knack with this particular grape: the complex nose offers well-balanced notes of elder flower and bell pepper, but we were somewhat let down by the palate, which, despite a good follow-through, does not open out. Of the reds, the Refosco, with scents of plum and fresh grass, and the Cabernet '96, although somewhat diminished by a lackluster structure, both deserve a mention.

○ Collio Pinot Bianco '98	🍷🍷	3*
○ Friuli Grave Sauvignon '98	🍷🍷	3*
○ Sauvignon '95	🍷🍷	5
● Collio Cabernet Franc '97	🍷	3
○ Collio Sauvignon '98	🍷	4
● Friuli Grave Cabernet '96	🍷	3
○ Friuli Grave Pinot Grigio '98	🍷	3
● COF Refosco P. R. '97	🍷	3

TORREANO DI CIVIDALE (UD)

JACUSS - IACUZZI
V.LE KENNEDY, 35/A
LOC. MONTINA
33040 TORREANO DI CIVIDALE (UD)
TEL. 0432/715147

The Iacuzzi brothers have chosen to change the name of their estate, partly to avoid repeated misunderstandings about who owns it. In substance, however, nothing has changed: there is still the usual sound management by the two brothers, who look after both the agronomic and the oenological aspects of their winery. Their great enthusiasm, determination to improve and interest in all new developments in the world of wine are plain for all to see. Hence their decision to seek higher quality by continuing to reduce the yields per hectare (and we fully understand how much of a sacrifice is involved in a substantial crop thinning operation on an estate of only nine hectares!). This year there is once again a fine range of well-made wines, without low points but with two high points, the Verduzzo Friulano and the Schioppettino. The former, yellow verging on gold, has proper if not intense baked apple and hazelnut aromas; after a decisive attack on the palate it reveals sweet and elegant fruit, well-integrated varietal tannins and a refreshing acidity on the finish that invites you to keep on drinking. The Schiopettino, made from a historical Friuli variety also known as ribolla nera, has come out very well in the Iacuzzis' version: ruby-hued and tinged with purple, it offers aromas of berry jam (blueberry, black currant and blackberry), tobacco and cinnamon, all mirrored on the palate, which closes on a grassy note with still slightly rough tannins. The well-executed Sauvignon displays green apple flavors. The Merlot has a promising nose, with scents of grass and red fruit, but the palate is thinned by tannins that are not yet fully softened. The Pinot Bianco and the Refosco are both characteristic and deserving of mention.

○ COF Verduzzo Friulano '97	🍷🍷	3*
○ COF Sauvignon '98	🍷	3
● COF Schioppettino '97	🍷	3
● COF Merlot '97		3
○ COF Pinot Bianco '98		3
● COF Refosco P. R. '97		3
○ COF Bianco Lindi Uà '97	🍸🍸	4

TORREANO DI CIVIDALE (UD)

VALCHIARÒ

VIA CASALI LAURINI, 3
33040 TORREANO DI CIVIDALE (UD)
TEL. 0432/712393

Characteristics shared by the five partners involved in running Valchiarò, headed by Lauro De Vincenti, include great affability, professional competence and good will. Emilio, Giampaolo, Armando and Galliano form, with Lauro, a team that is always happy to while away a few pleasant hours at table with you, but they do not hold back when there is work to be done, and their efforts are rewarded by the recognized quality of the wines they produce. This year we were struck in particular by the Tocai: the intense nose, with well-defined fruity aromas including pear and peach, is followed by a soft, full, even and alcohol-rich palate with quite good length. Three of the four reds they presented very nearly reached Two Glasses. The fragrance of the Merlot '97 is reminiscent of red fruit compote; this reappears on the successful palate, which is well balanced and ample. The Refosco dal Peduncolo Rosso '97 is redolent of red berry jam, but it's particularly interesting on a palate enriched by spicy notes of black and pink peppercorns that expands evenly into a long finish. The incredibly refreshing assemblage called El Clap '95 (which means stone in Friulian) is made from merlot, cabernet franc and refosco: the concentrated red fruit of the bouquet heralds the considerable concentration, substance and structure in the mouth and the plum and blackberry notes on the finish. The good Bianco La Clupa '97, a blend of tocai, pinot bianco, sauvignon and picolit, still shows toasty notes on the nose, but these are dominated on the palate by complex flavors of ripe white- and yellow-fleshed fruit; the finish is underpinned by appropriate acidity. The well-made Sauvignon, redolent of bell pepper, is supple and appealing in the mouth.

○	COF Tocai Friulano '98	🍷🍷	3*
○	COF Bianco La Clupa '97	🍷	3
●	COF Merlot '97	🍷	3
●	COF Refosco P. R. '97	🍷	3
○	COF Sauvignon '98	🍷	3
●	El Clap '95	🍷	4
●	COF Cabernet '97		3
●	Torre Quâl '95	🍸	3

TORREANO DI CIVIDALE (UD)

VOLPE PASINI

VIA CIVIDALE, 16
FRAZ. TOGLIANO
33040 TORREANO DI CIVIDALE (UD)
TEL. 0432/715151

When Emilio Rotolo took over ownership of the historic Volpe Pasini winery, we wondered which would prevail, his genius or his folly. This was a real question because he remade, or rather built from scratch, the cellar, equipping it with all the very best that modern technology can offer, and completely transformed the technical staff, appointing Flavio Zuliani chief oenologist and making the young Igor Erzetic cellarmaster. Meanwhile, he set about replanting the old vineyards and extending the estate. He stubbornly insisted on keeping the historic name of the winery, and we now find we must admit that he was right. With the help of Rosa Tomaselli, this Calabrian wine-maker, proud both of his origins and of Friuli, his new home, is already successfully dealing with a whole series of challenges and is eagerly lining up some new ones. He has reduced production to just two ranges (Zuc di Volpe and standard), and has turned out a series of really excellent wines. The splendid Ribolla Gialla, from the Zuc range, is full-bodied, tangy, soft and intense, with a pleasing toasty note on the nose. The Chardonnay Selezione `97 shows a balanced, intense and creamy bouquet; the same features are found on the rich, persistent palate. This vintage produced some great Pinot Grigios, but the Zuc '98 is a veritable champion. But their top wine - extraordinary, young and promising, elegant and full of personality - is the Bianco Le Roverelle. A blend with a good measure of picolit, matured in oak casks, it shows harmony and complexity, and also well-judged wood. They're working hard here to produce a range of important reds and, knowing Emilio, we can be sure they'll succeed.

○	COF Bianco Le Roverelle Zuc di Volpe '97	🍷🍷	5
○	COF Chardonnay Selezione Zuc di Volpe '97	🍷🍷	4
○	COF Pinot Grigio Zuc di Volpe '98	🍷🍷	4
○	COF Ribolla Gialla Zuc di Volpe '98	🍷🍷	4
●	COF Merlot '97	🍷	3
○	COF Pinot Bianco Zuc di Volpe '98	🍷	4
○	COF Tocai Friulano Zuc di Volpe '98	🍷	4
○	COF Chardonnay '98		3
○	COF Tocai Friulano '98		3
○	COF Bianco Le Roverelle Zuc di Volpe '96	🍸🍸	5

OTHER WINERIES

The following producers obtained good scores in our tastings with one or more of their wines:

PROVINCE OF GORIZIA

Maurizio Buzzinelli
Cormons, tel. 0481/60902
Collio Tocai Friulano '98,
Collio Cabernet Sauvignon Ronc dal Luis '97,
Collio Merlot Ronc dal Luis '97

Eredi Gradnik
Cormons, tel. 0481/61395
Collio Chardonnay '98,
Collio Tocai Friulano '98,
Collio Traminer '98

Albino Kurtin
Cormons, tel. 0481/60685
Collio Pinot Bianco '98,
Collio Pinot Grigio '98

Stanislao Mavric
Cormons, tel. 0481/60660
Collio Pinot Grigio '98,
Collio Merlot '98

Ronco di Zegla - Maurizio Princic
Cormons, tel. 0481/61155
Collio Chardonnay '98,
Collio Pinot Grigio '98

Tiare - Roberto Snidarcig
Cormons,
tel. 0481/60064
Collio Tocai Friulano '97,
Collio Pinot Nero '98

Sant'Elena
Gradisca d'Isonzo,
tel. 0481/92388
Friuli Isonzo Tatu Ris. '97,
Friuli Isonzo Bianco '98

Redi Vazzoler
Mossa, tel. 0432/80519
Collio Chardonnay '98,
Collio Pinot Bianco '98,
Collio Pinot Grigio '98

Il Carpino
S. Floriano del Collio,
tel. 0481/884097
Bianco Carpino '97,
Collio Chardonnay Vigna Runc '98

PROVINCE OF UDINE

Livio e Claudio Buiatti
Buttrio, tel. 0432/674317
COF Bianco Poianis Blanc '97,
COF Pinot Bianco '98,
COF Refosco P. R. '97

Flavio Pontoni, Buttrio, tel. 0432/674352
COF Pinot Grigio '98,
COF Merlot '98

Gigi Valle, Buttrio, tel. 0432/674289
COF Sauvignon '98,
COF Merlot Gigi Valle Ris. '92

Ronchi di Fornaz
Cividale del Friuli, tel. 0432/701462
COF Il Bianco Diverso '96,
COF Il Rosso Diverso '96

Nicola e Mauro Cencig
Manzano, tel. 0432/740789
COF Merlot '97,
COF Refosco P. R. '97,
COF Pinot Grigio '98

Gianpaolo ed Elisabetta Colutta
Manzano, tel. 0432/751208
COF Pinot Bianco '98,
COF Ribolla Gialla '98,
COF Rosso Frassinolo '97

Midolini, Manzano, tel. 0432/754555
COF Pinot Grigio '98,
COF Cabernet Franc '97,
COF Refosco P. R. '97

Aquila del Torre
Povoletto, tel. 0432/666428
COF Picolit '97,
COF Verduzzo Friulano '97

Ronco dei Pini, Prepotto, tel. 0432/713239
Collio Chardonnay '98,
COF Pinot Bianco '98,
COF Pinot Grigio '98,
COF Merlot '98

Brojli - Franco Clementin
Terzo di Aquileia, tel. 0431/32642
Friuli Aquileia Riesling '98

Albano Guerra - Dario Montina
Torreano di Cividale, tel. 0432/715077
COF Pinot Grigio '98,
COF Refosco P. R. '97

EMILIA ROMAGNA

Emilia Romagna is definitely becoming an important source of good wine. Its success was undreamed of until just a few years ago, and represents a now consolidated trend based on bold decisions and shrewd investments by an ever-growing number of producers. Recognition is due, also, to the intelligent attention provided by regional government agencies to private producers' efforts to improve quality, as it is to the wineries that have been able to make the most of their terroir and of the advice of consultant enologists who are famous throughout Italy. About a dozen wines from as many different producers made it all the way to the Three Glass finals. A not altogether unexpected "surprise" came from the Colli Bolognesi which, for several years now, have represented a sort of ongoing enological research station for the region. Here, apart from the confirmation of Tenuta Bonzara as one of the region's foremost estates with its Bonzarone Cabernet Sauvignon '97, the Vallana domain steps into the limelight this year with its extremely elegant Cabernet Sauvignon Riserva '97. Romagna, though with fewer Three Glass awards this year than last, has seen an overall increase in the quality of the wines on offer. Excellent performances were given here by wineries such as Tre Monti, La Palazza, Castelluccio, Cesari, Ferrucci and the Cantina di San Patrignano Terre del Cedro, a producer surely destined for outstanding success. These producers obtained significant results not only with wines made from "international" grape varieties (cabernet sauvignon and chardonnay) but also with traditional sangiovese-based wines which show a just balance between upfront fruit and skillful wine-making. Besides, in this region, the sangiovese variety has shown that it possesses specific characteristics which are capable of yielding wines of considerable structure and which are laden with rich, soft, fruity flavors. The real hot news, however, is the result obtained by Fattoria Zerbina, which is the first winery since we started judging the wines of this region to earn two Three Glass awards. These were for two wines of outstanding quality, the Marzieno '97 and the Albana Passito Scacco Matto '96. While we are on the subject: in view of the superb performance of this last wine and the generally positive results which many producers obtained with their Albana Passitos, we cannot but reiterate the great potential of this grape variety, especially in its Passito versions (raisin wine). Nor have we been wrong in pointing out the constant growth over the last few years of two wineries in the Colli Piacentini zone, La Stoppa and La Tosa. In the former case, we awarded our Three Glasses to the enchanting Vigna del Volta, a splendid wine made from semi-dried malvasia di Candia grapes. As for La Tosa, an estate which just goes from strength to strength, we gave our top award to their Cabernet Sauvignon Luna Selvatica, a wine of outstanding balance and undoubtedly the product of obsessive attention in the vineyard.

BERTINORO (FO)

VINI PREGIATI CELLI
V.LE CARDUCCI, 5
47032 BERTINORO (FO)
TEL. 0543/445183

Perhaps Celli's period of transition – from being a winery that only vinifies to becoming an all-around producer – has not yet been fully completed. The construction work involved in this transformation and the attention due to each of its priorities, from putting the finishing touches on the storage and tasting areas, to developing the vineyards, has greatly taxed the owners, Mauro Sirri and Emanuele Casadei. This may explain the results obtained, which are certainly worthy of some praise but which are not yet in line with this winery's true potential. One cannot deny, for example, that the Trebbiano di Romagna Poggio Ferlina '98 is one of the very best wines obtained from that grape variety in the whole of Romagna: it is an incisive, straightforward white, with a floral bouquet and a pleasantly acidulous flavour. The Albano Secco I Croppi '98 also showed well: it offers elegant scents of ripe fruit and, in line with tradition, a satisfying alcohol level and body. The Sangiovese Superiore Riserva Le Grillaie '96 is decent, but still well below the level of the best examples from previous vintages: its most interesting characteristics are its evolved ripe berry aromas and its rounded, fleshy fruit on the palate. The dominant note in the '97 Solara, the winery's Albana Passito, is its alcoholic warmth which, however, somewhat attenuates its perfumes of apricots and honey. Lastly, the straightforward Pagadebit '98 is fresh and appealing.

○	Albana di Romagna Secco I Croppi '98	🍷	2*
○	Trebbiano di Romagna Poggio Ferlina '98	🍷	2*
○	Albana di Romagna Passito Solara '97	🍷	4
●	Sangiovese di Romagna Sup. Le Grillaie Ris. '96	🍷	3
○	Pagadebit '98		1
●	Sangiovese di Romagna Sup. Le Grillaie '97	🍸	2

BERTINORO (FO)

FATTORIA PARADISO
VIA PALMEGGIANA, 285
47032 BERTINORO (FO)
TEL. 0543/445044

We have had tangible proof of the improving quality of this historic estate: the results obtained this year were really impressive and Graziella Pezzi, the daughter of the founder, has now really taken the helm of the winery, steering it determinedly in a new direction: she plans to re-equip the cellar and continue in the quest for excellence. However, the estate remains firmly committed to tradition. The Barbarossa '95, for example, is made from the indigenous grape of the same name. It is a red whose bouquet reveals hints of the large oak barrels in which it is aged, as well as wild berries and spice. On the palate, it is full-bodied, rounded and decidedly robust, but also remarkably elegant. The Albana Passito Gradisca '93 displays a deep golden color and offers intense scents of peach and apricot on the nose. It is a full, well-structured wines whose considerable level of alcohol provides it with a pleasing softness and balance. The Albana Dolce Vigna del Viale'98 is a fresh, fruity and moderately sweet wine, perhaps more in tune with the palate of the traditional Albana drinker. Lastly, there is the Castello Riserva Ugarte '95, a perfectly delicious example of an orthodox traditional style: it is rich, powerful, and almost arrogant in character, but also mischievously alluring.

○	Albana di Romagna Passito Gradisca '93	🍷🍷	5
●	Barbarossa '95	🍷🍷	3*
●	Castello Ris. Ugarte '95	🍷🍷	3*
○	Albana di Romagna Dolce Vigna del Viale '98	🍷	3

Slow Food 2000

Slow Food is an international movement founded in 1989 and active in 40 countries worldwide, with 60,000 members and about 500 Convivia (chapters).

Slow Food has a cultural agenda:
It promotes a **philosophy of pleasure**, protects small food producers who make quality products, counters the degrading effects of industrial and fast food culture which standardize tastes, has a **taste education** program for adults and children, works towards **safeguarding** traditional food and wine heritage, provides **consumer information** and promotes tourism that respects and cares for the environment.

Slow Food Events:
Each year Slow Food puts on important food and wine events for food enthusiasts and professionals: the biennial **Salone del Gusto** (the Hall of Taste) in Turin; the biennial **Cheese** in Bra; the **Luebeck Festival**, a food and drink event which celebrates German fare; **Wine Conventions; Tasting Sessions.**

Each **Convivium** organizes social meetings, tastings, cooking courses, trips, visits to restaurants, and lectures for its members. The twinning of Convivia from different countries promote the exchange of tastes and knowledge of different cultures.

An Ark to safeguard products and the planet of tastes:
An important project aimed at safeguarding and benefitting small-scale agricultural and food production, which risks dying out. Thousands of different kinds of *charcuterie*, cheeses, animal breeds and plants are in danger of disappearing forever: the homologation of tastes, the excessive power of industrial companies, distribution difficulties and disinformation are the causes of a process which could lead to the loss of an irreplaceable heritage of traditional recipes, knowledge and tastes. The Ark is a scientific research and documentation program which works towards relaunching businesses and outfits with important cultural and economic value.

Education of Taste:
The Slow Food Movement has taken action to realize one of the objectives of the **Ark Manifesto** to promote taste education in grade schools. Along with putting on numerous conferences on this subject, Slow Food published an instructional manual for teachers and parents on how to best teach children about enjoying and understanding their taste culture. Slow Food plans many more educational activities around the world during "**Weeks of Taste**".

Fraternal Tables to feed those who need assistance:
Slow Food funds **Fraternal Tables** dedicated to increasing international solidarity. **The Nicaragua Project** intends to recover agricultural land and improve production capacity in the rural area around the municipality of San Francisco Libre. The **Hekura Project** involves monthly support to the kitchen of a native American hospital for infectious diseases in Brazil. The **Zlata Project** funded two lunch programs to help resolve food emergencies, in particular concerning children, in Bosnia

Slow

Slow features in-depth and often off-the-wall stories about food culture across the globe, with related lifestyle topics of a truly international scope, unlike anything you've seen before on the newsstand... 160 well-designed pages in full color, with exciting photography and articles by top authors, gourmets, wine experts, and food & travel writers worldwide. Just take your pick: English, German, French, Spanish or Italian…

Italian Wines 2000

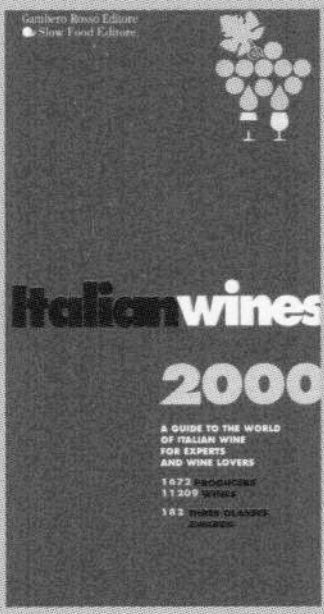

For the first time in English, the most complete, reliable and influential guide to the best Italian wines. Published by Slow Food and Gambero Rosso, it is now in its twelth edition. It describes the history and production of 1672 wine makers, describes and evaluates 11209 wines, awards 182 wines with "Tre Bicchieri" (Three Glasses): the élite of the great Italian wine-making tradition.
Price £16.99 or $ 24.95

Registration Form

Slow Food is aimed at food and wine enthusiasts, those who do not want to lose the myriad of tastes in traditional foodstuffs from around the world, and those who share the snail's wise slowness. Annual membership includes:
- a personal membership card
- four issues of the quarterly magazine, *Slow*
- the right to attend all events organized by the Slow Food movement throughout the world
- a 20% discount on all Slow Food publications

If you have any questions, please feel free to contact us. We are only a FAX, phone call or e-mail away. Phone: ++39 172 419611 - FAX: ++39 172 421293
E-mail: international@slow-food.com

I would like to:
❑ start a convivium ❑ become a member ❑ subscribe to "Slow"

Full Name

(of company or restaurant or other)

Street Address City

State/Prov./County Country Postal Code

Home Tel. Day Tel. Fax

Profession

I would prefer to receive Slow in: ❑ English ❑ German ❑ French ❑ Spanish ❑ Italian

membership fees to join *Slow Food*
U.K. £33.00
U.S. $60.00

Method of Payment

❑ Cash ❑ Check
❑ Credit Card: ❑ Visa ❑ AmEx ❑ Mastercard

|__|__|__|__||__|__|__|__||__|__|__|__||__|__|__|__|

|__|__/__|__| ✗

Exp. Date Signature

Cardholder Total Amount

Toll-free number in U.S. and Canada: 1-877-SLOW FOOD (756-9366)

BERTINORO (FO)

GIOVANNA MADONIA
VIA DE' CAPPUCCINI, 130
47032 BERTINORO (FO)
TEL. 0543/444361 - 0543/445085

Romagna's wine-making fortunes are tied to the increasing appearance on the scene of new figures like Giovanna Madonia: intelligent, dynamic, ambitious and driven by great passion, people who understand that, in order to achieve brilliant results, you have to invest and work without respite. This is the spirit animating the new enterprising generation of winegrowers in this area, especially where the estates are small, like this one. Giovanna has, on a small scale, done great things: the replanting project is the brainchild of the distinguished agronomist Remigio Bordini and wine-making has been entrusted to Attilio Pagli, one of the most skilled interpreters of state-of-the-art oenology in Italy. Excellent wines like the Sterpigno '97 (made from merlot) came, therefore, as no surprise. On the nose it offers intense scents of ripe red berries, but we were particularly impressed by the fruit on the palate, which is concentrated, rounded and elegant, shows extraordinary length and is not at all overset by the notable level of fine, soft tannins. The Sangiovese Superiore Fermavento '97 is so overwhelming in style that its balance is somewhat jeopardized. The '98 version is fresh and inviting on the nose, and shows remarkable softness on the palate. The Albana Amabile Neblina '98 is pleasant, too.

●	Forlì Merlot Sterpigno '97	🍷🍷	4
●	Sangiovese di Romagna Sup. Fermavento '97	🍷	3
●	Sangiovese di Romagna Sup. Fermavento '98	🍷	3
○	Albana di Romagna Amabile Neblina '98		3

BORGONOVO VAL TIDONE (PC)

TENUTA PERNICE
LOC. PERNICE
FRAZ. CASTELNOVO VAL TIDONE
29010 BORGONOVO VAL TIDONE (PC)
TEL. 0523/860050

The three holdings known as Pernice, Collinetta and Raballa fan out for some 24 hectares (at an altitude of 230 meters above sea level) around the nucleus of Maria Poggi Azzali's estate. The Tenuta Pernice, whose wines have been marketed since 1990, has always been recognized for the care it takes in producing semi-sparkling wines. Now, thanks to the input of the oenologist Giovanni Crosato and the availability of a thoroughly well-equipped cellar, two very impressive still reds are also made. These two wines amazed us with their typicity and clean, well-made style. The Collare Rosso '97, made from cabernet sauvignon and bonarda, just missed getting Two Glasses. Aged in oak casks of various sizes for 12 months, it has a handsome, deep color and a fruity, lightly spicy bouquet, and it displays smooth, ripe fruit on the palate. The '98 still Gutturnio also did well: it is purplish in color, and offers well-defined scents of red berries, as well as substantial body and appropriate acidity in the mouth. Among the traditional lightly sparkling wines, the Ortrugo is as appealing as ever: it has a straw-yellow color, a delicate nose and an extremely pleasing flavor. The Sauvignon Frizzante offers a sweet banana fragrance and fresh and invitingly quaffable fruit on the palate. Lastly, the Gutturnio Frizzante '98 displays a ruby color with purplish highlights; its bouquet is clean, and it reveals an appealing undertone of acidity on the palate.

●	Collare Rosso '97	🍷	3*
●	Colli Piacentini Gutturnio '98	🍷	3
○	Colli Piacentini Ortrugo Frizzante '98	🍷	2*
●	Colli Piacentini Gutturnio Frizzante '98		2
○	Colli Piacentini Sauvignon Frizzante '98		2
●	Collare Rosso '96	🍸	3

BRISIGHELLA (RA)

LA BERTA
VIA PIDEURA, 48
48013 BRISIGHELLA (RA)
TEL. 0546/84998

We are particularly impressed with the verve and dynamism of Costantino Giovannini, the young proprietor of this estate (which benefits from the advice of Stefano Chioccioli). He is determined to obtain brilliant results and, to this aim, is pursuing a path made up of small but decisive steps, like better vineyard management and improved winery equipment, increased contact and interchange with other producers and completion of the already appealing winery headquarters. Our faith in him has been amply repaid: the sign of progress this year is to be found in the broadening of the winery's range. The elegant chardonnay-based Pieve Alto '98 offers fresh floral hints on the nose, and is rich and inviting on the palate. The excellent Solano '97, a Sangiovese Superiore, displays a traditional bouquet; the palate is opulent and full-bodied, with chocolate and vanilla notes and, though a little bit resinous, it retains a distinctive country elegance. The Rosso Faenza Ca'di Berta '97, which is one of the new DOCs proliferating – almost unendingly – in this region, is made from cabernet sauvignon. It is ripe in flavor and perfumes, with reasonable body and an attractive easy-drinking style. We were also not at all disappointed by the extremely characteristic, powerful and well-structured Sangiovese Riserva Olmatello '96, although its nose is a bit dumb and its tannins are noticeable. The fresh and vinous Sangiovese '98 is at least worthy of mention. The Infavato Passito '96 was produced using new methods which enhance its sugar content and its complexity; it shows, as a result, a more intense color than usual and a notable softness and elegance.

●	Colli di Faenza Rosso Ca' di Berta '97	🍷🍷	4
●	Sangiovese di Romagna Sup. Solano '97	🍷🍷	3*
○	Infavato Passito '96	🍷	4
○	Colli di Faenza Pieve Alto '98	🍷	3
●	Sangiovese di Romagna Ris. Olmatello '96	🍷	3
●	Sangiovese di Romagna '98		2
●	Sangiovese di Romagna Ris. Olmatello '95	🍸🍸	3

CASALECCHIO DI RENO (BO)

TIZZANO
VIA MARESCALCHI, 13
40033 CASALECCHIO DI RENO (BO)
TEL. 051/577665 - 051/571208

This handsome estate, which comprises 230 hectares in the low foothills of Tizzano, has always been an important point of reference for the agricultural sector throughout the Bologna area. Owned for hundreds of years by the Marescalchi family, it was inherited at the beginning of the 20th century by the Visconti di Modrone. Today, after various vicissitudes, the 35 hectares of international grape varieties are starting to yield such positive results that, wisely, new plantings of the indigenous pignoletto grape have also been carried out. The common denominators among the wines produced are their cleanness, reliability and, no less important, their very good value for money. Among the wines we tasted this year there was an interesting Brut produced by the Charmat method from pignoletto grapes alone; it is an attractively fresh wine with good balance and satisfying body. The semi-sparkling Pignoletto Frizzante is pleasant and deliberately straightforward. It has a fine, fruity bouquet with notes of green apple, and is soft and typically almondy on the palate. The Pinot Bianco '98, with its characteristic toasty hint on the nose, is well made; in the mouth it is soft, rich and lingering. The Cabernet Sauvignon '97 is a nice surprise: it has a lovely ruby hue, and the bouquet is notable for its unusual notes of roasting coffee. On the palate it is well balanced, with good, rich fruit and appropriate tannins. The Riesling '98 and the Sauvignon '98 are fragrant, easy to drink and well executed. The still Barbera '98 is fresh and quaffable.

●	Colli Bolognesi Cabernet Sauvignon '97	🍷	3
○	Colli Bolognesi Pignoletto Brut	🍷	3
○	Colli Bolognesi Pignoletto Frizzante '98	🍷	2*
○	Colli Bolognesi Pinot Bianco '98	🍷	2
●	Colli Bolognesi Barbera '98		3
○	Colli Bolognesi Riesling Italico '98		3
○	Colli Bolognesi Sauvignon '98		3

CASTEL S. PIETRO TERME (BO)

UMBERTO CESARI

VIA STANZANO, 1120
FRAZ. GALLO BOLOGNESE
40050 CASTEL S. PIETRO TERME (BO)
TEL. 051/941896 - 051/940234

The evidence is there for all to see: this winery, which makes hundreds of thousands of bottles, has taken an irreversible step towards producing excellent wines. The symptoms of this trend, which were already evident at last year's tastings, have been amply confirmed. The admirably clean style of the wines is now accompanied by greater complexity and concentration. Longer aging in wood and greater care during vinification are probably the cause. And the entire range has benefited from this improvement in quality, with the white wines at the forefront. The Laurento '97, a white with intense scents of oak and vanilla, releases warm flavors of butter, vanilla and hazelnut on the palate; the fresh finish bodes well for its future development. The late-harvested Chardonnay '97 is a soft, mature wine with notes of honey and liqueur. The Albana Passito Colle del Re '94, with its uncloying sweetness and its inviting aromas of vanilla and honey, also impressed us. The Malise '98 (fresher and more attractive than usual) comes from a blend of pignoletto and chardonnay. The Liano '96, made from sangiovese and cabernet sauvignon, is a fine full-bodied and well-structured wine; it offers a broad bouquet with notes of vanilla combined with nuances of ripe fruit and spice. The interesting Sangiovese Riserva '96 displays a traditional fragrance, but is a bit tannic and aggressive. The Sangiovese Superiore Ca' Grande '98 has a herbaceous nose, whereas the Sangiovese di Romagna '98 is straightforward and appealing. Lastly, the Vigneto Parolino '98 is clean and reasonably well structured.

○ Albana di Romagna Passito Colle del Re '94	🍷🍷	4
○ Chardonnay Morandi '97	🍷🍷	4
○ Laurento '97	🍷🍷	4
● Liano '96	🍷🍷	4
○ Malise '98	🍷	3
● Sangiovese di Romagna '98	🍷	2*
● Sangiovese di Romagna Ris. '96	🍷	3
● Sangiovese di Romagna Sup. Ca' Grande '98	🍷	3
○ Trebbiano di Romagna Vigneto Parolino '98	🍷	2*
● Liano '95	YY	4

CASTELBOLOGNESE (RA)

STEFANO FERRUCCI

VIA CASOLANA, 3045/2
48014 CASTELBOLOGNESE (RA)
TEL. 0546/651068

Stefano Ferrucci is a very able producer whose ancient Roman posting station, transformed into winery headquarters, keeps turning out some very interesting wines indeed. If, a little mischievously, we must find fault, it's that the names on his labels rather remind us of a list of '60s B-movies which recount the deeds of Julius Caesar or the labors of Hercules. The outstanding characteristics of his wines are power and structure, witness the Bottale '95, a Sangiovese Riserva in which the dominant scents are of clean wood and violets. On the palate the wine is notably well balanced and long, with rounded fruit and very well-tamed tannins. The Sangiovese Riserva Domus Caia '96 also has a deep color and rich extract, but is even fuller and more attractive on the palate, with its hints of ripe red berries. The Domus Caia '97 displays intense, broad perfumes; its purple hue reveals its extreme youthfulness, but it has a surprisingly delicate cherry flavor and an unexpectedly soft rounded texture. The Sangiovese Superiore Centurione '98 offers aromas of plum and cherry and displays first-class fruit. The Albana Dolce '98 is striking in its richness and depth. These qualities are even more marked in the Domus Aurea '96, the Albana Passito (raisin wine) whose warm soft style attractively sets off its flavors of fruit and honey. The estate's other Passito, the Stefano Ferrucci '96, is made from malvasia grapes and is notable for its delicate perfumes that combine floral and varietal tones. The Albana Secco '98 is more straightforward than last year's version.

○ Albana di Romagna Passito Domus Aurea '96	🍷🍷	4
● Sangiovese di Romagna Bottale Ris. '95	🍷🍷	6
● Sangiovese di Romagna Domus Caia Ris. '96	🍷🍷	4
○ Albana di Romagna Dolce '98	🍷	3
● Sangiovese di Romagna Sup. Centurione '98	🍷	3
○ Stefano Ferrucci Passito '96	🍷	5
○ Albana di Romagna Secco '98		3
● Bottale '93	YY	5
● Domus Caia '95	YY	4

CASTELLO DI SERRAVALLE (BO)

VALLONA
VIA S. ANDREA, 203
LOC. FAGNANO
40050 CASTELLO DI SERRAVALLE (BO)
TEL. 051/6703058 - 051/6703066

The "grand maneuvers" of the Vallona winery are proceeding apace with the recent purchase of an estate in the Monte San Pietro area, where at least 10 hectares of vineyards are already being replanted. Something must be going right, because its Cabernet Sauvignon Selezione outshone its rivals and walked off with Three Glasses. A more than positive year, then, for young Maurizio Vallona who, apart from the Cabernet Sauvignon '97, presented an excellent range of whites and an interesting "normal" Cabernet Sauvignon. The Cabernet Selezione '97, however, is astonishingly elegant. Starting with its intriguing nose it shows that it's an extremely original wine: it offers varietal scents with intense, sweet notes, and the palate is succulent, soft and concentrated, with a long, lingering finish. The basic Cabernet Sauvignon '97 is very good too: it displays complex elegant perfumes with hints of cocoa. It has a well-balanced flavor, with soft tannins and good length. The magnificent Chardonnay Selezione '97, on the other hand, confirms their great talent at making whites: fermented in small oak casks, it offers a deep bouquet of ripe fruit well integrated with a delicate toasty note. The rich and beautifully balanced palate reveals a long, satisfying finish. The Chardonnay '98 is also very well made. It is vinified in stainless steel and is clean, harmonious and fine on the nose, and soft and elegant on the palate. The Sauvignon '98 and the Pignoletto Superiore '98 also easily earned One Glass each; both have very characterful bouquets, substantial fruit and the interesting, distinctive traits of Vallona's white wines. The Pignoletto Vivace '98 is correct and appealing, too.

●	Colli Bolognesi Cabernet Sauvignon Selezione '97	🍷🍷🍷	4
●	Colli Bolognesi Cabernet Sauvignon '97	🍷🍷	3*
○	Colli Bolognesi Chardonnay '98	🍷🍷	3*
○	Colli Bolognesi Chardonnay Selezione '97	🍷🍷	3*
○	Colli Bolognesi Pignoletto Sup. '98	🍷	3
○	Colli Bolognesi Pignoletto Vivace '98	🍷	2
○	Colli Bolognesi Sauvignon Sup. '98	🍷	3
●	Colli Bolognesi Cabernet Sauvignon '96	🍷🍷 (outline)	3
○	Colli Bolognesi Chardonnay '97	🍷🍷 (outline)	3

CASTELVETRO (MO)

VITTORIO GRAZIANO
VIA OSSI, 30
41014 CASTELVETRO (MO)
TEL. 059/799162

Vittorio Graziano never stands still for a moment. You lose sight of him for an instant, and there he is, inside the excavation (just completed) for the new made-to-measure cellar, which will be entirely under ground: he's building it right underneath his beloved vines. He has set himself a target: this is where the first vintage of the new millennium will be vinified. In the meantime he is getting ready for the release of a new wine which will undoubtedly be even more of a talking point in the zone than his Lambruscos, and they have been a center of attention for some time now. The wine in question is a still red from the '97 vintage, made from malbo gentile with the addition of small amounts of other varieties, which Vittorio has named Sassoscuro after the zone from which it comes. This wine is interesting and unusual: it is discreet rather than overwhelming and benefits from having been aged in small oak barrels. On the nose, its toasty notes are well integrated with its distinct aromas of chocolate, black cherry and alcohol. The palate is fat and powerful, but its fresh acidity and underpinning firm, well-balanced tannins give it length and promise. As usual, the Grasparossa, of which some 20 thousand bottles were produced this year, lives up to its reputation. Its intense ruby color with purple highlights precede the typical bouquet of a traditional Grasparossa: floral notes give way to red fruit and jammy tones, with agreeably rustic vegetal undertones. On the palate good extract and more than 12% alcohol make it attractively rich and rounded; its gentle effervescence and light tannins lead into a dry finish, just as tradition decrees. The Grasparossa's less complex sibling, the pleasant Ruspantino, is lighter and more straightforward.

●	Lambrusco Grasparossa di Castelvetro '98	🍷	2*
●	Sassoscuro '97	🍷	3
○	Spargolino Frizzante		3
●	Ruspantino		1

CIVITELLA DI ROMAGNA (FO)

PODERI DAL NESPOLI
VIA STATALE, 49
LOC. NESPOLI
47012 CIVITELLA DI ROMAGNA (FO)
TEL. 0543/989637

Is Civitella di Romagna actually at the end of the earth? And are the sandstone houses huddled around this winery really off the beaten track, on some far-off island only ever reached by the occasional traveler? Certainly not! It is true, however, that the Ravaioli family's estate seems to live up to the legend of being a secluded aristocratic hermitage, whose privacy would nevertheless be worth intruding upon with a visit. The wines are produced with rigorous respect for tradition: indeed in some cases they might be better off were they interpreted in a more modern and open-minded way. However, the estate's top wine, the Borgo dei Guidi '97, made from a blend of grapes in which sangiovese and cabernet sauvignon predominate, is no disappointment. On the nose it offers impressive fruity aromas, and on the palate one finds marked jam-like hints with intense overripe notes. With its good acidity and meaty fruit, it is an almost overwhelmingly full-flavored wine, and certainly has its own individual and unusual allure. Hints of overripeness, here to some extent uncontrolled, are also to be found in the Sangiovese Superiore Santodeno '98, which stands out from its peers in Romagna by virtue of its power and rich body. The Sangiovese Il Prugneto '97, perhaps less massive than its siblings but with more attractive fruit and an unexpected finesse, really confirms the potential of this estate. Lastly, the use of large, old oak barrels and late harvesting of the grapes are the salient features of the production of Il Nespoli '97; its mellow, sweetish notes are appealing on first impact but ultimately make the wine a bit tired and lackluster.

●	Borgo dei Guidi '97	🍷🍷	4
●	Il Nespoli '97	🍷	3
●	Sangiovese di Romagna Sup. Il Prugneto '97	🍷	2*
●	Sangiovese di Romagna Sup. Santodeno '98	🍷	2*
●	Sangiovese di Romagna Sup. Il Prugneto '98		2
●	Borgo dei Guidi '93	🍸🍸	4
●	Borgo dei Guidi '95	🍸🍸	4
●	Il Nespoli '95	🍸🍸	3

FAENZA (RA)

LEONE CONTI
VIA POZZO, 1
TENUTA S. LUCIA
48018 FAENZA (RA)
TEL. 0546/642149 - 0546/27130

The many positive characteristics of Leone Conti's wines are occasionally undercut by minor lapses in quality, caused probably by the intrinsic shortcomings of his vinification cellar. His broad and interesting range offers, above all, two excellent wines made from semi-dried grapes. The Non Ti Scordar di Me Albana Passito '96 is rendered warm, soft and intense by its robust level of alcohol and its fairly plump fruit. The Albana Passito Oro '98 was a real surprise: notes of noble rot are quite evident in its fresh, fruity bouquet. On the palate, one finds lingering sensations that range from honey to citrus fruit, candied citron peel and almond. The Albana Dolce Vignacupa '98 has an attractive flavor, whereas the Albana Secco Vignapozzo '98 shows some rough edges, although it does conform to the traditional well-structured, soft and concentrated style of Albana. The new Colli di Faenza Bianco '98 is a bit pungent, though it is interesting on the palate. Moving on to the reds, we must express our admiration of a slightly unusual wine whose name reveals Conti's passion for soccer: the Rossonero '97, a blend of 90% syrah and 10% sangiovese. It has a slightly rustic nose, but is succulent and ripe on the palate, with notes of plum, cherry and blackberry. The Il Capanno '98, made from the humble ciliegiolo grape, is pleasant, though a little short on extract; it too is reminiscent of red fruit, and cherry in particular. Lastly, there is a good Sangiovese di Romagna '98, which is tannic and robust.

○	Albana di Romagna Passito Non Ti Scordar di Me '96	🍷🍷	5
○	Albana di Romagna Passito Oro '98	🍷🍷	6
●	Rossonero '97	🍷🍷	4
○	Albana di Romagna Dolce Vignacupa '98	🍷	3
○	Albana di Romagna Secco Vignapozzo '98	🍷	3
○	Colli di Faenza Bianco '98	🍷	3
●	Il Capanno '98	🍷	2*
●	Sangiovese di Romagna '98	🍷	2*
○	Albana di Romagna Passito Non Ti Scordar di Me '95	🍸🍸	5

FAENZA (RA)

FATTORIA ZERBINA
VIA VICCHIO, 11
FRAZ. MARZENO
48010 FAENZA (RA)
TEL. 0546/40022

Great triumphs for Fattoria Zerbina: Cristina Geminiani's estate was the first ever in Emilia Romagna to have three wines go through to our final tastings and to win Three Glasses with two of them: the Albana Passito Scacco Matto and the Marzieno. The '96 version of the Scacco Matto shows a pale golden color and the intense, seductive aromas of fruit at the height of a hot summer. On the palate one finds alternating flavors of vanilla, almond, honey and citrus fruit, all beautifully amalgamated in the wine's extremely soft, long and persistent structure. This is a great wine that does honor both to Cristina and to her Tuscan consultant oenologist, Vittorio Fiore. The version of Arrocco from the '95 vintage, a year in which Scacco Matto was not produced, is also excellent: it shares the more important wine's notes of noble rot and attractive hints of vanilla. The '97 Marzieno, the estate's blend of cabernet sauvignon and sangiovese, is superb too. It is just a little rougher than the '95, though similar in its richness of extract; it displays an intense color and a powerful structure. The complex flavor leaves a long aftertaste with hints of wild berries, licorice and tobacco. The Sangiovese Superiore Torre di Ceparano '97 is certainly praiseworthy: it has an intense and characteristic nose, a well-structured and soft palate and a creamy finish. The Tergeno '97, made from chardonnay and sauvignon, is herbaceous and elegant in the mouth; the Sangiovese Ceregio '98 is attractively fruity and pleasantly quaffable.

●	Marzieno Ravenna Rosso '97	▼▼▼	5
○	Albana di Romagna Passito Scacco Matto '96	▼▼▼	5
○	Albana di Romagna Passito Arrocco '95	▼▼	5
●	Sangiovese di Romagna Sup. Torre di Ceparano '97	▼▼	4
○	Colli di Faenza Tergeno '97	▼	4
●	Sangiovese di Romagna Sup. Ceregio '98	▼	2*
●	Marzieno '95	▽▽▽	5
●	Marzieno '93	▽▽	3
●	Sangiovese di Romagna Sup. Pietramora Ris. '95	▽▽	5

FAENZA (RA)

ISTITUTO PROFESSIONALE
PER L'AGRICOLTURA E L'AMBIENTE
VIA FIRENZE, 194
48018 FAENZA (RA)
TEL. 0546/22932

It can happen that excellent wines are produced (almost just for fun) in the serene environment of a school, well away from the pressures of the marketplace. Here everything is small, from the few vineyards, entirely institute-owned, to the cellar, which lacks nothing (including barriques), and the well-equipped and efficient laboratory. The volume of wine produced is limited too: rarely more than a thousand bottles of each type. In this rarefied world there is a skilled wine-maker at work: Sergio Ragazzini, whose relative youth belies his considerable experience, and who gladly shares his knowledge with several of Romagna's wineries. The very absence of pressure as well as the school's strictly educational goals create fertile ground for research, even when it involves ignoring current consumer demands and experimenting with unusual grape varieties. Thus some very unusual new wines come into being, like the '97 Passito Rosso, made from malbo gentile, of which about 400 bottles were produced. It is a soft, enticing, almost resinous liqueur-like wine, which is extraordinarily lingering and really surprisingly delightful to drink. It is in some ways similar to Recioto or, even more, to port, but is more straightforward and easily quaffable than the latter. The no less interesting Albana Passito '97, which bears the apt name of Ultimo Giorno di Scuola (last day of school), is fruity, soft, warm, full yet delicate and sweet without cloying. The cellar, however, does not limit itself to dessert wines. The Rosso di Nero '97, made from pinot nero, is in fact an excellent wine. The nose is not perfectly well knit, but there is a charming, quite elegant palate with soft tannins. It is also worth remembering the Varrone '98, made from the indigenous burson grape: it reveals rich alcohol and a ripe flavor.

●	Amabile Persolino Rosso Passito '97	▼▼	4
○	Albana di Romagna Passito Ultimo Giorno di Scuola '97	▼	4
●	Rosso di Nero Ravenna Rosso '97	▼	3
●	Varrone Ravenna Rosso '98		1

FORLÌ

DREI DONÀ TENUTA LA PALAZZA
VIA DEL TESORO, 23
LOC. MASSA DI VECCHIAZZANO
47100 FORLÌ
TEL. 0543/769371

The entire Drei Donà family looks after this estate, with young Enrico at the forefront, particularly for marketing. They continue to acquire new vineyards, new wine-making equipment, more advanced computer technology and, of course, new markets. We'll describe the best of this year's wines, beginning with the Tornese '97, the most famous Romagna Chardonnay in Italy: it is a fine, elegant, lingering white, aged for a time in new oak. It just lacks some of the breadth that has so charmed us in the past. The Magnificat Cabernet Sauvignon '95, with an intense color and a broad, seductive bouquet, once again showed all of its breeding. The palate is powerful, rounded and moderately tannic. Oak, spice, licorice and wild berries combine in a full flavor that lingers in the mouth. Their other top red, the Pruno '95, is a fine expression of this area's most typical wine, Sangiovese. We particularly enjoyed this red, which may seem less fascinating and complex than the Magnificat but is certainly more immediate. It is a full-bodied, rounded, well-structured wine whose force, aromas and vigor are honed by the oak of the small barrels in which it is vinified and matures. A note of recognition is due to the fresh and modern Notturno '97, a young Sangiovese with characteristic perfumes, an intense violet cast and amazing quaffability.

○	Il Tornese Chardonnay '97	🍷🍷	4
●	Magnificat Cabernet Sauvignon '95	🍷🍷	5
●	Notturno Sangiovese '97	🍷🍷	3*
●	Sangiovese di Romagna Sup. Pruno Ris. '95	🍷🍷	5
○	Il Tornese Chardonnay '95	YYY	4
●	Magnificat Cabernet Sauvignon '94	YYY	5
○	Il Tornese Chardonnay '96	YY	4
●	Magnificat Cabernet Sauvignon '92	YY	5
●	Magnificat Cabernet Sauvignon '93	YY	5

FORMIGINE (MO)

BARBOLINI
VIA FIORI, 40
LOC. CASINALBO
41041 FORMIGINE (MO)
TEL. 059/550154

The Barbolini estate is certainly not falling behind. From its 24 hectares of vineyards come some 200 thousand bottles of semi-sparkling wine a year, of which only 20 thousand are white. There are some considerable novelties, however, on the drawing-board: for the first time, they intend to produce two still wines, a white and a red. Meanwhile, we tasted Il Civolino '98, a white obtained from trebbiano and scarsafoglia grapes. This well-made wine offers attractive herbaceous hints on the nose, similar in some ways to those of a sauvignon. The effervescence enhances the softness and appeal of the elegant palate. The Maglio '98 is a classic Lambrusco di Modena interpreted in a modern manner: the nose shows good intensity, but is slightly rustic. The generous, rounded palate leads into a not altogether dry finish. The Grasparossa '98 in the Amabile (mildly sweet) version has a distinctly floral fragrance with definite, attractive hints of ripe fruit. It is rich and sweet on the palate, which perfectly echoes the bouquet. Lastly, we should like to mention the Modena Capitale, which was conceived as a lighter, easier-drinking version of Lambrusco di Modena than Il Maglio. The result is a sound wine, with a bouquet of ripe apple and a fresher, leaner palate.

○	Bianco Il Civolino '98	🍷	2*
●	Lambrusco di Modena Il Maglio '98	🍷	2*
●	Lambrusco Grasparossa di Castelvetro Amabile '98	🍷	2*
●	Lambrusco di Modena Capitale '98		2

IMOLA (BO)

TRE MONTI
VIA LOLA, 3
40026 IMOLA (BO)
TEL. 0542/657122 - 0542/657116

Sergio Navacchia buzzes around among the crates of grapes during the harvest like an excited child, pausing for quite a while every so often to observe them and then to check how the new presses are working. In this way he can appreciate some of the tangible signs of the quite revolutionary wind of change brought about in the Imola hills by the estate's brilliant consultant oenologist, Donato Lanati. And, paradoxically, it is the young Navacchias, David and Vittorio, who attempt to curb the bubbling enthusiasm of their father, who is always ready to take up some new wine-making challenge. This zeal is justified, though, because Tre Monti has yet again produced a wide range of excellent wines, starting with the Thea '97, a splendid Sangiovese. Its richness is first revealed by its intense color. The complex and attractive aromas range from elegant oak to red fruit, licorice and tobacco. The palate is rounded, wonderfully structured and long: it's certainly one the best Sangioveses they have ever produced. There was an excellent performance too by the Boldo '98, a blend of sangiovese and cabernet sauvignon; it is a subtle, cerebral wine, with heady power and great refinement. The Turico '98 is a good example of what finesse, persistence and elegance are all about; it is a Cabernet Sauvignon, but conceived as a fruity, convivial wine. The whites provided some pleasant surprises. The Salcerella '98, made from albana and chardonnay, displays fresh, almost herbaceous aromas and a fuller, warmer, more elegantly evolved flavor than formerly. The Ciardo '98, also chardonnay-based, is clean, crisp and seductively quaffable. Their other wines, from the Trebbiano Vigna del Rio to the Albana Vigna della Rocca, are sound and well executed.

●	Colli d'Imola Boldo '98	🍷🍷	4
●	Colli d'Imola Cabernet Turico '98	🍷🍷	3*
○	Colli d'Imola Chardonnay Ciardo '98	🍷🍷	4
○	Colli d'Imola Salcerella '98	🍷🍷	4
●	Sangiovese di Romagna Sup. Thea '97	🍷🍷	4
○	Albana di Romagna Passito '96	🍷	4
○	Albana di Romagna Secco '98	🍷	3
○	Albana di Romagna Secco Vigna della Rocca '98	🍷	3
●	Sangiovese di Romagna Ris. '96	🍷	3
○	Trebbiano di Romagna Vigna del Rio '98	🍷	3
●	Colli d'Imola Boldo '97	🍸🍸🍸	4

LANGHIRANO (PR)

ISIDORO LAMORETTI
STRADA DELLA NAVE, 6
LOC. CASATICO
43013 LANGHIRANO (PR)
TEL. 0521/863590

Without a doubt, Isidoro Lamoretti deserves to be considered the standard-bearer of the Colli di Parma DOC, thanks to his many years of dedicated effort and the consistent quality of his wines. His Malvasia Colli di Parma and his Moscato were, as usual, among the best in their respective categories. The former is a lively, fresh semi-sparkling white with a characteristic bouquet; the latter a delicious partially fermented grape must. From his 20 hectares of splendid vineyards with a southeastern exposure in the hills near Casatico, Lamoretti also produces two other Colli di Parma DOCs which are certainly worth mentioning: a sound semi-sparkling Sauvignon and the Colli di Parma Rosso '98, which has a fruity bouquet and a fresh acidity. The remaining two Colli di Parmas were, on the other hand, strangely below par because of their less than straightforward aromas: we refer to the fizzy Vigna di Montefiore '97 and the still Vigna del Guasto, also a '97. In addition there are two new wines: a still red "vino da tavola", the Serbato, and a still Colli di Parma Sauvignon; both need a little fine-tuning before they are next released. Lastly, there is a new episode in the saga of the Vignalunga 71, a still red made from cabernet sauvignon and a tiny amount of merlot and aged in barrique. The '97 only just missed getting Two Glasses. On the nose it displays interesting mentholated aromas and some hints of cooked vegetables, while the palate is well balanced and substantial: not a very demanding red, but an eminently quaffable wine.

○	Colli di Parma Malvasia '98	🍷	3
○	Moscato '98	🍷	3
●	Vignalunga 71 '97	🍷	3
●	Colli di Parma Rosso '98		3
○	Colli di Parma Sauvignon '98		3
●	Colli di Parma Rosso Vigna di Montefiore '96	🍸🍸	3

MODIGLIANA (FO)

CASTELLUCCIO
VIA TRAMONTO, 15
47015 MODIGLIANA (FO)
TEL. 0546/942486

You need special ingredients to make a great dish, and the same is true of great wines. Take one distinguished oenologist like Attilio Pagli, new owners with a vast knowledge of the world of wine; shrewd and cautious investment and, obviously a suitable climate and soil. Based on the results of our tastings, these various ingredients seem to have been perfectly measured. The wines, overseen by the new owners throughout every phase of their production, are elegant and amazingly appealing to drink. The Ronco delle Ginestre '95 was left out of last year's review because it was still too massive and tannic, but it has acquired a new roundedness. The Sangioveses from the '96 vintage scored best of all. The Ronco delle Ginestre, their top wine, has a broad nose that shows hints of both vanilla and violets. Its long and complex palate displays nuances of spice, licorice and chocolate; it is a well-structured, imposing yet elegant wine, subtly underpinned by soft tannins. The Ronco dei Ciliegi displays stronger scents of red berries and offers some extraordinary taste sensations. The Ronco della Simia is less powerful but more elegant than its stablemates and exhibits a fine, aristocratic bouquet. The Le More '97 scored well, too: it is less cerebral than the preceding wines, but meaty and almost overwhelming on the palate. The whites also showed well: the nose of the Ronco del Re '97 is noteworthy for its delicate oaked aromas, while it reveals amazing freshness, softness and mineral notes on the palate. Lastly, the '97 Lunaria shows a vanilla fragrance and marked finesse and balance; it is a charming wine and offers very good value for money.

○	Lunaria '97	🍷🍷	3*
●	Ronco dei Ciliegi '96	🍷🍷	4
○	Ronco del Re '97	🍷🍷	5
●	Ronco della Simia '96	🍷🍷	5
●	Ronco delle Ginestre '95	🍷🍷	5
●	Ronco delle Ginestre '96	🍷🍷	5
●	Sangiovese di Romagna Le More '97	🍷🍷	3*
●	Ronco delle Ginestre '90	ΥΥΥ	5
●	Ronco dei Ciliegi '95	ΥΥ	5
○	Ronco del Re '96	ΥΥ	5
●	Ronco della Simia '95	ΥΥ	5
●	Ronco delle Ginestre '93	ΥΥ	5

MONTE S. PIETRO (BO)

TENUTA BONZARA
VIA S. CHIERLO, 37/A
40050 MONTE S. PIETRO (BO)
TEL. 051/6768324

This estate is now established not only as a major name in the Italian wine world but also as a destination for visitors with a love for wine and the countryside, situated as it is in the still uncontaminated area near Monte San Pietro in the Colli Bolognesi. Indeed Francesco Lambertini, the owner of Tenuta Bonzara, is well aware of the zone's enormous natural potential and, under the watchful eye of his talented oenologist Stefano Chioccioli, he has decided this year to plant another three hectares of new vineyards. At the moment annual production is roughly 65 thousand bottles, evenly split between whites and reds, and the high points are some wines made from merlot and cabernet sauvignon. It is in fact from these varieties that Lambertini produces two outstanding reds: the Cabernet Sauvignon Bonzarone, which won Three Glasses again this year, and the Merlot Rocca di Bonacciara. The former is further evidence of how well this grape can do in the Colli Bolognesi; it is dark, indeed almost opaque in color. The elegant nose offers notes of ripe red fruit well integrated with the oak. The positive palate, which has nicely amalgamated tannins, reveals an aristocratic structure. The Rocca di Bonacciara came very close to getting Three Glasses as well; it is just a little less elegant than the Bonzarone. The Merlot '98 is sound: it has a clean bouquet with hints of dry figs which are also to be found on the soft and reasonably long palate. The Sauvignon Le Carrate '98 releases scents of sage and elder flower, while the palate is crisp but not very meaty. The U Pasa '97 is a late-harvested Sauvignon Blanc, fermented and aged in barriques for 16 months. It has a floral nose and is warm and well balanced in the mouth, with hints of candied fruit. The range is completed by the Pignoletto '98, which was fermented for the first time in wood, and the Pinot Bianco '98, with a flowery bouquet and an agreeable quaffability.

●	Colli Bolognesi Cabernet Sauvignon Bonzarone '97	🍷🍷🍷	5
●	Colli Bolognesi Merlot Rocca di Bonacciara '97	🍷🍷	5
●	Colli Bolognesi Merlot '98	🍷	3
○	Colli Bolognesi Pignoletto Cl. Vigna Antica '98	🍷	3
○	Colli Bolognesi Pinot Bianco Borgo di Qua '98	🍷	3
○	Colli Bolognesi Sauvignon Le Carrate '98	🍷	3
○	U Pasa Passito '97	🍷	5
●	Colli Bolognesi Cabernet Sauvignon Bonzarone '96	ΥΥΥ	5

MONTEVEGLIO (BO)

San Vito
Via Monte Rodano, 6
Fraz. Oliveto
40050 Monteveglio (BO)
tel. 051/964521

In the late '60s Aldo Mazzanti decided to purchase a wine estate, and for some 20 years he divided his time between the family business and his winegrowing, limiting himself to producing a straightforward wine for himself and a small group of friends. Some time ago, things began to change at San Vito: assisted by Carlo Frascaroli, Mazzanti has initiated an ambitious project of up-dating the wine-making equipment and enlarging the winery. Furthermore, in the last three years he has replanted nine of the estate's 16 hectares, and now produces a total of some 90 thousand bottles, divided between Chardonnay, Cabernet Sauvignon and Pignoletto. This last wine, in both still and semi-sparkling versions, is still the estate's most important, from the point of view of both quantity and quality. The Pignoletto Frizzante showed especially well in our tastings. It offers ripe apple and floral scents, and the soft palate shows a generous mousse. The still Pignoletto '98 is also sound: it is still rather closed on the nose, but it opens up on the palate, displaying an unusual richness and fleshiness for this type of wine. The well-executed and generally harmonious Chardonnay '98 is clean and attractive on the nose, and the palate is well balanced. The Cabernet Sauvignon '98, the fruit of the estate's first replantings, was aged in stainless steel, with 30% spending a little while in new oak. The bouquet is toasty, with faint hints of coffee. The palate is rich, with reasonable concentration and good length.

●	Colli Bolognesi Cabernet Sauvignon '98	🍷	3
○	Colli Bolognesi Chardonnay '98	🍷	3
○	Colli Bolognesi Pignoletto Frizzante '98	🍷	2
○	Colli Bolognesi Pignoletto Sup. '98	🍷	2

OSPEDALETTO DI CORIANO (RN)

San Patrignano - Terre del Cedro
Via S. Patrignano, 53
47852 Ospedaletto di Coriano (RN)
tel. 0541/756436 - 0541/362362

It is a pleasure to find, with increasing frequency, the labels of this winery in the region's restaurants: the quality of the wines together with their extremely reasonable prices are naturally great attractions. We refer to the winery of San Patrignano, the largest therapeutic community for recovering drug abusers in Europe. Up here, in fact, where things have always been done in a very professional manner, Riccardo Cottarella has now been called in as oenological consultant, and as of last year the wineş are made using techniques more in harmony with the nature of the soil and the grape varieties, and with an appropriate use of barrels and barriques. We tasted the sangiovese-based Avi '97, a new wine whose release is scheduled for next year. It offers fine spicy hints on the nose, and the abundant tannins in the mouth are nicely tempered by the fatness of the body, all leading to an attractive rounded finish. The Zarricante, a Sangiovese Riserva '96, is excellent: it is a fruity wine with an intense color and broad perfumes; on the palate it is rich in extract, properly tannic, decidedly warm and well structured. The wood is again dominant in the trebbiano-based Vintàn '98, which offers interesting floral perfumes and a full and persistent flavor. The Tanimondi '98, a blend of trebbiano and sauvignon, is a white wine worthy of mention particularly because of its unusual structure and good balance. Lastly, the Sangiovese di Romagna '98, although a bit shy, is decidedly enjoyable.

●	Sangiovese di Romagna Sup. Zarricante Ris. '96	🍷🍷	3*
○	Tanimodi '98	🍷	3
○	Trebbiano di Romagna Vintàn '98	🍷	3
●	Sangiovese di Romagna '98		2
●	Sangiovese di Romagna Sup. Zarricante Ris. '95	YY	3

OZZANO TARO (PR)

MONTE DELLE VIGNE
VIA COSTA, 25-27
43046 OZZANO TARO (PR)
TEL. 0521/809105

The Monte delle Vigne estate is one of the most interesting producers in the Parma zone, partly because of the area it has under vine (a total of 25 hectares, owned and rented), partly because of its very good image and range of wines. We'll start at once with the Nabucco, made from barbera and merlot. This is something of a legendary wine, as it was the first barrique-aged red ever produced in the province of Parma. It was created in 1992 and, at least up to now, its best-ever vintage was the '93. The '97 version, tasted with the best reds of the region, netted Two Glasses. It is an interesting though still immature wine, in which the alcohol, acidity and tannins underpin intense but not yet entirely harmonious fruit. Continuing with the reds, which have always been Andrea Ferrari's most successful wines, we draw your attention to the Colli di Parma Rosso '98 from the Bottazza estate: the wine, although not notably characteristic, does offer attractive sweetness of fruit and a fresh easy-drinking style. The white Colli di Parma DOC wines from the '98 vintage, including the Malvasia and the Sauvignon from Tenuta Bottazza, definitely did not shine in their various categories because of evident defects on the nose. Lastly, the Malvasia Dolce '98, a pleasant partially fermented must, and the fruity Lambrusco '98 are both worthy of mention.

●	Nabucco '97	🍷🍷	4
●	Colli di Parma Rosso Tenuta Bottazza '98	🍷	3
●	Lambrusco dell'Emilia '98		2
○	Malvasia Dolce '98		3
●	Nabucco '96	🍷🍷 (white)	4

PREDAPPIO (FO)

PANDOLFA
VIA PANDOLFA, 35
LOC. FIUMANA
47010 PREDAPPIO (FO)
TEL. 0543/940073

This is a new entry in the Guide, a sign of the dynamic development currently taking place on the Romagna wine-making scene. This estate is developing rapidly, too, and is building a new cellar next to its stunning 18th century villa. It is a large property, of about 120 hectares, of which over 80 are under vine. Here, in addition to the more traditional plantings of cabernet sauvignon, they also cultivate nebbiolo which, from next year, will be vinified on its own. The enterprising Claudio Gimelli is undoubtedly the driving force behind the explosive upturn at this estate on Predappio hillside. To dominate this rather rough but fruitful land, considerable investments are being made in the vineyards, awaiting the great leap forward that will coincide with the initiation of the new cellar. However, things are already quite rosy, particularly as far as the reds are concerned. The Pezzolo '97, made from cabernet sauvignon, displays scents of wood, chocolate and licorice on the nose; the palate is full-bodied and rounded, and its persistence is really extraordinary. The Sangiovese Superiore Pandolfo '98 offers an intense color; the aromas do not yet seem properly mature, and the fruit on the palate is a little unusual. The Sangiovese di Romagna Canova '98, a slightly more rustic wine, has interesting notes of ripe fruit. The Cavina '98, the only white, is a Chardonnay with typical varietal character; it is a clean, fresh and appealing wine.

●	Pezzolo '97	🍷🍷	4
○	Forlì Chardonnay Cavina '98	🍷	2*
●	Sangiovese di Romagna Sup. Pandolfo '98	🍷	3
●	Sangiovese di Romagna Canova '98		2

REGGIO EMILIA

ERMETE MEDICI & FIGLI
VIA NEWTON, 13/A
FRAZIONE GAIDA
42040 REGGIO EMILIA
TEL. 0522/942135

This historic winery, established about a century ago, enters the Guide for the first time this year. Run for a long time by Ermete Medici, it is now brilliantly managed by his sons Valter and Giorgio. The up-to-the-minute cellar is located on the outskirts of Reggio Emilia, while the various contributing estates and the winery's own vineyards are to be found in a large valley near the river Enza. All of the 800 thousand bottles produced annually bear witness to constant, reliably good quality and reflect a modern approach to the zone's traditional wines. Concerto, their top wine, lives up to its reputation, even in comparative tastings. It is a Lambrusco made from lambrusco salamino and exhibits a fine deep ruby color and a very rich mousse. The attractive and lingering bouquet offers intense and singular fruity notes; the dry palate shows good structure and balance. The standard Lambrusco Reggiano is also interesting. It is rich and vinous on the nose, with delicate tones of violet and strawberry; in the mouth it is pleasantly succulent, fresh and well balanced. The Daphne '98, a semi-sparkling white made from malvasia, has a clean, lightly aromatic fragrance with intense ripe fruity notes. On the palate it is sound and fresh. Lastly, we mention the Nebbie d'Autunno '98, a sweet malvasia-based wine. It has very direct aromas and flavors and goes beautifully with sweet biscuits.

○	Colli di Scandiano e Canossa Malvasia Frizzante Secco Daphne '98	🍷	2*
●	Lambrusco Reggiano Secco	🍷	1*
●	Lambrusco Reggiano Secco Concerto '98	🍷	2
○	Malvasia dell'Emilia Frizzante Dolce Nebbie d'Autunno '98		2

RIMINI

SAN VALENTINO
VIA TOMASETTA, 11
FRAZ. S. MARTINO IN VENTI
47900 RIMINI
TEL. 0541/752231

This winery, which is making its debut in the Guide, has a long history: since the end of the 19th century it has been producing wines that reflect the genuine Romagna tradition. Its vineyards are situated on the gentle local slopes that were just recently officially recognized as Colli di Rimini DOC. San Valentino is one of the estates that have benefited most from this change, which has, in fact, made it possible to plant new grape varieties, further enriching the already ample range of estate wines. The Luna Nuova '97 is just such a new wine, made from cabernet sauvignon. It is a fresh, youthful and lively red with intense varietal characteristics; on the palate, which nicely echoes the bouquet, it offers good body, softness and elegance. The Sangiovese Superiore Scabi '97, which almost won Two Glasses, displays rich extract and color; its somewhat rustic perfumes lead to unusually good fruit and persistence on the palate. A rather dumb nose diminishes the red Colli di Rimini Eclissi di Sole '97, a blend of cabernet and sangiovese whose strong suit is its ripe and powerful flavor. The good Sangiovese Riserva Terra '95 reveals rich polyphenols that do not hide its notable fruit. The Sangiovese di Romagna Sbefi '98 is a good example of its type, if a little aggressive on the palate. The Fiore '98, a white made from the native rebola grape and chardonnay, has a lovely vanilla note. To conclude, the T.V.B. Rebola Dolce, the Trebbiano di Romagna Garbeia and the T.V.B. Rebola Secco, three '98s, all make for pleasant drinking.

●	Colli di Rimini Luna Nuova '97	🍷🍷	3*
●	Colli di Rimini Eclissi di Sole '97	🍷	3
○	Fiore '98	🍷	3
●	Sangiovese di Romagna Sbefi '98	🍷	3
●	Sangiovese di Romagna Sup. Terra Ris. '95	🍷	4
●	Sangiovese di Romagna Sup. Scabi '97	🍷	3
○	Colli di Rimini T.V.B. Rebola Dolce '98		3
○	Colli di Rimini T.V.B. Rebola Secco '98		3
○	Trebbiano di Romagna Garbeia '98		2

RIVERGARO (PC)

La Stoppa
Fraz. Ancarano
29029 Rivergaro (PC)
tel. 0523/958159

Last year Elena Pantaleoni's estate won Three Glasses with the cabernet sauvignon-based Stoppa '96, and this time it shines again with a series of excellent bottles, and two sweet wines in particular. The real star is the Malvasia Passito Vigna del Volta '97, a sunny Mediterranean wine surprising in its freshness and the persistence of its aromas. It offers scents of yellow peach and sweet cooked apricot with very intense notes of citrus fruit. The mouth-filling palate reveals great richness and depth, as well as astonishing length. One of the most interesting sweet wines from anywhere in Italy, it nets Three Glasses without any trouble. Close on its heels comes the extremely rare (only 500 bottles) Buca delle Canne '97, made from semillon with noble rot. It shows an attractive golden color and a not particularly powerful nose, but on the palate one finds sweet tones of honey, citrus fruit and jam set off by an attractive bitterish note on the finish. The Barbera '97 displays clean spicy and fruity notes on the nose; the palate is firm on the attack, and the fruity tone then spreads evenly, underpinned by the characteristic acidity of this grape. The nose of the Cabernet Sauvignon Stoppa '97 is somewhat diminished by sulfurous notes; the palate, while not particularly dense, is smooth, even and well balanced. The Macchiona '97, made from barbera and bonarda and partially aged in large barrels and in barriques, displays an intense color, but the solid substance, with floral aromas and some mineral hints, does not manage to get the better of the pronounced acidity. The Alfeo '97, made from pinot nero, has the color of ripe cherries; on the nose it offers animal and spicy notes, and the palate is light, with dry, astringent tannins.

○	Malvasia Passito Vigna del Volta '97	▼▼▼	4
○	Buca delle Canne '97	▼▼	5
●	Colli Piacentini Barbera della Stoppa '97	▼▼	4
●	Colli Piacentini Cabernet Sauvignon Stoppa '97	▼	4
●	Colli Piacentini Pinot Nero Alfeo '97	▼	4
●	Macchiona '97	▼	4
●	Stoppa '96	▽▽▽	5
●	Colli Piacentini Cabernet Sauvignon Stoppa '95	▽▽	5
●	La Stoppa '91	▽▽	5

RUSSI (RA)

Tenuta Uccellina
Via Garibaldi, 51
48026 Russi (RA)
tel. 0544/580144

This small estate now seems intent on becoming a regular guest in the Guide. Its vineyards are all in the heart of the historic Bertinoro area; they cover little more than 10 hectares, but are up to providing the raw material for a wide range of extremely interesting wines. Indeed, careful attention is lavished on every phase of production, from vineyard to cellar. The resultant wines are the fruit of enthusiastic dedication, experience and professional skill (although you won't find any of the great names of Italian oenology listed as consultant here). Once again it is the unorthodox Ruchetto, from the '95 vintage, that heads the list: the pinot nero grapes have yielded a particularly harmonious wine with an extraordinarily intense color. Its perfumes of cherry and plum introduce a remarkably structured and attractively rounded palate. The Albana Passito '97, which offers broad perfumes and a full, soft flavor, displays fruity notes, with apple to the fore. The Sangiovese Superiore '98 reveals surprising energy: it is a youthful wine, with good tannins that counterbalance its overripe fruity notes. The Regio '95, a sangiovese passito (from semi-dried grapes), is warm, festive and liqueur-like: it is a really pleasant surprise. To conclude, the Albana Dolce '98 is temptingly sweet, with a slightly bitter hint on the finish.

○	Albana di Romagna Passito '97	▼▼	4
●	Ruchetto dell'Uccellina '95	▼▼	4
○	Albana di Romagna Dolce '98	▼	2*
●	Regio '95	▼	4
●	Sangiovese di Romagna Sup. '98	▼	2*
●	Ruchetto dell'Uccellina '93	▽▽	4

S. ILARIO D'ENZA (RE)

Moro Rinaldo Rinaldini

Via Andrea Rivasi, 27
Fraz. Calerno
42040 S. Ilario d'Enza (RE)
tel. 0522/679190

Low espalier training, 3,500 vines per hectare, but above all the annual 80 thousand bottles of "metodo classico" sparkling wines give an indication that this is a dynamic producer of a kind that is difficult to find in these parts. Rinaldo Rinaldini is also thinking of producing still wines, and, with his customary skill and dedication, is experimenting with different vinification methods. Once again this year the Pjcol Ross, one of the best Lambrusco Spumantes from the area, stood out at our tastings. It offers an intense and clean bouquet, and a rich palate that perfectly echoes the nose. The Malvasia Brut displays the interesting aromatic characteristics of this grape variety, with singular overripe fruit notes that make it unique and intriguing. The white sparkling Lambrusco, on the other hand, is this year's debutant. It shows a generous mousse; the nose is intense but not perfectly straightforward, while the palate is fresh and attractive. We also noted the usual touch of overripeness (and marked notes of red fruit) in the Vecchio Moro, a monovarietal lambrusco grasparossa; it displays good structure on the palate and is an original and highly enjoyable interpretation of its type. Lastly, we mention the still Chardonnay '98, which is simple but agreeably quaffable.

● Colli di Scandiano e di Canossa Vecchio Moro	🍷	2
● Lambrusco Spumante Metodo Classico Pjcol Ross	🍷	2*
○ Colli di Scandiano e di Canossa Malvasia Secco Spumante	🍷	2
○ Colli di Scandiano e di Canossa Chardonnay '98		2
○ Lambrusco Bianco Metodo Classico		2

S. PROSPERO (MO)

Cavicchioli

P.zza Gramsci, 9
41030 S. Prospero (MO)
tel. 059/812411

Experiments are under way on a new Lambrusco di Sorbara that should be available in the near future, but the most significant addition to the list at Cavicchioli this year is the Lambrusco di Modena Nuova Cuvée. This wine, which takes its place in the range beside the classic Lambrusco, is a good example of what Cavicchioli is capable of. Both wines, in fact, won One Glass: the Cuvée , in particular, stands out for the intensity of its bouquet, which displays fragrantly fruity and floral tones. On the palate it is attractive, well balanced and long, and shows an elegant effervescence. The Lambrusco di Modena Classico, now in its third vintage, confirms all its attractive qualities, which are very similar to those of the Nuova Cuvée, on the palate at least. The good Grasparossa Tre Medaglie offers rich scents of fruit with hints of candy, and an appealingly well-balanced palate. The Vigna del Cristo '98, now a classic of the area, is still a little closed on the nose; the palate, however, is harmonious and reminiscent of red fruit and leads to a dry, persistent finish. The Sorbara Tre Medaglie shows a characteristic pale ruby hue and an impressive freshness in its perfumes and on the palate: in other words, it is an ideal accompaniment to cold meats in the summer.

● Lambrusco di Modena	🍷	2*
● Lambrusco di Modena Nuova Cuvée	🍷	2*
● Lambrusco di Sorbara Vigna del Cristo '98	🍷	3
● Lambrusco Grasparossa di Castelvetro Amabile Tre Medaglie	🍷	1*
● Lambrusco di Sorbara Tre Medaglie		1

SALA BAGANZA (PR)

VIGNETI CALZETTI
VIA S. VITALE, 47
LOC. S. VITALE BAGANZA
43030 SALA BAGANZA (PR)
TEL. 0521/830117

After two years in the Other Wineries section, this dynamic estate, always one of the best of the Colli di Parma DOC, is back in full view; all the wines presented this year by Sergio Calzetti, who is currently President of the Colli di Parma producers' consortium, were among the best of the zone. This family-run estate makes about 100 thousand bottles a year from 18 hectares under vine; the 10 hectares owned by the family border on the beautiful Boschi di Carrega regional Park. But let's get down to the fine range of wines we tasted. The Malvasia Conventino '98 has a lively mousse, and the floral notes on the nose are echoed on the palate. The Sauvignon '98, presented in a Bordeaux bottle, stands out clearly above its rivals thanks to its typical herbaceous perfumes (of sage in particular) and its balanced palate underpinned by nicely judged carbon dioxide. The Colli di Parma Rosso Conventino Campo delle Lepri '98 is also among the best of its type: it shows a brilliant ruby color, a lively mousse and attractive, fruity perfumes; the palate is both fresh and intense. The Malvasia Dolce '98, a partially fermented grape must, is good as well.

○ Colli di Parma Malvasia Conventino '98	🍷	2*
● Colli di Parma Rosso Conventino Campo delle Lepri '98	🍷	2
○ Colli di Parma Sauvignon '98	🍷	2*
○ Malvasia Dolce '98	🍷	2

SASSO MARCONI (BO)

FLORIANO CINTI
VIA GAMBERI, 48
FRAZ. S. LORENZO
40037 SASSO MARCONI (BO)
TEL. 051/845606 - 051/6751646

Floriano Cinti started winegrowing in 1979, but it was only in 1992 that he set up on his own. Today his estate includes 11 hectares under vine in the Tignano and San Lorenzo districts of Sasso Marconi, as well as three rented hectares at Montechiaro. Most of these vineyards are between 220 and 380 meters above sea level and are within the Colline Marconiane subzone, one of the best and least exploited parts of the Colli Bolognesi district. Total annual production is about 30 thousand bottles and, for the record, as of the '98 vintage they all show their sulfite content, according to official analysis, on the label of each wine. The Pignoletto Frizzante is one of the most structured and interesting of its type; it has a well-defined characteristic nose and a generous, fine mousse; the palate shows good balance and a long finish. The still version of the Pignoletto '98 almost earned Two Glasses, and shows the potential of this grape. The bouquet is intense and varietal and the palate is structured, balanced and lingering. The Sauvignon '98 is striking in its finesse, with subtle mineral hints and persistent varietal notes. The '98 Chardonnay, partially fermented in wood, displays an intense ripe fragrance with toasty notes; the palate is rich and individual. The well-made Cabernet Sauvignon has an intense nose of ripe fruit and a medium-bodied palate. The unusual but attractive Pignoletto Passito opens up new vistas for this variety.

● Colli Bolognesi Cabernet Sauvignon '97	🍷	3
○ Colli Bolognesi Chardonnay '98	🍷	3
○ Colli Bolognesi Pignoletto Cl.'98	🍷	3
○ Colli Bolognesi Pignoletto Frizzante '98	🍷	2
○ Colli Bolognesi Pignoletto Passito '98	🍷	4
○ Colli Bolognesi Sauvignon '98	🍷	3

SAVIGNANO SUL RUBICONE (FO)

Spalletti Colonna di Paliano
Via Sogliano, 100
47039 Savignano sul Rubicone (FO)
tel. 0541/943446

It was about time that this historic winery reclaimed its place in the Guide. After a few not altogether positive years in which its wines showed some slight faults, particularly on the nose, things have now changed. This large estate (220 hectares, of which 45 are under vine) is owned by Prince Colonna and his family and has its headquarters in the castle of Ribano, on the splendid Savignano hillside. It has presented a wide range of wines this year, mostly made with techniques that look askance at innovation and make great use of large Slovenian oak barrels. The major sign of change we noted at our tastings was the greater consistency of quality throughout the range. The reds are, as usual, their most important wines, starting with the Sabinio '98, made from cabernet sauvignon and sangiovese. Its shows a brilliant color and vinous perfumes, with aromas of ripe red fruit, and it's balanced and lingering in the mouth. The '96 Villa Rasponi is less successful: it reveals a more rustic character and a leaner body. The harsh and arrogant nose of the estate cru, the Sangiovese Superiore Rocca di Ribano '97, reveals its traditional vinification methods and the large oak barrels in which it matured. It is similarly unwilling to please on the palate, which is nevertheless substantial. The Sangiovese Superiore '98 is perhaps not especially elegant, but its good extract and robust tannins make it attractive. We must mention the Albana Dolce '98, which has a fresh, clean bouquet and an inviting flavor. Lastly, the Cagnina Dolce is enjoyable.

●	Sabinio '98	🍷🍷	2*
○	Albana di Romagna Dolce '98	🍷	2*
●	Sangiovese di Romagna Sup. '98	🍷	2
●	Sangiovese di Romagna Sup. Rocca di Ribano '97	🍷	3
●	Cagnina di Romagna '98		2
●	Sangiovese di Romagna Villa Rasponi Ris. '96		3

SCANDIANO (RE)

Casali
Via Scuole, 7
Fraz. Pratissolo
42019 Scandiano (RE)
tel. 0522/855441

As is the case every year, Casali presented a wide range of wines at our tastings. With each one we tried we became increasingly aware of how consistently good their quality is, with some highlights too that indicate further potential. The Casino dei Greppi '96, made this time just from cabernet, is satisfying: aged in wood, it displays an intense nose, a soft palate and well-balanced tannins. The Malvasia Secca Acaia '98 also showed well. Its bouquet is positive, distinct and fragrant; the palate is rich and well developed. The two sparkling wines, the Cà Besina Metodo Classico and the Villa Jano (Charmat method), are both well made. The former is slightly more complex and displays mature, toasty aromas derived from the five years it spent in contact with its lees. The latter is more vinous, with well-judged acidity and an excellent easy-drinking style. Of the Lambruscos, the Prà di Bosso '98 is the most straightforward and enjoyable. It has an aromatic nose and a vinous and rich palate. The Bosco del Fracasso '97, released a year after the harvest, offers spicy perfumes and a warm, mouth-filling palate. Lastly, the Spumante Roggio del Pradello is again well made, while the pleasant Malvasia Dolce '98 is aromatic and has just the right amount of effervescence.

○	Acaia Malvasia dell'Emilia Frizzante '98	🍷	2
●	Colli di Scandiano e di Canossa Casino dei Greppi '96	🍷	3
○	Colli di Scandiano e di Canossa Metodo Classico Cà Besina '94	🍷	4
○	Colli di Scandiano e di Canossa Spumante Villa Jano	🍷	3
●	Lambrusco Reggiano Bosco del Fracasso '97	🍷	2*
●	Lambrusco Reggiano Prà di Bosso '98	🍷	1*
●	Lambrusco Spumante Roggio del Pradello	🍷	3
○	Malvasia dell'Emilia Dolce '98	🍷	1*

TRAVO (PC)

IL POGGIARELLO
FRAZ. SCRIVELLANO DI STATTO
29020 TRAVO (PC)
TEL. 0523/957241 - 0523/571610

Paolo and Stefano Perini manage their 13 hectares under vine in the hills of the Val Trebbia with great competence and enthusiasm. These vineyards are divided up into plots, known locally as "perticati", hence the name that appears on this year's labels. The range of wines we tasted was good. The Sauvignon Perticato Il Quadri '98 displays a typical varietal nose; the medium-bodied palate, however, is somewhat blunted by the noticeable acidity and not yet fully integrated oak. The Chardonnay Perticato La Piana '98 has a golden color with greenish highlights; the fragrance is lightly resinous and the acidity on the palate is balanced by good, rich substance and well-judged wood. Among the reds, the Gutturnio Perticato Valandrea '96 displays attractive hints of spice on the nose which then carry through onto the not particularly broad but nevertheless well-structured palate; the finish is fresh and persistent. The Cabernet Sauvignon Perticato del Novarei '97 has come out very well indeed: it has a deep color and minty and varietal aromas which meld very well with its rich, tannic fruit. It also displays a slight vegetal hint which is not particularly elegant but does give it personality. The Pinot Nero Perticato Le Giastre '97 is dark ruby in color and offers aromas of red fruit with hints of coffee and tobacco; it reveals a particularly attractive balance among the acidity, alcohol and tannins on the palate.

●	Colli Piacentini Cabernet Sauvignon Perticato del Novarei '97	🍷🍷	4
●	Colli Piacentini Pinot Nero Perticato Le Giastre '97	🍷🍷	4
○	Colli Piacentini Chardonnay Perticato La Piana '98	🍷	3
●	Colli Piacentini Gutturnio Perticato Valandrea '96	🍷	3
○	Colli Piacentini Sauvignon Perticato Il Quadri '98	🍷	3
●	Colli Piacentini Pinot Nero Perticato Le Giastre '96	ΥΥ	4
●	Colli Piacentini Cabernet Sauvignon Perticato del Novarei '96	Υ	4

VERNASCA (PC)

LURETTA
LOC. PAOLINI, 3
FRAZ. BACEDASCO ALTO
29010 VERNASCA (PC)
TEL. 0523/895465 - 0523/976500

This estate made its debut in the Guide last year, and it is a pleasure to find our faith confirmed by this year's tastings. Indeed, Carla Asti and Felice Salamini presented a very interesting and uniformly appealing range. The lovely Malvasia Boccadirosa '98, for example, fully deserves its Two Glasses. It is modern in style and displays aromas of flowers and citrus fruit on the nose. On the palate it is fresh and well-balanced, with satisfying fruit which is well integrated with the oak. The Sauvignon '98 is more rustic and varietal: its perfumes include sage and tomato leaf, and these sensations along with mineral notes underpin a good persistent flavor. The Chardonnay '98 has a pale golden color with greenish highlights; it displays vegetal aromas on the nose and a restrained palate. And now for the reds. Here too they have not been able to resist the temptation of trying their hand at a Pinot Nero. The nose of the '97 version offers marked hints of tobacco and red fruit; this is an elegant wine whose development is definitely worth following. The name of the new wine made from a blend of barbera and bonarda is rather bizarre: Come la Pantera e i Lupi nella Sera (like a panther and wolves in the night). The '97 vintage shows an intense ruby hue and clean but still slightly closed aromas; the medium-bodied palate displays sweet notes on the finish.

○	Colli Piacentini Malvasia Boccadirosa '98	🍷🍷	3*
○	Colli Piacentini Chardonnay '98	🍷	3
●	Colli Piacentini Pinot Nero '97	🍷	3
○	Colli Piacentini Sauvignon '98	🍷	3
●	Come la Pantera e i Lupi nella Sera '97	🍷	3

VIGOLZONE (PC)

Conte Otto Barattieri di San Pietro

Fraz. Albarola
29020 Vigolzone (PC)
tel. 0523/875111

Count Barattieri's Vin Santo is still produced according to traditional methods that have been in use for over a century. It is made from specially selected malvasia grapes from old vines and does not undergo any type of chemical intervention. It is aged for nine long years before being bottled, naturally after having been subjected to the subtle and magical transformations caused by the miraculous lees which, with their over 150 years of life, contribute to making this wine unique. We tasted the '89 vintage of this Vin Santo (of which only a few hundred bottles were released) and, as always, we were stunned by it. An amber color introduces an extremely complex nose with nuances of tamarind, dried fig, hazelnut and honey. The palate is fat and viscous and has an extremely long finish. The Faggio, a wine made from semi-dried brachetto grown on old vines, also showed very well. It has a deep cherry red color and a dense palate rich in residual sugar and reminiscent of strawberry and cherry jam. The Barattieri Rosso '97 and the Pinot Nero Vignazzo '97 performed less well: both were unbalanced and lacked finesse. On the other hand, the Barbera Bocciarelli '97, with its characteristic perfumes, is sound. It displays both good acidity and softness on the palate, and a typical touch of bitterness on the finish. It is also worth mentioning the enjoyable Bonarda Dolce, which is fruity and fresh and is made even more appealing by its abundant violet purple mousse.

○	Colli Piacentini Vin Santo '89	🍷🍷	6
●	Il Faggio	🍷🍷	5
●	Colli Piacentini Barbera Vigneto Bocciarelli '97	🍷	4
●	Colli Piacentini Bonarda Dolce '98	🍷	3
●	Colli Piacentini Cabernet Sauvignon Barattieri Rosso '97		4
●	Colli Piacentini Pinot Nero Vigneto Vignazzo '97		4
○	Colli Piacentini Vin Santo '88	🍸🍸	6
●	Colli Piacentini Cabernet Sauvignon Barattieri Rosso '96	🍸	4

VIGOLZONE (PC)

La Tosa

Loc. La Tosa
29020 Vigolzone (PC)
tel. 0523/870727 - 0523/870168

We mentioned in last year's entry that the dynamic Stefano Pizzamiglio often swims against the current. Now his wines have undergone an alteration in style: some technical variations have taken place during vinification and changes have been made in the use of wood, but what definitely remains the same is his rigorous vineyard management and grape selection. The most obvious results are the extreme cleanness on the nose of the reds and the greater balance in the whites. Two absolutely first-class wines have emerged, giving liquid proof of the excellence attainable in this area. The first of these, the Cabernet Sauvignon Luna Selvatica '97, has an impenetrable color and offers extraordinarily well-defined aromas of ripe blackberry and raspberry; balsamic oak-derived notes enhance these sensations on the nose and join them on the dense, rich palate: Three Glasses well earned. The '98 version of the Malvasia Sorriso di Cielo is probably the best yet: its aromas of apricot, pineapple and peach keep the nose fresh despite 15% of alcohol. There is perfect harmony between the nose and the palate, which is round and substantial. The Sauvignon '98 is also interesting, with its aromas of ripe pineapple muted somewhat by the pronounced alcohol. On the palate it is fat and fleshy, but perhaps made excessively soft by the residual sugars. The Gutturnio '98 is even, with a soft, fruity nose, a well-balanced palate and a fresh finish. The lightly fizzy Valnure Frizzante '98, made from malvasia, trebbiano and ortrugo, is worthy of note; the nose is fair and it displays freshness and an attractive touch of sweetness on the palate.

●	Colli Piacentini Cabernet Sauvignon Luna Selvatica '97	🍷🍷🍷	5
○	Colli Piacentini Malvasia Sorriso di Cielo '98	🍷🍷	4
○	Colli Piacentini Sauvignon '98	🍷🍷	4
●	Colli Piacentini Gutturnio '98	🍷	3
○	Colli Piacentini Valnure '98	🍷	3
●	Colli Piacentini Cabernet Sauvignon Luna Selvatica '93	🍸🍸	4
●	Colli Piacentini Cabernet Sauvignon Luna Selvatica '95	🍸🍸	5
●	Colli Piacentini Gutturnio Vignamorello '96	🍸🍸	4
○	Colli Piacentini Malvasia Sorriso di Cielo '97	🍸	4

ZIANO PIACENTINO (PC)

GAETANO LUSENTI E FIGLIA
LOC. CASE PICCIONI DI VICOBARONE
29010 ZIANO PIACENTINO (PC)
TEL. 0523/868479

Gaetano Lusenti's estate is near Case Piccioni, on the road from Vicobarone to Ziano, in the heart of the Val Tidone winegrowing area; it consists of about ten hectares of vineyards, planted at altitudes varying between 300 and 350 meters. Lodovica, Gaetano's daughter, has quite transformed the winery, making it one of the most significant producers in the zone. The range of wines presented this year is sound, and points the way towards future improvement. The best wine is the still Gutturnio '97 which, after a disappointing '96, has managed to place itself once again at the top of its category. Its color is an intense ruby, and the floral notes on the nose are echoed on the palate, which is well balanced, fruity, soft and rounded. The Gutturnio Frizzante '98, on the other hand, has a nose marred by sulfurous notes, and the palate, though reasonably structured, has an astringent finish. The Villante '96, made from cabernet sauvignon, is similar to the '95: dilute in color, it offers ripe aromas and a palate that is balanced but rather lacking in depth. Among the semi-sparkling whites, the Ortrugo '98 is well balanced and supple and has a fresh and enchanting finish. The delicate Pinot Grigio '98 shows an onion-skin hue, an inviting fragrance and reasonable persistence on the palate. We conclude with the Filtrato Dolce di Malvasia '98: it is generous and aromatic on the nose and, on the palate, is immediate, flavorful and enlivened by well-balanced acidity.

●	Colli Piacentini Gutturnio '97	🍷	3
○	Colli Piacentini Ortrugo '98	🍷	3
○	Colli Piacentini Pinot Grigio '98	🍷	3
●	Il Villante Cabernet Sauvignon '96	🍷	4
●	Colli Piacentini Gutturnio Frizzante '98		3
○	Filtrato Dolce di Malvasia '98		3
●	Colli Piacentini Gutturnio Sup. '95	🍷 (outline)	2
●	Il Villante Cabernet Sauvignon '95	🍷 (outline)	4
●	Pinot Nero La Picciona '94	🍷 (outline)	4

ZOLA PREDOSA (BO)

MARIA LETIZIA GAGGIOLI
VIGNETO BAGAZZANA
VIA RAIBOLINI, 55
40069 ZOLA PREDOSA (BO)
TEL. 051/753489

Carlo Gaggioli has come a long way since this estate's first vineyards were planted in 1978. He began it as a hobby, but a passion for viticulture has always powered the activity of this dynamic producer who, in just over twenty years, has planted no fewer than 20 hectares of vines, producing a total of about 130 thousand bottles. Carlo is assisted by his daughter Letizia, and this year they have presented a range of wines of consistently good quality. We'll start with one of their classics, the elegant and individual Pinot Bianco Crilò '98: it has a clean bouquet, and the softness and persistence on the palate are underpinned by well-balanced acidity. The Pignoletto Superiore '98 is sound, as usual: it has a fruity nose and good intensity of flavor. The lightly fizzy Pignoletto Frizzante '98 is attractive on the nose, fresh on the palate and easy to drink. Both the Sauvignon '98 and the Chardonnay Lavinio '98 are characteristically varietal, well executed, gracefully fragrant, and balanced on the palate. Among the reds, we particularly mention the tasty Merlot '98, notable for its characteristic aromas of ripe fruit; it has a rounded palate and moderate length. The Cabernet Sauvignon '97, partially aged in medium-sized oak barrels, is attractive on the palate but still shows some imperfections on the nose.

●	Colli Bolognesi Cabernet Sauvignon '97	🍷	4
○	Colli Bolognesi Chardonnay Lavinio '98	🍷	3
●	Colli Bolognesi Merlot '98	🍷	3
○	Colli Bolognesi Pignoletto Frizzante '98	🍷	3
○	Colli Bolognesi Pignoletto Sup. '98	🍷	3
○	Colli Bolognesi Pinot Bianco Crilò '98	🍷	3
○	Colli Bolognesi Sauvignon Sup. '98	🍷	3

OTHER WINERIES

The following producers obtained good scores in our tastings with one or more of their wines:

PROVINCE OF BOLOGNA

Erioli, Bazzano, tel. 051/830103
Colli Bolognesi Chardonnay '97

Fattoria Cornacchia
Fontanelice, tel. 0542/92625
Sangiovese di Romagna Sup. '98,
Mussant '95

Santarosa
Monte S. Pietro, tel. 051/969203
Colli Bolognesi Pinot Bianco '98

Cantina dell'Abbazia
Monteveglio, tel. 051/6702069
Colli Bolognesi Merlot '98

PROVINCE OF FORLÌ

Colombina, Bertinoro, tel. 0543/460658
Sangiovese di Romagna Sup. Ris. '95

Braschi, Mercato Saraceno, tel. 0547/91061
Sangiovese di Romagna Sup.
Vigna del Monte '98

Nicolucci, Predappio, tel. 0543/922361
Sangiovese di Romagna
Predappio di Predappio Ris. '96

PROVINCE OF MODENA

Roberto Balugani
Castelvetro, tel. 059/791546
Lambrusco Grasparossa di Castelvetro '98

Manicardi, Castelvetro, tel. 059/799000
Lambrusco Grasparossa di Castelvetro
Ca' Fiore '98

Chiarli 1860, Modena, tel. 059/310545
Lambrusco di Modena Vecchia Modena

Maletti, Soliera, tel. 059/563876
Lambrusco di Sorbara Selezione '98

PROVINCE OF PARMA

Cantine dell'Asta
Parma, tel. 0521/482406
Colli di Parma Sauvignon '98

Forte Rigoni, Pilastro, tel. 0521/637678
Colli di Parma Malvasia '98

Cantine Ceci
Torrile, tel. 0521/810134
Lambrusco Antico Bruscone

Villa Bianca
Traversetolo, tel. 0521/842680
Colli di Parma Malvasia Vigna Caveriot '98

PROVINCE OF PIACENZA

Solenghi
Borgonovo Val Tidone, tel. 0523/860352
Colli Piacentini Bonarda Secco '98

Campana F.lli
Carpaneto Piacentino, tel. 0523/859448
Colli Piacentini Gutturnio Sup. Antiquum '98

Pusterla, Castell'Arquato, tel. 0523/896105
Colli Piacentini Cabernet Sauvignon '97

Campominosi
Vigolzone, tel. 0523/877853
Colli Piacentini Gutturnio
Vigna dei Cotorni Barrique '98

Molinelli
Ziano Piacentino, tel. 0523/863230
Colli Piacentini Gutturnio
Vigna Giacalva '94

Torre Fornello
Ziano Piacentino, tel. 0523/861001
Colli Piacentini Gutturnio Sup. Sinsäl '98

PROVINCE OF RAVENNA

Treré
Faenza, tel. 0546/47034
Albana di Romagna Dolce
Vigna della Calunga '98,
Albana di Romagna Secco
Vigna dello Sperone '98

Valli
Lugo, tel. 0545/24393
Sangiovese di Romagna Sup. '97

PROVINCE OF REGGIO EMILIA

Venturini e Baldini
Quattro Castella, tel. 0522/887080
La Papessa Bianco '98

TUSCANY

In this year's GuideThree Glasses have been awarded to 37 Tuscan wines, two more than in our last edition. There are also more reviews this time, 248 in all. But there's still a problem about Tuscan wines, particularly about their identity. Of these 37 top wines only eight, i.e. just over 20%, are DOC or DOCG wines. This tells us a lot. First of all, DOC and DOCG are to a great extent disregarded when it comes to making wine of the highest quality, with the lone exception of Brunello di Montalcino. The causes are many, but the main one is that the non-DOCs, the so-called super-Tuscans, appear on the market at prices that DOCs and DOCGs do not usually even begin to equal – except, once again, for Brunello di Montalcino (which helps one to understand the reason for the success of that appellation). The second factor, which is a direct consequence of the first, is that in Tuscany, obviously, the appellations do not seem to come fully to terms with the best wines, and their producers are often obliged to disregard them, or do not consider it expedient to follow them, for the reason we mentioned above. As a result everyone does pretty much as he pleases, and the wines most representative of production in this region include monovarietal sangioveses, blends of sangiovese and cabernet, of sangiovese and merlot, or Bordeaux-style cabernet and merlot blends, and great monovarietal wines made from international varieties such as the two already mentioned, and also syrah, pinot nero and chardonnay. They come from different parts of Tuscany and are very good, but they differ greatly amongst themselves and in only a few cases are they recognizably rooted in a specific terroir. This does not imply that we think it reasonable to assert that a Tuscan red means a pure sangiovese, as some would have it, and in fact we challenge anyone seriously to deny the intimate connection between Argiano's Solengo and the Montalcino district, or between Fonterutoli's Siepi and the Chianti Classico zone. Indeed this may be the path to follow in the future: characterizing a wine by means of its terroir, without racing madly ahead, but also without excluding as a matter of principle the inclusion of smaller percentages of non-native varieties. What, after all, would happen if by magic all of wine-growing Tuscany were suddenly to become a vast sangiovese vineyard? We feel that the average quality of the wines produced would not then improve without a long period of sangiovese research and selection, and this is work that has barely begun. Meanwhile we hope, first of all, that the regulations controlling super-Tuscans, which are such an important phenomenon, will acquire greater precision. It's quite ridiculous for these wines to be labeled just IGT, as if they were a kind of inferior DOC, comparable to the "vin de pays" in France. Our second hope is that the best Tuscan producers will give up a little of their individualism and begin to think of their wines as being part of a regional context, and not just little unique gems springing forth from their own individual cellars.

AREZZO (AR)

San Fabiano
Borghini Baldovinetti
Loc. San Fabiano, 33
52100 Arezzo (AR)
tel. 0575/370368

The sizable historic estate of San Fabiano covers 650 hectares at an average altitude of 300 meters above sea level. Here wines of two distinctly separate styles are produced. One includes great Tuscan classics, with Chianti at their head, followed by a white made from trebbiano, and by a Vin Santo: all very traditional wines. The second style is represented by a more modern red, their Armaiolo. This is the debut appearance of San Fabiano in the Guide, and it is in part to be explained by a nicely made Chianti '98, a grapy, fresh, quaffable wine with lots of fruit. But it would be pointless to deny that by far their most interesting bottle is their Armaiolo. The '97 is of a lovely brilliant ruby hue with vivid purple highlights. A clearly defined bouquet includes notes of red currant, raspberry and black currant that are not yet fully integrated with oaked tones (the wine spent about a year in barriques) which were still a little insistent at our tasting time. Dense extract, good basic substance, a full and soft fruitiness and a long finish characterize the palate. Its various elements have to blend further, but it is definitely a promising red and should be at its peak in two or three years.

● Armaiolo '97	**YY**	5
● Chianti '98		2

BARBERINO VAL D'ELSA (FI)

Casa Emma
Fraz. Cortine
50021 Barberino Val d'Elsa (FI)
tel. 055/8072859

You can't come in first all the time, and this is particularly true in an endeavor like wine-making which is so bound up with the variation from one vintage to another. Hence this year there are no Three Glass wines from Casa Emma, but their overall results are remarkably good just the same, thanks to the excellent work of the Bucalossi family, assisted by the oenologist Niccolò d'Afflitto. They have been persevering in their vineyard improvement program, and two hectares are already planted with new sangiovese vines. But let's get down to the wines. The '97 Chianti Classico is of a not too deep ruby color, and its fruity aromas of black currant, blackberry and blueberry, all very well blended and underpinned by a hint of vanilla, form a very elegant bouquet. The entry on the palate is just slightly dilute, with natural acidity emerging over close-knit tannins, balanced by alcohol. The agreeable finish is long and enchanting. The Chianti Classico Riserva '96 has a lovely rich and lively ruby color. Ripe succulent fruit dominates the nose, with cherry and plum to the fore, rounded off by elegant spicy tones. The attack on the palate is energetic, with acidity appearing in a fine blend with alcohol and tannins. The merlot-based Soloìo '96 was a little disappointing. The ruby hue is attractive, but the nose is definitely too forward, and there are some not very pleasing animal notes. The palate shows an appealing softness, but also a general lack of cohesion, and the finish is proper but not very exciting.

● Chianti Classico '97	**YY**	4
● Chianti Classico Ris. '96	**YY**	4
● Soloìo '96	**Y**	5
● Chianti Classico Ris. '93	YYY	4*
● Chianti Classico Ris. '95	YYY	4*
● Soloìo '94	YYY	5
● Chianti Classico '90	YY	3*
● Chianti Classico '93	YY	3*
● Chianti Classico '96	YY	3*
● Chianti Classico Ris. '90	YY	4
● Chianti Classico Ris. '94	YY	4
● Soloìo '95	YY	5
● Chianti Classico '92	Y	3
● Chianti Classico '94	Y	3
● Chianti Classico '95	Y	3

BARBERINO VAL D'ELSA (FI)

Isole e Olena

Loc. Isole, 1
50021 Barberino Val d'Elsa (FI)
tel. 055/8072763

Sometimes we suspect that we don't do full justice to the splendid job that Paolo De Marchi, the owner of this estate, has been doing for years. De Marchi is one of the very few producers who really go it alone, without the "magical" assistance of a roster of famous visiting consultants. He is agronomist, winemaker and business manager all rolled into one, and he wears these different hats with the modesty that only the genuinely competent possess. Having said this much, we must also say that this year his wines are extraordinary, and indeed we have given him two Three Glass awards. The first is for his Cepparello '97, a delicious 100% sangiovese, and an example of how this grape can give rise to great and elegant wines with well-defined, stylish aromas and smooth tannins. Of course it was an extraordinary year, but De Marchi really made the most of it. The Cabernet Sauvignon '96 from the Collezione Marchi (his designation for his non-native varietal wines) is splendid and characteristic, and has very fine tannins. Both of these wines reflect his respect for the raw material he works with. The Chianti Classico '97 is good, as usual, and among the best of it category. The Chardonnay '97 and the Syrah '96 are both, as expected, fine, but there's a little too much wood in each bouquet. All in all he has had no small triumph, and our hats are off.

● Cabernet Sauvignon '96	**YYY**	6
● Cepparello '97	**YYY**	5
● Chianti Classico '97	**YY**	4
○ Chardonnay '97	**Y**	5
● Syrah '96	**Y**	5
● Cabernet Sauvignon '88	YYY	6
● Cabernet Sauvignon '90	YYY	6
● Cabernet Sauvignon '95	YYY	6
● Cepparello '86	YYY	6
● Cepparello '88	YYY	6
● Chianti Classico '88	YYY	3*
● Cabernet Sauvignon '94	YY	5
● Cepparello '93	YY	5
● Cepparello '94	YY	5
● Cepparello '95	YY	5

BARBERINO VAL D'ELSA (FI)

Le Filigare

Loc. San Donato in Poggio
Via Sicelle
50020 Barberino Val d'Elsa (FI)
tel. 055/8072796

On the border between the provinces of Florence and Siena, in the heart of Chianti Classico country, lies Le Filigare, which was once the retreat where Carlo Burchi, a goldsmith by trade, spent his weekends; as his love for the vine increasingly asserted itself, however, it was gradually transformed into a really significant wine estate. Next year there will be a number of new creations from his cellar, and we'll be writing about them then. This year, as usual, he presented three wines, and they show the consistent quality that characterizes this producer. The Chianti Classico '97 has a brilliant ruby color and a light soft fragrance of red currant and cherry with pleasant balsamic notes. The attack on the palate is good and firm, with closely knit tannins well balanced by notable alcohol; mid palate is meaty, full-bodied and generous and there is an admirable finish. The Riserva '96 seems somewhat less successful, perhaps because of its year. It has a good ruby color still tinged with purple, and presents very simple aromas of ripe fruit. In the mouth the acidity is immediately evident in a not very powerful structure, but the wine is easy to drink. On the other hand, the sangiovese and cabernet sauvignon blend Podere Le Rocce '96 is back up to its customary high standard. It shows a dark ruby color and a good nose of various different fruits, with berries predominating. In the mouth it is soft and unaggressive; all its components seem to be in perfect balance.

● Chianti Classico '97	**YY**	4
● Chianti Classico Ris. '96	**YY**	5
● Podere Le Rocce '96	**YY**	5
● Podere Le Rocce '88	YYY	5
● Chianti Classico '88	YY	4
● Chianti Classico '95	YY	4
● Chianti Classico Ris. '85	YY	5
● Chianti Classico Ris. '88	YY	5
● Chianti Classico Ris. '90	YY	5
● Chianti Classico Ris. '91	YY	5
● Chianti Classico Ris. '93	YY	5
● Podere Le Rocce '90	YY	5
● Podere Le Rocce '91	YY	5
● Podere Le Rocce '93	YY	5
● Podere Le Rocce '94	YY	5

BARBERINO VAL D'ELSA (FI)

CASTELLO DELLA PANERETTA
STRADA DELLA PANERETTA, 37
50021 BARBERINO VAL D'ELSA (FI)
TEL. 055/8059003

Castello della Paneretta has become one of the most interesting producers in the whole Chianti Classico area. This is an estate on the rise, as was clear at our tastings, where it came very close to garnering our highest award. Their excellent Riserva Torre a Destra '96 stands out in their array of important wines. Intensely fragrant, it offers rich fruit underpinned by toasty oak. The palate is full and compact, with lively smooth tannins and a long, complex finish. The normal '96 Riserva, which nearly earned Two Glasses as well, is very successful in the mouth, but a little less so on the nose, where the vanilla lords it over the fruit. The '97 Chianti is similarly marked by wood, which is, in this case, somewhat smoky. Made only from the sangiovese grape, the Quattrocentenario is very good. It has a concentrated bouquet of spicy tones on a base of blackberry and sour cherry, and in the mouth it shows power, grip and a good progression. The very interesting sangiovese and canaiolo blend, Le Terrine '96, has an unusual nose, with mineral and animal notes, that does not suit everyone. You could hardly fail to like the palate, however, which is vigorous and full of body and character. This wine has a very strong personality, and opinions about it are always going to vary.

●	Chianti Classico Torre a Destra Ris. '96	🍷🍷	4
●	Le Terrine '96	🍷🍷	5
●	Quattrocentenario '96	🍷🍷	5
●	Chianti Classico '97	🍷	4
●	Chianti Classico Ris. '96	🍷	4
●	Chianti Classico '95	🍸🍸	4
●	Chianti Classico Ris. '90	🍸🍸	4
●	Chianti Classico Ris. '93	🍸🍸	4
●	Chianti Classico Ris. '95	🍸🍸	4
●	Chianti Classico Torre a Destra Ris. '95	🍸🍸	4
●	Quattrocentenario '95	🍸🍸	5
●	Chianti Classico '96	🍸	3
●	Le Terrine '93	🍸	5

BARBERINO VAL D'ELSA (FI))

I BALZINI
LOC. PASTINE
VIA COMUNALE DI PONETA
50021 BARBERINO VAL D'ELSA (FI)
TEL. 055/8075503

Vincenzo D'Istanto's I Balzini lies just outside the limits of the Chianti Classico zone. In theory this is a bit of bad luck, but it hasn't kept this estate from following its policy of producing good wine. Initially they made a range of different wines, almost playfully including whites produced from grapes not usually found in this area, such as gewürztraminer, but latterly they have concentrated on a single wine, a red of a more local identity, made from sangiovese and cabernet sauvignon. With little more than two hectares at their disposal, this seems a reasonable choice. Four people form the backbone of the estate. For some years Walter Filipputti has been assisting D'Istanto on the commercial side, while vines and cellar are cared for by two gifted wine technicians, Giulio Gambelli and Andrea Mazzoni. This year the '96 I Balzini Rosso echoes the pleasant sensations evoked by its predecessor last year. Of an intense ruby color still tinged with purple at the edge, it reveals, after an initial dominant vanilla tone, light and elegant hints of cherry and blackberry alternating with spicy notes, particularly clove and cinnamon. The palate shows a good impact, substance and juiciness, with tightly knit and concentrated tannins partially "tamed" by alcohol.

●	I Balzini Rosso '96	🍷🍷	6
●	I Balzini Rosso '95	🍸🍸	6
●	I Balzini Rosso '94	🍸	5

Enjoy Italy even more.

$18.95
4 issues

Gambero Rosso
the insider guide to
top wines
best restaurants
delightful hotels
recipes and routes
all chosen for you by our experts.

Treat yourself to a subscription to Gambero Rosso
Italy's top wine, travel and food magazine

If you want to subscribe, please call:
Speedimpex USA
35-02 48th Avenue
L.I.C. NY 1101-2421
800-969-1258
speedsub@aol.com

For any other information, call:
Gambero Rosso
New York
NY 10012
212-253 5653
gamberousa@aol.com

visit our website click on english
www.gamberorosso.it

Get to know Rom
the way we do.

Gambero Rosso's food and wine exper share their finds with you. We know that every minute matters.

$15

ROME

Everything you need to know about

291 places to eat - from a bite to a banqu
187 hotels - at every price
30 wine bars
196 food and wine shops

DISTRIBUITED IN THE USA AND CANADA BY
Antique Collector's Club, 91 Market Street Industrial Park, Wappinger's Falls, NY 12
ph 800-252-5231 info@antiquecc.com

BOLGHERI (LI)

Tenuta Belvedere

Loc. Belvedere, 140
57020 Bolgheri (LI)
tel. 0565/749735

The fact that the same number of Glasses has been given to the same Tenuta Belvedere wines over and over in recent years might suggest that the situation here is static, but this is very far from being the case, as we are in a position to explain. (This is one of the great advantages to offering a commentary, instead of reducing one's impressions to mere numbers or symbols.) The wines the Marquises Antinori produce from this property certainly do continue to be good, but in particular Guado al Tasso, their principal wine, has changed in a number of important ways. It now has an excellent nose of ripe and compact fruit without the hints of overripeness and occasional vegetal notes present in previous years. In the mouth the '96 Guado is still recognizable for its density and the silkiness of its tannins, but it has more character and grip and is less easygoing. The Rosato Scalabrone '98, a very successful wine in its category, came within an inch of Two Glasses. Its nose is exemplarily clean and fruity, with intense notes of raspberry and strawberry. The crisp and fragrant palate reveals a certain substance and excellent balance. The well-executed Vermentino '98 doesn't show much to the nose beyond cleanliness and a touch of yeast, but it comes into its own on the full-bodied, succulent and fairly long palate.

● Bolgheri Rosso Sup. Guado al Tasso '96	🍷🍷	6
⊙ Bolgheri Rosato Scalabrone '98	🍷	4
○ Bolgheri Vermentino '98	🍷	3
● Bolgheri Rosso Sup. Guado al Tasso '90	YYY	6
● Bolgheri Rosso Sup. Guado al Tasso '92	YY	4
● Bolgheri Rosso Sup. Guado al Tasso '93	YY	6
● Bolgheri Rosso Sup. Guado al Tasso '94	YY	6
● Bolgheri Rosso Sup. Guado al Tasso '95	YY	6
● Bolgheri Rosso Belvedere '96	Y	2*

BOLGHERI (LI)

Le Macchiole

Via Bolgherese
57020 Bolgheri (LI)
tel. 0565/763240

This is another memorable year for Eugenio Campolmi. His Paleo Rosso gets Three Glasses for the second consecutive year, a notable accomplishment, and his other wines are outstanding as well. But before we describe them, we should like to mention his extraordinary Messorio '97, a monovarietal merlot, which received a grade of 98 from a certain well-known American wine critic. As you can see, we have not even reviewed it, (and Eugenio himself wisely concurs), because so little of the wine was made: six or seven hundred bottles in all. This is an experiment which, however, has already demonstrated the enormous potential that merlot has in the Bolgheri area. Another wine in the experimental stage, his syrah-based Scrio, is quite promising in the '97 version, and we'll be writing about it next year. Returning to the Paleo, the '96 seems to be even more compact and harmonious than the '95, giving it superior elegance, more evident breeding and greater personality. The nose is rich and without defects; fruit is dominant and the oak well integrated. The concentrated and beautifully defined palate develops evenly and with perfect balance. The excellent Sauvignon Paleo '97 has intense aromas of pear, citrus fruit and vanilla, and a splendidly balanced and structured palate. The Bianco Le Contessine '98, a vermentino, is satisfactory if less brilliant this time around, while the Rosato is correct but little more.

● Bolgheri Rosso Sup. Paleo '96	🍷🍷🍷	6
○ Bolgheri Sauvignon Paleo '97	🍷🍷	4
○ Bolgheri Bianco Le Contessine '98	🍷	3
⊙ Bolgheri Rosato Le Contessine '98		2
● Bolgheri Rosso Sup. Paleo '95	YYY	6
● Bolgheri Rosso Sup. Paleo '94	YY	5
○ Bolgheri Sauvignon Paleo '95	YY	4
○ Bolgheri Sauvignon Paleo '96	YY	4
○ Paleo Bianco '93	YY	3*
○ Paleo Bianco '94	YY	3*
● Paleo Rosso '91	YY	5
● Paleo Rosso '92	YY	2*
● Paleo Rosso '93	YY	5

BOLGHERI (LI)

Tenuta dell'Ornellaia

Via Bolgherese, 191
57020 Bolgheri (LI)
tel. 0565/762140 - 0565/762141

In the sudden great rush to make a fortune on winegrowing in the Maremma (particularly in the Grosseto area, however) those who have for years believed and invested in this land have been consolidating their strong position harvest after harvest. Of course we are thinking of Lodovico Antinori, even if his wines are somewhat less exciting than usual this time. After its easily earned Three Glasses in '95, the Masseto in '96 is very well made, as it always is, but it lacks the verve and energy of its older brother. Of an intense, luminous ruby color, it has a powerful but severe and unbending impact on the nose, where notes of pencil lead, quinine, and licorice are lightly veiled by a slight hint of reduction. The palate is rich, full-bodied and mature, but once again somewhat aggressive because of not very fine-grained tannins; the finish, as usual, is very long. The Ornellaia '96 seems more successful; indeed it's one of the best Bolgheri wines of the year. It has a deep, brilliant ruby hue, and an intense, earthy and complex bouquet with a hint of reduction. On the palate it's well articulated and consistent, with plenty of extract; we await the harmonizing effect of a little more age: it's a very promising wine. The fruity and rich Poggio alle Gazze '98, a sauvignon, is a little shy on the nose but turns up trumps in the mouth. The IGT Le Volte '97, a blend of sangiovese and cabernet sauvignon, is an easy wine to get along with. Somewhat vegetal aromas lead on to a clean and straightforward palate.

●	Masseto '96	🍷🍷	6
●	Ornellaia '96	🍷🍷	6
○	Poggio alle Gazze '98	🍷🍷	4
●	Le Volte '97	🍷	3
●	Masseto '93	YYY	6
●	Masseto '94	YYY	6
●	Masseto '95	YYY	6
●	Ornellaia '93	YYY	6
●	Masseto '89	YY	6
●	Masseto '92	YY	6
●	Ornellaia '90	YY	6
●	Ornellaia '91	YY	6
●	Ornellaia '92	YY	6
●	Ornellaia '94	YY	6
●	Ornellaia '95	YY	6

BOLGHERI (LI)

Tenuta San Guido

Loc. Capanne, 27
57020 Bolgheri (LI)
tel. 0565/762003

After Sassicaia's umpteenth Three Glasses last year, we finished our review by saying that '96 had something exceptional in store for us. This prediction has been confirmed: the vintage '96 will be a classic. We never tire of saying that Sassicaia's great strength lies not so much in its richness of bouquet and palate, although that has long been remarkable, but in its confident and constant style, its unmistakable personality. The Tenuta San Guido has successfully created a model of cabernet, inspired, if you will, by the great wines of Bordeaux, but informed by the warmth and tannic fullness of a true Tuscan wine. The secret, if you can call it a secret, is right here: a faithful interpretation of its terroir, with no sleight of hand, no messing about in the cellar. Thus the '96 Sassicaia won't overwhelm you with its muscularity, but you'll probably be seduced by the purity of its aromas and the silky softness of its palate. Of an intense but not saturated ruby color, it opens on the nose with notes of spice and cedar, progressing through a rich gamut of fruit, including black currant and ripe blackberry. After a wonderfully restrained and delicate entry, the palate acquires a full, well-focused fruitiness. It is mature, elegant and full-bodied, and has a gentle finish, with extremely fine tannins, that just goes on and on.

●	Bolgheri Sassicaia '96	🍷🍷🍷	6
●	Bolgheri Sassicaia '95	YYY	6
●	Sassicaia '83	YYY	6
●	Sassicaia '84	YYY	6
●	Sassicaia '85	YYY	6
●	Sassicaia '88	YYY	6
●	Sassicaia '90	YYY	6
●	Sassicaia '92	YYY	6
●	Sassicaia '93	YYY	6
●	Bolgheri Sassicaia '94	YY	6
●	Sassicaia '86	YY	6
●	Sassicaia '87	YY	6
●	Sassicaia '89	YY	6
●	Sassicaia '91	YY	6

BUCINE (AR)

Fattoria Santa Maria di Ambra

Loc. Ambra
52020 Bucine (AR)
tel. 055/996806

The province of Arezzo has always been one of the areas most carpeted in vines in all of Tuscany, but there are very few producers here who seem determined to make wines of the highest quality. On the other hand, the remarkable potential of this extensive and varied terrain is always clear from our tastings. Perhaps what is principally lacking is something specifically characteristic of this terroir, which could unite producers in a joint project and bring the province into the public eye. These reflections bear some relationship to Vincenzo Zampi's beautiful estate, Santa Maria di Ambra, where for some years now he has been striving to make excellent wines. Only two examples were presented at our tastings, since his Chianti La Bigattiera Riserva '97 was not yet ready to be tasted. The very good Gavignano '96, two thirds cabernet and one third sangiovese, displays balanced and well-focused aromas with a laudable amount of fruit well integrated with and not disturbed by the distinct vegetal notes. The palate is dense and meaty, with compact and fine-grained tannins and no unobtrusive notes of oak. The Casamurli '96, a blend of sangiovese and malvasia nera, is less successful. Here the wood is strongly marked, blocking expression of the wine's inherent characteristics. Its customary energy is not in evidence, so its virtues are tied to the balance it shows on the palate. Next year we'll try the '97 and we feel sure that it will be something else again.

●	Casamurli '96	▼▼	4
●	Gavignano '96	▼	5
●	Casamurli '95	▽▽	5
●	Gavignano '92	▽▽	3
●	Gavignano '93	▽▽	3
●	Gavignano '95	▽▽	4
○	Chardonnay '97	▽	3
●	Chianti Ris. '88	▽	3
●	Chianti V. La Bigattiera Ris. '95	▽	3
●	Chianti V. La Bigattiera Ris. '96	▽	3
●	Chianti V. La Bigattiera Ris. '92	▽	2*
●	Gavignano '90	▽	4
●	Gavignano '94	▽	3

BUCINE (AR)

Fattoria Villa La Selva

Loc. Montebenichi
52021 Bucine (AR)
tel. 055/998203 - 055/998200

Villa La Selva has again done well this year. It is a competently managed estate and its entire range of wines is always very reliable. We feel we must repeat, however, that the great potential of this winery, in terms both of terrain and of the technical expertise available to it (Vittorio Fiore and Stefano Chioccioli are the consultant oenologists), is only partly realized. This is true even though a couple of their wines are within an ace of our highest award. We'll start, in fact, with their best wine, the sangiovese-based Felciaia '97, which is, as it has been in other years, an aristocratic red. It has a lovely intense ruby color, and greets the nose with spicy, restrained notes of oak, opening thereafter to a series of fruity tones, including blueberry, black currant, sour cherry and blackberry. In the mouth it is consistent, even, soft and very satisfying. The cabernet and sangiovese blend Selvamaggio '96 scored almost as high. It is very pure and fascinating, if somewhat vegetal in its bouquet. The palate is rich, full-bodied and mature, with a long finish that leaves you with well-amalgamated hints of wild berries and oak. Two rightly less ambitious wines are the Chianti Evento '96, a good example of its kind, simple and pleasing, and the rosé Tre Vaghissime Donne '98, which shows good substance and balance. The less successful sweet wines suggest that the search for a distinctive style for this category is still under way. The Anna dei Fiori '96, however, is reasonable and correctly made, but in need of greater focus on nose and palate. It could also do with less wood.

●	Felciaia '97	▼▼	5
●	Selvamaggio '96	▼▼	5
●	Chianti Evento '96	▼	3
⊙	Tre Vaghissime Donne '98	▼	4
○	Anna dei Fiori '96		5
●	Chianti Ris. '93	▽▽	5
●	Felciaia '93	▽▽	4
●	Felciaia '94	▽▽	5
●	Felciaia '95	▽▽	5
●	Selvamaggio '90	▽▽	5
●	Selvamaggio '91	▽▽	5
●	Selvamaggio '92	▽▽	5
●	Selvamaggio '93	▽▽	5
●	Selvamaggio '95	▽▽	5
●	Selvamaggio Ris. '90	▽▽	6

CAMPIGLIA MARITTIMA (LI)

LE VOLPAIOLE
VIA FONTE CARBOLI, 13
57021 CAMPIGLIA MARITTIMA (LI)
TEL. 0565/843194

The Val di Cornia is something of an exception for Tuscany, where wine estates are usually fairly big and owned by the old aristocracy or powerful investment groups. Here in Val di Cornia, so far at least, you can still find small or even tiny family-run wineries. Le Volpaiole, owned and run by a Swiss couple, Armin and Liliana Meili, is typical of this southern part of the province of Livorno. They have very few hectares under vine and make a limited amount of wine, all, happily, of just one kind. Their '95 and '96 had already impressed us, but the quantity produced was so small that we decided to relegate them to our list of Other Wineries. The '97, however, is too good to be left in the semi-anonymity to which we had consigned this appealing estate in Campiglia Marittima, and then too there are plans to increase production in the years to come. At our tastings everybody liked the Volpaiole Val di Cornia Rosso '97, and how could it have been otherwise? Even the color, an intense and dense ruby, promises great things. The bouquet is concentrated, with notes of coffee and toasty oak still apparent on a background of perfectly ripe black berries. On the palate it is decidedly soft, with tightly-knit vigorous tannins and a long finish that exactly reflects the nose.

●	Val di Cornia Rosso '97	ΨΨ	4

CAPANNORI (LU)

TENUTA DI VALGIANO
FRAZ. VALGIANO
55010 CAPANNORI (LU)
TEL. 0583/402271

It is a pleasure to report that this estate, which we in a sense discovered, continues to get better and better. Indeed our tastings revealed a great step forward: their premier wine, the Scasso dei Cesari '97, was so good that it came within a hair's breadth of winning Three Glasses. This is a powerful, dense and concentrated red that manages also to be extraordinarily drinkable and harmonious despite its 14% of alcohol, which might suggest a prize-winner for strength rather than a wine you would happily swallow. This result is even more significant when you think that Scasso dei Cesari is made almost entirely from sangiovese grapes grown in an area not yet known for producing important wines. But things are changing. The exceptional vintage, '97, made an important contribution, of course. But it is the determination at Valgiano to continue to learn and grow that convinces us that they are going to keep right on surpising and delighting us in the years to come. The single Glass that each of their other two wines received was a full one, and their scores do not really do justice to the performance of this estate. The aromas of the good Palistorti '97, with their jammy and spicy notes, have not yet settled down in perfect harmony. The soft and vigorous palate offers a full, fruity finish. The Giallo dei Muri '98 displays remarkable structure as well as fleshiness and warmth in the mouth, and a fruity bouquet (pear and citrus fruit) with mineral notes.

●	Scasso dei Cesari '97	ΨΨ	5
○	Colline Lucchesi Bianco Giallo dei Muri '98	Ψ	3
●	Colline Lucchesi Rosso dei Palistorti '97	Ψ	3
○	Colline Lucchesi Bianco Giallo dei Muri '97	YY	3*
●	Scasso dei Cesari '95	YY	4
●	Scasso dei Cesari '96	YY	4
●	Colline Lucchesi Rosso dei Palistorti '95	Y	2*
●	Colline Lucchesi Rosso dei Palistorti '96	Y	3
●	Scasso dei Cesari '94	Y	3

CAPRAIA E LIMITE (PO)

Enrico Pierazzuoli
Via Valicarda, 35
50050 Capraia e Limite (PO)
tel. 0574/574323

The young and dynamic Tuscan producer Enrico Pierazzuoli is in the unusual position of owning and running three different and by no means contiguous wineries: Tenuta Cantagallo in Montalbano, Le Farnete in Carmignano and Matroneo in Chianti Classico. For clarity's sake, it would probably be a good idea to have a separate entry for each of them, but questions of space and the proliferation of good producers force us to review all three together. Hence we shall get down at once to the most important wines on offer. The Carmignano Riserva '96 cut a fine figure thanks to good concentration and fair length and despite the noticeable wood on both nose and palate. There is no shortage of wood in the Carmignano '97 either, which, however, also showed fruitiness and an interesting finish. The appealing Chianti Riserva '95 offered delightful aromas of spice, red berries and flowers, as well as balance in the mouth. The Chianti '96 is pleasing particularly because of the well-delineated fruit on the nose. The palate is lively and intense, with a slightly dilute finish. The well-executed Montalbano Riserva is successful, apart, once again, from excessive wood. Both the Montalbano '97 and the Unico '95 are satisfyingly full-bodied; the former is, however, a bit overripe, and the latter wants more elegance on the palate. The decidedly good Riesling Carleto '98 displays very clearly articulated aromas but is still too young to be at its best. The long list concludes with the Vin Santo, which acquits itself very well, and the Gioveto '96, which is correct but a bit vegetal.

●	Carmignano Le Farnete Ris. '96	🍷🍷	4
○	Carleto '98	🍷	4
●	Carmignano Le Farnete '97	🍷	4
●	Chianti Cl. Matroneo '96	🍷	4
●	Chianti Cl. Matroneo Ris. '95	🍷	4
●	Chianti Montalbano '97	🍷	2*
●	Chianti Montalbano Ris. '96	🍷	3
●	Unico '95	🍷	4
●	Gioveto '96		3
○	Carleto '97	YY	4
●	Carmignano Le Farnete Ris. '92	YY	4
●	Carmignano Le Farnete Ris. '93	YY	4
●	Carmignano Le Farnete Ris. '94	YY	4
●	Chianti Montalbano Ris. '93	YY	3*
●	Chianti Montalbano Ris. '94	YY	4

CARMIGNANO (PO)

Fattoria Ambra
Via Lombarda, 85
50042 Carmignano (PO)
tel. 055/486488 - 055/8719049

Fattoria Ambra in Carmignano is a reputable and reliable winery, but this year's results are somewhat puzzling. The best red wines are from the '96 vintage, hardly a felicitous one in this area or indeed in Tuscany generally. All the Carmignanos, the regular version and the riservas, are substantial wines with good structure, and are also elegant and refined. Yet a certain slackening in mid palate suggests that they may not last as long as their older brothers. Let's consider them one by one. The standard Carmignano '96 has an intense and noble ruby color. At first the considerable fruit of the bouquet is hardly perceptible because of muffling reduction. But when the wine has had a few minutes to breathe, sulfurous notes are replaced by pleasant aromas of sour cherry and red currant. It develops confidently on the mouth-filling, full-bodied and tannic palate, where the general tone is austere rather than soft. The Riserva Le Vigne Alte, from the same vintage, has, predictably, more size and weight. Of a dark ruby hue, it displays clean, fresh, deep aromas that alternate between fruit and spice. The very harmonious palate offers fine tannins and excellent length. The Riserva Elzana '96 is similar but not quite as good. Its color is equally intense but bouquet and palate are somewhat skittish. The Barca Reale '98 is an agreeable red that is, however, usually more successful.

●	Carmignano Elzana Ris. '96	🍷🍷	4
●	Carmignano Le Vigne Alte Ris. '96	🍷🍷	4
●	Carmignano '96	🍷	4
●	Barco Reale '98		3
●	Carmignano '89	YY	3
●	Carmignano Elzana Ris. '95	YY	4
●	Carmignano Le Vigne Alte Ris. '94	YY	4
●	Carmignano Le Vigne Alte Ris. '90	YY	4
●	Carmignano Le Vigne Alte Ris. '95	Y	4
●	Carmignano Vigna S. Cristina in Pilli '95	Y	4

CARMIGNANO (PO)

CAPEZZANA

LOC. SEANO - VIA CAPEZZANA, 100
50042 CARMIGNANO (PO)
TEL. 055/8706005 - 055/8706091

There are changes afoot at the Capezzana estate. The Contini Bonacossi family, after spending years in a state of aloof contemplation, in stark contrast to the ferment of activity among other Tuscan producers in the '90s, has acquired new verve and enthusiasm, which prompts us to predict a richly successful future. They have also made an excellent choice in Stefano Chioccioli as their very able new consultant agronomist/oenologist . Turning to their wines, we consider first their Cabernet Ghiaie della Furba '97. It is not a very complicated wine, but it is exemplary for the neatness of its aromas of red and black berries with a bit of something vegetal, and a lovely well-balanced taste which is soft, round, long, and clean at the end. Their Carmignano Riserva '95 is convincing as well. Perhaps the nose is affected by the presence of wood, but in the mouth it is soft at the beginning, then fills the mouth, and finishes well. The Vin Santo Riserva '92 also receives Two Glasses. It is a frequent strong point of Capezzana's. This version has a golden color that is both brilliant and intense. It is elegant to the nose, and reveals suggestions of dried flowers, almond and fig. It is sweet and compact, and has good depth and length. Of the rest of the wine, the Carmignano '96 stands out for its pleasant fragrance and general harmoniousness. The Chardonnay '98 seems well made and a great bargain, and the Barca Reale '98 is pleasingly fruity.

●	Carmignano Villa di Capezzana Ris. '95	▼▼	5
●	Ghiaie della Furba '97	▼▼	5
○	Vin Santo di Carmignano Ris. '92	▼▼	5
●	Barco Reale '98	▼	3
●	Carmignano '96	▼	4
○	Chardonnay '98	▼	2*
●	Carmignano Villa di Capezzana Ris. '90	▽▽	5
●	Ghiaie della Furba '95	▽▽	5
○	Vin Santo di Carmignano Ris. '89	▽▽	5
○	Vin Santo di Carmignano Ris. '90	▽▽	5

CASTAGNETO CARDUCCI (LI)

GRATTAMACCO

LOC. GRATTAMACCO
57022 CASTAGNETO CARDUCCI (LI)
TEL. 0565/763840

Piermario Meletti Cavallari continues his own personal quest for excellence. To make a wine that is recognizably itself, and that expresses the positive qualities of the land from which it comes, is still the primary object of his present and future wine-making endeavors. There is no rush here at Grattamacco to do everything all at once, using familiar recipes to obtain wines that are full, soft, attractive and perhaps excellent, but certainly increasingly alike. He who would dedicate himself to the production of important wines must look to his vineyard. Anyone who doubts it should go see the carefully tended vineyards at Grattamacco: they are a veritable garden. We do not, of course, mean to say that everything is perfect: Piermario, like everyone else, has made mistakes, and we have not failed to point them out. But we share the convictions we have just described. He also believes that you shouldn't make wines just in order to win prizes with them, and we, who give out prizes, know how very true that is. But getting down to this year's tastings, we must say that the Grattamacco '96 has solid structure with evident good fruit that develops with the progression on the palate. Indeed the palate seems much better than the nose, which displays a touch of reduction that cannot be considered simply characterological. The Bianco '98 is unquestionably good: it is clean and pleasingly quaffable and altogether one of the most successful versions of this wine.

●	Bolgheri Rosso Sup. Grattamacco '96	▼▼	6
○	Bolgheri Bianco '98	▼	4
●	Grattamacco '85	▽▽▽	5
●	Bolgheri Rosso Sup. Grattamacco '95	▽▽	6
●	Grattamacco '86	▽▽	5
●	Grattamacco '87	▽▽	5
●	Grattamacco '88	▽▽	5
●	Grattamacco '89	▽▽	5
●	Grattamacco '90	▽▽	5
●	Grattamacco '91	▽▽	5
●	Grattamacco '92	▽▽	4
●	Grattamacco '93	▽▽	5
●	Bolgheri Rosso '96	▽	3

CASTAGNETO CARDUCCI (LI)

MICHELE SATTA
LOC. VIGNA AL CAVALIERE
57020 CASTAGNETO CARDUCCI (LI)
TEL. 0565/763894

There are no really big changes in Michele Satta's wines this year. We can say that the progress he has made in recent years has been maintained, and that things, if anything, are even better. The composition of some of his wines has changed, however. His Vigna al Cavaliere has had other red grapes added to its sangiovese base. His Costa di Giulia as well has an addition in its '98 version: a substantial amount of sauvignon blanc has come to join its vermentino. The Vigna al Cavaliere '97 has some very interesting qualities: it is different from usual, and perhaps less characteristic, but it has a greater overall richness, is densely tannic, deep and soft, and displays aromas of wild blackberry with a touch of toasty wood and a vegetal note. The Piastraia in its '97 version continues, reassuringly, to give much pleasure, and the different grapes which make it up, cabernet, merlot, syrah and sangiovese, function together with well-practiced teamwork. It has good concentration, offers spice and dark berries on the nose, and reveals notable strength, breadth and softness in the mouth. In the Costa di Giulia '98 the added sauvignon is noticeable. It is a wine of decent body and persistence, and presents an assortment of varietal characteristics: tropical fruit and apricot from the vermentino, and sage and lavender from the sauvignon. For Michele Satta the so-called lesser wines are equally important. The red Diambra and the Bolgheri Bianco share a pleasant fruitiness, good balance and quaffability.

●	Bolgheri Rosso Piastraia '97	▼▼	4
●	Vigna al Cavaliere '97	▼▼	5
○	Bolgheri Bianco '98	▼	3
●	Bolgheri Rosso Diambra '98	▼	3
○	Bolgheri Vermentino Costa di Giulia '98	▼	4
●	Bolgheri Rosso Piastraia '95	▽▽	3*
●	Bolgheri Rosso Piastraia '96	▽▽	4
●	Vigna al Cavaliere '90	▽▽	5
●	Vigna al Cavaliere '95	▽▽	4
●	Vigna al Cavaliere '96	▽▽	5
●	Bolgheri Rosso Diambra '93	▽	2*
●	Bolgheri Rosso Diambra '94	▽	1*
●	Piastraia '94	▽	3
●	Vigna al Cavaliere '94	▽	4

CASTELLINA IN CHIANTI (SI)

TENUTA DI BIBBIANO
VIA BIBBIANO, 106
53011 CASTELLINA IN CHIANTI (SI)
TEL. 0577/743065

We were very pleased last year to welcome into the Guide this centenarian estate, which is dedicated to making ever better wines. We can confirm that excellent work is still being done in both vineyards and cellar under the continued supervision of their experienced oenologist Giulio Gambelli. Nevertheless, to our surpise, the wines presented at our tastings this year were not completely convincing. The Chianti Classico Montornello '97 has a lively clear ruby color. On the nose it offers pleasantly fresh hints of mint, followed by aromas of ripe fruit (blackberry particularly) that are not very intense, but fine and delicate. The attack on the palate is a bit aggressive, with evident tightly knit tannins showing considerable staying power. The alcohol gives good support to the general structure, but the various components are not in perfect balance and don't seem sufficiently amalgamated. The finish is sufficiently long. The Vigna del Capannino Riserva '96 has a full and concentrated ruby color. The nose offers sweet jammy notes of ripe plum and cherry that are a bit too forward and not perfectly clean. The palate, though corresponding, wants grip and seems a bit dilute; the acidity stands out, and there's a general lack of harmony.

●	Chianti Cl. Montornello '97	▼	3
●	Chianti Cl. Vigna del Capannino Ris. '96	▼	5
●	Chianti Cl. Montornello '95	▽▽	3*
●	Chianti Cl. Vigna del Capannino Ris. '95	▽▽	5

CASTELLINA IN CHIANTI (SI)

CASTELLARE DI CASTELLINA
LOC. CASTELLARE
53011 CASTELLINA IN CHIANTI (SI)
TEL. 0577/740490

Castellare di Castellina presented an excellent range of wines this year, including, for the first time, a wine that made it to our finals, I Sodi di San Niccolò '95. But what seems most important is their evident great step forward in wine-making technique, which should improve even more when the new state-of-the-art cellar is ready. This is a very pleasing situation, and even though this time they merely came close to receiving Three Glasses, they have demonstrated that they are capable of producing a wine that will go all the way. For the moment, we'll content ourselves with this splendid version of I Sodi di San Niccoò, one of the best of recent years. Made almost entirely from sangiovese grapes, it offers intensely fruity aromas of a definition never heretofore achieved. It has a good full taste, and its body, though not enormous, is fine and well-balanced, right in line with the sangiovese wines of this part of Castellina in Chianti. Nor is the '94 version bad, although there's a more animal bouquet, and the wine seems less harmonious and concentrated. The very good Chianti Classico '97, on the other hand, is certainly one of the best of its category, and the first to be released of a number of '97s that seem to show extraordinary breeding. The Chianti Classico Vigna al Poggiale '96 is under par and somewhat thin. The Coniale '95, however, made from cabernet sauvignon, is excellent, and quite a departure for an estate so devoted to sangiovese. The series of wines finishes with the Chianti Classico Riserva '96, which despite its poor year does very well indeed.

●	Chianti Classico '97	𝐘𝐘	4
●	Chianti Classico Ris. '96	𝐘𝐘	5
●	Coniale '95	𝐘𝐘	6
●	I Sodi di San Niccolò '95	𝐘𝐘	6
●	I Sodi di San Niccolò '94	𝐘𝐘	6
●	Chianti Classico Vigna al Poggiale '96	𝐘	5
●	Chianti Classico '90	YY	4
●	Chianti Classico '95	YY	4
●	Chianti Classico Vigna al Poggiale '95	YY	5
●	Coniale '90	YY	6
●	Coniale '94	YY	6
●	I Sodi di San Niccolò '91	YY	5
●	I Sodi di San Niccolò '86	YY	5

CASTELLINA IN CHIANTI (SI)

CECCHI - VILLA CERNA
LOC. CASINA DEI PONTI
53011 CASTELLINA IN CHIANTI (SI)
TEL. 0577/743024

This famous producer of Chianti Classico has once again produced some first-rate wines. To start with the simplest, the Chianti Classico '97, which is very widely available in Italy, is well made, has a characteristic fruity nose and good body, and costs relatively little. It's a perfect wine for a picnic. The Messer Pietro di Teuzzo '97 is also good, finer and more concentrated than the preceding wine, but less lingering. The Riserva '96 Villa Cerna, from the Cecchi family's winery, is better, indeed one of the best of its year. It is elegant, well-structured and drinkable, as are all the best wines from the lower part of the Castellina zone. The Spargolo '96 is good, but not up to the level of previous vintages. It is made principally from sangiovese, which was not generally successful here in '96. But any doubts raised by wines from this year are completely swept away by the '96 Vigneto La Gavina, which is better than it has ever been before. Based almost entirely on cabernet sauvignon, it made it to our finals and very nearly received Three Glasses. It is a very elegant red with varietal aromas and nearly as much body as we would have liked. Furthermore, it is technically perfect. We'll conclude with the new wines from the Maremma, the Morellino di Scansano Valle delle Rose '97, which is simple, fragrant, and abounding in freshness, and the Riserva '95 version, which is more concentrated and complex.

●	Chianti Classico Villa Cerna Ris. '96	𝐘𝐘	4
●	Morellino di Scansano Val delle Rose Ris. '95	𝐘𝐘	4
●	Vigneto La Gavina '96	𝐘𝐘	5
●	Chianti Classico '97	𝐘	3
●	Chianti Classico Messer Piero di Teuzzo '97	𝐘	4
●	Chianti Classico Villa Cerna '97	𝐘	3
●	Morellino di Scansano Valle delle Rose '97	𝐘	3
●	Spargolo '96	𝐘	5
●	Chianti Classico Messer Piero di Teuzzo '95	YY	4
●	Spargolo '95	YY	4

CONCADORO

Loc. Concadoro, 67
53011 Castellina in Chianti (SI)
tel. 0577/741285

This estate is owned by the two Cerasi brothers. Originally from Rome, they have continued the work begun here by their father, and we, in turn, are glad to welcome them back into the Guide. They have 17 hectares under vine and another three that have been replanted and will become productive in the next few years. Concadoro follows organic principles in all stages of its wine production, with their director Benito Torricelli in charge of the vines, and Marco Chellini directing operations in the cellar. They have presented only two wines this year, having decided not to make a '96 Riserva. The Chianti Classico '97 has a dark, very clear ruby color. Vanilla has the upper hand at first in the bouquet, but then makes way for a ripe, rich, deep fruitiness. The entry on the palate is strong and immediate, and the succulent, densely knit tannins pleasingly support the even development through to the strong, delightfully tasty and long finish. The Vigna Gaversa '96 is a blend of cabernet sauvignon and sangiovese aged in barrique. Decidedly deep in color, it offers a ripe fruity nose with distinct notes of plum and raspberry. The palate is soft and velvety, and offers a succession of rich and lively sensations. The finish, which is pleasingly long, is very good.

● Chianti Cl. Vigna di Gaversa '96	🍷🍷	4
● Chianti Classico '97	🍷🍷	4
● Chianti Cl. Vigna di Gaversa '93	YY	4
● Chianti Classico Ris. '93	Y	4

CASTELLINA IN CHIANTI (SI)

★ CASTELLO DI FONTERUTOLI

Loc. Fonterutoli Via Rossini, 5
53011 Castellina in Chianti (SI)
tel. 0577/740476

Castello di Fonterutoli continues its march towards the top of the Italian wine world. Owned by the Mazzei family, this estate seems always to receive our highest award, and this year collects its twelfth Third Glass. This time the recipient is their '97 Siepi, made from equal parts of sangiovese and merlot. It is a monumental Tuscan red to which we have been awarding our top prize since 1993. It's obvious that we like it a lot. The '97, though, is especially convincing. That the year was a very good one goes without saying, but the concentration and the magical blending of the softness of the merlot with the acid spikiness of the sangiovese are just unbelievable. Furthermore, this is clearly a wine from the Chianti Classico region, even though it is made partly from a non-native grape. The Chianti Classico Castello di Fonterutoli Riserva '96 very nearly received a Third Glass too. It doesn't have the structure of the '95, but may be even better executed. Its acidic bite is fairly evident and makes it a little lean in the mouth. The Chianti Classico '97 is very good. It is full, drinkable, deliciously soft, and has, in our opinion, a long life ahead of it. Immediate in impact, very fruity, round and easy to drink, the Morellino di Scansano Belguardo '98 is a simple but extremely enjoyable red that has been very well made.

● Siepi '97	🍷🍷🍷	6
● Chianti Classico '97	🍷🍷	4
● Chianti Classico Castello di Fonterutoli Ris. '96	🍷🍷	5
● Morellino di Scansano Belguardo '98	🍷🍷	3*
● Chianti Classico Castello di Fonterutoli Ris. '95	YYY	5
● Concerto '90	YYY	5
● Concerto '93	YYY	5
● Concerto '94	YYY	5
● Siepi '93	YYY	5
● Siepi '94	YYY	6
● Siepi '95	YYY	6
● Siepi '96	YYY	6

Gagliole

Loc. Gagliole
53011 Castellina in Chianti (SI)
tel. 0577/740369

After only a year's absence, the winery of Thomas Bar, a Swiss lawyer who is ever more in love with all things Tuscan and who dedicates all his free time to his estate, reenters our guide. There is much to report. He has leased one estate, Siepi, which borders his, and bought another, Casina di Castagnoli. Its land, formerly planted to a great variety of grapes, has been completely restructured and replanted taking advantage of the most up-to-date viticultural techniques. Starting with the '99 version, fermentation takes place in oak barrels. The winery continues to follow an organic approach, and the wine-making is still entrusted to the oenologist Luca D'Attoma. Only one wine was presented at our tastings, the Gagliole '97, an IGT. It is a red made almost entirely from sangiovese with a touch of cabernet sauvignon. It has a clear deep ruby color, and an intensely fruity nose with plum and berries to the fore. In the mouth, it is not at all aggressive, as the tannins are restrained by a good bit of alcohol, while the acidity lends good support. There is a soft finish with a light and elegant touch of vanilla.

●	Gagliole Rosso '97	**YY**	5
●	Gagliole Rosso '95	YY	5
○	Gagliole Bianco '96	Y	4

La Brancaia

Loc. Brancaia
53011 Castellina in Chianti (SI)
tel. 0577/743084

We have been following the wines of this small but extraordinary producer in Castellina for years. This winery is the fruit of the passionate dedication of Bruno Widmehr, a successful Swiss adman, and of his collaboration with the Mazzei family of Fonterutoli and the oenologist Carlo Ferrini. From this little cellar, year after year, genuine oenological gems have been emerging, and this year is no exception. The Brancaia '97, sangiovese and merlot, shows really exceptional breeding. It is still very young and had, when we tasted it, just been bottled, so it showed, in addition to the concentration of a thoroughbred, some of the rough edges of an early adolescent. However, its great depth, progression on the palate, long finish and already fully evident wealth of aromas made it impossible to have any doubts: Three Glasses hands down. The '96 is a little leaner and more dilute, and has been almost all drunk up anyway. The Chianti Classico '97 is very interesting. It is soft, quaffable and concentrated, just as one would expect from this extraordinary vintage. This will be a year to remember for Brancaia, and a magnificent conclusion to the 20th century.

●	Brancaia '97	**YYY**	6
●	Brancaia '96	**YY**	6
●	Chianti Classico '97	**YY**	4
●	Brancaia '94	YYY	6
●	Brancaia '88	YY	6
●	Brancaia '90	YY	6
●	Brancaia '91	YY	6
●	Brancaia '93	YY	5
●	Brancaia '95	YY	6
●	Chianti Classico '95	YY	4
●	Chianti Classico '96	YY	4

Castello La Leccia

Loc. La Leccia
53011 Castellina in Chianti (SI)
tel. 0577/743148

So many wine producers are making such great strides so quickly, that we sometimes do not include everyone in the Guide as soon as we might. We are making up for lost time in the case of Castello La Leccia, which is certainly worthy of note. The estate covers 170 hectares, of which 20 are under vine. Francesco Daddi, the young proprietor, handles all aspects of the business, with some assistance on the oenological side from the highly experienced Franco Bernabei. The wines have a decisive character with round fruit, good strength and solidity. The supposedly simplest of his wines was the one that impressed us most: the Chianti Classico '97 easily walked off with Two Glasses. It is intensely fruity and pleasantly spicy on the nose, and even more expressive in the mouth, where it offers a captivating liveliness. Perhaps it's not very complicated, but it is ample and generous. The sangiovese Bruciagna '96 is also good and vigorous and nearly got Two Glasses as well, but was slightly handicapped by excessive oak, noticeable both in its spicy and toasty aromas and on the palate, which is still somewhat dominated by wood-derived tannins. The Riserva '96 suffers at the moment from the same handicap, although, like the other estate wines, it reveals first-class fruit. This quality bodes very well for the future of Castello La Leccia.

● Chianti Classico '97	▼▼	3*
● Bruciagna '96	▼	4
● Chianti Classico Ris. '96	▼	4

CASTELLINA IN CHIANTI (SI)

Fattoria Nittardi

Loc. Nittardi
53011 Castellina in Chianti (SI)
tel. 0577/740269

Among the estates that produce very good wines but have not yet made it to the top of their category, we, at any rate, would place Peter Femfert's Fattoria Nittardi. This should, of course, not be taken as a definitive criticism, and the personal preferences of the tasters always play their part. It can be said, however, that the wines made at this estate tend to place elegance and finesse before potency and concentration. Of course much depends on the zone of origin, and oenological history is full of examples of other areas where this has always been the case: one need but mention Margaux and Volnay, or the vineyards of Cannubi and Brunate in Barolo and La Morra. But let's return to the northern zone of the Castellina district, not far from Panzano, between Siena and Florence, in the heart of Chianti Classico country. We'll start with Femfert's Riserva '96, which shows good concentration with a touch of not yet perfectly integrated acidity, typical of wines made from sangiovese. Its nose reveals attractive fruit but also resinous and vegetal notes. The palate is good, after some harshness at the start. The more successful Chianti Classico Casanuova di Nittardi '97 is full-bodied and soft, with a light touch of sweet wood in the bouquet. It is a well-made modern red, and we look forward with pleasure to tasting the Riserva '97.

● Chianti Classico '97	▼▼	4
● Chianti Classico Ris. '96	▼▼	5
● Chianti Classico '90	▼	3
● Chianti Classico '92	▼	4
● Chianti Classico '94	▼	3
● Chianti Classico '91	▽▽	4
● Chianti Classico '93	▽▽	4
● Chianti Classico '95	▽▽	4
● Chianti Classico '96	▽▽	4
● Chianti Classico Ris. '88	▽▽	4
● Chianti Classico Ris. '90	▽▽	5
● Chianti Classico Ris. '93	▽▽	4
● Chianti Classico Ris. '94	▽▽	5
● Chianti Classico Ris. '95	▽▽	5

Podere Collelungo

Loc. Collelungo
53011 Castellina in Chianti (SI)
tel. 0577/740489

Collelungo in the Castellina district is one of the many new entries in this year's Guide. The estate is brand-new but already patently knows just what it wants to do. The property covers 82 hectares, of which nine are under vine at about 500 meters above sea level. Wine-making is in the hands of Alberto Antonini, who has made his debut with the '97 vintage. We admire the decision to concentrate on Chianti Classico and not bother with the over-proliferating super-Tuscans. So only two wines were presented: the Chianti Classico and the Roveto '97, a special selection which really stood out, giving us a good idea of what this winery is capable of. The color, a lively, intense ruby, foretells good structure, but it is the nose that is really intriguing, offering continual variations if the wine is allowed to breathe for a while. It is concentrated and of good depth, initially showing fruity, vegetal and woody notes, but then opening up with balsamic tones and hints of spice, oregano and other herbs. The palate reveals excellent depth and body, fine tannins and a good finish, notwithstanding the still marked presence of oak. The normal Chianti Classico is correct and well balanced, but a bit too vegetal.

● Chianti Classico Roveto '97	🍷🍷	4
● Chianti Classico '97		4

Rocca delle Macìe

Loc. Macìe
53011 Castellina in Chianti (SI)
tel. 0577/7321

This is the best year so far for Sergio Zingarelli's Rocca delle Macìe. Never had one of their wines made it to our finals, and this year two did: the Ser Gioveto and the Chianti Classico Fizzano Riserva, two '96s. The fact that both these wines are made from sangiovese and that '96 was not an exceptional year for this grape means that important changes have taken place in both vineyard and cellar. Only wine-makers with exceptional technical abilities succeed in making excellent wines in poor years. The '83 Tignanello was better than the '82; the Chardonnay Gaia e Rey from '84 better than the '83; indeed the Margaux '83 was as good as the '82, and so on. Thus Rocca delle Macìe is metamorphosing before our eyes from an essentially commercial producer to one of the important wine-makers of the Chianti Classico district. And about time, too. Proof of the transformation is to be found, as we were saying, in the rich and powerful Ser Gioveto '96, and the soft and concentrated Chianti Classico Fizzano Riserva '96, with corroborating evidence from the interesting Roccato '96, a blend of cabernet sauvignon and sangiovese which has good body and is clearly the result of extremely able cellar technique. And further evidence from the simple, fruity Rubizzo '98, an immediately likeable young red. The two basic Chiantis are somewhat less successful. The Riserva '96 isn't bad, but it doesn't have much body. The Chianti Classico '97 shows signs of overripeness on the nose, which can easily happen in a vintage like this one and is nothing much to worry about.

● Chianti Classico Fizzano Ris. '96	🍷🍷	4
● Roccato '96	🍷🍷	5
● Ser Gioveto '96	🍷🍷	5
● Chianti Classico Ris. '96	🍷	4
● Rubizzo '98	🍷	2*
● Chianti Classico '97		3
● Chianti Classico Fizzano Ris. '93	🍷🍷	5
● Chianti Classico Ris. '88	🍷🍷	4
● Chianti Classico Ris. '90	🍷🍷	4
● Roccato '93	🍷🍷	5
● Ser Gioveto '85	🍷🍷	5
● Ser Gioveto '86	🍷🍷	5
● Ser Gioveto '88	🍷🍷	5
● Ser Gioveto '94	🍷🍷	5
● Ser Gioveto '95	🍷🍷	5

Rodano

Loc. Rodano
53011 Castellina in Chianti (SI)
tel. 0577/743107

The Pozzesi family is still doing good work in Castellina in Chianti. Vittorio, the father, has gone back to being president of the Consorzio del Chianti Classico, very nearly a full-time occupation, but his son Enrico continues to do an excellent job as head of the winery. As we announced in last year's Guide, this year they have presented a new wine, the Lazzicante '96, a merlot. It has a deep ruby color and a delightful bouquet of ripe fruit, including black currant and blueberry. The tannins are foremost in the decisive attack on the palate, but they are soon transformed by the powerful alcohol, and show a dense-textured meaty softness. The finish is long, with a well-judged touch of acidity giving it a pleasant lightness. The Monna Claudia '96, a blend of cabernet sauvignon and sangiovese, presents a dense ruby color. Tertiary aromas of coffee, tobacco, and good toasty oak are the first to emerge on the nose, but after a while light animal notes rather stand out. The entry on the palate is correct and well balanced; initially noticeable acidity soon blends with the alcohol; the tannins are smooth and not too strong, but strong enough to balance the softer elements. The finish is long and even.

●	Lazzicante '96	▼▼	4
●	Monna Claudia '96	▼▼	4
●	Chianti Cl. Viacosta Ris. '86	▽▽	4
●	Chianti Cl. Viacosta Ris. '88	▽▽	4
●	Chianti Cl. Viacosta Ris. '90	▽▽	4
●	Chianti Cl. Viacosta Ris. '95	▽▽	4
●	Monna Claudia '88	▽▽	5
●	Monna Claudia '95	▽▽	4
●	Chianti Classico '90	▽	3
●	Chianti Classico '93	▽	3
●	Chianti Classico '94	▽	3

San Fabiano Calcinaia

Loc. Cellole
53011 Castellina in Chianti (SI)
tel. 0577/979232

Guido Serio, the proprietor of this beautiful estate, and Carlo Ferrini, his faithful consultant and our oenologist of the year, have not made a single mistake. They have presented four wines, each one better than the last, and all at the top of their separate categories. In terms of points received for wines presented, this producer is among the top five in Tuscany. Their Cerviolo Rosso '97, which received Three Glasses, is a blend of sangiovese (40%), merlot (30%) and cabernet sauvignon (30%). We liked the '96 version very much, but we recognize that we have even more to like in the '97. It has more body and the tannins seem imprisoned in a closely-woven soft velvet: it appears to caress the tongue. Its aromas have an extraordinary lucid elegance. It is an unforgettable wine. The barrique-aged Cerviolo Bianco '98, mostly chardonnay with some sauvignon, offers aromas of tropical fruit with some hints of sweet wood in the process of being absorbed. The palate is a knockout, rich, soft and seductive. There are very few Tuscan whites on this level. The Cellole Riserva '96, one of the two Chianti Classicos, is among the best from this tricky vintage, and the normal '97 is a small masterpiece. Quite immediate and pleasing, it has the palate of a really great, typical, varietal Chianti Classico.

●	Cerviolo Rosso '97	▼▼▼	5
○	Cerviolo Bianco '98	▼▼	5
●	Chianti Classico '97	▼▼	3*
●	Chianti Classico Cellole Ris. '96	▼▼	4
●	Cerviolo Rosso '96	▽▽▽	5
●	Cerviolo Rosso '91	▽▽	5
●	Cerviolo Rosso '95	▽▽	5
●	Chianti Classico '95	▽▽	3*
●	Chianti Classico '96	▽▽	3*
●	Chianti Classico Cellole Ris. '90	▽▽	4
●	Chianti Classico Cellole Ris. '93	▽▽	4
●	Chianti Classico Cellole Ris. '95	▽▽	4
●	Cerviolo Rosso '93	▽	4
●	Cerviolo Rosso '94	▽	5
●	Chianti Classico '91	▽	4

CASTELLINA IN CHIANTI (SI)

TENIMENTI ANGELINI - SAN LEONINO
LOC. SAN LEONINO
53011 CASTELLINA IN CHIANTI (SI)
TEL. 0577/7403108

We were glad to see that Tenimenti Angelini, which can be found in the southern part of Chianti Classico, merited a return to the Guide. They have more than 48 hectares under vine supervised by the oenologist Fabrizio Ciufoli, who works very closely with the director Mario Calzolari. The Chianti Classico '97 seems an excellent wine. It has a good lively ruby color with glints of purple. Its incisive and fresh fruity nose offers nuances of berries. The well-balanced palate shows the proper sinew that comes from the harmony achieved between acid and alcohol. The light tannins are well blended in, and if the finish is not as full as one might like, it is still long and tasty. The Salivolpe '95, an IGT, was a bit less convincing. It has good color, and rich aromas in which balsamic notes abound at first and then make way for a delightful variety of herbs. The palate is a little disappointing initially, because of a not very powerful attack, a slightly dilute sensation and a general lack of accord, but it comes back into its own with a decent finish. The '95 Riserva has a forward aspect, simple and not very varied aromas, and a direct but not very structured palate with acidity ruling the roost. The finish does not show much depth and is rather dry.

●	Chianti Classico '97	🍷🍷	3*
●	Salivolpe '95	🍷	4
●	Chianti Classico Ris. '95		4
●	Chianti Classico '90	ŸŸ	4
●	Chianti Classico Ris. '88	ŸŸ	4
●	Chianti Classico Ris. '90	ŸŸ	5
●	Chianti Classico '88	Ÿ	4
●	Chianti Classico '91	Ÿ	4

CASTELLINA IN CHIANTI (SI)

TRAMONTI
LOC. TRAMONTI
53011 CASTELLINA IN CHIANTI (SI)
TEL. 0577/740512

Last year we welcomed this winery with pleasure into the Guide last, and this year we are even more pleased to confirm its presence. The Kolk family, who run it, moved to Tuscany in 1995: what a propitious year to begin! Much of the property is still woodland, but the part under vine is slowly expanding as the planting of new vines continues. Whether because the year itself was helpful or because of increasing experience working among the vines and in the cellar, they have produced an excellent Chianti Classico '97. It has a deep, dark, gleaming ruby color. Toasty notes and vanilla are center stage at first in the bouquet, but sweet ripe fruit with berries and cherry to the fore soon edge them towards the wings. The palate is full-flavored, decided and very intense right from the attack, with a successful fusion of tannins and alcohol in the substantial body with its structure both robust and elegant. The long finish is a crescendo of pleasant complexity. The Kolks favor natural methods and avoid, where possible, intervention during the wine-making, They fine, for example, instead of filtering. We are very eager to see what next year brings, since this year's normal wine is so encouraging.

●	Chianti Classico '97	🍷🍷	4
●	Chianti Classico '96	ŸŸ	4

CASTELLINA MARITTIMA (PI)

Tenuta del Terriccio
Loc. Le Badie
Via Bagnoli
56100 Castellina Marittima (PI)
tel. 050/699709

For the third year in a row, Tenuta del Terriccio's Lupicaia gets our highest award. This fact says a lot about the potential of this terrain between Pisa and Livorno. It is an area in which the vine has returned to playing a leading role, and Tenuta del Terriccio has invested heavily in its vineyards. There are 30 hectares of already productive vines, and another 10 recently planted which will bring production in a few years up to the level its quality merits. Returning to the Lupicaia itself, we can only doff our caps. It resembles previous versions. The nose offers hints of black currant, blackberry, eucalyptus, and cocoa. And in the mouth it is even richer and more generous. It reveals power, harmony, enormous character, great length and formidable tannins. The Tassinaia '97 has also performed very well. From the same grapes as the Lupicaia, merlot and cabernet sauvignon, but with some sangiovese as well, this year's Tassinaia is probably the best yet, and is fuller and more concentrated and elegant than ever before. The very good Saluccio '97, a wood-fermented chardonnay, displays aromas of tropical fruit and roses, and a long, fat and voluptuous palate, without, however, the fresh acidity required for real greatness. The white Rondinaia '98 nearly got Two Glasses. The nose is still evolving, but the palate shows good weight and density. The Sauvignon Con Vento '98 is a little disappointing.

●	Lupicaia '97	🍷🍷🍷	6
○	Saluccio '97	🍷🍷	5
●	Tassinaia '97	🍷🍷	5
○	Con Vento '98	🍷	3
○	Rondinaia '98	🍷	4
●	Lupicaia '93	ΥΥΥ	5
●	Lupicaia '95	ΥΥΥ	6
●	Lupicaia '96	ΥΥΥ	6
●	Lupicaia '94	ΥΥ	6
○	Rondinaia '96	ΥΥ	4
○	Rondinaia '97	ΥΥ	4
●	Tassinaia '93	ΥΥ	4
●	Tassinaia '94	ΥΥ	5
●	Tassinaia '95	ΥΥ	5
●	Tassinaia '96	ΥΥ	5

CASTELNUOVO BERARDENGA (SI)

Castello di Bossi
Loc. Bossi in Chianti
53019 Castelnuovo Berardenga (SI)
tel. 0577/359330

Castello di Bossi has strengthened its position here as one of the most interesting emerging producers of excellent wine. It is a property with enormous potential, not only because of its excellent location, but also because it has 370 hectares of land, a quarter of which are under vine, which permits them to make a great quantity of wine, but also gives them a lot of choice in selecting the best grapes. The top of their range this year is certainly the Corbaia '95, a blend of cabernet sauvignon and merlot. The nose, which is intense, is still affected by the presence of wood, but fruity notes and mineral hints emerge. The palate is more harmonious and even. The entry is full-flavored, and smooth tannins give density to the mid palate; the finish is altogether appropriate: Two very generous Glasses. The '95 Riserva doesn't have the same degree of complexity, but it nevertheless merits its Two glasses because of the freshness of its fruit, and the pleasant rotundity in the mouth. The finish is a bit rough, but it is long, and should improve with further aging. The only disappointment is the '97 Chianti which, though it has plenty of body, shows overripeness on the nose and a not very balanced palate.

●	Chianti Classico Ris. '95	🍷🍷	4
●	Corbaia '95	🍷🍷	5
●	Chianti Classico '97		3
●	Chianti Classico Berardo Ris. '95	ΥΥ	5
●	Chianti Classico Ris. '94	ΥΥ	4
●	Corbaia '94	ΥΥ	5
●	Chianti Classico '94	Υ	3
●	Chianti Classico '95	Υ	3

Carpineta Fontalpino

Loc. Carpineta-Montaperti
53019 Castelnuovo Berardenga (SI)
tel. 0577/283228

Gioia Cresti, apart from being a delightful woman, grew up in the vineyards and the cellar, so she knows what she's about. It is only in the last few years, however, that she has dedicated herself full-time, together with her brother Filippo, to Carpineta Fontalpino, their historic family estate. It lies on the border between southern Chianti Classico and the vast Crete Senesi, and was clearly just waiting for their attention. The 10 hectares are planted almost entirely to red grapes, mostly sangiovese, but also some cabernet sauvignon and merlot. The two wines they presented this year made a very good impression and account for their debut in the Guide. All three of the above-mentioned varieties are included in their Do Ut Des '97, which showed estimable qualities. It has a very intense, fruity nose, with some still noticeable toasty oak-derived notes. The good progression on the palate pleasantly reveals lively tannins and leads to a juicy finish that echoes the bouquet. The Chianti Gioia '97 is simpler but quite delightful and well thought out. Notes of raspberry and black currant on the nose are followed by a fairly substantial and even palate.

● Do Ut Des '97	🍷🍷	4
● Chianti Colli Senesi Gioia '97	🍷	3

CASTELNUOVO BERARDENGA (SI)

Chigi Saracini

Via dell'Arbia, 2
53019 Castelnuovo Berardenga (SI)
tel. 0577/355113

If you know even just a smattering of Tuscan history you will probably have heard of the Chigi Saracinis. It turns out that, for some centuries, quite a number of them have concerned themselves with viticulture and even the making of wine. Today their propery in Castelnuovo Berardenga, which covers some 900 hectares, grows vines on about 70 of them. Their wine production methods are a good compromise between traditional ways and modern technique and style. They make the whole range of Tuscan wines, from light white to Chianti to Vinsanto. For their debut in our guide, we tasted only their reds. The Chianti Superiore '97 is surprisingly good, particularly considering its modest price. It is clean, fresh and fruity with a lively but restrained acidity. On the palate it is straightforward, but very tasty. The forthright Chianti Colli Senesi '98 is also very good, although it is slightly more tannic and acidic. The most successful of their wines is Il Poggiassai '97, a blend of cabernet and sangiovese which is particularly striking for its harmony on both nose and palate. It has an intense and glowing ruby color, and offers aromas of blueberry, red currant and blackberry, followed by a soft, full flavor with just the right amount of tannin. Because of this excellent debut, next year we will try our best to taste all their wines.

● Il Poggiassai '97	🍷🍷	4
● Chianti Colli Senesi '98	🍷	3
● Chianti Superiore '97	🍷	3

FATTORIA DI DIEVOLE
LOC. DIEVOLE
53019 CASTELNUOVO BERARDENGA (SI)
TEL. 0577/322613

Dievole arouses a lot of interest not only because of the style and originality of its offerings, but also because of its enormous potential, from which we are always expecting something really astonishing. They clearly have what it takes, and perhaps all they need do is concentrate on fewer wines. We tried three this year and found them quite successful, although none approached the highest level. Their Sangiovese Broccato '96 was very good. Despite the tricky vintage it shows a decent concentration and a soft and compact structure. The finish is certainly long enough but is a bit lacking in complexity. The biggest surprise came from the Chianti Classico Novecento '96, the only Dievole wine that easily won its Two Glasses. The nose is intense and richly fruity. In the mouth it is concentrated, dense and expansive, and the only defect of the long finish is limited aromatic definition. The Chianti '97 is not bad either. The color, like that of the other wines, is a very intense ruby. The interesting bouquet includes blackberry and vegetal hints. The palate is attractive, well balanced and fairly substantial.

●	Broccato '96	▼▼	4
●	Chianti Classico '97	▼▼	4
●	Chianti Classico Novecento '96	▼▼	4
●	Broccato '95	YY	4
●	Chianti Classico '96	YY	3*
●	Chianti Classico Novecento '93	YY	4
●	Chianti Classico Novecento '94	YY	4
●	Chianti Classico Novecento '95	YY	4
●	Chianti Classico Ris. '93	YY	4
●	Chianti Classico Ris. '95	YY	4
●	Broccato '93	Y	4
●	Broccato '94	Y	4
●	Chianti Classico '95	Y	3
●	Rinascimento '93	Y	4
●	Rinascimento '94	Y	4

★ FATTORIA DI FELSINA
STRADA CHIANTIGIANA, 484
53019 CASTELNUOVO BERARDENGA (SI)
TEL. 0577/355117

It is certainly nothing new for the Fattoria di Felsina, managed by Giuseppe Mazzocolin, to receive Three Glasses. This year's is the 13th we have given them, and the fifth for Fontalloro. We mention this not to gratify fans of statistics, but to underline how consisently excellent the wines are here. We should specify that although the prizes remain the same, we have noticed changes in style in certain of their wines, particularly the two sangioveses, Fontalloro and Chianti, which are less austere and more captivating than usual. Whether you consider that an improvement depends, of course, on your personal preferences. The Chianti has a pleasant sweet fruitiness throughout the palate, as well as a restrained note of wood. It is certainly good, but it doesn't have the grip and character that it has shown in some previous versions and is probably not superior to the '96 (a vintage of which they released neither the Riserva nor the Rancia). We must describe the greater charm and softness of the Fontalloro '95 in other terms. It is a wine with many years ahead of it, which nevertheless already shows enviable balance. Its structure is dense, concentrated and profound, yet also compact and elegant. It is a great wine. The cabernet-based Maestro Raro, on the other hand, is not at its usual high level. There is nothing wrong, despite some trifling defects on the palate, with its body and softness, but there are unexpected sulfurous notes on the nose. The very good chardonnay-based I Sistri is generously oak-toned on the nose and seductive, full, and lingering in the mouth.

●	Fontalloro '95	▼▼▼	6
●	Chianti Classico '97	▼▼	4
○	I Sistri '97	▼▼	4
●	Maestro Raro '95	▼▼	6
●	Chianti Classico Rancia Ris. '90	YYY	5
●	Chianti Classico Rancia Ris. '93	YYY	5
●	Chianti Classico Ris. '90	YYY	4*
●	Fontalloro '85	YYY	5
●	Fontalloro '86	YYY	5
●	Fontalloro '88	YYY	5
●	Fontalloro '90	YYY	5
●	Fontalloro '93	YYY	6
●	Maestro Raro '91	YYY	5
●	Maestro Raro '93	YYY	6
●	Fontalloro '94	YY	6

CASTELNUOVO BERARDENGA (SI)

Fattoria di Petroio

Loc. Quercegrossa
Via di Petroio, 43
53019 Castelnuovo Berardenga (SI)
tel. 0577/328045

This is a winery that seems to improve every year. They only make two wines, a Chianti Classico and a Riserva. This is worth noting because they are one of the very few producers who make only Chianti and don't dedicate even one of their 13 hectares under vine to the production of yet another super-Tuscan. This carefully reached decision of theirs, of which we entirely approve, does not in the least hinder them from making wines of a very high quality, indeed frequently better than many of the much-vaunted "table wines" or IGTs. Their Chianti Classico '97 easily found a place among the best ones we tasted this year. It shows a good intense ruby color, and a bouquet which is exemplary not so much for its complexity as for its clarity and fruitiness. The palate is broad and soft, with solid tasty tannins and a long, juicy finish. It's tempting to drink it up greedily right now, but it should be very satisfying in the future. The Riserva '96 is not so enthralling, and reflects in general the difference between the two vintages. Nonetheless it is very good, especially in its aromas, which are intense and quite rich, with notes of cherry jam and violet and well-judged nuances of oak. In the mouth, although it doesn't have a great deal of weight, it is even, well balanced and pleasing.

●	Chianti Classico '97	▼▼	3*
●	Chianti Classico Ris. '96	▼▼	4
●	Chianti Classico '90	▽▽	3*
●	Chianti Classico '91	▽▽	3*
●	Chianti Classico '93	▽▽	2*
●	Chianti Classico '95	▽▽	3*
●	Chianti Classico '96	▽▽	3*
●	Chianti Classico Ris. '90	▽▽	4
●	Chianti Classico Ris. '95	▽▽	4
●	Chianti Classico '94	▽	3
●	Chianti Classico Ris. '93	▽	4

CASTELNUOVO BERARDENGA (SI)

San Felice

Loc. San Felice
53019 Castelnuovo Berardenga (SI)
tel. 0577/359087 - 0577/359088

The wines from San Felice this year are not their usual brilliant selves. The quality is generally good, but the fact is that San Felice has accustomed us to much more. All it took was a slight decrease in quality, connected with the troublesome '96 vintage, and we felt disappointed. But perhaps we've been spoilt. The Riserva Poggio Rosso, for example, disoriented us somewhat: both color and body show the lovely depth of the best previous versions, but the aromas are unfocused and unbalanced. We note, however, the basic constant quality of the wine, and the potential of its structure, which may well, in time, overcome any present difficulties. We have fewer doubts about the Vigorello, which is pleasant enough and well balanced, but a little on the simple side, and characterized by a rather aggressive vegetal tone. The Chianti '97 is fair. It has a fruity nose with grassy nuances, and a pleasant amount of oak. The palate is even, moderately vigorous and, generally, characteristic and agreeable. The Riserva Il Grigio '96 reveals fruity and mineral notes on the nose, which carry through onto the even palate. Of the whites, the Belcaro is correct but not very expressive. The Ancherona, however, is good, with its golden straw color, clean and appealing fragrance of peach and white flowers, and good weight, balance and decent length in the mouth.

●	Chianti Classico Poggio Rosso Ris. '96	▼▼	5
○	Ancherona Chardonnay '97	▼	4
●	Chianti Classico '97	▼	3
●	Chianti Classico Il Grigio Ris. '96	▼	4
●	Vigorello '96	▼	5
○	Belcaro '98		3
●	Chianti Classico Poggio Rosso Ris. '90	▽▽▽	4
●	Chianti Classico Poggio Rosso Ris. '95	▽▽▽	5
●	Vigorello '88	▽▽▽	5
●	Vigorello '90	▽▽	5
●	Vigorello '93	▽▽	5
●	Vigorello '95	▽▽	5

CASTELNUOVO BERARDENGA (SI)

SELVOLE

LOC. SELVOLE
53010 CASTELNUOVO BERARDENGA (SI)
TEL. 0577/322662

One of the most beautiful estates in Chianti Classico has come back to life. Selvole, which lies in the western part of Castelnuovo Berardenga, in Vagliagli, with its clayey soil, was in a state of semi-abandonment. This was all the more unfortunate since this is an area that yields great powerful reds that sometimes resemble Brunello or the best Morellinos. However, Guido and Nobuko Busetto arrived from Cispiano a Castellina to take it in hand. Nobuko is Japanese and enamored both of Italy and of wine, and Guido is a well-known journalist who works for Il Sole 24 Ore. The first wines that they presented are surprising. The Riserva '96 in particular is excellent. It unites powerful alcohol and extract with a good level of acidity, which makes it very drinkable quite apart from its remarkable concentration. It's a little forward on the nose, but not excessively. And this is a '96, which was hardly a sterling vintage. The Chianti Classico '97 is not at all bad: it is a bit simpler and has quite forward aromas, but it's full-flavored and wonderfully soft. These are wines to which the Busettos were godparents, in a sense, as they had nothing to do with the vinification. Selvole, however, is one of the magic spots of Chianti Classico, and we are sure that in a very few years they will be making real oenological gems. We're taking bets.

●	Chianti Classico Ris. '96	▼▼	5
●	Chianti Classico '97	▼	4

CHIUSI (SI)

FICOMONTANINO

LOC. FICOMONTANINO
53043 CHIUSI (SI)
TEL. 0578/21180 - 06/5561283

There's another good range of wines from Ficomontanino. Certainly their area, around Chiusi, to the east of Siena, is not an established pilgrimage point for wine venerators, but the terrain has been shown to be quite hospitable both to traditional varieties and to glamorous foreigners like cabernet sauvignon. Their Chianti Colli Senesi Tutulus '97 reveals overall harmony, but given the excellent year, one could have hoped for more. It displays a brilliant light ruby color and scents, initially of laurel and geranium leaf, and then of a more acidic nature. The palate is fresh, somewhat acidulous, and well-structured; this is an austere, rather than a soft red. The Lucumone '97, 100% cabernet sauvignon, resembles its predecessors. There is no doubting the cleanness of its bouquet, its concentration or its depth. But the jammy notes suggest that the wine may be a little too mature. It is full-bodied, well-defined and spicy, a bit hollow at mid-palate, and moderate in length. The Sauvignon Porsenna '98 has good balance, good fruit and a good finish.

●	Lucumone '97	▼▼	5
●	Chianti Colli Senesi Tutulus '97	▼	3
○	Porsenna '98	▼	4
●	Chianti Colli Senesi Tutulus '95	▽▽	3
●	Chianti Colli Senesi Tutulus '96	▽▽	3
●	Lucumone '95	▽▽	5
●	Porsenna '97	▽▽	4
●	Lucumone '96	▽	5
●	Porsenna '96	▽	4

COLLE VAL D'ELSA (SI)

IL PALAGIO
LOC. CASTEL S. GIMIGNANO
53034 COLLE VAL D'ELSA (SI)
TEL. 0577/953004

Shortly after receiving his diploma from the wine school at Conegliano Veneto, Walter Sovran, a native of Friuli, took charge of this winery, which is part of the Zonin organization. That was in 1988. During these years, Walter, who is now 38, has brought the estate along very well. He finds that the most interesting thing about the vernaccia grape is that from it can be made either a fresh, fruity, simple wine, or a wine that has a lot of structure and complexity. An important white wine, in other words, that can handle being aged in new oak, and that begins to be presentable only a year after harvest time. That vernaccia can do this is amply demonstrated by his Gentilesca '98. It is fresh, harmonious, elegant, round and rich in fruit. It is not overblown, but well balanced, and has good structure and length. And, most importantly, it shows a well-judged use of new wood. This land and its oenologist also do well by the Sauvignon Il Palagio '98. It has clean and intense aromas that are elegantly varietal and fruity and seem to us much better than those of many other much more expensive rivals from central Italy. Its nose is characteristically suggestive of tomato leaf, and fresh, pleasantly vegetal notes are perceptible on the palate too, as well as good body and length. It is an excellent and very economical wine. The Chianti Colli Senesi '98 is good, and the Vernaccia di San Gimignano Abbazia di Monte Oliveto '98 is quite interesting as well.

○	Il Palagio Sauvignon '98	🍷🍷	2*
○	Vernaccia di S. Gimignano La Gentilesca '98	🍷🍷	4
●	Chianti Colli Senesi Il Palagio '98	🍷	2*
○	Vernaccia di S. Gimignano Abbazia di Monteoliveto '98	🍷	2*
○	Il Palagio Sauvignon '97	🍸🍸	2*
●	Chianti Colli Senesi Il Palagio '95	🍸	2*
○	Il Palagio Sauvignon '95	🍸	2*
○	Vernaccia di S. Gimignano Abbazia di Monteoliveto '97	🍸	2*
○	Vernaccia di S. Gimignano Abbazia Monteoliveto La Gentilesca '97	🍸	4

CORTONA (AR)

TENIMENTI D'ALESSANDRO
LOC. CAMUCIA
VIA DI MANZANO, 15
52044 CORTONA (AR)
TEL. 0575/618667

As relative outsiders the D'Alessandro brothers have in recent years astonished wine-makers from more famous areas with their intense and richly characterful wines. By now it is no longer a surprise to find their wines at the top of regional classifications. Theirs is now an established Tuscan estate and they have very clearly demonstrated that the Arezzo area has enormous potential. Their top wine, well known by all Italian wine lovers, is justly considered one of the best two or three Italian syrahs, and is in the running every year for our top award. After a year's pause, the Bosco again earns its Third Glass with the '97. It is an excellent red, both more forceful and more clearly defined than the '96. It shows a dark, luminous red color, and sensual aromas of red currant, ripe blackberry and pepper. The palate is harmonious and very soft, but also offers good acidity, excellent balance and an extremely long and corresponding finish. The Podere Fontarca, a blend of chardonnay and viognier, is also an excellent wine. In its broad array of aromas one finds lovely notes of tropical fruit. The palate reveals plenty of weight, good balance between acidity and alcohol, and a long finish. Another successful red is their Migliara '97, an IGT made from sangiovese which is making its debut in the Guide. Tasty, full-bodied, properly acidic, and intense, it has the particular merit of fidelity to the characteristics of its grape: laurel, violet and sour cherry all are present. The Podere il Vescovo '98, made from gamay, and the sauvignon-based Le Terrazze '98 seemed less convincing, and still somewhat muffled and closed. An honorable mention goes to the tasty Vin Santo '92.

●	Podere Il Bosco '97	🍷🍷🍷	5
●	Migliara '97	🍷🍷	5
○	Podere Fontarca '98	🍷🍷	4
○	Vin Santo '92	🍷	5
○	Le Terrazze '98		3
●	Podere Il Vescovo '98		3
●	Podere Il Bosco '95	🍸🍸🍸	5
○	Podere Fontarca '94	🍸🍸	4
●	Podere Il Bosco '94	🍸🍸	5
●	Podere Il Bosco '96	🍸🍸	5
●	Vigna del Bosco '92	🍸🍸	5
●	Vigna del Bosco '93	🍸🍸	4
○	Le Terrazze '97	🍸	3
○	Podere Fontarca '97	🍸	4
●	Podere Il Vescovo '97	🍸	3

FAUGLIA (PI)

FATTORIA DELL' UCCELLIERA
VIA PROVINCIALE LORENZANA
CUCIGLIANA, 1
56043 FAUGLIA (PI)
TEL. 050/662747

The vines planted experimentally a few years ago under the direction of their agronomist and oenologist Stefano Chioccioli are even now beginning to produce interesting results. Syrah, petit verdot, semillion, and viognier, to mention only those grapes less well known here in Italy, are already playing a part in the wines of the Fattoria dell'Uccelliera. The reds, of course, are still made principally from sangiovese, the traditional local grape. This year one of their red wines, the Castellaccio Rosso '97, very nearly received Three Glasses. It made a very strong impression during our tastings, with a rich expressiveness and completeness superior to what was offered by recent versions of the wine, which were already very good indeed. It has a very deep, brilliant color, rich in highlights. The bouquet of abundant perfectly mature fruit includes elegant notes of coffee. The velvety, supple palate reveals a finish with noble tannins and a reflection of the bouquet. The Castellaccio Bianco '98 does very well too. Its excellent structure works well with its aromas of citrus fruit and white flowers, and well-judged hints of vanilla, to make a wine that drinks well but has sufficient complexity. The '97 Chianti is a pleasure: it's very tasty, but also full-bodied and round. The white Ficaia '98 is just as good, with its aromas of pineapple and banana, and its good texture and balance in the mouth.

○ Castellaccio Bianco '98	🍷🍷	4
● Castellaccio Rosso '97	🍷🍷	4
● Chianti '97	🍷	3
○ Ficaia '98	🍷	3
○ Castellaccio Bianco '96	YY	4
● Castellaccio Rosso '93	YY	4
● Castellaccio Rosso '95	YY	4
● Castellaccio Rosso '96	YY	4
○ Castellaccio Bianco '97	Y	4
● Castellaccio Rosso '92	Y	4
● Chianti '94	Y	3
● Chianti '95	Y	3
● Chianti '96	Y	3
○ Ficaia '97	Y	3

FIRENZE

★ MARCHESI ANTINORI
P.ZZA DEGLI ANTINORI, 3
50123 FIRENZE
TEL. 055/23595

This is the most famous wine producer in Tuscany. However, enormous investments in Salento, Piedmont, Franciacorta, Umbria, Hungary, the U.S. and soon in other places, are turning them into an international wine colossus. This year's most important news is that they now own more than 2,000 hectares of vines, 1,500 of which are currently in production. This is an absolute record for Italy. Thus in two or three years' time, more than 60% of the wine they sell, which at this point is about 14 million bottles, will come from their own grapes. This is a significant figure and has meant much in terms of the structure of the organization. They produce a vast range of wines, of which we can, for obvious reasons, discuss only a few. We note that the basic wines are maintaining their traditional quality, while the best wines are getting better, particularly Solaia and Tignanello. This is in line with their organizational strategy. The Solaia '96, made from cabernet sauvignon plus 20% sangiovese, continues to be one of the greatest wines of Tuscany. This version is powerful, rich, and elegant, one of the best ever. The Tignanello '96, sangiovese plus 20% cabernet sauvignon, is better than the '95, which is significant since '95 was the superior vintage. The two '96 Chianti Classico Riservas, the Tenute del Marchese, and the Badia a Passignano, are both very good. The normal Badia a Passignano '97, a very interesting version, is also the last they intend to make. What a pity!

● Solaia '96	🍷🍷🍷	6
● Chianti Classico Badia a Passignano '97	🍷🍷	3*
● Chianti Classico Badia a Passignano Ris. '96	🍷🍷	5
● Chianti Classico Tenute del Marchese Ris. '96	🍷🍷	5
● Tignanello '96	🍷🍷	6
● Solaia '86	YYY	6
● Solaia '88	YYY	6
● Solaia '90	YYY	6
● Solaia '94	YYY	6
● Solaia '95	YYY	6
● Tignanello '85	YYY	6
● Tignanello '93	YYY	6

FIRENZE

MARCHESI DE' FRESCOBALDI
VIA S. SPIRITO, 11
50125 FIRENZE
TEL. 055/27141

With approximately 800 hectares under vine and dozens of different labels, Frescobaldi is something like an aircraft carrier of Tuscan, indeed Italian wine. In addition, they have had a reputation as a maker of fine wines for several centuries. We feel, however, that with such an enormous number of vines, many of which are blessed with splendid exposure and microclimate, they could make many great wines every year, and not just one or two. The Chianti Rufina Riserva Montesodi '97 is indeed superb and there is no doubt that it merits its Three Glasses. It has an intense, luminous ruby color, and a nose of black currant, pencil lead and toasted bread. In the mouth it is very harmonious, and has, thanks to a high level of extract, excellent structure and great length. It is not difficult to intuit that this wine was made from first-class grapes. Among the whites, the excellent Pomino il Benefizio '97 is fruity and wonderfully clear on the nose and also the palate, where it shows good body without heaviness. The delightful Pomino Rosso '96 offers a very fresh fruitiness and an even, clean finish. The Mormoreto '96 is more complicated and structured. Its very intense aromas are rather austere at this point; the earthy notes include some noble mineral nuances. The palate is robust, full and still quite closed, but promising. The Chianti Rufina Riserva '96 Nipozzano is a distinctive red, but the child of a poor year. Their Rèmole '98 is correct but modest.

●	Chianti Rufina Montesodi '97	🍷🍷🍷	6
●	Mormoreto '96	🍷🍷	6
○	Pomino Il Benefizio '97	🍷🍷	5
●	Pomino Rosso '96	🍷🍷	5
●	Chianti Rufina Nipozzano '96	🍷	5
○	Rèmole '98		3
●	Chianti Rufina Montesodi '88	YYY	6
●	Chianti Rufina Montesodi '90	YYY	6
●	Chianti Rufina Montesodi '96	YYY	6
●	Pomino Rosso '85	YYY	5
●	Chianti Rufina Montesodi '95	YY	6
●	Mormoreto '94	YY	6
●	Mormoreto '95	YY	6
○	Pomino Bianco '97	YY	4
○	Pomino Il Benefizio '96	YY	5

FOSDINOVO (MS)

PODERE TERENZUOLA
VIA VERCALDA, 4
54035 FOSDINOVO (MS)
TEL. 0187/68951

It may seem strange to review a winery in the Tuscany section that makes Colli di Luni Vermentino, a Ligurian specialty. But we are bound by the laws of geography, and political boundaries do not always follow wine-making practice. Not that it was unpleasant for us, after tasting a great number of Vermentinos from the Tuscan coast, to have a sip of a more classical, traditional sort, such as a Colli di Luni. The fact that the grape has been at home in Liguria and the part of Tuscany which borders on it for much longer, and that its growers have had more experience with it, certainly showed up in our tastings, at least in the case of the wine that Podere Terenzuola offered us. The proprietor, Ivan Giuliani, is a young man who has enthusiastically dedicated himself to making really good wine, and has therefore made substantial investments both in the vineyards, which he is extending, and in the cellar. But let's turn to the wine itself. The Colli di Luni Vermentino Fosso di Corzano '98 has an enticingly intense nose with floral notes of hedgerose and broom over a good base of apricot and tropical fruit. The entry on the palate is almost too sweet, but the wine quickly recovers, acquiring freshness which it keeps throughout the orderly progression to the long, extremely enjoyable finish which echoes the aromas.

○	Colli di Luni Vermentino Fosso di Corzano '98	🍷🍷	3*

FUCECCHIO (FI)

FATTORIA DI MONTELLORI
VIA PISTOIESE, 5
50054 FUCECCHIO (FI)
TEL. 0571/260641

The Fattoria di Montellori has given an excellent performance this year. All the wines that they presented have done well, and their super-Tuscan, the Salamartano '97, nearly received a Third Glass. It has good concentration and yet is elegant and harmonious. A very intense ruby color precedes excellently clean and distinct aromas: the oak is well blended with the plentiful fruit, although a clear note of green pepper clashes with the sensation of full ripeness. The really splendid palate is very soft and long, with noble smooth tannins. The Salamartano '96 is better than expected, given the year. It does show less concentration than the '97, but has a silky body, good balance and some finesse. The Vigna del Moro '97 does well too. It has interesting mineral notes and scents of sweet tobacco on the nose. In the mouth it is tannic, but round and dense. The Vin Santo doesn't have much personality, but is well made, and displays a bouquet of jam and candied fruit. The good chardonnay-based Castelrapiti Bianco '96, despite a nose dominated by toasty oak, offers a delightful soft full flavor. Their Sauvignon Costa Sant'Amato '98 seems a little simple in fragrance, but solid and substantial on the palate. And lastly, the Viognier Bonfiglio '98 is pleasant but a bit short.

●	Salamartano '96	🍷🍷	5
●	Salamartano '97	🍷🍷	5
○	Castelrapiti Bianco '96	🍷	5
●	Chianti Vigna del Moro '97	🍷	3
○	La Costa di Sant'Amato '98	🍷	4
○	Vin Santo dell'Empolese '95	🍷	5
○	Bonfiglio '98		4
●	Castelrapiti Rosso '92	YY	5
●	Castelrapiti Rosso '95	YY	4
●	Castelrapiti Rosso '93	YY	5
●	Salamartano '92	YY	5
●	Salamartano '93	YY	5
●	Salamartano '94	YY	5
●	Salamartano '95	YY	5
○	Vin Santo dell'Empolese '90	YY	5

GAIOLE IN CHIANTI (SI)

AGRICOLTORI
DEL CHIANTI GEOGRAFICO
VIA MULINACCIO, 10
53013 GAIOLE IN CHIANTI (SI)
TEL. 0577/749451

We know what is going to happen at our annual appointment with the wines from Agricoltori del Chianti Geografico. We admit that we are delighted to see small producers band together, and we know that Vittorio Fiore is a committed and capable oenologist. But since they have proven year after year that they make good, trustworthy wines, we know what to expect. Their Chianti Classico Montegiachi Riserva '96 is not as good as it normally is, but it was a very poor year. It is somewhat thinner and more evolved, and will have a shorter life than its predecessor. As usual, the Capitolare di Biturica I Vigneti del Geographico '97, which is made from sangiovese with some cabernet sauvignon, is very good. It equals or even betters the '96 version and has even more strength and depth. The Chianti Classico '97 is very properly made, and is one of the most easily found and trustworthy of its kind. It is a typical young Chianti Classico: it may not have a massive body, but it is irresistibly easy to drink. More concentrated, but also a bit rougher, the Chianti Classico Contessa di Radda '97 is a good version of this medium-bodied red.

●	I Vigneti del Geografico '96	🍷🍷	5
●	Chianti Cl. Montegiachi Ris. '96	🍷	4
●	Chianti Classico '97	🍷	3
●	Chianti Classico Contessa di Radda '97	🍷	3
●	Chianti Cl. Montegiachi Ris. '87	YY	3*
●	Chianti Cl. Montegiachi Ris. '88	YY	4
●	Chianti Cl. Montegiachi Ris. '90	YY	3*
●	Chianti Cl. Montegiachi Ris. '94	YY	4
●	Chianti Cl. Montegiachi Ris. '95	YY	4
●	Chianti Classico '90	YY	2*
●	I Vigneti del Geografico '95	YY	5
●	Chianti Classico '96	Y	2*
●	Chianti Classico Contessa di Radda '96	Y	3

★ Castello di Ama

Loc. Ama
53010 Gaiole in Chianti (SI)
tel. 0577/746031

Lorenza Sebasti and Marco Pallanti are in command of one of the most representative estates of the whole Chianti region. It's true that they haven't received Three Glasses for a few years, and there are various reasons for this. One is that Ama's vineyards are high up, and when the weather is not particularly favorable this can cause problems, particularly for the concentration of the wines. There are, however, various positive signs this year, and one is that the Chianti Classico Castello di Ama '97 is perhaps the best version ever. Since Marco and Lorenza decided to eliminate two of their four crus, (Bellavista and La Casuccia remain, San Lorenzo and Bertinga have been eliminated), the grapes from the eliminated crus are added to their normal Chianti, greatly to its benefit. The Chianti Classico La Casuccia '95 is very good: it's an extremely elegant red but it doesn't have an enormous amount of body. This is typical of the subzone of Ama and Lecchi. The Chianti Classico Bellavista '95 is interesting but less elegant, and perhaps a little thinner and harsh. The Vigna l'Apparita '95, the most famous merlot from the Chianti Classico, is just a step short of Three Glasses. We found it a bit closed on the nose and the structure is not fantastic. Do we love big wines too much? Maybe. But it's probably also true that where the world, like the world of wine here in Chianti, is constantly changing and improving, it is no easy matter to stay at the top, not even for capable and dedicated people like Marco and Lorenza.

● Chianti Cl. Bellavista '95	▼▼	6
● Chianti Cl. La Casuccia '95	▼▼	6
● Chianti Classico '97	▼▼	4
● Vigna l'Apparita Merlot '95	▼▼	6
● Chianti Cl. Bellavista '85	ΥΥΥ	6
● Chianti Cl. Bellavista '86	ΥΥΥ	6
● Chianti Cl. Bellavista '90	ΥΥΥ	5
● Chianti Cl. Bertinga '88	ΥΥΥ	6
● Chianti Cl. La Casuccia '88	ΥΥΥ	6
● Vigna l'Apparita Merlot '88	ΥΥΥ	6
● Vigna l'Apparita Merlot '90	ΥΥΥ	6
● Vigna l'Apparita Merlot '91	ΥΥΥ	6
● Vigna l'Apparita Merlot '92	ΥΥΥ	6
● Vigna l'Apparita Merlot '93	ΥΥ	6

GAIOLE IN CHIANTI (SI)

Badia a Coltibuono

Loc. Badia a Coltibuono
53013 Gaiole in Chianti (SI)
tel. 0577/749498

We had a lot of trouble getting hold of anything from Badia a Coltibuono. For one thing, the Chianti Classico Riserva '96 was bottled late, and for another, the Sangioveto '96, in accordance with the wise decision taken by Roberto and Emanuela Stucchi, will not be released. Hence we had to leave their page blank up to the last moment before we went to press. The results are not exciting, but we should remember that they have been making difficult decisions at the winery, that they have had to do without their most important wine, and that the year, 1996, was not a very good one. There is not much to worry about, however. The new vines and the up-to-the-minute cellar are clear signals about what Badia a Coltibuono is going to be doing in the next few years. In the meanwhile, the Chianti Classico Riserva '96 is a good wine. Part of it is the Sangioveto manqué, and therefore doesn't suffer much from the bad year. It offers its usual scents of ripe red fruit with some animal notes; the structure on the palate, while not enormous, is well balanced. We expected something more from the Chianti Classico '97. The same is true, more or less, of the Chianti Classico RS (which stands for Roberto Stucchi). In a year like '97 we usually find richer and more concentrated wines. Perhaps, however, the best barrels were saved for the '97 Sangioveto and Riserva, which will come out next year. That would be fun.

● Chianti Classico Ris. '96	▼▼	5
● Chianti Classico '97	▼	3
● Chianti Classico R. S. '97	▼	3
● Sangioveto '95	ΥΥΥ	6
● Chianti Classico '93	ΥΥ	3*
● Chianti Classico Ris. '82	ΥΥ	5
● Chianti Classico Ris. '85	ΥΥ	4
● Chianti Classico Ris. '88	ΥΥ	4
● Chianti Classico Ris. '90	ΥΥ	4
● Chianti Classico Ris. '95	ΥΥ	5
● Sangioveto '85	ΥΥ	6
● Sangioveto '86	ΥΥ	6
● Sangioveto '88	ΥΥ	6
● Sangioveto '90	ΥΥ	6
● Sangioveto '94	ΥΥ	6

GAIOLE IN CHIANTI (SI)

BARONE RICASOLI
LOC. BROLIO
53013 GAIOLE IN CHIANTI (SI)
TEL. 0577/7301

We're not to call it Castello di Brolio anymore. The property belongs to Barone Ricasoli and that will be the name of the winery from now on. (Actually Francesco Ricasoli, despite his descent from the Iron Baron, is anything but overbearing.) There have been changes in the wines as well. The Casalferro '97, which is a dream, is no longer only pure sangiovese: it also has just a little bit of merlot in it. In the spring of 2000 the '97 Chianti Classico Castello di Brolio will come out in a completely new version. It will be the great Château of Chianti Classico, for which it is genetically predisposed. Tasting it "en primeur" was a thrilling experience. The other wines presented are just splendid. Even the chardonnay-based Torricella '97, which we never liked much, is good this year. The Formulae '97, a monovarietal sangiovese with a youthful fragrance, is excellent. The Chianti Classico Brolio '97 is exceptional, and we find the Chianti Classico Rocca Guicciarda Riserva '96 a delightful surprise: although it's from a tricky vintage, it is just as good as the version that came out last year. This year is a triumph for one of Italy's best wineries. It has revived after a difficult period and does honor to its ancient and glorious tradition.

●	Casalferro '97	▼▼▼	5
●	Chianti Classico Brolio '97	▼▼	4
●	Chianti Classico Rocca Guicciarda Ris. '96	▼▼	4
●	Formulae '97	▼▼	3*
○	Torricella '97	▼▼	4
●	Casalferro '95	▽▽▽	5
●	Casalferro '96	▽▽▽	5
●	Casalferro '93	▽▽	5
●	Casalferro '94	▽▽	5
●	Chianti Classico Castello di Brolio Ris. '94	▽▽	4
●	Chianti Classico Castello di Brolio Ris. '95	▽▽	4

GAIOLE IN CHIANTI (SI)

CASTELLO DI CACCHIANO
FRAZ. MONTI IN CHIANTI
LOC. CACCHIANO
53010 GAIOLE IN CHIANTI (SI)
TEL. 0577/747018

Important changes have been made at Giovanni Ricasoli's winery. He has courageously and farsightedly decided to eliminate the special selection RF, leaving the Chianti Classico Millenio Riserva, which is produced only in top vintages, as the only top wine. This reflects a general change in policy which a number of producers in Chianti made last year: to concentrate on one principal wine which will reflect its terroir, instead of making a number of special wines in small quantities. This year we shall review just two wines, and wait until the next edition for the great reds. The Rosso di Toscana '98 is a simple wine of a deep purplish color with a very fresh and fruity nose. In the mouth the acidity is evident, and the wine is dry, tart and a bit short. The Vin Santo '93 is what a Vin Santo can and should be when it is well made. It has a light amber hue with deep gold highlights, and aromas of rare intensity in which a honeyed tone mingles perfectly with notes of almond and hazelnut, as well as very elegant hints of spice. The palate is enticing, fat, very velvety and sweet, with a very long, increasingly intense finish.

○	Vin Santo '93	▼▼	5
●	Rosso di Toscana '98		3
●	Chianti Cl. Millennio Ris. '90	▽▽▽	5
●	Chianti Cl. Millennio Ris. '88	▽▽	5
●	Chianti Cl. Millennio Ris. '95	▽▽	5
●	Chianti Classico '88	▽▽	3*
●	Chianti Classico '90	▽▽	3*
●	Chianti Classico '93	▽▽	3*
●	Chianti Classico '95	▽▽	3*
●	RF Castello di Cacchiano '88	▽▽	5
●	RF Castello di Cacchiano '90	▽▽	5
●	RF Castello di Cacchiano '93	▽▽	4
●	RF Castello di Cacchiano '95	▽▽	5
○	Vin Santo '86	▽▽	5
○	Vin Santo '91	▽▽	5

Colombaio di Cencio

Via Bandinelli
53017 Gaiole in Chianti (SI)
tel. 0577/749129

The history of this little estate, which, even as it makes its debut in the Guide walks off with Three Glasses, is linked to two people. One is Werner Wilhelm, the owner, a very successful German insurance executive. The other is the architect Jacopo Morganti, who was called upon to look after the buildings, and then stayed on to take care of everything else. At the moment he has 15 hectares of land under vine of which 11 are newly planted. They are in an especially felicitous part of the Gaiole district (very near Riecine and on the same road), and are kept like a garden. The consultant oenologist is the excellent Paolo Vagaggini, and the wines are very interesting indeed. The masterpiece is a blend of sangiovese and cabernet sauvignon aged for about 15 months in barriques. Called Il Futuro, it is from the '95 vintage. Its nose, which is extraordinarily elegant and well defined, releases notes of blackberry, raspberry, pencil lead and sour cherry. In the mouth it is full, rich, powerful and concentrated, with tannins that are compact and well marked but not overpowering. The progression of flavors is lengthy and laudable. This is a wine that astonished us both for the neatness of its technical accomplishment and also, for lack of a better word, its "soul". But that's not all: they have also presented two vintages of their Chianti Classico. The '95, obviously, is better since it is richer and more concentrated; the '96 being a little dilute and somewhat acidic, just as one would have thought. Both wines are praiseworthy for their cleanness. It seems to us that we're just at the beginning, and that in a couple of years this winery will be one of the stars of Chianti country. In fact we'd bet on it.

● Il Futuro '95	🍷🍷🍷	6
● Chianti Classico '95	🍷🍷	4
● Chianti Classico '96	🍷	4

GAIOLE IN CHIANTI (SI)

S. M. Lamole & Villa Vistarenni

Loc. Vistarenni
53013 Gaiole in Chianti (SI)
tel. 0577/738186

We noticed with pleasure that last year's change for the better here has been continued this year. The seven wines that Lamole and Vistarenni presented for our tastings did very well. Few of them were weak, and many were pleasant surprises. Among the latter their Riserva Campolungo '94 stood out. It has an intense ruby color showing no signs of age. The nose offers hints of vanilla, minerals and still richly present berries. The palate is well balanced, dynamic in its development, and long and pleasurable on the finish, which is just slightly dilute. The very good Riserva Lamole '95 is lively, dense and meaty, with plenty of concentrated fruit. The Riserva Villa Vistarenni '95, which almost got Two Glasses, has soft and even structure and decent length, but the nose is excessively woody, masking the personality of the wine. Decidedly more than merely good, the Riserva '96 also shows its oak, but in the company of fruity and vegetal scents. The masterful palate displays a soft roundness, good concentration and length. The Chianti Vistarenni '97 gave us pause. In the bottles available to us, at any rate, we found a noticeable acidity and signs of premature age. The Chianti Lamole '97, on the other hand, was full-flavored and lively and full of soft, tasty tannins.

● Chianti Cl. Campolungo Ris. '94	🍷🍷	4
● Chianti Cl. Lamole di Lamole '97	🍷🍷	3*
● Chianti Classico Lamole di Lamole Ris. '96	🍷🍷	4
● Chianti Classico Lamole di Lamole Ris. '95	🍷🍷	4
● Chianti Cl. Lamole di Lamole '96	🍷	4
● Chianti Cl. Villa Vistarenni Ris. '95	🍷	4
● Chianti Cl. Villa Vistarenni '97		3
● Chianti Cl. Villa Vistarenni '95	YY	4
● Codirosso '95	YY	5
● Chianti Cl. Lamole di Lamole '93	Y	4
● Chianti Cl. Lamole di Lamole '94	Y	4
● Chianti Cl. Villa Vistarenni Ris. '94	Y	4
● Chianti Classico Assolo '96	Y	3

GAIOLE IN CHIANTI (SI)

LE MICCINE

Loc. Miccine
53013 Gaiole in Chianti (SI)
tel. 0577/749526

Last year they appeared in our list of Other Wineries. This year they make their debut with an entry of their own. Work goes on apace in the open air, with a hectare of vineyard about to be replanted, bringing them up to seven hectares under vine, all renewed in recent years. Besides their sangiovese, they also grow malvasia nera, merlot and canaiolo, and the wine-making is entrusted to the distinguished oenologist Vittorio Fiore. Small oak casks have been chosen to age their 100% sangiovese Chianti, while the Chianti made from the traditional blend matures in once- or twice-used barriques. Two wines were available for our tastings: the Chianti Classico '97 made an excellent impression. It shows a very concentrated ruby color tinged with purple, and the bouquet is surprising for its elegance and finesse, as the sweetness of the vanilla is balanced by the scents of berries. The superb palate is dense and fruity, with tannins and alcohol in strengthening symbiosis, underpinned by good acidity. Its finish is robust, long and satisfying. The Chianti Classico Da Gino '97 is less convincing. It has a deep, almost impenetrable color, but its aromas suffer from an excessive amount of toasty wood that nearly covers everything else. There is some imbalance in the mouth, where the acidity seems too emphatic. There is plenty of structure, though, and the finish is pleasant and of decent length.

● Chianti Classico '97	🍷🍷	3*
● Chianti Classico Da Gino '97	🍷	4

GAIOLE IN CHIANTI (SI)

MONTIVERDI

Loc. Montiverdi
53013 Gaiole in Chianti (SI)
tel. 0577/749305 - 02/8378808

The Montiverdi winery, in the village of Montiverdi just within the borders of Gaiole in Chianti, has produced a decidedly interesting range of wines this year. Of the Longo family's 50 hectares more than 20 are under vine. Much of their production, followed in every phase by the oenologist Stefano Chioccioli, is devoted to Chianti Classico, of which they make about 100 thousand bottles every year. Our tastings revealed a consistently high general level of quality in their wines, all of which were excellent technically, and some of which were even better. Their Chianti Classico Questo '95 was particularly outstanding. It declaredly contains some cabernet sauvignon, a choice now permitted by DOC regulations. The nose reveals intense notes of berries as well as a noticeable vegetal tone, while the palate is concentrated and juicy, blessed with tasty tannins and an enviable freshness. The Chianti '96 is pleasantly fruity, and nicely designed on the medium-bodied palate. The interesting Riserva '96 came very close to receiving Two Glasses; the rather straightforward but very lively bouquet includes raspberry and sour cherry. This wine is tasty, well-balanced and easy to drink, wanting only greater depth. The other two wines we tasted, the Calesco '96, from sangiovese and merlot, and Le Borranine '96, from sangiovese and cabernet, are also well executed. They are both even and in keeping with this winery's style. We have a slight preference for the second, which seemed to be the denser of the two.

● Chianti Cl. Villa Maisano Questo '95	🍷🍷	4
● Calesco '96	🍷	5
● Chianti Classico '96	🍷	3
● Chianti Classico Ris. '96	🍷	4
● Le Borranine '96	🍷	5

RIECINE

Loc. Riecine
53013 Gaiole in Chianti (SI)
tel. 0577/749098

We must confess that we have a lot of respect for this estate. Not only are the wines excellent, but they have a distinct and pleasing aristocratic personality of their own that also manages to express the characteristics of their principal grape, sangiovese, and the soil from which it springs. The wines presented this year were more than satisfactory, particularly considering that two of them, La Gioia and the Chianti Riserva, were from the distinctly mediocre '96 vintage. La Gioia, the glorious Riecine sangiovese, this year is beguiling and almost gentle, but insistently dense and flavorful. Elegance is the keynote in this version; the tannins are carefully judged and the aromas of chocolate and berries fairly complex. A note of oak is clearly present, but, much to the credit of Sean O'Callaghan and Carlo Ferrini, without being aggressively intrusive. The Chianti '97 is also very good: indeed we preferred it, if only by a hair, to the Riserva. Its aromas are balanced and concentrated, with berries abundantly present. The palate is soft, warm and, thanks to its fresh acidity, lively, and the finish is long. The good Riserva '96 is well balanced, and has good weight in the mouth; but the tannins are still a little austere, and there's a touch too much wood.

●	Chianti Classico '97	TT	5
●	Chianti Classico Ris. '96	TT	6
●	La Gioia '96	TT	6
●	Chianti Classico Ris. '86	YYY	5
●	Chianti Classico Ris. '88	YYY	6
●	La Gioia '95	YYY	6
●	Chianti Classico '96	YY	5
●	Chianti Classico Ris. '90	YY	6
●	Chianti Classico Ris. '91	YY	5
●	Chianti Classico Ris. '93	YY	5
●	Chianti Classico Ris. '94	YY	5
●	Chianti Classico Ris. '95	YY	6
●	La Gioia '91	YY	5
●	La Gioia '93	YY	5
●	La Gioia '94	YY	5

ROCCA DI CASTAGNOLI

Loc. Castagnoli
53013 Gaiole in Chianti (SI)
tel. 0577/731004

Rocca di Castagnoli re-enters our selection of the best wineries with an essentially excellent performance. These results are particularly significant because this is a large producer (100 hectares under vine) with great potential which is at last clearly realized, even without the assistance of important vintages. We'll start with the most surprising and impressive of their fine range, the Chianti Classico Capraia Riserva '96, one of the best from the whole Chianti Classico zone. It shows superb structure, and is meaty and full-flavored, with its compact tannins nicely blended with its rich fruit. If they go on like this, we can expect extraordinary things from the next few versions. The muscular Cabernet Buriano '96 is no less interesting. It reveals concentrated scents of ripe black fruit, and the palate is massive, powerful and profound. The Stielle '96, two parts sangiovese and one part cabernet sauvignon, is also highly successful. It has an original nose of sour cherry, nettles and smoke, while in the mouth it is round and well sustained by its tannins, and then slightly bitter at the end. Their normal Chianti Classico '97, clearly a simpler wine, reveals fruity and vegetal notes and is most certainly good.

●	Buriano '96	TT	5
●	Chianti Classico Capraia Ris. '96	TT	4
●	Stielle '96	TT	5
●	Chianti Classico '97	T	3

GAIOLE IN CHIANTI (SI)

SAN GIUSTO A RENTENNANO
LOC. MONTI IN CHIANTI
53010 GAIOLE IN CHIANTI (SI)
TEL. 0577/747121

San Giusto a Rentennano is just the producer for lovers of wines that clearly represent the land from which they come. This year's tastings yet again displayed the excellence of the Martini di Cigala family's winery, despite the prevalence of wines from the disappointing '96 vintage. Their Percarlo '96, although not as fat or powerful as previous versions, reveals a superior personality, good concentration and plenty of fruit. The entry on the palate is unhesitating, the good development shows depth, and the spicy finish is lingering, with tannins sufficient to maintain the adequate, though not splendid, structure offered by that miserly year. The Chianti Classico is also excellent and a worthy representative of the '97 vintage. Its aromas are intense and elegant, fruity and flowery. On the palate it is full-flavored and solid, with a richly fruity finish. The Riserva '96 is good, and came very close to receiving Two Glasses; its lighter fruitiness underscores the agreeable woody tone, the alcohol and the somewhat dry tannins. It is a rigorous, classic wine of formidable character. Their merlot-based La Ricolma '96 is, alone of their wines, slightly disappointing. Its tannins and oak are both a bit aggressive, but we expect a lot from the versions to come in the next few years.

●	Chianti Classico '97	🍷🍷	4
●	Percarlo '96	🍷🍷	6
●	Chianti Classico Ris. '96	🍷	5
●	La Ricolma '96	🍷	6
●	Percarlo '88	ΥΥΥ	6
●	Chianti Classico Ris. '88	ΥΥ	5
●	Percarlo '85	ΥΥ	6
●	Percarlo '87	ΥΥ	6
●	Percarlo '90	ΥΥ	6
●	Percarlo '91	ΥΥ	6
●	Percarlo '92	ΥΥ	6
●	Percarlo '93	ΥΥ	6
●	Percarlo '94	ΥΥ	6
●	Percarlo '95	ΥΥ	6
○	Vin Santo '90	ΥΥ	6

GAIOLE IN CHIANTI (SI)

CASTELLO DI SAN POLO IN ROSSO
LOC. S. POLO IN ROSSO
53013 GAIOLE IN CHIANTI (SI)
TEL. 0577/746045 - 0577/746070

After a poor year in which the wines of Castello di San Polo in Rosso were not released, we can report a very successful showing. They are quite near Lecchi and Ama in Chianti, and at about 400 meters are much higher up than most Chianti vineyards. The property is owned by the Canessa family, and their consultant wine-maker is Maurizio Castelli, one of Italy's greatest oenologists when he puts his mind to it. This time Mother Nature has also put her mind to it, bestowing the particularly favorable '95 vintage. The Cetinaia '95 is a masterly version of this wine. Made only from sangiovese, it is extremely elegant in expressing its grape; hence there are clear notes of sour cherry and sweet violet, with background hints of tar and smoke. The palate, while not huge, is stylish: the tannins are sweet and closely knit, and the progression is particularly intriguing, not unlike that of a great Burgundy. Less complex, although still very interesting, the '95 Chianti Classico Riserva seems very well executed. The '96 Chianti Classico is more attenuated and acidic, but this was to be expected in these parts. Altogether a fine performance, and a very nearly triumphant return to the Guide.

●	Cetinaia '95	🍷🍷	6
●	Chianti Classico Ris. '95	🍷🍷	5
●	Chianti Classico '96	🍷	4
●	Cetinaia '85	ΥΥ	5
●	Cetinaia '86	ΥΥ	5
●	Cetinaia '88	ΥΥ	5
●	Cetinaia '90	ΥΥ	6
●	Cetinaia '93	ΥΥ	5
●	Cetinaia '94	ΥΥ	5
●	Chianti Classico '91	ΥΥ	4
●	Chianti Classico Ris. '86	ΥΥ	4
●	Chianti Classico Ris. '90	ΥΥ	5
●	Chianti Classico Ris. '91	ΥΥ	5
●	Chianti Classico '93	Υ	3
●	Chianti Classico Ris. '88	Υ	4

GAIOLE IN CHIANTI (SI)

San Vincenti
Loc. San Vincenti
Podere di Stignano, 27
53013 Gaiole in Chianti (SI)
tel. 0577/734047

With this year's range, San Vincenti has consolidated its position in the Guide. This is a winery we have followed with interest for a number of years, because we feel that their vineyards, although they total only six hectares, have a vocation to produce wines that are not only excellent but also faithful to their territory. They have essentially guaranteed continued high quality by placing technical control in the hands of Carlo Ferrini, who knows both the sangiovese grape and Chianti Classico very well indeed. The three wines we tasted did very well. The best of the three was the Sangiovese Stignano '96, which releases intense, concentrated aromas dominated by fruit (ripe blackberry and plum) with a subtle toasty note. The palate, which progresses nicely, is almost sweetly juicy, harmonious, not inelegant and only slightly hampered on the finish by slightly dry tannins. The Riserva '96 is also successful: it manages to show balance and character even though it doesn't have much structure. It is well made and very pleasurable, and offers fruit and fresh acidity. The Chianti '97 was only a step away from getting Two Glasses. It may be even fruitier than the Riserva but it shows slightly less aromatic complexity. In the mouth it displays fair density and a well-judged underpinning of oak.

●	Chianti Classico Ris. '96	🍷🍷	4
●	Stignano '96	🍷🍷	5
●	Chianti Classico '97	🍷	3
●	Chianti Classico '88	ΥΥ	3*
●	Chianti Classico Podere di Stignano '96	ΥΥ	3*
●	Chianti Classico Ris. '85	ΥΥ	4
●	Chianti Classico Ris. '88	ΥΥ	4
●	Chianti Classico Ris. '95	ΥΥ	4
●	Chianti Classico '90	Υ	3
●	Chianti Classico '91	Υ	4
●	Chianti Classico Ris. '91	Υ	3

GAMBASSI TERME (FI)

Villa Pillo
Via Volterrana, 26
50050 Gambassi Terme (FI)
tel. 0571/680212

The biggest surprises, at least in terms of wine, this year have come from lesser-known parts, showing that the map of the best wineries in Tuscany is still in the process of being drawn. When, for example, we consider the case of Villa Pillo, where the composition of the soil is congenial to vines, and the microclimate allows grapes to ripen perfectly without sacrificing any of their fragrance, we are forced to admit that great wines can be made near Gambassi too. The most conspicuous example is their Syrah which, taking advantage of the excellent '97 vintage, won Three Glasses without a dissenting voice. It is a soft and ample wine with great balance and length, and it gives optimal expression to the distinctive aromatic characteristics of its grape. It offers a well-timed succession of sensations: black fruit, pepper, spice, tobacco and mineral hints. Their Cabernet '97 is also very good. It overcomes the disadvantage of a slightly undefined nose with a meaty, round, and lingering palate. The more lightly structured but very pleasurable, fresh, and well-balanced Vivaldaia is a blend of the winery's principal red grapes. The Merlot also gets Two Glasses without even trying, and is broad, fruity, and persistent, if just a bit on the simple side. The Vin Santo is decent, and the Borgoforte sound and satisfactory.

●	Syrah '97	🍷🍷🍷	5
●	Cabernet Sauvignon '97	🍷🍷	5
●	Merlot '97	🍷🍷	5
●	Vivaldaia '97	🍷🍷	5
○	Vin Santo '93	🍷	6
●	Borgoforte '97		4
●	Cabernet Sauvignon '96	ΥΥ	5
●	Merlot '95	ΥΥ	5
●	Merlot '96	ΥΥ	5
●	Syrah '96	ΥΥ	5
●	Vivaldaia '95	ΥΥ	6
●	Borgoforte '94	Υ	4
●	Syrah '95	Υ	5
●	Vivaldaia '96	Υ	5

GHIZZANO DI PECCIOLI (PI)

TENUTA DI GHIZZANO
VIA DELLA CHIESA, 1
56030 GHIZZANO DI PECCIOLI (PI)
TEL. 050/20596 - 0587/630096

The Tenuta di Ghizzano has been very busy recently. It has increased the variety of wines produced and will shortly be increasing the number of bottles as well, thanks to new vines, some planted and others planned. From the current 10 producing hectares it will grow to 16, nearly all planted to red grapes, sangiovese in particular, followed by merlot, cabernet and some small plots dedicated to petit verdot and syrah. There has also been a change in oenologist: from Luca D'Attoma to Carlo Ferrini. We are expecting further improvement and consolidation of the estate style. At our tastings the Veneroso seemed excellent. It was not very expansive or defined on the nose, but the balanced, even and long palate made up for it. The extremely good merlot-based Nambrot '97 offers intense and concentrated aromas with notes of black fruit and roasting coffee. Full body, good balance, lively tannins annd a lovely finish characterize the palate. With a little more volume and fat it would have been a really great wine. The Chianti '98 is decidedly better than the average of its fellows. In addition to its customary straightforward quaffability it offers a touch of aromatic complexity that adds to its interest. A fragrance of fig jam and plum is the delightful prelude to the delectable sweet Vin Santo San Germano '95, which closes, with yet another Two Glasses, their very successful range of wines.

●	Nambrot '97	🍷🍷	6
●	Veneroso '96	🍷🍷	5
○	Vin Santo San Germano '95	🍷🍷	5
●	Chianti '98	🍷	3
●	Nambrot '96	ΥΥ	6
●	Veneroso '85	ΥΥ	5
●	Veneroso '86	ΥΥ	5
●	Veneroso '88	ΥΥ	5
●	Veneroso '90	ΥΥ	5
●	Veneroso '91	ΥΥ	4
●	Veneroso '93	ΥΥ	4
●	Veneroso '94	ΥΥ	4
●	Veneroso '95	ΥΥ	5
○	Vin Santo San Germano '94	ΥΥ	5
●	Chianti '97	Υ	2*

GREVE IN CHIANTI (FI)

CARPINETO
FRAZ. LUCOLENA
LOC. DUDDA
50022 GREVE IN CHIANTI (FI)
TEL. 055/8549062

Carpineto presented us with a long series of good wines this year. Nothing really let us down but, to tell the truth, we didn't find anything particularly exciting either. The Chianti Classico '97 was one of the most successful bottles, coming close to Two Glasses. A perfectly clean bouquet with a distinct black currant note is followed by a harmonious and quite firm palate. The Riserva '96, with its balanced, smooth and soft palate, is good too, but the vegetal notes on the nose and in the mouth are really somewhat excessive for a Chianti Classico. The Farnito Cabernet Sauvignon '96 was a bit disappointing: although it is harmonious and pleasing in the mouth, it has somewhat insistently grassy tones, which can in part be accounted for by the '96 vintage, plagued as it was by rain at the end of the season. The Dogajolo '98, which was intended to be a simple but agreeably fruity wine, is just that. The Nobile di Montepulciano '96 is both good and in keeping with the Carpineto style, which favors cleanness and balance. It is a very pleasant wine, with a fresh and fruity nose (black currant once again) and a medium-bodied and straightforward palate. There is more substance to be found in the Nobile di Montepulciano Riserva '95, which reveals a soft and vigorous palate, but suffers on the nose from, yet again, distinctly vegetal notes.

●	Chianti Classico '97	🍷	3
●	Chianti Classico Ris. '96	🍷	4
●	Dogajolo '98	🍷	3
●	Farnito Cabernet Sauvignon '96	🍷	5
●	Vino Nobile di Montepulciano '96	🍷	4
●	Vino Nobile di Montepulciano Ris. '95	🍷	4
●	Chianti Classico Ris. '93	ΥΥ	4
●	Chianti Classico Ris. '94	ΥΥ	4
●	Dogajolo '93	ΥΥ	4
●	Dogajolo '95	ΥΥ	3*
●	Farnito Cabernet Sauvignon '90	ΥΥ	5
●	Farnito Cabernet Sauvignon '91	ΥΥ	5
●	Farnito Cabernet Sauvignon '93	ΥΥ	5
●	Farnito Cabernet Sauvignon '95	ΥΥ	5
●	Vino Nobile di Montepulciano Ris. '94	ΥΥ	4

GREVE IN CHIANTI (FI)

CASTEL RUGGERO
LOC. ANTELLA
50011 GREVE IN CHIANTI (FI)
TEL. 055/6819237

It cannot be said that Niccolò d'Afflitto likes to take his ease. When he has done his work – and excellent work it is too – as consultant oenologist for various Tuscan wineries, he continues to busy himself with wine at his "country retreat", the family estate which belonged to a succession of famous Florentine families (the Guidis, for example) before passing to its current owners in the early 1900s. There are just two hectares under vine, in the northern part of Chianti Classico territory, and they are planted to sangiovese. The only wine presented this time was the Chianti Classico '97, since they didn't make a Riserva in '96. Ruby-hued with a definite purple cast, it opens on the nose with distinct notes of violet, to develop into a varied and harmonious fruity fragrance including berries, cherry and strawberry. On the palate the attack is not particularly impressive, being rather dilute and acidulous, but the development is smooth, the tannins are not too noticeable and the finish is well executed and long enough: it earns its One Glass without any trouble, but also without any excitement. We feel certain that next year's tastings will once again show the brio and energy we had grown accustomed to.

● Chianti Classico '97	▼	3
● Chianti Classico '90	▽▽	4
● Chianti Classico '93	▽▽	3*
● Chianti Classico Ris. '90	▽▽	4
● Chianti Classico Ris. '93	▽▽	4
● Chianti Classico Ris. '94	▽▽	4
● Chianti Classico Ris. '95	▽▽	4
● Chianti Classico '88	▽	4
● Chianti Classico '91	▽	4
● Chianti Classico '94	▽	3
● Chianti Classico '96	▽	3

GREVE IN CHIANTI (FI)

LA MADONNINA - TRIACCA
LOC. STRADA IN CHIANTI
V.LO ABATE, 1
50027 GREVE IN CHIANTI (FI)
TEL. 055/858003 - 0342/701352

At La Madonnina, one of the most important estates in Chianti Classico country, the vineyard replanting program is well under way. The Triacca family, which has long produced wine in its native Villa di Tirano near Sondrio (p. 190), is proceeding with its intelligent policy of investing in the modernization of its Tuscan property. We'll start with the cabernet sauvignon-based Il Mandorlo '95: a purplish tinge is still visible in the deep ruby color. The very interesting and agreeable bouquet offers notes of fresh ripe fruit. Abundant alcohol supports a good but not overwhelming body. The Chianti Classico Riserva '96, deep ruby in hue, offers intense aromas of blackberry and plum with faint spicy hints of cinnamon and clove. The not very impressive attack on the palate is lean, and the acidity and alcohol are not entirely harmonious. The estate cru, the Vigneto La Palaia Riserva '96, is better: a deep red color is answered by a lovely succession of fruity aromas, with cherry and black currant to the fore. The highly satisfactory palate is succulent, tasty and well delineated. The Chianti Classico '97 seemed the least successful of the lot. A lively color introduces a fresh fruity fragrance with a hint of violet. There's not much vigor in the mouth, where it's rather dilute and hardness prevails, but it manages nonetheless to be quite quaffable and fairly long.

● Chianti Classico V. La Palaia '96	▼▼	4
● Chianti Classico '97	▼	3
● Chianti Classico Ris. '96	▼	4
● Il Mandorlo '95	▼	4
● Chianti Classico '94	▽▽	3*
● Chianti Classico '95	▽▽	3*
● Chianti Classico Ris. '94	▽▽	4
● Chianti Classico Ris. '95	▽▽	4
● Chianti Classico '93	▽	3
● Chianti Classico '96	▽	3
● Chianti Classico Ris. '93	▽	4
● Chianti Classico V. La Palaia '95	▽	4
● Il Mandorlo '93	▽	4
● Il Mandorlo '94	▽	4
● Vino Nobile di Montepulciano '93	▽	4

GREVE IN CHIANTI (FI)

La Torraccia di Presura

Loc. Strada in Chianti
Via della Montagnola, 130
50022 Greve in Chianti (FI)
tel. 055/490563 - 055/489997

This winery, which lies on the Florentine edge of the Chianti Classico zone, continues to maintain its usual standard. There is certainly nothing wrong with this, but last year we had gotten our hopes up for a notable improvement in quality. So on the basis of our tastings, we can consider this a year of transition. They also presented a white wine this time, the Solitario '97, which we found quite pleasing. A pale straw color tinged with green introduces a simple, fruity, and sound nose, while the palate is fresh, crisply acidic and pleasurable. However, it was their reds we were looking forward to. The Chianti Classico Il Tarocco '97 was not completely convincing. It has a pleasant aspect in the glass, and a variety of aromas, with flowers and berries to the fore. In the mouth it is somewhat dilute and unsupported, agreeable but not intense. The '96 Riserva shows more structure. It has a dense, rich color, while the very elegant nose reveals a slightly overripe fruitiness together with sweet spicy notes. In the mouth it displays sufficient body, and its various elements are balanced and well distributed, with only the alcohol, perhaps, a bit dominant. It has a good juicy, if not excessively lengthy, finish. A blend of cabernet sauvignon and sangiovese, the Lucciolaio '96 has a bit too much vanilla, perhaps, on the agreeable nose, but the fruit is not completely covered by it. The not very powerful palate reveals noticeable acidity, not very strong alcohol and already smooth tannins.

●	Chianti Classico Il Tarocco '97	🍷	3
●	Chianti Classico Il Tarocco Ris. '96	🍷	4
●	Lucciolaio '96	🍷	5
○	Solitario '97	🍷	3
●	Chianti Classico Il Tarocco '96	🍷🍷	3*
●	Chianti Classico Il Tarocco '94	🍷	3
●	Chianti Classico Il Tarocco '95	🍷	3
●	Chianti Classico Il Tarocco Ris. '94	🍷	4
●	Lucciolaio '95	🍷	5

GREVE IN CHIANTI (FI)

Tenuta Montecalvi

Via Citille, 8
50022 Greve in Chianti (FI)
tel. 055/8544665

This has not been an easy year for Montecalvi. After the excellent '95 version, the '96 was a step backwards. The year itself, however, was a poor one, and did not yield grapes of the same quality. Particularly in the case of a wine based almost completely on sangiovese, it was difficult to make up for the dilution brought about by the constant rain during the last and crucial period of ripening. The great care with which Montecalvi manages its vineyards, though, has permitted them to make a wine that is well above average. Bernadette Doyle's winery should be followed carefully, because it has everything in place to make important wines beginning in 1997, which is a very promising year. Unfortunately Renzo Bolli, Bernadette's companion, has recently died, so cannot continue to take part in the work that he began; but their daughter, Jacqueline, has taken his place. The Montecalvi '96 has an intense and brilliant ruby color, and clean, consistent aromas of blackberry, cocoa and vanilla. The keynote of the palate is its balance, based on a notably dense and soft tannic underpinning, revealing the touch of a sure hand.

●	Montecalvi '96	🍷🍷	5
●	Montecalvi '94	🍷🍷	4
●	Montecalvi '95	🍷🍷	5
●	Montecalvi '93	🍷	4

GREVE IN CHIANTI (FI)

FATTORIA DI NOZZOLE
LOC. PASSO DEI PECORAI
VIA DI NOZZOLE, 12
50022 GREVE IN CHIANTI (FI)
TEL. 055/858018

We have only one wine from Nozzole to judge this year, but it's their best one, Il Pareto. It's a great red made only from cabernet sauvignon, and has been for some years now one of the best wines in Tuscany. It received Three Glasses in '88, '90 and '93. It went down to Two Glasses in '94 and, somewhat unexpectedly, in '95, which seemed to us to be somewhat overripe. The '96, however, is back on track. Perhaps it is less concentrated, but its aromas are well focused and its fruit is neat and elegant. There is a clearly evident note of wood and vanilla, but it is neither overbearing nor unpleasant. In the mouth it shows good body, an obvious touch of acidity, and fine, well-integrated tannins. Even if it is the fruit of a minor year, this is a well-executed red wine, and has returned to the style that made it a great one. With just a little more concentration, which is to say in a better year, it would easily be back at the level of the '93. The '88 and '90 are a different matter, but they were the two best versions ever made. The '97, however, could come close to them. We can but wait and hope to taste another great Pareto.

●	Il Pareto '96	🍷🍷	6
●	Chianti Cl. La Forra Ris. '90	YYY	4
●	Il Pareto '88	YYY	6
●	Il Pareto '90	YYY	6
●	Il Pareto '93	YYY	6
●	Chianti Cl. La Forra Ris. '88	YY	4
●	Chianti Cl. La Forra Ris. '93	YY	4
●	Chianti Cl. La Forra Ris. '94	YY	4
●	Chianti Cl. La Forra Ris. '95	YY	4
●	Chianti Classico '95	YY	3*
●	Il Pareto '89	YY	6
●	Il Pareto '94	YY	6
●	Il Pareto '95	YY	6
○	Le Bruniche '96	YY	3*

GREVE IN CHIANTI (FI)

PODERE POGGIO SCALETTE
LOC. RUFFOLI
50022 GREVE IN CHIANTI (FI)
TEL. 055/8549017

We expressed our disappointment, at the end of last year's review of this winery, that we had not yet been able to award them Three Glasses, but we also expressed our hopes that we would be able to do so in the coming year. Our hopes have been fulfilled. We should mention that Vittorio Fiore and his wife Adriana acquired this estate in 1991, and now run it together with their son Jurij. It covers 35 hectares, 12 of which are olive groves, while 12 are vineyards, at an altitude of from 350 to 500 meters, terraced in stone as they ascend, hence the name Poggio Scalette ("scalette" means little steps). Excellent for the cultivation of both vines and olive trees, this estate has the good fortune to include, in the vineyard that yields Il Carbonaione, examples of the celebrated and rare sangiovese di Lamole on vines planted in the 1920s. But let us turn to the delectable wine itself. Il Carbonaione '96 is an extraordinarily elegant and harmonious red. It has a dense, dark color that is also brilliant and vivid. Its nose is intense and profound, rich in black fruit and floral hints, as well, for the time being at least, as decidedly spicy, toasty ones from the oak. The palate is compelling, soft and vigorous, with excellent balance and dense tannins of great finesse, and a long, complex finish that reveals extraordinary personality.

●	Il Carbonaione '96	🍷🍷🍷	5
●	Il Carbonaione '92	YY	5
●	Il Carbonaione '93	YY	5
●	Il Carbonaione '94	YY	5
●	Il Carbonaione '95	YY	5

Castello di Querceto

Loc. Dudda
50020 Greve in Chianti (FI)
tel. 055/8549064

Castello di Querceto offered an impressive number of wines at our tastings this year. The reason for this profusion is that they do not want to put bottles on the market until they are ready to drink, and some years a number of different wines from different years are ready at the same time. But down to details: the Querciolaia '95 made an excellent impression. A blend of cabernet sauvignon and sangiovese, it has a deep, rich color. The nose releases a pleasant blend of fruit and spice, and the palate is soft, almost velvety, and harmonious. The Chianti Classico Riserva Il Picchio '94 shows a lovely clear ruby color and aromas of ripe fruit and fruit jam. In the mouth it offers strong, closely knit tannins well balanced by the abundant alcohol. Il Cento, we must admit, was disappointing. It was made from a special selection of sangiovese to celebrate the winery's 100th birthday. Although it has a deep color and consistent fruity aromas, it is unbalanced and incoherent on the palate. We distinctly felt that many more years of aging will be needed. Two versions of the Cignale, '94 and '95, mostly cabernet sauvignon with a bit of merlot, have been released. Both are dark and powerful, and made from first-class fruit, but both still need time to acquire proper balance. La Corte '95 is still clearly a thoroughbred. It has a lovely fragrance of berries and a tasty and inviting palate with tightly packed tannins that are not at all hard, but the finish is short. The Chianti Classico '96 and the Riserva '94 easily earn One Glass apiece, and both have good structure, but are on the acidulous side.

●	Chianti Classico Il Picchio Ris. '94	🍷🍷	4
●	Querciolaia '95	🍷🍷	5
●	Cento '95	🍷	6
●	Chianti Classico '96	🍷	3
●	Chianti Classico Ris. '94	🍷	4
●	Cignale '94	🍷	5
●	Cignale '95	🍷	5
●	La Corte '95	🍷	5
●	Chianti Classico '95	YY	3*
●	Chianti Classico Il Picchio Ris. '93	YY	4
●	Chianti Classico Ris. '90	YY	4
●	La Corte '94	YY	5
●	Querciolaia '90	YY	5

GREVE IN CHIANTI (FI)

Agricola Querciabella

Loc. Ruffoli
Via S. Lucia a Barbiano, 17
50022 Greve in Chianti (FI)
tel. 055/853834 - 055/853307

Querciabella is the best winery in Greve. We are not alone in thinking this, as the best Italian wine critics and several foreign experts share our opinion. Nor should this be a surprise. The technical direction is in the capable hands of Guido De Santi who has the extraordinary oenologist Giacomo Tachis as his consultant, and the father-and-son team of the owners, Giuseppe and Sebastiano Castiglioni, has considerable long-term vision. With this combination a positive result seems a sure thing. They are on the point of finishing a splendid new underground cellar, and plan to acquire more vineyards both in Chianti Classico and near Scansano. The wines this year are all fantastic. Let us begin with Batàr '97, Tuscany's best white, which is made almost completely from chardonnay. It has intensely fruity aromas, which have thoroughly absorbed the oak. The palate is full but not heavy, soft but not flabby, and concentrated without being cloying. This is the first time that a Tuscan white wine has received Three Glasses. The Camartina '95, made from cabernet sauvignon and sangiovese, is also very good. It is a masterful version, comparable to the '90. However it is worth waiting a bit before drinking this great red, since, although it has fruity aromas with a mineral slant, and a very full flavor, it is still shows some of the roughness of youth. The debut appearance of their Vin Santo Orlando '90, of which only a very few bottles were made, is surprisingly good. The Chianti Classico Riserva '96 and the Chianti Classico '97 are both well made and elegant, and the latter should have a very long life.

○	Batàr '97	🍷🍷🍷	5
●	Camartina '95	🍷🍷🍷	6
●	Chianti Classico '97	🍷🍷	4
●	Chianti Classico Ris. '96	🍷🍷	5
○	Vin Santo Orlando '90	🍷🍷	6
●	Camartina '88	YYY	5
●	Camartina '90	YYY	5
●	Camartina '94	YYY	5
●	Chianti Classico '95	YYY	4*
●	Chianti Classico Ris. '95	YYY	5
●	Camartina '87	YY	5
●	Camartina '91	YY	5
●	Camartina '93	YY	5
●	Chianti Classico '96	YY	4
●	Chianti Classico Ris. '90	YY	5

GREVE IN CHIANTI (FI)

Castello di Verrazzano
Loc. Verrazzano
50022 Greve in Chianti (FI)
tel. 055/854243

The somewhat difficult period that Castello di Verrazzano was apparently passing through in recent years has finally ended, and Luigi Cappellini's estate returns to Olympian heights in this year's Guide, thanks to his wonderful Sassello. This is all the more positive, since the fine performance of the rest of his range suggests that Sassello's triumph was not a matter of pure chance. This wine is a splendid example of a new style of sangiovese. It has a lovely color and a deep and concentrated bouquet with a solid fruity base successfully blended with woody notes. Its entrance on the palate reveals a decided character that harmonizes perfectly with a pervasive and elegant softness. It ends with a flourish, displaying the smooth compactness of its tannins and an excellent finish. The Riserva '96 confirms that they know what they're about at Castello di Verrazzano. It's a dense, concentrated wine with sound and lively fruit (such as we have seldom found in '96 riservas) supported by smooth but energetic tannins. Turning to the Chianti '97 we can do nothing but continue to sing their praises. It is, of course, simpler in style, and we detect the presence of some other grape varieties, which give it a fragrance of raspberry and black currant, expressed with exemplary cleanness and definition. The palate is meaty and well-balanced, harmonious and quite delightful.

● Sassello '97	▼▼▼	5
● Chianti Classico '97	▼▼	3*
● Chianti Classico Ris. '96	▼▼	4
● Chianti Classico Ris. '90	▽▽▽	5
● Bottiglia Particolare '90	▽▽	5
● Bottiglia Particolare '95	▽▽	5
● Chianti Classico '91	▽▽	3*
● Chianti Classico '94	▽▽	3*
● Chianti Classico Cinquecentenario Ris. '85	▽▽	5
● Chianti Classico Ris. '88	▽▽	4
● Sassello '90	▽▽	5
● Sassello '93	▽▽	5
● Sassello '95	▽▽	5
● Chianti Classico Ris. '94	▽	4
● Chianti Classico Ris. '95	▽	4

GREVE IN CHIANTI (FI)

Castello di Vicchiomaggio
Via Vicchiomaggio, 4
50022 Greve in Chianti (FI)
tel. 055/854079

Let us begin by saying that Villa Boscorotondo, in Panzano, is no longer part of the winery's holdings, and also that the winery's renewal is continuing apace. The castle now holds a cellar for aging wines which has been built according to present-day criteria, and John Matta, proprietor and oenologist, assisted by Giorgio Marone, continues the work of replanting. Our tastings, however, were less convincing than last year's. The Chianti Classico San Jacopo '97 displays a light ruby color, and aromas that include cherry and strawberry. In the mouth it appears a little dilute and undemanding, and the acidity is a bit dominant. The Chianti Classico La Prima Riserva '96 is made from sangiovese with just a touch of colorino and canaiolo. It has a deep, impenetrable color and lightly grassy aromas. While it is full-flavored and ample in the mouth, its tannins are still on the aggressive side, although the alcohol gives good support to the structure. The Chianti Classico Petri Riserva '96 seemed a little unbalanced. The nose is clearly and intensely fruity, with berries abundantly present, but the palate is still quite hard and shows excessively dry tannins. There is plenty of alcohol, however, and the finish is softer and very pleasant. The Ripa delle Mandorle '96 is better. Made from sangiovese and cabernet sauvignon, it is still quite woody on both nose and palate, although pleasing mature fruit can be glimpsed underneath. The Ripa delle More '96 is decidedly good. A pure sangiovese aged in barriques, it has glints of purple in its ruby color, a jammy fragrance, a good solid body with juicy tannins, and an excellent rising finish.

● Ripa delle More '96	▼▼	5
● Chianti Classico La Prima Ris. '96	▼	5
● Chianti Classico Petri Ris. '96	▼	5
● Chianti Classico San Jacopo '97	▼	3
● Ripa delle Mandorle '96	▼	5
● Ripa delle More '94	▽▽▽	5
● Chianti Classico La Prima Ris. '86	▽▽	5
● Chianti Classico La Prima Ris. '90	▽▽	5
● Chianti Classico La Prima Ris. '93	▽▽	5
● Chianti Classico La Prima Ris. '88	▽▽	5
● Chianti Classico La Prima Ris. '94	▽▽	5
● Chianti Classico La Prima Ris. '95	▽▽	5
● Chianti Classico Petri Ris. '90	▽▽	5
● Ripa delle More '90	▽▽	5
● Ripa delle More '95	▽▽	5

GREVE IN CHIANTI (FI)

Fattoria di Vignamaggio

Via di Petriolo
50022 Greve in Chianti (FI)
tel. 055/853007 - 055/853559

After last year's triumph, Three Glasses for the splendid Monna Lisa Riserva '95, we were expecting more of the same, although we are well aware that it is difficult both to achieve and to reproduce results on that level. But Vignamaggio made an almost subdued appearance at this year's tastings. Only two wines were presented, and, although certainly good, they were not outstanding, as if this estate had relaxed its efforts instead of being spurred on to greater heights. We hope to be proven wrong next year, but meanwhile here's what we found. We weren't greatly taken by the Chianti Classico, which just managed to carry off One Glass: not what one would have hoped for from Vignamaggio in a generally felicitous year like '97. The structure is good, it's soft and well-balanced, but also a bit short, and the not altogether clean aromas are overpowered by sulfurous notes. The Monna Lisa '96 is more successful, showing greater aromatic definition, although the oak lords it over the fruit to some extent. The palate is agreeable and characteristic, but it doesn't develop properly, and the drying oak-derived tannins make short work of the finish. So the '96 doesn't get very high marks, but it does have the excuse of a problematic vintage.

● Chianti Cl. Monna Lisa Ris. '96	▼	4
● Chianti Classico '97	▼	3
● Chianti Cl. Monna Lisa Ris. '95	YYY	4*
● Chianti Cl. Monna Lisa Ris. '85	YY	4
● Chianti Cl. Monna Lisa Ris. '88	YY	5
● Chianti Cl. Monna Lisa Ris. '90	YY	4
● Chianti Cl. Monna Lisa Ris. '94	YY	4
● Chianti Cl. Monna Lisa Ris. '93	YY	4
● Chianti Classico '96	YY	3*
● Gherardino '85	YY	5
● Gherardino '88	YY	5
● Gherardino '90	YY	5
● Gherardino '93	YY	5
● Gherardino '95	YY	5
● Vignamaggio '93	YY	5

GREVE IN CHIANTI (FI)

Viticcio

Via San Cresci, 12/A
50022 Greve in Chianti (FI)
tel. 055/854210

Last year we went so far as to offer some good-natured criticism of Viticcio because their two Chianti Classicos were not as good as their pair of super-Tuscans. They have answered us in the most effective way, i.e. with this year's wines, so now we can eat (or drink) our words and give them due credit: four wines, all extremely good, to the extent that it is virtually impossible to rank them. To tell the truth, we were most pleasantly surprised by the two Chianti Classicos, Riserva and non-Riserva. The Chianti '97 overflows with character. The nose is still a little dumb, but nevertheless concentrated and dense. As one might have predicted, the palate is full-bodied and substantial, with lots of fruit. The Riserva '96, which resembles it in style, has a more open bouquet, with notes of dark fruit and light spice, and a very well-balanced and meaty palate. The sangiovese-based Prunaio '96 reflects the characteristics of its vintage and is consequently not very full-bodied, but in compensation the notable general elegance it offers is really admirable. Classic aromas of red berries and violets complete the picture. The interesting Monile '96, two thirds cabernet with sangiovese and a hint of nebbiolo, shows most clearly the limitations of the '96 vintage. The bouquet displays a disproportionate amount of oak, with butter and hazelnut tones, and of vegetal notes. The palate is more successful, with its good structure and development and quite a long vanilla finish.

● Chianti Classico '97	▼▼	4
● Chianti Classico Ris. '96	▼▼	4
● Monile '96	▼▼	5
● Prunaio '96	▼▼	5
● Chianti Classico '95	YY	4
● Chianti Classico Ris. '90	YY	4
● Chianti Classico Ris. '91	YY	4
● Monile '91	YY	5
● Monile '93	YY	5
● Monile '94	YY	5
● Monile '95	YY	5
● Prunaio '90	YY	5
● Prunaio '93	YY	5
● Prunaio '94	YY	5
● Prunaio '95	YY	5

IMPRUNETA (FI)

Podere Lanciola II
Via Imprunetana, 210
50023 Impruneta (FI)
tel. 055/208324 - 055/352011

The Podere Lanciola II has gone a good part of the way towards realizing its ambitions. But although their best bottles are excellent, they have as yet to produce a really superb wine. The top of their line is again, of course, their substantial, intense and well-made sangiovese and cabernet blend, Terricci. The '96 version, from a vintage that was not very propitious hereabouts (and in most of the rest of the region as well), has a quite deep and limpid ruby hue. On the nose inviting fruity notes are followed by a slightly vegetal tone, accompanied by still rather noticeable sweet and spicy oak. The palate is tannic, with well-judged alcohol and lovely acidity. The Chianti Colli Fiorentini '97, a crisp and succulent wine, if a bit muffled in fragrance, is good; the Chianti Classico Le Masse di Greve is better: brilliant ruby in color, it offers toasty oak aromas followed by fruity notes; in the mouth it is full-bodied and tannic, carrying through consistently to mid palate and the finish, which is slightly bitter. Lastly, the good Vin Santo '94, traditional in style, is delicately sweet and quite complex, with interesting hints of dried chestnut and undergrowth.

●	Terricci '96	🍷🍷	4
●	Chianti Classico Le Masse di Greve '97	🍷	3
●	Chianti Colli Fiorentini '97	🍷	2*
○	Vin Santo '94	🍷	5
●	Terricci '86	🍷🍷	4
●	Terricci '88	🍷🍷	4
●	Terricci '95	🍷🍷	4
●	Chianti Classico Le Masse di Greve '96	🍷	3
●	Chianti Classico Le Masse di Greve Ris. '95	🍷	4
●	Chianti Colli Fiorentini '96	🍷	2
●	Chianti Colli Fiorentini Ris. '95	🍷	3
○	Vin Santo '91	🍷	5

LUCCA

Le Murelle
Fraz. Ponte del Giglio
Via per Camaiore
Trav. Via Cappella
55060 Lucca
tel. 0583/394055

After a few somewhat undistinguished years, Carla and Giampi Moretti's Le Murelle has acquired a voice of its own. Its position and the kind of wine it produces are both singular. The estate lies a dozen kilometers northwest of Lucca, in the Val Freddana, where there's plenty of sun during the day and really quite cold winds at night, hence a consistent and considerable variation in temperature. They have chosen to concentrate on making white wine, a reasonable choice given their climate, but quite unusual for Tuscany. Actually, an interesting red that Giampi Moretti has been preparing with the oenological assistance of Alberto Antonini should be released soon. But to get back to the whites: there are two, and their style is international, i.e. a sauvignon and a chardonnay. The good Chardonnay '98 has a somewhat backward bouquet, but the palate is both crisp and round, as well as structured and well-balanced. But we must confess that we feel more drawn to the decided personality of the Sauvignon. The '98 version has distinctly varietal aromas, sage and peach skin, which come across with clarity and intensity. The attack is only moderately vigorous, but the palate continues to open out all the way to a long finish that mirrors the bouquet.

○	Colline Lucchesi Sauvignon '98	🍷🍷	3*
○	Colline Lucchesi Chardonnay '98	🍷	3

LE PUPILLE

LOC. PERETA
58051 MAGLIANO IN TOSCANA (GR)
TEL. 0564/505129

The excellent Saffredi '97 easily scooped up Three Glasses, which is only what it deserves, as does this estate, which has held high the banner of Scansano for years, believing in its potential well before this area became the height of fashion. High marks to the good work of Elisabetta Geppetti, her husband Stefano Rizzi and the oenologist Riccardo Cotarella. This Saffredi '97 has a very dense, compact pigeon's blood ruby hue and a broad and intense nose with distinct notes of citron and undertones of black and red berries enriched by very elegant hints of spice. The opulent but never cloying palate offers extremely smooth tannins and a great finish that perfectly reflects the nose. Their other wines are good too, starting with the new Morellino cru, Poggio Valente '97. It is of an attractive ruby color and has a complex bouquet with clear fruity and spicy notes, and oak-derived tones in the foreground. The elegant palate shows character, and the tannins are well integrated. The '97 Solalto, a late-harvested wine of constant quality and fair price, also gets Two Glasses. The color is a rich straw verging on gold, and the bouquet includes well-delineated dried fruit, apricot and pineapple. The interesting Morellino Riserva '96 has a fruity nose that is somewhat smothered by wood. With its fine-grained and evenly distributed tannins it makes an impact on the palate.

●	Saffredi '97	🍷🍷🍷	6
●	Morellino di Scansano Poggio Valente '97	🍷🍷	5
●	Morellino di Scansano Ris. '96	🍷🍷	4
○	Solalto '97	🍷🍷	4
○	Vin Santo	🍷🍷	5
●	Morellino di Scansano '98	🍷	3
●	Poggio Argentato '98	🍷	3
●	Saffredi '90	♀♀♀	6
●	Saffredi '88	♀♀	5
●	Saffredi '89	♀♀	5
●	Saffredi '91	♀♀	5
●	Saffredi '93	♀♀	5
●	Saffredi '94	♀♀	5
●	Saffredi '95	♀♀	5

MANTELLASSI - SAN GIUSEPPE

LOC. BANDITACCIA, 26
58051 MAGLIANO IN TOSCANA (GR)
TEL. 0564/592037

It would be hard to find a better-known producer in the Maremma than Mantellassi of Magliano. For years their Morellino has been available practically everywhere in the area – wine shops, restaurants, pizzerias – and for years it has been excellent value for money. Mantellassi has now quietly undertaken a revamping of the style of its wines, and hence here it is again, after a period of non-appearance in the Guide. We'll start with their Morellino di Scansano San Giuseppe '98, a red that reflects the best qualities of this kind of wine: it's fresh, fragrant, fruity, and has lively, if slightly rustic tannins. The Morellino di Scansano Riserva '96 has daringly spent some aging time in little barrels, and this was evident at our tastings: an intense red hue leads to a woody fragrance with a slightly vegetal but agreeable nuance. The palate shows medium body, not very fine phenolics and a still somewhat insistent oaked tone, but it's tasty and of good substance. The other Morellino Riserva, the Le Sentinelle '95, is almost as pleasing but more forward. Garnet-hued, it opens on the nose with tertiary aromas of truffle and damp earth, together with animal notes and candied peel. It's rich, almost soft, in the mouth, and seems to be at its peak. The alicante-based Querciolaia '96 has a fairly intense ruby color, a decisive but not very clearly defined nose (at least at the moment) and remarkable structure with very clear but good oak-derived notes. With its length and tannic weight it should have the extract to keep going for years in the bottle.

●	Morellino di Scansano Ris. '96	🍷🍷	3*
●	Querciolaia '96	🍷🍷	4
●	Morellino di Scansano Le Sentinelle Ris. '95	🍷	4
●	Morellino di Scansano San Giuseppe '98	🍷	4

MANCIANO (GR)

LA STELLATA
VIA FORNACINA, 18
58014 MANCIANO (GR)
TEL. 0564/620190

When the fierce struggle to grab up every available corner of vineyard in the Tuscan Maremma was still a thing of the future, at least in Grosseto province, Manlio and Clara Divizia were already making their famous Bianco di Pitigliano Lunaia. Nine times out of ten that a thirsty diner ordered a cool white wine in a local restaurant it was Lunaia that appeared before him. Now things have changed, but the star of La Stellata is still this typical quaffable white. The '98 version is straightforward, in keeping with its dry and agreeable style. Pale straw yellow in hue, it has an intense pleasing fragrance with notes of citrus fruit. Good extract, fair balance and an appropriate finish characterize the palate. The successful Lunaia Rosso '97 has an attractive red color with cherry highlights, a pleasantly fruity nose, still a bit dumb because of its youth, but with an inviting lightly spicy undertone. In the mouth ripe fruit and full body lead to a long finish. Both of these wines, it should be remembered, offer very good value for money.

○ Bianco di Pitigliano Lunaia '98	🍷	3
● Lunaia Rosso '97	🍷	3
○ Bianco di Pitigliano Lunaia '93	🍷🍷	3*
○ Bianco di Pitigliano Lunaia '92	🍷	3
○ Bianco di Pitigliano Lunaia '94	🍷	2
○ Bianco di Pitigliano Lunaia '95	🍷	3
○ Bianco di Pitigliano Lunaia '96	🍷	3
○ Bianco di Pitigliano Lunaia '97	🍷	3
● Lunaia Rosso '93	🍷	2

MASSA MARITTIMA (GR)

MASSA VECCHIA
PODERE FORNACE
LOC. ROCCHE, 11
58024 MASSA MARITTIMA (GR)
TEL. 0566/915522

Fabrizio Niccolaini is a genuine "vigneron", a type not thick on the ground in Tuscany, and what he has done he has done himself. It would be altogether inappropriate to write a review of his estate listing the names of the proprietor, the oenologist, the agronomist and so on. Massa Vecchia consists entirely of Fabrizio and of his wife Patrizia Bartolini. And his wine conveys the fruit of his extremely individual quest and his firm convictions. You could perhaps question the occasionally unusual style of some of his wines, but there is no question about their individual personality. The first example is his vermentino, Ariento '97, which is matured, if you please, in casks of chestnut wood. Wine technicians of the new school would throw up their hands in horror but, in a blind tasting, it did quite well. Golden-hued, it has interesting and very individual aromas with notes of spice and pennyroyal. The entry on the palate is warm and firm and the general style is austere. We greatly admired his sweet wine, the aleatico-based Matto delle Giuncaie '97, with its characteristic black cherry and wildflower fragrances. The palate is a bit tannic, and there is some roughness, but it is also sweet, juicy and lingering. The other aleatico, Le Veglie di Neri '93, is more forward and somewhat unbalanced by medicinal notes, but it has a dry, singular, in no way run-of-the-mill palate. The interesting Patrizia Bartolini '97, made from late-harvested sauvignon, is redolent of vanilla and tomato leaf. The most 'normal' wine he offers is the cabernet, La Fonte di Pietrarsa '96, which displays a lovely intense ruby color, a clean bouquet with notes of dark fruit and vegetal nuances, and a soft, even palate with a long finish.

● Il Matto delle Giuncaie '97	🍷🍷	4
● La Fonte di Pietrarsa '96	🍷🍷	4
○ Monteregio di Massa Marittima Bianco Ariento '97	🍷	4
○ Patrizia Bartolini '97	🍷	4
● Le Veglie di Neri '93		4
● La Fonte di Pietrarsa '92	🍷🍷	4
● La Fonte di Pietrarsa '93	🍷🍷	4
● La Fonte di Pietrarsa '94	🍷🍷	4
● La Fonte di Pietrarsa '95	🍷🍷	4
● Terziere '93	🍷🍷	4
● Le Veglie di Neri '90	🍷	4
○ Patrizia Bartolini '96	🍷	4
● Terziere '96	🍷	4

MASSA MARITTIMA (GR)

Moris Farms
Loc. Curanuova
58024 Massa Marittima (GR)
tel. 0566/919135

The Moris Farms team is made up of first-class players: Andrea Paoletti, who looks after viticulture, and the distinguished oenologist Attilio Pagli, who watches over every phase of vinification. Our last tastings confirmed and reinforced our conviction that some of the most successful wines of the Maremma come from this lovely estate. This success consists not only in weight and concentration, but also, notably, in personality and style. This time we're starting our review not with their top wine, the celebrated Avvoltore, but with their basic red. The Morellino di Scansano '98, a simple and direct wine (as it should be), has an inviting fragrance of raspberry and cherry, and a not inconsiderable structure coexists easily with great quaffability. The Morellino Riserva '97 is of course a wine of greater scope. A dark dense ruby in color, it has intensely fruity aromas on a classic overripe base with notes of black cherry jam. Powerful extract, full body and a rich almost meaty quality characterize the palate. A lingering finish reveals mature tannins. And now for the Avvoltore '97: a lovely intense ruby hue which, dense as it is, still shows brilliant highlights is the prelude to a fruity bouquet, warm and very ripe, with notes of cherry, plum and blackberry jam. The oak is already quite well blended. In the mouth it's very powerful and fleshy, with solid and fine-grained tannins. Excellent, in a word.

●	Avvoltore '97	▼▼	5
●	Morellino di Scansano Ris. '97	▼▼	4
●	Morellino di Scansano '98	▼	2*
●	Avvoltore '94	▽▽	5
●	Avvoltore '95	▽▽	5
●	Morellino di Scansano Ris. '94	▽▽	4
●	Avvoltore '93	▽	5
●	Morellino di Scansano '94	▽	2*
●	Morellino di Scansano '95	▽	2*
●	Morellino di Scansano Ris. '93	▽	4

MATRAIA (LU)

Fattoria Colle Verde
Loc. Castello
55010 Matraia (LU)
tel. 0583/402256

Last year's debut in the Guide has been followed by a noteworthy performance from Francesca Pardini and Piero Tartagni's beautiful estate in the hills near Lucca. Had it not been for a series of hitches, making it impossible for us to taste their wines in previous years, they would probably have figured in these pages a good bit earlier. This year too, however, our review is incomplete, because neither their passito (raisin wine), Greco delle Gaggie, nor their trebbiano- and chardonnay-based Brania del Cancello was available for tasting in time. Nevertheless we did admire what was available, and most especially the distinguished Brania delle Ghiandaie '96. This red, a Colle Verde DOC which did not suffer particularly from the disadvantages of its vintage, got positive comments from everyone. An intense and lovely ruby color leads to a deep bouquet with a variety of mineral, dark fruit and licorice aromas. The entry on the palate is vigorous, there's a lot of body and concentration, and the mature tannins have a drying effect on the finish. This is a red wine made in an up-to-date manner, but it shows a touch of classic style that does not hurt it at all. The well-made Matraia Bianco '97 is characterful and distinctly appealing. The Matraia Rosso '97 is less winning, but certainly better than just acceptable.

●	Colline Lucchesi Rosso Brania delle Ghiandaie '96	▼▼	4
○	Colline Lucchesi Bianco Terre di Matraja '97	▼	3
●	Colline Lucchesi Rosso Terre di Matraja '97		3
○	Brania del Cancello '97	▽▽	4
●	Colline Lucchesi Rosso Brania delle Ghiandaie '95	▽▽	4
○	Greco delle Gaggìe '95	▽	4

MERCATALE VAL DI PESA (FI)

ISPOLI
VIA SANTA LUCIA, 2
50024 MERCATALE VAL DI PESA (FI)
TEL. 055/821613

This little estate has made a great debut in the Guide. In the 16th century it was the property of the Machiavellis, and now it belongs to the Mattheis family, husband and wife. Grapevines have been tended here at least since the 17th century, as contemporary documents show, and their position, between woods and olive groves 300 meters above sea level, is a good one. Organic principles guide production and the results this year are excellent. The Chianti Classico '97 is a vivid deep ruby red. Ripe concentrated fruit, such as blackberry and blueberry, is elegantly blended with vanilla in a bouquet enhanced by spicy hints of pepper and cinnamon. The attack on the palate is very well-balanced, not grand but steady, with acidity holding its own with the alcohol. The tannins are close-knit but soft and just properly succulent. The finish is long, harmonious and as it should be. The IGT Ispolaia is a sangiovese with a little cabernet sauvignon. The '96 displays a most inviting ruby hue still richly shot through with purple. The bouquet, after an initial fragrance of crushed red berries, opens to tertiary aromas, with coffee and chocolate slowly emerging. The entry on the palate is decided and powerful, and tannins announce their presence. In mid palate astringency recedes as balance is achieved with the alcohol and acidity, and the finish is long and lingering.

● Chianti Classico '97	🍷🍷	3*
● Ispolaia '96	🍷🍷	4

MERCATALE VALDARNO (AR)

PODERE IL CARNASCIALE
LOC. SAN LEONINO, 82
52021 MERCATALE VALDARNO (AR)
TEL. 055/9911142

It couldn't be said that Il Carnasciale is short on personality or originality. They make only one wine, bottled exclusively in magnums. It's just as well, under the circumstances, that the wine is their splendid Caberlot. This name gives a hint about the grape variety used, which is in fact a genetic mutation of cabernet with some of the characteristics of merlot, first discovered in the early '60s in an old vineyard in the Euganean Hills. And what a grape it is, to judge from the very concentrated and mature wine it gives rise to! It's no accident that the average yield is 750 grams (!) per vine. We must admit that the Caberlot '96 would easily have carried off Three Glasses if it were not the case that a mere thousand bottles are produced, and we have made it a policy not to give our highest award to wines that are essentially unfindable. But it is magnificent. In the glass it shows an intense saturated ruby hue. A very broad and well-defined range of aromas greets the nose, suggesting wild cherry, black currant, fresh plum and well-judged new oak (toasty bread and cinnamon). The attack on the palate is explosive, rich and full, and it follows through with absolute consistency. The tannins show exemplary finesse, the alcohol is warm, but not excessive. A superb red wine, in short, the short supply of which holds it down to 'only' Two Glasses. But soon the vineyard, which currently covers less than half a hectare, will be extended, and then Caberlot will most probably have the recognition it deserves.

● Caberlot '96	🍷🍷	6

MERCATALE VALDARNO (AR)

FATTORIA PETROLO
LOC. GALATRONA
52020 MERCATALE VALDARNO (AR)
TEL. 055/9911322 - 055/992965

Last year we finished our review by saying we suspected that Lucia Sanjust's Fattoria Petrolo might have some pleasant surprises in store for us. And indeed her Galatrona '97, which stood out at our tastings and won Three Glasses with ease, was a lovely surprise. Do we hear faint mutterings about our excessive fondness for merlot, cabernet and such? Well, just try tasting this wine, whatever your personal preferences may be, and we think you'll take off your hat to it. It's a great red with exceptional substance and a strong individual personality. The color is dark and dense; the nose is concentrated and richly, deeply fruity and, at the moment, pervaded by toasty oak. Its real nature is revealed on the palate: a powerful and vigorous attack, a very dense and broad mid palate and a finish that just goes on and on. The rest of the range is relegated somewhat to the background by this masterpiece, but the good classic sangiovese, Torrione '96, has admirable personality, good sweet fruit and a pleasing finish. There is, however, too much wood in this vintage, and it gets in the way of self-expression and harmony. The varieties used in the two estate champions are blended to make the Terre di Galatrona '97, which is clearly a simpler wine, but nevertheless an agreeable and satisfying one.

●	Galatrona '97	3 glasses (black)	6
●	Terre di Galatrona '97	1 glass (black)	4
●	Torrione '96	1 glass (black)	5
●	Chianti Titolato Ris. '90	2 glasses	4
●	Galatrona '95	2 glasses	6
●	Torrione '90	2 glasses	5
●	Torrione '94	2 glasses	5
●	Torrione '95	2 glasses	5
○	Vin Santo '93	2 glasses	5
●	Chianti Titolato '90	1 glass	2*
●	Chianti Titolato '91	1 glass	3
●	Galatrona '94	1 glass	6
●	Torrione '88	1 glass	5
●	Torrione '91	1 glass	5
●	Torrione '93	1 glass	5

MONTAGNANA VAL DI PESA (FI)

LE CALVANE
VIA CASTIGLIONI, 1
50020 MONTAGNANA VAL DI PESA (FI)
TEL. 0571/671073

This year Le Calvane didn't stop at proving itself yet again to be among the finest producers in the Florentine area: it also astonished us with the brilliant performance of its cabernet, the '96 Borro del Boscone. This is a wine of strong character and noteworthy concentration, and it came awfully close to top ranking. Its color is dark and concentrated, and an intense nose with a rich array of black berries and vegetal nuances is followed by a powerful attack on the palate and substantial body with imposing tannins. This is an excellent red that should last for years. We were surprised by how much we liked Il Trecione Riserva '96, which won Two Glasses, something of an anomaly for this category. It has medium body but was conceived as a wine that would please by dint of its great cleanliness and excellent balance. The well-made Chianti '98 has an agreeably fruity nose with notes of cherry and raspberry; the palate is correct, but a bit thin and short. The Sorbino '98 boasts the same aromatic distinctness that their other wines offer and, although simple, is well executed and very pleasant. A hair's breadth away from Two Glasses, the Vin Santo Zipolo d'Oro '92 is amber-colored and wafts a heady bouquet featuring notes of custard, dried fruits and candied peel. It has a fairly powerful attack and progresses well, with a fine corresponding finish.

●	Borro del Boscone '96	2 glasses (black)	5
●	Chianti Colli Fiorentini Il Trecione Ris. '96	2 glasses (black)	4
○	Sorbino '98	1 glass (black)	3
○	Vin Santo Zipolo d'Oro '92	1 glass (black)	4
●	Chianti Colli Fiorentini '98		3
●	Borro del Boscone '91	2 glasses	4
●	Borro del Boscone '94	2 glasses	4
●	Borro del Boscone '95	2 glasses	5
●	Chianti Colli Fiorentini Il Trecione Ris. '91	2 glasses	4
●	Chianti Colli Fiorentini Quercione '96	1 glass	3
●	Chianti Colli Fiorentini Quercione '97	1 glass	3

MONTALCINO (SI)

ALTESINO
LOC. TORRENIERI
53028 MONTALCINO (SI)
TEL. 0577/806208

The Altesino Vin Santo '94 is really splendid. This was our first chance to taste it, and the impact was immediate, pushing it to the top of their list this year. It has an intense and luminous color and a lovely rich nose, with tones of cocoa, dried fruit and candied peel. And it keeps its promise on the palate, where a slightly acid note underpins the good extract and beautifully balanced residual sugars. A very nice debut and Two Glasses, hands down. News from the red wine front is less brilliant but still quite satisfactory; indeed this producer had long since taught us to expect nothing less. We well remember that Altesino did not release a Brunello from the Montosoli cru in '94, because they felt the vintage was not up to standard. The '93 Riserva shows notable structure, with slightly spiky tannins disturbing the mid palate, but the finish is substantial. The bouquet includes agreeably intense notes of blackberry and cherry jam. The '94 Brunello has put its money on elegance, paying for its charm with diminished concentration, as you can see from its rather lightweight finish. The Alte d'Altesi and the Palazzo d'Altesi, both '96s, are very properly made and easily earn One Glass each. We slightly preferred the former.

○	Vin Santo '94	🍷🍷	6
●	Alte d'Altesi '96	🍷	5
●	Brunello di Montalcino '94	🍷	6
●	Brunello di Montalcino Ris. '93	🍷	6
●	Palazzo d'Altesi '96	🍷	5
●	Brunello di Montalcino '93	YY	5
●	Brunello di Montalcino Montosoli '93	YY	6
●	Brunello di Montalcino Ris. '88	YY	6
●	Brunello di Montalcino Ris. '90	YY	6
●	Quarto d'Altesi '95	YY	6
●	Alte d'Altesi '95	Y	5
●	Borgo d'Altesi '95	Y	4
●	Brunello di Montalcino '90	Y	5
●	Brunello di Montalcino Montosoli '90	Y	5
●	Palazzo d'Altesi '95	Y	4

MONTALCINO (SI)

TENUTA DI ARGIANO
LOC. S. ANGELO IN COLLE, 54
53020 MONTALCINO (SI)
TEL. 0577/844037

The vineyards of Montalcino are often sliced up into many small plots. Argiano is an exception, with almost 20 hectares under vine, no small matter in these parts. This should allow them to offset to some extent the difficulties of a problematic vintage and to produce good wines year after year. This time, however, their wines reflect varying degrees of success, ranging from absolute excellence to the simply acceptable. The '97 Rosso di Montalcino shows some uncertainties on both nose and palate; hence a fair wine, but rating no more than mention. The Brunello '97 is more successful. It has a good ruby color tinged with garnet. An initial trace of sulfur on the nose gives way to a warm heady tone, fading off on a faintly overripe jammy note. The palate has good body and solid tannins; it's long on finish but somewhat short on freshness. We have left till last the Argiano flagship, their Solenga. The '97 version is frankly superb. A dark, saturated red hue heralds an extraordinary richness, and indeed the nose offers an impressive range of fruit, from wild blackberry to blueberry and ripe plum, the whole perfectly blended with a nuance of smoky oak, present but safely under control. The density on the palate is remarkable; warmth and powerful extract, rather than elegance, are its strong suit: a rich, mature, intense and very long-lingering wine that commands Three Glasses.

●	Solengo '97	🍷🍷🍷	6
●	Brunello di Montalcino '94	🍷🍷	6
●	Rosso di Montalcino '97		3
●	Brunello di Montalcino Ris. '85	YYY	5
●	Brunello di Montalcino Ris. '88	YYY	6
●	Solengo '95	YYY	6
●	Brunello di Montalcino '85	YY	5
●	Brunello di Montalcino '87	YY	5
●	Brunello di Montalcino '88	YY	5
●	Brunello di Montalcino '90	YY	5
●	Brunello di Montalcino '92	YY	6
●	Brunello di Montalcino '93	YY	6
●	Brunello di Montalcino Ris. '90	YY	6
●	Brunello di Montalcino Ris. '91	YY	6
●	Solengo '96	YY	6

MONTALCINO (SI)

Castello Banfi
Castello di Poggio alle Mura
53024 Montalcino (SI)
tel. 0577/840111

There's nothing new about the great collection of Glasses for this great domain (154 hectares for Brunello alone). The news is that Pablo Harri, who has been in charge of production, left Banfi after the '99 harvest – but not before having turned out yet another superb wine: his Brunello di Montalcino Poggio all'Oro '93 is living proof that a wine doesn't have to be muscle-bound in order to become a champion. This is a really elegant wine, with a long-lingering palate that faithfully echoes the initial bouquet on the finish: notes of red fruit, black currant and cherry mingling with spicier scents of eucalyptus and vanilla. The flavors show an impeccable harmony, the acid/tannic component in perfect balance with the soft glycero/alcoholic side. In other words, this is a Brunello based on style rather than steroids. The Summus '96 is also very good, but this time stops just short of Three Glasses. The fruit of a sangiovese-syrah-cabernet sauvignon blend, it proffers a strong nose, with toasty notes of coffee and caramel underpinned by black and red fruit; the palate is beautifully balanced, with mouth-filling body and slightly prominent wood. As for Excelsus '95, that too teeters in a "Two-and-a-half" Glass position: a Bordeaux blend, it will want a bit more time in the bottle before it expresses its full potential. As usual, all the other wines are good and well made: the Rosso di Montalcino '97 joins the Two Glass category alongside the Mandrielle '96 and the Fontanelle '97. That Rosso di Montalcino '97 is a particular charmer, by the way: clearly etched fruity aromas based on ripe cherry, followed by an extremely drinkable balance of flavors.

●	Brunello di Montalcino Poggio all'Oro Ris. '93	🍷🍷🍷	6
●	Excelsus '95	🍷🍷	6
○	Fontanelle Chardonnay '97	🍷🍷	4
●	Mandrielle Merlot '96	🍷🍷	4
●	Rosso di Montalcino '97	🍷🍷	4
●	Summus '96	🍷🍷	6
●	Brunello di Montalcino '94	🍷	5
●	Toscana Centine '97	🍷	4
●	Brunello di Montalcino Poggio all'Oro '88	YYY	6
●	Brunello di Montalcino Poggio all'Oro Ris. '90	YYY	6
●	Excelsus '93	YYY	6
●	Summus '95	YYY	6

MONTALCINO (SI)

Fattoria dei Barbi
Loc. Podernovi
53024 Montalcino (SI)
tel. 0577/848277

We were reassured by the results of this year's tastings at the historic Barbi estate: the Vigna del Fiore is still their best wine; the Brunello '94 makes a very good showing considering the average for that year, and all the other wines we tasted were very satisfactory or at least well made, and certainly nothing to be ashamed of. So all's well at Barbi, just as we had expected. As we said, the Vigna del Fiore '93 was yet again the general favorite. It captures your interest from the very outset, with a range of rich and intense aromas including toasty oak, spice, aromatic herbs and licorice. After a mouth-filling entry, this wine opens up in a fine progression, and is balanced and clean in its finish, which lasts a bit more than the average. It has a stylistic rigor that certainly contributes towards its Two Glasses. To tell the truth, the Brunello di Montalcino '94 almost made it to that rank as well: some quite concentrated aromas based with a certain austerity on tertiary notes of leather, tobacco and blackberry jam lead up to a palate of considerable volume; the fabric of the tannins shows a degree of evolution and the finish is moderately long. The Rosso di Montalcino is somewhat difficult to judge: the palate is nice and rich but the nose is marked by elements of overripeness. At their new estate in the Maremma they have produced their very first Morellino di Scansano, which has made a promising debut, although with slight aromatic imperfections. As to the Brigante '95, it makes quite a good impression, but suffers from excessive vegetal tones and a bitter edge. And, last of all, the Brusco '97 is a well-made wine.

●	Brunello di Montalcino Vigna del Fiore Ris. '93	🍷🍷	6
●	Brigante dei Barbi '95	🍷	5
●	Brunello di Montalcino '94	🍷	5
●	Morellino di Scansano '98	🍷	3
●	Brusco dei Barbi '97		3
●	Brunello di Montalcino '93	YY	5
●	Brunello di Montalcino Ris. '88	YY	6
●	Brunello di Montalcino Vigna del Fiore Ris. '88	YY	6
●	Brunello di Montalcino Vigna del Fiore Ris. '90	YY	6
●	Brunello di Montalcino Vigna del Fiore Ris. '91	YY	6
●	Brunello di Montalcino Ris. '90	Y	6

MONTALCINO (SI)

Biondi Santi
Loc. Greppo
53024 Montalcino (SI)
tel. 0577/847121 - 0577/848087

In this review we are reporting on wines marketed by Jacopo Biondi-Santi, the last producer in the famous "founding family" of Brunello. So in addition to the Greppo Biondi-Santi wines we also cover those from the Poggio Salvi, another Montalcino label, as well as some fruits of the combined efforts of Jacopo Biondi-Santi and Vittorio Fiore, one of the best-known oenologists around. We sampled two Brunellos from the Greppo estate, a '93 and a '94, and were surprised to find that the better wine was the one from the supposedly less successful vintage. The '94 Brunello is of a ruby color tending to garnet, of medium density, with ripe aromas, including notes of tobacco and undergrowth, shot through with a light fruitiness. The attack is good, as is the progression, though the wine does not seem muscular, but does show finesse, without acidic or tannic excess. The Poggio Salvi Brunello di Montalcino '94 is also a well-made wine. No Hercules, but nicely built and easy to drink. The Aurico '96 is engaging: late-harvested, with intense notes of anise and apricot, it has a sweet but not cloying attack, thanks to a good acidity, and the finish is generous and leisurely, the flavors corresponding very nicely with the bouquet. Sassalloro continues on its upward course; the '97 version offers an aromatic complexity, where tones of blackberry and black currant mingle comfortably with the oak-derived caramel and vanilla notes. On the palate it reveals fine balance and an excellent, far-reaching finish.

● Aurico '96	▼▼	6
● Brunello di Montalcino '94	▼▼	6
● Sassoalloro '97	▼▼	5
● Brunello di Montalcino '93	▼	6
● Brunello di Montalcino Poggio Salvi '94	▼	6
● Brunello di Montalcino '83	▽▽▽	6
● Brunello di Montalcino '90	▽▽	6
● Brunello di Montalcino Poggio Salvi '93	▽▽	6
● Sassoalloro '93	▽▽	4
● Sassoalloro '94	▽▽	5
● Sassoalloro '95	▽▽	5
● Schidione '93	▽▽	6
● Schidione '94	▽▽	6

MONTALCINO (SI)

Campogiovanni
Loc. S. Angelo in Colle
53024 Montalcino (SI)
tel. 0577/864001 - 0577/864001

This year's was not one of Campogiovanni's most unforgettable performances. The only wine produced just barely squeaked through to a One Glass rating. This Brunello di Montalcino '94 has a garnet color and a nose of medium intensity, with some free-standing woody tones preceding the fruity aromas. The palate is all right, although its tannins are also somewhat separate from the rest: this in turn inhibits the finish, leaving it a bit rough and incomplete. Granted, '94 was not the best of years, but we still feel Campogiovanni could do better, and should. Their vines are rooted in a soil with excellent potential, and the ten hectares sloping down from S. Angelo in Colle towards the Maremma couldn't ask for a better exposure. This estate belongs to San Felice of Castelnuovo Berardenga, an important Chianti winery which has recently embarked on an experimental planting program, creating a new ultra-high-density vineyard with some ten thousand vines per hectare. This is an absolute first for Montalcino. The Campogiovanni cellar is admirably efficient and increasingly stocked with small French oak casks, which will be phasing out the more traditional barrels. This choice is a consequence of the very positive results obtained by S. Felice with its sangiovese.

● Brunello di Montalcino '94	▼	6
● Brunello di Montalcino '87	▽▽	5
● Brunello di Montalcino '88	▽▽	5
● Brunello di Montalcino '89	▽▽	5
● Brunello di Montalcino '90	▽▽	5
● Brunello di Montalcino Vigna del Quercione Ris. '90	▽▽	6
● Brunello di Montalcino '85	▽	5
● Brunello di Montalcino '86	▽	5
● Brunello di Montalcino '93	▽	6

MONTALCINO (SI)

Canalicchio di Sopra di Rosildo e Franco Pacenti

Via Canalicchio di Sopra
53024 Montalcino (SI)
tel. 0577/849277

Rosildo and Franco Pacenti are not fond of over-powerful wines; finesse and harmoniousness tend to characterize their offerings, and this year was no exception. Both the Brunellos and the Rosso – each according to its type, of course – are of medium body and medium concentration. Starting with the Rosso di Montalcino '97, we find a successful and highly drinkable wine, albeit with a few rough edges, as one might expect at this adolescent stage of its development. It shows a good bright ruby color and a nose of black cherry slightly veiled by a whiff of sulfur. The palate is characteristic, with a pleasing attack, but the tannins are still a bit harsh. A few years' patience should bring out the best in this wine. The Brunello di Montalcino '94 is somewhat shy and undefined on the nose: the dominant notes are a rather uncompromising licorice root, rhubarb and pencil lead. As for the palate, it has good extract, tannic at the core but fruity too, and a nice long bitterish finish. Although '94 may not have been the very best vintage, this wine ought to open up and come into its own with a few more years in the bottle. The Brunello Riserva '93 struck us as the best red of the house. A ruby hue with faint garnet highlights introduces a pleasantly progressing nose, with scents of toasted bread, sour cherry and bay leaf. On the palate it attacks with a warm, heady punch, proceeds on an intense and frankly tannic note, and finishes long and pleasantly bitter. It looks as though this wine has the raw material and balance it needs in order to go on improving for a good long time.

●	Brunello di Montalcino Ris. '93	🍷🍷	5
●	Brunello di Montalcino '94	🍷	4
●	Rosso di Montalcino '97	🍷	4
●	Brunello di Montalcino '93	🍸🍸	5
●	Brunello di Montalcino '92	🍸	5
●	Rosso di Montalcino '95	🍸	4
●	Rosso di Montalcino '96	🍸	4

MONTALCINO (SI)

Tenuta Caparzo

Loc. Torrenieri
53028 Montalcino (SI)
tel. 0577/848390 - 0577/847166

Caparzo has made a very good showing, with four different wines earning Two Glasses apiece. So it seems that those readjustments in management have had a far from negative impact on the cellar. The Turone-Fiore twosome, with the former running the business and the latter making the wine, is turning out to be one of the most dynamic teams in the area. Carpazo can rely on two fine crus: at Montosoli, on Montalcino's northern slope, where Brunello La Casa comes from, and at Castelgiocondo, further up the hill. Some fans will be disappointed at the absence of any Three Glass awards, but two of the Caparzo wines do stand at the summit of their respective categories this year. The Brunello di Montalcino La Casa '94 is a delicious wine. Of an intense ruby color, it has equally intense fruity scents, only slightly crowded by notes of caramel, vanilla, and roasted coffee. As for the palate, it is simply enchanting: closely knit and showing fine tannins and an excellent body (especially considering the vintage), it boasts a long and persuasive finish. We also liked the Moscadello '96 very much: it is a very successful, well-focused late-harvested wine, with overtones of candied fruit and dried apricot; in the mouth it has fine concentration, very nicely balanced by the fresh acidity that plays beautifully against its sweetness. It stands among the very best of this type. The quartet of Two Glass winners is completed by the juicy Rosso di Montalcino La Caduta in its impressive '97 version, and by the Brunello di Montalcino Riserva '93, a well-made and very harmonious wine. The other three wines we tasted rate One Glass apiece, further evidence of the great reliability of this estate.

●	Brunello di Montalcino La Casa '94	🍷🍷	6
●	Brunello di Montalcino Ris. '93	🍷🍷	6
○	Moscadello V. T. '96	🍷🍷	5
●	Rosso di Montalcino La Caduta '97	🍷🍷	4
●	Brunello di Montalcino '94	🍷	5
●	Ca' del Pazzo '95	🍷	5
●	Rosso di Montalcino '97	🍷	4
●	Brunello di Montalcino La Casa '88	🍸🍸🍸	6
●	Brunello di Montalcino La Casa '93	🍸🍸🍸	6
●	Brunello di Montalcino '88	🍸🍸	6
●	Brunello di Montalcino '93	🍸🍸	6
●	Brunello di Montalcino La Casa '85	🍸🍸	6
●	Brunello di Montalcino La Casa '86	🍸🍸	6
●	Brunello di Montalcino La Casa '91	🍸🍸	5
●	Brunello di Montalcino Ris. '88	🍸🍸	6

Casanova di Neri

Loc. Torrenieri
53028 Montalcino (SI)
tel. 0577/834029

If they took bets on wines, we would have no hesitation about putting good money on the future success of Giacomo Neri's work. Not that there's anything wrong with it right now – far from it; but the dedication and clarity with which he has charted his course assure us that the coming years will see a continuous rise in the fortunes of his Brunello. He can bank on the star quality of his new vineyards, sited in Castelnuovo dell'Abate, one of the most coveted spots in the whole Montalcino area and the focus of his future projects. The Riserva Cerretalto '93 is an authoritative Brunello with character to spare. Powerful and concentrated, it is a fine specimen of its type and its year, which did not generally yield great fleshiness, as witnessed by the clear oak-derived vanilla and toasty tones, and the still slightly acidic bite of the finish. The Tenuta Nuova '94 is less vigorous: it has a mellow, well-supported, compact structure, and is surely one of the best Brunellos from this inauspicious vintage. We take this as an indication of the excellence this estate promises, and will undoubtedly deliver, as soon as it can count on the support of a richer, more complete harvest. The Brunello di Montalcino did well: it is less solid than the two special selections, but successful all the same. well designed and balanced. The '97 Rosso was quite interesting too; it almost netted Two Glasses, having plenty of excellent stuffing and a very good outlook for improvement.

● Brunello di Montalcino Cerretalto Ris. '93	⯊⯊ (two black glasses)	6
● Brunello di Montalcino Tenuta Nuova '94	two black glasses	6
● Brunello di Montalcino '94	one black glass	5
● Rosso di Montalcino '97	one black glass	4
● Brunello di Montalcino Cerretalto Ris. '88	three white glasses	6*
● Brunello di Montalcino '88	two white glasses	6
● Brunello di Montalcino '89	two white glasses	6
● Brunello di Montalcino '90	two white glasses	5
● Brunello di Montalcino '91	two white glasses	6
● Brunello di Montalcino '93	two white glasses	5
● Brunello di Montalcino Tenuta Nuova '93	two white glasses	6

Fattoria del Casato Donatella Cinelli Colombini

Loc. Podernovi
53024 Montalcino (SI)
tel. 0577/848277

After having run the family business (the famous Barbi estate) for years, Donatella Cinelli Colombini has begun putting out her own label. La Fattoria del Casato is only one year old and is already getting good results, earning her a place in the Guide. Donatella's experience in this field is a guarantee for the future growth of her winery. She has received One Glass apiece for the wines we tasted: not a bad showing, especially since both the Brunellos come from the controversial '94 vintage. The Brunello di Montalcino Prime Donne is an interesting one, designed by a very skillful panel of women: it is in fact named for the group of experts who worked out the final blending. Its very deep intense ruby color wins it Two Glasses. The nose shows some slightly vegetal notes that mask the underlying fruity verve. It has a palate of medium intensity, a finish on the light side, and a touch too much tannin in need of greater maturity. The '94 Brunello takes a more classical approach; we meet again with that little vegetal note on the nose, but this time accompanied by a nuance of slightly overripe fruit; the palate betrays some not very fine tannins. The new wine here, the Leone Rosso '98, seems well focused: there's an intense fruitiness, fresh and clean, featuring notes of wild and other cherries. The palate is well balanced, free of any tannic excess and readily drinkable.

● Brunello di Montalcino Prime Donne '94	two black glasses	6
● Brunello di Montalcino '94	one black glass	6
● Leone Rosso '98	one black glass	4
● Brunello di Montalcino '93	two white glasses	5
● Brunello di Montalcino Prime Donne '93	two white glasses	6

MONTALCINO (SI)

CASTELGIOCONDO
LOC. CASTELGIOCONDO
53024 MONTALCINO (SI)
TEL. 055/27141

This estate has impressive potential: a good 130 hectares under vine, all registered as DOCG Brunello, and a technical staff which, under the able guidance of the oenologist Niccolò d'Afflitto, is more than up to the task. Castelgiocondo's star is certainly a rising one, especially in the light of their much talked-about alliance with the Mondavi winery of California. The tastings went well. We started with a '94 Brunello, which was pleasant and well made, but a bit anemic – no doubt the fault of the vintage. The ruby color is of medium intensity with a garnet tinge. As the nose develops, it releases a very fresh fruity note, followed by some less lively secondary aromas. The palate is well balanced, clean, and rich in alcohol, with medium-grained tannins well reined in, and a more acidic finish. The Rosso di Montalcino Campo ai Sassi was much more successful. This is a house classic, and the '97 version is tonic, fragrant, and harmonious. We particularly enjoyed the progression on the palate, supported as it is by soft, ripe extract (although the attack is just a bit acidic). This is head and shoulders above the previous version. Coming from such an undistinguished vintage, the Lamaione '96 is fortunate to have the softness of merlot to fall back on: round and tasty in the mouth, it shows a proper aromatic development, although some grassy tones reveal the earliness of the harvest. Castelgiocondo also presented a very glamorous "designer" wine, the Brunello F&F '93: this is a red born of the union of Frescobaldi (which owns this estate) and Gianfranco Ferré, the famous Italian fashion house. Since it is a one-shot deal (with a "unique label" made of a swatch of costly fabric), we will simply mention it in passing: it is an agreeable, well-made wine.

● Lamaione '96	▼▼	5
● Rosso di Montalcino Campo ai Sassi '97	▼▼	4
● Brunello di Montalcino '94	▼	5
● Brunello di Montalcino Ris. '88	▽▽▽	6
● Brunello di Montalcino Ris. '90	▽▽▽	6
● Brunello di Montalcino '89	▽▽	5
● Brunello di Montalcino '90	▽▽	5
● Brunello di Montalcino '93	▽▽	5
● Brunello di Montalcino '91	▽▽	5
● Lamaione '91	▽▽	5
● Lamaione '92	▽▽	5
● Lamaione '94	▽▽	5
● Lamaione '95	▽▽	5

MONTALCINO (SI)

CERBAIONA
LOC. CERBAIONA
53024 MONTALCINO (SI)
TEL. 0577/848660

Diego Molinari is most welcome back to the Guide, after his almost voluntary "exile" from our pages last year (he didn't make a Brunello '92) and after the mixed reactions to his Brunello '93. In the meantime, much has been happening at this ex-pilot's estate, where he is brilliantly assisted by his wife Nora. They had been experimenting with a wide variety of vines other than sangiovese, and have now narrowed down their choices, working mainly with cabernet sauvignon and merlot (as well as two others which Molinari prefers not to name: he says, "The important thing is to like the wine, not how it's made"). There are no doubts about the quality of the Cerbaiona '96, which is almost worth Two Glasses, in spite of its rather lackluster year of origin. It is intriguing and elegant on the nose, with a spicy touch to upgrade the otherwise muted primary fruit; the palate reveals good dense extract and nice smooth tannins. That wood-borne spiciness is something new at Cerbaiona; it comes from the Slovenian oak tonneaux (some 700 liters in capacity) they are now using for the aging process. After a few trials the more predictable barriques have been set aside: "We can get an interesting wine out of them, but nothing special. Kind of sweet for our taste" was all the explanation we got. It is in the '94 Brunello that we recognized the sober, austere style that has won Cerbaiona several Three Glass awards in the past. This wine needs a bit of breathing time before it comes into its own, but when it does, you get the classic nose, with notes of black and wild cherries, and that familiar suggestion of licorice hovering in the background, which is a sort of house trademark. A well-structured palate, with compact and legible tannins that fit nicely into the structure finishes nicely, with just the right degree of bitterness.

● Brunello di Montalcino '94	▼▼	6
● Cerbaiona '96	▼	5
● Brunello di Montalcino '85	▽▽▽	6
● Brunello di Montalcino '88	▽▽▽	6
● Brunello di Montalcino '90	▽▽▽	6
● Brunello di Montalcino '91	▽▽	6
● Brunello di Montalcino '89	▽	6
● Cerbaiona '93	▽	5

MONTALCINO (SI)

COL D'ORCIA
LOC. S. ANGELO IN COLLE
53020 MONTALCINO (SI)
TEL. 0577/808001

Under the able management of Edoardo Virano, Col d'Orcia has proven its reliability and its ability, in a good year, to turn out very interesting wines. Two eloquent examples are the Brunello di Montalcino Poggio al Vento and the Olmaia, made from cabernet. Not content to rest on its laurels, Col d'Orcia continues to invest in improvements both agronomic and oenological. The new high-density Banditella vineyard lies in the southern sector of Montalcino, at an altitude of 300 meters, in low-clay soil with streaks of marl. The result of a decade's worth of experimentation with sangiovese clones and soil types, Banditella will be the source of a new Brunello, to be aged in barriques. Technical innovations take the form of a new oenologist, Pablo Harri, well known in these parts for his work at the Banfi estate. And now for this year's tastings, which confirmed the high quality of Col d'Orcia's wines, even if they do not include a champion. For the first time in its illustrious history, the eagerly-awaited Brunello di Montalcino Poggio al Vento has failed to earn Three Glasses. This is mainly due to somewhat uncontrolled acidity and tannins; the attractive broad bouquet, on the other hand, includes notes of wild cherry, licorice and cherry jam. The '95 Olmaia performed much better: the nose offers intense toasty and mineral aromas with vegetal undertones; the palate, immediately powerful, displays good tannins and a convincing close. It is an excellent wine, and with a touch more elegance it would be even better. We had no trouble at all awarding Two Glasses to the Pescena '95, a passito (semi-dried) muscatel with beautifully balanced flavors and a fragrance of candied fruit and orange blossom.

●	Brunello di Montalcino Poggio al Vento Ris. '93	▼▼	6
○	Moscadello di Montalcino Vendemmia Tardiva Pascena '95	▼▼	5
●	Olmaia '95	▼▼	6
●	Brunello di Montalcino '94	▼	5
●	Rosso di Montalcino '97	▼	3
●	Brunello di Montalcino Poggio al Vento Ris. '85	▽▽▽	6
●	Brunello di Montalcino Poggio al Vento Ris. '88	▽▽▽	6
●	Brunello di Montalcino Poggio al Vento Ris. '90	▽▽▽	6
●	Olmaia '94	▽▽▽	5
●	Olmaia '93	▽▽	5

MONTALCINO (SI)

ANDREA COSTANTI
LOC. COLLE AL MATRICHESE
53024 MONTALCINO (SI)
TEL. 0577/848195

Andrea Costanti's estate is one of the most reliable in Montalcino. It produces very interesting wines and serves as a weathervane for the performance of a vintage on the market. Some seven hectares dedicated to Brunello lie right near the winery, up off the Torrenieri road to the east of Montalcino. Costanti's wines usually stand out for their great finesse and rich bouquets, rather than for their muscle, so we were surprised that, having tasted four wines, we could award only Two Glasses in all. To begin with, Costanti didn't make a normal Rosso di Montalcino '97, preferring to sacrifice it to the production of the "nobler" Brunello in such a favorable year. But he paid a price for that, as evinced by the simple honorable mention for his Rosso di Montalcino Calbello. The Brunellos fared better: they do get One Glass apiece, but that's not saying much in this case. The '94 releases an interesting but contradictory fragrance, with very youthful notes of fruit such as black currant and raspberry co-existing with very ripe tones of wild cherry. A slight defect on the nose fades away after the wine has had a chance to breathe. The palate is not very tightly knit, so the tannins stand out somewhat. The Brunello Riserva '93, on the other hand, almost collected Two Glasses with its youthful fruity aromas interspersed with prominent notes of toasty oak and cocoa, which are unusual for Costanti. On the palate, the attractive acidity blends well with the full-bodied flavor, making the wine quite agreeably drinkable.

●	Brunello di Montalcino '94	▼	6
●	Brunello di Montalcino Ris. '93	▼	6
●	Rosso di Montalcino Calbello '97		3
●	Vermiglio '98		4
●	Brunello di Montalcino '88	▽▽▽	6
●	Brunello di Montalcino '85	▽▽	6
●	Brunello di Montalcino '86	▽▽	6
●	Brunello di Montalcino '87	▽▽	6
●	Brunello di Montalcino '93	▽▽	6
●	Brunello di Montalcino '90	▽▽	6
●	Brunello di Montalcino '91	▽▽	6
●	Brunello di Montalcino Ris. '83	▽▽	6
●	Brunello di Montalcino Ris. '88	▽▽	6
●	Brunello di Montalcino Ris. '90	▽▽	6
●	Rosso di Montalcino '95	▽▽	4

DUE PORTINE - GORELLI

VIA CIALDINI, 53
53024 MONTALCINO (SI)
TEL. 0577/848098

Giuseppe Gorelli is an oenological craftsman, in the noblest sense of the word. He belongs to a category of small-scale winegrowers who, as opposed to the bigger Montalcino producers, take an artisan's approach to making wine. This is not opposition in the polemic sense; just a different way of seeing things, which is often apparent in the finished product. Gorelli's wines have character, and plenty of it, starting with the '94 Brunello di Montalcino, among the most enjoyable of the whole vintage. Its vivid ruby hue is intense and shot through with highlights. The attack on the nose is decisive, leading with a strong hint of wood (somewhat insistent, at the moment). Behind this first wave of new oak lurks a very ripe fruity aroma, followed by a creamy note that gives it an enveloping charm. In the mouth the fruit takes on an overripe note, while the wood draws back a bit. Long and soft, it is already drinking well, and it finishes on a note of milk chocolate. The Rosso di Montalcino '97 is among the best of its type: a deep and brilliant ruby color introduces light notes of overripe fruit in a very clean bouquet. On the palate this wine offers good balance, body, and sufficient length, but above all great drinkability: One overflowing Glass.

●	Brunello di Montalcino '94	**YY**	6
●	Rosso di Montalcino '97	**Y**	4
●	Brunello di Montalcino '88	YY	6
●	Brunello di Montalcino '89	YY	6
●	Brunello di Montalcino '90	YY	6
●	Brunello di Montalcino '92	YY	6
●	Brunello di Montalcino '93	YY	6
●	Rosso di Montalcino '90	YY	4
●	Rosso di Montalcino '91	YY	4
●	Rosso di Montalcino '92	YY	4
●	Rosso di Montalcino '93	YY	4
●	Rosso di Montalcino '96	YY	4
●	Rosso di Montalcino '95	Y	4
○	Vin Santo '89	Y	6

MONTALCINO (SI)

FANTI - LA PALAZZETTA

FRAZ. CASTELNUOVO DELL'ABATE
B.GO DI SOTTO, 25
53020 MONTALCINO (SI)
TEL. 0577/835631

Many Montalcino experts consider the Castelnuovo dell'Abate subzone to be one of the best, if not THE best, of the entire DOCG. It is here that Flavio Fanti, owner of the Palazzetta estate, has five hectares of vines. In the course of 1999 he planted another five, at a density which bespeaks an uncompromising commitment to high quality: some five thousand vines per hectare. The results at our tastings were again most convincing. With the help of the oenologist Maurizio Castelli, Fanti has released two very authoritative, rich and pleasurable red wines. We'll start with a highly expressive Rosso di Montalcino '97 which is, in fact, one of the best in its category. It is of a saturated ruby color, vivid and luminous, and has a muffled scent of toasty oak, followed by good, clean, intense fruit. Then it is full-bodied, soft, ripe, open and exceedingly drinkable, despite abundant tannins: Two well-earned Glasses. Fanti's Brunello made a good showing too. The '94 version is substantial, well proportioned and harmonious. The nose is primarily fruity, with, at the moment, somewhat insistent wood, which will probably blend in nicely before long. It is a vigorous wine, with good extract (especially the tannins) and energy, but also soft and ripe; it finishes on complex and satisfying notes of licorice and bitter herbs.

●	Brunello di Montalcino '94	**YY**	5
●	Rosso di Montalcino '97	**YY**	4
●	Brunello di Montalcino '93	YY	5
●	Rosso di Montalcino '96	YY	4

MONTALCINO (SI)

FANTI - SAN FILIPPO
LOC. SAN FILIPPO
53020 MONTALCINO (SI)
TEL. 0577/835523

Major changes have been taking place at the Fanti estate. Its owner, who is president of the recently merged Brunello and Rosso di Montalcino producers' consortia, has been busy in the barrel-room at San Filippo. He has been getting rid of the oldest barrels and bringing in smaller ones, such as tonneaux and barriques, in accordance with recent trends, which are also encouraged by the new DOCG regulations. Another innovation is the new consultant oenologist, Stefano Chioccioli, a technician known for his agronomical as well as oenological expertise. San Filippo will also be extending its vineyards, with denser plantings than before. And our tastings confirmed the felicity of the choices this house has been making. We start with an interesting Rosso di Montalcino '97, whose intense ruby color is tinged with purple. Its nose is richly fruity, with blackberry to the fore. The palate is intense, with a tightly-knit texture and just the right touch of acidity to make it easily quaffable. The two Brunellos on offer were slightly less successful: the Brunello di Montalcino Riserva '93 is of a moderately intense ruby hue veined with garnet; the nose, at first indistinct, then releases aromas of fruit and tobacco. The palate is smooth, with good tannins, and the wine is fairly easy to drink. Although the Brunello '94 also got One Glass, it seemed better, somewhat surprisingly given its vintage. Greater balance between fruity and earthy notes is already apparent on the nose and the livelier palate reveals sharpish but not unpleasant tannins. This one will improve over time.

●	Rosso di Montalcino '97	🍷🍷	4
●	Brunello di Montalcino '94	🍷	5
●	Brunello di Montalcino Ris. '93	🍷	6
●	Brunello di Montalcino '93	🍸🍸	5
●	Rosso di Montalcino '96	🍸🍸	4

MONTALCINO (SI)

TENUTA FRIGGIALI
LOC. FRIGGIALI
53024 MONTALCINO (SI)
TEL. 0577/849358 - 0577/849454

This estate now has 30 hectares dedicated to Brunello on the lovely hill above the church of Santa Restituta. This is the western part of Montalcino, and as we follow the Camigliano road down the hill we can see on our right the Pietranera and Pietrafocaia vineyards, which is where the best Friggiali wines come from. Gradual renovation of the cellar has included the purchase of barriques and tonneaux as well as the retirement of the oldest barrels, and the wines we tasted this year distinctly showed the effects. The '95 Pietrafocaia struck us as the best wine to come out of Friggiali in recent years. Made exclusively from sangiovese and aged some two years in small casks of French oak, it shows a compact, almost opaque ruby-violet color. The nose is ample and intriguing, with aromas of blackberry and blueberry blending perfectly with the oak-derived spicy notes. The palate is just as seductive, with its dense texture and soft tannins, and mirrors the bouquet. The Brunello di Montalcino '94 Pietranera also got Two Glasses: the nose, closed at first, soon opens to reveal well-defined fruit; the palate is fairly substantial, with well-balanced if not very fine tannins and a long-lasting finish: a very well-executed wine, and fully consistent with its vintage. Both the '97 Rosso di Montalcinos won One Glass, but we prefer the Pietranera, with its more impressive structure.

●	Brunello di Montalcino Pietranera '94	🍷🍷	6
●	Pietrafocaia '95	🍷🍷	5
●	Rosso di Montalcino '97	🍷	4
●	Rosso di Montalcino Pietranera '97	🍷	4
●	Brunello di Montalcino '94		5
●	Brunello di Montalcino '90	🍸🍸	5
●	Brunello di Montalcino '93	🍸🍸	5
●	Brunello di Montalcino Pietranera '93	🍸🍸	6
●	Rosso di Montalcino '93	🍸🍸	3*
●	Brunello di Montalcino '92	🍸	5
●	Pietrafocaia '93	🍸	5
●	Rosso di Montalcino '95	🍸	3
●	Rosso di Montalcino Pietranera '95	🍸	4

Eredi Fuligni
Via S. Saloni, 33
53024 Montalcino (SI)
tel. 0577/848039

Roberto Guerrini has cause to be pleased with his accomplishments. In just a few years he has made his family estate one of the most reliable in Montalcino, and, what's more, he has given his wines a well-defined style, based on elegance and a very rich aromatic range. His four DOCG hectares are situated in the northeastern zone of Montalcino, along the Buonconvento road. This year Fuligni has presented a new wine, the merlot-based San Giacomo '97, matured in barriques for over a year. It received rave reviews in some well-known American magazines, but we were not quite so enthusiastic when we tasted it. Notes of fur seemed to cover the fruit on the nose. It was more interesting in the mouth, with a good attack, a dense, full-bodied mid-palate progression and fine tannins. In any case, it's a promising start. The two Brunellos did better, especially the Riserva, as might have been expected from its year and provenance. This is a classic Fuligni wine, with a broad bouquet in which tones of wild cherry, blackberry and black currant blend well with a tobacco nuance. And the palate is well balanced, with a finish that echoes the nose. The '94 Brunello is very well made too; its moderately intense aromas include toasty notes and hints of cocoa, and the nicely dense palate reveals very elegant tannins. There was no Rosso di Montalcino Ginestreto this year; it was sacrificed at the Brunello altar because of the quality of the '97 harvest.

● Brunello di Montalcino '94	🍷🍷	6
● Brunello di Montalcino Ris. '93	🍷🍷	6
● San Giacomo '97	🍷	5
● Brunello di Montalcino '87	🍸🍸	5
● Brunello di Montalcino '88	🍸🍸	5
● Brunello di Montalcino '89	🍸🍸	5
● Brunello di Montalcino '90	🍸🍸	5
● Brunello di Montalcino '93	🍸🍸	5
● Brunello di Montalcino Ris. '88	🍸🍸	6
● Brunello di Montalcino Ris. '90	🍸🍸	6
● Rosso di Montalcino Ginestreto '95	🍸🍸	4
● Brunello di Montalcino '86	🍸	5
● Brunello di Montalcino '92	🍸	5
● Brunello di Montalcino '91	🍸	5
● Rosso di Montalcino Ginestreto '96	🍸	4

MONTALCINO (SI)

Greppone Mazzi
Tenimenti Ruffino
Loc. Greppone
53024 Montalcino (SI)
tel. 055/8368307 - 0577/849215

This estate is part of the Tenimenti Ruffini and is a regular in the Guide. Their ten hectares are all dedicated to Brunello. Recently they began a replanting program, taking advantage of the experience gained by the "parent" estate: restructuring involves planting many more vines per hectare, and careful selection of new clones which have already performed well in Ruffini's experimental vineyards. We expect to be seeing further improvements in quality here shortly: they have always presented well-made, sound and appealing wines which, however, wanted the personality that would propel them to greater heights. The '94 Brunello is in line with previous vintages, in spite of the unpropitious year. That the outcome is nonetheless successful is a testimony to the sure hand guiding the wine-making process and bringing out the best the grapes had to offer. This Brunello is of a ruby color tending toward garnet, and offers a very clean, intense fragrance of fresh wild cherry and cherries steeped in alcohol. In the mouth it is well balanced, medium-bodied and pleasantly drinkable. It seems to be a bit low on extract, which in turn somewhat shortens the palate, but the finish is happily not at all bitter. So it gets One full Glass, but we continue to expect more from Greppone Mazzi.

● Brunello di Montalcino '94	🍷	6
● Brunello di Montalcino Ris. '82	🍸🍸	6
● Brunello di Montalcino Ris. '83	🍸🍸	6
● Brunello di Montalcino Ris. '90	🍸🍸	6
● Brunello di Montalcino '91	🍸	5
● Brunello di Montalcino '93	🍸	5
● Brunello di Montalcino Ris. '85	🍸	6
● Brunello di Montalcino Ris. '88	🍸	6
● Brunello di Montalcino Ris. '91	🍸	6

MONTALCINO (SI)

IL POGGIONE
LOC. S. ANGELO IN COLLE
53020 MONTALCINO (SI)
TEL. 0577/864029

Every now and then a wine writer does well to sit back and think a bit. The various classifications, be they Glasses or stars or percentage points, all represent a system of quantifying quality which could too easily degenerate into a two-dimensional competition, ill befitting something as complex as wine, where so many factors come into play – human, cultural and historical, as well as business policy. For the producers can also get caught up in the process, grooming their wines to win prizes first of all. You will have understood by now that this is not the case with Il Poggione, where they hold to their course, in line with their established tradition. Theirs is a classical and constant style; any variations are imposed by the vagaries of the weather. Their quantities are like those of a Bordeaux château: some fifty hectares dedicated to Brunello, a limited number of labels. So anyone wanting to buy a Brunello from Fabrizio Bindocci's estate knows what to expect in terms of both quality and style. The '93 Riserva offers corroborating evidence, displaying aromatic complexity and depth. The attack on the palate is full and warm, with lots of densely knit tannins well integrated into the body, and an appropriately long finish. And the '94 Brunello is also up to expectations: its bouquet is a bit simpler and its palate is a bit less concentrated, but it's substantial and attractive. The fair '97 Rosso might have performed better given its year, but it is fresh, enjoyable and admirably lively.

●	Brunello di Montalcino Ris. '93	🍷🍷	5
●	Brunello di Montalcino '94	🍷	5
●	Rosso di Montalcino '97	🍷	4
●	Brunello di Montalcino '88	🍸🍸	5
●	Brunello di Montalcino '90	🍸🍸	5
●	Brunello di Montalcino '92	🍸🍸	5
●	Brunello di Montalcino Ris. '88	🍸🍸	6
●	Rosso di Montalcino '92	🍸🍸	3*
●	Rosso di Montalcino '93	🍸🍸	3*
●	Rosso di Montalcino '95	🍸🍸	3*
●	Brunello di Montalcino '89	🍸	5
●	Brunello di Montalcino '93	🍸	5
●	Brunello di Montalcino '91	🍸	5
●	Brunello di Montalcino Ris. '90	🍸	6
●	Rosso di Montalcino '96	🍸	3

MONTALCINO (SI)

LA FIORITA
LOC. CASTELNUOVO ABATE
53020 MONTALCINO (SI)
TEL. 0577/835521

La Fiorita is a small producer, with just under one hectare registered as DOCG at the moment and some newly planted vineyards soon to start producing. But their very good showing earned them a place in last year's Guide, and their offerings this year are further confirmation of their potential. The renowned oenologist Roberto Cipresso oversees the wine-making, and he certainly leaves his incisive and uncompromising imprint on the wines. We'll start with his most experimental red, the Quadratura del Cerchio (Squaring of the Circle) which is the fruit of an oenologico-philosophical odyssey, according to what Roberto tells us on the back label. The "third journey" (no indication of vintage) is a blend of primitivo di Manduria and sangiovese di Montalcino. It offers a wide panoply of aromas, ranging from the classic Montalcino fruitiness to what you might term a call of the wild. There is a strong impact on the palate, with rich, full flavor and young tannins that still need taming. The more traditional Brunello di Montalcino '94 shows a fine, intense and vivid ruby color with cherry-red highlights. The aromas are well delineated and direct, with a marked sweet tone from the new oak (at least at our tastings), but also distinct and enchanting fruit. The palate is full-flavored and well structured, with robust but fine tannins. This is a red wine with character and notable length, and it is already highly enjoyable. The slightly sweet touch on the finish is also due mainly to the wood and should retreat after a few years in the bottle. We look forward eagerly to future offerings, which should grow in both quantity and quality.

●	Brunello di Montalcino '94	🍷🍷	6
●	Quadratura del Cerchio Terzo Viaggio	🍷🍷	6
●	Brunello di Montalcino '93	🍸🍸	6
●	Quadratura del Cerchio Secondo Viaggio	🍸🍸	5

PODERE LA FORTUNA
LOC. PODERE LA FORTUNA
53024 MONTALCINO (SI)
TEL. 0577/848308

Despite a series of years that were not easy for Montalcino, Gioberto Zannoni's Podere La Fortuna has always managed to make headway, and is now one of the most interesting and reliable estates in the whole territory. Granted they enjoy certain natural advantages, such as the siting and microclimatic and geological characteristics of their vineyards, which favor the ripening process. And then there is the human element, in the form of extreme care and commitment both in the vineyard and in the cellar. But the proof of the pudding is in the eating. Their Brunello Riserva '93 has taken its place squarely among the very best of its type. Its ruby-garnet color is of a good intensity; the nose is concentrated and well defined, with prominent fruit and a dash of black pepper. The palate is meaty, full and well balanced, and reveals smooth, compact tannins. In a less than perfect vintage like '94, Zannoni's Brunello still managed to acquit itself well and earn a good rating. It does, however, lack the depth and complexity of better years. There is, in fact, a light vegetal tone with the black fruit and vanilla on the nose, but still the wine is successful thanks to its general harmony and solid structure. The '97 Rosso di Montalcino is acceptable, in spite of a rather indistinct phenolic nose. The palate, however, is attractive and grows in intensity as it progresses.

●	Brunello di Montalcino '94	🍷🍷	6
●	Brunello di Montalcino Ris. '93	🍷🍷	6
●	Rosso di Montalcino '97	🍷	4
●	Brunello di Montalcino '83	YY	6
●	Brunello di Montalcino '91	YY	6
●	Brunello di Montalcino '93	YY	6
●	Rosso di Montalcino '95	YY	4
●	Rosso di Montalcino '96	YY	4
●	Brunello di Montalcino '85	Y	6
●	Brunello di Montalcino '92	Y	6
●	Rosso di Montalcino '94	Y	4

MONTALCINO (SI)

LA PODERINA
LOC. CASTELNUOVO DELL'ABATE
53020 MONTALCINO (SI)
TEL. 0577/835737

After a couple of years in the Other Wineries section, La Poderina is back in full view. From its vineyards near the road to the marvelous abbey of St. Antimo it produces wines of remarkable elegance. And its technical team has managed to bring out this quality in all the reds they presented this year. We begin with an excellent '93 Riserva, which has no trouble picking up Two Glasses. Of a very dense ruby color tinged with purple, it offers a particularly fresh nose for its type: aromas of ripe wild cherry and berries blending nicely with notes of coffee. It is a pleasure on the palate as well, showing good extract, a satisfying overall balance and well-integrated tannins of considerable finesse. Pleasing spicy notes reappear on the substantial finish. The '94 Brunello is slightly less successful, hampered as it was by its less than felicitous vintage. But here, too, we can enjoy the new style of the house, based squarely upon a fresh fragrance (blackberry and black currant to the fore) and a solid architecture reflecting the terroir. It is an elegant rather than a powerful wine, smoothly tannic and appealingly quaffable. The '97 Rosso di Montalcino earns no more than a mention, however, due to some unwelcome notes in the bouquet.

●	Brunello di Montalcino Ris. '93	🍷🍷	6
●	Brunello di Montalcino '94	🍷	5
○	Moscadello '97	🍷	5
●	Rosso di Montalcino '97		4
●	Brunello di Montalcino Ris. '88	YYY	6
●	Brunello di Montalcino '88	YY	5
●	Brunello di Montalcino Ris. '90	YY	6
●	Brunello di Montalcino '89	Y	5
●	Brunello di Montalcino '90	Y	5

MONTALCINO (SI)

La Togata

Via del Poggiolo, 222
53024 Montalcino (SI)
tel. 0577/847107 - 06/42871033

The birth of a new label and the purchase of four and a half hectares of vineyard in the area between Argiano and Camigliano are some of the positive developments at La Togata. They have also moved operations to an impeccably restored farmhouse, thus solving their earlier problems of elbow room. Now they have separate spaces for vinification and the temperature-controlled aging-cellar. Their range has been enriched by the addition of a new red named Azzurreta, a pure sangiovese aged in barriques. The first year to be bottled was the '96, and it is quite balsamic on the nose, with notes of mint and eucalyptus that, for the moment at least, somewhat overshadow the varietal scents of bay leaf and wild cherry. Progression on the palate is as it should be, with a gentle attack and a fine overall elegance, thanks to the balance among the various components. A good debut, therefore, in not the easiest year. Now we come to the traditional wines, starting with a '94 Brunello di Montalcino, which easily earns Two full Glasses. Of a luminous ruby color, it offers a rich bouquet made up of intense notes of red fruit, spice and vanilla; its promise is fulfilled on the palate, where the extract is good and fine tannins contribute to the satisfying structure. The very well-executed '97 Rosso di Montalcino is clean, invitingly fruity and exceedingly drinkable.

●	Azzurreta '96	▼▼	5
●	Brunello di Montalcino '94	▼▼	6
●	Rosso di Montalcino '97	▼	3
●	Brunello di Montalcino '90	▽▽	6
●	Brunello di Montalcino '91	▽▽	6
●	Brunello di Montalcino '92	▽	5

MONTALCINO (SI)

Lisini

Fattoria di S. Angelo in Colle
53024 Montalcino (SI)
tel. 0577/864040

The historic Lisini estate is located in one of the wildest and most dramatically beautiful corners of the Montalcino area. In the woods and vineyards near the unpaved road that leads from Sant'Angelo in Colle to Castelnuovo dell'Abate you can often see pheasants, porcupines or wild boar. In addition to its scenic charms, this is one of the best-suited spots for Brunello production, enjoying a microclimate that protects the vines from serious deprivation even in the hottest and driest years. For quite a while the wines from this estate have stood out for their strength and balance, thanks to the sure hand of Franco Bernabei, one of the most renowned oenologists in all of Italy. Lisini presented three Brunellos this year, and we liked the '94 Ugolaia best. Of a lovely clear ruby color, it proffers an inviting bouquet made up of red fruit, sour cherry and wild cherry, all faintly overripe. The full-flavored palate reveals smooth tannins and a deep, mouth-filling finish. The '93 version was rather disappointing, however. There was something off-putting about the nose, in all the bottles we tried, which kept the fruit from unfolding properly. This was all the more regrettable, as the palate was very rich and charming. As for the Brunello di Montalcino '94, it did manage to get itself One Glass, but that's all. The ungenerous nose offers aromas of rhubarb, and there is a note of bitterness on the finish that keeps the wine from opening out as it should. Which brings us finally to the very interesting Prefillossero ("before phylloxera"), a red wine from a very old vineyard whose rootstock was unaffected by that notorious plague. It is a very well-made and tasty wine but it does not appear below because they make so little of it (some 300 bottles a year).

●	Brunello di Montalcino Ugolaia '94	▼▼	6
●	Brunello di Montalcino '94	▼	6
●	Brunello di Montalcino Ugolaia '93	▼	6
●	Brunello di Montalcino '88	▽▽▽	6
●	Brunello di Montalcino '90	▽▽▽	6
●	Brunello di Montalcino Ugolaia '91	▽▽▽	6
●	Brunello di Montalcino '87	▽▽	6
●	Brunello di Montalcino '89	▽▽	6
●	Brunello di Montalcino '91	▽▽	6
●	Brunello di Montalcino '93	▽▽	6
●	Brunello di Montalcino Ris. '85	▽▽	6
●	Brunello di Montalcino Ris. '86	▽▽	6
●	Brunello di Montalcino Ris. '88	▽▽	6
●	Brunello di Montalcino Ugolaia '90	▽▽	6
●	Rosso di Montalcino '90	▽▽	3*

LUCE

LOC. CASTELGIOCONDO
53024 MONTALCINO (SI)
TEL. 0577/848492

The multitudes of wine lovers who had with such eager anticipation greeted the appearance of Luce, a joint venture of Frescobaldi and Mondavi, have found their ardor somewhat damped over the past two years. The wines are certainly fine, but they have yet to capture a place at the top of their respective categories. And for good reason: their concentration is good, but not excellent. Their finesse is good but not excellent. And the value they offer for the money they cost (at least as regards the flagship, Luce) is good, but not really excellent either. We can but hope that these are simply teething troubles, rather than the result of actual policy choices. The '96 Luce follows in the footsteps of its predecessor. It offers a pronounced and very inviting nose with a ripe and sustained fruitiness, which does reappear on the palate, but the breadth and richness of extract, while considerable, are not yet outstanding. It is mouth-filling and even, and closes with pleasing cocoa overtones. Second son Lucente '97, made from sangiovese and merlot, has a brilliant ruby hue, saturated and intense. It is redolent of wild blackberry and black cherry; the tasty and direct palate is fresh, crisp and delicately tannic. The two new Danzante wines, one white and one red, are more reasonably priced. The '98 Bianco, made mostly from pinot grigio grown in northern vineyards (Trentino, Alto Adige and Friuli) is straightforward, crisp and quaffable. The fragrant Rosso '97, pure sangiovese (from the Marches), displays a fine red color, a scent of fresh strawberry, medium body and a slender finish.

●	Luce '96	🍷🍷	6
●	Lucente '97	🍷🍷	5
○	Danzante Bianco '98	🍷	3
●	Danzante Rosso '97	🍷	3
●	Luce '94	ΥΥΥ	6
●	Luce '93	ΥΥ	6
●	Luce '95	ΥΥ	6
●	Lucente '95	ΥΥ	5
●	Lucente '96	ΥΥ	5

MONTALCINO (SI)

MASTROJANNI

LOC. CASTELNUOVO DELL'ABATE
PODERI LORETO E SAN PIO
53020 MONTALCINO (SI)
TEL. 0577/835681

The Mastrojanni team has hit the bull's-eye again with an exceptional Brunello, winning Three Glasses with no dissenting voices. A round of applause for Antonio Mastrojanni and his technical consultants, the charismatic oenologist Maurizio Castelli and Andrea Machetti, who watches over the wines from day to day as they mature! The Brunello in question is the '93 Schiena d'Asino (donkey's back). It's got the classic color: a good, dense ruby with a garnet cast. The intensely fruity bouquet vaunts notes of sour cherry, wild cherry and blackberry jam with undertones of licorice. But where it really packs its wallop is on the palate: the attack and progression are simply superb, with the tannins woven perfectly into the velvety fruity structure, and the enormous, explosive finish just keeps on reverberating. The Brunello Riserva '93 is also very good, and easily wins its Two Glasses. It offers notes of leather and alcohol-steeped fruit on the nose, and good extract on the palate, although the tannins are slightly over-assertive. We felt a little less enthusiasm for the '94 Brunello, however: the bouquet has evolved a bit too far, muffling the fruit with a slightly earthy tone. The flavor is fine, though: rich and seductive, with a good balance. So a very nice range of reds puts Mastrojanni in the front ranks of this Montalcino subzone, Castelnuovo dell'Abate. Among the new developments at home we can report the restructuring of their cellar, which now includes a temperature-control system, and their decision to increase the number of barriques and tonneaux, which will be used both for their Brunellos and for the San Pio, their fair "table wine".

●	Brunello di Montalcino Schiena d'Asino '93	🍷🍷🍷	6
●	Brunello di Montalcino Ris. '93	🍷🍷	5
●	Brunello di Montalcino '94	🍷	5
●	San Pio '96		4
●	Brunello di Montalcino '90	ΥΥΥ	6
●	Brunello di Montalcino Ris. '88	ΥΥΥ	6
●	Brunello di Montalcino Schiena d'Asino '90	ΥΥΥ	6
●	Brunello di Montalcino '88	ΥΥ	6
●	Brunello di Montalcino '93	ΥΥ	5
●	Brunello di Montalcino Ris. '90	ΥΥ	6
●	San Pio '88	ΥΥ	5
●	San Pio '93	ΥΥ	5
●	San Pio '95	ΥΥ	5

MONTALCINO (SI)

MOCALI

Loc. Mocali, 273
53024 Montalcino (SI)
tel. 0577/849485

We can give a good report of Tiziano Ciacci's Mocali, which easily maintains the standing it has achieved in recent years. Indeed his vineyards are enviable both for management and position: they lie to the west of Montalcino, facing Castiglion del Bosco, on an airy hill of just a few hectares, overlooking the church of Santa Restituta. Some very well-built wines come from those three DOCG hectares. Two very different Brunellos, stylistically speaking, were on offer. The differences were mainly due to the type of barrel in which the wine was aged. The Brunello di Montalcino Riserva '93 is of an intense ruby color with light garnet highlights; its bouquet is clean and broad, with hints of mint to enrich the fragrance of fruit and spice. The palate is densely structured and gratifying, the tannins still young but of a good quality. The broad finish intriguingly echoes the nose. Then we have the very classical Brunello di Montalcino '94 (a year somewhat overestimated by the producers' consortium). This wine looks less dense than the other, with a garnet tendency, especially near the rim of the glass. Its bouquet includes a note of tobacco, in addition to the fruitier tone of cherries steeped in alcohol. The attractive palate is well constructed and very harmonious. It is not a muscular wine, but it has a long finish without a trace of bitterness. The equally good Rosso di Montalcino '97 vaunts a very soft attack, a smooth mid palate with no trouble from the tannic component and a creditable finish.

● Brunello di Montalcino Ris. '93	▼▼	5
● Brunello di Montalcino '94	▼	5
● Rosso di Montalcino '97	▼	3
● Brunello di Montalcino '93	▽▽	5

MONTALCINO (SI)

TENUTE SILVIO NARDI

Loc. Casale del Bosco
53024 Montalcino (SI)
tel. 0577/808269

The Tenute Silvio Nardi are eager to claw back lost ground, after having spent the '80s in a sort of hibernation. Emilia Nardi provides the needed energy behind this ambitious new approach, which was cautious at first but then proceeded to pick up enthusiasm and commitment and has now reached cruising speed. Given the vast extent of the Nardi estate, replanting the vineyards and restructuring the cellar have been Herculean tasks, but performed with complete conviction. And the resulting wines will be showing the good effects in the coming years. We shall already be seeing impressive results in the '95 Brunellos. This year's tastings, however, did not reveal any dramatic leaps forward. Only the '93 Riserva made it to the upper ranks: it received Two Glasses by virtue of its good body and overall balance. Skillfully designed by the oenologist Paolo Vagaggini, it is a smooth, well-made wine with perceptible notes of oak-derived vanilla, but as yet without noticeable personality. The '94 Brunello is about average for its vintage, which was egregiously overrated at the time. The nose lacks definition and is slightly muffled by oak. The palate is satisfying, balanced, and smooth in its development, but then a bit rough on the finish. The Rosso di Montalcino '97 was hard to rate, at least in the samples we tasted, because its otherwise admirable structure was diminished by definite traces of maderization.

● Brunello di Montalcino Ris. '93	▼▼	5
● Brunello di Montalcino '94	▼	5
● Rosso di Montalcino '97		4
● Brunello di Montalcino '90	▽▽	5
● Brunello di Montalcino '93	▽▽	5
● Brunello di Montalcino '92	▽	5
● Rosso di Montalcino '93	▽	4
● Rosso di Montalcino '95	▽	4
● Rosso di Montalcino '96	▽	4

SIRO PACENTI
LOC. PELAGRILLI, 1
53024 MONTALCINO (SI)
TEL. 0577/848662

This is one of the most dynamic Montalcino estates: experimentation with soil and vines, collaboration with prestigious centers of research, including foreign ones (e.g. the Institut d'Oenologie of Bordeaux) and careful trials with various types of wood for the aging process are only three examples of the efforts undertaken in the past five years or so by Giancarlo Pacenti, the young owner of this house. The vines grow on two opposite sides of town: one vineyard lies near headquarters, in the northernmost part of Montalcino, in an area known for producing wines of major fragrance and medium body; the other vineyard slopes away southwards, near Piancornello, a zone that usually means more muscular reds. As for the cellar, barriques have totally replaced the more traditional barrels, in keeping with the new DOCG regulations, of which Giancarlo was one of the most dedicated promoters. We were delighted by the Rosso di Montalcino and gave it Two (and a half) Glasses: it is one of the three best wines of its category. Very dense even in color, it has an immensely broad aromatic range, with notes of black cherry, black currant and blackberry mingled with balsamic nuances of eucalyptus. The palate is smooth and well balanced, with a generous and harmonious finish. The Brunello '94 is a curious phenomenon. Between the time it was first presented to the public in February and the time of our tastings (late May and late June) its nose had perceptibly altered: what had been highly expressive in the winter turned out to be closed and almost dumb in summertime. This may be just a transient phenomenon, but it cost the wine a number of points. In any case, the progression on the palate is admirable, with very soft and well-balanced tannins, and an attractive and long-lasting finish.

● Rosso di Montalcino '97	🍷🍷	5
● Brunello di Montalcino '94	🍷	6
● Brunello di Montalcino '88	🍷🍷🍷	6
● Brunello di Montalcino '89	🍷🍷	6
● Brunello di Montalcino '90	🍷🍷	6
● Brunello di Montalcino '91	🍷🍷	6
● Brunello di Montalcino '93	🍷🍷	6
● Brunello di Montalcino Ris. '90	🍷🍷	6
● Rosso di Montalcino '88	🍷🍷	4
● Rosso di Montalcino '90	🍷🍷	4
● Rosso di Montalcino '92	🍷🍷	4
● Rosso di Montalcino '93	🍷🍷	4
● Rosso di Montalcino '95	🍷🍷	4
● Rosso di Montalcino '96	🍷🍷	4

AGOSTINA PIERI
VIA FABBRI, 2
53014 MONTALCINO (SI)
TEL. 0577/375785

The first and only winery to get Three Glasses for a Rosso di Montalcino '95, this small estate was eagerly awaited by the panel for its final exams, i.e. its first Brunello . And the Brunello '94 has passed with flying colors, turning out to be one of the best of its year. First of all, it shows an intriguingly dense and brilliant ruby color. And then it comes forward with a generous bouquet composed of red and black fruit enveloped in a most delightful balsamic fragrance. Now to the palate, where the wine makes a solid entry, with good extract that lets it linger; the finish mirrors the nose and is really quite long, especially if you compare it with the average for that year. So congratulations to Agostina Pieri and to the oenologist, Vagaggini! But we told you so – we believed in the potential of this winery from the very outset. They say that Fortune is blind, but Misfortune sees all too well when it strikes. In the course of the '97 growing season, the Pieri vineyards were badly hurt by hail, which imposed some painful choices in the selection of the grapes. The Rosso di Montalcino '97 suffered from this setback: it is a good wine and well made, but it doesn't earn more than One Glass. Which is nothing to sneeze at, but after the performance of recent seasons, Pieri fans were looking forward to something better. Unfortunately there's no commanding Mother Nature. We were struck, however, by the finesse of the nose (wild cherry and black currant). This wine is medium-bodied, pleasant to drink and good on the finish.

● Brunello di Montalcino '94	🍷🍷	6
● Rosso di Montalcino '97	🍷	4
● Rosso di Montalcino '95	🍷🍷🍷	4*
● Rosso di Montalcino '94	🍷🍷	4
● Rosso di Montalcino '96	🍷🍷	4

MONTALCINO (SI)

Poggio di Sotto di Piero Palmucci
Fraz. Castelnuovo dell'Abate
Loc. Poggio di Sopra, 222
53024 Montalcino (SI)
tel. 0577/835502

Piero Palmucci is back in the Guide again, after only one year's absence. (Inevitable space limitations oblige us to make increasingly painful choices.) The Poggio di Sotto Brunello '94 is a very good wine. It fits the classical mold, starting from the ruby-garnet color; the rich range of aromas includes leather, tobacco and the note of wild cherry that characterizes Brunello di Montalcino. The palate is good, too: tannins and acidity are well blended in the velvety soft body, underpinned by substantial but restrained alcohol. We didn't get to taste the Rosso di Montalcino '97 because it hadn't yet been bottled. Palmucci likes to age this wine as well for a long time in wood, and our publishing deadlines rarely coincide with his maturation requirements. Poggio di Sotto is growing: they are increasing the area under vine and there are plans to expand the cellar, over which they live. The new vineyards are right nearby, at Castelnuovo dell'Abate, an area of great potential and in rapid development. In order to get the most out of the plots at his disposal, Pamlucci prefers small plantings at a variety of altitudes, thus minimizing the impact of difficult years. The success of the Brunello '94 is a proof of the wisdom of this strategy.

●	Brunello di Montalcino '94	🍷🍷	6
●	Rosso di Montalcino '94	YY	4
●	Brunello di Montalcino '91	Y	6

MONTALCINO (SI)

Castello Romitorio
Loc. Castello di Romitorio
53024 Montalcino (SI)
tel. 0577/897220

The wines of Castello Romitorio seem more successful and characterful every year. The estate belongs to the noted artist Sandro Chia, an outstanding exponent of the Transavanguardia movement, which originated in Italy in the late '70s. His works are exhibited throughout the world, and his wine labels are avidly sought by collectors. And two of his wines have earned Two Glasses apiece in this year's Guide: the Romito del Romitorio, a cabernet sauvignon, and the debutant Chardonnay. The '96 Romito del Romitorio sports a brilliant ruby color and a rather varietal nose, with suggestions of cedar and dark berries, while the medium-bodied palate shows balance and good tannins. Vegetal notes reappear on the finish, but the general effect is not unappealing. The '98 Chardonnay boasts a rich, glowing straw-yellow color. The nose opens with fruity tones of melon and banana, with added complexity from hints of butter, all enriched by an astute use of oak, which imparts notes of vanilla and cocoa. The attractive palate reveals a delightful, well-integrated crisp acidity. One step beneath it we find the '94 Brunello di Montalcino, which displays a ruby color tinged with garnet, and the classic bouquet of spice and undergrowth. The palate is not enormous, but the wine is pleasingly quaffable, thanks to proper balance and good unintrusive tannins. The '97 Rosso di Montalcino is somewhat less successful: with its inexpressive nose and lightweight palate it earns just an honorable mention.

○	Chardonnay '98	🍷🍷	5
●	Romito del Romitorio '96	🍷🍷	6
●	Brunello di Montalcino '94	🍷	6
●	Rosso di Montalcino '97		4
●	Brunello di Montalcino '93	YY	6
●	Romito del Romitorio '90	YY	5
●	Romito del Romitorio '96	YY	5
●	Brunello di Montalcino '88	Y	6
●	Rosso di Montalcino '92	Y	4
●	Rosso di Montalcino '96	Y	4

MONTALCINO (SI)

Salicutti

Podere Salicutti, 174
53024 Montalcino (SI)
tel. 0577/847003

Francesco Leanza is our discovery of the year. Sicilian by birth, Roman by adoption, he worked as a chemist in the capital for almost twenty years. Salicutti is a very small estate, with only one and a half hectares dedicated to Brunello, but it is growing – a bit: there will shortly be three hectares in production. His traditional vineyards, near the road to Castelnuovo dell'Abate, have a density of about 4,500 vines per hectare and are very well tended (Leanza is a dedicated practitioner of organic farming). His tiny cellar is full of brand-new barrels, barriques and tonneaux, cradling the wines we look forward to sampling when they are ready. As for his '97 Rosso di Montalcino, it is simply superb. It stands at the very top of its category and got very high scores indeed. Of a dense, vivid ruby hue, it boasts an ample bouquet, despite the noticeable wood-derived notes of vanillin, cocoa and coffee; the fruity tones (very ripe cherry and wild cherry) are pleasing and well defined. The palate shows great breeding, with considerable body that eschews heaviness thanks to the underpinning acidity. So it is a great Rosso di Montalcino, and a delightful surprise. We are eager to see how Leanza does with his Brunello, which seemed quite intriguing when we tasted it from the barrel.

●	Rosso di Montalcino '97	🍷🍷	4

MONTALCINO (SI)

Salvioni - La Cerbaiola

P.zza Cavour, 19
53024 Montalcino (SI)
tel. 0577/848499

We all know that Salvioni's Brunello is one of the most famous wines of Montalcino, and in just ten years it has become a veritable cult object for wine lovers, who squabble over the few bottles to come out of those two producing hectares. And it's there in the vineyards that the Salvionis have gradually created the basis of it all, with almost obsessive selection and ruthless and frequent summer pruning. In undistinguished vintages these techniques have produced true masterpieces, like the legendary '87 which, even at twelve years of age, is still a stunner. Unfortunately, however, you can't win them all, and the '94 Brunello La Cerbaiola is quite frankly somewhat disappointing. It's a good red wine, attractive and well made, but it can't command more than One Glass. The color is ruby tending to garnet, but we miss the characteristic Salvioni bouquet with those notes of tropical fruit and yellow peach that put it in a class of its own. This '94 Brunello releases light vegetal notes and very clean scents of blackberry, but they are all somewhat pale. The palate is elegant, the tannins show finesse and the finish is moderately long.

●	Brunello di Montalcino '94	🍷	6
●	Brunello di Montalcino '85	ΥΥΥ	6
●	Brunello di Montalcino '87	ΥΥΥ	6
●	Brunello di Montalcino '88	ΥΥΥ	6
●	Brunello di Montalcino '89	ΥΥΥ	6
●	Brunello di Montalcino '90	ΥΥΥ	6
●	Brunello di Montalcino '86	ΥΥ	6
●	Brunello di Montalcino '91	ΥΥ	6
●	Brunello di Montalcino '92	ΥΥ	6
●	Brunello di Montalcino '93	ΥΥ	6

MONTALCINO (SI)

TALENTI - PODERE PIAN DI CONTE

LOC. S. ANGELO IN COLLE
53020 MONTALCINO (SI)
TEL. 0577/864029

Pierluigi Talenti's death last September marked the end of an era at Montalcino, the era of the pioneers of modern Brunello. Anyone who follows Tuscan wine knows how important Talenti was in the development and growth of this premium red. Arriving in Montalcino in the late '50s, when there was just a handful of Brunello producers, he embarked upon a fruitful collaboration with the Franceschi family, owners of the Il Poggione estate, which, under Talenti's able guidance, became a benchmark winery. He waged a praiseworthy campaign to keep Brunello prices within limits (it has always been rather dear), thus making it possible for many more people to taste this celebrated wine. Over the years Talenti helped lots of producers with his valuable advice, and many a time he allowed those who were in trouble to buy grapes from vineyards he managed. So the memory of Pierluigi Talenti will long endure in the history of Montalcino, of Brunello, and in the hearts of many wine lovers. As for the wines we tasted this season, a few quick notes: these are good wines, correctly made and enjoyable, albeit not enormously concentrated.

● Brunello di Montalcino '94	🍷	6
● Brunello di Montalcino Ris. '93	🍷	6
● Rosso di Montalcino '97	🍷	4
● Brunello di Montalcino '88	YYY	5
● Brunello di Montalcino '85	YY	5
● Brunello di Montalcino '86	YY	5
● Brunello di Montalcino '87	YY	5
● Brunello di Montalcino '89	YY	5
● Brunello di Montalcino '90	YY	5
● Brunello di Montalcino Ris. '88	YY	6
● Brunello di Montalcino Ris. '90	YY	6
● Rosso di Montalcino '90	YY	4
● Brunello di Montalcino '93	Y	5
● Brunello di Montalcino '91	Y	5
● Brunello di Montalcino '92	Y	5

MONTALCINO (SI)

TENIMENTI ANGELINI - VAL DI SUGA

LOC. VAL DI SUGA
53024 MONTALCINO (SI)
TEL. 0577/804411

We start with very good news: the Brunello di Montalcino '93 Vigna di Spuntali follows right in the footsteps of its fraternal twin, the Vigna del Lago '93, which earned Three Glasses last year. With this success Val di Suga confirms its position as one of the best interpreters of this vintage, and one of the finest Brunello producers overall. This champion displays a very dense, intense "pigeon's-blood" ruby color, all the way out to the rim. The fragrance includes fruity notes of wild cherry, sour cherry and jam, with an interesting balsamic echo of oak, all perfectly integrated and never out of line. On the palate it has character to spare, and an excellent progression, with a broad, mouth-filling finish: this is a powerful wine, as you might expect from a Brunello grown on the Maremma side of Montalcino. For that is where the Spuntali vineyard lies, on the southern slope of the DOCG area, and it was one of the very first high-density vineyards in Montalcino. The reliability of Val di Suga, which belongs to the Angelini pharmaceutical group, is not limited to its special cru Brunellos: the '93 Brunello di Montalcino Riserva picked up Two Glasses without any trouble. It is made in the classical style, manifest from the outset in its garnet highlights; notes of tobacco blend with the broad and intense fruit of the bouquet. The palate is equally gratifying, the tannins slightly hard but not at all unpleasant. We awarded One Glass each to the Brunello '94 (a year in which neither of the two crus was produced) and the Rosso di Montalcino '97.

● Brunello di Montalcino Vigna Spuntali '93	🍷🍷🍷	6
● Brunello di Montalcino Ris. '93	🍷🍷	5
● Brunello di Montalcino '94	🍷	5
● Rosso di Montalcino '97	🍷	3
● Brunello di Montalcino Vigna del Lago '90	YYY	6
● Brunello di Montalcino Vigna del Lago '93	YYY	6
● Brunello di Montalcino '90	YY	5
● Brunello di Montalcino '93	YY	5
● Brunello di Montalcino Vigna Spuntali '89	YY	6
● Brunello di Montalcino Vigna Spuntali '90	YY	6

MONTECARLO (LU)

FATTORIA DEL BUONAMICO
VIA PROVINCIALE, 43
55015 MONTECARLO (LU)
TEL. 0583/22038

The Fattoria del Buonamico perfectly links the past, the present and the future of Montecarlo wines. A historic estate, it has managed to keep up with the times without losing touch with its roots, and to lay plans for improved growing methods in coming seasons. It, too, is planting new high-density low-yield vineyards which, together with the excellent work of recent years, assure us of even more impressive results in the near future. At our tastings we were quite struck by the Fortino '95, the only monovarietal syrah from Montecarlo. Syrah deserves more space in this zone: not only has it given brilliant results, but it was once a traditional variety here. The Fortino offers a characteristic bouquet of spice and dark berries with floral nuances. The soft and full-flavored palate has a good gradual development. The Cercatoja '95, a blend of cabernet and merlot, is excellent as well. It shows personality and some complexity, with a rounded, balanced and lingering palate. The pinot bianco-based Vasario '97 is intriguing: for the moment, the sweet sensations derived from its rich alcohol and aromas of vanilla and honey are dominant. But the wine shows good weight and should develop well, gaining in nose-palate harmony, after a little more time in the bottle. All of the Montecarlo '98 DOCs, both red and white, as well as the Cercatoja Rosato '98, were successful: even, fruity, and not without body. And to close, a word to the wise: Buonamico will be presenting a new wine next year, made from semillon and sauvignon, with noble rot: don't miss it!

●	Cercatoja Rosso '95	▼▼	5
●	Il Fortino Syrah '95	▼▼	5
⊙	Cercatoja Rosato '98	▼	3
○	Montecarlo Bianco '98	▼	3
●	Montecarlo Rosso '99	▼	3
○	Vasario '97	▼	4
●	Cercatoja Rosso '90	▽▽	5
●	Fort'Yrah '94	▽▽	5
●	Il Fortino Cabernet/Merlot '91	▽▽	5
●	Il Fortino Cabernet/Merlot '93	▽▽	5
●	Il Fortino Cabernet/Merlot '94	▽▽	5
●	Il Fortino Syrah '92	▽▽	5
○	Vasario '91	▽▽	5
○	Vasario '95	▽▽	5
○	Vasario '96	▽▽	4

MONTECARLO (LU)

FUSO CARMIGNANI
LOC. CERCATOIA
VIA DELLA TINAIA, 7
55015 MONTECARLO (LU)
TEL. 0583/22381

A bit of a character, Gino Fuso always has something new up his sleeve. The most recent innovation is his "transformation" of Montecarlo Bianco. He has banished the Pietrachiara label and replaced it with the name Stati d'Animo (states of mind), and, although it's still a DOC, it is quite different, not only in name but also in style and substance. His visit to California last year is probably to blame, but whatever the cause, Gino has converted to the fermentation of whites in wood. International taste, then, and quite out of line with the last few decades of Montecarlo, but this wine – even if the alterations in its flavor could have been predicted – has certainly turned out well. Of a lovely straw-yellow hue with greenish highlights, it has a clean fragrance with toasty and vanilla notes, and a quite full-bodied, even palate with a long finish. The Montecarlo Rosso di Fuso is a well-established success: intense in color and in its bouquet, which may be a bit too vegetal, it is mouth-filling, with a glorious structure for this type of wine; dense, smooth, broad and only slightly diminished on the finish by a faint grassy echo. It's a delight to drink. After those two Montecarlo '98s, which only just missed Two Glasses, here we are at the top of the line: For Duke, a blend of sangiovese and syrah. The '97 version is still young, and will be opening up further on the nose, but a major structure is already apparent, as is the excellent balance on the palate. This year's For Duke again shows body and great quaffability and, while not entirely above reproach in certain particulars, it has the undeniable virtue of belonging to the small group of wines with lots of personality.

●	For Duke '97	▼▼	5
○	Montecarlo Bianco Stati d'Animo '98	▼	3
●	Montecarlo Rosso Sassonero '98	▼	3
●	For Duke '90	▽▽	4
●	For Duke '94	▽▽	4
●	For Duke '95	▽▽	4
●	Montecarlo Rosso Sassonero '97	▽▽	2*
○	Vin Santo Le Notti Rosse di Capo Diavolo '95	▽▽	4
●	For Duke '93	▽	4
●	For Duke '96	▽	4
●	Montecarlo Rosso Sassonero '96	▽	2*
○	Vin Santo Le Notti Rosse di Capo Diavolo '94	▽	4

MONTECARLO (LU)

FATTORIA DI MONTECHIARI
VIA MONTECHIARI, 27
55015 MONTECARLO (LU)
TEL. 0583/22189

Many a winegrower comes up with a success in a good year, but it is by the leaner years that you can judge the true value of a wine or the house that produced it. Montechiari, you will have guessed, is a producer capable of rising above a mediocre vintage. After its Three Glass triumph with the '95 Cabernet, this estate has gone on to prove its mettle by producing an almost equally outstanding Cabernet '96. Not that we were actually surprised, though: you have but to note the care with which the vineyards are tended to realize that Montechiari is not a winery that leaves things to chance. This Cabernet '96 is a beauty: the color – a deep ruby – and the nose – very well focused, with notes of cocoa, black fruit and spice – are an excellent introduction to a substantial palate with good tannins and a remarkably long finish only slightly marred by a subtle trace of bitterness. The Pinot Nero '96 is quite intriguing: it packs an unusual punch for this variety. Fruit (black currant, cherry and black cherry jam) rules the roost on the intense nose, and the palate is rounded, soft and long-lasting. The good Chardonnay '97 shows admirable structure, a good amount of fat and a bouquet notable for its elegance. We also liked the mostly sangiovese-based Montechiari Rosso '96 despite dominant vegetal tones on the nose; the palate reveals evenness and depth.

●	Montechiari Cabernet '96	🍷🍷	6
●	Montechiari Pinot Nero '96	🍷🍷	5
○	Montechiari Chardonnay '97	🍷	4
●	Montechiari Rosso '96	🍷	4
●	Montechiari Cabernet '95	YYY	5
●	Montecarlo Rosso '96	YY	3*
○	Montechiari Chardonnay '96	YY	4
●	Montechiari Nero '95	YY	5
●	Montechiari Rosso '95	YY	4

MONTECARLO (LU)

WANDANNA
VIA DON MINZONI, 38
55015 MONTECARLO (LU)
TEL. 0583/228989 - 0583/22226

Wandanna has firmly established an excellent reputation. It produces a wide range of wines, in the uppermost ranks of which are their two standard-bearers, the Virente '96, a classic super-Tuscan blend consisting mainly of cabernet and merlot, and the Terre dei Cascinieri '97, a Montecarlo DOC: two very different labels and two very different styles. The Virente is built on balance and elegance. The fragrance is distinct and articulated, with nuances ranging from black fruit to spice, rounded out by subtle toasty notes of oak. The palate is not particularly powerful, but it is well balanced; the development of the flavor is even and smooth, all the way through to the stylish finish. The Terre dei Cascinieri, on the other hand, shows more grip, with a vigorous structure, good concentration, almost crunchy tannins and a solid fruit base: a champion in its category. The sauvignon-based Labirinto made a very good impression on its debut, almost getting Two Glasses. The clean bouquet offers notes of white-fleshed fruit; the palate is medium-bodied but develops very nicely and finishes well enough to suggest age-worthiness. The Terre dei Cascinieri Bianco shows good weight and a soft and rounded palate, although we'd have preferred a bit less oak and a bit more freshness. The other wines earn an honorable mention for their soundness and pleasing quaffability.

●	Montecarlo Rosso Terre dei Cascinieri '97	🍷🍷	4
●	Virente '96	🍷🍷	5
○	Labirinto '98	🍷	4
○	Montecarlo Bianco Terre dei Cascinieri '97	🍷	4
●	Montecarlo Rosso Terre della Gioiosa '98	🍷	2*
⊙	Cerasello '98		2
○	Montecarlo Bianco Terre della Gioiosa '98		2
●	Montecarlo Rosso Terre dei Cascinieri '96	YY	4
●	Virente '94	YY	5
●	Virente '95	YY	5

MONTECATINI VAL DI CECINA (PI)

FATTORIA SORBAIANO
VIA PROVINCIALE TRE COMUNI
56040 MONTECATINI VAL DI CECINA (PI)
TEL. 0588/30243

The '97 vintage was really excellent for the Rosso delle Miniere. For years now it has been performing very well, but we had begun to feel it had reached a plateau beyond which it was not about to rise. Of course the fact that the vineyards are sited up at around 400 meters above sea level means that they need the energy of the hottest seasons to bring out the very best in them. So it's no surprise that the '97 version mirrors in many aspects the excellent quality of the '90. It is a wine with solid structure and a smooth, balanced, long-lasting flavor. The aromas are concentrated and elegant; the wood is very well integrated, but some vegetal notes impinge on the ripeness of the fruit. The Lucestraia '97 made a very good showing with its well-rounded and full-flavored palate accompanied by a bouquet of honey, vanilla and tropical fruit. It well deserves its Two Glasses, but we feel it could aim still higher: with their unique microclimate, Sorbaiano could be producing an even more important white. They have, however, earned themselves the reputation of a fine and reliable winery, not least because of the attention they bestow upon the bottles at the bottom of their line, which are always not only sound but also structured and characterful. The intense and balanced Montescudaio Bianco '98 is particularly successful and the satisfactory '98 Rosso is a bit rustic, but energetic and agreeable.

○	Montescudaio Bianco Lucestraia '97	▼▼	4
●	Montescudaio Rosso delle Miniere '97	▼▼	4
○	Montescudaio Bianco '98	▼	2*
●	Montescudaio Rosso '98	▼	2*
●	Montescudaio Rosso delle Miniere '93	▽▽	4
●	Montescudaio Rosso delle Miniere '94	▽▽	4
●	Montescudaio Rosso delle Miniere '95	▽▽	4
●	Montescudaio Rosso delle Miniere '96	▽▽	4

MONTEFOLLONICO (SI)

VITTORIO INNOCENTI
VIA LANDUCCI, 10/12
53040 MONTEFOLLONICO (SI)
TEL. 0577/669537

Vittorio Innocenti is a very cultured and agreeable sort of man who runs his estate with great dedication and patience. He allows his wines all the time they need to mature in his small cellar, which is increasingly equipped with tonneaux (some American oak is now joining the classic French variety). The Montefollonico zone, home to the Innocenti vineyards, is partially contiguous with the Nobile di Montepulciano district, and produces wines of great structure which require more aging before their release. But patience is rewarded by longer-lived wines. A gratifying example of this was afforded us in a recent tasting of his legendary '88 Riserva which, at the ripe old age of 11, is still a truly great Nobile. Unfortunately, we went to press before we could try either the '96 Nobile di Montepulciano or the Acerone, which were both still in wood at the time of our tastings. What we did get to sample, however, afforded great pleasure, starting with the '93 Vin Santo. Of a rich golden color verging on amber, it offers intense perfumes of walnut skin, dried fruit and candied fruit, followed by an impressive palate with a fine balance between residual sugar and acidity. The Nobile di Montepulciano Riserva '95 gets just One Glass, as it was a bit closed at our tastings, with dominant licorice on the nose. After an intriguing attack, the palate suffered from excessive tannins, which limited its depth. But the finish, on which fruit reappears, is interesting. And, to close, the Chianti Colli Senesi '98 is delightful.

○	Vin Santo '93	▼▼	5
●	Chianti Colli Senesi '98	▼	3
●	Vino Nobile di Montepulciano Ris. '95	▼	5
●	Vino Nobile di Montepulciano Ris. '88	▽▽▽	5
●	Acerone '90	▽▽	5
●	Acerone '93	▽▽	5
●	Vino Nobile di Montepulciano '89	▽▽	4
●	Vino Nobile di Montepulciano '93	▽▽	3*
●	Vino Nobile di Montepulciano Ris. '90	▽▽	5
○	Vin Santo '90	▽	5
●	Vino Nobile di Montepulciano Ris. '94	▽	5

MONTEMURLO (PO)

TENUTA DI BAGNOLO
DEI MARCHESI PANCRAZI
VIA MONTALESE, 168
50045 MONTEMURLO (PO)
TEL. 0574/652058

You have to give Tuscan producers credit for their originality and individualism. They have shown these qualities time and again, and this year's tastings demonstrated them anew in the sometimes frenzied search for the right grape for a sudden leap in quality, even at the risk of obscuring full expression of the terroir. You might think this observation relevant to the Marchesi Pancrazi, but you'd be mistaken. It's no secret that pinot nero appeared here almost by chance, and that it turned out, over time and quite unexpectedly, to have a distinct affinity for the microclimate, and, most particularly, for the terrain. The vineyards are sited on the slopes below the first foothills of the Apennines, and are crisscrossed by subterranean streams that are absolutely incompatible with the cultivation of sangiovese, which comes out thin and acidulous. But this configuration happens to be very well suited to the vegetative and productive requirements of pinot nero. So this is a perfect environment for this fascinating variety, which is then most adroitly handled by Niccolò d'Afflitto, who knows it well and is drawn to it. And now to the tastings: let us state first off that the '97 is already in excellent form, with a bouquet of red fruit joined by floral nuances and mineral and animal hints. The palate is lively and rich, with an elegant evolution and a fruity finish. Nonetheless we would counsel patience with this wine, as it is sure to ripen to an even greater degree of complexity in the future. As for the San Donato '97, the estate's second wine, it is simple but juicy and dense.

●	Pinot Nero Villa di Bagnolo '97	▼▼	5
●	San Donato '97	▼	3
●	Pinot Nero Villa di Bagnolo '89	▽▽	5
●	Pinot Nero Villa di Bagnolo '91	▽▽	5
●	Pinot Nero Villa di Bagnolo '92	▽▽	5
●	Pinot Nero Villa di Bagnolo '93	▽▽	5
●	Pinot Nero Villa di Bagnolo '94	▽▽	5
●	Pinot Nero Villa di Bagnolo '95	▽▽	5
●	Pinot Nero Villa di Bagnolo '90	▽	5
●	Pinot Nero Villa di Bagnolo '96	▽	5

MONTEPULCIANO (SI)

AVIGNONESI
VIA DI GRACCIANO NEL CORSO, 91
53040 MONTEPULCIANO (SI)
TEL. 0578/757872 - 0578/757873

In its own way, it's an enchantress: Avignonesi's Vin Santo has reconfirmed its standing as one of Italy's best sipping wines. In spite of an inauspicious vintage, the '89 Vin Santo weaves a spell from the very outset: at first glance, it dazzles with its brilliant amber depths, and then entices with a bouquet of remarkable elegance, with notes of candied citrus peel and dried apricot, and light hints of toasted almond. All of which sets you up for an exquisite pleasure on the palate; the attack is both sweet and austere at the same time, and the body, while full, dense and long-lasting, never cloys, thanks to the admirable support of the acidity. After an interval of several years the Vin Santo Occhio di Pernice was also presented at our tastings. Made exclusively from red grapes, this wine certainly packs more than the "normal" punch; it has more residual sugars, but it is not underpinned to the same extent by acidity, so it seems perhaps too sweet. Among the dry wines, we liked the Rosso Avignonesi '97 best. Its intensely fruity nose and harmonious palate are impressive. This represents an important accomplishment for Avignonesi, as it confirms the value of the new high-density vineyards and the new vinification techniques, introduced that same year, which involve partial use of wooden vats for fermentation. We were also very pleased with the Marzocco '97, from chardonnay. This wine has now found its own distinct style, thanks to a balanced use of wood that doesn't distort, but does amplify, the characteristics of this variety. One last note: the most recent version of the Desiderio is pleasing; from '97 onwards it will no longer be made from merlot alone, but from a Bordeaux blend.

○	Vin Santo '89	▼▼▼	6
○	Il Marzocco '97	▼▼	4
●	Rosso Avignonesi '97	▼▼	3*
●	Vigna Capraia '97	▼▼	6
○	Vin Santo Occhio di Pernice '87	▼▼	6
○	Bianco Avignonesi '98	▼	3
●	Merlot Desiderio '96	▼	6
●	Vino Nobile di Montepulciano '96		5
○	Vin Santo '88	▽▽▽	6
●	Grifi '90	▽▽	5
●	Grifi '93	▽▽	5
●	Merlot '90	▽▽	5
●	Merlot '93	▽▽	6
●	Merlot Desiderio '95	▽▽	6
○	Vin Santo '86	▽▽	6

MONTEPULCIANO (SI)

Boscarelli

Loc. Cervognano
Via di Montenero, 28
53040 Montepulciano (SI)
tel. 0578/767277

An estate that presents interesting wines every time is Boscarelli. It has always been one of the best producers in the whole of Montepulciano, thanks to at least three factors: its siting in the glorious Cervognano zone, the guidance of the distinguished oenologist Maurizio Castelli and the dedication and ambition of the De Ferrari family. Hence Boscarelli turns out at least one wine at the top of its category every single year. Paola De Ferrari is the owner, and with the help of her two sons Luca and Niccolò she has been known to make some rather painful decisions in the interests of excellence (we're thinking of those rigorous early harvests). The decision not to make the '96 Boscarelli, their super-Tuscan, for the good of the Nobile, was a highly laudable one. It evinces a loyalty to the zone and its wines, in a region where many, too many, producers succumb to the $iren $ong of the $uper-Tuscans – and the devil take the hindmost. Boscarelli has presented three wines this year: in addition to the two '96 Nobiles there is also the De Ferrari '97, which was not sacrificed at the altar of the great vintage. Of the two Nobiles we not surprisingly preferred the house cru, the Vigna del Nocio, which was among the very best of the year. Of a deep ruby color, it offers a broad range of aromas, led by a lovely floral fragrance of violet, a sort of Boscarelli trademark, on a pleasantly fruity base, with notes of cherries steeped in alcohol. The palate is beautifully balanced, with excellent tannins and a very long-lasting finish. This wine has risen above the (alleged) shortcomings of its vintage. And just one rung below it is the Nobile di Montepulciano '96, whose nose is still slightly green and whose palate suffers from as yet inadequate integration of the tannins. But it still gets One Glass.

●	Vino Nobile di Montepulciano Ris. del Nocio '96	▼▼	5
●	De Ferrari '97	▼	3
●	De Ferrari '98	▼	3
●	Vino Nobile di Montepulciano '96	▼	4
●	Vino Nobile di Montepulciano Ris. '88	ΥΥΥ	5
●	Vino Nobile di Montepulciano Ris. del Nocio '91	ΥΥΥ	5
●	Boscarelli '95	ΥΥ	6
●	Vino Nobile di Montepulciano '94	ΥΥ	4
●	Vino Nobile di Montepulciano Ris. del Nocio '93	ΥΥ	5
●	Vino Nobile di Montepulciano Ris. del Nocio '95	ΥΥ	5

MONTEPULCIANO (SI)

Fattoria del Cerro

Loc. Acquaviva
Via Grazianella, 5
53040 Montepulciano (SI)
tel. 0578/767722

The improvements we noted in last year's Guide were evident again at this year's tastings: every single one of the Cerro wines is at the top of its respective category, confirming this estate's return to the Parnassus of Montepulciano. This year they have presented two new '97 reds: the Poggio Golo, a monovarietal merlot from the new high-density vineyards, and the Manero, a sangiovese aged in barriques and in 500-liter tonneaux. The extremely well-executed Manero offers a fine, rich and intensely fruity nose with clear notes of wild cherry sour cherry and red currant, as well as an enchanting oak-derived balsamic nuance, all mirrored on the remarkably elegant, delectable palate. The Poggio Golo also gets Two Glasses: it releases aromas of blackberry jam, blueberry and black currant with a touch of vanillin; in the mouth it is full-bodied, with a broad and velvety finish. Among the DOC wines, the Nobile di Montepulciano Antica Chiusina '95, the estate cru, bears the palm: it is the best local '95 presented this year and missed Three Glasses by a hair. It shows a ruby color tinged with "pigeon's blood", and a bouquet of red fruit and floral tones beautifully blended with the spiciness of the wood; the palate is captivatingly elegant and lingering, its noble tannins well integrated into the structure. Two Glasses, but not so full, go to the Vino Nobile di Montepulciano Riserva '95: it reveals the classic nose of violet and tobacco and is delightful to drink.

●	Manero '97	▼▼	5
●	Poggio Golo '97	▼▼	5
●	Vino Nobile di Montepulciano Ris. '95	▼▼	5
●	Vino Nobile di Montepulciano Vigneto Antica Chiusina '95	▼▼	5
○	Bravìolo '98	▼	2*
○	Cerro Bianco '98	▼	3
●	Rosso di Montepulciano '98	▼	3
●	Vino Nobile di Montepulciano '96	▼	4
●	Vino Nobile di Montepulciano '90	ΥΥΥ	4*
●	Rosso di Montepulciano '97	ΥΥ	3*
●	Vino Nobile di Montepulciano '95	ΥΥ	4
●	Vino Nobile di Montepulciano Ris. '93	ΥΥ	4

MONTEPULCIANO (SI)

CONTUCCI
VIA DEL TEATRO, 1
53045 MONTEPULCIANO (SI)
TEL. 0578/757006

This is one of the handsomest cellars of Montepulciano, situated as it is in the main square of the town, under the Contucci palace. Beneath the vaults (barrel vaults, of course) the wine is no longer kept in the red and black painted chestnut casks so dear to local tradition. These have given way to the more appropriate and functional ones made of Slovenian oak, with a capacity of 25 to 30 hectoliters apiece. This is part of the new estate policy, a path chosen by Alamanno Contucci, one of the most representative figures in the world of Vino Nobile, and current president of the local producers' association, the Consortium. The '96 vintage is the first to benefit – even if only partially – from this new production philosophy and, although the harvest was not enormously helpful, the difference is already apparent. Of the two Nobiles on offer, we preferred the standard version to the estate cru, the Pietrarossa, because of some aromatic uncertainties (a green scent that gets in the way of the underlying fruit) in the latter. This is a pity, because it is clear on the palate that first-class grapes went into this wine. The '96 Nobile di Montepulciano, on the other hand, displays a fine ruby color of medium density, followed by fresh and fruity (the characteristic cherry) scents, further enhanced by an inviting note of spice. It is pleasingly quaffable, with tannins present but kept well in check, and an interesting finish, free of those strains of bitterness evident in previous versions. Lastly, the straightforward and direct Rosso di Montepulciano '98 is quite attractive.

● Rosso di Montepulciano '98	▼	3
● Vino Nobile di Montepulciano '96	▼	4
● Vino Nobile di Montepulciano Pietrarossa '96	▼	4
○ Vin Santo '86	▽▽	6
○ Vin Santo '90	▽▽	4
● Vino Nobile di Montepulciano '90	▽▽	4
● Vino Nobile di Montepulciano Pietrarossa '90	▽▽	5
● Vino Nobile di Montepulciano Ris. '91	▽▽	4
● Vino Nobile di Montepulciano '93	▽	3
● Vino Nobile di Montepulciano '94	▽	4
● Vino Nobile di Montepulciano Pietrarossa '94	▽	4

MONTEPULCIANO (SI)

DEI
LOC. VILLA MARTIENA
53045 MONTEPULCIANO (SI)
TEL. 0578/716878

The enthusiastic and dedicated Caterina Dei, with the technical guidance of Niccolò d'Afflitto runs this family estate, which was established in 1985. After its first 15 years, Dei has grown to some 40 hectares under vine and has acquired a decidedly solid position on the market. Even with this impressive expansion, Caterina continues to see to every detail herself. The wines on offer this year confirm the reliability of the producer, although (rather like last year) the DOC wines seem to have trouble keeping up with the very successful super-Tuscan, the Sancta Catharina, a blend of prugnolo gentile, cabernet sauvignon and syrah aged in French oak tonneaux. The color is very dense, with violet highlights, and the lovely fragrance combines notes of blueberry and black currant in a perfect blend with the wood-derived balsamic nuances. All these charms lead right on to a commensurate pleasure on the palate, where the wine is compact and smooth, with elegant tannins well integrated into the velvety body and a long-lasting, elegant finish. As we said, it's a tough act to follow: both versions of the Nobile di Montepulciano are good, the '95 Riserva a nose ahead of the standard '96, as could have been expected. The Nobile Riserva '95 is of a moderately intense ruby color with an almost garnet rim, and offers well-defined aromas of red fruit jam. Once in the mouth, however, after a good attack, the not yet fully tamed tannins get in the way of a completely satisfying progression. The '96 Nobile shows a less interesting nose, with a slightly lactic tone inhibiting the fruit; the palate is not very densely knit, and this lets you down on the finish. But it is still agreeable to drink.

● Sancta Catharina '96	▼▼	5
● Vino Nobile di Montepulciano '96	▼	4
● Vino Nobile di Montepulciano Ris. '95	▼	4
● Rosso di Montepulciano '98		3
● Rosso di Montepulciano '93	▽▽	3*
● Rosso di Montepulciano '94	▽▽	3*
● Sancta Catharina '94	▽▽	5
● Sancta Catharina '95	▽▽	5
● Vino Nobile di Montepulciano '90	▽▽	4
● Vino Nobile di Montepulciano '91	▽▽	4
● Vino Nobile di Montepulciano '93	▽▽	4
● Vino Nobile di Montepulciano Ris. '90	▽▽	4
● Vino Nobile di Montepulciano Ris. '93	▽▽	4

MONTEPULCIANO (SI)

Fassati
Loc. Gracciano
Via di Graccianello, 3/A
53040 Montepulciano (SI)
tel. 0578/708708

Fassati is the Tuscan estate of Fazi Battaglia, the well-known Marche producer. It specializes in the production of red wines, which is quite appropriate to an estate of some 80 hectares in the Montepulciano district. Thirty-five of those hectares are dedicated to Nobile, while the other vineyards grow alternative varieties to prugnolo, like cabernet sauvignon, cabernet franc, merlot and syrah, a grape which is still somewhat rare in this zone. The new vineyards are planted quite densely, with about five thousand vines per hectare, and they include some native varieties such as mammolo, with which the winery is currently experimenting. Since they were presenting two years' wines at once, we had many different offerings to taste, but one definitely stood out, the Nobile di Montepulciano Salarco '95, one of the best of its type this year. Of a dense, intense ruby color, it releases wide-ranging and complex scents including red fruit (distinct wild cherry) and more evolved aromas like tobacco, further enriched by delightful notes of cocoa and eucalyptus. The palate is just as attractive, with a soft, dense attack, a good progression thanks to excellent tannins, and a finish that mirrors the bouquet. The very successful Nobile di Montepulciano '96 is at the summit of its category, with a nose still redolent of the wooden cask but not so much as to overpower the intense fruit, which should come out more clearly after a few additional months in the bottle. The appealing palate reveals great balance and elegance and a lingering finish. The Torre al Fante '94 was less of a success: a bit on the simple side (we accept its vintage as a partial excuse) although sound and pleasant.

●	Vino Nobile di Montepulciano '96	▼▼	4
●	Vino Nobile di Montepulciano Salarco '95	▼▼	5
●	Rosso di Montepulciano '98	▼	3
●	Torre al Fante '94	▼	5
●	Vino Nobile di Montepulciano Salarco '94	▼	5
●	Torre Al Fante '93	▽▽	5
●	Vino Nobile di Montepulciano '93	▽▽	4
●	Vino Nobile di Montepulciano '94	▽▽	4
●	Vino Nobile di Montepulciano '95	▽▽	4
●	Vino Nobile di Montepulciano Ris. '93	▽▽	5
●	Vino Nobile di Montepulciano Salarco '93	▽▽	5

MONTEPULCIANO (SI)

Podere Il Macchione
Via di Gracciano
53045 Montepulciano (SI)
tel. 0578/716493 - 0578/758595

We were all agog to try Robert Kengelbaker's Nobile di Montepulciano Riserva '95 after the knockout Three Glass '93 version from last year. Unfortunately this vintage turns out to be only distantly related. The nose does display the classic floral note, but without the support of that rich complexity we had hoped for; the palate is indeed rich, but the tannins are uncontrolled and a bit harsh, and have a stunting effect on the wine, which consequently does less well than the standard Vino Nobile '95 that we reviewed last year. Indeed the Caggiole version, from a great Montepulciano cru, does not show the elegance (usually a distinguishing feature) of the "normal" wine. On the other hand, the debut of the Rosso Abbadia, produced on the Abbadia estate near Montefollonico, is very interesting. The bouquet is richly fruity, with black cherry, black currant and blackberry to the fore, and an undertone of spice; the appealing palate reveals a lovely density, soft, well-integrated tannins, some freshness and a definite echo of the bouquet. The Rosso di Montepulciano '98 is too simple and forward to rate more than a mention.

●	Rosso Abbadia '97	▼▼	4
●	Vino Nobile di Montepulciano Le Caggiole Ris. '95	▼	5
●	Rosso di Montepulciano '98		3
●	Vino Nobile di Montepulciano Le Caggiole Ris. '93	▽▽▽	5
●	Vino Nobile di Montepulciano '90	▽▽	5
●	Vino Nobile di Montepulciano '95	▽▽	5
●	Vino Nobile di Montepulciano '91	▽▽	5
●	Vino Nobile di Montepulciano Ris. '90	▽▽	5
●	Vino Nobile di Montepulciano Ris. '91	▽▽	5
●	Vino Nobile di Montepulciano '94	▽	5

Fattoria La Braccesca

Loc. Gracciano - S. S. 326,15
53040 Montepulciano (SI)
tel. 0578/707058

The Montepulciano estate of the Antinoris is proceeding apace with its expansion: they now have some 140 hectares under vine, 30 of which are DOCG. The most recent plantings are very dense: more than five thousand vines per hectare, which the Antinori technical staff considers ideal for this area. The most important news is that they have finished building the new winery at Maestrelle near Valiano, the aristocrat of the Vino Nobile district. The old aging-cellar at the Badia (abbey) of Montepulciano will remain in use for some years to come. As expected, the wines presented by La Braccesca acquit themselves very well. The Nobile di Montepulciano '96 is admirable for its very classical bouquet, with distinct wild cherry and red berries and a floral nuance of violet. The body is not overwhelming, but the perfect harmony between the two bases of a wine, the acid-tannic component and its counterpart the glycero-alcoholic element, makes it particularly captivating. But the best estate wine this year is the Merlot, which, benefiting from the almost legendary '97 vintage, earns Two overflowing Glasses, thanks to a very intense color with a violet cast, a generous bouquet of yellow-fleshed fruit as well as varietal aromas, and a well-balanced palate with an ample finish. The Rosso di Montepulciano '98 is also successful and most enjoyably drinkable.

● Merlot '97	TT	5
● Vino Nobile di Montepulciano '96	TT	4
● Rosso di Montepulciano Sabazio '98	T	3
● Merlot '96	YY	5
● Rosso di Montepulciano Sabazio '97	YY	3*
● Vino Nobile di Montepulciano '90	YY	4
● Vino Nobile di Montepulciano '93	YY	4
● Vino Nobile di Montepulciano '95	YY	4
● Rosso di Montepulciano '93	Y	2*
● Rosso di Montepulciano '96	Y	2*
● Vino Nobile di Montepulciano '92	Y	4
● Vino Nobile di Montepulciano '94	Y	4

MONTEPULCIANO (SI)

La Calonica

Loc. Valiano
Via della Stella, 25
53040 Montepulciano (SI)
tel. 0578/724119

This estate lies in the Valiano area and enjoys the benefits of proximity to Lake Trasimeno, which means the winters are mild and the summers are never too dry. Estate news includes the acquisition of eight more hectares, to be planted to native varieties (sangiovese, called prugnolo gentile in these parts) as well as others the DOCG regulations allow in Nobile di Montepulciano (cabernet sauvignon and merlot). Ferdinando Cattani presented four wines for this year's tastings: in addition to his Girifalco and two "appellation" wines (the Nobile di Montepulciano '96 and the Rosso di Montepulciano '98) he also brought out his new red, La Calonica '98. And the debutant performed very well, winning points for freshness on the nose and for general charm. It may be a bit on the simple side, but it's delightful to drink and harmonious on the finish. The Nobile di Montepulciano '96 also gets One Glass, but a fuller one. It has a bright ruby color all the way to the rim, and aromas of black cherry accompanied by a greener, slightly vegetal note; the attack on the palate is fair, and the progression is good, although rough tannins get in the way somewhat. The Girifalco from the much-vaunted '97 vintage did not live up to expectations. The nose is distinct and very varietal, with wild cherry in the foreground and nuances of red fruit, but over-abundant tannins on the palate, while not actually bitter, certainly do not enhance the wine's quaffability, and do severely hamper the finish. As for the Rosso di Montepulciano '98, a lack of clarity on the nose reduces it to a mention only.

● Girifalco '97	T	6
● La Calonica '98	T	2*
● Vino Nobile di Montepulciano '96	T	4
● Rosso di Montepulciano '98		3
● Girifalco '93	YY	5
● Girifalco '95	YY	5
● Rosso di Montepulciano '91	YY	3*
● Vino Nobile di Montepulciano '90	YY	4
● Vino Nobile di Montepulciano '91	YY	4
● Girifalco '96	Y	5
● Rosso di Montepulciano '95	Y	3
● Sangiovese '95	Y	2*
● Vino Nobile di Montepulciano '92	Y	4
● Vino Nobile di Montepulciano '93	Y	4
● Vino Nobile di Montepulciano '95	Y	4

MONTEPULCIANO (SI)

Tenuta Lodola Nuova
Tenimenti Ruffino
Loc. Valiano
Via Lodola, 1
53023 Montepulciano (SI)
tel. 0578/724032

This estate is part of the Tenimenti Ruffino and has always produced wines that are pleasant and well made but somewhat lacking in personality. Now, to put this right, the Ruffino management is concentrating its efforts on the land, i.e. a gradual replanting of some of the vineyards. This is a recent development and involves the Valiano zone, which is highly prized for its ability to produce first-rate sangiovese. The density of the new plantings is medium-high, with about five thousand vines per hectare. Encouraged by the good results obtained so far, the winery is continuing to expand and now totals 30 hectares dedicated to the production of Vino Nobile di Montepulciano, out of a total of 50 hectares under vine. In addition to the traditional prugnolo gentile (the local name for sangiovese), the grapes grown include "international" varieties such as cabernet sauvignon and merlot, both of which are allowed in Nobile di Montepulciano by the new DOCG regulations. With its recent acquisitions, the winery has outgrown its existing cellar, and work is already under way on a new cellar adjacent to the new vineyards. So here, from this year's tastings, is the first wine produced within this new framework, the Rosso Montepulciano '98. Of a very deep, dark purplish color, it shows an intense, well-defined nose with a light vegetal note. With its attractive, pleasantly fresh palate and agreeably fruity finish, it can be considered one of the best wines of this vintage. The Nobile di Montepulciano '96 is clearly the product of this transition period. Overall, it is very well made, and shows a fruity nose with secondary floral notes (mainly oleander); in the mouth, however, it is somewhat simple, and not particularly full on the finish.

●	Rosso di Montepulciano '98	▼▼	3*
●	Vino Nobile di Montepulciano '96	▼	4
●	Vino Nobile di Montepulciano '93	▽▽	4
●	Vino Nobile di Montepulciano '95	▽▽	4
●	Vino Nobile di Montepulciano '94	▽	4

MONTEPULCIANO (SI)

Nottola
Loc. Bivio Nottola
53045 Montepulciano (SI)
tel. 0578/707060 - 0577/685240

This estate has been operating for quite a few years, but only recently has it begun work on the substantial innovations required to raise the standard – already good – of its wine. The owners, the Giomarelli family, have embarked on a major investment program, involving the purchase of new vineyards which are being replanted with not only local grapes, the engagement of the renowned oenologist Riccardo Cotarella as consultant, and the complete renewal of the barrel stock, with the addition of many barriques and tonneaux. This last year has also seen the construction of a new, very efficient and entirely temperature-controlled cellar adjacent to the original winery. The wines are still feeling the effects of this transitional period, but they showed well at our tastings. Although the estate has different ambitions for its two labels, for the time being they have scored alike. Nevertheless we were struck by the difference in style between the two. The Nobile di Montepulciano '96 is classic in style, with fruity aromas "covered" to some extent by greener notes, and flavors of average density, with tannins that need further aging. The finish is, not surprisingly, moderately long. The Nobile Vigna del Fattore, on the other hand, differs primarily on the nose, with its complex but somewhat conflicting aromas, where black currant jam sits alongside a rather pronounced vegetal tone. A good attack on the palate is followed by some fairly fine tannins. The wine then struggles a bit to develop, and the finish is somewhat dilute: all in all, a wine that is difficult to interpret, from a year that was itself controversial.

●	Vino Nobile di Montepulciano '96	▼	4
●	Vino Nobile di Montepulciano Vigna del Fattore '96	▼	5
●	Vino Nobile di Montepulciano Vigna del Fattore '95	▽▽	5
●	Rosso di Montepulciano '93	▽	2*
●	Rosso di Montepulciano '96	▽	3
●	Vino Nobile di Montepulciano '93	▽	4
●	Vino Nobile di Montepulciano '94	▽	4
●	Vino Nobile di Montepulciano Ris. '91	▽	4

Redi

Via di Collazzi, 5
53045 Montepulciano (SI)
tel. 0578/757102

The Redi project is a response to the determination of the Vecchia Cantina, the only cooperative winery in the Montepulciano district, to explore the new wine-making techniques and the real potential of the available resources. The 40 best hectares have thus been selected, from the approximately 980 available, for the production of the wines of the "new" Redi. The project has shown its worth right from the outset, producing wines with a striking personality whose quality, already good, will undoubtedly improve over time. Under the vaulted roof of the historic cellar lie hundreds of barriques and tonneaux, which are replacing the large old chestnut-wood barrels, in line with new policy. Let's consider the wines themselves: this year's novelty is called Riccio, the youngest – and the only white - of the line. Made from grechetto, viognier and sauvignon, it spends some months in barriques before bottling. It makes a good impression on the nose, offering notes of fruit and spice with laurel and medlar to the fore, and a significant but by no means intrusive contribution from the wood. The palate of this fairly substantial wine is well developed and underpinned by an agreeable acidity that enhances its quaffability. Of the reds, the Nobile di Montepulciano Briareo '96 is noteworthy. The result of a special selection, it has a dense ruby color and a fairly complex nose based on red fruit and wood-derived balsamic notes. It reveals a reasonably dense palate and a persistent finish. The estate's other DOC wines, the Nobile '96 and the Riserva '95, came in at the One Glass level; both are well made but still too short on personality to merit a higher score.

○ Riccio '97	🍷🍷	4
● Vino Nobile di Montepulciano Briareo '96	🍷🍷	5
● Vino Nobile di Montepulciano '96	🍷	4
● Vino Nobile di Montepulciano Ris. '95	🍷	5
● Rosso di Montepulciano '98		3
○ Vin Santo '90	🍸🍸	6
● Rosso di Montepulciano '97	🍸	3
● Vino Nobile di Montepulciano '95	🍸	4

MONTEPULCIANO (SI)

Massimo Romeo

Loc. Nottola di Gracciano
Via di Totona, 29
53045 Montepulciano (SI)
tel. 0578/716997

The wines produced by Massimo Romeo come from the Corsica estate in Gracciano, which is one of the best Montepulciano zones. The characteristics of the terrain, together with its altitude (about 450 meters above sea level), contribute to the strong character of the wines, which always have a good structure and a rather full bouquet that is part fruity, part floral. Romeo, for his part, seeks to enhance the characteristics of the terrain with low yields per hectare and fairly long maceration times. The wines are aged in barrels that are not overly large, about 25 hectoliters, and are replaced every nine years because, in the owner's words: "after that they have no more to offer". Recently, the cellar enriched its stock with 500- and 700-liter French oak tonneaux, used for the Riserva version of the Nobile and for the Lipitiresco, the standard-bearer of the estate. Romeo's tendency to favor rather muscular wines means that they can only really be savored after they have had some time in the bottle, a characteristic most clearly seen in the Lipitiresco. Even the '95 shows a degree of hardness on the palate, deriving from tannins that are rather more vigorous than the softer elements of the wine. Things will probably improve when the wine has spent more time maturing in the bottle, but for the time being it is difficult to judge how it will develop. We were happier with the Nobile di Montepulciano Riserva '95, in which an excellent harmony between the various components translates into a broader finish and a better follow-through from nose to mouth. The Nobile di Montepulciano '96 shows moderate structure and some sticking points on the nose that limit its range, but nevertheless the wine makes for balanced, agreeable drinking.

● Vino Nobile di Montepulciano Ris. '95	🍷🍷	5
● Lipitiresco '95	🍷	5
● Vino Nobile di Montepulciano '96	🍷	4
● Rosso di Montepulciano '98		3
● Lipitiresco '90	🍸🍸	4
○ Vin Santo '83	🍸🍸	6
○ Vin Santo '86	🍸🍸	5
● Vino Nobile di Montepulciano '91	🍸🍸	5
● Vino Nobile di Montepulciano '95	🍸🍸	5
● Vino Nobile di Montepulciano Ris. '88	🍸🍸	5
● Vino Nobile di Montepulciano '94	🍸	5
● Vino Nobile di Montepulciano Ris. dei Mandorli '94	🍸	5

MONTEPULCIANO (SI)

SALCHETO

Via di Villa Bianca, 15
53045 Montepulciano (SI)
tel. 0578/799031

This little estate continues to make progress and to produce wines that just get better and better. From its five hectares of vineyards devoted to Nobile di Montepulciano the Piccin husband-and-wife team and their new business partner Michele Manelli create wines with a strong link to the territory. You will not find cabernet sauvignon or merlot here, just prugnolo gentile. And, thanks to the new DOCG regulations, according to which pure prugnolo can be used for the Nobile, this grape will take up all of the seven additional hectares at the winery's disposal as of this year. In order to equip themselves for future production, they have also built a new cellar at Salcheto, where both 20- and 30-hectoliter Slovenian oak barrels and 500- and 700-liter sweeter French oak tonneaux, the latter for the Nobile Riserva, have been installed. And it is the Nobile di Montepulciano Riserva '95 that came over in our tastings as the estate's best wine, as might be expected from the quality of that vintage. A lovely intense ruby in color, it has a complex nose where the fruit is enhanced by a discreet, attractive balsamic nuance, a sign of great balance in the use of wood. The palate is impressive, thanks to very smooth, well-amalgamated tannins, and finishes on an intense and lingering note. The Nobile di Montepulciano '96 got a lower score, as its appealing nose contrasted with a palate where the tannins are not entirely integrated. The finish, however, closely echoes the nose and is nicely restrained and free from bitter notes.

● Vino Nobile di Montepulciano Ris. '95	🍷🍷	5
● Vino Nobile di Montepulciano '96	🍷	4
● Rosso di Montepulciano '97		3
● Salcheto '90	🍷🍷	4
● Vino Nobile di Montepulciano '91	🍷🍷	4
● Vino Nobile di Montepulciano Ris. '93	🍷🍷	5
● Rosso di Montepulciano '92	🍷	3
● Rosso di Montepulciano '96	🍷	3
● Vino Nobile di Montepulciano '94	🍷	4
● Vino Nobile di Montepulciano '95	🍷	4

MONTEPULCIANO (SI)

TENUTA SANTAVENERE - TRIACCA

S. S. per Pienza, 39
53045 Montepulciano (SI)
tel. 0578/757774

This is a welcome and well-deserved return to the Guide for the southernmost winery in the Triacca stable, a wine-producing colossus based in Valtellina. Enormous effort has been expended by the headquarters in Santavenere; of the 30 hectares with high-density planting only a few have been in production thus far, but with the '99 harvest the number rises sharply. The grapes grown here include merlot and cabernet sauvignon, in addition to sangiovese. During the coming year, once the bureaucratic delays have been dealt with, work should begin on the construction of the new cellar (the current one is decidedly undersized given the winery's new requirements). The wood used is of various dimensions, types and places of origin, with the number of barriques and tonneaux, key elements in the winery's new style, on the rise. As we await the results of these new developments, we can enjoy the already excellent Nobile di Montepulciano '96, which won its Two Glasses effortlessly. A fairly concentrated ruby in hue, with a slight tendency to garnet on the rim, it has an excellent range of aromas, from cocoa to wild cherry and vanilla, all pleasantly persistent. In the mouth the wine is not overly powerful, but proceeds elegantly from an encouraging attack on the palate, with attractively-textured tannins nicely enveloped by the glycero-alcoholic component, to a good finish with no trace of bitterness.

● Vino Nobile di Montepulciano '96	🍷🍷	4
● Vino Nobile di Montepulciano '94	🍷	4

MONTEPULCIANO (SI)

Tenimenti Angelini Tenuta Trerose

Fraz. Valiano
Villa Belvedere
53040 Montepulciano (SI)
tel. 0578/724018

This estate is part of the Tenimenti Angelini and now includes a remarkable 70 hectares or thereabouts under vine. Many of the vineyards are fairly young and have, for this zone, a considerable density of vines per hectare, in some cases 7-8 thousand. In addition to prugnolo gentile, other varieties are also grown: cabernet sauvignon for the reds, and viognier, sauvignon and chardonnay for the whites. Temperature-controlled steel vats have been chosen for vinification, while barriques are used on a grand scale for aging the wines. And in the glass, which is what really counts, the Tre Rose confirms its reputation as a reliable, capable winery that has managed to produce excellent wines even in years like '96 that were decidedly under par in these parts. This year the winery has won Two Glasses for each of two wines that are utterly different in character: the Nobile di Montepulciano Simposio '95 and the most unorthodox and distinctive of its offerings, the Busillis '97, made from viognier. The Simposio is a dense ruby-red in color, with an elegant nose featuring classic wild cherry and tobacco notes. The decidedly full-bodied palate, with its slightly pronounced but fine-textured tannins, leads into a good, lingering finish that echoes the nose. The Busillis has an attractive, intense straw-yellow color and a very interesting bouquet, with a well-expressed varietal note enriched by fragrances of white-fleshed fruit and a distinctive aromatic vein of camphor. The well-amalgamated wood is an unintrusive support to the flavors as they evolve, and the nicely judged acidity is evident but balanced. Four other Tre Rose wines netted One Glass each, a clear demonstration of the winery's overall soundness.

○	Busillis '97	🍷🍷	4
●	Vino Nobile di Montepulciano Simposio '95	🍷🍷	5
○	Vin Santo '	🍷	4
●	Vino Nobile di Montepulciano '96	🍷	4
●	Vino Nobile di Montepulciano La Villa '96	🍷	5
●	Vino Nobile di Montepulciano Ris. '95	🍷	5
●	Vino Nobile di Montepulciano La Villa '94	YY	4
●	Vino Nobile di Montepulciano La Villa '95	YY	5
●	Vino Nobile di Montepulciano Simposio '93	YY	5

MONTEPULCIANO (SI)

Terre di Bindella

Loc. Acquaviva
Via delle Tre Berte, 10/a
53040 Montepulciano (SI)
tel. 0578/767777

This estate saw many new developments during the year. The sale of the Borgo Scopeto Chianti holding brought in new capital, which was re-invested in the Montepulciano winery. The vineyards were extended, with the purchase of 12 hectares destined for high-density (about 7 thousand plants per hectare) vines, a choice based on the excellent results obtained from the winery's existing plots with a similar density. Over the next few years the number of hectares under vine will rise to 30, which should enable the winery to meet demand (at present a source of welcome difficulties) from its most enthusiastic customers. In the cellar the estate's new director, Andrea Mazzamurro, who has taken the place of the now retired Albano Ardessi, has introduced some changes, with the purchase of wooden vats for the vinification of the most important wines. Only two wines were presented at our tastings, since Bindella has not produced the Riserva del Nobile for some years and is concentrating its efforts on improving the quality of the standard Vino Nobile. The wines we tasted raised a few questions, no doubt because of the year, '96, which was not an easy one in this zone. Both the wines were slightly under par: the Nobile di Montepulciano '96 earned no more than a mention because of decidedly muffled aromas (which we found in both the samples we considered) held back in their development by a vegetal note, while in the mouth the tannins were somewhat detached from the whole. The Vallocaia '96 is better: it offers scents of red fruit jam and candied citrus peel, and a solid but rather aggressive tannic backbone that limits to some extent the evolution on the palate.

●	Vallocaia '96	🍷	5
●	Vino Nobile di Montepulciano '96		4
●	Vallocaia '90	YY	5
●	Vallocaia '94	YY	5
●	Vallocaia '95	YY	5
●	Vino Nobile di Montepulciano '90	YY	4
●	Vino Nobile di Montepulciano '91	YY	4
●	Vino Nobile di Montepulciano '92	YY	4
●	Vino Nobile di Montepulciano '94	YY	4
●	Vino Nobile di Montepulciano Ris. '90	YY	5
●	Vallocaia '93	Y	5
●	Vino Nobile di Montepulciano '93	Y	4
●	Vino Nobile di Montepulciano '95	Y	4

MONTEPULCIANO (SI)

Tenuta Valdipiatta
Via della Ciarliana, 25/a
53045 Montepulciano (SI)
tel. 0578/757930

Glasses have rained down on Valdipiatta this year, a further confirmation of the reputation of Sig. Caporali's winery as one of the best grape-growing and wine-producing estates of the zone. Their continuing quest for improvement, in both vineyard and cellar, is bearing excellent fruit. The new high-density vineyards should soon be coming on line, and a new cellar is under construction; this will include an area devoted to totally temperature-controlled vinification, where wooden vats will be placed. The storage rooms will also have humidity and temperature controls. But for tasters and fans alike the most striking development of the year is the birth of a new wine: the Trincerone, made from prugnolo gentile and colorino – and therefore a sort of homage to the native grapes – aged in barriques for about a year before bottling. The '97, the first Trincerone to come out, is an intense, dense ruby red in color, with fruity notes of blueberry and wild cherry on the nose, enriched by hints of spice and coffee. The attractive palate is underpinned by a fresh, very well controlled acidity. The Nobile di Montepulciano Riserva '95 is a wine of great structure and good length, which, however, has slightly uncontrolled, sharp-edged tannins that still need to mature for a good while in the bottle. The Nobile '96, with its enviable balance of flavors and rich, varietal nose, is excellent. Lastly, the Tre Fonti '96, with its attractive red berry fragrance and good persistence, is another appealing wine.

●	Tre Fonti '96	**YY**	5
●	Trincerone '97	**YY**	5
●	Vino Nobile di Montepulciano '96	**YY**	4
●	Vino Nobile di Montepulciano Ris. '95	**YY**	5
●	Rosso di Montepulciano '98		3
●	Vino Nobile di Montepulciano Ris. '90	YYY	5
●	Vino Nobile di Montepulciano '93	YY	4
●	Vino Nobile di Montepulciano '94	YY	4
●	Vino Nobile di Montepulciano '95	YY	4
●	Vino Nobile di Montepulciano Ris. '91	YY	4
●	Vino Nobile di Montepulciano Ris. '93	YY	5

MONTEPULCIANO (SI)

Villa S. Anna
Loc. Abbadia
53040 Montepulciano (SI)
tel. 0578/708017

How lucky are the wineries with problems like Villa Sant'Anna's, whose main worry is how to satisfy the demand from its fans all over the world! With this in mind Simonetta Fabroni, the owner, has recently purchased and rented other vineyards. But, as we know, winegrowing cannot be hurried, and production will rise just a little bit at a time. In the meantime, the cellar is being kept up to date with the purchase of new barrels and tonneaux in French oak. In this round of tastings Sant'Anna has again presented its key offering, the Vallone, after a year's absence (the '94 was considered unsuitable). A blend of cabernet sauvignon and sangiovese, it spends about 18 months in barriques and tonneaux before bottling. The '95 version certainly is a great success: it has fragrances of sour cherry jam with very appealing notes of coffee and black currant. And the palate is lovely too, with a soft, lightly alcoholic attack, after which the wine develops nicely in the mouth, with fine, well-integrated tannins. Another Two Glasses, although not so full, go to the Nobile di Montepulciano '96, which is an excellent wine for that inimical vintage. Of a bright and dense ruby color, it offers scents of red fruit and a very interesting spicy tone, and it is readily drinkable, notwithstanding the somewhat aggressive tannins. The Chianti Colli Senesi is appealing and quaffable, as is the Vin Santo '93 which, with its rich and balanced palate, would deserve a higher score were it not for its slightly dubious aromas, which we noted in both the bottles we tasted.

●	Vigna Il Vallone '95	**YY**	5
●	Vino Nobile di Montepulciano '96	**YY**	4
●	Chianti Colli Senesi '98	**Y**	3
○	Vin Santo '93	**Y**	5
●	Chianti '94	YY	2*
●	Chianti Colli Senesi '95	YY	2*
●	Vino Nobile di Montepulciano '94	YY	4
●	Vino Nobile di Montepulciano '93	YY	4
●	Chianti Colli Senesi '96	Y	3
●	Vigna Il Vallone '93	Y	5
○	Vin Santo '90	Y	5
●	Vino Nobile di Montepulciano '95	Y	4

MONTEPULCIANO STAZIONE (SI)

POLIZIANO

VIA FONTAGO, 11
53040 MONTEPULCIANO STAZIONE (SI)
TEL. 0578/738171

They say that you're never done with exams; for a wine-maker they are a yearly ritual. But some producers have become accustomed to passing them with ease, and often with top marks. Federico Carletti, owner of the Poliziano estate, is one of these. Although his winery is already something of a benchmark in the zone, and, let's say it out loud, one of the best in Italy, Carletti goes full out in his quest for further improvement, ably assisted, of course, by the highly skilled Carlo Ferrini, the oenologist with whom Carletti forms one of the leading teams on our wine-making scene. The most important new development here is the construction of a new cellar where vinification equipment will be housed, while the old cellar will be used for maturing the wines. Of the offerings we tasted this year the best was the truly marvelous Le Stanze '97. Dark purple and impenetrable to the eye, it offers an intense, full bouquet with scents of dark berries, pencil lead and eucalyptus. The palate is compact and rich, with an excellent tannic texture that marries perfectly with its seductive softness. The finish is full and deep, and seems to go on for miles. Two Glasses, and the prize for the best Nobile di Montepulciano '96, go to the Vigna Asinone, of which only a third of the usual number of bottles was produced. The great strength of this agreeably quaffable and satisfyingly lingering wine lies in its elegance, a reminder that our noblest wines do not need the muscles of a body-builder to win us over. The same score goes to the Morellino di Scansano Lohsa '98, produced by the Maremma branch of the winery.

●	Le Stanze '97	🍷🍷🍷	6
●	Morellino di Scansano Lohsa '98	🍷🍷	3*
●	Vino Nobile di Montepulciano Vigna dell'Asinone '96	🍷🍷	5
●	Vino Nobile di Montepulciano '96	🍷	4
●	Rosso di Montepulciano '98		4
●	Elegia '95	🍸🍸🍸	5
●	Le Stanze '93	🍸🍸🍸	5
●	Le Stanze '95	🍸🍸🍸	5
●	Vino Nobile di Montepulciano Vigna dell'Asinone '93	🍸🍸🍸	5
●	Vino Nobile di Montepulciano Vigna dell'Asinone '95	🍸🍸🍸	5
●	Vino Nobile di Montepulciano Vigna dell'Asinone Ris. '90	🍸🍸🍸	5

MONTESCUDAIO (PI)

POGGIO GAGLIARDO

LOC. POGGIO GAGLIARDO
56040 MONTESCUDAIO (PI)
TEL. 0586/630775

Poggio Gagliardo is one of the oldest wineries on the Tuscan coast. This is a real farm where a wide range of agricultural activities are carried out, although Sig. Surbone, the owner, naturally devotes his best efforts to wine production. We have been saying for years now that Poggio Gagliardo's best features are the consistent quality and the excellent execution of the wines that make up its long list. These two factors are in themselves positive, but the desire to achieve more has led the winery to try the path, already being followed by many Tuscan producers, of a cabernet- and merlot-based super-Tuscan that will probably come out in the next few years. However, there were already several good things in this year's tasting, starting with the Vigna Lontana '98, which did as well as last year's. This is a successful white with fragrances of pear, citrus fruit and vanilla, completed by a solidly structured, well-articulated palate with a convincing finish. After a couple of attempts the Rovo '97, a nicely concentrated wine with a good overall harmony and aromas of ripe blueberry, spice and toasty oak and a light vegetal nuance, has also netted Two Glasses. The other red, the Malemacchie '97, is satisfying but more evolved; this wine is balanced and well made, but of only average depth. The Linaglia '98, admirably clean as usual, with a substantial, gradually evolving palate, is fairly good. Lastly, the two properly executed Montescudaio wines also deserve a mention.

○	Montescudaio Bianco Vigna Lontana '98	🍷🍷	4
●	Montescudaio Rosso Rovo '97	🍷🍷	5
○	Montescudaio Bianco Linaglia '98	🍷	4
●	Montescudaio Rosso Malemacchie '97	🍷	4
○	Montescudaio Bianco '98		3
●	Montescudaio Rosso '98		3
○	Montescudaio Bianco Vigna Lontana '97	🍸🍸	4
●	Montescudaio Rosso Malemacchie '92	🍸🍸	3*
●	Montescudaio Rosso Rovo '93	🍸🍸	4
●	Montescudaio Rosso Rovo '94	🍸🍸	4
●	Montescudaio Rosso Rovo '96	🍸	4

MONTESPERTOLI (FI)

La Gigliola

Via S. Pietro in Mercato
50025 Montespertoli (FI)
tel. 0571/608001

This is the debut entry in the Guide of an estate located in a district that is undergoing something of an upheaval, with any number of wineries gearing themselves up to produce wines of increasingly high quality. The farm, owned by Anna Piazzini, has vineyards extending over about 50 hectares. The varieties grown are mainly the traditional ones, although some additional grapes, such as syrah and merlot, can also be found. Management of the vines and the vinification procedures are entrusted to Alberto Antonini, an oenologist who has also built up an excellent reputation for his work outside Italy. Two wines were presented at our tastings, a good Chianti and the remarkable Camporsoli red. The Chianti '98, a deep, intense ruby red in color, offers definite, clean fruity notes on the nose, with blackberry to the fore. The attack on the palate is soft, well balanced and reasonably mouth-filling, and the fairly full-bodied mid palate leads to quite a long finish, with tasty, closely knit and nicely smooth tannins. The Camporsoli '97 is made from a blend of 50% sangiovese with syrah and merlot. Matured in barriques for 12 months, it has an intense, almost impenetrable dark ruby color. On the nose it is concentrated and compact, with notes of black fruit, like plum and black currant, making their presence felt, accompanied by faint vegetal scents. In the mouth it is still youthful and medium-bodied, with lively tannins that are not overly smooth, but are tasty and agreeable. The finish is substantial, rich and lingering.

●	Camporsoli '97	🍷🍷	4
●	Chianti '98	🍷	3

MONTESPERTOLI (FI)

Fattoria Sonnino

Via Volterrana Nord, 10
50025 Montespertoli (FI)
tel. 0571/609198

After some years, the lovely Fattoria owned by Baron Alessandro De Renzis Sonnino makes a well-deserved return to the Guide. The quality of the wines presented is definitely encouraging, with some bottles, such as the Vinsanto and the Sanleone, of particular interest. We might say that the ups and downs in this winery's performance are perhaps still a touch too closely linked to the variability of the harvests. A greater degree of continuity still needs to be found even if, and here is the positive side of the coin, this same vulnerability to external conditions shows that the winery does not resort to artifice and compromise. The Sanleone '97, a blend of merlot, sangiovese and a touch of petit verdot, made a very positive impression. It failed by a mere hair's breadth to win Two Glasses, in part, perhaps, as a result of excessive caution suggested by the roughness of the tannins. This is, however, a structured, characterful wine with concentrated perfumes that include a good measure of fruit. The Vin Santo '95 is another very interesting wine, with an intense nose that includes medicinal scents of not very great elegance. The palate sweeps away any doubts: sweet on the attack, it is dense and powerful, and evolves very satisfactorily indeed. The acceptable but slightly disappointing Cantinino Vigneto di Fezzana '95 reveals some sulfurous notes on the nose and reasonable structure on the palate, but with some forward notes. The Chianti '98, on the other hand, is very successful, offering simple but very agreeable fresh scents of blackberry and raspberry. These are echoed on the balanced and pleasingly fruity palate.

○	Vin Santo del Chianti '95	🍷🍷	4
●	Chianti '98	🍷	2*
●	Sanleone '97	🍷	4
●	Cantinino Vign. di Fezzana '95		4
●	Cantinino Vign. di Fezzana '88	🍸🍸	4
●	Sanleone '93	🍸🍸	4
●	Sanleone '94	🍸🍸	4
●	Cantinino Vign. di Fezzana '90	🍸	4
●	Cantinino Vign. di Fezzana '93	🍸	4
●	Chianti Colli Fiorentini Castello di Montespertoli '94	🍸	2*
●	Chianti Titolato Castello di Montespertoli '91	🍸	2*

MONTEVARCHI (AR)

FATTORIA DI RENDOLA
LOC. RENDOLA, 85
52025 MONTEVARCHI (AR)
TEL. 055/9707594

After some years in the Other Wineries section, Sig. Keushguerian's Fattoria di Rendola has shown such steady improvement that it has earned a place of its own. The estate is of a good size, 19 hectares planted to merlot, chardonnay and sangiovese. Total production amounts to about 50 thousand very reasonably priced bottles. The main points to emerge from our tastings were the winery's consistency and technical expertise. The Chardonnay, which scored highest, was particularly successful. Of a brilliant green-tinged straw color, it shows an intense nose with good noticeable oak and delicate, unusual scents of spice, bay leaf and hazelnut. The fresh, well-balanced and medium-bodied palate boasts a delightful honey-toned finish. The Merlot '97, a well-designed, meaty wine held back by a somewhat simple nose notable for the cleanness of the fruit, just failed to get Two Glasses. One full Glass goes to the sangiovese-based La Pineta, a soft, substantial wine with good sweet fruit and fair length; its only flaw is the slightly intrusive oak.

○ Chardonnay '98	🍷🍷	4
● La Pineta '97	🍷	3
● Merlot '97	🍷	4

MONTOPOLI VALDARNO (PI)

VARRAMISTA
LOC. VARRAMISTA
VIA RICAVO, 31
56020 MONTOPOLI VALDARNO (PI)
TEL. 0571/468121

The excellence of Tuscan syrahs is by now beyond dispute, with more or less universal recognition of the fact that the grape has found a very favorable habitat in this region. Some bottles can hold their own against many a Rhône red, not to mention how well they do against their Australian counterparts. The best syrahs in Tuscany are made by just four or five wineries. Of these, Varramista's wine stands out for its consistently good quality, year after year, and even more for its elegance and the definition of its best varietal notes. Federico Staderini, the oenologist in charge of production, could almost be said to have specialized in the vinification of this noble grape, and the results are there for all to see. Each vintage we have tasted has successfully blended excellent concentration with finesse and freshness, something that cannot be taken for granted in our warm climes. The '97 version traces a similar path. A fairly intense, luminous ruby red in color, it makes an aromatic and clear impact on the nose, with notes of berries, white pepper and oriental spice, as well as faint secondary animal aromas. The palate, after a restrained but distinct entry, expands with intense, clean, and very tasty fruity notes. A slight lapse in extract at mid palate prevents this wine from getting Three Glasses, but it is still exemplary for its balance and harmony.

● Varramista '97	🍷🍷	5
● Varramista '95	🍷🍷 (outline)	5
● Varramista '96	🍷🍷 (outline)	5

ORBETELLO (GR)

RASCIONI CECCONELLO

FRAZ. FONTEBLANDA
LOC. POGGIO SUGHERINO
58010 ORBETELLO (GR)
TEL. 0564/885642

We welcome Rascioni Cecconello back to the Guide after a year's absence. The excellent behavior of the reds from the new vintages confirms that its time out was a perfectly natural fluctuation, linked to the varying quality of the individual vintages presented last year. The '95 version of the Poggio Capitana, made solely from sangiovese, has a good, clear, brilliant and fairly concentrated ruby color. The nose is initially muffled and indistinct, but with a few minutes' exposure to the air it opens out to release intense, well-defined notes of ripe fruit; some animal and vegetal nuances make for an aromatic spectrum that is robust but a bit unfocused. Fleshy, supple and softly tannic, the palate does better, from all points of view: cleanness, definition, balance and persistence. As is the case every year, the Poggio Ciliegio, the prototype for all the new-generation ciliegiolo wines from the Maremma, is Rascioni Cecconello's most successful wine. The '97 has a lovely ruby color with pure dark violet highlights. On the nose it displays noble notes of pencil lead, licorice and quinine nicely alternating with an intense, ripe and enveloping fruity timbre reminiscent of black currant. In the mouth it has considerable weight and balance; austere rather than yielding, thanks to its tannins (rather hard at present), it would seem to have great potential. The finish, not surprisingly, reveals a dominant bitterish note.

●	Poggio Ciliegio '97	▼▼	4
●	Poggio Capitana '95	▼	4
●	Poggio Ciliegio '95	♀♀	4
●	Poggio Capitana '93	♀	4

PALAIA (PI)

SAN GERVASIO

LOC. SAN GERVASIO
56036 PALAIA (PI)
TEL. 0587/483360

San Gervasio is one of the many estates created (or upgraded) in Tuscany in the last decade. It entered the Guide in the '98 edition, and is still on the right track and making continuous progress, as confirmed by this year's tastings; indeed we can now put it down not so much to favorable vintages as to growth in the skill and experience of the owners. There is nothing exceptional in the vinification techniques they use, which rely on practices that are now part of the wine-maker's lexicon: temperature control and controlled, not over-long maceration; maturation in small (and for the most part new) wood casks. The owners, the Tommasini siblings, make no secret of their ambition, as expressed in their close attention to the vineyards and in the irrepressible and contagious "wine fever" they seem to suffer from, to create wines of increasingly high quality. This year the key wine, A Sirio '97, made almost entirely from sangiovese, came out well in front of the others, good as they are – indeed it netted Two Glasses. A concentrated, elegant and characterful red, it has a well-designed palate based on the softness and sweetness of the tannins. Of the other wines, the Marna '98, a blend of vermentino and chardonnay that almost got Two Glasses, stands out, thanks to its distinct nose and substantial palate. The Chianti Le Stoppie '98, with its fruit and quaffability, is another success. The good Aprico '98, a rosé, is fragrant and medium-bodied. The Vin Santo is pleasing, despite somewhat excessive wood, while the San Torpé is acceptable.

●	A Sirio '97	▼▼	5
⊙	Aprico '98	▼	2*
●	Chianti Le Stoppie '98	▼	3
○	Marna '98	▼	4
○	Vin Santo '95	▼	4
○	S. Torpé Casina de' Venti '98		2
●	A Sirio '95	♀♀	4
●	A Sirio '96	♀♀	4
○	Marna '97	♀♀	4
●	Chianti Le Stoppie '96	♀	3
●	Chianti Le Stoppie '97	♀	3
○	Marna '96	♀	4

PANZANO IN CHIANTI (FI)

CAROBBIO
VIA S. MARTINO A CECIONE, 26
50020 PANZANO IN CHIANTI (FI)
TEL. 055/852136

Carobbio, whose excellent work in both vineyard and cellar is confirmed year after year, has presented another pair of excellent wines. Vineyard replanting, under the supervision of the agronomist Remigio Bordini, is almost finished, bringing the total area under vine to almost ten hectares. Unlike neighboring winegrowers, Carobbio still uses, in some plots, the gobelet training system, which is not very common nowadays. The consistent quality of their wines even in relatively poor years, thanks to the dedication of the oenologist Gabriella Tani and the able help of the winery's technical staff, is very impressive. A wise use of small barrels shows that it is possible to marry tradition to innovation, without depriving the resultant wine of its identity. The Chianti Classico '97, a full, unambiguous ruby red in color, initially offers deep aromas of roasting coffee and tobacco that eventually make way for fruitier notes. The even palate reflects the bouquet and leaves an agreeable aftertaste. The Riserva '96 has a limpid ruby color, and a slightly balsamic nose with full, simple fruity notes of plum and cherry. After a not particularly powerful attack on the palate, the complex, close texture of the tannins, meshing harmoniously with the alcohol, emerges, as does the marked but measured acidity.

●	Chianti Classico '97	🍷🍷	4
●	Chianti Classico Ris. '96	🍷🍷	5
●	Chianti Classico '88	🍸🍸	4
●	Chianti Classico '90	🍸🍸	4
●	Chianti Classico '93	🍸🍸	4
●	Chianti Classico '94	🍸🍸	4
●	Chianti Classico '95	🍸🍸	4
●	Chianti Classico Ris. '88	🍸🍸	5
●	Chianti Classico Ris. '90	🍸🍸	5
●	Chianti Classico Ris. '93	🍸🍸	5
●	Chianti Classico Ris. '95	🍸🍸	5
●	Leone del Carobbio '93	🍸🍸	5
●	Leone del Carobbio '94	🍸🍸	5
●	Pietraforte del Carobbio '93	🍸🍸	5
●	Pietraforte del Carobbio '95	🍸🍸	5

PANZANO IN CHIANTI (FI)

FATTORIA CASALOSTE
VIA MONTAGLIARI, 32
50020 PANZANO IN CHIANTI (FI)
TEL. 055/852725

A pause for thought? A year that is hard to interpret? We are not quite sure where to begin in our description of the wines presented this year by Giovan Battista d'Orsi, a keen winegrower who personally follows each step in the production of his wines, from the vineyard to the cellar, with, we are sure, the care that a father devotes to bringing up his children. We can only say that we were a bit disappointed by the results, especially the lack of harmony between the nose and the palate. But let's move on to the descriptions, which should give you a better idea of what we mean. The Chianti Classico '97 is very inviting in the glass, with a dense, pronounced ruby color. On the nose, after a fruity opening, the wood takes over, with still dominant vanilla tones that only subsequently spread out to make way for the fresh, balsamic and undoubtedly attractive other elements of the bouquet. The attack on the palate, initially decisive, with tannins that stand out authoritatively, does not follow through, leading to an abrupt, inharmonious and disconnected finish. The altogether more even Riserva '96 is better. It shows a full, bright ruby hue and aromas somewhat lacking in intensity. Notes of berries and cherry show an attractive finesse but insufficient power. The reasonably substantial palate is characterized by balance and elegance. The alcohol makes its presence felt, and the structure, although adequate, is not particularly impressive; a nicely persistent finish makes up to some extent for a slightly thin body. We await next year's wines.

●	Chianti Classico '97	🍷	3
●	Chianti Classico Ris. '96	🍷	4
●	Chianti Classico '95	🍸🍸	3*
●	Chianti Classico Don Vincenzo Ris. '95	🍸🍸	5
●	Chianti Classico Ris. '94	🍸🍸	4
●	Chianti Classico Ris. '95	🍸🍸	4
●	Chianti Classico '93	🍸	3
●	Chianti Classico '94	🍸	3
●	Chianti Classico '96	🍸	3

Cennatoio

Via di San Leolino, 35
50020 Panzano in Chianti (FI)
tel. 055/852134

We are grateful to Leandro Alessi for electing to work full-time as a winegrower, devoting his time and energy to the production of some very good wines indeed. The "conca d'oro" (golden valley), as the Panzano zone is known, is blessed with a particularly favorable microclimate and can without doubt reward these increased efforts, as our tastings this year confirm. The Chianti Classico '97 is a dense, intense ruby red in color. The nose has an impressive share of fresh fruits, cherry and plum in particular. The palate is light at first, but then opens out, enabling the tannins to unfold evenly and smoothly, with the acidity providing an agreeable counterpoint to the alcohol. The finish, which falls off slightly in intensity, is, however, persistent. The various components of the Riserva O'Leandro '95 are nicely melded, starting with its varied nose, in which the fruits have properly absorbed the oak. The palate too is successfully meshed, but does not offer great length. The Chianti Classico Riserva '96 stands out at once with its very intense color. On the nose it offers a wide, perfectly ripened, fresh fruit bouquet. It is less impressive in the mouth, because the alcohol is rather prominent. The sangiovese Etrusco '96, almost impenetrably dense in color, starts off with a slightly closed nose, which then opens out to form an appealing, well-defined bouquet. The palate is already nicely balanced, complex and free of harshness.

●	Chianti Classico '97	TT	3*
●	Etrusco '96	TT	5
●	Chianti Classico O'Leandro '95	T	4
●	Chianti Classico Ris. '96	T	4
●	Etrusco '94	YYY	5
●	Chianti Classico '93	YY	3*
●	Chianti Classico Ris. '91	YY	4
●	Chianti Classico Ris. '93	YY	4
●	Chianti Classico Ris. '94	YY	4
●	Chianti Classico Ris. '95	YY	4
●	Etrusco '93	YY	5
●	Etrusco '95	YY	5
●	Mammolo '93	YY	6
●	Rosso Fiorentino '93	YY	5
●	Rosso Fiorentino '95	YY	5

★ Tenuta Fontodi

Via San Leolino, 87
50020 Panzano in Chianti (FI)
tel. 055/852005

The '96 sangiovese wines from the Fontodi Estate in Panzano are slightly sharp as a result of their exuberant acidity. This is by no means a new development – one of the characteristics of Panzano reds is that they always have a high degree of fixed acidity. The Flaccianellos of '91, '93 and '95 are still somewhat tangy. However, in the '96 we found this feature more pronounced, perhaps because the vintage was more difficult and the alcohol and extracts did not fully balance the sharpness of the wine. Both the Chianti Classico Riserva '96 (the Vigna del Sorbo has as far as we know not yet been released) and the Flaccianello '96 have these minor limitations. The Chianti Classico '97 is an intriguing example of its category, again with some youthful sharpness, but with undeniably sweet polyphenols and a less acidity-dominated progression on the palate. In overall terms this is a smaller wine, but it seems to be more successful and better balanced. The excellent Syrah Case Via '96 shows some rustic notes on the nose. This is a powerful wine, with highly concentrated extract, fine, closely textured but evenly spread tannins and considerable length. It did not quite make Three Glasses, however. An initial reduced note on the nose compromises the varietal qualities to some extent. This may be a temporary defect, but the three bottles we tasted all had the same problem. For the first time the varietal and well-executed Pinot Nero Case Via '97 was quite interesting.

●	Chianti Classico '97	TT	4
●	Flaccianello della Pieve '96	TT	5
●	Pinot Nero Case Via '97	TT	5
●	Syrah Case Via '96	TT	5
●	Chianti Classico Ris. '96	T	5
●	Chianti Classico Vigna del Sorbo Ris. '86	YYY	5
●	Chianti Classico Vigna del Sorbo Ris. '90	YYY	5
●	Chianti Classico Vigna del Sorbo Ris. '94	YYY	5
●	Flaccianello della Pieve '88	YYY	6
●	Flaccianello della Pieve '90	YYY	6
●	Flaccianello della Pieve '91	YYY	5
●	Syrah Case Via '95	YYY	5

PANZANO IN CHIANTI (FI)

IL VESCOVINO
FRAZ. PIAZZOLE DI SOPRA
VIA CASE SPARSE
50020 PANZANO IN CHIANTI (FI)
TEL. 055/852512

After a couple of years in "purgatory" Riccardo Gosi and Antonella Mugnaini's attractive estate returns to the Guide. Which is not to say that the wines produced by Il Vescovino during this period were not good, but they have their own peculiar features, with a strong natural acidity that slows down the development of the wine, which therefore needs more time and a good degree of oxygenation. The sequence of two cool years like '95 and '96 evidently accentuated this natural tendency, endowing the wines with sharper flavors and putting a brake on their aromatic expansion. The '97 Chianti Classico Vigna Piccola, on the other hand, can already be savored to the full, and earned our admiration and a few more points in its score. On the nose it exhibits lively notes of fruit accompanied by subtle floral nuances; its entry on the palate is firm and a gradual and balanced development leads to a long, fruity finish with well-tamed tannins. In the Riserva '95 we find good substance and an appealing intensity of flavor, somewhat diminished by a trace of sulfur on the nose. There's the same problem with the Merlotto '95, which, however, reveals an intriguing and nicely dense palate with rounded, closely textured tannins and a reasonable finish. Cleaner on the nose, with notes of raspberry jam, the Merlotto '96 is, on the other hand, less complex and not so richly structured.

● Chianti Cl. Vigna Piccola '97	🍷🍷	3*
● Chianti Cl. Vigna Piccola Ris. '96	🍷	4
● Merlotto '95	🍷	5
● Merlotto '96	🍷	5
● Merlotto '94	🍷🍷	5
● Chianti Cl. Vigna Piccola '94	🍷	3

PANZANO IN CHIANTI (FI)

LA MASSA
VIA CASE SPARSE, 9
50020 PANZANO IN CHIANTI (FI)
TEL. 055/852701

If we commented last year that winning our highest award is nothing new for Giampaolo Motta's La Mass, what should we say this year, when the winery has hit its fifth consecutive bull's-eye? So let's consider something else, focusing our attention on the standard Chianti that, step by step, is definitely making its mark as an example to be followed: this is a fine, elegant but definitely quaffable wine. A round of applause is due to the owner and Carlo Ferrini, an oenologist who manages to bring out the very best in grapes. And now for the Giorgio Primo '97, a wine whose very color takes your breath away with is concentration and richness. The nose is decidedly intense, and the blend of the sweet toasty notes of oak with the aromas of red fruit is strikingly lively and sensual. The attack on the palate is impressive, with an immediate mouth-filling quality that reveals an extremely well-balanced wealth of extract. Mid palate is magnificent and silky, and the long finish is juicy and delicious. The Chianti Classico '97 has, once again, a lively, ruby-hued color, with complex fragrances, where fruit alternates with vanilla, and spice makes its presence felt without overstepping the mark. In the mouth, the alcohol fully complements the tannins in a magical balance, and the finish is smooth and consistent.

● Chianti Cl. Giorgio Primo '97	🍷🍷🍷	6
● Chianti Classico '97	🍷🍷	4
● Chianti Cl. Giorgio Primo '93	🍷🍷🍷	4*
● Chianti Cl. Giorgio Primo '94	🍷🍷🍷	5
● Chianti Cl. Giorgio Primo '95	🍷🍷🍷	5
● Chianti Cl. Giorgio Primo '96	🍷🍷🍷	5
● Chianti Cl. Giorgio Primo '92	🍷🍷	5
● Chianti Classico '90	🍷🍷	4
● Chianti Classico '92	🍷🍷	4
● Chianti Classico '93	🍷🍷	4
● Chianti Classico '94	🍷🍷	4
● Chianti Classico '95	🍷🍷	4
● Chianti Classico '96	🍷🍷	4
● Chianti Classico Ris. '90	🍷🍷	5

PODERE LE CINCIOLE
VIA CASE SPARSE, 83
50020 PANZANO IN CHIANTI (FI)
TEL. 055/852636

It's better than last year. It seems only right for us to start off by reassuring fans of the wines produced by Luca Orsini and Valeria Viganò, a couple that does not hold back on the energy and enthusiasm they put into their labors in the vineyard and in the cellar. Clearly each year is different; thus, last year's not entirely positive judgment fell within our task as tasters, and did not reflect on the highly professional - as always - work performed at this estate. After a year of sterling effort, restructuring has been completed. Two new hectares of vineyards, planted with selected clones of sangiovese, are about to start production, which will bring the total area under vine to about 11 hectares. And now to the wines, starting with the Chianti Classico '97: it shows a full, dense ruby color, and intense perfumes of fruit, with cherry and black currant to the fore, and light vanilla notes. It makes an excellent, well-supported entry on the palate, with strong but not dry tannins, and develops into a juicy, balanced, fairly long finish: One Glass with no trouble. The Riserva '96 Vigna del Pozzo gets Two Glasses, like the '95 last year. It presents a very attractive color, ruby that still has some traces of purple, and a bouquet that, after a light toasty nuance, opens out into fruitier notes of blueberry and blackberry, with faint hints of cherry. It makes a firm entry on the palate, with good pronounced acidity and closely textured but unaggressive tannins. The mid palate is sound, and the finish, long with no traces of heaviness, adds to the appealing quaffability of the wine.

● Chianti Classico Valle del Pozzo Ris. '96	**YY**	4
● Chianti Classico '97	**Y**	3
● Chianti Classico '93	YY	3*
● Chianti Classico '94	YY	3*
● Chianti Classico '95	YY	3*
● Chianti Classico Valle del Pozzo Ris. '95	YY	4
● Chianti Classico Valle del Pozzo Ris. '94	Y	4

PANZANO IN CHIANTI (FI)

LE FONTI
VIA LE FONTI
50020 PANZANO IN CHIANTI (FI)
TEL. 055/852194

It is a great pleasure for us to confirm a place in the Guide for this little estate in the heart of the Chianti Classico district, in a zone that is ideally suited to wine production. The owner, Conrad Schmitt, takes a personal interest in all the work of the winery, starting with the layout of the vineyards. It is obvious that great care and attention are lavished on the vines, but also on the cellar, so that it would be hard to fault the vinification technique. What is perhaps missing is that added something that would give the wines an extra dimension, but for the time being it seems more appropriate for us to remark on the consistent high quality achieved over the last two years. We were not able to taste the normal Chianti, which we will therefore review next year. So let's start with the Riserva '96, which shows an attractive vivid ruby hue. The bouquet is still dominated by a vanilla tone, which lingers pleasantly and then makes way for sweet, ripe, juicy fruit, from black currant to blueberry and blackberry. The fine attack on the palate immediately reveals an impressive balance, with lasting, firm, closely textured tannins that mesh nicely with the softer elements. The finish is very clean and prolonged. The Fontissimo '96, a blend of sangiovese and cabernet sauvignon which is becoming a classic for this zone, is notable for its very lively, bright purple color. The fragrance is youthful, intense and almost pungent. The palate is dominated by an acidity that does not overstep the mark, but provides the right degree of vigor in a robust body.

● Chianti Classico Ris. '96	**YY**	4
● Fontissimo '96	**YY**	5
● Chianti Classico Ris. '95	YY	4
● Fontissimo '91	YY	5
● Fontissimo '95	YY	5
● Chianti Classico '96	Y	4
● Chianti Classico Ris. '90	Y	3
● Chianti Classico Ris. '91	Y	4
● Chianti Classico Ris. '93	Y	4
● Fontissimo '93	Y	5

PANZANO IN CHIANTI (FI)

MONTE BERNARDI
VIA CHIANTIGIANA
50020 PANZANO IN CHIANTI (FI)
TEL. 055/852400

Stak and Sharon Aivaliotis clearly do not go in for half measures – indeed, their debut in the Guide coincides with their winning Three Glasses. A truly triumphant entry for an estate purchased by the Aivaliotis husband-and-wife team in 1988, with wines released starting with the '92 vintage. Vineyard yields are kept low and the style of vinification is decidedly international, with barriques used for all the wines in the range. In past tastings the wines were always distinguished by vigorous, concentrated structure that, however, appeared together with problems on the nose: these problems would seem, as of the '97 vintage, to have been solved once and for all. Hence this is a winery whose potential we were well aware of and which has not, all things considered, really taken us by surprise with its Three Glass Tzingana, a blend of cabernet and merlot. The color is extremely concentrated, as are the aromas: layer upon layer of black fruit accompanied by scents of coffee and cocoa and mineral hints. The palate is firm and powerful, with exceptionally dense tannins and a finish that just goes on and on expanding. This might seem like a display of muscles, pure and simple, but what really impressed and convinced us in this wine was the extremely well-considered execution and the perfect balance of all its components. The Sangiovese Sa'etta also did very well: it is elegantly woody, and balanced and smooth on the palate. The success of the '97s is confirmed by the Chianti, which is full-flavored and solid, though not overly long. The Riserva '96, with its somewhat flawed nose, is a leftover from the past. And to finish, a compliment and a criticism: the first goes to the oenologist Giorgio Marone, the second to the winery's pricing policy. As we said at the beginning, no half measures here.

●	Tzingana '97	🍷🍷🍷	6
●	Chianti Classico '97	🍷🍷	4
●	Sa'etta '97	🍷🍷	6
●	Chianti Classico Ris. '96		5

PANZANO IN CHIANTI (FI)

CASTELLO DEI RAMPOLLA
VIA CASE SPARSE, 22
50020 PANZANO IN CHIANTI (FI)
TEL. 055/852001

Luca and Maurizia have indeed taken up the mantle of Prince Alceo di Napoli, the noble vigneron with few equals in Tuscany. Certainly, living up to a legendary figure like their father cannot be easy. But with the almost paternal help of Giacomo Tachis, a prince among oenologists, they are – to say the very least – managing to produce great wines that the extremely rigorous Prince Alceo would have been proud of. This is especially true of the one named after him, which comes from vineyards that he chose to plant with cabernet sauvignon and petit verdot (Alceo hated the sangiovese grape): once again it is simply a dream. The '97 version of La Vigna di Alceo is richer and more powerful than the '96, and formidably concentrated, but does not perhaps have the magical balance that won the '96 the distinction of being proclaimed our Wine of the Year. It is still, however, absolutely one of the best Tuscan reds. The excellent Sammarco '96, cabernet sauvignon and sangiovese (but no more than 20% of the latter!), just missed joining the Vigna di Alceo with Three Glasses. Its failure - only just - to triumph can be blamed on a structure that was just a shade less rich and powerful than we would have expected. All the fault of that 20% sangiovese, old Alceo would have thundered. And yet the Chianti Classicos presented this year by Luca and Maurizia, made essentially from sangiovese grapes, were among the best ever. Both were elegant and quaffable, with fruity and floral notes that were simpler but more distinct in the basic '97 version. Two little masterpieces, in short, that need not blush in the company of the cabernet-based big guns.

●	La Vigna di Alceo '97	🍷🍷🍷	6
●	Chianti Classico '97	🍷🍷	4
●	Chianti Classico Ris. '96	🍷🍷	5
●	Sammarco '96	🍷🍷	6
●	La Vigna di Alceo '96	🍸🍸🍸	6
●	Sammarco '85	🍸🍸🍸	6
●	Sammarco '86	🍸🍸🍸	6
●	Sammarco '94	🍸🍸🍸	6
●	Chianti Classico Ris. '88	🍸🍸	5
●	Chianti Classico Ris. '93	🍸🍸	5
●	Chianti Classico Ris. '94	🍸🍸	5
●	Chianti Classico Ris. '95	🍸🍸	5
●	Sammarco '88	🍸🍸	6
●	Sammarco '93	🍸🍸	6
●	Sammarco '95	🍸🍸	6

Fattoria Sant'Andrea

Loc. Case Sparse
50020 Panzano in Chianti (FI)
tel. 055/8549090

This winery is better known as Panzanello, which is the name that appears on the labels of their bottles. The estate is located in one of the highest zones of the Panzano district and borders on Le Cinciole. It is owned by Andrea and Iole Sommaruga, a Roman couple who moved here after opting to change both lifestyle and work. With the aid of the consultant oenologist Gioia Cresti they began a couple of years ago (before then the grapes were sold to Castelli del Grevepesa) to vinify and produce on their own behalf. The jump in quality took place with the '97 harvest, a year in which the slightly sharp-edged, rather lean style of the Chianti Classicos of previous vintages seems magically to have become only a memory. The '97 version does not stand out in terms of complexity, but it has a sound, characteristic nose with a very appealing note of violet, and the flavors are softer and more concentrated than they used to be. This is due in part to the more favorable vintage, but also to a different and improved management of both the vineyards and the fermentation phase. There is, of course, a return to slightly tarter flavors with the Chianti Classico Riserva '95 and even more with the '96, which may well please the purists but decidedly reduces concentration and easy quaffability: the wines are thinner, with just a few too many rough edges and more acidic-tannic aggressiveness, qualities that may fade with time, but which for the moment dominate the palate of both of them.

●	Chianti Classico '97	🍷🍷	3*
●	Chianti Classico Ris. '95	🍷	4
●	Chianti Classico Ris. '96	🍷	4

PANZANO IN CHIANTI (FI)

Vecchie Terre di Montefili

Via S. Cresci, 45
50022 Panzano in Chianti (FI)
tel. 055/853739

This was another transitional year for an estate that nonetheless always presents really excellent wines at our tastings. But having got us used to the great bottles of previous years, they raised our expectations of excitement. We shall begin with the Vigna Regis '97, a blend of chardonnay, sauvignon and gewürztraminer. It exhibits an intense golden yellow color, and a bouquet of very warm buttery notes backed up by quite simple fruity tones of apple and banana. The palate immediately reveals a lively acidity that fits nicely into the harmonious whole. The Chianti Classico '97, a pronounced ruby red in color, has a nose of very intense balsamic notes and sweet, ripe fruit, with plum to the fore. The attack on the palate is substantial, with a good distribution of acidity and tannins; the finish is sound but not notably long. The Anfiteatro '96 again seems to be waiting in the wings: very lively in color, it offers elegant aromas of black currant and blueberry that are particularly sweet, spicy and inviting. The attack on the palate is soft, and then the tannins gradually come smoothly into play; the finish, while not powerful, is dry and agreeable. The Bruno di Rocca '96, a blend of sangiovese and cabernet sauvignon, is attractive in appearance, with its very pronounced lovely ruby hue. It offers tertiary aromas that start off with evolved animal tones and develop into deep and very elegant notes of chocolate and tobacco. In the mouth it exhibits good, closely textured tannins, which provide an appropriate juiciness underpinned by the warm, powerful alcohol. The finish falls off slightly, but is nonetheless agreeable.

●	Anfiteatro '96	🍷🍷	6
●	Bruno di Rocca '96	🍷🍷	6
●	Chianti Classico '97	🍷	4
○	Vigna Regis '97	🍷	4
●	Anfiteatro '94	YYY	6
●	Chianti Classico Anfiteatro Ris. '88	YYY	6
●	Chianti Classico Ris. '85	YYY	6
●	Anfiteatro '91	YY	6
●	Anfiteatro '93	YY	6
●	Anfiteatro '95	YY	6
●	Bruno di Rocca '91	YY	6
●	Bruno di Rocca '92	YY	6
●	Bruno di Rocca '93	YY	6
●	Bruno di Rocca '94	YY	6
●	Bruno di Rocca '95	YY	6

PANZANO IN CHIANTI (FI)

Vignole
Via Case Sparse, 14
50022 Panzano in Chianti (FI)
tel. 0574/592025 - 055/852197

The Nistri family has owned this winery for almost 30 years. Originally from Prato, they have always been in the wine business, but their overriding passion is this estate of almost 13 hectares, which has given them enormous satisfaction over the years. Traditional vinification techniques are used on carefully selected grapes, after which the must is matured in large barrels. Giorgio Marone, the consultant oenologist, is distinguished, as always, by his painstaking and conscientious approach. And so to the wines, with another encouraging outcome for the two we tasted. The Chianti Classico '97 shows a not very intense but limpid ruby color. Its varied aromas are mostly at the fruity end of the spectrum, with strawberry and cherry the most prominent, nicely underpinned by just the right degree of spice, with cinnamon to the fore. It is low in concentration and not overly powerful on the palate; however, it is well proportioned, with the nicely pronounced acidity making for a most enjoyable quaffability. The Riserva '96 is more complex: an intense, dense ruby in color, it offers a wide range of ripe fruity fragrances with a hint of jam. In the mouth it is already properly balanced, with initially dominant tannins that are then smoothed by the alcohol, which is substantial but not overwhelming. The rising finish is full-flavored and appealing.

●	Chianti Classico Ris. '96	▼▼	4
●	Chianti Classico '97	▼	3
●	Chianti Classico Ris. '85	YY	4
●	Chianti Classico Ris. '88	YY	4
●	Chianti Classico Ris. '95	YY	4
●	Chianti Classico '88	Y	3
●	Chianti Classico '90	Y	3
●	Chianti Classico '91	Y	3
●	Chianti Classico '93	Y	3
●	Chianti Classico '96	Y	3
●	Chianti Classico Ris. '90	Y	4

PANZANO IN CHIANTI (FI)

Villa Cafaggio
Via S. Martino in Cecione, 5
50020 Panzano in Chianti (FI)
tel. 055/8549094

Villa Cafaggio has shown a very high level of quality in all the wines presented, but, this year at least, there is no absolute champion (although they came close). We shall begin with the fine performance of the Chianti Classico '97, which shows a remarkably intense, brilliant color and a harmonious and varied nose, with scents of aromatic herbs, black fruit and oak and a faint vegetal note. The palate is concentrated, well articulated and long. The Riserva '96 is less rich but successful all the same. It focuses wisely on its lean elegance and on the fresh, well-defined vivacity of its fruit. The San Martino '96, sangiovese with a small amount of cabernet, is excellent. It reveals a very pure bouquet, including black cherry, cherry and a light vegetal note, and a substantial, steadily evolving palate with a long, attractive, spicy finish. To conclude our round-up of these excellent offerings, the Riserva Solatio Basilica '95 is a wine of great finesse with notes of black fruit and cocoa on the nose, and an extremely well-balanced and even palate.

●	Chianti Classico Solatio Basilica Ris. '95	▼▼	5
●	Chianti Classico '97	▼▼	4
●	Chianti Classico Ris. '96	▼▼	4
●	San Martino '96	▼▼	5
●	Cortaccio '93	YYY	6
●	Cortaccio '90	YY	6
●	Cortaccio '94	YY	6
●	Cortaccio '95	YY	6
●	San Martino '88	YY	5
●	San Martino '90	YY	5
●	San Martino '93	YY	5
●	San Martino '94	YY	5
●	San Martino '95	YY	5

PELAGO (FI)

TRAVIGNOLI
VIA TRAVIGNOLI, 78
50060 PELAGO (FI)
TEL. 055/8361089

This is a well-deserved return to the Guide, after just one year's absence, for the estate of the Busi family, winegrowers for over two centuries. Travignoli is one of the biggest estates of the Rufino group, with over fifty hectares under vine, set in a location that has everything going for it: the right altitude, southern exposure, suitable terrain. Travignoli's driving force is Giovanni Busi, Count Giampiero's son, who, having qualified as an oenologist at the Conegliano school, takes a personal interest in all the stages of production, from vineyard to cellar. The results obtained are, as we discovered during our tastings, excellent. The top of the range is the Tegolaia '97, an IGT made from sangiovese and cabernet sauvignon and matured in small oak casks. A very dense, almost impenetrable red in color, it has ripe, evolved fruity fragrances freshened by a light balsamic note. Its attack on the palate is not powerful, but it goes on to unfold in a balanced, harmonious fashion. The finish is soft and prolonged. The Riserva '97 is also very good, with well-matched perfumes of plum and cherry. The entry on the palate is smooth and even, the tannins are more pronounced, but not overly so, and the finish is tasty and juicy. The simple but sound Chianti '98 is ruby red in color with a marked purple tinge. Particularly rich in fruit on the nose, with notes of wild berries and strawberry, it is easily drinkable, with pronounced acidity; a vigorous wine, it has a dry, not overly long finish. The Vin Santo '90 is less satisfactory, with its somewhat maderized aromas and slightly flabby, dilute body that wants the fatness that would make it velvety.

●	Chianti Rufina Ris. '97	TT	3*
●	Tegolaia '97	TT	4
●	Chianti Rufina '98	T	2*
○	Vin Santo della Rufina '90		4
●	Tegolaia '94	YY	4
●	Chianti Rufina '96	Y	2*

POGGIBONSI (SI)

FATTORIA LE FONTI
LOC. S. GIORGIO
53036 POGGIBONSI (SI)
TEL. 0577/935690 - 035/711067

We were very pleased to see this estate, which has struck out along the path towards excellence, replicating its success. The owners are developing a passion for vineyard management; in coming years, with additional hectares coming into production, we shall see an important winery taking shape. There was an excellent overall result for the wines we tasted: they all won Two Glasses, thanks in great part to the painstaking work of the expert oenologist Paolo Caciornia. The Chianti Classico '97 is powerfully dark in color. Its very intense perfumes open on tertiary notes, with leather and tobacco overlying rich fruit, with plum and blackberry particularly distinct. The attack on the palate is good, soft – silky, even; it then makes way for firm, decided tannins that blend well with the substantial alcohol, giving a long, balanced finish. The Riserva '96, with purple highlights still appearing on the ruby background, displays ripe fruity notes and an inviting, sweet finish on the nose. The palate is substantial, with tannins unfolding nicely to provide, with the help of the rich alcohol, body and fullness. The rising finish is nicely underpinned by crisp acidity. The Vito Arturo '96 shows a limpid ruby color and very attractive fruity scents. The palate is a little muted at first, but then expands, with everything opening into a harmonious, beautifully balanced whole. The finish, while not powerful, is long.

●	Chianti Classico '97	TT	3*
●	Chianti Classico Ris. '96	TT	4
●	Vito Arturo '96	TT	4
●	Vito Arturo '95	YY	4
●	Chianti Classico '96	Y	3
●	Chianti Classico Ris. '95	Y	4

POGGIBONSI (SI)

MELINI
LOC. GAGGIANO
53036 POGGIBONSI (SI)
TEL. 0577/989001

The thing that most surprised – and in part disoriented – us this year in our tastings of the Melini wines is the change in style in some of its most classic reds. The Chianti Classico La Selvanella Riserva '96, in particular, is much more concentrated in color, with fruitier fragrances, and softer and richer flavors; as a result it is less acidic and sharp, less old-fashioned. According to Nunzio Capurso, the cellar director, this is the result of two factors: the entry into production of newly laid-out vineyards, which are more densely planted and produce lower yields per vine, and the replacement of part of the old stock of barrels with newer ones. This is very probably the case. The fact remains, however, that some fans of the old-style wines may turn up their noses at these developments. But we're not amongst them: we found the wines different but certainly not inferior. The more modern style is especially noticeable in the Chianti Classico Massovecchio Riserva '95, which may not be the most concentrated of wines, but is rounded and quaffable; and even more remarkable in the brand-new Merlot '98, which is varietal, extremely fruity and enchantingly drinkable. The Chianti Classico I Sassi '97, good and well made as usual, is an easy-drinking wine if ever there was one. The Vernaccia di San Gimignano Le Grillaie '98 deserves special mention. This wine is becoming one of their top bottles: it is beautifully structured and surprisingly concentrated for a wine of its type.

●	Chianti Cl. La Selvanella Ris. '96	ΨΨ	5
●	Chianti Classico Massovecchio Ris. '95	ΨΨ	4
●	Merlot '98	ΨΨ	4
○	Vernaccia di S. Gimignano Le Grillaie '98	ΨΨ	4
●	Chianti Classico I Sassi '97	Ψ	3
●	Chianti Cl. La Selvanella Ris. '86	ΥΥΥ	4*
●	Chianti Cl. La Selvanella Ris. '90	ΥΥΥ	4*
●	Chianti Cl. La Selvanella Ris. '88	ΥΥ	4
●	Chianti Cl. La Selvanella Ris. '93	ΥΥ	4
●	Chianti Cl. La Selvanella Ris. '94	ΥΥ	4
●	Chianti Cl. La Selvanella Ris. '95	ΥΥ	4
●	Chianti Classico Laborel Ris. '87	ΥΥ	3*
●	Chianti Classico Laborel Ris. '93	ΥΥ	3*

POGGIBONSI (SI)

ORMANNI
LOC. ORMANNI
53036 POGGIBONSI (SI)
TEL. 0577/937212

This is the well-deserved debut in the Guide of the Fattoria Ormanni, a traditional Chianti estate which, to tell the truth, has very nearly made the grade several times in recent years. The wines produced are indeed fairly traditional in style, with a robust structure that was not matched, in the past, by the same degree of elegance or by consistent quality throughout the range. In this year's tastings we noted greater clarity on the nose, which set off the considerable richness of the fruit, and rich, dense extract. We should add that Mr. Brini Batacchi's winery also has a lot going for it in terms of size and potential production levels, with about 35 hectares of vineyards at its disposal. But let's get down to the wines. The Chianti '97 makes up for the faint sulfurous notes on the nose with a convincing, fairly concentrated palate that boasts excellent balance and an expansive finish. The Riserva '95, a notably characterful and energetic wine, is very good. The concentrated bouquet shows very lively fruit and light vanilla notes, and the powerful palate reveals robust, sweet tannins and good depth. Lastly, the wine called Julius, named after Chianti's great master-taster, Giulio Gambelli: a blend of sangiovese with 25% merlot, it distinguished itself at our tastings, winning, thanks to its soft, balanced structure, Two Glasses.

●	Chianti Classico Ris. '95	ΨΨ	4
●	Julius '97	ΨΨ	5
●	Chianti Classico Ris. '97	Ψ	4

POGGIO A CAIANO (PO)

LA PIAGGIA

VIA CEGOLI, 47
59016 POGGIO A CAIANO (PO)
TEL. 05/8705401

La Piaggia, a little Carmignano estate owned by Mauro Vannucci, has worked away quietly over the last few years. Then, when the team finally emerged into the light of day, they hit their target right on the mark. Three vintages of Carmignano Riserva, the only wine produced, were presented, and three Two Glass awards were netted with ease. Sixteen thousand bottles of just one wine may not seem much but is in fact a perfectly respectable figure, while the winery's decision to devote its time and care to just one DOC label is altogether admirable. The wine, conceived with the technical help of Alberto Antonini, is certainly modern in style, with an intensive but well-gauged use of new barriques; it may not reflect the classic image of a Carmignano, but it is highly appealing nonetheless. The Riserva '96 was truly excellent: nobody considered giving it less than a very high mark. Of a quite concentrated dark red color, it has a deep bouquet with notes of roasting coffee on a compact background of berries, and an ample, velvety, long palate with soft layers of tannins underwriting its future development. The other vintages are very similar in style, but both have more pronounced vegetal notes; the '95 is perhaps sharper, and the '94, which is appealingly elegant, is just a touch more dilute on the finish.

●	Carmignano Ris. '94	🍷🍷	4
●	Carmignano Ris. '95	🍷🍷	4
●	Carmignano Ris. '96	🍷🍷	4

PONTASSIEVE (FI)

TENUTA DI BOSSI

VIA DELLO STRACCHINO, 32
50065 PONTASSIEVE (FI)
TEL. 055/8317830

In singing the praises of the Tenuta di Bossi's wines, we have to observe that once again their best bottles do not include the most characteristic wine of this zone, the Chianti Rufina. This often happens in Tuscany: producers, convinced by a market trend that dates back a decade or more, prefer to dedicate their closest attention to "table wines" rather than to the various DOCs and DOCGs. Some producers have been trying to reverse the trend, and to stage a return, with authoritative wines, to the more classically defined categories. But the temptation to display their skills by competing in the great ocean of "vini da tavola", or super-Tuscans, is awfully strong. Here at Bossi, Bonaccorso and Bernardo Gondi make excellent wines that also respect the characteristics of the terroir. But it was no surprise to see that the most satisfactory red is still the Mazzaferrata, a pure cabernet which performed beautifully once again in the '95 version. An intense cherry red in color, it has characteristic grassy scents accompanied by toasty notes of new wood. In the mouth it is full-bodied, clean and persistent. Our review of the Chianti Rufinas revealed a certain uniformity among the vintages. Even more importantly, we detected no clear distinction between the basic Rufina and the Riserva. The '97 has a ruby red color of average intensity, fresh and slightly acidic scents, and substantial acidity underpinning the palate. The Riserva '95 is rather forward, with pronounced woody aromas and a medium body. The Riserva '95 Villa Bossi is attractive, with a good body and length, but the Riserva '96 is better, richer and more balanced, with finer tannins. And lastly, we commend the excellent Vin Santo Riserva '94, which is full, almost fat, fragrant and sensual.

●	Mazzaferrata '95	🍷🍷	4
○	Vin Santo Rufina Ris. '94	🍷🍷	4
●	Chianti Rufina '97	🍷	3
●	Chianti Rufina Ris. '95	🍷	4
●	Chianti Rufina Ris. '96	🍷	4
●	Chianti Rufina Villa di Bossi Ris. '95	🍷	4
●	Chianti Rufina Ris. '90	🍸🍸	4*
●	Mazzaferrata '90	🍸🍸	4
●	Mazzaferrata '92	🍸🍸	4
●	Mazzaferrata '93	🍸🍸	4
●	Mazzaferrata '94	🍸🍸	4
○	Vin Santo Rufina '91	🍸🍸	5
○	Vin Santo Rufina '93	🍸🍸	4
○	Vin Santo Rufina Bernardo Gondi '88	🍸🍸	4

PONTASSIEVE (FI)

CASTELLO DEL TREBBIO
LOC. S. BRIGIDA
50060 PONTASSIEVE (FI)
TEL. 055/8304900

This is the debut entry to the Guide for the estate of the Baj-Macario family. The vineyards are in the Chianti Rufina and Chianti Colli Fiorentini districts and the castle was built in the 12th century by the Pazzi family, whose coat of arms, sculpted by Donatello, can still be seen in the courtyard. After the famous plot against Lorenzo the Magnificent, the castle was confiscated by the Medicis. In 1968 it was bought by the present owners, who totally renovated it. It has over 60 hectares under vine, out of a total of 350. Two of the estate's wines were presented at our tastings. The first, the Chianti Rufina Lastricato '97, of a lively, full, intense ruby color, offers a nicely complex bouquet, where ripe fruits blend with spicy notes in a harmonious and well-defined whole. The impact on the palate is soft and velvety, and is followed by harder elements that come to the fore without upsetting the overall harmony. The finish is correct but not particularly long. The Pazzesco '97 is a blend of 50% sangiovese with merlot and syrah. The attractive fragrance begins on sweet toasty notes from the wood and then opens into a rich, complex spiciness, with lively pepper accompanied by a warm coffee tone. In the mouth it is enticing, soft and smooth, with an excellent general balance, but perhaps just a trifle dilute. The finish is long and lingering.

●	Pazzesco '97	🍷🍷	4
●	Chianti Rufina Lastricato '97	🍷	3

PONTASSIEVE (FI)

LAVACCHIO
VIA DI MONTEFIESOLE, 85
50065 PONTASSIEVE (FI)
TEL. 055/8317472

One thing that emerged clearly from this year's tastings is the variability of styles to be found in Tuscany. Quality, we hasten to add, has improved considerably, but in a somewhat ad hoc manner, with marked degrees of individualism in the producers, who choose wines made from any and every grape variety to be their "top" bottles. There is no lack of originality at the Lavacchio farm either, where the quality of the white wines (which, by the way, are extremely reasonably priced) particularly attracted our favorable notice. We were especially impressed by the Oro del Cedro '98, made from late-harvested traminer, which offered an enviably rich, well-defined nose. Our tasting notes include aromas of rose, citrus fruit, celery, honey and sage. The flavors are balanced and elegant rather than powerful, and the finish is distinct and persistent. The Bianco del Cedro '98 is another very good wine, with intense perfumes of pear, vanilla and banana. The palate is balanced and agreeable, with good length. The interesting Chardonnay '98 is intense, nicely soft and structured, with well-gauged woody notes of excellent quality. It lightens a little on the finish, but still manages to win Two Glasses. The situation is less rosy with the reds, where the winery needs to move up a gear or two. The Chianti Rufina '97 and '96 are certainly acceptable and well made, but in no way special. The Riserva '96 is, however, quite good, with a nice weight in the mouth, and the Cortigiano, made from sangiovese and cabernet, is good too: it is nicely balanced but grassy and a touch forward.

○	Chardonnay '98	🍷🍷	3*
○	Oro del Cedro '98	🍷🍷	3*
○	Bianco del Cedro '98	🍷	2*
●	Chianti Rufina Ris. '96	🍷	3
●	Cortigiano '96	🍷	4
●	Chianti Rufina '96		2
●	Chianti Rufina '97		3

PONTASSIEVE (FI)

★ RUFFINO
VIA ARETINA, 42/44
50065 PONTASSIEVE (FI)
TEL. 055/83605

A double Three Glasses for the second year in a row! This result speaks for itself and earns the Ruffino winery a comfortable place in the top ranks of Italian wine-making. And this year also sees the conquest of a star, awarded for a total of ten Three Glasses. Not bad for a winery that until a few years ago had quite a different image, at least as far as the quality of its wines was concerned! And there's more news – for the first time, Ruffino has won our award with a white, the Cabreo La Pietra '97, a Chianti-district chardonnay fermented and matured in small casks. This is the best version ever, even better, in terms of the concentration and clarity of its varietal fragrances, than the legendary '83: it offers scents of peanut butter, exotic fruit and a very well-integraated woody note.
Magnificent – there is no other word for the Romitorio di Santedame '97, made from prugnolo and colorino – and you won't get grapes more native than that! This wine shows power, concentration, fine, even and sweet tannins, a noteworthy progression of flavors, and a long, lingering finish. The bouquet ranges from notes of black cherry to woody and vanilla undertones. A delight! Then comes the Cabreo Il Borgo '97, sangiovese with 20% cabernet sauvignon, a little less concentrated than we expected, and the Chianti Classico Santedame '97, fruity and fragrant on the nose, full and vigorous in the mouth. We close with a reasonably good version of the Nero del Tondo, the '97, in which the varietal notes of pinot nero are not expressed very strongly, and the traditional Chianti Classico Riserva Ducale Oro '95. It won Two Glasses, but we feel that a little more concentration and better-behaved wood would not be amiss.

○	Cabreo La Pietra '97	**YYY**	5
●	Romitorio di Santedame '97	**YYY**	6
●	Cabreo Il Borgo '97	**YY**	6
●	Chianti Cl. Ris. Ducale Oro '95	**YY**	5
●	Chianti Classico Santedame '97	**YY**	4
●	Nero del Tondo '97	**YY**	5
●	Cabreo Il Borgo '85	YYY	6
●	Cabreo Il Borgo '90	YYY	6
●	Cabreo Il Borgo '93	YYY	5
●	Cabreo Il Borgo '95	YYY	6
●	Cabreo Il Borgo '96	YYY	6
●	Chianti Cl. Ris. Ducale Oro '88	YYY	5
●	Chianti Cl. Ris. Ducale Oro '90	YYY	5
●	Romitorio di Santedame '96	YYY	5
●	Romitorio di Santedame '95	YY	5

PONTASSIEVE (FI)

FATTORIA SELVAPIANA
LOC. SELVAPIANA, 43
50065 PONTASSIEVE (FI)
TEL. 055/8369848

The Giuntini family is not given to resting on its laurels. It forges ahead enthusiastically with its work in the vineyard, without stopping to dwell on its illustrious past. It is thanks more than anything else to Marquis Francesco Giuntini's drive that they have succeeded in creating an oenological museum in the Rufina district. This year's tastings have provided some quite good results, but not, perhaps, the outstanding ones we were expecting. The Chianti Rufina '97, with its lovely bright ruby color, has attractive, fairly full perfumes of ripe fruit, with cherry and plum coming through most intensely. The flavors passed muster, although the structure suffers from a lack of vigor. Slightly dilute, albeit balanced, it has a pleasing, not too persistent finish. The Riserva '96 is better, with its intense, deep color indicating good concentration. The aromas are warm and full, with ripe fruit blending nicely with a light, fine spicy note. The attack on the palate is full-bodied, with pronounced acidity and well-knit tannins, the whole smoothed by alcohol into a long, tasty finish. The Riserva Fornace '96 is not quite so good: its nose seems less developed, with fruity scents alternating with notes of aromatic herbs. There is a lack of balance in the mouth, with slightly dry tannins that do not mesh well with the other elements. The finish is, however, nicely long. The Vin Santo della Rufina '93 brought the smile back to our lips, with its lovely amber color and scents of hazelnut standing out against light background notes of honey and almond. Fleshy, enchanting and rounded in the mouth, it has a lingering finish. Lastly, the Borro Lastricato '97, a quaffable white, is simple, even and sound – an agreeable and unpretentious wine.

●	Chianti Rufina Ris. '96	**YY**	4
○	Rufina Vin Santo '93	**YY**	5
●	Chianti Rufina '97	**Y**	3
●	Chianti Rufina Fornace Ris. '96	**Y**	5
○	Borro Lastricato '97		3
●	Chianti Rufina '91	YY	3*
●	Chianti Rufina Bucerchiale Ris. '90	YY	5
●	Chianti Rufina Bucerchiale Ris. '94	YY	5
●	Chianti Rufina Bucerchiale Ris. '95	YY	5
●	Chianti Rufina Fornace Ris. '94	YY	5
●	Chianti Rufina Ris. '88	YY	4
●	Chianti Rufina Ris. '90	YY	4
●	Chianti Rufina Ris. '95	YY	4

PORTOFERRAIO (LI)

ACQUABONA

LOC. ACQUABONA
57037 PORTOFERRAIO (LI)
TEL. 0565/933013

Little has changed in Elba wine-making. Compared to the rest of the region, where the pace is seriously dynamic, the tempo is a bit slow here. It is true that the new vineyards planted by the island's main wineries have only recently been laid out, which means they are not yet ready to express their potential. But taking the overview, we feel that the easy sales generated by the tourist trade do not provide much of a stimulus to speed up improvement. Acquabona is still, for the time being, the leading winery in the zone, thanks to its reliable quality, but a touch more drive in place of mere correctness of form would not, in our opinion, be amiss. The best of their range is again the good Aleatico '96, which approaches Two Glasses. A nicely concentrated ruby in color, it has an intense nose based on fruity notes of black cherry and blackberry, which are clean but not too complex. The palate is sweet, substantial, still tannic and very attractive. The Ansonica '98 is the best of the whites. Clean but somewhat neutral on the nose, it comes over better on the palate, thanks to the overall balance and the fairly good structure that make it an agreeable and quaffable wine. The Elba Bianco '98 is also clean and balanced, with yeasty notes on the nose and a well-made but short palate. Much the same could be said of the vermentino-based Acquabona di Acquabona '98, which has a slightly more incisive palate. Lastly, the Elba Rosso '98 is sound but light and dilute.

●	Aleatico dell'Elba '96	▼	6
○	Ansonica dell'Elba '98	▼	4
○	Acquabona di Acquabona '98		4
○	Elba Bianco '98		3
●	Elba Rosso '98		3
●	Aleatico dell'Elba '95	YY	6
●	Aleatico di Portoferraio '91	YY	6
●	Aleatico di Portoferraio '94	YY	6
○	Acquabona di Acquabona '97	Y	3
●	Aleatico di Portoferraio '92	Y	6
○	Ansonica dell'Elba '97	Y	4
○	Ansonica Passito '92	Y	5
●	Elba Rosso Ris. '94	Y	2*
●	Elba Rosso Ris. Camillo Bianchi '91	Y	3

RADDA IN CHIANTI (SI)

CASTELLO D' ALBOLA

LOC. PIAN D'ALBOLA, 31
53017 RADDA IN CHIANTI (SI)
TEL. 0577/738019

The only reason that none of Castello D'Albola's wines won Three Glasses is that the vintages here did not allow it. Albola is situated at a fairly high altitude, and "feels" the effects of the seasons particularly. Especially when, as in '96, conditions are far from ideal. But the way forward has been mapped out and Gianni Zonin, the owner of this splendid winery, has a strong sense of purpose and the best of intentions, and when such a man gets an idea into his head he is quite likely to see it through. We had a foretaste of the future with the Chianti Classico '97, a simple wine, certainly not particularly concentrated, but quite perfectly well made. Its fragrances are extremely well defined with clear and stylish fruity tones; the palate doesn't have great depth, but the wine is light, appealing and quaffable. The good Acciaiolo '96, made from sangiovese and cabernet sauvignon, does not show the complexity and breeding of the '95. It is very well made, but the acidity stands out too sharply and the general structure is a bit less concentrated. The bouquet is still extremely clean, not very ample but extremely well expressed, with notes of red fruit and vanilla and woody undertones. The Chardonnay Le Fagge '97 is reasonably good, still young, and simpler and fruitier than in the past. There must have been a change of style at the fermentation stage. The Chianti Classico Riserva '96 is not bad, but is a true product of its vintage. It has a medium body and simple but characteristic and sound perfumes. A sensational exception to the '96 rule is the Pinot Nero Le Marangole, one of the best of its kind in Italy. It has an elegant, varietal nose with characteristic scents of strawberry, and finesse on a palate without harshness.

●	Acciaiolo '96	▼▼	5
●	Le Marangole '96	▼▼	5
●	Chianti Classico '97	▼	3
●	Chianti Classico Ris. '96	▼	4
○	Le Fagge Chardonnay '97	▼	4
●	Acciaiolo '95	YYY	5
●	Acciaiolo '88	YY	5
●	Acciaiolo '93	YY	5
○	Le Fagge Chardonnay '91	YY	4
○	Le Fagge Chardonnay '93	YY	4
○	Le Fagge Chardonnay '95	YY	4
○	Le Fagge Chardonnay '96	YY	4
●	Le Marangole '95	YY	4
●	Chianti Classico '95	Y	3
●	Chianti Classico '96	Y	3

RADDA IN CHIANTI (SI)

Borgo Salcetino
Loc. Lucareli
53017 Radda in Chianti (SI)
tel. 0577/733541

The border between the Radda and Panzano districts, which coincides with the provincial border between Siena and Florence, runs through the center of the great Chianti Classico region. The village just on the edge is called Lucarelli and the best vineyards, the south-facing ones, can be found at Radda. We are fairly high up here, about 400 meters above sea level, and some famous estates are nearby. There is Melini's La Selvanella, and then there's the lovely Borgo Salcetino, which was bought a couple of years ago by the Livon family, owners, as all wine lovers know, of vast vineyards in the Gorizia zone of the Collio. Production in the Chianti Classico district is mostly in the hands of Tonino Livon, and he is already letting it be known that here too he has no intention of playing anything but a leading role. The first wines he presented for tasting are very promising, and we feel sure the future holds even better things in store. The Chianti Classico Lucarello Riserva '96, one of the best of its year, is very good. It has a slight excess of sweet wood on the nose and the fruit is still a bit muffled, but it's is only a matter of time. In the mouth, on the other hand, it offers fullness and a pleasing acidity that is already well integrated and prevents the wine from tasting heavy, although the extract is considerable. The interesting Chianti Classico '97 shows slightly sulfurous notes on the nose, but then opens up on a palate rich in extract. It's an appealing wine, a little simple perhaps, but inviting and drinkable.

●	Chianti Classico '97	🍷🍷	4
●	Chianti Classico Lucarello Ris. '96	🍷🍷	5

RADDA IN CHIANTI (SI)

Colle Bereto
Loc. Colle Bereto
53017 Radda in Chianti (SI)
tel. 0577/738083

There is a good performance from this estate on its return to the Guide after a brief absence. The Pinzauti family, the owners of a fashion accessory business, put a lot of enthusiasm and effort into their vineyards in an attempt to create wines with a distinctive personality, more elegant than muscular. Their consultant oenologist is the distinguished Niccolò d'Afflitto, who makes the most of the microclimatic features of the zone. We tasted five wines. Il Cenno '95 is a blend of sangiovese, malvasia nera and canaiolo and takes its name from one of the vineyards on the property. It has an intense, full ruby color, with purple nuances. Its nose is characterized by fresh, inviting balsamic notes, which open out into ripe, varied fruit. The palate is very supple and velvety and harmonious. Il Tocco '95, produced from the same blend but in a different zone, is ruby in color with a purple tinge. On the nose it is the initial tertiary notes that come over most strongly, with light but persistent scents of leather and tobacco. The palate is lively and fairly complex, with juicy, intense tannins and a nicely persistent finish. The Chianti Classico '96, with its lovely intense color, offers an appealing sequence of ripe fruity aromas. The attack on the palate is sound and harmonious, and it then develops steadily to a moderately long finish. The Riserva '94 has a slightly forward fragrance of jam, with a simple, slightly dilute but well-balanced palate. Lastly, the Colle Bereto 2000 is a blend of sangiovese, pinot nero and merlot. We found it unsatisfactory at our tastings: it seemed extremely disjointed, with an ill-defined bouquet and not much balance in the mouth.

●	Il Cenno '95	🍷🍷	5
●	Il Tocco '95	🍷🍷	5
●	Chianti Classico '96	🍷	3
●	Chianti Classico Ris. '94	🍷	4
●	Colle Bereto 2000		5
●	Chianti Classico Ris. '88	🍷🍷 (outline)	5
●	Chianti Classico Ris. '90	🍷🍷 (outline)	4
●	Il Tocco '88	🍷🍷 (outline)	6

RADDA IN CHIANTI (SI)

LIVERNANO
LOC. LIVERNANO
53017 RADDA IN CHIANTI (SI)
TEL. 0577/738353

Some may be surprised by the Three Glasses Livernano has won. In judging such a young and still generally unknown winery, there is always the risk that we might be dealing with a flash in the pan, the classic meteoric rise and fall. In this case, however, Livernano's wines already had the target well within their sights last year and, to be perfectly frank, we were expecting great things from the '97 vintage. Carlo Montanari's estate has, in the meantime, cut back its range by eliminating the Nardina and concentrating on just two reds, the Puro Sangue, a sangiovese, and the Livernano, a blend of equal measures of cabernet, merlot and sangiovese. The white wines are represented by a chardonnay, the Anima. The vineyards, modern in conception, are about 450 meters above sea level, with dense plantings and very low yields. The obvious aim is to obtain great wines, whatever it takes. The fact that the winery has achieved this aim in such a short time simply shows that Montanari's commitment is seconded by an area with a natural propensity for viticulture. The Livernano '97 is a truly marvelous wine: great concentration and depth, very aristocratic tannins, a velvety, complex palate. A star performer, in short, that found no detractors on our tasting panel. Next comes the Sangiovese Puro Sangue '97, which is not far behind it. The structure is powerful and firm and just needs a longer time in the bottle to absorb the oak better and express its full potential. The white Anima '97 is certainly good, but not overwhelming like the others. .

● Livernano '97	▼▼▼	6
● Puro Sangue '97	▼▼	6
○ Anima '97	▼	5

RADDA IN CHIANTI (SI)

FATTORIA DI MONTEVERTINE
LOC. MONTE VERTINE
53017 RADDA IN CHIANTI (SI)
TEL. 0577/738009

We are so fond of Sergio Manetti, the prophet of Montevertine, that we must declare immediately that, even if we are a little puzzled as we mull over our tastings of his wines in recent years, this does not cast the slightest shadow on the esteem and affection we feel for him. So, if he manages to sell these wines regardless, if so many people enjoy them, and, most important, if he himself is convinced by them, then we can even congratulate him in our hearts and think that he has, after all, the right to make his wines any way he likes. The fact that critics, and we in particular, do not entirely approve, must take second place. And since these wines are, when all is said and done, good, we invite everyone who admires them to continue to do so and not to pay any attention to what we think. Certainly, we would like the wines a little more concentrated, with slightly less forward perfumes. However, they have personality and are very recognizable. They are Sergio Manetti's wines, for better or worse. And what's more, this year we also had to factor into the equation the '96 vintage, which wasn't up to much. Thus the Le Pergole Torte, a pure sangiovese to which we have awarded Two Glasses, partly in recognition of its illustrious past, has a few sharp acidic-tannic edges that are not entirely supported by the structure, and offers perfumes that are already just a bit evolved. However, it is not bad: it has slight limitations of the sort that you might also find in a great Gevrey Chambertin in a "minor" year. But we cannot pretend that these limitations do not exist, at least as far as we are concerned. The same can be said, but even louder, of the Montevertine Riserva '96 and the Pian del Ciampolo '96, both of which are "smaller" than in previous years.

● Le Pergole Torte '96	▼▼	6
● Monte Vertine Ris. '96	▼	5
● Pian del Ciampolo '96	▼	4
● Le Pergole Torte '83	▽▽▽	6
● Le Pergole Torte '86	▽▽▽	6
● Le Pergole Torte '88	▽▽▽	6
● Le Pergole Torte '90	▽▽▽	6
● Le Pergole Torte '92	▽▽▽	6
● Monte Vertine Ris. '85	▽▽▽	5
● Il Sodaccio '90	▽▽	6
● Le Pergole Torte '85	▽▽	6
● Le Pergole Torte '93	▽▽	6
● Le Pergole Torte '94	▽▽	6
● Le Pergole Torte '95	▽▽	6
● Monte Vertine Ris. '90	▽▽	6

PODERE CAPACCIA

LOC. CAPACCIA
53017 RADDA IN CHIANTI (SI)
TEL. 0577/738385

Our assessment of the wines of the Podere Capaccia in Radda is a generous one this year, thanks more to the history of the wines from this estate than to the not entirely satisfactory scores they obtained this time around. There is no harm sometimes in forcing the issue a little, especially in consideration of what a producer has already achieved or is honestly trying to attain. This is the case with Giampaolo Pacini and his excellent consultant Vittorio Fiore. But what caused our hesitation? First of all, we should start by making it clear that we had to force the issue only a tiny bit, and that the wines we reviewed were both good. The features that gave us cause for concern were the slightly overripe tone on the nose and the detached acidity on the palate. It almost seems that in seeking a ripeness that the '96 vintage could not provide, they plumped for overripeness, with concentration of sugars, but of acidity too. This would also explain the evolution of the bouquets. But these are only hypotheses, an attempt to interpret the wines that does not necessarily reflect what actually happened. Nothing too serious, therefore, given that the wines, the Querciagrande in particular, and to a lesser extent the Chianti Classico Riserva, show excellent concentration on the palate and are more than respectable in terms of execution. We await the next vintage, the '97, which was excellent in this area, in the certainty that we shall meet with some first-class wines.

●	Chianti Classico Ris. '96	🍷🍷	5
●	Querciagrande '96	🍷🍷	5
●	Querciagrande '88	YYY	6
●	Chianti Classico '88	YY	4
●	Chianti Classico '90	YY	4
●	Chianti Classico '91	YY	4
●	Chianti Classico Ris. '86	YY	5
●	Chianti Classico Ris. '88	YY	5
●	Querciagrande '86	YY	6
●	Querciagrande '87	YY	6
●	Querciagrande '90	YY	6
●	Querciagrande '91	YY	6
●	Querciagrande '92	YY	6
●	Querciagrande '93	YY	6
●	Querciagrande '95	YY	6

POGGERINO

VIA POGGERINO, 6
53017 RADDA IN CHIANTI (SI)
TEL. 0577/738232

Our review confirms the consistently high quality of the wines produced by Piero Lanza's estate. Keeping to very high standards harvest after harvest is no easy undertaking, not least of all because of the diminutive size of the winery, but it is made possible by careful vineyard management, rigorous selection of the grapes, and precisely gauged vinification techniques. A new wine has arrived to enrich the winery's range: the Primamateria, a blend of equal measures of sangiovese and merlot matured in barriques and bottled only in magnums. Its salient features are a very intense color, a warm, rich fragrance and a full and lively palate. The aromas of ripe fruit suggest blackberry and plum, accompanied by spice. The palate is a touch aggressive, firm and even, with correctly evolving tannins and a fairly prolonged finish. The Chianti Classico '97 is also good, with its lively color and very incisive perfumes of fresh fruit such as cherry, strawberry and black currant. In the mouth, it is appealing and very juicy, with firm, smooth tannins and an even progression. The Bugialla '96 selection is again excellent: its slightly overripe aromas of jam, and vanilla nicely blended with cinnamon and cloves, form a bouquet of considerable finesse and elegance. The satisfying full-bodied attack on the palate reveals power and substance, with nicely contrasting tannins and alcohol and a beautifully meshed acidity. The finish is utterly enjoyable.

●	Chianti Cl. Bugialla Ris. '96	🍷🍷	5
●	Chianti Classico '97	🍷🍷	3*
●	Primamateria '97	🍷	5
●	Chianti Classico Ris. '90	YYY	5
●	Chianti Cl. Bugialla Ris. '94	YY	5
●	Chianti Cl. Bugialla Ris. '95	YY	5
●	Chianti Classico '90	YY	3*
●	Chianti Classico '91	YY	3*
●	Chianti Classico '93	YY	3*
●	Chianti Classico '94	YY	3*
●	Chianti Classico '95	YY	3*
●	Chianti Classico '96	YY	3*
●	Vigna di Bugialla '90	YY	5
●	Vigna di Bugialla '91	YY	5
●	Vigna di Bugialla '93	YY	5

Fattoria Terrabianca

Loc. S. Fedele a Paterno
53017 Radda in Chianti (SI)
tel. 0577/738544

Roberto Guldener's Fattoria Terrabianca has again produced two fine versions of the Campaccio '95, one normal and one special selection. Both wines derive from a blend of sangiovese and cabernet sauvignon and the second exhibits, in addition to a wax seal on the back of the bottle, superior qualities, including greater concentration and even softer tannins. We should point out, however, that the difference between the two is not enormous, and we are not absolutely certain that this division into two categories, established a few years ago, is warranted. But it's a legitimate choice and the wines are good. Both of them, however, are still a little less concentrated than they would need to be to net Three Glasses. The Chianti Classico Vigna della Croce Riserva '95 is elegant, very well made and a delight to drink. The barrique-aged Piano della Cappella '97, made from chardonnay, is not bad at all: the wood is not out of hand, the palate is moderately concentrated and the wine is attractive. In short, this is an admirable and reliable range and, we would emphasize, a masterfully executed one.

●	Campaccio '95	▼▼	5
●	Campaccio Sel. Speciale '95	▼▼	6
●	Chianti Classico Vigna della Croce Ris. '95	▼▼	4
○	Piano della Cappella '97	▼▼	4
●	Campaccio '89	▽▽	5
●	Campaccio '90	▽▽	5
●	Campaccio '91	▽▽	5
●	Campaccio '93	▽▽	5
●	Campaccio '94	▽▽	6
●	Campaccio Sel. Speciale '91	▽▽	6
●	Campaccio Sel. Speciale '93	▽▽	6
●	Piano del Cipresso '91	▽▽	5
●	Piano del Cipresso '94	▽▽	6
○	Piano della Cappella '95	▽▽	4

RADDA IN CHIANTI (SI)

Vignavecchia

Via Roma, 23
53017 Radda in Chianti (SI)
tel. 0577/738090

The Vignavecchia label is probably one of the best known in the Chianti Classico zone. In case you don't remember, it shows an elderly, white-bearded gent with a severe gaze who is none other than Odoardo Beccari, a 19th-century explorer and scientist who bought, a century and a half ago, the Fattoria di Vignavecchia, which has now come down to his current heirs. It's a label that we recall with pleasure because it reminds us of the first bottles of Chianti we ever drank. And it is just as great a pleasure for us now to dedicate a well-deserved review to this lovely property in the heart of the Chianti Classico area. The vineyards occupy about 15 hectares, of which almost 90% is dedicated to DOCG wines, and the remainder, about two and a half hectares, to cabernet sauvignon, merlot and chardonnay. The vineyards and the cellar have, since '95, been in the young but already expert hands of Francesco Staderini, and from that date, Vignavecchia can be said to have moved up a gear or so, with a completely renovated cellar and new vineyards. The first interesting results have also come through, as we happily discovered at this year's tastings. The pick of the batch was the Canvalle '96, a blend of two thirds cabernet and one third sangiovese which, in addition to a lovely vivid, dark color, exhibits an intense, elegant and even bouquet, with scents of black fruit and fresh vegetal notes. The palate is concentrated, ample, silky and long. The very good Chianti Riserva '96, although simpler and lighter, is admirable for its good fruit and excellent overall harmony. The Raddese '96, a monovarietal sangiovese, is only fair, but there's good reason to be pleased this year at Vignavecchia.

●	Canvalle '96	▼▼	5
●	Chianti Classico Ris. '96	▼▼	4
●	Raddese '96	▼	4
●	Canvalle '93	▽▽	5
●	Chianti Classico '90	▽▽	4
●	Raddese '90	▽▽	5
●	Canvalle '92	▽	5
●	Chianti Classico '91	▽	3
●	Chianti Classico Ris. '90	▽	5
●	Chianti Classico Ris. '91	▽	4
●	Raddese '93	▽	5

RADDA IN CHIANTI (SI)

CASTELLO DI VOLPAIA

LOC. VOLPAIA
P.ZZA DELLA CISTERNA, 1
53017 RADDA IN CHIANTI (SI)
TEL. 0577/738066

Anyone looking for more softness, more concentration, in a word more harmony, from the wines of Castello di Volpaia does not know Chianti Classico territory very well. The village of Volpaia, and the vineyards surrounding it, are in fact amongst the highest parts of the whole Chianti district. Here the sangiovese grapes sometimes have difficulty ripening, and the wines they yield are in any case high in acidity. These things also apply to many of the world's other winegrowing areas, with different grape varieties. What should we say of the great cabernets of Touraine, for example? Hence a few sharp edges in Volpaia's Chianti Classico fall entirely within the norm for the terroir and are certainly not to be considered technical limitations. And in particular vintages, like the '88, they are also less obvious. In others, they are almost unbearably pronounced. It would be easy nowadays, with cleverly gauged additions of other grapes, to soften those edges. But this is not part of the production philosophy of Giovanella Stianti and Carlo Mascheroni who, like their consultant Maurizio Castelli, are serious-minded people. This year did not go at all badly. The Coltassala '95 does not stand out for its complexity, for the time being at least, nor does it have a body-builder's physique. But it's a textbook of breeding and displays elegance and finesse on both the nose and the palate. The very interesting Chianti Classico '97, the fruit of an outstanding vintage for this region, is very interesting: fruity, most agreeable, above all very Chianti Classico. The Riserva '96, thinner and more acidic, was less satisfactory. The Balifico '95, a blend of sangiovese and cabernet sauvignon from which we expected more complexity, was a bit disappointing.

●	Chianti Classico '97	🍷🍷	4
●	Coltassala '95	🍷🍷	5
●	Balifico '95	🍷	5
●	Chianti Classico Ris. '96	🍷	5
●	Balifico '86	🍷🍷	5
●	Balifico '87	🍷🍷	5
●	Balifico '88	🍷🍷	5
●	Balifico '91	🍷🍷	5
●	Chianti Classico Ris. '93	🍷🍷	4
●	Chianti Classico Ris. '94	🍷🍷	4
●	Chianti Classico Ris. '95	🍷🍷	5
●	Coltassala '85	🍷🍷	5
●	Coltassala '90	🍷🍷	5
●	Coltassala '91	🍷🍷	5
●	Coltassala '94	🍷🍷	5

RAPOLANO TERME (SI)

CASTELLO DI MODANELLA

LOC. SERRE
53040 RAPOLANO TERME (SI)
TEL. 0577/704604

We shall be hearing a lot about Castello di Modanella in coming years: its wines are not only carefully made but are also of personality. The estate, which has found a wise balance between dynamic innovation and preservation of the best elements of tradition, uses up-to-date agronomic and oenological techniques. A good example of their thoughtful reproposal of local varieties is the Poggio l'Aiole, a monovarietal canaiolo. The '97 version has an attractive, moderately intense bright ruby color. The aromas, still slightly closed, include a hint of licorice root. In the mouth this red is tannic and reasonably full-bodied, and develops more on the mid-palate than on the not overly long finish. The Sangiovese Campo d'Aia '96, the fruit of a vintage that was decidedly under par, is, not surprisingly, less impressive than the '95. It shows a not very concentrated light ruby hue and dominant new oak on the nose, with just a suggestion of fruit. The palate is simple, clean and somewhat light, with an astringent finish. Their top wine, the Cabernet Le Voliere '96, on the other hand, is as good as it has been in recent years. An intense, saturated red color introduces scents of black currant and bell pepper accompanied by pronounced notes of toasty oak. Tannic on the palate, it shows power and length, but not great finesse. This year we also tasted the Poggio Mondino '96, a slightly rustic red. Aromas of roasting coffee are made pungent by a strong sulfurous note. In the mouth it is rough and astringent, but well-structured. Lastly, we mention the Poggio Elci '98, a very simple malvasia.

●	Le Voliere Cabernet Sauvignon '96	🍷🍷	4
●	Campo d'Aia '96	🍷	3
●	Poggio l'Aiole '97	🍷	3
●	Poggio Mondino '96	🍷	3
○	Poggio Elci '98		2
●	Campo d'Aia '95	🍷🍷	3
●	Le Voliere Cabernet Sauvignon '95	🍷🍷	4

RIBOLLA (GR)

I CAMPETTI
VIA COLLACCHIA
58036 RIBOLLA (GR)
TEL. 0564/579663

With the debut in the Guide of I Campetti there is an increase in the number of estates in the Monteregio DOC district, an area that has become a magnet for many of the great names of Italian wine-making. The I Campetti farm, on the other hand, is one of a core group of local producers who played a key role in enhancing the reputation of this territory in less prosperous times. In this family-run winery, the Falciani siblings divide up all the work amongst themselves. I Campetti's claim to originality lies in the choice of wines produced in the 10 hectares of vineyards. These include, in addition to the Monteregio di Massa Marittima DOC, the distinctive Almabruna, 100% viognier. The '98 reveals personality and intriguing scents of aromatic herbs, exotic fruit and Mediterranean wildflowers. The palate is well structured, rounded and full-flavored, and the bouquet is echoed faithfully on the fairly long finish. Very different in style, L'Accesa '98, made from malvasia di candia, has no lack of weight on the palate but shows rather ripe fruity notes and an acidic finish. The Nebbiaie '98 is simpler but undoubtedly sound, balanced and agreeable. The Rosato is acceptable and quite easy to drink, as is the Montereggio Rosso Castruccio, which is slightly vegetal and not entirely clean in fragrance. The Montereggio Baccio '96, however, proved to be very satisfying indeed, and almost won Two Glasses. It offers an intriguing bouquet, with notes of fruit and black pepper and, in the mouth, density, full flavor and an attractively lingering finish.

○	Almabruna '98	🍷🍷	4
●	Montereggio di Massa Marittima Rosso Baccio '96	🍷	4
○	L'Accesa '98		3
○	Montereggio di Massa Marittima Bianco Nebbiaie '98		2
●	Montereggio di Massa Marittima Rosso Castruccio '97		3

ROCCALBEGNA (GR)

VILLA PATRIZIA
FRAZ. CANA
LOC. VILLA PATRIZIA
58050 ROCCALBEGNA (GR)
TEL. 0564/982028

The Villa Patrizia team is an expert one: Romeo Bruni, with his children Patrizia, Maurizio and Tiziano, cover all aspects of the winery, with the help of the renowned consultant oenologist Luca D'Attoma. We would add that the terrain, is, thanks to the great potential it holds, one of the most sought after in all of Tuscany, but this is hardly news. The Morellino di Scansano '98, with its moderately intense ruby color, starts out with an indistinct nose, to open out more clearly into fruity tones of black cherry and red currant. It is a little green in the mouth but the weight of the extract is, on the whole, excellent, the balance good and the finish faultless. The Orto di Boccio '95, a red made from sangiovese, merlot and cabernet, did not entirely justify our excitement of last year: intense, deep, rich and complex in both its aromas and its flavors, it has, however, a sulfurous nuance that detracts from its elegance. The simple Albatraia '98 shows some positive similarities. A deep ruby red in color, it offers intense notes of lavender on the nose, with an undertone of fruit; it has an acidic attack on the palate, after which it expands somewhat, to become quite harmonious and long. The Alteta, a blend of chardonnay and sauvignon that was Villa Patrizia's best wine last year, put on another good performance. The '97 offers an attractive bouquet of sweet fruit with intense, clean woody notes, and a full-bodied palate, less soft and more austere this time, with complex bitter nuances and an alcohol-rich finish. Finally, the good white Sciamareti '98 is fruity, grapey, clean and appealing, while the Villa Patrizia Bianco '98 seemed a trifle elementary.

○	Alteta '97	🍷🍷	4
●	Albatraia '98	🍷	1*
●	Morellino di Scansano '98	🍷	2*
●	Orto di Boccio '95	🍷	4
○	Sciamareti '98	🍷	2*
○	Villa Patrizia Bianco '98		2
○	Alteta '96	🍸🍸	4
●	Albatraia '96	🍸	1*
●	Morellino di Scansano '96	🍸	2*
●	Morellino di Scansano '97	🍸	3
●	Orto di Boccio '94	🍸	4
○	Sciamareti '96	🍸	2*
●	Villa Patrizia Rosso '96	🍸	3

ROCCATEDERIGHI (GR)

MELETA
LOC. MELETA
58028 ROCCATEDERIGHI (GR)
TEL. 0564/567155

Erica Suter, the owner of Meleta, has put together a most creditable team. Agronomic and oenological consultants as well as cellar technicians all work in the knowledge that they have a real treasure house of vines and climatic conditions here. The results, as the string of Two Glass awards adorning the last few editions of the Guide shows, are in general very impressive. This year's wines are a little less sure in style, perhaps because of a pair of vintages that were far from ideal. The first wine is a new one, the Bianco della Rocca. The '97, an attractive golden yellow in color with glowing highlights, is woody, sweet and very inviting on the nose. The Pietrello d'Oro '98 presents a not very concentrated brilliant ruby hue. The nose is rather closed at first, but with some breathing time it opens out into fruity notes. The palate is simple, soft and grapey. The Pietrello '97 cannot be said to be above reproach, as it revealed a certain harshness at our tastings. And so we arrive at Meleta's flagship wine, the Rosso della Rocca. The '96, of a very deep, intense ruby color, shows quite a lot of sulfur on the nose. It improves markedly on the palate, where it reveals abundant weight, ripe fruit, softness and balance. It suffers, therefore, from a lack of follow-through from nose to mouth. This is not a serious failing, but it keeps the wine from scoring higher. Once again we found the Vin Santo, this time the '95 vintage, very successful: sweet and ripe, with sensuous notes of honey and crème caramel. The Rocchigiano '98, a rosé, is very pleasant, while the Vermentino Lucertolo '98 is sound but simple.

○	Vin Santo '95	▼▼	5
○	Bianco della Rocca '97	▼	5
●	Pietrello d'Oro '98	▼	4
⊙	Rocchigiano '98	▼	2*
●	Rosso della Rocca '96	▼	5
○	Lucertolo '98		2
●	Pietrello '97		4
●	Merlot '94	▽▽	6
●	Pietrello d'Oro '90	▽▽	4*
●	Rosso della Rocca '91	▽▽	5
●	Rosso della Rocca '92	▽▽	5
●	Rosso della Rocca '93	▽▽	5
●	Rosso della Rocca '94	▽▽	5
●	Rosso della Rocca '95	▽▽	5
○	Vin Santo '94	▽▽	5

RUFINA (FI)

FATTORIA DI BASCIANO
V.LE DUCA DELLA VITTORIA, 159
50068 RUFINA (FI)
TEL. 055/8397034

A new line-up of Two Glass awards for the wines of the Fattoria di Basciano confirms the very positive trend perceptible from our tastings in recent years. Paolo Masi works with great enthusiasm and care, and the result is wines with irreproachably clean, fresh fruit, and, in the best examples, abundant personality. We shall start with the Chianti Rufina '97, a brilliant example of its category: fresh, fruity, well-defined, grapey but not simple, full-bodied and lingering. The Chianti Rufina Riserva '96, is, naturally, even better, although the gap between it and its humbler relative, which benefited from a better vintage, is not very great. A notably intense, dense red color introduces primary aromas of fruit that are simple, perfectly clean and inviting. In the mouth it exhibits good extract, a slight slackening on the mid palate, and lingering fruity notes (wild cherry, strawberry and black currant) on the finish. The two cabernet and sangiovese reds did better, largely because of their greater complexity. The Corto '97 (90% sangiovese, 10% cabernet) is even better than the '96: its concentrated, saturated ruby color leads to intensely fruity fragrances of blackberry, blueberry and black cherry, accompanied at the moment by somewhat intrusive notes of oak. The palate is ripe, full, fresh, very tasty and remarkably long. I Pini '97 (equal measures of sangiovese and cabernet) is in some ways similar. The nose opens on the same sweetly woody and ripely fruity notes. In the mouth, however, the wine shows a less firm structure and a faintly bitter finish. Lastly, the Vin Santo '94 is also attractive.

●	Chianti Rufina Ris. '96	▼▼	2*
●	I Pini '97	▼▼	3*
●	Il Corto '97	▼▼	3*
●	Chianti Rufina '97	▼	2*
○	Vin Santo Rufina '94	▼	3
●	Chianti Rufina Ris. '95	▽▽	2*
●	I Pini '96	▽▽	3
●	Il Corto '96	▽▽	3
●	Chianti Rufina '95	▽	2
●	Chianti Rufina '96	▽	2
●	Chianti Rufina Ris. '94	▽	2
●	I Pini '94	▽	3
●	I Pini '95	▽	3
●	Il Corto '94	▽	3
●	Il Corto '95	▽	3

S. CASCIANO VAL DI PESA (FI)

Castelli del Grevepesa
Loc. Mercatale Val di Pesa
Via Grevigiana, 34
50024 S. Casciano Val di Pesa (FI)
tel. 055/821911

The style of the wines produced by this great Chianti cooperative winery is fairly classic. All the wines have evolved aromas that can be enticing and even complex. The acidic-tannic "edges" that are such characteristic features of the sangiovese grape are not at all masked. If anything, the winery tries to present their wines when they're a little more mature (this year the '95 vintage, which most producers brought out over a year ago, was their leading player). The results are nearly always satisfactory, and sometimes decidedly good. The best in the series this time were, in our opinion, the Coltifredi and the Guado al Luco, both '95s. The first is almost pure sangiovese; the second also has a little cabernet sauvignon. These wines are fairly similar in style: their perfumes are already complex, intense, and mature, while the structure on the palate overshadows the substantial acidity that, like the salt in a well-made dish, underpins the flavors without calling attention to itself. The rest of their wide and varied range reveals excellent cellar technique. The '97 Chianti Classico Clemente VII and the Lamole '95 are both quite interesting and true benchmark wines for the winery. The other two Chianti Classico crus, the Pianacci '95 and the Castello di Bibbione '95, which we tasted for the first time, are fair. The Grevepesa Riserva '96 is slightly muffled on the nose, but it won One Glass anyway, in recognition of its "career".

●	Coltifredi '95	▼▼	5
●	Guado al Luco '95	▼▼	5
●	Chianti Cl. Castelgreve Ris. '96	▼	4
●	Chianti Cl. Castello di Bibbione '95	▼	5
●	Chianti Cl. Clemente VII '97	▼	4
●	Chianti Cl. Lamole '95	▼	5
●	Chianti Cl. Pianacci '95	▼	5
●	Chianti Cl. Castelgreve Ris. '88	▽▽	4
●	Chianti Cl. Castelgreve Ris. '90	▽▽	4
●	Chianti Cl. Castelgreve Ris. '95	▽▽	4
●	Chianti Cl. Montefiridolfi '90	▽▽	4
●	Chianti Cl. Vigna Elisa '90	▽▽	5
●	Chianti Cl. Clemente VII '88	▽▽	5
●	Guado al Luco '93	▽▽	5

S. CASCIANO VAL DI PESA (FI)

Fattoria Corzano e Paterno
Fraz. S. Pancrazio
Via Paterno, 8
50026 S. Casciano Val di Pesa (FI)
tel. 055/8248179 - 055/8249114

The most striking feature to emerge from our tastings of the wines of Corzano e Paterno was their consistent excellence: the overall average was higher than in the past, and we did not find the customary gap between their top wine, the Corzano, and all the others. Of course variations in vintages were not without effect, but for four wines out of four to win Two Glasses is unusual and admirable. The Corzano '96, made from sangiovese and cabernet, clearly shows the characteristics of its vintage, and hence does not express its habitual energy and complexity. But it nevertheless displays exemplary balance, wonderfully clean fruity and vegetal aromas, and perfectly judged tannins in a nicely substantial body. The surprising Chianti '97 offers a concentrated bouquet of mineral and jammy notes, and a succulent, intense palate, with crisp tannins and a good finish. The excellent Vin Santo '93, classic in style and almost amber in color, exhibits fragrances of fruit and dried flowers and a sweet, even palate with good crisp acidity. To finish, the Aglaia '98, a chardonnay, also hit the mark. Of a vivid straw yellow hue, it offers scents of fresh spice and exotic fruit together with a smoky note. These are echoed on the palate, which is fairly full and even, and nicely underpinned by the fruit and acidity; the finish is good and long.

○	Aglaia '98	▼▼	4
●	Chianti Terre di Corzano '97	▼▼	3*
●	Il Corzano '96	▼▼	5
○	Vin Santo '93	▼▼	5
●	Chianti Terre di Corzano Ris. '90	▽▽	4
●	Chianti Terre di Corzano Ris. '95	▽▽	4
●	Il Corzano '88	▽▽	5
●	Il Corzano '95	▽▽	5
○	Vin Santo '90	▽▽	5
●	Chianti '96	▽	3
●	Chianti Terre di Corzano '94	▽	3

Tenuta Castello Il Corno

Via Malafranca, 20
50026 S. Casciano Val di Pesa (FI)
tel. 055/8248009

There is no doubting the fact that Maria Giulia Frova, owner and guiding spirit of the Tenuta Il Corno, is an unusual person. As if the work involved in her estate's agricultural production were not enough, she is also involved in numerous other projects and cultural activities. This is probably possible because she trusts - and rightly so - her oenologist Claudio Gori, who is also carrying out very interesting experiments on some colorino clones that are part of Il Corno's surprising viticultural wealth. These experiments have now taken liquid form with the bottling of the most recent vintages of their monovarietal Colorino. We tasted the '96 and have to admit that we really liked it. This is certainly a wine with its own particular characteristics, which are not easy to find elsewhere, and it does undeniably have some rustic touches. But it's full of character (a good one, fortunately), and it leaves its mark on your memory. Of the other wines we tasted I Gibbioni '97, a cabernet, is particularly good, with its intense bouquet of vegetal, mineral and oak-derived smoky notes. The palate is very soft and well balanced, with a long but slightly vegetal finish. The '96 version is also fairly good, with well-defined perfumes and flavors; however it has a decidedly vegetal tone and is a bit short. The San Camillo '97, densely flavored and considerably tannic, is good. The last of Il Corno's worthy range is the Chianti Classico '97, which was more than satisfactory notwithstanding the disproportionate presence of oak.

●	Colorino '96	▼▼	4
●	I Gibbioni '97	▼▼	4
●	Chianti Classico '97	▼	3
●	Chianti Colli Fiorentini San Camillo '97	▼	3
●	I Gibbioni '96	▼	4

S. CASCIANO VAL DI PESA (FI)

La Sala

Via Sorripa, 34
50026 S. Casciano Val di Pesa (FI)
tel. 055/828111

This was another successful performance by the wines of La Sala, a small but important estate in the somewhat underrated district of San Casciano Val di Pesa in the Chianti Classico region. The clever and enthusiastic owner, Laura Baronti, is realizing her dream of creating a model cellar and producing really great wines. And on tasting her Riserva '96, we had to concede that she is not all that far away from her goal. This is a very interesting wine, perhaps the best Chianti Classico we have ever tasted from La Sala. It combines a soft seductiveness, mouth-filling and velvety, with excellent concentration and complex perfumes in which wood and varietal fruit mesh perfectly. It is undeniably paying the price of a rather poor year, with the result that its length is nothing to write home about, but this is the only defect we were able to find. The Campo all'Albero '96, which includes a little cabernet sauvignon along with the sangiovese, is also very good, somewhat on the simple side, perhaps, but extremely well executed. The Chianti Classico '97 is less satisfactory: it is slightly acidulous – which is rather strange for such a rich and "southern" year. Perhaps the answer is simpler than might first appear: the best batches of sangiovese may have gone into the '97 Riserva and Campo all'Albero. In which case the future holds some surprising wines indeed. We'll just have to wait and see.

●	Campo all'Albero '96	▼▼	5
●	Chianti Classico Ris. '96	▼▼	4
●	Chianti Classico '97	▼	3
●	Campo all'Albero '94	▽▽	4
●	Campo all'Albero '95	▽▽	4
●	Chianti Classico '96	▽▽	3*
●	Campo all'Albero '93	▽	4
●	Chianti Classico '90	▽	3
●	Chianti Classico '91	▽	3
●	Chianti Classico '93	▽	3
●	Chianti Classico '95	▽	3
●	Chianti Classico Ris. '90	▽	4
●	Chianti Classico Ris. '93	▽	4
●	Chianti Classico Ris. '95	▽	4

FATTORIA LE CORTI - CORSINI
VIA SAN PIERO DI SOTTO, 1
50026 S. CASCIANO VAL DI PESA (FI)
TEL. 055/820123

What a good wine the Chianti Classico Don Tommaso '97 is! This is the first entirely successful wine we have tasted from Duccio Corsini and Carlo Ferrini: an elegant red, with good concentration and very fruity scents with a light, beautifully blended vanilla and woody undertone. And the tannins particularly delighted us with their sweetness, dense texture and finesse. So why only Two Glasses? First of all, we should say that the wine made it through to the finals and was only eliminated at the last tasting, so it came awfully close to Three Glasses. Its only drawback is its weight, the concentration of its flavors: good but not extraordinary. It might have passed muster even so, but this wine came from the '97 vintage, which was particularly rich, so our expectations, in terms of body, were higher. The problem will really only be solved when they complete the changes in their vineyard management, including reduced yield per vine and more rigorous selection. For the time being this masterfully made wine is about as good as it could be, given the raw material available, and in the zone between San Casciano and Mercatale hugely structured wines are hard to come by. At the moment, at any rate. The other wines of the range are good. The Chianti Classico Cortevecchia Riserva '96 is a little under par and has some acidic-tannic roughness. The Chianti Classico '97 is extremely good: straightforward, very fruity, and great to drink - what more could you ask for?

● Chianti Classico '97	🍷🍷	3*
● Chianti Classico Don Tommaso '97	🍷🍷	5
● Chianti Cl. Cortevecchia Ris. '96	🍷	5
● Chianti Cl. Cortevecchia Ris. '95	YY	5
● Chianti Classico '93	YY	4
● Chianti Classico Don Tommaso '94	YY	5
● Chianti Classico Don Tommaso '95	YY	5
● Chianti Classico Don Tommaso '96	YY	5
● Chianti Classico Ris. '93	YY	4
● Chianti Cl. Cortevecchia Ris. '94	Y	4

S. CASCIANO VAL DI PESA (FI)

ANTICA FATTORIA MACHIAVELLI
LOC. S. ANDREA IN PERCUSSINA
50026 S. CASCIANO VAL DI PESA (FI)
TEL. 0577/989001

The Machiavelli winery at Sant'Andrea in Percussina is an excellent confirmation of the renaissance taking place in Italian wine production. It is owned by the Gruppo Italiano Vini, the biggest wine-making group in Italy, which has a turnover of over 350 billion lire per year. And yet it is constantly up in the top league of Tuscan producers, which is not an easy achievement. This means, in short, that a sort of multinational wine company is actually interested in devoting a part of its energies to producing first-rate wine. And it does so with a truly surprising degree of consistency and professional skill. A case in point is the Chianti Classico Vigna Fontalle Riserva '95, which we tasted this year (we apologize for our error in last year's Guide – we had actually reviewed the '94 but we said it was the '95, which in fact was nowhere near ready for release). It is a great red, powerful and rich, with compact, densely knit but very smooth tannins, and also an intense, complex bouquet in which black cherry, vanilla, blackberry and raspberry alternate and blend with great finesse: a masterpiece, in short and a worthy example of the very best that Chianti Classico can offer. When we uncovered the bottle of this extraordinary, captivating and extremely elegant red after our blind tastings, we were simply astonished. And, to keep the Vigna Fontalle company, they have made the best pinot nero in Tuscany, Il Principe '96, which is full, rounded and concentrated. Indeed it seems more like a great red Chianti than a pinot nero. It is less concentrated than the '95, but remarkable all the same. Our hearty congratulations, for both the wines, to Nunzio Capurso, one of the greatest oenologists in Chianti and an Olympian of Italian wine-making.

● Chianti Cl. V. di Fontalle Ris. '95	🍷🍷🍷	5
● Il Principe '96	🍷🍷	5
● Il Principe '95	YYY	4*
● Ser Niccolò Solatio del Tani '88	YYY	4*
● Chianti Cl. V. di Fontalle Ris. '88	YY	4
● Chianti Cl. V. di Fontalle Ris. '90	YY	4
● Chianti Cl. V. di Fontalle Ris. '93	YY	4
● Chianti Cl. V. di Fontalle Ris. '94	YY	4
● Il Principe '94	YY	4
● Ser Niccolò Solatio dei Tani '87	YY	5
● Ser Niccolò Solatio del Tani '93	YY	5
● Chianti Classico Conti Serristori Ris. '94	Y	3
● Ser Niccolò Solatio del Tani '94	Y	5

S. CASCIANO VAL DI PESA (FI)

FATTORIA POGGIOPIANO
VIA DI PISIGNANO, 26/30
50026 S. CASCIANO VAL DI PESA (FI)
TEL. 055/8229629

A banner year for Poggiopiano – the Rosso di Sera has won its second Three Glass award in an almost breathtaking manner. There can be no doubting the progress that Alessandro and Stefano Bartoli's estate has made, not only in the quality of the wines, which just get better and better, but also in organization and management. The number of hectares under vine has risen to seven, with a clear prevalence of sangiovese, while modern techniques, such as temperature-controlled vinification and the use of small wooden barrels, hold sway in the cellar. It should be noted that no-one would expect a wine as rich and concentrated as the Rosso di Sera '97 to come out of a zone like San Casciano or from vineyards with a partly northern exposure, and, furthermore, that this is one of those cases that demonstrate the rarely understood potential of the colorino grape as an ideal complement to sangiovese. But let's move on to our tasting notes. The color, dark ruby, is extremely intense. The nose confirms the impression that we are dealing with something out of the ordinary: it has depth, layer upon layer of black fruit and notes of cocoa and coffee. Nor does the wine slow down on the palate: it is concentrated, dense and very, very soft, with an exceptional polyphenolic richness and a long finish. The Chianti Classico '97 is good, albeit quite far behind its super-Tuscan stablemate; it displays a balanced, firm structure, but we had hoped for something more from this excellent vintage.

●	Rosso di Sera '97	▼▼▼	5
●	Chianti Classico '97	▼	4
●	Rosso di Sera '95	▽▽▽	5
●	Rosso di Sera '96	▽▽	5
●	Chianti Classico '95	▽	3
●	Chianti Classico '96	▽	3

S. GIMIGNANO (SI)

BARONCINI
LOC. CASALE, 43
53037 S. GIMIGNANO (SI)
TEL. 0577/941961

Bruna and Stefano Baroncini have successfully extended their range from Vernaccia di San Gimignano to other classics of Tuscan wine-making such as Brunello di Montalcino, Vino Nobile di Montepulciano and, most recently, Morellino di Scansano. The most interesting of the wines they produce at San Gimignano is the Vernaccia Riserva Dometaia, which has become a classic, and is maintaining its customary high standards with the '97. It has a lovely deep straw color, and an intense, fresh bouquet in which sweet ripe fruit and a delicate floral note are accompanied by a characteristic and elegant note of fresh almond. In the mouth it is full, soft and richly structured, with balanced acidity and a long finish with a crescendo of flavors. Another white, La Faina '97, made from overripe trebbiano, came over on retasting as a rich, deep wine, and the Vernaccia Poggio ai Cannici '98 from the Sovestro line displays a lovely bright straw color and fresh, intense scents of flowers and white-fleshed fruit. In the mouth it is soft and nicely full, and an agreeable characteristic bitter note appears on the finish. We found the '98 Chianti Colli Senesi from the Sovestro line reasonable; it is not tremendously structured but offers freshness and quaffability. A big step forward, on the other hand, has clearly been made by the Maremma wines from their Aia della Macina estate. The Morellino Terranera Riserva '96 has quite rich extract, and is a wine of considerable concentration, softness and depth. Less structured but no less fine and elegant, the Morellino Vigneto Roggetone '98 is richly fruity and harmonious, with fine, smooth tannins.

●	Morellino di Scansano Terranera Ris. Aia della Macina '96	▼▼	4
●	Morellino di Scansano Vign. Roggetone Aia della Macina '98	▼▼	3*
○	Vernaccia di S. Gimignano Dometaia Ris. '97	▼▼	3*
●	Chianti Colli Senesi S. Vigna S. Domenico Sovestro '98	▼	2*
○	Vernaccia di S. Gimignano Poggio ai Cannici '98	▼	2*
○	Vernaccia di S. Gimignano Dometaia Ris. '95	▽▽	3*
○	La Faina '97	▽▽	3
●	Morellino di Scansano Aia della Macina '97	▽	3

S. GIMIGNANO (SI)

CASA ALLE VACCHE
LOC. LUCIGNANO, 73
53037 S. GIMIGNANO (SI)
TEL. 0577/955103

Fernando and Lorenzo Ciappi are beginning to stand on their own legs, showing vintage after vintage that they are no longer at the mercy of the year but that their good results are a matter of estate policy. Two full Glasses go to their Chianti Colli Senesi Cinabro '97 (which was erroneously included in last year's edition of the Guide). It has a bright dark ruby color that extends right up to the rim, and on the nose it releases sweet notes of vanilla that are well amalgamated with the fruit. The palate is full, softly fruity and satisfyingly substantial, with a long, lingering finish. In short, a wine worthy of the Colli Senesi. Another good performance, this time from the Chianti Colli Senesi '98: an intense ruby in hue, it offers a rich bouquet of black fruit and spicy nuances, while the palate is soft and agreeable. This was an interesting debut for the Aglieno, a well-made IGT with aromas of red fruit and some vegetable nuances; the palate is substantial, with slightly rough tannins that a little time in the bottle will no doubt take care of. The Vernaccia di San Gimignano Crocus '98 also nets Two Glasses: straw-colored with golden highlights, it shows a complex fragrance of fruit and flowers; in the mouth it is appealing, substantial, soft and rather long. The Vernaccia '98 is also good: it has an intense floral nose and a well-balanced, soft palate, with a typically bitter finish – a nicely characteristic wine. The Vernaccia I Macchioni '98 is a little under par, with its vegetal nose and not very well-balanced palate.

● Chianti Colli Senesi Cinabro '97	🍷🍷	4
○ Vernaccia di S. Gimignano Crocus '98	🍷🍷	3*
○ Aglieno '98	🍷	3
● Chianti Colli Senesi '98	🍷	2*
○ Vernaccia di S. Gimignano '98	🍷	2*
○ Vernaccia di S. Gimignano I Macchioni '98		3
● Chianti Colli Senesi '95	🍸	1*
● Chianti Colli Senesi '96	🍸	1*
● Chianti Colli Senesi '97	🍸	1*
● Chianti Colli Senesi Cinabro '93	🍸	3
● Chianti Colli Senesi Cinabro '95	🍸	3
● Chianti Colli Senesi Cinabro '97	🍸	3

S. GIMIGNANO (SI)

CASALE - FALCHINI
VIA DI CASALE, 40
53037 S. GIMIGNANO (SI)
TEL. 0574/28123 - 0577/941305

Riccardo Falchini's Casale is part of a historic group (dating from 1964) of San Gimignano wineries that has given a modern stamp to the Vernaccia tradition. It returns to the limelight with full honors, after a sojourn in the Other Wineries section, thanks to a really outstanding range of wines. We very much liked the Riserva '97 version of the Vigna a Solatio. It has a lovely intense straw color, and a nose rich in elegant ripe fruit (melon and peach) mixed with toasty notes from the wood. The palate opens out with just the right degree of freshness and fullness. Falchini surprised us with a selection of Vernaccia matured in barrique, Ab Vinea Doni '98. An intense straw yellow in color, it charms the nose with scents of exotic fruit that are followed by buttery, honeyed notes. The satisfying palate is structured and elegant. The Vernaccia '98 is less intriguing, but still deserves One Glass: it has a stylish nose of flowers and almond, and the latter is attractively echoed on both mid palate and finish. On the red front, too, the expert house touch is confirmed by a double release of the Campora, '94 and '95. The former, already mentioned in last year's edition of the Guide, is attractive in color, with aromatic notes of red fruit and woody nuances. It is satisfyingly warm, soft and well balanced on the palate. The Campora '95 is just as appealing: perhaps a little grassy on the nose, it has good substance in the mouth, with a perceptible but unintrusive note of toasty oak. The red "table wine", the Paretaio '96, is a step lower down the scale, but still pleasant. The Chianti Colombaia '97 is a bit forward for its year. The Vin Santo '93 and the Millesimato, made from vernaccia, are both good.

○ Vernaccia di S. Gimignano Ab Vinea Doni '98	🍷🍷	4
● Campora '94	🍷🍷	6
● Campora '95	🍷🍷	6
○ Vernaccia di S. Gimignano Vigna a Solatio Ris. '97	🍷🍷	3*
○ Vernaccia di S. Gimignano Vigna a Solatio '98	🍷	2*
○ Vin Santo del Chianti '93	🍷	4
● Chianti Colli Senesi Titolato Colombaia '97		2
● Paretaio '96		3
● Campora '88	🍸🍸	6
● Campora '90	🍸🍸	6
● Campora '91	🍸🍸	6

VINCENZO CESANI
LOC. PANCOLE, 82/D
53037 S. GIMIGNANO (SI)
TEL. 0577/955084

Vincenzo Cesani and his wife Lucia have spent a lifetime laboring in their lovely vineyards in the Pancole district near San Gimignano. Originally from the Marche, they arrived here more than 30 years ago and decided that this was where they wanted to put down their roots. During this time many things have changed in the world of wine: production philosophy, cellar technology, vineyard management. And they have been working away all this time, pruning and tying their vines, one by one, determined to rise above the local average. One new development of recent years is that it is now possible to make great reds at San Gimignano, as well as the traditional Vernaccia. And so here we are with the revelation of the year: the Luenzo '97, sangiovese (with a little colorino) fermented and matured in wood, made with the advice of the consultant oenologist Paolo Caciornia. It is dark ruby, almost black, in color, dense and all but impenetrable. The two previous vintages were already very good, but the '97 is on another level. It offers intense, rich perfumes of ripe red fruit, cherry and pencil lead, with spicy notes and elegant hints of perfectly toasted wood. Although powerful, luscious and finely tannic in the mouth, it is also harmonious and incredibly long: Three Glasses hands down. Their other wines are equally interesting and carefully made: the Vernaccia Sanice '98 displays freshly soft fruity tones on the nose and on the palate, where it is harmonious and full, with fine flavors of aromatic herbs and ripe fruit and a very well-judged measure of spicy new wood; the Vernaccia '98 is soft, fruity and full, while the Chianti '98 is admirable for its intense nose and good extract.

●	Luenzo '97	🍷🍷🍷	5
○	Vernaccia di S. Gimignano Sanice '98	🍷🍷	4
●	Chianti Colli Senesi '98	🍷	2*
○	Vernaccia di S. Gimignano '98	🍷	2*
●	Luenzo '95	🍸🍸	4
●	Luenzo '96	🍸🍸	4
●	Chianti Colli Senesi '93	🍸	2*
●	Chianti Colli Senesi '94	🍸	2*
○	Vernaccia di S. Gimignano '97	🍸	2*
○	Vernaccia di S. Gimignano Sanice '96	🍸	4
○	Vernaccia di S. Gimignano Sanice '97	🍸	4

S. GIMIGNANO (SI)

GUICCIARDINI STROZZI
FATTORIA DI CUSONA
53037 S. GIMIGNANO (SI)
TEL. 0577/950028

Do you know for how many centuries there has been a Fattoria di Cusona? A parchment from 994 provides evidence that the total is ten centuries at least. Girolamo Strozzi, who is nothing like as old, has presented a wide range of remarkably good wines this year, mainly reds. We shall start with the Selvascura '97, a blend of merlot and 10% colorino that fell just short of our top award. A dark ruby in color, it has a complex nose with notes of black currant, blackberry and black cherry, and nuances of vanilla that testify to the well-judged wood. In the mouth it is highly concentrated, powerful and soft, with rich fruit and an elegant, lingering finish. Sumptuous! The Millanni '96 gets Two Glasses, like the '95, and is if anything even better. The color is inkily intense. It is round on the nose, with vegetal notes, blackberry and wood. On the palate it is concentrated and soft, with sweet tannins and a long finish. The Millanni '97 is a complex wine: the nose releases notes of dark berries and a touch of spice; in the mouth, where the great potential of the '97 vintage shines through, it expresses its youthfulness to the full. The consistently good Sodole '97 is worthy of note: it offers intensity and attractive notes of violet, berries and spice. Of the whites, we particularly enjoyed the Vernaccia Riserva '97 with its intense, sweet perfumes and good body. The Vernaccia Perlato '98, however, is slightly under par and a bit monotonous; it develops evenly on the palate, but the finish is short. The Vernaccia Titolato '98 has a good, if unusual, personality; the Vernaccia San Biagio '98 is fair. To close, the Chianti Colli Senesi Titolato '98 is fresh and immediate.

●	Millanni '96	🍷🍷	6
●	Millanni '97	🍷🍷	6
●	Selvascura '97	🍷🍷	5
○	Vernaccia di S. Gimignano Ris. '97	🍷🍷	4
●	Chianti Colli Senesi Titolato '98	🍷	3
●	Sodole '97	🍷	5
○	Vernaccia di S. Gimignano Titolato '98	🍷	3
○	Vernaccia di S. Gimignano Perlato '98		4
○	Vernaccia di S. Gimignano S. Biagio '98		3
●	994 Millanni '94	🍸🍸	6
●	Millanni '95	🍸🍸	6
●	Sodole '93	🍸🍸	5

S. GIMIGNANO (SI)

Il Lebbio
Loc. S. Benedetto, 11/c
53037 S. Gimignano (SI)
tel. 0577/944725

In last year's Guide we mentioned the possibility that a new red might be in the wings at Il Lebbio. And here we are with our tasting notes for the Cicogio '98, a blend of ciliegiolo, colorino and sangiovese that easily crossed the Two Glass threshold. Its color is a rather dense red; the nose is rich in notes of ripe fruit (blackberry and blueberry), while the palate is juicy, full, soft and structured, and the limpid flavors and aromas reappear on the beautifully intense finish. The other red of the same year, I Grottoni, whose predecessor was last year's revelation, was slightly under par, albeit still quite good. Of an intense ruby hue, it is initially closed on the nose, but then opens out on winning notes of ripe berries (raspberry and black currant). The attractively expressive, full-bodied palate has a slightly rough finish as a result of somewhat uncontrolled tannins. The fairly good Chianti '98 is pleasant, characteristic and easy to drink. The Malvasia '98, an unusual wine in Vernaccia territory, won One Glass. It has faint perfumes of grapefruit and lemon, and a simple, correct, pleasant palate that distinctly displays the characteristics of its grape. The finish, while clean, is not particularly long. Lastly, the basic '98 Vernaccia is properly made.

●	Cicogio '98	🍷🍷	3*
●	I Grottoni '98	🍷	3
○	Malvasia '98	🍷	2*
●	Chianti '98		2
○	Vernaccia di S. Gimignano '98		2
●	I Grottoni '97	♀♀	2*
●	Chianti '97	♀	2*

S. GIMIGNANO (SI)

La Lastra
Loc. Santa Lucia
Via R. De Grada, 9
53037 S. Gimignano (SI)
tel. 0577/941781

Nadia Betti and Renato Spanu arrived in San Gimignano in the summer of 1980, after graduating from the Istituto Agrario at San Michele all'Adige. What should have been a short holiday turned out to be a fundamental life choice. After working for various producers, Nadia and Riccardo started up their own small, carefully tended estate, La Lastra. Here they try to create their ideal of Vernaccia, but the winery serves above all to show their clients (Nadia is an agronomic consultant) what can be achieved with very high-density planting, which in fact produces extremely sound, rich grapes. The Vernaccia Riserva, in Nadia and Riccardo's view, is one of the most fascinating whites in the world, and all we can say is that after tasting the '97 vintage we feel ready to second this daring claim. This is a white that has richness, density, a good structure and exuberantly fresh aromatic tones, with an excellent woody timbre that is elegant and harmonious and in no way weighs down the wine. The Vernaccia '98 is simpler in style but is still one of the best of its kind. It has a wealth of fresh, ripe, sweet fruit, with a discreet floral note, and good structure and well-judged alcohol; it is concentrated, rounded and full, and of considerable finesse and persistence. The Rovaio '98, a red made from sangiovese, cabernet and merlot which we tasted while it was still maturing and which we'll review next year, is very promising; the Chianti Colli Senesi '98, soft and immediate, is also good.

○	Vernaccia di S. Gimignano '98	🍷🍷	2*
○	Vernaccia di S. Gimignano Ris. '97	🍷🍷	3*
●	Chianti Colli Senesi '98	🍷	2*
○	Vernaccia di S. Gimignano Ris. '95	♀♀	3*
○	Vernaccia di S. Gimignano Ris. '96	♀♀	3*
●	Chianti Colli Senesi '95	♀	4
●	Chianti Colli Senesi '96	♀	4
●	Chianti Colli Senesi '97	♀	4
●	Rovaio '95	♀	4
●	Rovaio '96	♀	5
○	Vernaccia di S. Gimignano '96	♀	3
○	Vernaccia di S. Gimignano '97	♀	3

S. GIMIGNANO (SI)

La Rampa di Fugnano
Loc. Fugnano
53037 S. Gimignano (SI)
tel. 0577/941655

With a masterful stroke Gisela Traxler and her husband Herbert Erhebold, Swiss in origin but transplanted years ago to San Gimignano, have established their place in the narrow circle of the best wine producers in Italy – and, what's more, after a couple of years' absence from the Guide. A return in the grand style, in short. The wine that bears the palm is the merlot-based Gisèle '97, a small masterpiece of concentration and elegance. It shows an impenetrably dark ruby hue, and is intense and extremely elegant on the nose, where scents of fully ripe sweet red and black berries blend with delicate vegetal strains, a sweet note of chocolate and a spicy, measured touch of new wood. In the mouth the wine is ample, deep, extremely elegant and dense. The engaging notes of ripe, succulent fruit are underpinned by well-judged acidity and highlight the abundant but extraordinarily smooth, fine tannins. Extremely long on the finish, this is the fruit of a great harvest from one of La Rampa's new vineyards, which has perfect exposure and has been densely planted and "forced" into very low yields. The fact that these two years were in no way wasted can be seen also from another wine made by the couple and their consultant oenologist, Paolo Caciornia. This is the Sangiovese Bombereto '97. Of considerable depth and softness, it suggests a great wine, even if it does not quite manage to attain the elegance and balance of the Gisèle. It wouldn't surprise us, in the future, to see it taking its place with the merlot in the top ranks. The Vernaccia Riserva Privato '97 is good, as is the rest of the range.

●	Gisèle '97	▼▼▼	5
●	Bombereto '97	▼▼	5
●	Chianti Colli Senesi Via dei Franchi '97	▼	3
●	Chianti Colli Senesi Via dei Franchi '98	▼	3
○	Vernaccia di S. Gimignano '98	▼	3
○	Vernaccia di S. Gimignano Privato Ris. '97	▼	4
●	Bombereto '92	▽	3
●	Bombereto '93	▽	4
●	Chianti Colli Senesi Via dei Franchi '93	▽	2*
●	Chianti Colli Senesi Via dei Franchi '95	▽	3

S. GIMIGNANO (SI)

Mormoraia
Loc. S. Andrea
53037 S. Gimignano (SI)
tel. 0577/940096

Despite its extreme youth this estate, which belongs to Giuseppe Passoni, who is Milanese, and to his wife Franca, has achieved great things. It must have been destiny, as once Giuseppe, a businessman and former rally driver, had arrived in San Gimignano, he quite fell in love with this corner of Tuscany and decided to stay here as a major player. And this is how the 20 hectares under vine (but many more are planned) in the S. Andrea district came into being, the modern winery (which is in the process of being enlarged) was built, and Franco Bernabei was called in to provide his valuable oenological advice: all the ingredients, in short, for a success story. And this year's tastings simply confirm how well and with what scrupulous attention to even the tiniest detail Giovanni has worked throughout these years. The Vernaccia Riserva, making its debut with the '97 version, is one of the best in its category. It has a deep, green-tinged straw color, an intense nose of vanilla and ripe fruit with stylish toasty nuances, and a fresh, fat and balanced palate with lingering fruity notes of pineapple and banana. The Ostrea '97, made from vernaccia and chardonnay and matured in barrique, has a good structure, a full, elegant body and an inviting, rich, gradual development on the palate, where it displays a fruity freshness given added charm and complexity by the spicy tones of the wood. The Vernaccia '98 is also excellent, while the Neitea '96, a red made from sangiovese and cabernet sauvignon in wood, pays the price of a poor year. It is very good, rich and elegant but lacks the concentration of the '95. The '97, however, already has the makings of a great wine.

●	Neitea '96	▼▼	4
○	Ostrea '97	▼▼	4
○	Vernaccia di San Gimignano '98	▼▼	3*
○	Vernaccia di San Gimignano Ris. '97	▼▼	4
●	Neitea '95	▽▽	4
○	Ostrea '95	▽▽	4
○	Ostrea '96	▽▽	4
○	Vernaccia di San Gimignano '96	▽	3
○	Vernaccia di San Gimignano '97	▽	3

S. GIMIGNANO (SI)

PALAGETTO

VIA MONTEOLIVETO, 46
53037 S. GIMIGNANO (SI)
TEL. 0577/943090 - 0577/942098

Simone Niccolai runs Palagetto, made up of three properties that together account for 17 hectares of vineyards, with great skill and managerial flair. In just a few years he has raised the winery to an excellent level, thanks in no small measure to the masterly technical advice of the oenologist Paolo Salvi. The wine that most impressed us was once again the red Sottobosco '97, classed as a "table wine". It has a very deep, luminously bright ruby color. The nose offers an intense spectrum of aromas that include quinine, wood, licorice and tobacco; the structure and rich alcohol on the palate, which is supple and soft on the entry, emerge as the flavors develop and lead through to a persistent finish. In this year's tasting the Vernaccia Riserva '97, which glided effortlessly over the Two Glass threshold, also put in a fine performance. A strong straw yellow in color, it releases intense floral, honeyed and almond scents; in the mouth it is expressive, decisive and fruity, with almond notes rounding off the long, persistent finish. The Vernaccia Vigna Santa Chiara is again clearly a skillfully made wine. A fairly deep straw yellow in color, it has penetrating, attractively fruity perfumes, accompanied by floral notes. The palate is appealing, soft and balanced, with a bitter-sweet finish. The '98 version of the basic Vernaccia is less expressive but well made. And to finish, the good Chianti Colli Senesi '98 is pleasantly fruity and of exemplary cleanness.

●	Sottobosco '97	🍷🍷	5
○	Vernaccia di S. Gimignano Ris. '97	🍷🍷	4
●	Chianti Colli Senesi '98	🍷	3
○	Vernaccia di S. Gimignano Vigna Santa Chiara '98	🍷	3
○	Vernaccia di S. Gimignano '98		3
●	Chianti Colli Senesi '95	🍸	1*
●	Sottobosco '94	🍸	3
●	Sottobosco '95	🍸	4
●	Sottobosco '96	🍸	4
○	Vernaccia di S. Gimignano '96	🍸	3
○	Vernaccia di S. Gimignano '97	🍸	3
○	Vernaccia di S. Gimignano Vigna Santa Chiara '96	🍸	3

S. GIMIGNANO (SI)

GIOVANNI PANIZZI

LOC. RACCIANO - S. MARGHERITA
53037 S. GIMIGNANO (SI)
TEL. 0577/941576 - 02/90938796

Under the spell of the Tuscan countryside, Giovanni Panizzi left Milan and a job in information science in 1979. It took ten years to reorganize the vineyards and cellar before his first harvest. His Vernaccia Riserva wines, matured in new wood, are probably the best interpretations we have of this grape. Thus far, no-one has managed to do better, but perhaps his Vernaccia needs just a little more concentration and depth in order to take its place beside the other great whites of the world. Giovanni is convinced that to give this wine a further boost, serious work needs to be done on replanting the old vineyards, a task with which he is making excellent progress. In the meantime, we advise you to savor every last drop of the excellent Vernaccia Riserva '97, one of the best ever produced. It has a strong, green-tinged straw yellow color and intense, sweet aromas of candied fruit, sweet pastry and vanilla. Outstandingly elegant on the palate, it exhibits good concentration, with an imposing structure and very clean fruit, enhanced by well-gauged spicy notes of new wood. Panizzi's '97 is also one of the best Chianti dei Colli Senesis we have ever tasted: luscious and rich, it releases soft fruity notes on the nose and on the palate, where it is concentrated and rich in smooth tannins. We gave good marks to the red Ceraso '98, the Vernaccia '98 and the Bianco di Gianni '97, made from chardonnay and vernaccia and not very distinct on the nose but quite well structured.

●	Chianti Colli Senesi '97	🍷🍷	4
○	Vernaccia di S. Gimignano Ris. '97	🍷🍷	5
○	Bianco di Gianni '97	🍷	5
●	Ceraso '98	🍷	3
○	Vernaccia di S. Gimignano '98	🍷	4
○	Vernaccia di S. Gimignano Ris. '94	🍸🍸	5
○	Vernaccia di S. Gimignano Ris. '95	🍸🍸	5
○	Vernaccia di S. Gimignano Ris. '96	🍸🍸	5
●	Ceraso '95	🍸	3
●	Ceraso '96	🍸	3
●	Chianti Colli Senesi '93	🍸	2*
●	Chianti Colli Senesi '95	🍸	3
●	Chianti Colli Senesi '96	🍸	4

S. GIMIGNANO (SI)

FATTORIA PARADISO
LOC. STRADA, 21/A
53037 S. GIMIGNANO (SI)
TEL. 0577/941500

A doctor by profession, Vasco Cetti was for some years the president of the Vernaccia Producers' Consortium, as well as winegrower on his lovely estate, the Fattoria Paradiso. We have been saying for quite a while that the wines he produces are one of the area's unfulfilled promises. They suffer in particular, in our opinion, from their maker's untiring desire to experiment and, at times, from the impatience that, for better or worse, is part of his personality. Over the years Vasco has had some remarkable successes, but these have rarely been followed through the following year. The Basolo Solivo '88, for example, was an important wine because it clearly demonstrated the potential of this terroir to yield great reds, while, for the whites, the Vernaccia Biscondola '93 was of similar distinction. Vasco does not always accept our criticisms willingly, but that's the way it is. However, we would like to see two of the wines we tasted this year becoming "classics" of this winery and of San Gimignano. The first is the Saxa Calida '96, a Bordeaux-style blend of great depth and irrepressible intensity. So dense in color that it's almost black, it is concentrated, rich in fruit and smooth tannins, elegant, mouth-filling, harmonious and very long. The other is the Bottaccio '97, a sangiovese. This is a red of indisputable breeding, hugely rich in extract, fruity and succulent, elegant and complex in its spicy notes and fine tannins. The rest of the wide range of wines produced by the Fattoria Paradiso is good. Of course he could do even better.

●	Bottaccio '97	🍷🍷	4
●	Saxa Calida '96	🍷🍷	4
●	Chianti Colli Senesi '98	🍷	2*
○	Docciola '98	🍷	3
○	Lo Cha '97	🍷	4
●	Paterno II '96	🍷	4
○	Vernaccia di S. Gimignano '98	🍷	3
●	Chianti Colli Senesi '95	🍸	2*
●	Chianti Colli Senesi '96	🍸	2*
●	Chianti Colli Senesi '97	🍸	2*
●	Paterno II '94	🍸	4
●	Paterno II '95	🍸	4
●	Saxa Calida '93	🍸	4
●	Saxa Calida '94	🍸	4
●	Saxa Calida '95	🍸	4

S. GIMIGNANO (SI)

FATTORIA SAN DONATO
LOC. S. DONATO, 6
53037 S. GIMIGNANO (SI)
TEL. 0577/941616

Umberto Fenzi possesses in no small measure the enthusiasm of the able vigneron. Ever since he took over at the helm of this winery, with the help of the oenologist Paolo Salvi, results have been excellent and quality constant. A case in point is the Vernaccia Riserva '97 Benedetta, which has a bright, intense straw yellow color. Its aromas are complex, elegant and fresh, characterized by fruit and almond; on the palate the wine is concentrated, soft and well balanced, and the moderately long finish offers a mouth-filling almond flavor. The Vernaccia '98 Selezione was not so good, perhaps because we tasted it just after its bottling. It only just made it over the One Glass threshold. Pleasing to the eye with its almost golden yellow hue, it has an intense nose, with a note of good wood currently lording it over the ripe fruit. It is smooth and moderately concentrated on the palate, and the finish is somewhat short. The good Chianti Colli Senesi '98 is redolent of cherry and spice; it is nicely concentrated in the mouth, with a fruity tone and a soft, appealing finish. To conclude, the Vernaccia di San Gimignano '98 is correctly made, with faint mineral notes on the nose and a quite well-balanced palate.

○	Vernaccia di S. Gimignano Ris. '97	🍷🍷	4
●	Chianti Colli Senesi '98	🍷	3
○	Vernaccia di S. Gimignano Sel. '98	🍷	4
○	Vernaccia di S. Gimignano '98		3
○	Vernaccia di S. Gimignano Sel. '97	🍸🍸	4
●	Chianti Colli Senesi '95	🍸	2*
●	Chianti Colli Senesi '96	🍸	2*
○	Vernaccia di S. Gimignano '97	🍸	3
○	Vernaccia di S. Gimignano Ris. '96	🍸	4
○	Vernaccia di S. Gimignano Sel. '96	🍸	4

S. GIMIGNANO (SI)

FATTORIA SAN QUIRICO
LOC. PANCOLE, 39
53037 S. GIMIGNANO (SI)
TEL. 0577/955007

The Fattoria San Quirico's presence in the Guide is by no means constant, and we honestly don't know why this should be the case. Andrea Vecchione has at his disposal 25 hectares in the Pancole district, which is one of the best in the area, an up-to-the-minute cellar, and the advice of the expert consultant oenologist Luigino Casagrande. The potential for excellence is here – all you need do is really believe in it. This said, we noted another improvement during this year's tastings. The Vernaccia Riserva '97 I Campi Santi missed Two Glasses by a mere hair's breadth, while the Riserva '96 made it over the threshold. Both have a more modern style than they used to, but perhaps an even sharper break with the past could be made. An intense straw yellow in color, the Riserva '97 has attractively complex fruity and floral scents. After a soft attack on the palate, the wine develops with good balance. The finish, moderate in length, beautifully echoes the bouquet, and wants just a bit more concentration. The Riserva 96, on the other hand, has a sweet nose with elegantly evolved nuances balanced by notes of sage and elder flower. In the mouth it shows character, good depth and balance, and is markedly long. The Vernaccia '98 is one of the best of its kind. The nose develops steadily, with floral and fruity scents alternating; the palate is fresh, soft and medium-bodied and it finishes with the classic almond note. Lastly, the Chianti Colli Senesi '96 is correctly made; although agreeable, it is somewhat forward, and shows already smooth tannins.

○	Vernaccia di S. Gimignano I Campi Santi Ris. '96	🍷🍷	4
○	Vernaccia di S. Gimignano '98	🍷	2*
○	Vernaccia di S. Gimignano I Campi Santi Ris. '97	🍷	4
●	Chianti Colli Senesi '96		3
○	Vernaccia di S. Gimignano I Campi Santi Ris. '92	🍸🍸	4
●	Chianti Colli Senesi '95	🍸	3
○	Vernaccia di S. Gimignano '96	🍸	2*

S. GIMIGNANO (SI)

SIGNANO
VIA DI SAN MATTEO, 101
53037 S. GIMIGNANO (SI)
TEL. 0577/940164

Manrico Biagini does not like wines matured in barriques, because, he claims, it gives them a "taste of the carpenter's workshop". Yet it would seem that he has gained a degree of confidence and familiarity with small oak barrels – indeed the Vernaccia Selezione '97 has won Two Glasses and is the most interesting wine presented by Signano this year. An intense golden-hued straw yellow in color, it clearly reveals the spice of the barrique on the nose, together with notes of ripe fruit. The attack on the palate is soft and the development even, leading up to a fairly long finish. Of the Vernaccia Poggiarelli '98, the Vernaccia Riserva '97 and the basic Vernaccia '98, the last-named is the most successful. It has a straw yellow color of medium intensity and its perfumes are well defined, sound and delicately fruity. Fresh, pleasing and balanced on the palate, it is not overly long. The Vernaccia Riserva '97 is a little austere, with reticent scents ranging from mineral to floral. The palate has a mature flavor, a good body and a reasonably good finish with a characteristic almond note. The Vernaccia Poggiarelli is rather tired on the palate, although its varietal features still show through. The Chianti Colli Senesi Poggiarelli '97, on the other hand, is again very good. A strong ruby in color, it offers a fragrance of red fruit with intense balsamic and vanilla notes; the well-structured palate reveals substantial – and still somewhat rough – tannins. The Chianti Colli Senesi '98 does not have the same intensity of expression, but is nonetheless correctly made and pleasantly quaffable. Lastly, the Vin Santo '90 is pleasing and characteristic.

○	Vernaccia di S. Gimignano Sel. '97	🍷🍷	4
●	Chianti Colli Senesi Poggiarelli '97	🍷	4
○	Vernaccia di S. Gimignano '98	🍷	2*
○	Vernaccia di S. Gimignano Ris. '97	🍷	3
○	Vin Santo '90	🍷	4
●	Chianti Colli Senesi '98		2
○	Vernaccia di S. Gimignano Poggiarelli '98		3
●	Chianti Colli Senesi Poggiarelli '94	🍸	3
●	Chianti Colli Senesi Poggiarelli '95	🍸	4
●	Chianti Colli Senesi Poggiarelli '96	🍸	4

S. GIMIGNANO (SI)

TERUZZI & PUTHOD
LOC. CASALE, 19
53037 S. GIMIGNANO (SI)
TEL. 0577/940143

Enrico Teruzzi and his wife Carmen Puthod are founder members of San Gimignano's "Milanese colony". Their first harvest was in 1974. Twenty-five years later, thanks in part to their dedication, Vernaccia has undergone a profound transformation. And it has also conquered the international market. In their cellar the most avant-garde technological procedures are tested, involving both equipment and the software for running it. Each stage of production (Teruzzi & Puthod markets something like a million and a half bottles a year) is entirely computer-controlled, and the history of each bottle that leaves the cellar can be reconstructed from harvest time to the moment of delivery to the customer. This year once again their leading wine is the Terre di Tufi, in the '97 version. It has a strong, brilliant straw yellow color, intense scents of ripe fruit with a hint of extremely fine vanilla and flowers, and a palate that is elegant, full, dense and soft, and richly structured like a great Vernaccia, with the additional exotic touch of new wood and of the vermentino and chardonnay grapes that go to complete the blend. The Carmen, a white made from sangiovese matured in new wood, of which we tasted the '97 and '98 versions, is again excellent. The former is a touch fatter and more opulent, while the latter's winning card is the freshness of its fruit and its admirably judged wood. The Vernaccia Vigna a Rondolino '98 has a good soft, fruity character, and the basic freshly quaffable Vernaccia (of which almost 500 thousand bottles are produced) is the DOCG benchmark.

○	Carmen '97	🍷🍷	4
○	Carmen '98	🍷🍷	4
○	Terre di Tufi '97	🍷🍷	5
●	Peperino '98	🍷	3
○	Vernaccia di S. Gimignano '98	🍷	3
○	Vernaccia di S. Gimignano Vigna a Rondolino '98	🍷	4
○	Carmen '93	🍸🍸	4
○	Carmen '94	🍸🍸	4
○	Carmen '95	🍸🍸	4
○	Carmen '96	🍸🍸	4
○	Terre di Tufi '93	🍸🍸	5
○	Terre di Tufi '94	🍸🍸	5
○	Terre di Tufi '95	🍸🍸	5
○	Terre di Tufi '96	🍸🍸	5

S. GIMIGNANO (SI)

F.LLI VAGNONI
LOC. PANCOLE, 82
53037 S. GIMIGNANO (SI)
TEL. 0577/955077

The Vagnoni family's dynamic estate is yet again amongst Italy's top wine producers. Every year when Luigi, who comes from the Marche – and it shows, in his unstinting work in the vineyard and scrupulous attention to detail in the cellar – bottles the Mocali, their key wine, he allows his thoughts to wander for a moment to the top prize, but he doesn't let this show. This year we were denied the pleasure of tasting it because the wine was still maturing in the bottle, so we'll discuss it in next year's edition. We were surprised when we tasted the Sodi Lunghi '97, a red made from sangiovese, canaiolo and cabernet. A purplish ruby in color, it releases notes of rich fruit on the nose, with a hint of tobacco and leather rounded off by sweet vanilla; the soft attack on the palate leads into good concentration and smooth tannins on the mid palate, followed by a mouth-filling finish. The Chianti Colli Senesi '98 is rather dark in color, nicely clean on the nose, with notes of cherry and undergrowth, and well articulated on the palate, after a soft, nicely weighty attack. The Vernaccia '98, whose strong point is the ripeness of its the grapes, is quite admirable. The bouquet is characterized by notes of banana and apple, while the well-judged acidity on the palate is counterbalanced by glycerin and alcohol, which confer a full, balanced flavor. The Vin Brusco del Solatio '98, a fresh white made from trebbiano and malvasia, is interesting, fairly substantial and quaffable. The Rosato '98 reveals good structure, as usual.

●	I Sodi Lunghi '97	🍷🍷	4
●	Chianti Colli Senesi '98	🍷	3
○	Vernaccia di S. Gimignano '98	🍷	3
⊙	Rosato '98		2
○	Vin Brusco del Solatio '98		2
○	Vernaccia di S. Gimignano Mocali '96	🍸🍸	4
○	Vernaccia di S. Gimignano Mocali '97	🍸🍸	4
●	Chianti Colli Senesi '95	🍸	3
●	Chianti Colli Senesi '97	🍸	3
●	I Sodi Lunghi '93	🍸	3
●	I Sodi Lunghi '95	🍸	4
●	I Sodi Lunghi '96	🍸	4
○	Vernaccia di S. Gimignano '97	🍸	3

S. PANCRAZIO (LU)

LA BADIOLA
VIA DEL PARCO, 10
55100 S. PANCRAZIO (LU)
TEL. 0583/30633

With the regularity of a Swiss clock, the wines of La Badiola deliver their usual impeccable cleanness and fruity quaffability. These are wines that can be drunk with pleasure: they are not given to exaggerated displays of hyper-concentration with massive doses of tannins and wood, as can happen with some examples of the "over-oaked" style, which are, alas!, all too frequent at our annual tastings. The range of wines has been enriched by a monovarietal Merlot that faithfully reflects the winery's style, which means that it is soft, rounded and excellently balanced; it shows attractive notes of black fruit, and was held back from crossing the Two Glass level only by a slightly excessive vegetal tone. We continue, however, to award the winner's crown to the Vigna Flora, a blend of cabernet and merlot which in the '97 version comes well up to expectations. A lovely dark, almost black red in color, it is concentrated and elegant on the nose, notwithstanding its pronounced vegetal aromas. The palate is decidedly tasty, very soft and smooth, and it would be really difficult not to like it. The Colline Lucchesi Rosso '98 also hits the mark: a successful wine that easily nets its One Glass and boasts not only the usual appealing qualities of La Badiola's wines, but also much more body than one generally finds in its category and an admirable bouquet. The whites too made a positive impression: the Stoppielle '98 is fairly good, and the Colline Lucchesi Bianco '98 more than correct.

●	Vigna Flora '97	TT	3*
●	Colline Lucchesi Rosso '98	T	2*
●	Merlot '97	T	4
○	Stoppielle '98	T	3
○	Colline Lucchesi Bianco '98		2
○	Vigna Flora '92	YY	3*
●	Vigna Flora '93	YY	3*
●	Vigna Flora '96	YY	3*
○	Colline Lucchesi Bianco '97	Y	2*
●	Colline Lucchesi Rosso '93	Y	2*
●	Colline Lucchesi Rosso '97	Y	2*
○	Stoppielle '97	Y	3

SAMBUCA DI TAVARNELLE (FI)

IL POGGIOLINO
VIA CHIANTIGIANA, 32
50020 SAMBUCA DI TAVARNELLE (FI)
TEL. 055/8071635

The Pacini family's estate is slightly off the beaten track, on the eastern part of the slope linking Tavarnelle and San Donato in Poggio, on the border of the Chianti Classico district. This year sees its first appearance in the Guide. Run with constancy and commitment by Fausto Castellini, it benefits from the technical expertise of the noted oenologist Attilio Pagli. Three wines were presented at our tastings. The Chianti Classico '97, which won Two Glasses, is excellent. Of an intense ruby hue, it offers a very elegant bouquet, with extremely fruity perfumes, rather like freshly squeezed mixed red fruit, with secondary notes of violet. The palate is lively without being overwhelming, and the balance is good, with not particularly harsh tannins. The acidity is well judged and the agreeable finish boasts length and depth. The Riserva '96 has a ruby color of no great intensity, and mature, forward and not entirely clear jammy scents. In the mouth, however, it is fairly substantial, with firm, closely textured, unaggressive tannins, rich alcohol and pronounced acidity, and a finish that, while not terribly long, is as it should be. Le Balze '95 is a sangiovese-based IGT matured in barriques. Limpid in appearance, it has simple, not particularly intense perfumes of fresh fruit. After a good entry the palate reveals not very graceful tannins, that are a little dry and too prominent. The finish, however, is good, with a proper and pleasing persistence.

●	Chianti Classico '97	TT	3*
●	Chianti Classico Ris. '96	T	4
●	Le Balze '95	T	4

SAN VINCENZO (LI)

PODERE SAN MICHELE
LOC. CADUTA, 3/A
57027 SAN VINCENZO (LI)
TEL. 0565/798038

There's a widespread prejudice in the wine world against coastal zones. And here we are once again, giving a positive review to a winery that proves these traditional beliefs to be unfounded. Marino Socci's estate is near San Vincenzo, a famous seaside resort that, thanks to the presence of Fulvio Pierangelini's legendary Gambero Rosso restaurant, is also well known to lovers of good food. The Podere San Michele is run, with wholehearted enthusiasm, by the brother-and-sister team Giorgio and Tiziana, who began, six or seven years ago, to put their minds to seriously boosting quality by betting on their own potential. And they have succeeded. The most prevalent grapes here are sangiovese, and to a lesser extent cabernet sauvignon, syrah and viognier. The oenologist is Luca D'Attoma, vinification techniques are modern in style, with well-judged and never overly long maceration times, and a preference for small wooden barrels. Their first wine, in order both of importance and date of birth, is the Allodio Rosso, almost 100% sangiovese, which first came out with the '95 harvest and of which we tasted the '97 version this year: an intense red, with abundant fruit and a not yet altogether focused nose, but endowed with density, concentrated tannins and an attractive personality. The Allodio Bianco '98 has made a successful debut: it's an agreeable viognier-based wine whose personality comes through pleasingly in its succulent, reasonably full and lingering palate with delightful notes of exotic fruit, chamomile, and broom.

●	Allodio Rosso '97	🍷🍷	4
○	Allodio Bianco '98	🍷	4

SAN VINCENZO A TORRI (FI)

UGGIANO
VIA EMPOLESE
50020 SAN VINCENZO A TORRI (FI)
TEL. 055/769087

The rapid pace of improvement in many Tuscan wineries has moved the threshold for access to a place in the Guide higher and higher. Having overcome these obstacles, Giuseppe Losapio's estate, located in the hilly territory bordering the Chianti Classico area, is making its debut here. The grapes on the estate are mainly sangiovese and cabernet sauvignon, which are the principal components of the wines we tasted this year. The Cabernet Rodaro '94, a vigorous, characterful wine, stands out above the rest. It shows an intense garnet-hued ruby red color, and a concentrated nose with scents of blackberry jam and toasty oak, as well as light tertiary notes of leather and sweet tobacco. The palate is powerful, progressive, full and persistent. This wine falls somewhat short of elegance, and has over-emphatic wood, but is solid and substantial. The Falconieri '95 performed reasonably well. A blend of four parts cabernet with one part sangiovese, it is less rich in structure and slightly more forward. The flavor is rounded and well balanced, accompanied by spice, quinine and coffee on the nose. The Chianti Classico Riserva '95 was not at all bad either; its perhaps over-forward color and nose are countered to some extent by a soft, balanced palate. The Colli Fiorentini is acceptable and correctly made, although it's obviously on a downward slope. The Orvieto Classico, vintage '94, is, however, open to question: it is completely dominated by wood, but the effect is not unpleasant.

●	Rodaro '94	🍷🍷	5
●	Chianti Ris. '95	🍷	4
●	Falconieri '95	🍷	4
●	Chianti Colli Fiorentini '95		3
○	Orvieto Classico Madonnino '94		3

SCANSANO (GR)

ERIK BANTI
LOC. FOSSO DEI MULINI
58054 SCANSANO (GR)
TEL. 0564/508006

If there exists a producer who is scrupulous, indeed painstaking to the nth degree, then that producer is Erik Banti. His love for precision is renowned both in the Maremma, where he has played something of a ground-breaking role, and in the rest of the Italian wine-making world. These gifts have enabled him to create some of the best wines of the Maremma, wines that are very closely linked to their territory, or to use a more exact, albeit foreign word, to the terroir. The wines we tasted this year were perhaps less dazzling than usual, but they were still well executed. The Morellino di Scansano '98, although slightly fermentative, shows good body and the right degree of fruit; its bouquet however, is adversely affected by muffled, rustic notes of fusel oil. The Morellino di Scansano Ciabatta '96 is more engaging, with its lovely ruby color and spicy, robustly fruity and intense fragrance. It has a medium-bodied, warm palate with delicate overripe notes. The Carato '97, of a deep bright ruby color, has the typical sangiovese nose of bay leaf, faint vegetal notes, and a hint of geranium. On the palate it is fruity, nicely weighty, balanced and persistent. And so we reach the newcomer, the Anno I, vintage '97. It has an attractive, fairly deep ruby color. The nose displays notes of sweet, spicy oak, which at the moment are a bit insistent. The corresponding palate is soft, full-bodied and mature, with a nicely persistent finish. A final note: the Aquilaia '97, which we are not reviewing because the sample we tasted was not definitive, showed promise.

●	Anno I '97	🍷	4
●	Carato '97	🍷	3
●	Ciabatta '96	🍷	4
●	Morellino di Scansano '98		3

SIGNA (FI)

FOSSI
VIA DEGLI ARRIGHI, 4
50058 SIGNA (FI)
TEL. 055/8732174

Enrico Fossi is not afraid of a challenge. He does not accept compromises or half measures: indeed he has even ruled out blends: the numerous wines his estate produces are all, by his choice, monovarietal. For Fossi the issue is very clear-cut: no clouding the issue by mixing different grapes or vintages. For our part, we feel that the idea would be debatable if we were in Chianti Classico country or another of the celebrated historic wine-making districts of Tuscany, but in the case in question we are in a zone without a great oenological tradition which could actually do with some daring choices to characterize local production. We tasted four red wines, but Fossi also produces two whites, a sauvignon and a chardonnay, which were not ready in time for our tastings. The sangiovese grape is represented by the Vignavento '95, which was quite interesting and intense on the nose, albeit with somewhat excessive oak. The palate is powerful and decisive, the finish attractive and spicy. It very nearly got Two Glasses. The Sassoforte '95, a cabernet that has concentrated perfumes with toasty notes of spice, coffee and hazelnut, is very good. The flavor is soft, supple and solid, with smooth tannins that make their presence felt. The Syrah '95 is also excellent, with its characteristic nose of mineral, tobacco and plum jam. The palate is warm, full and characterful, but just a little rough on the finish. The merlot-based Portico '96, a vigorous, spirited wine that was a trifle inelegant, does not lack concentration.

●	Sassoforte '95	🍷🍷	5
●	Syrah '95	🍷🍷	5
●	Portico '96	🍷	5
●	Vignavento '95	🍷	5

SINALUNGA (SI)

TENUTA FARNETA
LOC. FARNETA, 161
53048 SINALUNGA (SI)
TEL. 0577/631025

The soft pedal was in use for this year's performance by Tenuta Farneta. Even their traditional champion, the full-bodied Bongoverno, is quieter than usual. Both reds and whites are correctly produced, and in some cases original and intriguing. But the peaks of expression attained in the past (the superb Bongoverno '86 and '88, the supremely flavorsome Bentivoglio '93) are not paralleled in this edition of the Guide. The '96 version of the Bentivoglio, which normally provides just about the best value for money in the whole of Tuscany, is still reliable and well made, but a bit simpler than in the past. Of a moderately intense ruby red color, it has grapey and, in part, overripe fruity aromas. In the mouth it is full-bodied, with notes of quinine and pencil lead providing a degree of variety in the not very long but clean finish. The Bongoverno '95, the product of a year that was anything but mediocre, has weight and complexity, but lacks drive. The color, a fairly intense ruby, is already somewhat forward. This impression is confirmed on the nose, which offers notes of roasting coffee, sweet oak and ripe fruit, but also a light animal undertone and hints of undergrowth. The tertiary notes, which provide elegance and complexity, are repeated on the well-measured palate, but, all things considered, somewhat precociously, in view of its year. The finish, long, even and irreproachable, is excellent. A few rapid notes on the other two wines: the Chianti '98 is agreeable but modest, and the Farneta, a white of the same year, is more successful, although quite a bit simpler.

●	Bongoverno '95	▼▼	6
●	Bentivoglio '96	▼	3
○	Farneta Bianco '98	▼	2*
●	Chianti '98		2
●	Bentivoglio '89	▽▽	2*
●	Bentivoglio '91	▽▽	2*
●	Bongoverno '85	▽▽	6
●	Bongoverno '86	▽▽	6
●	Bongoverno '88	▽▽	6
●	Bongoverno '90	▽▽	6
●	Bongoverno '91	▽▽	6
●	Bongoverno '92	▽▽	6
●	Bongoverno '93	▽▽	6
●	Bongoverno '94	▽▽	6
●	Chianti '97	▽	2

CASTELLO DI FARNETELLA
FRAZ. FARNETELLA
RACCORDO AUTOSTRADALE
SIENA-BETTOLLE, KM 37
53040 SINALUNGA (SI)
TEL. 0577/663520

The lovely Farnetella estate, which in the last edition of the Guide won its first Three Glasses with an elegant, distinctly styled wine, the Poggio Granoni '93, has once again presented an excellent range. The wines tasted this year were full of character, and only one, the Pinot Nero, seemed to need substantial improvement. The '94 version of the winery's top red will not, alas, be released; this vintage is being skipped because it does not come up to the high standards set by the directors of production, the famous duo Giuseppe Mazzocolin-Franco Bernabei (the names behind the success of the Fattoria di Felsina, in the Chianti Classico zone). So we'll have to do without the Poggio Granoni. But we can console ourselves with another couple of very successful bottles. We'll start with the Sauvignon '97, which is yet again one of the best whites of the region. Fresh, pure, beautifully clean and very drinkable, but also structured, it is a model of balance. It has a nicely intense yellow color, distinct but not overwhelming varietal aromas, and a flavorsome, full-bodied, fragrant and long palate. The Chianti Colli Senesi '97 is another very agreeable wine, whose strong points are its freshness and its easy-going drinkability: it has a clean, intense, fruity nose with notes of black cherry jam, and an attractive, fresh palate of medium length. We were a little less happy with the Nero di Nubi, Farnetella's pinot nero. The '95 vintage already shows evolved tertiary notes, and is a trifle dry on the palate, where it lacks the sensual fruity softness characteristic of this grape. But as we know, there is no variety more difficult to vinify than pinot nero.

○	Sauvignon '97	▼▼	4
●	Chianti Colli Senesi '97	▼	3
●	Nero di Nubi '95	▼	5
●	Poggio Granoni '93	▽▽▽	6
●	Chianti Colli Senesi '96	▽▽	3
○	Sauvignon '91	▽▽	4
○	Sauvignon '95	▽▽	4
●	Chianti Colli Senesi '91	▽	3*
●	Nero di Nubi '92	▽	5
●	Nero di Nubi '93	▽	5
●	Nero di Nubi '94	▽	5
○	Sauvignon '92	▽	4
○	Sauvignon '93	▽	4
○	Sauvignon '94	▽	4
○	Sauvignon '96	▽	4

SOVANA (GR)

SASSOTONDO
LOC. PIANI DI CONATI, 52
58010 SOVANA (GR)
TEL. 0546/614218

You can bet your bottom dollar that in the space of just a few years prices for the vineyards in upper Maremma will be catching up with those of Chianti and Montalcino. This zone has climatic conditions that are, on average, undeniably superior to the Maremma coastal plain, and is currently attracting a lot of attention from the great (and small) names of Italian wine-making, eager to snap up some property here. Those who understood the great potential of this part of Tuscany before the rush started include Carla Benini and Edoardo Ventimiglia, the owners of the Sassotondo estate. Having fled from the city (Rome) and landed in the Sovana countryside, the two wisely decided a few harvests ago to call on the services of the skilled agronomist Remigio Bordini and the renowned oenologist Attilio Pagli. The results were immediately encouraging. But let's see about this year's wines. The Sassotondo Rosso '98 is very good: the aromas are surprisingly intense, although the bouquet is simple, with inviting notes of raspberry and white pepper; the palate is vital and full-bodied. The rather simple Bianco di Pitigliano '98 is less exciting, although properly made. The two key reds, the San Lorenzo and the Franze, are excellent. The San Lorenzo '97, a monovarietal ciliegiolo (from a wonderful vine over thirty years old), shows a deep ruby color and intense scents of new oak and ripe black cherry; the palate is soft but substantial and the finish is long. The wood, still strong, should tone down with age. Lastly, the sangiovese-based Franze '97 is good but less winning: an attractive ruby in color, it has slightly muffled but characteristically varietal, warm perfumes; in the mouth it reveals good extract and balance.

●	San Lorenzo '97	🍷🍷	4
●	Sassotondo Rosso '98	🍷🍷	3*
○	Bianco di Pitigliano '98	🍷	3
●	Franze '97	🍷	3
○	Bianco di Pitigliano '97	🍷 (white glass)	3
●	Sassotondo Rosso '97	🍷 (white glass)	3

SUVERETO (LI)

LORELLA AMBROSINI
LOC. TABARO, 95
57028 SUVERETO (LI)
TEL. 0565/829301

A year's pause and here is Ambrosini making a prompt return to the pages of the Guide. Improvement at this estate had slowed down somewhat for reasons linked both to a couple of harvests that left a lot to be desired, and to the natural ups and downs that characterize young wineries. This year's tastings confirmed this interpretation and it seems to us that, starting with the '97 vintage, the pace has picked up again and is, indeed, getting faster, starting with the Riflesso Antico, from montepulciano, which has an attractively vivid, intense ruby color followed by concentrated perfumes of black fruit and still pronounced notes of toasty oak. The palate is full, solid, and slightly vegetal, and the finish is densely packed with soft tannins. How different from the '96, which is more forward, with wood lording it over the fruit and the rather thin structure! The difference between the '96 and '97 versions of the Subertum is less pronounced. The '96, moderately intense in color, offers fair fruit on the nose and a balanced, attractive palate, with vegetal and toasty notes emerging on the finish. Predictably richer and more intense, the '97 is characterized by a bouquet of ripe fruit and blackberry jam; the palate is soft, dense and ample in its development. The Vermentino Armonia also shows attractive fruit, and a balanced, nicely weighted palate with a slightly salty finish. We were very pleasantly surprised by the Tabarò Rosso, which is distinctly appealing both on the nose, with its black fruit, spice and pepper, and in the mouth, where it is soft and fairly well structured and offers a good finish. Closing this rich range, the Tabarò Bianco, though simple, shows some depth.

●	Riflesso Antico '97	🍷🍷	5
●	Subertum '97	🍷🍷	5
●	Subertum '96	🍷	5
○	Val di Cornia Bianco Armonia '98	🍷	4
○	Val di Cornia Bianco Tabarò '98	🍷	3
●	Val di Cornia Rosso Tabarò '98	🍷	3
●	Riflesso Antico '96		5
●	Riflesso Antico '94	🍷🍷 (white glasses)	4
●	Riflesso Antico '93	🍷 (white glass)	4
●	Subertum '94	🍷 (white glass)	4
●	Val di Cornia Rosso Ambrosini '93	🍷 (white glass)	2*

SUVERETO (LI)

Gualdo Del Re

Loc. Notri, 77
57028 Suvereto (LI)
tel. 0565/829888 - 0565/829361

Gualdo del Re has a feature that is common to many Tuscan wineries: new plantings in the vineyards which will, in a short time, result in an increase in both output and quality. The share allocated to red grapes will increase, with sangiovese dominating the scene, followed by merlot, cabernet and even pinot nero (a daring step where there's a microclimate like that of the Tuscan coast). We are, however, well aware that there is a special place in Nico Rossi's heart for his sangiovese, the Gualdo del Re, which to tell the truth we found slightly under par this year. The '96 was certainly not the best vintage for this grape and the Gualdo, although good, suffers from a conflict between the ripe notes of jam on the nose and the slightly detached acidity of the finish on the palate. However, some bottle-age ought to resolve this slight dissonance, of which there is no trace in the Federico Primo, a blend of cabernet, merlot and sangiovese that we particularly liked this year. The bouquet is concentrated, harmonious and compact, with layers of black fruit and notes of coffee that emerge clearly. In the mouth it is extremely soft, silky and elegant, and just a bit light on the finish. Another surprise was the Lumen '98, a pinot bianco fermented for the first time in barrique. It reveals intensity and finesse on the nose, with notes of citrus fruit, vanilla and pear, and lives up to its promise on the substantial, well-balanced palate. A quick run over the other wines: the Vigna Valentina and the Rosso '98 are fairly good, and the Bianco is more than satisfactory.

●	Federico Primo '96	🍷🍷	5
○	Lumen '98	🍷🍷	4
●	Val di Cornia Gualdo del Re Ris.	🍷	5
○	Vigna Valentina	🍷	3
●	Val di Cornia Rosso '98	🍷	2*
○	Val di Cornia Bianco '98		2

SUVERETO (LI)

Montepeloso

Loc. Montepeloso, 82
57028 Suvereto (LI)
tel. 0565/828180

Montepeloso is situated in one of the most sought-after parts of the Suvereto area. The characteristics of the terrain and the microclimate confer powerful structure on the wines which, in addition to high levels of sugars and extract, also have noteworthy acidity, particularly marked in the sangiovese. Hence wines like the Nardo, a sangiovese with 20% cabernet, definitely seem a little cantankerous, especially when they're young. This feature is more pronounced in the '96 version, which is more evidently harsh, despite the robustness of the body. Most importantly, the wine does not manage entirely to shake off the initial sulfurous aromas. Powerful and concentrated, the '97 Nardo displays a very unusual bouquet, with clear mineral and earthy notes and a fruity and slightly vegetal undertone. The palate is rich and vigorous, with firm tannins and decided acidity: a wine of considerable potential that needs more time before it can be enjoyed to the full. In spite of its powerful structure (there is no place for so-called "feminine" wines at Montepeloso), the Gabbro '97, a pure cabernet sauvignon newcomer, is, in marked contrast, already an open book. The nose is deep, although not overly fine, with a black fruit background and notes of quinine and tar. The palate is massive and muscular, but develops silkily to a long, persistent finish. The Val di Cornia Rosso, which shows depth and substantial alcohol, is more than satisfactory; the Bianco is sound and well executed.

●	Gabbro '97	🍷🍷	5
●	Nardo '97	🍷🍷	6
●	Nardo '96	🍷	6
●	Val di Cornia Rosso '98	🍷	4
○	Val di Cornia Bianco '98		3
●	Nardo '95	🍸🍸	5
●	Val di Cornia Rosso Montepeloso '95	🍸🍸	4
●	Nardo '94	🍸	5
●	Val di Cornia Rosso Montepeloso '94	🍸	4

SUVERETO (LI)

Tua Rita

Loc. Notri, 81
57028 Suvereto (LI)
tel. 0565/829237

Rita Tua's estate is going through a restructuring period, with all the benefits and drawbacks that this entails. The benefits lie primarily in the extension of the area under vine, which now amounts to about ten hectares, with a resulting increase in output. Drawbacks lurk in the (brief) handover period between one oenologist and another, a phase that every winery has to handle with care. Luckily, one highly skilled oenologist, Luca D'Attoma, has been succeeded by another, the equally expert and capable Stefano Chioccioli. Hence high wine-making standards are certain to continue in the future. For the time being our comments refer to wines still "signed" by D'Attoma, as Chioccioli has only been working with Rita Tua since the '99 harvest. Her most famous red, the Giusto di Notri, winner of numerous awards, is lovely in the '97 version, although it lacks the aromatic and gustatory definition that would have taken it to the top. Intense, concentrated, full and tasty on the palate, it has perfumes that are a little disjointed and not altogether distinct. It is an excellent red, all the same, and is flanked by the Redigaffi '97, a merlot of which only about 2,000 bottles are made. The excellent palate is fat, ripe, extremely long and very promising, but this wine too is a little less successful – a bit muffled – on the nose. Of the other wines a fine Sileno '98 is worthy of note: a white made mainly from riesling and chardonnay, with appealing notes of ripe pear; and the Perlato del Bosco Rosso '97 is pleasant and well made. The Perlato del Bosco Bianco '98 is straightforward, one-dimensional and quaffable.

●	Giusto di Notri '97	TT	5
●	Redigaffi '97	TT	6
●	Perlato del Bosco Rosso '97	T	4
○	Sileno '98	T	4
○	Perlato del Bosco Bianco '98		3
●	Giusto di Notri '94	YYY	5
●	Redigaffi '96	YYY	6
●	Giusto di Notri '92	YY	5
●	Giusto di Notri '93	YY	5
●	Giusto di Notri '96	YY	5
●	Perlato del Bosco Rosso '96	YY	4
●	Redigaffi '95	YY	6
○	Sileno '96	YY	4

SUVERETO (LI)

Villa Monte Rico

Loc. Poggio al Cerro
57028 Suvereto (LI)
tel. 0565/829550

We were curious to assay the real value of Monte Rico in a problematic year like the '96. Well, we can only say that Signora Reichenberg's wine has proved its worth, confirming its high quality and distinctive style. The '95 was certainly a few steps up the scale in terms of vigor and breadth, but if such differences did not exist between one vintage and another we would not be producing an annual Guide. Meanwhile it is reasonable to expect greater things from the '97 when it is ready, as there can be no denying that this was a very good year indeed, at least for sangiovese. In fact Monte Rico's wine, like that of other producers, serves to underline the interesting potential of this typically Tuscan grape in Val di Cornia, an area still in search of an oenological identity, torn as it is between the course mapped out by producers, in neighboring Bolgheri, with cabernet and merlot, and its own quest for improved quality with the sangiovese grape. In Monte Rico they have never been in any doubt and, while it is true that sangiovese needs more patience, it is equally likely that in the future they will be proved to be dead right. The '96 shows a ruby red color with a slight garnet tinge on the rim, and an interesting nose dominated by black cherry, with hints of tobacco and earth and some spicy, toasty notes from the oak. The palate does not reveal the power of the best vintages but is nicely rounded and balanced; the wood is still somewhat pronounced on the attractive finish.

●	Villa Monte Rico '96	TT	5
●	Villa Monte Rico '95	YY	5

Podere La Cappella
Loc. S. Donato in Poggio
Strada Cerbaia, 10/A
50028 Tavarnelle Val di Pesa (FI)
tel. 055/8072727

Bruno Rossini's Podere La Cappella clearly deserves to keep the place in the Guide it won last year. An affable Veronese transplanted to Tuscany almost ten years ago, Rossini also grows fruit according to strict organic principles, but who knows, his love for the vine may convince him to carve out a bit more room for new vineyards. Meanwhile, he has six hectares under vine, and another hectare ready for planting. Two wines were presented at our tastings this year. The Chianti Classico Querciolo '97 displays a lovely intense, full, limpid ruby red hue. The nose opens on fruity scents, cherry in particular, with vanilla forming an elegant counterpoint. The palate is soft, almost buoyant, and velvety, with substantial alcohol underpinning the sweet, smooth tannins. The appropriate finish has just the right length. The Corbezzolo '97, made mainly from sangiovese and matured in small oak casks, is almost impenetrably red in color, such is its concentration. The bouquet includes very ripe berries (blackberry, black currant and blueberry) beautifully blended with sweet toasty notes. The palate is soft, enticing and full-bodied, with powerful but well-judged tannins. The finish is long, intense and pleasing. The merlot we mentioned last year was used to complete the other blends, but given the excellent results obtained in the last few vintages, it will in future be bottled on its own. Next year we shall already be able to taste the '98. We look forward to it.

● Corbezzolo '97	▼▼	5
● Chianti Classico Querciolo '97	▼	4
● Corbezzolo '96	▽▽	5
● Chianti Classico Querciolo '96	▽	4

Montecchio
Via Montecchio, 4
50020 Tavarnelle Val di Pesa (FI)
tel. 055/8072907

Only one wine was presented this year by the Fattoria di Montecchio, an estate that entered the Guide last year and that we fully expected to see consolidating its position, something it has lost no time in doing. Indeed, the Chianti Classico '97 is a great success. Its intense, bright ruby color heralds a significant structure, which is confirmed on the nose: concentrated and rich, with lots of black fruit complemented by subtle spice and perceptible but well-judged notes of oak. The equally satisfactory palate is full and round, with tannins that are already well incorporated into the body of the wine, and a wonderfully lingering finish. Two ample Glasses, then, which raise our hopes for the Riserva of the same year when it comes out. Altogether the outlook is excellent for Montecchio, and quantity could also be quite interesting, given that it covers some 273 hectares, of which 36 are under vine. It is clear that we shall have to wait a few years before it can extend its range of first-class wines, since apart from the 10 hectares planted to sangiovese and merlot in '95 with a density of over six thousand vines per hectare, the rest of the vineyards are still laid out in the traditional '70s style and are hence less promising. To these will be added, by the end of '99, a further eight hectares divided equally among cabernet, merlot and syrah. These are significant plans, indicative of the best intentions.

● Chianti Classico '97	▼▼	4
● Chianti Classico '96	▽▽	4
● Chianti Classico Ris. '95	▽▽	4

TAVARNELLE VAL DI PESA (FI)

POGGIO AL SOLE
LOC. SAMBUCA VAL DI PESA
50028 TAVARNELLE VAL DI PESA (FI)
TEL. 055/8071504

We just cannot hide our admiration for Giovanni Davaz's winery. We found ourselves once again this year tasting a series of excellent wines, a sign that nothing is left to chance at Poggio al Sole. Every wine is properly representative of its category and is followed with the closest attention, both in the vineyards, which cover about 15 hectares, and in the cellar, where widespread use is made of small wooden casks. The Chianti Casasilia is not as rich as the '95, but very good all the same; the Seraselva is solid but still young; there is no arguing about the Syrah '97 and, lastly, the standard Chianti Classico is a pleasant surprise. But let's proceed in order. The Casasilia '96, as we said, easily replicates its past performances and offers an intelligent interpretation of the vintage at its disposal, by focusing on harmony and elegant quaffability, although it does offer density, concentration and depth. The intense aromas display notes of cocoa and toasty oak. The Chianti '97 is also quite good; it has no lack of substance and shines above all for its nicely rounded flavors and attractive fruit. The Seraselva '96, a blend of cabernet sauvignon and merlot, has a robust, intense nose, with notes of blackberry and bell pepper. Although the tannins are still a bit unruly, the body is big enough to take them in stride, quite absorbing their harshness. The very good Syrah '97 shows a concentrated, compact nose with notes of coffee, spice and aromatic herbs. The palate is supple and soft, with a vegetal note emerging on the long finish.

● Chianti Cl. Casasilia Ris. '96	▼▼	5
● Chianti Classico '97	▼▼	4
● Seraselva '96	▼▼	5
● Syrah '97	▼▼	5
● Chianti Cl. Casasilia '93	▽▽	5
● Chianti Cl. Casasilia '94	▽▽	5
● Chianti Cl. Casasilia Ris. '95	▽▽	5
● Chianti Classico '95	▽▽	3*
● Chianti Classico Ris. '95	▽▽	4
● Chianti Classico Ris. '91	▽▽	4
● Seraselva '94	▽▽	5
● Seraselva '95	▽▽	5
● Syrah '96	▽▽	5
● Chianti Classico '96	▽	3
● Chianti Classico Ris. '94	▽	4

TERRICCIOLA (PI)

BADIA DI MORRONA
LOC. LA BADIA
56030 TERRICCIOLA (PI)
TEL. 0587/658505

The hills near Pisa known as the Colline Pisane are part of the vast Chianti DOC district, which covers a large part of the winegrowing area of Tuscany. But when we taste the Vigna Alta we are pleasantly reminded of the wines of Montalcino. This is, in fact, a solid wine with a strong personality, obtained from a classic Tuscan blend of sangiovese with a small percentage of canaiolo. The Vigna Alta originates in old vineyards with a very low yield; it has a bright color with good concentration, and very intense aromas of black fruit with mineral nuances. The attack on the palate is powerful and almost sweet, the development is irresistible, and the long finish, which reveals notes of fruit and spice, is still slightly hard , as is right and proper for a young sangiovese. It came very close to netting Three Glasses, which it would certainly have won with just a pinch more restraint and elegance. The N'Antia, a blend of cabernet, merlot and sangiovese, is similar in quality but quite different in style: it's a concentrated red with an elegant, silky long palate. And these are both '96s, so we can expect fireworks from the next vintage. It should be noted that the estate already produces a goodly number of bottles, and will receive a further boost when the newly planted vines – 10 hectares of very promising vineyards with excellent exposure – come on line. The other wines are somewhat overshadowed, although we did like the well-structured wood-fermented chardonnay, La Suvera, and the San Torpé Felciaio '98 is admirably fresh, inviting and well balanced. The Chianti is not as good as the highly successful '97, but is sound and agreeable all the same.

● N'Antia '96	▼▼	5
● Vigna Alta '96	▼▼	6
○ La Suvera '98	▼	3
○ S. Torpè Felciaio '98	▼	2*
● Chianti Sodi del Paretaio '98		2
○ La Suvera '94	▽▽	3
● N'Antia '91	▽▽	5
● N'Antia '93	▽▽	5
● N'Antia '94	▽▽	5
● N'Antia '95	▽▽	5
● Vigna Alta '94	▽▽	5
● Chianti Sodi del Paretaio '94	▽	2*
● Chianti Sodi del Paretaio '96	▽	2*
● Chianti Sodi del Paretaio '97	▽	2*
● N'Antia '92	▽	5

VAGLIA (FI)

Camposilio
Loc. Montorsoli
Via Basciano, 8
50030 Vaglia (FI)
tel. 055/696456

After its debut entry to the Guide last year, the winery owned by the passionately dedicated Alessandro Rustioni has turned in another excellent performance. In tandem with oenologist Francesco Naldi, Rustioni has succeeded in creating a wine that has gradually got better and better and is becoming increasingly well known, thanks in great part to the constant, indeed almost obsessive attention given by the producer to every step of the production process. He also has laudably shown his confidence in the potential of an area considered by many to be oenologically marginal. His has been a ground-breaking role that is undoubtedly a thankless one, leading to head-on clashes with obtuse thinkers but which might serve as an example to anyone thinking of tracing the same route. The village of Vaglia is north of Florence but the winery is right on the borders of the city, which means that the vineyards are just a few kilometers from the city center. The wine bears the same name as the winery, and is a blend of cabernet sauvignon and sangiovese. A very intense, dense ruby red in color, it offers intense perfumes, with nicely pronounced balsamic notes, which then make way for the rich fruit of black currant and blueberry. The attack on the palate is mouth-filling and juicy, with closely textured tannins emerging in a structure that is complex, full and well balanced. We await new developments for next year, thanks to the merlot vines that have come into production and which, judging from our early tastings, are providing a raw material worthy of the utmost respect.

●	Camposilio '96	▼▼	5
●	Camposilio '95	▽▽	5
●	Camposilio '94	▽	5

VINCI (FI)

Cantine Leonardo
Bivio di Streda
Via Provinciale Mercatale, 921
50059 Vinci (FI)
tel. 0571/902444

The confirmation we expected from the Cantine Leonardo was not long in coming: all the wines presented for our tasting lived up to their promise. The Sant'Ippolito '97, made from merlot and a smaller amount of syrah, confirms its standing as a significant wine. Although, to be frank, after the excellent debut of the '96 we were expecting something even more outstanding, from a year that was generally considered superior. But as we said the quality is all there, the color is intense and concentrated, the perfumes rich, with notes of plum jam and vanilla. The palate is full, robust and balanced, with a good but not very long finish and moderate complexity, but these limitations are related in part to the youth of the vines. The Sangiovese SanZio '97, with its lively fruit, solid structure, and soft tannins, is equally good. One full Glass goes to each of the other three wines presented. We shall give pride of place to the most surprising in value for money terms, the Chianti '98, which is an example to be followed by all those seeking to produce easily accessible wines. This wine is very well made, from good raw material, and exhibits a rich, well-defined fruitiness, in addition to a rounded quality that is not easy to find in this category. The Ser Piero '98, a chardonnay in which intense notes of vanilla and exotic fruits can be detected, along with a balanced flavor that holds up well, is also good. The Vin Santo '94, which has the classic scents of dried fruits married to a fairly expressive, medium-bodied palate, is no disappointment.

●	Sant'Ippolito '97	▼▼	5
●	SanZio '97	▼▼	4
●	Chianti '98	▼	2*
○	Ser Piero '98	▼	3
○	Vin Santo Tegrino d'Anchiano '94	▼	4
●	Sant'Ippolito '96	▽▽	4
●	SanZio '96	▽▽	4
●	Chianti '97	▽	2*
○	Vin Santo Tegrino d'Anchiano '93	▽	4

OTHER WINERIES

The following producers obtained good scores in our tastings with one or more of their wines:

PROVINCE OF AREZZO

Santa Vittoria
Foiano della Chiana, tel. 0575/66807
Scannagallo '97,
Vin Santo '94

Villa Cilnia
Pieve al Bagnoro, tel. 0575/365017
Chianti Colli Aretini Ris. '95,
Vocato '95

PROVINCE OF FIRENZE

Petreto
Bagno a Ripoli, tel. 055/6519021
Pourriture Noble '96

Casa Sola
Barberino Val d'Elsa, tel. 055/8075028
Chianti Classico '97,
Chianti Classico Ris. '95

Monsanto
Barberino Val d'Elsa, tel. 055/8059000
Chianti Cl. Il Poggio Ris. '96,
Fabrizio Bianchi Chardonnay '97

Quercia al Poggio
Barberino Val d'Elsa, tel. 055/8075278
Chianti Classico '97,
Chianti Classico Ris. '96

Spadaio e Piecorto
Barberino Val d'Elsa, tel. 055/8072915
Chianti Classico '97

Fattoria di Bibbiani
Capraia e Limite, tel. 0571/57338
Chianti Montalbano '98

Il Cavaliere, Dicomano, tel. 055/8386340
Chianti Rufina Frascole '97

Terreno
Greve in Chianti, tel. 055/854001
Chianti Classico '97,
Chianti Classico Ris. '96

Solatione
Mercatale Val di Pesa, tel. 055/821082
Chianti Classico '96,
Chianti Classico Ris. '95

Petrognano
Montelupo Fiorentino, tel. 0571/542001
Montevago '97

Castello di Poppiano
Montespertoli, tel. 055/82315
Tricorno '95

La Doccia
Panzano in Chianti, tel. 055/8549049
Chianti Classico '96

Le Bocce
Panzano in Chianti, tel. 055/852153
Chianti Classico '97,
Chianti Classico Ris. '96

Colognole, Rufina, tel. 055/8319870
Chianti Rufina '97,

Il Mandorlo
S. Casciano Val di Pesa,
tel. 055/8228211
Chianti Classico Ris. '95

Tenuta La Novella, S. Casciano Val di Pesa,
tel. 055/8337749
Chianti Classico '97

Frimaio
San Donato in Poggio, tel. 055/8077253
Chianti Classico '97

Villa Buonasera
Strada in Chianti, tel. 055/8547932
Chianti Classico Ris. '95

Fattoria La Ripa
Tavarnelle Val di Pesa, tel. 055/8072948
Santa Brigida '97

PROVINCE OF GROSSETO

La Parrina
Albinia, tel. 0564/862636
Parrina Rosso Ris. '97

Coliberto
Massa Marittima, tel. 0566/919039
Monteregio di Massa Marittima Rosso '97

Tenuta Roccaccia
Pitigliano, tel. 0564/616256
Fontenova '98

I Botri, Scansano, tel. 0564/507921
Morellino di Scansano '97

Provveditore
Scansano, tel. 0564/599237
Morellino di Scansano Primo Ris. '96

PROVINCE OF LIVORNO

Ceralti
Bolgheri, tel. 0565/763989
Bolgheri Rosso Alfeo '97

Jacopo Banti
Campiglia Marittima, tel. 0565/838802
Val di Cornia Poggio Angelica '98

Cipriana
Castagneto Carducci, tel. 0565/877153
Bolgheri Rosso San Martino '97

Cecilia, Isola d'Elba, tel. 0565/977322
Elba Bianco '98

Podere San Luigi
Piombino, tel. 0565/220578
San Luigi '96

Bulichella
Suvereto, tel. 0565/829892
Val di Cornia Tuscanio '97

Il Falcone, Suvereto, tel. 0565/829294
Boccalupo '96

Martelli e Busdraghi
Suvereto, tel. 0565/829401
Val di Cornia Rosso Incontri '97

PROVINCE OF LUCCA

Camiliano, Lucca, tel. 0583/490420
Nerio '93

Cohens e Gervais, Lucca, tel. 0583/90431
Tempietto '97

Fattoria del Teso
Montecarlo, tel. 0583/286288
L'antico del Teso '96,
Montecarlo Rosso Anfiteatro di Lucca Ris. '96,

Fattoria La Torre
Montecarlo, tel. 0583/22330
Altair '98,
Stringaio '97

Vigna del Greppo
Montecarlo, tel. 0583/22593
Montecarlo Rosso Carlo IV Ris. '95

PROVINCE OF PISA

Torre a Cenaja, Crespina, tel. 050/643739
Rosso Toscano '97

I Giusti e Zanza, Fauglia, tel. 0585/44354
Dulcamara '96

Fattoria di Sassolo
San Miniato, tel. 0571/460001
Vin Santo San Torpé Fiorile '94

Elyane & Bruno Moos, Soiana, tel. 0587/654180
Soianello '98

PROVINCE OF PRATO

Artimino, Carmignano, tel. 055/8792051
Carmignano Ris. Medicea '95

PROVINCE OF SIENA

Bucciarelli
Castellina in Chianti, tel. 0577/749756
Chianti Classico Ris. '96,
Gandino '96

Casina di Cornia
Castellina in Chianti, tel. 0577/743052
L'Amaranto '97

La Castellina
Castellina in Chianti, tel. 0577/741238
Reale '95

Lilliano
Castellina in Chianti, tel. 0577/743070
Anagallis '97

Fattoria dell'Aiola
Castelnuovo Berardenga, tel. 0577/322615
Logaiolo '96,
Rosso del Senatore '97

Le Trame
Castelnuovo Berardenga, tel. 0577/359116
Chianti Classico '97

Pacina
Castelnuovo Berardenga,
tel. 0577/355044
Chianti Colli Senesi '96

Poggio Bonelli
Castelnuovo Berardenga,
tel. 0577/355382
Tramonto d'Oca '95

Castello di Meleto
Gaiole in Chianti, tel. 0577/749217
Chianti Classico Ris. '96

Fattoria Valtellina
Gaiole in Chianti, tel. 0577/731005
Convivio '96

Podere Il Palazzino
Gaiole in Chianti, tel. 0577/747008
Chianti Cl. Grosso Sanese '96

Rietine
Gaiole in Chianti, tel. 0577/731110
Chianti Classico Ris. '95

Rocca di Montegrossi
Gaiole in Chianti, tel. 0577/747267
Vin Santo del Chianti Classico '93

Cantina di Montalcino
Montalcino, tel. 0577/848704
Brunello di Montalcino '94

Castello di Camigliano
Montalcino, tel. 0577/844068
Brunello di Montalcino Ris. '93

Castiglion del Bosco
Montalcino, tel. 0577/807078
Brunello di Montalcino '94

La Fornace, Montalcino, tel. 0577/848465
Brunello di Montalcino '94

La Fuga, Montalcino, tel. 0577/816039
Brunello di Montalcino Ris. '93

La Gerla, Montalcino, tel. 0577/848599
Birba '96,
Brunello di Montalcino Ris. '93

La Torre, Montalcino, tel. 0577/844073
Brunello di Montalcino '94,
Brunello di Montalcino Ris. '93

Lambardi, Montalcino, tel. 0577/848476
Brunello di Montalcino '94

Oliveto, Montalcino, tel. 0577/835542
Rosso di Montalcino Roccolo '97

Palagetto, Montalcino, tel. 0577/943090
Brunello di Montalcino La Bellarina '94

Pieve Santa Restituta
Montalcino, tel. 0577/848610
Brunello di Montalcino Rennina '94

Poggio Antico, Montalcino, tel. 0577/848044
Brunello di Montalcino Ris. '93

Uccelliera, Montalcino, tel. 0577/835729
Brunello di Montalcino '94

Canneto, Montepulciano, tel. 0578/757737
Vino Nobile di Montepulciano '96

Fanetti, Montepulciano, tel. 0578/757266
Principesco '97

La Ciarliana, Montepulciano, tel. 0578/758423
Vino Nobile di Montepulciano '96

Le Casalte
Montepulciano, tel. 0578/799138
Vino Nobile di Montepulciano Ris. '95

Lombardo, Montepulciano, tel. 0578/708321
Vino Nobile di Montepulciano Ris. '95

Casale
Montepulciano Stazione, tel. 0578/738257
Vino Nobile di Montepulciano '96

Podere Terreno Alla Via Della Volpaia
Radda in Chianti, tel. 0577/738312
Chianti Classico '97

Cantine Ravazzi
San Casciano dei Bagni, tel. 0578/56008
Vigna Rossa '96

Cappella di Sant'Andrea
San Gimignano, tel. 0577/940456
Vernaccia di San Gimignano Rialto '98

Fattoria di Pietrafitta
San Gimignano, tel. 0577/943200
San Gimignano Rosso La Sughera '97,
Vernaccia di S. Gimignano V. Borghetto '98

Fontaleoni
San Gimignano, tel. 0577/950193
Vernaccia di S. Gimignano V. Casanuova '98

Podere Arcangelo
San Gimignano, tel. 0577/944986
Vernaccia di S. Gimignano V. del Lago '98

Belriguardo
Siena, tel. 0577/45524
La Clausura '97

Poggio Salvi
Sovicille, tel. 0577/349045
Campo del Bosco '97

MARCHE

Wine production in the Marche has been growing and improving for some time in historically well-known areas that include large estates and small producers, but also in districts less in the spotlight. That said, we must admit that weather conditions leading up to the '98 harvest had a significant effect on the year's white wines. In particular, a long spell of dry summer weather led to rather early ripening and a drop in grape acidity. The consequences are particularly evident in many of this year's Verdicchios, which were already drinkable, in some cases, early in the summer: they tend to be rich in alcohol but without enough acidic underpinning. The situation is better for the reds, especially those where harvesting was carried out in successive stages throughout October. But let's see what our tastings revealed, starting with a wine that returns to Three Glass status, a fabulous Verdicchio dei Castelli di Jesi Contrada Balciana 1997, from the Sartarelli estate. On tasting it, more than a few have thought it Alsatian, and its complexity and opulence certainly justify the comparison, but its individual character is true to Jesi. Another Verdicchio with an undisputed Three Glasses is the markedly rich and yet admirably balanced Podium '97 from Garofoli. This estate also presented several other seriously good wines (Serrafiorese, for instance, which is stylistically similar to the Contrada Balciana), confirming its position as one of the region's best all-rounders. Another is Umani Ronchi, whose Pelago '96 and special riserva Verdicchio Plenio '95 we particularly admired. Still among the Verdicchios, the consistently excellent quality of the whole range offered by La Monacesca (in Matelica) can't be ignored; neither can the development of Vigna Novali '96 from Terre Cortesi Moncaro, which we reviewed last year; nor should we neglect further evidence of the high standards of Vallerosa Bonci. Moving on to the reds, compliments are due first to Fattoria Le Terrazze in Numana, whose steady progress has now been crowned by their Three Glass winner, the outstanding Caos, a powerful and elegant red. And their special selection Rosso Conero Sassi Neri '97 was not far behind. Next comes the stellar performance of Oasi degli Angeli, which, at its debut appearance in the Guide, has surged ahead and won Three Glasses straight off for its monovarietal montepulciano Kurni, one of the best reds in Italy, with just one defect: a mere 1500 bottles were produced. Another highlight from this year's tastings was the cabernet-based Akronte, from the Boccadigabbia estate, which has kept up standards despite the infelicitous '96 vintage. The Rosso Piceno Superiore Vigna Monteprandone from Saladini Pilastri deserves a mention, as does Anghelos from Tenuta De Angelis and Rosso Conero '98 from Lanari, which is, by the way, one of the best examples of value for money in the entire country.

ANCONA

LANARI
VIA POZZO, 142
FRAZ. VARANO
60029 ANCONA
TEL. 071/2861343

We had already been quite comfortably spoilt by the Lanaris' way of running their estate, their meticulous care in vineyard and cellar: in '95, for example, not one bottle was released for sale because the wine wasn't considered up to the estate's standards. But we would never have imagined that in such a short time they could produce the wines they've presented from the '97 and '98 vintages. To achieve these by no means chance results they had the assistance of the technical skills of Giancarlo Soverchia and also two fine harvests. Il Casino, a Marche Bianco produced from a blend of moscato, malvasia and trebbiano, unites a firm structure, unusual softness and drinkability with an artfully multi-faceted aroma (citrus fruits, mint, fresh green leaves). The standard Rosso Conero '98 has an almost impenetrable but fluid black color and offers notes of wild cherry, blackberry and plum over a vegetal and grapey ground bass. The entry on the palate is very powerful but not at all harsh, with a perfect balance between highly concentrated fruit, well-judged acidity and amazingly smooth tannins. This and its clean, well-defined finish give the impression that the wine, already good, will unveil even greater gifts as it evolves and matures. Fibbio '97, a Rosso Conero special selection matured in small barrels, has a deep, dense, dark violet hue; a definite fragrance of ripe cherry and blueberry merges with a lightly spicy tang of nutmeg, licorice and tobacco. It is soft on the palate, with great structure and elegant concentration, smooth tannins, mellowness and a pleasing finish.

●	Rosso Conero '98	🍷🍷	3*
●	Rosso Conero Fibbio '97	🍷🍷	4
○	Casino '98	🍷	3
●	Rosso Conero '97	🍷🍷 (white)	3

ANCONA

MARCHETTI
VIA DI PONTELUNGO, 166
60131 ANCONA
TEL. 071/897386

Although the Marchetti estate has been appearing in the Guide for only a few years, it has considerable experience behind it and is fairly representative of how Rosso Conero has evolved in the past decade. Starting with a traditional orientation which produced acidic, tannic, long-lasting wines that did not always develop elegantly (a fairly common failing in these parts), producers have shifted to a more modern vinification style, aiming at sweetness of fruit and smoothness on the palate, and thereby giving the wines an attractive elegance. For Marchetti in particular the change has been remarkable, especially in the last two years. The Rosso Conero '98, moderately priced and appealingly quaffable, has a good structure that melds perfectly with its ripe tannins and the complex bouquet dominated by ripe wild cherry and light sweet spice. The Rosso Conero Villa Bonomi Riserva '97 has notes of wild cherry and cinnamon and a touch of rhubarb; it makes a decided attack on the palate, with tannins present but well under control, indeed blended nicely with the considerable body of the wine and its distinctive freshness. Marchetti also produces Verdicchio; however if '98 was notable for reds it was anything but for its whites. The two Verdicchios, both the basic version and the special selection Villa Bonomi, have little varietal character and fleeting perfumes; they fare better on the palate where they reveal fairly marked structure, although crispness is in short supply. Overall they are reasonably meaty and balanced, thanks to their succulence rather than their acidity: they are drinking well now but we wouldn't bet on their longevity.

●	Rosso Conero '98	🍷🍷	3
●	Rosso Conero Villa Bonomi Ris. '97	🍷🍷	4
○	Verdicchio dei Castelli di Jesi Cl. '98	🍷	1*
○	Verdicchio dei Castelli di Jesi Cl. Sup. Villa Bonomi '98	🍷	3
●	Rosso Conero Villa Bonomi Ris. '96	🍷🍷 (white)	3
●	Rosso Conero '97	🍷 (white)	2

ANCONA

ALESSANDRO MORODER
FRAZ. MONTACUTO, 112
60029 ANCONA
TEL. 071/898232

Since 1984 Alessandro Moroder, together with his wife Serenella, has been directly involved with this Montacuto estate which has been in the family since 1837. In the last few years the Moroders have refurbished their cellar and renewed their barrel stocks, and they boast the oenological advice of Franco Bernabei. As of two years ago they have an attractive hostelry and restaurant for those who wish to stay a while and sample the various Moroder products. Amongst these, however, wine has pride of place, and in recent years it has had lots to be proud of, particularly the Rosso Conero special selection called Dorico, which has walked off with Three Glasses on several occasions. The latest version of this wine is due out shortly. In the meantime we tasted an excellent example of their standard Rosso Conero, the '97. Although it slips down very easily it has substance and character, and if it doesn't exactly shine on the nose, it is soft and pleasing in the mouth. In addition to Rosso Conero, their main wine, they have long been producing an admirably fruity rosé, Rosa di Montacuto, of which the '98 is a good example. For several years now there has also been Oro di Moroder, made from semi-dried trebbiano, moscato and malvasia grapes. Its lovely golden color, balanced sweetness and well-delineated aromas make it a most successful dessert wine.

●	Rosso Conero '97	🍷🍷	3*
○	L'Oro di Moroder	🍷	4
⊙	Rosa di Montacuto '98		2
●	Rosso Conero Dorico '90	🍷🍷🍷 (white)	4
●	Rosso Conero Dorico '93	🍷🍷🍷 (white)	4
●	Rosso Conero Dorico '92	🍷🍷 (white)	4
●	Rosso Conero Dorico '95	🍷🍷 (white)	4

APPIGNANO (MC)

VILLA FORANO
C.DA FORANO, 40
62010 APPIGNANO (MC)
TEL. 0733/57102

This new and promising estate in the province of Macerata fully merits its debut in the Guide. Last year we mentioned a '97 from this property of the Lucangelis in our Other Wineries section, and our recent retasting of the same wine showed that it has developed beautifully. This year's whites are perhaps less full and creamy in the mouth – a typical characteristic of the vintage – but they're expressive and technically faultless. The most important white, the special selection Monteferro Colli Maceratesi '98, is striking in its floral sweetness on the nose, the balanced contrast between crispness and softness on the palate and its inviting drinkability. The normal Colli Maceratesi '98 is less concentrated but just as crisp and easy to drink. The well-made and dense Rosso Piceno got high marks at our tastings, while the Rosso Piceno Villa Forano '97 did even better because of its greater concentration, its warm if slightly vegetal fragrance and a generous, almost creamy palate supported by just the right amount of silky tannins, which keep it going strong right through to the finish.

○	Colli Maceratesi Bianco Monteferro '98	🍷🍷	3
●	Rosso Piceno Villa Forano '97	🍷🍷	3
○	Colli Maceratesi Bianco Villa Forano '98	🍷	2

ASCOLI PICENO

ERCOLE VELENOSI
VIA DEI BIANCOSPINI, 11
63100 ASCOLI PICENO
TEL. 0736/341218

Angela and Ercole Velenosi have succeeded in attracting market attention by means of constant and determined improvement in the quality of their wines, and this year's releases are a further example. Wines like the Falerio Vigna Solaria '98 make years of hard work seem worthwhile. Produced from fully ripened grapes, it has an intense nose with a broad array of floral aromas; on the palate it is fat, with acidity well integrated into plentiful alcohol and a long finish. This is clearly a wine to lay down: it won't peak for a while. Although from a difficult vintage, the '96 Rosso Piceno Superiore cru Roggio del Filare is no less important: of a fine ruby color, it has an oaky nose with notes of clove and cherry and, on the palate, good concentration with tannins and extract properly harmonized by its time in barrique. The wines from the Brecciarolo range, the 'younger brothers' of the above, are both good and moderately priced. There are fine results from non-local varieties too: the Villa Angela Chardonnay '98 has an intense fragrance reminiscent of banana and melon, and a crisp and notably succulent palate, while Il Barricato '97, another chardonnay, asserts its significant structure and alcohol over the oak-derived vanilla. Their bubbly wine, the excellent Velenosi Brut Metodo Classico, came very close to Two Glasses, while Linagre was better than ever before and reaped One Glass.

○	Falerio dei Colli Ascolani Vigna Solaria '98	🍷🍷	3*
○	Il Barricato di Villa Angela '97	🍷🍷	4
●	Rosso Piceno Sup. Roggio del Filare '96	🍷🍷	4
○	Villa Angela Chardonnay '98	🍷🍷	3*
○	Falerio dei Colli Ascolani Il Brecciarolo '98	🍷	2*
○	Linagre Sauvignon di Villa Angela '98	🍷	3
●	Rosso Piceno Sup. Brecciarolo '96	🍷	3
○	Velenosi Brut Metodo Classico	🍷	4
○	Il Barricato di Villa Angela '96	🍷🍷 (outline)	4
●	Rosso Piceno Sup. Roggio del Filare '95	🍷🍷 (outline)	3

BARBARA (AN)

SANTA BARBARA
BORGO MAZZINI, 35
60010 BARBARA (AN)
TEL. 071/9674249

The Santa Barbara estate changed track about 10 years ago when Stefano Antonucci, having taken it over, determinedly embarked on a complete overhaul of production methods. From the current range the standard Verdicchio and the special selection Pignocco Bianco are both well executed, as far as a tricky year in the Castelli di Jesi zone would allow. The former is characterized by a mainly vegetal tone, the latter by a generous bouquet and denser fruit. Still among the Verdicchio dei Castelli di Jesi special selections, Le Vaglie '97 shows itself a wine of depth, with high alcohol and quite a broad palate. The very interesting Verdicchio Riserva Stefano Antonucci '97 is better balanced than in previous vintages, with a richness both in its wide sweep of aromas and in its full-bodied but crisp palate. The Verdicchio line is rounded off by the clean, straightforward Nidastore '98. Now for the reds: the Pignocco Rosso '98, from an unusual blend of local and non-local grape varieties, is quite irresistibly drinkable, while the San Bartolo '97, from montepulciano and cabernet, seems a successful alternative to a young Chianti. However, the Rosso delle Marche Stefano Antonucci, a merlot with some cabernet sauvignon, impressed us most. The '97, which is now available, has a lovely dark hue and a distinctive fresh bouquet of flowers and berries. The palate is still developing, but is already an admirable blend of complexity and quaffability. To close, the Muscatell, made, not surprisingly, from the moscato grape, is as well executed as ever.

●	Rosso delle Marche Stefano Antonucci '97	🍷🍷	4
○	Verdicchio dei Castelli di Jesi Cl. Le Vaglie '97	🍷🍷	3*
○	Verdicchio dei Castelli di Jesi Cl. Stefano Antonucci '97	🍷🍷	4
○	Muscatell '98	🍷	3
●	Pignocco Rosso '98	🍷	3
●	San Bartolo '97	🍷	3
○	Verdicchio dei Castelli di Jesi Cl. '98	🍷	2
○	Verdicchio dei Castelli di Jesi Nidastore '98	🍷	3
○	Verdicchio dei Castelli di Jesi Pignocco '98	🍷	2

BARCHI (PS)

VALENTINO FIORINI
VIA CAMPIOLI, 5
61030 BARCHI (PS)
TEL. 0721/97151

This noteworthy estate in the Colli Pesaresi has made considerable strides in the vinification of Bianchello. This is a DOC that has had difficulty in establishing its identity and a place for itself in the market. Despite the dryness of the year, the two '98 Bianchellos show admirable crispness and fair structure. The Bianchello DOC Sant'Ilario '98 has a clear, bright straw yellow color, a not very distinctive nose and noticeable acidity that needs rounding out. The Tenuta Campioli '98 is better. It has a gold-tinged straw yellow hue and a nose redolent of ripe apricot and white flowers. Greater structure promotes a balance between body and fragrance on the palate, and the finish does not disappoint. The surprising Rosso Bartis '97 is a successful blend of sangiovese, here in something more than a minor role, with montepulciano and cabernet sauvignon. A brilliant limpid ruby hue leads to aromas in which the cabernet sauvignon's herbaceous quality knits well with the fruitiness of the other varieties and the odd spicy note. Smooth tannins and elegance greet the palate, where red berries and a delightful warm softness prevail. Lastly, the Monsavium cannot be considered a vin santo, although this is what they had in mind. It has the color of old gold and an intense fragrance revealing a controlled amount of maderization and aromas of dried fig and hazelnut; the palate has an appropriate softness in which a light succulence blends with hints of dried fruit, leading to an extremely clean finish: it's more like a manzanilla sherry than a vin santo.

●	Colli Pesaresi Rosso Bartis '97	🍷🍷	4
○	Bianchello del Metauro Tenuta Campioli '98	🍷	3
○	Monsavium Passito	🍷	4
○	Bianchello del Metauro Vigna Sant'Ilario '98		2

BELVEDERE OSTRENSE (AN)

LUCIANO LANDI
VIA GAVIGLIANO, 16
60030 BELVEDERE OSTRENSE (AN)
TEL. 0731/62353

Luciano Landi's estate is back in the Guide, as it deserves to be. In addition to the perfectly acceptable bulk wine, of which and from which it makes most, it has produced two admirable '98 DOCs: Verdicchio dei Castelli di Jesi and Lacrima di Morra d'Alba. Although '98 was not a brilliant year, an excessive metabolization of the acids caused by the hot, dry weather having deprived the whites of the fragrance they need for their development, Landi, with the technical assistance of Sergio Paolucci, has made well-structured wines ready for drinking. But we wouldn't bet on their having a long life span, despite their coming from carefully selected grapes. The Verdicchio has a straw yellow color and subtle, rather tenuous aromas; it's fairly crisp and harmonious on the palate, with a well-defined, typically bitterish finish. The Lacrima, a red wine for drinking young and fresh, is better, counting as it does on some excellent primary aromatic components which can save the nose, even in difficult years. This year's example has a typically varietal and persistent fragrance; its fair structure boasts a good balance of freshness, alcohol and ripe tannins. Saturno, an experiment with semi-dried lacrima grapes begun in '97, seems to have taken a clear direction: of a dark violet red hue, it parades varied aromas ranging from violets to sweet spice underpinned by good structure. Just a tiny extra touch of residual sugar would give it a finishing touch of full sensual softness.

●	Lacrima di Morro d'Alba '98	🍷🍷	3*
●	Saturno Passito '98	🍷	4
○	Verdicchio dei Castelli di Jesi Cl. '98	🍷	2*

CASTEL DI LAMA (AP)

Tenuta De Angelis
Via S. Francesco, 10
63030 Castel di Lama (AP)
tel. 0736/87429

It happens ever more often that certain areas, be they entire zones or single vineyards, reveal their innate potential to produce one splendid wine. The Tenuta De Angelis is a case in point. This year the whole range is good but one wine really stands out. This is their Anghelos '97, a blend of montepulciano, sangiovese and cabernet sauvignon. In its debut appearance the wine immediately shows its stuff: it's dark, concentrated, purplish in hue, with aromas of sour cherry jam and ripe dark berries and notes of spice on the nose; the palate is soft and long, with all its components in good balance. Next comes the Rosso Piceno '98, which also shows good depth of color (brilliant ruby). The nose is ripely fruity and intensely grapey, as befits its youth; the palate is admirably substantial and well-executed. The very good Falerio dei Colli Ascolani '98 is of a straw hue verging on green; fruity aromas and a lingering palate complete the picture. The Rosso Piceno Superiore '95, which we reviewed last year, is still definitely holding its own.

●	Anghelos '97	🍷🍷	4
●	Rosso Piceno '98	🍷🍷	2*
○	Falerio dei Colli Ascolani '98	🍷	1*
●	Rosso Piceno Sup. '95	🍸	2

CASTELPLANIO (AN)

Fazi Battaglia
Via Roma, 117
60032 Castelplanio (AN)
tel. 0731/813444

This renowned estate in Castelplanio, the erstwhile creator of the well-known amphora bottle, now has 340 hectares of vineyard scattered throughout the Castelli di Jesi area. Although Verdicchio is still, of course, the focus of most of their efforts, a series of reds is making quite some headway, promising interesting developments. Their Rutilus, for example, an IGT sangiovese designed for easy drinking, is very well made and invitingly fruity. Similarly, the attractive '98 Rosso Conero shows good concentration and well-defined typical montepulciano notes of plum and wild cherry. The Rosso Conero Passo del Lupo Riserva '94 obviously has more body; this is a structured, soft wine which has been aged with expert care. Indeed, the estate's technical staff, which consists of the oenologist Dino Porfiri and the agronomists Mario Ghergo and Antonio Verdolini, with, in recent years, Franco Bernabei as consultant, has given special attention to the development of the new wines, both red and white. The Arkezia, for example, is produced only in those years when the verdicchio grape develops botrytis cinerea (noble rot); we reviewed the '96 last year. Then there is San Sisto, a Verdicchio special selection. The '95 vintage, now available, keeps its various components, including the oaky ones from its time in small barrels, in excellent balance. The '98 vintage of the traditional selection Le Moie is as successful as ever despite the difficult year. Both the Titulus, their bottom of the line Verdicchio, and the sparkling verdicchio-based Brut are reliable, as usual.

○	Verdicchio dei Castelli di Jesi Cl. San Sisto Ris. '95	🍷🍷	4
●	Rosso Conero '98	🍷	3
●	Rosso Conero Passo del Lupo Ris. '94	🍷	4
●	Rutilus Marche Sangiovese '98	🍷	2*
○	Verdicchio dei Castelli di Jesi Cl. Sup. Le Moie '98	🍷	3
○	Verdicchio dei Castelli di Jesi Cl. Titulus '98	🍷	3
○	Fazi Battaglia Brut	🍷	3
○	Arkezia Muffo di San Sisto '96	🍸	5

CINGOLI (MC)

Tavignano

Lucangeli Aymerich di Laconi
Loc. Tavignano
62011 Cingoli (MC)
tel. 0733/617303

The Verdicchio dei Castelli di Jesi appellation includes, for the most part, vineyards in the province of Ancona. One exception is Cingoli, in the neighboring province of Macerata but right on the border. Here, high in the hills, the vines bask in excellent exposures and fine climatic conditions. This is the case with the fortunate vineyards of Tavignano, an estate that has been going for several years and is working single-mindedly for excellence. So far they have produced only white wines, but some new reds are promised for later. In total, annual production comes to around 40 thousand bottles of Verdicchio, split among various styles. We tasted the '98 of their top special selection, Misco, and found it one of the best of the vintage. The wine has a lively yellow color laced with hints of pale green, a fragrance of ripe fruit and a well-knit palate with substantial structure. The other selection, Vigneti di Tavignano, again '98, is almost as good; the bouquet is different, featuring greener notes (linden blossom and green apple), and the palate has the characteristic almondy tone. A new release this year joins the two crus: a selection of overripe verdicchio grapes called Sante Lancerio, for drinking with dessert or just sipping at the end of the meal. The '95 vintage, with its attractive yellow hue highlighted with gold, its rich nose and sweet palate, is definitely an interesting experiment and worth working on in the future, given its obvious promise.

○	Verdicchio dei Castelli di Jesi Cl. Selezione Misco '98	🍷🍷	3*
○	Verdicchio dei Castelli di Jesi Cl. Tenuta di Tavignano '98	🍷🍷	2*
○	Verdicchio dei Castelli di Jesi Cl. Sante Lancerio '95	🍷	4
○	Verdicchio dei Castelli di Jesi Cl. Selezione Misco '97	🍷🍷 (white)	3*
○	Verdicchio dei Castelli di Jesi Cl. Tenuta di Tavignano '97	🍷🍷 (white)	2

CIVITANOVA MARCHE (MC)

Boccadigabbia

C.da Castelletta, 56
62012 Civitanova Marche (MC)
tel. 0733/70728

Akronte, a monovarietal cabernet sauvignon aged in small French oak barrels, comes from a small vineyard situated just a few hundred meters from the sea. Even in a year like '96, which is well known to be unexceptional, the wine won over everyone at our tastings. It didn't manage to win Three Glasses but is nonetheless a lovely wine, especially in its inviting array of aromas, with blackcurrant, bell pepper and coffee in splendid succession. The palate that follows is dense and powerful but already very elegant. It may not last forever, but for present drinking it's absolutely great. So is the sangiovese-based Saltapicchio '96. This is a wine it's very difficult to stop drinking, thanks to a really satisfying roundness. This is true as well of the elegant white Monsanulus from the Villamagna estate recently acquired by Alessandri. The very good Rosso Piceno '97 is less distinguished than the Saltapicchio but similar in style. The good news continues with the whites, from the simple Garbì '98 (chardonnay and trebbiano), crisp and easy drinking, to Aldonis '98 (a chardonnay aged in stainless steel), ultra-fruity and mouth-filling, passing by way of Montalperti '97 (oaked Chardonnay), very fully structured but too woody, and the selection La Castelletta '98 (pinot grigio), flowery and very well balanced. We need hardly say, in conclusion, that this is a range of wines with few rivals in the region. Hats off, once again, and with feeling, to Elvio Alessandri, owner of the estate, and Giovanni Basso and Fabrizio Ciufoli, the consultant oenologists.

○	Aldonis Marche Chardonnay '98	🍷🍷	3*
○	La Castelletta Pinot Grigio '98	🍷🍷	3
○	Monsanulus Marche Bianco '98	🍷🍷	4
●	Akronte '96	🍷🍷	6
●	Saltapicchio Marche Sangiovese '96	🍷🍷	5
○	Garbì '98	🍷	3
○	Montalperti Marche Chardonnay '97	🍷	4
●	Rosso Piceno '97	🍷	3
●	Akronte '92	🍷🍷🍷 (white)	5
●	Akronte '93	🍷🍷🍷 (white)	5
●	Akronte '94	🍷🍷🍷 (white)	5
●	Akronte '95	🍷🍷🍷 (white)	5
●	Girone '95	🍷🍷 (white)	3

CUPRA MARITTIMA (AP)

OASI DEGLI ANGELI
C.DA SANT'EGIDIO, 50
63012 CUPRA MARITTIMA (AP)
TEL. 0735/778569

When veteran wine tasters and reviewers like ourselves come upon an oenological phenomenon like Oasi degli Angeli we are, as you can readily imagine, well pleased. It is partly the joy of discovery, of course, but there's something more: the enlivening confirmation that aiming at excellence, which we have always promoted, is indeed the mainspring of modern winemaking. The reason for all this enthusiasm is Kurni '97, a great discovery that fully merits its Three Glasses. This magnificent wine, 100% montepulciano, has remarkable structure, warmth and softness, and reveals mouth-filling weight and silky tannins; black cherry, mint, leather, rhubarb and coffee compose the bouquet, to which a broad and engrossing palate corresponds. Their second wine is the white Esedra '97, a monovarietal trebbiano expertly aged in small oak casks. With one sure blow it does in all the usual prejudices about how you can't make anything but a characterless wine out of trebbiano: Esedra exhibits a wide range of fascinating aromas: white flowers, caramel, citrus fruit and anise blend, underpinned by powerful alcohol. The warm yet sinewy palate mirrors the nose. There is no doubt that the creators of these wines, Marco Casolanetti and Eleonora Rossi, partners in life as in work, assisted by their consultant oenologist Giovanni Basso, are staking their all on great quality. The '98 vintage, which is still in the barrel, can already attest that this year's results were not just a flash in the pan.

●	Kurni '97	ŶŶŶ	6
○	Esedra '97	ŶŶ	5

CUPRAMONTANA (AN)

VALLEROSA BONCI
VIA TORRE, 13
60034 CUPRAMONTANA (AN)
TEL. 0731/789129

The Castelli di Jesi area was not spared the extreme heat of the summer of 1998: the verdicchio grapes yielded structured, alcoholic wines at the expense of fragrance and acidity, and acidity is essential for balance in a wine. So the San Michele '98, even though again one of the best Verdicchios of the vintage, shows its origins. At the time of tasting it offered most enjoyable aromas of ripe apple and a delightfully rich palate with broad structure and personality and a long almondy finish. In short it was a real pleasure. But it didn't equal the fantastic '96 and '97 vintages. Le Case '98, a partly barrique-aged Verdicchio, has elegant and variegated floral aromas leading to a sweetly spicy note, all carried through onto the round, enchanting palate: an easy Two Glasses. Last of the '98s, the attractive Focus is a simpler Verdicchio selection, well made and less demanding. The fully oak-aged Verdicchio, Barré '96, clearly reveals where it spent its time: distinct but pleasing vanilla scents are echoed on the firm and still fresh palate with its good finish. The Bonci Brut is as pleasing as ever and the Rosso Piceno Vallerosa '98 rates a mention, while the new vintage of the raisin wine Rojano, the '96, is still maturing. Our conclusion must be that the estate, thanks in part to Sergio Paolucci's oenological know-how, has yet again produced an excellent range of wines.

○	Verdicchio dei Castelli di Jesi Cl. Sup. Barré Ris. '96	ŶŶ	4
○	Verdicchio dei Castelli di Jesi Cl. Sup. Le Case '98	ŶŶ	4
○	Verdicchio dei Castelli di Jesi Cl. Sup. San Michele '98	ŶŶ	4
○	Verdicchio dei Castelli di Jesi Cl. Focus '98	Ŷ	2*
○	Verdicchio Spumante Brut Bonci	Ŷ	3
●	Rosso Piceno Vallerosa '98		2
○	Verdicchio dei Castelli di Jesi Cl. Sup. San Michele '96	YYY	4
○	Verdicchio dei Castelli di Jesi Cl. Sup. San Michele '97	YYY	4

CUPRAMONTANA (AN)

Colonnara Viticultori in Cupramontana

Via Mandriole, 6
60034 Cupramontana (AN)
tel. 0731/780273

This year Colonnara celebrated its 40th anniversary with justifiable pride for what it has accomplished since its establishment, in the heart of Verdicchio dei Castelli di Jesi country, in 1959. Today this wine cooperative includes some 200 small growers, and the production of Verdicchio, in various styles, remains its chief activity, for which it calls on the advice of two of the most esteemed oenologists of Franciacorta, Cesare Ferrari and Corrado Cugnasco. The Cuprese, from selected verdicchio grapes grown on the higher slopes between Cupramontana, Staffolo and Maiolati, has always been their flagship wine. The '98 vintage boasts a striking nose with notes of linden blossom and hazelnut; the taste, still somewhat closed at the time of tasting, has good weight. We also retasted several earlier vintages of Cuprese, confirming that it is a wine for keeping; it is, by the way, also a great bargain. The oak-aged Romitello '97 was not yet ready at the time of our tastings, so we'll review it next year. The basic Verdicchio '98 seemed properly executed, with vegetal tones and a crisp palate. There are also two sparkling Verdicchios: the creamy Colonnara Metodo Classico, which shows a particular finesse, and the cuve close method Colonnara Brut, which further confirms that they have a way with bubblies here. The range concludes with the red Tornamagno '95, a blend of sangiovese grosso, sangiovese montanino and montepulciano matured in small French oak barrels. It is redolent of red berries and shows good structure.

○	Verdicchio dei Castelli di Jesi Cl. Sup. Cuprese '98	▼▼	3*
●	Tornamagno '95	▼	3
○	Verdicchio dei Castelli di Jesi Cl. '98	▼	2*
○	Verdicchio dei Castelli di Jesi Colonnara Brut	▼	3
○	Verdicchio dei Castelli di Jesi Colonnara Metodo Classico '91	▼	4
○	Verdicchio dei Castelli di Jesi Cl. Sup. Cuprese '95	▽▽	3
○	Verdicchio dei Castelli di Jesi Cl. Sup. Cuprese '97	▽▽	3

FABRIANO (AN)

Enzo Mecella

Via Dante, 112
60044 Fabriano (AN)
tel. 0732/21680

Year after year Enzo Mecella's estate succeeds in presenting really interesting wines; indeed he is one of the most reliable and consistent producers in the entire region. There isn't much to say however about the Verdicchio di Matelica Pagliano '98; quite pale in the glass, it offers very slight structure, although it still is easy to drink. The Casa Fosca '98 is much more successful and the special selection Antico di Casa Fosca is even better, indeed the best of the whites. It has a good, soft structure, full of personality, with hints of almond, citrus fruit and white flowers; wood has been used really masterfully, but then we're used to that here. There is good news from the reds too, starting with the Rosso Conero I Lavi, vintage '97. This reveals good body although it lacks a distinctive nose. Indeed the Braccano '97 (ciliegiolo with a little merlot) beats it: aromas of raspberry, cherry and meat lead to a well-structured but perhaps overly bitter palate. However, it is the Rosso Conero Rubelliano that, as usual, stands out from the pack. The '97 has an extremely satisfying bouquet of black cherry enhanced by just the right amount of oak; in the mouth it is warm, generous and recognizably a montepulciano, with excellent carry-through from the nose and remarkable length. This was a great year.

●	Braccano '97	▼▼	4
●	Rosso Conero Rubelliano '97	▼▼	4
○	Verdicchio di Matelica Antico di Casa Fosca '98	▼▼	3*
●	Rosso Conero I Lavi '97	▼	2
○	Verdicchio di Matelica Casa Fosca '98	▼	3
○	Verdicchio di Matelica Pagliano '98		2
●	Braccano '95	▽▽	4

FANO (PS)

Claudio Morelli
V.le Romagna, 47/b
61032 Fano (PS)
tel. 0721/823352

This year Claudio Morelli's estate, which has long been one of the most reliable in the province of Pesaro, has produced a selection of well-made but not exactly brilliant wines, particularly as far as Bianchello del Metauro is concerned. The most successful of these three whites is the Borgo Torre '98, thanks to its slightly more substantial structure. The San Cesareo and La Vigna delle Terrazze, the two other '98s, are no more than acceptable, with faint floral fragrance and lightweight palates. Let's turn to the reds, for which the estate has ambitious plans. We tasted a good Sant'Andrea in Villis '97, which is a Colli Pesaresi Sangiovese DOC, characterized by a dignified bouquet, a little floral and a little fruity, and fair length. The appealing Suffragium '96, ruby verging on garnet in color, is an attempt to put the inviting nose of vernaccia di Pergola on top of the considerable body of montepulciano. The result is agreeable but, the '96 vintage being what it was, it succeeds only in part. The Solare, a wine from semi-dried grapes, is a new arrival. The '97 shows a lovely yellow color tinged with gold. The bouquet doesn't stint on fruit (peach, ripe apricot and banana in particular), which is joined by spicy (cinnamon) notes. The nicely knit palate with well-judged residual sugar is supported by a good amount of alcohol.

○ Bianchello del Metauro Borgo Torre '98	🍷	3
● Colli Pesaresi Sangiovese Sant'Andrea in Villis '97	🍷	3
○ Solare Passito '97	🍷	4
● Suffragium '96	🍷	3
○ Bianchello del Metauro La Vigna delle Terrazze '98		2
○ Bianchello del Metauro San Cesareo '98		2

JESI (AN)

Mario e Giorgio Brunori
V.le della Vittoria, 103
60035 Jesi (AN)
tel. 0731/207213

As usual there is a range of pleasing wines from the Brunori family which, year after year, manages to maintain high standards and, above all, to produce wines of a clearly individual character. This year we tasted the Verdicchios from '98, an extremely hot year hereabouts, with resultant low acidity generally. The Brunori wines, however, seem to have managed to help themselves to only the best characteristics that this in many ways positive vintage had to offer. The basic Verdicchio, for example, has a clean, well-defined floral fragrance and a certain structure in which the asperity that the verdicchio grape often produces has been smoothed away. And the selection San Nicolò, made from the best grapes to be found in the eponymous vineyard, seems even better as soon as you see it. The aromas are quite intense and distinct; the floral tone of Verdicchio dei Castelli di Jesi comes across with great clarity, and is reflected on a palate supported by good structure. The wine usually takes home Two fully deserved Glasses, and this year is no exception.

○ Verdicchio dei Castelli di Jesi Cl. San Nicolò '98	🍷🍷	3*
○ Verdicchio dei Castelli di Jesi Cl. '98	🍷	2
○ Verdicchio dei Castelli di Jesi Cl. San Nicolò '97	🍷🍷 (outline)	3

LORETO (AN)

GIOACCHINO GAROFOLI
VIA ARNO, 9
60025 LORETO (AN)
TEL. 071/7820163

The reliability of this producer is not a matter of chance but the result of constant dedication and hard work. This year, despite their different vintages, we found pleasing similarities in the quality of the three Verdicchios we tasted. The Macrina '98 has a delicate fragrance of acacia blossom and a clean, soft, fairly concentrated palate. The Podium '97, which has yet again walked off with Three Glasses, has distinct and lasting floral aromas, but also notes of hazelnut and green apple; on the palate it's concentrated, rich and powerful, but with a soft, elegant structure and a delicately almondy finish. The excellent barrique-aged Verdicchio Serra Fiorese Riserva '96 offers clear notes of citrus fruit, elder blossom and acacia that are not overshadowed by the well-judged oak-derived toasty notes; in the mouth it is balanced, powerful and opulent, yet still extremely crisp. The rosé Kòmaros '98 has a lovely onion skin color and aromas of ripe fruit; the palate is reasonably structured. The Rosso Piceno Colle Ambro '97 gains complexity from its aromas of sweet spice; a soft, well-expressed and balanced palate follows. The Rosso Conero Vigna Piancarda '97, of a deep ruby hue, offers a grapey fragrance with notes of red berries and light spice; it is attractively soft and fairly elegant on the palate. The Rosso Conero Riserva Grosso Agontano '96, dark ruby in color, has rather muffled fruity aromas; it is still a little harsh on the palate, where the tannins are not yet integrated into the concentrated structure. Although it has not yet acquired perfect balance, this wine has what it takes to develop well and to last.

○	Verdicchio dei Castelli di Jesi Cl. Sup. Podium '97	🍷🍷🍷	3*
●	Rosso Conero Grosso Agontano Ris. '96	🍷🍷	4
○	Verdicchio dei Castelli di Jesi Cl. Serra Fiorese Ris. '96	🍷🍷	4
●	Rosso Conero Vigna Piancarda '97	🍷	3
●	Rosso Piceno Colle Ambro '97	🍷	3
○	Verdicchio dei Castelli di Jesi Cl. Sup. Macrina '98	🍷	3
⊙	Kòmaros '98		3
○	Verdicchio dei Castelli di Jesi Cl. Sup. Podium '95	YYY	4
○	Verdicchio dei Castelli di Jesi Cl. Sup. Podium '96	YYY	4

MAIOLATI SPONTINI (AN)

MONTE SCHIAVO
VIA VIVAIO
FRAZ. MONTESCHIAVO
60030 MAIOLATI SPONTINI (AN)
TEL. 0731/700385 - 0731/700297

This estate in Maiolati Spontini has, with the help of the oenologist Piero Lorenzetti, been making lots of progress and has presented a fine range of wines this year. The late-harvested grapes for the Verdicchio Palio di San Floriano '98 come from the Fossato vineyards near San Marcello. The resulting wine, matured partly in stainless steel vats, partly in large oak casks, is one of the best Verdicchios dei Castelli di Jesi of the year. It has both depth and freshness, as well as notable balance. The basic Verdicchio is also very well made, while the special selection Coste del Molino again combines easy drinkability with original nuances of taste. The '97 vintage of the Bando di San Settimio, although not extraordinarily complex, does carry through nicely from nose to palate. We shall be following the development of the Verdicchio Le Giuncare Riserva '97; at the moment the bouquet is variegated and the palate well-knit, if not overly full. The Passito Arché, made from semi-dried verdicchio grapes, is a wine of well-dosed sweetness. Among the reds, the Rosso Conero Bottaccio '98 is striking in its rich bouquet of fragrant fruit and its inviting quaffability. The Rosso Conero Conti Cortesi '97 may not have the body of the Bottaccio, but the estate's consistent oenological style is apparent in the full expression of the wine's fruit and its softness on the palate. The successful Lacrima di Morro d'Alba '98 shows, in its bouquet, its fine lively color and its engaging taste, all the floral and fruity richness one expects from this appellation. This winery has great hopes for its most important red, the relative newcomer Esio, a blend of montepulciano and cabernet.

○	Verdicchio dei Castelli di Jesi Cl. Sup. Palio di S. Floriano '98	🍷🍷	2*
●	Esio Marche Rosso '97	🍷🍷	4
●	Lacrima di Morro d'Alba '98	🍷	3
●	Rosso Conero Bottaccio '98	🍷	3
●	Rosso Conero Conti Cortesi '97	🍷	3
○	Verdicchio dei Castelli di Jesi Cl. Coste del Molino '98	🍷	2*
○	Verdicchio dei Castelli di Jesi Cl. Le Giuncare Ris. '97	🍷	3
○	Verdicchio dei Castelli di Jesi Cl. Passito Arché '97	🍷	3
○	Verdicchio dei Castelli di Jesi Cl. Sup. Bando di S. Settimio '97	🍷	3
○	Verdicchio dei Castelli di Jesi Cl. '98		2

MATELICA (MC)

BELISARIO CANTINA SOCIALE
DI MATELICA E CERRETO D'ESI
VIA MERLONI, 12
62024 MATELICA (MC)
TEL. 0737/787247

The Belisario cooperative winery, directed by the oenologist Roberto Potentini, once more shows its skill at making white wine, with a range of admirable Verdicchios di Matelica, but this is nothing new. The brightest star is without doubt their Cambrugiano '96, with its deep straw yellow hue, delicate aromas of anise and white flowers and elegant palate with a balanced sweet almondy finish: a really lovely wine. The Vigneti del Cerro '98, attractively tinged with green in the glass, offers an intense and lasting bouquet of acacia blossom and apple. Despite its youth, it shows sinew and succulence on the palate, as well as almond on the finish. The Cinque Annate al Duemila '97, produced with controlled oxidation of the must, displays an impressively intense bouquet of ripe fruit and linden blossom; on the palate, however, the somewhat fragile structure is dominated by strong acidity that the wine's high alcohol does not completely balance out. The subtle, reticent Ritratti '98 is, as ever, well made, as is the undemanding Esino Bianco Ferrante '98. The Passito Carpe Diem '95 does not yet hit the spot. Amber-hued, with aromas of fruit seeped in alcohol, on the palate it is over-acidic and too forward. The cooperative also presented two reds: while there was good, straightforward drinking to be had from the Colferraio '98, we await better things in the future from the San Leopardo '96.

○ Verdicchio di Matelica Cambrugiano Ris. '96	🍷🍷	3*
○ Verdicchio di Matelica Vigneti del Cerro '98	🍷🍷	3*
○ Verdicchio di Matelica Cinque Annate al Duemila '97	🍷	3
○ Verdicchio di Matelica Ritratti '98	🍷	1*
● Colferraio '98		1
○ Esino Bianco Ferrante '98		1
● San Leopardo '96		3
○ Verdicchio di Matelica Passito Carpe Diem '95		4

MATELICA (MC)

LA MONACESCA
C.DA MONACESCA, 1
62024 MATELICA (MC)
TEL. 0733/812602

Casimiro Cifola, the owner of this estate, his son Aldo, who has been delighting us with wonderfully full-bodied white wines for more than ten years, and Roberto Cipresso, their consultant oenologist, have produced a really remarkable bottle with the '97 Mirum. As usual it begins to make an effect as soon as you see its atypically deep concentrated straw yellow color tinged with youthful green. The aromas are no less impressive, ranging from acacia, almond and anise to orange; and the exceptionally full-bodied, rich, even and consistent palate does its part as well. Like all its elders it will doubtless have no trouble continuing to be enormously satisfying for at least five years more. The very successful Chardonnay Ecclesia is pleasingly varietal and expressive of its terroir. The result is soft and satisfying, like all great chardonnays, but with a specific mineral tone that gives it a distinctly individual personality. Next year will see the release of a new red wine, made from a blend of merlot and sangiovese grosso. Early tastings suggest that it will not let down the side. La Monacesca has again shown that it is one of the best producers of white wine, not only in the Marche, but in all of Italy.

○ Ecclesia Marche Chardonnay '98	🍷🍷	3*
○ Mirum '97	🍷🍷	4
○ Verdicchio di Matelica '98	🍷🍷	3*
○ Verdicchio di Matelica La Monacesca '98	🍷🍷	3*
○ Mirum '94	🍷🍷🍷 (outline)	4
○ Mirus '91	🍷🍷🍷 (outline)	4
○ Verdicchio di Matelica La Monacesca '94	🍷🍷🍷 (outline)	4
○ Ecclesia Marche Chardonnay '97	🍷🍷 (outline)	3
○ Mirum '95	🍷🍷 (outline)	4
○ Mirus '93	🍷🍷 (outline)	4

MONTECAROTTO (AN)

Terre Cortesi Moncaro

Via Piandole, 7/A
60036 Montecarotto (AN)
tel. 0731/89245

For the past few years this estate, run by the expert Giulio d'Ignazi with additional oenological advice from Marco Monchiero, has been producing red wines as well as its traditional Verdicchios. We'll start with the Verdicchio dei Castelli di Jesi Vigna Novali '96, which last year won Two Glasses and has since triumphantly developed into an absolute champion. A lovely yellow color, verging on bright gold, is followed by a complex and ripe but not excessively forward bouquet and a broad and satisfying palate. While awaiting the next release of this great wine we tasted the '98 Verdicchios, starting with the Verde di Ca' Ruptae, which we found properly varietal; the distinct vegetal notes on the nose lead to a crisp palate with medium structure. The selection Le Vele is succulent and sinewy; its wealth of fragrance is in part due to innovative vinification techniques that almost entirely exclude exposure to oxygen. The Verdicchio Biologico (organically produced), with its straightforward nose and clean, crisp palate, is also laudable, despite the tricky vintage. The last of the more important whites from this estate at Montecarotto is the Passito Tordiruta, which earned its Two Glasses with its overall balance and an opulence nowhere near cloying. This year's reds are the Terre Cortesi Riserva '96, which is a Rosso Conero DOC, and the Barocco '96 (montepulciano and cabernet sauvignon in equal proportions). Both wines show character and depth; the latter offers greater complexity and will probably go on developing for a longer time.

○	Verdicchio dei Castelli di Jesi Cl. Passito Tordiruta '96	▼▼	4
●	Barocco Marche Rosso '96	▼	4
●	Rosso Conero Terre Cortesi Ris. '96	▼	3
○	Verdicchio dei Castelli di Jesi Cl. Biologico '98	▼	3
○	Verdicchio dei Castelli di Jesi Cl. Le Vele '98	▼	3
○	Verdicchio dei Castelli di Jesi Cl. Sup. Verde di Ca' Ruptae '98	▼	3
○	Verdicchio dei Castelli di Jesi Cl. Sup. Verde di Ca' Ruptae '97	▽▽	3
○	Verdicchio dei Castelli di Jesi Cl. Sup. Vigna Novali '96	▽▽	3

MONTEGRANARO (AP)

Rio Maggio

C.da Vallone, 41
63014 Montegranaro (AP)
tel. 0734/889587

Rio Maggio, run by the brothers Simone and Pierpaolo Santucci, made its debut in the Guide last year and this year's results consolidate its position. The oenologist Giancarlo Soverchia is in charge of the technical orientation of this estate, whose well-made and affordable wines have been attracting attention for some time. The straw yellow Falerio '98 has subtle floral aromas, a somewhat forward and hence not overly fragrant, full-bodied but short palate. The Falerio selection Telusiano '98, also straw yellow in color, displays quite developed notes of apple and ripe yellow plum on the nose; considerable acidity makes it crisp and fairly long in the mouth, although its impact is not great. The deep straw yellow Chardonnay Artias '98 is redolent of banana and ripe fruit; perfectly ripened grapes have produced a well-structured palate. The Sauvignon Ombra '98, which is, as usual, interesting, has a straw yellow color with greenish-gold highlights; the characteristic green leaf and peppermint aroma is interwoven with ripe fruit and the palate is fragrant, well balanced and fairly powerful, with an elegantly clean finish. The Rosso Piceno DOC '98 has a dense ruby hue tinged with violet, a still grapey nose and a soft, concentrated palate with smooth tannins. The selection Granarijs represents a step forward for a Rosso Piceno, which can so often be harsh and aggressive. This dark scarlet wine, instead, has an enticing nose with a note of cherry and a sweetly smooth, concentrated palate with a long, aromatic finish. An interesting Pinot Nero is on its way for tasting next year.

○	Ombra Marche Sauvignon '98	▼▼	3*
●	Rosso Piceno Granarijs '97	▼▼	4
○	Artias Marche Chardonnay '98	▼	3
○	Falerio dei Colli Ascolani '98	▼	2*
○	Falerio dei Colli Ascolani Telusiano '98	▼	3
●	Rosso Piceno '98	▼	2

MORRO D'ALBA (AN)

Mario Lucchetti
Via Santa Maria del Fiore, 17
60030 Morro d'Alba (AN)
tel. 0731/63314

The small DOC Lacrima di Morro d'Alba has been growing recently. Until a short time ago only about 30 hectares altogether were devoted to satisfying the demand for this unique, enchanting and notably drinkable wine. Among the estates dedicated to producing Lacrima di Morro d'Alba, Mario Lucchetti's fairly new one is particularly noteworthy and owes its debut in the Guide to its successful interpretations of this local wine. Lucchetti has nine hectares under vine, of which all have excellent exposure and five are already in production; the other four, all planted to lacrima di Morro d'Alba, have been bearing fruit for three years. Careful work in the vineyards, from pruning to selection of the best grapes from the older plots, and similar precision in the up-to-the-minute cellar allow the oenologist Alberto Mazzoni to produce wines of admirable substance and cleanness. The Selezione di Lacrima '98, one of the best examples of its kind in recent years, stands out particularly for its well-defined and fragrant fruity and grapey bouquet. It is further graced with a lovely deep color, somewhere between violet and black, and a balanced palate. The basic version, distinctly varietal in character and only a little less intense on the nose, is almost as good.

● Lacrima di Morro d'Alba Selezione '98	🍷🍷	3*
● Lacrima di Morro d'Alba '98	🍷	2*

MORRO D'ALBA (AN)

Stefano Mancinelli
Via Roma, 62
60030 Morro d'Alba (AN)
tel. 0731/63021

Lacrima has really captured the imagination of the wine-drinking public, becoming almost a cult wine, thanks in great part to the efforts of the Mancinelli estate. Run by Stefano Mancinelli with the advice and assistance of Roberto Potentini, the winery produces exemplarily characteristic versions of this red that parade a wealth of aromas worthy of a botanical garden, from sweet violet to rose, elder blossom and broom. And this richness of bouquet, a delightful mainstay of the wine even in difficult vintages, is the secret of its success. Mancinelli also produces Verdicchio and we're starting our review with them. The basic Verdicchio '98 reveals the unpropitious vintage in its fleeting aromas, amongst which hazelnut can only just be identified; the palate is attractive but rather short. The Santa Maria del Fiore version has more of a nose, with notes of medlar and broom, and a fuller palate, with just a touch of freshness and a fairly long finish. The Lacrima has its usual bright purple color and distinct aromas of fruit and flowers, but the palate, although pleasingly crisp, is not as rich as the nose would lead one to believe. The Sensazioni di Frutto, a version more dependent on expertise in cellar techniques, has an intense violet color, a richer, warmer nose with notes of balsam and spice, and a palate with noticeable, still rough tannins that, despite the good concentration, maintain their astringency. Further balance would go some way towards assuring long life to this wine. Lastly, the extremely well-executed Rosso Piceno San Michele '98, after a not very promising nose, offers a fragrant tone of red berries on the palate.

● Lacrima di Morro d'Alba Sensazioni di Frutto '98	🍷🍷	3*
● Lacrima di Morro d'Alba '98	🍷	3
● Rosso Piceno S. Michele '98	🍷	2
○ Verdicchio dei Castelli di Jesi Cl. '98	🍷	2
○ Verdicchio dei Castelli di Jesi Cl. Podere S. Maria del Fiore '98	🍷	3
● Lacrima di Morro d'Alba S. Maria del Fiore '97	🍷🍷 (white glasses)	2
● Lacrima di Morro d'Alba Sensazioni di Frutto '97	🍷🍷 (white glasses)	3

NUMANA (AN)

CONTE LEOPARDI DITTAJUTI
VIA MARINA II, 26
60026 NUMANA (AN)
TEL. 071/7390116

Count Piervittorio Leopardi, assisted as usual by his consultant oenologist Romeo Taraborrelli, has produced a creditable range of wines this year. We'll start with the whites: the Calcare Sauvignon '98, matured in stainless steel vats, offers fair structure and a predominantly herbaceous bouquet. The Villa Marina Sauvignon, on the other hand, is fermented and aged in barriques for 14 months and boasts an excellent soft structure; at the moment, oak rules the roost, particularly on the nose. The Bianco del Coppo '98 certainly does not disgrace itself in this company: despite less body, it has even better-defined varietal character than the other two and is supremely drinkable. This year the estate has also presented a vintage sparkling wine, the Spumante Brut Metodo Classico, which spent a full 38 months on its yeasts. Although it has fair structure we were not entirely convinced by a bouquet where yeast calls the tune and the perlage is somewhat aggressive. It is promising, however, although still a callow youth. Both the Rosso Coneros were good. The Vigneti del Coppo '97 has quite enchanting floral aromas and a most attractive palate, while the selection Pigmento has good structure, although at the time of our tastings it still had some rough edges which time should smooth away.

● Rosso Conero Pigmento '95	🍷🍷	4
○ Calcare Sauvignon '98	🍷	3
○ Bianco del Coppo Marche Sauvignon '98	🍷	3
○ Brut Conte Leopardi Ris. '95	🍷	4
● Rosso Conero Vigneti del Coppo '97	🍷	3
○ Villa Marina Marche Sauvignon '97	🍷	4
● Rosso Conero Pigmento '93	🍸🍸	4
● Rosso Conero Pigmento '94	🍸🍸	4
● Rosso Conero Vigneti del Coppo '96	🍸	3

NUMANA (AN)

FATTORIA LE TERRAZZE
VIA MUSONE, 4
60026 NUMANA (AN)
TEL. 071/7390352

With the '97 vintage Antonio and Giorgina Terni have produced two fabulous wines of international standing: an extraordinary Rosso Conero and a super-Marchean (apologies for the neologism), both of which do honor to this estate. With viticultural assistance from Leonardo Valenti and oenological support from Attilio Pagli, success seems a bygone conclusion, but credit is due to the owners as well for having had the courage and tenacity to opt for low yields. The amazing Chaos (montepulciano, syrah and merlot) could not fail to get Three Glasses. Of a dark and impenetrable violet color with well-defined, slowly receding 'legs', it offers a bouquet in which oaky tones do not mask ripe blackberry, wild cherry and notes of pepper, clove, cocoa and roasted coffee; the palate is remarkable for smoothness, together with a depth of concentration dominated by ripe fruit and tannin; it lingers on with notes of ripe plum and chocolate. The almost equally impressive Rosso Conero Sassi Neri '97 has a nearly opaque ruby color, a warm, deep bouquet with a rich array of aromas of herbs, sweet spice and tobacco, and a dense, evenly structured palate with smooth tannins and a soft meatiness. The Rosso Conero '97, of a clear ruby tending to garnet hue, boasts an ample bouquet of red berries and spice, and good length and carry-through on the palate. The Le Cave Chardonnay '98, the best wine the estate has so far produced from this variety, has an attractive yellow color and a full, crisp palate with a honeyed fruitiness. As usual, the montepulciano-based "metodo classico" sparkling wine, Donna Giulia, is exemplary: a lively and fragrant tipple.

● Chaos Marche Rosso '97	🍷🍷🍷	5
○ Le Cave Marche Chardonnay '98	🍷🍷	3*
● Rosso Conero '97	🍷🍷	3*
● Rosso Conero Sassi Neri '97	🍷🍷	5
○ Spumante Donna Giulia	🍷	4
● Rosso Conero Sassi Neri '95	🍸🍸	4
● Rosso Conero Sassi Neri '96	🍸🍸	3

OFFIDA (AP)

San Giovanni
C.da Ciafone, 41
63035 Offida (AP)
tel. 0736/889032

A range of successful wines and a general surge forward have brought this estate back into the Guide. Established by Silvano Di Lorenzo in 1979, San Giovanni has the good fortune to be located in Ciafone, known to knowledgeable red wine lovers as one of the best grape-growing areas of the whole province. Today Silvano's son Giovanni is in charge, and is assisted by the oenologist Narcisi and, as of the '99 harvest, by the advice of Attilio Pagli. Some 30 of their 48 hectares are under vine and recently the proportion of grapes for red wine has increased. Since this is a district capable of producing wines of great concentration it is reasonable to suppose that that will be the focus of their energies. Indeed, they have already presented two admirable reds, the Rosso Piceno Superiore Leo Guelfus '97 and the montepulciano-based Rosso del Nonno '97. Both are technically faultless, distinct in their aromas (cherry in the first case, wild cherry and plum in the second) and soft on a palate that mirrors the bouquet, although it could do with a little more concentration. The Rosato Riccardo is good, as is the Falerio '98 (another wine from their Leo Guelfus range) which offers an intense and lasting fragrance and a rich, succulent palate. The interesting '97 Falerio Sur Lies is, somewhat unusually for this wine, made for keeping, at least for a while. It displays a really enticing bouquet and its only blemish is a rather short finish. To end on a sweet note, they have now perfected the Dulcis in Fundo, produced with botrytized grapes (noble rot), which is good drinking after a meal or even as an aperitif, in the French manner.

○	Falerio dei Colli Ascolani Leo Guelfus '98	🍷🍷	3*
○	Dulcis in Fundo '96	🍷	4
○	Falerio dei Colli Ascolani Vigna Chiara Sur Lies '97	🍷	3
●	Rosso del Nonno '97	🍷	4
●	Rosso Piceno Sup. Leo Guelfus '97	🍷	3
⊙	Rosato Riccardo '98		2

OFFIDA (AP)

Villa Pigna
C.da Ciafone, 63
63035 Offida (AP)
tel. 0736/87525

We start the round-up of Villa Pigna's latest releases with the whites. First up is the Colle Malerbi, a chardonnay which was presented for the first time last year and has proven itself to be well constructed. The '98 version is also a focused wine, with a vivid almost straw yellow hue and notes of hazelnut on the nose; a palate of medium body is supported by good acidity and length. The Falerio Selezione '98, another good white, has a limpid greenish-yellow color and a floral and fruity bouquet; it is decidedly drinkable and appropriately long. The well-made standard Falerio '98 shows floral and mineral aromas and softness in the mouth. Of the reds, apart from the Cabernasco '97, which we reviewed last year and tasted again this, the pick of the crop is the montepulciano-based Rozzano '97. It has a good deep ruby color (an indication of concentration) and assorted aromas of vanilla and red berries; good structure and admirable length characterize the palate. Two further '97s, the basic Vellutato and the Rosso Piceno Superiore, can both be drunk now with ease. From '96, a year which wins no prizes, we tasted the Vellutato Superiore, which despite the evident shortcomings of this vintage does display an attractive spicy nose, and the Rosso Piceno Superiore Selezione, which is already quite forward, both in its color and in its aromas of ripe fruit. We finish our review with a white, the riesling and chardonnay blend Rugiasco '98. It has an inviting fruity fragrance and a well-knit palate underpinned by balanced acidity.

○	Falerio dei Colli Ascolani Selezione '98	🍷🍷	2*
●	Rozzano '97	🍷🍷	4
○	Colle Malerbi '98	🍷	2
○	Falerio dei Colli Ascolani '98	🍷	2
●	Rosso Piceno Sup. '97	🍷	2
○	Rugiasco '98	🍷	2
●	Vellutato '97	🍷	2
●	Vellutato Selezione '96	🍷	3
●	Rosso Piceno Sup. Selezione '96		3
●	Cabernasco '97	🍷🍷 (98)	3
●	Rozzano '96	🍷🍷 (98)	4

OSIMO (AN)

UMANI RONCHI
S.S. 16, KM. 310+400, 74
60027 OSIMO (AN)
TEL. 071/7108019

The on-going enlargement of the cellar in Osimo, to be completed in 2000, is another positive sign at Umani Ronchi, one of the best-established Italian estates in both the domestic and the international markets. The winery owns 100 hectares under vine in the Castelli di Jesi area, where the Castelbellino cellar is located, and another 50 in Rosso Conero country; in addition they rent a further 40. Some are planted to the traditional verdicchio and montepulciano, but they have also done very well with their chardonnay, sauvignon, cabernet sauvignon and merlot. One of their considerable successes is Pelago, a blend of cabernet, merlot and montepulciano aged for 14 months in French oak. The elegance and complexity of the '96 vintage, in which spicy notes blend with hints of cocoa, make it once more the estate's leading wine. The other and simpler Rosso Conero, Serrano '97, displays a bouquet of red berries and a fresh palate. The grapey Montepulciano d'Abruzzo Jorio '97 is characteristically redolent of plum and wild cherry and shows balance on the palate. The sangiovese-based Medoro '97, which links a spicy attractiveness with a youthful vinous quality, promises a good development. Among the whites, the Verdicchio Plenio Riserva '95 did very well at our tastings: it shows excellent balance between fruit and oak without any aggressiveness. And the Verdicchio Casal di Serra Riserva '98 was one of the best of its year, both on the palate and in its aromas, which, although a little closed, offer notes of hazelnut, apple and pineapple. The new versions of Maximo, an excellent dessert wine, and Le Busche, from verdicchio and chardonnay, amply maintain their high standards, while the Verdicchio Villa Bianchi '98 and the fruity Bianchello del Metauro '98 are well executed.

○	Le Busche '97	▼▼	4
○	Maximo '97	▼▼	4
○	Verdicchio dei Castelli di Jesi Cl. Plenio Ris. '95	▼▼	4
●	Pelago '96	▼▼	5
○	Verdicchio dei Castelli di Jesi Cl. Sup. Casal di Serra '98	▼▼	3*
○	Bianchello del Metauro '98	▼	2
●	Medoro Marche Sangiovese '97	▼	3
●	Montepulciano d'Abruzzo Jorio '97	▼	3
●	Rosso Conero Serrano '97	▼	3
○	Verdicchio dei Castelli di Jesi Cl. Villa Bianchi '98	▼	3
●	Pelago '95	▽▽	4
●	Rosso Conero Cùmaro '95	▽▽	4

OSTRA VETERE (AN)

F.LLI BUCCI
VIA CONA, 30
60010 OSTRA VETERE (AN)
TEL. 071/964179 - 02/6570558

The reason that the list below contains quantities of white glasses, referring to wines we reviewed last year, is that the new vintages of the Villa Bucci Riserva and the standard Verdicchio had not yet been released when the Guide went to press. However, regular readers will know that the name Fratelli Bucci indicates something out of the ordinary and a guarantee of high and recognizably individual quality. They will also be aware that Ampelio Bucci is never in any rush to put his complex and lasting wines on the market, wines that have it in them to continue developing over quite a long time. The estate has 15 hectares planted to verdicchio and another five where they grow grapes for red wine (mainly sangiovese and montepulciano). Five vineyards contribute to their Verdicchios, each with its own particular altitude and exposure, and each one's grapes are vinified separately before assemblage. We are in a position to say that the buttery quality and almondy note that were just suggested on the palate of the '97 Verdicchio last year have now come out beautifully. The Villa Bucci Riserva '95 currently offers a complex bouquet featuring hazelnut and hints of citrus fruit, and a variegated palate, richly suggestive and well structured, yet not in the least aggressive. The Rosso Piceno Pongelli '97, the only new release, is somewhat atypical for this area, being easy to drink and fairly elegant, especially on the palate.

●	Rosso Piceno Tenuta Pongelli '97	▼	3
○	Verdicchio dei Castelli di Jesi Cl. '96	▽▽	3
○	Verdicchio dei Castelli di Jesi Cl. '97	▽▽	3
○	Verdicchio dei Castelli di Jesi Cl. Villa Bucci '90	▽▽	5
○	Verdicchio dei Castelli di Jesi Cl. Villa Bucci '92	▽▽	4
○	Verdicchio dei Castelli di Jesi Cl. Villa Bucci '94	▽▽	4
○	Verdicchio dei Castelli di Jesi Cl. Villa Bucci Ris. '95	▽▽	5

PESARO

FATTORIA MANCINI
STRADA DEI COLLI, 35
61100 PESARO
TEL. 0721/51828

This year provides further proof of the excellent raw material available to the Fattoria Mancini, and of their determination to do their best with it. The estate is located in the San Bartolo park, just inland from Pesaro, and the vineyards are planted to albanella, sauvignon blanc, montepulciano, trebbiano and sangiovese; some particular plots (nine hectares out of the total 34) are dedicated to the cultivation of pinot nero, the pride of the estate. The Roncaglia '98 (85% albanella with pinot nero) is pleasingly drinkable, thanks largely to its distinct freshness, although its nose is a little dumb at first. The Roncaglia Valserpe '97 is a blend of pinot nero, albanella and trebbiano aged in barriques. It has almost forward mineral and ripe fruit aromas, greater structure on the palate than the basic Roncaglia and a well-defined, clean finish. The Pinot Nero Impero '97, whose grapes are grown on vines yielding only around 30 quintals per hectare, is light ruby in color and displays a fragrance of geranium, juniper and sweet spice not muffled by toasty oak; the decidedly attractive palate reflects the nose and displays fine tannins: a Pinot that is well worth Two Glasses. The appealing Colli Pesaresi Sangiovese '98 has a pleasing grapiness and carries through nicely from nose to palate, while the '97 Focara Rosso, the first vintage to be aged in barrique, is definitely a more important wine. The delightfully drinkable, fragrant rosé version of the '98 Pinot Nero is more pleasing to the palate than satisfying to the nose. We close with the Valserpe '98 which, unlike the '97, is not a DOC; it's a blend of albanella, white-vinified pinot nero and a small amount of sauvignon with a complex bouquet and a broad and mouth-filling palate.

● Impero Marche Pinot Nero '97	▼▼	4
○ Valserpe '98	▼▼	3*
○ Colli Pesaresi Bianco Roncaglia '98	▼	2
○ Colli Pesaresi Bianco Roncaglia Valserpe '97	▼	2
⊙ Marche Pinot Nero '98	▼	3
● Colli Pesaresi Focara Rosso '97	▼	3
● Colli Pesaresi Sangiovese '98		2

POGGIO S. MARCELLO (AN)

SARTARELLI
VIA COSTE DEL MULINO, 26
60030 POGGIO S. MARCELLO (AN)
TEL. 0731/89732 - 0731/89571

The astounding thing about Sartarelli wines is the elegance and finesse they display despite alcohol levels comparable to those of full-bodied reds. But whether it's due to the exposure of the vineyards, the late harvest of the grapes or a seemingly unfailing vinification method, this estate seems always to turn out good wines. Let's start with the standard Verdicchio '98, a wine of exemplary style with fairly intense and fragrant varietal aromas and a well-balanced, crisply tart and concentrated palate. The Tralivio '98, with the distinctive Verdicchio greenish straw yellow color, boasts a rich bouquet including hazelnut, Golden Delicious apple and wisteria. On the palate it is lively, soft and extremely concentrated, with a delicately almondy finish. The Contrada Balciana '97 shows once more how versatile Verdicchio can be. Produced in '94 and '95 but not in '96, it now returns in fabulous form: the color is deep yellow with green and gold nuances; the bouquet practically explodes with ripe apple, honey, thyme, clove and musk; the appealingly unctuous, soft, fat palate shows remarkable concentration, finesse and elegance and an appealingly bitter finish. This version has great character and fully earns its Three Glasses. Our hats are off to Patrizio Chiacchierini and his wife Donatella Sartarelli who, by reducing yields, harvesting sequentially throughout September and October and constantly perfecting their cellar technique, continue to bring forth such gems.

○ Verdicchio dei Castelli di Jesi Cl. Sup. Contrada Balciana '97	▼▼▼	4
○ Verdicchio dei Castelli di Jesi Cl. '98	▼▼	2*
○ Verdicchio dei Castelli di Jesi Cl. Sup. Tralivio '98	▼▼	3
○ Verdicchio dei Castelli di Jesi Cl. Sup. Contrada Balciana '94	▽▽▽	4
○ Verdicchio dei Castelli di Jesi Cl. Sup. Contrada Balciana '95	▽▽▽	4
○ Verdicchio dei Castelli di Jesi Cl. Sup. Tralivio '97	▽▽	3

RIPATRANSONE (AP)

Tenuta Cocci Grifoni

C.da Messieri, 12
Fraz. S. Savino
63030 Ripatransone (AP)
tel. 0735/90143

Guido Cocci Grifone, legendary winegrower of the Piceno area, who is assisted by his daughters Paola and Marilena, is a point of reference for local producers. After studying and experimenting with the pecorino and passerina grapes, he is now working on a new red, to be released next year, which, to judge from our first tastes from the barrel, seems very promising indeed. But to get down to what he actually presented, the Podere Colle Vecchio '98 has a mineral nose with notes of wet grass and hay, and good body with considerable structure. The Falerio Vigneti San Basso '98, straw yellow tinged with green, is redolent of hazelnut and green apple, while the palate shows good balance between softness and acidity. The unfailingly appealing Passerina Brut, as good as ever, provides further proof of the suitability of this variety for making sparkling wine. The Rosso Piceno Superiore Vigna Messieri, after a few years below par, is back up to scratch with the '97. Its fairly concentrated ruby hue leads to a nose with lots of ripe fruit and notes of coffee and vanilla; the long palate promises good development over time. Both standard versions of the local DOCs are sound, more notably the Rosso Piceno Superiore '97.

○ Podere Colle Vecchio '98	▼▼	3*
● Rosso Piceno Sup. Vigna Messieri '97	▼▼	3*
○ Falerio dei Colli Ascolani Vigneti S. Basso '98	▼	2
○ Passerina Brut	▼	3
● Rosso Piceno Sup. '97	▼	3
○ Falerio dei Colli Ascolani '98		2
○ Podere Colle Vecchio '97	▽▽	3
● Rosso Piceno Sup. Vigna Messieri '95	▽▽	3
● Rosso Piceno Sup. Vigna Messieri '96	▽	3

RIPATRANSONE (AP)

Le Caniette

Via Canali, 23
63038 Ripatransone (AP)
tel. 0735/9200

After last year's debut in the Guide, this estate has lived up to its promise. Let's consider the whites: the Lucrezia '98, a Falerio selection, displays notes of chamomile and ripe damson on the nose; the palate is structured and lingering. The second Falerio, Veronica '98, is crisp and more immediate, with an unusual floral nose. The Vagnoni family is proceeding with its efforts to make something of Vin Santo di Ripatransone: the '95 is the second vintage of their Sibilla Ellespontica, produced entirely from semi-dried passerina grapes. Of a deep golden color, it offers a toasty bouquet of dried fruit, nuts and dates. It has taken a great leap forward since last year's version and is now unquestionably one of the best raisin wines in the Marche. Now for the reds: the Morellone '97, of a lovely concentrated red color, offers aromas of red berries mixed with vanilla and leather, but also, alas, a sulfurous note; the long palate has a slightly bitter finish. The other Rosso Piceno, Rosso Bello '97, has a light ruby color and oaky notes, revealing its brief stay in wood. It is agreeably easy to drink.

○ Falerio dei Colli Ascolani Lucrezia '98	▼▼	2*
○ Sibilla Ellespontica '95	▼▼	4
○ Falerio dei Colli Ascolani Veronica '98	▼	2
● Rosso Piceno Morellone '97	▼	3
● Rosso Piceno Rosso Bello '97		2

SERRA DE' CONTI (AN)

CASALFARNETO
VIA FARNETO, 16
60030 SERRA DE' CONTI (AN)
TEL. 0731/889001

Casalfarneto, a relative newcomer to the Guide, has not disappointed us: its wines have body and sinew, even in very hot, dry years like '98. The key to this is consistently wide daily temperature variations during September and an assemblage of grapes from vineyards with different exposures. The 23 hectares under vine are planted principally to verdicchio, but there's been a recent planting of montepulciano, sangiovese, cabernet sauvignon and merlot. The '98 vintage represents the third year of production in their up-to-the-minute cellar set up in a farmhouse on the property. The two '98s, each a version of Verdicchio dei Castelli di Jesi Classico Superiore DOC, are called Gran Casale and Fontevecchia. The former, of which 12 thousand bottles have been produced, shows a clear and bright deep straw yellow color with highlights ranging from green to pale gold and notable legs, indicating richness of structure. The deep and complex nose features aromas of linden blossom, tropical fruit and apple, as well as a delicate vegetal hint. The elegant palate balances a pleasingly fragrant quality with a meaty structure; it develops with intensity to an appropriately varietal slightly bitter finish. The Fontevecchia, 40 thousand bottles strong, is an exemplary Verdicchio Classico. Its clearly green-tinged straw hue introduces well-defined aromas of fresh fruit and acacia flowers. The generous palate is supported by reasonable structure which, together with a refreshing acidity, makes for agreeable drinking and a cleanly delineated finish.

○ Verdicchio dei Castelli di Jesi Cl. Sup. Fontevecchia '98	🍷🍷	2*
○ Verdicchio dei Castelli di Jesi Cl. Sup. Gran Casale '98	🍷🍷	3*
○ Verdicchio dei Castelli di Jesi Cl. Gran Casale '97	♀♀	3

SPINETOLI (AP)

SALADINI PILASTRI
VIA SALADINI, 5
63030 SPINETOLI (AP)
TEL. 0736/899534

This estate, established in the early '70s, just when the local wines won their DOC status, has provided very convincing evidence of a desire to aim now for excellence in all its wines. Furthermore, viticulture here has become rigorously organic. Last year's leading wine, the Rosso Piceno selection Vigna Piediprato '97, was in the vanguard of Piceno wines made in a more modern style. The currently available new version, the '98, had the oenologist Domenico D'Angelo as midwife, with the advice of Roberto Cipresso, and it too captured our attention at the first glance. Its color is dense and dark; the bouquet, not yet altogether open, is very elegant, and the palate is smooth, concentrated and stylish. A companion bottle is the new Rosso Piceno Superiore selection, Vigna Monteprandone '97, which was identified at our tastings as one of the best Marche reds: it is concentrated and complex both in its aromas of spice, plum and wild cherry, and on its broad, soft palate. We greatly admired the standard Rosso Piceno '98, a wine of exemplary style and quaffability. The two Falerio dei Colli Ascolani '98s, the basic version and the cru Vigna Palazzi, are both good. The former is crisper, the latter has more substance, with riper fruitiness and fuller body. A final white deserves our attention: the Pregio del Conte Bianco, made from different grapes (80% fiano and falanghina). An inviting citrus bouquet leads to a structured and soft palate.

● Rosso Piceno Sup. Vigna Monteprandone '97	🍷🍷	4
● Rosso Piceno Vigna Piediprato '98	🍷🍷	3*
○ Pregio del Conte Bianco '98	🍷🍷	2*
○ Falerio dei Colli Ascolani '98	🍷	1
○ Falerio dei Colli Ascolani Vigna Palazzi '98	🍷	2
● Rosso Piceno '98	🍷	3
● Rosso Piceno Vigna Piediprato '97	♀♀	3

STAFFOLO (AN)

Fattoria Coroncino
C.da Coroncino, 7
60039 Staffolo (AN)
tel. 0731/779494

After last year's triumphal Three Glasses for the Gaiospino '97, Fattoria Coroncino has presented four wines, all of which are up to its habitual high standards and give evidence of constantly improving admirable methods, including exemplary reduction of yields, rigorous grape selection and impeccable vinification techniques. But all of this is second nature to Lucio and Fiorella Canestrari, whose dedication to excellence has led them to produce, with enviable regularity, elegant, soft, powerful and distinctly varietal wines. The '98 vintage was certainly not favorable to white grapes: an oppressively hot and humid summer with very little rain and not much relief at night tended to 'cook' the grapes, which lost acidity. Nevertheless this estate turned up trumps. Le Lame, a straw-colored pure trebbiano, has a delicate but noticeable bouquet with banana to the fore, and a crisp, soft palate with an elegant finish. The Verdicchio dei Castelli di Jesi Staffilo '98, the estate's bread and butter, is straightforward and characteristic, both in its green-toned straw yellow hue and in its distinct floral aromas, nicely balanced by a crisp structure. Yet its price is modest. The Verdicchio Bacco '98, one step up in bouquet and structure, is a little closed at first, but then discloses its full panoply of aromas and tastes. The Coroncino '98 shows quite remarkable structure and concentration. Its fully expressed rich aromas include green leaves, ripe fruit, apple and linden blossom, while the palate is soft and well balanced between its abundant alcohol and fragrant acidity. The '98 Gaiospina, the estate's leading wine, is still maturing in the cellar.

○	Verdicchio dei Castelli di Jesi Cl. Sup. Il Coroncino '98	🍷🍷	3*
○	Le Lame '98	🍷	3
○	Verdicchio dei Castelli di Jesi Cl. Staffilo '98	🍷	1*
○	Verdicchio dei Castelli di Jesi Cl. Sup. Bacco '98	🍷	2
○	Verdicchio dei Castelli di Jesi Cl. Sup. Gaiospino '97	🍷🍷🍷	3
○	Verdicchio dei Castelli di Jesi Cl. Sup. Gaiospino '96	🍷🍷	3

STAFFOLO (AN)

Fonte della Luna
Via S. Francesco, 1
60039 Staffolo (AN)
tel. 0731/779307

The Verdicchio dei Castelli di Jesi on offer is becoming ever richer and more various. Many small estates have begun to make a name for themselves, reducing their quantity of bulk wine, bottling more and improving quality. Those with a clear strategy, willingness to invest and technical ability are most likely to succeed. Medoro Cimarelli's Fonte della Luna is such a one, and makes its debut in the Guide thanks to splendid results at our blind tastings. Medoro's son Luca is in charge in the cellar, and, with the help of the agronomist and oenologist Giancarlo Soverchia, he has produced brilliant wines, available at amazingly affordable prices. The standard Verdicchio dei Castelli di Jesi has the full spectrum of classic Verdicchio characteristics: a yellow hue verging on brilliant green; an array of aromas with prominent white flowers and peach; a firm structure with a rich, extremely soft palate. Perhaps it wants a little more crispness, but this is typical of '98 Verdicchios because of the dry, hot year. The Fra Moriale, a special selection that shows what power this grape is capable of, has a deep straw yellow color with highlights ranging from grey to greenish gold; the direct and extremely intense aromas suggest dried apricot and quince; remarkable structure blends with a general softness and an opulent, satisfying fruitiness. Il Grizio is a Rosso Piceno made from montepulciano and sangiovese. The distinct notes of ripe cherry on the nose are echoed on the seductively velvety palate; silky tannins are perfectly balanced by a notable structure, which bodes well for its development.

●	Rosso Piceno Grizio '98	🍷🍷	3*
○	Verdicchio dei Castelli di Jesi Cl. Fra Moriale '98	🍷🍷	3*
○	Verdicchio dei Castelli di Jesi Cl. '98	🍷	2*

OTHER WINERIES

The following producers obtained good scores in our tastings with one or more of their wines:

PROVINCE OF ANCONA

Antonio Canestrari, Apiro, tel. 0733/611315
Verdicchio dei Castelli di Jesi Cl.
Moja Cupa '98

Umberto Socci
Castelplanio, tel. 071/9160725
Verdicchio dei Castelli di Jesi Cl. Sup.
Deserto '98

Anna Maria Strozzi
Castelplanio, tel. 0731/813006
Verdicchio dei Castelli di Jesi Cl. Sup.
Tenuta dell'Ugolino '98

Mancini, Maiolati Spontini, tel. 0731/702975
Verdicchio dei Castelli di Jesi Cl.
Santa Lucia '98

Crognaletti, Montecarotto, tel. 0731/779307
Verdicchio dei Castelli di Jesi Cl.
Vigneto delle Oche '98

Donatella Paoloni
Montecarotto, tel. 0731/889004
Verdicchio dei Castelli di Jesi Cl.
Sabbionare '98

Poggio Montali
Monteroberto, tel. 0731/702825
Verdicchio dei Castelli di Jesi Cl. Sup. '98

Malacri, Offagna, tel. 071/7107002
Rosso Conero '97

Marconi, S. Marcello, tel. 0731/267374
Verdicchio dei Castelli di Jesi Cl.
Corona Reale '98

Maurizio Benigni
S. Paolo di Jesi, tel. 0731/704042
Verdicchio dei Castelli di Jesi Cl.
La Scappia '98

Amato Ceci
S. Paolo di Jesi, tel. 0731/779052
Verdicchio dei Castelli di Jesi Cl. Sup.
Vignamato '98

Angelo Accadia
Serra S. Quirico, tel. 0731/85172
Verdicchio dei Castelli di Jesi Cl. Cantori '98

Esther Hauser, Staffolo, tel. 0731/770203
Cupo Rosso '97

F.lli Zaccagnini & C.
Staffolo, tel. 0731/779892
Verdicchio dei Castelli di Jesi Cl. '98

PROVINCE OF ASCOLI PICENO

Cantina di Castignano
Castignano, tel. 0736/822216
Gramelot '98

Aurora, Offida, tel. 0736/880902
Rosso Piceno Sup. '97

La Cantina dei Colli Ripani
Ripatransone, tel. 0735/99940
Rosso Leo Ripanus '97

San Savino, Ripatransone, tel. 0735/90107
Moggio '97

PROVINCE OF MACERATA

Saputi, Colmurano, tel. 0733/508137
Rosso Piceno Castru Vecchiu '97

Castiglioni - F.lli Bisci
Matelica, tel. 0737/787490
Verdicchio di Matelica '98

Fattoria dei Cavalieri
Matelica, tel. 0737/84024
Verdicchio di Matelica
Fattoria dei Cavalieri '98

San Biagio, Matelica, tel. 0737/83997
Grottagrifone '97

Lanfranco Quacquarini
Serrapetrona, tel. 0733/908103
Vernaccia di Serrapetrona Secco '98

Massimo Serboni
Serrapetrona, tel. 0733/904088
Vernaccia di Serrapetrona Secco Ris. '97

PROVINCE OF PESARO

Fattoria Ligi
Pergola, tel. 0721/734351
Vernaculum Grifoleto '98

Anzilotti Solazzi
Saltara, tel. 0721/895491
Bianchello del Metauro '98

UMBRIA

Umbria is moving forward fast, almost dizzyingly fast. Last year three wines achieved Three Glasses, which is a good performance for such a small region. This year there are five. This is, making allowances for relative size, like Piedmont's 50, which is as good as it gets (at the moment). After years of more or less veiled criticisms about the lack of a clear orientation towards quality and the non-existence of a sensible plan of development, here are the first answers. Of course the high spots are still isolated, though less so than it might appear; but each award reflects an individual success. For two of the winners, La Palazzola with its Merlot and Còlpetrone with its Sagrantino, this is a new honor. A further two, Antinori's Castello della Sala, now gathering up its tenth recognition, and the Caprai from Montefalco, with its fourth successive trophy, cause more surprise when they don't reach the prizewinners' rostrum than in years like this when they do. The fifth, Giovanni Dubini's Il Palazzone estate, is welcome back with the Armaleo after a brief interval; their return is a confirmation of an achieved level of excellence. Of course they can always feel the effects of a poor vintage, but their foundations are quite firm. These five producers were certainly not working in concert. They have simply placed themselves in a sort of top-level oenological Gulf Stream, in which there is an international exchange of ideas and techniques, alliances are formed, fairs and tastings are attended and, generally, cross-fertilization takes place among estates. This is what has been missing in Umbria – and still is for many producers, those who stay holed up in their estates like feudal lords without the desire or the courage to be pitted against the best, be it regionally or from further afield. However, such attitudes are becoming ever rarer. The wine world changes quickly and the Umbrians, whether from private estates or cooperatives, seem to have noticed. Within the region, Montefalco is again an emerging terroir, as is Orvieto, which, apart from the starry classic Cervaro, is gaining ever more prestige from its reds. In addition, Colli del Trasimeno, after years of stasis, is finally making headway. Several of its estates have received important recognition at home and abroad, and others may well soon join them. But a ferment of new ideas and projects has stirred up the whole region and no zone is excluded. This year's stars are Caprai with the Sagrantino di Montefalco 25 Anni '96, Castello della Sala with the Cervaro della Sala '97, Còlpetrone with the Sagrantino di Montefalco '96, La Palazzola at Stroncone with the Merlot '97 and Palazzone in Orvieto with the Armaleo '97: five outstanding wines to remind us that Umbria is one of the top wine-making areas in Italy - and hence in the world.

AMELIA (TR)

Cantina Sociale dei Colli Amerini
Loc. Fornole
Strada Amerina km 7.100
05020 Amelia (TR)
tel. 0744/989721

This cooperative deals in big numbers: its range includes numerous wines, it produces large numbers of bottles and it has collected a vast number of Glasses. We'll start at the top, with the Colli Amerini Rosso Superiore Carbio '97 and the Merlot dell'Umbria Olmeto '97: both are concentrated and elegant and easily win Two Glasses apiece; the Merlot is also remarkably good value for money. The One Glass wines are the Chardonnay dell'Umbria Amiro '98, which is fresh, intense and attractive; the Chardonnay dell'Umbria Rocca Nerina '97, with lots of power but a slight imbalance between fruit and oak; and the Grechetto dell'Umbria Il Vignolo '98, a fine example of the variety's potential. The Grechetto Villa Gioconda '97 is less exciting: here too the oak has resisted blending. The Malvasia dei Colli Amerini La Corte '98 gives a delightful repeat performance. It is fresh, fragrant and structured. The Sangiovese dell'Umbria Il Torraccio '97 seemed slightly below par. The Colli Amerini Terre Arnolfe Rosso '98 is a young fresh red of excellent quality and very good value, while the Aleatico dell'Umbria Bartolomeo '97 is an attractive red dessert wine. A mention goes to the clean, fragrant Colli Amerini Rosato Terre Arnolfe '98, the only Umbrian rosé in the Guide. Lack of space brings us to a halt, leaving just enough room to note that this range of wines is always among the most reliable in the region.

●	Colli Am. Rosso Sup. Carbio '97	🍷🍷	4
●	Merlot dell'Umbria Olmeto '97	🍷🍷	3*
●	Aleatico dell'Umbria Bartolomeo '97	🍷	4
○	Chardonnay dell'Umbria Amiro '98	🍷	2*
○	Colli Am. Chardonnay Rocca Nerina '97	🍷	3
○	Colli Am. Grechetto Il Vignolo '98	🍷	2*
○	Colli Am. Grechetto Villa Gioconda '97	🍷	3
○	Colli Am. Malvasia La Corte '98	🍷	2*
●	Colli Am. Rosso Terre Arnolfe '98	🍷	2*
●	Sangiovese del'Umbria Torraccio '97	🍷	3
⊙	Colli Am. Rosato Terre Arnolfe '98		2

BASCHI (TR)

Barberani - Vallesanta
Loc. Cerreto
05023 Baschi (TR)
tel. 0744/950113

The '97 vintage, a great one for Calcaia, brings Two Glasses to Barberani. The wine is certainly the flagship of the estate: an enormously rich, fat Orvieto Classico Muffa Nobile (noble rot). The result is all the more remarkable given the traditional blend: 85% consists of local grapes (procanico, verdello, grechetto, malvasia and drupeggio). Its length and complexity make it an ideal accompaniment to aged or blue cheeses as well as, of course, desserts. Unfortunately, the situation is different for the '97 Foresco, a red from sangiovese and cabernet which has come close to Three Glasses in past years. A vintage like '97 could have nudged it up into the company of central Italy's great wines. But the wine shone neither for power nor for concentration at our tastings and it gets One Glass. The interesting barrique-aged Moscato Passito Villa Monticelli '98 furnishes further proof of the estate's aptitude for dessert wines. The Orvieto Classico Castagnolo '98 and the Grechetto '98 did well too. Both are fresh and characteristic whites that admirably express the qualities of the area and of the local varieties. To round up, we mention the Polago '98, a young red from sangiovese (70%) and montepulciano (30%) which had the same difficulties as the estate's other reds.

○	Orvieto Classico Sup. Calcaia '97	🍷🍷	5
●	Foresco '97	🍷	4
○	Grechetto '98	🍷	3
○	Moscato Passito Villa Monticelli '98	🍷	6
○	Orvieto Classico Castagnolo '98	🍷	3
●	Polago '98		3
●	Foresco '93	🍸🍸	4
○	Moscato Passito Villa Monticelli '97	🍸🍸	6
○	Orvieto Classico Sup. Calcaia '92	🍸🍸	5
○	Orvieto Classico Sup. Calcaia '93	🍸🍸	5
○	Orvieto Classico Sup. Calcaia '94	🍸🍸	5
○	Orvieto Classico Sup. Calcaia '95	🍸🍸	5
●	Foresco '94	🍸	4
●	Foresco '95	🍸	4
●	Foresco '96	🍸	4

BEVAGNA (PG)

F.LLI ADANTI
LOC. ARQUATA
06031 BEVAGNA (PG)
TEL. 0742/360295

Adanti, near Bevagna, nestled between the hillsides of Arquata and Colcimino, is again producing wines worthy of its long-standing reputation and is back in the Guide after several years' absence. The winery, built on the ruins of an old monastery, has excellent up-to-the-minute equipment. On their roughly 20 hectares under vine they grow quite a variety of grapes, from the traditional grechetto and sagrantino to barbera and sangiovese and the inevitable 'international' varieties, chardonnay, merlot and cabernet. We'll start with the Rosso dell'Umbria Arquata '94, which may have been released a little late but is still a good, fresh, clean, heady and appropriately tannic wine. The Rosso di Montefalco, from the fine '97 vintage, wants more definition on the nose but has attractive spicy notes and a soft, lean palate. The Bianco di Montefalco '98 is straightforward and pleasantly quaffable. Our favorite was the fragrant Sagrantino Passito '95, with its overripe notes of stewed prunes on the nose and a very fruity and lingering palate with good extract. The standard Sagrantino '95 rates a mention, but we expected more from it.

●	Sagrantino di Montefalco Passito '95	🍷🍷	5
○	Bianco di Montefalco '98	🍷	3
●	Rosso dell'Umbria Arquata '94	🍷	3
●	Rosso di Montefalco '97	🍷	3
●	Sagrantino di Montefalco '95		5
●	Rosso dell'Umbria Arquata '91	🍷🍷 (past)	4
●	Rosso di Montefalco '91	🍷 (past)	2*
●	Sagrantino di Montefalco '90	🍷 (past)	3
●	Sagrantino di Montefalco Passito '89	🍷 (past)	4

BEVAGNA (PG)

FATTORIA MILZIADE ANTANO
LOC. COLLE ALLODOLE
06031 BEVAGNA (PG)
TEL. 0742/360371

It is a pleasure, after his return to the Guide last year, to be writing again about this enthusiastic producer from the Montefalco district. The estate concentrates on reds and has rung up good scores for all its DOC wines, starting with the excellent versions – three this time – of Rosso di Montefalco. The ruby-hued '95 shows distinct aromas of red fruit and notes of incense and bay on the nose, and good body and balance in the mouth. The standard '97 displays a dark purplish red color, a fruity bouquet of blackberry and attendant berries, and a broad, powerful and tannic palate with rich notes of ripe red fruit. The excellent '97 Riserva is redolent of berries and, on the palate, clean, ample and well-structured. The two versions of Sagrantino di Montefalco won One Glass each. The '94 is traditional in style: ruby in color, overripe on the nose, warm and tannic in the mouth, while the '96 has a richer and more elegant bouquet of fresher red fruit, and good structure and softness on the palate. We close with the remarkable Sagrantino di Montefalco Passito '96 which, with its richness of fragrance and its warm, properly tannic palate, easily walks off with Two Glasses.

●	Rosso di Montefalco '97	🍷🍷	3*
●	Rosso di Montefalco Ris. '97	🍷🍷	3*
●	Sagrantino di Montefalco Passito '96	🍷🍷	5
●	Rosso di Montefalco '95	🍷	3
●	Sagrantino di Montefalco '94	🍷	5
●	Sagrantino di Montefalco '96	🍷	5
●	Sagrantino di Montefalco '95	🍷🍷 (past)	5
●	Sagrantino di Montefalco Passito '94	🍷🍷 (past)	5
●	Rosso di Montefalco '94	🍷 (past)	3

CANNARA (PG)

Di Filippo
Via Conversino, 160
06033 Cannara (PG)
tel. 0742/72310

Here is a surprising debut in the Guide for a little-known estate in the province of Perugia. Without exception, all the wines presented did very well at our tastings. Di Filippo proudly adheres to strict organic principles throughout every stage of production, from vineyard management to the various phases of wine-making and aging. The range includes quite a wide selection of regional wines. To start, there is an excellent Rosso dell'Umbria, the Madrigale '96, a blend of merlot, montepulciano and sangiovese that shows great harmony and depth. Dark ruby in hue, it offers intense aromas of ripe berries with a hint of tar and pencil lead. The rich palate shows good extract and medium-knit, non-astringent tannins. It fully earns its Two Glasses. The very attractive Colli Martini Sangiovese Properzio '97 is clean, fragrant, lively and forthright, if not particularly complex. The other two reds we tasted, the Terre di San Nicola '96 (merlot, montepulciano, barbera) and the Villa Conversino '98 (sangiovese, montepulciano, barbera, ciliegiolo) are properly made and simpler. Of the whites we particularly liked the succulent Grechetto Terre di San Nicola '98, with its well-judged alcohol. The Villa di Conversino Bianco, also '98, seems a little less appealing.

●	Madrigale '96	🍷🍷	4
○	Colli Martani Grechetto Terre di S. Nicola '98	🍷	2*
●	Colli Martani Sangiovese Properzio '97	🍷	3
●	Terre di S. Nicola Rosso '96	🍷	3
●	Villa Conversino Rosso '98	🍷	1*
○	Villa Conversino Bianco '98		1

CASTEL VISCARDO (TR)

Cantina Monrubio
Fraz. Monterubiaglio
Loc. Le Prese, 22
05014 Castel Viscardo (TR)
tel. 0763/66064

Cantina Monrubio is the new name of Vi.C.Or in Castel Viscardo. This large cooperative winery, founded in 1957, includes 300 member growers and has for some years been one of the most interesting and dynamic co-ops in the region. Their successful wines in recent years are the result of a shift in policy favoring high quality, which shift was accelerated and focused by the arrival of the celebrated and skilled consultant oenologist Riccardo Cotarella to direct the cellar. The wine that impressed us most at this year's tastings was the red Monrubio '98, a blend of sangiovese with ciliegiolo, montepulciano and small quantities of merlot and pinot nero. After fermentation it is aged for a few months, first in barriques, then in bottles. It shows a dark ruby color and an intense nose with scents of ripe red fruit, sweet spice and licorice; the palate is rich, concentrated, and soft and the tannins show finesse. The estate's other red, the Palaia '97, from merlot, pinot nero and cabernet, shows a lovely vivid color with a youthful purple cast, and considerable depth and richness, but it needs a few more months of aging to acquire balance. Of the whites, all Orvieto DOC '98s, we particularly liked the Soana with its bright green-tinged color, bouquet of attractive fruit and elegant vegetal and herbal nuances, and crisply acidic and fruity palate. The Salceto and the Roio also got One Glass each.

●	Monrubio '98	🍷🍷	2*
○	Orvieto Classico Roio '98	🍷	2*
○	Orvieto Classico Salceto '98	🍷	2*
○	Orvieto Classico Sup. Soana '98	🍷	2*
●	Palaia '97	🍷	3
●	L'Olmaia '96	YY	4
○	Orvieto Classico Roio '97	Y	1*
○	Orvieto Classico Salceto '97	Y	2*
○	Orvieto Classico Sup. Fiorile '97	Y	3

CASTIGLIONE DEL LAGO (PG)

FANINI
C.DA CUCCHI
LOC. PETRIGNANO DEL LAGO
06060 CASTIGLIONE DEL LAGO (PG)
TEL. 075/9528116

Further evidence of the progress being made by Umbrian wineries is the second appearance of Fanini in the Guide. Situated on the slopes near Lake Trasimeno, this interesting estate has again produced a good selection of wines. The best, as before, is the Robbiano '97, a 100% chardonnay fermented and aged for about six months in Allier barriques. It shows a deep straw yellow color; the intense and complex bouquet features distinct notes of white-fleshed fruit and well-judged oak; the broad, fat palate offers good body and excellent balance between its fruit and the sweet oak-derived tone. It is an excellent white wine, both complex and powerful. Fanini's only red is good too: the Colli del Trasimeno Morello del Lago '96, from sangiovese, gamay and canaiolo. Of a ruby hue, it opens on the nose with intense and lingering fruity tones, which are given complexity by secondary notes of oriental spice. The palate is fruity, clean and intense, perhaps a touch less structured than the '95, but still most enjoyable. To finish, the Colli del Trasimeno Bianco Albello del Lago '98 (from trebbiano toscano, malvasia and grechetto) receives no more than a mention as it is slightly disappointing on both nose and palate.

○	Chardonnay Robbiano '97	🍷🍷	3*
●	Colli del Trasimeno Rosso Morello del Lago '96	🍷	3
○	Colli del Trasimeno Bianco Albello del Lago '98		2
○	Chardonnay Robbiano '96	🍷🍷 (white)	3*
●	Colli del Trasimeno Rosso Morello del Lago '95	🍷🍷 (white)	3*

CITTÀ DELLA PIEVE (PG)

DUCA DELLA CORGNA
VIA PO' DI MEZZO
06064 CITTÀ DELLA PIEVE (PG)
TEL. 075/9652493 - 075/9653210

The Cantina del Trasimeno is one of the Umbrian cooperatives that have recently made a serious move towards high quality. With a strong base of 270 member growers and the valuable advice of the consultant Andrea Mazzoni, they produce some 250 thousand bottles a year. In these pages we consider only their special line, Duca della Corgna, the result of a project involving the most highly prized and best sited vineyards in the Colli del Trasimento district, which are then managed with extreme care by those growers who have chosen to take part: dense plantings, hard pruning, rigorous thinning and low yields per vine are the order of the day. Only these vineyards may yield Duca della Corgna wines, which are all barrel-aged and then further aged in the bottle, in the recently restored medieval cellar of what was once the Ducal Palace in Città della Pieve. At this year's tastings we particularly admired the Colli del Trasimeno Rosso Corniolo '97, a richly structured, soft wine with fine tannins, elegance and good concentration: an easy Two Glasses. The very good Gamay '97 (starting with the '98 vintage, Gamay and Grechetto will be Colli del Trasimeno DOCs), shows intense, fruity aromas, and good structure in the mouth, with attractive tones of spice and vanilla.

●	Colli del Trasimeno Rosso Corniolo '97	🍷🍷	3*
●	Gamay dell'Umbria '97	🍷	3

CIVITELLA DEL LAGO (TR)

TENUTA DI SALVIANO
LOC. SALVIANO
05020 CIVITELLA DEL LAGO (TR)
TEL. 0744/950459

This was not a great year for Tenuta di Salviano, which had always impressed us with the quality and consistency of its wines. The top bottle of this lovely winery, which is in a beautiful medieval village in the heart of the Umbrian countryside, is the Orvieto Classico, and the '98 does comfortably reach One Glass. Fresh and captivating on the nose, with notes of apple and white-fleshed fruit, it is a little disappointing on the palate, which, despite careful vinification, is somewhat thin. It is, however, clean, balanced, soft and a pleasure to drink, but without its usual concentration. The red Turlò '97 also gets One Glass but it shows more energy. Its color is a bright deep ruby and the nose releases appealing notes of berries. Once again, though, a little more concentration and length would have been welcome: it finishes before yielding the breadth of sensations one would expect from a '97 red. This seems a transitional year for the estate. On the basis of the excellent wines presented in previous years, we feel it's reasonable to expect that next year will see a return to high standards.

○	Orvieto Classico Salviano '98	🍷	3
●	Rosso dell'Umbria Turlò '97	🍷	3
○	Orvieto Classico Salviano '95	🍸🍸	2*
○	Orvieto Classico Salviano '96	🍸🍸	3*
○	Orvieto Classico Salviano '97	🍸🍸	3*
○	Vin Santo	🍸🍸	5
●	Lago di Corbara Rosso '95	🍸	2*
●	Lago di Corbara Rosso Turlò '97	🍸	3

CORCIANO (PG)

PIEVE DEL VESCOVO
VIA G. LEOPARDI, 82
06073 CORCIANO (PG)
TEL. 075/6978874

The delightful Iolanda Tinarelli hides (well, partially hides) a will of iron. Her plans for grape-growing and wine-making are simple: a quest for the highest quality, nothing more. The wines of Pieve del Vescovo reflect this attitude. There may not yet have been any Three Glass wines (although Iolanda and her oenologist Riccardo Cotarella have come close several times), but what really matters is that the estate produces wines of high quality with remarkable consistency year after year. Among the most constant is the Lucciaio (mainly merlot with sangiovese, canaiolo and gamay), a really tasty Colli del Trasimeno Rosso. The '97 is rich, full-bodied, soft and elegant, with well-expressed tannins. The ample, fragrant and firm palate has an excellent long finish: Two Glasses without the shadow of a doubt. The standard Colli del Trasimeno Rosso, also a '97, naturally has less complexity and depth but it still shows well, being fresh, succulent, medium-bodied and quite long and quaffable. Of the Colli del Trasimeno whites the Etesiaco '98 stands out, as you might imagine, but the normal version is quite noticeable too. Both are clean and very well made, with abundant crisp acidity and well-judged alcohol, but they are somewhat simple on nose and palate.

●	Colli del Trasimeno Rosso Lucciaio '97	🍷🍷	4
○	Colli del Trasimeno Bianco '98	🍷	2*
○	Colli del Trasimeno Bianco Etesiaco '98	🍷	3
●	Colli del Trasimeno Rosso '97	🍷	2*
○	Colli del Trasimeno Bianco Etesiaco '94	🍸🍸	2*
●	Colli del Trasimeno Rosso '97	🍸🍸	2*
●	Colli del Trasimeno Rosso Lucciaio '94	🍸🍸	3*
●	Colli del Trasimeno Rosso Lucciaio '95	🍸🍸	3*
●	Colli del Trasimeno Rosso Lucciaio '96	🍸🍸	4

FICULLE (TR)

★ CASTELLO DELLA SALA
LOC. SALA
05016 FICULLE (TR)
TEL. 0763/86051

Castello della Sala was the great leader of the changeover in Umbrian viticulture from quantity to quality. It is here that wines that were (and still are) models of style for regional wine-making came into existence. Renzo Cotarella, who has long piloted this estate and is now responsible for all of Antinori's wines, created whites that influenced many producers, both in and beyond the region. That said (and not for the first time), we come to the results of our tastings. The Cervaro della Sala has won, yet again, Three Glasses. The '97 is a worthy heir of its distinguished forebears. It shows a brilliant, warm gold color; the bouquet strikes a clever balance between fruity notes of pineapple, apricot and banana and the mineral notes of flint; there is wonderful harmony on the palate, even though, at the time of our tastings, the oak tone was somewhat insistent: it is ripe, round and firm with a long and corresponding finish. The stripling Chardonnay '98, remarkably harmonious, lively and full, seemed excellent as well. The '96 Pinot Nero, perforce a Mediterranean rather than a Burgundian interpretation, has weight, restraint and good fruit. The Sauvignon '98 displays well-tamed varietal notes and is succulent and crisp. As usual, special praise is due to the Muffato which, in its '97 version, is full, sensual and fragrant, and very nearly got Three Glasses. Lastly, the Orvieto Classico '98 is succulent and good drinking.

○	Cervaro della Sala '97	3 filled glasses	5
○	Chardonnay della Sala '98	2 filled glasses	3*
○	Muffato della Sala '97	2 filled glasses	5
●	Pinot Nero '96	2 filled glasses	5
○	Orvieto Cl. Castello della Sala '98	1 filled glass	2*
○	Sauvignon della Sala '98	1 filled glass	3
○	Cervaro della Sala '88	3 outline glasses	5
○	Cervaro della Sala '89	3 outline glasses	5
○	Cervaro della Sala '90	3 outline glasses	5
○	Cervaro della Sala '92	3 outline glasses	5
○	Cervaro della Sala '93	3 outline glasses	5
○	Cervaro della Sala '94	3 outline glasses	5
○	Cervaro della Sala '95	3 outline glasses	5
○	Cervaro della Sala '96	3 outline glasses	5
○	Muffato della Sala '93	3 outline glasses	5

GUALDO CATTANEO (PG)

CÒLPETRONE
FRAZ. MARCELLANO
LOC. MADONNUCCIA
VIA DELLA COLLINA, 4
06035 GUALDO CATTANEO (PG)
TEL. 0578/767722

Two years ago we wrote that this estate was a revelation; last year we said it was going full steam ahead. This time we can say that it is now among the top producers in Umbria and has, with its Sagrantino '96, won Three Glasses. Còlpetrone belongs to the SAI group and has five hectares under vine (another 13 will start producing next year), under the able management of the young oenologist Lorenzo Landi. The vineyards are planted to the local sagrantino di Montefalco, but also to sangiovese and merlot. The estate has again presented two wines, the exceptional Sagrantino di Montefalco '96 and the Rosso di Montefalco '97, its little brother (but not so little as all that, judging from its score). The former is indeed a revelation. It shows an intense, luminous violet-red hue; the nose has a clear and powerful attack and offers distinct aromas of red fruit and sweet spice; on the palate it is complex, rich and broad, with noble tannins and light, elegant tones of oriental spice. The Rosso di Montefalco, perhaps the best version yet, is excellent. Of a ruby color with a purple cast, it offers inviting fruity aromas of wild blackberry and black currant, accompanied by sweet notes of oak; the broad palate shows good body with elegant tannins and a remarkably clean and long finish. Our congratulations!

●	Sagrantino di Montefalco '96	3 filled glasses	4*
●	Rosso di Montefalco '97	2 filled glasses	3*
●	Rosso di Montefalco '95	2 outline glasses	3*
●	Sagrantino di Montefalco '95	2 outline glasses	4
●	Rosso di Montefalco '93	1 outline glass	3
●	Rosso di Montefalco '96	1 outline glass	3
●	Sagrantino di Montefalco '93	1 outline glass	4

MONTECASTRILLI (TR)

Fattoria Le Poggette

Loc. Le Poggette
05026 Montecastrilli (TR)
tel. 0744/940338

Fattoria Le Poggette, owned by Giorgio Lanzetta, covers 450 hectares, of which 12 are under vine, near Montecastrilli in the province of Terni. The consultant oenologist is the able Claudio Gori. Two wines were presented for tasting this year, both red. We'll start with the succulent Colli Amerini Rosso Superiore '97, made from sangiovese with a small addition of canaiolo. Of a brilliant ruby hue, it offers intense and lingering fruity scents (cherry and sour cherry), rich vegetal tones and light notes of fine spice on the nose. The structured and fruity palate reveals distinct suggestions of plum and cherry and a good tannic finish. It's an admirable wine that once again easily reaches One Glass. The top estate wine, however, is still the Montepulciano Rosso '96 selection, a monovarietal montepulciano d'Abruzzo that ages for18 months in small oak barrels. It shows a luminously bright, intense ruby hue, rich fruity scents with elegant notes of pepper and clove, and sweet oak-derived nuances. Remarkable body, elegant fruit and soft, noble tannins characterize the palate, which has a corresponding, restrained and long finish.

●	Montepulciano '96	▼▼	5
●	Colli Amerini Rosso Superiore '97	▼	3
●	Montepulciano '95	▽▽	5
●	Colli Amerini Rosso Superiore '96	▽	3

MONTEFALCO (PG)

Antonelli - San Marco

Loc. San Marco, 59
06036 Montefalco (PG)
tel. 0742/379158

This established Montefalco estate has considerably improved its range in the past few years and is going to be worth watching. Three of the wines won Two Glasses, a result which is unusually good for Montefalco (for anywhere, come to that) and recognizes the excellent work of the whole Antonelli family and their technical staff. The Sagrantino di Montefalco Passito has always been very carefully made and the '95 is rich, concentrated, powerful and yet - revealing great wine-making skill – elegant. It's a most impressive wine and the best of its category. The very good Sagrantino di Montefalco '96, with its quite distinct sensations of red fruit and its moderate intensity, also garnered Two Glasses. The excellent Grechetto Vigna Tonda '97 may well be the best oak-aged Grechetto we tasted this year. Its Two Glasses arrive thanks to an excellent oak-fruit balance and considerable concentration. The Grechetto Colli Martani '98 and the Trebbiano dei Colli Martani San Marco '98, two whites with medium body and intensity, are good, not for the first time. The only jarring note is the '97 Rosso di Montefalco which rates only a mention. In this company it disappoints.

○	Colli Martani Grechetto Vigna Tonda '97	▼▼	3*
●	Sagrantino di Montefalco '96	▼▼	4
●	Sagrantino di Montefalco Passito '95	▼▼	4
○	Colli Martani Grechetto '98	▼	2*
○	Colli Martani Trebbiano S. Marco '98	▼	2*
●	Rosso di Montefalco '97		3
●	Sagrantino di Montefalco '94	▽▽	4
●	Sagrantino di Montefalco '95	▽▽	4
●	Sagrantino di Montefalco '92	▽	3
●	Sagrantino di Montefalco '93	▽	4
●	Sagrantino di Montefalco Passito '93	▽	4

MONTEFALCO (PG)

Arnaldo Caprai - Val di Maggio
Loc. Torre
06036 Montefalco (PG)
tel. 0742/378802 - 0742/378523

Oenological Umbria may never have seen such a meteoric ascent as that of Caprai in Montefalco. In the past six or seven years this estate has gone from honest anonymity to national and international acclaim, with prizes, medals, awards and goodness knows what all else raining down on it – not without reason, since the wines are indeed excellent. It is all due to the hard work of Marco Caprai and his able team, of which the most celebrated member is the oenologist Attilio Pagli. We'll start with the almost predictable triumph of the Sagrantino del Montefalco 25 Anni: the '96 shows the great power of its predecessors. Of a dense dark red, it makes a forceful impact on the nose with its notes of ripe blackberry, wild cherry and sorb apple beautifully blended with nuances of pencil lead and cocoa. On the palate it is, as usual, massive, full-flavored, soft, very fruity and very long. It hardly needs saying that it gets Three Glasses. Its little brother, the Sagrantino '96, has many of the same features without the same depth, but with not inconsiderable weight: Two Glasses, brimful. Coming back down to earth, we find the Colli Martani Grechetto Grecante '98 and the Montefalco Bianco '98, which are both fresh and attractive. We tasted two versions of the Rosso di Montefalco, the '96 and the '97, and found them very similar: clean, appealingly fruity and straightforward but not simple. The '96 Riserva is richer and more complex, as you might expect. It reveals an intense bouquet and a full body, and has the extract and balance to last for several years in the bottle. The Sagrantino Passito '96 is well executed.

●	Sagrantino di Montefalco 25 Anni '96	▼▼▼	6
●	Rosso di Montefalco Ris. '96	▼▼	5
●	Sagrantino di Montefalco '96	▼▼	6
○	Colli Martani Grechetto Grecante '98	▼	3
○	Montefalco Bianco '98	▼	3
●	Rosso di Montefalco '96	▼	3
●	Rosso di Montefalco '97	▼	3
●	Sagrantino di Montefalco Passito '96	▼	6
●	Sagrantino di Montefalco 25 Anni '94	▽▽▽	6
●	Sagrantino di Montefalco 25 Anni '95	▽▽▽	6

MONTEFALCO (PG)

Rocca di Fabbri
Loc. Fabbri
06036 Montefalco (PG)
tel. 0742/399379

After its debut in the Guide last year, Rocca di Fabbri has again collected a good number of Glasses, a confirmation of a general level of achieved excellence. The Rosso dell'Umbria '97, (they've been thinking about changing the name), succeeded on all counts. A barrique-aged blend of equal parts of cabernet sauvignon and sagrantino, it shows a deep ruby color with vivid purple highlights and, on the nose, clear fruity tones of red currant and bitter cherry and wild cherry. The palate is also richly expressive, thanks to dense extract (notable close-knit tannins in particular). Warm, well-paced and full, it lingers long. Next comes the Rosso di Montefalco '96, good on both nose and palate, with well-expressed aromas of red fruit and an inviting quaffability. The Sagrantino di Montefalco '96 easily takes its place among the One Glass wines: it's properly made and succulent, without being particularly complex or exciting. The Pinot Nero '97 seems a pleasing but somewhat simple version of a variety well known to be extremely tricky to grow and to vinify. The Grechetto dei Colli Martani '98 rates a mention.

●	Rosso dell'Umbria '97	▼▼	4
●	Pinot Nero dell'Umbria '97	▼	5
●	Rosso di Montefalco '96	▼	3
●	Sagrantino di Montefalco '96	▼	4
○	Colli Martani Grechetto '98		3
●	Pinot Nero dell'Umbria '90	▽▽	5
●	Cabernet Sauvignon '90	▽	3
○	Colli Martani Grechetto '97	▽	3
●	Colli Martani Sangiovese Satiro '93	▽	2*
○	Colli Martani Trebbiano '97	▽	3
●	Rosso di Montefalco '95	▽	3
●	Sagrantino di Montefalco '90	▽	3

ORVIETO (TR)

BIGI
LOC. PONTE GIULIO, 3
05018 ORVIETO (TR)
TEL. 0763/316224 - 0763/316391

The '98 Orvieto Classico Torricella is one of the best versions ever and easily earns Two Glasses. This is yet another triumph for Fabrizio Bardi, who shows extraordinary skill in expressing the potential of this terroir. The wine is direct, intense and remarkably balanced, fruity on the nose and warm in the mouth. The very interesting Marrano '97, a barrique-aged white from grechetto, receives only One Glass because the structure, the concentration and the overt oak detract from its elegance. The attractive Grechetto dell'Umbria '98 is a fresh and fruity version with good intensity despite its lightness: One Glass without hesitation. The good news continues: the standard Orvieto '98 also gets One Glass. This is the estate's principal wine and possibly the Orvieto best known to the general public, so it is a delight to be able to recommend it as one of the most reliable wines of central Italy. Red wines continue to gain importance in the Orvieto area and Bigi's are certainly interesting. The Sangiovese Tenuta di Corbara '98 easily earns One Glass and might still improve; wood and fruit are well balanced and there is a good level of intensity. The very appealing Sangiovese dell'Umbria '98, aged in stainless steel, is captivatingly fragrant and fresh.

○	Orvieto Classico Vigneto Torricella '98	🍷🍷	3*
○	Grechetto dell'Umbria '98	🍷	2*
○	Marrano '97	🍷	4
○	Orvieto Classico '98	🍷	2*
●	Sangiovese dell'Umbria '98	🍷	2*
●	Sangiovese Tenuta Corbara '98	🍷	3
○	Marrano '93	YY	4
○	Marrano '94	YY	4
●	Sangiovese dell'Umbria '97	YY	2*
○	Orvieto Classico Vigneto Torricella '97	Y	2*

ORVIETO (TR)

CO.VI.O.
FRAZ. SFERRACAVALLO
LOC. CARDETO, 18
05019 ORVIETO (TR)
TEL. 0763/343189 - 0763/341286

The cooperatives that are fighting for quality are not all in the north – as Orvieto's Co.Vi.O admirably shows. It has about 400 member growers and an annual production of a million bottles (with the Cardeto label), and has gained the respect even of small producers thanks to the almost craftsmanlike care with which the wine is produced. With the magic touch of Riccardo Cotarella, good reds and whites are turned out in goodly number. One of the best of the batch this year is the red Fantasie del Cardeto '96, a selection of local grapes that shows cleanness, aromatic intensity and great softness. The Orvieto '97 Vendemmia Tardiva (late harvest) is also excellent: soft, almost fat, and richly redolent of tropical fruit with inviting hints of citrus. One Glass was earned by each of a long series of '98 whites. These go from the balanced Chardonnay to the more succulent Grechetto, the characteristic standard Orvieto, the enchanting Orvieto Classico Jazz and the Orvieto Classico Febeo (a little less supple but still appealing and quaffable). Of the reds, the Cardeto Rosso '98, from sangiovese, montepulciano, canaiolo and ciliegiolo, is a lean wine made to be easily drinkable; the Pinot Nero seemed fair but not very distinctive. Lastly, the Aleatico Malcorino '98, a structured sweet red made by drawing off the must, is simple and well executed.

●	Fantasie del Cardeto Rosso '96	🍷🍷	3*
○	Orvieto Classico Dolce V. T. Cardeto '97	🍷🍷	4
●	Aleatico Malcorino '98	🍷	3
●	Cardeto Rosso '98	🍷	1*
○	Chardonnay Cardeto '98	🍷	1*
○	Grechetto Cardeto '98	🍷	1*
○	Orvieto Classico Cardeto '98	🍷	1*
○	Orvieto Classico Febeo '98	🍷	2*
○	Orvieto Classico Jazz '98	🍷	2*
●	Pinot Nero '98	🍷	4
●	Fantasie del Cardeto Rosso '95	YY	3*
○	Orvieto Classico Dolce V. T. Cardeto '96	YY	4
○	Orvieto Classico Febeo '94	YY	2*

ORVIETO (TR)

DECUGNANO DEI BARBI
LOC. FOSSATELLO DI CORBARA, 50
05019 ORVIETO (TR)
TEL. 0763/308255

Claudio and Marina Barbi's Decugnano dei Barbi is rightly considered a valuable part of the Umbrian world of wine, and this year it has again presented a very successful and varied range. The estate, near Lake Corbara, has about 25 hectares under vine which yield 100-120 thousand bottles annually. The Brut Metodo Classico vintage '95, although not particularly complex, is properly made: this is always a reliable wine. The entire Orvieto Classico line is admirably cleanly executed and quaffable; the most notable are the Orvieto Classico Secco Barbi '98, which is excellent value for money, and the '98 "IL", rich, soft, mellow, fragrant and lingering, and probably the best vintage ever of this wine. Of the reds, the '96 "IL" stands out for character and incisiveness: it is dense in color, well-defined and articulated on the nose, and full-bodied, balanced, appropriately tannic and long. Both the Lago di Corbara Decugnano dei Barbi '97 and the Lago di Corbara Barrique Barbi '96 are admirably quaffable, harmonious and elegant. The well-made Umbria Sangiovese Pojo del Ruspo '97 is succulent but a bit rustic. A wine to finish with is the excellent Pourriture Noble '97, long one of Umbria's best sweet whites: it shows a glowing golden yellow hue and a sensual fragrance of candied fruit and dried flowers. On the palate, with its restrained sweetness, it is fleshy, soft, clean, even and very inviting.

● "IL" '96	🍷🍷	5
○ Orvieto Classico Pourriture Noble '97	🍷🍷	5
○ Orvieto Classico "IL" '98	🍷🍷	4
○ Decugnano dei Barbi Brut M. Cl. '95	🍷	5
● Lago di Corbara '97	🍷	3
● Lago di Corbara Barrique Barbi '96	🍷	3
○ Orvieto Classico Barbi '98	🍷	2*
○ Orvieto Classico Decugnano dei Barbi '98	🍷	3
● Pojo del Ruspo Barbi '97	🍷	3
● "IL" '93	🍸🍸	5
● "IL" '94	🍸🍸	5
● "IL" '95	🍸🍸	5

ORVIETO (TR)

LA CARRAIA
LOC. TORDIMONTE, 56
05018 ORVIETO (TR)
TEL. 0763/304013

Despite the oft-cited improvement in Umbrian wineries it is still not easy to find an estate like La Carraia, which, instead of presenting, whether by chance or by plan, just one notable wine surrounded by a collection of mediocrities, produces an extremely good range year after year. Of course they are subject to the variability of their vintages, but Odoardo Gialletti's wines, for which the esteemed oenologist Riccardo Cotarella is the midwife, are all extremely reliable. This year once again there are several Two Glass wines. First there's the Orvieto Classico Poggio Calvelli, a small masterpiece of freshness, full flavor and quaffability, sold, what's more, at a highly competitive price. There is also a good, if simpler, standard Orvieto. There are no complaints about the Sangiovese '98 or the Fobiano '97. The '98 Sangiovese is not unlike the splendid '97 vintage: an intense and brilliant ruby hue, aromas of sour cherry and ripe blackberry and an appropriately tannic, vibrant, long palate. The '97 Fobiano, from merlot (90%) and cabernet, is the estate's leading wine. Once again it is fragrant, rich, powerful, structured, broad and soft on the palate, with a beautifully well-defined and lingering finish. Our compliments!

● Fobiano '97	🍷🍷	4
○ Orvieto Classico Poggio Calvelli '98	🍷🍷	3*
● Sangiovese dell'Umbria '97	🍷🍷	3*
○ Orvieto Classico '98	🍷	2*
● Fobiano '95	🍸🍸	4
● Fobiano '96	🍸🍸	4
● Sangiovese dell'Umbria '97	🍸🍸	3*
○ Orvieto Classico Poggio Calvelli '96	🍸	3
○ Orvieto Classico Poggio Calvelli '97	🍸	3

ORVIETO (TR)

TENUTA LE VELETTE
LOC. LE VELETTE, 23
05019 ORVIETO (TR)
TEL. 0763/29090

In the last edition of the Guide we described Le Velette as a real revelation. It is a pleasure to be able to confirm the verdict this year. The estate, run by Corrado and Cecilia Bottai, covers 95 hectares right in the center of the Orvieto Classico zone and has a wonderful cellar dug out of the tufa in Etruscan times. This year they have once more succeeded brilliantly in expressing the great potential of their terroir. We'll start our review of their ample range with the tasty Orvieto Classico '98, a straightforward and well-made white. The clean Velico '98, a more ambitious (barrique-fermented) Orvieto, is not quite as successful: notes of oak are rather evident on the nose and there is only medium body. The third Orvieto, the Lunato '98, is another of the fresh and quaffable whites. The Sauvignon Traluce is tangy, not overly rich and quite attractive. The Calanco '96, a wine of great softness, predictably stands out among the reds. Dense dark ruby in color, it displays elegant and intense fruity aromas quite well integrated with the notes of oak. The palate is powerful, full-bodied, even and very long. We also liked the Rosso di Spicca '98, which is a simpler wine. The two sweet whites, the Raggio '95 (from trebbiano, grechetto, chardonnay and sauvignon) and the Orvieto Amabile, are both sound and well balanced. The simple attractiveness of the Rosato Monaldesco is also worth highlighting.

●	Calanco '96	🍷🍷	5
○	Il Raggio '95	🍷	3
⊙	Monaldesco '98	🍷	2*
○	Orvieto Classico '98	🍷	2*
○	Orvieto Classico Amabile '98	🍷	2*
○	Orvieto Classico Sup. Lunato '98	🍷	3
○	Orvieto Classico Velico '98	🍷	3
●	Rosso Orvietano Rosso di Spicca '98	🍷	2*
○	Traluce '98	🍷	4
●	Calanco '95	ΥΥΥ	5
●	Calanco '91	ΥΥ	4
○	Traluce '96	ΥΥ	3*
●	Calanco '93	Υ	4
●	Rosso di Spicca '97	Υ	2*

ORVIETO (TR)

PALAZZONE
LOC. ROCCA RIPESENA, 68
05019 ORVIETO (TR)
TEL. 0763/344921

A further confirmation of the excellence of Giovanni Dubini's estate, which was established in the '70s and has 22 hectares under vine and the ubiquitous Riccardo Cotarella as consultant, is a fabulous Armaleo, which, after a year's break (the '96 was not produced), returns to the Olympus of Italian wine and claims Three Glasses. This elegant red, made from cabernet sauvignon and cabernet franc and aged for about a year in barrique, has a dark violet-tinged color and an ample and lingering nose with distinct but restrained vegetal scents and subtle spicy nuances. The palate is soft, and shows notable extract and elegant tannins. The fresh and quaffable Rubbio '98 displays inviting notes of red fruit. The Orvieto Campo del Guardiano seemed the best of the whites. It has a deep straw color, a delicately fruity nose and a well-structured, intense, beautifully clean palate. The Orvieto Terre Vineate '98, rich in aromas of white peach, well-structured and intense, is also successful, as is the Grechetto '98, with its enticing scents of rennet apple and its finesse on the palate. The selection L'Ultima Spiaggia '98 is unusual: a monovarietal viognier aged in barrique for some months. It shows a deep straw color, intense, complex aromas of apricot and a broad and balanced palate. To finish, the '98 Muffa Nobile, a barrique-fermented sauvignon, is excellent, as is its wont.

●	Armaleo '97	🍷🍷🍷	5
○	Muffa Nobile '98	🍷🍷	4
○	Orvieto Cl. Campo del Guardiano '97	🍷🍷	3*
○	Grechetto L'Ultima Spiaggia '98	🍷	3
○	Orvieto Cl. Terre di Vineate '98	🍷	3
●	Rubbio '98	🍷	3
○	Viognier L'Ultima Spiaggia '98	🍷	3
●	Armaleo '95	ΥΥΥ	4*
●	Armaleo '92	ΥΥ	5
●	Armaleo '94	ΥΥ	4
○	Muffa Nobile '95	ΥΥ	5
○	Muffa Nobile '96	ΥΥ	4
○	Muffa Nobile '97	ΥΥ	4
○	Viognier L'Ultima Spiaggia '96	ΥΥ	3*

PANICALE (PG)

LA FIORITA - LAMBORGHINI
LOC. PANICAROLA
06064 PANICALE (PG)
TEL. 075/8350029

It is not every day that the celebrated American critic Robert Parker gives a wine 97 points. But that's just what happened to a bottle from La Fiorita, the estate of Patrizia Lamborghini. (Yes, it's the same Lamborghini: she was, in fact, his wife.) It is the Campoleone '97, an explosive red from merlot and sangiovese (half and half), aged for a year or so in French oak barriques and then transferred to 4,000 bottles. Our opinion, however, while certainly favorable, is not nearly so enthusiastic. It seemed an excellent red wine, very powerful, intensely fruity, very long, very tannic, very woody, but perhaps not quite elegant or harmonious enough to go beyond Two Glasses. Tastes vary, of course. Its vigor and richness of extract are certainly extraordinary. The Colli del Trasimeno Trescone '97, from sangiovese, ciliegiolo and merlot, is an extremely pleasing second wine. The color is an intense ruby red; the nose at first lacks clarity but then opens out to fresh and lively fruity notes. The palate has good weight, balance, well-judged fine-textured tannins and a very harmonious if rather simple finish. Since '98 was an even better vintage in these parts, we have come to two conclusions. First, we can expect great things from this estate. And second, Parker may well need to raise the top limit of his scoring range.

●	Rosso dell'Umbria Campoleone '97	🍷🍷	5
●	Colli del Trasimeno Trescone '97	🍷	3

PENNA IN TEVERINA (TR)

RIO GRANDE
LOC. MONTECCHIE
05028 PENNA IN TEVERINA (TR)
TEL. 0744/993102 - 06/66416440

Here's a poser for you: who is the consultant oenologist for this lovely estate in the countryside near Terni? Yes, it's Riccardo Cotarella. Their 12 hectares of vineyard near the Lazio border yield excellent grapes, which are then vinified with state-of-the-art technology. The Casa Pastore is Rio Grande's top red, and there are two good whites, the Colle delle Montecchie and the Campo Antico. We'll start with their flagship, the Bordeaux blend (90% cabernet sauvignon, 10% merlot) Casa Pastore. The '97 shows a dense and brilliant ruby color. Notes of blackberry, wild cherry and fresh blueberry appear on the nose and easily hold their own against the unintrusive, well-integrated hint of oak. The development on the palate is smooth and even, showing richness, full body, well-judged tannins and a pleasing bitter cherry nuance on the finish. The Colle delle Montecchie '98, from chardonnay with just a little sauvignon, has a fresh and lively fragrance and a simple, direct, tasty palate with moderate length. The Campo Antico '98 comes from the same grapes but in different proportions (the sauvignon accounts for 30%). It is faintly herbaceous on the nose and is well executed and quaffable.

●	Casa Pastore Rosso '97	🍷🍷	4
○	Campo Antico '98	🍷	3
○	Colle delle Montecchie Bianco '98	🍷	3
●	Casa Pastore Rosso '95	🍸🍸	4
○	Chardonnay Colle delle Montecchie '94	🍸🍸	3*
○	Chardonnay Colle delle Montecchie '95	🍸🍸	3*
●	Casa Pastore Rosso '93	🍸	3
●	Casa Pastore Rosso '94	🍸	4
●	Casa Pastore Rosso '96	🍸	4
○	Chardonnay Colle delle Montecchie '96	🍸	3
○	Chardonnay Colle delle Montecchie '97	🍸	3

PERUGIA

GISBERTO GORETTI
LOC. PILA - STRADA DEL PINO, 4
06070 PERUGIA
TEL. 075/607316

After their good debut in the Guide last year, Stefano and Gianluca Goretti have presented a slightly less successful range. This may well be due to bad luck with the weather, especially for their leading wine, the Colli Perugini Rosso l'Arringatore, a blend of sangiovese, montepulciano, ciliegiolo and merlot, which was lovely in the '95 version. The '96 seems less so. Of a moderately vivid ruby color, it shows an agreeable bouquet of red fruit, simpler than that of its predecessor. The palate, after an acidic attack, opens to fruitier notes, but without ever seeming ripe or mouth-filling; the finish is neither short nor long. The Fontanella Rosso '97, the same blend but without the ciliegiolo, is a more direct, easily drinkable wine with a faintly bitter finish. The most admirable of the whites is the well-executed, fragrant and harmonious Chardonnay dell'Umbria '98. The succulent and rather tangy Grechetto dell'Umbria '98 is also well made. The other whites are somewhat anonymous, but the Fontanella Bianco, from trebbiano toscano, malvasia del Chianti and garganega, although simple, has a sort of rustic appeal.

○	Chardonnay dell'Umbria '98	🍷	2*
●	Colli Perugini Rosso L'Arringatore '96	🍷	3
●	Fontanella Rosso '97	🍷	2*
○	Grechetto dell'Umbria '98	🍷	2*
○	Fontanella Bianco '98		1
●	Colli Perugini Rosso L'Arringatore '95	🍷🍷 (prev.)	3*
○	Chardonnay dell'Umbria '97	🍷 (prev.)	2*
○	Grechetto dell'Umbria '97	🍷 (prev.)	2*

SPELLO (PG)

F.LLI SPORTOLETTI
VIA LOMBARDIA, 1
06038 SPELLO (PG)
TEL. 0742/651461

Remo and Ernesto Sportoletti's estate has had its profile in the Guide for years and is unquestionably an important producer, indeed perhaps the only important one, in the Assisi DOC district. It has 20 hectares under vine in the lovely countryside between the hills of Spello and Assisi, and Riccardo Cotarella as consultant oenologist. We were particularly struck by the wines this year. For a start, both versions of the Villa Fidelia, red and white, were very good, better than ever before in fact, and get Two Glasses apiece. The '98 Bianco has a vivid straw color, a nose rich in fruity notes and sweet tones of oak, and a warm, intense, medium-bodied palate with a good balance between fruit and wood. The '97 Rosso shows an intense violet-ruby hue, copious aromas of berries with hints of bay and fine spice, and a broad, well-structured, properly tannic and fruity palate with a distinct flavor of blackberry and black currant. The straw yellow Bianco '98 releases generous scents of white-fleshed fruit with notes of damson and peach and is crisp and intense in the mouth. The violet-red Rosso '98 displays vegetal tones and light sweet spice on the nose; the palate is harmonious and lingering. The Grechetto d'Assisi '98, straw yellow in color, is also excellent; an elegant fragrance of tropical fruit precedes a clean, intense and structured palate. The Assisi Rosato '98 receives only a mention, as despite its fruit it shows little structure.

○	Villa Fidelia Bianco '98	🍷🍷	4
●	Villa Fidelia Rosso '97	🍷🍷	4
○	Assisi Grechetto '98	🍷	2*
○	Bianco di Assisi '98	🍷	2*
●	Rosso di Assisi '98	🍷	2*
⊙	Rosato di Assisi '98		2
○	Villa Fidelia Bianco '95	🍷🍷 (prev.)	4
●	Villa Fidelia Rosso '91	🍷🍷 (prev.)	4
●	Rosso di Assisi '96	🍷 (prev.)	1*
○	Villa Fidelia Bianco '96	🍷 (prev.)	4
●	Villa Fidelia Rosso '94	🍷 (prev.)	4
●	Villa Fidelia Rosso '96	🍷 (prev.)	5

STRONCONE (TR)

La Palazzola
Loc. Vascigliano
05039 Stroncone (TR)
tel. 0744/607735 - 0744/272357

For some time now, wines from Stefano Grilli's interesting estate near Terni have been regular entrants in our Three Glass finals. But this year, not only was there impeccable quality across the board, but the '97 Merlot, one of the house jewels, was so superb it could not fail to receive our top award. It has a vivid dark violet-red color. The fruity bouquet is rich in elegant notes of blackberry, sour cherry, cocoa and pencil lead. The palate is soft, long and structured, with plentiful but fine and unintrusive tannins. The Rubino '97 is not far behind. It too shows a wealth of complex fruity aromas, but with nuances of spice and licorice. In the mouth it is intense, soft and appropriately tannic. The pale ruby Pinot Nero '97 is fairly characteristic of its variety, while the Cerquolo '98 is fresh, appealing and intense. The two whites, the Palazzotto '98 and the Verdello '98, are both clean and well-structured and get One Glass each. The best of the bubblies is the Riesling Brut '95, a "metodo classico" that shows both complexity and finesse. The appealing fresh Moscato Demi Sec is also good. The estate's newest wine, the excellent Vino Passito '96, displays a warm amber hue and complex aromas of white chocolate and spice, while the '97 Vendemmia Tardiva is as elegant as ever.

●	Merlot '97	TTT	5
●	Rubino '97	TT	5
○	Vino Passito '96	TT	5
●	Cerquolo '98	T	3
○	Il Palazzotto '98	T	3
○	La Palazzola V. T. '97	T	5
○	Moscato Demi Sec	T	4
●	Pinot Nero '97	T	4
○	Riesling Brut M. Cl. '95	T	4
○	Verdello '98	T	3
○	La Palazzola V. T. '96	YY	5
●	Merlot '95	YY	4
○	Riesling Brut M. Cl. '94	YY	4
●	Rubino '95	YY	4
●	Rubino '96	YY	5

TORGIANO (PG)

Cantine Lungarotti
Via Mario Angeloni, 16
06089 Torgiano (PG)
tel. 075/9880348

We won't say much about the death of Giorgio Lungarotti. His historical importance for wine, not just in Umbria but throughout Italy, is known to everyone. Such a heritage is a great honor, and also a great responsibility, for those who come after, but Chiara Lungarotti and Teresa Severini Lungarotti, who had been working with him for a number of years, have already shown that they are well up to the task. This year's range includes some wines from a splendid vintage, i.e. '90. We'll start with the standard-bearing Rubesco Riserva Vigna Monticchio, with which Lungarotti was often so pleased. The long-awaited '90 lives up to expectations. It shows a fairly vivid ruby color with garnet highlights, and sensual scents of bitter cherry and black currant accompanied by nobly evolved notes of damp earth and undergrowth, and very restrained wood; the ample palate reveals fine, ripe tannins. In short, the wine is excellent, and its strong suit, as always, is elegance rather than power. The San Giorgio, from the same vintage, is slightly less successful: a fairly forward ruby hue with a garnet rim introduces somewhat indistinct tertiary aromas and an elegant and aristocratic but not entirely harmonious palate. We also liked the appealing Brut, the well-made and quaffable Torgiano Bianco Torre di Giano '98 and their new red wine, the tasty, straightforward and immediate Giubilante. We were, however, somewhat puzzled by the Torgiano cru Vigna il Pino '96.

●	Torgiano Rosso Vigna Monticchio Ris. '90	TT	5
○	Brut M. Cl.	T	4
●	Giubilante '97	T	4
●	San Giorgio '90	T	5
○	Torgiano Bianco Torre di Giano '98	T	3
●	Torgiano Rosso Vigna Monticchio Ris. '78	YYY	6
●	Cabernet Sauvignon '95	YY	4
●	Il Vessillo '93	YY	4
●	San Giorgio '86	YY	5
●	San Giorgio '88	YY	5
●	Torgiano Rosso Vigna Monticchio Ris. '88	YY	5

OTHER WINERIES

The following producers obtained good scores in our tastings with one or more of their wines:

PROVINCE OF TPERUGIA

Tili
Capodacqua Assisi,
tel. 075/8064370
Assisi Rosso '95,
Marilù '95,
Muffa Reale '94

Il Poggio
Castiglione del Lago,
tel. 075/9589923
Colli del Trasimeno Bianco '98,
Colli del Trasimeno Rosso '98

Villa Po' del Vento
Città della Pieve,
tel. 0578/299950
Colli del Trasimeno Rosato '98,
Colli del Trasimeno Rosso '97

Terre dei Trinci
Foligno, tel. 0742/320165
Rosso di Montefalco '95,
Sagrantino di Montefalco '95

Cantina Intercomunale del Trasimeno
Magione, tel. 075/840298
Colli del Trasimeno Rosso Barca '97

Umbria Viticoltori Associati
Marsciano, tel. 075/8748989
Colli Perugini Bianco '98,
Colli Perugini Rosso '97

Ruggeri
Montefalco, tel. 0742/379294
Rosso di Montefalco '97,
Sagrantino di Montefalco Passito '95

Il Ramaccio
Petrignano del Lago, tel. 075/9528148
Assolato '97

Spoletoducale
Petrognano di Spoleto, tel. 0743/56224
Rosso di Montefalco '96,
Rosso Pievano '97,
Sagrantino di Montefalco '94

Chiorri, S. Enea, tel. 075/607141
Colli Perugini Rosato '98,
Colli Perugini Rosso '98,
Saliato Rosso '97

Cantina Sociale Tudernum
Todi, tel. 075/8989403
Colli Martani Grechetto di Todi '98,
Colli Martani Sangiovese '95

PROVINCE OF TERNI

Poggio del Lupo
Allerona Scalo, tel. 0763/68850
Brut Poggio al Lupo,
Orvieto Classico Secco '98

Petrangeli, Orvieto, tel. 0763/304189,
Umbria Rosso Canto '97

Tordimaro, Orvieto, tel. 0763/304085
Orvieto Classico '98,
Umbria Bianco '98

LAZIO

Lazio is facing the new millennium in fairly good form. The '98 vintage was climatically uneven. In some zones, such as the hills surrounding Rome and lower Lazio, incessant rain at the end of the summer caused humidity problems for the grapes, and as a result many wines are aromatically fainter than usual, especially the whites. But, as usual, Lazio as a whole cannot be considered as a whole, since it is so varied. There is no startling news this year, but there are definitely signs of movement. Once again Falesco's Montiano has won its Three Glasses, which it is again enjoying in solitary splendor, although other contenders are getting close. The nearest is a sumptuous Vigna del Vassallo from Paola di Mauro in Marino, already the first great red of the Castelli Romani and now glorying in the new look given it by one Riccardo Cotarella. Next in line are a fleshy Vigna del Cavaliere from Casale Marchese, the work of its oenologist Sandro Facca; a worthy Quattro Mori from Castel di Paolis, the result of the ministrations of one of the great oenologists of our time, Franco Bernabei; and an interesting La Petrosa from the classic Frascati producer, Conte Zandotti. From the homeland of Marcello Mastroianni and Vittorio De Sica come an excellent Duca Cantelmi from Giovanni Palombo at Atina, one of the greatest surprises of the 1999 Vinitaly wine fair, and a fine Torre Ercolana from Colacicchi in Anagni – even though the Trimani family, the owners of this tiny but distinguished estate, insist on keeping the wine for over six years before releasing it. Casale del Giglio in Borgo Montello is doing very well, as we expected, and has produced a beautifully made Cabernet Sauvignon. The Pietra Pinta holding, near Cori, makes its first appearance in the Guide with an admirably realized red, the Colle Amato. Prompted by Riccardo Cotarella's guidance, the Cantina di Cerveteri is also taking part in this revival of Lazio's reds with a successful Vigna Grande Rosso and an innovative Tertium from an unusual but intriguing grape blend. The Trappolini family's estate in Castiglione in Teverina has also made its contribution with the appealing Paterno. As far as the whites are concerned, there is a debutant, the full-bodied Malvasia del Lazio Rumon from Conte Zandotti, which can hold its own beside the fine old trooper, the Malvasia Terre dei Grifi from Fontana Candida. Another newcomer is the admirable Somigliò from Giovanni Palombo. Lastly, there are familiar names, back again with good performances.

ANAGNI (FR)

COLACICCHI
LOC. ROMAGNANO
03012 ANAGNI (FR)
TEL. 06/4469661

The news is that the long wait for the new vintages is finally over. Francesco Trimani, who runs the Colacicchi estate (and a famous wine shop in Rome) together with his siblings and his father Marco, has made it clear that the wines will be released when they are good and ready, not when they are still young and green and count on customers to age them. So we can finally review the Romagnano Bianco '97, from malvasia puntinata, passerina and romanesco, vinified in part with skin contact. While retaining its usual firm, solid style, it shows a striking aromatic wealth, great elegance and harmony and an incredibly fresh palate. The Romagnolo Rosso '96, from cabernet, merlot and cesanese, with one year's oak aging, does not have the complexity of a great red but is nevertheless richly suggestive and fairly elegant on both nose and palate, with a broad bouquet and fair depth. However, the '93 Torre Ercolana is again in great form. A change in the proportion of cabernet has given a decisive jolt to the wine's style. It has a pronounced nose with scents of licorice, oak and ground coffee and hints of bitter cherry. The good structure on the palate reveals noticeable tannins, and the finish is long. It needs further aging, however.

○	Romagnano Bianco '97	YY (black)	4
●	Torre Ercolana '93	YY (black)	5
●	Romagnano Rosso '96	Y (black)	4
○	Romagnano Bianco '92	YY	4
○	Romagnano Bianco '93	YY	3*
○	Romagnano Bianco '94	YY	4
●	Torre Ercolana '87	YY	5
●	Torre Ercolana '88	YY	6
●	Torre Ercolana '90	YY	5
●	Torre Ercolana '91	YY	5
○	Romagnano Bianco '96	Y	4
●	Romagnano Rosso '91	Y	4
●	Romagnano Rosso '93	Y	4
●	Romagnano Rosso '95	Y	4

ATINA (FR)

GIOVANNI PALOMBO
C.SO MUNANZIO PLANCO
03042 ATINA (FR)
TEL. 0776/610200 - 0776/610639

"The genius of wine is in the vine" says an old proverb that Giovanni Palombo has printed on his labels. But when a wine nudges Three Glasses at its first release there has to be some genius in the cellar too. The wine in question is the Cabernet Duca Cantelmi '97 and the "genius" is Roberto Mazzer, a young, promising oenologist who has been taken on to direct this small but excellently equipped cellar. The Duca Cantelmi is truly impressive. It makes a great impact on the nose with its rich notes of spice, coffee and red fruit and a subtle balsamic note from the tiny percentage of syrah. The palate, with its sinew, great intensity and rare elegance, confirms the promise. Of course there are other jewels in the Palombo crown. For example, the Colle della Torre '97, from 90% merlot and 10% cabernet, has a good array of vegetal aromas and fair structure which might want just a bit more concentration. The wine is, however, still certainly worthy of its Two Glasses. And then the Rosso delle Chiaie '98, from cabernet. It's an easily quaffable wine, but by no means banal. Noticeable ripe tannins support a good structure. The "genius" has been busy with the whites too. The Somigliò '98 offers strikingly intense, rich, varietal aromas of sauvignon and semillon. With a little more length on the palate it would be perfect. The Bianco delle Chiaie '98, from malvasia and vermentino, is most attractive drinking at an excellent price.

●	Cabernet Duca Cantelmini '97	YY (black)	5
●	Colle della Torre '97	YY (black)	4
●	Rosso delle Chiaie '98	Y (black)	3
○	Somigliò '98	Y (black)	3
○	Bianco delle Chiaie '98		2
●	Colle della Torre '97	YY	4
●	Rosso delle Chiaie '97	Y	3

BOLSENA (VT)

ITALO MAZZIOTTI
L.GO MAZZIOTTI, 5
01023 BOLSENA (VT)
TEL. 0761/799049

There has been a great leap ahead. Signora Flaminia Mazzioti, the owner, together with her husband Alessandro Laurenzi, of this lovely estate on the gentle slopes flanking Lake Bolsena, has, after some rather stationary years, decided to go all out for excellence. With advice and encouragement from Marino Fontana and Paolo Peira she has brought out five wines this year. To start there is a well-made '98 Est Est Est di Montefiascone with delicate and stylish aromas. Next comes the selection Filò '98, from procanico, malvasia bianca and rossetto, which offers softness enlivened by a subtle but captivating citric tone. Then an intriguing version, the '97, of Canuleio. It's a classic local blend that ages on its lees in oak. Although it does not have the concentration of the '94, it does have good structure, complex aromas ranging from toasted hazelnut to vanilla, and a soft and fresh finish. For the first time the Mazziottis have presented two reds. (It's almost as if there had been a secret agreement among the producers of the region to make this the year of the reds.) The first, the Filò '98, is a sangiovese-merlot blend, graceful and easily drinkable, but with a fairly firm structure and a rich selection of aromas. The other red, the Volgente '98, from merlot, sangiovese and montepulciano, is considerably more interesting. Aged for about a year in small oak casks, it offers an ample and varied bouquet with scents of red fruit, tobacco and spice, although it still shows some of the harshness of youth. Nevertheless it has good substance and it shows.

●	Volgente Rosso '97	▼▼	4
○	Est Est Est di Montefiascone Canuleio '97	▼	4
○	Est Est Est di Montefiascone '98		2
○	Est Est Est di Montefiascone Filò '98		2
●	Filò Rosso '98		2
○	Est Est Est di Montefiascone Canuleio '94	▽▽	4
○	Est Est Est di Montefiascone '96	▽	2*
○	Est Est Est di Montefiascone '97	▽	2*
○	Est Est Est di Montefiascone Canuleio '92	▽	3

BORGO MONTELLO (LT)

CASALE DEL GIGLIO
STRADA CISTERNA-NETTUNO, KM 13
04010 BORGO MONTELLO (LT)
TEL. 06/5742529 - 06/5746359

Antonio Santarelli, the owner, and Paolo Tiefenthaler, the oenologist, make a winning team at this important estate and have never deviated from their commitment to quality. Indeed all the wines in Casale del Giglio's vast range are always reliably good. The Satrico '98, although just a bottom-of-the-line wine, shows well and is richer on nose and palate than previous versions. The same applies to the '98 Chardonnay and the '98 Sauvignon. These are essentially easy-drinking, fairly varietal wines sold at very fair prices. The Antinoo '96, an oak-aged chardonnay, is in another category. Affected by the capricious year, it has lost a bit of its freshness but retains good fruit-oak balance. The rosé Albiola benefited in '98 from more shiraz which has given it more grip and body. Of the reds, the Merlot '97 and the Petit Verdot '97 both have delightful varietal aromas, good body and fair length. The '97 Shiraz has tones of rich, ripe fruits and spice on the nose and excellent nose-palate harmony. Of their top reds the star is the Cabernet Sauvignon '96. It has a dense, enchanting bouquet, lots of body, just the right amount of tannins and a dense texture. The Madreselva '95, a classic Bordeaux blend, and the Mater Matuta '95, from syrah and petit verdot, are both very good. You could never have found such wines in these parts a few years ago,

●	Cabernet Sauvignon '96	▼▼	4
●	Madreselva '95	▼▼	4
●	Mater Matuta '95	▼▼	4
⊙	Albiola '98	▼	2*
○	Antinoo '96	▼	3
○	Chardonnay '98	▼	2*
●	Merlot '97	▼	3
○	Satrico '98	▼	2*
○	Sauvignon '98	▼	2*
●	Shiraz '97	▼	2*
○	Antinoo '95	▽▽	3*
○	Chardonnay '97	▽▽	2*
●	Madreselva '94	▽▽	3*
●	Merlot '96	▽▽	3*
●	Shiraz '96	▽	2*

CASTIGLIONE IN TEVERINA (VT)

TRAPPOLINI
VIA DEL RIVELLINO, 65
01024 CASTIGLIONE IN TEVERINA (VT)
TEL. 0761/948381

After an uncertain period the Trappolini family seems to have found the right path. We used to be somewhat puzzled by the fluctuating quality of the wines from this estate, which now has apparently reached a turning point. Even the '98 Est Est Est di Montefiascone has a richness of fruity and varietal aromas and a fresh, lively palate. The Orvieto S. Egidio '98 is also more successful, with its harmonious fusion of grapey and fruity notes. The captivating monovarietal Grechetto Brecceto '98 shows a soft texture with characteristic faintly bitter aromatic tones. The Chardonnay dell'Umbria '98 is particularly good. Vinified and aged in new barriques, it is admirably close-knit and reveals an ideal balance between fruit and vanilla, remarkable freshness and fair length. The star of the reds is the Paterno '96 from 100% sangiovese. Broad and intense on the nose, it shows an elegant, complex and appropriately tannic palate. However, the wine that particularly delighted and surprised us at this year's tastings was a splendid aleatico, the Idea '98. It stands out for the fragrance of its fruity and floral tones, reminiscent of dried rose and raspberry and blackberry jam. It is warm and silky on the palate, but also sweet, succulent, fresh and balanced.

○	Chardonnay '98	🍷🍷	3*
●	Idea '98	🍷🍷	4
●	Paterno '96	🍷🍷	3*
○	Grechetto dell'Umbria Brecceto '98	🍷	3
○	Est Est Est di Montefiascone '98		2
○	Orvieto Sant'Egidio '98		3
○	Grechetto dell'Umbria Brecceto '95	🍷	3
●	Paterno '92	🍷	3

CERVETERI (RM)

CANTINA COOPERATIVA DI CERVETERI
VIA AURELIA, KM 42.700
00052 CERVETERI (RM)
TEL. 06/9905677

This has been a good year for the Cantina di Cerveteri. The whites have regained a certain vigor and in place of last year's occasional flabbiness we now find an attractive acidity and a good range of primary aromas. The Cerveteri Fontana Morella '98 is as pleasing on the palate as on the nose, with an attractive, light, smooth, fresh fruity note. The selection Vigna Grande '98 is more impressive, fresh, and abundantly fruity, and easily earns One Glass. This cooperative, which is still assisted by the fine oenologist Riccardo Cotarella, has now presented a 100% Malvasia del Lazio, from the '98 vintage: it is attractively aromatic, although substantial alcohol has the upper hand. The red Cerveteri Fontana Morella '98 is good of its kind: a youthful grapiness makes it just right for those who like undemanding wines. The Cerveteri Rosso Vigna Grande '97 is something else again. Although it doesn't have the depth of the '95, it boasts a fine array of spicy and herbaceous aromas, elegant structure and a certain nobility. There's also a new red, the good and well-balanced Tertium '97, a blend of malvasia nera, sangiovese and cabernet, which reveals an intriguingly complex and very concentrated nose; tannins of some finesse and a good acidic underpinning suggest that it should develop well over time.

●	Cerveteri Rosso Vigna Grande '97	🍷🍷	3*
○	Cerveteri Bianco Vigna Grande '98	🍷	2*
●	Tertium '97	🍷	3
○	Cerveteri Bianco Fontana Morella '98		1
●	Cerveteri Rosso Fontana Morella '98		1
○	Malvasia del Lazio '98		2
●	Cerveteri Rosso Vigna Grande '95	🍷🍷	3*
●	Cerveteri Rosso Vigna Grande '94	🍷	3

CIVITELLA D'AGLIANO (VT)

TENUTA MOTTURA
LOC. RIO CHIARO, 1
01020 CIVITELLA D'AGLIANO (VT)
TEL. 0761/914501

It may seem odd to start with a dessert wine, but when the wine in question is Sergio Mottura's Muffo '97 it seems wrong not to. It is a not unusual blend of procanico and grechetto, the two classic varieties of this zone straddling Lazio and Umbria. The grapes are late-harvested and vinified with the greatest care in the fine cellar below Civitella d'Agliano. The result is a warm, silky wine with scents of honey, ripe and dried figs and peach blossom, with a solid structure and a lingering finish. But let's consider the wines that made this estate famous, first of all the Orvieto Vigna Tragugnano. The '98, from a propitious vintage, is exuberant and characterful, with scents of dill and wildflowers alternating with very elegant fruit. Next is the monovarietal Grechetto Poggio della Costa '98, which also makes an impact on both nose and palate; it shows solid substance and excellent balance. Then there is Sergio's experiment, of which he is very proud: the Latour a Civitella, a white aged in barriques provided by Louis Latour, the famed French cooper. Changes in its vinification (which is overseen by the oenologist Marco Monchiero) have made the '97 much more balanced. The fruit-oak relationship favors primary aromas and freshness is assured by crisp acidity. The result is a wine of considerable body and length.

○	Grechetto Latour a Civitella '97	▼▼	4
○	Grechetto Poggio della Costa '98	▼▼	3*
○	Muffo '97	▼▼	3*
○	Orvieto Vigna Tragugnano '98	▼	2*
○	Grechetto Latour a Civitella '96	▽▽	4
○	Grechetto Poggio della Costa '94	▽▽	3*
○	Grechetto Poggio della Costa '95	▽▽	3*
○	Grechetto Poggio della Costa '97	▽▽	3*
○	Muffo '95	▽▽	4
○	Muffo '94	▽	4
●	Rosso di Civitella Magone '93	▽	4
●	Rosso di Civitella Magone '94	▽	4

CORI (LT)

COOPERATIVA COLLE SAN LORENZO
VIA GRAMSCI, 52
04010 CORI (LT)
TEL. 06/9677151

A small but splendid estate on the gentle slopes of the Monti Lepini is making its debut in the Guide. Colle San Lorenzo, which has been run by the Ferretti family since 1962, was already renowned for its extra virgin olive oil, which can be found in some of the most famous Italian restaurants in the U.S. Since they could count on the grapes of many member growers, they decided to see if they could make a go of it with wine too. The first results are encouraging, in part because the estate receives technical assistance from the Istituto Sperimentale of Conegliano (in the Veneto) and that of Velletri. The best white is easily the Chardonnay del Lazio '98 which has a fair array of varietal aromas buttressed by a contribution from the curiously named variety, incrocio Manzoni 6.0.13. The wine is fresh and attractive drinking although not very long. The Cori Rosso '97, a blend of merlot and petit verdot partially fermented in small oak casks, is densely knit and substantial, and manages coolly to keep its various aromas in balance. More length and complexity would be welcome, however. The Colle Amato '97, from cabernet and syrah, is decidedly more interesting, possibly one of Lazio's great reds. It is warm and mellow, elegantly structured, rich in nuances of spice and red fruit, with the "foxy" hint typical of syrah. They say in Italy that the morning tells you if the day will be fine...

●	Colle Amato '97	▼▼	3*
○	Chardonnay del Lazio '98		2
●	Cori Rosso Costa Vecchia '97		2

FRASCATI (RM)

CASALE MARCHESE
VIA DI VERMICINO, 34
00044 FRASCATI (RM)
TEL. 06/9408932

Well, what do you think? They've decided to make a great red at Casale Marchese, or so it would seem from our tastings. With the arrival of the oenologist Sandro Facca at the estate there seems to have been a major change in production philosophy: Casale Marchese, formerly noted for its Frascati, has now presented the excellent Vigna del Cavaliere '96, a blend of merlot, cabernet, montepulciano and cesanese barrique-aged for a few months. It displays a full bouquet including balsamic scents, ground coffee, spice and ripe red fruit, as well as solid structure and great elegance: Two full Glasses. The Rosso di Casale Marchese '98, a different interpretation of the same grape blend, didn't seem at all bad either. It knows no oak, but is vinified and aged in stainless steel, which has enhanced the fragrance of its primary aromas and made it particularly enchanting to drink. We come down to earth with the '98 Frascati Superiore and, to some extent, the Cortesia '98: there is work to be done on both. The Frascati shows some strange aromatic notes that upset its freshness and balance, while the Cortesia has a fine subtle sweetness but is a little too fleeting. Yet it would take so little to turn them around.

● Vigna del Cavaliere '96	▼▼	4
● Rosso di Casale Marchese '98	▼	3
○ Cortesia di Casale Marchese '98		3
○ Frascati Superiore '98		2
○ Cortesia di Casale Marchese '93	▽▽	3*
○ Cortesia di Casale Marchese '94	▽▽	3*
○ Cortesia di Casale Marchese '95	▽▽	3*
○ Frascati Superiore '93	▽▽	2*
○ Frascati Superiore '94	▽▽	2*
○ Frascati Superiore '95	▽▽	2*
● Rosso di Casale Marchese '97	▽▽	3*
○ Frascati Superiore '96	▽	2*
○ Frascati Superiore '97	▽	2*

GROTTAFERRATA (RM)

CASTEL DE PAOLIS
VIA VAL DE PAOLIS, 41
00046 GROTTAFERRATA (RM)
TEL. 06/9413648 - 06/94316025

The arrival of Franco Bernabei as consultant oenologist chez Santarelli has resulted in an immediate restyling of the whole production. The reds have reaped most benefit from the change, gaining the concentration and structure they have sometimes lacked in the past. The '97 Campo Vecchio Rosso, for example, from syrah, merlot, petit verdot and cabernet sauvignon, has a dark ruby color and intense, soft aromas with an appealing spicy tone. The palate is balanced and has good tannin and extract. The fascinating '97 Quattro Mori from the same grape blend is better than ever before. Of a dense, opaque dark ruby hue, it is spicy and powerful on the nose with sweet, exuberant tones of ripe black fruit. The palate boasts warmth, depth, rich structure and ripe tannins, and leads into a vanilla finish with a balsamic nuance. Among the whites an excellent Selve Vecchie '97, an elegant blend of sauvignon and chardonnay, fat, harmonious and full, stands out. The Frascati Superiore Vigna Adriana '98 displays good balance and has intense, floral scents with lavender and citrus to the fore; the palate is more delicate and fresher than in the past. The Frascati Superiore '98 shows attractive floral aromas with pleasing hints of dried fruit. The palate is round and fat, finishing with delicately aromatic notes. The Frascati Campo Vecchio, round and structured, is also excellent. The Moscato Rosa Rosathea '98, varietal and sweet but a little too forward, is less successful than earlier versions.

○ Frascati Sup. V. Adriana '98	▼▼	5
● Quattro Mori '97	▼▼	5
○ Selve Vecchie '97	▼▼	6
● Campo Vecchio Rosso '97	▼	4
○ Frascati Sup. Campo Vecchio '98	▼	3
○ Frascati Superiore '98	▼	4
● Rosathea '98	▼	5
○ Frascati Sup. V. Adriana '96	▽▽	5
○ Frascati Sup. V. Adriana '97	▽▽	5
○ Muffa Nobile '94	▽▽	5
○ Muffa Nobile '97	▽▽	5
● Quattro Mori '93	▽▽	5
● Quattro Mori '94	▽▽	5
● Quattro Mori '96	▽▽	5
● Rosathea '95	▽▽	5

MARINO (RM)

Paola Di Mauro - Colle Picchioni
Via Colle Picchione di Marino, 46
00040 Marino (RM)
tel. 06/93546329

This is the second year that Riccardo Cotarella has been the consultant oenologist here, and it seems that the wines of Paola and Armando Di Mauro are gaining elegance and concentration. The 92 points that Robert Parker gave the Vigna del Vassallo '97 are a confirmation. He called it "the little Cheval Blanc of Lazio", drawing attention to the fact that it is a blend of cabernet sauvignon, cabernet franc and merlot, just like the great Saint-Emilion. We are perhaps slightly less enthusiastic: we'd like it yet more concentrated and with denser and more even polyphenols. But there is no doubt that this is the best red the estate has produced in recent years. It offers a bouquet of black currant and sour cherry and an elegant and delicate palate, not imposing but very well balanced. The '96 is just a bit more dilute and there's a slight acidic edge – the result of an inferior vintage. The Marino Etichetta Oro is, as usual, the best of the whites. The '98 is fatter and more concentrated on the palate and has distinct scents of pear and Golden Delicious apple. The two base wines, the Marino Etichetta Verde '98 and the Colle Picchioni Rosso '97, are well made but not outstanding.

○	Marino Colle Picchioni Oro '98	▼▼	4
●	Vigna del Vassallo '96	▼▼	5
●	Vigna del Vassallo '97	▼▼	5
●	Colle Picchioni Rosso '97	▼	3
○	Marino Etichetta Verde '98	▼	3
●	Vigna del Vassallo '85	▽▽▽	5
●	Vigna del Vassallo '88	▽▽▽	5
○	Le Vignole '92	▽▽	4
○	Le Vignole '93	▽▽	4
○	Marino Colle Picchioni Oro '97	▽▽	4
●	Vigna del Vassallo '90	▽▽	5
●	Vigna del Vassallo '92	▽▽	5
●	Vigna del Vassallo '93	▽▽	5
●	Vigna del Vassallo '95	▽▽	5
●	Colle Picchioni Rosso '93	▽	3

MARINO (RM)

Gotto d'Oro
Fraz. Frattocchie
Via del Divino Amore, 115
00040 Marino (RM)
tel. 06/9302221

Gotto d'Oro is one of the most important producers in the Castelli Romani. With its several million bottles a year this winery shows unusual success in combining good average quality with significant quantity. All the wines are reliable, the Frascati and Marino particularly so, and showed well in the '98 vintage too. The Frascati selection in the Bordeaux bottle, which is sold only in wine shops and restaurants, shows a fine golden straw color and intense aromas of apple and wildflowers. The palate is fresh, full, well structured and fairly long. The Marino Superiore is not dissimilar. The bouquet is softer and sweeter and the palate, though supported by fresh acidity, is fat, round and rich in ripe fruit. The Castelli Romani '98, from montepulciano, sangiovese, cesanese and merlot, has a bright and youthful ruby color. The nose is fresh and fruity with notes of berries, while the palate is soft, easy and only lightly tannic. The aim is not a fully structured red but a very fresh and fruity wine that can be drunk right through the meal or, in hot weather, served cool with fairly strong-flavored fish dishes. The Malvasia del Lazio is also fragrant and interesting.

●	Castelli Romani '98	▼	2*
○	Frascati Superiore '98	▼	2*
○	Marino Superiore '98	▼	2*
○	Malvasia del Lazio '98		2
●	Castelli Romani '97	▽	2*
○	Frascati Superiore '95	▽	2*
○	Frascati Superiore '96	▽	2*
○	Frascati Superiore '97	▽	2*
○	Marino Superiore '95	▽	2*
○	Marino Superiore '96	▽	2*
○	Marino Superiore '97	▽	2*

MONTEFIASCONE (VT)

FALESCO
S. S. CASSIA NORD, KM 94.155
01027 MONTEFIASCONE (VT)
TEL. 0761/826332

The Montiano '97 is not a wine that is easily forgotten. It manages to provide sensations that, on the palate, become almost overwhelmingly exciting. It is as warm and silky as only a great wine can be, and shows enormous body and complexity, with its spicy, herbaceous and balsamic notes: Three Glasses for the fourth time in a row. Riccardo "the genius" Cotarella has even been willing to improve the "little" Vitiano, made principally from cabernet, giving the '98 a breadth of herbaceous aromas with exquisite hints of chocolate and coffee, and a firm, elegant structure: Two Glasses. There's something new about the whites too. The basic Est Est Est '98 has retained its usual sober style emphasizing freshness and aroma rather than structure, but the '98 Poggio dei Gelsi has concentrated on softness rather than freshness, and as a result the aromas are a little fainter and the structure seems fuller and fatter. The '98 Grechetto is the best version yet. Its brief sojourn in oak has not affected its nose, and it is substantial, elegant and soft. After a short absence, the Vendemmia Tardiva, made from classic grapes of the zone picked overripe, is now back and the '97 again seems intriguing. This little brother of a Sauternes unites the greater wine's qualities with the more classic nuances of honey, sweet pear and white flowers; it seems to have a velvety freshness and is not at all cloying.

● Montiano '97	🍷🍷🍷	5
○ Est Est Est di Montefiascone Poggio dei Gelsi '98	🍷🍷	3*
○ Est Est Est di Montefiascone Vendemmia Tardiva '97	🍷🍷	4
○ Grechetto '98	🍷🍷	3*
● Vitiano '98	🍷🍷	2*
○ Est Est Est di Montefiascone Falesco '98	🍷	1*
● Montiano '94	ΥΥΥ	5
● Montiano '95	ΥΥΥ	5
● Montiano '96	ΥΥΥ	5
● Montiano '92	ΥΥ	5
● Montiano '93	ΥΥ	5
● Vitiano '97	ΥΥ	2*

MONTEPORZIO CATONE (RM)

FONTANA CANDIDA
VIA FONTANA CANDIDA, 11
00040 MONTEPORZIO CATONE (RM)
TEL. 06/9420066

Perhaps we repeat ourselves, but the wines from this colossus of the Lazio wine scene continue to appeal to us. Behind their appeal lies a profound understanding of a terroir that yields very uneven raw material, which the expert oenologist Franco Bardi is a past master at selecting. How else can the consistent success of the Frascati Santa Teresa '98 be explained? It always came out among the top wines of its category at our blind tastings. Its most striking features are the fragrance of its aromas, its exciting freshness and its elegance: Two Glasses with ease. And what about the Malvasia del Lazio '98 from the Terre dei Grifi line? It's a lesson for those who persist in not understanding the aromatic potential of this kind of wine. The bouquet is rich and complex, with notes of banana and sage supported by a soft freshness. The Frascati Superiore '98 from the same line is more than acceptable. Rigorous selection of typical local grapes and expert vinification have enhanced the fragrance, adding very intense fruity notes to the floral tones; the palate is full-flavored and succulent, with a most appealing fresh acidity. To understand the true worth of a winery you have to taste its base-level wines, and the Fontana Candida workhorse, Frascati Superiore '98, is exemplary in its cleanness and freshness.

○ Frascati Sup. Santa Teresa '98	🍷🍷	2*
○ Malvasia del Lazio '98	🍷🍷	2*
○ Frascati Sup. Terre dei Grifi '98	🍷	2*
○ Frascati Superiore '98	🍷	2*
○ Frascati Sup. Santa Teresa '93	ΥΥ	2*
○ Frascati Sup. Santa Teresa '94	ΥΥ	2*
○ Frascati Sup. Santa Teresa '95	ΥΥ	2*
○ Frascati Sup. Santa Teresa '96	ΥΥ	2*
○ Frascati Sup. Santa Teresa '97	ΥΥ	2*
○ Frascati Sup. Terre dei Grifi '95	ΥΥ	2*
○ Malvasia del Lazio '95	ΥΥ	2*
○ Malvasia del Lazio '96	ΥΥ	2*
○ Malvasia del Lazio '97	ΥΥ	2*
○ Frascati Sup. Terre dei Grifi '97	Υ	2*
○ Frascati Superiore '97	Υ	2*

MONTEPORZIO CATONE (RM)

Villa Simone

Via Frascati Colonna, 29
00040 Monteporzio Catone (RM)
tel. 06/3213210 - 06/9449717

Piero Costantini, a latter-day Cincinnatus, seems to have definitively chosen the peace of the countryside over the "battleground" of his wine shop in Rome. Thus, surrounded by his vineyards, he is now concentrating on producing the wines that have brought him fame. There have been no visible changes at the estate but this year's wines have a more toned-down complexity. In the Frascati Villa Simone, for example, the aromas from the malvasia puntinata don't satisfy completely, leaving a sensation of almost sweet softness. We do not mean that it isn't a good wine, just that we note a loss of energy. The '98 Frascati Vigna dei Preti, however, shows its habitual freshness. It has never been muscular: its appeal has always been in its fresh, light, aromatic style; it's a lean wine, certainly, but a delightfully approachable one. The '98 Frascati Vigneto Filonardi once more leads the pack. Either its vineyard of origin enjoys an ideal microclimate or, since it's so small, calls forth particularly loving care. The wine seems to have little in common with its lesser siblings, so great is the breadth of its bouquet. It even has a crisp acidity, something that can't be counted on in the wines of the Castelli Romani: Two well-deserved Glasses. The Cannellino '98 was not released in time for our tastings, so we'll be reviewing it next year.

○	Frascati Sup. Vign. Filonardi '97	▼▼	3*
○	Frascati Sup. V. dei Preti '98	▼	2*
○	Frascati Sup. Villa Simone '98		2
○	Frascati Sup. Cannellino '91	▽▽	5
○	Frascati Sup. Cannellino '92	▽▽	5
○	Frascati Sup. Cannellino '97	▽▽	5
○	Frascati Sup. V. dei Preti '94	▽▽	2*
○	Frascati Sup. V. dei Preti '95	▽▽	2*
○	Frascati Sup. V. dei Preti '97	▽▽	2*
○	Frascati Sup. Vign. Filonardi '93	▽▽	3*
○	Frascati Sup. Vign. Filonardi '94	▽▽	3*
○	Frascati Sup. Vign. Filonardi '95	▽▽	3*
○	Frascati Sup. Vign. Filonardi '97	▽▽	3*
○	Frascati Sup. Villa Simone '93	▽▽	2*
○	Frascati Sup. Villa Simone '95	▽▽	2*

ROMA

Conte Zandotti

Via Vigne Colle Mattia, 8
00132 Roma
tel. 06/20609000 - 06/6160335

At last the wines of Conte Zandotti have made a very good showing. Last year's criticisms, polite though they were, caused some mutterings at the estate but we seem to have been right, and the '98s have a much wider range of aromas and distinctly more complex structure than before. Even the Frascati Superiore offers clearly perceptible delightful aromas of fruit and warm and soft notes, in a perfect nose-palate balance. The extraordinary Rumon, an excellent Malvasia del Lazio '98 in its debut appearance, shows an ample bouquet with classic almond notes and attractive hints of honey and spice; it also has good sinew, and persistence on both nose and palate: a well-earned Two Glasses. And hearty congratulations to the oenologist Marco Ciarla, who is making such a difference at this estate. The '98 Frascati Cannellino is a delicate wine that seems to favor gentle harmony rather than voluptuous richness in its sweet tones of apple and wildflowers. La Petrosa '98 is the intriguing result of an experiment with (mainly) cabernet and sangiovese. Bottled after six months in barrel, it is fairly firm, warm and mouth-filling and reveals notes of red fruit and spice. The selection De Copa was not released in time for this year's Guide.

○	Frascati Superiore '98	▼▼	2*
●	La Petrosa '98	▼▼	4
○	Malvasia del Lazio Rumon '98	▼▼	3*
○	Frascati Cannellino '98	▼	3
○	Frascati Cannellino '95	▽▽	3*
○	Frascati Cannellino '96	▽▽	3*
○	Frascati Superiore '94	▽▽	2*
○	Frascati Superiore '95	▽▽	2*
○	Frascati Cannellino '93	▽	3*
○	Frascati Cannellino '94	▽	3
○	Frascati Cannellino '97	▽	3
○	Frascati Cannellino De Copa '97	▽	3
○	Frascati Superiore '96	▽	2*
○	Frascati Superiore '97	▽	2*
○	Frascati Superiore De Copa '97	▽	3

OTHER WINERIES

The following producers obtained good scores in our tastings with one or more of their wines:

PROVINCE OF FROSINONE

Antonello Coletti Conti
Anagni, tel. 0775/728610
Cesanese del Piglio Hernicus '98,
Passerina del Frusinate Hernicus '98

Marcella Giuliani
Anagni, tel. 06/44235908
Cesanese del Piglio Alagna '98

Giuseppe Iucci
Cassino, tel. 0776/311883
Merlot di Atina Tenuta La Creta '98

La Selva
Paliano, tel. 0775/533125
Cesanese del Piglio '98,
Passerina del Frusinate '98

Cantina Sociale Cesanese del Piglio
Piglio, tel. 0775/502355
Cesanese del Piglio Etichetta Oro '98,
Cesanese del Piglio Etichetta Rossa '98

Vigneti Massimi Berucci
Piglio, tel. 06/68307004
Cesanese del Piglio Casal Cervino '98,
Passerina del Frusinate '98

PROVINCE OF LATINA

Cantina Sociale Cincinnato
Cori, tel. 06/9679384
Rosso dei Dioscuri '98

Pouchain
Ponza, tel. 06/30365644
Vino di Bianca '98

PROVINCE OF ROMA

Cantina San Marco
Frascati, tel. 06/9422689
Frascati Sup. Sel. '98

Casale Mattia
Frascati, tel. 06/9426249
Frascati Sup. '98

Casale Vallechiesa
Frascati, tel. 06/9417270
Frascati Sup. Vallechiesa '98

L'Olivella
Frascati, tel. 06/9424527
Frascati Sup. Racemo '98

Tenuta di Pietra Porzia
Frascati, tel. 06/9464392
Frascati Sup. Regillo Etichetta Nera '98

Baldassarri
Genzano, tel. 06/9396106
Colli Lanuvini Sup. '98

Cantina Sociale La Selva
Genzano, tel. 06/9396085
Colli Lanuvini Sup. Fontanatorta '98

Cantina Sociale San Tommaso
Genzano, tel. 0 6/9375863
Colli Lanuvini Sup. Castel San Gennaro '98

Camponeschi
Lanuvio, tel. 06/9374390
Carato Bianco '98,
Carato Rosso '97,
Colli Lanuvini Sup. '98

Tenuta Le Quinte
Montecompatri, tel. 06/9438756
Montecompatri Colonna Sup. Virtù Romane '98

Torre In Pietra
Torrimpietra, tel. 06/61697070
Terre di Breccia Rosso '97

CO.PRO.VI
Velletri,
tel. 06/9587444
Velletri Bianco Villa Ginnetti '98,
Velletri Rosso Ris. '96

Cesare Loreti
Zagarolo,
tel. 06/9575956
Zagarolo Sup. Vigneti Loreti '98

PROVINCE OF VITERBO

Cantina Oleificio Sociale di Gradoli
Gradoli,
tel. 0761/456087
Aleatico di Gradoli Ris.

Cantina Sociale Colli Cimini
Vignanello,
tel. 0761/754591
Greco di Vignanello '98

ABRUZZO AND MOLISE

Quality in Abruzzo is on the rise, as is, consequently, the number of estates included in the Guide, which has doubled in three years. The flagship wine of the region is still Montepulciano d'Abruzzo, a rich, full-bodied red that, with the technological advances of the region's wineries, is acquiring an increasingly modern style, allowing it to compete without a handicap with the great bottles of the world. This is already true of the wines from the two standard-bearers of the region, the "legendary" Edoardo Valentini of Loreto Aprutino and Gianni Masciarelli who, in addition to his customary great Villa Gemma, has come up with an excellent Chardonnay named after his wife Marina Cvetic. This latter wine is a perfect demonstration of how the soil and climate of Abruzzo can produce great grapes which go on to become great wines. It should be mentioned that these two men represent the grand tradition and the pull of modernity respectively and, as such, are emblematic of a region that has only recently been moving decisively in the right direction. Then there are fine performances from names we knew and also some new profiles. It is certainly worth highlighting the good showing of a pair of the established estates. One is Illuminati, which again this year has some wines in pole position (Lumen and Zanna, particularly) and a very good range in general. The other is Luigi Cataldi Madonna, who, in the province of L'Aquila, has succeeded in producing a Cerasuolo such as one hardly ever sees any more, and a Montepulciano d'Abruzzo, the Tonì, that had us all sitting up in our seats. We welcome to the Guide the historic Bosco estate, Faraone, a small but very good estate in Teramo province, and the cooperative wineries of Casal Bordino and Miglianico, the only co-ops so far to follow the example of Cantina Tollo and set their sights on high quality. In the province of Teramo the reliable names are still Montori, Nicodemi, Lepore, Barone Cornacchia and Orlandi Contucci Ponno, although they seem not yet to have fully realized that they are on the cutting edge of Abruzzese wine-making. In Molise, Di Majo Norante seems to be on the right track, with three or four reds of notable depth. There is great ferment in Molise, as in Abruzzo, with a new generation of oenologists constantly on call and cellars being re-equipped right and left, and in the next few years we should start seeing the fruits of all these efforts. A final thought: there remains a danger, albeit a still distant one, that the desire to improve, to change a way of thinking, to move towards the taste of the market with overly soft and agreeable wines – international in style, possibly even somewhat artificial – will compromise the typical characteristics and individual personality of Abruzzese and Molisano wines. And distinctive traits are surely essential for a place on the world stage.

BOLOGNANO (PE)

CICCIO ZACCAGNINI

C.DA POZZO
65020 BOLOGNANO (PE)
TEL. 085/8880195

There is good reason to be pleased at the Zaccagnini estate, particularly given the promise of the new vineyard and the results of the experiments that their oenologist Concezio Marulli has carried out. For now the highlight is, once again, the Montepulciano d'Abruzzo San Clemente, this time the '97, aged half in large casks, half in barriques. The color is an intense red, and the nose, initially slightly closed, soon opens out to notes of red fruit (red currant); the palate is soft, meaty and mouth-filling, and finishes on a note of licorice. We were almost as happy with the Montepulciano d'Abruzzo Castello di Salle '96, which shows good substance and distinct and delightfully fruity notes on the palate, but a somewhat less well-defined nose, and the Capisco Rosso '95, which, despite its full body, is dominated by wood and has a somewhat uneven palate. The '98 San Clemente, a barrique-fermented chardonnay, is not as good as the '97 (which is still intriguing); it is certainly one of the best in its category, but it is already showing signs of age. Their second line has improved, as can be seen from the good Montepulciano d'Abruzzo '97, the successful Montepulciano d'Abruzzo Cerasuolo '98 and the crisp and succulent Myosotis '98, one of the best Abruzzese rosés this year. The Bianco di Ciccio '98, from trebbiano and chardonnay, is good too, as is the Ibisco Bianco '98, an attractive monovarietal riesling.

●	Montepulciano d'Abruzzo Abbazia S. Clemente '97	▼▼	4
○	Bianco di Ciccio '98	▼	3
●	Capsico Rosso '95	▼	4
○	Chardonnay Abbazia S. Clemente '98	▼	4
○	Ibisco Bianco '98	▼	3
●	Montepulciano d'Abruzzo '97	▼	3
●	Montepulciano d'Abruzzo Castello di Salle '96	▼	3
⊙	Montepulciano d'Abruzzo Cerasuolo '98	▼	3
⊙	Myosotis Rosé '98	▼	3
○	Chardonnay Abbazia S. Clemente '97	▽▽	4
●	Montepulciano d'Abruzzo Abbazia S. Clemente '96	▽▽	4

CAMPOMARINO (CB)

DI MAJO NORANTE

C.DA RAMITELLO, 4
86042 CAMPOMARINO (CB)
TEL. 0875/57208

This historic Molise estate has definitely benefited from the advice of their new consultant oenologist Riccardo Cotarella: this year their wines are more concentrated, more modern and fresher. And there are interesting new developments, such as the first release of the Don Luigi, an aglianico with a touch of prugnolo, a very promising red. But all the Di Majo wines did well, from the low-priced Molì '98, admirably concentrated and enjoyably drinkable, to the highest-scoring reds, the Prugnolo and the Ramitello, both from '97. The ruby-hued Prugnolo offers intense, ripe fruity aromas and good structure, guaranteeing depth on the palate. The Ramitello, from montepulciano and aglianico, has a more concentrated color, enticing notes of red fruit on the nose and a lovely softness on the palate that melds almost perfectly with the spicy oak-derived notes and the admirably smooth tannins. The other red from aglianico, the Contado '97 is also good, while the best of the whites is the Greco '98, with its intense scents of citrus fruit and white flowers, and good length on the palate. The Biblos '97, an oak-fermented blend of falanghina and greco with a modern style, is similarly good, as is the Fiano '98, with its fresh, fruity notes, good body and excellent definition on both nose and palate. The '94 Apianae, however, a white dessert wine from moscato, is a bit below its normal standard and the other whites, although worthy of mention, seem to have suffered from a tricky vintage.

●	Biferno Rosso Ramitello '97	▼▼	3*
●	Prugnolo '97	▼▼	3*
●	Aglianico Contado '97	▼	3
○	Biblos '97	▼	4
●	Biferno Molì Rosso '98	▼	1*
●	Don Luigi '97	▼	4
○	Fiano '98	▼	3
○	Greco '98	▼	3
○	Apianae '94		3
○	Biferno Molì Bianco '98		1
○	Falanghina '98		3
○	Ramitello Bianco '98		3
○	Apianae '93	▽▽	4
○	Biblos '95	▽▽	4
●	Biferno Rosso Ramitello '96	▽▽	3*

CASALBORDINO (CH)

COOPERATIVA CASALBORDINO

C.DA TERMINE, 38
66021 CASALBORDINO (CH)
TEL. 0873/918107 - 0873/918420

This is the debut in the Guide of this important cooperative, a recognition of the new path that they have been following, as we've noticed, in the last few years. Their president Alberto Tiberio and their skilled oenologist Beniamino Di Domenica have succeeded where many other large co-ops haven't even ventured: in establishing medium- and long-term agreements with their member growers, so as to be able to produce good wines at reasonable prices. This process is, of course, still in its early stages and much remains to be done. But some encouraging signs are two wines from the Contea di Bordino line that repeat good performances and two newcomers that are modern in style. The Montepulciano d'Abruzzo Badia dei Miracoli '97, a barrique-aged red, is interesting but could still be improved: its nose is somewhat oak-dominated and its palate, despite good fullness of extract, doesn't quite hang together. The Contea di Bordino '98 is successful, as usual. It shows an intense ruby color, captivating aromas of ripe bitter cherry and red currant and, on the palate, good body and well-judged wood. The Trebbiano d'Abruzzo '98, fresh and attractively fruity on both nose and palate, also receives One Glass, as does the Castel Verdino '98, a barrique-fermented chardonnay. The latter offers a more complex bouquet, a fuller flavor and better balance, although the finish is rather bitter. Both fresh and quaffable versions of the Montepulciano d'Abruzzo Cerasuolo are appreciably improved.

○	Castel Verdino '98	🍷	4
●	Montepulciano d'Abruzzo Badia dei Miracoli '97	🍷	4
●	Montepulciano d'Abruzzo Contea di Bordino '97	🍷	3
○	Trebbiano d'Abruzzo Contea di Bordino '98	🍷	3
⊙	Montepulciano d'Abruzzo Cerasuolo Contea di Bordino '98		3
⊙	Montepulciano d'Abruzzo Cerasuolo Villa Adami '98		2

COLONNELLA (TE)

LEPORE

C.DA CIVITA
64010 COLONNELLA (TE)
TEL. 0861/70860 - 085/4222835

We've always believed in the potential of this estate, its owners Gaspare Lepore and Giampiero Cichetti and their oenologist Umberto Svizzeri, and we continue to feel that they will definitively prove us right sooner or later. But this year we can again report only a timid step forward. The two whites from the native passerina grape are well made without being exciting: the classic version has a fruity bouquet, and the structure on the palate is underpinned by fair acidity; the new, barrique-fermented version offers a forward nose and reasonable body; it seems a good start, and much can still be done with it. The Montepulciano d'Abruzzo '97, after initial uncertainty on the nose, hints at red fruit, and the palate, although pleasingly substantial, has a somewhat insistent aftertaste of bitter licorice. The '95 Luigi Lepore selection, from montepulciano, shows even more concentrated color and fruit and a well-structured palate with solid tannins, but the finish is a bit rough. The Trebbiano d'Abruzzo and the Cerasuolo, both '98s, are properly made, while the Passito (unusually from montepulciano), although not very complex, offers pleasing notes of blackberry, cherry and sour cherry on both nose and palate.

●	Montepulciano d'Abruzzo '97	🍷	3
●	Montepulciano d'Abruzzo Luigi Lepore '95	🍷	5
○	Passera delle Vigne '98	🍷	3
○	Passerina Do '98	🍷	4
●	Passito dei Lepore '95	🍷	5
⊙	Montepulciano d'Abruzzo Cerasuolo '98		3
○	Trebbiano d'Abruzzo '98		3
●	Montepulciano d'Abruzzo '94	♀	2*
●	Montepulciano d'Abruzzo '96	♀	3
●	Montepulciano d'Abruzzo Luigi Lepore Ris. '93	♀	5
●	Montepulciano d'Abruzzo Ris. '92	♀	3
●	Passito dei Lepore '95	♀	5

CONTROGUERRA (TE)

DINO ILLUMINATI
C.DA S. BIAGIO, 18
64010 CONTROGUERRA (TE)
TEL. 0861/808008

Quality continues to improve at Dino Illuminati's well-known estate, particularly as regards the Montepulciano d'Abruzzos. We'll start with the brilliant Lumen '95, which seems dense and powerful even in the glass. The intense nose offers fruity and herbaceous notes (there's a touch of cabernet sauvignon) blended beautifully with the oak, and the palate reveals already smooth tannins and a broad, long finish. The Montepulciano d'Abruzzo Zanna '95 is just as good; it shows a more traditional style, with very ripe fruit dominating both nose and taste. The entry on the palate is soft, broad and reminiscent of blackberry and black currant; licorice takes over on the finish. These two wines are fine examples of two divergent styles that Claudio Cappellacci and Giorgio Marone have perfected, and between them is the Riparosso '98, which amazed us with its concentration and aromatic richness. The Nicò '95, from late-harvested montepulciano, is almost as good. It is soft and seductive, and develops evenly with lots of fruit and complex spice. All the whites are well executed, fresh and quaffable, although there are no stars among them. However, there is good potential in the Trebbiano d'Abruzzo Daniele '97, from barrique-fermented trebbiano, and in the Controguerra Ciafrè '98, an interesting blend of passerina, garganega and trebbiano. Both the Cenalba Chardonnay '98 and the sparkling Brut metodo classico are as appealing as ever.

●	Montepulciano d'Abruzzo Lumen '95	🍷🍷	5
●	Montepulciano d'Abruzzo Riparosso '98	🍷🍷	2*
●	Montepulciano d'Abruzzo Zanna Vecchio '95	🍷🍷	4
○	Brut Metodo Classico	🍷	4
○	Chardonnay Cenalba '98	🍷	3
○	Ciafré '98	🍷	3
⊙	Montepulciano d'Abruzzo Cerasuolo Campirosa '98	🍷	2*
●	Nicò '95	🍷	5
○	Trebbiano d'Abruzzo Costalupo '98	🍷	2*
○	Trebbiano d'Abruzzo Daniele '98	🍷	4

CONTROGUERRA (TE)

CAMILLO MONTORI
PIANE TRONTO, 23
64010 CONTROGUERRA (TE)
TEL. 0861/809900

Despite the '96 vintage, probably the worst of the decade in these parts, Camillo Montori, now assisted by his daughters Laura and Beatrice, has bravely presented both his top wines, the Leneo Moro and the Montepulciano d'Abruzzo Fonte Cupa. The first, a blend of montepulciano with a little cabernet, is appearing for the first time as a Controguerra DOC. Of a bright ruby hue, it is characterized by a light fragrance of ripe fruit and black cherries steeped in alcohol, with faint vegetal notes. After a soft attack on the palate it develops with good tannins and fair depth to an enjoyable finish. The Fonte Cupa does not boast great breadth of bouquet but does have good ripe fruit on the palate and a fairly long finish. The '98 Trebbiano d'Abruzzo from the Fonte Cupa line is enjoyable but a little less rich than usual. The Leneo d'Oro '97 shows a quite intense straw color, and notes of ripe fruit with light mineral nuances on the nose; the palate offers good texture but could be longer. The Montepulciano d'Abruzzo '97 deserves special comment. It was reviewed last year and will be available until April 2000. Tasting it again, we found it confirmed our previous assessment of a good wine from a fine vintage, rich and open on the nose, with clearly defined fruit; the tannins have improved. The two Cerasuolos, rosés from montepulciano, and the standard Trebbiano d'Abruzzo could all do better.

○	Leneo d'Oro '97	🍷	4
●	Leneo Moro '96	🍷	4
●	Montepulciano d'Abruzzo Fonte Cupa '96	🍷	4
⊙	Montepulciano d'Abruzzo Cerasuolo '98		2
⊙	Montepulciano d'Abruzzo Cerasuolo Fonte Cupa '98		3
○	Trebbiano d'Abruzzo '98		2
○	Trebbiano d'Abruzzo Fonte Cupa '98		3
●	Leneo Moro '94	🍷🍷 (white)	5
●	Leneo Moro '95	🍷🍷 (white)	5
●	Montepulciano d'Abruzzo Fonte Cupa '94	🍷🍷 (white)	4*

FRANCAVILLA A MARE (CH)

Franco Pasetti
C.da Pretaro, 61
Via S. Paolo
66023 Francavilla a Mare (CH)
tel. 085/61875

The declared aim of the brothers Mimmo and Rocco Pasetti is to dedicate ever more of their energies to improving the quality of their wines. This encouraging statement is in line with the trend in several of the region's estates and is a further instance of how much Abruzzese winegrowers believe in their land's potential. With their investments in their new vineyards in Collecorvino, some of which are just starting to produce, the Pasettis will be able to count on even better grapes. While we await the release of some new experimental wines, we note that the Montepulciano d'Abruzzo Tenuta di Testarossa '95 has not yet quite earned Two Glasses. It shows a deep ruby hue, and a bouquet rich in ripe red fruit somewhat dominated by toasty notes from the new oak tonneaux. The soft, full, spicy palate does not reveal great complexity. On the other hand, the economical version, the Montepulciano d'Abruzzo Fattoria Pasetti '97, shows all the hallmarks of a splendid vintage and of faultless vinification. The color is ruby red with a purplish rim; the nose, closed at first, soon opens to clearly defined fruity notes; in the mouth it shows good structure and balance, with attractive hints of ripe citrus peel and licorice. The inexpensive Trebbiano d'Abruzzo '98 is clean, well made, lightly redolent of flowers and medium-bodied, but the Cerasuolo, from montepulciano, does not have its usual freshness.

●	Montepulciano d'Abruzzo '97	🍷	2*
●	Montepulciano d'Abruzzo Tenuta di Testarossa '95	🍷	4
○	Trebbiano d'Abruzzo '98	🍷	2*
⊙	Montepulciano d'Abruzzo Cerasuolo '98		2
●	Montepulciano d'Abruzzo '96	🍷 (empty glass)	2*
●	Montepulciano d'Abruzzo Tenuta di Testarossa '94	🍷 (empty glass)	4

GIULIANOVA (TE)

Faraone
Loc. Colleranesco
S. S. 80, 290
64020 Giulianova (TE)
tel. 085/8071804

This debut in the Guide is a recognition of years of patient work on the part of Giovanni Faraone, one of the first in Abruzzo to use native grapes to make sparkling wine, and one of the few to experiment with new ways of making white wines from trebbiano and passerina. The '95, '96 and '97 vintages of his inexpensive Trebbiano d'Abruzzo Le Vigne are still marvelously enjoyable today, and the latest version, the '98, seems similarly likely to last for years. It displays quite an intense straw yellow color, a rich variety of fruity and floral aromas, and a fragrant palate with lingering notes of citrus fruit, fresh apple and minerals underpinned by crisp acidity. The other white, the good Trebbiano d'Abruzzo Santa Maria dell'Arco '97, is aged in small oak barrels that have given it a deeper color and a more complex nose. On the palate, however, it is somewhat less fresh and structured, and the fruit is slightly forward. Recent improvements in the two reds and the Cerasuolo, all from montepulciano, are evident, but we think there's still more to be done: the fruit on the nose is sometimes masked by other components, and grape selection could be more rigorous. The Brut metodo classico (vintage '95, dégorgement '99), from passerina and trebbiano, shows a fairly fine perlage and a rich if not elegant nose with notes of yellow flowers and just ripe fruit that reappear on the palate and linger on the finish.

○	Brut Metodo Classico '95	🍷	4
●	Montepulciano d'Abruzzo '97	🍷	3
○	Trebbiano d'Abruzzo Le Vigne '98	🍷	2*
○	Trebbiano d'Abruzzo S. Maria dell'Arco '97	🍷	4
⊙	Montepulciano d'Abruzzo Cerasuolo Le Vigne '98		2
●	Montepulciano d'Abruzzo S. Maria dell'Arco '95		4

LORETO APRUTINO (PE)

EDOARDO VALENTINI
VIA DEL BAIO, 2
65014 LORETO APRUTINO (PE)
TEL. 085/8291138

If he were French, a man like Edoardo Valentini would long since have been awarded the Légion d'honneur for his contributions to his region's viticulture. In Italy he cannot even get a grant to help him replant ten hectares of vineyard destroyed by the heavy snows of December '98. He would have had to grow varieties other than trebbiano and montepulciano and with training systems other than his customary pergola. What did it matter if his way yielded fabulous wines? In law, it is the letter that counts, not the particularities of an individual case. But Valentini is not a man who gives way to despair or self pity: he has already found a way of dealing with the vineyard problem. However, the consistency and scrupulousness with which he treats everyone and everything, including his wines, led him to make another difficult decision this year: not to release a single bottle. He finds them all still too young and wants to wait a few more months. After all, he has been waiting for at least three years for the Trebbiano, so what does it matter if he adds a further six months? The only thing he cares about is that the wines be just as he wants them. And we feel the same way.

●	Montepulciano d'Abruzzo '77	🍷🍷🍷	6
●	Montepulciano d'Abruzzo '85	🍷🍷🍷	6
●	Montepulciano d'Abruzzo '88	🍷🍷🍷	6
●	Montepulciano d'Abruzzo '90	🍷🍷🍷	6
●	Montepulciano d'Abruzzo '92	🍷🍷🍷	6
○	Trebbiano d'Abruzzo '88	🍷🍷🍷	5
○	Trebbiano d'Abruzzo '92	🍷🍷🍷	5
○	Trebbiano d'Abruzzo '95	🍷🍷🍷	5
●	Montepulciano d'Abruzzo '87	🍷🍷	6
●	Montepulciano d'Abruzzo '93	🍷🍷	6
⊙	Montepulciano d'Abruzzo Cerasuolo '96	🍷🍷	5
○	Trebbiano d'Abruzzo '90	🍷🍷	6
○	Trebbiano d'Abruzzo '93	🍷🍷	5
○	Trebbiano d'Abruzzo '94	🍷🍷	5

MIGLIANICO (CH)

CANTINA MIGLIANICO
VIA SAN GIACOMO, 40
66010 MIGLIANICO (CH)
TEL. 0871/951262 - 0871/950240

Miglianico is among the few cooperative wineries that are determined to produce first-class wines as soon as possible. Of these, it is the one that has made the fastest progress. The credit is due both to its oenologist Carmine Mancini, and to its directors, who have managed to "convert" many of its 450 member growers to the co-op's new mission: bottling. (Almost half their wine now goes into bottles). Having found a particularly good site in the hills near Montupoli, they initiated a process of viticultural selection and reorganization, as well as improvement in cellar technology. All of this has led to Miglianico's first entry in the Guide. Of the two wines named after their founder, Don Vincenzo Pizzica (the first president of the co-op and still the parish priest), the Montepulciano d'Abruzzo Fondatore '96 missed Two Glasses by a hair's breadth. It shows a deep color with an orange rim, and a dense array of aromas of ink and ripe sour cherry with balsamic notes. The entry on the palate is a little austere, with tannins still a bit harsh, but there are masses of evident fruit, albeit somewhat forward. The Trebbiano d'Abruzzo Fondatore '96, an oak-fermented white, has had more difficulty in staying the course. However, the more economical line, Montupoli, continues to show well: the Montepulciano d'Abruzzo '97 has a rich bouquet, plentiful good fruit and balanced development on the palate; and the Trebbiano d'Abruzzo '98 offers light but soft and harmonious fruit.

●	Montepulciano d'Abruzzo Fondatore '96	🍷	4
●	Montepulciano d'Abruzzo Montupoli '97	🍷	2*
○	Trebbiano d'Abruzzo Montupoli '98	🍷	2*
⊙	Montepulciano d'Abruzzo Cerasuolo Montupoli '98		2
○	Trebbiano d'Abruzzo Fondatore '96		4

NOCCIANO (PE)

Nestore Bosco

C.da Casali, 7
65010 Nocciano (PE)
tel. 085/847345

For the Bosco estate, a debut in the Guide represents a recognition of an entire career rather than just one year's production, since they have been making wine, bottling it and exporting it all over the world for decades. Especially their two Montepulciano d'Abruzzos, or rather three, as of this year. From their splendid cellar in Nocciano we now have Pan (a symbol of abundance, captured on the label by Pietro Cascella), a wine from which you expect great complexity; instead, it shows a not very intense ruby color, and a still youthful bouquet of fruit and rose, but good structure well blended with the oak. The traditional version from the same vintage, '95, is as usual a rustic wine, in the best sense of the word. The nose releases robust scents of cherry and sour cherry steeped in alcohol; the attack on the palate is bitter, the tannins are very smooth and the imposing structure makes for an unhurried finish. The less expensive, easily quaffable '98, which we tasted just a few weeks after its bottling, has the same characteristics but with less power. It displays an intense, vivid ruby red with a purplish cast, and a light, youthful fragrance of red fruit with herbaceous notes; in the mouth it is rich with still forceful tannins and fair length. The Bosco family has never concentrated particularly on its whites and this year has seen no change on that front, while the Montepulciano d'Abruzzo Cerasuolo '98 and the Grappolo '98, from montepulciano, sangiovese and merlot, are a little less good than last year's.

●	Montepulciano d'Abruzzo '95	🍷	4
●	Montepulciano d'Abruzzo '98	🍷	2*
●	Montepulciano d'Abruzzo Pan '95	🍷	5
○	Il Grappolo Bianco '98		2
●	Il Grappolo Rosso '98		2
⊙	Montepulciano d'Abruzzo Cerasuolo '98		2
○	Trebbiano d'Abruzzo '98		2

NOTARESCO (TE)

Bruno Nicodemi

C.da Veniglio, 8
S. P. 19
64024 Notaresco (TE)
tel. 085/895493 - 085/895135

This is considered one of the loveliest estates of the region, viticulturally speaking, and is widely expected to improve significantly in the near future. But this was not the decisive year. All the wines presented were clearly well executed but they lacked that additional excitement that Nicodemi's best wines have within their reach. The Montepulciano d'Abruzzo Bacco '95, for example, is a successful, characterful red. The color is a fairly deep ruby with bright highlights. The nose offers distinct and even fruit and the medium-bodied palate is pleasingly fruity, but the finish has too much alcohol for balance. The '98 version of the Trebbiano d'Abruzzo Bacco is again good. Of a bright straw color, it shows an attractive array of fresh and well-defined aromas and a palate underpinned by attractive acidity and intense citrus notes. The more economical Trebbiano d'Abruzzo, while less structured and important, displays a good breadth of appealing floral notes. The other wines in this range are equally good: the Montepulciano d'Abruzzo Cerasuolo '98 has a pleasing fresh, fruity fragrance, a cherry note on the palate and an aftertaste of bitter almond; the Montepulciano d'Abruzzo '97 is a bright, lively red with a fruity, herbaceous and vegetal nose, and a palate with good body and structure.

●	Montepulciano d'Abruzzo '97	🍷	2*
●	Montepulciano d'Abruzzo Bacco '95	🍷	5
⊙	Montepulciano d'Abruzzo Cerasuolo '98	🍷	2*
○	Trebbiano d'Abruzzo '98	🍷	2*
○	Trebbiano d'Abruzzo Bacco '98	🍷	4
●	Montepulciano d'Abruzzo Bacco '93	YY	5
●	Montepulciano d'Abruzzo Bacco '94	YY	5
●	Montepulciano d'Abruzzo Bacco '91	Y	3
●	Montepulciano d'Abruzzo Colli Venia '95	Y	2*

OFENA (AQ)

TENUTA CATALDI MADONNA
LOC. PIANA, 1
67025 OFENA (AQ)
TEL. 0862/954252 - 085/4911680

In recent years Luigi Cataldi Madonna's estate has been particularly generous with pleasant surprises. The house team, enriched two years ago by the arrival of the oenologist Giovanni Ballo and Bruna Musso for business management, has done very well in a very short time. The '95 version of the Montepulciano d'Abruzzo Tonì is probably the best ever. Of a deep ruby hue, it offers a great variety of aromas of ripe fruit, roasting coffee and chocolate enriched by hints of spice. The palate perfectly mirrors the bouquet, and vaunts an admirable fusion of woody tones with the rich dense extract; sour cherry, black currant and licorice linger on the long finish. The youthful, fruity, easy-drinking base version of the Montepulciano d'Abruzzo '97 is excellent value for money. The new red, the Malandrino '97, from montepulciano and cabernet sauvignon, combines pleasing quaffability with a well-articulated substantial structure. The flagship of the estate has always been the Cerasuolo, which has been available also in the Pié delle Vigne version for a couple of years. It is deeper in color and richer on the nose, with more of a red fruit fragrance, than the standard version; the bouquet reappears clearly on the palate and then lingers. The traditional whites are also showing as well as ever: the delicately fragrant Trebbiano d'Abruzzo '97 is fresh and harmonious on the palate and the Pecorino '98 shows notes of ripe apple on the nose and a rich, succulent palate. Lastly, the successful Vigna Cona '98, from sauvignon, is full, varietal and balanced.

⊙	Montepulciano d'Abruzzo Cerasuolo Pié delle Vigne '98	**YY**	3*
●	Montepulciano d'Abruzzo Tonì '95	**YY**	5
●	Malandrino '97	**Y**	4
●	Montepulciano d'Abruzzo '97	**Y**	3
○	Pecorino '98	**Y**	4
○	Trebbiano d'Abruzzo '98	**Y**	2*
○	Vigna Cona Bianco '98	**Y**	3
⊙	Montepulciano d'Abruzzo Cerasuolo '98		2
●	Montepulciano d'Abruzzo Tonì '91	YY	4*
●	Montepulciano d'Abruzzo Tonì '93	YY	5
●	Montepulciano d'Abruzzo '96	Y	3*
●	Montepulciano d'Abruzzo Tonì '90	Y	3
●	Vigna Cona Rosso '95	Y	4

POPOLI (PE)

LORENZO FILOMUSI GUELFI
VIA MARCONI, 28
65026 POPOLI (PE)
TEL. 085/98353

Lorenzo Filomusi Guelfi's good work is showing results, and with the restructuring of the cellar further improvements should appear, perhaps including a new version of the Montepulciano d'Abruzzo. The care customarily given to the excellent vineyards at Ceppete has again been rewarded by perfect grapes, vinified as usual with a skillful hand. We'll start with a fine Montepulciano d'Abruzzo '97, of a fairly deep ruby red color with brilliant highlights. The nose releases broad notes of sour cherry and ripe cherries steeped in alcohol; the palate has good body, noticeable tannins and fairly dense fruit. It's a good red wine, and with a couple of years in bottle it should be even better. Once more this year the quaffable Montepulciano d'Abruzzo Cerasuolo is one of the most successful of its kind. It shows a luminous, not very intense cherry-red hue and a youthful nose with enchanting notes of red fruit, echoed on the fresh, clean palate that finishes on a characteristic bitter almond tone. The good white Scuderie del Cielo '98, from chardonnay, sauvignon and malvasia, offers light fruity and floral scents of apple, banana and broom, and a fresh, even, medium-bodied palate with a balanced finish.

○	Le Scuderie del Cielo '98	**Y**	3
●	Montepulciano d'Abruzzo '97	**Y**	3
⊙	Montepulciano d'Abruzzo Cerasuolo '98	**Y**	3
●	Montepulciano d'Abruzzo '93	YY	3*
●	Montepulciano d'Abruzzo '90	Y	3
●	Montepulciano d'Abruzzo '91	Y	3
●	Montepulciano d'Abruzzo '92	Y	3

ROSCIANO (PE)

MARRAMIERO
C.DA S. ANDREA, 1
65010 ROSCIANO (PE)
TEL. 085/8505766

The wines we tasted this year provide ample confirmation that Marramiero is a producer worthy of note. This young winery is run by the young Enrico Marramiero and Antonio Chiavaroli, with help in the cellars from Romeo Taraborrelli, one of the region's most active oenologists. The best wines come from their better range (for which a new barrel-room was created); for the more economical range, Dama, there is still a bit of work to be done. We'll start with the impressive Montepulciano d'Abruzzo Inferi '95, a full-bodied barrique-aged red. Well-modulated balsamic and fruity notes on the nose are followed by a wonderfully restrained and soft attack on the palate, which develops with substantial extract and tannic heft to the full finish. The Altare '97, the first of three whites from trebbiano, again shows well-judged oak, an intense straw color, a rich fruity nose with notes of peach and appealing toasty tones, and a full-bodied, crisply acidic palate that promises a fairly long life. The Trebbiano d'Abruzzo Anima '98 also earns its One Glass. It has less complexity but offers fresh scents of apple and white flowers, and a fragrant, medium-bodied palate. Two of the three wines from the Dama line receive only a mention, as does the metodo classico Brut. A vat tasting of the '97 Montepulciano d'Abruzzo was extremely promising.

●	Montepulciano d'Abruzzo Inferi '95	▼▼	4
○	Trebbiano d'Abruzzo Altare '97	▼	4
○	Trebbiano d'Abruzzo Anima '98	▼	3
○	Marramiero Brut		4
⊙	Montepulciano d'Abruzzo Cerasuolo Dama '98		2
○	Trebbiano d'Abruzzo Dama '98		2
●	Montepulciano d'Abruzzo Inferi '93	▽▽	4
●	Montepulciano d'Abruzzo Inferi '94	▽▽	4
○	Chardonnay Punta di Colle '97	▽	3
○	Trebbiano d'Abruzzo Altare '95	▽	3
○	Trebbiano d'Abruzzo Altare '96	▽	4
○	Trebbiano d'Abruzzo Anima '95	▽	3

ROSETO DEGLI ABRUZZI (TE)

ORLANDI CONTUCCI PONNO
C.DA VOLTARROSTO
VIA PIANA DEGLI ULIVI, 1
64026 ROSETO DEGLI ABRUZZI (TE)
TEL. 085/8944049

This estate, run by Marina Orlandi Contucci with Donato Lanati as consultant oenologist, has never disguised its "international" leanings: nearly 30 years ago they chose to plant cabernet sauvignon, sauvignon blanc, chardonnay and merlot side by side with the traditional montepulciano and trebbiano. This year the Liburnio, a cabernet-based blend, again stands out. The '95 is striking in its intensity of color, progression on the nose (quinine, black currant, bitter cherry and vegetal notes) and its full-bodied and even palate. The Colle Funaro '96 has a typically varietal cabernet profile with bell pepper notes on the nose and, more elegantly, also on the palate, but without great power. The whites, in a new development, are softer than before. The Roccesco '98, a monovarietal chardonnay, seems the most successful: it offers delicate but distinct aromas of apple, banana and citrus fruit, which are echoed on the full-bodied palate. The Trebbiano d'Abruzzo Colle della Corte '98 is lighter but still well made and fragrant. About the Montepulciano d'Abruzzo '97: we have nothing against wines that are modern in manner; but perhaps the characteristic nature of this classic Abruzzese red have been sacrificed in the Orlandi Contuci Ponno version in favor of an exaggeratedly international style.

●	Liburnio '95	▼▼	5
●	Cabernet Sauvignon Colle Funaro '96	▼	3
○	Chardonnay Roccesco '98	▼	3
●	Montepulciano d'Abruzzo La Regia Specula '97	▼	3
○	Trebbiano d'Abruzzo Colle della Corte '98	▼	2*
⊙	Montepulciano d'Abruzzo Cerasuolo Vermiglio '98		2
●	Cabernet Sauvignon Colle Funaro '95	▽▽	3*
●	Liburnio '93	▽▽	5
○	Sauvignon Ghiaiolo '97	▽	3

S. MARTINO SULLA MARRUCINA (CH)

GIANNI MASCIARELLI
VIA GAMBERALE, 1
66010 S. MARTINO SULLA MARRUCINA (CH)
TEL. 0871/85241

We're glad to be in a position to write this review. We feel certain that Gianni Masciarelli will remember 1999 for a long time. He was in danger of dying, and then the family of his wife Marina Cvetic risked death in the Nato bombing of Belgrade. Next, Gianni walked off with Three Glasses for two of his wines, and perhaps there's yet more news, also splendid, but it would be tempting fate to say what. If we wanted to be catty we'd point out that Gianni goes in for excess. We think, however, that excess can be positive, and so it is in his case. As for this year's range, there are two stunners. For a start, the '94 Montepulciano d'Abruzzo Villa Gemma is one of the best versions yet: powerful, fat and maybe tending to excess (well, why not?). Then the Chardonnay Marina Cvetic '97 is simply fabulous: full-flavored, varietal, with perfectly melded oak and well-delineated, elegant aromas of tropical fruit. The rest of the range is exemplary, with our special compliments for one of the best Trebbiano d'Abruzzos (the '97) he has ever made, second only to the legendary '91. Then there is the new cellar, his newly planted vineyard at such a high density (8,000 vines per hectare) that he passed it off as a tomato plot to stop his neighbors from calling him a lunatic, and so on. What can one say except long live excess?

○	Chardonnay Marina Cvetic '97	🍷🍷🍷	4*
●	Montepulciano d'Abruzzo Villa Gemma '94	🍷🍷🍷	6
●	Montepulciano d'Abruzzo Marina Cvetic '97	🍷🍷	4
○	Trebbiano d'Abruzzo Marina Cvetic '97	🍷🍷	5
●	Montepulciano d'Abruzzo '97	🍷	2*
⊙	Montepulciano d'Abruzzo Cerasuolo '98	🍷	3
○	Villa Gemma Bianco '98	🍷	3
●	Montepulciano d'Abruzzo Villa Gemma '92	🍸🍸🍸	5
●	Montepulciano d'Abruzzo Villa Gemma '93	🍸🍸🍸	5

SPOLTORE (PE)

FATTORIA LA VALENTINA
VIA COLLE CESI, 10
65010 SPOLTORE (PE)
TEL. 085/4478158

Entrusting the technical direction of the cellar to Luca d'Attoma has not brought great changes as yet, but Sabatino Di Properzio, the young and capable manager, knows that this is not a short-term project. In the meantime the new cellar equipment (technology and oak) has arrived and experiments are going ahead. Some are quite curious, such as the Montepulciano d'Abruzzo made in conjunction with the Veneto winegrower Stefano Inama. The wines that showed best this year were the reds from montepulciano. The Montepulciano d'Abruzzo '97 scores for its attractive scents of ripe fruit and delicate herbaceous notes, and for its soft, well-balanced and long palate. However, the special selection Spelt '94 did not exceed One Glass because the classic ripe red fruit was not clearly expressed on either nose or palate, although the wine was well structured overall. The two non-DOC wines, the Lusinga and the Punta Rossa, were well delineated. The late-harvested Lusinga has clear balsamic and spicy (mint, rhubarb, pepper) notes, but on the palate, despite its fullness, there is a slight alcohol imbalance and a persistent bitterish note. The more restrained, direct and elegant Punta Rossa displays hints of anise and ripe fruit. The Cerasuolo seemed to lack its usual liveliness, as did the two whites from trebbiano d'Abruzzo. In the base version this lack of freshness is compensated by attractive fruity notes of ripe apple on both nose and palate. The '98 Vigneto Spilla once more has the noticeably forward character that it shows every year – some would find it a defect.

●	Lusinga	🍷	2*
●	Montepulciano d'Abruzzo '97	🍷	2*
●	Montepulciano d'Abruzzo Spelt '94	🍷	3
●	Punta Rossa	🍷	2*
○	Trebbiano d'Abruzzo '98	🍷	2*
⊙	Montepulciano d'Abruzzo Cerasuolo '98		2
○	Trebbiano d'Abruzzo Vigneto Spilla '98		2
●	Montepulciano d'Abruzzo Ris. '93	🍸🍸	3*
●	Montepulciano d'Abruzzo '96	🍸	2*
●	Montepulciano d'Abruzzo '95	🍸	2*
●	Montepulciano d'Abruzzo Ris. '92	🍸	3
○	Trebbiano d'Abruzzo Vigneto Spilla '96	🍸	2*

TOLLO (CH)

CANTINA TOLLO
VIA GARIBALDI
66010 TOLLO (CH)
TEL. 0871/961726

Cantina Tollo deserves great credit for having forged the way forward in Abruzzo and for having been an encouraging example for the region's more than 30 cooperative wineries. That today it is no longer alone in searching for a balance between good quality and fair pricing simply sheds further luster on the program set in place years ago by Tommaso Perantuono (Tollo's president) and Giancarlo Di Ruscio (cellarmaster), and on the efforts of the technical personnel led by Goffredo Agostini. This year all the wines are again exemplary value for money. The '95 Montepulciano d'Abruzzo Cagiolo, Tollo's top wine, is stylish and almost balsamic on the nose and quite full-bodied and soft on the palate, but not particularly long. As usual the Colle Secco wines are successful and enjoyable: the Trebbiano d'Abruzzo is fragrant and surprisingly rich and the two Montepulciano d'Abruzzos each easily claims One Glass. The small difference between the two is in the greater elegance and more modern style of the Rubino. Of the three Valle d'Oro wines, the red combines quaffability and structure while the Cerasuolo, the rosé from montepulciano, seems to have a subscription to international prizes thanks to its beautifully clean cherry fragrance, its fresh palate and its subtly almondy finish. The Cagiolo Bianco '98 is appealing, but perhaps its structure is a little too slender to support the oak.

●	Montepulciano d'Abruzzo Cagiòlo '95	Y	4
⊙	Montepulciano d'Abruzzo Cerasuolo Valle d'Oro '98	Y	1*
●	Montepulciano d'Abruzzo Colle Secco '97	Y	2*
●	Montepulciano d'Abruzzo Colle Secco Rubino '97	Y	2*
●	Montepulciano d'Abruzzo Valle d'Oro '97	Y	1*
○	Trebbiano d'Abruzzo Colle Secco '98	Y	2*
○	Cagiòlo Bianco '98		3
●	Montepulciano d'Abruzzo Cagiòlo '94	YY	3*

TORANO NUOVO (TE)

BARONE CORNACCHIA
C.DA TORRI
64010 TORANO NUOVO (TE)
TEL. 0861/887412

It seems that Piero Cornacchia's historic, export-oriented estate has now found continuity and constancy. Both new and old vineyards, situated in fine positions on the hills of Torano Nuovo, yielded reds of deep color and good structure even in the difficult '97 vintage, although they were not hugely complex. The best is the Montepulciano d'Abruzzo Vigna Le Coste '95, with its rich notes of red fruit on the nose and good entry on the palate, where it reveals softness and substance. But even the base Montepulciano d'Abruzzo '97 has a clean, fruity nose with notes of bay, and a notable palate despite untamed tannins. The good Poggio Varano '97, also from montepulciano, is somewhat uncertain on the nose, but the palate is light and fresh, with ripe fruit and fair length. Both the Montepulciano d'Abruzzo Cerasuolo '98 and the Villa Torri Chardonnay are properly executed but could be improved. The former shows a slightly ill-defined nose and a rather anemic palate, and the latter has still to find its balance. Encouraging things from the Trebbiano d'Abruzzo: the '97 has a straw yellow color with a greenish tinge, a good pungent, floral nose, and a faintly acidulous but direct palate, making for pleasurable drinking.

●	Montepulciano d'Abruzzo '97	Y	2*
●	Montepulciano d'Abruzzo Poggio Varano '97	Y	4
●	Montepulciano d'Abruzzo Vigna Le Coste '95	Y	4
○	Trebbiano d'Abruzzo '98	Y	2*
○	Chardonnay Villa Torri '98		2
⊙	Montepulciano d'Abruzzo Cerasuolo '98		2
●	Montepulciano d'Abruzzo Poggio Varano '96	YY	3*
●	Montepulciano d'Abruzzo '97	Y	2*
●	Montepulciano d'Abruzzo Vigna Le Coste '96	Y	3

OTHER WINERIES

The following producers obtained good scores in our tastings with one or more of their wines:

PROVINCE OF CAMPOBASSO

Borgo di Colloredo
Campomarino,
tel. 0875/57453
Biferno Rosso Gironia '95

PROVINCE OF CHIETI

Spinelli
Atessa, tel. 0872/897916
Montepulciano d'Abruzzo Terra d'Aligi '97

Santoleri
Guardiagrele,
tel. 0871/82250 - 983301
Montepulciano d'Abruzzo Crognaleto '94

Agriverde
Ortona, tel. 085/9032101
Montepulciano d'Abruzzo '97

Citra
Ortona, tel. 085/9031342
Montepulciano d'Abruzzo Caroso '94,
Montepulciano d'Abruzzo Villa Torre '97

Sarchese Dora
Ortona, tel. 085/9031249
Montepulciano d'Abruzzo
Rosso di Macchia '95

Buccicatino, Vacri, tel. 0871/720273
Montepulciano d'Abruzzo '97

Torre Zambra
Villa Magna, tel. 0871/300121
Montepulciano d'Abruzzo '96

PROVINCE OF L'AQUILA

Praesidium, Prezza, tel. 0864/45103
Montepulciano d'Abruzzo '96

PROVINCE OF PESCARA

Chiarieri
Pianella, tel. 085/973313 - 971365
Montepulciano d'Abruzzo Hannibal '95

Roxan, Rosciano, tel. 085/8505683
Montepulciano d'Abruzzo '98

PROVINCE OF TERAMO

Di Giovampietro
Gulianova, tel. 085/8002569
Montepulciano d'Abruzzo
Castel Musiano '98

F.lli Barba, Pineto, tel. 085/8990104
Montepulciano d'Abruzzo '93,
Montepulciano d'Abruzzo '97

Casal Thaulero
Roseto degli Abruzzi, tel. 085/894531
Montepulciano d'Abruzzo Vigna Pauli '95

CAMPANIA

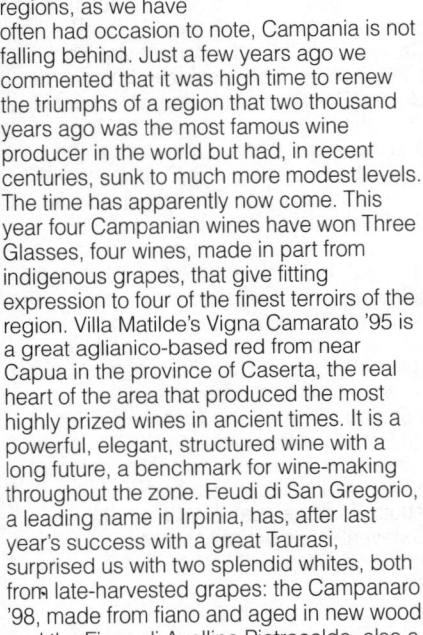

Campania is, in terms of wine, one of the most dynamic regions in southern Italy. In an era when the world's oenological center of gravity is moving steadily towards the hotter, sunnier regions, as we have often had occasion to note, Campania is not falling behind. Just a few years ago we commented that it was high time to renew the triumphs of a region that two thousand years ago was the most famous wine producer in the world but had, in recent centuries, sunk to much more modest levels. The time has apparently now come. This year four Campanian wines have won Three Glasses, four wines, made in part from indigenous grapes, that give fitting expression to four of the finest terroirs of the region. Villa Matilde's Vigna Camarato '95 is a great aglianico-based red from near Capua in the province of Caserta, the real heart of the area that produced the most highly prized wines in ancient times. It is a powerful, elegant, structured wine with a long future, a benchmark for wine-making throughout the zone. Feudi di San Gregorio, a leading name in Irpinia, has, after last year's success with a great Taurasi, surprised us with two splendid whites, both from late-harvested grapes: the Campanaro '98, made from fiano and aged in new wood, and the Fiano di Avellino Pietracalda, also a '98. Both are powerful, rich, highly concentrated, and lively on the nose, and point the way to new developments in Irpinian wine-making. And then the '97 Montevetrano, a red from the province of Salerno that has risen to international fame. This is its fourth award in five years, a performance that few Italian wines can equal. It's a blend of cabernet and merlot with a small percentage of aglianico: a great wine, international in style, but still intimately connected to its terroir and its tradition. No Campanian producer would want to sever that connection, or cancel that memory. Indeed, if we look at the wines that engendered most enthusiasm apart from the Three Glass winners, we find that they all have indigenous grapes as a significant part of their make-up. Galardi's excellent Terra di Lavoro, for example, from piedirosso and aglianico, and the Taurasis of Feudi di San Gregorio, Terredora and Caggiano are all elegant, powerful wines that are sketching a new profile for the great wines of the south. And from Ischia to Sannio, from the Cilento to the Amalfi coast, wherever people talk about important wines and improvement in quality, they recognize that it must all be based on the invaluable terroir and the rich patrimony of varieties that make this region special – as they have done for thousands of years.

ATRIPALDA (AV)

ANTONIO, CARLO E PIETRO
MASTROBERARDINO
VIA MANFREDI, 75/81
83042 ATRIPALDA (AV)
TEL. 0825/626123

Antonio Mastroberardino is one of the most prominent figures on the Campanian wine scene. From his state-of-the-art cellar at Atripalda he has sent forth wines that are now considered Italian classics. Fiano di Avellino, Greco di Tufo and Taurasi all owe their international fame to him and his amazing enthusiasm. And it was these three wines out of his now vast range that pleased us most at our tastings. Antonio, with the help of his sons Carlo and Pietro, has produced an excellent Taurasi Radici '95. It has a vivid deep ruby color and intense aromas of ripe blackberry, cherry and black currant elegantly integrated with delicate spicy tones and heady notes of alcohol. In the mouth it is warm and deep, with lots of fruit and plentiful but smooth, ripe tannins; the fruit on the long finish is rendered more complex by elegant nuances of old wood. The Lacryma Christi del Vesuvio '98, a monovarietal piedirosso, displays a concentrated dark ruby hue and an intense sweet bouquet of ripe plum and blackberry. The palate is round, warm, rich in smooth tannins, balanced, intense and long. Of the whites, we particularly liked the Fiano d'Avellino Vignadora '98, with its elegant floral nose and fruity, well-structured palate. The Fiano di Avellino Radici '98 and the Greco di Tufo Vignadangelo '98 are less complex but well executed and stylish; the former displays fresh, delicately vegetal perfumes and a good acid bite on the palate, and the latter is floral on the nose and fresh and full-flavored in the mouth.

○	Fiano di Avellino Vignadora '98	▼▼	4
●	Lacryma Christi Rosso '98	▼▼	3*
●	Taurasi Radici '95	▼▼	5
●	Aglianico Avellanio '97	▼	2*
○	Delizie d'Irpinia Passito '96	▼	4
○	Fiano di Avellino '98	▼	4
○	Fiano di Avellino Radici '98	▼	4
○	Greco di Tufo '98	▼	4
○	Greco di Tufo Vignadangelo '98	▼	3
●	Taurasi Radici '90	▽▽▽	6
○	Fiano di Avellino Radici '95	▽▽	4
○	Fiano di Avellino Vignadora '95	▽▽	4
●	Taurasi Radici '93	▽▽	5
●	Taurasi Radici '94	▽▽	5
●	Taurasi Ris. '86	▽▽	6

CASTELVENERE (BN)

FATTORIA CIABRELLI
VIA ITALIA
82030 CASTELVENERE (BN)
TEL. 0824/940565

Fattoria Ciabrelli has been run by Antonio Ciabrelli since his father passed it on to him in 1976, which is when he started bottling his wine. The estate is at Castelvenere in the province of Benevento, in the heart of the Sannio zone. There are five hectares under vine planted almost entirely to traditional varieties, and from them he produces six wines, two Solopaca DOCs and four Beneventano IGTs. Of the Solopacas we particularly liked the Bianco Vigna di Castelvenere '98. Of a brilliant straw color, it offers a clean, well-expressed bouquet of Golden Delicious apple and white peach; the palate reveals good body, fair finesse and moderate intensity and length. The Solopaca Rosso Vigna di Castelvenere '98 rates only a mention. The very good Barbera del Beneventano has quite intense, well-defined aromas of blackberry and ripe cherry, and character, good structure and soft tannins on the palate, which echoes the bouquet. The '98 Aglianico was good too, with its sweet fragrance of ripe plum and soft, balanced and fairly long palate. From a blend of aglianico, barbera and montepulciano Antonio Ciabrelli produces the Rosso del Beneventano '98, a fresh wine with a great immediate appeal, redolent of berries and lean but harmonious in the mouth. To close, the Falanghina del Beneventano is properly made but a bit thin and evanescent.

●	Aglianico del Beneventano '98	▼	3
●	Barbera del Beneventano '98	▼	2*
●	Beneventano Rosso '98	▼	2*
○	Solapaca Bianco Vigne di Castelvenere '98	▼	2*
○	Falanghina del Beneventano '98		3
●	Solopaca Rosso Vigne di Castelvenere '98		2
●	Solapaca Rosso Vigne di Castelvenere '94	▽▽	2*
●	Solopaca Rosso Vigne di Castelvenere '93	▽	3
●	Solopaca Rosso Vigne di Castelvenere '95	▽	2*

CASTELVENERE (BN)

ANTICA MASSERIA VENDITTI
VIA SANNITICA, 98
82030 CASTELVENERE (BN)
TEL. 0824/940306

Nicola Venditti's estate is back in the Guide after a couple of years' absence, and it's more than welcome, as one of the wines was awarded Two Glasses and a further two came very close. Nicola, winegrower and oenologist, cultivates his own vines according to the dictates of organic farming. The soil is fertilized naturally and the grapes are picked by hand and immediately vinified to avoid the need for chemical additives. The vineyards lie within the Solopaca DOC zone, and the Solopaca Bianco della Vigna Bacalàt '98 emerged as the best Venditti wine this year. It has a brilliant pale straw color with a greenish cast; the nose releases notes of fresh tropical fruit (pineapple and papaya); the palate is fresh, fairly full-bodied, balanced and delightfully fruity, with a hint of apricot. The finish is moderately long. The ruby-hued Sannio Barbera Barbetta Vàndari '98 also showed well. The intense aromas of plum and ripe cherry are given greater complexity by spicy notes and a delicate hint of incense; good balance, appropriate tannins and lots of acidity and fruit characterize the palate. The Sannio Bianco '98, from the local indigenous clones grieco and cerreto, opens on the nose with intense fruity aromas that give way to greener nuances with a hint of sage and a fresh balsamic note. In the mouth it offers structure, full flavor, nice intensity and fair persistence. The other wines are all good too.

○	Solopaca Bianco Vigna Bacalàt '98	🍷🍷	3*
●	Sannio Barbera Barbetta Vàndari '98	🍷	2*
○	Sannio Bianco '98	🍷	1*
○	Sannio Falanghina Vàndari '98		2
●	Sannio Rosso '98		1
●	Solopaca Rosso Bosco Caldaia '97		3
●	Solopaca Rosso Bosco Caldaia '93	🍸🍸	3*
●	Solopaca Rosso Bosco Caldaia '95	🍸	3
●	Solopaca Rosso Vigna Marraioli '93	🍸	3

CELLOLE (CE)

VILLA MATILDE
S. S. DOMITIANA, KM. 4,700
81030 CELLOLE (CE)
TEL. 0823/932088 - 0823/932134

Three Glasses have arrived at Villa Matilde, the first of what we hope will be a long series of similar triumphs. They are, among other things, a recognition of the devotion and enthusiasm that Salvatore Avallone and his sister Maria Ida have long dedicated to their family estate. The arrival of the distinguished consultant oenologist Riccardo Cotarella was an important turning point in the style of the wines: they acquired greater purity of style and expressive intensity, and entered the company of the best wines of southern Italy. The champion is a fabulous red from aglianico, the Vigna Camarata '95. Its ruby color is so dense and dark it looks almost black. The intense and complex nose releases a rich array of aromas ranging from a variety of berries to vanilla and chocolate, with stylish notes of toasty oak, pencil lead and tobacco. The fleshy, elegant, succulent and fresh palate offers extraordinary concentration and depth, clean, refreshing fruit and extremely fine-grained tannins. The long and complex finish displays a wide range of soft nuances of berries and vanilla. The wine is a delight right now, but it has great aging potential. The Falerno del Massico Rosso '97 won Two Glasses for its marvelous nose-palate harmony, velvety tannins and overall warm softness. The Falerno del Massico Bianco Vigna Caracci '98, although not as concentrated as the '97, shows soft tones of white-fleshed fruit and vanilla on the nose and good structure on the palate. The rest of the range is also excellent, from the Falerno del Massico Bianco '98 to the Terre Cerase '98, a good rosé.

●	Vigna Camarato '95	🍷🍷🍷	5
●	Falerno del Massico Rosso '97	🍷🍷	3*
○	Falanghina di Roccamonfina '98	🍷	3
○	Falerno del Massico Bianco '98	🍷	3
○	Falerno del Massico Bianco Vigna Caracci '98	🍷	4
⊙	Terre Cerase Rosato '98	🍷	3
○	Falerno del Massico Bianco Vigna Caracci '96	🍸🍸	4
○	Falerno del Massico Bianco Vigna Caracci '97	🍸🍸	4
●	Falerno del Massico Rosso '96	🍸🍸	3*
●	Vigna Camarato '85	🍸🍸	6
●	Vigna Camarato '88	🍸🍸	6
●	Vigna Camarato '92	🍸🍸	4

FORIO (NA)

D'AMBRA VINI D'ISCHIA
LOC. PANZA
S. S. 270
VIA MARIO D'AMBRA
80075 FORIO (NA)
TEL. 081/907210 - 081/907246

One of the best-known names in Campanian oenology has entered a new phase. Established in 1888 , D'Ambra was brought to great renown by Don Mario D'Ambra, gentleman, businessman and great legendary figure. On his death in 1985 the estate passed to his nephews, Corrado and Andrea, and in these 15 years they have worked incredibly hard to raise the quality of the wines and, with steadfast dedication, to save the vineyards of Ischia from the threat of abandonment and the unbridled encroachment of concrete. This year the two cousins have finally decided to go their separate ways. Corrado, who took care of the commercial side, will be running a wine shop full time at Ischia Porto; Andrea, the oenologist, will run the estate. And he will continue to plant vineyards and experiment with new ways of harnessing the potential of the island's typical grapes. This year's range seemed a little subdued. All of the many wines were irreproachably executed, but none really excited us, not even the '98 Tenuta Frassitelli, excellent though it was: but then, this biancolella-based white has in other vintages reached the dizzy heights of Three Glasses. The new estate wine, the white Arime '98, 50% rilla from the Forio vineyards with equal parts of biancolella and forastera, was subjected to batonage, a technique involving leaving the wine on its lees for a long period; it has depth and character but lacks the elegance and freshness that would have pushed it up a notch. We eagerly await further vintages, as we do the important red wine Don Mario Riserva, a monovarietal guarnaccia, of which we hear great things.

○ Biancolella Tenuta Frassitelli '98	▼▼	4
○ Arime '98	▼	4
○ Biancolella Vigne di Piellero '98	▼	3
○ Ischia Biancolella '98	▼	3
○ Ischia Forastera '98	▼	2*
● Ischia Per"e Palummo '98	▼	2*
● Ischia Per"e Palummo Tenuta Montecorvo '98	▼	4
○ Biancolella Tenuta Frassitelli '90	▽▽▽	2*
○ Cimentorosso '97	▽▽	3*
● Ischia Per"e Palummo Tenuta Montecorvo '94	▽▽	4
○ Tenuta Frassitelli '97	▽▽	4
○ Vigne di Piellero '97	▽▽	3*

FORIO (NA)

CANTINE DI PIETRATORCIA
LOC. FORIO
VIA PROVINCIALE PANZA, 267
80075 FORIO (NA)
TEL. 081/908206 - 081/997406

The ancient winegrowing tradition of Ischia has been sadly battered in the last 30 years. Vineyards under assault from the incursions of concrete from unlicensed construction are in danger of disappearing, while others painstakingly carved out on the rocky terraces of Monte Epomeo run the risk of abandonment in favor of the more lucrative attractions of the tourist industry. In a bid to halt the tide, three old Ischian families, the Iaconos, the Regines and the Verdes, have united forces and set up a new estate, Pietratorcia. There are seven hectares of vineyard, all planted to traditional varieties such as the white biancolella and forastera and the red per"e palummo and guarnaccia. With the valuable advice of experts from the Istituto Agrario di San Michele all'Adige, Pietratorcia produces eight different wines. The Pietratorcia Rosso Riserva '97, a wood-aged blend of piedirosso and guarnaccia making its debut this year, was our favorite. It shows a fine deep ruby color, captivating aromas of ripe cherry, spice and vanilla, and, on the palate, remarkable harmony, good structure, elegant tannins and a long finish. The more immediate, fruity red, Tifeo '98, is less structured but wonderfully fresh, as is the Ischia Rosso '97 Vigne di Ianno Piro, which is vinous and spicy on the nose and full-bodied on the palate. The excellent white Ischia Riserva '97 has great elegance and a soft, full structure, while the good Ischia Bianco Superiore Vigne di Chignole '98 is floral, rounded and full. All the other wines in this wide range are also properly executed.

○ Ischia Bianco Ris. '97	▼▼	5
● Pietratorcia Rosso Ris. '97	▼▼	5
○ Ischia Bianco '98	▼	3
○ Ischia Bianco Sup. Vigne del Cuotto '98	▼	4
○ Ischia Bianco Sup. Vigne di Chignole '98	▼	4
● Ischia Rosso Vigne di Ianno Piro '97	▼	3
○ Meditandum '98	▼	5
● Tifeo Rosso '98	▼	3
○ Ischia Bianco Sup. Vigne del Cuotto '97	▽	4
○ Ischia Bianco Sup. Vigne di Chignole '97	▽	4

FURORE (SA)

Cuomo

Via G. B. Lama, 14
84010 Furore (SA)
tel. 089/830348 - 0336/610544

Once again the Cuomo wines, lovingly produced by Andrea Ferraioli and his wife Marisa Cuomo, have done extremely well. These are, we feel, the best Costa d'Amalfi Docs to be found, and the reason is the painstaking care that Marisa and Andrea devote to their vineyard, which is on terraces carved out of the coastal rocks, 300-500 meters above the sea. The number of whites has increased this year. In addition to the customary Ravello and Furore there is now a Furore selection, the Fiorduva '98. Of a deep straw color, it offers an intense floral bouquet dominated by broom with sweet notes of ripe white-fleshed fruit, and noteworthy structure on the concentrated, elegant, fresh palate that boasts a long aromatic finish. The standard Furore '98 is appealingly fresh and structured in the mouth; soft tones of white peach appear on both nose and palate. Of the reds the Furore Riserva '96 showed particularly well and easily reached Two Glasses. It has a dark ruby hue, a shapely bouquet of ripe fruit melding elegantly with spicy oak-derived notes, and body, softness and elegance on the palate. The Ravello Riserva '96 is less appealing despite its good structure, because it is too forward on the nose. To finish, the Furore Rosso '98 is a not very concentrated but light, fresh and quaffable wine.

○	Costa d'Amalfi Furore Bianco Fiorduva '98	▼▼	4
●	Costa d'Amalfi Furore Rosso Ris. '96	▼▼	4
○	Costa d'Amalfi Furore Bianco '98	▼	3
●	Costa d'Amalfi Furore Rosso '98	▼	3
○	Costa d'Amalfi Ravello Bianco '98	▼	3
●	Costa d'Amalfi Ravello Rosso Ris. '96	▼	4
○	Costa d'Amalfi Furore Bianco '95	▽▽	3*
●	Costa d'Amalfi Furore Rosso Ris. '95	▽▽	4
●	Costa d'Amalfi Ravello Rosso Ris. '95	▽▽	4
●	Costa d'Amalfi Furore Rosso '97	▽	3

GALLUCCIO (CE)

Telaro

Cooperativa Lavoro e Salute
Loc. Cinque Pietre
81045 Galluccio (CE)
tel. 0823/925841

The Lavoro e Salute cooperative winery was set up in 1987 when the Telaro brothers got together with a group of other young winegrowers determined to live and promote a healthier, more balanced life with the help of organic farming. Hence the name Lavoro e Salute (Work and Health). The co-op is near Galluccio in the province of Caserta, an area once famous for its wines; after its heyday in the early 1600s it gradually sank into obscurity until recently, when its revival was officially sanctioned by the new DOC Galluccio. Luigi Telaro looks after the vineyards and his brother Pasquale, an oenologist, coordinates wine-making activities. The other brothers deal with administration, sales and their country guest accommodation (agriturismo). Their 35 hectares under vine, planted mostly to local varieties but including some experimental plots, yield a full range of DOC and IGT wines. The best we tasted this year is the excellent Aglianico di Roccamonfina '97. It shows a fine dark ruby color; elegant and complex scents of ripe red fruit blended with stylish notes of medicinal herbs, spice and balsamic hints; and a broad, powerful palate, rich in soft tannins and fruity succulence. It's an important red, and it heads the range of clean and carefully made wines. We hope that future vintages will be just as successful.

●	Aglianico di Roccamonfina '97	▼▼	3*
○	Falanghina di Roccamonfina '98	▼	3
○	Galluccio Bianco '98	▼	3

GUARDIA SANFRAMONDI (BN)

CORTE NORMANNA
CONTRADA SAPENZIE, 20
82034 GUARDIA SANFRAMONDI (BN)
TEL. 0824/817008 - 0824/817004

Alfredo and Gaetano Falluto ably and enthusiastically continue their family's more than 70-year-old tradition. Their estate includes 18 hectares under vine at Guardia Sanframondi within the Sannio DOC zone, planted mainly to traditional varieties: falanghina, greco, fiano, malvasia and trebbiano for the whites; and aglianico, sangiovese and agostinella, but also cabernet sauvignon, for the reds. Corte Normanna, which is in the process of converting to an organic regime, has the valuable advice of the consultant oenologist Roberto Mazzer. The fresh, clean Solopaca Bianco Guiscardo '98, a blend of trebbiano, malvasia and falanghina, is noteworthy: the distinct, intense and persistent aromas of white peach carry through onto the lean, crisp, fruity palate, making for an enjoyably quaffable wine. The well-constructed Falanghina del Sannio '98 also boasts distinct and inviting scents of white-fleshed fruit, with Golden Delicious apple to the fore; the straightforward palate shows good body and fair length. The Aglianico del Sannio '98 is appealing for its intensity, its fragrance of red fruit and its freshness; on the palate it is warm, tannic and mouth-filling. The Solopaca Rosso Riccardo '98 achieves only a mention: the nose is rather heady and the structure on the palate is not up to coping with some bitter notes.

●	Sannio Aglianico '98	🍷	4
○	Sannio Falanghina '98	🍷	4
○	Solopaca Bianco Guiscardo '98	🍷	3
●	Solopaca Rosso Riccardo '98		3

GUARDIA SANFRAMONDI (BN)

DE LUCIA
C.DA STARZE
82034 GUARDIA SANFRAMONDI (BN)
TEL. 0824/817705

De Lucia is one of the most interesting estates in the Benevento area. The owners are three cousins, Enrico, Cosimo and a second Enrico De Lucia, and they have Riccardo Cotarella, one of Italy's most noted oenologists, as consultant. The vineyards, which they cultivate themselves, lie in the Sannio and Solopaca DOC zones and yield a comprehensive range of the area's DOCs. Our favorite this year was the Sannio Aglianico Adelchi '97, which shows a fine dense ruby hue and intense, inviting aromas of blackberry, black currant and ripe cherry shading into spice and toasty new oak. The palate reveals good extract, noticeable but finely grained tannins, rich fruit, substantial alcohol and length. Of the whites, the Solopaca Bianco Vassallo '98 easily deserves its Two Glasses. A brilliant pale straw color with a greenish cast introduces a complex fruity and floral nose with a distinct aromatic note of sage; the palate shows good texture, fairly substantial fruit and the vegetal and balsamic notes encountered in the bouquet. The Sannio Greco '98 displays some of the freshness and delicately vegetal tones of the Vassallo as well as intensity and fairly ample fruity and floral notes. All the other wines are good as well.

●	Aglianico Adelchi '97	🍷🍷	4
○	Solopaca Bianco Vassallo '98	🍷🍷	3*
●	Sannio Aglianico '98	🍷	3
○	Sannio Falanghina '98	🍷	3
○	Sannio Greco '98	🍷	3
●	Solopaca Rosso Vassallo '98	🍷	2*
○	Sannio Coda di Volpe '98		3
●	Sannio Aglianico '97	🍸🍸	3*
○	Sannio Falanghina '97	🍸🍸	3*
○	Sannio Greco '97	🍸🍸	3*
●	Sannio Aglianico '96	🍸	3
●	Solopaca Rosso '95	🍸	2*
●	Solopaca Rosso '96	🍸	2*
●	Solopaca Rosso Vassallo '97	🍸	2*

MANOCALZATI (AV)

VEGA - D'ANTICHE TERRE
C.DA LO PIANO
S. S. 7 BIS
83030 MANOCALZATI (AV)
TEL. 0825/675358

The estate of Gaetano Ciccarella, Carmine Cornacchia and Saverio Iandoli, with its 35 hectares of vineyard cultivated with dedication and enthusiasm, has previously come up with wines that placed it in the vanguard of producers in Irpinia. Last year no stunning bottles emerged but the wines were all good. This year the estate has held its place in the Guide but there was nothing to rave about. We hope that this is just a chance occurrence, due to the vintage rather than to any dropping off of interest on the part of the owners. We write these things because we can remember wonderful wines like the '96 Fiano which we believe they are still capable of producing. The '98 resembles it in some ways but doesn't have all its power and concentration. The color is a pale straw, and the fruity bouquet reveals yellow plum and damson, interlaced with green vegetal notes. The palate is crisp, clean and medium-bodied but perhaps too simple in its distinct tones of white peach. The straightforward and well-made Rosso dell'Irpinia Coriliano '98, from aglianico, piedirosso and sciascinoso, offers a fragrance of ripe cherry and a lean, fresh, appropriately tannic palate. The Bianco Eliseo di Serra '98 shows an ill-defined nose and the Greco di Tufo '98 is light, and somewhat muffled on both nose and palate: both were less good than previous versions.

● Coriliano '98	▼	2*
○ Fiano di Avellino '98	▼	4
○ Eliseo di Serra '98		3
○ Greco di Tufo '98		3
○ Fiano di Avellino '96	▽▽	4
● Coriliano '94	▽	3
● Coriliano '96	▽	2*
○ Eliseo di Serra '95	▽	3
○ Eliseo di Serra '96	▽	3
○ Fiano di Avellino '95	▽	4
○ Greco di Tufo '95	▽	3
○ Greco di Tufo '96	▽	3
● Irpinia Rosso Coriliano '96	▽	2*
● Taurasi '94	▽	4

MONTEFUSCO (AV)

MONTESOLÆ - COLLI IRPINI
VIA SERRA DI MONTEFUSCO
83030 MONTEFUSCO (AV)
TEL. 0825/963972

Montesolæ was the idea of a young agronomist, Rosa Pesa, who formed a company in 1994 with two other women, Federica Costanza and Sabina Gubitosa, to set it up. Within just a few years the three partners, all from Irpinia, have succeeded in creating one of the most interesting wineries of the zone, equipped with state-of-the-art technology and now producing significant quantities of wine. Indeed, the first, 'experimental' harvest was in 1995 and resulted in barely 850 hectoliters of wine, while the '98 vintage yielded 7,000 hectoliters. The broad range includes the classic wines of Irpinia as well as those of neighboring Sannio. Top place in this year's tastings went to the white Splendore '98, a blend of trebbiano, coda di volpe, fiano and chardonnay vinified in stainless steel, which is . a joy to drink. Intense, well-defined and lingering aromas of tropical fruit, with hints of pineapple and passion fruit, precede an extremely fresh, fruity, lean palate. The Irpinia Bianco '98, from fiano, coda di volpe and trebbiano, with notes of peach and damson, seemed just as fruity and delightful. One Glass goes to the Fiano d'Irpinia '98 with its fresh bouquet of lemon balm and acacia honey and notable crispness on the palate. The Fiano di Avellino '98 earns its One Glass with its good structure and stylistic purity. Among the reds the Aglianico dell'Irpinia '97 gains similar recognition. It has a good nose of cherry and other red fruit and the palate shows medium body and good balance.

○ Fiano di Avellino '98	▼	3
○ Irpinia Bianco '98	▼	2*
○ Irpinia Fiano '98	▼	2*
● Irpinia Rosso Aglianico '97	▼	2*
○ Splendore '98	▼	2*
○ Falanghina del Beneventano '98		2
○ Greco di Tufo '98		3
○ Sannio Falanghina '98		3

MONTEFUSCO (AV)

TERREDORA
VIA SERRA
83030 MONTEFUSCO (AV)
TEL. 0825/968215 - 0825/963022

Walter, Paolo, Lucio and Daniela Mastroberardino's estate Terredora, with its more than 100 hectares under vine in the most beautiful sites in Irpinia, has in past years come up with some of the best wines of Campania, both red and white. This year, though, the range seemed less impressive. We trust this is just accidental, especially because this estate is deeply rooted in the oenological culture of this area, almost as deeply as its historic vines. From such an estate we expect great wines, not just good ones. We are, however, somewhat consoled by two of the most stimulating whites produced in Campania this year. The Fiano di Avellino Terre di Dora '98 is simply delicious: it offers elegant, finely-tuned scents of fresh fruit featuring apricot and peach, delicate hints of citrus peel and the unmistakable floral nuance of a classic fiano. On the palate it is full, fruity and rich in crisp acidity, and the long and elegant finish boasts an attractive fresh note of grapefruit. The Greco di Tufo Terra degli Angeli '98 has a delightful aromatic note of clary and a balsamic hint interwoven with clean scents of white-fleshed fruit. On the palate it shows the crispness and firm structure that have always distinguished it. The good standard Fiano di Avellino, with appealing vegetal tones on the nose and a dry, stylish but slightly thin palate, came close to Two Glasses. Most of the other wines in this vast, (perhaps too vast) and diversified range are very well executed. But we want more!

○	Fiano di Avellino Terre di Dora '98	🍷🍷	4
○	Greco di Tufo Terra degli Angeli '98	🍷🍷	3*
○	Fiano di Avellino '98	🍷	4
○	Fiano di Avellino Campo Re '98	🍷	4
○	Greco di Tufo '98	🍷	3
○	Greco di Tufo Loggia della Serra '98	🍷	3
●	Irpinia Aglianico Il Principio '97	🍷	4
●	Taurasi Fatica Contadina '95	🍷	5
●	Irpinia Aglianico '98		3
○	Irpinia Bianco Falanghina '98		3
⊙	Irpinia Rosato Rosaenovae '98		3
●	Taurasi Fatica Contadina '94	🍸🍸	5

MONTEMARANO (AV)

SALVATORE MOLETTIERI
VIA MUSANNI, 19/B
83040 MONTEMARANO (AV)
TEL. 0827/63424

Salvatore Molettieri personally tends the seven hectares of vineyard that his family has owned for generations at Cinque Querce near Montemarano. The vines, aglianico and coda di volpe, grow at 500 meters in clayey and calcareous soil and have good southeastern exposure. This is the heartland of the Taurasi zone and, hot on the heels of last year's excellent showing, the '95, like many other Taurasis from this vintage, does not earn Two Glasses. It is a good wine and has a fine deep ruby color, but notes of oak and bitter hints of rhubarb and quinine gain the upper hand over the fruit on the nose, while the palate, although warm and richly tannic, lacks the fatness that would make it quite irresistible. The Molettieri banner is, however, held high by the Cinque Querce '97, an excellent aglianico-based red that, unlike the Taurasi with its three years in wood and six months in bottle, doesn't spend more than 10 months maturing, between the barrique and the bottle. The propitious vintage and Salvatore's skill have together given us a dark ruby wine with attractive berry aromas seasoned with a delicate hint of spice and vanilla. The palate is well-calibrated, structured, warm and fruity, with harmonious tannins and appropriate length: Two Glasses without any trouble. The Cinque Querce Bianco '98 seemed a little tired and over-evolved: perhaps overripe grapes diminished the acidity. We look forward to seeing what Salvatore can do with next year's vintage.

●	Cinque Querce Rosso '97	🍷🍷	4
●	Taurasi Vigna Cinque Querce '95	🍷	5
○	Cinque Querce Bianco '98		3
●	Cinque Querce Rosso '96	🍸🍸	3*
●	Taurasi Vigna Cinque Querce '94	🍸🍸	4
○	Cinque Querce Bianco '97	🍸	3

PONTE (BN)

OCONE
VIA DEL MONTE, 56
82030 PONTE (BN)
TEL. 0824/874040 - 0824/874328

Domenico Ocone, the owner of this classic and beautiful estate established at the beginning of the century, is one of the most energetic and competent winegrowers in Campania and produces good whites and excellent reds. For example, the Aglianico del Taburno Diomede '96 is a concentrated, elegant, complex, lingering red of considerable breeding. Ocone's skills with reds are also displayed in the Aglianico del Taburno Vigna Pezza La Corte '95. This comes from one of the estate's best vineyards, with well-drained gravelly soil, a southwestern exposure and an altitude of 350 meters. It shows an intense dark ruby color and a soft, fruity, elegant and complex nose: the sweet scents of black plum and vanilla reveal the perfect ripeness of the grapes and the skill with which they were vinified. The palate is soft, deep and rich in tones of black cherry and blackberry, with delicate spicy nuances and vanilla echoed from the bouquet. The intriguing Taburno Piedirosso '98 is not such an imposing wine but is extremely enjoyable, with its attractive aromas of cherry and vanilla and the freshness of its fruit. The best of the whites are the Taburno Coda di Volpe '98, which is balanced and full-bodied, and the clean Taburno Falanghina Vigna del Monaco '98, with its good bite of acidity.

●	Aglianico del Taburno Vigna Pezza la Corte '95	🍷🍷	4
○	Coda di Volpe del Taburno '98	🍷	3
○	Falanghina del Taburno Vigna del Monaco '98	🍷	4
●	Piedirosso del Taburno '98	🍷	4
○	Falanghina del Taburno '98		4
○	Greco del Taburno '98		4
●	Aglianico del Sannio Vigna Pezza la Corte '91	🍸🍸	4
●	Aglianico del Taburno '94	🍸🍸	4
●	Aglianico del Taburno Diomede '96	🍸🍸	4
●	Aglianico del Taburno Vigna Pezza la Corte '93	🍸🍸	4
●	Aglianico del Taburno '95	🍸	4

PRATOLA SERRA (AV)

CASA DELL'ORCO
VIA LIMATURO, 54
83039 PRATOLA SERRA (AV)
TEL. 0825/967038

The picturesque name (House of the Ogre) of this estate comes from a legend connected with a prehistoric settlement just here, in what is now the village of San Michele, between Pratola Serra and Montefalcione in the heart of Irpinia. Indeed the row of three great menhirs in the midst of the vineyards is believed to represent Silpa, a local shepherd, the fair Matulpa, his beloved, and Cronopa, the ogre who held her in thrall and was consequently slain by Silpa. The Musto family, whose connection to this estate is very nearly prehistoric as well, has recently built a new winery and completely reorganized production. They now have about 20 hectares under vine, but new plantings are under way. Interest is focused, not surprisingly in these parts, on Fiano d'Avellino and Greco di Tufo, both of which were quite interesting in their '98 versions. The Fiano has an attractive fragrance of white-fleshed fruit with delicate vegetal hints; the palate offers structure, crisp acidity, substantial alcohol, rich fruit and good length. The simpler and more immediate appeal of the Greco is based on its pleasing fruity notes of white peach and damson. In the mouth the fresh acidity is most notable, but there is a certain structure as well. The range concludes with two well-made One Glass Irpinia IGTs, the fiano-based white Matulpa and the red Silpa from aglianico: both are enjoyable drinking. Next year Casa dell'Orco will be releasing its first Taurasi, a '96.

○	Fiano di Avellino '98	🍷	4
○	Greco di Tufo '98	🍷	4
○	Matulpa '98	🍷	3
●	Silpa '98	🍷	3

PRIGNANO CILENTO (SA)

ALESSANDRO DE CONCILIIS E FIGLI
LOC. QUERCE, 1
84060 PRIGNANO CILENTO (SA)
TEL. 0974/831090

In just a few short years Bruno De Conciliis has catapulted this estate into the small group of leading southern Italian wineries. Before his involvement in the family farm run by his father Alessandro and his siblings Luigi and Paola, wine had had a subordinate role and there were just seven hectares under vine. There are now 22, yielding 150 thousand bottles a year. The family is intent on producing really good wine, so they have taken on Saverio Petrilli as consultant oenologist. How close they have come to reaching their goal can be seen from the Naima '97, from 100% aglianico, which has remarkable fullness, depth and cleanness of fruit. It is aged in new oak, which gives it complexity and elegant spicy notes on both the nose and the surprisingly concentrated and balanced palate. In the Zero '97 there are small proportions of other red grapes joining the aglianico, and the resultant wine shows breadth and concentration, starting with the nose, which releases fresh notes of blackberry and other dark fruit, pencil lead and ink, interlaced with spicy hints and well-judged, stylish oaked tones. The palate is elegant, structured, well balanced, rich in fat glycerin and long. Both these wines have, at their debut, claimed a place near that of Italy's greatest reds: a fine performance that also bodes well for future vintages. The other wines are carefully made and surprisingly inexpensive.

●	Naima '97	TT	5
●	Zero '97	TT	5
○	Donna Luna '98	T	3
●	RA Passito '97	T	5
○	Tempadoro '97	T	2*
●	Temparubra '98	T	2*
●	Temparubra '97	YY	2*
○	Donna Luna '97	Y	3
○	Tempadoro '97	Y	2*
○	Vigna Perella '97	Y	3

QUARTO (NA)

CANTINE GROTTA DEL SOLE
VIA SPINELLI, 2
80010 QUARTO (NA)
TEL. 081/8762566

The Martusciello family continues in its invaluable efforts to preserve the Campanian wine heritage. Several historic wines owe their continued existence to the Grotta del Sole, which for years has been dedicated to saving them from oblivion: Lettere, for example, and Gragnano della Penisola Sorrentina and Asprinio di Aversa, all threatened by the tendency to give up working the land, especially near the coast, and to abandon traditional training systems such as the tree-supported "alberata aversana". The experienced oenologist Gennaro Martusciello has presented an impressive range of local wines, ranging from the Campi Flegrei bottles to the classic Greco di Tufo and Fiano di Avellino. Among the most interesting are the Lacryma Christi del Vesuvio Rosso '97, with a full body and the sweetness of ripe red fruit; the Fiano di Avellino '98, fresh, structured and well balanced; and the grapey, fruity, lightly sparkling Gragnano della Penisola Sorrentina '98. It's also worth tasting the good Piedirosso dei Campi Flegrei '98, with its sweet tones of black fruit and hints of spice; the easily enjoyable '98 Greco di Tufo; and the Lacryma Christi del Vesuvio Rosato '98, with its attractive cherry-red color and inviting suggestions of berries. The Asprinio di Aversa '98, from vines with that traditional tree-based training five meters above the ground, is among the best of its denomination: rich in crisp acidity and very well-defined fruity tones.

○	Asprinio d'Aversa '98	T	3
○	Fiano di Avellino '98	T	4
●	Gragnano '98	T	3
○	Greco di Tufo '98	T	4
⊙	Lacryma Christi Rosato '98	T	3
●	Lacryma Christi Rosso '97	T	4
●	Piedirosso '98	T	4
○	Campi Flegrei Falanghina '98		4
●	Campi Flegrei Rosso Montegauro Ris. '95		5
●	Lettere '98		3
●	Campi Flegrei Piedirosso '97	Y	3
●	Lacryma Christi Rosso '97	Y	3

S. CIPRIANO PICENTINO (SA)

MONTEVETRANO
VIA MONTEVETRANO
84099 S. CIPRIANO PICENTINO (SA)
TEL. 089/882285

However you happen to feel about it, the example of the intrepid Silvia Imparato has perceptibly galvanized wine-making throughout Campania. And indeed in the past two or three years we have witnessed an exponential growth in the number of first-class wines in the region, and most of them are barrique-aged reds. Skeptics may say that this is hardly all thanks to Silvia Imparato, that Campania has ancient oenological tradtions. This is quite true, but it is also true that if this small estate (which now produces more than 10 thousand bottles a year) had not shown the way, we would probably still be reviewing over-alcoholic, over-evolved, tired Campanian reds. Montevetrano, by contrast, is vigorous, vital, extremely fragrant and elegant, and has already become a national classic. Once again it has walked off with Three Glasses, an award that seems more justified than ever, since we found the '97 the best Montevetrano yet – and that is no small compliment. The brilliant and aristocratic intense ruby hue introduces a bouquet that already shows surprising definition and aromatic depth, although at this early stage in the wine's life there are still assertive herbaceous notes. It is on the palate, though, that the '97 really reveals its breeding: full-bodied, extremely clearly delineated, ripe and meaty, it has very elegant tannins and extraordinarily well-integrated oak, and the finish just goes on and on. This is a wine that could hold up its head in the company of any other bottles, from Italy or elsewhere. What more need we say?

● Montevetrano '97	▼▼▼	5
● Montevetrano '93	▽▽▽	5
● Montevetrano '95	▽▽▽	5
● Montevetrano '96	▽▽▽	5
● Montevetrano '94	▽▽	5

S. MARCO DI CASTELLABATE (SA)

LUIGI MAFFINI
LOC. CENITO
84071 SAN MARCO DI CASTELLABATE (SA)
TEL. 0974/966345

Luigi Maffini is one of the young bloods on the Campanian wine scene. Five years ago the winery consisted of an old vineyard planted to fiano and a shed where he and his father, agronomists both, made wine for the family as a hobby. Then Luigi, who is a perfectionist, became increasingly captivated by the beauty of the Cilento coast, perceived its enormous potential as a wine-making zone and moved there permanently, bound and determined to create a proper wine estate. This is only his third vintage, but the results are already excellent. He makes two standard wines, Kràtos and Klèos. The Kràtos is a fiano-based white with 10% greco, and the '98 shows a fine brilliant straw color and intense, distinct aromas dominated by white-fleshed fruit with undertones of sage and tomato leaf; the palate is fleshy, elegant, concentrated, fresh and lingering. The ruby-hued Klèos '98, an equal blend of piedirosso and aglianico, releases soft scents of ripe red fruit with spicy nuances; in the mouth it is full-bodied, soft, fruity, appropriately tannic and long. But Luigi Maffini's most fascinating wine is the Cenito, a monovarietal piedirosso made in tiny quantities (just 3,500 bottles) and now at its second vintage. It has a dense dark ruby hue, a sweet, fresh and harmonious fragrance of berries, and a broad, fat, powerful and warm palate with aristocratic notes of ink and pencil lead that make it complex and fascinating. Not bad for a beginner!

● Cenito '98	▼▼	6
● Klèos '98	▼▼	3*
○ Kràtos '98	▼▼	3*
● Cenito '97	▽▽	5
● Klèos '97	▽▽	2*
○ Kràtos '97	▽▽	2*

S. SEBASTIANO AL VESUVIO (NA)

DE FALCO VINI
VIA FIGLIOLA
80040 SAN SEBASTIANO AL VESUVIO (NA)
TEL. 081/7713755

With its average annual production of 250 thousand bottles De Falco Vini is one of the largest producers in the province of Naples. At its tiller are Angelo De Falco and his son Gabriele. With Gabriele's arrival in the family business came renewed interest in the improvement of their best wines, particularly those from the area of Vesuvius. The winery owns no vineyards but buys its grapes from carefully selected growers to achieve its well-made range. This year we have given One Glass to the Lacryma Christi del Vesuvio '98, from piedirosso and aglianico. It has intense and lingering fruity aromas and a harmonious, smoothly tannic and soft palate. The straightforward Aglianico del Beneventano '97 is of similar quality: the fruity nose reveals overripe cherries, and the palate is balanced, medium-bodied and appropriately tannic. The Falanghina del Beneventano '98, of an appealing bright pale straw color, displays a floral fragrance and a direct style on the medium-structured and notably acidic palate. The Greco di Tufo '98 offers appealing fruity scents, fair balance and medium length. The other wines are also of interest.

○ Falanghina del Beneventano '98	🍷	3
○ Greco di Tufo '98	🍷	4
● Lacryma Christi Rosso '98	🍷	3
● Sannio Aglianico Beneventano '97	🍷	3
● Gragnano '98		4
○ Lacryma Christi Bianco '98		3

SESSA AURUNCA (CE)

GALARDI
PROV.LE SESSA - MIGNANO
81030 SESSA AURUNCA (CE)
TEL. 0823/708034

Galardi represents a small miracle of enterprise, inventiveness, enthusiasm, and passion for wine and the land it comes from. A group of cousins and their respective spouses (Roberto and Maria Luisa Selvaggi, Arturo and Dora Celentano, Francesco Catello) decided to replant the vineyards on their family property and to vinify the fruit of their labors. At the start they themselves probably didn't believe that they could get so far so quickly. However, the advice of their consultant Riccardo Cotarella, one of the most skilled oenologists working in Italy, made a significant difference, and out came Terra di Lavoro, which is among the most interesting reds in the entire south. It is made from aglianico with 20% piedirosso and ages for a year in new French oak barriques. The '97 is its fourth vintage and probably the best so far. The famous American critic Robert Parker gave it a stratospheric mark and we find it extremely good too. It has spectacular concentration, so dense and thick that it's stunning. The nose is incredibly rich in aromas of red fruit and oak-derived spicy notes; on the palate it is juicy, fat, concentrated, richly tannic, and enlivened by balsamic and spicy tones on the finish. It has many of the characteristics of an absolute champion, but we found it slightly lacking in balance and elegance on the palate and a little muffled on the nose, so our highest award is not yet within its grasp. Power without restraint is less attractive. At least that's our opinion.

● Terra di Lavoro '97	🍷🍷	5
● Terra di Lavoro '94	YY	5
● Terra di Lavoro '95	YY	5
● Terra di Lavoro '96	Y	5

SORBO SERPICO (AV)

FEUDI DI SAN GREGORIO
LOC. CERZA GROSSA
83050 SORBO SERPICO (AV)
TEL. 0825/986266

There are several surprises from this splendid estate. The first is that the distinguished oenologist Riccardo Cotarella has agreed to be their consultant starting with the '99 vintage. He will work with a group from the University of Naples led by Professor Luigi Moio, forming what should be a very strong technical team. Meanwhile the wines presented this year, especially the whites, were formidable. Indeed, two were awarded Three Glasses, both made from late-harvested, partially botrytis-affected fiano grapes: the Campanaro '98 and the Fiano Pietracalda '98. Both have very intense aromas of fresh almond and ripe fruit, with light notes of noble rot slightly more evident in the Campanaro. The power on its palate is better supported by an acidity that interacts with the wine's great softness and roundness. The Pietracalda, on the other hand, is even fatter and more velvety, but it has less grip. They are both splendid. Just a half-step down is the Greco di Tufo Cutizzi '98, which is also late-harvested. Once again there is abundant ripe fruit on the nose and a lingering, mouth-filling softness on the palate. Of the standard whites, the fresh and fragrant Falanghina '98 is excellent; and the Greco di Tufo '98 and Fiano di Avellino '98 are both good; all three are technically irreproachable. The two '95 Taurasis are less exciting: we still prefer the standard version to the Piano di Montevergine, but both show slightly aggressive acidity. In part this comes from the aglianico grape itself, but the problem is exacerbated by regulations requiring high fixed acidity, and then long aging to insure that the wines are not too thin.

○	Campanaro '98	▼▼▼	5
○	Fiano di Avellino Pietracalda V. T. '98	▼▼▼	4*
○	Falanghina '98	▼▼	3*
○	Fiano di Avellino '98	▼▼	3*
○	Greco di Tufo '98	▼▼	3*
○	Greco di Tufo Cutizzi V. T. '98	▼▼	4
●	Taurasi '95	▼▼	4
●	Taurasi Piano di Montevergine '95	▼▼	5
●	Taurasi '94	▽▽▽	5
○	Campanaro '96	▽▽	4
○	Campanaro V. T. '96	▽▽	5
●	Serpico '95	▽▽	6
●	Serpico '96	▽▽	6

TAURASI (AV)

ANTONIO CAGGIANO
C.DA SALA
84030 TAURASI (AV)
TEL. 0827/74043

Antonio Caggiano has lost his heart to his native land, Irpinia. He spent years in reconstruction after the 1980 earthquake, and where it was not possible to restore the buildings to their original state he carefully put architraves and arches, balustrades and banisters into storage to await the right occasion. Antonio is also a dedicated winegrower and some years back he decided to aim for excellence, without compromise. So he replanted most of his splendidly sited vineyards, with guyot training and 8,000 vines per hectare, a density previously unheard of in an area where widely spaced plantings are the norm. Advice from the distinguished consultant oenologist Luigi Moio has been a determining factor and now Antonio makes an excellent range of wines in his lovely cellar, built from stones he painstakingly reclaimed from the rubble of the earthquake. The most interesting of this year's batch is the Taurasi Macchia dei Goti '95. It displays a depth and concentration that most other reds in the area can't even aspire to. It is soft, complex, tannic and balanced, and should have a great future. The red Salae Domini '97 is an aglianico that spends less time in new oak than DOC regulations require for Taurasi. It reveals impeccable fruit, incredible fullness and an elegant spicy finish. The Taurì '97, is a more straightforward and accessible aglianico that nonetheless offers attractive structure and good depth. The Fiagrè and the Mel, a raisin wine, are both from greco and fiano, and both interesting.

●	Salae Domini '97	▼▼	5
●	Taurasi Vigna Macchia dei Goti '95	▼▼	6
●	Taurì '97	▼▼	4
○	Fiagrè '98	▼	4
○	Mel '97	▼	6
○	Fiagrè '96	▽▽	3*
●	Salae Domini '96	▽▽	5
●	Taurasi Vigna Macchia dei Goti '94	▽▽	5
●	Taurì '95	▽▽	3*
●	Taurì '96	▽▽	3*
○	Fiagrè '97	▽	3
●	Salae Domini '95	▽	5

TORRECUSO (BN)

ORAZIO RILLO
C.DA FONTANAVECCHIA
82030 TORRECUSO (BN)
TEL. 0824/876275

The Rillo wines presented this year provide happy confirmation of last year's favorable impression. The estate includes eight hectares under vine in the Taburno DOC district and produces 45 thousand bottles split among four wines. Our favorite this time was the Aglianico del Taburno Vigna Cataratte Riserva '95. It displays an intense ruby hue and an elegant bouquet of ripe red fruit with remarkably intense notes of toasty new oak and coffee. The entry on the rich, full-bodied palate shows a characteristic berry tone expressed with great immediacy; the mid palate is in a more evolved and complex key, with the fruit beautifully balanced by tannins and structure. The wine fully merits its Two Glasses and is not that far from Three. The excellent Aglianico del Taburno '96 has also carried off Two Glasses. It is not so impressive as the Cataratte, which it however quite resembles: it's a sort of Cataratte in miniature. Here too we found fruit, smooth tannins and acidity in excellent balance, yielding good aromatic length. The Aglianico del Taburno Rosato '98 is good and the Falanghina del Taburno '98 decidedly interesting with its rich nose of fresh, floral notes with lemon balm to the fore, and the fruity tone of Golden Delicious apple. It is crisply acidic, varietal, fresh and invitingly quaffable.

●	Aglianico del Taburno '96	▼▼	3*
●	Aglianico del Taburno Vigna Cataratte Ris. '95	▼▼	5
●	Aglianico del Taburno Rosato '98	▼	3
○	Falanghina del Taburno '98	▼	3
●	Aglianico del Taburno Vigna Cataratte Ris. '94	▽▽	5
●	Aglianico del Taburno '95	▽	3
⊙	Aglianico del Taburno Rosato '97	▽	2*

VITULAZIO (CE)

VILLA SAN MICHELE
VIA APPIA KM. 198
81050 VITULAZIO (CE)
TEL. 0823/963775 - 081/666773

The oenologist Franco Pastore, with the help of the Faculty of Agriculture of the University of Naples, produces a carefully honed series of red and white wines on the Galeno family's estate at Vitulazio, which year by year are becoming better known for reliability, attractiveness and value for money. Villa San Michele covers more than 100 hectares, 34 of which are under vine and accommodate an experimental University project on the indigenous grapes of Campania. The Aglianico Terre del Volturno is again a well-made, balanced red, rich in notes of ripe red fruit, with plum in their lead. This wealth of good fruit is echoed on the substantial, full-flavored palate, together with a nice acidic bite. The Falanghina '98 shows a bright straw color and an ample array of attractive fruity aromas on a background of delicate floral tones. The palate is strong, fresh, fruity, succulent and well-textured. This year the Piedirosso and the Greco, both '98s, are a little below par: they seem to lack the cleanliness and concentration (particularly the Greco) of previous versions. But the metodo classico sparkling wines: the Don Carlos Brut (pinot bianco, greco and chardonnay), the Don Carlos Demi Sec (same grape blend, more "dosage") and the Greco Brut with its elegant floral and yeasty tones, are all as good as ever and One Glass goes to each.

●	Aglianico '97	▼	3
○	Don Carlos Brut	▼	4
○	Don Carlos Demi Sec	▼	4
○	Falanghina '98	▼	3
○	Greco Brut	▼	5
○	Greco '98		3
●	Piedirosso '97		3
○	Greco '96	▽▽	3*
●	Aglianico '96	▽	2*
○	Don Carlos Brut	▽	4
○	Don Carlos Demi Sec	▽	4
○	Falanghina '97	▽	2*
○	Greco '97	▽	2*

OTHER WINERIES

The following producers obtained good scores in our tastings with one or more of their wines:

PROVINCE OF AVELLINO

Bonaventura
Aiello del Sabato,
tel. 0825/666020
Fiano di Avellino '98

Marianna
Grottolella,
tel. 0825/627252
Fiano di Avellino '98,
Irpinia Coda di Volpe '98

Colli di Lapio
Lapio,
tel. 0825/982191 - 982184
Fiano di Avellino '98

Romano, Nicola
Lapio,
tel. 0825/982189
Irpinia Bianco Lapideum '98

Vadiaperti
Montefredane,
tel. 0825/36263 - 607270
Irpinia Coda di Volpe '98

Giulia
Prata di Principato Ultra,
tel. 0825/961219
Greco di Tufo '98,
Irpinia Rosso Albinalia '97

Di Meo
Salza Irpinia,
tel. 0825/981419
Greco di Tufo '98,
Taurasi '95

Guido Marsella
Summonte,
tel. 0825/691446
Fiano di Avellino '97

Struzziero, Giovanni
Venticano,
tel. 0825/965065
Fiano di Avellino '98,
Greco di Tufo '98,
Taurasi Campoceraso '94

PROVINCE OF BENEVENTO

Cantina del Taburno
Foglianise,
tel. 0824/871338
Aglianico Taburno Ris. 92,
Falanghina del Taburno '98,
Taburno Rosso '97

Mustilli
S. Agata dei Goti,
tel. 0823/717433
Corte Artus '97,
S. Agata dei Goti Aglianico Cesco di Nece '95,
S. Agata dei Goti Piedirosso '97

Cantina Soc. di Solopaca
Solopaca,
tel. 0824/977921
Solopaca Bianco '98,
Solopaca Rosso Sup. '95

PROVINCE OF CASERTA

Vestini - Campagnano
Caiazzo,
tel. 0823/862770
Terre del Volturno Pallagrello Bianco '98,
Terre del Volturno Pallagrello Rosso '97

Fattoria del Prattico
Rocca D'Evandro,
tel. 081/7690031
Falanghina Vigna del Prete '98,
Galluccio Aglianico '98

Cantine Caputo
Teverola, tel. 081/5033955
Asprinio d'Aversa Brut - I Normanni,
Greco Demi Sec Terre del Volturno -
I Normanni,
Lacryma Christi del Vesuvio Bianco '98,
Lacryma Christi del Vesuvio Rosso '97

Cicala
Teverola, tel. 081/8118103
Sannio Aglianico '97
Sannio Falanghina '98

PROVINCE OF NAPOLI

Cantina Farro
Bacoli, tel. 081/8545555
Falanghina dei Campi Flegrei '98,
Piedirosso dei Campi Flegrei '98

Sorrentino
Boscotrecase,
tel. 081/8584194
Lacryma Christi del Vesuvio Rosso '97,
Passito Fior di Ginestra '97

La Caprense
Capri,
tel. 081/8376835
Capri Bianco Bordo '98,
Capri Bianco Punta Vivara '98,
Capri Rosso Solaro '98

PROVINCE OF SALERNO

Marino
Agropoli,
tel. 0974/821719
Cilento Bianco '98,
Cilento Rosato '98,
Cilento Rosso '98

San Giovanni
Castellabate,
tel. 089/237331 - 224896
Fiano '98

Episcopio
Ravello,
tel. 089/857244
Costa d'Amalfi Ravello Bianco '98,
Costa d'Amalfi Ravello Bianco
V. San Lorenzo '98,
Costa d'Amalfi Ravello Rosso '97

Sammarco, Ettore
Ravello, tel. 089/872774
Costa d'Amalfi Ravello Bianco
Selva delle Monache '98
Costa d'Amalfi Ravello Rosso
Selva delle Monache '97

Ianniello-Scorziello
Roccadaspide, tel. 089/756037,
Castel San Lorenzo Barbera Bios '98

Barone
Rutino, tel. 0974/830007
Paestum Rosso '98

Apicella, Giuseppe
Tramonti, tel. 089/876075,
Costa d'Amalfi Tramonti Rosso '97

BASILICATA

Basilicata, in wine terms, is the region of Aglianico, both wine and grape. Aglianico del Vulture is the glory of Lucanian (from the ancient name of the region) oenology. The variety is a noble one, whose pedigree is the subject of much current research: it could, we hear, turn out to be indigenous to the area, contradicting the long-held belief that its name is a corruption of "ellenico" (Hellenic) and indicates that it was imported from Greece. Wine-making fortunes in the region or, more precisely, in the province of Potenza, have been inextricably linked to this wine, but this has turned out to be something of a limitation. The land of Horace and of this great red has not exactly stood out for its entrepreneurial, experimental or revivalist spirit – at least until a few years ago. Now it seems that things are beginning to move. D'Angelo and Paternoster have long set a high standard for this wine, high enough, indeed, to attract a discriminating public. They were thus able to sell beyond the confines of the region and export to far-flung markets, leaving the others to sell locally or at best to neighboring areas. Next the cooperative wineries started to wake up, as did a few small private estates, and suddenly the Vulture district is in a ferment of activity. While Sasso, in the midst of thorough restructuring, has temporarily ceased production, we welcome a newcomer to the Guide, Basilium at Acerenza, a cooperative that has been steadily working towards improved quality and has produced an excellent range this year. Only limited space has prevented us from dedicating a detailed review to Di Palma in Rionero, an estate fairly new to the market that has got off to an excellent start: low yields, a modern cellar and aging in new oak have all contributed to their fine Aglianico del Vulture Nibbio Grigio '97. On the other hand Cantina della Riforma Fondiaria in Venosa seemed below par, but we hope it will soon be returning to these pages. Pisani in Viggiano, 600 meters high in the Agri valley, is maintaining standards. For the first time we tasted some interesting wines from the province of Matera. The Dragone brothers are aiming for excellence and have already produced some quite well-made wines. Their best is a red from primitivo, reflecting the wine culture of nearby Puglia. We hope their winery will not remain an isolated phenomenon.

ACERENZA (PZ)

Basilium
C.da Pipoli
85011 Acerenza (PZ)
tel. 0971/741449

This year Basilium at Acerenza, one of the most important cooperative wineries of the region, has come out with a range of reds of such quality that it immediately joins Basilicata's best producers. The standard-bearer is the excellent Aglianico del Vulture Valle del Trono '96, aged in 5-hectoliter oak casks. It displays a lovely dense dark ruby color and intense, sweet and captivating aromas of ripe red fruit beautifully blended with elegant notes of coffee and well-judged toasty oak. The palate is round, fat, rich in extract and succulently fruity with elegant tannins and great length. Its Two overflowing Glasses are well earned. The selection I Portali '97 is equally good. The nose releases very well-defined and clean notes of blackberry, cherry and sour cherry, while the palate, of an impeccably clean modern style, is warm and deep with velvety tannins and a spicy tobacco finish. The Pipoli '97, the other Aglianico, is a simpler, (but not very much so) version of its "bigger brothers" and also shows pleasingly fruity notes, good body and plentiful softness. The special selection Greco I Portali '98 offers refreshing tones of white-fleshed fruit; we found Il Levantino '98, from chardonnay and pinot grigio, properly made but less fascinating.

●	Aglianico del Vulture Valle del Trono '96	🍷🍷	4
●	Aglianico del Vulture I Portali '97	🍷🍷	3*
●	Aglianico del Vulture Pipoli '97	🍷	2
○	Greco I Portali '98	🍷	2*
○	Levantino '98		1

BARILE (PZ)

Consorzio Viticoltori
Associati del Vulture
S. S. 93
85022 Barile (PZ)
tel. 0972/770386

This consortium, set up at the end of the '70s, includes five co-operative wineries and a few member growers, all possessing vines on the slopes of Monte Vulture, in the classic Aglianico heartland. It has a production capacity of 20 thousand hectoliters a year, 5,000 of which age in oak casks. The average quality is quite impressive, an example being the excellent Aglianico selection, Carpe Diem '95, which we retasted this year and found as good as we said it was last time. The '96 is not quite so successful but is still a richly structured, warm, harmonious wine with a wealth of spicy notes and austere tannins; it may be a little old-fashioned, but it's all the more appealing for it. The Aglianico del Vulture '97 has a rather dark ruby color and a rich bouquet of cherry and ripe plum shot through with delicate vegetal tones. The palate is warm, structured, tannic, well balanced and as full-bodied as a proper Aglianico should be. The aromatic and varietal sparkling Moscato is interesting; the rather sweet bubbly red Ellenico, from aglianico, is a little less so.

●	Aglianico del Vulture '97	🍷	2*
●	Aglianico del Vulture Carpe Diem '96	🍷	3
○	Moscato Spumante	🍷	2*
●	Aglianico Spumante Ellenico		2
●	Aglianico del Vulture '96	🍷🍷 (outline)	2*
●	Aglianico del Vulture Carpe Diem '93	🍷🍷 (outline)	3*
●	Aglianico del Vulture Carpe Diem '95	🍷🍷 (outline)	3*
●	Aglianico del Vulture '94	🍷 (outline)	2*

BARILE (PZ)

Paternoster

Via Nazionale, 23
85022 Barile (PZ)
tel. 0972/770224 - 0972/770658

The estate of the Paternoster brothers Vito, Sergio and Anselmo is a model for producers in the Vulture district. Its clean wines, modern in style, rich in structure and very characteristic, are exemplary. The best wine we tasted this year is again the Aglianico del Vulture Don Anselmo. The '94 shows a fine ruby color and aromas of ripe red fruit and spice; the palate offers admirably tight-knit and velvety tannins and rich fruit and alcohol. The Aglianico del Vulture '96, dark ruby in hue, offers a lovely bouquet of ripe cherry with a delicate vegetal note; fairly astringent tannins on the palate don't seem to detract from the balance and general appeal. The '97 is decidedly better: the color is more concentrated; and the nose reveals a wealth of fruit, toasty oak and spice; the palate is fat, ripe, harmonious and balanced: one of Paternoster's best standard Aglianicos yet. Another appealing '97 is the white Bianco di Corte, from oak-aged fiano. It has a fresh, delicately vegetal and vanilla-toned nose, and a palate with some finesse although it is neither hugely intense nor very long. The intriguing Moscato Clivus '98 is a sparkling wine distinctly redolent of apricot and white flowers, with the typical moscato notes of sage and musk; in the mouth it is sweet and crisp, with a pleasing light fizz.

●	Aglianico del Vulture '97	▼▼	4
●	Aglianico del Vulture Don Anselmo Ris. '94	▼▼	5
●	Aglianico del Vulture '96	▼	3
○	Bianco di Corte '97	▼	3
○	Clivus Moscato della Basilicata '97	▼	2*
●	Aglianico del Vulture '94	▽▽	3*
●	Aglianico del Vulture '95	▽▽	3*
●	Aglianico del Vulture Don Anselmo Ris. '88	▽▽	5
●	Aglianico del Vulture Don Anselmo Ris. '93	▽▽	5
●	Aglianico del Vulture '93	▽	3
●	Aglianico del Vulture Don Anselmo Ris. '90	▽	5

RIONERO IN VULTURE (PZ)

D'Angelo

Via Provinciale, 8
85028 Rionero in Vulture (PZ)
tel. 0972/721517

Year after year D'Angelo proves itself one of the best estates of southern Italy. It keeps abreast of the times, modernizing its cellar and its vineyards, and experimenting with aging in new oak, for instance, without ever sacrificing its own distinct personality or the characteristics of the area. Mainly reds – great reds – are produced. The leading wine is Canneto, a 100% aglianico from vineyards in Rionero, harvested late and aged for 15 months in small oak barrels. The '95 has a dark, almost impenetrable hue. The rich and generous bouquet offers notes of berries, tobacco, toasty oak and spice. The palate is concentrated, rich, fat and beautifully balanced, giving it remarkable elegance despite its relative youth: kept well it could easily live at least another 15 years. The '97 Aglianico del Vulture may not be a champion of finesse but it's bursting with body and structure. It has a slightly rustic feel but is very well made nonetheless. The white Vigna dei Pini '98 is a touch less intense and clean than the '97. It has a seductive floral fragrance with notes of orange flower and wisteria, but on the palate the blend of chardonnay, pinot bianco and incrocio Manzoni seems a little forward. The Riserva Vigna Caselle '95 was not released in time for our tastings: we'll be speaking about it next year.

●	Canneto '95	▼▼	5
●	Aglianico del Vulture '97	▼	4
○	Vigna dei Pini '98	▼	3
●	Aglianico del Vulture '90	▽▽	3
●	Aglianico del Vulture '95	▽▽	3
●	Canneto '90	▽▽	5
●	Canneto '91	▽▽	5
●	Canneto '93	▽▽	5
●	Canneto '94	▽▽	5
○	Vigna dei Pini '94	▽▽	3
○	Vigna dei Pini '97	▽▽	3*
●	Aglianico del Vulture '93	▽	3
●	Aglianico del Vulture '94	▽	3
●	Aglianico del Vulture Vigna Caselle Ris. '93	▽	4

RIONERO IN VULTURE (PZ)

Armando Martino

Via Luigi La Vista, 2/a
85028 Rionero in Vulture (PZ)
tel. 0972/721422

Tasting the wines of Armando Martini gives us the pleasing sensation of traveling backwards in time. The color, the bouquet, even the structure of the wines are all reminiscent of what a good Lucanian producer of the old school used to offer. The Aglianico del Vulture Oraziano '93, for instance, has a ruby color with orange highlights, elegant but rather forward aromas of undergrowth and berry jam, and an attractive, warm, tannic, full-bodied but excessively astringent and forward palate. The Aglianico del Vulture '97 is also old-fashioned in style, but cleaner and more inviting; it shows fair concentration, a dense-knit texture and evident smooth tannins. The Donna Lidia '98, from aglianico, is an immediately appealing rosé with a lovely cherry-red color and an intense fragrance of rose hip more like moscato than aglianico. The palate is almost sweet and just pétillant, with delicate aromatic nuances. The lightly sparkling Carolin, from aglianico, and a rather thin and forward Brut seemed less successful. The Chardonnay '98, redolent of rennet apple, is fairly well made, but the oak-aged white Oraziano '97 is less attractive: the nose is a little tired and the palate wants balance.

●	Aglianico del Vulture '97	▼	3
●	Aglianico del Vulture Oraziano '93	▼	4
○	Basilicata Chardonnay '98	▼	3
⊙	Donna Lidia Rosato '98	▼	3
○	Basilicata Bianco Oraziano '97		4
●	Aglianico del Vulture '93	▽	3
●	Aglianico del Vulture '94	▽	3
●	Aglianico del Vulture '95	▽	3
●	Carolin '93	▽	2*
●	Carolin '95	▽	2*

VIGGIANO (PZ)

Pisani

C.da San Lorenzo
85059 Viggiano (PZ)
tel. 0975/352603

In a region dominated by aglianico, Raffaele Pisani, who has planted everything but, has nevertheless found his niche. His estate produces some 270 thousand bottles of good wine annually from certifiably organically cultivated vineyards planted high in the Valle dell'Agri, at Viggiano in the province of Potenza. The red varieties are cabernet sauvignon, cabernet franc, merlot, freisa and ciliegiolo; the whites are malvasia, cortese and chardonnay. The leading wine is the red Concerto, a barrique-aged Bordeaux blend. The '97 shows a dark ruby hue; the nose is still a little closed but nevertheless releases notes of ripe blackberry, cocoa, vanilla and toasty oak. The palate is warm, mouth-filling, soft, generously fruity and quite intriguing. The Basilicata Rosso '98 is also made from merlot and cabernet sauvignon. It has a concentrated color, a clean, rich bouquet of red fruit, and a fresh, fruity, full-bodied palate with smooth tannins and a fairly elegant rounded finish.

●	Basilicata Rosso '98	▼	2*
●	Basilicata Rosso Concerto '97	▼	4

PUGLIA

Wine-making Puglia has really got cracking, and this last year has seen big changes. Italy's most prolific producer of wines is casting off the role of poor relation and dispenser of cheap undistinguished wine, and has realized, with a stirring of pride, that much of its land and its plurimillennial gobelet-trained vineyards can yield fabulous grapes. But maybe "realized" isn't the correct word. They've always known it down here, but most didn't dare believe in it and act accordingly. And now some people do, despite the risks. Three Pugliese wines went all the way to the top this year. The '95 Salice Salentino Donna Lisa Riserva has repeated the success of last year. It is a fascinating, complex wine, the fruit of a great terroir. The other two are first-timers. One is the Vigna del Feudo '97, a superb red from Felline in Manduria, an estate whose wines had been hovering around the top rank for a couple of years. All the work of the last few years has been captured in the wine: the painstaking care of the vineyards, an excellent site, the successful blend of primitivo, montepulciano, cabernet and merlot and an expert hand in the cellar. The real surprise was the '98 Zinfandel from Sinfarosa, an estate which forms part of the Accademia dei Racemi, a consortium, created by Pervini, that includes numerous up-and-coming wine companies. The wine is fantastic, and the idea of calling a Primitivo DOC that could stand its ground with the great Californians "Zinfandel" is amusingly provocative. These three wines were accompanied at our finals by another five or six that missed Three Glasses only because of vintage or other tangential problems, wines like Vallone's Graticciaia, Candido's Duca d'Aragona and Masseria Pepe's Dunico, which is also a primitivo. These riches show that Puglia can still turn out "classic" wines, like the great Patriglione at its best, and is also able to harness the same ancient grape varieties to produce wines of a more modern and international style. Maybe that's its particular charm, a charm that many are starting to feel. Antinori, for example, has bought two Pugliese estates totaling 600 hectares in the course of one year and is said to be looking for another. Gruppo Italiano Vini is also apparently viewing properties in the area, as are various other Italian and foreign investors. So Puglia is on the move, and the direction is forward. The only sad note is the death of Cosimo Taurino, one of the leading figures of Puglia's recent history. We feel sure that his family will find the strength and courage to continue along the path he laid out.

ALEZIO (LE)

ROSA DEL GOLFO
VIA GARIBALDI, 56
73011 ALEZIO (LE)
TEL. 0833/281045

Young Damiano Calò, with dignified determination, is following in his father's footsteps. Mino Calò had performed the Herculean task of building up a successful winery in southern Italy and creating an international market for its wines, quite apart from identifying the winery (starting with its name) with rosé, which is hardly the most marketable of categories. And in fact his Rosa del Golfo, an excellent blend of negroamaro and malvasia nera, took its place with the best Italian rosés of the last 30 years, a position it has subsequently maintained by dint of showing a remarkably consistent high quality. This year it again receives Two Glasses, brimful. The '98 shows a brilliant deep rose color with flashes of coral and an intense, rich fragrance of berries with hints of Mediterranean scrub; the palate vaunts a full, soft structure and abundant fruit supported by lovely crisp acidity; the finish is long and elegant. The red Portulano is, like the rosé, a blend of negroamaro with 10% malvasia nera. The concentration of the '97 is given away by its dark ruby color. Rich aromas of ripe red fruit, vanilla and tobacco precede a warm, full-bodied, tannic palate that also reveals balance and finesse. A long, complex finish puts the final touch to a fascinating wine. The Bolina '98 is an agreeable white made from verdeca. There is nothing complex or important about it, but if you're looking for a dry, fresh, delicately fruity, soft and inviting wine that will be fun to drink and won't cost you a pot of money, this is your ticket.

⊙	Salento Rosato Rosa del Golfo '98	🍷🍷	3*
●	Salento Rosso Portulano '97	🍷🍷	3*
○	Salento Bianco Bolina '98	🍷	3
○	Salento Bianco Bolina '95	ΥΥ	2*
○	Salento Bianco Bolina '96	ΥΥ	3*
○	Salento Bianco Bolina '97	ΥΥ	3*
⊙	Salento Rosato Rosa del Golfo '96	ΥΥ	3*
⊙	Salento Rosato Rosa del Golfo '97	ΥΥ	3*
●	Salento Rosso Portulano '93	ΥΥ	2*
●	Quarantale '88	Υ	5

ANDRIA (BA)

RIVERA
C.DA RIVERA
S. S. 98, KM 19.800
70031 ANDRIA (BA)
TEL. 0883/569501 - 0883/569510

Rivera, owned by the de Corato family, produces a vast range of excellent wines, all in significant quantities. As a result, in addition to being one of the historic Pugliese producers, Rivera is also amongst the best known outside the region. It has consistently kept up to date with wine-making technology and continues to produce some of Puglia's best reds. Il Falcone, a Castel del Monte Rosso Riserva, is its most prestigious wine. The '96 easily reached Two Glasses despite the vintage. It has a deep ruby color shot through with purple, and intense, distinct fruity aromas supported by alcohol and interwoven with notes of oak, tar and tobacco that make it complex and enticing. The structured, warm palate has good extract, soft tannins, masses of fruit and attractive herbaceous nuances; the finish is long and fruity. The Moscato di Trani Piani di Tufara '97 is again quite intriguing. It shows a bright deep straw color and a richly floral nose with lavender to the fore. The palate is sweet and fresh, with elegant notes of orange blossom honey, candied citrus peel and orange marmalade. The Castel del Monte Rosso Rupicolo '97, from uva di Troia and montepulciano, comes quite close to Two Glasses with its good concentration, softness and clean fruit. The Castel del Monte Rosé '98, from bombino nero, fresh and fruity just as it should be, is excellent, as usual, and all the rest of the range is exemplary.

●	Castel del Monte Rosso Il Falcone Ris. '96	🍷🍷	4
○	Moscato di Trani Piani di Tufara '97	🍷🍷	4
●	Castel del Monte Aglianico Cappellaccio Ris. '96	🍷	4
○	Castel del Monte Pinot Bianco Terre al Monte '98	🍷	3
⊙	Castel del Monte Rosé di Rivera '98	🍷	2*
●	Castel del Monte Rosso Rupicolo di Rivera '97	🍷	2*
○	Castel del Monte Sauvignon Terre al Monte '98	🍷	3
○	Castel del Monte Terre al Monte Preludio n. 1 '98	🍷	4

AVETRANA (TA)

SINFAROSA
S. S. 174, KM 3
74020 AVETRANA (TA)
TEL. 099/9711660

Primitivo is one of the leading players in the revival of Pugliese wine. It is modern in nature, and with its rich fruit and spicy tones, its warm softness and its elegant, rounded tannins, it has international appeal. Formerly only wine merchandizers seemed aware of this: they would use this precious liquid to soup up feeble wines with prestigious names, in Italy and elsewhere. This is now history, and Primitivo has carved out its own reputation. If the zinfandel grape, which is neither more nor less than primitivo mysteriously cropping up on the West Coast of the U.S., can yield the most characteristic of California's reds, surely primitivo can aspire to an important role on its home territory. The proof is a terrific red that this year gets Three Glasses: the Zinfandel (watch out, America!) made by Sinfarosa, an attractive estate in Avetrana, within the Manduria DOC zone, that has ten hectares of gobelet-trained primitivo vines with an average age of 40. The owners, Antonio Spedicato, Arcangelo My and Celestino Scarciglia, have entrusted the wine-making to the oenologist Fabrizio Perrucci. The result is a wine of great breeding, elegant on the nose, concentrated and full on the palate, seductively rich in notes of red and black fruit and spicy hints of pepper, toasty oak, vanilla and bitter chocolate, and perfectly balanced throughout. The excellent Primitivo del Tarantino '98 is just one small step below; it too is full-bodied, spicy and softly enthralling.

● Primitivo di Manduria Zinfandel '98	🍷🍷🍷	4*
● Primitivo '98	🍷🍷	4

CELLINO SAN MARCO (BR)

LIBRA
C.DA BOSCO, 13
72020 CELLINO SAN MARCO (BR)
TEL. 0831/619211

Albano Carrisi is attached to the land and especially to his native land, Salento; despite a highly successful artistic career he has never wanted to leave it. In the 1960s he created a large property of 150 hectares within the Salice Salentino zone, which he manages with his brother Franco. Half of it is under vine, planted to negroamaro, montepulciano, primitivo, chardonnay and sauvignon, and there are also 2,500 olive trees that yield an excellent extra virgin oil. Wine production is in the hands of the oenologist Giuseppe Rizzo and runs to about 700 thousand bottles a year. Our favorite of this year's wines is the Salice Salentino Albano Carrisi '96. It has a lovely deep ruby color and an enchanting nose with notes of ripe red fruit, tobacco and spice that meld with very faint hints of new oak. The full, velvety and fat palate reveals excellent structure, elegant tones of ripe red fruit and good length. The Nostalgia '96, a blend of primitivo and negroamaro, displays an attractive concentrated color, an elegant bouquet of berry jam, a warm, balanced, harmonious palate, and tobacco and licorice on the finish. The attractively fruity Felicità '98, mainly from sauvignon, shows sweet notes of ripe white-fleshed fruit, good body underpinned by crisp freshness, and a certain length. The Mediterraneo '98, a rosé from negroamaro and primitivo, is less fascinating but well made.

● Nostalgia Rosso '96	🍷🍷	3*
● Salice Salentino Albano Carrisi '96	🍷🍷	2*
○ Felicità Bianco '98	🍷	3
⊙ Rosato Mediterraneo '98		3
● Nostalgia Rosso '94	🥂	3
⊙ Rosato Mediterraneo '96	🥂	3

CORATO (BA)

SANTA LUCIA
STRADA COMUNALE SAN VITTORE, 1
70033 CORATO (BA)
TEL. 080/8721168

Giuseppe and Roberto Perrone Capano, father and son, are two successful Neapolitan professionals with a passion for wine. The Santa Lucia estate is the natural result and has become a solid business with a serious output, both quantitatively (over 100 thousand bottles) and qualitatively. Last year the wines showed very well and this year's results reveal that it was not just a flash in the pan. For example, the Castel del Monte Rosso '97 is excellent. It has a fine deep ruby color with a garnet cast, and a stylish nose characterized by notes of fully ripe berries with an undertone of spice. The entry on the palate is elegant and full-flavored; mid palate is perfectly even and reveals good structure, soft tannins and appealing fruit. The long finish leaves the mouth clean and warm. The good Castel del Monte Rosso Riserva '96 shows concentration, body and some elegance, but without the finesse of the '95. The successful Vigna del Pozzo '97, a red from uva di Troia, malbec and montepulciano, has good depth but slightly hard tannins. This last is also a feature of the Castel del Monte Rosso Vigna del Melograno '98, a wine of great concentration but somewhat unbalanced and over-extracted.

●	Castel del Monte Rosso '97	🍷🍷	2*
●	Castel del Monte Rosso Ris. '96	🍷	4
●	Vigna del Pozzo '97	🍷	2*
●	Castel del Monte Rosso Vigna del Melograno '98		2
●	Castel del Monte Rosso Ris. '95	♀♀	3*
⊙	Castel del Monte Rosato Vigna Lama di Carro '97	♀	2*
●	Castel del Monte Rosso '94	♀	2*
●	Castel del Monte Rosso '95	♀	2*
●	Castel del Monte Rosso '96	♀	2*
●	Castel del Monte Rosso Ris. '92	♀	3
●	Murgia Rosso '96	♀	2*
●	Vigna del Pozzo Ris. '95	♀	2*

CORATO (BA)

TORREVENTO
LOC. CASTEL DEL MONTE
S. S. 170, KM 28
70033 CORATO (BA)
TEL. 080/8980973 - 080/8980929

Torrevento, with 25 hectares of producing vineyards, another 10 recently planted and a further 25 planned for the near future, still does not produce enough grapes for its needs. The secret of the success of its 600 thousand bottles of wine a year is in the special relationship it has developed with a group of growers, whose vines it follows through all their annual stages, thereby guaranteeing grapes of prime quality. The oenologist Lino Carparelli handles the wine-making and Torrevento looks after the sale of the wines from Carparelli's own estate, I Pastini, in Locorotondo. The Castel del Monte Rosso Vigna Pedale '96 was reviewed last year and retasted this, and is still a wine of great structure and elegance. This year, though, the standard-bearer is the excellent Moscato di Trani Dulcis in Fundo '97, which bewitched us with its freshness and the balance achieved among its sweetness, acidity and aromatic notes, and with its intense aromas of arbutus, Mediterranean scrub, myrtle and wild honey. The Torre del Falco '96 is a powerful, concentrated red, rich in body and structure; its only defect is a not very well delineated nose; nonetheless it is soft, fat and fairly long. The Castel del Monte Rosato '98 offers delightful scents of red fruit, predominantly cherry, and good balance. The Castel del Monte Bianco, redolent of apple, is crisp and soft in the mouth. From the I Pastini line we recommend the excellent Primtivo del Tarantino '97, a red of considerable depth and balance produced from 50-year-old gobelet-trained vines; and the good Murgia Rosso '97, from cabernet and montepulciano.

○	Moscato di Trani Dulcis in Fundo '97	🍷🍷	4
●	Primitivo del Tarantino I Pastini '97	🍷🍷	3*
○	Castel del Monte Bianco '98	🍷	2*
⊙	Castel del Monte Rosato '98	🍷	2*
●	I Pastini Rosso '97	🍷	3
●	Torre del Falco '96	🍷	3
●	Castel del Monte Rosso '97	♀♀	1*
●	Castel del Monte Rosso Vigna Pedale Ris. '94	♀♀	2*
●	Castel del Monte Rosso Vigna Pedale Ris. '96	♀♀	2*
●	Murgia Rosso I Pastini '96	♀♀	2*
●	Primitivo del Tarantino I Pastini '96	♀♀	2*
●	Castel del Monte Rosso '93	♀	2*

FASANO (BR)

Borgo Canale
Loc. Selva
V.le Canale di Pirro, 23
72015 Fasano (BR)
tel. 080/4331351

Borgo Canale has long been one of the important producers in Puglia. After several difficult years and a complete administrative shake-up it is now re-emerging with excellent market prospects. The main shareholders are the Marchitelli family, with Tito as president and his son Mauro as manager. Borgo Canale owns no vineyards, so its grapes are supplied by numerous growers on long-term contracts whose vines are supervised throughout their annual growth cycle. Some 700 thousand bottles are produced annually, and whites are the specialty. The oenologist is the young Nicola Carparelli, and he has presented an excellent sweet Moscato, the Gotha '98, which has a brilliant amber hue, extremely inviting aromas of cooked fruit and sweet pastry, and a sweet and properly acidic palate suggestive of caramel and plum tart. The Puglia Rosso Maestro '97, from montepulciano and uva di Troia, is also appealing, with its good concentration of fruit, attractive softness and youthful, vinous, freshness. The Rosa di Selva '98 has a fine light cherry-toned color, an intense cherry fragrance and an attractive, fresh and lively fruitiness. Two whites, the Locorotondo and the Divo, the latter from bianco d'Alessano and falanghina, are slightly less successful. The lightly sparkling Agorà is one of the most popular whites of the region. Youthful management, careful cellar technique, the thoughtful design of the labels and well-planned sales policies make this one of the most solid and dynamic estates of the region.

●	Maestro '97	🍷	3
○	Moscato Dolce Gotha '98	🍷	4
⊙	Rosa di Selva '98	🍷	2*
○	Agorà Bianco '98		2
○	Locorotondo '98		2
●	Maestro '97	🍸🍸	3*
○	Chardonnay del Salento Robur '94	🍸	4
○	Divo '93	🍸	4
○	Divo '94	🍸	4

GALATINA (LE)

Valle dell'Asso
Via Guidano, 18
73013 Galatina (LE)
tel. 0836/561470

With the Valle dell'Asso estate, Luigi Vallone continues a family activity that started early in the 20th century. There are now 50 hectares under vine in Galatina, divided among the DOC districts of Galatina, Copertino and Salice Salentino. The vines range from newly planted to 50-year-old gobelet-trained; negro amaro accounts for about 80% of the total, but there are also primitivo, aglianico, cabernet sauvignon and cabernet franc; the white grapes are predominantly chardonnay, with fiano, garganega and malvasia. Annual production is about 200 thousand bottles but there is potential for considerable growth as there are also still considerable bulk sales. Of the wines Luigi Vallone produces with the help of the oenologist Elio Minoia, we particularly admired the Salento Rosso '97, made mainly from negroamaro and primitivo. It has a fine ruby color, an intense nose with distinct tones of plum and cherry, and good body, fresh fruit, proper acidic balance, smooth tannins and fair harmony on the palate. The interesting Galatina Rosato '98 shows an intense rosé color, good structure, depth and softness, delicate herbaceous tones and the merest hint of tannins. The Galatina Rosso '97 is pleasingly full-bodied, perhaps a little too rustic, but warm and mouth-filling on the finish. The rather forward Copertino Rosso '97 is less interesting, as is the properly made and faintly fruity Salento Bianco '98.

●	Copertino Rosso '97	🍷	3
⊙	Galatina Rosato '98	🍷	3
●	Galatina Rosso '97	🍷	3
●	Salento Rosso '97	🍷	1*
○	Salento Bianco '98		1

GUAGNANO (LE)

COSIMO TAURINO
S. S. 605 SALICE-SANDONACI
73010 GUAGNANO (LE)
TEL. 0832/706490

Puglia has lost one of its heroes. Cosimo Taurino, the pharmacist from Guagnano who loved the wine of his native land above all else, did not see the end of the '99 harvest. Cosimo did a lot for Pugliese wine. He firmly believed that the land could yield great wines and when no one took him seriously he took up the cudgels and transformed his family estate into a model of southern Italian oenology. He was a man of great intuition, in both the production and marketing of wine. He also showed great perseverance against all odds, and against the opinions of others, which he eventually succeeded in changing. Patriglione, his great red from negroamaro, converted us all 15 years ago, even the difficult American market, where Taurino soared to star status. Today, with southern Italian wine production surging forward, many of his techniques, like overripening and grape selection, are taken for granted, but 20 years ago they were anything but. This year there were only two wines available for tasting apart from the excellent '93 Patriglione, which we reviewed last year. The Notarpanaro '94, of a dense dark ruby color, reveals intense aromas of ripe black fruit and Mediterranean scrub, and a warm, full, round, alcohol-rich and structured palate. The Salice Salentino Riserva '96 shows good concentration, fair balance throughout, plentiful alcohol and tannins, and a delicately bitter note on the finish. We feel sure that the Taurino family will find the strength and courage to continue Cosimo's work and we eagerly await the new vintages of Patriglione.

●	Notarpanaro '94	🍷🍷	4
●	Salice Salentino Rosso Ris. '96	🍷	3
●	Patriglione '85	YYY	5
●	Patriglione '88	YYY	5
●	Notarpanaro '86	YY	3*
●	Notarpanaro '88	YY	3*
●	Notarpanaro '90	YY	3*
●	Notarpanaro '93	YY	4
●	Patriglione '93	YY	5
○	Salento Chardonnay '97	YY	3*
●	Salice Salentino Rosso Ris. '88	YY	3*
●	Salice Salentino Rosso Ris. '90	YY	3*
●	Salice Salentino Rosso Ris. '93	YY	3*
●	Salice Salentino Rosso Ris. '94	YY	3*

LATIANO (BR)

LOMAZZI & SARLI
C.DA PARTEMIO
S. S. 7 BRINDISI - TARANTO
72022 LATIANO (BR)
TEL. 0831/725898

Lomazzi & Sarli, a richly traditional name in Pugliese oenology, is owned by the Dimastrodonato family and covers about 100 hectares under vine in the Brindisi DOC area. In the last few years the estate has been seriously engaged in a major revamping that should, according to Pino Dimastrodonato, who manages it, raise it within a few years to the level of the region's best producers. The first phase of this project is the conversion of the vineyards, abandoning the old pergola system in favor of high-density espalier training. This year the estate's technical director, the oenologist Lino Carparelli, has produced a good range of wines, lead by the Primitivo del Salento Latias '98 and the Brindisi Rosso Solise '96. The Primitivo has a dark, almost black ruby color, and a sweet, intense nose that releases classic notes of ripe plum and blackberry with hints of chocolate and pastry fresh from the oven. The soft, fleshy palate is rich in smooth tannins, fruity and warm, and spicy on the finish. The Solise has a more traditional stamp but still shows good extract, a firm structure, balance, elegant tannins, overall harmony and complex balsamic notes on the finish. We liked the robust, warm and inviting Salento Rosso Terra di Tacco '97; the delicately aromatic but slightly lean Malvasia del Salento Partemio '98 seemed interesting; the other wines are properly executed.

●	Primitivo del Salento Latias '98	🍷🍷	3*
●	Brindisi Rosso Solise '96	🍷	2*
○	Malvasia del Salento Partemio '98	🍷	3
●	Salento Rosso Terra di Tacco '97	🍷	2
⊙	Salento Rosato Terra di Tacco '98		2

LECCE

AGRICOLE VALLONE
VIA XXV LUGLIO, 7
73100 LECCE
TEL. 0832/308041

Graticciaia is a sort of southern Amarone. Like the celebrated Veneto wine it is rich in alcohol, warm, concentrated, complex and capable of very long aging; and it too comes from late-harvested grapes that are further dried on racks called "graticci" – hence its name – before pressing. The grapes are, of course, negroamaro and malvasia nera, the leading players in the Salento area. The '94 is probably the best ever, thanks to the oenologist Severino Garofono. It has a dense dark, almost black ruby color. The nose releases a wealth of rich, complex aromas, from the sweet notes of blackberry jam to berries and ripe plum, and on to bitter chocolate, mint and vanilla. The palate is dense and soft, perfectly balanced, harmonious, clean, fruity and quite long. This is a classic wine from Maria Teresa and Vittoria Vallone, and is already breathing hotly on Three Glasses. The Brindisi Rosso Vigna Flaminio '96 offers some of the characteristics of the great Vallone wine, although in miniature, particularly the delightful concentration of ripe black fruit, which here too results from a fairly late harvest. It is an intriguing wine with scents of ripe cherry, tobacco and spice, lots of ripe tannins and an amazingly reasonable price. The '96 Salice Salentino Vereto has its usual soft full flavor, while the Sauvignon Corte Valesio '98 is attractive and intriguingly vegetal. We found the Brindisi Rosato Vigna Flaminio '98 disappointing.

●	Brindisi Rosso V. Flaminio '96	▼▼	2*
●	Graticciaia '94	▼▼	5
●	Salice Salentino Vereto '96	▼	2*
○	Sauvignon del Salento Corte Valesio '98	▼	2*
⊙	Brindisi Rosato V. Flaminio '98		2
●	Brindisi Rosso V. Flaminio '94	▽▽	2*
●	Brindisi Rosso V. Flaminio '95	▽▽	2*
●	Graticciaia '90	▽▽	5
●	Graticciaia '92	▽▽	5
●	Graticciaia '93	▽▽	5
●	Salice Salentino Rosso '93	▽▽	2*
●	Salice Salentino Rosso '94	▽▽	2*
●	Salice Salentino Vereto '95	▽▽	2*

LEVERANO (LE)

CONTI ZECCA
VIA CESAREA
73045 LEVERANO (LE)
TEL. 0832/922606 - 0832/925613

The 800-hectare Conti Zecca estate, with 320 hectares under vine, is now definitely oriented towards quality. Modernization of the vineyards and cellars, and renewal of the barrel stock, including the introduction of new oak barriques, are just some of the more obvious signs of the work that Antonio Romano, the estate's manager and oenologist, has recently carried out. The arrival of Giorgio Marone as consultant has had a major positive impact on the wines, which are sold at remarkably fair prices. The most interesting wine we tasted this year was certainly the Nero '97, a red from negroamaro, malvasia nera and cabernet. Of a dark ruby hue, it offers a rich bouquet of red fruit, chocolate and spice, and a warm, velvety, ripe, elegant and soft palate. The Salice Salentino Cantalupi '96 displays a wealth of aromatic notes of Mediterranean scrub and blackberry jam, and an attractively round and deep palate. The Leverano Vigna del Saraceno Riserva '96 seduced us with its full flavor, its cleanness, the finesse of its tannins and its sweet fruit. The Malvasia Vigna del Saraceno '97 is an important late-harvested white with a deep golden hue, rich in aromatic notes and hints of citrus peel on the nose, and fat, soft, full, crisp and amazing balanced on the palate. The estate's other wines are all good and also excellent value for money

○	Leverano Malvasia Vigna del Saraceno '97	▼▼	3*
●	Leverano Rosso Vigna del Saraceno Ris. '96	▼▼	2*
●	Nero '97	▼▼	4
●	Salice Salentino Rosso Cantalupi '96	▼▼	2*
○	Leverano Bianco Vigna del Saraceno '98	▼	2*
⊙	Leverano Rosato Vigna del Saraceno '98	▼	2*
○	Salento Bianco Donna Marzia '98	▼	1*
●	Salento Rosso Donna Marzia '97	▼	1*
○	Salice Salentino Bianco Cantalupi '98	▼	2*
●	Salento Rosso Donna Marzia '96	▽▽	2*

LIZZANO (TA)

CANTINA SOCIALE DI LIZZANO
C.SO EUROPA, 37/39
74020 LIZZANO (TA)
TEL. 099/652013

The Cantina Sociale di Lizzano is a large cooperative winery that is currently undergoing major reorganization. The range of wines produced is fairly wide but, strangely, there is a considerable qualitative divide between those based on primitivo and those coming under the Lizzano DOC. While the former are characterful, concentrated and well executed, all the Lizzano wines leave something to be desired, despite the apparent good quality of the grapes. We hope that this gap will soon be narrowed, allowing the full range positive reviews. For now, we console ourselves with an excellent Primitivo del Tarantino '98, of a fine dark ruby color and rich in complex aromas of ripe red fruit, herbs, licorice and pencil lead. The palate is deep, fat and rich, with exuberant soft tannins that blend into a full, fruity body. The Primitivo di Manduria Dolce Monte Manco '96 has a very concentrated ruby hue and an intense nose that releases soft notes of berry and cherry jam, tobacco and spice. The sweet and balanced palate is dense, fat, opulent, full and long.

●	Primitivo del Tarantino '98	1*
●	Primitivo di Manduria Dolce Monte Manco '96	4

LOCOROTONDO (BA)

CANTINA DEL LOCOROTONDO
VIA MADONNA DELLA CATENA, 99
70010 LOCOROTONDO (BA)
TEL. 080/4311644

The Cantina del Locorotondo is one of the biggest cooperatives of the region and has always stood out for its carefully produced and reliable wines. Curiously enough, although they concentrate on whites, it was the reds that emerged particularly at our tastings this year. The Casale San Giorgio '97, for instance, is a very successful blend of negroamaro and primitivo with a dark ruby color, an intense bouquet of ink, tobacco and dark fruit, and a well-structured palate with notes of chocolate and spice on the finish. It is an exemplary combination of modern technique and traditional character and came close to reaching Two Glasses. The Primitivo di Manduria Terre di Don Peppe '97, fat, round and full, with lots of fruit and smooth tannins, is another interesting red. The Valle d'Itria Rosso Roccia '98 has a well-expressed straightforward, youthful, fresh character that makes for balanced and enjoyable drinking. The '98 rosé version is also attractive and quaffable. The '98 whites, all DOC Locorotondos, whether the special selections such as the Vigneti in Tallinajo and the Riserva del Presidente or the standard DOC, all seemed less successful than in previous years. This is a pity because they were always really quite good. We hope it was just a brief lapse and that they will be back up to scratch with the next vintage.

●	Casale San Giorgio '97	2*
○	Moscato Olimpia '98	3
○	Moscato Spumante Olimpia	3
●	Primitivo di Manduria Terre di Don Pepe '97	5
⊙	Roccia Rosato '98	1*
●	Roccia Rosso '98	1
●	Casale San Giorgio '96	2*
○	Locorotondo In Tallinajo '97	2*
○	Moscato Olimpia '97	3

MANDURIA (TA)

FELLINE
VIA N. DONADIO, 20
74024 MANDURIA (TA)
TEL. 099/9711660

After inching ever closer over the last three years Felline has at last seized Three Glasses with a fabulous red wine, the Vigna del Feudo '97. Since its inception, Felline has produced wines that stood out both for their own excellence and for the amazing value for money they offered. Gregorio Perrucci and his brother Fabrizio, assisted by the oenologist Roberto Cipresso, obtain the grapes for their three wines from their 33 hectares of vineyard, mostly gobelet-trained, in the countryside near Acuti di Manduria. The Vigna del Feudo is a blend of primitivo (60%), montepulciano (30%) and equal parts of cabernet sauvignon and merlot, grown partly with free-standing espalier training and partly on gobelet-trained vines. The '97 is of an impenetrably dark ruby color and releases amazingly intense and elegant aromas of red fruit and spice with stylish toasty notes. The palate offers elegance and finesse, and the beautifully clean, succulent fruit, the smooth, caressing tannins and complex new-oak-derived nuances are in perfect balance. The nose is exactly mirrored on the palate, which is remarkably long. This magnificent wine is accompanied by two other excellent reds: the '98 Primitivo di Manduria is just as good as the excellent vintage that preceded it. On the nose it displays attractive hints of green and black peppercorns and pencil lead; in the mouth it is fruity, soft and concentrated, finishing on notes of chocolate, ripe cherry and pencil lead. The Alberello '98, an equal blend of primitivo and negroamaro, has an exuberant bouquet and a richly fruity, warm, powerful palate with soft, rounded tannins.

●	Vigna del Feudo '97	🍷🍷🍷	4*
●	Primitivo di Manduria '98	🍷🍷	3*
●	Salento Rosso Alberello '98	🍷🍷	2*
●	Primitivo di Manduria '96	♈♈	4
●	Primitivo di Manduria '97	♈♈	4
●	Salento Rosso Alberello '97	♈♈	3*

MANDURIA (TA)

PERVINI
VIA SANTO STASI PRIMO
Z. I. - C.DA ACUTI
74024 MANDURIA (TA)
TEL. 099/9711660

Perrucci Vini, better known as Pervini, is making a big impact on the Pugliese wine scene. This is not just because of the quality of its wines: it is also the leading light of the Accademia dei Racemi, an association of several small estates that have been saved from abandonment, and, with the help of some renowned oenologists, (as well as Fabrizio Perrucci, the resident oenologist) are all producing again, and with notable success. The list of wines produced is long and studded with excellent names. The peaks this year were the Primitivo di Manduria '97: stylish and harmonious, with mouth-filling fruit and hints of white pepper and chocolate; and the fleshy and balanced Bizantino Rosso, from negroamaro and primitivo, which has great extract and smooth tannins, with notes of spicy oak, tobacco and coffee on the finish. The Primitivo Primo Amore '97 is soft, concentrated and redolent of blackberry, walnut skin, cocoa and sour cherry; the Primitivo I Monili is full-bodied, fruity, soft and long. Both are excellent, as is the rest of the range. Pervini also markets the wines of two small wineries, Casale Bevagna, which makes a sensational Salice Salentino Te Deum '98, complex, structured, soft and rich in ripe fruit; and Antica Masseria Torre Mozza, a tiny estate owned by a Swiss couple, Rina and Raymund Amstutz. They produce the aristocratic Sole Leone '96, a blend of negroamaro, malvasia nera and cabernet, and the fascinating Finibusterre '97, a cabernet sauvignon from 60-year-old gobelet-trained vines.

●	Finibusterre Antica Maseria Torre Mozza '97	🍷🍷	6
●	Primitivo del tarantino I Monili '97	🍷🍷	2*
●	Primitivo di Manduria Archidamo '97	🍷🍷	3*
●	Primitivo di Manduria Primo Amore '97	🍷🍷	3*
●	Salento Rosso Bizantino '97	🍷🍷	2*
●	Salice Salentino Rosso Te Deum Casale Bevagna '98	🍷🍷	4
●	Sole Leone Antica Maseria Torre Mozza '96	🍷🍷	6
●	Galante Rosso '97	🍷	1*
○	Salento Chardonnay Bizantino '98	🍷	2*
⊙	Salento Rosato Bizantino '98	🍷	2*

MARUGGIO (TA)

MASSERIA PEPE
LOC. CASTIGNO
74020 MARUGGIO (TA)
TEL. 099/9711660

This is prime time for primitivo. There is much talk of its origins (it seems to have been established that zinfandel – the American grape – is just another way of pronouncing it) and of its characteristics, and at last there is a new wave of producers who are offering more "modern" interpretations and generally exploring all the potentials of the variety and of the Pugliese terroirs. One of these young lions is Alberto Pagano, born in 1911 and a pharmacist by calling. Last year Dr. Pagano decided to vinify the excellent grapes from his property in Maruggio (in Primitivo di Manduria country) himself, calling in his son-in-law, the fellow pharmacist and passionate winegrower Mario Calò, to help him out. The result is two excellent versions of this great red. The first is the Portile '98, a beautifully clean and concentrated Primitivo del Salento with a deep ruby hue and intense aromas of ripe dark fruit. On the palate it is meaty, fruity, richly structured and well supported by an acidic backbone and evident tannins of great finesse; the tone is soft, spicy and remarkably powerful. But the real star is the Dunico, a Primitivo di Manduria '98, from a terrific vineyard where vine roots sink into the sands of the Maruggio coastline. The wine is similar to the Portile, but it goes further: its full body and depth of fruit and spice, shot through with sweet notes of cocoa, vanilla and cherry liqueur, make it a model Primitivo. After this success, Alberto has, with astonishing determination and enthusiasm, just finished planting a new vineyard of three hectares adjacent to Dunico – a fact that speaks for itself.

● Primitivo di Manduria Dunico '98	🍷🍷	5
● Primitivo Portile '98	🍷🍷	4

RUTIGLIANO (BA)

VIGNETI DEL SUD
VIA CAVALIERI DI VITTORIO VENETO, 6
70018 RUTIGLIANO (BA)
TEL. 055/23595

Antinori has gone down south. And it has landed in style. This celebrated Florentine producer, with vineyards in the best zones of Tuscany, has, in little over a year, added 600 hectares under vine in Puglia to its holdings. After expanding long since to Umbria (but Umbria is practically their back yard) and Piedmont, the Antinoris saw it was high time to look southwards, in line with the trend that has recently seen a great deal of investment in Puglia and Sicily. They have bought two separate estates that figure together under the name Vigneti del Sud. The first is Tormaresca, a property of about 100 hectares in the Castel del Monte DOC area, at Minervino Murge in the province of Bari. Tormaresca previously belonged to Gancia, the giant producer at Canelli in Piedmont, and the vineyards are planted to aglianico, cabernet and merlot for the reds, and to chardonnay for whites. The second estate is at San Pietro Vernotico in the heart of Salento, with 500 hectares growing mainly negroamaro. There is still a lot of restructuring going on but the excellent red and white Tormarescas from the '98 vintage are already available and are both spectacular value for money. The first is a monovarietal chardonnay fermented and aged for several months in small oak barrels. It shows a deep straw color, sweet scents of ripe apple, yellow peach and apricot, and a structured, full-flavored, fruity palate with pleasing crisp acidity. The Rosso, a blend of the three red varieties, has a fine ruby color and a bouquet of red fruit with a noticeable vegetal note. The palate, while not particularly concentrated, reveals good balance and soft tannins.

○ Tormaresca Bianco '98	🍷🍷	2*
● Tormaresca Rosso '98	🍷	2*

SALICE SALENTINO (LE)

LEONE DE CASTRIS
VIA SENATORE DE CASTRIS, 50
73015 SALICE SALENTINO (LE)
TEL. 0832/731112

This year Salice Salentino Donna Lisa Riserva is again one of the best reds made in Italy. The '95 stood out in our blind tastings, easily exceeding the threshold score for Three Glasses, just as the '93 did last year. It presents a dense dark ruby color and an ample array of sweet, ripe aromas ranging from berry and cherry jam to tamarind, with the softly balsamic notes of new oak. On the palate it is dense, fat, elegantly structured and harmonious, echoing the fruit of the bouquet. It boasts enormous body, abundant tannins of notable finesse and a very long finish. This great red crowns a reliable range which has offered unwavering quality through the years, the result of the intelligent hard work of Salvatore Leone de Castris, a major figure on the Italian wine scene, his son Piernicola and the oenologist Leonardo Pinto. The Salice Salentino Majana '97 is also excellent. It is round, full and rich in fruity aromas and spicy notes of toasty oak and tobacco. De Castris' classic rosé, the Five Roses '98, it too from a blend in which negroamaro plays the main role, is equally good. A brilliant deep rosé color introduces a fragrance of raspberry, blueberry and red currant, and a fruity, well-structured palate rich in crisp acidity. The Salice Salentino Bianco Donna Lisa '98, which is structured and refreshing, the Salice Salentino Bianco Imago '98, another chardonnay, the Salice Salentino Riserva '96 and the sweet Aleatico del Salento Negrino '97 all caught our attention.

●	Salice Salentino Rosso Donna Lisa Ris. '95	TTT	5
⊙	Five Roses '98	TT	3*
●	Salice Salentino Rosso Majana '97	TT	2*
●	Aleatico Negrino '98	T	4
●	Salento Bianco Verdeca Messapia '98	T	3
○	Salice Salentino Bianco Donna Lisa '98	T	4
○	Salice Salentino Bianco Imago '98	T	2*
●	Salice Salentino Rosso Ris. '96	T	3
●	Salice Salentino Rosso Donna Lisa Ris. '93	YYY	4*
●	Salice Salentino Rosso Donna Lisa Ris. '92	YY	4

SANDONACI (BR)

FRANCESCO CANDIDO
VIA A. DIAZ, 46
72025 SANDONACI (BR)
TEL. 0831/635674

The Candido estate, at Sandonaci in the Brindisi province, is one of the finest wineries in Puglia. With the aid of Severino Garofano as consultant oenologist it produces a wide, carefully honed range of wines. Leading the list, as usual, is the Duca d'Aragona. The '93, a blend of negroamaro and montepulciano, is one of the most interesting reds of the region. A dark ruby hue with a garnet cast precedes intense aromas of blackberry and cherry jam and a hint of tar. The warm, mouth-filling and velvety palate mirrors the fruit of the bouquet, whose stylish development is accompanied by intense spicy notes. The excellent Cappello di Prete, a blend of negroamaro and malvasia nera, is remarkably elegant and intense, one of the most stylistically consistent wines of the south and certainly one of its greatest bargains. The '95, which we reviewed last year, is still extremely good. The same goes for the Paule Calle '97, a passito (raisin) wine from malvasia. Re-tasting it one year on serves to confirm its depth and complexity and the elegance of its floral and fruity tones. The Salice Salentino Bianco '98 is crisp, soft and rich in notes of white-fleshed fruit, while the Vigna Vinera '98, a white from oak-aged sauvignon, shows good body and attractive fruit but less concentration and elegance than the '97. The Casina Cucci '98 is properly made and easy to drink and the Salice Salentino Rosato le Pozzelle shows good depth, but we found the sweet Salice Salentino Aleatico a little too forward.

●	Duca d'Aragona '93	TT	5
○	Chardonnay del Salento Casina Cucci '98	T	2*
○	Salento Bianco Vigna Vinera '98	T	2*
○	Salice Salentino Bianco '98	T	2*
⊙	Salice Salentino Rosato Le Pozzelle '98	T	2*
●	Cappello di Prete '92	YY	3
●	Cappello di Prete '93	YY	3*
●	Cappello di Prete '94	YY	3*
●	Cappello di Prete '95	YY	3*
●	Duca d'Aragona '90	YY	5
●	Duca d'Aragona '91	YY	5
●	Duca d'Aragona '92	YY	5
●	Salice Salentino Rosso Ris. '94	YY	2*

SAVA (TA)

Cantina e Oleificio Sociale di Sava

S.S. 7 ter, Km. 17,800
74028 Sava (TA)
tel. 099/9726139

Primitivo immediately brings to mind the DOC district of Manduria in the province of Taranto. But within this Primitivo di Manduria district is the area of Sava, which has several distinct characteristics of its own. For one thing, the primitivo clones that grow here are slightly different, then there are fewer grapes on the bunch, and winegrowers here "instinctively" tend to favor lower yields and later harvests. The primitivo from these vines, which are mostly gobelet-trained, acquires great concentration and lends itself to late harvesting. The Primitivo di Manduria Terre di Miele '94 from the Cooperativa e Oleificio Sociale is exemplary. This cooperative, established in 1960, is directed by the oenologist Bruno Garofano and includes 800 small producers with a total of 850 hectares under vine. Theirs is the traditional Primitivo, full-bodied, concentrated and almost sweet, the sort of wine that, with dried figs, once formed the lunch of farm workers, giving them the energy they needed for their hard labor. We like it for its fleshiness and the intensity and cleanness of its jammy scents, with cherry and plum to the fore, and notes of chocolate and spice. The '94 Primitivo has "only" 14% alcohol, is rich in fresh, fruity tones of blackberry and blueberry, and has a soft, warm, full-bodied, balanced palate with abundant ripe tannins. To close, the successful Chardonnay del Salento '98, redolent of peach and apricot, is clean and remarkably refreshing in the mouth.

●	Primitivo di Manduria Terra di Miele '94	🍷🍷	3*
●	Primitivo di Manduria '94	🍷	2*
○	Salento Chardonnay '98	🍷	1*
●	Primitivo di Manduria Terra di Miele '88	Y	3

SAVA (TA)

Pichierri - Vinicola Savese

Via I. Prato, 1
74028 Sava (TA)
tel. 099/9726232

Don't be put off by the old-fashioned labels that adorn the wines from this historic estate in Sava! These wines have been a model in the Manduria zone for over 40 years. Today the winery is run by Luigi Pichierri, a representative of the third generation. The range is vast, going from the traditional Primitivo di Manduria to dry and sweet sparkling wines, but for us the most interesting wines are the classics: the Primitivos. We were particularly pleased with the Primitivo di Manduria Passione '97, a sweet wine with 6% residual sugar and 15.5% alcohol. It is one of those wines of a somewhat unfashionable style, perhaps, and quite innocent of market trends, which are a part of the most ancient wine-making tradition and definitely worth preserving, when they are well made and interesting like this one, because they have much to offer. This particular example displays great concentration in its sweet, powerful and fruity bouquet (blackberry and cherries steeped in alcohol), which carries through onto the soft palate where it merges with the wine's sweetness and its nuances of vanilla and chocolate. It has denseness and substantial alcohol but it's balanced, rich and long. The Primitivo di Manduria Mamma Teresa '94 is dry, but shows admirable substance and spicy notes of white pepper, tobacco and chocolate on the tannic and full-bodied palate, which finishes on notes of fruit and licorice. The meaty and spicy Primitivo Le Petrose '98 is also good, as is the fat and concentrated Primitivo Vermiglio '98.

●	Primitivo di Manduria Passione '97	🍷🍷	6
●	Primitivo del Tarantino Le Petrose '98	🍷	2*
●	Primitivo del Tarantino Vermiglio '98	🍷	1*
●	Primitivo di Manduria Mamma Teresa '94	🍷	4
●	Primitivo di Manduria Terrarossa '95	Y	3
●	Primitivo di Manduria Tradizione del Nonno '92	Y	3
●	Primitivo di Manduria Tradizione del Nonno '95	Y	3

TRICASE (LE)

Castel di Salve
Fraz. Depressa - P.zza Castello, 8
73039 Tricase (LE)
tel. 0833/771012

Francesco Marra from Salento and the Englishman Francesco Winspeare both have a boundless passion for wine, and between them these two good-natured young men own some 500 hectares of land, of which 36 are under vine. A while ago they acquired an old, abandoned winery and re-equipped it to vinify the wine of their newly established Castel di Salve. At first they sold the wine, made from negroamaro, sangiovese, malvasia nera and montepulciano – the classics – in bulk. Then they decided to launch an attack on the upper end of the market. So they drastically reduced grape yields, bought equipment for cold maceration and temperature-controlled fermentation, and the inevitable French oak barriques. With two consultant oenologists, Andrea Boaretti and Fabrizio Perrucci (a name to conjure with in Salento), the project started to take off and three excellent wines have emerged. The Sangiovese di Puglia Volo di Alessandro '98 has an attractive dense dark ruby color and an intense nose with notes of berries, vegetal nuances and a hint of spice. On the palate it is warm and mouth-filling, with lots of ripe fruit and fine-grained velvety tannins. The Negroamaro del Salento Armecolo '98 manages to express the power and concentration of negroamaro with an admirable softness, cleanness of fruit and roundness of tannins. The Priante, an oak-aged blend of all the estate's varieties, shows a dark ruby hue, a bouquet of berry and cherry jam with notes of spice and ink, and a deep, soft, concentrated and full-bodied palate.

●	Armecolo '98	ΨΨ	3*
●	Priante '98	ΨΨ	3*
●	Il Volo di Alessandro '98	Ψ	3

TUGLIE (LE)

Michele Calò & Figli
Via Masseria Vecchia, 1
73058 Tuglie (LE)
tel. 0833/596242

In the mid-'50s Michele Calò established a small winery in Tuglie, his native village, and then set up a wine-selling business in Lombardy. This enabled him to expand production and build a larger cellar. His wines are now among the best known and most esteemed of Salento. A large part of the output of Michele's winery, in which he now has the help of his sons Fernando and Giovanni, goes into the Mjère line, and the top of the line is the Alezio Rosato. The '98 was not up to the excellent '97: although it is interesting, fresh and fruity, it lacks the richness and balance that would have won it Two Glasses. The Mjère Rosso '97, from negroamaro with 10% malvasia nera, is structured, soft and appropriately tannic, with some fruit and moderate length. The Mjère Bianco, on the other hand, has a not very well-defined nose and finishes rather short. But the Vigna Spano, a selection of negroamaro and malvasia nera grapes grown in the Spano vineyard at Sannicola produced only in the best years, keeps the banner flying. The '96 displays a dark ruby color and intense, complex aromas of ripe red fruit (cherry and plum) blended with exotic spice and the balsamic, spicy notes of old oak. It shows volume on the palate and an even progression with clean, ripe fruit, abundant smooth tannins, softness, full body and length.

●	Vigna Spano '96	ΨΨ	5
⊙	Alezio Rosato Mjere '98	Ψ	3
●	Alezio Rosso Mjere '98	Ψ	4
○	Salento Bianco Mjere '98		3
⊙	Alezio Rosato Mjere '97	ΥΥ	3*
⊙	Alezio Rosato Mjere '95	ΥΥ	2*
●	Alezio Rosso Mjere '90	ΥΥ	3*
●	Alezio Rosso Mjere '92	ΥΥ	3*
●	Alezio Rosso Mjere '94	ΥΥ	3*
●	Alezio Rosso Mjere '95	ΥΥ	3*
●	Alezio Rosso Mjere '96	ΥΥ	3*
○	Salento Bianco Mjere '95	ΥΥ	2*
●	Vigna Spano '90	ΥΥ	4
●	Vigna Spano '93	ΥΥ	4

OTHER WINERIES

The following producers obtained good scores in our tastings with one or more of their wines:

PROVINCE OF BARI

Botromagno
Gravina di Puglia, tel. 080/3265865
Gravina '98

Cardone
Locorotondo, tel. 080/4311624
Puglia Primitivo Primaio '98

Cooperativa Riforma Fondiaria
Ruvo, tel. 080/9501611
Terre di Talos Rosso

Nugnes
Trani, tel. 0883/586837
Moscato di Trani Dolce Naturale '96

Coppi
Turi, tel. 080/8915049
Puglia Primitivo Vinacciero '98

PROVINCE OF BRINDISI

Cantina Due Palme
Cellino San Marco, tel. 0831/619728
Salice Salentino Selvarossa Ris. '96

Tenuta La Mea
Cellino San Marco, tel. 0831/617689
Bella Mojgan '97,
Salice Salentino '97

Santa Barbara
San Pietro Vernotico, tel. 0837/652749
Brindisi Rosso '96,
Salento Barbaglio '95

PROVINCE OF FOGGIA

Antica Enotria
Cerignola, tel. 0885/424688
Aglianico della Daunia '96

D'Alfonso Del Sordo
San Severo, tel. 0882/221444
Daunia Casteldrione '96

D'Arapri
San Severo, tel. 0882/333927
Brut Metodo Classico,
Pas Dosé Metodo Classico,
Rosé Metodo Classico

PROVINCE OF LECCE

Cantina Sociale Copertino
Copertino, tel. 0832/947031
Salento Chardonnay Cigliano '98

Masseria Monaci
Copertino, tel. 0832/947512
Copertino Eloquenzia '97

Cantele
Lecce, tel. 0832/307018
Salice Salentino Ris. '95

Duca Guarini di Poggiardo
Scorrano, tel. 0836/460288
Salento Sauvignon Mura '98,
Salento Primitivo Vigne Vecchie '98

PROVINCE OF TARANTO

Agricola Pliniana
Manduria, tel. 099/8794273
Primitivo di Manduria '96

Consorzio Produttori Vini
Manduria, tel. 099/97305332
Primitivo di Manduria Il Sonetto '97

Soloperto
Manduria, tel. 099/9794286
Primitivo di Manduria '96

Miali
Martina Franca,
tel. 080/4303222
Castel del Monte Rosato '98

CALABRIA

Oenological Calabria is still a promise yet to be fulfilled. This year, as in the past, the general standard of wines at our tastings was acceptable and we tried many good and even very good bottles, but they give no real idea of the region's vast potential. Although this is now the moment when the southern parts of Italy and of the other wine-producing countries are surging ahead, with a huge revival of interest in all the warmer, sun-drenched viticultural regions of the world, Calabria seems lost in a time warp of its own, light years away from the ferment coursing through the wine sector world-wide. The fact that there are just six full entries for Calabria should speak for itself. The region desperately needs a critical mass of top-level producers and, numerically, there is no shortage of estates to supply them. Neither is it a lack of DOCs nor the land that is holding things back: the region has stupendous terrains and an incredible variety of climates. Significantly, though, in the estates that have made it to these pages one thing stands out: all have expert oenologists working in their cellars. This should make other producers think hard. So Calabria still appears to be in need of a breath of fresh air. But does it make sense to talk of fresh air in a zone that has excellent viticultural traditions dating back several thousand years? And what sort of fresh air? Is it really necessary to use international varieties when you have before you the native greco and gaglioppo? Should one change beautiful 30-40-year-old gobelet-trained vines for more "modern" systems? Let us hope not. Instead, "fresh air" should mean looking at the old in a new way, and doing away only with those old things that are not worth keeping, as Librandi, Odoardi and Fattoria San Francesco have done, and as Cantine Lente and the newcomers to the Guide, Statti and Vivacqua, are now doing. What a pity that such legendary names as Caparra & Siciliani and Ippolito are not yet on the same wavelength. Caparra & Siciliani has produced a good Cirò Bianco, the Curiale '98, and Ippolito a more than acceptable Cirò Rosso Classico Riserva '85 which certainly rate a mention in these pages, but just one wine apiece is not really sufficient. It's the same story with Enotria, a large cooperative with an excellent cellar and 120 hectares under vine and whose sole interesting wine this year is a '98 Cirò Bianco. If you look for them you can find good wines here and there, but they are still isolated pearls in a sea of mediocrity. Two estates beginning to emerge from this sea are Serracavallo, which has a good Valle del Crati Rosato, and Lidia Matera, with a quite attractive Valle del Crati Rosso Terre Nobili '98. To finish there are two very good sweet wines from Vintripodi, the Greco di Bianco '96 and the Mantonico di Bianco '96, which represent a Calabrian tradition that must not be allowed to vanish.

CIRÒ (KR)

FATTORIA SAN FRANCESCO
LOC. QUATTROMANI
88071 CIRÒ (KR)
TEL. 0962/32228

Francesco Siciliani's Fattoria San Francesco is going through what can only be described as a renaissance. New cellars have been built and the able oenologist Fabrizio Ciufoli has arrived from Tuscany to be their consultant. Thus, in this year's tastings, the '97 Cirò Rosso Classico Superiore Ronco dei Quattroventi, the estate's flagship wine, came perilously close to Three Glasses. This monovarietal gaglioppo is in fine form, with a dense deep ruby hue and intense scents of red and black fruit, pencil lead and vanilla and elegant hints of spice. The soft, fat palate delightfully echoes the blackberry, blueberry and wild strawberry notes of the bouquet and reveals fine tannins, good balance and appropriate length. A second extremely appealing wine, one of the few Italian rosés to attain Two Glasses with ease, is the Cirò Rosato, this too from gaglioppo. It displays an intense and brilliant rosé hue and a fragrant and inviting nose with notes of raspberry, blueberry, red currant and ripe cherry; the palate has fair structure but is strikingly soft, fruity and fresh, indeed virtually irresistible. The Cirò Rosso Donna Madda '97 also performs well, with its fine deep ruby color suggestive of concentration, appealing fragrance of ripe black fruit, and soft, structured palate with fine tannins and fair length. The Cirò Bianco '98 is fresh, fruity and redolent of flowers and green apple; the Cirò Rosso Classico '98 is a little less successful but still good; the lightly sparkling Martà is agreeably fresh and light.

⊙	Cirò Rosato '98	🍷🍷	2*
●	Cirò Rosso Classico Ronco dei Quattro Venti '97	🍷🍷	4
○	Cirò Bianco '98	🍷	2*
●	Cirò Rosso Classico Sup. Donna Madda '97	🍷	3
●	Cirò Rosso Classico Ronco dei Quattro Venti '92	YY	4
●	Cirò Rosso Classico Sup. '91	YY	3*
●	Cirò Rosso Classico Sup. Donna Madda '92	YY	3*
●	Cirò Rosso Classico Sup. Donna Madda '93	YY	4
●	Cirò Rosso Classico Sup. Donna Madda '95	YY	4

CIRÒ MARINA (KR)

LIBRANDI
C.DA S. GENNARO
S. S. 106
88072 CIRÒ MARINA (KR)
TEL. 0962/31518 - 0962/31519

The '95 Gravello came within an ace of matching the success of the '93 by winning Three Glasses, and is, in fact, an excellent wine. The color is a dense dark ruby tinged with purple. The nose releases intense, sweet scents of ripe fruit enriched by toasty, smoky tones from the new barriques. The palate is warm, deep, balanced and round with fine tannins and fair length: indeed one thinks "Ah, lovely!", but then one also wishes it had just a touch more concentration and length. This year Donato Lanati succeeded Severino Garofano as consultant oenologist and, rewardingly for both, the entire range is of high quality, keeping Librandi firmly among southern Italy's top estates. For example, the sweet Le Passule '95 has a fine golden straw color and a rich bouquet of sweet pastry and peach jam; in the mouth it is sweet, stylish and long, and fascinating notes of apricot and vanilla emerge on the finish. The Critone '98, a blend of chardonnay and sauvignon, is indisputably the best white of the region. It captivates with the fullness of its aromas, its excellent structure and persistent fruitiness. The Cirò Bianco '98, with its abundant citrus and tropical fruit on the nose, and the Cirò Rosato '98, with its fruit, balance and good texture, are slightly less concentrated but just as attractive. The '95 Cirò Riserva Duca di Sanfelice showed less well than in previous vintages. It is tannic and structured but too forward for its age. The '98 rosé Terre Lontane and the '97 Cirò Rosso Classico are very good, as is their wont.

○	Critone '98	🍷🍷	3*
●	Gravello '95	🍷🍷	5
○	Le Passule '95	🍷🍷	4
○	Cirò Bianco '98	🍷	2*
⊙	Cirò Rosato '98	🍷	2*
●	Cirò Rosso Classico '97	🍷	2*
●	Cirò Rosso Duca Sanfelice Ris. '95	🍷	4
⊙	Terre Lontane '98	🍷	3
●	Gravello '89	YYY	5
●	Gravello '90	YYY	5
●	Gravello '93	YYY	5
●	Gravello '88	YY	5
●	Gravello '91	YY	5
○	Le Passule '90	YY	3*

COSENZA

GIOVAN BATTISTA ODOARDI
V.LE DELLA REPUBBLICA, 143
87100 COSENZA
TEL. 0984/29961

Gregorio Odoardi's Scavigna from his Vigna Garrone cru is a red of international standard, made from an intelligent blend of aglianico, merlot, cabernet sauvignon and cabernet franc. The '97 vintage is as successful as the fine '96 and offers a dense, deep, dark ruby hue and intense aromas of perfectly ripe blueberry, black currant and blackberry shot through with nuances of mint and a balsamic note. The palate is full-bodied, concentrated and smoothly tannic with lots of fruit and a long vanilla finish. It goes without saying that we expect further significant achievements over the next few years from this estate, which is overseen by the consultant oenologist Luca d'Attoma. The Scavigna Rosato '98, from gaglioppo, nerello cappuccio, sangiovese and pinot nero, and the white Scavigna Pian della Corte '98, an unusual blend of chardonnay, pinot bianco and riesling italico, are both excellent. The Pian della Corte shows a fine greenish-straw color, a fresh, fruity nose and, in the mouth, structure, a good acidic grip and body. The Rosato is invitingly fresh and fruity with its scents of raspberry and blackberry. However, the Valeo '98, a sweet wine from zibibbo produced only in half bottles, is slightly less expressive than the previous version. The new vintage of the Savuto Superiore Vigna Mortilla has not been released, so we had another taste of the '95 and found that it's keeping very well indeed.

● Scavigna Vigna Garrone '97	🍷🍷	5
○ Scavigna Pian della Corte '98	🍷	4
⊙ Scavigna Rosato '98	🍷	3
○ Valeo '98	🍷	4
● Savuto Sup. Vigna Mortilla '88	YY	3
● Savuto Sup. Vigna Mortilla '93	YY	4
● Savuto Sup. Vigna Mortilla '95	YY	4
● Savuto Sup. Vigna Vecchia '87	YY	3
● Savuto Sup. Vigna Vecchia '88	YY	4
○ Scavigna Pian della Corte '97	YY	4
● Scavigna Vigna Garrone '96	YY	4
○ Valeo '91	YY	5
○ Valeo '93	YY	5
○ Valeo '95	YY	5
○ Valeo '97	YY	5

LAMEZIA TERME (CZ)

CANTINE LENTO
VIA DEL PROGRESSO, 1
88046 LAMEZIA TERME (CZ)
TEL. 0968/28028

Salvatore Lento's beautiful estate in the province of Catanzaro counts 30 hectares under vine within the Lamezia DOC zone and is becoming known as one of the best in Calabria. The range, though vast, is overseen by the oenologist Zaffina and is of good quality. The standard-bearer is the red Federico II, a cabernet sauvignon aged in new oak. The '96 displays a dark ruby color and an intense bouquet of red fruit and incense with balsamic hints. The palate is fat, full, round, rich in ripe tannins and altogether delightful. From a selection of vintages of Lamezia Rosso Riserva, all made from nerello mascalese, cappuccio, gaglioppo and greco nero, the '93 showed best. It has a fairly deep ruby hue, a sweet fragrance of berry jam, and a good palate with fair structure and substantial alcohol. The appealing Lamezia Rosso Tenuta Romeo '97 is full-flavored, fairly warm and fruity, but the acidity is a little out of kilter. Of the whites, we liked the Contessa Emburga '98, an oak-aged sauvignon rich in structure and aromatic notes, with a round, fat palate shot through with vegetal hints; the soft Lamezia Greco '98, richly redolent of tropical fruit with a delicate note of rosewood; and a well-made Lamezia Bianco Tenuta Romeo '98.

● Federico II '96	🍷🍷	4
○ Lamezia Bianco '98	🍷	2*
○ Lamezia Greco '98	🍷	2*
● Lamezia Rosso '97	🍷	2*
● Lamezia Rosso Ris. '93	🍷	4
● Lamezia Rosso Ris. '84	YY	3*
● Lamezia Rosso Ris. '91	YY	3*
● Lamezia Rosso '91	Y	3
● Lamezia Rosso '92	Y	1*
● Lamezia Rosso Ris. '90	Y	3
● Lamezia Rosso Ris. '92	Y	3

LAMEZIA TERME (CZ)

STATTI
TENUTA LENTI
88046 LAMEZIA TERME (CZ)
TEL. 0968/456138 - 0968/453655

This estate has been in the Statti family for centuries. It stretches over 500 hectares, of which 30 are under vine; much of the rest is dedicated to the cultivation of olives, citrus fruit and seed crops, and to livestock rearing. A few years ago the brothers Alberto and Antonio Statti decided to renew the vineyards and re-equip the cellar. The vineyards are now planted to gaglioppo, greco nero, merlot and cabernet sauvignon for the reds and greco bianco, mantonico, malvasia, trebbiano, chardonnay and sauvignon for the whites. The oenologist Fabrizio Zardini from Brescia is in charge of wine-making, and the average annual production is about 200 thousand bottles. The white Ligeia '98, from chardonnay and sauvignon blanc, is a soft, rich, fresh and harmonious wine with a greenish-straw color, aromas of basil and tomato leaves, and a fleshy, full-flavored, elegant, balanced and pleasingly long palate. Another "table wine", the red Cauro '97, is a blend of gaglioppo and cabernet sauvignon given several months in new barriques. It is warm, tannic and characterful and, although not yet perfectly balanced, it is admirable for its restrained fruit and soft fullness on the palate. The Lamezia Greco '98 is fresh, fruity, aromatic and rather like sauvignon on the nose, which shows an intense note of Pantelleria oregano. The fleshy palate reveals hints of gooseberry and pineapple. The Arvino '97, another blend of gaglioppo and cabernet, is pleasantly fruity and notably fresh.

○	Ligeia '98	🍷🍷	3*
●	Cauro '97	🍷	5
○	Lamezia Greco '98	🍷	3
●	Arvino '97		3

LUZZI (CS)

VIVACQUA
C.DA SAN VITO
87040 LUZZI (CS)
TEL. 0984/543404

Luigi and Menuccia Vivacqua own a lovely estate in the province of Cosenza at San Vito di Luzzi, now also the name of one of Calabria's latest DOCs. The 120-hectare property is run on organic lines. Much of it is dedicated to olive groves and seed crops, but Luigi and Menuccia have recently returned to wine production, which was once a family tradition. They have created a new cellar, fitted it out with modern equipment and taken on Severino Garofano as consultant. Five wines are produced, three of them DOCs. The Marinò Rosso '97, mainly from gaglioppo and greco nero, has an attractive dark ruby color, a clean, rich bouquet of ripe blackberry and cherry, and a well-structured, full palate with noticeable tannins that however show finesse and lead into a warm, harmonious finish. The Chardonnay Donna Aurelia '98 is fresh and richly fruity, with notes of rennet apple and white-fleshed peach, on the nose, and crisp, soft, fruity and lively on the palate: altogether very appealing. The fresh, dry Rosato '98 was easily our favorite of the three DOCs. It shows a pale rosé color and an attractively rounded, balanced palate with crisp acidity and fresh hints of red fruit in a well-balanced structure.The San Vito di Luzzi Rosso, from the same blend of gaglioppo, greco nero, malvasia nera and sangiovese, is straightforward and fruity, while the '98 Bianco, from malvasia, mantonico and greco, did not seem particularly exciting.

○	Donna Aurelia Chardonnay '98	🍷	3
●	Marinò Rosso '97	🍷	3
⊙	San Vito di Luzzi Rosato '98	🍷	3
●	San Vito di Luzzi Rosso '98		3

SICILIA

For the second year running we find ourselves writing a very positive review of Sicily, at least of those producers – and their number is becoming substantial – who have set their sights high and are attempting to maximize the potential of their terrain. Of course it isn't all rosy. A large proportion of Sicily's vineyards still turn out anonymous, standardized wines, and real entrepreneurial spirit is not exactly widespread. However there do exist some significant producers who make us quite hopeful for the future, and there are native grape varieties, like grecanico, inzolia and nero d'avola, that could become the basis of Sicilian viticulture in the new century. And then a growing number of young producers, like the Planetas, the Rallos, the Tascas, the Firriatos, Gaetana Jacono and Giusto Occhipinti, are dedicated professionals in a new world, that of Sicilian wine of high quality. And that's not all. Leaving aside the entry of Donnafugata and the minuscule Pantelleria estate of D'Ancona into the Three Glass club, and a pair of Three Glass awards for Planeta, the real news this year is the arrival of one of the giants of Sicilian wine production, Settesoli, in Italian wine's upper class. Settesoli is a co-operative in Menfi that vinifies over 50 million kilos of grapes and bottles over 100 thousand hectoliters of wine (the rest, sadly, is still sold in bulk). Settesoli's giant step upward is not just an isolated case: it means that major changes are taking place at the heart of Sicilian wine-making. Meanwhile large Italian commercial groups such as Zonin, GIV and Marzotto-Santa Margherita have bought or are buying hundreds and hundreds of hectares in the island's best vine-growing areas. This could result in a complete transformation of the Sicilian wine world, and the dream of its becoming a sort of Mediterranean California may well come true a lot sooner than we now think. For the moment we can but record this year's unprecedented number – six – of Three Glass awards: two to Planeta and one each to Donnafugata, D'Ancona, Murana and Abbazia di Sant'Anastasia. Other notable names such as Tasca, Benanti, COS and Duca di Salaparuta didn't quite make it, not because they are intrinsically less good than the prizewinners, but because they had less favorable vintages to cope with. It is also worth noting that, with the exception of what takes place on the island of Pantelleria, there are more so-called "international" wines, made primarily from chardonnay and cabernet sauvignon, than wines derived from indigenous grapes. Among the new names are two surprises, Firriato in Paceco and the Cantina Sociale di Trapani, which have presented wines that are both well made and very economical. It's worth keeping an eye on them over the next few years. We are already closely observing Spadafora, which as of this year has taken on Luca D'Attoma, one of Italy's most promising young oenologists, as consultant.

ACATE (RG)

CANTINE TORREVECCHIA
C.DA TORREVECCHIA
97011 ACATE (RG)
TEL. 091/6882064 - 0932/990951

Market demand has led this large estate, owned by Giuseppe and Daniela Favuzza, to increase its range by the addition of two wines, one based on an indigenous variety, frappato, and one made from an "international" grape, syrah, which, however, is believed by many to have been well established in Sicily, near Siracusa, around the year 1000. In any event, it is Casale dei Biscari '96, a monovarietal nero d'avola, that is again Torrevecchia's top wine. It has a good intense ruby color and releases spicy aromas of sour cherries steeped in alcohol. With just a little more concentration on the palate it would be as good as the '95, but it's a very attractive wine as it is, and so is the '97 Bianco Biscari, a blend of inzolia and chardonnay. It has a fully fruited nose with delicate vanilla notes that suggest toasted hazelnut. The debut of the intriguing Syrah, a '98, is decidedly good: it's concentrated and offers appealing notes of black currant and coffee. The well-made red Pietra di Zoe '98, a frappato, did very well too. The three whites, Chardonnay, Alcamo and Inzolia, reflect the less than perfect vintage but are nevertheless fresh and fruity. All the wines are good value for money.

○	Bianco Biscari '97	🍷	3
●	Casale dei Biscari '96	🍷	4
●	Pietra di Zoe '98	🍷	1*
●	Syrah '98	🍷	3
○	Bianco d'Alcamo '98		1
●	Cerasuolo di Vittoria '97		2
○	Chardonnay '98		1
●	Frappato '98		3
○	Inzolia '98		1
○	Bianco Biscari '96	YY	3*
●	Casale dei Biscari '93	YY	3*
●	Casale dei Biscari '94	YY	3*
●	Casale dei Biscari '95	YY	3*
●	Pietra di Zoe '96	Y	2*
●	Pietra di Zoe '97	Y	2*

ACATE (RG)

CANTINA VALLE DELL'ACATE
C.DA BIDINI
97011 ACATE (RG)
TEL. 0932/874166

This is a somewhat disappointing year for Gaetana Jacono's Cantina Valle dell'Acate. The quality of the wines had been increasing so dramatically that what used to be merely one of the better co-operatives of the area has become one of the most renowned producers of the entire region. We had hoped for something more from the Frappato'98, and we were expecting a definitive upswing for the Cerasuolo di Vittoria...But let's look at the wines one by one. It must be admitted that the Frappato is still a gem of its type, even if the one we tasted this time seemed less concentrated and the aromas of sour and black cherry were less distinct and intense than in the past. But it's an enthralling wine all the same, soft, immediate and very easily drinkable. While we confidently await the release of the '98 Cerasuolo di Vittoria we have to say that the '97 shows no appreciable improvement over the previous vintage and displays little more than proper execution. The inzolia and chardonnay blend Bidis, making its third appearance with the '97, again shows its customary concentration, aromatic scents and attractive notes of vanilla, as well as a firm yet delicate structure reminiscent of the original version, the '95. We finish our review with the Inzolia '98 and the Milaro '98, two unpretentious wines produced for easy and agreeable drinking. They are both well made and good value for money.

○	Bidis '97	🍷	2*
●	Frappato '98	🍷	2*
●	Cerasuolo di Vittoria '97		2
○	Inzolia '98		1
●	Milaro '98		1
●	Frappato '97	YY	2*
○	Bidis '95	Y	2*
○	Bidis '96	Y	2*
●	Cerasuolo di Vittoria '94	Y	2*
●	Cerasuolo di Vittoria '95	Y	2*
●	Cerasuolo di Vittoria '96	Y	3
●	Frappato '95	Y	2*
●	Frappato '96	Y	2*
●	Milaro '97	Y	3

ALCAMO (TP)

ANTONINO MELIA
VIA ENEA, 18
91011 ALCAMO (TP)
TEL. 0924/507860

At the beginning it was like a gamble: a compatible trio of brothers, Antonino, Giuseppe and Vincenzo Melia, a farmer, an oenologist and an agronomist respectively, decided to realize an old dream by producing Ceuso Custera. They even penned a sort of manifesto: "A great wine is the fruit of a desire to create something out of the ordinary, beyond what monetary investment can achieve. The creative urge fuels the workings of the imagination until they take shape as a project." The minuscule Melia estate, after only its second vintage, is already a star in the Sicilian wine scene, thanks to the passionate dedication of the three brothers and the excellent quality of their wine, the Ceuso Custera, a very successful blend of nero d'avola, merlot and cabernet sauvignon aged in barriques for a year. The '97 displays a lovely dense ruby color and a broad, complex array of aromas dominated by red berries, alcohol-steeped cherries and notes of cinnamon and spice; it keeps its promise on the big, substantial palate which is mouth-filling and round and reveals attractive, soft and vigorous tannins. Our compliments to the Melia brothers!

●	Ceuso Custera '97	🍷🍷	5
●	Ceuso '96	🍸🍸	5

CASTELBUONO (PA)

ABBAZIA SANT'ANASTASIA
C.DA SANTA ANASTASIA
90013 CASTELBUONO (PA)
TEL. 0921/671959

Among the many oenological miracles that Giacomo Tachis, oenologist supreme, has had a hand in over the years, we have, for a while now, had to include the wines from this Sicilian estate. It is all the more remarkable because no one would have thought that an area like the Cefalù district, which is certainly not known for distinguished wines, could produce such superb ones. True, the varieties used are mainly "imported" (cabernet sauvignon and chardonnay predominate), but then there is little choice in such a zone. The Litra '97, mostly cabernet sauvignon, is again simply excellent and has walked coolly off with Three Glasses. Like its predecessor it is an extremely powerful red. The decidedly intense fragrance is composed of ripe red berries and vanilla with lightly balsamic and mineral notes. Intensity and concentration are at home on the palate too, where tannins are present but not aggressive and the finish never seems to stop. The excellent Baccante '98 is a barriqued chardonnay that had just been bottled when we tasted it. Even so, it displayed aromas of ripe fruit with a light vanilla note, and a palate of true Mediterranean opulence and structure. The standard estate wines, the Passomaggio '97 (nero d'Avola and merlot) and the Santa Anastasia Rosso '97 (100% nero d'Avola), were a little below par but perfectly acceptable.

●	Litra '97	🍷🍷🍷	6
○	Baccante '98	🍷🍷	5
●	Passomaggio '97	🍷	4
●	Santa Anastasia Rosso '97	🍷	3
●	Litra '96	🍸🍸🍸	5
○	Baccante '97	🍸🍸	5
●	Passomaggio '95	🍸🍸	4
●	Passomaggio '96	🍸🍸	4
●	Santa Anastasia Rosso '96	🍸🍸	3*
○	Zurrica '97	🍸🍸	3*
○	Cinquegrani '96	🍸	4
●	Santa Anastasia Rosso '95	🍸	3

CASTELDACCIA (PA)

Duca di Salaparuta - Vini Corvo
Via Nazionale, S. S. 113
90014 Casteldaccia (PA)
tel. 091/945111 - 02/77399211

Duca di Salaparuta did well this year. It hasn't gathered in any more Three Glass awards, but compared with recent performances there has been distinct progress. Besides, the success that Corvo wines continue to have on the Italian marketplace cannot be simply a matter of chance. Of the bottles we tasted this time, we particularly recommend the '95 Duca Enrico, a good example of this famous red made mostly from nero d'Avola. Of a deep garnet color, it displays forward complex aromas with notes of ripe red fruit, leather and vanilla. In the mouth it is soft and full-bodied, with an attractive note of acidity and good concentration. The Bianca di Valguarnera '97, made from inzolia, is less typical; intensely grassy and vegetal aromas reminiscent of sauvignon precede a medium-bodied palate with an echo of the balsamic and vegetal notes on the finish. The agreeable Terre d'Agala '96, made mainly from frappato, is a little lighter and more forward than the glorious '94, the best version yet. The three base wines, Corvo Bianco '98, Corvo Glicine '98 and Corvo Rosso '97, are all properly made, as usual, and the Rosso is especially appealing. The Colomba Platino '98 is slightly under par, rather thinner than in the past. Overall, this is a reliable range.

○	Bianca di Valguarnera '97	🍷🍷	5
●	Duca Enrico '95	🍷🍷	6
○	Corvo Bianco '98	🍷	2*
○	Corvo Colomba Platino '98	🍷	3
○	Corvo Glicine '98	🍷	2*
●	Corvo Rosso '97	🍷	2*
●	Terre d'Agala '96	🍷	3
●	Duca Enrico '84	🍷🍷🍷	6
●	Duca Enrico '85	🍷🍷🍷	6
●	Duca Enrico '86	🍷🍷🍷	6
●	Duca Enrico '87	🍷🍷🍷	6
●	Duca Enrico '88	🍷🍷🍷	6
●	Duca Enrico '90	🍷🍷🍷	6
●	Duca Enrico '92	🍷🍷🍷	6
●	Duca Enrico '93	🍷🍷	6

COMISO (RG)

Vitivinicola Avide
C.da Mendolilla
S. P. 7 km 1.5
97013 Comiso (RG)
tel. 0932/967456

Giovanni Demostene and Giovanni Calcaterra, uncle and nephew, have been making a success of this estate in southeast Sicily. Their flagship wine is Cerasuolo di Vittoria, and it was the reds in general that most interested all our tasters. Their grapes come from vineyards scattered about near Bastonaca and Mortilla, between Comiso and Vittoria, and are vinified by the oenologist Giovanni Rizzo. The '95 Cerasuolo di Vittoria Barocco is the best version of recent years. It has well-defined scents of ripe fruit and is richly aromatic, soft and balanced, with a pleasing bitter note on the finish. But its younger brother, Cerasuolo di Vittoria Etichetta Nera '97, shouldn't be underestimated. An intense, warm fragrance precedes good concentration on the palate; this wine is also a great bargain. The whites were on a lower level. We expected more from the Vigne d'Oro '97, a barrique-aged inzolia, which did, however, have an attractive nose; the Dalle Terre di Herea '98, although fruity on the nose, is dry on the palate and rather thin.

●	Cerasuolo di Vittoria Barocco '95	🍷🍷	4
●	Cerasuolo di Vittoria Etichetta Nera '97	🍷	2*
○	Dalle Terre di Herea Bianco '98		2
○	Vigne d'Oro '97		3
○	Vigne d'Oro '96	🍷🍷	3*
●	Cerasuolo di Vittoria Barocco '91	🍷	4
●	Cerasuolo di Vittoria Barocco '92	🍷	4
●	Cerasuolo di Vittoria Barocco '93	🍷	4
●	Cerasuolo di Vittoria Barocco '94	🍷	4
●	Cerasuolo di Vittoria Etichetta Nera '95	🍷	2*
●	Cerasuolo di Vittoria Etichetta Nera '96	🍷	2*
○	Dalle Terre di Herea Bianco '97	🍷	2*

ERICE (TP)

FAZIO WINES
FRAZ. FULGATORE
VIA CAPITAN RIZZO, 39
91010 ERICE (TP)
TEL. 0923/811700 - 0923/811701

Fazio Wines, together with Firriato, Nuova Agricoltura and the Cantina Sociale di Trapani, are four newly prominent wine producers who have shed glory on the province of Trapani, which is, viticulturally speaking, the most important province in Sicily and one of the biggest in Italy. Fazio Wines, owned by the brothers Enzo and Mimmo Fazio who follow an ancient family tradition, has more than 600 hectares of vineyard spread over the countryside near Erice. They have fitted out the winery with up-to-date equipment and, with advice from the young, enthusiastic oenologist Giacomo Ansaldi, have produced the first bottles with the estate label. The team is completed by Lilly Fazio, who looks after marketing and the commercial side. Their top wine is the lovely '98 Cabernet Sauvignon, opaque ruby in color. A spicy, complex nose with well-defined notes of black pepper and licorice precedes a full-bodied, extremely soft palate with delightful velvety tannins. The Torre dei Venti '98, 100% nero d'Avola, is well made, moderately concentrated, succulent and harmonious. The Merlot seemed fair, while the whites, Müller Thurgau and Sauvignon, rate no more than a mention – at least for now.

● Cabernet Sauvignon '98	🍷🍷	4
● Torre dei Venti Rosso '98	🍷	3
● Merlot '98		4
○ Müller Thurgau '98		2
○ Sauvignon Blanc '98		3
○ Torre dei Venti Bianco '98		2

LICATA (AG)

BARONE LA LUMIA
FRAZ. POZZILLO
92027 LICATA (AG)
TEL. 0922/891709

The wines of Barone La Lumia bring back tastes and aromas that we thought had been lost forever. They are what wines of 50 years ago must have been like when they were well made. Today they are in danger of seeming a little outdated technically, although they can't be said to lack personality or varietal characteristics. The Signorio Rosso, for example, in the '95 version, again displays all the traditional qualities of a great nero d'Avola. Of an intense and very concentrated garnet color, it offers a nose of red berries and leather, but also spicy and forward notes. The palate shows strong character, indeed even some harshness, because of the presence of both slightly aggressive tannins and rather high acidity, which are typical of this grape. It's a somewhat 'vertical' wine, as they say in the trade, but full of old-fashioned charm. This year's two whites, the Signorio Bianco and the Cadetto, both '98s, are better adapted to the modern taste but also less characterful. They display a fruity fragrance (more intense and pleasing in the former) and a light, attractive palate with good balance but not an awful lot of body.

○ Signorio Bianco '98	🍷	3
● Signorio Rosso '95	🍷	3
○ Cadetto Bianco '98		2
○ Signorio Bianco '95	🍸	2*
○ Signorio Bianco '97	🍸	2*
● Signorio Rosso '93	🍸	3
● Signorio Rosso '94	🍸	3
● Stemma '97	🍸	2*

MARSALA (TP)

ALVIS - RALLO
VIA VINCENZO FLORIO, 2
91025 MARSALA (TP)
TEL. 0923/721633 - 0923/721635

We were almost overwhelmed by the flood of wines submitted for tasting by this prolific winery. We managed, however, to consider them carefully one by one and came to the conclusion that real progress has been made, although the range is perhaps a bit vast. But what matters is that all the wines be properly made, and so they are, as you can tell from the number of Glasses they have collected this year. We don't have the space, unfortunately, to review each wine separately, but we particularly want to say that the Passito di Pantelleria Mare d'Ambra is, we feel, one of the best in its category, and also to point out that the Nero d'Avola '97 clearly demonstrates that the estate's skills are not restricted to fortified and raisin wines. This is confirmed by all the good dry whites, and by the Vesco Rosso '97, a blend of cabernet sauvignon and nero d'Avola. In addition, the entire range is excellent value for money.

○	Passito di Pantelleria Mare d'Ambra	🍷🍷	4
○	Grillo '98	🍷	2*
○	Marsala Sup. Semisecco Anima Mediterranea	🍷	3
○	Moscato di Pantelleria	🍷	3
●	Nero d'Avola '97	🍷	2*
○	Vesco Inzolia '98	🍷	2*
●	Vesco Rosso '97	🍷	3
○	Marsala Sup. Ambra Semisecco	🍸	3
○	Vesco Bianco '97	🍸	3
●	Vesco Rosso '96	🍸	4

MARSALA (TP)

MARCO DE BARTOLI
C.DA FORNARA, 292
91025 MARSALA (TP)
TEL. 0923/962093 - 0923/918344

With a mixture of effort, stubbornness, angry determination and boundless passion, Marco De Bartoli somehow manages to keep his estate on its feet and produce his wines despite all the troubles that surround him. The "legal difficulty" that has pitted him against the local bureaucracy, leading to the partial sequestration of one of his cellars, is still not resolved despite the inordinate time the case has been dragging on. De Bartoli has already suffered huge damages and if, as we hope, he is ultimately judged innocent of most of the administrative lapses with which he has been charged, his losses will also be completely unjustified. However, we are powerless to do anything but hope that justice runs its course without further delay. But let's consider his wines. Marco has presented a very good Moscato Passito di Pantelleria Bukkuram, which is concentrated, sweet and well developed. Then there's a fabulous Vecchio Samperi 30 Anni. This classic of Marsala wine-making does honor to the land from which it springs, as well as to the splendid and renowned winegrower Marco De Bartoli, who, let it be said again, laid the foundations of the great revival of Sicilian wine. We want him to know, in this difficult period, that we haven't forgotten.

○	Moscato Passito di Pantelleria Bukkuram	🍷🍷	5
○	Vecchio Samperi Ris. 30 Anni Solera	🍷🍷	6
○	Marsala Sup. Oro Vigna La Miccia '90	🍸🍸	4
○	Marsala Sup. Oro Vigna La Miccia '91	🍸🍸	4
○	Marsala Superiore	🍸🍸	4
○	Moscato Passito di Pantelleria '91	🍸🍸	5
○	Pietranera '97	🍸🍸	4
○	Vecchio Samperi	🍸🍸	4
○	Vecchio Samperi Ris. 20 Anni Solera	🍸🍸	5
○	Vigna La Miccia	🍸🍸	4

MARSALA (TP)

TENUTA DI DONNAFUGATA
VIA SEBASTIANO LIPARI, 18
91025 MARSALA (TP)
TEL. 0923/999555

This is the first time that Donnafugata, whose better range has been making enormous progress in the last two or three years, has won Three Glasses, which it undeniably deserved for the Chiarandà del Merlo '98, a chardonnay fermented and aged in Allier barriques. The wine is as elegant and aristocratic as Burt Lancaster in "The Leopard", with a golden straw hue and very nearly perfectly melded aromas of tropical fruit and vanilla. The stylish, full-bodied palate offers a reflection of the bouquet on the finish. But this is not the only surprise that Giacomo and Gabriella Rallo, the fortunate owners of Tenuta di Donnafugata, have prepared for us. Their Milleunanotte '95 is just a whisper away from the top award. This is a splendid red, mainly from night-harvested nero d'Avola. The excellent Tancredi '97 is a blend of nero d'Avola and cabernet sauvignon; the very successful Passito di Pantelleria Ben Ryé '98 is sweet, concentrated and distinctly redolent of date and raisin; the soft, delicate and delightfully quaffable Contessa Entellina Vigna di Gabri '98, from inzolia and chardonnay, should be borne in mind. This year's list ends with the Contessa Entellina Chardonnay La Fuga '98, a simple and properly made white.

○ Contessa Entellina Chiarandà del Merlo '98	▼▼▼	5
○ Contessa Entellina Vigna di Gabri '98	▼▼	3*
● Milleunanotte '95	▼▼	6
○ Passito di Pantelleria Ben Ryé '98	▼▼	4
● Tancredi '97	▼▼	5
○ Contessa Entellina Chardonnay La Fuga '98	▼	3
○ Chiarandà del Merlo '94	▽▽	4
○ Chiarandà del Merlo '95	▽▽	4
○ Chiarandà del Merlo '96	▽▽	4
○ Passito di Pantelleria Ben Ryé '97	▽▽	5
● Tancredi '96	▽▽	5

MARSALA (TP)

VINICOLA ITALIANA FLORIO
VIA VINCENZO FLORIO, 1
91025 MARSALA (TP)
TEL. 0923/781111

Not many new wines were presented by Florio this year, but numerous corroborative retastings confirm that this reliable estate is still a good representative of the important and celebrated Marsala district. Indeed it is in great part due to large and legendary wineries like Florio that the oenological glory of Marsala continues to exist, after all the long dark years of systematic attempts to tarnish the image and quality of its wines. The memory of Marsala all'Uovo (a bottled eggy confection) and banana-flavored Marsala lingers on (and in a few cases is more than just a memory). But on to more serious matters, i.e. the two wines presented this year. The very interesting Vecchioflorio Riserva '91 has a complex bouquet with intense aromas of cocoa and leather and a decidedly full flavor with a lightly sweet tone. The '87 Baglio Florio, flagship of the estate, is both more austere and less concentrated than earlier versions. Both wines are very well executed and admirable.

○ Marsala Sup. Vecchioflorio Ris. '91	▼▼	4
○ Marsala Vergine Baglio Florio '87	▼	5
○ Marsala Soleras Oro Baglio Florio '79	▽▽	6
○ Marsala Sup. Targa Ris. '89	▽▽	4
○ Marsala Sup. Targa Ris. '88	▽▽	4
○ Marsala Vergine Baglio Florio '85	▽▽	5
○ Marsala Vergine Baglio Florio '86	▽▽	5
○ Marsala Vergine Terre Arse '86	▽▽	4
○ Marsala Vergine Terre Arse '87	▽▽	4
○ Morsi di Luce '95	▽▽	4
○ Marsala Sup. Vecchioflorio '94	▽	3*

MARSALA (TP)

Carlo Pellegrino
Via del Fante, 37/39
91025 Marsala (TP)
tel. 0923/951177

The biggest news from Pellegrino this year is that they have released the first Delia Nivolelli wines, Trapani's brand-new DOC. They are a Chardonnay and a Müller Thurgau, both '98s, well made and fairly varietal. The chardonnay grape seems to be less bothered by the local torrid summers, while müller thurgau can easily become overripe. Nevertheless these are both delightfully drinkable wines. The rest of the vast range is, as usual, reliable. However, one wine does stand out, the Passito di Pantelleria '98, which easily wins Two Glasses and takes its place among the best of its type. It has an intense amber hue, a characteristic bouquet of raisin and date, and a full, very sweet but not cloying palate that lasts forever. It would be a dream with a true Sicilian cassata or one of the marzipan sweets made in these parts. The classic, very dependable Marsala Vergine Soleras is not at all bad either. The Etna Rosso Ulysse '96, from their Duca di Castelmonte line, is decidedly good. It comes from a disappointing vintage but has made up for it.

○	Passito di Pantelleria '98	🍷🍷	4
●	Cent'Are Rosso '97	🍷	3
○	Delia Nivolelli Chardonnay '98	🍷	3
○	Delia Nivolelli Müller Thurgau '98	🍷	3
●	Etna Rosso Ulysse '96	🍷	3
○	Gorgo Tondo Bianco '98	🍷	3
○	Marsala Vergine Soleras	🍷	3
●	Gorgo Tondo Rosso '96	🍷🍷 (white)	3*
○	Marsala Vergine Vintage '62	🍷🍷 (white)	5
●	Cent'Are '92	🍷 (white)	3
●	Cent'Are Rosso '95	🍷 (white)	3
●	Etna Rosso Duca di Castelmonte '92	🍷 (white)	2*
●	Etna Rosso Ulysse '94	🍷 (white)	3

MENFI (AG)

Settesoli
S. S. 115
92013 Menfi (AG)
tel. 0925/77111

When a large co-operative winery that vinifies about 50 million kilos of grapes from some 9 thousand hectares under vine manages to present a range as good as this year's Settesoli offerings, it means that something important is taking place. In particular, it means that the uprooting of vineyards can come to a halt at last, that those who labor in the vineyard can receive a fair return for their work and that there is hope for the future of winegrowing in Sicily. It's a sort of bloodless revolution involving thousands of families in southwest Sicily. Settesoli, its president Diego Planeta and its oenologist Carlo Corino are working to achieve and consolidate all of this and we cannot but support them. And what of the wines? They are all noteworthy and one is extraordinary: the Nero d'Avola/Cabernet '98, a red that could hold its own with wines of far greater fame and much higher price. The monovarietal Nero d'Avola '98 is nearly as good, less structured perhaps but certainly a delicious red and characteristic of this part of Sicily. The Feudo dei Fiori '98, from inzolia and chardonnay, is as interesting as ever and misses its second Glass by a hair. All the others are very well executed, including the ones we haven't mentioned for reasons of space.

●	Nero d'Avola '98	🍷🍷	3*
●	Nero d'Avola/Cabernet '98	🍷🍷	3*
●	Bonera '95	🍷	3
○	Feudo dei Fiori '98	🍷	2*
○	Grecanico/Chardonnay '98	🍷	2*
●	Nero d'Avola/Merlot '98	🍷	3
●	Rosso di Sicilia '97	🍷	2*
●	Bonera '94	🍷🍷 (white)	3*
○	Feudo dei Fiori '97	🍷🍷 (white)	2*
○	Porto Palo Bianco '97	🍷 (white)	2*
●	Soltero Rosso '95	🍷 (white)	2*

MESSINA

Colosi
Via Militare Ritiro, 23
98100 Messina
tel. 090/53852

This estate, run by Pietro Colosi with the help of his oenologist son Piero and Piero's wife Lidia Labate, who is in charge of administration and public relations, is back in the Guide this year. It has seven hectares under vine at Gramignazzi, near Malfa, on the island of Salina. The vines are rooted in structurally difficult soil and are cultivated in the most traditional way, by hand; protection from wind and the sea salt it carries is provided by low dry-stone walls. Our favorite of the wines presented was the Malvasia delle Lipari Naturale '97, deep golden yellow in color, redolent of ripe apricot and warm, sweet and aromatic in the mouth. The '97 Malvasia Passita has its usual characteristics but is a little understated, but we were immediately taken by the Passito di Pantelleria '97, with its particularly elegant and not at all cloying palate, in its debut appearance. The Moscato di Pantelleria '97 is good too. It is lighter and less concentrated but still well executed, as are the table wines Salina Bianco '98 and Salina Rosso '98. This latter, a blend of various subvarieties of nerello such as cappuccio and mascalese, is grapey and fully flavored.

○	Malvasia delle Lipari Naturale '97	🍷🍷	5
○	Passito di Pantelleria '97	🍷🍷	4
○	Malvasia delle Lipari Passita '97	🍷	5
○	Moscato di Pantelleria '98	🍷	4
●	Salina Rosso '98	🍷	1*
○	Salina Bianco '98		1
○	Malvasia delle Lipari Naturale '95	🍸🍸	5
○	Malvasia delle Lipari Passita '96	🍸🍸	4
○	Malvasia delle Lipari Naturale '96	🍸	4
○	Malvasia delle Lipari Passita '95	🍸	5

MESSINA

Palari
Loc. S. Stefano Briga
98123 Messina
tel. 090/694281

Salvatore Geraci hasn't managed a repeat performance. This year his Faro Palari '97, although excellent, just missed winning Three Glasses. Geraci, who is a true gentleman, indeed a true country gentleman with excellent manners, and maybe something of a dandy, didn't take it at all badly. "The only thing I regret," he said, "is that this year I won't have the excuse of the Three Glass presentation ceremonies to travel all over the world." He will probably console himself by driving his Jaguar along the coast road between Messina and Taormina, which is for him like taking a turn through the property, or by sporting his newest panama hat or the white linen suit he wears in summer, but never in the evening. And the Palari, that magical red he produces at Santo Stefano Briga (between Messina and Taormina of course) with the help of Donato Lanati, the Piedmontese oenologist who makes a hobby of striking out on new paths? The '97 is not at all bad. It is a bit more forward and softer than the '96 but it has less grip and less character. Made mostly from nerello mascalese, it was aged in barriques for about 18 months (too long?). Still, it's wonderful drinking and we feel sure that Geraci will score another bull's-eye soon. The same general comments apply to the Rosso del Soprano, Faro's little brother. The '97 is a little less concentrated than the '96 but definitely not bad.

●	Faro Palari '97	🍷🍷	6
●	Rosso del Soprano '97	🍷	4
●	Faro Palari '96	🍸🍸🍸	5
●	Faro Palari '94	🍸🍸	5
●	Faro Palari '95	🍸🍸	5
●	Rosso del Soprano '95	🍸🍸	4
●	Rosso del Soprano '96	🍸🍸	4

MILAZZO (ME)

GRASSO
VIA ALBERICO, 5
98057 MILAZZO (ME)
TEL. 090/9261082

Last year we were favorably impressed by Alessio Grasso's Moscato Passito di Pantelleria; this time we also very much liked his well-made table wines. Hence this clearly deserved debut appearance in the Guide for Grasso, whose 10 hectares planted to inzolia, catarratto and nero d'Avola are scattered through the countryside, at an altitude of 200 meters, between Furnari and Rodi Milici, facing the Aeolian Islands. For some years now Fabrizio Zardini has been the estate oenologist, and his wines have been getting better vintage after vintage. We particularly admired the white Capobianco '98, an elegant blend of catarratto and inzolia with a fruity nose and a harmonious palate; it also shows good structure and concentration – remarkable when one considers the grapes from which it is made. The Caporosso '97, from nero d'avola and sangiovese picked when fully mature early in October, has a distinct personality: it shows good substance, intriguing complexity on both nose and palate and softness from careful aging in large barrels. To finish where we began, the zibibbo-based Moscato Passito di Pantelleria Ergo '95, aromatic and intense, has good sugar concentration and balance.

○	Capobianco '98	🍷🍷	2*
●	Caporosso '97	🍷	2*
○	Passito di Pantelleria Ergo '95	🍷	5
○	Passito di Pantelleria Ergo '93	🍷🍷 (outline)	4

MONREALE (PA)

AZIENDE AGRICOLE POLLARA
C.DA MALVELLO
90046 MONREALE (PA)
TEL. 091/8462922

For the second year running the wines presented by the Pollara family estate (the former IVICOR) located between Corleone and Roccamena did well at our tastings. Apparently, grafting with various "improving" vine varieties, hard pruning and low yields per hectare, all unthinkable around here just a few years ago, are beginning to produce results. The most interesting wine this year was the nero d'Avola-based Principe di Corleone Rosso '98, with its complex fragrance and warm, harmonious palate. The '96 Cabernet Sauvignon, which enjoys six months in oak barrels, was better on the richly ripe-fruited nose than the previous vintage and showed moderate length in the mouth. The '98 Chardonnay Vigna di Corte '98 may be a little less concentrated than last year's but is attractively fruity and well-balanced. The Alcamo Bianco '98, a good example of its kind, is well executed and free of the harshness that catarratto, its main grape, can give, thanks to a well-judged addition of damaschino. The properly made Giada (from damaschino and other local varieties) offers a lightly fruity fragrance, but the Pinot Bianco '98 was not quite up to expectations. It's an admirable range, but we're still waiting for the outstanding wine we think they have it in them to produce.

○	Alcamo Principe di Corleone '98	🍷	2*
●	Cabernet Sauvignon Principe di Corleone '96	🍷	3
○	Chardonnay Vigna di Corte '98	🍷	3
●	Principe di Corleone Rosso '98	🍷	2*
○	Giada Bianco '98		2
○	Pinot Bianco '98		2
○	Alcamo Principe di Corleone '97	🍷 (outline)	2*
●	Cabernet Sauvignon Principe di Corleone '96	🍷 (outline)	3
○	Chardonnay Vigna di Corte '97	🍷 (outline)	2*
○	Pinot Bianco Principe di Corleone '97	🍷 (outline)	2*

PACECO (TP)

FIRRIATO
VIA TRAPANI, 4
91027 PACECO (TP)
TEL. 0923/882755

Firriato is the big surprise of this year's tastings, and it walks right into the Guide, backed up by some impressive statistics. Annual production exceeds three and a half million bottles, 70% of which are exported. An unusual international team, led by Australian Master of Wine Kim Milne and including experts from California, Australia and New Zealand, works in perfect harmony with the Marsala-born oenologist Giuseppe Pellegrino. The estate, owned by the brothers Girolamo and Salvatore Di Gaetano, with the enthusiastic, dynamic Michele Cirillo as business manager, presented eight wines for tasting and they all got at least One Glass, a good indication that the aim at Firriato is to make excellent wine. The splendid Santagostino Bianco '98, a briefly barriqued blend of catarratto and chardonnay, displays delicate notes of flowers and white-fleshed fruits on the nose and a soft, mouth-filling palate. The Santagostino Rosso '97, no less good, is a successful blend of nero d'Avola and syrah with engaging spicy aromas and caressingly velvety tannins. The other wines are all well made, modern in style and excellent value for money.

○	Santagostino Bianco '98	🍷🍷	4
●	Santagostino Rosso '97	🍷🍷	4
○	Altavilla della Corte Bianco '98	🍷	2*
●	Altavilla della Corte Rosso '97	🍷	3
○	Bianco d'Alcamo '98	🍷	1*
●	Etna Rosso '96	🍷	2*
○	Primula Bianco '98	🍷	1*
●	Primula Rosso '97	🍷	1*
○	Altavilla della Corte Bianco '97	🍸	1*

PALERMO

AZIENDE VINICOLE MICELI
VIA AMMIRAGLIO SALVATORE
DENTI DI PIRAINO, 7
90142 PALERMO
TEL. 091/6396111

Aziende Vinicole Miceli is the new name for the wine production branch of the renowned M.I.D., which markets these wines, together with others from numerous top estates. M.I.D. was created by the late lamented Ignazio Miceli, an irreplaceable figure who loomed large not only in Sicily, but throughout the world of wine. Highlights among the new wines include the Yrnm '98, made entirely from zibibbo grapes from the island of Pantelleria. It abounds in fresh, alluring aromatic notes on the nose as well as on the appealing palate, which also reveals a delicate, savory mineral tone reminiscent of the volcanic rock of that island. We liked the easily drinkable Organza '98 too, a blend of indigenous Sicilian grapes, modern in style, with delicate scents of flowers and fruit, most notably white damson. The sweet, sparkling, extremely fragrant Garighe, made from zibibbo, is as engaging as ever and goes beautifully with fruit and custard tart. The '97 vintage of Nero d'Avola is once again a well-made, appealing wine with fairly intense aromas typical of its grape. The newest arrival, Yanir, is a strong Moscato Passito di Pantelleria with a brilliant amber color and good concentration and length. The whites are somewhat below par, but then the '98 vintage in Sicily was no friend to white wine. The whole range offers excellent value for money.

○	Garighe Zibibbo '98	🍷	3
●	Nero d'Avola '97	🍷	2*
○	Organza '98	🍷	2*
○	Passito di Pantelleria Yanir	🍷	5
○	Yrnm '98	🍷	4
○	Bianco d'Alcamo '98		1
●	Fiammato '98		3
○	Grecanico '98		2
○	Bianco d'Alcamo '97	🍸	1*
○	Garighe Zibibbo '97	🍸	2*
○	Grecanico '97	🍸	1*
○	Passito di Pantelleria Tanit	🍸	3

PALERMO

SPADAFORA

VIA A. DE GASPERI, 58
90146 PALERMO
TEL. 091/514952 - 091/518544

There is an admirable range of wines this time from Francesco Spadafora's estate, indeed the best in recent years. The grapes come from 100 hectares under vine between Camporeale and Alcamo and the oenologists Maggio and D'Attoma supervise the vinification. Once again we were particularly impressed by the reds. The surprisingly good Schietto '97, a cabernet sauvignon selection, displays a fine deep red color, well-defined fruity aromas and full flavor. The equally appealing Vigna Virzì '98, a blend of nero d'Avola and syrah, easily beats its recent predecessors with its fragrance of ripe fruit and soft, velvety, mouth-filling palate. The third red, Don Pietro '98, has even and intense fruity aromas with hints of spice, a rounded, lingering palate and a compelling drinkability. The white Divino '98, made from inzolia and grillo grapes, is balanced and concentrated, while Vigna Virzì Bianco '98 and Bianco d'Alcamo '98 are maintaining standards, if not creating a furor. Last in the cast, the acceptable catarratto-based sweet Incanto has a walk-on role.

● Don Pietro Rosso '98	▼▼	2*
● Schietto '97	▼▼	3*
● Vigna Virzì Rosso '98	▼▼	2*
○ Divino '98	▼	2*
○ Bianco d'Alcamo '98		1
○ Incanto '97		3
○ Vigna Virzì Bianco '98		2
● Don Pietro Rosso '95	▽▽	3*
● Don Pietro Rosso '96	▽▽	3*
○ Don Pietro Bianco '94	▽	2*
○ Don Pietro Bianco '96	▽	2*
● Don Pietro Rosso '94	▽	3
● Vigna Virzì Rosso '95	▽	2*

PANTELLERIA (TP)

SALVATORE MURANA

C.DA KHAMMA, 276
91017 PANTELLERIA (TP)
TEL. 0923/915231

It is no longer a novelty when Salvatore Murana's Passito di Pantelleria Martingana succeeds in walking off with Three Glasses. This time he has done it with a monumental version, the '96, which easily scores as high as its worthiest predecessors. It is a great passito (dried grape wine) in the best traditions of the estate: sweet, powerful and concentrated. In addition, the nose seems fruitier and less oxidized than in the past, and, despite the great concentration of sugar, the palate is not at all cloying. Richness of extract, almost infinite length and an alluring and by no means commonplace softness make it an extraordinary wine. The Passito di Pantelleria Khamma, also '96, scored almost as high. It is less imposing and even somewhat simpler than the Martingana but it offers the varietal aromas of the zibibbo grape in all their fragrance. These two wines do honor to Pantelleria, where viticulture is a perpetual struggle, and to a producer who has become one of the glories of Italian wine-making. They also prove that Murana-Pantelleria is a winning combination, representing the zenith of sweet wine production in Italy.

○ Moscato Passito di Pantelleria Martingana '96	▼▼▼	6
○ Moscato Passito di Pantelleria Khamma '96	▼▼	6
○ Moscato Passito di Pantelleria Martingana '93	▽▽▽	6
○ Moscato Passito di Pantelleria Martingana '94	▽▽▽	6
○ Moscato Passito di Pantelleria Khamma '94	▽▽	6
○ Moscato Passito di Pantelleria Martingana '89	▽▽	6
○ Moscato Passito di Pantelleria Mueggen '97	▽▽	5

PANTELLERIA (TP)

NUOVA AGRICOLTURA
C.DA BARONE
91017 PANTELLERIA (TP)
TEL. 0923/670214

All the gods of the Phoenicians, the ancient colonizers of Pantelleria, must have been mobilized this year in favor of the wine producers of this glorious volcanic island. Indeed the Guide bears evidence, quite apart from the well-known names, of a number of other winegrowers who share a determination to make first-rate wine. Such is the case with Nuova Agricoltura, a 13-member co-operative equipped with up-to-the-minute technology that affords optimum conditions for vinification and bottling. Giacomo D'Ancona, (don't we know that name from somewhere?) is the consultant oenologist here, a new role for him, and the results speak for themselves. The very good amber-hued Rihali Passito '97 releases delicious, balanced balsamic and dried zibibbo grape aromas; it has a seductive sweetness in the mouth that it spins out to intriguing length. The Rihali Moscato '97 is intense and fragrant, while the well-made, soft and caressing Zibibbo Khania '98 is a dry, refreshing, aromatic wine that would be ideal with couscous "alla Pantelleria", made with fish and vegetables.

O	Passito di Pantelleria Rihali '97	🍷🍷	5
O	Moscato di Pantelleria Rihali '97	🍷	4
O	Zibibbo Khania '98	🍷	2*
O	Passito di Pantelleria '93	🍸	4

PANTELLERIA (TP)

D'ANCONA
C.DA KADDIUGGIA
91017 PANTELLERIA (TP)
TEL. 0923/913016

At their third appearance in the Guide, Giacomo and Solidea D'Ancona have won Three Glasses with the Passito Solidea '98, the top wine of their tiny estate. We're happy for them and for Pantelleria, but we also have the satisfaction of having long said that this "Island of the Winds" really is a gold mine for Italian oenology. The exceptional climate easily yields wines of great concentration and extraordinary aromatic richness. You just need to understand that marvelous grape they call zibibbo and learn how to let it express itself with proper vinification. And "the kids", (who hardly total 60 years between them), really seem to know how to do it. Their Passito Solidea '98, of a glorious bright amber hue, offers distinct, generous and concentrated aromas dominated by notes of acacia honey, date and dried fig; the soft, mouth-filling, sensual palate is unmistakably Mediterranean. It is a real masterpiece and it bears the mark of Giacomo D'Ancona, the great but shy craftsman of Pantelleria wine. The good Moscato '98 displays delicate color and fragrance; the fresh and fruity dry Zibibbo Solidea '98 is still a bit closed.

O	Passito di Pantelleria Solidea '98	🍷🍷🍷	5
O	Moscato di Pantelleria Solidea '98	🍷	4
O	Zibibbo Solidea '98	🍷	2*
O	Bianco Scluvaki '97	🍸🍸	3*
O	Moscato di Pantelleria	🍸🍸	3*
O	Passito di Pantelleria	🍸🍸	3*
O	Passito di Pantelleria Solidea '93	🍸🍸	5
O	Passito di Pantelleria Solidea '95	🍸🍸	5
O	Scirocco '96	🍸🍸	2*
O	Bianco Sciuvaki '96	🍸	3

ROSOLINI (SR)

COOPERATIVA INTERPROVINCIALE
ELORINA
VIA BELLINI, 17
96019 ROSOLINI (SR)
TEL. 0931/857068

This valiant cooperative in southeastern Sicily is keeping its place in the Guide although we have a few reservations. The Eloro Pachino '97 is a completely different animal from its spectacular predecessor. It is true that these were very different vintages and some lack of concentration was only to be expected. But why those forward, overripe tones on the nose? And why that excess of alcohol, separated from the other components on the palate? It's quite possible that they had a late harvest, in the hopes of counterbalancing the excessive acidity that nero d'Avola grown in the Pachino zone shows in certain years. Well, it's a venial sin (when committed only once). Great wine can and should be made here. The co-op's second wine, Eloro Rosso, also a '97, is reasonable. It has less structure but better-defined aromas and a balanced, if slightly simple palate. But we are still of good hope. We look forward to a great red from Pachino, as do all who love the Mediterranean wines of the south.

● Eloro Rosso '96	🍷	3
● Eloro Rosso Pachino '96	🍷	4
● Eloro Rosso Pachino '96	🍷🍷	4
● Eloro Rosso '96	🍷	3
● Eloro Rosso Pachino '95	🍷	4

S. CIPIRELLO (PA)

CALATRASI - TERRE DI GINESTRA
C.DA PIANO PIRAINO
90040 S. CIPIRELLO (PA)
TEL. 091/8576767 - 091/8578080

The wines listed below are just a sampling of the vast range produced by Calatrasi this year. Indeed, there are three different ranges: the D'Istinto line, which seemed best to us, as well as most innovative, Terre di Ginestra, the classic label, and Terrale, which includes both Sicilian and Pugliese wines and is probably meant to be the most commercially viable line. We have chosen the best from each range, but we must say that the average quality of all the wines was quite satisfactory. The particularly good D'Istinto Syrah '97 is a further confirmation of how well this grape does in Sicily. It is a characteristic red with spicy aromas and good weight. The Terre di Ginestra Rosso '98 was terrific despite very recent bottling. It vaunts an intensely fruity fragrance and a palate that has smoothed out all rough edges: a wine that doesn't have enormous body but is an absolute delight to drink. The D'Istinto Catarratto/Chardonnay '98 and the D'Istinto Sangiovese '97 are both reasonable. The most successful wine from the Terrale range was the Sicilia Rosso '98; the others, especially those from Puglia, seemed less interesting.

● D'Istinto Syrah '97	🍷🍷	4
● Terre di Ginestra Rosso '98	🍷🍷	3*
○ D'Istinto Catarratto/Chardonnay '98	🍷	3
● D'Istinto Sangiovese '97	🍷	4
● Terre di Sicilia Rosso '98	🍷	3
● Terrale Nero d'Avola/Nerello '98		3
● Pelavet Rosso '95	🍷🍷	4
○ D'Istinto Bianco '97	🍷	3
○ D'Istinto Catarratto/Chardonnay '97	🍷	3
● D'Istinto Nero d'Avola Nerello Mascalese '97	🍷	3
● D'Istinto Sangiovese/Merlot '97	🍷	3
● Terre di Ginestra Rosso '93	🍷	2*
● Terre di Ginestra Rosso '96	🍷	2*

SALINA (ME)

HAUNER
FRAZ. LINGUA DI SALINA
98050 SALINA (ME)
TEL. 090/9843141

This celebrated estate in Lingua di Salina now has 12 hectares planted to malvasia and corinto nero. Gjona, Alda, Ida and Carlo junior, the heirs of Carlo Hauner who founded it in 1963, are its guarantee for the future. They have modern vinification equipment, with stainless steel vats and a refrigeration plant, and they benefit from the assistance of Gianfranco Sabatino and Pippo Siracusano, who organize their commercial strategy, and of the oenologist Ferrara for wine-making. But let's consider the wines. The Malvasia delle Lipari Naturale is produced from bunches of grapes that are picked when they have already begun to dry, and which then continue the process on cane mats in the sun. We liked the '97 more than the previous vintage. A classic honey-yellow hue introduces good concentration on the nose, with generous aromatic notes of ripe summer fruit such as apricot and fig. The very good Passito version, also '97, offers abundant aromatic scents and a rich palate shot through with hints of marmalade. We found the Malvasia delle Lipari Passito from the '93 vintage fragrant, aromatic and sweet but not cloying. The Salina Bianco '98 and the Salina Rosso '97 are properly made, as usual.

○	Malvasia delle Lipari Naturale '97	▼▼	5
○	Malvasia delle Lipari Passita '93	▼	5
○	Malvasia delle Lipari Passita '97	▼	5
○	Salina Bianco '98		1
●	Salina Rosso '97		1
○	Malvasia delle Lipari Passita '95	▽▽	5
○	Malvasia delle Lipari Passita '96	▽▽	5
○	Malvasia delle Lipari Naturale '95	▽	4
○	Salina Bianco '97	▽	3
●	Salina Rosso '96	▽	3

SAMBUCA DI SICILIA (AG)

PLANETA
C.DA ULMO E MAROCCOLI
92017 SAMBUCA DI SICILIA (AG)
TEL. 0925/80009

Planeta is one of the most astounding phenomena on the Italian wine scene. In just four short years of existence the estate has become not just famous but one of the leading players. The formula is apparently no more than enthusiasm plus professional competence, its creators three bright, enterprising youngsters, Alessio, Francesca and Santi Planeta, with a combined age of about 85 years. The wine world could well do with more like them. This year they have racked up two Three Glass awards, one for the '98 Chardonnay (we haven't mentioned the '97, which was about as good, because it has disappeared even from the most out-of-the-way wine shops), the other for the Santa Cecilia '97, a blend of 80% nero d'Avola and 20% syrah. The Chardonnay, sensational, as usual, displays a bouquet of rare intensity with notes of vanilla and tropical fruit, and a rounded, concentrated palate, thanks in part to its more than 14° of alcohol. The Santa Cecilia has an exciting balance between acidity, a typical characteristic of nero d'Avola, and roundness of extract; the nose presents lightly balsamic and spicy notes on a background of red fruit and vanilla. The Cabernet Sauvignon (more clearly varietal and greater concentration) is better than the Merlot from the '97 vintage, while the opposite was distinctly the case for the '95s. The very interesting La Segreta Rosso '97 is a blend of nero d'Avola and merlot, but the two '98 whites, the Alastro (grecanico and chardonnay) and the La Segreta Bianca (same grápes, slightly different proportions) were a little below par, being cruder and shorter than we expected. Perhaps with a few months' bottle age...

○	Chardonnay '98	▼▼▼	5
●	Santa Cecilia '97	▼▼▼	5
●	Cabernet Sauvignon '97	▼▼	5
●	La Segreta Rosso '97	▼▼	3*
●	Merlot '97	▼▼	5
○	La Segreta Bianco '98	▼	3
○	Alastro '98	▼	4
○	Chardonnay '96	▽▽▽	5
○	Alastro '96	▽▽	4
●	Cabernet Sauvignon '95	▽▽	5
○	Chardonnay '95	▽▽	5
○	La Segreta Bianco '97	▽▽	3*
●	La Segreta Rosso '95	▽▽	3*
●	La Segreta Rosso '97	▽▽	3*
●	Merlot '95	▽▽	5

TRAPANI

CANTINA SOCIALE DI TRAPANI

C.DA OSPEDALETTO FONTANELLE
91100 TRAPANI
TEL. 0923/539349

Roberto Adragna, (ardent winegrower and dynamic president of this cooperative), his children Francesca (who handles public relations) and Goffredo (business manager), as well as all the 120 member growers, can be justifiably proud. One of the surprises of this year's tastings was the performance of this cooperative situated at the gates of Trapani, just below the mountain of Erice. After all, it is not every day that wines from a Sicilian cooperative are so harmonious, full-bodied and well executed. Part of the credit for this success belongs to Giovanni Centonze, a young oenologist from Trapani, who also oversees the members' vineyards, which are in the countryside near Kinisia, Rocca del Giglio and also Valderice, where cabernet sauvignon is planted. And it is from this 'foreign' variety that the co-op produces the soft and velvety Forti Terre di Sicilia Cabernet Sauvignon, rich in extract, full-bodied, balanced and very concentrated. The Forti Terre di Sicilia Rosso '98, from cabernet sauvignon and nero d'Avola, is no less impressive, with its intense aromas and light balsamic and vegetal notes followed by a round, appealingly grapey palate. In addition the wine is remarkably economical – as is its white counterpart, Forti Terre di Sicilia Bianco '98 (inzolia, catarratto and chardonnay). Richly fruity in fragrance and soft and easy to drink, it nevertheless reveals surprisingly good structure. We certainly hope that these wines, the result of careful planning and constant dedication, will serve as an inspiration for other local producers.

●	Forti Terre di Sicilia Cabernet Sauvignon '97	YY	3*
●	Forti Terre di Sicilia Rosso '98	YY	1*
○	Forti Terre di Sicilia Bianco '98	Y	1*

VALLELUNGA PRATAMENO (CL)

TASCA D'ALMERITA

C.DA REGALEALI
90029 VALLELUNGA PRATAMENO (CL)
TEL. 0921/544011 - 0921/542522

It has been a hard year for this famous Sicilian estate. After the death of the founding father Giuseppe Tasca, creator of Regaleali, there was the loss of Ignazio Miceli, one of the greatest figures on the Italian wine scene. He helped develop the worldwide demand for these wines, and was one of the first to understand how to create a market for really good Italian wines. He was also a great man in many ways that had nothing to do with his work. Now Count Giuseppe Tasca's son Lucio is carrying on his father's and Miceli's work with skill and determination. This should be stressed, even in a year when they add no new Three Glass awards to their large collection. The '96 Cabernet Sauvignon, although more forward and less concentrated than in the past, is still very interesting: it shows great elegance on nose and palate and notably smooth tannins. We expected a little more from the '97 Chardonnay, which is powerful and concentrated but a bit forward, with aromas of overripe fruit. The intriguing Nozze d'Oro '97, a well-structured white from sauvignon tasca, a variety unique to the estate, is also slightly forward on the nose. The '97 version of the classic Rosso del Conte is undeniably good, as is the '97 Rosso Novantasei, which in fact was first made in '96 but is more distinctive this year. The metodo classico sparkling wine, Almerita Brut '96, is surprisingly good, and the two Regalealis, the Bianco '98 and the Rosso '97, are both very well executed, as is the brand-new Leone d'Almerita '98, made from chardonnay and inzolia.

○	Almerita Brut '96	YY	5
●	Cabernet Sauvignon '96	YY	6
○	Chardonnay '97	YY	6
○	Nozze d'Oro '97	YY	4
●	Rosso del Conte '97	YY	5
●	Rosso Novantasei '97	YY	4
○	Leone d'Almerita '98	Y	3
○	Regaleali Bianco '98	Y	2*
●	Regaleali Rosso '97	Y	3
●	Cabernet Sauvignon '90	YYY	6
●	Cabernet Sauvignon '92	YYY	6
●	Cabernet Sauvignon '95	YYY	6
○	Chardonnay '94	YYY	6
○	Chardonnay '95	YYY	6
○	Chardonnay '93	YYY	6

VIAGRANDE (CT)

BENANTI
VIA G. GARIBALDI, 475
95029 VIAGRANDE (CT)
TEL. 095/7893533

The '96 vintage was not very good in Sicily and the weather was at its most capricious in the east, in the lands around Etna. This explains why even an estate like Benanti, with its up-to-the-minute equipment and excellent management, seemed to tread water. This is not to say that they did badly, but for a model Sicilian estate they fell a little short of expectations. The Lamoremio, a blend of cabernet sauvignon, nero d'Avola and nerello mascalese, is again the best of the range and was not greatly affected by the mediocrity of the vintage. It presents distinctive, complex aromas with light lactic notes and a full, tannic and long palate. All the others were no more than fair: the Etna Superiore Pietramarina '96 was more closed on the nose and harsher on the palate than the '95, and the Etna Rosso Rovittello '96 was clearly less concentrated than in previous years. What does remain is extreme technical proficiency informed by a thorough respect for "oenological basics", a sine qua non of any producer today.

●	Lamoremio '96	🍷🍷	5
○	Etna Bianco Bianco di Caselle '98	🍷	3
○	Etna Bianco Sup. Pietramarina '96	🍷	5
●	Etna Rosso Rosso di Verzella '97	🍷	3
●	Etna Rosso Rovittello '96	🍷	5
○	Etna Bianco Sup. Pietramarina '93	ΥΥ	4
○	Etna Bianco Sup. Pietramarina '95	ΥΥ	4
●	Etna Rosso Rovittello '93	ΥΥ	5
●	Etna Rosso Rovittello '94	ΥΥ	5
●	Etna Rosso Rovittello '95	ΥΥ	5
●	Lamoremio '95	ΥΥ	5

VITTORIA (RG)

COS
P.ZZA DEL POPOLO, 34
97019 VITTORIA (RG)
TEL. 0932/864042

We are extremely sorry that we couldn't try the '97 Cerasuolo di Vittoria Sciri, which wasn't ready in time for our tastings. It will be available in the new year and, if past experience is anything to go by, it should be even better than the '96, the master creation of Titta Cilia and Giusto Occhipinti, the two genial and easy-going owners of an estate which has always held aloft the banner of Sicilian wine of high quality. The technically impeccable Ramingallo '98, produced exclusively from the indigenous inzolia, did very well. Delicate and wonderfully well-defined aromas of flowers and fruit carry through onto the palate, where the wine develops confidently, revealing soft attractiveness and good length. The '97 Cerasuolo di Vittoria (frappato and nero d'Avola) is less successful than usual. Although as inviting and well made as ever it is less concentrated and the bouquet is not very intense or expressive. The intriguing new Aestas Siciliae '98, from moscato, is gentle and delicate and reveals the sweetness of the grape together with a trace of supple, exciting Mediterranean sensuality.

○	Ramingallo '98	🍷🍷	3*
○	Aestas Siciliae '98	🍷	2*
●	Cerasuolo di Vittoria '97	🍷	4
●	Cerasuolo di Vittoria V. di Bastonaca '98	🍷	2*
○	Le Vigne di Cos Bianco '97	🍷	4
●	Cerasuolo di Vittoria '94	ΥΥ	3*
●	Cerasuolo di Vittoria '95	ΥΥ	3*
●	Cerasuolo di Vittoria '96	ΥΥ	3*
●	Cerasuolo di Vittoria Sciri '95	ΥΥ	4
●	Cerasuolo di Vittoria Sciri '96	ΥΥ	4
●	Cerasuolo di Vittoria V. di Bastonaca '95	ΥΥ	4
●	Le Vigne di Cos Rosso '95	ΥΥ	4
○	Ramingallo '97	ΥΥ	3*

OTHER WINERIES

The following producers obtained good scores in our tastings with one or more of their wines:

PROVINCE OF CATANIA

Barone Scammacca del Murgo
Catania, tel. 095/7130090
Etna Bianco '98

Barone di Villagrande
Milo, tel. 095/7082175
Etna Bianco '98

PROVINCE OF MESSINA

Paone
Scala Torregrotta,
tel. 090/9981101
Malvasia delle Lipari Passito '96

PROVINCE OF PALERMO

Rapitalà
Palermo,
tel. 091/332088
Alcamo Rapitalà Grand Cru '97

SARDINIA

The world of wine in Sardinia has recently been like a vat in ferment. Estates are increasing the area under vine, coming out with new wines, changing the style of their range or taking on new markets. These are all signs of the change and regeneration that is recharging the Sardinian wine scene with vitality and renown. But there is still lots to be done, thanks in particular to the rich assortment of indigenous grape varieties. Why not, for example, bring back varieties like bovale, of which there are various forms, or caricagiola, pascale di Cagliari, gregu nieddu, caddiu, carenisca, retagliadu, nieddu mannu and girò, all of which were once used either singly or in blends to produce interesting reds on this island? There is hardly any doubt that with today's technical know-how one could get excellent results, just as is already happening with cagnulari, carignano, monica and nieddera, although quantities are still small. There are further opportunities to salvage the grape patrimony with the white varieties albaranzeli, arvesiniadu, monica bianca, greco bianco, cuscussedda and retagliadu biancu, which could bring exciting new wines to light. The same holds for dessert wines. Indeed, it can't be said often enough that Sardinia could boast a rich and varied range of excellent wines of unusual individuality. This year's tastings, though, did not reveal any particular peaks. Despite the usual talking up of the vintage, the "grande année" to close the century has not materialized. The grapes were highly rated but the wines less good than expected. Perhaps the oenologists can explain why. Our tastings tell us that little else has changed, essentially. The wines of Sella & Mosca and Argiolas remain top-notch, both continue to have international success and both win Three Glasses, the former for the Marchese di Villamarina '95, the latter for the Turriga '94. Good things continue to arrive from the co-operatives (Cantine Sociali) of Gallura, the land of Vermentino di Gallura, the island's only DOCG. Leading the field is the one in Tempio Pausania with its extraordinary Piras and Canayli Vermentinos, then comes the Monti cooperative with Funtanaliras, followed by the Berchidda co-op with a good Vigne Storiche, all from '98. Among the private estates Capichera, Mancini and Pedra Majore stand out, the last being the new estate of the Isoni family. There is nothing new from the province of Oristano, but near Nuoro the robust reds based on cannonau are beginning to go places. Wines from the private estates of Gabbas, Arcadu and Loi and the co-ops of Dorgali, Oliena and Jerzu are also showing well. The dessert wine sector brings comforting results too. Apart from Vernaccia di Oristano, there has been notable success for Argiolas with Angialis and for Sella & Mosca with Anghelu Ruju and the nasco-based Monteluce. Then Villa di Quartu's Moscato di Cagliari, Meloni Vini's Donna Jolanda line, Picciau's Nasco, Gian Vittorio Naìtana's Malvasia Murapiscados and the new Latinia, based on nasco, from the Cantina Sociale in Santadi are all just as interesting.

ALGHERO (SS)

CANTINA SOCIALE
SANTA MARIA LA PALMA
LOC. SANTA MARIA LA PALMA
07041 ALGHERO (SS)
TEL. 079/999008

The image of this co-op is still linked with the drainage and reclamation of the area just after the Second World War. The vines are protected from the mistral by rows of eucalyptus, or by interspersed olive trees close to the low Mediterranean scrub. This land, with its diversity and its climate, produces excellent grapes, most of which are vinified by this coop. For many years Santa Maria La Palma has aimed at well-made, clean, easy drinking, affordable wines and its well-organized sales department has brought them to some of Europe's most important markets. But the wines must surely be able to express the area's potential better than they do. Every so often there is a new wine, always attractive and well priced, but never a stunner. They produce vermentino-based white, for the most part. The Vermentino di Sardegna Aragosta is the best known. The '98 is fairly fruity on the nose and harmonious on the palate. The Alghero Cantavigna Rosato and Vermentino di Sardegna I Papiri are both light but made attractive by the presence of carbon dioxide. The good white from the Vigne del Mare line is immediate and balanced, although not up to last year's; the '96 red, released last year, is still on sale. The development this year is with Cannonau di Sardegna. There is a new label and the wine has taken a stride forward to match: the grapes are better selected and more carefully vinified and there is a period in French oak. The '97 has a good nose and a succulent and tasty palate. The rosé Alghero Punta Rosa '98 is delicate, lively and lean.

⊙	Alghero Punta Rosa '98	🍷	1*
●	Cannonau di Sardegna Le Bombarde '97	🍷	2*
○	Vermentino di Sardegna Aragosta '98	🍷	2*
○	Alghero Bianco Vigne del Mare '98		1
○	Vermentino di Sardegna I Papiri '98		3
⊙	Alghero Cantavigna '98		2
●	Cannonau di Sardegna Le Bombarde '93	YY	2*
○	Alghero Bianco Vigne del Mare '97	Y	2*
●	Alghero Rosso Vigne del Mare '96	Y	2*

ALGHERO (SS)

TENUTE SELLA & MOSCA
LOC. I PIANI
07041 ALGHERO (SS)
TEL. 079/997700

It's a hundred years old but doesn't look it. Sella & Mosca proudly cherishes its glorious history, and is now the object of reverential visits like the great maisons of France. It is currently replanting several hundred of its hectares. Once more the Marchese di Villamarina has earned itself Three Glasses. The '95 has a deep ruby hue, an ample and intense nose with notes of hay, black currant and sour cherry, and extremely elegant hints of spice. The palate is full, soft, complex and rich, keeps all its components in perfect balance and then just keeps on going. The latest arrival is called Raim, which means "grapes" in Catalan. It is a red from carignano, merlot and cabernet sauvignon, aged for 12 months in large old barrels. It has the stuff of a young Bordeaux, with soft tannins and a pleasing immediacy but elegance too. The Cannonau di Sardegna Riserva '96 has a forward bouquet with a distinct spiciness and hints of violet and jam, and body and good length on the palate. A warm, full Vermentino di Gallura Monteoro '98 joins the range of whites. The Torbato Terre Bianche '98, rich in fragrance with hints of pistachio and flowers, and soft on the palate, is excellent. The Arenarie '98 and the Vermentino di Sardegna La Cala '98 are attractively fresh and acidulous. Two Glasses go to the Anghelu Ruju Riserva '91 with its broad, intense bouquet including captivating scents of herbal infusions and ripe black berries. To conclude, there's a new Riserva version of the '94 Tanca Farrà which is particularly concentrated and intense, and certainly worthy of notice.

●	Alghero Marchese di Villamarina '95	🍷🍷🍷	6
○	Alghero Le Arenarie '98	🍷🍷	3*
○	Alghero Torbato Terre Bianche '98	🍷🍷	3*
●	Anghelu Ruju Ris. '91	🍷🍷	4
●	Raim '96	🍷🍷	3*
●	Alghero Tanca Farrà Ris. '94	🍷🍷	4
○	Vermentino di Gallura Monteoro '98	🍷🍷	3*
⊙	Alghero Oleandro '98	🍷	2*
●	Cannonau di Sardegna Ris. '94	🍷	3
○	Vermentino di Sardegna La Cala '98	🍷	3
●	Alghero Marchese di Villamarina '93	YYY	6

ARZACHENA (SS)

TENUTE CAPICHERA
LOC. CAPICHERA
07021 ARZACHENA (SS)
TEL. 0789/80612

There are big changes in the air at this Gallura estate. The most important involves an increase of the area under vine. The new more rational plantings are being planned with drip irrigation and with careful selection of vines and training systems. A further development is the uprooting of older vines which no longer regularly yield vermentino characteristics, and their replacement with new vines. It is no novelty that the Ragnedda brothers manage to sell most of their wine, often before the harvest, at prices notably higher than the local norm. Their most representative wine is Vermentino di Gallura Capichera '98, which easily gained Two Glasses. Fresh on both nose and palate, with a fragrance of tropical fruit, it is soft, clean and harmonious in the mouth. Just behind it is the '98 Vendemmia Tardiva (late-harvested) version of which about 13 thousand bottles were produced. The grapes are aged partly in new, partly in once-used barriques. Spiciness and length are more evident than in the Capichera. The unoaked "younger brother", Vigna 'Ngena '98, is simpler but well made: it's easy to drink and enjoyable, even with its bite of acidity. The red Assajè '98, from carignano, shows an attractive ruby color with a marked purplish cast, a blackberry nose and good concentration on the palate.

○	Vermentino di Gallura Capichera '98	▼▼	5
○	Vermentino di Gallura V. T. '98	▼▼	5
●	Assajè Rosso '98	▼	4
○	Vermentino di Gallura Vigna 'Ngena '98	▼	4
○	Vermentino di Gallura Capichera '95	▽▽	5
○	Vermentino di Gallura V. T. '96	▽▽	5
○	Vermentino di Gallura V. T. '97	▽▽	5
○	Vermentino di Gallura Vigna 'Ngena '94	▽▽	4
●	Assajè Rosso '97	▽	4
○	Vermentino di Gallura Vigna 'Ngena '97	▽	4

BERCHIDDA (SS)

CANTINA SOCIALE GIOGANTINU
VIA MILANO, 30
07022 BERCHIDDA (SS)
TEL. 079/704163 - 079/704939

This cooperative winery is back in the Guide with bells on. It now has a wide-awake dynamism that was not there before, so looking around to see what was going on elsewhere must have been salutary. We've always believed in the potential of their area and we're pleased with this year's results. The 350 member growers cultivate 350 hectares under vine, some of which are still gobelet-trained, with yields of not more than 6,000 kilos per hectare. Among the most intriguing and satisfying of the newer wines is the Vermentino di Gallura Vigne Storiche '98, now at its second release. The '97 was labeled "superiore" and had 13.5% alcohol. The '98, though, is a "normale" and also more interesting. The bouquet is of moderate intensity but distinct fruitiness, and on the palate the fruit really comes out, with the typical almondy note of old-fashioned Vermentino di Gallura. Its balance and attractiveness win the wine Two Glasses. One Glass, however, goes to the Vermentino di Gallura Superiore '98, a simple but notably soft wine. The Vermentino di Gallura '98 has a faint nose and a slightly thin palate. The new, fresh, attractive and lightly bubbly Tancarè is also worthy of mention. The red Nastarrè '98, from pascale, malaga, nebbiolo, monica and cagnulari, shows a simple fruitiness on the nose and fair balance in the mouth. It's not an imposing and persistent wine, but it is attractive and quaffable.

○	Vermentino di Gallura Vigne Storiche '98	▼▼	4
●	Nastarrè '98	▼	1*
○	Vermentino di Gallura Sup. '98	▼	2*
○	Tancaré		2
○	Vermentino di Gallura '98		1

CABRAS (OR)

Attilio Contini
Via Genova, 48/50
09072 Cabras (OR)
tel. 0783/290806

"Vernaccia. But not only." These words, highlighted in Contini's new brochure, reveal how strongly the estate feels about changing course. The continuing fall in Vernaccia consumption has pushed Paolo and his brother Antonio to diversify their range. They now produce new blends that include vernaccia grapes, and well-known wines like Cannonau and Vermentino. But they also make an important local red that producers here would do well to consider: Nieddera. We tasted the '96, the latest to be released. It has broad, intense and complex aromas with notes of Mediterranean scrub and hints of blackberry and licorice. It also boasts concentration and length on the palate: Two Glasses. The Vernaccia di Oristano '90 is the best we found this year. It has an intrinsic harmony that is particularly evident in the nicely heady bouquet of almond and toasted hazelnut. The palate is warm, soft and long. The white Pontis, from moscato grown in upper Gallura, again earns One Glass. The '98 is simple and direct, with proper nose-palate balance. The Vermentino di Sardegna '98 is good, especially on the nose; the palate wants a little more concentration. The lightly spicy Cannonau di Sardegna '97 is dry and well made; the Karmis '98, based on vernaccia, is less interesting.

●	Nieddera Rosso '96	🍷🍷	2*
○	Vernaccia di Oristano Ris. '90	🍷🍷	3*
○	Pontis '98	🍷	3
○	Vermentino di Sardegna '98	🍷	2
●	Cannonau di Sardegna '97		3
○	Karmis '98		2
○	Vernaccia di Oristano Ris. '71	YYY	5
○	Antico Gregori	YY	6
○	Elibaria '93	YY	2*
○	Karmis '96	YY	2*
●	Nieddera Rosso '91	YY	3*
○	Vernaccia di Oristano '88	YY	3*
○	Vernaccia di Oristano Ris. '80	YY	3*
○	Karmis '97	Y	2*
●	Nieddera Rosso '95	Y	3

CARDEDU (NU)

Alessandro Loi & Figli
S. S. Orientale Sarda km. 124.200
08040 Cardedu (NU)
tel. 070/657259

Ogliastra is unquestionably one of the best areas in Sardinia for Cannonau. This is not only because until a few years ago it was the only variety cultivated here but also because the cannonau grape lucky enough to grow in this earth enjoys particularly propitious soil and climatic conditions. For a long time the wine was made in a traditional way that no longer corresponds to the tastes of consumers. Often the wine was perfectly acceptable, but at times it seemed old as soon as it was bottled; this was a problem shared by private producers and cooperatives. Much is now changing and this estate, run by the Loi brothers with boundless enthusiasm, is no exception. The vineyards have been replanted, in part to red varieties considered innovative in these parts, and the cellar has been completely restructured. Cannonau is and will remain the estate's principal care, although the wider range of varieties now grown could give rise to other major wines. The brothers are already doing good things, but they are still in the experimental phase of their quest for the best way to bring out the characteristics of traditional Cannonau. The '96 Riserva seemed the most complete of the range. Although its bouquet is not extremely rich, it has characteristic notes of walnut skin; the palate is warm, clean and still a little tannic: in two or three years it should be at its peak. The Cannonau di Sardegna Alberto Loi Riserva '95 is different but still intriguing: it releases appealing aromas of blackberry and cherry on the nose, and the palate has more depth and also seems younger because of its good acidity and still harsh tannins. To conclude, the Cannonau di Sardegna Cardedo '96 is fair.

●	Cannonau di Sardegna Alberto Loi Ris. '95	🍷	4
●	Cannonau di Sardegna Ris. '96	🍷	4
●	Cannonau di Sardegna Cardedo '96		3
●	Cannonau di Sardegna Alberto Loi Ris. '93	YY	4
●	Cannonau di Sardegna Cardedo '95	Y	3
●	Cannonau di Sardegna Sa Mola Rubia Ris. '96	Y	3

DOLIANOVA (CA)

CANTINA SOCIALE DOLIANOVA
LOC. SANT'ESU
S. S. 387 - KM. 17,150
09041 DOLIANOVA (CA)
TEL. 070/740643

Lots of wines and lots of labels would seem to be the philosophy of this cooperative, one of the largest in Sardinia. Practically all the region's categories are embraced in its huge range. Those produced in the largest quantities are the whites Vermentino di Sardegna and Nuragus di Cagliari. We found both '98s well made but not particularly exciting. The same could be said of the Vermentino di Sardegna Naeli '98 and the Capidiana Chardonnay '98 from the Vigne Sarde line. The Dolicante '98, made from sauvignon blanc, is distinctly better. It has a fresh, attractive fragrance reminiscent of tropical fruit and a soft palate with some length. Of the reds the Falconaro '97 is excellent: it is not quite up to the standard of last year's but easily gets Two Glasses nonetheless. The aromas are faint but well knit and clean; the palate has good body and fair length. The successful Cannonau di Sardegna '97 is notable for its softness and balance. On the other hand, the Monica di Sardegna is fragile, almost enervated. We gladly gave Two Glasses to the Moscato di Cagliari '96, which is full and enticing on both nose and palate. It should be noted that this zone, to the north and east of Cagliari, used to be known for its excellent dessert wines, particularly Moscato, Malvasia and Girò. The reappearance of these traditional varieties is an encouraging sign for the future. To close, the sparkling wines Caralis Brut and Scaleri Démi sec, both based on malvasia, deserve mention.

● Falconaro '97	🍷🍷	3*
○ Moscato di Cagliari '96	🍷🍷	4
○ Dolicante '98	🍷	3
● Cannonau di Sardegna '97	🍷	2
○ Capidiana Chardonnay '98		4
○ Caralis Brut		3
○ Nuragus di Cagliari '98		2
○ Scaleri Démi sec		3
⊙ Sibiola Rosato '98		2
○ Vermentino di Sardegna '98		2
○ Vermentino di Sardegna Naeli '98		2
○ Dolicante '96	🍸🍸	3*
● Falconaro '96	🍸🍸	3*
● Falconaro '95	🍸	3
● Monica di Sardegna '96	🍸	2*

DORGALI (NU)

CANTINA SOCIALE DI DORGALI
VIA PIEMONTE, 11
08022 DORGALI (NU)
TEL. 0784/96143

We have long regretted a sort of stasis in Sardinian cooperative wineries. And although the Cantina Sociale di Dorgali is in Cannonau country in the province of Nuoro, where some movement has been perceptible, this co-op has not yet reached its turning point. Now, however, the distinguished oenologist Franco Bernabei has been summoned to the bedside of the patient, although we haven't quite understood whether it's Cannonau or the wineries – or perhaps both – that are languishing in need of treatment. The most interesting new wine to emerge this year is the Noriolo '97, a red made from cannonau with some sangiovese grosso, refosco, aglianico, pinot nero and cabernet, all grown in a newly acquired co-op vineyard. Of a fairly intense, concentrated ruby color, it is still young and shows herbaceous notes on the nose and a still tannic palate that has, however, good structure: it should definitely improve after some months in bottle. Other varieties, both indigenous and imported, have also been planted and will be used, either singly or in blends, to produce new reds. Of the more traditional wines we liked the Filieri Rosso '98 and the rosé version from the same year, the Filieri Rosato. Both are attractive and properly made, with medium extract and fair length. There is also a simple, maybe too simple, white called Calaluna.

● Filieri Rosso '98	🍷	2*
● Noriolo '97	🍷	4
⊙ Filieri Rosato '98		2
● Cannonau di Sardegna '94	🍸	3
● Cannonau di Sardegna Filieri '95	🍸	2*
● Filieri Rosso '96	🍸	2*
● Filieri Rosso '97	🍸	2*

JERZU (NU)

CANTINA SOCIALE DI JERZU
VIA UMBERTO I, 1
08044 JERZU (NU)
TEL. 0782/70028

It has long been known that the zone of Ogliastra is one of the best for Cannonau. Differences in terrains and microclimates make it possible to diversify the production of red wines, and also to make much better ones. But often there's a tendency to vinify en masse, so as to have quantities of a homogeneous wine that will be easily saleable at home and abroad. Nevertheless, suddenly this co-op seems to have been jolted out of the inertia that has afflicted it too for years, at least so it seems from its new wine Radames, made from cannonau, carignano and cabernet and barrique-aged for about 12 months. The '97 has intense, persistent aromas with notes of vanilla from the young wood. The tannins are fairly astringent on the palate, and one notes the freshness of a young wine that is still evolving: it is very likely to improve as it matures. The Cannonau di Sardegna Riserva '95 is more complete although not very distinguished on the mildly spicy nose; the palate is soft and full and the alcohol properly substantial. The Cannonau di Sardegna '97 has a faint, moderately persistent fragrance; the palate is too warm for perfect balance. Like many other wineries, both private and co-operative, the Cantina di Jerzu has enlarged its range with wines that are typical of other zones, including, of course, Vermentino. This seems rather like producing a white wine in Brunello country.

●	Cannonau di Sardegna '97	🍷	2*
●	Cannonau di Sardegna Ris. '95	🍷	3
●	Radames '97	🍷	4
●	Cannonau di Sardegna Ris. '91	🍷🍷	3*
●	Cannonau di Jerzu Dolce Pardu '90	🍷	3
●	Cannonau di Sardegna '92	🍷	2*
●	Cannonau di Sardegna '93	🍷	2*
●	Cannonau di Sardegna '95	🍷	2*
●	Cannonau di Sardegna '96	🍷	2*
●	Pardu Dolce '91	🍷	3

MAGOMADAS (NU)

GIANVITTORIO NAITANA
VIA ROMA, 2
08010 MAGOMADAS (NU)
TEL. 0785/35333

This small estate which is dedicated to the revival of Malvasia della Planargia has had another good year. Gianvittorio Naìtana is lucky enough to be working in one of the most beautiful and renowned areas for this grape. His little vineyards are close to the sea at altitudes varying between 60 and 260 meters. The soil composition doesn't vary much, all containing a goodly amount of limestone: just right for yielding the best Malvasia, the old vignerons would say, and so do we, having often tasted the local wines over the years. Malvasia is an extraordinary wine and full of personality. However, excessive fragmentation of the land and the obstinate individualism of some producers have stymied its development. More collaboration would help restore it to the place it deserves: maybe action by local agencies is needed here. There is a further problem: DOC regulations stipulate a minimum of two years' aging, thus excluding the possibility of a young DOC version. We think they could happily co-exist, both being characteristic, although the fresh and easily quaffable one would still be generally preferred. Naìtana's Planargia Murapiscados '98 has more to it than the '97; it is richer on the nose, with clearly defined, captivating notes of ripe apricot; the palate is soft, delicately sweet and mouth-filling; harmony and the excellent carry-through from bouquet to palate make the wine particularly elegant.

○	Planargia Murapiscados '98	🍷🍷	4
○	Planargia Murapiscados '96	🍷🍷	4
○	Planargia Murapiscados '97	🍷🍷	4

Cantina Sociale del Vermentino

Via S. Paolo, 1
07020 Monti (SS)
tel. 0789/44012

Some 350 member growers provide the grapes of this cooperative winery. Vermentino predominates, but they also grow small amounts of cannonau, monica, pascale and malaga, all red. We were happier with what we tasted this year. The Vermentino di Gallura Funtanaliras '98 made it to Two Glasses. It is a white with a powerful structure and perfect balance between nose and palate. The lovely fruity bouquet offers notes of apple and lemon balm; the palate is fresh, succulent, concentrated and long. The Vermentino di Gallura Aghiloia '98 is, as usual, a good, simple, direct white: it comes closest to the traditional style of the local Vermentino, as we have had occasion to remark before. It is neither overly intense nor very persistent on the nose, but is more interesting on the palate, which is full and round, with notes of fresh almond and fair length. The Vermentino di Gallura S'Eleme '98 was the figurehead wine before the appearance of Funtanaliras. Now it has a less exalted role but is still a well executed wine. The red Abbaìa '98, a blend of cannonau, pascale di Cagliari and other local varieties, is very like the '96: it does not show great body but is properly made and clean on both nose and palate.

○	Vermentino di Gallura Funtanaliras '98	▼▼	3*
●	Abbaìa '98	▼	1
○	Vermentino di Gallura S'Eleme '98	▼	1*
○	Vermentino di Gallura Sup. Aghiloia '98	▼	2*
○	Vermentino di Gallura Sup. Aghiloia '94	▽▽	2*
○	Vermentino di Gallura Sup. Aghiloia '96	▽▽	2*
●	Abbaìa '94	▽	1*
●	Abbaìa '96	▽	1*
●	Abbaìa '97	▽	1*
●	Abbaìa '93	▽	1*

Pedra Majore

Via Roma, 106
07020 Monti (SS)
tel. 0789/43185

The Isoni brothers, who own this estate, carry on a venerable tradition. It is in the heart of Gallura and has over 60 hectares under vine, of which 50 are planted to vermentino, eight to moscato and a further seven to a mix of indigenous and experimental red varieties (including cabernet and merlot). What they have in mind is producing first-class wine, and as of this year they have the help of illustrious experts: Attilio Scienza gives viticultural advice and Donato Lanati is their consultant oenologist. The results of these contributions will begin to appear with the '99 vintage. The cellar can hold about 5,000 hectoliters and has up-to-the-minute equipment. As for the wines we tasted, it should be remembered that this is a transitional year. They are all more than acceptable and several are quite interesting. The Vermentino di Sardegna Le Conche '98 has a pale straw color and lightly vegetal aromas but the palate is still a little crude, not very concentrated and rather short. The Vermentino di Gallura I Graniti '98 has more to it. The bouquet, while not overwhelming, is even and delicately fruity, while the palate is crisp, succulent and balanced. The Murighessa '98, a red made mainly from indigenous grapes, is intriguing but still young. The sparkling Moscato La Eltica and the extremely concentrated and soft Moscato Passito Mirju '98 are attractive enough to warrant One Glass each. All in all, not bad for a first appearance in the Guide!

○	Mirju Passito '98	▼	5
○	Moscato Spumante La Eltica	▼	4
●	Murighessa '98	▼	3
○	Vermentino di Gallura I Graniti '98	▼	3
○	Vermentino di Sardegna Le Conche '98		2

NUORO

GIUSEPPE GABBAS
VIA TRIESTE, 65
08100 NUORO
TEL. 0784/31351 - 0784/33745

There have been some changes at this well-known estate at the foot of Supramonte in Barbagia. Some of the vineyards are about to be replanted and work has begun on a vinification cellar. The grapes will thus no longer be vinified by Censar in Villasor, but will be taken care of at home as soon as they're picked. Claudio Gori is still the estate oenologist and continues to use traditional methods such as very long maceration. Results seem to prove him right. The Lillovè '98, from cannonau with small amounts of other indigenous grapes, sees no oak. The color is an intense, deep ruby and the very rich fruity bouquet is distinctly reminiscent of cherry and sour cherry. The palate is very fresh and notably full-bodied. The Dule '98, a blend of 50% cannonau with cabernet sauvignon, montepulciano and sangiovese, had a long maceration and, in part, six months of barrique-aging. It is a superb, rich, almost opulent yet well-balanced red with intense, clearly defined spicy scents. The attack on the palate is fresh and distinct, and although slightly rough tannins still need time to soften, the wine has remarkable body and structure.

●	Cannonau di Sardegna Lillovè '98	🍷🍷	3*
●	Dule '98	🍷🍷	4
●	Cannonau di Sardegna Lillovè '96	🍸🍸	3*
●	Cannonau di Sardegna Lillovè '97	🍸🍸	3*
●	Dule '94	🍸🍸	4
●	Dule '95	🍸🍸	4
●	Dule '96	🍸🍸	4
●	Dule '97	🍸🍸	4
●	Cannonau di Sardegna Lillovè '93	🍸	2*
●	Cannonau di Sardegna Lillovè '94	🍸	2*
●	Cannonau di Sardegna Lillovè '95	🍸	2*

OLBIA (SS)

PIERO MANCINI
LOC. CALA SACCAIA
08026 OLBIA (SS)
TEL. 0789/50717

Coming in to land at Olbia airport you can see the large green sign for the Mancini winery just a few yards from the sea. The vineyards, though, are elsewhere, inland. We admire the determination of Alessandro and Antonio Mancini, who are both personally involved in the cultivation of the vine and in wine-making. Their vines produce excellent grapes and their cellar is beautifully equipped for the production of great white wines. But a bad vintage is a bad vintage, and there's not much that the most modern equipment can do about it. And if a poor year happens to coincide with the release of a new wine there may be disappointments in store. This is what has happened with the new Vermentino di Gallura Vignalta '98, a good white wine from which we were expecting something more. It does not have great richness on the nose; the palate, which is somewhat more interesting, is straightforward and well executed, with a good finish. The traditional Vermentino di Gallura Cuccaione is also well made and has greater body and better texture on the palate. The reds seemed more intriguing, particularly the Cannonau di Sardegna '97. Of a deep ruby hue, it has a penetrating fragrance of ripe berries and a warm, full palate with excellent acid-alcohol balance. The Saccaia, with no vintage indication (quite properly), has moderately intense, complex and attractive aromas, a harmonious, velvety palate and fair length.

●	Cannonau di Sardegna '97	🍷🍷	3*
●	Saccaia	🍷	3
○	Vermentino di Gallura Cuccaione '98	🍷	3
○	Vermentino di Gallura Vignalta '98	🍷	4
●	Saccaia '94	🍸🍸	3
●	Saccaia '96	🍸🍸	3*
●	Cannonau di Sardegna '96	🍸	3
○	Pinot Chardonnay Brut '94	🍸	3
○	Pinot Chardonnay Brut '95	🍸	3
●	Saccaia '92	🍸	3
●	Saccaia '93	🍸	3
●	Saccaia '95	🍸	2*
○	Vermentino di Gallura Cuccaione '97	🍸	3

SANTADI (CA)

CANTINA SOCIALE DI SANTADI
VIA SU PRANU, 12
09010 SANTADI (CA)
TEL. 0781/950012 - 0781/950127

The '98 vintage was not a great one for Santadi, but only as regards their standard whites. The wine that impressed us most is the Villa di Chiesa '98, a briefly barrique-aged blend of vermentino and chardonnay. It offers a complex, varied and sensuous bouquet with slightly insistent oak. The full-flavored palate finishes on a note of roasted hazelnut. The Villa di Chiesa '97 is also excellent; it's slightly less concentrated but still full, deep, balanced and fascinating. The succulent Villa Solais '98 is fresh and fruity and gets One Glass. The Nuragus di Cagliari Pedrera '98 is notably richer and more intense, has attractive fruity notes on the nose and is clean and crisp on the palate. There have been a few developments with the reds too. The now famous Carignano del Sulcis Terre Brune remains the leading wine. The '95 is excellent, flawless and substantial but less rich in bouquet and less structured than the '94. The Carignano del Sulcis Riserva Rocca Rubia '95 has a somewhat forward color; dried fruit and oak stand out on the nose and the palate is dry and warm. The Carignano del Sulcis Tre Torri '98 seems more balanced and harmonious: it's an immediately appealing wine without undue pretensions, which is also true of the Monica di Sardegna Antigua '98. The Araja '97 and the Baie Rosse '96 are not quite as good as last year's versions. For the first time Santadi has presented a dessert wine, the nasco-based Latinia, which seems perfumed, warm, full and very rich in ripe fruit.

○	Latinia '97	▼▼	6
●	Terre Brune '95	▼▼	6
○	Villa di Chiesa '97	▼▼	3*
○	Villa di Chiesa '98	▼▼	3*
●	Araja '97	▼	3
●	Carignano del Sulcis Baje Rosse '96	▼	4
●	Carignano del Sulcis Rocca Rubia Ris. '95	▼	5
●	Carignano del Sulcis Tre Torri '98	▼	2*
●	Monica di Sardegna Antigua '96	▼	2*
○	Nuragus di Cagliari Pedraia '98	▼	2*
○	Villa Solais '98	▼	2*
●	Terre Brune '93	▽▽▽	6
●	Terre Brune '94	▽▽▽	6

SELARGIUS (CA)

MELONI VINI
VIA GALLUS, 79
09047 SELARGIUS (CA)
TEL. 070/852822

One hears a lot about organic produce, and it's not all positive. We don't feel it's our place to pontificate on the subject, but we are called upon to judge the wines submitted for tasting by this estate. They are more than acceptable, well made and attractive, but they cannot be said to be exciting. The reds from the Germoglio line have a somewhat delicate structure and high acidity, especially the Cannonau di Sardegna '95. The Germoglio whites are weak on the nose and rather short. The Vermentino di Sardegna '98 from the Natura range is better, especially on the nose. The full, structured Cannonau di Sardegna Le Ghiaie '95 recalls the old style of Cannonau and really gets one interested, as do the dessert wines from the Donna Jolanda line. Among these, the Nasco di Cagliari '94 has intense aromas of dried and tropical fruit and a broad, clean, concentrated palate. The Moscato di Cagliari '94 is meaty and fat, and strongly varietal on both nose and palate. We tasted the dry version of the Malvasia di Cagliari '94: time has made considerable changes in its varietal characteristics. The semi-sweet version would probably have done a better job of preserving its essential bouquet. The palate, however, was warm, heady and round.

○	Nasco di Cagliari Donna Jolanda '94	▼▼	4
●	Cannonau di Sardegna Le Ghiaie '95	▼	3
○	Malvasia di Cagliari Donna Jolanda '94	▼	4
○	Moscato di Cagliari Donna Jolanda '94	▼	4
○	Vermentino di Sardegna Natura '98		3
●	Cabernet di Sardegna '92	▽▽	4
○	Moscato di Cagliari Donna Jolanda '91	▽▽	4
●	Cannonau di Sardegna Le Ghiaie '91	▽	3

SENORBÌ (CA)

CANTINA SOCIALE DELLA TREXENTA
V.LE PIEMONTE, 28
09040 SENORBÌ (CA)
TEL. 070/9808863 - 070/9809378

Many changes are under way at this cooperative winery, especially in the vineyards, where native varieties and imported grapes now grow side by side. They are committed, here, to improving and promoting local wines, but they also carefully watch the market. Things are slowly getting better. Having, as usual, tasted the entire range, we can say that the best wines are those of the "new wave". For a start, the good Tanca su Conti '95, a blend of carignano and montepulciano given 18 months in barrique and a further six in bottle, is still young and fresh; vegetal notes appear on the nose and the palate confirms that the wine is still developing: it is full-bodied, fairly tannic, warm and long. The '98 Monica di Sardegna is slightly less good than the '97 but is still an attractive, well-made, balanced wine and good value for money. Both the Cannonau di Sardegna Corte Adua '96 and the Cannonau di Sardegna Baione '95 are interesting; the latter, from gobelet-trained vines, has a more concentrated bouquet and reasonable structure. The whites are not bad at all, especially the Monteluna Chardonnay '98 with its fruity bouquet and linear palate. The Nuragus di Cagliari '98 is immediate and refreshing. The Vermentino di Sardegna Donna Leonora '98 is rather short, but the Moscato di Cagliari Simieri '95 got quite close to Two Glasses: rich in intense, lingering aromas, it has a full, slightly honeyed, pleasing palate.

●	Cannonau di Sardegna Baione '95	▼	3
●	Monica di Sardegna Duca di Mandas '98	▼	2*
○	Monteluna Chardonnay '98	▼	2*
○	Moscato di Cagliari Simieri '95	▼	4
○	Nuragus di Cagliari Tenute San Mauro '98	▼	1*
●	Tanca Su Conti '95	▼	4
●	Cannonau di Sardegna Corte Adua '96		3
○	Vermentino di Sardegna Donna Leonora '98		2
●	Monica di Sardegna '97	▽▽	1*
●	Tanca Su Conti '91	▽▽	5
●	Segolai Rosso '95	▽	1*

SERDIANA (CA)

ANTONIO ARGIOLAS
VIA ROMA, 56/58
09040 SERDIANA (CA)
TEL. 070/740606

It may not be startling, but the Argiolas estate has again presented a range of splendid wines. The Turriga '94 is as superb as usual. It has become a classic of Sardinian and indeed Italian oenology, and a major collector of Three Glass awards. This version has a deep, intense ruby color and ample and complex aromas with notes of ripe berries and well-integrated oak. There is remarkable structure on the palate, which is harmonious and stylish, with good tannins and great length. As for the whites, Two Glasses go to the Argiolas '98, which shows a richly vegetal, aromatic and fruity nose and a well-developed flavor; another Two to the Vermentino di Sardegna Costamolino '98, where the lavender and rosemary notes of the bouquet reappear in delightful alternation on the palate. The Nuragus di Cagliari S'Elegas '98 offers harmony, balance and good value for money. Among the other reds, the Kore '97, Turriga's "younger brother" made from bovale, carignano, cannonau, syrah and merlot, is a most pleasant surprise. It's already very good and its future is even rosier. The bouquet is still evolving: notes of oak are still apparent, and the palate is full, meaty and rounded. The Cannonau di Sardegna Costera '97 is as well made and traditional as ever, as is the Monica di Sardegna Perdera '97, which is considerably better than the previous vintage. Even the rosé Serralori, in its simplicity, is delicately fruity on the nose and fresh in the mouth. A treat to finish: the Angialis '96 is a white of sensual sweetness with intoxicating and complex aromas of honey and candied fruit. The palate is sweet, warm, balanced, fat and long.

●	Turriga '94	▼▼▼	6
○	Angialis '96	▼▼	5
○	Argiolas '98	▼▼	3*
●	Kore '97	▼▼	5
○	Vermentino di Sardegna Costamolino '98	▼▼	2*
●	Cannonau di Sardegna Costera '97	▼	3
●	Monica di Sardegna Perdera '97	▼	2*
○	Nuragus di Cagliari S'Elegas '98	▼	2*
⊙	Serralori Rosato '98	▼	2*
●	Turriga '90	▽▽▽	6
●	Turriga '91	▽▽▽	6
●	Turriga '92	▽▽▽	6
●	Turriga '93	▽▽▽	6

TEMPIO PAUSANIA (SS)

Cantina Sociale Gallura

Via Val di Cossu, 9
07029 Tempio Pausania (SS)
tel. 079/631241

The Gallura cooperative winery is still one of Sardinia's best. Each year it turns out good wines at exceptional prices. Its director and oenologist Dino Addis is constantly engaged in improving quality; regular supervision of the co-op's vineyards and those of its member growers has contributed to its upswing. The Vermentino di Gallura Superiore Canayli '98 continues to gather praise: elegant and fruity on the nose, it is even more delightful on the palate, where it is full-flavored and structured but also crisp and enticing, yielding a harmony that we have seldom found in Gallura wines. The Vermentino di Gallura '98 isn't a poor cousin, although it doesn't have the same structure; it boasts a rich, fresh, lively nose with fruity and vegetal notes, all of which is mirrored on the palate. The experiments in barrique-aging to make the Balajana '98 have yielded interesting results. It's like rediscovering the old-fashioned country folk's Vermentino, but cleaned and properly dressed, with an almond fragrance and a full, round palate. The Vermentino di Gallura Mavriana '98 and the Campos Rosato (rosé) are both good and get One Glass apiece, but the red Karana Nebbiolo dei Colli del Limbara '98 receives Two Glasses. It is as pleasing on the nose as on the palate, and is fresh and youthful, and rich in notes of berries and pomegranate. The very well-made Moscato di Tempio Pausania is as fragrant and elegant as a classic sparkling Moscato should be, and rich in fully varietal aromas.

○ Balajana '98	▼▼	4
● Karana Nebbiolo dei Colli del Limbara '98	▼▼	1*
○ Vermentino di Gallura Piras '98	▼▼	1*
○ Vermentino di Gallura Sup. Canayli '98	▼▼	2*
⊙ Campos Rosato del Limbara '98	▼	1*
○ Moscato di Tempio Pausania '98	▼	4
○ Vermentino di Gallura Mavriana '98	▼	1*
● Dolmen '94	▽▽	4
● Dolmen '95	▽▽	4
● Karana Nebbiolo dei Colli del Limbara '97	▽▽	1*
○ Vermentino di Gallura Piras '97	▽▽	2

USINI (SS)

Giovanni Cherchi

Via Ossi, 18/20
07049 Usini (SS)
tel. 079/380273

We can't exactly say we're disappointed, but after many tastings Giovanni Cherchi's Vermentinos still don't seem to have the fragrance, the finesse and the elegance that until recently distinguished them from all their peers. Something should be done, in the vineyards or the cellar: this is the producer who, with just a very few colleagues, made a name for Vermentino di Sardegna in Italy and abroad. The wine we always most admired, the Tuvaoes, is not as good as it was a few years ago and the '98 offers less on the nose than on the palate. The Vermentino di Sardegna '98 is better, but even here the bouquet, after an initial burst of fresh flowers, fades away. The palate is fresh and succulent, with a vegetal note of tomato leaf. The Billia is not very intense and shows merely average structure. Things are better with the reds, particularly the Luzzana '97, from cannonau and cagnulari, which has good carry-through from nose to palate. The nose is a little herbaceous at first, and then opens to attractive jammy notes; the palate is full, soft and appropriately tannic. The medium-bodied, fairly long Alghero Cagnulari '98 is worthy of mention. Incidentally, they are now making some grappas and a new passito (raisin) wine which, from early tastings, seems quite promising.

● Luzzana '97	▼	4
○ Vermentino di Sardegna '98	▼	2*
● Alghero Cagnulari '98		2
○ Billìa		1
○ Vermentino di Sardegna Tuvaoes '98		4
● Cagnulari di Sardegna '94	▽	2*
● Cannonau di Sardegna '93	▽	3
● Luzzana '91	▽	4
● Luzzana '93	▽	4
● Luzzana '94	▽	4
● Luzzana '96	▽	4
○ Vermentino di Sardegna '97	▽	2
○ Vermentino di Sardegna Tuvaoes '96	▽	4

OTHER WINERIES

The following producers obtained good scores in our tastings with one or more of their wines:

PROVINCE OF CAGLIARI

Gigi Picciau
Pirri, tel. 070/560224
Nasco di Cagliari '95,
Vermentino di Sardegna '97

Villa di Quartu
Quartu Sant'Elena, tel. 070/826997
Moscato di Cagliari

Cantina Sociale di Sant'Antioco
Sant'Antioco, tel. 0781/83055
Carignano del Sulcis Ris. '96

Fattoria Mauritania
Santadi, tel. 070/401465
Barrua '97

PROVINCE OF NUORO

Columbu
Bosa, tel. 0785/373380
Malvasia di Bosa '95

Arcadu
Oliena, tel. 0784/288417
Cannonau di Sardegna '98,
Su Gucciu '97

Cantina Sociale Oliena
Oliena,
tel. 0784/287509
Cannonau di Sardegna
Nepente di Oliena '98

Cantina Sociale di Sorgono
Sorgono,
tel. 0784/60113
Mandrolisai Rosso '98

PROVINCE OF ORISTANO

Cantina Sociale Marrubiu
Marrubiu,
tel. 0783/859213
Arborea Sangiovese '98

Cantina Sociale Terralba
Terralba,
tel. 0783/81824
Terralba Bovale '98

PROVINCE OF ASSARI

Tenute Soletta
Florinas,
tel. 079/438160
Cannonau di Sardegna Firmadu '97

Arcone
Sassari, tel. 079/233721
Arcone '97

INDEX OF WINES

INDEX OF PRODUCERS